Concise International Arbitration

KLUWER LAW INTERNATIONAL

Concise International Arbitration

Edited by:
Loukas A. Mistelis

AUSTIN   BOSTON   CHICAGO   NEW YORK   THE NETHERLANDS

Published by Kluwer Law International,
P.O. Box 316, 2400 AH Alphen aan den Rijn, The Netherlands
sales@kluwerlaw.com
http://www.kluwerlaw.com

Sold and distributed in North, Central and South America by
Aspen Publishers, Inc.,
7201 McKinney Circle, Frederick, MD 21704, USA

Sold and distributed in all other countries by
Turpin Distribution Services Ltd.,
Stratton Business Park,
Pegasus Drive, Biggleswade,
Bedfordshire SG18 8TQ, United Kingdom

Suggested citation:
[Author name], in Mistelis, *Concise Int'l Arbitration*, [Document name] …,
art. …, note …

Disclaimer:
The chapters do not necessarily reflect the views of the contributors' law firms.

© 2010 Kluwer Law International
ISBN 978-90-411-2609-2

All rights reserved. No part of this publication may be reproduced, stored in a retrieval system, or transmitted in any form or by any means, mechanical, photocopying, recording or otherwise, without prior written permission of the publishers.

Permission to use this content must be obtained from the copyright owner. Please apply to Permissions Department, Wolters Kluwer Legal, 111 Eighth Avenue, 7th Floor, New York, NY 10011-5201, United States of America. E-mail: permissions@kluwerlaw.com

Printed in the United Kingdom

FOREWORD

International Arbitration is a rather idiosyncratic area of study and practice: in continental Europe it started as an area of practice populated predominately by academics while in the common law was embraced mainly by practitioners who manifested academic aspirations and credibility. Moreover, it is an area of legal practice where the proliferation of academic and legal writing in the last twenty-five years is rather unparalleled both in terms of quantity and quality.

International arbitration is also an area of law with very few absolutes. Sources of substantive law have a different dynamic than in domestic litigation and arbitration: in addition to traditional positive law, soft (transnational) rules of law have firmly established themselves as applicable norms for arbitral decision-making. Arbitral procedural rules are an anthology of international treaty rules, arbitration rules (soft law) and domestic rules, which are mainly enabling default rules for the organisation and conduct of proceedings and in rare occasions mandatory.

Domestic perceptions are often challenged and arbitration practitioners find themselves working in many different jurisdictions and with different laws. As a result (successful) international arbitration practitioners are cosmopolitan and internationalist in outlook and disposition: they have a good grounding in one legal system but are capable and even enthusiastic about working in different systems. However, it is not always easy to have access to foreign arbitration laws or in the 'legal system' of different arbitration institutions.

Although the market for information on international arbitration is growing increasingly competitive, until now there has been a singular lack of a short, direct guide of manageable size that focuses on answering the essential questions that inevitably arise when practitioners work in an array of jurisdictions, under differing rules and different conventions.

Concise International Arbitration is an article-by-article commentary and offers the reader a swift understanding of all provisions of the leading arbitration instruments. It is the first commentary of this type and part of Kluwer Law International's 'Concise' series. A concise commentary is particularly aimed at busy practitioners who require a succinct but authoritative commentary on the most often used instruments. In this book, leading practitioners offer a systematic and accessible commentary of the 1958 New York Convention on the Recognition and Enforcement of Foreign Arbitral Awards, the 1965 ICSID Convention on the International Centre for the Settlement of Investment Disputes, the UNCITRAL Arbitration Rules; the ICSID Rules; the ICC Arbitration Rules; the LCIA Arbitration Rules, AAA-ICDR International Arbitration Rules; CIETAC (China International Economic and Trade Arbitration Commission) Arbitration Rules, 1985/2006 UNCITRAL Model Law on International Commercial Arbitration, the Chinese Arbitration Law 1994; the English Arbitration Act 1996, the French Code of Civil Procedure and Swiss Private International Law Act.

The law is stated as at April 2010, with the exception of the ICSID Convention and ICSID Rules where the law is stated as in 2009. It is envisaged that there will be regular new editions to reflect changes in law and practice.

This is a collective project and many thanks are due. First, I wish to express my thanks to all contributors who worked on their parts with enthusiasm and self-discipline and commentary-writing is a different short of writing than traditional legal writing. I found all contributions to be insightful, concise and authoritative. Second, I would like to thank the editorial team, John Ribeiro at the School of International Arbitration and Steve Lambley at Kluwer. Finally, my sincere thanks are due to Gwen de Vries, for the idea of this book and Eleanor Taylor and Vincent Veschoor for the co-ordination of the project at Kluwer Law International.

London and Athens
1 May 2010
LM

TABLE OF CONTENTS

Foreword	v
About the Authors	ix

Part I. Conventions

Convention on the Recognition and Enforcement of Foreign Arbitral Awards (New York Convention), 1958	1
Convention of the Settlement of Investment Disputes between States and Nationals of Other States (Washington/ICSID Convention), 1965	33

Part II. Rules

United Nations Commission on International Trade Law (UNCITRAL) Arbitration Rules, 1976	171
International Centre for Settlement of Investment Disputes (ICSID) Rules of Procedure for Arbitration Proceedings (Arbitration Rules), 2006	231
International Chamber of Commerce (ICC) Rules of Arbitration, 1998	305
London Court of International Arbitration (LCIA) Arbitration Rules, 1998	401
American Arbitration Association (AAA) International Centre for Dispute Resolution (ICDR) International Arbitration Rules, 2009	467
China International Economic And Trade Arbitration Commission (CIETAC) Arbitration Rules, 2005	513

Part III. Laws

United Nations Commission On International Trade Law (UNCITRAL) Model Law On International Commercial Arbitration, 1985/2006	581
Arbitration Law of the People's Republic of China, 1994	657
English Arbitration Act 1996 (Chapter 23), 1996 – Arbitration Law in England, Wales and Northern Ireland	719

Table of Contents

French Code of Civil Procedure (Book IV: Arbitration), 1981	873
Swiss Private International Law Act (Chapter 12: International Arbitration), 1989	911
List of References	981
Index	1079

ABOUT THE AUTHORS

Denis Bensaude, Paris

Denis Bensaude is a member of the New York and Paris Bars and a former Counsel of the ICC International Court of Arbitration. He began his career practicing in capital markets and mergers and acquisitions before moving into the field of international litigation and arbitration and joining the ICC in 1999. In 2002, he returned to private practice and established his own firm in 2004. He now regularly acts as arbitrator and counsel in international arbitrations, whether ad hoc or institutional under the auspices of the LCIA, the PCA and the ICC, as well as French institutions. Denis is a member of the International Arbitration Commissions of the ICC and the International Law Association and is on the ICDR roster of neutrals. Fluent in English and French, Denis has written numerous articles on international arbitration and, since 2009, publishes quarterly commentaries and abstracts on French court decisions on international arbitration.

Stavros Brekoulakis, School of International Arbitration, Queen Mary University of London

Stavros Brekoulakis is a lecturer in International Dispute Resolution at Queen Mary, University London, member of the School of International Arbitration, Centre for Commercial Law Studies. He teaches on the LLM courses of International Comparative and Commercial Arbitration, International Commercial Construction, International Commercial Litigation and Conflict of Laws. He is also the academic director of the Diploma Course (taught by distance learning) in International Arbitration. He is a member of the Athens Bar having practiced shipping law and dispute resolution. His academic research and writing focuses on international commercial arbitration, conflict of laws, multiparty and complex dispute resolution, issues on jurisdiction of tribunals and national courts, and enforcement of awards and national judgments. He has received his LLB from Athens (with distinction), his LLM from King's College London and his PhD from Queen Mary University of London.

Stephen R. Bond, Covington & Burling LLP, London*

Stephen Bond is senior of counsel in the Covington & Burling LLP's London office. He specializes in international commercial arbitration and is European Chair of the firm's Arbitration Practice Group. He has served as an advocate or arbitrator in dozens of international arbitrations under the rules of

---

* The author would like to thank Anya Rodriguez Roos for her kind assistance in the preparation of the chapter on the ICC Rules of Arbitration.

the International Chamber of Commerce, the London Court of International Arbitration, the Stockholm Arbitration Institute, the Japanese Commercial Arbitration Association, the Vienna Centre, and UNCITRAL. Mr. Bond's experience includes disputes in the energy, international joint venture, construction, technology, sales and distribution fields.

Domenico Di Pietro, Chiomenti Studio Legale, Rome

Domenico Di Pietro was educated in Rome and Queen Mary University of London and joined Chiomenti Studio Legale in 2007. From 2000 to 2007 he worked with Mayer, Brown, Rowe & Maw LLP in London. His main area of practice is domestic and international arbitration, both ad hoc and administered, with specific focus on ICC (International Chamber of Commerce) cases and foreign investment disputes, especially before ICSID (International Center for Settlement of Investment Disputes). He has published extensively in the areas of contract law, public international law and international arbitration, including two books on the New York Convention. He teaches international arbitration at Roma III.

John Fellas, Hughes Hubbard & Reed LLP, New York

John Fellas is a partner in the New York office of Hughes Hubbard & Reed LLP, practicing in international litigation and arbitration. He has practiced in both the U.S. and England; he is a member of the New York Bar and a Solicitor of the Supreme Court of England and Wales. He has served as counsel, and as chair, sole arbitrator and co-arbitrator, in arbitrations under the AAA, ICC and ad hoc rules. He also serves on the Mediation Panel of the District Court for the Southern District of New York. He has also been retained to act as an expert witness on U.S. law in proceedings in other countries. He has been recognized for his practice in international arbitration and in commercial litigation. In 2006, Global Arbitration Review identified him as one of 45 leading international arbitration practitioners under the age of 45. He received a B.A. (Hons.) from the University of Durham, England, and both an LL.M. and an S.J.D. from the Harvard Law School.

Jacomijn van Haersolte-van Hof, Amsterdam

Jacomijn van Haersolte-van Hof has her own 'boutique firm' and acts as counsel and arbitrator in international and national proceedings; her practice is partly devoted to disputes involving foreign states or state entities. She acts as counsel and advisor, and as arbitrator. She advises on the possibilities to litigate. As experienced litigator, she is acting in front of national and international tribunals and in Dutch courts. Moreover, she is conducting cases in Dutch or English. She has a good knowledge of French and a basic knowledge of German. She is experienced in so-called 'kort geding' (injunction) proceedings, in particular in connection with and in support of arbitral proceedings as well as attachment proceedings. She has particular experience in cases involving states and assets belonging to foreign states, where international and diplomatic immunities play an important role. She is also highly experienced in setting aside proceedings of arbitral awards, and enforcement proceedings of foreign awards and judgments. As arbitrator Jacomijn van Haersolte-van Hof's caseload is varied. Her independent position ensures her capacity to act as arbitrator as well as counsel.

Daniel Kalderimis, Chapman Tripp, Wellington

In 2009, Daniel returned to Chapman Tripp after seven years abroad in New York and London. In New York, Daniel was a Fulbright Scholar and Associate-in-Law at Columbia Law School. In London, Daniel was a senior associate in the leading international arbitration group of Freshfields Bruckhaus Deringer LLP. Daniel is widely published in the field of international economic law and makes frequent presentations on topics in this field. Most recently, he has co-authored, with two of his former colleagues, a guide to the ICSID Convention and Arbitration Rules relating to international investment disputes. Daniel was recently selected as one of the world's pre-eminent commercial arbitration specialists by Global Arbitration Review's International Who's Who of Commercial Arbitration 2010. He was the only lawyer from a full-service firm to be included in the New Zealand chapter.

Loukas A. Mistelis, School of International Arbitration, Queen Mary University of London

Loukas Mistelis is an acknowledged authority in international dispute resolution. He has been listed as one of the 'leading lights in international arbitration', 45 under 45 and is also listed on the Who's Who Commercial Arbitration since 2007. He is the Clive Schmitthoff Professor of Transnational Law and Arbitration at the Centre for Commercial Law Studies and the Director of the School of International Arbitration, Queen Mary University of London. He is also Visiting Professor, NYU in London, and was a Visiting Scholar at Columbia University Law School and at Keio University Law School. He teaches International and Comparative Commercial Arbitration, International Trade and Investment Dispute Settlement, International Commercial Litigation and ADR. He was educated in Greece, France, Germany and Japan and is fluent in English, German and Greek, has good knowledge of French and basic knowledge of Polish, Russian and Spanish. His publications include 50 referred articles and ten books. He has practiced law in Germany, Greece and the UK, having also acted as a consultant in Cambodia, Japan, Moldova, Nigeria, Poland, Ukraine, and Vietnam. He has substantial arbitration experience, under ICC, ICISD, LCIA, UNCITRAL, SCC and Moscow Rules.

About the Authors

Simon Nesbitt, Hogan Lovells LLP, London*

Simon Nesbitt is a partner in Hogan Lovells international arbitration group. He originally qualified as an English solicitor with Lovells in London in 1994. Following a period on secondment in-house to a major client of the firm, he moved to Lovells' Paris office. While in Paris, Simon took the French Bar examinations and was admitted as an avocat à la cour in 1997. He returned to London in 1998 and has since focused exclusively on international arbitration. His arbitration experience extends to cases conducted under all of the major institutional rules, including ICSID, ICC, SIAC and LCIA as well as ad hoc arbitrations. He is experienced in all aspects of court proceedings ancillary to arbitration proceedings, such as pre-arbitral injunctions, and challenges to and the enforcement of arbitral awards. He acts for clients from a wide range of industry sectors, including oil and gas, banking and financial services, commodities trading and distribution, food and beverage, pharmaceutical and telecoms industry. Simon speaks fluent English, French and Italian and is admitted as a solicitor-advocate.

Silvia Noury, Freshfields Bruckhaus Deringer LLP, London

Sylvia is Counsel in Freshfields' international arbitration group, having practised in the London, Paris and New York offices. Sylvia has represented states and corporations in a variety of commercial and investment treaty arbitrations, including under the auspices of ICSID, under UNCITRAL Rules and under the auspices of the ICC, AAA and LCIA, both in English and Spanish. Sylvia has acted in disputes under various legal systems (civil law, common law and international law) in sectors as diverse as oil, gas, electricity, mining, water concessions, telecommunications, construction contracts, alcoholic beverages, tobacco and financial services. She was cited by LATINLAWYER 250 as a 'recognised name' in the field of Latin American arbitration and by Chambers Latin America as an 'Up-and-coming individual' in the area of international arbitration. Sylvia is a visiting lecturer at the London School of Economics' LLM programme and has spoken and published widely in the field of arbitration. Before joining Freshfields, Sylvia completed an internship at the Buenos Aires office of Marval, O'Farrell & Mairal. She holds a first-class law degree from the University of Cambridge.

Marily Paralika, White & Case LLP, Paris

Marily Paralika specializes in international arbitration. She has experience of arbitral proceedings conducted under the auspices of the ICC, as well as ad hoc proceedings. Industry sectors in which she has advised include construc-

---

* The author gratefully acknowledges the invaluable assistance of Jerome Finnis (Senior Associate, Hogan Lovells LLP) and Giles Hutt (Professional Support Lawyer, Hogan Lovells LLP).

tion. Prior to joining White & Case, Marily was Assistant Counsel to the International Court of Arbitration of the ICC, where she oversaw thousands of arbitrations, spanning almost all industry sectors and regions. In addition to her work in international arbitration, Marily has non-contentious experience advising clients on general corporate matters. Prior to moving to France in 2003, she worked at a leading Greek law firm in the corporate department. Marily is currently the Greek National Commissioner to the ICC. She is also a member of the LCIA Young International Arbitration Group, Arbitralwomen and the Comité Français de l'Arbitrage.

Georgios Petrochilos, Freshfields Bruckhaus Deringer LLP, Paris

Avocat à la Cour and Advocate of the Greek Supreme Court, Georgios Petrochilos is a partner in Freshfields' international arbitration and public international law groups and is based in Paris. Georgios specializes in public international law and international arbitration, with a particular emphasis on energy-related matters. His extensive arbitration experience includes acting as counsel or advisor for numerous clients, under the arbitration rules of the ICC, UNCITRAL, LCIA, SCC, PCA, ICSID, and ICSID Additional Facility. He has represented governments, international organizations, and private parties on a broad range of cases involving long-term energy contracts, investment protection, boundary disputes, entitlement to natural resources, and immunities from jurisdiction. As arbitrator or secretary to tribunals, he has been involved in cases under the UNCITRAL, LCIA, SCC, and Cairo Regional Centre Rules. Georgios has served as advisor to the UNCITRAL Secretariat and represents Greece as a delegate to UNCITRAL. Georgios is also a rapporteur for the Institute for Transnational Arbitration. He has published extensively on subjects related to international law and international arbitration. Georgios holds degrees from the Universities of Athens, Strasbourg, and Oxford, including a doctorate in international arbitration law.

Matthew Secomb, White & Case LLP, Paris

Matthew Secomb specializes in international arbitration with a focus on construction and energy-related disputes. He has been involved in international commercial arbitrations, under most of the major institutional rules as well as in ad hoc arbitrations. Prior to joining White & Case in 2006, Matthew was counsel to the International Court of Arbitration of the International Chamber of Commerce, where he oversaw thousands of arbitrations, spanning almost all industry sectors and regions. In addition to his work in international arbitration, Matthew has experience advising clients on construction (both contentious and non-contentious) and general corporate matters. Prior to moving to France in 2001, he worked at a leading Australian law firm in both the construction and corporate law groups. Matthew is a member of the ICC Commission on Arbitration.

About the Authors

Georg von Segesser, Schellenberg Wittmer, Zürich

Georg von Segesser is a partner in Schellenberg Wittmer's Dispute Resolution Group in Zurich. He has acted as chairman, co-arbitrator, sole arbitrator and counsel in over two hundred domestic and international arbitrations (ICC, Swiss Rules, LCIA, UNCITRAL and others) and as co-director of the Claims Resolution Tribunal for Dormant Accounts in Switzerland. In 1972, he graduated from Lucerne College and Zurich University. After serving as a district court clerk in 1971-72, he worked as an associate and partner in a large Zurich law firm from 1973 until 1982, and in 1974-75 served as a foreign associate in a leading New York law firm. In 1982, he was as one of the founding partners who established Schellenberg Wittmer. He has authored publications on international arbitration, property and trust law, and cultural and art law. He is a member of the Swiss Arbitration Association, IBA, LCIA, the German Institution of Arbitration, the Chartered Institute of Arbitrators (Fellowship), and arbitration institutions in Austria, Kuala Lumpur, and Hong Kong, the ICDR of the American Arbitration Association, and the Society of Trust and Estate Practitioners. He is president-elect of the International Academy of Estate and Trust Law.

Audley Sheppard, Clifford Chance LLP, London*

Audley Sheppard is a Partner and Global Head in the International Commercial Arbitration and International Law Groups of Clifford Chance LLP in London. He was recently named in Practical Law Co's global list of 'Which lawyer?'s top 20 arbitration specialists'. Audley has LLB (Hons) and BComm from Victoria University of Wellington, New Zealand, and an LLM from the University of Cambridge. England. He is a Fellow of the Chartered Institute of Arbitrators and a Fellow of the Institute of Advanced Legal Studies. Audley's positions include: Rapporteur of the International Arbitration Committee of the International Law Association (1996-2006); Co-Chair of the Arbitration Committee of the International Bar Association (2006-07), following a year as Senior Vice-Chair and three years as Newsletter Editor; Member on the ICC Commission on International Arbitration (2000-present). Audley is on the Steering Committee of BIICL's Investment Treaty Forum and is a co-editor of BIICL's Investment Treaty Law: Current Issues (vol. 1, 2006) (with Dr Federico Ortino and Hugo Warner). He is on the Editorial Boards of the International Arbitration Law Review and the IBA's Business Law International.

---

* The author thanks James Dingley, Nola Donachie, James Egerton-Vernon, Jagdev Kenth, Cameron Scholes and Sachin Trikha of Clifford Chance LLP for their assistance.

About the Authors

Dorothée Schramm, Schellenberg Wittmer, Zürich

Dorothée Schramm is an associate in Schellenberg Wittmer's International Arbitration Group in Geneva. Her main areas of practice include domestic and international commercial arbitration and litigation, private international law, and Swiss and German contract and tort law. Admitted to the bar in Switzerland in 2007, she graduated from the University of Göttingen, Germany, in 2001 and obtained a doctorate of laws from the University of Lucerne in 2004. Between 2001 and 2004, she worked as a research and teaching assistant at the University of Lucerne and from 2004 until 2008 she worked as a part-time lecturer at the University of Lucerne. She continues to teach arbitration and advocacy skills at the university. She has published mainly in the areas of international arbitration and private international law, addressing issues of jurisdiction in international matters and the recognition and enforcement of foreign decisions. She is a member of several professional associations, including the Swiss Arbitration Association, the German Institution of Arbitration, the Austrian Arbitration Association, the International Bar Association, the Société Suisse de Droit International (SVIR), ArbitralWomen, and the Ordre des Avocats of Geneva.

Laurence Shore, Gibson Dunn & Crutcher LLP, New York

Laurence Shore is a dual U.S./U.K. qualified partner in the New York office of Gibson, Dunn & Crutcher. He is Co-chair of the firm's International Arbitration Practice Group. Mr. Shore's practice focuses on international arbitration. He has been the lead advocate in a large number of arbitration cases under, for example, the ICC, LCIA, AAA, UNCITRAL and Swiss Rules. He also has sat as an arbitrator in cases under the ICC, ICDR, Cairo Regional Centre, and LCIA Rules. In addition to his work as an arbitration practitioner, Mr. Shore has tried cases in the United States courts and in England's High Court. He holds the appointment of Visiting Professor in the School of International Arbitration, Queen Mary, University of London. Prior to joining Gibson Dunn, Mr. Shore was the global head of international arbitration at a major law firm in London. Mr. Shore earned his Juris Doctor degree in 1989 from Emory University School of Law. He previously earned Master of Arts and Doctor of Philosophy degrees in History from The Johns Hopkins University. Mr. Shore received his Bachelor of Arts degree from the University of North Carolina-Chapel Hill. He writes on international commercial and investment arbitration.

Jingzhou Tao, Jones Day, Beijing

Jingzhou Tao has more than 25 years of experience in advising Fortune 500 companies on China-related matters. His areas of practice include international mergers and acquisitions, arbitration, and corporate work. He has acted as counsel, chair, or party-nominated arbitrator in international arbitration

About the Authors

proceedings involving letters of credit, construction projects, management contracts, joint ventures, technology transfers, trademark licensing agreements, agency agreements, and international sales of goods. Jingzhou is member of the ICC International Court of Arbitration, the LCIA, and the Advisory Committee of China International Economic and Trade Arbitration Commission. He is chair of the Commission on International Commercial Arbitration of ICC China, an adjunct professor at Peking University Law School, and a Fellow of the Chartered Institute of Arbitrators. In addition, he is a listed arbitrator for the Court of Arbitration for Sport, the HKIAC, the CIEATAC, and the Beijing Arbitration Commission. He is author of several books in English and French on Chinese law. He also has written articles on matters related to Chinese arbitration, foreign investment, and foreign trade.

CONVENTION ON THE RECOGNITION AND ENFORCEMENT OF FOREIGN ARBITRAL AWARDS (NEW YORK CONVENTION), 1958*

(Done in New York, 10 June 1958)

[Introductory remarks]

1. General. The New York Convention on the Recognition and Enforcement of Foreign Arbitral Awards is arguably the most successful instrument, not only in the area of private dispute resolution, but also in the area of private and commercial law in general. It has 144 Member States, the more recent additions being Cook Islands in 2009 and Rwanda in 2008. In this respect, the Convention brings together countries with very different legal cultures and levels of economic development heralding a true product of early globalisation and projecting international arbitration as one of the few, and oldest, areas of global legal practice. Although the Convention, adopted by diplomatic conference on 10 June 1958, was prepared by the United Nations prior to the establishment of UNCITRAL – the specialist United Nations Commission on International Trade Law, which started its operation in 1966 – promotion of the Convention is an integral part of UNCITRAL's work. The Convention is widely recognised as the foundation of international commercial arbitration, imposing on courts of Contracting States a public international law obligation to give effect to an agreement to arbitrate when seized of an action in a matter covered by an arbitration agreement and also to recognise and enforce awards made in other States, subject to specific limited exceptions. Consequently, the Convention deals with the recognition and enforcement of foreign arbitral awards, the recognition and enforcement of arbitration agreements and creates a uniform legal regime of the grounds on which enforcement of an award may be resisted. The three areas that the Convention does not cover or harmonise are left to domestic legislation and one can only hope that these systems will gradually converge. These areas are: (a) public policy, (b) what matters are capable of settlement by arbitration (arbitrability) and (c) procedure relating to recognition and enforcement of awards.

2. History and Status. In 1953, the International Chamber of Commerce (ICC) suggested a new treaty to modernise international commercial arbitration and the regime created by the Geneva Protocol of 1923 and the Geneva Convention of 1927. The old regime distinguished between enforceability of arbitration agreements and arbitration awards. The problem was the so-called double exequatur, since awards were enforceable only in the State where the

---

* Reproduced with permission of the United Nations Commission on International Trade Law (UNCITRAL). The text reproduced here is valid at the time of reproduction. As amendments may from time to time be made to the text, please refer to the website <http://www.uncitral.org> for the latest version.

award was made and leave for enforcement was needed in any other State. This issue is now addressed by the New York Convention that ensures enforceability of arbitration awards internationally. The ICC proposal was taken up by the United Nations Economic and Social Council (ECOSOC) and led to the adoption of the New York Convention of 1958. The Convention entered into force on 7 June 1959. The current status of ratification may be found at the UNCITRAL website and specifically at <www.uncitral.org/uncitral/en/uncitral_texts/arbitration/NYConvention_status.html>. The preparatory documents (*travaux préparatoires*) of the Convention which may well have a bearing on its (historical) interpretation are available from <www.uncitral.org/uncitral/en/uncitral_texts/arbitration/NY Convention_travaux.html>.

3. Sources. Despite the great popularity of the Convention there are fairly few books published on the topic in English. A few publications can be referred to in the context of this concise commentary:

- Marc Blessing (ed.), *The New York Convention of 1958. A Collection of Reports and Materials* delivered at the ASA Conference held in Zürich on 2 February 1996, ASA 1996
- Domenico Di Pietro and Martin Platte, *Enforcement of International Arbitration Awards. The New York Convention of 1958* (Cameron May 2001)
- Emmanuel Gaillard and Domenico Di Pietro (eds), *Enforcement of Arbitration Agreements and International Arbitral Awards. The New York Convention in Practice* (Cameron May 2008)
- Giorgio Gaja (ed.), *New York Convention* (Oceana, 1978-1996)
- Loukas Mistelis and Stavros Brekoulakis (eds), *Arbitrability. International and Comparative Perspectives* (Kluwer 2009)
- United Nations (eds.), *Enforcing Arbitral Awards under the New York Convention. Experience and Prospects* (1999)
- Albert Jan van den Berg, *The New York Arbitration Convention of 1958. Towards a Uniform Judicial Interpretation* (Kluwer 1981)
- Albert Jan van den Berg, *Consolidated Commentary on New York Convention*, part of ICCA Yearbook but also available at <www.kluwerarbitration.com>, since 1976.

[Scope of Application]

Article I

1. This Convention shall apply to the recognition and enforcement of arbitral awards made in the territory of a State other than the State where the recognition and enforcement of such awards are sought, and arising out of differences between persons, whether physical or legal. It shall also apply to arbitral awards not considered as domestic awards in the State where their recognition and enforcement are sought.

2. The term 'arbitral awards' shall include not only awards made by

arbitrators appointed for each case but also those made by permanent arbitral bodies to which the parties have submitted.

3. When signing, ratifying or acceding to this Convention, or notifying extension under article X hereof, any State may on the basis of reciprocity declare that it will apply the Convention to the recognition and enforcement of awards made only in the territory of another Contracting State. It may also declare that it will apply the Convention only to differences arising out of legal relationships, whether contractual or not, which are considered as commercial under the national law of the State making such declaration.

1. Scope of Application: the Territorial Criterion. The Convention determines its scope of application by adopting a 'territorial criterion'. It applies to arbitral awards rendered in a State other than the State where recognition and enforcement are sought. During the negotiation of the Convention, it was considered whether other alternative criteria based on traditional conflict of laws elements should be adopted in order to determine which awards should fall within the scope of application of the Convention. Eventually, the territorial criterion was adopted because it allowed for an objective standard that was in line with the degree of detachment from domestic laws, which international arbitration is generally believed to be entitled to.

2. Qualification of the Territorial Criterion. In order to pursue the Convention's general pro-enforcement bias, it was agreed that it would be desirable to allow the application of the Convention to arbitral awards that – by strict application of the territorial criterion – would be outside of the Convention's scope. This was considered as a necessary step to protect the enforcement of arbitral awards rendered in the country of recognition and enforcement which, because of factual or legal circumstances, are characterised by a degree of detachment from that jurisdiction. The determination as to which arbitral awards should not be considered as 'domestic awards' was left to the legislation of the State where recognition and enforcement are sought. In this way the Convention allows for delocalised or denationalised arbitration and the recognition and enforcement of awards rendered under such regimes.

3. Definition of Arbitral Awards. Interestingly, the Convention does not provide a definition of the term 'award'. This is not a moot issue since it cannot be assumed that any means of dispute resolution other than domestic court proceedings should per se qualify as 'arbitration' under the Convention. Similarly, it should not be taken for granted that any orders issued by an arbitral tribunal could be enforced under the New York Convention. It is submitted that to be within the scope of the Convention an arbitral award should (i) be issued in a means of dispute resolution genuinely alternative to the jurisdiction of domestic courts (the so-called 'alternativity test') and (ii) finally settle one or more of the issues submitted to the jurisdiction of an arbitral tribunal (the so-called 'finality test').

4. Reservations. One of the main tools for the Convention's undeniable success, is the fact that it allows Contracting States to 'mould', at least to a certain extent, the Convention's provisions to avoid any clash with the core principles of each Contracting State's domestic law. One example of this can be found in the two reservations available to Contracting States under art. I.

5. Reciprocity Reservation. The first reservation allows Contracting States to limit the application of the Convention to awards made in another Contracting State. Therefore, an award made in a non-Contracting State would not benefit from enforcement under the Convention in a State which has adopted this reservation. Seventy States have made a reciprocity reservation. Nowadays this reservation has lost much of its significance because of the widespread adoption of the Convention (in 144 States).

6. Commercial Reservation. The second reservation allows Contracting States to limit recognition and enforcement to awards relating to commercial relationships, either contractual or not. This reservation was made available in order to facilitate the signing of the Convention by countries whose national legal systems only allowed referral to arbitration of commercial disputes. In fact, forty-four States have made use of this reservation. The test as to whether a matter is to be considered as a 'commercial' one is to be carried out by using the law of the place where enforcement of the award is sought. In practice, the commercial reservation has given rise to few isolated problems even though its potential in this regard is much higher than that of the reciprocity reservation. One notable example is the US case *BV Bureau Wijsmuller* where a US District Court considered the salvage of a US warship outside the scope of the Convention as such activities are normally considered as 'non-commercial' in international law. Some domestic courts of States that have adopted the commercial reservation have at times adopted a rather narrow interpretation of their own notion of 'commercial'. In *Societè d'Investissement Kal*, the Tunisian courts were called upon to deal with a dispute between a company and two architects that had been retained to draw up urbanisation plans for a resort. The contract contained a clause referring all disputes to ICC arbitration in Paris. A dispute arose concerning the payment of outstanding fees and an ICC arbitral tribunal rendered an award in favour of the architects. The architects sought enforcement of the award in Tunisia, where the Court of Appeal confirmed the lower court's decision and denied enforcement. The Court of Appeal explained that Tunisia had adopted the commercial reservation and architectural and urbanisation works were not commercial matters under Tunisian law. The Supreme Court upheld the decision of the Court of Appeal. It is important to stress, however, that the majority of domestic courts seem prepared to construe the commercial reservation rather narrowly. An example of such approach is a much quoted case entertained by the courts of India in *RM Investment & Trading Co*. The local High Court had held that the rendering by a company of consultancy services for promoting a related commercial deal should not be regarded – pursuant to

Indian law – as a commercial transaction. The decision was reversed by the Supreme Court of India which held that: 'While construing the expression commercial it has to be borne in mind that the aim of the Convention is to facilitate international trade by means of facilitating suitable alternative ways of settlement of international disputes and therefore any expression adopted in the Convention should receive, consistent with its literal and grammatical sense, a liberal construction. The expression commercial should therefore be construed broadly having regard to the manifold activities which are integral part of international trade nowadays.' Needless to say, this approach is not common to all jurisdictions and it might not be even common to all the courts within the same jurisdiction. Indeed, some domestic courts might stick to the definition of 'commercial' available under domestic law and make no allowance to reflections on the needs and principles of international trade. It would therefore be highly advisable to perform a preliminary assessment of this issue when drafting the arbitration clause and when planning enforcement.

[Arbitration agreements]

Article II

1. Each Contracting State shall recognise an agreement in writing under which the parties undertake to submit to arbitration all or any differences which have arisen or which may arise between them in respect of a defined legal relationship, whether contractual or not, concerning a subject matter capable of settlement by arbitration.

2. The term 'agreement in writing' shall include an arbitral clause in a contract or an arbitration agreement, signed by the parties or contained in an exchange of letters or telegrams.

3. The court of a Contracting State, when seized of an action in a matter in respect of which the parties have made an agreement within the meaning of this article, at the request of one of the parties, refer the parties to arbitration, unless it finds that the said agreement is null and void, inoperative or incapable of being performed.

1. Scope. Despite the fact that the Convention's title seems to focus on recognition and enforcement of arbitral awards, a good part of the Convention, and certainly its most controversial aspect, deals with enforcement of arbitration agreements. It is interesting to note that art. II, which deals with the issues of validity and enforcement of arbitration agreements, was a last-minute addition to the Convention's text. Some of the uncertainties connected to such provisions are therefore 'blamed' on the fact that comparatively little time was devoted to the negotiation of art. II.

2. Content of the agreement to arbitrate. Art. II(1) of the Convention imposes upon Contracting States the public international law obligation to recognise agreements in writing by which the parties have agreed to submit their future or existing disputes to arbitration (arbitration clauses and submission agreements). Art. II(1) employs the word 'differences' which can be assumed to be equivalent to, if not wider than 'disputes'. The words 'whether contractual or not' are considered to be aimed at entailing claims in tort. It is important to note that such a general obligation imposed upon Contracting States is limited with respect to disputes that can be validly submitted to arbitration. The most problematic aspect of art. II resides in what constitutes an 'agreement in writing'. The definition of what is an agreement in writing can be found under art. II(2) of the Convention where it is explained that the term 'agreement in writing' shall include an arbitral clause in a contract or an arbitration agreement, signed by the parties or contained in an exchange of letters or telegrams.

3. Matter capable of settlement by arbitration (arbitrability). The New York Convention imposes upon its Member States an obligation to recognise arbitration agreements provided that they are intended to settle disputes that are arbitrable. This is a 'ratione materiae' notion, which is normally referred to as 'objective' arbitrability as it is independent of the quality of the parties or their will. Art. II does not indicate which law should be taken into account in order to assess the arbitrability of a given dispute. On one hand, it is suggested that the issue of arbitrability should be resolved in accordance with the lex fori, i.e. the law of the courts that have been seized with the question as to whether an arbitration agreement deals with a matter capable of being settled through arbitration. On the other hand, it is suggested that the issue of arbitrability should be settled through the application of the law applicable to the arbitration agreement. In other words, the validity of the arbitration clause should be determined in all respects on the basis of the same law, whether the issue is one of arbitrability or whether it is an issue of validity of the parties' consent. As far as the practice of arbitration tribunals is concerned, the majority of cases seem to follow the view that the issue of arbitrability should be settled with reference to the law in force at the place of arbitration, even though in some cases, tribunals have avoided taking a clear-cut position on the issue where it had been ascertained that the dispute would have been arbitrable under each of the laws that the transaction was connected to. An interesting approach in this regard was adopted in *Meadows Indemnity*. The court observed that 'reference to the domestic laws of only one country, even the country where enforcement of an award will be sought', does not resolve whether a claim is 'capable of settlement by arbitration under Article II(1) of the Convention'. The court continued that such determination must be made 'on an international scale, with reference to the laws of the countries party to the Convention'. It has, however, been observed that in the majority of cases, courts have determined the question of arbitrability according to their domestic law. This is normally done without any conflicts of law analysis, even though a number of decisions have been resolved by applying the provisions of art. V(2)(a).

4. Agreement in writing. The Convention contains two alternative requirements of form in order to comply with its definition of 'in writing'. An arbitration agreement must be either (i) signed by the parties or (ii) contained in an exchange of letters or telegrams. The reference to 'letters or telegrams' is certainly obsolete and out of touch with modern business practice. However, it has given rise to very few problematic issues. Most domestic courts accept the idea that the reference to such 'old fashioned' means of communication should be read in the light of developing technology as also suggested by the UNCITRAL Secretariat in its note of 14 December 2005. This was formally adopted by the United Nations Commission on International Trade Law on 7 July 2006 as the 'Recommendation regarding the interpretation of article II, paragraph 2, and article VII, paragraph 1, of the Convention'. Accordingly, the Commission recommends that art. II(2) should be applied (and be interpreted) in a dynamic way recognising that the circumstances described therein are not exhaustive. Furthermore, the Commission recommends that art. VII(1) should be applied to allow any interested party to avail itself of rights it may have, under the law or treaties of the country where an arbitration agreement is sought to be relied upon, to seek recognition of the validity of such an arbitration agreement. In the case of *Chloe Z Fishing Co.* it was held that the means of communication employed at art. II(2) should be read to include other forms of written communication regularly adopted to conduct business in the various contracting parties. It would, however, be incautious to assume that such an approach is unqualifiedly accepted in all jurisdictions. In a decision rendered by the Norwegian Court of Appeal (Hålogaland Court of Appeal 16 August 1999) it was indeed held that a contract that had been concluded by exchange of emails making reference to a charter party did not comply with the requirements of validity of arbitration agreements under the Convention. The most problematic issues with regard to the interpretation of art. II, however, arise in connection with the issue of actual signature and exchange of documents containing a clause (which need not to be signed). A strict application of the Convention's provisions would exclude several common business practices such as where a written contractual offer containing an arbitration clause is accepted and given effect through performance (so-called tacit acceptance).

5. Incorporation by reference. A considerable number of business contracts are frequently entered into by reference to contractual provisions contained in a separate document. The provisions referred to are normally contractual provisions of industry-specific trade associations or the general conditions of trade elaborated by one of the parties. Usually, the document which the parties make reference to contains, amongst other provisions, an arbitration clause. Whether such reference has the effect of validly concluding an arbitration agreement has been the subject of debate. Art. II does not deal directly with incorporation of arbitration clauses by reference. Therefore, it is unclear whether art. II(2) only applies to cases where the arbitration clause is contained in the documents exchanged by the parties or whether it also applies to cases where: a) although the documents exchanged do not contain an arbitration clause, they nonetheless make express reference to an arbitration clause contained in another document (so-called relatio perfecta), or b) the documents exchanged by the parties do not contain an arbitration clause but make reference to a document containing one, although there is no express reference to it in the exchange of documents (so-called relatio imperfecta). The case law on art. II seems to suggest that domestic courts are inclined to uphold the validity of incorporation of arbitration clauses to which the parties have made express reference. More uncertain is the fate of clauses where there is only a general reference to the document or set of rules in which the arbitration clauses are contained. Some decisions tend to affirm the validity of arbitration clauses where the document in which they are contained is either known or available to the parties. Most decisions upholding the validity of arbitration clauses incorporated without specific reference tend to do so by placing importance on the status of the parties and particularly on whether the parties are experienced traders that are used to entering into contracts governed by certain rules or are aware of the outcome generated by the reference. Although such case law is regarded as complying with the pro-enforcement bias of the Convention, it is not possible to assume that a similar conclusion should be reached by any courts under any circumstances. The silence of art. II on the issue may produce inconsistent case law. As a matter of fact, some courts have denied the validity of incorporation where the reference was not specific or where it was not possible to ascertain whether the parties were in a position to foresee the outcome of the incorporation. The arbitration statutes of a considerable number of Contracting States have adopted provisions that are much clearer on the issue of incorporation, at least with regard to issues of express reference. The majority of such statutes, however, are silent on the issue of general reference to a document containing an arbitration clause (relatio imperfecta). The case law on such statutes too seems to generally favour enforcement in the presence of evidence as to the parties' actual or deemed awareness of the existence of an arbitration clause in the document incorporated by reference.

6. Assignment. Assignment of a contract is a recurrent feature in international business. Assigned contracts often contain arbitration clauses. It is not a settled issue whether the assignment of a contract automatically results in the valid assignment of the arbitration agreement contained in the contract. The issue is rather complex as it entails the question of whether it is possible to assign both benefits and burdens of an arbitration clause. In other words, whether assignees can validly start arbitration proceedings against original counterparties and whether signatories can validly start arbitration proceedings against non-signatory assignees. The New York Convention does not explicitly address such an issue. It is therefore left to the relevant applicable law (or laws) to solve the problem. Many jurisdictions seem to advocate a commercially minded approach that takes into account the characteristics of modern trade as well as the pro-enforcement bias of the Convention. Most notably, in this latter regard the Paris Court of Appeal in *Bomar Oil NV* v *Entreprise d'Actvitiés Pétrolières* observed that since the New York Convention's 'drafters were desirous to facilitate the resolution of disputes by means of arbitration in the field of international trade', it was appropriate to look at any available evidence of consent, including commercial practices, in order to determine whether an arbitration agreement had been entered into between the parties. From other corners it has, however, been suggested that any too speculative interpretation of the Convention may lead to results that may be inconsistent with the intention of the Convention's Contracting States. It is highly advisable that where an assignment is likely to take place or in any event where it does take place, the parties structure the relevant contracts in order to address such an issue.

7. Null and void, inoperative or incapable of being performed. The third paragraph of art. II requires domestic courts of Contracting States to stay any legal proceedings in breach of an arbitration agreement. This obligation is not an absolute one. First of all, it is for the interested party to object to the jurisdiction of the domestic court pointing out the existence of a valid arbitration agreement. Therefore, a domestic court is not in a position to raise the issue on its own motion. Secondly, the obligation to stay the proceedings does not operate if the domestic court finds that the arbitration agreement is null and void, inoperative or incapable of being performed. The double description 'null and void' used in the English version should be construed in accordance with the common law countries' practice, according to which the two terms are actually the description of a single phenomenon whose existence is not conditional to the coming into play of two different requirements. The concept of what it is 'null and void' may change radically depending on the approach taken by the jurisdiction concerned. Indeed, in order to ascertain whether an arbitration agreement is null and void, reference should be made to the law by which the arbitration agreement is governed. However, it might be assumed that the words 'null and void' may be generally interpreted as referring to circumstances where the arbitration agreement is affected by some invalidity, such as lack of consent due to misrepresentation, duress, fraud or undue influence. The 'inoperative' defence makes reference to cases where the arbitration agreement, even though existing, has no effect or has ceased to have effect. This type of defect in an arbitration agreement may be caused by a plethora of reasons such as: the validity of the arbitration agreement is conditional, the arbitration agreement is explicitly or implicitly revoked or modified, or because of issues of res judicata. As opposed to cases of inoperativity, where the agreement has ceased to have binding effect between the parties, incapability of performance entails cases where, even though both existence and binding force of the agreement are not in dispute, the arbitration agreement lacks clarity or intelligibility and therefore cannot be performed, i.e. cases where the arbitration cannot be effectively set into motion. Some of the issues that have given rise to incapability of performance are the following: inconsistency, uncertainty (when the arbitration clause is too vaguely worded) and deadlock clauses (such as where the clause makes reference to institutions or individual that are no longer available).

[Obligation to recognise and enforce arbitral awards]

Article III

Each Contracting State shall recognise arbitral awards as binding and enforce them in accordance with the rules of procedure of the territory where the award is relied upon, under the conditions laid down in the following articles. There shall not be imposed substantially more onerous conditions or higher fees or charges on the recognition or enforcement of arbitral awards to which this Convention applies than are imposed on the recognition or enforcement of domestic arbitral awards.

1. General. Art. III imposes a general obligation on signatory States to recognise arbitral awards made in other countries, subject to procedural requirements no more onerous than those applicable to domestic awards. Furthermore, it is one of a number of provisions stipulating that the award needs to be binding (*Fertilizer Corporation of India*, 957-958).

2. Presumption of validity of awards. Art. III presumes the validity of awards and places the burden of proving invalidity on the party opposing enforcement. This has been consistently upheld. (See e.g., Queensland, 29 October 1993; *Rosseel*; Geneva CA, 14 April 1983; Corte di Cassazione 7 June 1995; *Iran v Gould, Inc*, 1364 n. 11.)

3. No definition of 'award'. Art. III does not introduce nor support a definition of 'award'. It merely provides for its main characteristics: awards are binding and enforceable. The overarching principles embodied within 'under conditions laid down in the following articles' are, first, awards are binding; secondly, awards are not subject to any review; and thirdly there is no need for confirmation of awards. Various provisions of the Convention employ some of these terms. This discussion is more appropriately considered under art. V.

4. Reference to law of forum. The general obligation to recognise Convention awards as binding under art. III confirms the application of the procedural law of the forum to those aspects incidental to the enforcement, which are not regulated by the Convention. Examples are discovery of evidence, estoppel or waiver, set-off or counterclaim against award, the entry of judgment clause, period of limitation for enforcement of a Convention award, and interest on the award (Van den Berg, *Consolidated*).

5. Procedural requirements for recognition and enforcement. Art. III is generally the starting point for the requirement that the courts are not to engage in a substantive review of the facts. Awards need not be confirmed at the seat of arbitration before enforcement can be sought abroad (no double exequatur). Signatory States may not impose procedural requirements that are more onerous, or a fee or charge that it is higher than those applicable to the recognition and enforcement of domestic arbitral awards. The Convention thus does not contain substantive requirements providing for either expeditious or efficient procedural mechanisms for enforcing Convention awards; it merely requires signatory States to use procedures no more cumbersome than their domestic enforcement procedures.

6. Jurisdiction to enforce an award. The question of whether a court of a Contracting State has jurisdiction to enforce an award depends, in principle, on rules of jurisdiction. Applications to have foreign awards declared enforceable presupposes that the court has jurisdiction over the respondent, although a case can be made in favour of the proposition that the Convention itself provides a basis for jurisdiction. England is a country where no jurisdictional requirements are imposed for enforcement of an award under the Convention. *Rosseel*: 'The English Court is bound by a statute, arising from treaty obligations, to enforce the award'.

7. Assets in the jurisdiction. The presence of assets in the jurisdiction is not a precondition to the enforcement of the award (Van den Berg, *Consolidated, 1996*, 301 Procedure for Enforcement, in General). However, the existence of assets within a country would be sufficient to establish jurisdiction for enforcement actions. The award creditor will have to investigate where assets of the unsuccessful party are located and where enforcement proceedings will be simpler. Unlike setting aside proceedings, which can, in principle, only be held at the place of arbitration, enforcement proceedings are generally possible more or less anywhere assets are located. This allows for forum shopping. Such discretion in relation to choosing a forum for enforcement proceedings is welcome. In the US, however, courts have exercised their discretion not to enforce an award where they considered that they were not the appropriate forum (forum non conveniens) (*Monde Re* v *Naftogaz*: Ukraine was the natural forum for enforcement; the State of Ukraine invoked the Foreign Sovereign Immunity Act, *Base Metal* v *OJSC*; *Glencore* v *Shivnath Rai Harnarain*; *Dardana* v *Yugaskneftegaz*).

8. Equal treatment of domestic and foreign awards. An Italian court (Corte d'Appello di Napoli 13 December 1974) rejected the argument that from the reference in art. III that 'no substantially more onerous conditions ... than for domestic awards' it would follow that a foreign award would have to be assimilated to a domestic award and that, for this reason, art. 825 of the Italian CCP would also apply to a foreign award. A clear distinction between the two types of awards should be made. The Italian Supreme Court in another case dealt with the allegation that the Court of Appeal had, in violation of art. III, directed the respondent to pay the costs of the enforcement proceedings because national law would not allow to award costs in domestic enforcement proceedings (Corte di Cassazione 3 April 1987). The Supreme

Court rejected the contention, reasoning that art. III concerns the costs to be borne by the party requesting recognition and that it does not derogate from the principle apportioning the costs in proceedings arising from the other party's opposition to the recognition of the award.

[Formalities required to obtain recognition and enforcement]

Article IV

(1) To obtain the recognition and enforcement mentioned in the preceding article, the party applying for recognition and enforcement shall, at the time of the application, supply:
- **(a) The duly authenticated original award or a duly certified copy thereof;**
- **(b) The original agreement referred to in article II or a duly certified copy thereof.**

(2) If the said award or agreement is not made in an official language of the country in which the award is relied upon, the party applying for recognition and enforcement of the award shall produce a translation of these documents into such language. The translation shall be certified by an official or sworn translator or by a diplomatic or consular agent.

1. General. The formalities required for obtaining recognition and enforcement of awards to which the Convention applies are simple and minimal. The party seeking recognition and enforcement is merely required to produce to the relevant court the duly authenticated original award or a duly certified copy; and the original arbitration agreement, referred to in art. II, or a duly certified copy thereof. If the award and the arbitration agreement are not in the official language of the country in which recognition and enforcement is sought, certified translations are needed. However, courts in several countries do not insist on submission of translations, if the award was made in easily accessible foreign language.

2. Authenticated award/original arbitration agreement. An authenticated award or a certified copy is essential as it is evidence of the entitlement of the party seeking enforcement. The fact that art. IV additionally requires the submission of the arbitration agreement referred to in art. II does not imply any obligation on the party seeking enforcement to establish the formal validity of the arbitration agreements (Di Pietro/Platte, *Enforcement of International Arbitration Awards*, 125; Van den Berg, *New York*, 250). *Dardana Ltd* v *Yukos* held that the presentation of a prima facie valid arbitration agreement is required. This shifts the burden of proof to the respondent wishing to resist enforcement, but see the stricter approach followed in Hålogaland Court of Appeal 16 August 1999, where enforcement was refused due to lack of an arbitration agreement (the correspondence was contained in emails and the court held that under the Convention the party had not submitted a valid arbitration clause for enforcement). In the case of an ICC arbitration, no copy of the arbitration agreement will be required, provided the parties sign the terms of reference.

3. Authentication. The required authentication refers generally to the signing of the award by the tribunal and the document being genuine. Certification is an assurance that the submitted documents are a true copy of the original. The Convention is silent as to how this certification should be effected, in terms of form or legal requirements. As a general rule it is the law of the place of enforcement that stipulates how the award should be authenticated and certified, e.g., by a notary, consular or judicial authorities of the place where the award was made. The few reported cases suggest that the enforcing courts have taken a rather liberal attitude in respect of authentication and certification (Van den Berg, *New York*, 250-258). This is evidenced by a decision of the German Federal Court (BGH 17 August 2000: the arbitration proceedings were based on an undertaking to arbitrate contained in the Treaty of Friendship between Germany and Poland so that it was impossible to submit a copy of an arbitration agreement. The respondent alleged that the copy of the award submitted was not duly certified. The Federal Court considered art. IV to be a rule establishing a standard of proof. As long as the authenticity of the award was not challenged, the non-fulfilment of the form requirements does not constitute a ground to refuse enforcement). International conventions regarding the recognition of international documents for civil procedure may also be of use (e.g. the Hague Convention Abolishing the Requirement of Legalisation of Foreign Public Documents, 5 October 1961).

5. Translation of originals. The party seeking enforcement also must produce a translation of the award and the agreement if they are in a language other than the official language of the court in which enforcement is sought. The translation must be certified by an official translator or by a diplomatic or consular authority. Courts normally accept a translation made in the country where the award was made or in the country where enforcement is sought (Van den Berg, *New York*, 258-262).

6. Time for submission of documents. The two documents may be submitted at the same time as the application for enforcement. If this is not the case it can be rectified by subsequent submission of the arbitration agreement and such 'delay' cannot be a ground to deny enforcement (OGH 17 November 1965; *Baruch Foster*).

7. No further requirements. Once the necessary documents have been supplied, the court will grant recognition and enforcement unless one or more of the grounds for refusal, listed in the Convention, are present. Permission for enforcement from the courts in the country where the award was made is not required. This was different under the 1927 Geneva Convention that required that the award had become final in the country in which the award was made.

8. Most applications are successful. Despite the simplicity, cases are from time to time reported in which the application for enforcement fails. For example, the decisions of the Corte di Cassazione, in *Lampart*, and the Bulgarian Supreme Court's decision in *National Electricity*.

9. Liberal approach. Equally, some jurisdictions take a liberal and pragmatic approach to the fulfilment of formal requirements. For example, a Geneva court recognised a Chinese award that had not been translated into French, noting that the spirit of the Convention was to reduce the obligations for the party seeking questions relating to the authenticity of the arbitration agreement or the award lay on the party opposing recognition (*R. SA v A. Ltd*).

[Grounds to refuse enforcement of foreign arbitral awards]

Article V

1. Recognition and enforcement of the award may be refused, at the request of the party against whom it is invoked, only if that party furnishes to the competent authority where the recognition and enforcement is sought, proof that:

    (a) The parties to the agreement referred to in article II were, under the law applicable to them, under some incapacity, or the said agreement is not valid under the law to which the parties have subjected it or, failing any indication thereon, under the law of the country where the award was made; or

    (b) The party against whom the award is invoked was not given proper notice of the appointment of the arbitrator or of the arbitration proceedings or was otherwise unable to present his case; or

    (c) The award deals with a difference not contemplated by or not falling within the terms of the submission to arbitration, or it contains decisions on matters beyond the scope of the submission to arbitration, provided that, if the decisions on matters submitted to arbitration can be separated from those not so submitted, that part of the award which contains decisions on matters submitted to arbitration may be recognised and enforced; or

    (d) The composition of the arbitral authority or the arbitral procedure was not in accordance with the agreement of the parties, or, failing such agreement, was not in accordance with the law of the country where the arbitration took place; or

    (e) The award has not yet become binding on the parties, or has been set aside or suspended by a competent authority of the country in which, or under the law of which, that award was made.

2. **Recognition and enforcement of an arbitral award may also be refused if the competent authority in the country where recognition and enforcement is sought finds that:**
   (a) **The subject matter of the difference is not capable of settlement by arbitration under the law of that country; or**
   (b) **The recognition or enforcement of the award would be contrary to the public policy of that country.**

1. General. The obligation on a national court to recognise and enforce arbitration awards (as provided in art. III) is subject to limited exceptions. Recognition and enforcement may be refused only if the party against whom enforcement is sought can show that one of the exclusive grounds for refusal enumerated in art. V(1) has occurred. The court may refuse enforcement ex officio if the award violates that enforcing State's public policy pursuant to art. V(2). All grounds for refusal of enforcement must be construed narrowly; they are exceptions to the general rule that foreign awards must be recognised and enforced. Consequently, the Convention sets maximum standards so that Contracting States cannot adopt legislation that adds grounds for resisting recognition and enforcement. Except for the public policy defence, the second look at the award during the enforcement stage is confined to the procedural issues listed in art. V(1). A re-examination of the merits of the award is not allowed by the Convention. Finally, it is important to point out the permissive language in arts. V(1) and V(2). A court may, but is not obliged to, refuse enforcement if one of the exceptions is satisfied. Even if one ground that would justify refusal of enforcement is proven by the resisting party, the court has a residual discretion to enforce the award (*China Nanhai Oil Joint Service*). In some countries, however, the 'may' in art. V is interpreted as a 'shall', leaving no discretion to the courts if one of the grounds to refuse enforcement exists (BGH 2 November 2000).

2. Overview of grounds. Art. V(1) grants to national courts the discretion to reject or annul an award tainted with procedural irregularity. The courts even have the discretion to partially enforce an award if the decisions on matters submitted to arbitration can be separated from those not so submitted. Art. V(1) enumerates following grounds on which enforcement may be resisted: (a) invalidity of arbitration agreement, (b) incapacity of a party to enter into an arbitration agreement, (c) violation of due process, (d) arbitration acted beyond its jurisdiction, (e) improper constitution of tribunal and serious departure from agreed procedure, and (g) the award is not yet final or binding or is subject to a setting-aside procedure.

3. Invalidity of arbitration agreement. The defence of invalidity of the arbitration agreement pursuant to art. V(1)(a) has given rise to considerable case law. Enforcement has been refused where the arbitration agreement was ambiguous, (*Eastern Mediterranean Maritime*) or not validly assigned (*IMP Group*). While it is obvious that substantive validity must be determined according to the law chosen by the parties or, in the absence of a choice, by the law of the place of arbitration, different views exist as to the relevant form requirements. There is support for the view which considers that the reference in art. V(1)(a) to 'the agreement referred to in Article II' requires that formal validity, which is often inseparably linked to the question of consent, be determined on the basis of art. II (*Harry L Reynolds*: no written form was complied with). Reliance on more favourable national form requirements is excluded where recognition is sought under the New York Convention. It can then only be relied upon where enforcement is sought under a more favourable national regime. The alternative view is that formal validity is governed by the law chosen by the parties or the law of the place of arbitration. The reference to art. II is considered a superfluous additional description of the arbitration agreement. This has the advantage that form requirements which are more lenient than art. II can be taken into account within the framework of the Convention. Art. II is only considered to be a maximum standard above which the national legislator cannot go. Therefore, if the validity of the arbitration is an issue, it might be easier to rely on national rules rather than enforcement under the Convention (*Owerri Commercial*, where enforcement was based on the Dutch regime rather than on the New York Convention). If the Convention is to be relied on, a dynamic interpretation of its provisions should be adopted.

4. Incapacity. One type of incapacity relates to arbitrations involving a State party which invokes the defence of sovereign immunity. Sovereign immunity is restricted to cases in which a State acts in its governmental capacity (acta iure imperii). It is not applicable if the State participates in commercial life (acta iure gestionis). Furthermore, a State may always waive its immunity. The Italian Supreme Court decision in *Société Arabe des Engrais Phosphates et Azotes* is arguably the most advanced position in this area and the concept of international capacity contemplated is particularly suitable for international commercial disputes. Despite this modern view State parties may still in certain parts of the world be successful in resisting enforcement by invoking the lack of capacity to enter into an arbitration agreement (a particularly unfortunate example is the Syrian case in *Fougerolle* where the Syrian Administrative Tribunal refused to enforced ICC awards as 'non-existent' because the Syrian Council of State had not advised on the arbitration clause). The capacity of a party to enter into an arbitration agreement may also be restricted by the necessity of special permissions for foreign trade transactions (BGH 23 April 1998) or the lack of authority of the person signing the arbitration agreement (Court of Cassation Dubai 25 June 1994, where the person agreeing on the arbitration clause was acting under a power of attorney which, according to the view of the court, did not cover the submission to arbitration; for an unsuccessful reliance on this ground see *Dalmine SpA*; *Union de Cooperativas Agricolas Epis Centre (France)* v *La Palentina SA (Spain)*; see also *Agrimpex*: enforcement was refused due to lack of written power of attorney to conclude the arbitration agreement).

5. Violation of due process. According to art. V(1)(b), recognition and enforcement of the award may also be refused if the party resisting enforcement furnishes proof that he 'was not given proper notice of the appointment of the arbitrator or of the arbitration proceedings or was otherwise unable to present his case'. This is a due process defence and the paragraph particularly contemplates the right to be heard. The rationale of this defence is to ensure that certain standards of fairness are observed by the arbitration tribunal. Art. V(1)(b) provides for two dimensions in relation to fairness of proceedings. First, proper notice must be given; second, each party must be able to present his case. The Convention is not specific enough as to the benchmark of fairness; apparently observance of standards set by the law chosen by the parties to govern the arbitration, or alternatively by the law at the place of arbitration, would suffice (Van den Berg, *New York*, 298). However the view that art. V(1)(b) is a genuinely international rule is also convincing. Ultimately the question of violation of due process is a matter of fact which the parties will have to prove. This ground to refuse enforcement may overlap with the international public policy defence of art. V(2)(b). This is because fairness and observance of due process are often seen as international public policy of many States. However, according to art. V(2)(b) the only relevant public policy is that of the enforcing State.

6. Violation of due process: proper notice. Proper notice always must be given. This covers lack of notice or where notice of proceedings was received after the award had been rendered. Such cases are rare. (USA: *Sesotris SAE*; Germany: BayOLG 16 March 2000, where the enforcement of a Russian award was refused because the respondent was actually only informed about the proceedings after the award was rendered as service was constructive rather than real). Short time notices do not normally violate the requirement of proper notice as they are typical in certain industry and trade sectors (Obergericht Basel, 3 June 1971). The most important issue is whether the notice was timely and appropriate (Italy: *Bauer & Grobmann*, the award was refused enforcement because one month's notice was deemed inadequate: the respondent's area had been hit by an earthquake; Hong Kong: *Guangdong New Technology*, the award was recognised despite late notice because the party was not prejudiced). This is a matter of fact but it is worth noting that several of the formal requirements will be invoked by national laws. However, often a more liberal interpretation of national law requirements is needed. In any event, not only must notice of proceedings be proper, but also other notices, such as disclosure of the names of arbitrators.

7. Violation of due process: unable to present a case. This defence has been clearly defined in a decision of *Generica*. It is clear that an arbitrator must provide a fundamentally fair hearing. The US Court of Appeals for

Seventh Circuit held in *Generica* that a fundamentally fair hearing is one that 'meets "the minimal requirements of fairness" – adequate notice, a hearing on the evidence, and an impartial decision by the arbitrator'. Standards of fairness have been discussed in other US cases such as the often cited *Parsons*. Normally reference is also given to the national law standards of impartiality and independence of the tribunal: some national laws afford parties a full opportunity (e.g. art. 18, UNCITRAL Model Law) to present their case; other laws afford a reasonable opportunity (e.g. section 33(1)(a), English Arbitration Act). Specific issues which can amount to a ground for challenge of an award include the fact that a party has not been able to participate in the taking of evidence or in discovery proceedings (*Polytek*), that a party had been denied the right to introduce certain evidence (*Iran Aircraft Industries*; in *Laminoires* the award was nevertheless enforced), or to comment on an expert's report submitted to the tribunal (*Paklito* v *Klockner*) or that the standards of adversarial proceedings adopted by the tribunal deprived a party of its fundamental right to defence (OLG Hamburg 3 April 1975; in BGH 18 January 1990 the award was recognised despite the fact that the tribunal did not consider all arguments). However, it is only required that the tribunal gives the parties the opportunity to present their case. Whether the party actually makes use of it or not, and in which way, does not generally affect the enforceability of the award (Germany: OLG Hamburg 30 June 1998; USA: *Fitzroy Engineering Ltd*; Hong Kong: *Sam Ming Forestry Economic Co,* the award was enforced even though the beneficiary did not participate in the proceedings). It is essential that there is a duty on the parties to raise an objection promptly. This implies that objection should be raised during the arbitration first if the relevant facts are known to the party objecting. Otherwise the party may be estopped from raising the objection before the enforcing court as this undermines the purpose of the New York Convention (*Sonatrach*).

8. Arbitrators have acted beyond their jurisdiction. Recognition and enforcement of the award may be refused, under art. V(1)(c), if the award deals with a difference not contemplated by or not falling within the terms of the submission to arbitration, or it contains decisions on matters beyond the scope of the submission to arbitration, provided that, if the decisions on matters submitted to arbitration can be separated from those not so submitted, that part of the award containing decisions on matters submitted to arbitration may be recognised and enforced. While the presumption is that the tribunal acted within its powers (*Sojuznefteexport*), this provision covers two different issues. First, the case where the tribunal rendered a decision outside its jurisdiction or without jurisdiction (extra petita), and secondly, where the tribunal has exceeded its jurisdiction (ultra petita). In either case it is assumed there is an arbitration agreement which in principle confers jurisdiction on the tribunal, albeit not in respect of matters decided by it. This ground may cover the non enforcement of the award or a severable part of it.

9. Arbitrators have acted beyond their jurisdiction: extra petita. This defence has rarely been successfully invoked. The defence covers cases where the tribunal has decided matters outside the jurisdiction conferred upon it by the parties. This may be the case, for example, when the tribunal awards consequential damages while the contract between the parties expressly excluded this type of damages (*Fertilizer Corporation of India*: the court found the justification of the award of damages colourful and satisfactory and confirmed the award; *Ministry of Defense and Support*). This is also the case when the tribunal awards remedies not specified in the contract despite the objection of one party (*Millicom*).

10. Arbitrators have acted beyond their jurisdiction: ultra petita. This defence has also rarely been successfully invoked; there is a strong presumption that arbitrators have not exceeded their authority. Courts have looked beyond the wording of the claims submitted to establish whether tribunals awarded more than requested. In this instance, the Convention wishes to safeguard the part of the award that has not been tainted by the ultra petita objection. In an Italian case the court held that only the part of the award that is consistent with the mandate of the tribunal is enforceable but not the remaining part of the award, which exceeded the tribunal's jurisdiction (*Simer SpA*).

11. Irregular procedure or composition of tribunal. Art. V(1)(d) introduces two grounds on which enforcement may be refused. It establishes the supremacy of party autonomy over the law of the place of arbitration and allows a national court to refuse recognition and enforcement where the composition of the arbitral authority or the arbitral procedure was not in accordance with the agreement of the parties, or, failing such agreement, was not in accordance with the law of the country where the arbitration took place. Art. V(1)(d) has rarely been invoked before courts. One notable exception is a decision of the Supreme Court of Hong Kong. The dispute was whether the composition of the tribunal was in accordance with the agreement of the parties (*China Nanhai Oil Joint Service*). The arbitrators were supposed to be on the Beijing list whereas they were actually on the Shenzhen list. The court rejected the request to refuse enforcement as the arbitrators were on CIETAC list and the parties had agreed to CIETAC arbitration. Furthermore, the court held that as the objection was not raised during the arbitration, the party was estopped from raising this ground at the enforcement stage. The fact that an arbitrator did not speak one of the languages requested by the parties was also not seen as sufficient to prevent enforcement of an award (OLG Dresden 20 October 1998). In another unsuccessful attempt to invoke this defence, a party argued that the arbitrators had acted as amiables compositeurs. The Belgian court held that this was not the case and enforced the award (*Inter-Arab Investment Guarantee Corp*). In another case, an award was refused enforcement because the proceedings were bifurcated into liability and damages phases contrary to the applicable arbitration rules (Appelationsgericht

Basel 6 September 1968). Furthermore, a number of court decisions confirm the view that if the procedure adopted by the tribunal conforms with the applicable arbitration rules or with the law governing the arbitration there can be no ground to refuse enforcement (*Industrial Risk Insurers*). Also the lack of oral hearing is not sufficient to establish refusal of enforcement (OLG Hamburg).

12. Award is not binding, or has been suspended or set aside. The final ground to refuse recognition and enforcement, under art. V(1), is in sub-para (e) where the award has not yet become binding on the parties or has been set aside or suspended by a competent authority of the country in which, or under the law of which, that award was made. Here again there are two separate reasons: the award is not yet 'binding', and the award has been set aside or suspended.

13. Award is not binding. The drafters of the Convention intentionally chose the expression 'not binding' and not the word 'final' (as was the case with the 1927 Geneva Convention). The reason was simply to avoid the problem of the party seeking enforcement having to request leave for enforcement by the courts at the place of arbitration (Van den Berg, *New York*, 333-337). However, the meaning of the term 'binding' has generated debate. The main issue is whether the term 'binding' is an autonomous term or is subject to national law determination. As the drafters of the New York Convention wanted to depart from the national characterisation envisaged by the Geneva Convention, an autonomous interpretation of 'binding' is preferred. An award can be binding notwithstanding the fact that some additional formalities are required to make it enforceable where it was made (*Resort Condominiums*). Consequently an award may not be refused enforcement because, inter alia, formal time limits imposed by the law of the place of arbitration have not yet expired, or confirmation of the award is required in court at the place of arbitration and this has not yet been given (*Fertilizer Corporation of India*), or the award needs to be deposited with the court at the place of arbitration (*Compagnie de Saint Gobain-Pont*). Furthermore, if the award is not subject to a genuine appeal on the merits to a second arbitration tribunal or court, it must be considered 'binding'. Partial awards are binding and hence enforceable.

14. Award has been suspended or set aside. If the party resisting enforcement has successfully applied for a suspension or setting aside of the award, the enforcement court may adjourn its decision pursuant to art. VI. To the extent that the New York Convention does not harmonise the rules on which challenge of awards may be effected, the local standard for annulment of awards may well differ and become an impediment to the effectiveness of arbitration. The enforcing court has discretion to enforce the award despite the fact that it was successfully challenged at the place of arbitration. Awards annulled at the place of arbitration have been enforced in the US, France and Austria (see art. VII, note 4). Pursuant to art. IX European Convention the annulment of the award in the country of origin is a ground to refuse enforcement only if the award was annulled for one of the reasons listed in art. V(1)(a)–(d) New York Convention. Accordingly, an annulment because the award contravenes the public policy of the country of origin does not hinder enforcement in another Contracting State. There is discretion exercised by courts in recognising and enforcing awards set aside at the place of arbitration. This practice is justified as a matter of art. VII and more favourable positions in national law or international conventions.

15. Violation of public policy of country of enforcement. Art. V(2) provides further grounds on which recognition and enforcement of an award may be resisted. Both grounds listed in sub-paragraphs (a) and (b) fall under the heading public policy defence. In relation to this paragraph the court may ex officio raise the issue of public policy; no request of a party is necessary. The two aspects of public policy envisaged relate to whether the subject matter of the dispute is capable of settlement by arbitration in the enforcing State (arbitrability) and whether the recognition and enforcement of the award would violate the international public policy of the enforcing State. There are as many shades of international public policy as there are national attitudes towards arbitration.

16. Violation of public policy of country of enforcement: arbitrability. A national court may refuse recognition and enforcement if the subject matter cannot be settled by arbitration on its own territory. The concept of arbitrability has expanded considerably in recent decades as a consequence of a general policy favouring arbitration (Mistelis/Brekoulakis, *Arbitrability*). Consequently, in countries with a wide concept of arbitrability, such as the US, the courts have repeatedly noted this policy (*Sonatrach*). Ultimately they exercise their discretion not to refuse enforcement of awards on grounds of non-arbitrability under the law of the US if the case has an international element (*Parsons*). There are very few cases in which enforcement of an award has been refused for lack of arbitrability of the underlying dispute (*Audi-NSU*; *BV Bureau Wijsmuller*; *Sherk Enterprises*).

17. Violation of public policy of country of enforcement: enforcement violates public policy. This ground to resist enforcement, as for all other grounds in art. V, must be construed narrowly. In fact, only violation of the enforcement State's public policy with respect to international relations (international public policy or ordre public international) is a valid defence. This defence is only available 'where the enforcement would violate the forum state's most basic notions of morality and justice' (*Parsons*). The public policy exception set out in art. V(2)(b) is an acknowledgment 'of the right of the State and its courts to exercise ultimate control over the arbitral process' (ILA). It is difficult, if not impossible, to define the concept of public policy. In the context of enforcement of foreign awards it has been just as difficult to define public policy. The English Court of Appeal in *DST* v *Rakoil* observed that 'Considerations of public policy can never be exhaustively defined, but they should be approached with extreme caution. ... It has to be shown that there is some element of illegality or that the enforcement of the award would be clearly injurious to the public good or, possibly, that enforcement would be wholly offensive to the ordinary reasonable and fully informed member of the public on whose behalf the powers of the state are exercised.' In 2000 and 2002, the International Law Association Committee on International Commercial Arbitration published a report and a resolution on public policy as a bar to the enforcement of foreign arbitration awards. The report offers a guidance for the classification of public policy grounds as procedural or substantive. Accordingly, possible procedural public policy grounds include fraud in the composition of the tribunal; breach of natural justice; lack of impartiality; lack of reasons in the award; manifest disregard of the law; manifest disregard of the facts; and annulment at place of arbitration. The report further lists as substantive public policy grounds mandatory rules/lois de police; fundamental principles of law; actions contrary to good morals; and national interests/foreign relations. This classification although it has merit, may not be universally accepted as it emerges from case law in a limited number of countries. Furthermore, public policy has by its very nature, a dynamic character, so that any classification may crystallise public policy only at a certain period of time (ILA). Widely accepted examples of violations of international public policy (Lalive, *Public Policy*) include biased arbitrators, lack of reasons in the award, serious irregularities in the arbitration procedure, allegations of illegality (*Soleimany*), corruption or fraud (*Westacre*; *European Gas Turbines*), the award of punitive damages (Japan Supreme Court 11 July 1997) and the breach of competition law (*Eco Swiss*). It is generally rare that an award is successfully refused enforcement in a State because of violation of its international public policy. The international trend emerging from courts throughout the world is to take a robust view of the application of the New York Convention. It has been largely applied to ensure that the foreign award is enforced and this seems to be consistent. Only in very limited circumstances will an award be refused enforcement. For example, the Supreme Court of Korea also gave a narrow interpretation to the public policy principle in *Adviso*. The court accepted that art. V(2) gave the competent court power to refuse enforcement of a foreign award if the award would be contrary to the public policy of that country and stated that the 'basic tenet of this provision is to protect the fundamental moral beliefs and social order of the country where recognition and enforcement is sought from being harmed'. The Supreme Court felt, however, that regard should be given to international public order as well as domestic concerns. The exception in art. V(2) must therefore be interpreted narrowly. The mere fact that the particular foreign legal rules applied in an arbitration award violated mandatory provisions of Korean law did not of itself constitute a valid reason to refuse enforcement. In a Swiss decision, the court acknowledged that the Swiss public policy defence had a more restricted application when foreign arbitral awards were being considered. It noted that 'a procedural defect in the course of the foreign arbitration does not lead necessarily to refusing enforcement even if the same defect would have resulted in the annulment of a Swiss award (with the obvious exception of the violation of fundamental principles of our legal system, which would contrast in an unbearable manner with our feeling of justice)' (Camera di Esecuzione Tessin). The Hong Kong Court of Final Appeal confirmed that there must be compelling reasons before an award can be set aside in accordance with the public policy provisions of the New York Convention. The court said in *Hebei* that 'the reasons must be so extreme that the award falls to be cursed by bell, book and candle. But the reasons must go beyond the minimum which would satisfy setting aside a domestic judgement or award.' This very much echoes the US District Court's decision of 25 June 1999 (*Seven Seas*) where it concluded that enforcement of an arbitration award could only be found contrary to public policy if 'it would violate our most basic notions of morality and justice'. Only in very extreme cases will the foreign award be set aside on public policy considerations. All these cases illustrate how the courts make a distinction between the rules they may have applied in a domestic situation and those taken into account when enforcing a foreign award, a different standard being imposed on foreign as opposed to domestic awards. This distinction is expressed in the New French Code of Civil Procedure where it permits an international arbitration award to be set aside 'if the recognition or execution is contrary to international public policy (ordre public international)' (art. 1502(5)).

[Discretion of national courts to adjourn enforcement decision pending setting aside proceedings]

Article VI

If an application for the setting aside or suspension of the award has been made to a competent authority referred to in article V (1)(e), the authority before which the award is sought to be relied upon may, if it considers it proper, adjourn the decision on the enforcement of the award and may also, on the application of the party claiming enforcement of the award, order the other party to give suitable security.

1. General. Art. VI of the Convention provides that, in the presence of an application for the setting aside or suspension of an arbitral award at the place of arbitration, the court of the place where recognition and enforcement are sought may adjourn the relevant decision. It may also, on the application of the enforcing party, order the resisting party to give suitable security. The permissive meaning of the word 'may' means that, also in this regard, the court has discretion whether or not to actually issue any such orders.

2. Practice. A case that is frequently cited to describe the interplay between art. V(1)(e) and art. VI is *Fertilizer Corporation of India*, relating to an award that had been rendered in India by an ICC tribunal. In that case the tribunal had found in favour of FCI, a State corporation. The award was challenged by the losing party (IDI) before the courts of India while the winning party moved to enforcement in the USA. The losing party, a US company, opposed the enforcement in the US arguing that the award had not yet become binding under Indian law. Alternatively, the losing party sought a stay of enforcement pending the outcome of the setting aside proceedings in India. The US District Court rejected all of IDI's arguments against enforcement. As for the binding nature of the award, the court held that the award should be considered binding for the purposes of the Convention if no further recourse is possible on the merits. In this regard the court differentiated between recourse to a court of law to set aside the award and an appeal on the merits that in some countries might be available in the absence of a waiver by the parties to that effect. The District Court, however, granted the request for stay of the enforcement proceedings pending the challenge before the courts of India and, upon request by the winning party, requested IDI to post security.

[Most favourable laws]
Article VII

1. The provisions of the present Convention shall not affect the validity of multilateral or bilateral agreements concerning the recognition and enforcement of arbitral awards entered into by the Contracting States nor deprive any interested party of any right he may have to avail himself of an arbitral award in the manner and to the extent allowed by the law or the treaties of the country where such award is sought to be relied upon.

2. The Geneva Protocol on Arbitration Clauses of 1923 and the Geneva Convention on the Execution of Foreign Arbitral Awards of 1927 shall cease to have effect between Contracting States on their becoming bound and to the extent that they become bound, by this Convention.

1. General. Art. VII states that the Convention shall not deprive any party of the more favourable provisions that might be available under (i) bilateral and multilateral treaties or (ii) the law of the country where such award is sought to be relied upon.

2. Most favourable law. 'More favourable' in this context means more 'pro-enforcement oriented'. The mandatory 'shall' of the provision implies that if there is a more favourable local law, and a party wishes to rely on it, the court should have no discretion as to whether the more favourable provision should be applied or not. The provision is helpful and necessary since, under international law, the Contracting States are bound to apply the Convention, and in the absence of this article it could have been argued that the more favourable domestic law is superseded by the international treaty. While the Convention still supersedes less favourable law, i.e. law that imposes stricter requirements on the enforcing party, art. VII opens the door for more 'arbitration friendly' statutes. An example of more favourable domestic law might be found by looking at the provisions of the UNCITRAL Model Law, or the French Court of Civil Procedure which contains a more favourable regime in relation to awards set aside in their country of origin. In art. 1502 of the French NCPC, for example, this is not recognised as a separate ground to refuse enforcement. An example of more favourable international instruments can be found in the European Arbitration Convention of 1961, which, amongst other things, restricts the number of grounds for the challenge of arbitral awards rendered abroad (art. IX of the European Convention). The application of certain provisions of a more favourable treaty or domestic law should not by itself exclude the application of the New York Convention. It should therefore be possible to apply the New York Convention at the same time as any other applicable treaty or domestic law that might be available where the different instruments apply different degrees of protection with regard to different aspects.

3. The Geneva Protocol on Arbitration Clauses of 1923 and the Geneva Convention on the Execution of Foreign Arbitral Awards. Under the auspices of the League of Nations, the ICC elaborated the Geneva Protocol of 1923, which was soon superseded by the Geneva Convention. The Protocol was limited in range and effect as it differentiated arbitration agreements and awards and provided that only agreements were to be recognised and enforced internationally whereas awards only done so in the State where the awards was made. The Geneva Convention widened the scope of the Protocol however the main problem of this second attempt was the so-called 'double exequatur' requirement which has been dealt in art. V (see art. V). With the adoption of the New York Convention and its more arbitration friendly provisions the two 'Geneva' instruments have become redundant.

4. Examples from practice. Pursuant to art. IX European Convention, the annulment of the award in the country of origin is a ground to refuse enforcement only if the award was annulled for one of the reasons listed in art. V(1)(a)–(d) New York Convention. Accordingly, an annulment because the award contravenes the public policy of the country of origin does not hinder enforcement in another Contracting State (Paulsson, *Disregarding LSAS*). French courts are by law under an obligation to enforce a foreign award even if it was set aside in the country of origin. The nullification of the award is not recognised as a ground to refuse enforcement (*Hilmarton*). Courts in Austria (*Kajo Erzeugnisse*: the Austrian Supreme Court applied the European Convention as a more favourable law) and the US (*Chromalloy*) have also recognised awards set aside at the place of arbitration. Such cases are exceptional, rather than the norm. The discretion exercised by courts in recognising and enforcing awards set aside at the place of arbitration has been welcomed by many writers and criticised by others (see more discussion in Lew/Mistelis/Kroll, *Comparative and International Commercial Arbitration*). In any event, the practice is justified as a matter of art. VII and more favourable positions in national law or international conventions.

[Signature, ratification]
Article VIII

1. This Convention shall be open until 31 December 1958 for signature on behalf of any Member of the United Nations and also on behalf of any other State which is or hereafter becomes a member of any specialised agency of the United Nations, or which is or hereafter becomes a party to the Statute of the International Court of Justice, or any other State to which an invitation has been addressed by the General Assembly of the United Nations.

2. This Convention shall be ratified and the instrument of ratification shall be deposited with the Secretary-General of the United Nations.

1. General. Art. VIII specifies which States may be signatories to the Convention. It provides that the Convention is open for signature by States that are members of the United Nations but it is also open to States that become a member of any of the specialised agencies of the United States or becomes a party to the Statute of the International Court of Justice. Other States may be invited by the General Assembly of the United Nations. It is a matter for the United Nations General Assembly to decide when and on what conditions a State may be invited to join the New York Convention. According to the art. 93(2) of the UN Charter, the General Assembly will determine conditions typically upon the recommendation of the Security Council.

2. Signature. The signing of the Convention is not by itself sufficient in order for that State to become a party to the Convention. The State must also ratify, accept or approve the Convention. The original text of the Convention with the signatures of the first States is available at <www.uncitral.org/pdf/1958NYConvention.pdf>.

3. Ratification, acceptance or approval. There is no substantive difference between ratification, acceptance and approval. They are three common methods by which a State can express its consent to be bound by a treaty. Any instrument of ratification, acceptance or approval has to be transmitted to the Convention's depositary, namely the Secretary-General of the United Nations World Bank.

4. Status of the Convention. The Convention is in force in 144 States. A wide range of legal cultures are represented and indeed all geographical regions. An up-to-date list of ratifications may be obtained by the United Nations Treaty Series and also from <www.uncitral.org>.

[Accession]
Article IX

1. This Convention shall be open for accession to all States referred to in Article VIII.

2. Accession shall be effected by the deposit of an instrument of accession with the Secretary-General of the United Nations.

1. Accession: general. States that did not take part on the negotiation of the Convention or have not been able to sign it while the Convention was open for signature, may accede to the Convention at any time. As a matter of fact more than 100 States have joined the Convention by way of accession. Accession is effected by way of deposit of the necessary instrument with the Secretary-General of the United Nations, the depositary for the Convention.

[Territorial application declaration]
Article X

1. Any State may, at the time of signature, ratification or accession, declare that this Convention shall extend to all or any of the territories for the international relations of which it is responsible. Such a declaration shall take effect when the Convention enters into force for the State concerned.

2. At any time thereafter any such extension shall be made by notification addressed to the Secretary-General of the United Nations and shall take effect as from the ninetieth day after the day of receipt by the Secretary-General of the United Nations of this notification, or as from the date of entry into force of the Convention for the State concerned, whichever is the later.

3. With respect to those territories to which this Convention is not extended at the time of signature, ratification or accession, each State concerned shall consider the possibility of taking the necessary steps in order to extend the application of this Convention to such territories, subject, where necessary for constitutional reasons, to the consent of the Governments of such territories.

1. General. Art. X provides that the Convention will apply to all territories for whose international relations a Contracting State is responsible, unless a written notice of territorial exclusion has been given to the depositary. Art. X is a standard-type clause found in many treaties, especially those pre-dating 1960 (see further *UN HFCMT,* p. 80).

2. Dependent territories. At the time the Convention was concluded, several Contracting States, most notably in Europe, possessed overseas or dependent territories. For this reason the Convention affords flexibility to a Contracting State to exclude from the application of the Convention any territories for whose international relations it has responsibility. For example, the UK acceded to the Convention on 24 September 1975 and extended the territorial application of the Convention, for the case of awards made only in the territory of another Contracting State, to the following territories on several different dates: Gibraltar (24 September 1975), Isle of Man (22 February 1979), Bermuda (14 November 1979), Cayman Islands (26 November 1980), Guernsey (19 April 1985), Jersey (28 May 2002). Similarly, upon resumption of sovereignty over Hong Kong on 1 July 1997, the Government of China extended the territorial application of the Convention to Hong Kong, Special Administrative Region of China, subject to the statement originally made by China upon accession to the Convention. On 19 July 2005, China declared that the Convention shall apply to the Macao Special Administrative Region of China, subject to the statement originally made by China upon accession to the Convention. China acceded to the Convention in 1987. On 24 April 1964, the Netherlands declared that the Convention shall apply to the Netherlands Antilles and on 10 February 1976, Denmark declared that the Convention shall apply to the Faroe Islands and Greenland.

3. Operation. If overseas, dependent, etc., territories have not been excluded from the scope of the Convention, they will be covered, by operation of art. X. (The converse arrangement, whereby such territories are excluded unless contrary notice has been given, is also current in treaty practice; see, e.g., art. 63 ECHR.) States often nonetheless adopt the practice of specifically extending the Convention to their dependent territories by way of implementing legislation.

4. The depositary of the Convention. Pursuant to art. VIII(2), the Secretary-General of the United Nations is specified as the depositary to which written notice of territorial exclusion under art. X must be submitted. Once a notice of territorial exclusion has been received it is the responsibility of the depositary to notify all Contracting States of the notice to exclude in accordance with art. XV.

5. Timing of a notice of territorial exclusion. A notice of territorial exclusion can be given at the time of ratification, acceptance or approval, or subsequently.

6. Application of the Convention upon the independence of a territory. In principle, the Convention would cease to apply upon independence of a territory for whose international relations another State was until that time responsible. However, that is not an issue regulated by the Convention, but rather by the law on State succession or specific treaties. This is a broader question of customary international law which is not settled (note that art. 16 VCSS provides that a newly independent State is not bound to maintain in force, or to become a party to, any treaty by reason of the fact that on the date of the succession the treaty was in force in the territory to which the succession relates, but this rule may not represent customary international law). Some Contracting States' former territories have since become Contracting States in their own right, including Bosnia and Herzegovina, Croatia, Mauritius, Montenegro, Serbia and Slovenia. By contrast upon resumption of sovereignty over Hong Kong on 1 July 1997, the Government of China extended the territorial application of the Convention to Hong Kong, Special Administrative Region of China, subject to the statement originally made by China upon accession to the Convention and on 19 July 2005, China declared that the Convention shall apply to the Macao Special Administrative Region of China, subject to the statement originally made by China upon accession to the Convention.

[Federal or non-unitary States]

Article XI

In the case of a federal or non-unitary State, the following provisions shall apply:
  (a) **With respect to those articles of this Convention that come within the legislative jurisdiction of the federal authority, the obligations of the federal Government shall to this extent be the same as those of Contracting States which are not federal States;**
  (b) **With respect to those articles of this Convention that come within the legislative jurisdiction of constituent States or provinces which are not, under the constitutional system of the federation, bound to take legislative action, the federal Government shall bring such articles with a favourable recommendation to the notice of the appropriate authorities of constituent States or provinces at the earliest possible moment;**
  (c) **A federal State Party to this Convention shall, at the request of any other Contracting State transmitted through the Secretary-General of the United Nations, supply a statement of the law and practice of the federation and its constituent units in regard to any particular provision of this Convention, showing the extent to which effect has been given to that provision by legislative or other action.**

1. General. In respect of federal or non-unitary States, there is a distinction made between articles of this Convention that fall within the jurisdiction of the federal authority and those that fall under the jurisdiction of constituent States or provinces of the federation. In the former case, the Convention applies to federal States in the same way as it applies to non-federal (unitary

States). A typical example is the United States, where international law is a matter of federal jurisdiction and the Convention applies to the entire territory via its incorporation in the Federal Arbitration Act. Another example is Germany where this is a matter of federal jurisdiction. In the latter case, the federal State is under a public international law obligation to bring these articles of the Convention to the attention of the appropriate authorities and to recommend that appropriate action is taken at the earliest possible moment to comply with the international obligation of the State.

2. Notifications. It is the obligation of a federal State to notify the Secretary-General of the United Nations of any information showing the extent to which effect has been given to this provision by legislative or other (e.g. administrative) action.

[Entry into force]
Article XII

1. This Convention shall come into force on the ninetieth day following the date of deposit of the third instrument of ratification or accession.

2. For each State ratifying or acceding to this Convention after the deposit of the third instrument of ratification or accession, this Convention shall enter into force on the ninetieth day after deposit by such State of its instrument of ratification or accession.

1. General. The Convention entered into force on 7 June 1959, ninety days after the deposit of the fourth instrument of ratification. The first four ratifications were by Egypt, Israel, Morocco and Syria. Several other ratification followed in 1960 and 1961 including those by Austria, Belarus, Cambodia, Finland, France, Germany, Greece, Hungary, India, Japan, Madagascar, Norway, Poland, Romania, Russian Federation (then USSR), Thailand and Ukraine.

[Denunciation]
Article XIII

1. Any Contracting State may denounce this Convention by a written notification to the Secretary-General of the United Nations. Denunciation shall take effect one year after the date of receipt of the notification by the Secretary-General.

2. Any State which has made a declaration or notification under Article X may, at any time thereafter, by notification to the Secretary-General of the United Nations, declare that this Convention shall cease to extend to the territory concerned one year after the date of the receipt of the notification by the Secretary-General.

3. This Convention shall continue to be applicable to arbitral awards in respect of which recognition or enforcement proceedings have been instituted before the denunciation takes effect.

1. General. Art. XIII provides for Contracting States' right to denounce the Convention by written notice, such denunciation to take effect one year later. Denunciation is a procedure initiated unilaterally by a State to terminate its legal engagements under a treaty.

2. The depositary of the Convention. A notice of denunciation must be submitted to the Secretary-General of the United Nations that, pursuant to art. X, is the depositary for the Convention. Once a notice of denunciation has been received it is the responsibility of the depositary to notify all signatory States of the Convention of the notice of denunciation in accordance with art. XV. At the time of writing, no notice of denunciation from a Contracting State had been received by the depositary.

3. One-year period. In treaty relations generally, a stand-still period before denunciation takes effect is designed to provide time for the denouncing Contracting State to wind up its membership implications and to allow the other Contracting States a period in which to formulate arrangements responsive to the denunciation. In addition, and more importantly, stand-still periods proceed from the premise that there should be no surprise in treaty relations. The Convention shall continue to be applicable to arbitral awards in respect of which recognition or enforcement proceedings have been instituted before the denunciation takes effect.

[Reciprocity]
Article XIV

A Contracting State shall not be entitled to avail itself of the present Convention against other Contracting States except to the extent that it is itself bound to apply the Convention.

1. General. For the Convention to be made available by a Contracting State against another Contracting State the principle of reciprocity applies. In such a case the Convention will apply to the enforcement of arbitral awards rendered both in private and public (inter-State) dispute resolution. There is no published practice as regards the application of the Convention for the enforcement of awards between States.

[Notifications]

Article XV

The Secretary-General of the United Nations shall notify the States contemplated in Article VIII of the following:
- (a) Signatures and ratifications in accordance with Article VIII;
- (b) Accessions in accordance with Article IX;
- (c) Declarations and notifications under Articles I, X, and XI;
- (d) The date upon which this Convention enters into force in accordance with Article XII;
- (e) Denunciations and notifications in accordance with Article XIII.

1. General. Art. VIII designates the Secretary-General of the United Nations as the Convention's depository. The Secretary-General receives instruments of ratification, acceptance or approval of the Convention (arts. VIII, IX, and XII) as well as amendments, denunciations (art. XIII), and various declarations and notifications (arts. I, X and XI). The Secretary-General is also charged with the transmittal of certified copies of the Convention to the Contracting States and to accede to the Convention.

[Official languages]

Article XVI

1. This Convention, of which the Chinese, English, French, Russian and Spanish texts shall be equally authentic, shall be deposited in the archives of the United Nations.

2. The Secretary-General of the United Nations shall transmit a certified copy of this Convention to the States contemplated in Article VIII.

1. General. The Convention originally had five equally authentic texts. A sixth one has been added so that the text of the convention exists in all six official languages of the United Nations (Arabic, Chinese, English, French, Russian and Spanish). The Convention is now under the auspices of the United Nations Commission on International Trade Law.

CONVENTION OF THE SETTLEMENT OF INVESTMENT DISPUTES BETWEEN STATES AND NATIONALS OF OTHER STATES (WASHINGTON/ICSID CONVENTION), 1965*

(Done in Washington, 18 March 1965)

[Preamble]

The Contracting States

Considering the need for international cooperation for economic development, and the role of private international investment therein;

Bearing in mind the possibility that from time to time disputes may arise in connection with such investment between Contracting States and nationals of other Contracting States;

Recognising that while such disputes would usually be subject to national legal processes, international methods of settlement may be appropriate in certain cases;

Attaching particular importance to the availability of facilities for international conciliation or arbitration to which Contracting States and nationals of other Contracting States may submit such disputes if they so desire;

Desiring to establish such facilities under the auspices of the International Bank for Reconstruction and Development;

Recognising that mutual consent by the parties to submit such disputes to conciliation or to arbitration through such facilities constitutes a binding agreement which requires in particular that due consideration be given to any recommendation of conciliators, and that any arbitral award be complied with; and

Declaring that no Contracting State shall by the mere fact of its ratification, acceptance or approval of this Convention and without its consent be deemed to be under any obligation to submit any particular dispute to conciliation or arbitration,

Have agreed as follows:

1. The Contracting States … have agreed as follows. The travaux préparatoires (preparatory work) of the Convention is contained in the Convention's History. The History documents negotiations attended by legal experts from 86 countries that took place in cities around the world in the years 1961 to 1965.

---

* Reproduced with permission of the International Centre for Settlement of Investment Disputes (ICSID). The text reproduced here is valid at the time of reproduction and covers developments through the summer of 2008. As amendments may from time to time be made to the text, please refer to the website <http://icsid.worldbank.org> for the latest version.

Volume 1 of the History contains a review of the formulation of the Convention and an article-by-article analysis of the successive drafts of the Convention. Volumes 2, 3 and 4 contain documents concerning the origin and formulation of the Convention. The History texts are published in English, French and Spanish. On 18 March 1965 the Executive Directors adopted a resolution approving the final text of the Convention and the Report of the Executive Directors (*History,* Vol. II, p. 1039). On 14 October 1966 the Convention entered into force. At the time of writing, there were 155 signatory States to the Convention. Of these, 143 States had deposited their instruments of ratification, acceptance or approval of the Convention to become Contracting States.

2. Considering the need for international cooperation for economic development, and the role of private international investment therein. The Convention's primary aim is the promotion of economic development. As economic development is fostered by private international investment, the Convention seeks to promote an atmosphere of mutual confidence in which such investment can flourish and thereby stimulate the flow of private international capital into those countries wishing to attract it (see the Report of the Executive Directors, paras. 9 and 10 and Paulsson, *ICSID's Achievements and Prospects*, p. 381).

3. Bearing in mind the possibility that from time to time disputes may arise in connection with such investment between Contracting States and nationals of other Contracting States. In order to attain this atmosphere of mutual confidence, the Convention offers a procedural framework for the settlement of disputes. These disputes will be settled in accordance with the Convention provided that the following requirements are met: the dispute must arise directly out of an investment; one party to the dispute must be a Contracting State while the other must be a national of another Contracting State; and the Contracting State and the national must have specifically contracted to settle the dispute under the Convention (see art. 25(1)). If these requirements are not met, the disputes may be settled in accordance with the Additional Facility, adopted by the Council in 1978. Settlements before the Additional Facility are not governed by the Convention.

4. Recognising that while such disputes would usually be subject to national legal processes, international methods of settlement may be appropriate in certain cases. Under general principles of the conflict of laws, the courts and tribunals of the host State would typically have jurisdiction over disputes between that State and a foreign investor. However, perceptions of bias, the complexity of the disputes in question and delay have lead to a reluctance on the part of investors to have their disputes settled by national courts (Schreuer, *Commentary*, p. 6). Similarly, the national courts of the investor's home State are unlikely to be an appropriate forum, with those courts often lacking territorial jurisdiction over the dispute (Schreuer, *Commentary*, p. 7). In the absence of a desirable domestic forum, and in consideration of the fact that both States and investors mutually benefit from agreeing to a method of settlement (Report of the Executive Directors, para. 10), international settlement appears to be the most viable option. However, the International Court of Justice is only accessible to States (art. 34(1) of the Statute of the International Court of Justice, accessible at <www.icj-cij.org>) and the avenue of diplomatic protection requires the investor to have exhausted all local remedies (Brownlie, *Principles*, pp. 472-473). International arbitration under the Convention preserves sovereignty to the extent that States must consent to the jurisdiction of the Convention (see art. 26) and may attach conditions to that consent. Parties to the dispute are given considerable freedom to tailor and appoint their arbitral tribunal (see art. 37(2)) and select the substantive and procedural rules to be applied to their dispute (see arts. 42 and 44).

5. Attaching particular importance to the availability of facilities for international conciliation or arbitration to which Contracting States and nationals of other Contracting States may submit such disputes if they so desire. Although the Convention offers the parties to a dispute the option of either conciliation or arbitration, in practice, most parties choose arbitration. At the time of writing, only six conciliations had been brought under the Convention and of these none have ever been made public. When compared with litigation, arbitration is perceived as a more attractive alternative for the following reasons: neutrality; efficiency; privacy and confidentiality; the ability to appoint arbitral tribunals that have expertise in the relevant (and often technically complex) fields of the disputes. Arbitration within the specific context of the Convention offers these benefits in conjunction with a set of rules and procedure, institutional support and a means of enforcement. As outlined above, the parties retain a considerable amount of autonomy in the submission of their disputes to the Centre and in the conduct of the proceedings themselves, preserving the sovereignty of States. By consenting to jurisdiction under the Convention, host States receive the added benefit of protection from other forms of foreign or international litigation and interference by the investor's home State (see arts. 26 and 27). For the foreign investors, the benefit is having direct access to an effective and enforceable international dispute resolution mechanism. This mutually beneficial environment stimulates foreign investment and economic development, which are the aims of the Convention. Schreuer notes how the Convention promotes these aims even in the absence of actual utilisation of its procedure: 'the mere availability of an effective remedy tends to affect the behaviour of parties to potential disputes' (Schreuer, *Commentary*, p. 9).

6. Desiring to establish such facilities under the auspices of the International Bank for Reconstruction and Development. Art. I(ii) of the World Bank's Articles of Agreement states that one of the purposes of the World Bank is to promote private foreign investment (accessible at <www.worldbank.org>). The Convention has a corresponding purpose and the Centre, established under the Convention, enacts this purpose while maintaining close administrative ties to the World Bank (Schreuer, *Commentary*, p. 10 and art. 6 and art. 17).

7. Recognising that mutual consent by the parties to submit such disputes to conciliation or to arbitration through such facilities constitutes a binding agreement which requires in particular that due consideration be given to any recommendation of conciliators, and that any arbitral award be complied with. The binding nature of consent to arbitration or conciliation under the Convention is evident in numerous provisions, including: when the parties have given their consent, they cannot withdraw that consent unilaterally (art. 25(1)); the parties shall cooperate in good faith with any conciliation commission in order to enable the commission to carry out its function, and shall give most serious consideration to its recommendations (art. 34(1)); if the parties fail to constitute a tribunal within ninety days after notice of registration of the request or within the period agreed by the parties, the Chairman shall appoint any arbitrators not yet appointed (art. 38); any challenge to the jurisdiction of the tribunal shall be determined by the tribunal (art. 41); if a party fails to appear or present his case, the tribunal may still render its award (art. 45(2); annulment under art. 52 is the only avenue available to challenge an award (Schreuer, *Commentary*, p. 11); the award shall be binding on the parties and shall not be subject to any appeal or to any other remedy except those provided for in the Convention. Each party shall abide by and comply with the terms of the award except to the extent that enforcement shall have been stayed pursuant to the relevant provisions of the Convention (art. 53(1)); and each Contracting State shall recognise and award rendered pursuant to the Convention as binding and enforce the pecuniary obligations imposed by that award within its territories as if it were a final judgment of a court in that State (art. 54(1)).

8. Declaring that no Contracting State shall by the mere fact of its ratification, acceptance or approval of this Convention and without its consent be deemed to be under any obligation to submit any particular dispute to conciliation or arbitration. Importantly, participation in the Convention does not, on its own, establish consent to the Centre's jurisdiction (Schreuer, *Commentary*, p. 11). Art. 25 requires that the parties to a dispute consent to the jurisdiction of the Centre in writing in respect of that dispute (see art. 25). An increasingly common way for this to happen is by way of the 'standing offer' to arbitrate under the Convention contained in bilateral investment treaties which is accepted by an investor commencing ICSID arbitration under the relevant BIT.

CHAPTER I. INTERNATIONAL CENTRE FOR SETTLEMENT OF INVESTMENT DISPUTES

Section 1. Establishment and Organisation

[The establishment of the Centre]

Article 1

(1) There is hereby established the International Centre for Settlement of Investment Disputes (hereinafter called the Centre).

(2) The purpose of the Centre shall be to provide facilities for conciliation and arbitration of investment disputes between Contracting States and nationals of other Contracting States in accordance with the provisions of this Convention.

1. General. Art. 1 establishes the Centre and provides its purpose.

2. Background. At the time of drafting the Convention it was made clear that the Centre was to be an administrative organ and not a judicial one (see *History*, Vol. II p. 103). It was decided that the Centre would only 'facilitate' conciliation and arbitration and would refrain from actually undertaking those activities itself (see *History*, Vol. II, pp. 104, 110 to 111, 129, 241 and 953; Schreuer, *Commentary*, pp. 12-13).

3. The Centre's activities. In order to facilitate conciliation and arbitration, the Centre undertakes various activities including: adopting rules and regulations; assisting with the constitution of conciliation commissions and arbitral tribunals; communicating documents and information to the parties to the dispute; drafting model clauses; maintaining a Panel of Conciliators and a Panel of Arbitrators (see art. 3); providing services and facilities for the conduct of proceedings; and screening and registering requests for conciliation/arbitration (Schreuer, *Commentary*, p. 13).

4. Research and publication. The Centre also undertakes the research and publication of information. While these additional activities were explicitly referred to in the first draft of the Convention, they were removed from the final draft (*History*, Vol. II, pp. 660, 676 to 678, 681, 687 to 688, 691, 750, 934). The Centre's publications include: the ICSID Review – Foreign Investment Law Journal; ICSID Basic Documents; List of Contracting States and Other Signatories to the Convention; Members of the Panels of Conciliators and of Arbitrators. Some of the Centre's publications are now available to download at ICSID's website: <icsid.worldbank.org>.

5. Advice on drafting laws and arbitration provisions. The Centre's Secretariat provides States with advice on drafting investment laws and arbitration laws (Schreuer, *Commentary*, p. 14). The Centre has also assisted States and foreign investors with the drafting of model BITs and the arbitration provisions of investment contracts (see the ICSID Annual Reports for the years 1998 through to 2002 accessible at <icsid.worldbank.org>).

ICSID Convention, art. 2

[The seat of the Centre]

Article 2

The Seat of the Centre shall be at the principal office of the International Bank for Reconstruction and Development (hereinafter called the Bank). The seat may be moved to another place by decision of the Administrative Council adopted by a majority of two-thirds of its members.

1. General. Art. 2 provides the seat of the Centre.

2. Principle office. The principal office of the World Bank is located at 1818 H Street, NW, Washington, DC, 20433, USA. Accordingly, this address is the seat of the Centre.

3. Movement of the Centre. At time of publication, no attempt has ever been made to move the seat of the Centre.

4. Place of the proceedings. As a default position, proceedings will be held at the seat of the Centre, although, subject to certain limitations, the parties to a dispute may decide to hold proceedings at a different location (Schreuer, *Commentary,* p. 15). It is common for proceedings to be held at the World Bank's offices in Paris located at 66, Avenue d'Iéna 75116 Paris, France. E.g., in *Helnan Hotels* v *Egypt*, the parties elected to have a hearing on the jurisdictional issues take place in the World Bank's Paris office.

5. Relationship between the Centre and the World Bank. The Centre was given a purely administrative role in order to counter potential arguments that the close relationship between the Centre and the World Bank (see note 6) might lead to potential conflicts of interest between the judicial activities of the Centre and the fiscal lending activities of the World Bank (see *History*, Vol. II, pp. 92, 108, 111, 115, 117 to 132, 248, 477 to 478, 559). In *CMS* v *Argentina* (FA), Argentina argued that as the International Finance Corporation, an affiliate of the World Bank, granted certain loans to one of the companies that was the subject of the dispute, there arose a conflict of interest for an ICSID tribunal operating under the auspices of the World Bank. The tribunal firmly rejected this argument.

6. Legal ties between the Centre and the World Bank. The Governors of the World Bank are ex officio members of the Council unless a State designates otherwise (see art. 4). The President of the World Bank will be ex officio the Chairman of the Council (see art. 5). Under the Memorandum of Administrative Arrangements entered into by the World Bank and the Centre on 13 February 1967, the World Bank provides office space, services and facilities to ICSID (see art. 6). In addition, the administrative budget of the Secretariat is fully funded by the World Bank (see art. 17).

[The structure of the Centre]

Article 3

The Centre shall have an Administrative Council and a Secretariat and shall maintain a Panel of Conciliators and a Panel of Arbitrators.

1. General. Art. 3 provides that the Council, the Secretariat and two separate Panels be established for the Centre.

2. Further details. Details about the Council are contained in arts. 4 to 8. Details about the Secretariat are contained in arts. 9 to 11. Details about the Panels are contained in arts. 12 to 16.

Section 2. The Administrative Council

[The composition of the Council]

Article 4

(1) The Administrative Council shall be composed of one representative of each Contracting State. An alternate may act as representative in case of his principal's absence from a meeting or inability to act.

(2) In the absence of a contrary designation, each governor and alternate governor of the Bank appointed by a Contracting State shall be ex officio its representative and its alternate respectively.

1. General. Art. 4 details the composition of the Council, which will have one representative from each Contracting State. An alternate representative may only act where the principal representative is absent or unable to act.

2. Overlap with the Governors of the World Bank. The Council will, unless a Contracting State makes a contrary designation, be composed of the same persons who act as the Governors of the World Bank. The persons who act as Governors of the World Bank will usually be the finance ministers of their respective Contracting States. In practice, the Council has almost always been composed of the same Governors of the World Bank that represent the Contracting States, with occasional representation from the non-Members of the World Bank (see Schreuer, *Commentary*, p. 19).

[The Chairman of the Council]

Article 5

The President of the Bank shall be *ex officio* Chairman of the Administrative Council (hereinafter called the Chairman) but shall have no vote. During his absence or inability to act and during any vacancy in the office of President of the Bank, the person for the time being acting as President shall act as Chairman of the Administrative Council.

1. General. Art. 5 provides that the President of the World Bank shall, by virtue of office, also be Chairman of the Council.

2. Powers of the Chairman. The Chairman presides over meetings of the Council but is unable to vote at such meetings. Details of the Chairman's powers are to be found in various parts of the Convention, and these powers are: to nominate to the Council candidates for the office of Secretary-General and Deputy Secretary-General (see art. 10); to designate a maximum of ten persons to the Panel of Conciliators and the same number to the Panel of Arbitrators (see art. 13); to appoint a conciliator (or conciliators) at the request of either party to a dispute in the event that the parties fail to appoint a conciliator (see art. 30); to appoint an arbitrator (or arbitrators) at the request of either party to a dispute in the event that the parties fail to appoint an arbitrator (see art 38); to appoint the three members of an ad hoc committee (see art. 52); to appoint a conciliator or an arbitrator on the resignation of a party-appointed conciliator or arbitrator (see art. 56); and to decide on a proposal to disqualify a sole conciliator or arbitrator or a majority of the conciliators or arbitrators (see art. 58) (Schreuer, *Commentary*, p. 21).

3. Appointment of an 'acting' President of the World Bank. The Articles of Agreement of the World Bank do not contain express provisions for the appointment of an 'acting President'. At the time of drafting the Convention, this discrepancy led to some debate (see Schreuer, *Commentary*, p. 20). In practice, the President of the World Bank appoints an acting President of the World Bank on an ad hoc basis if necessary.

[The role of the Council]

Article 6

(1) Without prejudice to the powers and functions vested in it by other provisions of this Convention, the Administrative Council shall
- **(a) adopt the administrative and financial regulations of the Centre;**
- **(b) adopt the rules of procedure for the institution of conciliation and arbitration proceedings;**
- **(c) adopt the rules of procedure for conciliation and arbitration proceedings (hereinafter called the Conciliation Rules and the Arbitration Rules);**
- **(d) approve arrangements with the Bank for the use of the Bank's administrative facilities and services;**
- **(e) determine the conditions of service of the Secretary-General and of any Deputy Secretary-General;**
- **(f) adopt the annual budget of revenues and expenditures of the Centre;**
- **(g) approve the annual report on the operation of the Centre.**

The decisions referred to in sub-paragraphs (a) (b) (c) and (f) above shall be adopted by a majority of two-thirds of the members of the Administrative Council.

(2) The Administrative Council may appoint such committees as it considers necessary.

(3) The Administrative Council shall also exercise such other powers and perform such other functions as it shall determine to be necessary for the implementation of the provisions of this Convention.

1. General. Art. 6 provides for the powers and functions of the Council.

2. Powers and functions of the Council. The powers and functions of the Council under art. 6 are by no means exhaustive. The Council's other powers and functions include the following: to move the seat of the Centre to another place by a decision adopted by a majority of two-thirds of the Council's members (see art. 2); to appoint such committees as it considers to be necessary (see art. 6(2)); to exercise such other powers and perform such other functions as it shall determine to be necessary for the implementation of the provisions of this Convention (see art. 6(3)); to establish, by a majority of two-thirds of its members, a procedure whereby the Chairman may seek a vote of the Council without convening a meeting of the Council (see art. 7(4)); to elect the Secretary-General and any Deputy Secretary-General by a majority of two-thirds of its members upon the nomination of the Chairman (see art. 10(1)); to adopt rules determining the proportion of the Centre's expenditure to be met by Contracting States which are not members of the World Bank (see art. 17); to decide, by a majority of two-thirds of its members, to circulate any proposed amendment to the Convention to all Contracting States for ratification, acceptance or approval (see art. 66(1)); and to invite, by a majority of two-thirds of its members, any State that is not a member of the World Bank but is a party to the Statute of the International Court of Justice to sign the Convention (see art. 67).

3. Administrative and Financial Regulations. The Council adopted the Provisional Administrative and Financial Regulations in 1967 (6 ILM 225 (1967)). These provisional regulations were replaced by the Administrative and Financial Regulations, adopted on 25 September 1967 (7 ILM 351 (1968)). The Administrative and Financial Regulations have been periodically revised, including a significant revision on 26 September 1984. The Administrative and Financial Regulations address the procedures of the Council and the organisation and functions of the Secretariat. The parties are not able to modify or derogate from regulations in the Administrative and Financial Regulations except to the extent that modification or derogation is provided for in a particular regulation (Schreuer, *Commentary,* pp. 24-25).

4. The Institution Rules. The Council adopted the Provisional Institution Rules in 1967. These provisional rules were replaced by the Rules of

Procedure for the Institution of Conciliation and Arbitration Proceedings (Institution Rules) on 25 September 1967 (7 ILM 351, 363 (1968)). The Institution Rules were revised on 26 September 1984. The Institution Rules supplement the registration of a request for conciliation or arbitration under arts. 28 and 36. The parties are not able to modify or derogate from the rules in the Institution Rules except to the extent that modification or derogation is provided for in a particular rule (Schreuer, *Commentary,* p. 25).

5. The Rules of Procedure. At the time of drafting the Convention, it was emphasised by Dr. Broches that the Rules of Procedure would be optional since they are subject to modification or exclusion by the parties (see *History,* Vol. II, pp. 76, 79, 107, 110, 249. 357, 383, 479, 481, 692, 693 to 694). This idea is echoed in the language of arts. 33 and 44 that state that those articles only apply 'except as the parties otherwise agree'. The Council adopted the Provisional Conciliation Rules and Provisional Arbitration Rules in February 1967 (6 ILM 225, 246, 260 (1967)). These provisional rules were replaced by the Conciliation Rules and Arbitration Rules on 25 September 1967 (7 ILM 351, 365, 376 (1968)). The Conciliation Rules and Arbitration Rules were revised on 26 September 1984. In accordance with art. 33 and the 'intertemporal rule' in art. 44, the old rules will continue to apply in regard to any consents to conciliation or arbitration given before the revision of the Conciliation Rules and Arbitration Rules (Schreuer, *Commentary,* p. 26).

6. Use of the Bank's facilities and services. The World Bank and the Centre entered into a Memorandum of Administrative Arrangements on 13 February 1967 under which the Centre's staffing and administrative costs (including travel, office accommodation and equipment) are met by the World Bank. In return, and only to the extent that it is received by the Centre itself, any income that the Centre generates from charging parties for the use of the Centre's facilities under art. 59 will go towards reimbursing the World Bank (see art. 17).

7. Conditions of service of the Secretary-General and Deputy Secretary-General. The Council will determine the conditions of service of the Secretary-General and the Deputy Secretary-General at the time they are elected to office (Schreuer, *Commentary,* p. 29).

8. Annual budget. The fiscal year for ICSID runs from 1 July to 30 June. Under Reg. 17 of the Administrative and Financial Regulations, the Secretary-General should submit the budget at the ICSID annual meeting for approval by the Council and may submit a supplementary budget at any time during the financial year. The financial statements of the Centre are also included in the annual report and give details of the following: the value of the assets due to the Centre from parties to arbitration proceedings; the value of the Centre's share in pooled cash and investments; the value of advances paid to the Centre by parties to arbitration proceedings; the value of investment income due to parties to arbitration proceedings; the amount of revenue and support generated by the Centre from arbitration proceedings, in-kind contributions and sale publications; the amount of expenses related to arbitration proceedings, services provided by the World Bank as in-kind contributions and administrative expenses paid to the Bank; and statements of cash flows. The total budget for the year ending 30 June 2007, excluding expenditures relating to particular proceedings since these are met by the parties, amounted to USD 23.5 million.

9. Annual report. The Secretariat of the Centre is tasked with preparing the Centre's annual report which is then approved by the Council. The annual report will usually contain, inter alia, information regarding: Contracting States and other signatories to the Convention; the number of cases administered by the Centre in that fiscal year; the details of disputes before the Centre in that fiscal year; the names and nationalities of designees appointed to the Panels during that fiscal year; the publications put forward by the Centre during that fiscal year and any developments to existing publications put forward by the Centre; conferences hosted or participated in by the Centre and any training administered by the Centre; the meetings of the Council; and the finances of the Centre.

10. Certain decisions to be taken by two-thirds majority voting. In order for the Council to adopt any of the Administrative and Financial Regulations, the Institution Rules, the Conciliation Rules or the Arbitration Rules, a two-thirds majority is necessary. Art. 7(2) is concerned with voting by the Council in general (Schreuer, *Commentary*, p. 30).

11. Exercise of 'other functions' necessary for implementing the Convention. The wording of art. 6 makes it clear that the Council has restricted power to exercise any 'other functions' as it may only exercise 'other functions' (i.e. other than those covered elsewhere in the Convention) that are necessary for the implementation of the Convention (Schreuer, *Commentary*, p. 30). In 1978, the Council adopted the Additional Facility to expand the activities of the Secretariat of the Centre by allowing it to administer proceedings that do not fall within the provisions of the Convention (Schreuer, *Commentary*, p. 31). The Additional Facility Rules explicitly state that proceedings of the Additional Facility are not governed by the Convention. As Schreuer notes, the fact that the Additional Facility operates outside the Convention makes it difficult to argue that it is 'necessary for the implementation of the provisions of this Convention' (Schreuer, *Commentary*, p. 31).

[The decisions of the Council]

Article 7

(1) The Administrative Council shall hold an annual meeting and such other meetings as may be determined by the Council, or convened by the Chairman, or convened by the Secretary-General at the request of not less than five members of the Council.

ICSID Convention, art. 7

(2) Each member of the Administrative Council shall have one vote and, except as otherwise herein provided, all matters before the Council shall be decided by a majority of the votes cast.

(3) A quorum for any meeting of the Administrative Council shall be a majority of its members.

(4) The Administrative Council may establish, by a majority of two-thirds of its members, a procedure whereby the Chairman may seek a vote of the Council without convening a meeting of the Council. The vote shall be considered valid only if the majority of the members of the Council cast their votes within the time limit fixed by the said procedure.

1. General. Art. 7 provides procedural rules for the Council's activities, such as meetings of the Council, voting in the Council, quorums of the Council and the establishment of a decision-making procedure that dispenses with the need for holding a meeting of the Council.

2. Meetings. For reasons of expediency, the meetings of the Council are held in conjunction with the annual meeting of the World Bank's Board of Governors (Reg. 1(1) Administrative and Financial Regulations). The Secretary-General is, however, able to convene a meeting at the request of a minimum of five members of the Council (art. 7(1)). The Administrative and Financial Regulations provide details of meetings, such as: the notice for meetings (Reg. 2 Administrative and Financial Regulations); the agenda for meetings (Reg. 3 Administrative and Financial Regulations); the presiding officer of meetings (Reg. 4 Administrative and Financial Regulations); and the secretary of the Council and records of proceedings (Reg. 5 Administrative and Financial Regulations).

3. Standard voting procedure. Art. 7(2) provides for a standard voting procedure by which decisions of the Council are made by simple majority of votes cast and wherein each member of the Council is allowed only one vote. Further detail on this voting procedure is provided by Reg. 7 Administrative and Financial Regulations.

4. Quorum. Under art. 7(3), more than 50% of the entire membership of the Council must be present for a meeting of the Council to be quorate.

5. Two-thirds majority voting. Certain matters under the Convention are expressly required to be decided by a two-thirds majority of the members of the Council. In the case of those decisions, the majority will be cast on the basis of the entire membership of the Council rather than on the basis of the votes cast (i.e. the standard voting procedure of art. 7(2), above). The matters required to be decided by a two-thirds majority are: moving the seat of the Centre from the principle office of the World Bank (art. 2); adopting the Administrative and Financial Regulations; the Institution Rules; the Conciliation Rules and the Arbitration Rules (art. 6 (1)); adopting the annual budget (art. 6(1)); adopting a procedure whereby the Chairman may seek a vote of the Council without convening a meeting of the Council (art. 7(4)); electing the Secretary-General and any Deputy Secretary-General (art. 10(1)); deciding on a proposed amendment of the Convention (art. 66(1)); and inviting non-members of the World Bank to sign the Convention (art. 67).

6. Voting without a meeting. There is an exceptional procedure, under Reg. 7(3) of the Administrative and Financial Regulations, to accommodate the situation where the Council wishes to take an action which should not be postponed until the next annual meeting and does not warrant the calling of a special meeting. In such a case, the Secretary-General shall transmit to each member a motion embodying the proposed action. The members then have twenty-one days in which to cast their vote. This procedure has never been used. There is a similar procedure under Reg. 7(4) of the Administrative and Financial Regulations to accommodate the situation where a two-thirds majority of the Council is required and all of the members of the Council are not present. In such cases, the Council, with the concurrence of the Chairman, may solicit the votes of the members by the same procedure outlined above. This procedure has also never been used.

7. The Administrative and Financial Regulations. Regs. 1 to 7 of the Administrative and Financial Regulations provide further detail to develop the rules contained in art. 7.

[Remuneration from the Centre]
Article 8

Members of the Administrative Council and the Chairman shall serve without remuneration from the Centre.

1. General. The members of the Council and the Chairman are not entitled to be remunerated by the Centre for holding those offices.

2. Other remuneration. Under art. 4(2), unless the States parties make a contrary designation, the members of the Council will be composed of the same persons who act as the Governors of the World Bank. The persons who act as Governors of the World Bank are usually the finance ministers of their respective States and are therefore remunerated by their respective States (Schreuer, *Commentary,* p. 36).

3. Expenses. At the time of drafting the Convention, it was emphasised that art. 8 does not prevent members of the Council or the Chairman from being provided with subsistence allowances. Accordingly, they will be reimbursed for reasonable expenses incurred while fulfilling their duties to the Centre, such as travel expenses and per diem allowances (see *History,* Vol. II, pp. 251, 319, 389, 481, 482, 715 to 716).

4. Tax exemption. Art. 24(2) provides that no tax shall be levied on any expenses paid by the Centre to the members of the Council or the Chairman.

Section 3. The Secretariat

[The composition of the Secretariat]

Article 9

The Secretariat shall consist of a Secretary-General, one or more Deputy Secretaries-General and staff.

1. General. Art. 9 provides for the composition of the Secretariat.

2. Background. At the time of drafting the Convention, Dr. Broches expressed his concern that allowing for the appointment of multiple Deputy Secretaries-General could result in overstaffing (see *History*, Vol. II, pp. 117, 718). Dr. Broches proposed that language be included in the Report of the Executive Directors (4 ILM 524 (1965)) to the effect that only one Deputy Secretary-General was likely to be needed (*History*, Vol. II, pp. 718-719, 954, 968). This language reads: 'In the interest of flexibility the Convention provides for the possibility of there being more than one Deputy Secretary-General, but the Executive Directors do not now foresee a need for more than one or two full time high officials of the Centre.'

3. The Secretariat. The ICSID annual report for the year ending 30 June 2007 shows that the Secretariat is staffed by one Secretary-General, eight Senior Counsel and Counsel, six Consultants, three Paralegals and five support staff (accessible at <icsid.worldbank.org>).

4. Former and current Secretaries-General. At the time of writing, the complete list of the names of the former and current Secretary-Generals is: Aron Broches: 2 February 1967 to 2 October 1980; Heribert Golsong: 3 October 1980 to 30 September 1983; Ibrahim F.I. Shihata: 1 October 1983 to 24 July 2000; Ko-Yung Tung: 25 July 2000 to 23 July 2003; Roberto Dañino: 24 September 2003 to 31 January 2006 (resigned); Scott White (acting Secretary-General): 1 February 2006 to 19 September 2006; Ana Palacio: 20 September 2006 to 15 April 2008 (resigned); and Nassib G. Ziadé (acting Secretary General): since 16 April 2008.

5. Former and current Deputy Secretaries-General. Antonio R. Parra was the first person elected to the office of Deputy-Secretary General. He was elected on 30 September 1999 and held the office until 30 September 2005. Nassib G. Ziadé was then elected to the office on 22 October 2007 and remains in office at the time of writing.

6. Prohibition on serving on Panels or tribunals. By virtue of a prohibition in Reg. 13 of the Administrative and Financial Regulations, the Secretary-General, the Deputy Secretary-General and the staff of the

Secretariat are not allowed to sit on the Panels or act as members of any commission or tribunal.

[The Secretary-General and the Deputy Secretary-General]
Article 10

(1) The Secretary-General and any Deputy Secretary-General shall be elected by the Administrative Council by a majority of two-thirds of its members upon nomination of the Chairman for a term of service not exceeding six years and shall be eligible for re-election. After consulting the members of the Administrative Council, the Chairman shall propose one or more candidates for each such office.

(2) The offices of Secretary-General and Deputy Secretary-General shall be incompatible with the exercise of any political function. Neither the Secretary-General nor any Deputy Secretary-General may hold any other employment or engage in any other occupation except with the approval of the Administrative Council.

(3) During the Secretary-General's absence or inability to act, and during any vacancy of the office of Secretary-General, the Deputy Secretary-General shall act as Secretary-General. If there shall be more than one Deputy Secretary-General, the Administrative Council shall determine in advance the order in which they shall act as Secretary General.

1. General. Art. 10 provides the procedure by which the Secretary-General and the Deputy Secretary-General will be elected and the terms upon which they shall hold office.

2. Chairman's role. Reg. 8 of the Administrative and Financial Regulations allows the Chairman to propose the names of one or more candidates for the office of Secretary-General or any Deputy Secretary-General. The Chairman should at the same time make proposals with respect to following: the length of the term of service; the approval for any of the candidates to hold, if elected, any other employment or engage in any other occupation; and the approval for any of the conditions of service. In practice, the Chairman has only ever proposed one candidate at a time and that candidate has invariably been elected by the Council. Whilst the term of service for the inaugural Secretary-General (elected at the Inaugural Meeting of the Council on 2 February 1967) was set at twenty months, all subsequent Secretaries-General have had their term of service fixed at six years (Schreuer, *Commentary*, p. 40).

3. Incompatibility with political functions. Art. 10(2) provides an absolute prohibition on any persons undertaking the office of Secretary-General or Deputy Secretary-General from undertaking any political function.

4. Approval required for other employment or occupation. Reg. 8(b) of the Administrative and Financial Regulations provides that the Chairman will make proposals with respect to the approval of any other employment or occupation of the nominee at the time of proposing the candidates for the office of Secretary-General and Deputy Secretary-General. Historically, all Secretaries-General have also concurrently held the office of General Counsel of the World Bank and the Deputy Secretary-General has been a senior lawyer at the Centre (Schreuer, *Commentary*, p. 41). The current Deputy Secretary-General, Nassib G. Ziadé, served as ICSID's Chief Counsel before he was elected to the office of Deputy Secretary-General on 22 October 2007.

5. Acting Secretary-General. Under Reg. 9(1) of the Administrative and Financial Regulations, if at the time of the election of a Deputy Secretary-General there is more than one Deputy Secretary-General, the Chairman has the responsibility of proposing to the Council the order in which the Deputies shall act as Secretary-General pursuant to art. 10(3). Unless the Council makes a decision to the contrary, the order will be that of seniority in office. At the time of writing there has never been a need for the Chairman to propose the order of the Deputy Secretaries-General since there has never been an occasion in which there has been more than one serving Deputy Secretary-General.

6. Absence or inability of Secretary-General and Deputy Secretaries-General. In the case of either absence, vacancy or an inability to act by both the Secretary-General and any Deputy-Secretaries General, Reg. 9(2) of the Administrative and Financial Regulations provides that senior members of the staff of the Centre may be designated to act.

[The role of the Secretary-General]

Article 11

The Secretary-General shall be the legal representative and the principal officer of the Centre and shall be responsible for its administration, including the appointment of staff, in accordance with the provisions of this Convention and the rules adopted by the Administrative Council. He shall perform the function of registrar and shall have the power to authenticate arbitral awards rendered pursuant to this Convention, and to certify copies thereof.

1. General. Art. 11 provides a non-exhaustive list of the Secretary-General's powers and functions. Other powers and functions are provided for elsewhere under the Convention, the Administrative and Financial Regulations, the Institution Rules, the Conciliation Rules and the Arbitration Rules.

2. Representational powers and functions. The Secretary-General is the Centre's representative in its external relations. Accordingly, the Secretary-General may enter into agreements on the Centre's behalf, an example of which is the Memorandum of Administrative Arrangements entered into with the World Bank in 1967 (see art. 6(1)(d), and Schreuer, *Commentary*, p. 44).

3. Internal powers and functions. The internal powers and functions of the Secretary-General include: convening a meeting at the request of a minimum of five members of the Council (pursuant to art. 7(1)); advising the Chairman regarding the Chairman's designation of persons to the Panels pursuant to art. 13(2); advising the Chairman regarding the Chairman's appointment of conciliators, arbitrators and members of ad hoc committees pursuant to arts. 30, 38, 52(3) and 56(3); advising the Chairman regarding the Chairman's disqualification of conciliators and arbitrators pursuant to art. 58; and transmitting any proposed amendments of the Convention to the Council pursuant to art. 65 (Schreuer, *Commentary*, p. 44).

4. Administrational powers and functions. The Secretary-General has responsibility for the administration of the Centre. This includes: appointing members of staff (Reg. 10 Administrative and Financial Regulations); making arrangements with the World Bank for the participation of members of the Secretariat in the Staff Retirement Plan of the World Bank as well as in other facilities and contractual arrangements established for the benefit of the staff of the Bank (Reg. 11(2) Administrative and Financial Regulations); directing the Deputy Secretaries-General (Reg. 12(1) Administrative and Financial Regulations); dismissing members of the Secretariat and imposing disciplinary measures (Reg. 12(2) Administrative and Financial Regulations); preparing and submitting the Centre's budget to the Council and executing the budget (Reg. 17 of the Administrative and Financial Regulations); and calculating any assessment on the parties to the Convention under art. 17 of the Convention and Reg. 18 of the Administrative and Financial Regulations. Under these provisions, if the Centre's expenditure cannot be met out of charges under art. 59 and other receipts, art. 17 provides that the Contracting States will meet the Centre's expenditure in proportion to each Contracting State's subscription to the World Bank. Reg. 18 of the Administrative and Financial Regulations explains how the assessment of each State's contribution should be calculated. These assessments will be calculated by the Secretary-General immediately after the adoption of the annual budget and shall promptly be communicated to all Contracting States. The assessments shall be payable as soon as they are thus communicated. The Secretary-General also has responsibility for arranging for the Centre's accounts to be audited once each year and, on the basis of this audit, submitting a financial statement to the Council for consideration at the annual meeting (Reg. 19 of the Administrative and Financial Regulations).

5. Record keeping functions. The Secretary-General is responsible for keeping a record of information on the Contracting States including the dates of signature, the dates of ratification, the dates of the Convention's entry into force and the dates of any notice of denunciation (see Reg. 20 of the Administrative and Financial Regulations). The Secretary-General also maintains a related record of information for each Contracting State, which is regularly updated and published as 'Contracting States and Measures Taken by them for the Purpose of the Convention' (ICSID/8) (available at the Centre's website at <www.worldbank.org/icsid>). This document details: a list of Contracting States and the dates the Convention entered into force for each of them; designations by Contracting States regarding constituent subdivisions or agencies under art. 25(1) and (3); notifications concerning classes of disputes considered suitable or unsuitable for submission to the Centre pursuant to art. 25(4); designations of courts or other authorities competent for the recognition and enforcement of awards rendered pursuant to art. 54(2); legislative or other measures relating to the Convention pursuant to art. 69; and exclusions of territories by Contracting States under art. 70. Additionally the Secretary-General is responsible for maintaining: a list of the members of the Panels including details of the member's address, their nationality, the terminal date of their designation, the designating authority and the member's qualifications (art. 16(3) and Reg. 21 of the Administrative and Financial Regulations); a register of requests for arbitration/conciliation with any related significant procedural developments such as any request for the supplementation, rectification, interpretation, revisions or annulment of the award, and any stay of enforcement (arts. 28 and 36 and Reg. 23 of the Administrative and Financial Regulations; and an archive pursuant to Reg. 28(1) of the Administrative and Financial Regulations containing the original texts of the requests and of all instruments and documents filed or prepared in connection with any proceeding, including the minutes of any hearing, and the original text of any report by a commission or of any award or decision by a tribunal or committee. Under Reg. 28(2) of the Administrative and Financial Regulations, the Secretary-General must provide, on the agreement of the parties to particular proceedings, certified copies of reports and awards as well as of other instruments, documents and minutes.

6. Registrar functions. The activities in connection with which the Secretary-General acts as registrar include: receiving and registering requests for conciliation and arbitration pursuant to arts. 28 and 36 of the Convention and under Rules 1, 5, 6, 7 and 8 of the Institutional Rules. The Secretary-General will, upon receiving such a request, determine whether the dispute is within the jurisdiction of the Centre; dispatching certified copies of awards to the relevant parties (art. 49 and Rule 48 of the Arbitration Rules); receiving and registering requests for a supplementary decision on, or the rectification of, an award (art. 49 and Rule 49 of the Arbitration Rules); receiving requests for the interpretation, revision and annulment of awards (arts. 50 to 52 and Rules 50 to 52 of the Arbitration Rules); and receiving and registering requests for the resubmission of a dispute after annulment (art. 52(6) and Rule 55 of the Arbitration Rules).

7. Administrative support during proceedings. During conciliation/arbitration proceedings, support is provided by the Secretary-General (along with the staff of the Secretariat). This support includes: providing a venue for conciliation and arbitration proceedings at the seat of the Centre or making arrangements and providing supervision if the proceedings are held elsewhere (arts. 62 and 63; Reg. 26 of the Administrative and Financial Regulations; Rule 13 of the Conciliation Rules; Rule 13 of the Arbitration Rules); appointing a Secretary for each commission, tribunal and committee (Reg. 25 of the Administrative and Financial Regulations); providing such other assistance as may be required in connection with all meetings of commissions, tribunals and committees, in particular in making translations and interpretations from one language to another and duplicating documents (Reg. 27 of the Administrative and Financial Regulations); and making arrangements during proceedings for hearings, minutes to be noted and draft procedural orders to be prepared (Schreuer, *Commentary*, p. 46). Pursuant to Reg. 24 of the Administrative and Financial Regulations, the Secretary-General is the official channel of written communications among the parties, the conciliation commission/arbitral tribunal/committee, and the Chairman. As Schreuer notes, there are many provisions contained in the Conciliation Rules and Arbitration Rules stipulating that notifications be transmitted by or through the Secretary-General (see Rules 1 to 6, 8 to 11, 18, 30, 33, 41, 49 to 52, 54 and 55 of the Arbitration Rules, for example; Schreuer, *Commentary*, p. 47).

8. Fees and charges. Pursuant to arts. 59 and 60 of the Convention and Rule 28 of the Arbitration Rules, the Secretary-General is responsible for determining the amount payable to the Centre for the cost of proceedings. In order to make this determination, the Secretary-General will consult with the commission or tribunal as to fees and expenses. The Secretary-General, with the Chairman's approval, will also determine the fees of conciliators/arbitrators/committee members (Schreuer, *Commentary*, p. 47).

9. Other administrative powers. The Secretary-General has the following additional administrative powers: the Secretary-General must be consulted by the conciliation commission or the arbitral tribunal on holding proceedings outside of the Centre itself (if the Centre has not made previous arrangements at that venue) (art. 63(b); Rule 13 of the Conciliation Rules; Rule 13 of the Arbitration Rules); the Secretary-General can request a prehearing conference (Rule 21 of the Arbitration Rules); the Secretary-General has various powers to discontinue proceedings such as where the parties fail to pay advances and charges (Reg. 14 of the Administrative and Financial Regulations) or where the parties agree to settle, request a discontinuance, or fail to take any steps in the proceedings (Rules 43 to 45 of the Arbitration Rules); the Secretary-General must be consulted on sessions (Rule 13 of the Conciliation Rules; Rule 13 of the Arbitration Rules); the Secretary-General must be consulted on any procedural language that is not an official language of the Centre (Rule 22 of the Conciliation Rules; Rule 21 of the Arbitration Rules); the Secretary-General must be consulted on copies of instruments (Rule 23 of the Arbitration Rules) (Schreuer, *Commentary,* p. 47).

10. Publication of information. The Secretary-General shall appropriately publish information about the operation of the Centre, including the registration of all requests for conciliation or arbitration and in due course an indication of the date and method of the termination of each proceeding. If both parties to a proceeding consent, the Secretary-General shall arrange for the publication of conciliation commission reports, arbitral awards and the minutes and records of proceedings (art. 48(5); Reg. 22 of the Conciliation Rules; Rule 33(3) of the Conciliation Rules; Rule 48(4) of the Arbitration Rules). Some of the more important publications made by the Secretariat are also listed in art. 1, note 4. They include the ICSID Review – Foreign Investment Law Journal; ICSID Basic Documents; List of Contracting States and Other Signatories to the Convention; Members of the Panels of Conciliators and of Arbitrators; and are available to download or order at <www.worldbank.org/icsid>.

11. The Additional Facility. The Secretary-General has a number of functions to perform under the Additional Facility, which was set up in 1978 in order to deal with certain proceedings outside the Convention's scope (see art. 11). These functions are regulated by the Rules Governing the Additional Facility for the Administration of Proceedings by the Secretariat of the International Centre for Settlement of Investment Disputes (Additional Facility Rules), published January 2003 and accessible at <www.worldbank.org/icsid>. Under art. 4 of the Additional Facility Rules, any agreement providing for conciliation or arbitration proceedings under the Additional Facility requires the approval of the Secretary-General.

12. Power to act as appointing authority for non-ICSID arbitration. The Secretary-General may be designated as appointing authority for disputes that do not fall under the Convention or the Additional Facility, such as in the case of agreements to arbitrate under the United Nations Commission on International Trade Law Arbitration Rules 1976 (the UNCITRAL Rules) (accessible at <www.uncitral.org>). The Secretary-General is not obliged to accept such a designation. Accordingly, it is prudent for his consent to be sought in advance by the parties at the time of drafting of the arbitration agreement. The specific circumstances in which the Secretary-General is to act should be made clear in the arbitration agreement (Schreuer, *Commentary*, pp. 48-49). It must be borne in mind that the designation of the Secretary-General as appointing authority in non-ICSID arbitration will be entirely unconnected to the application of the Convention to such a dispute and the Convention and the relevant rules and regulations will therefore not apply to the dispute, nor will the facilities or services provided by the Centre be automatically available.

Section 4. The Panels
[The Panels]
Article 12

The Panel of Conciliators and the Panel of Arbitrators shall each consist of qualified persons, designated as hereinafter provided, who are willing to serve thereon.

1. General. Art. 12 and the four articles that follow it (arts. 13 to 16) are concerned with the manner and terms of designation of the Panels that the Centre is obliged to maintain under art. 3.

2. Purpose of the Panels. The Panels are appointed to assist the parties to a dispute under the Convention in finding suitable conciliators/arbitrators. However, the parties are not obliged to appoint a member of either Panel. Pursuant to arts. 31 and 40, the parties may appoint a conciliator/arbitrator that is not a member of the Panels, provided that any such appointee has the qualities that are required of panel members under art. 14.

3. Panel members must be qualified and willing to serve. The qualifications required for panel members to serve are detailed in art. 14. Reg. 21(3) of the Administrative and Financial Regulations requires the Secretary-General to request a confirmation of the designated panel member's willingness to serve (Schreuer, *Commentary*, p. 51)

4. Chairman may select appointees from the Panels. The only time at which the Chairman may select from the Panels is when he is exercising his powers either to appoint members of the conciliation commission or the arbitral tribunal where the parties have failed to appoint within ninety days (arts. 30 and 38) or to fill a vacancy following the death or resignation of a conciliator or arbitrator (art. 56(3) of the Convention, Rule 11(2) of the Conciliation Rules and Rule 11(2) of the Arbitration Rules). Likewise, the Chairman is limited to selecting from the Panels when exercising his powers of appointment to an ad hoc committee (under art. 52(3)). As Schreuer notes, although the Chairman's powers of appointment are limited, he does enjoy the power to designate up to ten persons to each of the Panels in the first place pursuant to art. 13(2) (Schreuer, *Commentary*, p. 51)

5. Consolidated list of Panel members. In practice, the members of the Panels often overlap (Schreuer, *Commentary*, p. 51). Due to this overlap the Centre maintains a consolidated list of the members of both Panels which it publishes and updates as ICSID/10 (Members of the Panels of Conciliators and Arbitrators) (available via the Centre's website at <www.worldbank.org/icsid>)

[Designation to the Panels]
Article 13
(1) Each Contracting State may designate to each Panel four persons who may but need not be its nationals.
(2) The Chairman may designate ten persons to each Panel. The Persons so designated to a Panel shall each have a different nationality.

1. General. Art. 13 provides the number of designations that may be made to each of the Panels by each Contracting State and the Chairman.

2. Right or duty of a Contracting State? By virtue of the wording of art. 13(1), the designation of members to the Panels by States is a right and not a duty. However, in order for the Panels to effectively function, each Contracting State must exercise this right (Schreuer, *Commentary*, p. 53). Shihata and Parra note that the failure of countries to make their full designation makes the Chairman's role to appoint arbitrators in the absence of a fully constituted tribunal (under art. 38) a more difficult one (Shihata/Parra, *The Experience of ICSID*, p. 310). It is perhaps for this reason that Reg. 21 of the Administrative and Financial Regulations requires the Secretary-General to invite any State that has the right to make one or more designation to make such designations.

3. Exercise of the Contracting State's designation rights. At the time of writing, 98 States had made designations. Of the 510 designations made, 206 were made to the Panel of Arbitrators, 171 were made to the Panel of Conciliators and 133 were made to both Panels. At the time of writing, there were 155 signatory States to the Convention. Of these, 143 States had deposited their instruments of ratification, acceptance or approval of the Convention to become ICSID Contracting States. As may be surmised from a comparison between the number of Contracting States and the number of persons serving as arbitrators, about half of the Contracting States have not or have only partly made use of their right to make designations.

4. The Chairman's List. The Chairman will use his right of designation under art. 13 on the advice of the Secretary-General. He may use this right to designate to the Panels a suitable person for the needs of a particular proceeding where there is a shortage of eligible candidates on the List of Members of the Panels (Schreuer, *Commentary*, p. 513). Once designated to either of the Panels, the member designated by the Chairman will serve for six years (Schreuer, *Commentary*, p. 55). As Schreuer notes, the Chairman's right of designation has been very useful, not least because some panel members have official functions that do not allow them the necessary time to serve on a commission or tribunal (Schreuer, *Commentary*, p. 51).

5. Nationality. Contracting States are allowed to designate both nationals and non-nationals to the Panels. At the time of drafting the Convention, Dr. Broches explained that some countries might not be able at the outset to find sufficiently eminent people willing to serve on the Panels and should be allowed to draw on nationals of other States with which they have some affinity (see *History,* Vol. II, p. 970). Presently, Bahrain is an example of a State that has designated a non-national, having appointed Mr. Jan Paulsson, a French national, to the Panel of Arbitrators. However, most Panel members are nationals of the Contracting State that has designated them (Schreuer, *Commentary*, p. 55). Although art. 13 allows for the appointment of a State's nationals to the Panel of Arbitrators, this does not imply that a State's national will be appointed to a particular tribunal. In fact, art. 39 prohibits arbitrators of the same nationality as the parties (or co-nationals) from forming a majority on a tribunal. Art. 52(3) prohibits any member of an ad hoc committee that has been appointed in order to oversee an annulment request from being the same nationality as any member of the tribunal which rendered the award. Additionally, art. 52(3) prohibits any ad hoc committee member from being the same nationality as any of the original tribunal members and from being a national of the State who was the State party to the dispute or a national of the State whose national was a party to the dispute. However, there are no such limitations on the appointment of nationals (or co-nationals) to be members of a conciliation committee (Schreuer, *Commentary*, p. 55). Shihata and Parra use the term co-national to describe the situation where a tribunal member has the same nationality as one of the parties to the proceedings (Shihata/Parra, *The Experience of ICSID*, p. 311).

[The required qualities of the Panel members]
Article 14

(1) Persons designated to serve on the Panels shall be persons of high moral character and recognised competence in the fields of law, commerce, industry or finance, who may be relied upon to exercise independent judgment. Competence in the field of law shall be of particular importance in the case of persons on the Panel of Arbitrators.

(2) The Chairman, in designating persons to serve on the Panels, shall in addition pay due regard to the importance of assuring representation on the Panels of the principal legal systems of the world and of the main forms of economic activity.

1. General. Art. 14 provides a list of the qualities that the members of the Panels must have, depending on whether they were designated by the Contracting State or by the Chairman.

2. Non-lawyers serving on the Panel of Arbitrators. Although art. 14(1) does not establish a prohibition on non-lawyers serving on an arbitral tribunal, Schreuer points out that a lack of qualified layers serving on an arbitral tribunal will make the drafting of an arbitral award in accordance with art. 48 more difficult and will therefore make an annulment more likely under art. 52(1) since 'the Tribunal was not properly constituted' (see art. 52 and Schreuer, *Commentary*, p. 57).

3. Administrative and Financial Regulations. Pursuant to Reg. 21(2) of the Administrative and Financial Regulations, all designations must contain a statement of the designee's qualifications with particular reference to any competence in law, commerce, industry and finance.

4. Independent judgment. At the time of drafting the Convention, it was noted that the independence of judgment of the Panel members was decisive for the effectiveness of the ICSID machinery (*History*, Vol. II, p. 56). It was emphasised that this independence related to not only general independence of judgment, but additionally the ability to act with complete impartiality on a dispute by dispute basis (*History*, Vol. II, p. 386). Under Rule 6 of the Arbitration Rules, before or at the first session of the tribunal, each arbitrator must sign a declaration asserting his independence and disclosing all past and present business relationships with the parties and any other circumstance that might call into question that member's reliability for independent judgment (see Rule 6(2) of the Arbitration Rules).

5. Challenge to a Contracting State's designation. At the time of drafting the Convention, Dr. Broches noted that the designation of Panel members was entirely at the discretion of the States and, accordingly, no one could challenge the designation of the members (*History*, Vol. II, p. 728). Nevertheless, art. 57 allows a party to propose to a conciliation commission or an arbitral tribunal the disqualification of any of its members 'on account of any fact indicating a manifest lack of the qualities required by paragraph 1 of art. 14.

6. The Chairman's List. In addition to the requirements of art. 14(1), two further requirements are necessary in cases wherein a Panel member has been proposed by the Chairman under art. 14(2). These are that the Panels must represent the world's principal legal systems and the main forms of economic activity. At the time of drafting of the Convention, Dr. Broches explained that the need for representation of the world's principle legal systems derived from the fact that arbitration clauses sometimes refer to principles of law common to a certain group of countries (*History,* Vol. II p. 728). There was general agreement that art. 14(2) should function with a view to ensuring balanced representation on the Panels (*History,* Vol. II pp. 145, 253, 318 to 319, 386, 488, 662). Dr. Broches further explained that the expression 'the main forms of economic activity' covered such sectors of the economy as banking, industry, agriculture and the like (*History*, Vol. II, at p. 487).

7. Nationalities on the Chairman's List. At the time of writing, the following nationalities are represented on the Chairman's List: Australian, American, Beninese, Canadian, Chilean, Egyptian, French, Indian and Swiss.

[The terms of the Panel members]

Article 15

(1) Panel members shall serve for renewable periods of six years.

(2) In case of death or resignation of a member of a Panel, the authority which designated the member shall have the right to designate another person to serve for the remainder of that member's term.

(3) Panel members shall continue in office until their successors have been designated.

1. General. Art. 15 provides details about the service of Panel members.

2. Expiry of six years. After the expiry of six years, the Contracting States will be given the opportunity to either redesignate their current Panel members, or make alternative designations. In other words, a Panel member will not have his membership automatically terminated (Schreuer, *Commentary*, p. 61).

3. Continuance of service upon appointment to a commission or tribunal. Art. 56(2) states that a member of a conciliation commission or an arbitral tribunal shall continue to serve in that capacity notwithstanding that he shall have ceased to be a member of the Panels.

4. Death or resignation of a Panel member. Upon the death or resignation of a Panel member, whichever of the Contracting States or the Chairman made the original designation will designate a replacement designee. In such a circumstance, the replacement designee will only serve for the balance of the previous designee's term of office (Schreuer, *Commentary*, p. 61).

[Serving on both Panels]

Article 16

(1) A person may serve on both Panels.

(2) If a person shall have been designated to serve on the same Panel by more than one Contracting State, or by one or more Contracting States and the Chairman, he shall be deemed to have been designated by the authority which first designated him or, if one such authority is the State of which he is a national, by that State.

(3) All designations shall be notified to the Secretary-General and shall take effect from the date on which the notification is received.

1. General. Art. 16 provides for a designee to be able to serve on both the Panel of Conciliators and the Panel of Arbitrators; for the status of a designee upon designation by more than one authority; and details to whom a designation shall be notified.

2. Serving on both Panels. In practice it is very common for the same person to serve on both Panels and as such the Centre maintains a consolidated list for both Panels (see art. 12). With the exception of the greater emphasis on a legal background in the case of the Panel of Arbitrators, the qualifications and requirements for Panel members are practically the same as under art. 14(1).

3. Multiple designations. Although a designation by the Contracting State of the designee's nationality prevails over any other designation of that same person, in practice the designation of one person by several authorities is not likely. This is because, as Schreuer notes, the Contracting States and the Chairman are notified of the names of the existing Panel members (Schreuer, *Commentary*, p. 62).

4. The notification process. Pursuant to art. 16(3), designations are notified to the Secretary-General. It is the Secretary-General's duty, under Reg. 21(4) of the Administrative and Financial Regulations, to maintain a list of the members of the Panels, indicating for each member: his address; his nationality; the terminal date of the current designation; the designating authority; and his qualifications.

5. Effective date of designation. While art. 16(3) states that a designation shall take effect from the date at which the notification was received by the Secretary-General, it should be borne in mind that in the case of a designee who is to replace a current Panel member, then any such designation shall be effective from the expiry of the term of office of the previous panel member (Schreuer, *Commentary*, p. 62).

Section 5. Financing the Centre

[Financing of the Centre]

Article 17

If the expenditure of the Centre cannot be met out of charges for the use of its facilities, or out of other receipts, the excess shall be borne by Contracting States which are members of the Bank in proportion to their respective subscriptions to the capital stock of the Bank, and by Contracting States which are not members of the Bank in accordance with rules adopted by the Administrative Council.

1. General. Art. 17 provides for the expenditure of the Centre to be met from the charges for the use of the Centre's facilities and from other receipts. Any excess is to be met by the Contracting States. This is separate from the fact that the parties must bear the costs of the conciliation and arbitration proceedings that they are involved in pursuant to art. 61.

2. World Bank as underwriter. Prior to the adoption of the Convention, the Executive Directors of the World Bank gave an undertaking to provide the Centre with office accommodation free of charge as long as the Centre had its seat at the World Bank's headquarters. The Executive Directors also gave an undertaking to underwrite, within reasonable limits, the basic overhead expenditure of the Centre for a period of years to be determined after the Centre was established (see the Report of the Executive Directors, para. 17 and *History* Vol. II, pp. 953-954 and 970-971).

3. World Bank covers administrative expenditure in practice. In actual practice, the Centre's entire administrative expenditure has been covered by the World Bank. Under the Memorandum of Administrative Arrangements of 13 February 1967 between the Centre and the World Bank, the Bank agrees to bear the cost of the Centre's staff and the Centre's administrative costs (see also art. 6, note 6). As Schreuer notes, the World Bank is effectively providing a subsidy to the Centre by covering the Centre's entire overhead expenditure. Since the Contracting States are in practice not required to fund any excess expenditure, this means that the Centre can offer a relatively low cost for ICSID proceedings (Schreuer, *Commentary*, p. 66).

4. Revenue from charges for the use of the Centre and other receipts. In return for the World Bank covering its entire administrative expenditure, the Centre makes partial payment to the World Bank by remitting any revenues that it receives from the fees for lodging requests pursuant to art. 59 and Reg. 16 of the Administrative and Financial Regulations and from selling its publications. The Report and Financial Statement of 28 September 2007 shows that the values of the revenues collected from the fees for lodging requests and the sale of publications for the year ended 30 June 2007 were USD 1,887,264.00 and USD 66,816.00, respectively. The Report and Financial Statement of 28 September 2007 also shows that the value of the services provided by the World Bank to the Centre for the period 30 June 2006 to 30 June 2007 was USD 3,492,168.00. This value is comprised of staff services (including benefits) and administrative costs (such as contractual services, administrative services, communications and information technology, office accommodations and travel).

5. Provision for administrative expenditure to be met by Contracting States. If the Centre's expenditure cannot be met out of charges under art. 59 and other receipts, art. 17 provides that the Contracting States will meet the Centre's expenditure in proportion to each Contracting State's subscription to the World Bank. Reg. 18 of the Administrative and Financial Regulations provides the rules as to how the assessment of each State's contribution should be calculated. Each State that is not a member of the World Bank shall be assessed a fraction of the total assessment equal to the fraction of the budget of the International Court of Justice that that State would have to bear if that budget were divided only among the Contracting States in proportion to the then current scale of contributions applicable to the budget of the Court. The balance of the total assessment shall be divided among the Contracting States that are members of the World Bank in proportion to their respective subscription to the capital stock of the World Bank. The assessments will be calculated by the Secretary-General immediately after the adoption of the annual budget and shall promptly be communicated to all Contracting States. The assessments shall be payable as soon as they are thus communicated.

[The legal personality of the Centre]
Article 18

The Centre shall have full international legal personality. The legal capacity of the Centre shall include the capacity
    (a) to contract;
    (b) to acquire and dispose of movable and immovable property;
    (c) to institute legal proceedings.

1. General. Art. 18 provides for the Centre to be an autonomous international institution.

2. Capacity to contract. The Centre enters into contracts in its own name for the publication of its publications and periodicals (see art. 1, note 4).

3. Capacity to acquire and dispose of property. Although the Centre has the ability to acquire and dispose of property, it does not actually own any property and has no financial resources to call its own. The Centre relies on the World Bank for its staff services (including benefits) and administrative costs (such as contractual services, administrative services, communications and information technology, office accommodations and travel). In return for this assistance, the Centre provides the World Bank with the totality of its revenues collected from the fees for lodging requests and the sale of publications (see arts. 2, 66 and 17 for further discussion of the Centre's relationship with the World Bank).

4. Legally distinct from the World Bank. As the Centre has full international legal personality and is a separate legal personality to the World Bank, it follows that the treaties that cover the World Bank's status, immunities and privileges are not applicable to the Centre (Schreuer, *Commentary*, p. 67).

5. Centre is not a Specialised Agency under the UN Charter. The Centre is not classed as a Specialised Agency under the United Nations Charter and as such the Convention on the Privileges and Special Immunities of the Specialised Agencies does not apply to the Centre (Schreuer, *Commentary*, p. 67).

Section 6. Status, Immunities and Privileges

[Immunities and privileges of the Centre]

Article 19

To enable the Centre to fulfil its functions, it shall enjoy in the territories of each Contracting State the immunities and privileges set forth in this Section.

1. General. Art. 19 is an introduction for the following five articles that establish more precisely the immunities and privileges that are afforded to the Convention (see the commentary on arts. 20 to 24, below).

[Immunity of the Centre]

Article 20

The Centre, its property and assets shall enjoy immunity from all legal process, except when the Centre waives this immunity.

1. General. Art. 20 provides that the Centre is immune from suit unless it chooses to waive that immunity.

2. Claiming immunity against counterclaims. A the time of drafting the Convention, it was agreed that the Centre would not invoke its immunity in the case of counterclaims arising in cases which the Centre had instituted itself (see *History*, Vol. II pp. 724, 741, 748). The Report of the Chairman of the Legal Committee on Settlement of Investment Disputes expressly stated that the Centre should not invoke its immunity, and should exercise its power to waive the immunity of any person covered by arts. 21 and 22, in the case of counterclaims directly connected with the principle claim in proceedings instituted by the Centre or such person (*History*, Vol. II, p. 935).

3. Waiver of immunity. Regs. 32(1)(a) and 32(3)(c) of the Administrative and Financial Regulations allow the Secretary-General and the Council, respectively, to waive the immunity of the Centre but fail to elucidate the circumstances in which this will be done. See art. 21, note 4 for various other instances in which immunity may be waived.

[Immunity of persons appointed by the Centre]

Article 21

The Chairman, the members of the Administrative Council, persons acting as conciliators or arbitrators or members of a Committee appointed pursuant to paragraph (3) of Article 52, and the offices and employees of the Secretariat

(a) **shall enjoy immunity from legal process with respect to acts performed by them in the exercise of their functions, except when the Centre waives this immunity;**
(b) **not being local nationals, shall enjoy the same immunities from immigration restrictions, alien registration requirements and national service obligations, the same facilities as regards exchange restrictions and the same treatment in respect of travelling facilities as are accorded by Contracting States to the representatives, officials and employees of comparable rank of other Contracting States.**

1. General. Art. 21 provides for certain individuals connected to the Centre to enjoy various immunities and privileges.

2. Immunity from legal process. Those persons referred to in art. 21 will enjoy immunity from all legal proceedings, including criminal proceedings, providing that the proceedings relate to acts performed by those persons in the exercise of their functions for the Centre. As Schreuer notes, akin to the position under Secs. 18 and 20 of the Convention on the Privileges and Immunities of the United Nations (accessible at <www.un.org>), such persons will not benefit from immunity from legal process related to actions of a private nature that are not connected with the activities of the Centre (Schreuer, *Commentary*, p. 72).

3. Claiming immunity against counterclaims. As noted in art. 20, it has been agreed that the Centre will not invoke its immunity in the case of counterclaims arising in proceedings which the Centre has instituted.

4. Waiver of immunity. Under Regs. 32 (1) and (3) of the Administrative and Financial Regulations, the immunity of the Centre may be waived by the Secretary-General or the Council (see art. 20, note 3). The Chairman may, pursuant to Reg. 32(2) of the Administrative and Financial Regulations, waive the immunity of the Secretary-General and the Deputy Secretary-General, and also that of the members of a conciliation commission, arbitral tribunal or committee. The Council may, pursuant to Reg. 32(3) of the Administrative and Financial Regulations, waive the Chairman's immunity and that of the members of the Council and any person listed in Regs. 32(1) and (2).

[Immunity of parties and witnesses]

Article 22

The provisions of Article 21 shall apply to persons appearing in proceedings under this Convention as parties, agents, counsel, advocates, witnesses or experts; provided, however, that sub-paragraph (b) thereof shall apply only in connection with their travel to and from, and their stay at, the place where proceedings are held.

1. General. Art. 22 provides for certain individuals connected to the Centre to enjoy various immunities and privileges.

2. Purpose of immunities and privileges. The purpose of providing immunities and privileges to those individuals listed in art. 22 is to ensure the proper functioning of proceedings under the auspices of the Centre (*History*, Vol. II, p. 147).

3. Persons to whom the immunities and privileges apply. The text of art. 22 is clear as to who it will apply. Accordingly, a witness will, by virtue of the text of art. 22, automatically receive immunity (*Sempra* v *Argentina* (FA)). However, the immunities and privileges may be granted to persons other than those contemplated by the drafters of the Convention. In the case of *Libananco Holdings* v *Turkey* (DPI), the tribunal applied arts. 21 and 22 to accord immunity to the parties, their counsel and witnesses, and further held that the immunities could be extended to escrow agents.

4. Application only in connection with travel to and from, and stay at, place of proceedings. The individuals listed in art. 22 may only enjoy the same immunities from immigration restrictions, alien registration requirements and national service obligations, the same facilities as regards exchange restrictions and the same treatment in respect of travelling facilities as are accorded by Contracting States to the representatives, officials and employees of comparable rank of other Contracting States in connection with their travel to and from, and their stay at, the place where proceedings are held. Under Reg. 31 of the Administrative and Financial Regulations, the Secretary-General can ensure that these immunities and privileges are recognised by issuing certificates to the individuals listed in art. 22 indicating that they are travelling in connection with a proceeding under the Convention. The provisions of art. 22 are not always adhered to: in *Tradex* v *Albania*, the hearing had to be postponed after the United Kingdom denied visas to witnesses of Albanian nationality who were intending to give evidence.

5. Waiver of immunity. Reg. 32(2)(c) of the Administrative and Financial Regulations states that the Chairman may waive the immunity of the individuals listed in art. 22 if a recommendation for such waiver is made by the commission, tribunal or committee concerned. Under Reg. 32(3)(b) of the Administrative and Financial Regulations, the Council may waive the immunity of the individuals listed in art. 22 even if no recommendation for such a waiver is made by the commission, tribunal or committee concerned.

[Archives and official communications of the Centre]
Article 23

(1) The archives of the Centre shall be inviolable, wherever they may be.

ICSID Convention, art. 24

(2) With regard to its official communication, the Centre shall be accorded by each Contracting State treatment not less favourable than that accorded to other international organisations.

1. General. Art. 23 provides for the inviolability of the Centre and ensures the equal and favourable treatment of its official communications.

2. The archives of the Centre. Every draft of the Convention contained a provision ensuring that the archives of the Centre would remain inviolable (*History*, Vol. I, pp. 100 and 102). In 1964, it was decided that the text 'wherever they may be' should be inserted into the provision (*History*, Vol. II., pp. 743-744). Although the archives are inviolable, they are by no means confidential. Under art. 11, the Secretary-General keeps a record of information on the Contracting States and the members of the Panels, maintains a register of requests for arbitration and conciliation and archives the original text of all documents filed or prepared in connection with any proceeding and the original text of any report by a commission or of any award or decision by a tribunal or committee (see art. 11). The Secretary-General publishes this information and, if both parties proceeding consent, the Secretary-General may arrange for the publication of conciliation commission reports, arbitral awards and the minutes and records of proceedings (see art. 11, note 10 and art. 48(5); Reg. 22 of the Administrative and Financial Regulations; Rule 33(3) Conciliation Rules; Rule 48(4) Arbitration Rules). At the time of writing, there have been no known problems concerning the inviolability of the Centre's archives.

3. Official communications. While the first three drafts of the Convention accorded the Centre's official communications treatment no less favourable than that accorded to the official communications of the Contracting States, the final draft was limited to treatment no less favourable than that accorded to other international organisations (see *History*, Vol. I, p. 102). The proposal to include a reference to 'documents in transit' to art. 23(2) was opposed by a majority (*History*, Vol. II, p. 744). Art. 23(2) is relevant to issues such as priority of transmission, transmission rates and taxes and freedom from censorship (Schreuer, *Commentary*, p. 78).

[Tax exemptions]

Article 24

(1) The Centre, its assets, property and income, and its operations and transactions authorised by this Convention shall be exempt from all taxation and customs duties. The Centre shall also be exempt from liability for the collection or payment of any taxes or customs duties.

(2) Except in the case of local nationals, no tax shall be levied on or in respect of expense allowances paid by the Centre to the Chairman or members of the Administrative Council, or on or in respect of salaries,

expense allowances or other emoluments paid by the Centre to officials or employees of the Secretariat.

(3) No tax shall be levied on or in respect of fees or expense allowances received by persons acting as conciliators, or arbitrators, or members of a Committee appointed pursuant to paragraph (3) of Article 52, in proceedings under this Convention, if the sole jurisdictional basis for such tax is the location of the Centre or the place where such proceedings are conducted or the place where such fees or allowances are paid.

1. General. Art. 24 relates to taxation under the Convention of the Centre, its employees and conciliators/arbitrators/ad hoc committee members.

2. Taxation of the Centre. The text of art. 24(1) was copied from the World Bank's and International Monetary Fund's Articles of Agreement (*History*, Vol. II, p. 744) and remained virtually unchanged throughout the drafting process (*History*, Vol. I, p. 104). At the time of drafting the Convention, it was explained that the word 'transactions' refers to such matters as purchases of office equipment and the like (*History*, Vol. II, p. 389). The phrase 'its operations and transactions authorised by this Convention' refers to the fact that the Centre might want to enter into various contracts. An example of a liability for the collection or payment of any taxes or customs duties that the Centre would be exempt from is the liability for withholding taxes that is imposed upon employers by many countries (*History*, Vol. II, p. 745).

3. Taxation of the Centre's employees. All of the drafts of the Convention provided a tax exemption for persons paid by the Centre. The earlier drafts provided an exemption in respect of salaries but the later (and final) provisions restricted the exemption to taxes in respect of expense allowances paid by the Centre (*History*, Vol. I, p. 106). At the time of drafting the Convention, it was explained that art. 22(2) should be interpreted in the same sense as the corresponding provisions in the Articles of the World Bank, the International Monetary Fund, the International Development Association and the International Finance Corporation (*History*, Vol. II, pp. 391-392). Schreuer notes that the phrase 'officers or employees of the Secretariat' includes the Secretary-General and the Deputy Secretary-General (Schreuer, *Commentary*, p. 81).

4. Taxation of conciliators, arbitrators and ad hoc committee members. Every draft of the Convention contained a provision prohibiting the taxation of fees, salaries or expense allowances received by conciliators or arbitrators. Only the final draft included a reference to committee members (*History*, Vol. I, pp. 108 and 110). Art. 24(3) does not confer a tax exemption, but merely seeks to avoid taxation based solely on the location of the Centre, the place where the proceedings are held, or the place of the payment (*History*, Vol. II, pp. 147-148, 390, 652, 746 and 756). Art. 24(3) only applies to fees and expense allowances of conciliators, arbitrators and ad hoc committee members. The parties' counsel, witnesses and experts will not benefit from this provision (Schreuer, *Commentary*, p. 81).

CHAPTER II. JURISDICTION OF THE CENTRE

[Jurisdiction of the Centre]

Article 25

(1) The jurisdiction of the Centre shall extend to any legal dispute arising directly out of an investment, between a Contracting State (or any constituent subdivision or agency of a Contracting State designated to the Centre by that State) and a national of another Contracting State, which the parties to the dispute consent in writing to submit to the Centre. When the parties have given their consent, no party may withdraw its consent unilaterally.

(2) 'National of another Contracting State' means:
  (a) any natural person who had the nationality of a Contracting State other than the State party to the dispute on the date on which the parties consented to submit such dispute to conciliation or arbitration as well as on the date on which the request was registered pursuant to paragraph (3) of art. 28 or paragraph (3) of art. 36, but does not include any person who on either date also had the nationality of the Contracting State party to the dispute; and
  (b) any juridical person which had the nationality of a Contracting State other than the State party to the dispute on the date on which the parties consented to submit such dispute to conciliation or arbitration and any juridical person which had the nationality of the Contracting State party to the dispute on that date and which, because of foreign control, the parties have agreed should be treated as a national of another Contracting State for the purposes of this Convention.

(3) Consent by a constituent subdivision or agency of a Contracting State shall require the approval of that State unless that State notifies the Centre that no such approval is required.

(4) Any Contracting State may, at the time of ratification, acceptance or approval of this Convention or at any time thereafter, notify the Centre of the class or classes of disputes which it would or would not consider submitting to the jurisdiction of the Centre. The Secretary-General shall forthwith transmit such notification to all Contracting States. Such notification shall not constitute the consent required by paragraph (1).

1. General. Art. 25 defines the limits of ICSID's jurisdiction. In order for the Centre to have jurisdiction over a dispute: the dispute needs to be of a legal nature; the dispute has to arise directly out of an investment; the dispute must be between a Contracting State (or any constituent subdivision or agency of a Contracting State designated to the Centre by that State) and a national of another Contracting State; and consent to ICSID jurisdiction has to be given in writing by the parties to the dispute. The activities of the Centre encompass both conciliation and arbitration. Art. 25 does not differentiate between the two methods of dispute settlement. It is up to the parties to indicate if they wish to refer their dispute to conciliation, arbitration or to conciliation followed, in case of failure, by arbitration.

2. The existence of a dispute. A dispute may be defined as 'a disagreement on a point of law or fact, a conflict of legal views or interests between parties' (ICJ *East Timor* case and the references to prior case-law). In *Maffezini* v *Spain*, the tribunal concluded that 'there tends to be a natural sequence of events that leads to a dispute. It begins with the expression of a disagreement and the statement of a difference of views. In time these events acquire a precise legal meaning through the formulation of legal claims, their discussion and eventual rejection or lack of response by the other party. The conflict of legal views and interests will only be present in the latter stage, even though the underlying facts predate them.' The failure to respond to a demand is sufficient to establish the existence of a dispute (*AARL* v *Sri Lanka*). The mere acknowledgement of the claimant's rights without any further action is not sufficient to settle the dispute (*AGIP* v *Congo*). Another distinction that has to be made is that between 'disputes' and 'divergences'. This distinction is illustrated in the *Helnan Hotels* v *Egypt* case where the Tribunal concluded that 'although, the terms "divergence" and "dispute" both require the existence of a disagreement between the parties on specific points and their respective knowledge of such disagreement, there is an important distinction to make between them as they do not imply the same degree of animosity. Indeed, in the case of a divergence, the parties hold different views but without necessarily pursuing the difference in an active manner. On the other hand, in case of a dispute, the difference of views forms the subject of an active exchange between the parties under circumstances which indicate that the parties wish to resolve the difference, be it before a third party or otherwise. Consequently, different views of parties in respect of certain facts and situations become a "divergence" when they are mutually aware of their disagreement. It crystallises as a "dispute" as soon as one of the parties decides to have it solved, whether or not by a third party.' The Centre cannot decide on legal questions in abstracto. Purely theoretical disputes fall out of the Centre's jurisdiction (Schreuer, *Commentary*, p. 102). The claimants must establish that they have a justiciable legal interest in the dispute. Although the Convention does not place any temporal limitations on the jurisdiction of Centre, the parties' consent to the jurisdiction of the Centre may contain such limitations (see note 21).

3. Legal nature of the dispute. The Convention does not define the term 'legal dispute'. The Report of the Executive Directors clarified its meaning by pointing out that 'while conflicts of rights are within the jurisdiction of the Centre, mere conflicts of interests are not. The dispute must concern the existence or scope of a legal right or obligation, or the nature or extent of the reparation to be made for breach of a legal obligation.' In one instance, an ICSID tribunal concluded that the legal nature of a dispute resulted from the fact that it concerned legal rights and obligations under an agreement between the parties (*Alcoa Minerals* v *Jamaica*; see also *DIPENTA-LESI* v *Algeria*). Choosing conciliation as a method of dispute settlement does not necessarily imply that the dispute does not have a legal nature (Schreuer, *Commentary,* p. 109).

4. Excluded disputes. During the drafting of the Convention there were some attempts to exclude certain types of disputes, such as disputes that could affect the sovereign powers of States, had major political significances or affected or could affect vital interests, security or national policy (*History*, Vol. II, pp. 257, 466, 468, 470, 500, 501, 548, 565, 699, 700, 708, 838). However, no such limitations exist in the final version of the Convention and this has been recognised by a number of ICSID tribunals (*Amco* v *Indonesia* (I) (DA); *CSOB* v *Slovakia*). States can exclude certain types of disputes by notification to the Centre pursuant to art. 25(4). A notification under art. 25(4) is not a reservation to the Convention (Report of the Executive Directors, para. 31). Such notifications cannot be interpreted as the expression of a State's consent to jurisdiction (*SPP* v *Egypt* (DJ)) nor can they limit the State's ability to give consent in respect of a dispute falling into one of the excluded classes (Schreuer, *Commentary*, p. 343). In the event that a Contracting State has specifically consented to arbitrate a certain dispute which would otherwise have been excluded pursuant to art. 25(4), such specific consent will prevail (*History*, Vol. II, p. 824). The notifications under art. 25(4) are mere statements of intent (Schreuer, *Commentary*, p. 1273). Specific consent, once given, cannot be withdrawn by a notification under art. 25(4).

5. List of exclusions under art. 25(4). To date there have been seven notifications of exclusions pursuant to art. 25(4) (*Contracting States and Measures Taken by Them* (ICSID Document ICSID/8, available on the ICSID website at <www.worldbank.org/icsid>)). Jamaica excluded disputes 'arising directly out of an investment relating to minerals or other natural resources' (8 May 1974). Papua New Guinea consented only to disputes 'which are fundamental to the investment itself' (14 September 1978), though the impact of this is rather unclear (Schreuer, *Commentary*, p. 121). UAE excluded 'all questions pertaining to oil and to acts of sovereignty' (8 May 1980). Turkey consented only to disputes regarding investments that 'obtained necessary permission, in conformity with the relevant legislation of the Republic of Turkey on foreign capital, and that have effectively started' and excluded all disputes relating to 'the property and real rights upon the real estates' (3 March 1989); which has been given effect to in, e.g., the 2006 France–Turkey BIT (see Protocol, ad art. 8). China gave its consent only for disputes arising from expropriations and nationalisations (7 January 1993). Guatemala excluded 'any dispute that arises from a compensation claim against the State for damages due to armed conflicts or civil disturbances' (16 January 2003). Ecuador excluded from the Centre's jurisdiction disputes resulting from an investment relating to 'the exploitation of natural resources, such as oil, gas, minerals or others' (4 December 2007).

6. The directness requirement. The Centre only has jurisdiction over disputes that arise directly out of an investment. The requirement of directness does not relate to the nature of the investment itself but rather to the relationship between the dispute and the investment. Jurisdiction can exist even in respect of indirect investments as long as the dispute arises directly out of such investments (*Fedax* v *Venezuela* (DJ)). Directness is an objective criterion for establishing the Centre's jurisdiction. Therefore, even if parties agree on the fact that a certain dispute arose directly out of an investment, a tribunal, or commission, is entitled to satisfy itself as to its own jurisdiction (Schreuer, *Commentary*, p. 114). Investments can comprise complex operations and involve various transactions expressed in diverse agreements which are not always directly linked to the investment. Tribunals have taken the view that such complex operations should not be regarded narrowly, and that the term 'investment' should be interpreted to include the overall operation (*Holiday Inns* v *Morocco*; *Fedax* v *Venezuela* (DJ); *CSOB* v *Slovakia* (DJ)). Art. 2(b) of the Additional Facility Rules provides for an alternative dispute settlement mechanism which is available in relation to disputes which do not arise directly from an investment. This provision encompasses transactions that do not qualify as investments. Ordinary commercial disputes are, however, excluded.

7. The concept of investment. The term 'investment' is not defined in the Convention. It is left to the parties to determine which types of investments they wish to bring to ICSID (*Joy Mining* v *Egypt*, (DJ)). On one view, the fact that the Convention does not offer any definition should not be interpreted as allowing parties to define any operation as an 'investment' (*Joy Mining* v *Egypt* (DA)). That view suggests that the requirement of an investment is constitutional in nature under the Convention, and has an objective meaning. Investment treaties typically define the term 'investment' (see, e.g., art. 1 of the UK model BIT; art. 1139 NAFTA). The term 'investment' may also be defined by the law of the host State (see, e.g., art. 1 of the Albanian Law on Foreign Investments). In *Zhinvali* v *Georgia*, the tribunal's jurisdiction was based only on Georgian investment law. In that case, the tribunal had to decide if 'development costs' could be considered investments. The tribunal declined jurisdiction, concluding that there was no specific agreement between parties to treat development costs as investments and that, under Georgian law, development costs could not be regarded as investments (see also *Mihaly* v *Sri Lanka*). An investor and a host State may also specifically agree that a particular operation will constitute an investment (1993 ICSID Model Clause 3). ICSID tribunals have identified certain features that an activity must have in order to qualify as an investment for the purposes of art. 25: a certain duration; a regularity of profit and return; an element of risk; substantial commitment; and significant contribution to the development of the host State (*Salini* v *Morocco* (DJ), *Joy Mining* v *Egypt*, (DA); see also *Biwater* v *Tanzania*; *MHS* v *Malaysia*). It is clear that, even if one accepts these criteria as relevant, their presence has to be evaluated in the entire circumstances of a given case. That is not a tick-box exercise. Nor are these criteria exhaustive in any way. In any event, the terms in which the parties agreed that a given investment should be subject to the Centre's jurisdiction are of primordial importance. Going beyond, or against, the parties' agreement in that regard must be highly exceptional – if possible at all. In *LESI-DIPENTA* v *Algeria* the tribunal concluded that it is not necessary for an investment to be made in the host State so long as it was made in the context of a project which was to be realised in the host State. Many BITs specifically limit their application, including consent to the jurisdiction of the Centre, to investments made 'in the territory' of the host State (*SGS* v *Philippines*; *SGS* v *Pakistan*).

8. Contracting State. The Centre only has jurisdiction if both the host State and the investor's State of nationality are Contracting States. The critical date for assessing the fulfilment of this jurisdictional requirement is the date of the institution of ICSID proceedings. This requirement is fulfilled if consent to jurisdiction is given prior to the ratification of the Convention but the Convention enters into force before the institution of proceedings (*Holiday Inns* v *Morocco*; see also *Amco* v *Indonesia* (I) (DA); *LETCO* v *Liberia*; *Cable TV* v *St. Kitts and Nevis*). Parties to a dispute may have recourse to the Additional Facility if either, but not both, the host State or the investor's State of nationality are Contracting States. However, an agreement to submit a dispute to conciliation or arbitration under the Additional Facility is subject to the approval of the Secretary-General. If neither the host State nor the investor's State of nationality are Contracting States, the only way in which the parties can have recourse to ICSID arbitration is on an ad hoc basis (1993 ICSID Model Clause 22).

9. Constituent subdivisions or agencies of a Contracting State. It is not uncommon for investment agreements to be entered into by an entity that exercises public functions but has legally distinct personality from the Government. Similarly, provinces and authorised sub-regions of the host State may enter into such agreements. The extension of party status was designed to cover a wide range of entities. The expression 'constituent subdivision' covers any territorial entity beneath the level of the State that has full international personality (Schreuer, *Commentary*, p. 151). The term 'agency' should be interpreted in a functional way so that the relevant requirement should be performance of public/governmental functions (Schreuer, *Commentary,* p. 151).

10. State designation requirement. In addition to satisfying these objective criteria, there must also be designation to the Centre (*Cable TV* v *St Kitts* *and Nevis*; for a list of designations see *Contracting States and Measures Taken by Them* (ICSID Document ICSID/8, available on the ICSID website at <www.worldbank.org/icsid>)). The Convention does not specify the form or manner of such designation. Express notifications are advisable (Schreuer, *Commentary*, p. 154). Clear designation in the national legislation of the host State or in a BIT should be sufficient. Designation in an agreement with the investor will not suffice, although notification to the Centre of an agreement containing such a designation will be sufficient (Schreuer, *Commentary*, p. 153). The institution of proceedings may be regarded as the critical date for designation; however, there may be exceptional circumstances that will allow designation even after the commencement of proceedings (*Klöckner* v *Cameroon*, (I) (DA)). The Convention is silent on whether or not designations, once given, may be withdrawn. It would appear on general principles that if consent is already given by the constituent subdivision or agency, unilateral withdrawal of designation should not be possible (Schreuer, *Commentary*, p. 158). Finally, it should be noted that the host State's failure to designate a constituent subdivision or agency pursuant art. 25(3) does not deprive an investor of the right to bring a claim against the host State in relation to an investment contract entered into between an investor and a constituent subdivision or agency of the State, provided that the State has consented to the jurisdiction of the Centre (*Vivendi* v *Argentina* (I); and see more generally *Maffezini* v *Spain* and *Salini* v *Morocco* regarding rules of attribution as a matter of international responsibility).

11. National of another Contracting State. The Centre has jurisdiction only over disputes between a State and a national of another Contracting State. Disputes between States or between private investors are excluded (*Maffezini* v *Spain* (DJ)). Multipartite arbitrations are possible despite the usage of the singular form in the expression 'a national of another Contracting State'. Tribunals determined that the concept of 'national' is not limited to privately owned companies and does not depend on whether the company is partially or even fully controlled by the State (*CSOB* v *Slovakia*). The relevant test is whether the company in question is acting as an agent for the Government or is discharging a governmental function (Broches, *The Convention*, pp. 345, 354). Under the Convention, only investors that are nationals of a Contracting State have the right to bring a claim before the Centre. The critical date for becoming a Contracting State is the time of the institution of proceedings and not the date of consent to the Centre's jurisdiction (*Holiday Inns* v *Morocco*). At the time of the institution of proceedings, the identification of the State of nationality becomes mandatory and a simple statement that 'the investor is a national of another Contracting State' would no longer suffice (Rule 2(1)(d) of the Institutional Rules).

12. Natural persons. The Convention establishes both a positive and a negative requirement as to the nationality of natural persons. The positive requirement is that only natural persons who are nationals of a Contracting State may commence proceedings. The negative requirement is the non-possession of the host State's nationality: this is an absolute bar to commencing ICSID proceedings. The proposition that the rule in art. 25(2)(a) is to be read subject to customary international law rules on (inter alia) involuntary acquisition of nationality and effectiveness of nationality finds some, but limited, support in the negotiating history of the Convention and the jurisprudence of ICSID tribunals. Generally, those customary international law rules were developed in the context of diplomatic protection, and though it will readily be admitted that the Convention neither was built nor operates in a vacuum, the appropriateness of any customary international law rule has to be demonstrated in a specific manner. There is some support for disregarding involuntary acquisitions/conferrals of nationality (*Champion Trading* v *Egypt* (DJ)). As for effective nationality, the position is that the parties' arbitration agreement will be the starting, and in most cases the finishing, point (cf. *Siag* v *Egypt* (DJ)); *Micula and ors* v *Romania* (DJ)).

13. Natural persons: determination of nationality. The determination of nationality is made in accordance with the national law of the granting State. Special circumstances (fraud and patent error) may allow tribunals to go behind national law (*Soufraki* v *Egypt* (DJ)). There was broad consensus during the drafting of the Convention that a certificate of nationality should constitute only prima facie evidence of nationality (*History*, Vol. II, pp. 256, 394-395, 504, 508, 543, 582; Schreuer, *Commentary*, p. 268). A contractual clause inserted in the investment agreement concerning the investor's nationality creates a strong presumption in favour of the existence of the stipulated nationality (1993 ICSID Model Clause 6) but cannot create a nationality that does not exist (Schreuer, *Commentary*, p. 269). A company may not avail itself of the nationalities of both its parent and subsidiary companies. In *Banro* v *Congo*, the tribunal held that Banro was not free to submit to the Congo both diplomatic intervention on the part of the Canadian Government (availing itself of the nationality of its parent company), and an arbitration proceeding before an ICSID tribunal by availing itself of the American nationality of one of its subsidiaries.

14. Natural persons: critical dates. Both nationality requirements must be met at two distinct dates: the date of consent to arbitration and the date of registration of the Request for Arbitration (*Siag* v *Egypt* (DJ)). The Convention does not in terms require continuous nationality, and continuity of nationality between those dates will in any event normally be presumed.

15. Juridical persons. Juridical persons must have the nationality of another Contracting State. However, art. 25(2)(b) provides an exception, in cases of 'foreign control'. This curb on nationality principles is of significant importance in the light of the ICJ decision in *Barcelona Traction* and, more recently, *Diallo*. (It is also replicated in many BITs.) The concept of 'juridical persons' is not defined by the Convention. The entity in question must have legal personality under the legal system of the State whose nationality is claimed. Associations which lack legal personality will not qualify as juridical persons under art. 25 (*LESI-DIPENTA* v *Algeria*).

16. Juridical persons: determination of nationality. Domestic laws require either incorporation or a 'siège social' in the country. The question has arisen, based on the 'control' language in the Convention, whether nationality by incorporation may be disregarded when the entity in question is owned/controlled by nationals of the host State. It has been answered in the negative (*Tokios Tokelès* v *Ukraine*, (DJ)). ICSID tribunals have adopted the test of incorporation or seat in determining the nationality of a juridical person (*Kaiser Bauxite* v *Jamaica*, *Amco* v *Indonesia* (I) (DA)). The question of nationality may be also clarified through an agreement between parties (1993 ICSID Model Clause 6). Such an agreement, though advisable, cannot create a nationality that does not exist (*MINE* v *Guinea* (FA)).

17. Juridical persons: critical date. The nationality requirements for juridical persons have to be fulfilled only on the date of consent to arbitration. Any change in the juridical person's nationality after the date of consent is irrelevant for the purposes of establishing the Centre's jurisdiction. The question of continuous nationality (see *Loewen Group* v *US*) does not arise under the ICSID Convention per se.

18. Juridical persons under foreign control. If a juridical person has the nationality of the host State, art. 25(2)(b) allows the parties to agree to treat it as a national of another Contracting Party on the basis of foreign control. The Convention does not contain any provision regarding the form of the agreement. Such an agreement may be explicit (1993 ICSID Model Clause 7). The identification of the nationality of the controlling entity in the arbitration agreement is not necessary (*Amco* v *Indonesia* (I) (DJ); *SOABI* v *Senegal*; see also Rule 2 of the Institutional Rules). On implicit agreements regarding foreign control see *Holiday Inns* v *Morocco*; *Amco* v *Indonesia* (I) (DJ); *LETCO* v *Liberia*. The nationality of the controlling persons or entity has to be that of another Contracting State (*SOABI* v *Senegal*). Acceptance of foreign-controlled entities may also be the result of specific provisions inserted either in the national legislation of the host State (Investment Code of Zaire, 1986; Uganda Investment Code, 1991) or in a BIT. An agreement on foreign control creates only a presumption that foreign control exists. This presumption is not absolute; it may be rebutted if foreign control manifestly does not actually exist (*Vacuum Salt* v *Ghana*). Some BITs also allow an entity of a third State to be treated as a national of another Contracting Party because of foreign control (see, e.g., the Switzerland–Argentina and Sweden–Romania BITs).

19. Juridical persons under foreign control: indirect foreign control. It is not unusual for international groups of companies to have complex internal structures including chains of subsidiaries. A question arises as to whether such indirect foreign control is sufficient for the application of art. 25(2)(b). The practice on this issue is not uniform. In *Amco* v *Indonesia* (I), the tribunal refused to look beyond the first level of control. On the other hand, in *SOABI* v *Senegal*, the company in question was controlled by a Panamanian company which was itself under the control of Belgian nationals. Panama was not a Contracting State, so the question of indirect control was fundamental. The tribunal accepted that SOABI was in fact controlled by Belgian nationals and thus upheld its jurisdiction (see also Schreuer, *Commentary*, p. 318). Despite this different approach, the tribunal's reasoning led to a decision that it had jurisdiction over the dispute.

20. Juridical persons under foreign control: the meaning of 'control'. The Convention left the term undefined in order to give parties latitude in that regard (*Vacuum Salt* v *Ghana*; *Aucoven* v *Venezuela*). During the drafting of the Convention it was noted that a mere majority holding of shares would not necessarily be decisive (*History*, Vol. II, pp. 359, 360, 396, 447, 448, 538); but see *Aguas del Tunari* v *Bolivia*. On this basis, and on the relevant case-law (*Amco* v *Indonesia*; *Klöckner* v *Cameroon*; *SOABI* v *Senegal*; *LETCO* v *Liberia*; *Vacuum Salt* v *Ghana*), it may be concluded that determination of control is to take account of several factors, such as voting rights and management control (Schreuer, *Commentary*, pp. 318-323). The analysis is in every case a mixed one, of fact and law, where the law relevant is that of the State of incorporation or 'siège social' (lex societatis). It should also be noted that 'control', here, does not simply mean absolute control. It may be accepted that in a specific case there may be more than one controlling entity. In national legislation, the term 'control' is often defined to mean a majority equity interest (*Mozambique Law of Investment* 1993; for a more flexible interpretation see Tanzanian 1990 National Investment Act). BIT provisions also generally provide a narrower definition than that permitted by the Convention (UK model BIT – majority share ownership; see also Schreuer, *Commentary*, p. 323).

21. Juridical persons under foreign control: critical dates for foreign control. It is undisputed that foreign control must exist at the time of consent, but this may not be sufficient. ICSID tribunals have focused on foreign control at the time of consent but have also been concerned with subsequent changes (*Amco* v *Indonesia* (I) (DJ); *SOABI* v *Senegal*). Some BITs provide that foreign control must also exist 'before the dispute arises' (UK model BIT).

22. Parties' consent. Participation in the Convention does not impose any obligation on Contracting States to consent to arbitration or conciliation.

23. Parties' consent: form of consent. In practice, consent may be expressed in three different ways. The first method is by a clause inserted in an agreement with a foreign investor (*CDC* v *Seychelles*, *MINE* v *Guinea*). Such consent can relate to future disputes (*Holiday Inns* v *Morocco*) or to a dispute that has already arisen (*MINE* v *Guinea, Compania des Desarollo de Santa Elena SA* v *Costa Rica*). The Report of the Executive Directors states that both forms are covered by the Convention (para. 24 of the Report). A second method is a special arbitration provision in the national law of the host State (*SPP* v *Egypt* (DJ), *Tradex* v *Albania* (DJ); *Zhinvali* v *Georgia*; see also *Amco* v *Indonesia* (I) (DJ). The legal provision containing the host State's offer to arbitration must be in force at the time of its acceptance by the investor (*Tradex* v *Albania* (DJ)). A third method is an arbitration provision in BITs or multilateral treaties or regional treaties (art. 1120 NAFTA; art. 26 ECT). In these cases, the arbitration provision represents only an offer of the host State to arbitration. In order to perfect the consent, the investor must accept the State's offer. The investor may accept the offer by simply instituting arbitration (*Generation Ukraine* v *Ukraine*). A written communication to the State as early as possible is advisable mainly because it offers comfort to the investor that the host State will not seek to withdraw its offer. (Nevertheless, questions arise as to whether an offer may be unilaterally withdrawn by giving notice of denunciation of the Convention; see art. 71.)

24. Parties' consent: scope of consent. Particular problems may arise in defining the scope of the consent to arbitration when that consent is effected through the host State's legislation or through a BIT. Some offers to consent to arbitration in national laws are very narrow. For example, the 1993 Albanian Law on Foreign Investments limits the consent to disputes arising out of or relating to expropriation (*Tradex* v *Albania* (DJ)). The *Tradex* tribunal held, however, that it had jurisdiction to determine whether expropriation had occurred. The same is true of some BITs, (e.g. the United Kingdom–USSR BIT), though the general tendency is to provide very broad consent encompassing 'all disputes concerning investments'. The decisions of tribunals interpreting the scope of these broad types of clauses is divided. Most tribunals have concluded that the phrase 'all disputes concerning investments' extends not only to a claim for violation of the applicable BIT but also to a claim based on an investment contract (*Salini* v *Morocco* (DJ); *Vivendi* v *Argentina* (I) (DA); *SGS* v *Philippines*). In *SGS* v *Pakistan*, the tribunal declined jurisdiction concluding that the wording 'disputes with respect to investments' contained in art. 9 of the Switzerland–Pakistan BIT does not necessarily imply that 'both BIT and purely contractual claims are intended to be covered by the Contracting Parties' (*SGS* v *Pakistan*, (DJ)). The question will be affected by the existence of an umbrella clause in a BIT (see also Schreuer, *Consent to Arbitration*, pp. 10-15), if it is accepted that contractual breaches in such cases will also constitute treaty violations (see Dolzer/Stevens, *Bilateral Investment Treaties*; *MTD* v *Chile* (DA); see also *Noble Ventures* v *Romania* (FA); *CMS* v *Argentina* (FA)). At any rate, umbrella clauses differ in form, and some of them may not have the effect of making a violation of an investment contract a violation of the BIT (*Salini* v *Jordan* (DJ)).

25. Parties' consent: consent under most-favoured nation clauses. The question has been addressed in a number of cases, in which the claimants either tried to avoid certain procedural limitations in the applicable BITs or to extend the scope of the consent to arbitration in the BIT. Regarding procedural limitations and requirements (e.g. prior limitation of local-court proceedings), tribunals have held that the claimants were entitled to rely on the most-favoured nation (MFN) clause in the applicable BIT in order to invoke the more favourable dispute settlement clause of another BIT (*Maffezini* v *Spain* (DJ); *Siemens* v *Argentina* (DJ)). Where the claimant sought to rely on an MFN clause to extend the scope of consent, the attitude of tribunals has typically been more conservative. In *Salini* v *Jordan*, the tribunal was asked to apply an MFN clause to extend the scope of the applicable arbitration clause to contract claims, but it refused to do so on the basis that the MFN clause in question 'does not apply insofar as dispute settlement clauses are concerned'. However, in *RosInvest* v *Russian Federation*, the tribunal found that the MFN clause of the United Kingdom–USSR BIT extended to the dispute resolution mechanism of the Denmark–Russia BIT (although note that the latter BIT provided for UNCITRAL or SCC, but not ICSID, arbitration). The leading case regarding ICSID arbitration probably remains *Plama Consortium Limited* v *Bulgaria* (DJ), in which the tribunal held that clear and unambiguous consent to ICSID arbitration could not be reached if the agreement to arbitrate was incorporated by reference (see *Plama Consortium Limited* v *Bulgaria* (DJ), paras. 198 and 199).

26. Parties' consent: time of consent. In cases where the host State makes an offer to arbitrate in its national legislation or in an international treaty, the time of consent to arbitration is determined by the investor's acceptance of the offer (see also Rule 2(3) Institutional Rule). This acceptance may occur at the latest at the date of the Request for Arbitration. A manifest absence of consent is an absolute bar to the pursuance of the proceedings. Proceedings instituted on the basis of forum prorogatum (basically, an invitation by an investor to the host State to accept the jurisdiction of the Centre in respect of one or more claims set forth in the Request for Arbitration) have been admitted according to the principle in *Klöchner* v *Cameroon* in an obiter dictum. Nonetheless, the screening mechanism of the Centre makes this practically difficult. In the case where not all of the jurisdictional requirements were met on the date that consent is perfected (e.g. the respondent State is not yet a Contracting State) the date of consent will be the date on which all the conditions have been met (Schreuer, *Commentary*, p. 226; *Holiday Inns* v *Morocco*; *Aucoven* v *Venezuela*).

27. Parties' consent: irrevocability of consent. Once perfected, consent may no longer be withdrawn unilaterally. The principle of irrevocability of consent is affirmed in the Preamble to the Convention and the Report of the Executive Directors (para. 11 of the Report). The parties may jointly agree to terminate their consent to jurisdiction at any time.

28. Parties' consent: prohibition of indirect withdrawal of consent. Notification of the exclusion of a class of disputes under art. 25(4) may not be relied upon to withdraw or limit prior consent (*Alcoa* v *Jamaica*; *Kaiser Bauxite* v *Jamaica*; *Reynolds* v *Jamaica*). Denunciation of the Convention will not affect consent that has already been given (see art. 72, notes 4-5). Similarly, once consent has been given by a designated constituent subdivision or agency, such consent cannot be withdrawn or vitiated by a revocation of the designation of the subdivision or agency (but difficulties will inevitably arise if the designated entity ceases to exist). If consent to jurisdiction is limited to investments approved by the host State, once approval and consent have been given, the consent becomes effective and irrevocable. A subsequent revocation of the authorisation cannot nullify the consent to arbitration (*SPP* v *Egypt* (DJ)). Furthermore, the invocation of the invalidity of the investment agreement will not of itself nullify consent to arbitration contained therein. The arbitral tribunal or the commission will have to decide on the alleged invalidity of the arbitration agreement (see art. 45 (1), Arbitration (Additional Facility) Rules). This approach follows the doctrine of the severability of the arbitration agreement, which is based on the assumption (to put it no higher) that when parties agree to submit their disputes to an arbitral tribunal, they agree to so submit all their disputes including those relating to the validity of the agreement. Principles of estoppel, by now well recognised in practice and theory, may also be used to counter an assertion by the respondent State that its consent was vitiated, in form or substance, *ab initio* (see, e.g., *Benteler* v *Belgian State*; see also Paulsson, *May a State Invoke its Internal Law*).

[Exclusive remedy]
Article 26
Consent of the parties to arbitration under this Convention shall, unless otherwise stated, be deemed consent to such arbitration to the exclusion of any other remedy. A Contracting State may require the exhaustion of local administrative or judicial remedies as a condition of its consent to arbitration under this Convention.

1. General. Art. 26 establishes the exclusivity of ICSID arbitration once consent is given, provided that the parties have not agreed otherwise. Art. 26 also provides that Contracting States may require the exhaustion of local remedies as a condition of their consent to ICSID arbitration in a given case.

2. Scope. Art. 26 applies only to arbitration proceedings. It operates from the moment that consent is perfected and does not depend upon the institution of ICSID proceedings. Art. 26 applies until the proceedings have been finalised. If the Secretary-General finds that the claim is manifestly outside the jurisdiction of the Centre or the ICSID tribunal decides that it lacks jurisdiction over the claim, art. 26 will no longer apply and other remedies may be pursued. In case no ICSID arbitration has been instituted and a non-ICSID tribunal is seised of a claim, the latter tribunal must decide whether there is consent to ICSID arbitration, in which case it will have to decline jurisdiction (*MINE* v *Guinea*; see also Schreuer, *Commentary*, p. 349).

3. The meaning of 'any other remedy'. It is clear that the formulation 'any other remedy' encompasses all types of recourse taken before national courts or any other non-ICSID arbitration bodies. There has been some debate on whether it extends also to non-legal remedies. In *Amco* v *Indonesia* the tribunal rejected the respondent's argument that by articulating a certain point of view about the case in a newspaper article, the claimant had violated art. 26. The tribunal concluded that this was not the case (*Amco* v *Indonesia* (*DPM*)). Nevertheless, the second sentence of art. 26 expressly refers to 'administrative or judicial remedies' and there is no indication in the drafting history of the Convention that 'remedies' should have different meanings in the two sentences of art. 26. From art. 27, it is clear that such remedies include diplomatic protection. As to such protection, the theoretical possibility exists of diplomatic protection being exercised on the basis of a third nationality (that of a non-Contracting State) in parallel with proceedings under the Convention: art. 27 does not apply to non-Contracting States. For obvious reasons, this would be ill-advised, even if the formulation of art. 27 might on its face make it possible. In *Banro* v *Congo*, the claimant had sought diplomatic protection by Canada early on, before seeking to create ICSID jurisdiction by way of an assignment to a US entity (the claim failed on jurisdictional grounds).

4. Parties' consent. Art. 26 allows parties to agree on other dispute settlement procedures in addition to ICSID arbitration. This may result directly from the parties' agreement (1993 ICSID Model Clause 12) or from the national legislation or international treaties concluded by the host State. In *Amco* v *Indonesia*, the tribunal rejected Indonesia's contention that by cooperating in domestic court proceedings and not requesting a stay of them, the claimant had waived its right to institute international arbitration. The tribunal pointed out that there was no identity between the parties in the national and international proceedings and that the object in the international dispute was not the same as that in the national dispute (*Amco* v *Indonesia* (I) (DJ)). It may be concluded that failure to protest the institution of domestic proceedings may be interpreted as a waiver of the exclusive-remedies rule but it does not amount to renunciation of ICSID arbitration.

5. Exhaustion of local remedies. Contracting States may require the exhaustion of local remedies as a condition of their consent to ICSID arbitration. This may be by agreement between the host State and the investor (1993 ICSID Model Clause 13), through BITs or through national legislation (an example was to be found in Papua New Guinea's 1978 Investment Disputes Convention Act, repealed in 1982). Provisions of this kind may be found in some BITs (Romania–UK 1976; Romania–Germany 1979; Romania–Egypt 1976). A method of announcing a requirement of exhaustion of local remedies as a condition of consent is by notifying the Centre in this respect.

Guatemala notified the Centre that it 'will require the exhaustion of local administrative remedies as a condition of its consent to arbitration under the Convention' (16 January 2003; see *Contracting States and Measures Taken by Them*). Israel made a similar statement but subsequently withdrew it. In case exhaustion of local remedies is required, it may still be dispensed with if there are no reasonably available local remedies to provide effective redress (see *Finnish Ships Arbitration*; *Ambatielos* case; see also Amerasinghe, *State Responsibility*; see also the ILC Draft Articles on Diplomatic Protection (2006), art. 14).

6. Attempt to settle the dispute in domestic courts for a certain time. Some BITs provide for the mandatory attempt to first settle the dispute in the domestic courts of the host State for a certain period of time (art. 10(3)(a) of the Argentina–Germany BIT provides for a period of eighteen months). It can be argued that the most likely effect of such a provision is delay in the settlement of the dispute. ICSID tribunals have concluded that such provisions are not an application of art. 26 (*Maffezini* v *Spain* (DJ); *Siemens* v *Argentina* (DJ)) and that such provisions turn out to be 'nonsensical from a practical point of view' (*Plama Consortium Limited* v *Bulgaria* (DJ)). It may be possible to avoid the effects of such clauses invoking an MFN clause (*Maffezini* v *Spain* (DJ); see also art. 25, note 25)

7. Fork-in-the-road clauses. Fork-in-the-road provisions typically offer the investor a choice between the host State's domestic courts and international arbitration (Argentina-US BIT, art. VII). Once the choice has been made, it becomes final, operating as a waiver of the other option. The test to be applied is derived from a lis pendens analysis. (*Genin* v *Estonia*; see also *Olguín* v *Paraguay* (DJ); *Champion Trading* v *Egypt*; *Azurix* v *Argentina*, (DJ); *Pan American* v *Argentina* (DJ)). Two disputes are said to be identical only if there is identity as to the parties, object and cause of action (*Benvenuti* v *Congo*) though difficulties will arise when technically different causes of action are pleaded to obtain a very similar relief in substance (see *Vivendi* v *Argentina* (DA) on the distinction between BIT and contract claims).

[Diplomatic protection]
Article 27

(1) No Contracting State shall give diplomatic protection, or bring an international claim, in respect of a dispute which one of its nationals and another Contracting State shall have consented to submit or shall have submitted to arbitration under this Convention, unless such other Contracting State shall have failed to abide by and comply with the award rendered in such dispute.

(2) Diplomatic protection, for the purposes of paragraph (1), shall not include informal diplomatic exchanges for the sole purpose of facilitating a settlement of the dispute.

ICSID Convention, art. 27

1. General. Art. 27 prohibits Contracting States (by definition it does not apply to third States) from giving diplomatic protection to their nationals in cases that fall under the jurisdiction of the Centre. Art. 27 also provides that a Contracting State may offer diplomatic protection if the respondent State has failed to abide by or comply with an award. Diplomatic protection, in the sense of art. 27, does not include 'informal diplomatic exchanges' between Contracting States for the purpose of facilitating the settlement of a dispute.

2. Scope. Art. 27 applies only to arbitration proceedings. Unlike art. 26, it is mandatory, in the sense that parties cannot derogate from it through agreement (*Aucoven* v *Venezuela*). Violation of art. 27 will not affect the jurisdiction of the Centre or the competence of the tribunal but it may prevent another international court dealing with a claim in violation of art. 27 to exercise its jurisdiction. It will certainly raise a discrete claim for breach of the Convention as between two Contracting States.

3. International claims. Typical forms of exercising diplomatic protection are by bringing a claim before an international court or tribunal, or by special settlement agreement (in the past, often a lump-sum settlement agreement). Numerous BITs contain special dispute-settlement clauses concerning the Contracting States. Dr. Broches argued that such clauses should cover only abstract questions of interpretation of a treaty and that such inter-State arbitrations should not affect ICSID awards that have already been rendered (*History*, Vol. II, pp. 65, 66). However, parallel proceedings might lead to contradictory decisions. One practical way to avoid this is by inserting a provision in BITs barring inter-State arbitration where ICSID arbitration has been instituted or is available (German model BIT; see also Schreuer, *Commentary*, pp. 404-405).

4. Temporal aspects. Art. 27 excludes the possibility of diplomatic protection from the moment of the parties' consent to arbitration (*Aucoven* v *Venezuela*). During the drafting of the Convention there were some attempts to exclude diplomatic protection only from the moment of institution of proceedings but none of these attempts succeeded (*History*, Vol. II, pp. 763, 765). If the host State has offered consent to ICSID arbitration but the investor has not yet accepted it, art. 27 does not apply. A BIT may provide that diplomatic protection will not be exercised where there is an offer to ICSID arbitration (UK model BIT).

5. Non-compliance with awards. Diplomatic protection in this case is limited to seeking compliance with an award. Art. 27 does not in terms authorise a State to pursue diplomatic protection where an award has dismissed a claim (Schreuer, *Commentary*, p. 413).

6. Informal diplomatic exchanges. The second paragraph of art. 27 was included in the Convention in order to avoid a strict interpretation of the meaning of 'diplomatic protection'. It should not be read as an exception to the first paragraph. There are some BITs that provide that dispute settlement should first be attempted by diplomatic means and only if these means prove to be unsuccessful should arbitration proceedings be instituted (1980 Belgium/Luxemburg–Cameroon Treaty, art. 10).

CHAPTER III. CONCILIATION

Section 1. Request for Conciliation

[Request for conciliation]

Article 28

(1) Any Contracting State or any national of a Contracting State wishing to institute conciliation proceedings shall address a request to that effect in writing to the Secretary-General who shall send a copy of the request to the other party.

(2) The request shall contain information concerning the issues in dispute, the identity of the parties and their consent to conciliation in accordance with the rules of procedure for the institution of conciliation and arbitration proceedings.

(3) The Secretary-General shall register the request unless he finds, on the basis of the information contained in the request, that the dispute is manifestly outside the jurisdiction of the Centre. He shall forthwith notify the parties of registration or refusal to register.

1. General. Art. 28 addresses the institution of conciliation proceedings. It is substantially identical to art. 36, which concerns institution of arbitral proceedings. It describes the written request that must be submitted to the Secretary-General. The request should contain information relating to the issue in dispute, the identity of parties and the parties' consent to conciliation. The Secretary-General will transmit the submitted request to the other party or, in case he finds that the dispute is manifestly outside the jurisdiction of the Centre, notify the parties of the refusal to register the request.

2. Institution of conciliation proceedings. Conciliation under the Convention has been resorted to on only six occasions (*SESAM* v *CAR*; *Togo Electricité* v *Togo*; *TG* v *Nigeria*; *SEDITEX* v *Madagascar* (I); *Tesoro* v *Trinidad & Tobago*; *SEDITEX* v *Madagascar* (II)). The decisions of conciliation committees to date have never been made public. Given the similarities between arts. 28 and 36, the considerations that are relevant to the institution of arbitral proceedings are also relevant to the institution of conciliation proceedings.

ICSID Convention, art. 29

Section 2. Composition of the Conciliation Commission
[Composition of the conciliation commission]
Article 29

(1) **The Conciliation Commission (hereinafter called the Commission) shall be constituted as soon as possible after registration of a request pursuant to Art. 28.**

(2) (a) **The Commission shall consist of a sole conciliator or any uneven number of conciliators appointed as the parties shall agree.**

    (b) **Where the parties do not agree upon the number of conciliators and the method of their appointment, the Commission shall consist of three conciliators, one conciliator appointed by each party and the third, who shall be the president of the Commission, appointed by agreement of the parties.**

1. General. Art. 29 sets forth the procedure for the constitution of the conciliation commission. It is substantially identical to art. 37, which deals with the constitution of the arbitral tribunals. Art. 29 provides for the parties' freedom to decide on the number of conciliators but provides that there should always be an uneven number, and that in case the parties do not reach an agreement the commission will consist of three conciliators. In this case, each party will appoint its own conciliator and the third one will be appointed by agreement of the parties.

2. Constitution of the conciliation commission. The details concerning the constitution of the conciliation commission are set out in the Rules 1 to 7 of the Conciliation Rules. These rules are similar to the corresponding rules dealing with arbitration (Rules 1 to 7 of the Arbitration Rules). Although there are some differences, the observations regarding art. 37 are also broadly applicable with respect to art. 29.

3. Number of conciliators. Art. 29 provides that the conciliation commission shall consist of a sole conciliator or any uneven number as the parties agree upon. In the limited number of conciliations that have taken place, the conciliation commission has consisted of either a sole conciliator (*Tesoro* v *Trinidad and Tobago*) or three conciliators (*SEDITEX* v *Madagascar II*).

4. Parties' nationals acting as conciliators. A key difference between the constitution of a conciliation commission and an arbitral tribunal is the possibility to have nationals or co-nationals of the parties as members of the conciliation commission. Dr. Broches concluded that it might be helpful to have conciliators who are nationals of the parties to enhance the prospects of settlement (*History*, Vol. II, pp. 266, 329, 510, 511, 569). In consequence, there are no provisions regarding the nationality of conciliators in the Convention. Practice shows that parties sometimes appoint co-nationals as conciliators (*SEDITEX* v *Madagascar II*).

5. Incapacity. There is no provision similar to Rule 1(4) of the Arbitration Rules prohibiting a person who has previously acted as conciliator or arbitrator in the case to be later appointed as an arbitrator.

[Appointment by the Chairman]
Article 30

If the Commission shall not have been constituted within 90 days after notice of registration of the request has been dispatched by the Secretary-General in accordance with paragraph (3) of Art. 28, or such other period as the parties may agree, the Chairman shall, at the request of either party and after consulting both parties as far as possible, appoint the conciliator or conciliators not yet appointed.

1. General. Art. 30 provides a mechanism for the constitution of the conciliation commission by the Centre in the event that the parties are unable to agree on the appointment of conciliators in a timely manner. Art. 30 is substantially identical with the first sentence of art. 38 regarding arbitration.

2. Appointment by the Chairman. During the drafting of the Convention there was some debate on the purpose of art. 30, given that the conciliation procedure is voluntary. Dr. Broches pointed out that parties would accept nominations from a third party and would have to cooperate once a commission has been set up (*History*, Vol. II, pp. 409, 413, 783). Art. 30 does not establish any nationality requirements for the conciliators (see also Rule 4 of the Conciliation Rules). There is no practice on the application of art. 30. The considerations which apply in relation to art. 38 are also relevant to the application of art. 30.

[Conciliators' qualities]
Article 31

(1) Conciliators may be appointed from outside the Panel of Conciliators, except in the case of appointments by the Chairman pursuant to Art. 30.

(2) Conciliators appointed from outside the Panel of Conciliators shall possess the qualities stated in paragraph (1) of Art. 14.

1. General. Art. 31 provides for the possibility that the parties may appoint conciliators from outside the existing Panel of Conciliators. This does not apply in case the appointment is made by the Centre pursuant to art. 30. Conciliators who are selected from outside the Panel must possess the qualities set forth in art. 14(1). This article is substantially identical to art. 40, which deals with arbitral proceedings. The considerations which are relevant to the application of art. 40 may be relevant to the application of art. 31.

2. Qualities of conciliators. A conciliator chosen from outside the Panel of Conciliators must be a person of high moral character and recognised competence in the fields of law, commerce, industry or finance, who may be relied upon to exercise independent judgement (art. 14(1)).

Section 3. Conciliation Proceedings

[Conciliation proceedings]

Article 32

(1) The Commission shall be the judge of its own competence.
(2) Any objection by a party to the dispute that that dispute is not within the jurisdiction of the Centre, or for other reasons is not within the competence of the Commission, shall be considered by the Commission which shall determine whether to deal with it as a preliminary question or to join it to the merits of the dispute.

1. General. Art. 32 reiterates the well-established principle that international tribunals or commissions should be judges of their own competence (compétence de la compétence). It provides that any objection made by a party regarding the jurisdiction of the Centre will be considered by the commission either as a preliminary question or by joining it to the merits of the dispute. Obviously, an objection may be held not to constitute a proper objection to jurisdiction or admissibility of a claim precluding examination of the claim at the threshold. Art. 32 is substantially identical to art. 41 concerning arbitral proceedings.

2. Decision on jurisdiction. The details concerning the commission's power to rule on its own competence are addressed by Rule 29 of the Conciliation Rules. In comparison to the corresponding rule regarding arbitral tribunals under Rule 41 of the Arbitration Rules, Rule 29 is less formal. A decision by a commission stating that it lacks jurisdiction must be rendered in a reasoned report (Rule 29(5) of the Conciliation Rules). In *Tesoro* v *Trinidad and Tobago*, the respondent objected to the jurisdiction of the Centre. The sole conciliator decided to join the question of jurisdiction to the merits, where he finally concluded that the Centre had jurisdiction over the claim. The considerations which are relevant to the application of art. 41 may also be relevant to the application of art. 32.

[Rules of procedure]

Article 33

Any conciliation proceeding shall be conducted in accordance with the provisions of this Section and, except as the parties otherwise agree, in accordance with the Conciliation Rules in effect on the date on which the parties consented to conciliation. If any question of procedure arises

which is not covered by this Section or the Conciliation Rules or any rules agreed by the parties, the Commission shall decide the question.

1. General. Art. 33 provides that conciliation proceedings are to be conducted in accordance with the ICSID Conciliation Rules. However, the parties are free to derogate from these rules by agreement. The commission may decide on questions which are not covered by the Conciliation Rules or the agreement of the parties. Art. 33 is substantially identical to art. 44 concerning arbitral proceedings.

2. Conciliation procedure. The more flexible nature of conciliation is reflected in the rules governing procedural aspects. The Convention's provisions regarding conciliation procedure do not address all of the issues that are addressed by the arbitral procedural rules. Rectification, interpretation, revision and annulment are not relevant to conciliation proceedings. The questions relating to the taking of evidence, default of a party, ancillary claims, provisional measures and awards are discussed in different terms than is the case in arbitration (see art. 34). The provisions covering written statements, hearings, witnesses and evidence (Rules 25 to 28 of the Conciliation Rules) are substantially more flexible. There are no provisions in the Conciliation Rules dealing with the question of remedies and procedures which apply after the commission's report.

[Conciliation proceedings and the commission's report]
Article 34

(1) It shall be the duty of the Commission to clarify the issues in dispute between the parties and to endeavour to bring about agreement between them upon mutually acceptable terms. To that end, the Commission may at any stage of the proceedings and from time to time recommend terms of settlement to the parties. The parties shall cooperate in good faith with the Commission in order to enable the Commission to carry out its functions, and shall give their most serious consideration to its recommendations.

(2) If the parties reach agreement, the Commission shall draw up a report noting the issues in dispute and recording that the parties have reached agreement. If, at any stage of the proceedings, it appears to the Commission that there is no likelihood of agreement between the parties, it shall close the proceedings and shall draw up a report noting the submission of the dispute and recording the failure of the parties to reach agreement. If one party fails to appear or participate in the proceedings, the Commission shall close the proceedings and shall draw up a report noting that party's failure to appear or participate.

1. General. Art. 34 addresses the procedure to be adopted by the conciliation commission. The commission may recommend terms of settlement to the parties, and the parties are required to cooperate in good faith with the commission. Any agreement between parties will be recorded in the commission's report. If it is unlikely that parties will reach agreement or if one of the parties fails to appear, the commission must close the proceedings.

2. The functions of the conciliation commission. The conciliation procedure differs from arbitration. It is not adversarial but rather a process of facilitating a settlement between the parties. Conciliation may be used when parties desire to carry on their cooperation in relation to the investment. This basic function of conciliation was reflected in all the draft texts of the Convention (*History*, Vol. I, pp. 162, 164) and it is reiterated in the Report of the Executive Directors, which records that 'the differences between the two sets of provisions reflect the basic distinction between the process of conciliation which seeks to bring the parties to agreement and that of arbitration which aims at a binding determination of the dispute by the Tribunal' (para. 37). The functions of conciliators have been described in *Tesoro* v *Trinidad and Tobago* as: 'to examine the contentions raised by the parties, to clarify the issues, and to endeavour to evaluate their respective merits and the likelihood of their being accepted, or rejected, in Arbitration or Court proceedings, in the hope that such evaluation may assist the parties in reaching an agreed settlement' (see also Rule 22 of the Conciliation Rules).

3. Conciliation proceedings. The principle of due process does apply in conciliation proceedings. Both parties have the right to be heard by the commission. However, ex parte communications with each of the parties are not prohibited (Rule 22 of the Conciliation Rules, Note A). The Conciliation Rules offer limited guidance as to the sequence of written and oral submissions. Rule 25(1) provides that the parties should initially give written statements but that either party may at any stage of the proceedings file such written statement as it deems useful or relevant. Rule 22(3) provides that the commission may request oral explanations from the parties at any stage of the proceedings. Under Rule 28(1) the parties may request at any stage of the proceedings that the commission hear witnesses and/or experts (*Tesoro* v *Trinidad and Tobago*; *SEDITEX* v *Madagascar II*; see Schreuer, *Commentary*, pp. 432-433).

4. Terms of settlement. Art. 34 provides that the commission may at any stage of the proceedings and 'from time to time' recommend terms of settlement. This is one of the essential functions of the commission (*History*, Vol. I, pp. 162, 164). The recommendations may concern specific terms of final settlement as well as provisional measures. The recommendations must be reasoned.

5. Parties' good faith. The obligation to cooperate in conciliation proceedings is detailed in Rule 23 of the Conciliation Rules and confirmed in the Convention's Preamble. In contrast to arbitration proceedings (see art. 45), the non-participation of one of the parties to the conciliation proceedings will lead to the closure of the proceedings and to a note in the commission's report recording this fact.

6. Nature of the recommendations. The commission's recommendations are not binding. Though the parties are not obliged to give effect to the recommendations, they must consider them in good faith (*History*, Vol. II, pp. 1254, 155, 328, 785, 786, 791). The parties may agree in advance to accept the commission's recommendations. Such an agreement will not transform the recommendation into an award, and the recommendation will not be enforceable according to art. 54. It is therefore advisable to insert an arbitration clause in such an agreement.

7. The commission's report. The report of the commission is the final document in conciliation proceedings. If the parties reach agreement, the report shall contain the terms of the agreement. Under Rule 30(1) of the Conciliation Rules, the parties may agree that the report shall record in detail the terms of their agreement. Pursuant to Rule 33(3), the report will not be published without the parties' consent. To date, none of the conciliation reports has been published.

[Non-invocation in subsequent proceedings]
Article 35

Except as the parties to the dispute shall otherwise agree, neither party to a conciliation proceeding shall be entitled in any other proceeding, whether before arbitrators or in a court of law or otherwise, to invoke or rely on any views expressed or statements or admissions or offers of settlement made by the other party in the conciliation proceedings, or the report or any recommendations made by the Commission.

1. General. Art. 35 prevents the invocation of any statements or admissions made during conciliation proceedings in any subsequent arbitration or court proceedings. This gives effect to a rule of customary international law, expressly endorsed by the PCIJ and other courts and tribunals. Unless parties agree otherwise, they cannot rely on any views expressed in the conciliation proceedings or on any statements or offers to settlement made before the conciliation commission.

2. Application. The purpose of art. 35 is to encourage parties to be forthcoming and flexible in conciliation procedures, by offering a guarantee that positions taken by them during conciliation proceedings will not be used against them in any subsequent arbitration or court proceedings (*History*, Vol. II, pp. 154, 155, 328, 414). However, if any agreement is reached by the parties to accept the recommendation of the conciliation commission, that agreement may be invoked in subsequent proceedings.

3. Parties' agreement. Art. 35 allows the parties to agree that any materials produced for the purposes of the conciliation procedure may be used in subsequent proceedings. Such agreement may be made in advance of or during the conciliation proceedings and it may also be part of an agreement reached pursuant to art. 34(2) (Rule 34 of the Conciliation Rules).

CHAPTER IV. ARBITRATION

Section 1. Request for Arbitration

[Request for arbitration]

Article 36

(1) Any Contracting State or any national of a Contracting State wishing to institute arbitration proceedings shall address a request to that effect in writing to the Secretary-General who shall send a copy of the request to the other party.

(2) The request shall contain information concerning the issues in dispute, the identity of the parties and their consent to arbitration in accordance with the rules of procedure for the institution of conciliation and arbitration proceedings.

(3) The Secretary-General shall register the request unless he finds, on the basis of the information contained in the request, that the dispute is manifestly outside the jurisdiction of the Centre. He shall forthwith notify the parties of registration or refusal to register.

1. General. Art. 36 deals with the commencement of arbitration proceedings. It describes the written request that must be submitted to the Secretary-General by the claimant in order to initiate arbitration proceedings and the steps the Secretary-General must take to determine whether the request for arbitration is within the Centre's jurisdiction. The Institution Rules (authorised by art. 6(1)(c)) contain specific and detailed rules for this initial stage of arbitration and should be read together with art. 36.

2. Application. ICSID proceedings are initiated by a written request for arbitration submitted by the investor, or the host State, to the Secretary-General of ICSID. By contrast, UNCITRAL arbitrations are initiated by a notice delivered directly to the respondent (art. 3, UNCITRAL Rules). Arbitrations commenced under the ICSID Additional Facility Rules require the specific approval of the Secretary-General, but are not addressed here as they are not governed by the Convention.

3. Who can submit a request for arbitration. Requests are submitted by the claimant. Usually in practice, the claimant in ICSID proceedings is an investor and the respondent is the host State. A host State can, of course, submit a request. Rule 2 of the Institution Rules allows for a request by a host State's subdivision or agency, within the terms of the jurisdictional requirements of art. 25(1) and (3). An investor does not require any authorisation from its

State of nationality to institute proceedings. Rule 1(2) of the Institution Rules provides that a request may be made jointly by both parties.

4. Format of the request. Rule 1(1) of the Institution Rules sets out the formal requirements of the request. First, the request should be made in writing to the Secretary-General and be drafted in English, French or Spanish. The choice of language for the request does not affect the choice of the procedural language for the arbitration proceedings. Secondly, the request must be dated. Thirdly, the request must be signed by the requesting party or its duly authorised representative. If the request is signed by a representative, the request should enclose proof of the authorisation (e.g. power of attorney or letter of engagement). Fourthly, the request shall indicate whether it relates to a conciliation or an arbitration proceeding. Rule 4 of the Institution Rules requires that one original and five copies of the request should be submitted. The Secretariat may request additional copies.

5. Content requirements. Rule 2 of the Institution Rules lists the information that must be included in the request. Broadly, this information should include the names, contact details and nationality of the parties, written evidence of consent to arbitrate, information on the dispute and evidence of authorisation to file a request. Where the respondent is a State, the request should usually specify as the respondent an authorised legal representative of that State, such as the President, the Minister for Foreign Investment or the Attorney-General. The request does not have to be set out in any particular manner, but must contain all of the information listed in Rule 2 of the Institution Rules. Since the Institution Rules are not subject to modification by the parties, the required information must be provided even in the case of a joint request.

6. Optional information. Rule 3 of the Institution Rules provides that the request may set out any agreement between the parties regarding the number of conciliators or arbitrators and the method of their appointment. Art. 37(1) provides that the tribunal shall be constituted as soon as possible after the registration of the request. It is advisable therefore to indicate any agreements at the earliest possible stage. In addition, a request would usually outline the merits of the claim. The request is a good advocacy opportunity as it will be the first document the Secretary-General and, in due course, the tribunal, will read regarding the dispute.

7. Lodging fee. Reg. 16 of the Administrative and Financial Regulations requires a non-refundable lodging fee to be paid upon submission of a request for arbitration by the party filing the request, or by both parties in case the request is made jointly. At the time of writing, the fee is USD 25,000. Under Rule 5(1) of the Institution Rules, the Secretary-General will not take any action other than acknowledge receipt of the request until the lodging fee has been paid. The fee should be paid to ICSID (through the International Bank for Reconstruction and Development) by wire transfer. ICSID's bank details are available on its website. A copy of the wire transfer order should be included with the request.

8. Where to send the request. In accordance with art. 2, the Centre's seat is at the principal office of the World Bank. A hard copy of the request should be sent to the Secretary-General of ICSID at MSN U3-301, 1818 H Street, NW, Washington, DC, 20433, USA. An electronic copy of the request and its annexes should be submitted either on a CD-ROM to the above postal address or sent by e-mail to: ICSIDsecretariat@worldbank.org. ICSID provides a detailed guide to filing a request on-line at: <icsid.worldbank.org/ICSID/ICSID/HowToFileReq.jsp>.

9. Supporting documentation. Any documentation filed in support of a request that is not in one of the Centre's official languages must be accompanied by a translation (Reg. 30(3), Administrative and Financial Regulations). Any documentation supporting the request must comply with the requirements under Reg. 30 of the Administrative and Financial Regulations on matters such as form, copies and language.

10. Acknowledgement of receipt and copy sent to respondent. Under Rule 5 of the Institution Rules, the Secretary-General will send the requesting party an acknowledgement of receipt of the request. Provided the claimant has paid the lodging fee, the Secretary-General will also transmit a copy of the request and supporting documentation to the respondent. The respondent does not need to respond to the request at this stage.

11. Time limit. Neither the Convention nor the Institution Rules provide for any time limits within which a request must be made. However, claimants should be wary of limitation periods that otherwise apply to the case. If the claim arises from a contract, the governing law of the contract will determine the limitation period. If the claim arises out of a BIT, the BIT may impose a limitation period, or other procedural requirements, for initiating ICSID arbitrations. It is unclear to what extent international law includes a rule of 'laches', by which remedies will be denied due to a lapse of time in bringing a claim. An arbitral tribunal addressed this principle in the *Ambatielos* case, but denied a British submission that the relevant claim should be rejected due to undue delay by Greece.

12. Consulting the Centre, supplementing and amending a request. The fact that the Convention and the Institution Rules require a formal request does not rule out informal communication between the claimant and the Centre. The Secretary-General will consult with the requesting party if the request does not conform to the requirements of the Convention or the Institution Rules or if additional information is necessary. Consultation with the Centre prior to lodging the request is encouraged as it can be helpful to clarify any issues at an early stage and avoid the cost, or disappointment, of a request being rejected. The Secretary-General will usually give the party concerned an opportunity to supplement or correct their request before a decision is taken on its registration.

13. Registration requirements. Once the request has been submitted to the Centre, the Secretary-General is under an obligation to register it if it complies with all formal filing requirements, subject to the Secretary-General's jurisdiction screening powers (art. 36(3), reviewed below at note 14; see, e.g., *Aguas del Tunari SA* v *Republic of Bolivia*). The formal filing requirements comprise: filing of the information and documentation required by Rule 2 of the Institution Rules; compliance of the supporting documentation with Reg. 20 of the Administrative and Financial Regulations; and payment of the lodging fee. The registration process takes between a few weeks and several months and is completed by entry of the request into the Arbitration Register (see below note 17).

14. Secretary-General's screening power under Art. 36(3): 'manifestly outside the jurisdiction of the Centre'. Art. 36(3) provides that the Secretary-General shall register a request which complies with formal filing requirements unless it finds that the dispute is manifestly outside the Centre's jurisdiction. The rationale for this screening power is to prevent the waste of time, effort and expense that would result from setting up a tribunal, only for the tribunal to find that it evidently lacked competence or that the request had been submitted for purely vexatious reasons (see generally *History*, Vol. II, pp. 771, 772, 774 and 775). This power is not exercised lightly. Equally, it does not anticipate the tribunal's assessment of its own jurisdiction as to the dispute before it. Thus, a discussion paper produced by the Secretariat dated 22 October 2004 noted that this power does not extend to the merits of the dispute or to cases where jurisdiction is merely doubtful but not manifestly lacking.

15. Respondent's observations. Although the art. 36(3) screening power is the exclusive responsibility of the Secretary-General, as a matter of practice, the Secretary-General will send a copy of the request to the respondent and may take account of any observations made. Even if the respondent does not take advantage of this opportunity, the respondent still retains the right to contest jurisdiction before the tribunal (art. 41 and Rule 41 of the Arbitration Rules). The amended Rule 41(5) of the Arbitration Rules (effective from April 2006) provides that a party may, within thirty days of the constitution of the tribunal, file an objection that a claim is manifestly without merit. After giving the parties an opportunity to present their observations, the tribunal is required to rule on the objection at its first session or shortly thereafter.

16. Refusal of registration. The Secretary-General rarely refuses to register a request for arbitration. This partly results from pre-registration consultation between the requesting party and the Centre to clarify what additional information may be necessary. Registration has, however, been refused on grounds such as a lack of consent to arbitrate under ICSID, the absence of a legal dispute, non-ratification of the Convention by the investor's home State and the absence of an investment. A decision by the Secretary-General not to register a request for arbitration is not subject to review. A party may at any time submit a new request based on the same claim; however, the procedure under art. 36 and the Institution Rules must be followed, including payment of a lodging fee. If the Secretary-General registers the new request, this does not in any way bind the tribunal as to its jurisdiction (see note 14) (art. 41).

17. Notification of registration. Registration occurs on entry of the request into the Arbitration Register kept by the Secretary-General in accordance with Reg. 23 of the Administrative and Financial Regulations. On the same day the Secretary-General must notify the parties of the registration (Rule 6(1)(a) of the Institution Rules). Rule 7 of the Institution Rules provides the details regarding the particulars of a notice of registration.

18. Effect of registration. The arbitration proceedings are considered to have been formally instituted on the date of registration. As a result, art. 37(1) requires the tribunal to be constituted 'as soon as possible' after the date of registration (see also Rule 6(2) of the Institution Rules).

19. Withdrawal of request. A claimant may unilaterally withdraw its request only up to the registration date (Rule 8 of the Institution Rules). Thereafter, the proceedings may only be discontinued with the respondent's consent. The lodging fee will not be refunded in case of a withdrawal. Withdrawal of the request does not constitute withdrawal of a consent to arbitrate in general, and of the object of the request in particular (art. 25(1)). Therefore the requesting party does not prejudice the other party by unilaterally withdrawing its request: the other party can issue its own request if it so wishes.

Section 2. Constitution of the Tribunal

[Composition and constitution of the tribunal]

Article 37

(1) The Arbitral Tribunal (hereinafter called the Tribunal) shall be constituted as soon as possible after registration of a request pursuant to Article 36.

(2) (a) The Tribunal shall consist of a sole arbitrator or any uneven number of arbitrators appointed as the parties shall agree.

(b) Where the parties do not agree upon the number of arbitrators and the method of their appointment, the Tribunal shall consist of three arbitrators, one arbitrator appointed by each party and the third, who shall be the president of the Tribunal, appointed by agreement of the parties.

1. General. Art. 37 deals with the basic principles for the constitution of a tribunal and the appointment of arbitrators by the parties (see also Rules 1-6 of the Arbitration Rules).

2. Formalities. There are three mandatory formalities under the Convention for a tribunal to be properly constituted: the tribunal must consist of a sole arbitrator or an odd number of arbitrators (art. 37(2)(a)); the majority of arbitrators must not be nationals of the parties unless each arbitrator is appointed by agreement of the parties (art. 39); and arbitrators appointed from outside the Panel of Arbitrators must have met the necessary qualifications required of those on the Panel of Arbitrators (the Panel of Arbitrators is discussed in arts. 12 to 16 and art. 40, note 4) (art. 40(2)). Improper constitution of the tribunal is a ground for annulment of the resulting award (art. 52(1)(a)). The Secretariat monitors the constitution of tribunals carefully.

3. Procedure for constituting the tribunal: by the parties' previous agreement. The main source for the composition and method of constitution of a tribunal is the agreement of the parties. If the parties have reached an agreement before the institution of proceedings, its contents should either be set out in the request for arbitration or be communicated by the parties to the Secretary-General as soon as possible after registration of the request.

4. Procedure for constituting the tribunal: by the parties' agreement after a dispute has arisen. Rule 2 of the Arbitration Rules sets out a procedure by which parties who have not agreed upon the number of arbitrators and the method of their appointment prior to registration of the request must exchange proposals. The procedure is designed to bring the parties to agreement within sixty days, although this period is often extended. The agreement, if any, and all related correspondence, must be transmitted through or copied to the Secretary-General as and when they are made (Rule 2(2) of the Arbitration Rules).

5. Procedure for constituting the tribunal: by the art. 37(2)(b) default procedure. If the parties cannot agree on a specific procedure pursuant to Rule 2 of the Arbitration Rules, a three-member tribunal will be constituted (art. 37(2)(b)). Rule 3 of the Arbitration Rules provides that each party names one arbitrator and the two parties seek to agree on the third arbitrator to be president of the tribunal. Whilst there are no specific time limits in Rule 3, if ninety days after the Secretary-General's dispatch of the notice of registration (or some longer agreed period) the tribunal has not been constituted, either party may request the Centre (through the offices of the Chairman) to appoint any arbitrators not yet appointed, including the president (art. 38 and Rule 4 of the Arbitration Rules). Any such appointment is made from the Panel of Arbitrators, although it is common at this stage for the Secretariat to propose non-Panel arbitrators to be appointed with the mutual consent of the parties. The Chairman must use his best efforts to make an appointment within thirty days. Both parties are to be consulted as far as possible during this process.

6. Timing for constitution of the tribunal. A tribunal must be constituted as soon as possible after registration of a request for arbitration (art. 37(1) and Rule 1(1) of the Arbitration Rules). The appointment process frequently involves delay and non-cooperation, especially from respondent parties. Accordingly, 'as soon as possible' should be understood as a relative term: in general it takes between three to twelve months to constitute a tribunal (or an average of just over five months, from registration to constitution). It is rare for a tribunal to be constituted in less than ninety days. The process of constituting the tribunal is complete with the Secretary-General gives the parties notice of the acceptance by all arbitrators of their appointments (art. 37(1)). From this point on, all formal communications will usually be directly with the tribunal, copied to the Centre (see Reg. 24 of the Administrative and Financial Regulations).

7. Number of arbitrators. The tribunal must have an uneven number of arbitrators. This rule is designed to avoid a deadlock in case the arbitrators cannot form a majority on a decision. In theory, the parties may choose any uneven number of arbitrators. Parties to date have always chosen three arbitrators, or, less commonly, a sole arbitrator. Other instruments governing international arbitration either mandate or express a strong preference for an uneven number of arbitrators. For example, art. 5 of the UNCITRAL Rules and art. 8(1) of the ICC Arbitration Rules require that either a sole arbitrator or three arbitrators be appointed.

8. Designation of the president. Art. 37(2)(b) provides that the third arbitrator should be the tribunal's president. This provision is mandatory. It is in the interests of impartiality that an arbitrator who has been appointed by just one of the parties should not preside over the tribunal.

9. Appointing authority. It is possible for the parties to ask a neutral official such as the Chairman, the Secretary-General or a well-regarded third party such the President of the International Court of Justice to act as an appointing authority for the arbitrators.

10. Acceptance and replacement of an arbitrator. Rule 5 of the Arbitration Rules sets out the procedure for the acceptance of appointments. The appointment of an arbitrator only takes effect on the arbitrator's acceptance. The arbitrator has no duty to accept an appointment (even if he is a member of the Panel of Arbitrators). The Secretary-General has a duty to inquire whether an arbitrator appointed by a party, or by agreement of the parties, wishes to accept the appointment and must inform the parties and, if necessary, the Chairman or other appointing authority, if an arbitrator approached has refused to accept an appointment. A party which has appointed an arbitrator is free to change that appointment at any time prior to the constitution of the tribunal (see Rule 7 of the Arbitration Rules). Rules 5, 6 and 7 of the Arbitration Rules govern the details of the appointment and replacement of arbitrators.

[Appointment by the Chairman]
Article 38

If the Tribunal shall not have been constituted within 90 days after notice of registration of the request has been dispatched by the Secretary-General in accordance with paragraph (3) of Article 36, or such other period as the parties may agree, the Chairman shall, at the request of either party and after consulting both parties as far as possible, appoint the arbitrator or arbitrators not yet appointed. Arbitrators appointed by the Chairman pursuant to this Article shall not be nationals of the Contracting State party to the dispute or of the Contracting State whose national is a party to the dispute.

1. General. Should the parties fail to appoint arbitrators in accordance with art. 37, art. 38 provides a fall-back procedure whereby appointments are made by the Chairman (the President of the World Bank as per art. 5). Articles 6(2)(3) and 7(2)(3) of the UNCITRAL Rules contain comparable provisions. Because of the short time limits that apply to constituting the tribunal, art. 38 is frequently used.

2. What triggers the art. 38 procedure? As the art. 38 procedure may be applied regardless of whether one of the parties has been uncooperative, there are a number of instances which may trigger its application: a party may have failed to make its unilateral appointment or the parties may be unable to agree on a joint appointment; the members of the tribunal already appointed by the parties may be unable to agree on the appointment of a third member (or of further members if the tribunal is to consist of more than three arbitrators); an external appointing authority may have failed to make an appointment pursuant to an agreement between the parties; or the parties may have missed the ninety-day time limit provided by art. 38 and Rule 4 of the Arbitration Rules.

3. The ninety-day time limit. The ninety-day time limit begins to run from the date of dispatch of the notification of registration of the request. The parties may extend this time limit by agreement at any time before the tribunal's constitution (even if the ninety days have elapsed), or agree to reduce the ninety-day time limit. Once the ninety days have elapsed, the art. 38 procedure is not automatically triggered: as long as neither party has made a request to the Chairman under art. 38 to appoint an arbitrator, the parties may continue with their efforts to constitute the tribunal without the Chairman's intervention. In practice, the time limit of ninety days is difficult to meet and the constitution of a tribunal often takes considerably longer. Under Rule 2(3) of the Arbitration Rules, the parties have sixty days to agree the composition of the tribunal and the method of appointing arbitrators. This then leaves thirty days for the actual appointment of arbitrators, which is a lengthy process involving preliminary consultations with prospective appointees, communication between the parties and notifications to the Secretary-General, as well as acceptance by the persons nominated as arbitrators (under Rule 5 of the Arbitration Rules, appointees have fifteen days to accept or decline).

4. Upon request of a party. In order to trigger art. 38, one of the parties must request that the Chairman make an appointment. The request must be made in writing to the Chairman (Rule 4(1) of the Arbitration Rules). The Chairman acts upon the recommendation of the Secretary-General and the decision is ultimately communicated to the parties through the Secretary-General in accordance with Reg. 24(1) of the Administrative and Financial Regulations.

5. Content of the art. 38 request. The request must contain precise information on any agreement between the parties regarding the composition of the tribunal and the appointment of arbitrators and whether any appointments have already been made. If the parties have not reached any agreement, the Chairman will proceed to appoint an arbitrator on the basis of the procedure set out in art. 37(2)(b).

6. Consultation. Under art. 38, the Chairman must consult both parties, as far as possible, either orally or in writing, so as to avoid appointments that are objectionable to either of them. Whilst the Chairman may disregard the objections of a party, in practice the Chairman rarely does so. The obligation to consult both parties extends to any arbitrators not yet appointed. Therefore, if a party fails to appoint its own party-nominated arbitrator, the other party gains the procedural right to be consulted on the appointment of that arbitrator by the Chairman. The Chairman must make an effort to consult, but failure to elicit a constructive response from a party will not affect the Chairman's power to make the appointment.

7. Chairman's obligation to appoint arbitrator(s). Under Rule 4 of the Arbitration Rules, the Chairman is under an obligation to make appointments if so requested and does not have the discretion not to appoint an arbitrator. The Chairman must make the appointment within thirty days of the request, unless the parties agree otherwise. In effect, given the ninety-day and thirty-day time limits, a party could theoretically press for the constitution of a tribunal within 120 days from the registration of the request for arbitration.

8. Appointments and designations. If only one party has made an appointment and there is no agreement on the president, the Chairman will have to make two appointments: one appointment for the party that failed to unilaterally appoint an arbitrator and the other in the absence of an agreement on the third arbitrator. In such a case, the Chairman also has to designate one of these arbitrators appointed by him as president of the tribunal. However, a designation as president is not necessary if both parties have made their appointments but no agreement has been reached on the third arbitrator. In this case, the third arbitrator appointed by the Chairman will be the president.

9. Nationality of arbitrators. The Chairman is more limited in his choice than the parties in that he may not appoint a national or co-national of one of the parties. In addition, under art. 40(1), he must appoint an arbitrator who is on the Panel of Arbitrators, unless specific agreement to the contrary is reached (sometimes the Secretariat may propose names outside of the Panel due to the specific needs of the case, but any such appointment requires the express consent of the parties). ICSID's 2007 Annual Report lists 512 members of the Panels. A complete list of all Panel members is available on the ICSID website at <www.worldbank.org/icsid>. The prohibition against appointing a national only applies if the appointment by the Chairman is made pursuant to the art. 38 procedure. If the Chairman acts as appointing authority under an agreement between the parties, this exclusion does not apply.

10. Acceptance by the appointed arbitrator. An appointment by the Chairman is subject to acceptance by the appointed arbitrator. It is for the Secretary-General to seek this acceptance (art. 37, and Rule 5(2) of the Arbitration Rules) and to inform the parties of appointments made by the Chairman.

[Nationality of arbitrators]
Article 39

The majority of the arbitrators shall be nationals of States other than the Contracting State party to the dispute and the Contracting State whose national is a party to the dispute; provided, however, that the foregoing provisions of this Article shall not apply if the sole arbitrator or each individual member of the Tribunal has been appointed by agreement of the parties.

1. General. The question of the nationality of arbitrators is controversial. Some argue that arbitrators of the same nationality as the parties might not be impartial. Others believe national arbitrators provide insight into the issues and parties and can inspire trust in the process (*History*, Vol. II, p. 983). Art. 39 mitigates the effect of nationality-based appointments by stipulating that the majority of arbitrators must not be of the same nationality as either of the parties. This means that most ICSID tribunals do not include any national of either party.

2. No majority of national arbitrators. Art. 39 does not exclude national arbitrators, it merely states that they must not form a majority of the tribunal. For a three-member tribunal, Rule 1(3) of the Arbitration Rules prevents a national of either party to the dispute from being appointed as an arbitrator by a party without the agreement of the other party. Otherwise, the party acting first would appoint a national and preclude the other party from doing so. This means that if the tribunal is to consist of five arbitrators, then either party may appoint one national arbitrator since two national arbitrators would not be a majority in a five person tribunal. While Art. 39 is mandatory, the Arbitration Rules can be modified, and the parties can therefore agree that one party may unilaterally appoint its own national or co-national as arbitrator. The Chairman, when acting under art. 38, may not appoint any national arbitrators.

3. Arbitrator's nationality. The Convention and the Arbitration Rules are particularly strict with regard to national arbitrators. Art. 6(4) of the UNCITRAL Rules states that regard should be had to 'such considerations as are likely to secure the appointment of an independent and impartial arbitrator and shall take into account as well the advisability of appointing an arbitrator of a nationality other than the nationalities of the parties'. For arbitrators who have dual or multiple nationalities, the parties may focus on the arbitrator's dominant nationality, but it may be safer to avoid appointing an arbitrator if there is any danger of breaching art. 39.

4. Investor's nationality. Art. 39 assumes that the nationality of the investor is obvious. Rule 2(1)(d) of the Institution Rules requires the request for arbitration to specify the nationality of the investor. Questions may still arise, particularly if the parties have agreed under art. 25(2)(b) to treat a national of the host State as a national of another Contracting State because of foreign control. The tribunal in *Rompetrol* considered, in the context of art. 25, that an investor registered outside Romania could bring an ICSID claim against Romania even though the investor was effectively controlled by Romanians (*Rompetrol*, paras. 80-84).

5. Agreement of the parties. In order to fall within the 'agreement of the parties' exception in art. 39 it is necessary to secure the direct agreement of the parties on every single appointment. The reference to 'agreement of the parties' in art. 39 does not relate to a general agreement on the composition of a tribunal and the method of appointment. The parties may not agree on the appointment of a presiding arbitrator and grant each other the right to appoint national arbitrators. Rather, the direct appointment of the parties on every single appointment is necessary. Due to the requirement to identify the appointees by name, a prior agreement by the parties to appoint a national arbitrator would not suffice.

6. Non-compliance. There are several consequences of non-compliance with the nationality requirements of art. 39. For example, under art. 57 a party may propose the disqualification of an arbitrator if he was ineligible for appointment under art. 39 (or under art. 38, which prohibits the Chairman from appointing national arbitrators). In addition, under art. 52(1)(a) the resulting award may be subject to annulment if the tribunal was not properly constituted.

[Qualities of arbitrators]
Article 40

(1) Arbitrators may be appointed from outside the Panel of Arbitrators, except in the case of appointments by the Chairman pursuant to Article 38.

(2) Arbitrators appointed from outside the Panel of Arbitrators shall possess the qualities stated in paragraph (1) of Article 14.

1. General. Art. 40(1) deals with appointments from the Panel of Arbitrators kept by the Centre in accordance with arts. 12 to 16. A complete list of all Panel members is available on the ICSID website at <www.worldbank.org/icsid>. Refer to arts. 12 to 16 for more details regarding the Panel.

2. Appointment by the parties. The Panel assists the parties in the selection of appropriate individuals as arbitrators. The parties are free, unilaterally or by joint agreement, to appoint arbitrators who are not on the Panel. If the parties have agreed that their two party-appointed arbitrators may appoint the president, those arbitrators may jointly appoint a person from outside the Panel.

3. Appointment by the Chairman. When acting under art. 38, the Chairman may only appoint Panel members, unless the parties agree otherwise. If the Chairman is acting as appointing authority, the Chairman is free to appoint arbitrators who are not on the Panel. The Chairman has the power under art. 13(2) to designate ten persons to the Panel. The Chairman may exercise this power if there is an absence or shortage of eligible candidates for a particular arbitral tribunal. If an arbitrator has been appointed by the Chairman under art. 38 in accordance with art. 40(1), he continues to be a member of the tribunal even if his term of office as a Panel member expires during the arbitration. When appointing arbitrators to an ad hoc committee under art. 52(3), the Chairman is also restricted to appointing Panel members only.

4. Qualities of arbitrators. Art. 14(1) lists the qualities that a person must have in order to be eligible to serve on the Panel: high moral character; recognised competence in the fields of law, commerce, industry or finance; and reliability to exercise independent judgment. Art. 40(2) requires that non-Panel appointees also have these qualities. There are similar provisions in other international arbitration rules, in particular as to the need for independence. For example, art. 10 of the UNCITRAL Rules requires that an arbitrator be impartial and independent.

5. Post-appointment. The prohibition against conflicts of interest and the disclosure obligation continue after appointment. If any doubts arise during the course of arbitration proceedings as to an arbitrator's independence and impartiality, the arbitrator is expected to reveal them promptly. This is now uncontroversial as the 2006 amendments to Rule 6(2) of the Arbitration

Rules expressly stipulate that the obligation to declare conflicts of interest is a continuing obligation. As an extra precaution, Rule 1(4) of the Arbitration Rules prevents an arbitrator from taking part in the same dispute twice at different stages, whether before the facts came before ICSID, or in annulment proceedings.

6. Improper appointment. Any appointment that violates the Convention or Arbitration Rules may result in the disqualification of the arbitrator under art. 57. The other members of the tribunal make the decision on an arbitrator's disqualification (art. 58). Where the members are evenly divided, the Chairman has a casting vote. An improper appointment of an arbitrator could lead to the annulment of the resulting award of the tribunal under art. 52. In view of the complexity of the appointment provisions, and the importance of ensuring valid appointments, tribunals will often ask parties at the first procedural meeting to confirm and agree that the tribunal has been validly constituted (see Broches, *Explanatory Notes and Survey*, para. 101).

Section 3. Powers and Functions of the Tribunal
[Decision on jurisdiction]
Article 41

(1) The Tribunal shall be the judge of its own competence.
(2) Any objection by a party to the dispute that that dispute is not within the jurisdiction of the Centre, or for other reasons is not within the competence of the Tribunal, shall be considered by the Tribunal which shall determine whether to deal with it as a preliminary question or to join in to the merits of the dispute.

1. General. This article embodies the general principle that a tribunal has the power to determine its own competence. The fact that the Secretary-General has not exercised his screening power under art. 36(3) and that the tribunal has been constituted, does not mean that a tribunal is bound to accept jurisdiction. Art. 41 provides the framework, together with Rule 41 of the Arbitration Rules, for what is commonly known as the 'jurisdictional phase' of ICSID proceedings. The jurisdictional phase has become a major feature of many ICSID cases, mostly because of State-respondent parties to BIT arbitrations routinely objecting to jurisdiction. The jurisdiction of an ICSID tribunal may be challenged on a subject-matter basis (e.g. that the dispute does not arise directly out of an investment pursuant to art. 25; or that the tribunal lacks jurisdiction under the contract or applicable investment treaty containing the agreement to arbitrate) and/or on a personal basis (e.g. that the claimant is not a national of a Contracting State). These issues are discussed more fully in art. 25. A tribunal's final award on jurisdiction, when issued, is subject to all the provisions of the Convention relating to awards, including the remedy of annulment (as to which see art. 52).

2. Tribunal as judge of its own competence. Art. 41 gives the tribunal the exclusive power to decide upon matters of its jurisdiction. Thus, art. 41 prevents parties from bringing jurisdictional challenges to the ICSID arbitration process in other fora, such as the International Court of Justice, the Secretary-General of ICSID or domestic courts. The tribunal is still bound by law: as the ad hoc committee in *Soufraki* v *UAE* (DA) warned, 'compétence compétence is, of course, not a license for judicial self-levitation. An ICSID tribunal cannot create jurisdiction for itself where none has been granted by the Convention and the Parties to the dispute.'

3. International Court of Justice. Under art. 64, disputes arising between Contracting States concerning the interpretation or application of the Convention shall be referred to the ICJ, unless the dispute is settled by negotiation. It is clear that this provision does not mean that a party to ICSID proceedings can frustrate those proceedings by seeking to refer to the ICJ any question relating to the competence of a tribunal (*History*, Vol. II, p. 906). No case concerning the competence of an ICSID tribunal (or, indeed, any other question arising from the Convention) has ever been brought before the ICJ.

4. Secretary-General of ICSID. The Report of the Executive Directors on the Convention confirms what is now settled practice; a tribunal is free to decline jurisdiction even if the Secretary-General has found that the dispute is not manifestly outside the Centre's jurisdiction. This principle was initially confirmed by the ICSID tribunal in the case *Holiday Inns* v *Morocco* (DJ), where it found that 'registration does not of course preclude a finding by the Tribunal that the dispute is outside the jurisdiction of the Centre'.

5. Domestic courts. Art. 26 provides that, unless otherwise stated, consent to ICSID arbitration shall exclude other remedies. This follows from the fact that the Convention is a 'complete, exclusive and closed jurisdictional system, insulated from national law' (*Broches Article*, p. 288). From the moment ICSID proceedings have been instituted, domestic courts of ICSID Contracting States must defer to the tribunal's decision on its own jurisdiction. In *Mobil* v *NZ* (NZ), art. 41 was one of the grounds on which the New Zealand High Court ordered a stay of proceedings until the ICSID tribunal had ruled on its jurisdiction. ICSID tribunals do not rely on domestic courts to enforce art. 26 and they will grant costs against parties that have pursued parallel proceedings (*LETCO* v *Liberia*).

6. Review of the tribunal's decision on jurisdiction. In *Klöckner* v *Cameroon* (II) (DA) the ad hoc committee stated that arbitrators have the power to determine their own jurisdiction, subject only to the check of the ad hoc committee in post-award annulment proceedings. Requests for annulment for jurisdictional reasons will normally allege that the tribunal manifestly exceeded its powers in accordance with art. 52(1)(b). If the decision on jurisdiction was joined to the merits of the case and the tribunal's decision on jurisdiction is contained in the award, the award is clearly also subject to annulment.

7. Jurisdictional objections by a party. Rule 41(1) of the Arbitration Rules requires that any objection that a dispute is not within the jurisdiction of the Centre or within the competence of the tribunal be made as early as possible. Jurisdictional objections are sometimes filed immediately upon registration, in which case they will be dealt with as the first order of business when the tribunal is constituted. A party cannot file objections to jurisdiction after the time limit for filing of the counter-memorial has passed (Rule 41(3) of the Arbitration Rules).

8. Raising of a jurisdictional objection suspends proceedings on merits. Once a formal objection to jurisdiction has been filed, the tribunal may then decide to suspend the proceedings on the merits in accordance with Rule 41(3) of the Arbitration Rules. In practice, this almost always happens. ICSID tribunals routinely suspend proceedings on the merits upon receipt of an objection to jurisdiction (e.g. *Continental Casualty* v *Argentina* (DJ) and *Rompetrol* v *Romania*). The tribunal may set time limits for the parties' submissions on the objections to jurisdiction as well as decide its own procedure for determining the objection, which can include written or oral proceedings, or both. Rule 41(2) of the Arbitration Rules states that the tribunal also has the power to consider jurisdictional questions on its own initiative. Failure of the parties to raise jurisdictional objections may be interpreted as implicit consent to jurisdiction, although tribunals are wary of finding that jurisdictional challenges should have been raised earlier (e.g. *Helnan Hotels* v *Egypt*).

9. Right to make observations. During the jurisdictional phase of the arbitration, the parties have the right to submit observations to the tribunal. Increasingly, the observations follow a similar process to the merits phase of the case in the form of an 'objection, answer, reply and rejoinder' procedure.

10. Uncontested proceedings. In default proceedings, a tribunal must examine jurisdiction on its own initiative (Rule 42(4) of the Arbitration Rules). The failure of a tribunal to account for the jurisdictional basis of its award may expose that award to annulment. For example, in *Kaiser Bauxite* v *Jamaica* (DJ), Jamaica failed to appear and the tribunal nonetheless examined its own jurisdiction.

11. Choice between a preliminary decision and a joinder to the merits. The tribunal may deal with jurisdictional questions in one of two ways: either as a separate preliminary issue or part of the award on the merits. Once an award on the merits has been rendered, the decision on jurisdiction becomes part of the final award for the purposes of annulment and recognition. Dealing with jurisdictional questions as preliminary issues will in many cases be more efficient in terms of costs and time.

12. Addressing an objection to jurisdiction as a preliminary question. In practice, ICSID tribunals have tended to address jurisdictional issues primarily as preliminary questions. Where this route is selected, the duration of the ISCID arbitration is likely to be delayed by up to a year. Most high-profile BIT arbitrations now have a lengthy jurisdictional phase before the merits are reached. ICSID tribunals which find that they do have jurisdiction will usually issue a preliminary decision (and not a final award) on jurisdiction, which will then be incorporated into a final award after the merits phase. This is done either by reference, by reciting the conclusions, or relevant parts, of the preliminary decision or by attaching the decision on jurisdiction to the final award. Preliminary decisions on jurisdiction can be challenged at the time of the final award through the annulment procedure. Where, however, the tribunal finds it lacks jurisdiction, it must issue a final award, which is immediately subject to annulment proceedings (Rule 41(6) of the Arbitration Rules).

13. Joinder to the merits. A tribunal may decide to join the jurisdictional question to the merits of the dispute where the answer to the jurisdictional questions depends on testimony and other evidence that can only be obtained through a full hearing of the case. For example, in *Tradex* v *Albania* (DJ), it was found that the issue in both the jurisdictional phase and the merits phase was whether Albania's actions amounted to expropriation.

14. **Jurisdiction and merits.** The jurisdictional issues in an arbitration are conceptually different to the merits issues. Consideration of the merits issues will determine which party is 'right', but consideration of the jurisdictional issues will determine whether the tribunal is an appropriate forum to consider the merits issues at all. In practice, the line between jurisdiction and merits is not always clear cut. In order to determine jurisdiction, the tribunal will often have to look at substantive issues in order to define the scope of its competence (*Inceysa* v *El Salvador*). The tribunal in *Continental Casualty* v *Argentina* (DJ), when discussing the jurisdiction phase of the case, extended the principle from *Inceysa* v *El Salvdor* and found that, although for decisions on questions of jurisdiction the facts asserted by the claimant are normally assumed, if it can be shown that the claim has 'no factual basis even at a preliminary scrutiny' then the tribunal '[will] not be competent to address the subject matter of the dispute' (*Continental Casualty* v *Argentina* (DJ), para. 45).

[**Applicable law**]

Article 42

(1) The Tribunal shall decide a dispute in accordance with such rules of law as may be agreed by the parties. In absence of such agreement, the Tribunal shall apply the law of the Contracting State party to the dispute (including its rules on the conflict of laws) and such rules of international law as may be applicable.

(2) The Tribunal may not bring in a finding of non liquet on the ground of silence or obscurity of the law.

ICSID Convention, art. 42

(3) The provisions of paragraphs (1) and (2) shall not prejudice the power of the Tribunal to decide a dispute ex aequo et bono if the parties so agree.

1. General. Art. 42(1) provides the mechanism for the determination of the appropriate rules of law for a particular dispute. It preserves the freedom of the parties to choose the applicable law, but also provides a default regime in the event that the parties fail to do so. If the parties agree, the tribunal can decide according to good faith or equitable principles – ex aequo et bono (art. 42(3)). Art. 42(2) prevents a tribunal from declaring that there is no applicable law and therefore from refusing to make a finding.

2. Scope. Art. 42 refers to the substantive law that is to be applied to the ICSID arbitration proceedings. The Convention regulates questions of procedural law too (art. 44). Art. 42 does not cover all aspects of the arbitration; for example the question of nationality for art. 25 is governed by the law of the State whose nationality the investor claims. In *CMS* v *Argentina* (DA), the tribunal confirmed that art. 42 is designed for the resolution of disputes on the merits and, as such, it is in principle independent from decisions on jurisdiction, which are governed solely by art. 25 (affirmed in *Noble Energy and Machalapower* v *Ecuador* (DJ)).

3. Choice of law or choice of rules. Art. 42(1) refers to 'rules of law' rather than to systems of law. It is generally accepted, therefore, that the parties do not have to adopt an entire system of law, but are free to combine, select and exclude rules or sets of rules of different origins. The parties will remain subject to certain mandatory or core provisions of the host State's laws such as criminal or labour law. There is no requirement of a reasonable connection between the transaction and the law chosen.

4. Freedom of the parties to choose: in general. Art. 42(1) grants the parties substantial deference in choosing the law that they consider would best regulate their relationship. The parties will generally have agreed on a choice of law clause in their investment agreement, or they may agree the governing law in the course of arbitration proceedings (as was the case in *Benvenuti* v *Congo*). The parties may choose a law they are familiar with, one they trust or one closely connected to the contractual relationship. The State party may insist on the application of its own domestic law as a matter of principle and national prestige. Complex international investment agreements, such as energy and concession contracts, will often choose an applicable law similar to that provided for as the default rule in art. 42, as the reference to international law protects the 'internationalisation' of contractual stabilisation clauses. It is rare for investment agreements to be governed by the law of the investor's home country. However, this is done from time to time, particularly with loan contracts, where there is a practice of submitting the agreement to the law of the lender's country of nationality (see, e.g., *SPP* v *Egypt* (DA)).

5. Freedom of the parties to choose: right to choose international law. The parties may choose that international law be applied either in connection with a national law or on its own. In practice, ICSID tribunals have considered international law even in the presence of an agreement on choice of law that does not incorporate it. For example, in *SPP* v *Egypt* (DA), the tribunal found that although the parties had implicitly agreed to apply Egyptian law, they had not entirely excluded the direct application of international law.

6. Implicit choice of law. Art. 42 leaves open the possibility that the parties can be taken to have chosen a law, even though they have not expressly so provided (*History*, Vol. II, pp. 418, 570). In any well-drafted international investment agreement the applicable law will be expressly stated.

7. Choice of law by reference to domestic legislation. National investment laws providing for ICSID jurisdiction may contain a clause specifying the applicable law. However, the mere fact that jurisdiction is based on a provision of the host State's law cannot be taken as a choice of the host State's law as the governing law of the transaction. In addition, it has not been accepted that the recital in an agreement of a provision of domestic law or even of an entire piece of legislation constitutes a choice of that jurisdiction's law (*SPP* v *Egypt* (DA)).

8. Choice of law by reference to the parties' submissions. Tribunals may use the parties' submissions to help them discover the choice of law. In *Amco* v *Indonesia* (I) (DA), the tribunal held that, as both parties had sought to justify their position with reference to Indonesian law and international law, these were the chosen laws.

9. Choice of law in BIT cases. In ICSID arbitrations commenced under investment treaties, there is often no express choice of law, save for the substantive investment protections contained in the investment treaty itself (as an example of a BIT which does include an express choice of law clause, see art. 9(7) of the Switzerland–Argentina BIT, which provides for a combination of applicable treaties, the law of the host State and international law). Where there is no express choice of law clause contained in a BIT, art. 42 does not apply, except possibly by way of analogy or example, to the interpretation of that BIT. Tribunals seeking to fill gaps have usually invoked public international law principles. Sometimes, as with the 2004 US Model BIT, this is justified on the basis of directions in the investment treaty text. However, the traditional approach to the interpretation of a BIT would apply art. 31 of the Vienna Convention on the Law of Treaties, which provides the established classical rules, also reflected in customary international law, for the interpretation of international agreements. Art. 31(3)(c) of the Vienna Convention specifically provides that relevant principles of international law between the Contracting Parties are to be taken into account in interpreting a treaty between those parties, and was expressly applied in *Siemens* v *Argentina* (DJ). This was also the approach taken in by the tribunal in *AARP* v *Sri Lanka*, one of the earliest ICSID cases.

10. Absence of agreement on choice of law. In order to apply the default rule in art. 42(1), the tribunal must determine that the parties have not agreed on a choice of law. This is a high threshold: the tribunal can review the contractual document governing the parties' relationship for an explicit or implicit choice of law clause, look at the parties' subsequent conduct for any implicit agreement on the choice of law and look at the parties' submissions to the tribunal in the course of the proceedings to infer agreement on a choice of law.

11. Default rule on applicable law: law of the State party and applicable international law. Art. 42(1) states that where the parties have failed to choose the governing law, the tribunal will apply the law of the State party to the dispute and any applicable international law. The certainty provided is a unique feature of the ICSID Convention. For example, art. 17(1) of the UNCITRAL Rules directs the tribunal to apply those rules and principles that they determine to be appropriate.

12. Default rule on applicable law: interpretation. The default rule in fact refers to two different systems of law: the law of the State party to the dispute and applicable international law. Art. 42(1) does not explain how they are to be reconciled. There is evidently a significant interpretation issue, which has not yet been definitively clarified. Traditionally, art. 42(1) has been interpreted in a 'corrective manner', meaning that international law is invoked to trump, rather than merely supplement, any inconsistent provisions in domestic law; see for example *Klöckner* v *Cameroon* (II) (DA). Under this approach, a tribunal may render its award on the basis of the host State's domestic law, even if it finds no positive support in international law, but only so long as there is no contrary rule of international law. In some recent decisions, international tribunals have sought to apply a 'middle ground' approach, which is neither supplementary nor corrective, but seeks to apply shared principles from both legal systems; see, e.g., *CMS* v *Argentina* (FA). Such decisions appear to suggest a case-by-case analysis of which rule – domestic or international – should prevail in case of a conflict. This middle ground is still somewhat ill-defined.

13. Default rule on the applicable law: meaning of 'international law'. The Report of the Executive Directors states that the term 'international law' should be understood in the sense given to it by art. 38(1) of the Statute of the ICJ. Art. 38(1) refers to treaties, custom, general principles of law, judicial decisions and academic writings. The ad hoc committee in *Wena* v *Egypt* (DA) accepted the possibility of a broad approach to the role of international law and that the arbitral tribunal has 'a certain margin and power of interpretation'.

14. Limits on the application of the host State's law. The most important limits on the application of the host State's law arise from the applicable rules of international law (see note 10). Other possible limits to the application of the host State's law concern the status and capacity of the parties, e.g. some domestic legal systems impose limitations on the power of the State and its agencies to enter into arbitration agreements. Note that the legal status and capacity of the foreign investor should not be subject to the control of the host State's law but must continue to be governed by the law of the State of incorporation.

15. Changes in the host State's law. For the investor, the most risky aspect of choosing the host State's law as the governing law is the prospect of subsequent changes in that law which will affect the investment, such as changes in taxation, minimum wages, environmental standards and other aspects of the regulatory framework relied on by the investor. Investors have sought to protect themselves from such changes by negotiating the insertion of a stabilisation clause into the investment contract whereby the host State undertakes to leave the investor unaffected by subsequent changes of the local law. In the absence of a stabilisation clause, the law chosen is understood to include subsequent amendments. The law and practice on the interpretation of stabilisation clauses is complex, but it is clear that any stabilisation clause should be supported by reference to international law.

16. Tribunal may make a finding of non liquet. Art. 42(2) prevents a tribunal from refusing to come to a decision on the basis that the law is not sufficiently clear. Art. 48(3) requires the tribunal to consider every question put to it and reinforces art. 42(2). Where the parties have agreed a choice of law, the tribunal must first exhaust the possibilities of answering the questions put to it under the chosen rules of law. If the chosen laws provide no answer, the tribunal will have recourse to the residual rule in the second sentence of art. 42(1). As stated above, lacunae in the choice of law can be dealt with by looking at the general legal context (including international law) and broader principles. In addition, the tribunal may refer to non-binding authority such as judicial decisions, scholarly writings or codes of conduct to clarify any obscurities.

17. Power of parties to authorise the tribunal to decide ex aequo et bono. Art. 42(3) provides that the parties may authorise a tribunal to disregard the rules of law otherwise applicable under art. 42(1) and come to a decision that is equitable, just and fair.

18. Agreement of the parties to the tribunal deciding ex aequo et bono. The parties must agree that the tribunal will decide ex aequo et bono. The agreement can be made in the investment agreement, it may be authorised under a BIT, or the parties can come to an agreement on its use once the dispute has become apparent or the arbitration has commenced.

19. Non-compliance with art. 42. Failure to apply art. 42 properly may mean that the tribunal's resulting award is annulled (see art. 52, note 7).

In *Klöckner* v *Cameroon* (II) (DA) the ad hoc committee confirmed that non-compliance with art. 42 could constitute an excess of powers and consequently lead to nullity. Similarly in *MTD* v *Chile* (DA), the tribunal stated that a failure to apply the law to which a tribunal is directed by art. 42(1) can constitute a manifest excess of powers.

[Evidence]

Article 43

Except as the parties otherwise agree, the Tribunal may, if it deems it necessary at any stage of the proceedings,
  (a) call upon the parties to produce documents or other evidence, and
  (b) visit the scene connected with the dispute, and conduct such inquiries there as it may deem appropriate.

1. General. Art. 43 specifically empowers an ICSID tribunal to take evidence on its own initiative, subject to the parties' agreement. Art. 43 should be read subject to Rules 33 and 34 of the Arbitration Rules, which provide more detailed guidelines.

2. Except as the parties otherwise agree. The parties are free to vary the terms of art. 43 or to agree for other specific rules to govern the taking of evidence. If the parties do not wish to present evidence, they may submit to the tribunal an agreed statement of facts together with a request to render an award purely on the legal issues in dispute. Rule 21 of the Arbitration Rules provides that a pre-hearing conference may be arranged for an exchange of information and the stipulation of uncontested facts to expedite proceedings.

3. Discretion of the tribunal. Rule 34 of the Arbitration Rules provides that the tribunal has complete discretion as to the admissibility and probative value of any evidence adduced and has the power to summon further evidence.

4. At any stage of the proceedings. The tribunal may request further information and evidence as the need arises. For example, in *AGIP* v *Congo*, the tribunal requested the production of documents before it had received memorials because the claimant's records had been seized by the Congo in the course of the nationalisation. Further, the tribunal remains free to accept evidence from the parties (even after the expiry of time limits – see *Benvenuti* v *Congo*) and to examine evidence up to the time it renders the award. Rule 38 of the Arbitration Rules provides that, even after closure of the proceeding, the tribunal may reopen it in order to take new evidence. This was done in *Klöckner* v *Cameroon* (I) (DA). If new evidence arises after an award has been rendered, the award can be revised under art. 51.

5. Call upon the parties to produce. Whilst the parties will generally provide the relevant evidence on their own initiative, the tribunal may request further information from the parties when it considers that the evidence supplied remains incomplete. The tribunal does not have any procedural right to request judicial assistance or help from national authorities to obtain evidence. Under Rule 39(5) of the Arbitration Rules the parties may agree that provisional measures may be requested from domestic courts. Such requests, however, may only be made by the parties. Professor Schreuer expresses the view that, ignoring the travaux préparatoires of art. 43, nothing in the article prevents a tribunal directly inviting a witness to appear before it and testify. However, a tribunal clearly has no power to compel such a witness to do so (Schreuer, *Commentary*, p. 654). Similarly, a tribunal may directly approach independent experts and request reports from them (*AMT* v *Zaire*). But again, a tribunal cannot order third parties, including experts, to provide evidence.

6. Form. There is no prescibed form which the tribunal must follow to call upon the parties to produce the evidence. In the context of visits and inquiries, however, Rule 37 of the Arbitration Rules requires the tribunal to make a procedural order under Rule 19 of the Arbitration Rules.

7. Legal effect of procedural orders. Whilst procedural orders do not have the same status as awards in terms of recognition and enforcement under arts. 53 and 54, Rule 34(3) of the Arbitration Rules creates a duty on the part of the parties to cooperate with the tribunal in the production of evidence. If the parties fail to cooperate, the tribunal may draw the appropriate inferences in the resulting award, in accordance with general international arbitration practice. Adverse costs awards may also be made.

8. Documents. Rule 34(2)(a) of the Arbitration Rules refers to documents, witnesses and experts. In requests for additional documentation, tribunals usually ask for financial statements and accounts, memoranda and notes or correspondence.

9. Witnesses. The attendance of a witness will generally be arranged by the parties as the tribunal has no power to compel their attendance. Rule 35 of the Arbitration Rules governs the examination of witnesses. Witnesses will normally testify before the tribunal and in the presence of the parties, although this rule may be waived (see Rule 35 of the Arbitration Rules).

10. Experts. The testimony and examination of experts is governed by the same rules as for witnesses (they are expressly mentioned in Rules 34 to 36 of the Arbitration Rules). Rule 35(3) of the Arbitration Rules requires each expert to make a declaration before making his statement. Both the tribunal and parties can ask an expert to provide evidence.

11. Rules of evidence. ICSID arbitration is not governed by formal rules of evidence. Rule 33 of the Arbitration Rules provides that each party is to communicate to the Secretary-General precise information regarding the evidence that it intends to produce and that it intends to request the tribunal to call for. Rule 34(1) of the Arbitration Rules grants tribunals the discretion to assess the probative value of any evidence put to it.

12. Expenses. Under art. 61(2), the tribunal decides how and by whom expenses are to be paid and Rule 28(1)(b) of the Arbitration Rules provides that the tribunal may decide that the related costs shall be borne entirely or in a particular share by one of the parties. Therefore if one party is responsible for the need to obtain evidence, that party may be liable for all or a large portion of the cost of doing so; e.g., in *SOABI* v *Senegal*, the tribunal accepted both Senegal's demand that SOABI's accounts be audited because SOABI had failed to explain its figures, and that the related costs be borne by SOABI.

13. Visiting the scene connected with the dispute. Rule 34(2)(b) of the Arbitration Rules authorises the tribunal to visit any place connected with the dispute or to conduct inquiries there. Rule 37 of the Arbitration Rules requires a separate procedural order, made under Rule 19 of the Arbitration Rules, for any visits and inquiries. If a particular visit or inquiry is undertaken upon a request of a party, that party may be liable for any connected costs. Schreuer interprets the specific mention of visits in the Convention to mean that Contracting Parties cannot deny the tribunal or parties' representatives access to territory for this purpose (Schreuer, *Commentary*, p. 664). Arbitrators, parties, experts and witnesses have immunities whilst engaged in visits (arts. 21 and 22).

14. Evidence-taking in international arbitration generally. Provisions empowering tribunals to take evidence are, of course, a standard feature of international arbitration rules. See, for example, arts. 16, 24, 25 and 27 of the UNCITRAL Rules, ICC Rules 63 to 75 and LCIA rules 15 and 20 to 22. The non-binding IBA Rules on the Taking of Evidence in International Commercial Arbitration, which are often used as guidelines (if not adopted) by ICSID tribunals, contain detailed procedures for the submission of documentary evidence (see art. 3), the taking of witness evidence (see art. 4) and on-site inspections (see art. 7). Revisions are presently under consideration which may adapt the IBA Rules to relate more directly to ICSID arbitrations.

[Rules on procedure]

Article 44

Any arbitration proceeding shall be conducted in accordance with the provisions of this Section and, except as the parties otherwise agree, in accordance with the Arbitration Rules in effect on the date on which the parties consented to arbitration. If any question of procedure arises which is not covered by this Section or the Arbitration Rules or any rules agreed by the parties, the Tribunal shall decide the question.

1. General. Art. 44 is the procedural counterpart to the substantive choice of law provision of art. 42(1). Art. 44 directs the tribunal and the parties to use ICSID's Arbitration Rules as in effect at the date on which the parties consented to arbitration (the most recent revision was in April 2006), in addition to the procedural rules contained in the Convention. Art. 44 creates a comprehensive and self-contained system that is insulated from national rules of procedure. Accordingly, the place of proceedings has no influence on procedure before an ICSID tribunal. The parties are free to adapt the Arbitration Rules (subject to certain limits), or even to substitute their own rules, although this would usually be an impractical decision.

2. Any arbitration proceeding. The Arbitration Rules come into force for each dispute once the tribunal is constituted. In addition, they regulate certain post-award procedures including proceedings before an ad hoc committee (Rule 53 of the Arbitration Rules). Art. 44 also applies to proceedings before a tribunal to which the case is resubmitted after annulment under art. 52(6).

3. Conducted in accordance with the provisions of 'this Section'. Art. 44 provides that any arbitration shall be conducted in accordance with the provisions of 'this Section', which is a reference to Section 3 of Chapter IV of the Convention containing arts. 41 to 47, which deal with the tribunal's power to determine its own jurisdiction, applicable law, the taking of evidence, default proceedings, incidental or additional claims, counterclaims and provisional measures. However, in addition to Section 3 of Chapter IV, procedural rules are contained in arts. 48, 49, 50, 51, 56, 57, 58, 60, 61 and 63. The parties cannot derogate from arts. 37 to 40, 56 and 59 to 61 relating to the composition of the tribunal.

4. Except as the parties otherwise agree. Whilst the parties may agree to vary the Arbitration Rules, the Convention's procedural provisions as referred to in this Section are mandatory. In addition, the Institution Rules and the Administrative and Financial Regulations cannot be derogated from by the parties, save to the extent permitted by a particular rule or regulation. Accordingly, to the extent that an Arbitration Rule restates the substance of a relevant Convention article, it may not be amended by the parties. Although, in principle, the parties can agree to apply procedural rules other than the Arbitration Rules, the Arbitration Rules were drafted specifically for the Convention and other rules may not be as effective.

5. In accordance with the Arbitration Rules. The Arbitration Rules are subject to the Convention. In the unlikely event of a conflict, the Convention prevails. The Institution Rules govern the procedure for the submission of the request for arbitration, the registration of the request and the dispatch of the notice of registration to the parties. All proceedings from the tribunal's constitution are governed by the Arbitration Rules. The Administrative and Financial Regulations deal in the main with the internal procedure of the Centre but some touch upon arbitration procedure with regard to costs, means of communication, the place of the proceedings and time limits. The Institutional Rules and the Administrative and Financial Regulations are always applied in their most recent version.

6. Which version of the Arbitration Rules? The original Arbitration Rules came into force in 1968; they were amended in September 1984 and April 2006. Art. 44 is expressed so that the Arbitration Rules as they existed at the time of consent to arbitration apply, as opposed to the date on which the request was filed or the proceeding registered. As a result, any change to the Arbitration Rules subsequent to the date of consent will be ignored. The parties are not constrained by this aspect of art. 44, however, and can agree to apply the Arbitration Rules in their most recent form rather than as in force at the time of consent. In practice, this is done by advance agreement between the parties. Once an arbitration is underway, it becomes difficult to agree changes to the procedural framework.

7. Residual power of the tribunal to decide procedural matters not covered by the Convention or the Arbitration Rules. The final sentence of art. 44(1) authorises the tribunal to make decisions on procedure where the rules do not cover the procedural issue at hand and the established methods of interpretation for treaties and other legal documents fail to yield an answer to the question of procedure under consideration. If the tribunal then finds that the rules genuinely do not cover the situation, it may not, however, go beyond the framework of the Convention, the Arbitration Rules and the parties' procedural agreements. Art. 44 is sometimes invoked by tribunals, for instance in *Aguas Argentinas* v *Argentina*, the tribunal concluded that art. 44 granted it the power to admit amicus curiae submissions from suitable non-parties in appropriate cases.

[Default of a party]

Article 45

(1) Failure of a party to appear or to present his case shall not be deemed an admission of the other party's assertions.

(2) If a party fails to appear or to present his case at any stage of the proceedings the other party may request the Tribunal to deal with the questions submitted to it and to render an award. Before rendering an award, the Tribunal shall notify, and grant a period of grace to, the party failing to appear or to present its case, unless it is satisfied that that party does not intend to do so.

1. General. Where a party does not cooperate in the arbitral proceedings the cooperating party can ask the tribunal to continue the proceedings and render an award (art. 45 and Rule 42 of the Arbitration Rules). This default procedure does not lead to a 'default award'. The tribunal must still make a reasoned decision and can find in favour of the non-cooperating party.

2. Failure to appear is not deemed an admission of the other party's case: jurisdictional issues. In default proceedings, a tribunal must satisfy itself of the Centre's jurisdiction and its own competence, whereas in contested proceedings it will normally restrict itself to dealing with jurisdictional objections raised by the parties. In both *Kaiser Bauxite* v *Jamaica* (DJ) and *LETCO* v *Liberia*, the tribunal was forced to make an examination of jurisdiction on its own initiative because the respondent party that would normally challenge jurisdiction was not cooperating.

3. Failure to appear is not deemed an admission of the other party's case: merits issues. In the merits phase of the proceedings, the place of the tribunal becomes even more difficult as it has to act as an examiner of the evidence put forward by the cooperating party. This position may not help the cooperating party – the tribunal will be forced to take a critical view of arguments it may have easily accepted if it did not have such a responsibility to examine.

4. What constitutes default? The most orthodox instances of default are a failure to appear at all, or failure to make advance payments in accordance with Reg. 14(3) of the Administrative and Financial Regulations. It is possible that making consistently weak filings or repeatedly missing deadlines will be interpreted as an effective default.

5. Request by party. Rule 42(1) of the Arbitration Rules provides that if a party fails to appear or to present its case at any stage of the proceeding, the other party may request the tribunal to deal with the questions submitted to it and to render an award. If the cooperating party is the claimant, it may request the tribunal to decide in its favour on the merits. If the cooperating party is the respondent, it may request the tribunal to discontinue the proceeding altogether (Rule 44 of the Arbitration Rules). If there is no request by the other party that the tribunal render an award or discontinue the proceeding and no further steps are taken by either party during six consecutive months, the proceeding must be discontinued for failure of the parties to act (Rule 45 of the Arbitration Rules).

6. At any stage of the proceeding. Default may occur at any stage of the proceeding. Art. 45 covers all stages and aspects of procedure before the tribunal and extends up to the time of the discontinuance of the proceeding. Art. 45 also covers the jurisdictional phase. It is therefore possible for a party to be in default even if it is later found that the tribunal lacked jurisdiction. If the proceeding is not discontinued, the application of art. 45 extends to proceedings for the interpretation, revision and annulment of the resulting award.

7. Discretion of the tribunal. It is up to the tribunal to determine whether default has occurred. Declaring a party in default is a measure of last resort, which the tribunal should apply once it has concluded that there is no realistic chance that the uncooperative party will cooperate. In exercising its discretion, the tribunal may take into consideration special circumstances affecting the defaulting party. For example, in *AMT* v *Congo*, the Congo said that its failures were due to the 'unfortunate and disastrous' consequences of the political situation in the country at the time.

8. Tribunal to deal with the questions submitted to it and to render an award. Art. 45(2) reiterates the obligation under art. 48(3) that an award must deal with every question submitted to the tribunal. Unless the proceeding is discontinued, the tribunal's duty to deal with the questions submitted to it in default proceedings applies in the same way as in contested proceedings. If the tribunal finds that it has jurisdiction, it must decide on the substantive questions before it in the form of an award on the merits. If it declines jurisdiction, that decision also will be given in the form of an award.

9. Grace period. Rule 42 of the Arbitration Rules provides that a grace period should be given to an uncooperative party which should not exceed sixty days. The commentary on Rule 42 of the Arbitration Rules provides further detail with regard to grace periods.

10. Non-compliance with art. 45. A tribunal's failure to abide by the rules of art. 45 may expose the resulting award to annulment under art. 52.

[Ancillary claims]

Article 46

Except as the parties otherwise agree, the Tribunal shall, if requested by a party, determine any incidental or additional claims or counterclaims arising directly out of the subject-matter of the dispute provided that they are within the scope of the consent of the parties and are otherwise within the jurisdiction of the Centre.

1. General. Art. 46 and Rule 40 of the Arbitration Rules allow the claimant to raise incidental or additional claims and the respondent to raise counterclaims that relate to the same facts as in the main proceedings. The art. 46 procedure can generate considerable cost savings in complex cases and allows parties to be more strategic in the way they conduct the arbitration. Rule 40 of the Arbitration Rules prescribes that an incidental or additional claim is to be presented not later than a party's reply, and a counterclaim must be presented no later than a party's counter-memorial, absent extenuating circumstances. By way of analogy, art. 19(3) of the UNCITRAL Rules contains a similar provision that allows the respondent to make a counterclaim arising out of the same contract or rely on a claim arising out of the same contract for the purpose of a set-off.

2. Except as the parties otherwise agree. The parties may vary or exclude the tribunal's power to deal with ancillary claims in their consent agreement or subsequently. Only the parties can initiate ancillary claims, the tribunal may not do so on its own motion.

3. Obligation to decide. The tribunal has no discretion to refuse to consider ancillary claims. Failure to deal with an ancillary claim could lead to annulment for a manifest excess of powers under art. 52(1)(b) or failure to state reasons in the award under art. 52(1)(e).

4. Incidental or additional claims or counterclaims. The distinction between incidental and additional is not legally significant. Broadly, an incidental claim arises as a consequence of the primary claim, whereas an additional claim is an amendment to the original pleading. Typical incidental claims include claims against third parties, interest claims and motions relating to costs in the arbitration. A counterclaim is a claim made by the respondent.

5. Arising directly out of the subject-matter of the dispute. Ancillary claims must be so close to the primary claim as to require the adjudication of the ancillary claim before the primary claim can be finally settled. This close connection is distinct from the 'arising directly out of' condition of jurisdiction in art. 25. The 'arising directly out of' clause in art. 46 presupposes jurisdiction. In *CMS* v *Argentina* (DJ), the tribunal concluded that CMS's claims were of the nature of ancillary claims which, in accordance with art. 46 of the Convention and Rule 40 of the Arbitration Rules; arose directly out of the dispute; were within the scope of the consent of the parties; and were otherwise within the jurisdiction of the Centre.

6. Within the scope of the consent of the parties and jurisdiction of the Centre. The tribunal can only adjudicate once consent has been given by the parties. In cases where jurisdiction is based on a general offer by the host State contained in its legislation or a treaty, consent will be restricted to the extent of the investor's acceptance of the offer. If the investor accepts the offer by instituting proceedings, such consent exists only to the extent necessary to deal with the investor's request. It may be possible for a respondent State party to assert an ancillary claim which is sufficiently closely connected to the investor's claim, but art. 46 cannot be used to extend the jurisdiction of the tribunal beyond the scope of the parties' consent and a State cannot therefore rely on its general consent to arbitration to extend the tribunal's jurisdiction.

7. Timing. Rule 40(2) of the Arbitration Rules states than an incidental or additional claim shall be presented during the course of the written proceedings and no later than in the reply. A counterclaim must be presented no later than in the counter-memorial. A tribunal may authorise a later submission but this requires a specific decision by the tribunal after having heard any objections from the other party. Upon presentation of an ancillary claim by one party, the other party must be given an opportunity to file observations subject to any time limits fixed by the tribunal.

ICSID Convention, art. 47

[Provisional measures]

Article 47

Except as the parties otherwise agree, the Tribunal may, if it considers that the circumstances so require, recommend any provisional measures which should be taken to preserve the respective rights of either party.

1. General. It is common for international arbitration rules to give a tribunal the power to grant provisional measures (e.g. see art. 26(1) of the UNCITRAL Rules, which provides a broader power than in ICSID arbitrations for the tribunal to grant such measures, not limited to the preservation of rights of the parties). Art. 47 should be read in conjunction with Rule 39 of the Arbitration Rules, which provides a detailed procedural framework for the granting of provisional measures. Rule 39(6) of the Arbitration Rules restricts the parties from seeking provisional relief before domestic courts, unless they have agreed otherwise in their consent to arbitrate. This effectively means that provisional measures cannot be obtained from a domestic court in BIT proceedings commenced under the Convention (unless this is expressly provided for in the relevant BIT).

2. 'Recommend' or 'order'? There has been a long-standing debate as to whether the use of the word 'recommend' in art. 47 means that a tribunal lacks the power to 'order' provisional measures. At an early stage in the drafting history of the Convention, the word 'order' was used, only to be replaced by the word 'recommend' so as to avoid difficult questions as to the enforcement of injunctions against State parties (Broches, *Explanatory Notes and Survey*, para 100). Art. 47 of the Additional Facility Arbitration Rules, in contrast, provides that the tribunal has the power to 'order' provisional measures upon the request of the parties. Recently, however, ICSID tribunals have held that they do have the power to issue binding orders for provisional measures. Thus, in *Maffezini* v *Spain*, the tribunal stated that 'the word "recommend" is of equivalent value as the word "order"' and even more strongly that 'the Tribunal's authority to rule on provisional measures is no less binding than that of a final award'. This interpretation has been affirmed by other ICSID tribunals, for example *Tokios Tekelès* v Ukraine and *Occidental* v *Ecuador* (DPM).

3. Except as the parties otherwise agree. The parties are free to exclude art. 47, vary the measures available to the tribunal or expressly stipulate that provisional measures will be binding between them.

4. Discretion of the tribunal to recommend provisional measures. Whilst the tribunal has the power to recommend measures on its own initiative, in practice it is generally an interested party who will initiate action under art. 47. The tribunal is also able to recommend measures not specifically requested by a party but, again, this will be rare in practice. Under Rule

39(3) of the Arbitration Rules, the tribunal may at any time modify or revoke provisional measures if they are no longer required by the circumstances.

5. If the tribunal considers the circumstances so require. There is little assistance from the travaux préparatoires to the Convention regarding the circumstances which would justify provisional measures (*History*, Vol. II, pp. 337 *et seq.*, 515, 573). There are situations in which the requirements of necessity and urgency are normally present, such as stopping the destruction of evidence; creating conditions that will allow compliance with a final award and costs order; preventing a party from seeking relief through domestic tribunals in breach of the consent to arbitrate; and preventing escalation of the dispute during the arbitration.

6. Urgency of provisional measures. Under Rule 39(1) of the Arbitration Rules a party may request provisional measures from the moment proceedings are instituted. Rule 39(3) of the Arbitration Rules allows the Secretary-General to fix time limits for the making of submissions relating to a request for provisional measures, so that it can be promptly considered by the tribunal upon its constitution. Rule 39(2) of the Arbitration Rules requires tribunals to deal with provisional measures motions as a matter of priority. Rule 16(2) of the Arbitration Rules allows the tribunal to take a decision by correspondence between the members. However, even in such an expedited procedure, both parties must be heard before provisional measures may be recommended. In *Occidental* v *Ecuador* (DPM), the tribunal, applying a traditional formulation of the provisional measures test, found a requirement that the measures be urgently needed to prevent irreparable harm. That interpretation has been cast into doubt since *City Oriente* v *Petroecuador* where the test was recast as requiring that the 'harm spared by the petitioner by such measures must be significant and that it exceed greatly the damaged caused to the party affected thereby'. Subsequent to *City Oriente* v *Petroecuador*, the tribunal in *Paushok* v *Mongolia* cited *Occidental* v *Ecuador* (DPM) and confirmed the application of the 'irreparable harm' test to arbitrations taking place under UNCITRAL rules. It is unclear if the formulation in *City Oriente* v *Petroecuador* will be applied by future ICSID tribunals

7. Circumstances in cases before ICSID tribunals. The Convention and the Arbitration Rules do not specify what types of provisional measures may be recommended. Under Rule 39(1) of the Arbitration Rules, a party must specify the provisional measures it is seeking. The measures to be requested and ultimately recommended will depend on the particular dispute. Provisional measures must be directed to the parties, who are the only entities over which the tribunal has jurisdiction. Some examples are given in notes 7-10.

8. Preservation of evidence. In *Biwater* v *Tanzania*, the claimants were concerned about access to paper records during the arbitration (*Biwater* v *Tanzania* Procedural Order No. 1). The tribunal found that '[i]t is uncontroversial that the Arbitral Tribunal's powers under art. 47 include the power to recommend the preservation of evidence.' Although noting the significant overlap in this context between provisional measures orders under art. 47 and orders in relation to evidence under art. 43, the tribunal granted the provisional measures to preserve evidence.

9. Preserving confidentiality. The respondents in *World Duty Free* v *Kenya* secured a recommendation as a provisional measure that all reports of the case be accurate, on the basis that the dispute would be otherwise aggravated. A similar provisional measure was ordered in *Biwater* v *Tanzania* (Procedural Order No. 3), to restrict leaks being made to the press. Biwater sought an order preventing Tanzania from disclosing certain information such as the Minutes of Session, Procedural Orders and documents disclosed in the proceedings. Tanzania argued that as the danger of an aggravation or exacerbation of the dispute had yet to manifest itself in concrete terms, the tribunal was not warranted to impose a provisional measure. The tribunal held that its mandate extended to reducing the risk of future aggravation and exacerbation of the dispute. Equally, however, the tribunal recognised the interests of transparency and public information. Accordingly, the parties were prohibited from disclosing to third parties the minutes and records of the hearings, any documents produced in the hearings, any of the pleadings and any correspondence between the parties and the tribunal. The parties were, however, permitted to engage in general discussion about the case in public, provided that any such public discussion was necessary and not used as an instrument to antagonise the parties or create undue pressure. However, a similar claim in *Amco* v *Indonesia* had been rejected on the basis that there was no evidence that the newspaper reports would in fact have exacerbated the dispute (*Amco* v *Indonesia* (DPM)). In *CMS* v *Argentina* (DPM), the claimant requested that the tribunal issue a formal order declaring that the hearings were private and that Argentina cease publishing excerpts of the hearing in the press, again on the basis that this was likely to exacerbate the dispute. The application was rejected on the basis that the claimant failed to demonstrate that it had suffered prejudice or irreparable damage.

10. Security for costs. In *Atlantic Triton* v *Guinea*, the tribunal confirmed that it was acceptable to request provisional measures for a financial guarantee if there were concerns that the other party may not be able to honour an eventual award. It is notoriously difficult for parties to succeed in claims for security for costs. For example, in *Casado and Allende Foundation* v *Chile*, it was held, after a careful examination of the ICSID convention and comparative practice, that in certain circumstances security for costs would be available. However, that statement was made with considerable hesitation. The tribunal felt that the silence of the ICSID Convention when it came to security for costs 'seems to entail a certain presumption that such a measure is not authorised or included [in the ICSID Convention]'. The measures sought were in fact rejected.

11. Anti-suit injunctions. Anti-suit injunctions were sought in the first case brought before an ICSID tribunal. In *Holiday Inns* v *Morocco* (DJ), the tribunal's decision did not specifically request that Morocco's actions in its domestic courts be withdrawn, but it did ask the parties to refrain from actions which were contrary to the contract between them. The issue has arisen more recently in *SGS* v *Pakistan*. The tribunal in *SGS* v *Pakistan* was faced with a situation where the Supreme Court of Pakistan had granted an anti-suit injunction preventing the claimant pursuing its case under the Convention. The tribunal recommended that the Government of Pakistan refrain from initiating domestic contempt proceedings, ensure contempt proceedings were not initiated by third parties and, in the case of contempt proceedings initiated by a third party, inform the domestic court of the status of the ICSID arbitration.

12. Protected rights. The Convention and the Arbitration Rules do not specify which of the parties' rights may be protected by provisional measures. Under Rule 39(1) of the Arbitration Rules, a party requesting provisional measures must specify the right it is seeking to be preserved. Rights that have been invoked include non-aggravation of the dispute, non-frustration of the eventual award, preservation and production of evidence, confidentiality of proceedings and preservation of the exclusive nature of ICSID arbitration under art. 26. In *Plama Consortium Limited* v *Bulgaria*, the tribunal stated that the rights to be preserved must relate to the requesting party's ability to have its claims in the arbitration fairly considered and determined. In *City Oriente* v *Petroecuador* (DPM), the tribunal stated that art. 47 provides authorisation for the passing of provisional measures that prohibit any action that affects the 'disputed rights, aggravates the dispute, frustrates the effectiveness of the award or entails having either party take justice into their own hands'. In that case, the tribunal adopted provisional measures prohibiting Ecuador from: instituting any judicial proceedings against City Oriente and/or its employees or officers; demanding that City Oriente pay any amount as a result of the application of the relevant law; or engaging in any conduct that may directly or indirectly affect the legal situation agreed upon under the relevant contract.

13. Provisional measures and jurisdiction. Giving priority to a request for provisional measures may mean that a tribunal will have to deal with such a request before having ruled on its own jurisdiction. Consequently, a party may find a provisional measure being made against it by a tribunal whose jurisdiction it is contesting. The tribunal in *Occidental* v *Ecuador* (DPM) determined that whilst the absence of a complete examination of jurisdiction issues will not preclude the recommendation of provisional measures, the tribunal must establish that it has at least prima facie jurisdiction.

14. Provisional measures not award. A recommendation for provisional measures does not constitute an award and so is not subject to annulment or enforcement proceedings under the Convention.

15. Provisional nature. Provisional measures are only recommended for the duration of the proceedings, and can be modified or revoked at any time.

16. Obtaining provisional measures from a court. Rule 39(6) of the Arbitration Rules provides that provisional measures can only be requested from a national court or any other authority if the parties have so agreed in the agreement recording their consent to arbitration. As no such agreement is generally to be found in investment treaties (or, indeed, in most investor-State contracts), the arbitral tribunal is the only body that can award provisional measures in an ICSID BIT arbitration. This was recognised by the English Court of Appeal in *Ecuador* v *Occidental* (UK) and *ETI Telecom* v *Bolivia* (UK). In contrast, where a BIT arbitration is conducted under the UNCITRAL Rules, provisional measures can be sought from domestic courts pursuant to art. 26(3).

17. Enforcement of provisional measures by a court. In order to obtain a domestic court order to enforce provisional measures granted by ICSID tribunals, the domestic court will need to be persuaded that ICSID 'recommendations' are in fact binding orders. Given the current trend in the cases cited in note 2, this should not be difficult. Further, domestic courts have shown that they will consider ICSID provisional measures orders that relate to the domestic proceedings. In *MINE* v *Guinea* (Geneva), the Swiss courts took into account the ICSID provisional measure directed at MINE recommending that it discontinue proceedings against Guinea in the national courts.

Section 4. The Award

[Award]

Article 48

(1) The Tribunal shall decide questions by a majority of the votes of all its members.

(2) The award of the Tribunal shall be in writing and shall be signed by the members of the Tribunal who voted for it.

(3) The award shall deal with every question submitted to the Tribunal, and shall state the reasons upon which it is based.

(4) Any member of the Tribunal may attach his individual opinion to the award, whether he dissents from the majority or not, or a statement of his dissent.

(5) The Centre shall not publish the award without the consent of the parties.

1. General. Art. 48 addresses a number of matters principally related to the award, including: majority decisions, separate opinions and the form, content and publication of the award.

2. Application. Art. 48(1) applies to preliminary and procedural questions as well as to questions that arise in the award itself, in addition to the rectification, interpretation, revision and annulment of the award under arts. 49, 50, 51 and 52. The remainder of art. 48 on its own terms applies only to awards. Although the Convention fails to provide a definition of 'award', Schreuer defines an award as a final decision of the tribunal by which it disposes of all questions before it (Schreuer, *Commentary*, p. 792). Other decisions of the tribunal are not awards (such as preliminary decisions on jurisdiction, decisions to recommend provisional measures, procedural orders and decisions on requests for the supplementation, rectification, interpretation and revisions of awards) (Schreuer, *Commentary*, p. 793). The provisions of art. 48 are mandatory and cannot be modified or dispensed with by the parties.

3. Decision by majority. Every draft of the Convention contained a rule that an ICSID tribunal should decide by majority (*History*, Vol. I, p. 209). Dr. Broches has explained that 'majority' means a simple majority, i.e. half of the members of the tribunal plus one (*History*, Vol. II, p. 270). Accordingly, a majority will always be attainable as ICSID tribunals may only consist of a sole arbitrator or any uneven number of arbitrators (art. 37(2)(a)). Neither the Convention nor the Arbitration Rules provide for the contingency where a tribunal fails to reach a majority decision. However, Schreuer notes that the mandatory language of art. 48(1) suggests that the tribunal is under a duty to deliberate until a majority has been reached (Schreuer, *Commentary*, p. 789). In practice, a member may be required to vote in favour of a decision even though he has expressed a different opinion, purely with the aim of reaching a majority (*Guinea-Bissau* v *Senegal*). The tribunal can make its decision either by voting in person or by correspondence (Rule 16 of the Arbitration Rules). If the tribunal makes its decision by correspondence, every member must be consulted. However, so long as a majority is reached, every member need not respond (Rule 16(2), Arbitration Rules; Schreuer, *Commentary*, p. 786). If the tribunal makes its decision in person, except if the parties agree otherwise, the presence of a majority of the members of the tribunal shall be required at its sittings (Rule 14(2) of the Arbitration Rules). Abstention shall count as a negative vote (Rule 16(1) of the Arbitration Rules). No decision shall be made during a vacancy of a tribunal member (Rule 10(2) of the Arbitration Rules).

4. Award must be in writing and signed. The award must be in writing. There is no requirement that the tribunal deliver the award orally (*History*, Vol. II, at pp. 826-827 and 939). Further details on the form of the award are set out in Rule 47 of the Arbitration Rules. The award must contain, inter alia, the names of the parties, the names of their agents/counsel/advocates, the names of the tribunal members and the details of the proceedings (date, place, summary, statement of facts). The requirements of form set out in art. 48 and Rule 47 of the Arbitration Rules also apply to the final decisions of ad hoc committees on annulment (art. 54(2); Rule 53 of the Arbitration Rules). The award must be signed and dated by the tribunal members who voted for it. The signing must take place within 120 days of the decision, although this period may be extended by an additional sixty days (Rule 46 of the Arbitration Rules). The date at which the last signature is added is the date relevant to the Secretary-General's duty to dispatch a certified copy of the award to the parties (art. 49(1) and Rule 48(1) of the Arbitration Rules). The date at which these copies are dispatched is the date of the award for the purposes of the time limits applicable to requests for supplementation, rectification, revision and annulment.

5. Award must deal with every question and state reasons. The requirement that, in its award, the tribunal must deal with every question submitted to it and state the reasons upon which the decision is based are general principles of the law of arbitration (Schreuer, *Commentary*, pp. 798 and 800). The requirement to state reasons is a particularly important one, since failure to do so is a ground for annulment under art. 52(1)(e). At the time of drafting the Convention, Dr. Broches explained that the reader must be able to follow the reasoning of the tribunal both on points of fact and of law (*History*, Vol. II, p. 515). This principle has been interpreted differently by annulment committees over the years. In what has been described as the first generation of annulment decisions, early ad hoc committees held that a failure by the tribunal to deal with every argument, and give reasons for upholding or rejecting each one, could expose the award to annulment for failure to state reasons. Moreover, contradictory, dubious or hypothetical reasoning could also result in annulment (*Klöckner* v *Cameroon* (I) (DA); *Amco* v *Indonesia* (I) (DA)). In the second generation of annulment decisions, ad hoc committees narrowed the scope for review of the tribunal's reasoning, but confirmed that contradictory reasons could still lead to annulment (*MINE* v *Guinea* (DA); *Klöckner* v *Cameroon* (II) (DA)). The third generation of annulment decisions represent an ever higher water mark. Recent ad hoc committees have held that an award should only be annulled where no reasons are provided or where the reasons provided are so contradictory as to cancel each other out. not simply where they are inappropriate, unconvincing or inadequate (*Lucchetti* v *Peru* (DA); *CMS* v *Argentina* (DA)). In particular, the ad hoc committees in *Wena* v *Egypt* (DA) and *Vivendi* v *Argentina* (I) (DA) emphasised that their role was limited to reviewing issues of jurisdiction and procedure and not the merits of a case. An examination of the reasons should thus not mask a re-examination of the merits, since this would amount to an appeal in violation of art. 53(1). It should be noted that since art. 48(3) only applies to awards, its requirements will not necessarily apply to other decisions, such as decisions recommending preliminary measures.

6. Individual opinions. Both concurring and dissenting opinions are allowed under art. 48(4) and Rule 47(3) of the Arbitration Rules. Art. 48(4) appears to allow for a mere statement to be given in dissent, but to require a full opinion if the tribunal member is in the majority. Concurring opinions are permitted to be brief and confined to a small number of points (*SOABI* v

Senegal). The requirements of art. 48(3) relating to reasoned awards do not apply to dissenting statements or opinions (Schreuer, *Commentary*, p. 817).

7. Publication of award. Art. 48(5) states that the Centre shall not publish the award without the consent of the parties. Rule 48(4) of the Arbitration Rules provides the additional requirement that the Centre shall promptly include in its publications excerpts of the legal reasoning of the tribunal. The award, or excerpts thereof, will be published in the ICSID Review – Foreign Investment Law Journal or on the Centre's website (<www.worldbank.org>). Accordingly, the public has access to the decisions and/or reasoning of ICSID tribunals, forming a body of case law that can be utilised in future ICSID (and other) proceedings. While the decision of one ICSID tribunal is not binding on another, past decisions can be used as persuasive authority and guidance as to how a new tribunal could deal with the same or a similar issue. Tribunal members are bound to protect the confidentiality of proceedings and the privacy of deliberations (Rules 6(2) and 15 of the Arbitration Rules). These rules apply only to the Centre and the tribunal and not the parties. Accordingly, the parties are free to publish the award or release information regarding proceedings pending before a tribunal (*Amco* v *Indonesia* (I)), provided that in doing so they do not exacerbate the dispute (*CMS* v *Argentina*, (DPM)) (see art. 47). In *Biwater* v *Tanzania* Procedural Order No. 3, the parties were prohibited from disclosing to third parties the minutes and records of the hearings, any documents produced in the hearings, any of the pleadings and any correspondence between the parties and the tribunal. The parties were, however, permitted to engage in general discussion about the case in public, provided that any such public discussion was necessary and not used as an instrument to antagonise the parties or create undue pressure. However, orders have been made in the past to protect the confidentiality of disputes. In the recent case of *Azpetrol* v *Azerbaijan* the tribunal made a confidentiality order, the details of which have not been made public.

[Dispatch, supplementation and rectification]

Article 49

(1) The Secretary-General shall promptly dispatch certified copies of the award to the parties. The award shall be deemed to have been rendered on the date on which the certified copies were dispatched.

(2) The Tribunal upon the request of a party made within 45 days after the date on which the award was rendered may after notice to the other party decide any question which it had omitted to decide in the award, and shall rectify any clerical, arithmetical or similar error in the award. Its decision shall become part of the award and shall be notified to the parties in the same manner as the award. The periods of time provided for under paragraph (2) of Article 51 and paragraph (2) of Article 52 shall run from the date on which the decision was rendered.

ICSID Convention, art. 49

1. General. Art. 49 addresses the dispatch of the award, and its supplementation and rectification in the event of minor omissions or errors.

2. Application. Art. 49 expressly applies to awards. Art. 52(4) extends the operation of art. 49 to decisions of ad hoc committees and art. 52(6) extends its application to awards issued by a new tribunal in a resubmitted case. Decisions on applications for interpretation, revision and annulment of awards must be dispatched by the Secretary-General in accordance with art. 49(1). Under art. 49(2), decisions on the rectification and supplementation of an award become part of the award and will therefore also be subject to the provisions in art. 49(1). Preliminary decisions are, however, not subject to art. 49(1) and may be certified and dispatched by the Secretary of the tribunal (Schreuer, *Commentary*, p. 832). At the time of writing, twelve proceedings on rectification and supplementation had been initiated: *LETCO* v *Liberia* (DSR); *Amco* v *Indonesia* (DSR); *Maffezini* v *Spain* (DSR); *Genin* v *Estonia*; *Vivendi* v *Argentina* (DSR); *Noble Ventures* v *Romania* (DSR); *Inceysa* v *El Salvador* (DSR); *Soufraki* v *UAE* (DSR); *Enron* v *Argentina* (DSR); *Lucchetti* v *Peru* (DSR); *Ares* v *Georgia*; *LG&E* v *Argentina* (DSR).

3. Certification and transmission of award. Art. 49(1) corresponds with art. 11, which gives the Secretary-General the power to authenticate awards and certify copies thereof. Rule 48 of the Arbitration Rules provides further detail as to the Secretary-General's duty under art. 49. The Secretary-General must: authenticate the original text of the award, along with any individual opinions and statements of dissent; deposit the original in the Centre's archives; dispatch certified copies of the award to the parties; and note the date of dispatch on the original and all copies of the award. A copy of the award is certified when the Secretary-General attaches a certificate that precisely identifies the case and states words to the effect that the copy is a true copy. If there are separate opinions, these should be noted in the certificate before it is signed and dated by the Secretary-General. In practice, the Secretary-General will usually dispatch the award within six to twenty-five days of the date the last tribunal member signs the award or any separate opinion, whichever is the later (Schreuer, *Commentary*, p. 832). Reg. 28 of the Administrative and Financial Regulations provides further detail as to the certification and dispatching of copies of the award.

4. Date of award. Arts. 49(2), 51(2) and 52(2) set time limits for the rectification, supplementation, revision and annulment of awards. The date of the award will be crucial to the calculation of these time limits. Under art. 49(1), the date of the award is the date it is dispatched to the parties. Under Rule 48(1) of the Arbitration Rules, the date of dispatch will be noted by the Secretary-General on the original text and all copies of the award.

5. Request for supplementation and rectification of award. The purpose of art. 49(2) is to enable the parties to request the tribunal to remedy technical errors or minor omissions in the award. Art. 49(2) does not, however, provide a mechanism by which the parties can challenge the substance or validity of the tribunal's or ad hoc committee's decision. Since omissions are by definition questions which the tribunal has failed to decide, art. 49(2) relates closely to the requirement in art. 48(3) that the award must deal with every question submitted to the tribunal. An example of a minor omission which was remedied under this provision was a tribunal's failure to list the name of one of the parties' representatives in the award (*Noble Ventures* v *Romania* (DSR)). An example of an omission which was not considered to be capable of remedy under this provision was a tribunal's failure to update the quantum of compensation (*LG&E* v *Argentina* (DSR)). In this case, the claimant sought a supplementary decision to update the quantum of compensation on the basis that the tribunal had found that the respondent's liability was ongoing, but calculated damages only until the last written pleading. The tribunal decided that as it had already looked at the issue of quantum at length in the award, supplementation was not an available remedy. Instead, the parties could claim any additional damages by starting new ICSID proceedings. Technical errors may be clerical, arithmetical or similar errors. Again, only errors that are minor are capable of rectification: for example, reference to the claimant rather than the respondent was considered to be minor by one tribunal (*Vivendi* v *Argentina* (DSR)), but a tribunal's decision to award interest only until the date of the award and not the date of payment was not considered to be minor by another (*Enron* v *Argentina* (DSR)). There can be no rectification of substantive findings or the weight and credence accorded by a tribunal or ad hoc committee to the arguments and evidence presented by the parties (*Vivendi* v *Argentina* (DSR)). If a question is not merely technical or minor but concerns an issue that is fundamental to the case, such as major facts or arguments, annulment is the appropriate remedy (Schreuer, *Commentary*, p. 853). The misuse of art. 49(2) may provoke criticism from the tribunal or ad hoc committee that rendered the award or decision on annulment. If a claimant seeks to use art. 49(2) as a means to reargue substantive aspects of a decision, it may find itself subject to a cost order for the entirety of the fees and expenses incurred in connection with the request (*Vivendi* v *Argentina* (DSR)).

6. Procedure. Rule 49 of the Arbitration Rules provides further detail as to the procedure to be followed in respect of a request for supplementation or rectification. Under Rule 49, only a party may make such a request. The party's request must be specific and must be filed separately from any request for interpretation, revision or annulment. The time limit for filing such a request is forty-five days, which will be calculated from the date the award is dispatched to the parties. Once the Secretary-General registers the request, the other party must be notified (Rule 49(2)(b) of the Arbitration Rules). Schreuer notes that while art. 49(2) fails expressly to provide the other party to the dispute with a chance to respond, allowing the other party to be heard is a fundamental procedural requirement (Schreuer, *Commentary*, p.

845). Thus, in practice, the other party will be given the chance to submit observations (see, e.g., *LG&E* v *Argentina* (DSR)). Only the tribunal or ad hoc committee that rendered the original award or annulment decision may supplement or rectify that award or decision. If the original tribunal or ad hoc committee is unavailable, supplementation and rectification cannot occur and the parties' only recourse will be to utilise the provisions for interpretation, revision or annulment under the Convention to address the deficiency. Under Rule 49(3) of the Arbitration Rules, the tribunal may determine which procedure it will use to determine the application for supplementation or rectification. Under Rule 16(2) of the Arbitration Rules, the tribunal may choose to decide by correspondence. Under Reg. 28(2) of the Administrative and Financial Regulations, the original and any certified copy of the award must be updated with any decision on supplementation or rectification. The provisions on time limits, dates, signatures and separate opinions and the requirements for authentication and dispatch in Rules 46 to 48 will also apply to decisions on supplementation and rectification.

7. Effect on time limits. Since a decision on the supplementation or rectification of an award will form part of the original award, it will cause the time limits for applications for revision and annulment to run anew. This will be the case even where the tribunal decides not to supplement or rectify its original decision. A party may therefore secure a tactical advantage by issuing a request for supplementation or rectification merely to extend the time limit for revisions and annulment. As Schreuer notes, the Secretary-General may only refuse to register a request under art. 49(2) if the forty-five-day time limit has not been complied with. There is no scope for refusal of a request that is manifestly lacking in merit or devoid of relevance (Schreuer, *Commentary*, p. 855). There is also no scope under Rule 54 of the Arbitration Rules for the parties to request a stay of enforcement pending a supplementary decision or a decision on rectification.

Section 5. Interpretation, Revision and Annulment of the Award

[Interpretation]

Article 50

(1) If any dispute shall arise between the parties as to the meaning or scope of an award, either party may request interpretation of the award by an application in writing addressed to the Secretary-General.

(2) The request shall, if possible, be submitted to the Tribunal which rendered the award. If this shall not be possible, a new Tribunal shall be constituted in accordance with Section 2 of this Chapter. The Tribunal may, if it considers that the circumstances so require, stay enforcement of the award pending its decision.

1. General. Art. 50 provides a procedure for the authoritative interpretation of an award, where a dispute exists between the parties as to its meaning or scope.

2. Application. Unlike art. 40, art. 50 does not apply to decisions of ad hoc committees on annulment (art. 52(4)). At the time of writing, only two interpretation proceedings had been initiated: *Wena* v *Egypt* and *Tanzania Electric* v *Independent Power Tanzania*.

3. Request for interpretation. Art. 50 together with Rules 50 and 51 of the Arbitration Rules establish the conditions for and procedure to be followed in an application for interpretation. There must be a dispute between the original parties as to the meaning or scope of the award capable of interpretation, which should be sufficiently concrete. The dispute should not contain abstract or theoretical arguments or raise new arguments (Schreuer, *Commentary*, p. 858). The parties should express a difference of opinion on definite points in relation to the award's meaning or scope, and the dispute must have at least some practical relevance to the award's implementation (*Wena* v *Egypt*). In this case – the only concluded application for interpretation – Wena requested an interpretation of the consequences of the tribunal's finding of expropriation, i.e. that Wena had been totally and permanently deprived of its interest in a particular asset as from a certain date, which the tribunal duly provided. However, the tribunal refused to decide on the issue of whether Wena could incur liability in respect of those expropriated rights, since this issue had not been decided with binding force in the award. Neither art. 50 nor Rule 50 prescribe any time limit in which a request for interpretation must be made. Accordingly, any number of requests for interpretation may be made at any time. Furthermore, the only grounds upon which the Secretary-General may refuse to register a request for interpretation is if it does not relate to an award. Any request for rectification, revision or annulment must be made separately to a request for interpretation. Under Rule 50(2) of the Arbitration Rules, the Secretary-General must notify the parties once he registers an application for interpretation and transmit a copy to the other party. Under Rule 53, the provisions of the Arbitration Rules apply mutatis mutandis to decisions on interpretation. Accordingly, the other party will have a right to respond to the request for interpretation. Similarly, the provisions on signature, dates, separate opinions, authentication and dispatch will apply (Rules 47 and 48 of the Arbitration Rules).

4. Effect of a decision on interpretation. Any decision on interpretation will be added to certified copies of the award (arts. 48 and 49; Reg. 28(2) of the Administrative and Financial Regulations). However, at the time of drafting the Convention, the majority of delegates opposed a provision being inserted into art. 50(1) to the effect that the interpretation given to the award by the tribunal will have effect as part of the original award (*History*, Vol. II, p. 847). Accordingly, a decision on interpretation will not be subject to the provisions on supplementation and rectification, revision or annulment. Schreuer notes that art. 53(2) states that for the purposes of recognition and enforcement, however, the award will be interpreted in accordance with any decision rendered under art. 50 (Schreuer, *Commentary*. p. 862).

5. Decision by the tribunal which rendered the award. Rule 51 of the Arbitration Rules sets out the procedure by which the Secretary-General will approach the original tribunal for a decision on interpretation of an award. Under Rule 51(2), a decision on interpretation can only be made if each of the original tribunal members, including those in the majority and those in dissent, agree to it. Once the tribunal members have agreed to make a decision on interpretation, they are again bound, under art. 49 and Rules 47 and 53 of the Arbitration Rules, to make that decision and provide reasons for it. If the original tribunal cannot be reconstituted, the Secretary-General must notify the parties and invite them to constitute a new tribunal. The parties can choose whether or not to follow the Secretary-General's recommendation to appoint the same number of tribunal members and employ the same method of selection as was used in the original proceedings. Schreuer notes that this means that some of the original members may be employed in the new tribunal, so long as the requirement for an uneven number of arbitrators is met (art. 37(2)(a); Schreuer, *Commentary*, p. 865).

6. Stay of enforcement of the award. Under Rule 54 of the Arbitration Rules, either party may request a stay of enforcement at any time before the final resolution of an application for interpretation. The tribunal has a discretionary power under art. 50(2) to agree to order the stay (*History*, Vol. II, pp. 723, 845, 846, 885, 887, 987), and if the stay is granted, may modify or terminate that stay at any time. The Secretary-General is bound to notify the parties of any stay of enforcement (Rule 54 of the Arbitration Rules). No provisional stays (pending the reconstitution or constitution of the tribunal) may be ordered. The request will automatically terminate on the date on which the final decision on interpretation is rendered.

[Revision]

Article 51

(1) Either party may request revision of the award by an application in writing addressed to the Secretary-General on the ground of discovery of some fact of such a nature as decisively to affect the award, provided that when the award was rendered that fact was unknown to the Tribunal and to the applicant and that the applicant's ignorance of that fact was not due to negligence.

(2) The application shall be made within 90 days after the discovery of such fact and in any event within three years after the date on which the award was rendered.

(3) The request shall, if possible, be submitted to the Tribunal which rendered the award. If this shall not be possible, a new Tribunal shall be constituted in accordance with Section 2 of this Chapter.

(4) The Tribunal may, if it considers that the circumstances so require, stay enforcement of the award pending its decision. If the applicant requests a stay of enforcement of the award in his application, enforcement shall be stayed provisionally until the Tribunal rules on such request.

1. General. Art. 51 provides a mechanism for the revision of awards on the ground of discovery of some fact of such a nature as decisively to affect the award.

2. Application. Art. 51 only applies to the final decision of the tribunal and will not apply to any of its preliminary decisions. Art. 51 will also apply to an award issued by a new tribunal following an annulment. Art. 51 will not apply to decisions of ad hoc committees (art. 52(4)). At the time of writing, three proceedings on revision had been initiated: *AMT* v *Congo* (Revision); *Siemens* v *Argentina* (Revision); *Casado and Allende Foundation* v *Chile* (Revision).

3. Request for revision. Every draft of the Convention contained a provision for the revision of awards (*History*, Vol. I, pp. 222-230). Art. 51 does not require the existence of a dispute for its operation (see art. 50, above). At the time of drafting, it was suggested that art. 51 should contain a provision for revision in the event that the award is manifestly erroneous in law or where the tribunal did not adjudicate on certain matters submitted for its consideration. Both these suggestions were dismissed and accordingly revision may only take place on the basis of a new fact (*History*, Vol. II, pp. 847-848). Schreuer suggests that the phrase 'of such a nature as decisively to affect the award' means that the fact must be of such a nature that it would have led the tribunal to make a different decision had it been known (Schreuer, *Commentary*, p. 874). In *Siemens* v *Argentina* (Revision), Siemens secured a favourable award which Argentina initially sought to have annulled. Following the constitution of an ad hoc committee on annulment, Argentina filed an application for revision of the award with the original tribunal. The new fact upon which Argentina based this application was the testimony of a Siemens executive in a German court that the contract that was the subject of the dispute was procured by means of bribery. At the time of writing, the outcome of the request was still pending (as was a request for revision in *Casado and Allende Foundation* v *Chile* (Revision); an earlier request for revision in the case of *AMT* v *Congo* was settled). Under art. 51, the fact must have been unknown to both the tribunal and the applicant at the date on which the award was rendered (Rule 50(1)(c)(ii) of the Arbitration Rules). The other party's knowledge is irrelevant to the operation of art. 51. It is only the applicant's ignorance that has bearing on a decision for revision. The decision on whether or not the applicant's ignorance was due to negligence rests with the tribunal. At the time of drafting the Convention, Dr. Broches noted that there would probably be a presumption of the absence of knowledge and that the burden of proof would be on the party resisting the application for revision to prove that the tribunal or the other party had such knowledge (*History*, Vol. II, p. 518).

4. Procedure. A request for revision must come from the one of the parties to the original proceedings. Rule 50 of the Arbitration Rules sets out in detail the procedure to be followed in such a request. Once a party discovers a fact that could form the basis for a revision, it must make its request for revision within ninety days of that discovery. If the party fails to meet the ninety-day time limit, the Secretary-General will refuse to register its request (Rule 50(3)(a) of the Arbitration Rules). The Secretary-General will refuse to register a request irrespective of when the fact was discovered if the application is made more than three years after the award was rendered (Rule 50(3)(a) of the Arbitration Rules). Schreuer notes that in light of these time limits, it is advisable that the date on which the new fact was discovered be specified in the request (Schreuer, *Commentary*, p. 872). The Secretary-General also has grounds for refusal where a request fails to relate to an award. If a party fails to comply with any of the other requirements of Rule 50(1)(c)(ii) (e.g. fails to confirm that the fact in question was not known to the applicant and that this was not due to the applicant's negligence), the Secretary-General may request the party to provide further details on that issue. Schreuer notes that the Secretary-General is not under a duty to determine the veracity of the party's claim (Schreuer, *Commentary*, p. 873). Under Rule 50(2) of the Arbitration Rules, the Secretary-General must notify the parties once he registers a request for revision and transmit a copy to the other party. Under Rule 53, the provisions for the Arbitration Rules apply mutatis mutandis to decisions on revision. Accordingly, the other party will have a right to respond to the request for revision. Similarly, the provisions on signature, dates, separate opinions, authentication and dispatch will apply (Rules 47 and 48 of the Arbitration Rules). Any decision on revision will be added to certified copies of the award (arts. 48 and 49; Reg. 28(2) Administrative and Financial Regulations). Art. 53(2) states that for the purposes of recognition and enforcement, the award will be interpreted in accordance with any decision made under art. 51. A decision on revision will not be subject to the provisions on supplementation and rectification, revision or annulment. A request for revision of an award must be made separately from any request for interpretation, rectification or annulment (*Siemens* v *Argentina* (Revision)).

5. Decision by the tribunal that rendered the award. Rule 51 of the Arbitration Rules sets out the procedure by which the Secretary-General will approach the tribunal for a decision on revision of an award. Under Rule 51(2), a decision on revision can only be made if each of the original tribunal members, including those in the majority and those in dissent, agree. Once the tribunal members have agreed to make a decision on revision, they are again bound, under art. 49 and Rules 47 and 53 of the Arbitration Rules, to provide reasons for their decision. If the original tribunal cannot be reconstituted, the Secretary-General must notify the parties and invite them to constitute a new tribunal. The parties can choose whether or not to follow the Secretary-General's recommendation to appoint the same number of tribunal members and employ the same method of selection as was used in the original proceedings. Schreuer notes that this means that some of the original members may be employed in the new tribunal, so long as the requirement for an uneven number of arbitrators is met (art. 37(2)(a); Schreuer, *Commentary*, p. 865).

6. Stay of enforcement of the award. The tribunal may stay the enforcement of the award pending a decision on revision in two circumstances. The first is where the applicant requesting a revision simultaneously requests a stay of enforcement (see *Siemens* v *Argentina* (Revision), in which the award was already subject to a provisional stay in the context of pending annulment proceedings and a separate stay was requested by Argentina in its request for revision). In such a case, enforcement must be automatically stayed until the tribunal rules on the request (Rule 54(2) of the Arbitration Rules). At the time of drafting the Convention, Dr. Broches explained that this provision was included in view of the fact that, while in domestic courts when an appeal is made against an enforceable decision there is always a judicial authority available to consider an urgent request to stay enforcement, in the case of ICSID, the tribunal may not be easily reconstituted to consider the request. In those circumstances, fairness dictates that the losing party should have an absolute right of suspension of execution until the tribunal can be reconstituted (*History*, Vol. II, p. 988). The second circumstance is following the reconstitution of the tribunal. At this stage, under Rule 54 of the Arbitration Rules, either party may request a stay of enforcement at any time before the final resolution of the request for revision. Either party may also request continuation, modification or termination of an existing stay. Thirty days after the tribunal's reconstitution, any stay of enforcement that is in operation due to the applicant's original request will lapse unless it is confirmed by the tribunal (Rule 54(2) of the Arbitration Rules). The tribunal may only grant a stay once it has heard both parties. Upon granting a stay of enforcement, the tribunal has the discretion to decide whether that stay will relate to all or part of the award. Once the tribunal has made a decision on revision, any stay of enforcement will be automatically terminated (Rule 54(2) of the Arbitration Rules). Other procedures may also be stayed pending a decision on the revision of an award. In *Siemens* v *Argentina* (Revision), both parties requested that Argentina's application for the annulment of the award be suspended while its application to revise the award was considered.

[Annulment]

Article 52

(1) Either party may request annulment of the award by an application in writing addressed to the Secretary-General on one or more of the following grounds:

ICSID Convention, art. 52

    (a) that the Tribunal was not properly constituted;
    (b) that the Tribunal has manifestly exceeded its powers;
    (c) that there was corruption on the part of a member of the Tribunal;
    (d) that there has been a serious departure from a fundamental rule of procedure; or
    (e) that the award has failed to state the reasons on which it is based.

(2) The application shall be made within 120 days after the date on which the award was rendered except that when annulment is requested on the ground of corruption such application shall be made within 120 days after discovery of the corruption and in any event within three years after the date on which the award was rendered.

(3) On receipt of the request the Chairman shall forthwith appoint from the Panel of Arbitrators an ad hoc Committee of three persons. None of the members of the Committee shall have been a member of the Tribunal which rendered the award, shall be of the same nationality as any such member, shall be a national of the State party to the dispute or of the State whose national is a party to the dispute, shall have been designated to the Panel of Arbitrators by either of those States, or shall have acted as a conciliator in the same dispute. The Committee shall have the authority to annul the award or any part thereof on any of the grounds set forth in paragraph (1).

(4) The provisions of Articles 41-45, 48, 49, 53 and 54, and of Chapters VI and VII shall apply mutatis mutandis to proceedings before the Committee.

(5) The Committee may, if it considers that the circumstances so require, stay enforcement of the award pending its decision. If the applicant requests a stay of enforcement of the award in his application, enforcement shall be stayed provisionally until the Committee rules on such request.

(6) If the award is annulled the dispute shall, at the request of either party, be submitted to a new Tribunal constituted in accordance with Section 2 of this Chapter.

1. General. Art. 52 provides a mechanism for the annulment of the award: the strongest sword in the armoury of the remedies provided in arts. 49 to 52. This mechanism is similar in effect to an application to set aside a commercial arbitration award in national courts in jurisdictions which adhere to the New York Convention. The effect of annulment is to cancel the award (in whole or part) and provide the parties with a second chance to arbitrate the same issues again before a new ICSID tribunal (known as an ad hoc committee). Since the Convention is self-contained, the parties cannot apply to national courts to set aside an ICSID award.

2. Application. Only awards, awards recording settlement and decisions supplementing or rectifying awards may be subject to annulment. Decisions on jurisdiction and decisions on provisional measures may only be annulled once they have been incorporated into the award, except where, in its decision, the tribunal accepts the objections to its jurisdiction and terminates the proceedings (see art. 41 and Rule 41(6) of the Arbitration Rules). Decisions on interpretation and revision of the award and decisions of ad hoc committees may not be annulled. Annulment is the remedy most resorted to by parties to ICSID arbitration.

3. Statistics on annulment: applications. At the time of writing, thirty proceedings on annulment had been initiated. In fifteen of these proceedings, the foreign investor made the application for annulment (*Klockner* v *Cameroon* (I) (DA); *Vivendi* v *Argentina* (I) (DA); *Philippe Gruslin* v *Malaysia* (DA); *Joy Mining* v *Egypt* (DA); *RFC* v *Morocco* (DA); *Soufraki* v *UAE* (DA); *Lucchetti* v *Peru* (DA); *Vivendi* v *Argentina* (II) (DA); *LG&E* v *Argentina* (DA); *Ahmonseto* v *Egypt* (DA); *MCI* v *Ecuador* (DA); *Fraport* v *Philippines* (DA); *Transgabonais* v *Gabon* (DA); *Vieira* v *Chile* (DA); *Malaysian Salvors* v *Malaysia* (DA)). In another thirteen proceedings, the State made the application (*Amco* v *Indonesia* (I) (DA); *MINE* v *Guinea* (DA); *SPP* v *Egypt* (DA); *Wena Hotels* v *Egypt* (DA); *CDC* v *Seychelles* (DA); *Repsol* v *Petroecuador* (DA); *Mitchell* v *Congo*; *MTD* v *Chile* (DA); *CMS* v *Argentina* (DA); *Azurix* v *Argentina* (DA); *Siemens* v *Argentina*; *Sempra* v *Argentina* (DA); *Enron* v *Argentina* (DA)). In the remaining two proceedings, both the foreign investor and the State made the application for annulment (*Klockner* v *Cameroon* (II) (DA); *Amco* v *Indonesia* (II) (DA)).

4. Statistics on annulment: success. Of the published concluded cases on annulment to date, only two were entirely successful (i.e. the ad hoc committee annulled the tribunal's award in its entirety) (*Klockner v Cameroon* (I) (DA); *Mitchell v Congo* (DA)). Four awards were partially annulled (*Amco v Indonesia* (I) (DA); *MINE v Guinea* (DA); *Vivendi v Argentina* (I) (DA); *CMS v Argentina* (DA)). The remaining twelve concluded cases were either unsuccessful (i.e. the ad hoc committee rejected the application for annulment), discontinued or remain unpublished (*Klockner* v *Cameroon* (II) (DA); *Amco* v *Indonesia* (II) (DA); *SPP* v *Egypt* (DA); *Philippe Gruslin* v *Malaysia*; *Wena Hotels* v *Egypt* (DA); *Joy Mining* v *Egypt* (DA); *CDC* v *Seychelles* (DA); *Repsol* v *Petroecuador* (DA); *RFC* v *Morocco* (DA); *MTD* v *Chile* (DA); *Soufraki* v *UAE* (DA); *Lucchetti* v *Peru* (DA)).

5. Grounds for annulment. The grounds of annulment are exhaustively listed in art. 52(1). These grounds are very limited and relate to fundamental principles of justice and due process, i.e. they are concerned with the legitimacy of the arbitration process rather than the outcome. Annulment is therefore not an appeal on the merits and the ad hoc committee constituted to rule on the annulment cannot amend the award or substitute its views for those of the original tribunal. The first generation of annulment decisions appear to have strayed from this principle since they re-examined the awards subject to annulment on the merits (*Klöckner* v *Cameroon* (I) (DA); *Amco* v *Indonesia* (I) (DA)). The second generation of ad hoc committees were more restrained in their review (*Klöckner* v *Cameroon* (II) (DA); *Amco* v *Indonesia* (II) (DA); *MINE* v *Guinea* (DA)). However, the third and most recent generation of annulment decisions have confirmed the principle that an ad hoc committee may rarely intervene in the award of a previous tribunal, and only if there has been a substantial violation of one of the grounds listed in art. 52. According to recent case law, the principles of review under art. 52 are limited to issues of jurisdiction and procedure; ad hoc committees are not permitted to reconsider the merits of the claim (*Wena* v *Egypt* (DA); *Vivendi* v *Argentina* (I) (DA); *RFC* v *Morocco* (DA); *CDC* v *Seychelles* (DA); *Mitchell* v *Congo* (DA); *Lucchetti* v *Peru* (DA); *MTD* v *Chile* (DA); *CMS* v *Argentina* (DA)). The interpretation of some of the grounds in art. 52(1) has nonetheless proved to be a contentious matter.

6. First ground: improper constitution of the tribunal. A review of the published cases suggests that this ground has never been invoked in an application for annulment. Examples of issues that may arise with the constitution of the tribunal include the members' qualifications and character (see art. 14, which provides that arbitrators must be independent and competent) and nationalities (see arts. 38 and 39, which prohibit arbitrators of certain nationalities being appointed). Schreuer notes that while the drafting history to this ground is somewhat contradictory, a party should raise the issue of improper constitution as early as possible but should only submit an application for annulment once the award has been issued (Schreuer, *Commentary*, p. 929; *History*, Vol. I, pp. 230 and 232 and Vol. II, pp. 432, 850 to 853, 872). The party should also exhaust the remedies available during the proceedings (e.g. under arts. 57 and 58, regarding the replacement and disqualification of arbitrators) unless the facts only come to light once the proceedings have closed. However, the Secretary-General does not have the power to refuse registration of a request for annulment where these remedies have not been exhausted; it is simply good practice to do so.

7. Second ground: manifest excess of powers. At the time of drafting the Convention, Dr. Broches explained that this provision was intended to refer to cases where a decision of the tribunal went beyond the scope of agreement of the parties (i.e. lacked competence) or decided points which had not been submitted to it or had been improperly submitted to it (i.e. limits of its competence) (*History*, Vol. II, p. 850). Tribunals have defined 'manifest' as: incapable of being arguable; what is clear and seen readily; what is obvious; what is self evident; what is plain on its face (*Wena* v *Egypt* (DA); *CDC* v *Seychelles* (DA); *MTD* v *Chile* (DA); *Soufraki* v *UAE* (DA)). A tribunal may manifestly exceed its powers by making a decision where it has incorrectly assumed jurisdiction over a question (*Klöckner* v *Cameroon* (I) (DA)). A tribunal may equally exceed its powers if it fails to exercise a jurisdiction that it possesses. However, only if the failure to exercise a jurisdiction is clearly capable of making a difference to the outcome of the award can it be considered a manifest excess of power (*Vivendi* v *Argentina* (I) (DA)). Another way in which a tribunal may manifestly exceed its powers is where it fails to render its award on the basis of the applicable law. Dr. Broches highlighted at the time of drafting the Convention that failure to apply the right law would constitute an excess of power if the parties had instructed the tribunal to apply a particular law (*History*, Vol. II, p. 851). Similarly, failure to apply the law applicable under art. 42(1) may result in annulment (*Amco* v *Indonesia* (I) (DA); *MINE* v *Guinea* (DA)). Ad hoc committees have sought to distinguish between a failure to apply the law and errors in the application of the law; it is only the former that will permit annulment. Thus, even where a tribunal defectively applies the law, the award will not be annulled (*MINE* v *Guinea* (DA); *MTD* v *Chile* (DA); *CMS* v *Argentina* (DA)). However, if a tribunal resorts to equitable principles without the authority of the parties to do so, the tribunal may have exceeded its powers (*Klöckner* v *Cameroon* (I) (DA); *Amco* v *Indonesia* (I) (DA); *MINE* v *Guinea*). A tribunal is likely to have acted within its powers when applying international law, even in the absence of the agreement of the parties (see art. 42; Schreuer, *Commentary*, pp. 962-963 and *Amco* v *Indonesia* (I) (DA); *Wena* v *Egypt* (DA)). However, a tribunal was held to have exceeded its powers by refusing to consider the merits of a treaty claim on the basis that it overlapped with a contractual claim which it could not consider (*Vivendi* v *Argentina* (I) (DA)). A party should raise the issue of manifest excess of powers as early as possible in the proceedings or as soon as it discovers the facts pointing to this issue.

8. Third ground: corruption on the part of the tribunal. To date, this ground has not been raised in any published annulment proceedings. In the absence of case law on this provision, Schreuer suggests the following principles will apply: corruption must be established and not inferred; for bias to constitute corruption, there must have been acceptance of an improper payment by the tribunal member in question; unauthorised communication between a tribunal member and a party outside of the official channels of proceedings would not, by itself, constitute corruption; and a failure completely and truthfully to comply with Rule 6 of the Arbitration Rules which requires tribunal members to give a statement of any past or present professional, business or other relationship with the parties (if any) would not, by itself, constitute corruption (Schreuer, *Commentary*, pp. 967-968).

9. Fourth ground: serious departure from a fundamental rule of procedure. There are two requirements for the application of this ground: the departure must have been 'serious' and the rule in question must have been 'fundamental' (*MINE* v *Guinea*; *Wena* v *Egypt* (DA); *Vivendi* v *Argentina* (I) (DA)). The emphasis in art. 52(1)(d) is clearly on the manner in which the tribunal proceeded and not on the content of its decision (*Vivendi* v *Argentina* (I) (DA)). At the time of drafting the Convention, it was explained that the rules of procedure which will be considered fundamental by the ad hoc committee are those embodying the principles of natural justice such as the rule that both parties must be heard and that there must be adequate opportunity for rebuttal (*History*, Vol. II, pp. 423, 480, 517, see also *Wena* v *Egypt* (DA)). Schreuer notes that impartiality and the observance of the rules of evidence are examples of fundamental rules of procedure (Schreuer, *Commentary*, p. 972). A further example of what may constitute a fundamental rule of procedure is the tribunal's obligation to deliberate, while an example of what will not is the tribunal's obligation to base its decision on an argument developed by the parties (*Klöckner* v *Cameroon* (I) (DA); *Amco* v *Indonesia* (I) (DA); and *Amco* v *Indonesia* (II) (DA)). The drafters of the Convention did not give any guidance as to what constitutes a 'serious departure'. In *MINE* v *Guinea* (DA), the ad hoc committee stated that a serious departure is one that has deprived the party of the benefit of the protection which the rule was intended to provide. In *Wena* v *Egypt* (DA), the tribunal stated that in order for a departure to be serious, the violation of the rule must have caused the tribunal to reach a decision substantially different from that which it would have had the rule been observed. Recently, it has been held that this ground for annulment may not be used broadly and applicants who based their requests on anything other than serious rules of procedure (such as due process requirements) will be the subject of criticism (*Vivendi* v *Argentina* (I) (DA)). A party should state its objection as soon as it becomes aware of a violation of proper procedure. If it fails to, the Secretary-General will not have the power to refuse the registration of its request, however the ad hoc committee may refuse to allow that party to rely on this violation as a ground of annulment (*Klöckner* v *Cameroon* (II) (DA)).

10. Fifth ground: failure to state reasons on which award is based. The tribunal is obliged to give reasons for its decision (see art. 48, note 5). Thus, it is unlikely that the situation will ever arise where a tribunal entirely fails to give reasons; however, a tribunal may give reasons that are inadequate, incomplete or contradictory. The first generation of annulment decisions interpreted this ground for annulment broadly. In these cases, the ad hoc committees looked to the adequacy of the tribunal's decision (that is, whether the reasons given by the tribunal were capable of providing a basis for the decision) (*Klöckner* v *Cameroon* (I) (DA); *Amco* v *Indonesia* (I) (DA)). In the second generation of annulment decisions, the ad hoc committees interpreted this ground more narrowly, holding that reasons will be sufficient where the committee is able to follow how the tribunal got from Point A to Point B; (*MINE* v *Guinea* (DA); *Klöckner* v *Cameroon* (II) (DA); *Amco* v *Indonesia* (II) (DA)). Recently, ad hoc committees have held that it is well accepted both in the cases and the literature that this ground concerns a failure to state any reasons for a particular decision and not the failure to state correct, appropriate or convincing reasons: 'provided that the reasons given by a tribunal can be followed and relate to the issues that were before the tribunal, their correctness is beside the point of art. 52(1)(e)' (*Vivendi* v *Argentina* (I)

(DA), see also *Wena* v *Egypt* (DA); *Lucchetti* v *Peru* (DA); *CMS* v *Argentina* (DA)). Thus, this third generation of decisions have marked a turning point in the interpretation of this ground of annulment. Ad hoc committees are now limited to reviewing issues of jurisdiction and procedure and are prohibited from looking to the merits of a case. Schreuer notes the difficulty an ad hoc committee faces when assessing the tribunal's reasoning whilst avoiding any examination of the merits (Schreuer, *Commentary*, p. 986). However, an examination of the reasons cannot be a re-examination of the merits, as this would amount to an appeal in violation of art. 53(1).

11. Procedure. It is clear from the text of art. 52(1) that one of the parties to the original arbitration, or both parties jointly, must initiate annulment proceedings; neither the Centre nor any third party has the power to do so. Art. 52(1) permits the applicant to rely on more than one ground for annulment in its request, which is the norm in practice as demonstrated in the case law. A party may waive its right to request annulment in certain circumstances (*Amco* v *Indonesia* (I) (DA)). However, a party cannot be said to have waived its right to request annulment where it was not aware of the facts that form the basis of the application. Rule 27 of the Arbitration Rules deems a party to have waived its right to request annulment if it fails to make a timely objection to a set of circumstances that could constitute a ground for annulment. A request for annulment may only be made in respect of an award. It may not be made in respect of other decisions such as preliminary decisions on jurisdiction (unless the decision upholds the objections to jurisdiction thereby ending the proceedings), decisions to recommend provisional measures, procedural orders and decisions on the interpretation and revision of awards. Decisions on annulment are not themselves subject to annulment (Schreuer, *Commentary*, p. 916). Awards may be annulled in whole or in part. Severable parts of the award which are not themselves annulled will stand, a situation expressly contemplated in art. 52(3) (*Vivendi* v *Argentina* (I) (DA); *CMS* v *Argentina* (DA)). Rules 50 and 52 of the Arbitration Rules set out the procedure to be followed in a request for annulment and require, inter alia, that the party requesting annulment state in detail the grounds for its request. Reg. 16 of the Administrative and Financial Regulations prescribes that the party requesting annulment of the award must pay a non-refundable fee which, at the time of writing, was USD 10,000. Pursuant to art. 52(4), the provisions of arts. 41 to 45, 48, 49, 53 and 54 and Chapters VI and VII (applicable to proceedings before the original tribunal) shall apply mutatis mutandis to annulment proceedings.

12. Time limits. Pursuant to art. 52(2), the application shall be made within 120 days (c.f. forty-five or ninety days for applications for rectification or revision). For all grounds of annulment other than the corruption of the tribunal, the time limit is calculated from the date on which the award was rendered. If a party makes a request for supplementation or rectification, the time limit for an application for annulment will be extended (art. 49(2)).

ICSID Convention, art. 52

If the party fails to submit a detailed request for annulment within 120 days, the Secretary-General shall refuse to register the request (Rules 50(3)(b) and (c) of the Arbitration Rules); however registration by the Secretary-General does not guarantee that the ad hoc committee will find that art. 52(2) has been complied with (*Amco* v *Indonesia* (I) (DA)). Merely stating the grounds for annulment within the time limit and promising further submissions to be submitted outside the time limit will not satisfy art. 52(2) (*Amco* v *Indonesia* (I) (DA)). Where there was corruption on the part of a member of the tribunal, the time limit is calculated from the date the corruption is discovered by the party making the application. Accordingly, an application for annulment on this ground should indicate the date of discovery. Pursuant to Rule 50(3)(b) of the Arbitration Rules, the Secretary-General shall refuse to register the application if it is not made within 120 days of that date and in any event within three years after the date on which the award was rendered (or any subsequent decision or correction). Again, registration by the Secretary-General does not guarantee that the ad hoc committee will find that the time limit has been complied with. Once the annulment proceedings are underway, a party may be able to raise a new ground for annulment where the facts that form the basis of that ground have only recently come to light (Schreuer, *Commentary*, p. 1038).

13. Constitution of ad hoc committee. Unlike decisions on interpretation and revision under arts. 50 and 51, a decision on annulment can only be made by a tribunal that is entirely different to that which made the original decision. The new tribunal, known as the ad hoc committee, will be appointed by the Chairman, who by virtue of art. 5 is also the President of the World Bank. The ad hoc committee will be chosen from the Panel of Arbitrators (see art. 12) by the Chairman, usually after consultation with the parties. Rule 52 of the Arbitration Rules sets out the procedure for appointment. Members of the committee must not be: a member of the tribunal which rendered the original award; a person of the same nationality as any member of the tribunal which rendered the original award; a national of the State party to the dispute or of the State whose national is a party to the dispute; an arbitrator designated to the Panel of Arbitrators by either the State party to the dispute or the State whose national is a party to the dispute; or a person who has acted as a conciliator in the same dispute. The committee will consist of three members and shall be deemed constituted on the date the Secretary-General notifies the parties that all the members have accepted their appointment (Rule 52(2) of the Arbitration Rules). In practice, the three members will choose which of them will act as the president of the committee (Schreuer, *Commentary*, p. 1014). Schreuer notes that it is important that ad hoc committees give consistent decisions and posits that this has been achieved in part by appointing the same arbitrators to the ad hoc committees in different cases (Schreuer, *Commentary*, pp. 1014-1016; e.g., *MINE* v *Guinea* (DA); *Klockner* v *Cameroon* (II) (DA); *Amco* v *Indonesia* (II) (DA)).

14. Stay of enforcement of the award. The enforcement of an award may be stayed pending a decision on annulment. The Secretary-General will automatically grant a provisional stay of enforcement upon registration of an application for annulment, unless it is made outside of the time limit in art. 52(2). Once the ad hoc committee is constituted, a party may request a continuance of the provisional stay. If the parties fail to request a continuance within thirty days of the constitution of the ad hoc committee, the provisional stay will automatically terminate (Rule 54(2) of the Arbitration Rules). Rule 54 of the Arbitration Rules sets out the procedure to request for a stay of enforcement. Once a stay is obtained, either party may request that it be terminated (Rule 54(3) of the Arbitration Rules). The committee is likely to terminate the stay where the situation that justified the stay in the first place is no longer present (Schreuer, *Commentary*, p. 1061). In the absence of a stay, the original award is enforceable throughout the annulment proceedings unless the parties agree otherwise (*SPP* v *Egypt* (DA)). The following factors may be considered by an ad hoc committee when deciding whether or not to grant a stay of enforcement: whether the party seeking the stay has a prima facie case; whether the party seeking the stay will grant security (e.g. in the form of a bank guarantee or bond); whether the party resisting the stay is likely promptly to adhere to the original award if it is upheld; whether the parties have ulterior motives for requesting a stay; whether the parties will suffer irreparable injury should the stay be refused (Schreuer, *Commentary*, pp. 1056-1057). Recently, the ad hoc committee in *Enron* v *Argentina* (Stay Decision) held that a requested stay should be granted unless the committee finds that there are very exceptional circumstances why this should not occur. To date, ad hoc committees have granted all requests for stays in annulment proceedings, often conditioning the stay on the provision of security. In *Enron* v *Argentina* (Stay Decision), the ad hoc committee noted that neither the Convention nor the Arbitration Rules expressly state that an ad hoc committee may grant a request for a stay subject to conditions. However, the committee held that there was what amounts to a jurisprudence constante to the effect that a stay may be made conditional on the provision of security. The committee noted that previous ad hoc committees had been called upon to exercise their power under art. 52(5) on eleven known occasions (*Amco* v *Indonesia* (I) (Stay Decision); *MINE* v *Guinea* (Stay Decision); *Amco* v *Indonesia* (II) (Stay Decision); *SPP* v *Egypt* (Stay Decision); *Wena* v *Egypt* (Stay Decision); *Mitchell* v *Congo* (Stay Decision); *CDC* v *Seychelles* (Stay Decision); *MTD* v *Chile* (Stay Decision); *Repsol* v *Petroecuador* (Stay Decision); *CMS* v *Argentina* (Stay Decision); *Azurix* v *Argentina* (Stay Decision)). On each of those occasions, a continuation of the stay was ordered. On five of those occasions, the continuation of the stay was ordered on the condition that the State seeking the stay provided security (*Amco* v *Indonesia* (I) (Stay Decision); *Amco* v *Indonesia* (II) (Stay Decision); *Wena* v *Egypt* (Stay Decision); *CDC* v *Seychelles* (Stay Decision); *Repsol* v *Petroecuador* (Stay Decision)). In three of those cases, the State provide the requisite security (*Amco* v *Indonesia* (I); *Amco* v *Indonesia* (II); *Wena* v *Egypt*) while in the remaining two, the State failed to provide the security and the stay was consequently terminated (*CDC* v *Seychelles*; *Repsol* v *Petroecuador*). In another five, the ad hoc committees declined to make an order for security (*MINE* v *Guinea* (Stay Decision); *Mitchell* v *Congo* (Stay Decision); *MTD* v *Chile* (Stay Decision); *CMS* v *Argentina* (Stay Decision); *Azurix* v *Argentina* (Stay Decision)). In the last remaining case, the provision of security was agreed between the parties (*SPP* v *Egypt* (Stay Decision)). Ad hoc committees have declined to order security where to do so would impose financial hardship on the State (*MINE* v *Guinea* (Stay Decision); *Mitchell* v *Congo* (Stay Decision)), or where the State has given assurances as to payment (*CMS* v *Argentina* (Stay Decision), particularly if these assurances are supported by a proven track-record of compliance (*MTD* v *Chile* (Stay Decision)). Ad hoc committees have noted that any perceived requirement to post security should be examined carefully as it might deter developing countries from submitting annulment applications (*Mitchell* v *Congo* (Stay Decision); *Azurix* v *Argentina* (Stay Decision)). The ad hoc committee will conduct a balancing exercise to determine whether the burden on the State of posting security outweighs the risk on the investor of ultimate non-enforceability.

15. Resubmission of dispute. If the award is annulled, pursuant to art. 52(6), either or both of the parties is entitled to submit the dispute to a new tribunal constituted in accordance with arts. 37 to 40. Schreuer states that the text of art. 52(6) suggests that the parties may not introduce new claims when submitting the dispute to the new tribunal (Schreuer, *Commentary*, p. 1071). Where only part of the award has been annulled, the portion of the award that has not been annulled will be res judicata and will accordingly bind the new tribunal. Any findings in the original award not challenged in the annulment proceedings will similarly bind the new tribunal (*Amco* v *Indonesia* (II)). At the time of writing, three new tribunals constituted under art. 52(6) had issued new awards, in the cases of *Klöckner* v *Cameroon* (II); *Amco* v *Indonesia* (II) and *Vivendi* v *Argentina* (II). In *MINE* v *Guinea*, the case was resubmitted under art. 52(6) after the tribunal's decision was annulled but the parties decided to settle and their request for resubmission was discontinued. Schreuer notes that as the resubmitted dispute must be brought between the parties to the original proceedings, problems may arise in the cases of State succession and altered corporate structures (Schreuer, *Commentary*, p. 1066).

16. Costs. In the vast majority of annulment decisions, ad hoc committees have ordered each party to bear its own costs incurred in the annulment phase and one half of the costs incurred by the Centre. However, this practice is not without exception. In the case *of CDC* v *Seychelles*, the ad hoc committee ordered the respondent to pay both the claimant's and the Centre's costs as punishment for making an application that was fundamentally lacking in merit. In the case of *Repsol* v *Petroecuador*, the ad hoc committee ordered the respondent to bear all of the costs incurred by the Centre and half of the costs incurred by that claimant since the arguments raised were neither valid nor complex and the respondent delayed the proceedings by refusing to make the advance payment.

Section 6. Recognition and Enforcement of the Award
[Binding force of the award]
Article 53

(1) The award shall be binding on the parties and shall not be subject to any appeal or to any other remedy except those provided for in this Convention. Each party shall abide by and comply with the terms of the award except to the extent that enforcement shall have been stayed pursuant to the relevant provisions of this Convention.

(2) For the purposes of this Section, 'award' shall include any decision interpreting, revising or annulling such award pursuant to Articles 50, 51 or 52.

1. General. Pursuant to art. 53, the award is final, binding and not subject to appeal and each party shall abide by and comply with that award, unless enforcement has been stayed.

2. Application. Art. 53 applies to awards, including any decision interpreting, revising or annulling such award, but does not apply to preliminary decisions (other than those preliminary decisions on jurisdiction which dispose of the case). Art. 53 also does not apply to provisional measures or procedural orders.

3. The binding nature of the award. At the time of drafting the Convention, the binding nature of the arbitral award was consistently emphasised (*History*, Vol. II, pp. 54-55, 57, 58, 74, 80, 110, 161, 304, 344, 347, 424, 428, 430, 502, 505, 521, 574, 763, 819, 916, 989). Under art. 53, the award is binding on the parties to the arbitration, and under art. 54, each Contracting State must recognise an award under the Convention. Art. 53 thus only creates obligations that are binding on the parties to the arbitration, and not State parties in general.

4. No appeal. The parties may only challenge an award using the mechanisms provided by the Convention (arts. 49(2), 50, 51 and 52). Art. 53 is mandatory: the parties may not agree to modify it and thereby introduce other avenues of appeal. The award may not be attacked in national courts (*MINE* v *Guinea*) or before the ICJ (*History*, Vol. II, pp. 274, 438, 440). Once all the remedies available under the Convention have been exhausted, the parties may not seek relief for the same claim in another forum as the dispute is res judicata (Schreuer, *Commentary*, p. 1085). This will not be the case where an ICSID tribunal declines to exercise jurisdiction over a dispute.

ICSID Convention, art. 53

5. Compliance with the award. The obligation to abide by and comply with the award contained in art. 53 is automatic. If a party turns to a court or other authority to disobey an ICSID award, it will be in breach of art. 53. At the time of drafting the Convention, a provision requiring compliance was included in all drafts (*History*, Vol. II, pp. 242, 244). To date, voluntary compliance by Contracting States with ICSID awards has been the norm. In fact, the drafting history of the Convention suggests that the drafters believed that if any party would be in danger of defaulting, it would be the investor (e.g. on an award for costs). The price of non-compliance by the State, in terms of losing its reputation in the international community as a safe place for investment, was considered so high that the judicial protection of the investor and the mechanism for enforcement provided under art. 54 were deemed to be less important (*History*, Vol. II, pp. 379, 424 and 989). Voluntary compliance by States may also be attributed, in part, to the indirect impact that failure to comply with an ICSID award may have on access to World Bank funding, or international credit in general. In addition to the commercial repercussions, there are serious legal consequences; failure to pay an ICSID award (after the exhaustion of challenge rights under the Convention) is not simply a breach by a State of its obligation to the investor, but a breach of the State's international obligations towards the other Contracting States. If a State fails to comply with an award, action may be taken under arts. 27 and 64. Under art. 27, an investor may call for diplomatic protection from its own State once the host State of its investment has failed to abide by and comply with an award, but not before. Consequently, in the event of non-compliance, a parallel diplomatic incident could be created. Moreover, under art. 64, any dispute between Contracting States concerning the application of the Convention which is not settled by negotiation shall be referred to the ICJ for resolution, which could escalate the dispute even further. For these reasons, to date, the tendency of Contracting States has overwhelmingly been to abide by and comply with awards as the drafters had hoped (Alexandrov, *Enforcement*, p. 10). To date, only Congo, Liberia, Senegal, Kazakhstan and Argentina have refused to pay ICSID awards rendered against them. The case of Argentina is a unique one. In the last four years, nine final awards have been rendered in ICSID cases against Argentina with some thirty more claims waiting in the wings. In view of this deluge of claims, Argentina has adopted a policy of applying for the annulment of all awards rendered against it. In May 2007, the first of these annulment proceedings culminated in a decision partially upholding the award, including the damages in full (*CMS* v *Argentina* (DA)). However, Argentina has yet to comply with this award. Argentina's rationale for not doing so was explained in the annulment proceedings in *Siemens* v *Argentina* and *Enron* v *Argentina* (Stay Decision). In response to Siemens' and Enron's argument that Argentina had defaulted on the CMS award in breach of art. 53 (and so should be required to post a bond in subsequent proceedings), Argentina argued that CMS (and other investors with awards in their favour) must enforce those awards before the Argentine courts in accordance with art. 54. Argentina considered that art. 53 must be read in light of art. 54, which provides that Contracting States are obliged to recognise and enforce ICSID awards through their own courts; Argentina viewed its obligation thus not to comply voluntarily with the award, but to recognise and enforce the award in its own courts once the investor seeks to enforce it there. This position has been rejected by the US government, among others. Commentators virtually unanimously consider that the obligation of recognition and enforcement through a Contracting State's courts in art. 54 only applies once a party to the arbitration defaults on its obligation to comply voluntarily with the award under art. 53. This position was accepted in *Enron* v *Argentina* (Stay Decision), where the ad hoc committee noted that nothing in the language of arts. 53 and 54 suggests that the obligation within art. 53(1) must be read as being subject to the enforcement mechanisms established pursuant to art. 54(1). The Committee found that the word 'party' in art. 53(1) clearly referred to a party to the award, while art. 54(1) addressed 'each Contracting State' to the Convention. By this rationale, a State's obligations under art. 54 cannot be relied on as a reason not to comply with its obligation of voluntary compliance under art. 53.

6. Suspension or modification of the award. If an ad hoc committee has granted a stay of enforcement under art. 52(4), the obligation to comply with the award will be suspended until the stay has ended (*MINE* v *Guinea* (DA)). The same applies if a tribunal has granted a stay under art. 50(2) on an application for interpretation, or under art. 51(4) on an application for revision. However, if a request for supplementation or rectification is made under art. 49, the obligation to comply will remain in force. The only means by which the obligation to comply may be suspended is where a stay is issued pursuant to the Convention (Alexandrov, *Enforcement*, p. 2). Once an award has been interpreted, revised, supplemented or rectified, the parties are obliged to comply with this modified version. If a party complies with an award that is later modified, underperformance or overperformance will have to be calculated and adjusted. Once the award has been annulled, the parties are no longer obliged to comply with the award. Where an award has only been partially annulled, the parties will only be obliged to comply with the unannulled part of the award (Schreuer, *Commentary*, p. 1096).

[Enforcement of the award]

Article 54

(1) Each Contracting State shall recognise an award rendered pursuant to this Convention as binding and enforce the pecuniary obligations imposed by that award within its territories as if it were a final judgment of a court in that State. A Contracting State with a federal constitution may enforce such an award in or through its federal courts and may pro-

vide that such courts shall treat the award as if it were a final judgment of the courts of a constituent state.

(2) A party seeking recognition or enforcement in the territories of a Contracting State shall furnish to a competent court or other authority which such State shall have designated for this purpose a copy of the award certified by the Secretary-General. Each Contracting State shall notify the Secretary-General of the designation of the competent court or other authority for this purpose and of any subsequent change in such designation.

(3) Execution of the award shall be governed by the laws concerning the execution of judgments in force in the State in whose territories such execution is sought.

1. General. Under art. 54(1), each Contracting State is obliged to recognise a final ICSID award and enforce the monetary obligations in the award on the same basis as a final judgment of a court in that State. Art. 54 provides both a general obligation and procedural directions for the implementation of that obligation.

2. Application. The general obligation imposed by art. 54 applies to all Contracting States whether or not they were a party to the arbitration (either directly or by virtue of the nationality of the investor). Accordingly, the recognition and enforcement of an award may be sought in all 143 Contracting States. This allows for 'forum shopping' whereby the enforcing party can identify Contracting States in which the losing party has attachable assets and then seek to have the award recognised and enforced in the courts of those States. If a Contracting State refuses to recognise or enforce an award, it will be in breach of its obligations under the Convention. Under art. 64, the aggrieved State (either the respondent State or the State of the investor in the arbitration) could refer the resulting dispute with the non-enforcing Contracting State to the ICJ. If the courts of the respondent State refuse to recognise or enforce the award, that State will be in violation of both art. 53 (the obligation to comply with the award) and art. 54 (the obligation to recognise and enforce). As the ad hoc committee noted in *Enron* v *Argentina* (Stay Decision), art. 54 does not require a party to an award to use the enforcement machinery established pursuant to the provision as a condition of its compliance with the award under art. 53. Art. 54 applies to final awards and also to decisions on jurisdiction (Schreuer, *Commentary*, p. 1111). If the parties reach a settlement and their settlement is embodied in an award under Rule 43(2) of the Arbitration Rules, art. 54 will also apply to that award. Decisions on interpretation, revision and annulment (under arts. 50, 51 and 52) will be subject to art. 54 as will decisions on supplementation and rectification (as they are incorporated into the final award under art. 49(2)).

3. Recognition of the award. A party will only need to have recourse to the mechanism of court recognition provided in art. 54 where the other party has refused to comply voluntarily with an award. Once a State recognises an award in its courts, the award becomes legally binding in that State, enforceable and res judicata between the parties. States may not impose in their domestic courts conditions for recognition over and above those prescribed by the Convention. A domestic court is essentially limited to determining that the award is authentic, and may not subject an award to an appeal of any kind – not a review of the jurisdiction of the tribunal, nor a review of the merits, nor a review of the fairness of the proceedings. The process of recognition must be distinguished from the process of enforcement. Unlike in the case of enforcement, States may not rely on sovereign immunity to resist the recognition of an award (*Benvenuti* v *Congo* (France); *SOABI* v *Senegal* (France)). Moreover, both awards for pecuniary measures and non-pecuniary measures, such as specific performance, are subject to recognition – again, this is not the case for enforcement. There may be cases where for tactical reasons a party applies to a domestic court for the recognition but not the enforcement of the award. For example, in *Enron* v *Argentina* and *Sempra* v *Argentina*, the investors sought immediate recognition of their award against Argentina (prior to any annulment proceedings being commenced) in the US courts in order to attract the interest applicable to US court judgments, since they had not been granted post-award interest by the arbitral tribunal.

4. Enforcement of the award. Schreuer notes that despite the use of the words 'enforcement' and 'execution' in art. 54, a study of the French and Spanish texts reveals that the words are entirely interchangeable (Schreuer, *Commentary*, pp. 1122-1123). Under art. 54(3), the enforcement or execution of the award in a State's courts will be governed by that State's domestic law concerning the execution of judgments, which is logical since the award is to be enforced 'as if it were a final judgment of a court in that State'. Some domestic laws may provide limited grounds on which their courts can refuse to enforce a final judgment, e.g., in the US, under Rules 60(b) of the Federal Rules of Civil Procedure, on the grounds (inter alia) of mistake, newly discovered evidence and fraud (Baldwin/Kantor/Nolan, *Limits of Enforcement of ICSID Awards*, p. 8). Art. 54(3) does not require that States create new procedures to facilitate the enforcement of awards, they need only utilise existing procedures. This includes that State's laws on sovereign immunity, as spelled out in art. 55, which provides that nothing in art. 54 shall be construed as derogating from the law in force in any Contracting State relating to immunity of that State or of any foreign State from execution. Unlike in the case of recognition, only the pecuniary obligations of an award are subject to enforcement. Thus, non-pecuniary measures, such as specific performance, cannot be enforced. However, the inability to enforce does not detract from the effect of res judicata of the award. Due to the tendency of States to comply voluntarily with ICSID awards, there is little precedent of the enforcement of awards under art. 54. To date, judicial enforcement proceedings have been brought in five cases: *LETCO* v *Liberia* (NY); *LETCO* v *Liberia* (DC); *Benvenuti* v *Congo* (France); *SOABI* v *Senegal* (France); *AIG* v *Kazakhstan* (UK); *CMS* v

Argentina (NY and Switzerland). In the two French cases, the French courts drew a distinction between the enforcement of an award and the execution of an award against certain assets, stating that considerations of sovereign immunity applied only to the latter. The French courts also imported a concept of ordre public into enforcement proceedings at odds with the Convention's drafting history (*Benvenuti* v *Congo* (France); *SOABI* v *Senegal* (France); Baldwin/Kantor/Nolan, *Limits to Enforcement*, p. 7). The US courts have permitted enforcement of ICSID awards, but refused to grant orders for execution on the grounds of sovereign immunity (*LETCO* v *Liberia* (NY); *LETCO* v *Liberia* (DC)) and on the basis that attachable assets could not be identified with sufficient certainty (*CMS v Argentina* (NY)). The English courts have also applied principles of sovereign immunity to resist the execution of an award (*AIG v Kazakhstan* (UK)), whilst the Swiss courts have applied principles of the division of State and provincial assets to refuse execution (*CMS v Argentina* (Switzerland)).

5. Enforcement in States with federal constitutions. Under art. 54(1), if a Contracting State has a federal system (such as the US, Switzerland or Germany) then the award may be treated as a final judgment of a court of a constituent State of that Contracting State. Schreuer expresses doubt as to whether this provision would allow federal States to treat awards like decisions of their constituent States and thereby apply mechanisms of review to the decision (Schreuer, *Commentary*, p. 1133).

6. Procedure for recognition and enforcement. Art. 54(2) provides the procedure for the recognition and enforcement of awards, which is straightforward. Under art. 54(2), a party is required to furnish a copy of the award that has been certified by the Secretary-General to the court or other authority of the State in which it is seeking to have the award recognised or enforced. A party may not furnish an award that is subject to a stay of enforcement. Schreuer notes that 'only a party to the original ICSID arbitration may initiate the procedure under art. 54(2). This would exclude action by an interested third party. ... The requirement that only one of the original parties may initiate a proceedings for the recognition and enforcement of an award may also lead to problems of State succession or corporate succession.' (Schreuer, *Commentary*, pp. 1135-1136). The procedure in art. 54(2) may be initiated in more than one State. Under art. 69, Contracting States should have legislative measures in place to recognise and enforce the award once the parties have furnished it. Under art. 54(2), each Contracting State shall notify the Secretary-General of the designation of the competent court for the purpose of art. 54. At the time of writing, 98 of the 143 Contracting States had made designations. A list of the designations made by Contracting States (ICSID/10) is available at <www.worldbank.org/icsid>. Schreuer notes that since the vast majority of the leading commercial and financial States have made their designations, the failure of other States to make their designations should not have too great an impact on the effective enforcement of awards (Schreuer, *Commentary*, p. 1137).

7. Stay of enforcement. Where a party has obtained a stay of enforcement, a Contracting State's obligation to enforce the award under art. 54 will be suspended for so long as the stay is in place (*MINE* v *Guinea* (Stay Decision); *Amco* v *Indonesia* (II) (Stay Decision); *CMS* v *Argentina* (Stay Decision); *Enron* v *Argentina* (Stay Decision); Report of the Executive Directors, para. 42; Schreuer, *Commentary*, pp. 1112-1113). If a party fails to secure a stay of enforcement, the award may be recognised and enforced, despite the fact that there are pending proceedings for interpretation, revision or annulment.

[State or sovereign immunity]

Article 55

Nothing in Article 54 shall be construed as derogating from the law in force in any Contracting State relating to immunity of that State or of any foreign State from execution.

1. General. Art. 55 clarifies art. 54, providing that the mechanisms provided therein shall not derogate from the laws of the Contracting State where recognition and enforcement is sought relating to State or sovereign immunity.

2. Application. Art. 55 applies to the execution but not the recognition of awards. State immunity should be raised as a defence at the time the award is executed against specific assets, not in the context of legal enforcement (*Benvenuti* v *Congo* (France), *SOABI* v *Senegal* (France)). While immunity against execution may be raised pursuant to this provision, art. 55 does not provide immunity against suit or jurisdiction, which is waived by each Contracting State upon signature of the Convention.

3. Non-derogation from the law on State immunity. The extent to which an award may be executed in a given State will depend on that State's domestic law (see art. 54(3)), including its laws on State immunity. Since the time at which the Convention was drafted, domestic laws on State immunity have developed considerably. The laws on State immunity in each Contracting State differ. While most States permit the execution of awards and domestic judgments against property used for a commercial purpose or activity (see, e.g., the US FSIA, the UK SIA; the Canadian SIA), some States grant other States absolute immunity from execution in their courts (see, e.g., the case of Russia which still arguably practices the theory of absolute immunity for the State: Shaleva, *The Public Policy Exception*, p. 88). Execution against property serving a sovereign purpose will not be permitted (see Schreuer, *Commentary*, pp. 1149). In order to determine whether State property serves a commercial or sovereign purpose, a court will consider how the State has used the property in addition to how the property originated. In *LETCO* v *Liberia* (NY), a New York court applying the US FSIA found that the levy and collection of taxes intended to serve as funds for the support and maintenance of governmental functions was an exercise of powers particular to the sovereign, and refused to grant the execution order requested. However, if the taxes had been used for other (commercial) purposes, this finding may not have been the same. Under domestic legislation, blanket exceptions often apply to property belonging to a State's central bank, military and diplomatic missions. In *AIG v Kazakhstan* (UK), the English court, applying the UK SIA, held that the property of a State's central bank was entirely immune from enforcement, regardless of whether the property was used for commercial purposes (as argued by AIG). In *LETCO v Liberia* (DC), a court in Washington DC, applying the US FSIA, refused to permit the execution of an award against the bank accounts of the Liberian embassy and the Liberian central bank. The court noted that the concept of commercial activity, in the context of the enforcement of awards, should be construed narrowly because sovereign immunity remains the rule rather than the exception. In the cases of *Benvenuti v Congo* (France) and *SOABI v Senegal* (France), the losing States successfully avoided execution based on sovereign immunity defences in the French courts. In *Benvenuti v Congo* (France) the Paris Cour d'appel rejected the claimant's attempt to enforce its award against the assets of the Banque Commerciale Congolaise (BCC) on the basis that the BCC was a separate entity whose funds were not available to satisfy an award against the People's Republic of the Congo itself. In *SOABI v Senegal* (France), the Cour d'appel held that sovereign immunity continued to protect the relevant Senegalese assets as the claimant had failed to prove that they were used for commercial activities. Accordingly, the court held that the execution of the award against the relevant assets would contravene the international ordre public of immunity. Thus, the French courts appear to have imported a concept of ordre public into enforcement proceedings at odds with the Convention's drafting history (Baldwin/Kantor/Nolan, *Limits to Enforcement*, p. 7; see art. 54, note 4). These cases highlight the potential challenges that investors may face when they seek forcibly to execute their awards. However, in some cases, execution proceedings may lead to an out-of-court settlement which will not necessarily become public.

4. Waiver of immunity. An investor may seek to argue that a State has waived its immunity against execution. However, in most legal systems, in the absence of an express waiver of immunity against execution this will not succeed; in particular, consent to arbitration will not be deemed to constitute an implicit waiver of immunity against execution (*LETCO v Liberia* (NY); *LETCO v Liberia* (DC)). Domestic laws may also prescribe requirements for an effective waiver which should be taken into account.

5. Subdivision, agency and State owned entities. Schreuer notes that a State's constituent subdivision or agency, if a party to the arbitration under art. 25, may be subject to the recognition and enforcement of awards. Whether such a subdivision or agency can claim State immunity will depend on the domestic law applied to the enforcement proceedings. Investors may also seek to enforce awards against the assets of a State-owned entity or

State agency. Again, whether this is possible will depend on domestic law, e.g., principles of alter ego liability under US law (*FNCB* v *Bancec*; *Bridas* v *Turkmenistan*) or piercing of the veil under UK law (*Norsk Hydro* v *Ukraine*; *Svenska* v *Lithuania*), which will depend on the degree of control exerted on the State-owned entity or State agency, and issues of fraud and injustice.

CHAPTER V. REPLACEMENT AND DISQUALIFICATION OF CONCILIATORS AND ARBITRATORS

Article 56

[Replacement of conciliators and arbitrators]

(1) After a Commission or a Tribunal has been constituted and proceedings have begun, its composition shall remain unchanged; provided, however, that if a conciliator or an arbitrator should die, become incapacitated, or resign, the resulting vacancy shall be filled in accordance with the provisions of Section 2 of Chapter III or Section 2 of Chapter IV.

(2) A member of a Commission or Tribunal shall continue to serve in that capacity notwithstanding that he shall have ceased to be a member of the Panel.

(3) If a conciliator or arbitrator appointed by a party shall have resigned without the consent of the Commission or Tribunal of which he was a member, the Chairman shall appoint a person from the appropriate Panel to fill the resulting vacancy.

1. General. Art. 56 is based on the principle of non-frustration of proceedings and seeks to avoid vacancies by establishing a straightforward replacement procedure. The first paragraph of art. 56 sets out the principle of immutability of a tribunal or commission and the replacement procedure for arbitrators and conciliators. Art. 56(2) provides that membership in a tribunal or commission is not affected by the expiry of a term on the Panel of Arbitrators or the Panel of Conciliators. The last paragraph of art. 56 establishes a special replacement procedure for cases of resignation without the consent of the tribunal or commission. Art. 56 does not apply to ad hoc committees constituted in accordance with art. 52.

2. The principle of immutability. The principle of immutability applies from the time that the commission or the tribunal has been constituted. The commission or tribunal is considered to be constituted from the date on which the Secretary-General notified the parties that all the conciliators or arbitrators have accepted their appointments (see art. 37). There are certain exceptions to the immutability principle. According to art. 56 these exceptions are: the death of a conciliator or arbitrator; the incapacity of a conciliator or arbitrator; and the resignation of a conciliator or arbitrator. arts. 57 to 58 provide for one further exception to the immutability principle, namely the disqualification of a conciliator or arbitrator. Such exceptions lead to vacancies which lead to the suspension of proceedings. The proceedings are suspended until the vacancy is filled (see Rule 10 of the Arbitration Rules and Rule 12 of the Arbitration Rules). The principle of immutability may also prevent parties from appointing counsel whose participation in the proceedings would force an arbitrator to resign due to a conflict of interest (*HEP* v *Slovenia*). Such situations will naturally be exceedingly rare, and the application of the principle will depend on the circumstances of the case (e.g. the timing of the purported appointment of counsel).

3. Rules for filling vacancies. Art. 56 provides that the procedure for filling vacancies should be the same as for the constitution of the arbitral tribunal or that of the conciliation commission (see also Rule 11 of the Arbitration Rules). Art. 56(3) contains an exception in cases of resignation of a party-appointed arbitrator or conciliator without the consent of the tribunal or commission. In such case, the Centre shall appoint a person from either the Panel of Arbitrators or the Panel of Conciliators (*Holiday Inns* v *Morocco*). The exception is to avoid the possibility of collusion between an arbitrator or conciliator and the appointing party (*History*, Vol. I, paras. 258, 260; Vol. II, paras. 872, 992). This exception does not apply to arbitrators or conciliators appointed by agreement between the parties, by the Centre or by any other appointing authority.

4. Vacancy caused by incapacity. Incapacity relates to mental or physical inability to participate in the commission's or tribunal's works. Filling vacancies is subject to the procedure used in cases of disqualification (see Rule 8 of the Arbitration Rules). There must be a proposal by one of the parties and a vote of the remaining members of the commission or tribunal. If the proposal refers to the majority of members or if the remaining members are divided, the decision will be made by the Centre (see Rule 9 of the Arbitration Rules).

5. Vacancy caused by resignation. Resignation of an arbitrator or conciliator must always be reasoned. This is premised on the principle that acceptance of appointment entails an obligation to serve (see Rule 8 of the Arbitration Rules). Neither the Convention nor the Rules specify legitimate grounds for resignation.

6. Vacancy caused by death. The death of a commissioner or tribunal member does not call for a decision by the commission or tribunal. It automatically entails the filling of vacancy procedure described in the relevant Rules of Procedure (e.g. Rule 11 of the Arbitration Rules; see generally *Holiday Inns* v *Morocco*; *Adriano Gardella* v *Cote d'Ivoire*; *LESI-DIPENTA* v *Algeria*).

7. Expiry of term on a Panel. Art. 56(2) provides for the non-termination of the arbitrator's or conciliator's membership of the tribunal or commission upon expiration of his term on the relevant Panel. Any other solution would imply that in selecting arbitrators or conciliators special attention should be paid not to select a person whose term on the Panel is to expire before the anticipated end of the proceedings (Schreuer, *Commentary*, p. 1191), which would conflict with the rule of immutability.

Article 57

[Proposal to disqualify]

A party may propose to a Commission or Tribunal the disqualification of any of its members on account of any fact indicating a manifest lack of the qualities required by paragraph (1) of Article 14. A party to arbitration proceedings may, in addition, propose the disqualification of an arbitrator on the ground that he was ineligible for appointment to the Tribunal under Section 2 of Chapter IV.

1. General. Art. 57 is the first of the two articles dealing with the question of disqualification of arbitrators or conciliators. It deals with the initiation of the proceeding to disqualify. Art. 57 is important in the light of art. 52(1)(a) concerning the parties' right to request the annulment of the award on the ground that the tribunal was not properly constituted (see art. 52, note 6). A timely proposal for disqualification would preclude a later request for annulment and, conversely, holding back on a disqualification proposal may well jeopardise the chances of an annulment application. Art. 57 applies to both arbitration and conciliation but does not apply to an ad hoc committee.

2. The proposal to disqualify. Only parties to the proceedings may make such a proposal. Neither the commission or tribunal nor the Centre may initiate a disqualification procedure. The proposal for disqualification can only be made after the constitution of the commission or tribunal. The proposal must be made as soon as the party concerned learnt of the grounds in support of disqualification (see Rule 9 of the Arbitration Rules).

4. Grounds for disqualification. There are two sets of grounds for disqualification. The first relates to both conciliators and arbitrators while the second relates only to arbitrators. The first set includes any fact indicating a manifest lack of the qualities required by art. 14(1). According to that article, the required qualities are: high moral character; recognised competence in the fields of law, commerce, industry or finance; and reliability to exercise independent judgment. Designation to the Panel entails the presumption that the designated person has the required qualities. Such presumption can be rebutted, but the burden of proof is very heavy. A conflict of interest is the most likely cause for a lack of independence. The lack of independence has to be 'manifest', so that a simple 'possibility' of partiality will not suffice (*Amco* v *Indonesia* (I) (DA)). Recent and high-profile cases in which a State has attempted to disqualify a particular arbitrator can be found in *Aguas Argentinas* v *Argentina* and *Interagua* v *Argentina* (see art. 58). The second set of grounds refers to the nationality requirements for arbitrators, namely arts.

37 to 40. These requirements vary depending on whether the appointment is made by the Centre or the parties (see arts. 38 and 39). A violation of these eligibility criteria is in practice unlikely (Schreuer, *Commentary*, p. 1201). Possible problems may however appear if the investor's nationality is unclear or in cases of dual nationality of arbitrators or parties.

Article 58

[Decision to disqualify)

The decision on any proposal to disqualify a conciliator or arbitrator shall be taken by the other members of the Commission or Tribunal as the case may be, provided that where those members are equally divided, or in the case of a proposal to disqualify a sole conciliator or arbitrator, or a majority of the conciliators or arbitrators, the Chairman shall take that decision. If it is decided that the proposal is well-founded the conciliator or arbitrator to whom the decision relates shall be replaced in accordance with the provisions of Section 2 of Chapter III or Section 2 of Chapter IV.

1. General. Art. 58 is the second article that addresses the question of disqualification. It deals with the procedure on a proposal to disqualify a conciliator or arbitrator and with the filling of a vacancy in case there is a decision to disqualify. It does not apply to an ad hoc committee.

2. The decision to disqualify. The decision on any proposal to disqualify a conciliator or an arbitrator is made by the other members of the Commission or tribunal. Where the members are evenly divided, the Chairman has a casting vote. The Chairman also decides on the proposal in situations involving either a sole conciliator or arbitrator, or a majority of conciliators or arbitrators (see Rule 9 of the Arbitration Rules). As a recent example, in *Aguas Argentinas* v *Argentina*, Argentina filed a challenge to an arbitrator on the basis that she lacked the requisite impartiality. Because the arbitrator in question rejected Argentina's allegations, it fell to the two remaining arbitrators to rule on the challenge. They rejected the challenge on two bases: first, Argentina had failed to make the challenge in a timely and prompt fashion; secondly, the challenge itself lacked substance. The remaining arbitrators held that, contrary to the submissions of Argentina, an arbitrator cannot be disqualified on the grounds of bias merely because he or she sat on the tribunal in an earlier case which was resolved in a manner adverse to the party in question. In any event, they noted that the present dispute before the tribunal was different from the previous case that had been decided against Argentina.

3. Replacement procedure. If the proposal to disqualify is accepted, the proceedings are suspended until a new conciliator or arbitrator is appointed. The procedure is substantively identical to the one set forth in art. 56(1) (see art. 56 and Rule 11 of the Arbitration Rules).

CHAPTER VI. COST OF PROCEEDINGS

[Charges of the Centre]

Article 59

The charges payable by the parties for the use of the facilities of the Centre shall be determined by the Secretary-General in accordance with the regulations adopted by the Administrative Council.

1. General. Art. 59 provides that the charges payable for use of the Centre's facilities shall be determined by the Secretary-General, in accordance with the regulations adopted by the Administrative Council.

2. Applicable Administrative Council regulations. The regulations referred to in art. 59 are the Administrative and Financial Regulations adopted by the Administrative Council. The Secretary-General has adopted a Schedule of Fees which specifies the current charges.

3. Lodging fee. The lodging fee is a non-refundable fee paid by parties in connection with the following types of requests: institution of arbitration or conciliation procedures (arts. 28, 36); supplementation or rectification of an award (art. 49); interpretation of an award (art. 50); revision of an award (art. 51); annulment of an award (art. 52); and resubmission of a dispute after annulment (art. 52(6)). Currently, the lodging fee for the institution of arbitration or conciliation is USD 25,000 (Schedule of Fees art. 1). For the other types of requests, the fee is USD 10,000 (Schedule of Fees art. 2). The Secretary-General will not take any action until payment of the lodging fee has been received (Rule 5(1)(b) of the Institutional Rules).

4. Administrative charges. The Centre charges fees in connection with the out-of-pocket administrative expenses such as for interpreters, reporters and secretaries. The current fee is set to USD 20,000 and is calculated on an annual basis (Schedule of Fees art. 4). A secretary is appointed for each commission, tribunal or ad hoc committee by the Secretary-General (Reg. 25 of the Administrative and Financial Regulations). The Schedule of Fees also provides for advance deposits of costs (Reg. 15 of the Administrative and Financial Regulations).

[Fees and expenses]

Article 60

(1) Each Commission and each Tribunal shall determine the fees and expenses of its members within limits established from time to time by the Administrative Council and after consultation with the Secretary-General.

ICSID Convention, art. 60

(2) Nothing in paragraph (1) of this Article shall preclude the parties from agreeing in advance with the Commission or Tribunal concerned upon the fees and expenses of its members.

1. General. Art. 60 addresses the remuneration of arbitrators and conciliators. This article applies also to ad hoc committees (art. 52(4)). The fees and expenses of the commission or tribunal can be determined by agreement with the parties. If there is no agreement, the commission or tribunal can determine the fees and expenses which will apply provided that those fees and expenses are within the specified limits.

2. Limits established by the Centre. The Administrative and Financial Regulations delegate the determination of the relevant limits to the Secretary-General, with the approval of the Chairman (Reg. 14 of the Administrative and Financial Regulations). The current version of the Schedule of Fees, published on 1 January 2008, provides for a fee of USD 3,000 per day of meeting or other work performed by arbitrators, conciliators or ad hoc committee members in connection with the proceedings. Additionally, they are entitled to reimbursement of travel expenses as well as subsistence allowances and any other expenses reasonably incurred (Reg. 14 of the Administrative and Financial Regulations). The fees specified in the Schedule of Fees are intended to provide an upper limit. However, they are usually regarded as automatically applicable (Schreuer, *Commentary*, pp. 1214-1215). Although there has been some criticism that ICSID fees are relatively low compared to rates observed in some commercial arbitration cases, it has been pointed out that the work performed should be regarded as performance of a public service (Schreuer, *Commentary*, p. 1215).

3. Agreement on fees and expenses. Parties can set fees higher or lower than the amounts set in the Schedule of Fees by agreement with the commission or tribunal. In practice the agreed fees are higher than those provided by the Schedule of Fees. The agreement has to be entered into between all parties and all the members of the commission or tribunal. An agreement entered into between one of the parties and an arbitrator appointed by it would lead to the annulment of the award (art. 52(1)(c)).

4. Payment of fees. The payment of fees and expenses is made exclusively by the Centre and not by or through the parties to the proceeding (Reg. 14 of the Administrative and Financial Regulations). The payments made by the Centre are funded by the advance payments made by the parties (Reg. 14(3) of the Administrative and Financial Regulations).

ICSID Convention, art. 61

[Apportionment of expenses]

Article 61

(1) In the case of conciliation proceedings the fees and expenses of members of the Commission as well as the charges for the use of the facilities of the Centre, shall be borne equally by the parties. Each party shall bear any other expenses it incurs in connection with the proceedings.

(2) In the case of arbitration proceedings the Tribunal shall, except as the parties otherwise agree, assess the expenses incurred by the parties in connection with the proceedings, and shall decide how and by whom those expenses, the fees and expenses of the members of the Tribunal and the charges for the use of the facilities of the Centre shall be paid. Such decision shall form part of the award.

1. **General.** Art. 61 addresses apportionment of costs between the parties in ICSID proceedings. The article deals with three types of costs: charges payable to the Centre; fees and expenses of conciliators or arbitrators; and costs incurred by the parties.

2. **Costs in conciliation proceedings.** In conciliation proceedings, the charges for use of the Centre's facilities and the fees and expenses of conciliators are always borne equally by the parties. Each party bears any other costs it might incur. The Convention does not provide for the possibility of agreement between parties on a different method of apportioning costs. The commission does not have any discretionary power in the apportionment of costs for conciliation (*Tesoro Petroleum Corporation* v *Trinidad and Tobago*).

3. **Costs in arbitration proceedings.** Art. 61(2) deals with three types of costs arising in arbitration proceedings: charges for the use of the Centre's facilities; fees and expenses of the tribunal members; and expenses incurred by the parties in connection with the proceedings. The last category includes the costs of legal representation of the parties. Neither the Convention nor the Rules provide any substantive criteria for the tribunal's decision on how costs should be apportioned (Schreuer, *Commentary*, p. 1224). The practice of ICSID tribunals in awarding costs is neither clear nor uniform (Schreuer, *Commentary*, p. 1225). Some tribunals have applied the principle that costs follow the event (*AGIP* v *Congo*; *SPP* v *Egypt* (DA)). In other cases costs have been awarded against parties as a sanction for procedural misconduct (*LETCO* v *Liberia*). In the majority of cases tribunals have decided that parties should bear costs equally and that each party should bear its own expenses whether because both parties acted in good faith (*Fedax* v *Venezuela*) or because both parties had been partly successful and partly unsuccessful (*Tradex* v *Albania* (DJ)). In *Noble Ventures Inc.* v *Romania*, the tribunal dismissed the claims in their entirety but split the costs between the parties, since it considered, inter alia, that the claimant had succeeded on some points

Petrochilos, Noury and Kalderimis

of argument. Tribunals may require one party to bear the costs of a particular part of the proceedings (Rule 28 of the Arbitration Rules). It follows that a party that requests a special measure to be taken by the tribunal, or makes a preliminary objection, may ultimately have to bear the costs of such a request or objection (*AMT* v *Zaire*; *SOABI* v *Senegal*).

4. Reasons for decision on costs. According to the last part of art. 61(2), the decision on costs is part of the award (see also Rule 47(1)(j) of the Arbitration Rules). One ICSID tribunal held that art. 61(2) confers full discretion in deciding the apportionment of costs and that tribunals are not under any obligation to provide substantive reasoning for their decision on costs (*MINE* v *Guinea*, (DA)). This reasoning is open to criticism primarily because the use of a discretionary power and the obligation to provide reasons for a decision are distinct (*Amco* v *Indonesia* (DA); see also Schreuer, *Commentary*, p. 1231). Failure to state reasons for part of an award may lead to annulment of that part of an award (art. 52).

5. Advance payments. Parties are required to make certain advance payments (Reg. 14(3) of the Administrative and Financial Regulations). Each party shall pay half of each required advance. All advance payments together with their specific apportionment are provisional in the sense that the final award will decide by whom and in what proportion costs will be paid.

6. Decision on costs part of the award. A decision on costs is a necessary part of every award (Rule 47(1)(j) of the Arbitration Rules). Interim decisions are not awards and therefore do not have to address the question of costs in that phase. As a decision that a tribunal lacks jurisdiction is an award, it must include a decision on costs. Decisions on rectification, interpretation and revision become part of the award to which they relate and therefore must include a decision on additional costs in connection with these proceedings. The decisions of ad hoc committees on annulment applications should contain a decision on costs as well. A settlement may be embodied in an award and this should also contain an agreement on costs. Orders noting the proceedings' discontinuance will not normally contain a decision on costs. In such cases, the parties should settle the issue of costs between themselves. Decisions on costs are subject to rectification and supplementation (*LETCO* v *Liberia*). They are also subject to interpretation, revision or annulment pursuant to arts. 50, 51 and 52 (*MINE* v *Guinea*). The decision on costs is final and binding upon the parties and is subject to recognition and enforcement (*History*, Vol. II, pp. 436, 873). Costs resulting from subsequent enforcement proceedings can be claimed only in the domestic court or authority before which recognition and enforcement is sought.

CHAPTER VII. PLACE OF PROCEEDINGS

[Proceedings at seat of the Centre]

Article 62

Conciliation and arbitration proceedings shall be held at the seat of the Centre except as hereinafter provided.

1. General. Art. 62 provides that arbitration and conciliation proceedings are to be held at the seat of the Centre unless otherwise provided.

2. Place of Proceedings. The legal place or seat of proceedings in ICSID arbitration or conciliation has little legal relevance. The procedure to be applied is independent of the law of the place of proceedings and is entirely governed by the provisions of the Convention and the Rules (and international law). Remedies against awards are also exclusively governed by the Convention, and are not brought before domestic courts. The choice of a venue for the proceedings is typically a matter of convenience. It is advisable, for obvious reasons, to conduct proceedings on the territory of a Contracting State (Schreuer, *Commentary*, p. 1243).

3. Seat of the Centre. Unless the parties agree otherwise, the place of the proceedings is the seat of the Centre, which is the principal office of the World Bank in Washington DC (see art. 2, note 4). The Secretary-General makes the necessary arrangements for the holding of the proceedings (Reg. 26 of the Administrative and Financial Regulations).

[Proceedings at another place]

Article 63

Conciliation and arbitration proceedings may be held, if the parties so agree,
- **(a) at the seat of the Permanent Court of Arbitration or of any other appropriate institution, whether private or public, with which the Centre may make arrangements for that purpose; or**
- **(b) at any other place approved by the Commission or Tribunal after consultation with the Secretary-General.**

1. General. Art. 63 sets out the conditions which must be satisfied in order for proceedings to be held at a venue other than the Centre, with the agreement of the parties. In addition, there must be either an arrangement with the appropriate institutions, such as the Permanent Court of Arbitration (PCA), or approval by the commission or the tribunal following consultation with the Secretary-General.

2. Parties' agreement. The parties' discretion is bound by the conditions set in art. 63(a) and (b). The parties have to agree either on the seat of an appropriate institution with which there is an existing arrangement or, if the arbitration is to held at another place, the parties must obtain the approval of that place from the commission or tribunal. The agreement may take place either before the institution of proceedings by inserting the place of arbitration in the consent to ICSID arbitration clause (1993 Model Clause 19) or during the proceedings, typically at the First Session.

3. Factors affecting the decision. Parties might take into account factors such as whether: the place of proceedings should be in the territory of a Contracting State; the place should be of convenience for all the parties and for the members of the tribunal or commission; the place should be a neutral venue; or the place should provide for easy access, especially for witnesses (Schreuer, *Commentary*, p. 1252). In practice, parties agree that the tribunal may meet and deliberate not only in the place selected for the proceedings but also at other places that are convenient to its members (*SOABI v Senegal*).

4. Arbitration at other institutions. The PCA is not the only institution envisaged by art. 63. The inclusion of the expression 'other appropriate institution, whether public or private' was accepted in order to allow arrangements with both public and private institutions (*History*, Vol. II, pp. 665, 678, 881, 940). The Report of the Executive Directors concluded in connection with the Centre's arrangements that they: 'are likely to vary with the type of institution and to range from merely making premises available for the proceedings to the provision of complete secretariat services.' (para. 44 of the Report). The arrangements typically provide for the provision of meeting rooms, offices and equipment, as well as the services of interpreters, translators and other personnel.

5. Existing arrangements. The Centre has entered into agreements pursuant to art. 63(a) with the following institutions: the PCA; the Regional Centre for Commercial Arbitration, Kuala Lumpur (where special legislation was enacted by Malaysia for such purposes); the Regional Centre for Commercial Arbitration, Cairo; Australian Commercial Disputes Centre, Sydney; the Australian Centre for International Commercial Arbitration, Melbourne; the Singapore International Arbitration; the Gulf Cooperation Council Commercial Arbitration Centre, Manama, Bahrain; the Regional Centre for Commercial Arbitration, Lagos, Nigeria; and the German Institution of Arbitration (DIS).

6. Other places of arbitration or conciliation. Art. 63(b) provides for the possibility of agreement on a different place for the proceedings, subject to approval by the commission or tribunal (see also Rule 13(3) of the Arbitration Rules). Consultation with the Secretary-General is also required (see also Reg. 26(1) of the Administrative and Financial Regulation). It is not unusual for parties to agree on one of the World Bank's regional offices, often in Paris.

7. Multi-seat proceedings. The wording of art. 63 is broad enough to include the possibility of holding proceedings in more than one place. In practice, tribunals have met at different locations in connection with the same proceedings (*Benvenuti* v *Congo*). In all cases, the conditions set out in art. 63 have to be met. The possibility of multi-seat proceedings is envisaged by art. 43(b), which deals with on-site visits ('descente sur les lieux') (see also Rule 37 of the Arbitration Rules and Reg. 26(2) of the Administrative and Financial Regulations). In a number of cases, parties agreed that the tribunal should meet alternately in the capital of the host State and in the capital of the investor's home State (Schreuer, *Commentary*, p. 1258).

CHAPTER VIII. DISPUTES BETWEEN CONTRACTING STATES

[International Court of Justice]

Article 64

Any dispute arising between Contracting States concerning the interpretation or application of this Convention which is not settled by negotiation shall be referred to the International Court of Justice by the application of any party to such dispute, unless the States concerned agree to another method of settlement.

1. General. Art. 64 confers upon the ICJ compulsory jurisdiction over disputes between Contracting States regarding the interpretation or application of the Convention.

2. Reservations. The Convention does not contain any provisions on reservations. On general principles of compatibility, it is doubtful that a State could validly make a reservation excluding the jurisdiction of the ICJ (see art. 68, note 3). Although Turkey made a declaration in connection with art. 64 expressing a preference for negotiations (see *Contracting States and Measures Taken by Them* (ICSID Document ICSID/8, available on the ICSID website at <www.worldbank.org/icsid>)) this interpretative declaration does not have the tenor of a reservation to the Convention.

3. Scope of the ICJ's jurisdiction. The disputes over which the ICJ has jurisdiction include those relating to: the obligation to cooperate with the Centre; compliance with ICSID awards; recognition and enforcement of ICSID awards; immunities of the Centre; privileges granted to certain persons under the Convention; the duty of national courts not to interfere in ICSID proceedings; the duty not to provide diplomatic protection in a situation where the dispute has already been submitted to the ICSID (*History*, Vol.

II, pp. 354, 403, 533, 906, 994, 1030). No dispute has been submitted to the ICJ to date.

4. Compliance with awards. Although ICSID proceedings do not extend to the enforcement of awards, the investor's State of nationality may bring a claim before the ICJ if the host State refuses to comply with an award (see art. 53). A claim in the ICJ against a State of enforcement, which was not a party to the ICSID proceedings, is also possible.

5. Disputes outside the scope of ICJ jurisdiction. Art. 64 does not confer jurisdiction on the ICJ to review a decision of an ICSID tribunal or to act as a court of appeal. Similarly, the ICJ has no jurisdiction to pronounce upon the nullity or revision of an arbitral award. The internal remedies of award review and annulment provided for by the Convention are exclusive (see arts. 51 and 52). Art. 27 prevents a State from bringing a diplomatic protection claim on the merits in the ICJ in respect of a dispute which one of its nationals and another Contracting State have consented to submit to arbitration (see art. 27).

6. Advisory opinions. Art. 64 only deals with the subject of contentious proceedings in the ICJ and does not address the question of the ICJ's jurisdiction to give advisory opinions. Art. 96 of the UN Charter allows UN organs and specialised agencies, authorised to do so by the UN General Assembly, to request advisory opinions on legal questions arising within the scope of their activities. The World Bank is a specialised agency of the UN which is authorised, under art. 96 of the UN Charter, to request advisory opinions from the ICJ. However, ICSID is a separate international institution.

7. Disputes between States and the Centre. Art. 64 only addresses the question of disputes between Contracting States and does not include disputes between a Contracting State and the Centre. Such a dispute could be settled by negotiations or ad hoc arbitration (Schreuer, *Commentary*, p. 1264).

CHAPTER IX. AMENDMENT

[Amendments to the Convention]

Article 65

Any Contracting State may propose amendment of this Convention. The text of a proposed amendment shall be communicated to the Secretary-General not less than 90 days prior to the meeting of the Administrative Council at which such amendment is to be considered and shall forthwith be transmitted by him to all the members of the Administrative Council.

1. General. Art. 65 specifies how the procedure for amending the Convention is to be initiated. It provides that any Contracting State may propose an amendment by transmitting the proposal to the Secretary-General who will then transmit the proposal to the members of the Council. The proposal must be transmitted to the Secretary-General ninety days prior to the Council meeting. No proposal has been made to date though amendments relating to an appeal-system process were studied in recent years.

[Decision on amendment]
Article 66

(1) If the Administrative Council shall so decide by a majority of two-thirds of its members, the proposed amendment shall be circulated to all Contracting States for ratification, acceptance or approval. Each amendment shall enter into force 30 days after dispatch by the depositary of this Convention of a notification to Contracting States that all Contracting States have ratified, accepted or approved the amendment.

(2) No amendment shall affect the rights and obligations under this Convention of any Contracting State or of any of its constituent subdivisions or agencies, or of any national of such State arising out of consent to the jurisdiction of the Centre given before the date of entry into force of the amendment.

1. General. Art. 66(1) specifies the procedure for amending the Convention. Art. 66(2) provides that any amendment will not affect rights and obligations arising out of consent to jurisdiction given prior to the amendment taking effect.

2. Adoption of amendments. In order for an amendment to enter into force, it must first be approved by a two-thirds majority of the Administrative Council. The amendment must then be ratified, accepted or approved by all Contracting States. This procedure rules out the possibility of amendments being effective only as between a limited number of States agreeing to them.

3. Effects of amendments. An amendment is to enter into force thirty days after it has been circulated by the Word Bank to all Contracting States. From the entry into force of the amendment, the Convention applies as amended. However, the amended version of the Convention will not be applicable if consent to jurisdiction has been given prior to the entry into force of the amendment. This exception is in accord with other provisions of the Convention (arts. 70, 71, 72) and is underpinned by the notion that consent, once given, must be preserved as given (see art. 25, note 27).

CHAPTER X. FINAL PROVISIONS

[Signature of the Convention]

Article 67

This Convention shall be open for signature on behalf of States members of the Bank. It shall also be open for signature on behalf of any other State which is a party to the Statute of the International Court of Justice and which the Administrative Council, by a vote of two-thirds of its members, shall have invited to sign the Convention.

1. General. Art. 67 specifies which States may be signatories to the Convention. It provides that the Convention is open for signature by States that are members of the World Bank. The Council, by a two-thirds vote of its members, may invite a State which is not a member of the World Bank to sign the Convention, if that State is a party to the Statute of the ICJ.

2. Non-members of the World Bank. In order to be eligible to be invited by the Council to sign the Convention, a State must be a party to the Statute of the ICJ. All members of the UN are ipso facto parties to the Statute of the ICJ (art. 93(1) of the UN Charter). States that are not members of the UN may become a party to the Statute of the ICJ on conditions determined in by the General Assembly upon the recommendation of the Security Council (art. 93(2) of the UN Charter). The Administrative Council invited Switzerland (1967) and Seychelles (1977) to sign the Convention, which they did.

3. Signature. The signing of the Convention is not by itself sufficient in order for that State to become a party to the Convention. The State must also ratify, accept or approve the Convention (art. 68).

[Ratification and entry into force]

Article 68

(1) This Convention shall be subject to ratification, acceptance or approval by the signatory States in accordance with their respective constitutional procedures.

(2) This Convention shall enter into force 30 days after the date of deposit of the twentieth instrument of ratification, acceptance or approval. It shall enter into force for each State which subsequently deposits its instrument of ratification, acceptance or approval 30 days after the date of such deposit.

1. General. Art. 68 provides that, in addition to signing, a State must ratify, accept or approve the Convention.

2. Ratification, acceptance or approval. There is no substantive difference between ratification, acceptance and approval. They are three common methods by which a State can express its consent to be bound by a treaty. Any instrument of ratification, acceptance or approval has to be transmitted to the Convention's depositary, namely the World Bank (see art. 73).

3. Reservations to the Convention. The Convention does not contain any specific provisions on reservations, either permitting or excluding them. As consent to jurisdiction is voluntary, there was no need for such a provision (*History*, Vol. II, pp. 311, 362, 363). As the Convention was concluded before the Vienna Convention on the Law of Treaties entered into force, the provisions of that Convention regarding reservations are not per se applicable to the ICSID Convention (art. 4, Vienna Convention on the Law of Treaties). Customary international law provides that reservations to treaties are possible as long as they are compatible with the treaty's object and purpose (*Reservations to the Convention on Genocide*, ICJ Advisory Opinion). No Contracting State has ever made a reservation to the Convention. (On Turkey's declaration, see art. 64, note 2.) Notifications under art. 25(4) cannot be regarded as reservations (see art. 25, note 4).

4. Status of the Convention. The Convention entered into force on 14 October 1966. To date, the total number of Contracting States is 143. Notable non-parties include Canada (signatory; ratification Bill tabled in March 2007), Russia (signatory), Mexico, Brazil, India, Iran, Poland and South Africa.

[Implementing legislation]
Article 69
Each Contracting State shall take such legislative or other measures as may be necessary for making the provisions of this Convention effective in its territories.

1. General. Art. 69 requires Contracting States to take such measures as are necessary in order to carry out their obligations under the Convention.

2. Domestic implementation of the Convention. The measures that are necessary in order to implement the Convention depend on the constitutional structure and domestic laws of the implementing State. Enactment of domestic legislation will usually be required, even in States whose legal orders permit the direct application of international treaties such as the Convention.

3. Examples of legislative measures. Implementing legislation typically addresses the enforcement of awards pursuant to art. 54 of the Convention, including the national procedure for recognition and enforcement of awards (Schreuer, *Commentary*, p. 1278). Some national legislation specifically excludes the review of ICSID awards by national courts by providing that the generic arbitration legislation does not apply (see, e.g., Sec. 9, NZ Act; Sec. 3(2), UK Act; Sec. 15(2), Ireland Act; and Sec. 3(a), US Act). Other legislation addresses the question of taking of evidence (see, e.g., Sec. 3(1),

UK Act; and Sec. 15(1), Ireland Act) and other issues, such as privileges and immunities (see, e.g., Sec. 8, Australia Act; and art. 4, Denmark Act). Art. 69 does not address the issue of consent to jurisdiction (art. 25). Even though a State can consent to the jurisdiction of the Centre through the enactment of legislation, such a measures is not 'necessary' to carry out the obligations set out in the Convention. A list of national legislation enacted pursuant to art. 69 of the Convention may be found in *Contracting States and Measures Taken by Them* (found on the ICSID website at: <icsid.worldbank.org/ICSID/FrontServlet?requestType=ICSIDDocRH&actionVal=Contracting Measures&reqFrom=Main>).

[Notice of territorial exclusion]

Article 70

This Convention shall apply to all territories for whose international relations a Contracting State is responsible, except those which are excluded by such State by written notice to the depositary of this Convention either at the time of ratification, acceptance or approval or subsequently.

1. General. Art. 70 provides that the Convention will apply to all territories for whose international relations a Contracting State is responsible, unless a written notice of territorial exclusion has been given to the depositary. Art. 70 is a standard-type clause found in many treaties, especially those pre-dating 1960 (see further *UN HFCMT,* p. 80).

2. Dependent territories. At the time the Convention was concluded, several Contracting States, most notably in Europe, possessed overseas or dependent territories. For this reason the Convention affords flexibility to a Contracting State to exclude from the application of the Convention any territories for whose international relations it has responsibility.

3. Operation of art. 70. If overseas, dependent, etc., territories have not been excluded from the scope of the Convention, they will be covered, by operation of art. 70. (The converse arrangement, whereby such territories are excluded unless contrary notice has been given, is also current in treaty practice; see, e.g., art. 63 ECHR.) States often nonetheless adopt the practice of specifically extending the Convention to their dependent territories by way of implementing legislation. In *SPP* v *Egypt* (DJ), p. 120, where the claimants were Hong Kong entities, the tribunal found that the dispute was with a national of a Contracting State (the UK) since Hong Kong was a territory for whose international relations the UK had responsibility, in accordance with art. 70. The tribunal went on to note that the UK had expressly extended the application of the Convention to Hong Kong in 1967.

4. The depositary of the Convention. Pursuant to art. 73, the World Bank is specified as the depositary to which written notice of territorial exclusion under art. 70 must be submitted. Once a notice of territorial exclusion has been received it is the responsibility of the depositary to notify all Contracting States of the notice to exclude in accordance with art. 75(d).

5. Timing of a notice of territorial exclusion. A notice of territorial exclusion can be given at the time of ratification, acceptance or approval, or subsequently. For example, the UK ratified the Convention on 19 December 1966 and subsequently, in June 1973, gave notice under art. 70 to exclude the British Indian Ocean Territory, the Pitcairn Islands, the British Antarctic Territory, and the Sovereign Base areas of Cyprus.

6. Publication of a notice of territorial exclusion. The ICSID Secretariat publishes all the currently effective notices of territorial exclusion received by the depositary under art. 70 as *ICSID/8-B* (available at the World Bank's website <icsid.worldbank.org/ICSID/Index.jsp>).

7. Withdrawal of a notice of territorial exclusion. At the time the Convention was being prepared, the question of whether a notice of territorial exclusion could be withdrawn after it had been submitted to the depositary was raised. Dr. Broches was firmly of the opinion that the wording of the Convention would allow for a Contracting State to exclude a dependent territory from the application of the Convention and subsequently withdraw that notice of exclusion, for example, where there had not been enough time for a Contracting State to consult the legislature of the dependent territory (*History*, Vol. II, p. 1007). Subsequent practice has confirmed this reading. The Kingdom of the Netherlands originally restricted the application of the Convention to the Netherlands (i.e. the territory in Europe), but in 1970 withdrew the restriction, following which the Convention extended to Suriname (now independent) and the Netherlands Antilles. Similarly, Denmark excluded the Faroe Islands by a notification dated 15 May 1968 but restored the application of the Convention to those territories on 30 October 1968.

8. Application of the Convention upon the independence of a territory. In principle, the Convention would cease to apply upon independence of a territory for whose international relations another State was until that time responsible (see *History*, Vol. II pp. 284, 443-4). However, that is not an issue regulated by the Convention, but rather by the law on State succession or specific treaties. This is a broader question of customary international law which is not settled (note that art. 16 VCSS provides that a newly independent State is not bound to maintain in force, or to become a party to, any treaty by reason of the fact that on the date of the succession the treaty was in force in the territory to which the succession relates, but this rule may not represent customary international law). Some Contracting States' former territories have since become Contracting States in their own right, including Mauritius, St. Lucia and Swaziland. By contrast Suriname, which became independent from the Kingdom of the Netherlands in 1975, did not become a party to the Convention.

9. Interaction of territorial application of the Convention and applicable BITs. Where ICSID jurisdiction regarding a dispute in a dependent territory is based on a dispute resolution provision contained in a BIT, care must be taken to ensure that both the Convention and the BIT extend to the territory in question. For example, while the Convention extends to dependent territories of the UK unless specifically excluded, BITs signed by the UK are generally drafted so as not to extend to dependent territories, unless specifically covered by a separate Exchange of Notes. Thus the Convention extends to Bermuda, for instance, but the UK–Russian Federation BIT does not.

[Denunciation of the Convention]

Article 71

Any Contracting State may denounce this Convention by written notice to the depositary of this Convention. The denunciation shall take effect six months after receipt of such notice.

1. General. Art. 71 provides Contracting States with the possibility of denouncing the Convention by written notice, such denunciation to take effect six months later. The issues surrounding a denunciation of the Convention are complicated, particularly where the Contracting State seeking to denounce the Convention has already given its consent to ICSID jurisdiction within the terms of art. 25 or art. 72.

2. Denunciation as an unconditional right. Denunciation is a procedure initiated unilaterally by a State to terminate its legal engagements under a treaty (see further *UN HFCMT*, pp. 109-111). During the preparation of the Convention, Dr. Broches expressed the opinion that the right of withdrawal from the Convention was an unconditional right that could be exercised at any time, without providing reasons (*History*, Vol II, pp. 534-5).

3. The depositary of the Convention. A notice of denunciation must be submitted to the World Bank which, pursuant to art. 73, is the depositary for the Convention. Once a notice of denunciation has been received it is the responsibility of the depositary to notify all signatory States of the Convention of the notice of denunciation in accordance with art. 75(f).

4. Notices of denunciation received by the depositary. At the time of writing, only one notice of denunciation from a Contracting State had been received by the depositary. This notice of denunciation was transmitted by Bolivia on 2 May 2007 pursuant to art. 71, and an announcement was published on the World Bank's website in the following terms: 'On May 2, 2007, the World Bank received a written notice of denunciation of the Convention on the Settlement of Investment Disputes between States and Nationals of Other States (the ICSID Convention) from the Republic of Bolivia. In accordance with art. 71 of the ICSID Convention, the denunciation will take effect six months after the receipt of Bolivia's notice, i.e. on November 3, 2007.'

5. Denunciation forthcoming. In April 2007 the members of Alternativa Bolivariana para los Pueblos de Nuestra América (ALBA) announced their intention to withdraw from the World Bank (including the Convention) and the IMF. At the time, ALBA comprised Bolivia, Cuba (which is not a Contracting State), Nicaragua and Venezuela. Following ALBA's announcement, only Bolivia sent a notice of denunciation to the depositary; however, on 12 February 2008 the Venezuelan National Assembly passed a non-binding recommendation that the Government withdraw from the Convention, and on 14 April 2008, the Attorney-General of Nicaragua reiterated Nicaragua's intention to withdraw from the Convention.

6. Six-month period. In treaty relations generally, a stand-still period before denunciation takes effect is designed to provide time for the denouncing Contracting State to wind up its membership implications (such as monetary contributions and representation to collective bodies) and to allow the other Contracting States a period in which to formulate arrangements responsive to the denunciation. In addition, and more importantly, stand-still periods proceed from the premise that there should be no surprise in treaty relations.

[Consequences of notices of territorial exclusion and denunciation]
Article 72

Notice by a Contracting State pursuant to Articles 70 or 71 shall not affect the rights or obligations under this Convention of that State or of any of its constituent subdivisions or agencies or of any national of that State arising out of consent to the jurisdiction of the Centre given by one of them before such notice was received by the depositary.

1. General. Art. 72 is a derogation provision which addresses the situation where a Contracting State, or any of its constituent subdivisions or agencies, or a national of that Contracting State, has provided consent to the jurisdiction of ICSID before the Contracting State issues a notice of denunciation or territorial exclusion. Art. 72 seeks to limit the ability of that Contracting State to denounce the Convention or exclude territories in such a hypothesis and thereby frustrate acquired rights and obligations. Art. 72 must be read in the light of art. 25(1) which provides that once a party has consented to ICSID jurisdiction, such consent cannot unilaterally be withdrawn.

2. Context. The protective scope of art. 72 operates from the time of receipt of a notice of denunciation (rather than the time at which denunciation takes effect which is six months after receipt of the notice, pursuant to art. 71), in respect of 'rights or obligations … arising out of consent'. Accordingly, it is crucial to define 'consent' for art. 72 purposes (see notes 4 et seq.).

3. Rights and obligations under the Convention. The rights and obligations referred to in art. 72 include the commencement of arbitration or conciliation proceedings as well as compliance with an ICSID award pursuant to art. 53 (see Schreuer, *Commentary*, p. 1286).

4. Consent to the jurisdiction of the Centre. As noted in connection with art. 25, consent may be given by way of a contractual arbitration clause; a submission agreement executed after a dispute has arisen (compromis); or separately by the Contracting State, on the one hand, and the investor, on the other, such that the investor accepts and perfects the Contracting State's offer to submit the dispute to ICSID arbitration given, for example, in national legislation or a BIT. Where consent is given by the first two instruments, it cannot be unilaterally withdrawn by denouncing the Convention. Even after denunciation has been notified and taken effect, the parties' rights and obligations under the Convention will remain intact, so far as these 'aris[e] out of consent to the jurisdiction of the Centre'. However, where consent is given separately by the parties in the third hypothesis, and the relevant BIT or national legislation has not been terminated at the time of the denunciation, the position is more complicated. The question that arises is whether the unilateral offer of ICSID jurisdiction contained in a BIT or national legislation is 'consent' for art. 72 purposes – such that the investor's acceptance can validly be given within the six-month period which is required under art. 71 for the denunciation to take effect (or indeed after that period has expired).

5. Consent: bilateral or unilateral? On one view, consent must be bilateral, such that the Contracting State's offer of ICSID jurisdiction in legislation or a BIT must be accepted by the investor in order to be perfected (Schreuer, *Commentary*, p. 1286). This view relies on art. 25(1), the basic jurisdictional provision in the Convention, which expressly requires the *parties* to a dispute to provide written consent in order to submit the dispute to ICSID. Dr. Broches similarly emphasised that consent to ICSID arbitration requires one or more additional separate actions, noting that 'a party's consent becomes irrevocable only after both parties to the dispute have given their consent' (see Broches, *Explanatory Notes and Survey*, paras. 31 and 38). Likewise, the Preamble to the Convention itself proclaims the centrality of bilateral consent: 'Recognising that *mutual* consent by the parties to submit such disputes to conciliation or to arbitration through such facilities constitutes a binding agreement ...' (emphasis added). This is echoed in Rule 2(3) of the ICSID Institution Rules, which provides that the "[d]ate of consent' means the date on which the *parties* to the dispute consented in writing to submit it to the Centre; *if both parties did not act on the same day*, it means the date on which the second party acted' (emphasis added). The contrary view is to the effect that the offer of ICSID arbitration contained in national legislation or a BIT in fact constitutes the Contracting State's consent, which requires no perfection. Thus, once given, this consent cannot be unilaterally withdrawn, unless the instrument in which it is contained is also terminated (see Gaillard,

NYLJ, p. 3). While such termination may be easily achieved where national legislation is concerned (and often with immediate effect), it may be more difficult in the context of BITs, not least because of 'survival' clauses protecting existing investments for ten to fifteen years after termination of the BIT. Moreover, certain BITs, such as the Belgium/Luxembourg–Bolivia BIT, specifically provide that the parties 'irrevocably' consent to submit disputes with investors to ICSID arbitration. This raises the question as to whether denunciation of the Convention while the BIT remains in force is simply a breach of the BIT (to be pursued at the inter-State level) or, in addition, non-opposable to a Belgium/Luxembourg investor (with the consequence that ICSID jurisdiction is still intact). No jurisprudence yet exists to shed light on this debate, since the first denunciation of the Convention took place on 2 May 2007 (see art. 71, notes 5 and 6). However, some of these issues will be considered in *ETI Telecom* v *Bolivia*, which was registered by ICSID on 31 October 2007, days before Bolivia's notice of denunciation of 2 May 2007 took effect.

6. Implications of art. 72 for BITs. From a practical perspective, it is important to bear in mind that, even if art. 72 does not apply to preserve an investor's ability to accept an offer of ICSID arbitration made in national legislation or a BIT, other dispute resolution options in that legislation or BIT will naturally not be affected by the Contracting State's denunciation. Most BITs contain an offer to arbitrate under a selection of dispute resolution rules (ICSID, ICSID Additional Facility, UNCITRAL, SCC or ICC). The non-ICSID avenues will remain available unless the Contracting State validly terminates the offer of arbitration in national legislation or the BIT.

[Depositary of the Convention]

Article 73

Instruments of ratification, acceptance or approval of this Convention and of amendments thereto shall be deposited with the Bank which shall act as the depositary of this Convention. The depositary shall transmit certified copies of this Convention to States members of the Bank and to any other State invited to sign the Convention.

1. General. Art. 73 designates the World Bank as the Convention's depository. The World Bank receives instruments of ratification, acceptance or approval of the Convention as well as amendments, denunciations (art. 71) and notices of exclusion (art. 70) or designation (art. 25). The World Bank is also charged with the transmittal of certified copies of the Convention to the Contracting States and to all States that are eligible, pursuant to art. 67, to accede to the Convention.

[Registration of the Convention]

Article 74

The depositary shall register this Convention with the Secretariat of the United Nations in accordance with Art. 102 of the Charter of the United Nations and the Regulations thereunder adopted by the General Assembly.

1. General. Art. 74 requires the World Bank to register the Convention with the UN Secretariat in accordance with art. 102 of the United Nations Charter, which provides that 'every treaty and every international agreement entered into by any Member of the United Nations after the present Charter comes into force shall as soon as possible be registered with the Secretariat and published by it'. The Convention was registered with the UN Secretariat on 17 October 1966 and was published in the United Nations Treaty Series Vol. 575.

[Notification]

Article 75

The depositary shall notify all signatory States of the following:
  (a) signatures in accordance with Article 67;
  (b) deposits of instruments of ratification, acceptance and approval in accordance with Article 73;
  (c) the date on which this Convention enters into force in accordance with Article 68;
  (d) exclusions from territorial application pursuant to Article 70;
  (e) the date on which any amendment of this Convention enters into force in accordance with Article 66; and
  (f) denunciations in accordance with Article 71.

1. General. According to art. 75, the World Bank, as depositary of the Convention pursuant to art. 73, shall notify the Contracting States of legally relevant facts relating to the treaty: deposits of instruments of ratification, acceptance and approval; the Convention's entry into force date; territorial exclusions pursuant to art. 70; the date of entry into force of amendments; and denunciations.

UNITED NATIONS COMMISSION ON INTERNATIONAL TRADE LAW (UNCITRAL) ARBITRATION RULES, 1976*

(Resolution 31/98, Adopted by the General Assembly on 15 December 1976)

SECTION 1. INTRODUCTORY RULES

[Scope of application]

Article 1

(1) Where the parties to a contract have agreed in writing that disputes in relation to that contract shall be referred to arbitration under the UNCITRAL Arbitration Rules, then such disputes shall be settled in accordance with these Rules subject to such modification as the parties may agree in writing.

(2) These Rules shall govern the arbitration except that where any of these Rules is in conflict with a provision of the law applicable to the arbitration from which the parties cannot derogate, that provision shall prevail.

1. Scope. Art. 1(1) sets out the scope of application of the UNCITRAL Arbitration Rules 1976. It requires that the parties agree in writing that their dispute shall be referred to arbitration under the Rules before such dispute can be settled in accordance with them. The requirement for writing was included to increase the chances of an award under the Rules being enforceable, as the New York Convention and various domestic laws contain a similar requirement.[1] The drafters chose not to define the phrase 'agreement in writing' as it was decided that this question should be left to the applicable national law.[2] The question of whether or not a 'legal person of public law' could enter into an agreement to arbitrate was similarly left open.

2. Modifications. Art. 1(1) explicitly allows the parties to modify the Rules, provided that such modifications are agreed in writing. A prime example of a tribunal making use of a modified version of the Rules is the specially adapted

---

* Reproduced with permission of the United Nations Commission on International Trade Law (UNCITRAL). The text reproduced here is valid at the time of reproduction. As amendments may from time to time be made to the text, please refer to the website <http://www.uncitral.org> for the latest version.
1. UNCITRAL, *Report on Ninth Session* (1976), UN Doc A/31/17, para. 9, 7 U.Y.B. at 67; UNCITRAL, *Report on Eighth Session* (1975), UN Doc A/10017, para. 18, 7 U.Y.B. at 26.
2. UNCITRAL, *Report on Ninth Session* (1976), UN Doc A/31/17, para. 10, 7 U.Y.B. at 67.

set of the Rules used by the Iran-US Claims Tribunal. For a further example of the use of a modified version of the Rules, see the modifications agreed by the parties in the NAFTA *Glamis Gold* arbitration. The Rules are adaptable for different types of disputes; art. 1 deliberately does not limit their applicability to a specific type, although they were designed with international commercial arbitration in mind. There is nothing to prevent the Rules from being used for domestic arbitration or disputes involving non-contractual issues, such as tort or public international law. In the ad hoc *Larsen* arbitration, the tribunal acting under the aegis of the Permanent Court of Arbitration found 'no reason why the UNCITRAL Rules cannot be adapted to apply to a non-contractual dispute', including disputes where one of the parties is alleged to be a state. The flexibility of the Rules is demonstrated by the frequent references to them in BITs; see for example the Dutch Model BIT.

3. Conflict with domestic law. Art. 1(2) sets out the relationship between the Rules and other applicable laws, such as, in particular, the domestic law of the place of arbitration. The Rules shall govern an arbitration except to the extent that any of them is in conflict with 'a provision of law applicable to the arbitration from which the parties cannot derogate', in which case such provision shall prevail. In the ad hoc *Wintershall* (Partial) arbitration, the tribunal held that the arbitration would be governed by the Rules subject to any mandatory provisions of the Netherlands Arbitration Law, which would prevail in the event of conflict with the Rules.

[Notice, calculation of periods of time]
Article 2

(1) For the purposes of these Rules, any notice, including a notification, communication or proposal, is deemed to have been received if it is physically delivered to the addressee or if it is delivered at his habitual residence, place of business or mailing address, or, if none of these can be found after making reasonable inquiry, then at the addressee's last-known residence or place of business. Notice shall be deemed to have been received on the day it is so delivered.

(2) For the purposes of calculating a period of time under these Rules, such period shall begin to run on the day following the day when a notice, notification, communication or proposal is received. If the last day of such period is an official holiday or a non-business day at the residence or place of business of the addressee, the period is extended until the first business day which follows. Official holidays or non-business days occurring during the running of the period of time are included in calculating the period.

1. When notice becomes effective. The effect of art. 2(1) is that any notice, including notifications, communications and proposals, will be effective upon receipt. The question then arises as to when 'receipt' takes place. As the drafters have specifically chosen not to include a presumption of receipt, a notice is deemed to have been received on the day that it is delivered.

2. Delivery. Delivery may be by physical delivery to the addressee; delivery to the addressee's habitual residence, place of business or mailing address; or, if none of these can be found after reasonable enquiry, delivery to the addressee's last-known residence or place of business. Presumably notice may also be delivered to the contractually agreed notification address.

3. Types and means of communication. The broad language of art. 2(1) allows the rule to cover a wide range of types of communication, as well as a wide range of means of communication. However, the broad wording does mean that the concepts of actual receipt and notice are not specifically defined in the article, and that the applicable law is relevant in this context.[3] The parties may supplement art. 2 with a specific set of rules for the serving of documents and giving of notice if they so wish, in accordance with art. 1(1).

4. Calculation of time periods. Art. 2(2) sets out the rule for calculating periods of time. Periods of time under the Rules begin to run on the day after receipt of a notice or other communication. Most of the cases that have come before the Tribunal regarding art. 2 concern 'Refusal Cases', where a request for filing a Statement of Claim has been made outside the deadline stated in the Tribunal's specially tailored version of the Rules. The Tribunal has consistently enforced these deadlines strictly; for example, claims which were delayed by a severe storm and arrived one day after the stated deadline were refused in the *Cascade* arbitration. However, the Tribunal's strict approach is a consequence of the jurisdictional nature of the particular filings and should therefore not be extrapolated to regular submissions in ad hoc arbitrations.

5. Holidays and non-business days. If the last day of a time period is an official holiday or a non-business day at the addressee's residence or place of business, that period is extended until the first business day which follows. Official holidays or non-business days occurring during the running of the period of time are included when calculating the period.

[Notice of arbitration]
Article 3

(1) The party initiating recourse to arbitration (hereinafter called the 'claimant') shall give to the other party (hereinafter called the 'respondent') a notice of arbitration.

(2) Arbitral proceedings shall be deemed to commence on the date on which the notice of arbitration is received by the respondent.

---

3. *Summary Record of the 2nd Meeting of the Committee of the Whole (II)*, UNCITRAL, 9th Session, UN Doc A/CN.9/9/C.2/SR.2, at 5-6, para. 21 (1976).

(3) **The notice of arbitration shall include the following:**
   (a) **A demand that the dispute be referred to arbitration;**
   (b) **The names and addresses of the parties;**
   (c) **A reference to the arbitration clause or the separate arbitration agreement that is invoked;**
   (d) **A reference to the contract out of or in relation to which the dispute arises;**
   (e) **The general nature of the claim and an indication of the amount involved, if any;**
   (f) **The relief or remedy sought;**
   (g) **A proposal as to the number of arbitrators (i.e. one or three), if parties have not previously agreed thereon.**
(4) **The notice of arbitration may also include:**
   (a) **The proposals for the appointments of a sole arbitrator and an appointing authority referred to in article 6, paragraph 1;**
   (b) **The notification of the appointment of an arbitrator referred to in article 7;**
   (c) **The statement of claim referred to in article 18.**

1. Notice of arbitration. Art. 3(1) provides that a claimant must send a notice of arbitration to a respondent in order to initiate arbitral proceedings. Note that the national law or treaty governing the arbitration may impose additional notice requirements. The purpose of the notice of arbitration is to ensure that the respondent is informed that arbitral proceedings have been started and that a claim will be submitted.[4] Note that the Rules do not make provision for the respondent to reply to the notice of arbitration with a 'short answer', nor for a statement identifying any counter-claim.

2. Commencement of proceedings. Art. 3(2) specifies the exact point in time at which proceedings will be deemed to have commenced (the date on which the respondent receives the notice of arbitration), in order to provide a reference point for national law provisions on prescription of rights or limitation of actions.

3. Contents of the notice. Art. 3(3) lists the information which must be included in a valid notice of arbitration under the Rules. It explicitly demands that the dispute be referred to arbitration. The claimant is also required to provide information on the identity of the parties, the arbitration clause or agreement invoked, the contract at issue, the general nature of the claim and amount involved and the relief or remedy sought. The claimant must make a proposal regarding the number of arbitrators if this has not previously been agreed. The purpose behind this list is to ensure that the respondent receives

---

4. *Report of the Secretary-General on the Preliminary Draft Set of Arbitration Rules*, UNCITRAL, 8th Session, UN Doc A/CN.9/97 (1974), reprinted in (1975) VI U.Y.B. 163, 167 (Commentary on Draft Article 3).

sufficient information to apprise himself of the 'general context of the claim asserted against him'[5] and 'to enable him to decide on his future course of action'.[6]

4. Optional content. Claimants are not restricted to supplying only the information listed in art. 3 in the notice of arbitration. Under art. 3(4) a claimant may also include, if relevant, his proposal for appointing a sole arbitrator and appointing authority pursuant to art. 6(1). In cases where three arbitrators will be used, the claimant may notify the respondent of his appointment of an arbitrator pursuant to art. 7.

5. Statement of claim. The notice of arbitration should not be confused with the subsequent statement of claim required by art. 18. In *Ethyl Corporation*, the NAFTA tribunal confirmed that the notice of arbitration and statement of claim are separate and elaborated the different content requirements for each. However, pursuant to art. 3(4)(c), a claimant may append his statement of claim to the notice if he so chooses, thus satisfying his obligations under art. 18.

[Representation and assistance]
Article 4

The parties may be represented or assisted by persons of their choice. The names and addresses of such persons must be communicated in writing to the other party; such communication must specify whether the appointment is being made for purposes of representation or assistance.

1. Representation. This article provides that both parties may appoint representatives who will be deemed to act on their behalf before the arbitral tribunal. The acts of the representatives shall be binding on the appointing party. A representative is not required to be licensed to practice law.

2. Assistance. Arbitrating parties may also be assisted in proceedings before the arbitral tribunal by one or more persons of their choice. Such persons, unless they are also appointed as representatives, are not deemed to act before the tribunal on behalf of the appointing party, to bind the appointing party or to receive notices, communications or documents on behalf of the appointing party. Any such assistant is not required to be licensed to practice

---

5. *Report of the Secretary-General on the Preliminary Draft Set of Arbitration Rules*, UNCITRAL, 8th Session, UN Doc A/CN.9/97 (1974), reprinted in (1975) VI UNCITRAL Ybk 163, 167 (Commentary on Draft Article 3, para. 2).
6. *Report of the Secretary-General on the Revised Draft Set of Arbitration Rules*, UNCITRAL, 9th Session, Addendum 1 (Commentary), UN Doc A/CN.9/112/Add.1 (1975), reprinted in (1976) VII UNCITRAL Ybk 166, 168 (Commentary on Draft Article 4, paras. 1 & 3).

law. This article seems to limit to some extent the category of people who assist to those persons who assist 'in the proceedings'. This would exclude people such as travel agents. In *Starrett Housing* the Tribunal held that the Rules do not prevent an attorney from using assistants, nor from assigning them to argue before the Tribunal.

3. Communication to the other party. The requirement of communicating the names and addresses of both representatives and assistants to the other party is maintained in this article. However, it is unlikely that the drafters intended for such a wide provision; this would imply that the names and addresses of all supporting staff assistants, such as translators, paralegals and perhaps even travel agents, should be provided. Although the travaux préparatoires are unclear on the matter, a better view is that only the identity of the legal assistants should be disclosed.

4. Requirement for a power of attorney. With respect to the issue of authority to represent an appointing party, the drafters rejected the suggestion to require a power of attorney of a person purporting to act on behalf of a party. The general view is that no power of attorney is required (see *International Technical Products*) but before the Tribunal, most parties appear to have provided it voluntarily. In special situations the Tribunal has imposed strict requirements, such as those involving withdrawals of claims or specific (and perhaps reasonable in light of the circumstances) requests for authorisations. In practice, powers of attorney submitted usually take the form of letters from parties that simply announce that a certain person or law firm will act as a representative.

SECTION II. COMPOSTION OF THE ARBITRAL TRIBUNAL

[Number of arbitrators]

Article 5

If the parties have not previously agreed on the number of arbitrators (i.e. one or three), and if within fifteen days after the receipt by the respondent of the notice of arbitration the parties have not agreed that there shall be only one arbitrator, three arbitrators shall be appointed.

1. General. This article provides for the situation where the parties have failed to agree upon the number of arbitrators to be appointed. If, within fifteen days of receipt by the respondent of the notice of arbitration, no agreement has been reached on this point, a panel of three arbitrators will be appointed.

2. Fifteen days. The parties may agree to modify the provisions of this article in accordance with art. 1 should they require a period longer than fifteen days. Presumably, such modifications may be made at any time, including after the initiation of proceedings.

3. Three arbitrators. The drafters concluded that a three-member panel was most appropriate in default of agreement otherwise by the parties, as arbitral tribunals established ad hoc to hear international commercial disputes were customarily composed of three arbitrators, and the presence of three arbitrators also ensures that the tribunal will possess a sufficient degree of competence and expertise. Furthermore, each of the two party-appointed arbitrators will usually be of the nationality of the nominating party, bringing to the tribunal a special knowledge of the commercial law and practice of that country.[7]

[Appointment of a sole arbitrator]

Article 6

(1) If a sole arbitrator is to be appointed, either party may propose to the other:
  (a) The names of one or more persons, one of whom should serve as the sole arbitrator; and
  (b) If no appointing authority has been agreed upon by the parties, the name or names of one or more institutions or persons, one of whom would serve as appointing authority.

(2) If within thirty days after receipt by a party of a proposal made in accordance with paragraph 1 the parties have not reached agreement on the choice of a sole arbitrator, the sole arbitrator shall be appointed by the appointing authority agreed upon by the parties. If no appointing authority has been agreed upon by the parties, or if the appointing authority agreed upon refuses to act or fails to appoint the arbitrator within sixty days of the receipt of a party's request therefor, either party may request the Secretary-General of the Permanent Court of Arbitration at The Hague to designate an appointing authority.

(3) The appointing authority shall, at the request of one of the parties, appoint the sole arbitrator as promptly as possible. In making the appointment the appointing authority shall use the following list-procedure, unless both parties agree that the list-procedure should not be used or unless the appointing authority determines in its discretion that the use of the list-procedure is not appropriate for the case:
  (a) At the request of one of the parties the appointing authority shall communicate to both parties an identical list containing at least three names;
  (b) Within fifteen days after the receipt of this list, each party may return the list to the appointing authority after having deleted

---

7. UNCITRAL, *Report on Ninth Session* (1976), UN Doc A/31/17, paras. 27-29, 7 U.Y.B. at 68; UNCITRAL, *Report on Eighth Session* (1975), UN Doc A/10017, para. 39, 6 U.Y.B. at 28-29.

> the name or names to which he objects and numbered the remaining names on the list in the order of his preference;
> (c) After the expiration of the above period of time the appointing author ity shall appoint the sole arbitrator from among the names approved on the lists returned to it and in accordance with the order of preference indicated by the parties;
> (d) If for any reason the appointment cannot be made according to this procedure, the appointing authority may exercise its discretion in appointing the sole arbitrator.
>
> **(4) In making the appointment, the appointing authority shall have regard to such considerations as are likely to secure the appointment of an independent and impartial arbitrator and shall take into account as well the advisability of appointing an arbitrator of a nationality other than the nationalities of the parties.**

1. General. Art. 6 deals with the procedure for selecting an arbitrator in the event that the parties decide that a sole arbitrator will preside. Where agreement has been reached that a sole arbitrator will preside, either party may propose an arbitrator or list of potential arbitrators to the other under art. 6(1). No limits are placed on whom the parties may propose or appoint. If no agreement is reached within thirty days of receipt by either party of a proposal by the other party, either party may request that a third party, the 'appointing authority', appoint the sole arbitrator. The appointing authority is necessarily also competent to examine whether the preconditions necessary for an appointment have been satisfied (as stated by the tribunal in the *Sapphire* arbitration).

2. Appointing authority. A definition of 'appointing authority' was deliberately excluded from the Rules, in order to leave the authority's selection to the parties' discretion.[8] The travaux préparatoires reflect the fact that if the appointing authority is an institution, there will be benefits in terms of continuity and expertise, without excluding the possibility of using an individual.[9] Under art. 6(2), if the parties are unable to agree on an appointing authority, or if the appointing authority agreed upon refuses to act or fails to appoint the arbitrator within sixty days of the receipt of a party's request therefor, appointment of the appointing authority falls, at the request of either party, to the Secretary-General of the Permanent Court of Arbitration at The Hague. The practice of the Secretary-General reflects a trend towards appointing individuals as well as institutions as appointing authorities, albeit with a majority of institutions being appointed. Initially, the Secretary-General did

---

8. UNCITRAL, *Report on Ninth Session* (1976), UN Doc A/31/17, para. 37, 7 U.Y.B at 69.
9. *Summary Record of the 15th Meeting of the Committee of the Whole (II)*, UNCITRAL, 9th Session, UN Doc A/CN.9/9/C.2/SR.15 (1976) at 4.

not act as an appointing authority itself, but since 1999 it has become willing to act as such.

3. Challenge to the appointing authority. The Rules do not provide for challenge by a party to either the appointing authority or the Secretary-General. However, a party may challenge the arbitrator chosen by those entities in accordance with arts. 10 to 12.

4. The list-procedure. When requested by a party, the appointing authority must appoint the sole arbitrator 'as promptly as possible', using the list procedure set out in art. 6(3). The list-procedure consists of: (a) the appointing authority communicating to both parties an identical list of at least three names (this list should include the full names, addresses and nationalities of the proposed arbitrators, and a description of their qualifications, in accordance with art. 8(2)); (b) the parties returning the lists to the authorities within fifteen days of receipt, having deleted the names to which they object and numbered the remaining names in order of preference; and (c) the authority selecting a sole arbitrator from the approved names on the list, taking into account the order of preference. If no common ground can be found under the list-procedure, then the appointing authority may exercise its discretion in appointing a sole arbitrator, having regard to such considerations as are likely to secure the appointment of an independent and impartial arbitrator, and in particular to the advisability of appointing an arbitrator of a different nationality to that of the parties.

5. Liability of arbitral institutions. The Rules do not contain an explicit provision on liability of arbitrators, the appointing authority, and/or the Secretary-General. However, the absence of an explicit right to object to certain decisions does not automatically imply an exclusion of liability. The source of the liability will depend upon the relevant national law, notably the lex loci for claims based in tort and the lex contractus for claims based in contract.

[Appointment of a three-person panel]

Article 7

(1) If three arbitrators are to be appointed, each party shall appoint one arbitrator. The two arbitrators thus appointed shall choose the third arbitrator who will act as the presiding arbitrator of the tribunal.

(2) If within thirty days after the receipt of a party's notification of the appointment of an arbitrator the other party has not notified the first party of the arbitrator he has appointed:

   (a) **The first party may request the appointing authority previously designated by the parties to appoint the second arbitrator; or**
   (b) **If no such authority has been previously designated by the parties, or if the appointing authority previously designated refuses to act or fails to appoint the arbitrator within thirty days after receipt of a party's request therefor, the first party**

may request the Secretary-General of the Permanent Court of Arbitration at The Hague to designate the appointing authority. The first party may then request the appointing authority so designated to appoint the second arbitrator. In either case, the appointing authority may exercise its discretion in appointing the arbitrator.

(3) If within thirty days after the appointment of the second arbitrator the two arbitrators have not agreed on the choice of the presiding arbitrator, the presiding arbitrator shall be appointed by an appointing authority in the same way as a sole arbitrator would be appointed under article 6.

1. Right to appoint. Art. 7 deals with the procedure for selecting arbitrators in the event that the parties decide that a three-person panel will preside. Each party may appoint one arbitrator to this panel and, except for the provision for challenge by the other party contained in arts. 10 to 12, no limits are placed on this choice. For an application of art. 7(1) by an ad hoc tribunal see *CME Czech Republic*.

2. Refusal by a party to exercise its right to appoint. Art. 7(2) anticipates the possibility that a party will refuse to exercise its right to appoint an arbitrator. Thirty days after a party receives notice of the other party's appointment of an arbitrator, the notified party's right to appoint ceases (or continues only at the sufferance of the other party). The party who has appointed its arbitrator may then request the appointing authority to appoint the opposing party's arbitrator. The appointing authority may use its discretion for this appointment. If no appointing authority has been designated, or if the designated authority refuses to act or fails to do so within thirty days, the party may ask the Secretary-General to designate the appointing authority.

3. Appointment of presiding arbitrator. The two 'party' arbitrators will choose a third arbitrator to act as the presiding arbitrator of the tribunal. Under art. 7(3), if the two arbitrators have not agreed on a presiding arbitrator within thirty days of the appointment of the second party arbitrator, then, at the request of either or both parties, the presiding arbitrator shall be appointed by the appointing authority using the procedure for appointment of a sole arbitrator set out in art. 6.

[Appointment by the appointing authority]

Article 8

(1) When an appointing authority is requested to appoint an arbitrator pursuant to article 6 or article 7, the party which makes the request shall send to the appointing authority a copy of the notice of arbitration, a copy of the contract out of or in relation to which the dispute has arisen and a copy of the arbitration agreement if it is not contained in the

contract. The appointing authority may require from either party such information as it deems necessary to fulfil its function.

(2) Where the names of one or more persons are proposed for appointment as arbitrators, their full names, addresses and nationalities shall be indicated, together with a description of their qualifications.

1. General. This article ensures that an appointing authority appointed under art. 6 or 7 has sufficient information about any proposed arbitrator(s) to complete its tasks. The approach to this provision should be functional: the point is that the appointing authority should know what the dispute at hand involves.[10]

2. Appointing authority. The function of the appointing authority is either to appoint an arbitrator in circumstances where the parties or the party-appointed arbitrators have failed to agree, or to give a decision on the challenge of an arbitrator by a party. The authority is designated by the parties in accordance with art. 6. A definition of 'appointing authority' was deliberately excluded from the Rules, in order to leave its selection to the parties' discretion. For further discussion of the nature of the appointing authority see art. 6, note 2.

3. Information required. The party requesting that the appointing authority appoint an arbitrator must provide the authority with a copy of the notice of arbitration, a copy of the contract out of or in relation to which the dispute has arisen, and a copy of the arbitration agreement (if not contained in the contract). The notice should contain sufficient information to apprise the authority of what the dispute involves, particularly as the Rules do not prescribe that the respondent be given the opportunity to provide a 'short answer' and a request for counter-claim.

4. Details of proposed arbitrators. The appointing authority must also be given the full name, address and nationality of any proposed arbitrator, together with a description of their qualifications.

[Disclosure]

Article 9

A prospective arbitrator shall disclose to those who approach him in connection with his possible appointment any circumstances likely to give rise to justifiable doubts as to his impartiality or independence. An arbitrator, once appointed or chosen, shall disclose such circumstances to the parties unless they have already been informed by him of these circumstances.

---

10. *Summary Record of the 4th Meeting of the Committee of the WHOLE (II)*, UNCITRAL, 9th Session, UN Doc A/CN.9/9/C.2/SR.4 at 7, para 51 (1976).

1. Pre-appointment disclosure. The arbitrator himself is deemed to be the best judge of whether circumstances exist that are likely to give rise to justifiable doubts as to his impartiality or independence. A prospective arbitrator is therefore under an obligation to disclose any such circumstances at the earliest stage possible – the pre-appointment stage – when first approached regarding an arbitration. The disclosure must be to whomever approaches the arbitrator regarding the arbitration, and thus can include a non-party such as the appointing authority.

2. Duty of continuing disclosure. Although the travaux préparatoires are not clear on the point, it is generally accepted that the arbitrator or prospective arbitrator's duty to disclose under art. 9 is a continuous obligation, and that such arbitrator or potential arbitrator must inform the parties if new circumstances arise at any point that may call into question his impartiality or independence. The commentary to the preliminary draft of art. 8, which states that 't[he] obligation to disclose in these circumstances is extended to the pre-appointment stage', supports the view that the drafters believed that the duty to disclose necessarily exists after appointment. A continuing duty would be consistent with the policies underlying art. 9 and with disclosure requirements in other rules of arbitral procedure, such as art. 7(3) of ICC Rules of Arbitration and art. 5.3 of the LCIA Rules. The duty of disclosure during this second stage may also have been intended to catch cases where relevant circumstances arise after an appointment.

3. Circumstances giving rise to justifiable doubts. The circumstances which should be disclosed are those which are 'likely' to give rise to 'justifiable doubts' as to an arbitrator's impartiality and independence, and thus constitute grounds for challenge under art. 10(1), which is worded in parallel terms. The disclosure requirement under art. 9 is broader than the grounds for challenge of an arbitrator under art. 10(1): not everything required to be disclosed under the Rules will ultimately justify a challenge. A balance must be struck between the necessity for sufficient disclosure and the fact that overly broad disclosure may trigger unnecessary challenges, which could be used as a tool to obstruct proceedings.

4. Content. As to the content of any disclosure, the Rules allow for the use of supplementary sources such as the IBA Guidelines on Conflicts of Interest in International Arbitration, or the relevant national rules on challenges and disclosure.

5. Challenge. Disclosure at both the pre- and post-appointment stages helps avoid the selection of an arbitrator who may be successfully challenged at a later point. Acceptance of an arbitrator in full knowledge of any pertinent circumstances also potentially estops the accepting party from seeking to challenge the arbitrator on the basis of those circumstances (see art. 10(2)), or to challenge the award in the appropriate domestic court. The Rules do not address the issue of what consequences flow from a failure to disclose.

Disclosure and challenge are distinct mechanisms for an arbitrator and a party respectively.

[Standard for challenge]
Article 10
(1) Any arbitrator may be challenged if circumstances exist that give rise to justifiable doubts as to the arbitrator's impartiality or independence.

(2) A party may challenge the arbitrator appointed by him only for reasons of which he becomes aware after the appointment has been made.

1. Grounds for challenge. Art. 10 provides that a party may challenge an arbitrator if circumstances exist which give rise to justifiable doubts as to the arbitrator's impartiality or independence. The challenging party need not establish a lack of impartiality or independence, but rather justifiable doubts regarding those qualities.

2. Circumstances. The drafters considered the inclusion of a list setting out examples of circumstances which could give rise to 'justifiable doubts'. The two specific examples which seemed to them to clearly raise such doubts were a financial or personal interest in the outcome of the arbitration, or family or commercial ties with either party or with a party's counsel or agent.[11] However, the decision was taken to leave the language of art. 10(1) sufficiently broad, as to encompass a wide variety of situations. Circumstances put forward as the basis for challenges in Tribunal arbitrations have included: a relationship with the parent corporation of a party; physical assault on a fellow arbitrator; an arbitrator's handling of proceedings; breach of confidentiality of deliberations; and previous advocacy on behalf of a country formerly adverse to a sovereign party. It was held in the Decision of the Appointing Authority on the Second Challenge by Iran of Judge Briner that the substance of arbitrators' confidential in camera deliberations may not be considered by an appointing authority in deciding a challenge.

3. Failure to disclose as grounds for challenge. Failure by an arbitrator to disclose under art. 9 may give rise to, but does not per se establish, justifiable doubts as to impartiality or independence. In the Argentine water arbitrations, the co-arbitrators discussed the grounds for challenge in the UNCITRAL proceedings. It was held that Doctor Kaufmann-Kohler's failure to disclose

---

11. *Report of the Secretary-General on the Preliminary Draft Set of Arbitration Rules*, UNCITRAL, 8th Session, UN Doc A/CN.9/97 (1974), reprinted in (1975) VI UNCITRAL Ybk 163, 171 (Commentary on Draft Article 8); UNCITRAL, *Report on Eighth Session* (1975), UN Doc A/10017, paras. 70-72, reprinted in (1975) VI UNCITRAL Ybk 24, 32 (Commentary on Draft Article 8, para. 2).

the fact (of which she was unaware) of her service as a non-executive member of the Supervisory Board of the investment bank UBS, which in turn held shares in the claimant companies, did not provide sufficient grounds for removing her as an arbitrator in the disputes.

4. Issue conflicts. The question has recently arisen as to whether 'issue conflicts' constitute sufficient grounds for the removal of an arbitrator. In the *Telekom Malaysia Berhad* arbitration, based on the UNCITRAL Rules, Ghana's challenge to Professor Gaillard on the basis that he was acting counsel in an ICSID annulment proceeding where similar issues of law had arisen, and where Gaillard would be required to take a position adverse to that taken by Ghana in the arbitration, was dismissed by the Secretary-General of the Permanent Court of Arbitration as appointing authority. However, the challenge was later upheld by the Dutch courts, which had jurisdiction based on the seat of arbitration.

5. Justifiable doubts. The inclusion of the word 'justifiable' in art. 10(1) is intended to establish an objective standard for impartiality and independence. The appointing authority in Challenge Decision of 11 January 1995 held that a party's subjective doubts will be an insufficient ground for challenge; any such doubts must be objectively reasonable. The same objective standard applies to both party-appointed and non-party-appointed arbitrators.[12]

6. Impartiality and independence. Impartiality is generally taken to mean that an arbitrator will not favour one party more than the other, and so refers to an arbitrator's independent disposition. Independence is taken to mean that the arbitrator is free from external control (see the case law of the European Court of Human Rights regarding art. 6 of the European Convention on Human Rights on the topic of independence and impartiality). In a challenge decision of 11 January 1995, the appointing authority in question held that the standard of independence or impartiality should be the same whether the challenge is raised at the start or later on in the proceedings. In 2007, the Belgian courts rejected a request by the Republic of Poland to remove Judge Schwebel from the ad hoc tribunal hearing the *Eureko* arbitration (in a non-UNCITRAL case). Poland had complained that the relationship between Schwebel and the law firm Sidley Austin, which was concurrently representing other claimants in other cases against Poland, cast doubt on his independence and impartiality.

7. Relationship with art. 13. Art. 13 provides that arbitrators may be removed under the challenge procedure for failure to act or in the event that it becomes factually or legally impossible for an arbitrator to perform his duties, effectively providing an additional ground for challenge.

---

12. *Report of the Secretary-General on the Revised Draft Set of Arbitration Rules*, UNCITRAL, 9th Session, Addendum 1 (Commentary), UN Doc A/CN.9/112/Add.1 (1975), reprinted in (1976) VII UNCITRAL Ybk 166, 170 (Commentary on Draft Article 9, para. 1).

8. Awareness of reasons for challenge. A party may challenge an arbitrator he has himself appointed, but only on the basis of reasons of which he becomes aware after the appointment has been made.

[Notification of challenge]

Article 11

(1) A party who intends to challenge an arbitrator shall send notice of his challenge within fifteen days after the appointment of the challenged arbitrator has been notified to the challenging party or within fifteen days after the circumstances mentioned in articles 9 and 10 became known to that party.

(2) The challenge shall be notified to the other party, to the arbitrator who is challenged and to the other members of the arbitral tribunal. The notification shall be in writing and shall state the reasons for the challenge.

(3) When an arbitrator has been challenged by one party, the other party may agree to the challenge. The arbitrator may also, after the challenge, withdraw from his office. In neither case does this imply acceptance of the validity of the grounds for the challenge. In both cases the procedure provided in article 6 or 7 shall be used in full for the appointment of the substitute arbitrator, even if during the process of appointing the challenged arbitrator a party had failed to exercise his right to appoint or to participate in the appointment.

1. A party. As art. 11(1) commences with the words 'a party', only a party to proceedings may challenge an arbitrator.

2. Time limit for challenge. Art. 11(1) sets out the period within which a challenge must be made. A notice of challenge must be sent within fifteen days of the appointment of the challenged arbitrator being notified to the challenging party, or within fifteen days of the circumstances constituting the basis of the challenge becoming known to the challenging party. If the pertinent facts become known to the challenging party via an art. 9 post-appointment disclosure, then the fifteen-day period will run from the date of the disclosure rather than the date of appointment. As only an 'arbitrator' may be challenged, the fifteen-day period cannot commence prior to the date of appointment. The drafters made clear that after the time limit expires the right to challenge is waived.[13] The notice of challenge must be sent within fifteen days rather than received within that time limit.

---

13. *Report of the Secretary-General on the Revised Draft Set of Arbitration Rules*, UNCITRAL, 9th Session, Addendum 1 (Commentary), UN Doc A/CN.9/112/Add.1 (1975), reprinted in (1976) VII UNCITRAL Ybk 166, 170 (Commentary on Draft Article 10, para. 1).

3. Circumstances becoming known. It is difficult to prove when the circumstances giving rise to a challenge became known to a challenging party. The matter of who should bear the burden of proof on this question has not been addressed, although it is arguable that by analogy with art. 24(1) it should be the party bringing the challenge.

4. Notice. Art. 11(2) requires that notice of the challenge should be sent to the other party, the arbitrator being challenged, and the other members of the arbitral tribunal. The notice must be in writing and must state the reasons for the challenge, although it need not necessarily provide evidence. If no justification is provided, a challenge may be declared inadmissible. The Decision of the Appointing Authority on the Objections by Iran to Judge Mangård states that to be admissible a challenge must both be intended to be a challenge under the UNCITRAL Rules and must meet the formalities required. The purpose of the notice is to enable the other party to decide if he will agree to the challenge, and the challenged arbitrator to decide whether to withdraw.[14]

5. Procedure if challenge is accepted. Art. 11(3) sets out the procedure for appointing a substitute arbitrator if either the challenge is accepted or the challenged arbitrator steps down. In these instances, the procedures for the appointment of the original arbitrator – under art. 6 for a sole arbitrator and art. 7 for a three-member panel – should be followed. If a party's arbitrator is successfully challenged, that party will have the right to appoint a replacement arbitrator, even if he failed to exercise his right to appoint during the process of appointing the successfully challenged arbitrator.

[Challenge decision]
Article 12
(1) If the other party does not agree to the challenge and the challenged arbitrator does not withdraw, the decision on the challenge will be made:
- **(a) When the initial appointment was made by an appointing authority, by that authority;**
- **(b) When the initial appointment was not made by an appointing authority, but an appointing authority has been previously designated, by that authority;**
- **(c) In all other cases, by the appointing authority to be designated in accordance with the procedure for designating an appointing authority as provided for in article 6.**

---

14. *Report of the Secretary-General on the Revised Draft Set of Arbitration Rules*, UNCITRAL, 9th Session, Addendum 1 (Commentary), UN Doc A/CN.9/112/Add.1 (1975), reprinted in (1976) VII UNCITRAL Ybk 166, 170 (Commentary on Draft Article 10, para. 2).

(2) If the appointing authority sustains the challenge, a substitute arbitrator shall be appointed or chosen pursuant to the procedure applicable to the appointment or choice of an arbitrator as provided in articles 6 to 9 except that, when this procedure would call for the designation of an appointing authority, the appointment of the arbitrator shall be made by the appointing authority which decided on the challenge.

1. Decision on the challenge. Art. 12(1) states that an appointing authority will resolve a challenge in the event that the challenge is disputed by the other party or the challenged arbitrator does not withdraw. Subsections (a) to (c) set out the three possible means by which this authority may be appointed. If an appointing authority made the original appointment of the arbitrator under challenge, then the challenge will be decided by that authority. If the arbitrator under challenge was not appointed by an appointing authority but the parties have already designated an appointing authority, then that pre-designated authority shall decide the challenge. In all other cases, an appointing authority will be designated in accordance with art. 6 in order to resolve the challenge.

2. Role of national courts. Note that the applicable national arbitration law may contain mandatory rules on court review/jurisdiction over challenges. In the *Telekom Malaysia Berhad* arbitration, Ghana's challenge to Professor Gaillard was dismissed. Ghana therefore filed a challenge with the District Court of The Hague (The Hague being the seat of the arbitration). The District Court ruled that, under Dutch law, Gaillard's 'issue conflict' was a circumstance raising justifiable doubts about his impartiality, and ordered that Ghana's challenge should be upheld if Gaillard did not resign within ten days of the judgment.

3. The decision making process. Art. 12 does not prescribe a specific process for the resolution of a challenge by an appointing authority; the appointing authority may use its discretion in each individual case. This is reflected in the differing ways in which challenges have been dealt with during Tribunal arbitrations. During the Iranian challenge to Judge Mangård, initiated on 1 January 1982, the designated appointing authority took an informal approach, requesting views from both the Judge himself and the State Agents on certain points, through oral discussions and by letter. Later challenges to Judge Briner were more formalised and a series of memoranda and reply memoranda were exchanged.

4. Appointment of a substitute arbitrator. The procedures set out in arts. 6 to 9 will govern the appointment of a substitute arbitrator should a challenge succeed. The only exception is that where these articles require the designation of an appointing authority, the appointing authority which ruled upon the challenge shall be used.

[Replacement of an arbitrator]
Article 13

(1) In the event of death or resignation of an arbitrator during the course of the arbitral proceedings, a substitute arbitrator shall be appointed or chosen pursuant to the procedure provided for in articles 6 to 9 that was applicable to the appointment or choice of the arbitrator being replaced.

(2) In the event that an arbitrator fails to act or in the event of the de jure or de facto impossibility of his performing his functions, the procedure in respect of the challenge and replacement of an arbitrator as provided in the preceding articles shall apply.

1. Death or resignation. Art. 13(1) sets out the procedure for replacement of an arbitrator in the event of resignation or death. Should resignation or death occur, a substitute arbitrator shall be chosen using the same appointment procedure as was used for the original arbitrator. In effect, this means that if a sole arbitrator resigns, then the appointment procedure will be governed by art. 6, and if a party-appointed arbitrator or presiding arbitrator resigns, then the appointment procedure will be governed by art. 7.

2. Resignation. Though debated during the drafting, the view taken by the Committee was that a resigning arbitrator need not provide reasons for his resignation.[15] However, the applicable national law may impose restrictions in this respect, and it was recognised by the drafters that UNCITRAL arbitrators resigning without justifiable reason may be liable for damages, as domestic legal systems widely recognise limits on rights of resignation. The Rules do not provide any guidance on the duties of a resigning arbitrator as regards the tribunal, and in particular are silent regarding when a resignation becomes effective. This can be problematic with regard to abrupt resignations, as the appointment of a substitute arbitrator under arts. 6 to 9 may take time.

3. Failure to act. Art. 13 distinguishes cases of death or resignation from more diverse circumstances where an arbitrator fails to act or circumstances where it becomes legally or physically impossible for an arbitrator to perform his functions. Under art. 13(2), to replace an arbitrator in circumstances of failure to act or incapacitation, a party must institute a challenge procedure in accordance with arts. 10 to 12. Art. 13(2) therefore effectively creates a further ground for challenge in addition to that set out in art. 10. In its Decision on the Challenge by Iran to Judge Arangio-Ruiz, the Appointing Authority held that 'fails to act' covers the situation where an arbitrator is not completely inactive, but consciously neglects his duties in such a way that his conduct falls below the standard to be reasonably expected of him.

---

15. *Summary Record of the 5th Meeting of the Committee of the Whole (II)*, UNCITRAL, 9th Session, UN Doc A/CN.9/9/C.2/SR.5, at 5, paras. 31-32.

The drafters chose not to fix a specific time limit for establishing when an arbitrator has failed to act, leaving the issue to the discretion of the authority deciding the challenge.[16]

4. Incapacitation. The term 'de jure or de facto impossibility of performing his functions' was chosen to emphasise the fact that art. 13(2) extends 'to all circumstances that made it legally or physically impossible for an arbitrator to perform his functions'.[17] It was felt that 'incapacitated', the phrase originally chosen, was unduly ambiguous as it was not clear that it covered both legal and physical incapacity.

5. Continuing in the absence of an arbitrator. The Rules do not address the question of whether a tribunal may proceed in truncated fashion in the unauthorised absence of an arbitrator. The ad hoc tribunal in the *Himpurna (Final)* arbitration held in the particular circumstances that a tribunal 'has not only the right, but the obligation, to proceed when, without valid excuse, one of its members fails to act, withdraws … or even purports to resign'.

[Repetition of hearings in the event of the replacement of an arbitrator]
Article 14

If under articles 11 to 13 the sole or presiding arbitrator is replaced, any hearings held previously shall be repeated; if any other arbitrator is replaced, such prior hearings may be repeated at the discretion of the arbitral tribunal.

1. General. Art. 14 sets out the procedural rule regarding the repetition of previously held hearings when an arbitrator is replaced.

2. Sole or presiding arbitrator. The article recognises the special role played by the sole or presiding arbitrator and provides that all hearings must be repeated if either the sole or presiding arbitrator is replaced.

3. Any other arbitrator. If any arbitrator other than the sole or presiding arbitrator is replaced, it is for the arbitral tribunal to decide on the necessity of rehearing(s). There is no clear consensus in the travaux as to whether it is the entire, newly constituted tribunal that must decide on the issue of repetition, or merely the replacing members or the original members of the tribunal.[18]

---

16. *Summary Record of the 5th Meeting of the Committee of the Whole (II)*, UNCITRAL, 9th Session, UN Doc A/CN.9/9/C.2/SR.5, at 5, para. 35.
17. UNCITRAL, *Report on Ninth Session* (1976), UN Doc A/31/17, para. 70, reprinted in (1976) VII UNCITRAL Ybk 66, 71 (Commentary on Draft Article 12, para. 2).
18. UNCITRAL, *Report on Eighth Session* (1975), UN Doc A/10017, para. 94, 6 U.Y.B. at 34 (Commentary on Draft Article 11, para. 2).

Art. 14 applies to both replacements arising out of art. 13 and to replacements resulting from a challenge brought under arts. 11 or 12.[19]

4. Hearing. It should be noted that art. 14 requires only the repetition of hearings previously held and not the granting of a new hearing at which new evidence may be submitted. The article specifies that 'any' hearing should be repeated when the sole or presiding arbitrator is replaced, and thus applies not only to final hearings, but also to any other hearing such as interim hearings or those concerned with jurisdiction.

SECTION III. ARBITRAL PROCEEDINGS

[General provisions]

Article 15

(1) Subject to these Rules, the arbitral tribunal may conduct the arbitration in such manner as it considers appropriate, provided the parties are treated with equality and that at any stage of the proceedings each party is given a full opportunity of presenting his case.

(2) If either party so requests at any stage of the proceedings, the arbitral tribunal shall hold hearings for the presentation of evidence by witnesses, including expert witnesses, or for oral argument. In the absence of such a request, the arbitral tribunal shall decide whether to hold such hearings or whether the proceedings shall be conducted on the basis of documents and other materials.

(3) All documents or information supplied to the arbitral tribunal by one party shall at the same time be communicated by that party to the other party.

1. General. Art. 15 sets out fundamental principles which must be taken into account by an arbitral tribunal during UNCITRAL proceedings and when applying the more specific norms set out in the Rules.

2. Subject to these rules. Art. 15(1) gives the tribunal a discretion to conduct the arbitration 'in such a manner as it considers appropriate'; thus allowing a large degree of procedural flexibility. However, this discretion is subject to certain limitations. The tribunal's freedom is 'subject to these Rules' and therefore limited by the more specific provisions of the Rules. Nevertheless, where the Rules do not provide guidance a tribunal may develop particulars in accordance with the overarching principles set out in art. 15. In the *Methanex* (Decision) and *UPS* (Decision) NAFTA arbitrations, the respective tribunals held that their decisions to allow amicus submissions by

---

19. *Summary Record of the 5th Meeting of the Committee of the Whole (II)*, UNCITRAL, 9th Session, UN Doc A/CN.9/9/C.2/SR.5, at 7, paras. 46, 48 and 57.

third parties fell within their powers over the conduct of the arbitration under art. 15(1). A tribunal may fill any lacunae in the Rules by 'borrowing' procedural models in whole or part from a legal system or another set of rules (by incorporating such rules or referring to them as 'guidelines'). For example, in the ad hoc *CME Czech Republic* arbitration, the tribunal decided to apply the IBA Rules on Taking Evidence in International Commercial Arbitration to the extent appropriate.

3. Equality. The tribunal is also guided by the requirement that the parties be treated with equality. The travaux préparatoires indicate that this provision is not necessarily aimed at guaranteeing a mechanical application of equality in all circumstances, but rather is aimed at guaranteeing equality in the material sense of justice and fairness.[20] For example, a tribunal need not insist on mechanical equality between the parties' languages in all circumstances, provided that this does not prejudice either party's right to present its case and receive justice on the basis of material equality. Conversely, in *Foremost Tehran Inc*. the Tribunal held that if one party were permitted to present an extensive memorial and exhibits without allowing the other party to file a memorial then 'the delicate balance of equality would be tipped' and material inequality of treatment would result.

4. Opportunity to present case. The principle of equality is closely tied to the requirement that 'at any stage of the proceedings each party is given a full opportunity of presenting his case.' Denial of such an opportunity may lead to the non-enforcement of the award, as happened to the Tribunal's award in *Avco*. The US courts refused to enforce this award because Avco had been denied the right to introduce certain evidence before the Tribunal.

5. Other limitations. The tribunal's discretion will also be limited by any modifications to the Rules agreed in writing by the parties under art. 1(1). Under art. 1(2), the arbitrators may not derogate from mandatory provisions of the law applicable to the arbitration.

6. Right to a hearing. Under art. 15(2), the tribunal shall hold hearings at the request of either party 'at any stage of proceedings'. These hearings are not only for the presentation of witness evidence, but also for oral argument. The right to a hearing does not necessarily have to be exercised at the start of proceedings. It is not clear whether there are any limitations on the right. Whereas the Tribunal has interpreted the right to a hearing as being dependent on whether the question relates to 'procedural matters', a tribunal in an ad hoc arbitration should not proceed from such a general distinction between the substantive and the procedural unless authorised by the parties.

7. Communication of documents. Art. 15(3) extends the principle of equality set out in art. 15(1) to the parties' own conduct, requiring them to

---

20. UNCITRAL, *Report on Eighth Session* (1975), UN Doc A/10017, para. 99, reprinted in (1975) VI UNCITRAL Ybk 24, 35.

communicate any information they supply to the tribunal to the other party at the same time. Any such information should be communicated in accordance with the provisions of art. 2.

[Place of arbitration]
Article 16

(1) Unless the parties have agreed upon the place where the arbitration is to be held, such place shall be determined by the arbitral tribunal, having regard to the circumstances of the arbitration.

(2) The arbitral tribunal may determine the locale of the arbitration within the country agreed by the parties. It may hear witnesses and hold meetings for consultation among its members at any place it deems appropriate, having regard to the circumstances of the arbitration.

(3) The arbitral tribunal may meet at any place it deems appropriate for the inspection of goods, other property or documents. The parties shall be given sufficient notice to enable them to be present at such inspection.

(4) The award shall be made at the place of arbitration.

1. General. Art. 16 gives the parties freedom to choose the place of arbitration. Place in this context denotes the country or distinct jurisdiction in which the arbitration will take place. If the parties fail to make a choice, the arbitrators will do so, 'having regard to the circumstances of the arbitration'. The consequences of the choice of place are extremely important. The place will usually determine the lex arbitri, which determines matters of mandatory arbitration law. Furthermore, any award shall be made in the place of arbitration, which is of significance for the enforceability of that award.

2. Choice of place by the parties. Under art. 16(1), the parties have the right to determine the place of arbitration prior to the commencement of proceedings, or even thereafter (in the *Glamis Gold* NAFTA arbitration the parties agreed on the place of arbitration after the commencement of proceedings in their Agreement on Certain Procedural Matters). If the parties fail to make a choice, the tribunal will come to a decision on the matter.

3. Choice of place by the tribunal. A tribunal choosing the place of arbitration must have 'regard to the circumstances of the arbitration' when making its choice. The UNCITRAL Notes on Organizing Arbitral Proceedings at para. 22 enumerate a number of non-binding 'factual and legal factors' that may influence choice of place. These include considerations of neutrality, practical considerations, legal considerations flowing from the law in the country of arbitration, and legal considerations relating to enforcement outside that country. In the *Canfor Corp.* (Decision) arbitration, the NAFTA tribunal considered the factors set out in the UNCITRAL Notes when coming to a decision on place, whilst also making clear that it was not required to do so and was free to disregard them without giving reasons if it saw fit.

4. Choice of venue by the tribunal. The specification of a locale, or venue, within the place of arbitration (that is a city or other exact locality within the chosen country or other distinct jurisdiction) does not entail legal consequences in addition to those flowing from the choice of place. Art. 16(2) states that a tribunal may choose a venue within the country agreed upon as the place of arbitration. However, the article does not address the question of whether a tribunal may choose a venue outside the place of arbitration. In *Himpurna*, invoking art. 16(2) and alleging this provision as the basis for the authority to do so, the tribunal felt it necessary to move the hearing from the seat of arbitration in Jakarta to The Hague, without changing the legal seat of arbitration. Indonesia sought an injunction (unsuccessfully) in the Dutch courts to try to prevent the tribunal from holding hearings in The Hague. Under art. 16(2), hearings of witnesses and consultation meetings may be held at any location deemed appropriate by a tribunal, having regard to the circumstances of the arbitration.

5. Choice of venue by the parties. Art. 16 does not preclude the parties from determining the venue for themselves.

6. Regard to the circumstances of the arbitration. A tribunal must 'have regard to the circumstances of the arbitration' when choosing locations for hearings and consultations. The intention behind this provision is to dissuade arbitrators from choosing attractive or glamorous meeting places with no link to the arbitration.

7. Inspection of goods, property and documents. Under art. 16(3) the tribunal may hold meetings for the inspection of goods, other property or documents in any place that it considers appropriate. Any such inspection must take place in accordance with the law of the place in which the goods are situated.

8. The award. Art. 16(4) states that the award shall be made at the place of arbitration. A party to an international arbitration must be prepared for the possibility of having to seek enforcement of the award outside the place of arbitration. Enforcement will usually take place via international agreements, such as the New York Convention (which attaches special significance to the rules and law of the country where the award was made). It is therefore sensible to choose a place of arbitration that is a signatory to the Convention, or to ensure the existence of a bilateral treaty between the place of arbitration and the likely place of enforcement.

9. Practical considerations. In addition to the above-described legal considerations, the parties should ensure that the place of arbitration is suitable from a practical point of view and boasts suitable facilities. It is worth noting that if no appointing authority has yet been chosen, then the place of arbitration will determine or at least influence the nationality of any appointing authority designated by the Secretary-General.

[Language]

Article 17

(1) **Subject to an agreement by the parties, the arbitral tribunal shall, promptly after its appointment, determine the language or languages to be used in the proceedings. This determination shall apply to the statement of claim, the statement of defence, and any further written statements and, if oral hearings take place, to the language or languages to be used in such hearings.**

(2) **The arbitral tribunal may order that any documents annexed to the statement of claim or statement of defence, and any supplementary documents or exhibits submitted in the course of the proceedings, delivered in their original language, shall be accompanied by a translation into the language or languages agreed upon by the parties or determined by the arbitral tribunal.**

1. Language. Art. 17(1) gives the parties autonomy to determine the language of proceedings by mutual agreement. Where the parties have not agreed, the tribunal shall, 'promptly after its appointment', determine the working language(s). The decision should be among the tribunal's first acts and a decision regarding language should be a precondition for any exchange of pleadings. The decision concerning the language of the proceedings applies to all written statements by the parties, as well as to oral proceedings. The question of annexes and exhibits to statements is dealt with at art. 17, note 3 below.

2. Multiple languages. Either the parties or the tribunal may determine that proceedings be conducted in more than one language. Where two languages are used, and this is particularly relevant for arbitrations involving a state or state entity, documents and decisions should generally be issued in both languages simultaneously. In *Computer Sciences Corporation*, the Tribunal refused to allow a Post-Hearing Memorial received in Farsi only, rather than in both Farsi and English. However, there are instances of the Tribunal accepting the submission of a document in one language only as sufficient for the purposes of calculating time limits, as the principle of equality of treatment set out in art. 15 is not automatically violated by a deviation from formally identical treatment. By way of example, in *Hood Corporation*, the Tribunal held that, to give full effect to the purpose of art. 37 (dealing with the possibility of requesting an additional award), the date on which a request for such additional award was made was the date on which the requesting submission, even if only in one language, was received. Such request may not be acted upon, however, until the other language version is received and such other version must be received within a reasonable period. The parties may waive the requirement for the use of two languages in respect of a particular document.

3. Translation of documents and exhibits. Art. 17(2) allows a tribunal discretion as to whether annexes, exhibits and supplementary documents require translation into the language(s) of proceedings. Such documents may be submitted in their original language unless a tribunal requires otherwise.

4. Consequences. The consequences of failure to produce a document in the language(s) required will depend upon the discretion of the tribunal in question. If correction is possible without undue prejudice to the other party or the overall proceedings, the party may be allowed the opportunity to correct the defect.

[Statement of claim]

Article 18

(1) **Unless the statement of claim was contained in the notice of arbitration, within a period of time to be determined by the arbitral tribunal, the claimant shall communicate his statement of claim in writing to the respondent and to each of the arbitrators. A copy of the contract, and of the arbitration agreement if not contained in the contract, shall be annexed thereto.**

(2) **The statement of claim shall include the following particulars:**
   (a) **The names and addresses of the parties;**
   (b) **A statement of the facts supporting the claim;**
   (c) **The points at issue;**
   (d) **The relief or remedy sought.**

The claimant may annex to his statement of claim all documents he deems relevant or may add a reference to the documents or other evidence he will submit.

1. Practicalities. Art. 18 sets out the requirements for the statement of claim. The statement of claim must be in writing and communicated to the respondent and all the arbitrators. The mode of communication used must be one of those set out in art. 2(1). The statement may be appended to the notice of arbitration, in which case it should be communicated to the arbitrators as soon as they have been appointed. If submitted as a separate document, the statement must be communicated within a period of time determined by the arbitral tribunal. In accordance with art. 23, this period should not exceed forty-five days. In practice, either the parties and/or the tribunal will be likely to change this time limit.

2. Mandatory contents. A copy of the contract and of the arbitration agreement (if not contained in the contract) must be annexed to the statement. The claimant must also include the names and addresses of the parties, a statement of the facts supporting the claim, the points at issue, and the relief or remedy sought. However, these elements need not be fully elaborated;

the important point is that the statement informs the tribunal of the 'essence of the claim', as stated by the NAFTA tribunal in the *UPS* arbitration. A statement of claim must be specific enough to allow the respondent to reply adequately in his statement of defence.

3. Optional contents. The claimant may annex a list of all relevant documents or the documents themselves to the statement of claim, although the Rules do not oblige him to do so.

4. Sanctions for inadequate statement of claim. If the claimant fails to submit a statement of claim which fulfils the requirements of art. 18 within the time limit set by the arbitral tribunal, the consequences set out in art. 28(1) may in principle apply. That is, if no 'sufficient cause' is demonstrated for the claimant's failure, then the tribunal may issue an order terminating proceedings. However, it is accepted that a tribunal may and should allow a claimant who has submitted a defective statement to cure the shortcomings by submitting supplementary information, as was requested by the NAFTA tribunal in *Methanex* (Partial), and that only rarely should such defects justify the termination of proceedings under art. 28. In *Cyrus Petroleum* (Award), the Tribunal dismissed the claim on the ground that neither the claim nor the claimant's subsequent filings detailed the substance of the claimant's allegations or provided any evidence to support them, despite the Tribunal allowing ample time for correction of these defaults.

[Statement of defence]

Article 19

(1) Within a period of time to be determined by the arbitral tribunal, the respondent shall communicate his statement of defence in writing to the claimant and to each of the arbitrators.

(2) The statement of defence shall reply to the particulars (b), (c) and (d) of the statement of claim (article 18, para. 2). The respondent may annex to his statement the documents on which he relies for his defence or may add a reference to the documents or other evidence he will submit.

(3) In his statement of defence, or at a later stage in the arbitral proceedings if the arbitral tribunal decides that the delay was justified under the circumstances, the respondent may make a counter-claim arising out of the same contract or rely on a claim arising out of the same contract for the purpose of a set-off.

(4) The provisions of article 18, paragraph 2, shall apply to a counter-claim and a claim relied on for the purpose of a set-off.

1. Practicalities. Art. 19 requires that, once a statement of claim has been submitted under art. 18, the respondent must submit a statement of defence to both the claimant and each arbitrator within a period prescribed by the tribunal. The period set should not normally exceed forty-five days (see art. 23) unless the parties have agreed otherwise.

2. Contents. The intention behind art. 19 is that the statement of defence responds to the information contained in the statement of claim. If a purported statement of claim does not fulfil the requirements of art. 18, then there may be no duty to submit a statement of defence under art. 19. In *Cyrus Petroleum*, the respondent contended that it was unable to respond to an 'obscure and unclear' statement of claim. The Tribunal ordered the claimant to respond to these objections and when the claimant failed to do so within the allotted time, the Tribunal informed the parties that it 'intended to decide the case on the basis of the pleadings and documents before it' and subsequently dismissed the claim.

3. Optional contents. Under art. 19(2) the respondent may annex or reference any documents or evidence on which he is relying to his statement of defence, but he is not obliged to do so. The wording of the subsection makes it clear that failure to annex such documents will not prejudice the respondent's right to provide additional or substitute documents at a later stage in proceedings.

4. Counter-claims and claims for the purpose of set-off. Article 19(3) gives the respondent the right to present claims arising out of the same contract that the original claim is based upon, by way of counter-claim or set-off claim. A counter-claim is a separate claim which can remain valid even if the original claim has been dismissed, whereas a set-off claim is a purely defensive claim which may not exceed the amount originally claimed.

5. Late claims. Counter-claims and set-off claims should be presented in the statement of defence, and may only be made at a later time if the tribunal decides that the delay was justified under the circumstances. Late counter-claims have frequently been rejected by the Tribunal where no explanation for the delay is given (see *Intrend International*) and the burden of justifying any delay rests on the respondent, as stated by the Tribunal in *Harris International Telecommunications*. Exceptions are, however, conceivable when the delay is minimal. The Tribunal noted in *Anaconda-Iran* that a delay of one or two days would not ordinarily result in a counter-claim's dismissal. Factors which the Tribunal has considered when deliberating on late counter-claims include: the reasons for the delay, possible prejudice to the claimant if the late submission is accepted, and the effect of the delay on the proceedings as a whole. The Tribunal has viewed 'prejudice' as prejudice in the procedural sense, rather than substantive prejudice caused by the strength of a counter-claim. For example, in *Harris International Telecommunications*, the Tribunal stated that it would be particularly reluctant to accept late counter-claims shortly before a hearing. Conversely, in *American Bell* a late, but prima facie meritorious counter-claim was allowed as the other party had sufficient time to respond to it before the hearing. The delay was justified in *American Bell* by the volume of records surrounding the case.

6. Arising out of the same contract. Any counter-claim or set-off claim must arise out of the same contract as that on which the main claim is based. If the parties wish to dispense with the requirement for a link between the main contract and any set-off claim, as is permitted by certain legal systems, they must amend art. 19(3) accordingly. To arise from the same contract, a counter- or set-off claim cannot be based on a contract which is not covered by the arbitration clause or agreement, notwithstanding a close connection with the subject matter of the claim.[21] If the arbitration clause or agreement is formulated to cover non-contractual claims, art. 19(3) should be modified accordingly.

7. Structure. Art. 19(4) prescribes that a counter-claim or claim for set-off shall follow the structure of the statement of claim as prescribed by art. 18(2).

[Amendments to the claim or defence]
Article 20

During the course of the arbitral proceedings either party may amend or supplement his claim or defence unless the arbitral tribunal considers it inappropriate to allow such amendment having regard to the delay in making it or prejudice to the other party or any other circumstances. However, a claim may not be amended in such a manner that the amended claim falls outside the scope of the arbitration clause or separate arbitration agreement.

1. Amendments. Art. 20 sets out the possibilities for amendment of the parties' statements of claim or defence. The preliminary draft of the article was more restrictive than the version finally adopted, allowing for amendments only with the permission of the arbitrators.[22] This approach was rejected in favour of allowing either party to make amendments, albeit with the proviso that the arbitrators retain the power to disallow amendments.[23]

---

21. UNCITRAL, *Report on Eighth Session*, UN Doc A/10017, paras. 136-37, reprinted in (1975) VI UNCITRAL Ybk 24, 37-38: a suggestion in discussions concerning the Preliminary Draft that the phrase 'same contract' be replaced with the phrase 'same transaction' was rejected.
22. *Report of the Secretary-General on the Preliminary Draft Set of Arbitration Rules*, UNCITRAL, 8th Session, UN Doc A/CN.9/97 (1974), 6 U.Y.B. at 173 (Commentary on Draft Article 16).
23. UNCITRAL, *Report on Eighth Session* (1975), UN Doc A/10017, para. 126, 6 U.Y.B. at 37.

2. Outside the scope of the arbitration clause or agreement. A claim may not be amended in such a manner that the amended claim falls outside the scope of the arbitration clause or agreement. The amended claim should not fall outside the subject matter of the dispute, and the amendment should not alter the substance of the claim originally made so that it would in effect become a new claim.[24] Many cases concerning this point involve amendments which introduce a new claimant to proceedings. If the new entity is not a party to the agreement forming the basis of the arbitration, its introduction will not normally be within the scope of the arbitration clause or agreement. However, in *AMF Corporation*, the Tribunal allowed the introduction of a new party as it was clear from the circumstances that the original claim concerned on its face the new party, which was owned and controlled by the party in whose name the original claim was submitted. It is possible in some instances to bring a new party into proceedings by way of amendment, as in the Tribunal case of *Fedders Corporation*, provided that the amendment is within the limits of the arbitration agreement (i.e. the new party is bound by the agreement) and also meets the other conditions set out in art. 20.

3. Grounds for disallowing amendments. An amendment found to fall within the arbitration clause or agreement should be accepted by a tribunal unless it is inappropriate to do so on grounds of delay, prejudice to the other party, or any other circumstances. The Tribunal has rejected amendments on the basis of (unjustified) delay (see, for example, *Nazari*). An amendment prejudices another party where it is raised so late as to deprive that party of the chance to properly defend itself. In *Malek*, the Tribunal held that filing an amendment eight months after the filing of the Statement of Claim and one month before the Defence did not, in the circumstances, constitute an unreasonable or prejudicial delay. The reaction of the other party to an amendment is an important factor; the Tribunal cited the absence of any objection from the potentially prejudiced parties as a factor in favour of accepting a Supplementary Statement of Claim and Supplementary Statement of Counter-claim in the *Sylvania* arbitration. Objections based on the nature of a proposed amendment are assessed on their merit in light of all the circumstances. Prejudice may be more easily established where an amendment raises new factual or legal issues, as was held to be the case regarding the proposed amendment in *Harris International Telecommunications*. In the *Westinghouse* arbitration, a request at the final hearing for declaratory relief in addition to the monetary relief previously sought was rejected on the basis that it raised new factual and legal issues.

4. Procedure. If an amendment is ultimately held to be frivolous, the amending party may be responsible for costs incurred by the other party

---

24. UNCITRAL, *Report on Eighth Session* (1975), UN Doc A/10017, paras. 130-131, 6 U.Y.B. at 37; UNCITRAL, *Report on Ninth Session* (197[6]), UN Doc A/31/17, para. 96, 6 U.Y.B. at 73.

in relation to it. In the *Methanex* (Partial) case before the NAFTA tribunal, Methanex was permitted to amend its claim subject to an order that regardless of the outcome of the arbitration, Methanex would bear the wasted costs thrown away by its amendment.

[Pleas as to the jurisdiction of the arbitral tribunal]
Article 21

(1) The arbitral tribunal shall have the power to rule on objections that it has no jurisdiction, including any objections with respect to the existence or validity of the arbitration clause or of the separate arbitration agreement.

(2) The arbitral tribunal shall have the power to determine the existence or the validity of the contract of which an arbitration clause forms a part. For the purposes of article 21, an arbitration clause which forms part of a contract and which provides for arbitration under these Rules shall be treated as an agreement independent of the other terms of the contract. A decision by the arbitral tribunal that the contract is null and void shall not entail ipso jure the invalidity of the arbitration clause.

(3) A plea that the arbitral tribunal does not have jurisdiction shall be raised not later than in the statement of defence or, with respect to a counter-claim, in the reply to the counter-claim.

(4) In general, the arbitral tribunal should rule on a plea concerning its jurisdiction as a preliminary question. However, the arbitral tribunal may proceed with the arbitration and rule on such a plea in their final award.

1. Power to determine jurisdiction. Art. 21(1) empowers a tribunal to rule upon any objection to its jurisdiction, and thus rule upon any objection raised regarding the validity of the arbitration agreement. It is clear from the travaux préparatoires that the article 'is designed to cover all objections to the jurisdiction of the arbitrators, irrespective of the grounds for and the extent of, such objections'.[25] Note, however, that questions as to the competence and jurisdiction of a tribunal are ultimately a matter for the relevant national court to settle in accordance with the lex fori[26] (hence the reference to the applicability of national law to the Rules in art. 1(2)). Any award by an ar-

---

25. *Report of the Secretary-General on the Revised Draft Set of Arbitration Rules*, UNCITRAL, 9th Session, Addendum 1 (Commentary), UN Doc A/CN.9/112/Add.1 (1975) reprinted in (1976) VII UNCITRAL Ybk 166, 174 (Commentary on Draft Article 19, para. 1).
26. UNCITRAL, *Report on Eighth Session* (1975), UN Doc A/10017, para. 141 (1975), reprinted in (1975) VI UNCITRAL Ybk 24, 38.

bitral tribunal may theoretically be subject to challenge under the applicable national law for excess of jurisdiction.

2. Existence or validity of contract. Art. 21(2) states that an arbitration clause is an agreement separate from the contract in which it is contained. It follows that where a contract containing an arbitration clause is allegedly null and void, the validity of the arbitration clause contained within that contract will not be affected by the alleged nullity of the contract. The competence of the arbitrators to come to a decision on jurisdiction will therefore not be undermined.

3. Time limits. Art. 21(3) states that objections to the jurisdiction of a tribunal shall be raised no later than in the statement of defence (and no later than in the reply to a counter-claim in respect of a counter-claim). Taken alone, art. 21(3) seems to suggest that the time limits on jurisdictional objections are mandatory. For example, in the *Chevron* v *National Iranian Oil* arbitration, the Tribunal found that a jurisdictional objection raised eight months after the statement of defence was filed, without evidence or reason sufficient to raise substantial doubt as to the claimant's nationality, was not raised in accordance with art. 21. However, the travaux préparatoires suggest that a tribunal may, by utilising its discretion over procedure under art. 15, or by allowing an amendment, permit objections at a later date.[27]

4. Preliminary question. Art. 21(4) states that a tribunal should usually rule on objections to jurisdiction as a preliminary question, whilst allowing a tribunal a discretion as to whether to follow this general rule. The intention behind the general rule was to ensure that proceedings were conducted efficiently, bearing in mind that an early resolution of jurisdictional issues could yield substantial cost savings. The NAFTA tribunal during the *Methanex* (Partial) arbitration, when considering whether to hear an objection to jurisdiction as a preliminary question, weighed up the potential costs savings in terms of both time and money against the practicality of splitting the proceedings into two, given that the jurisdictional issues were to a large extent intertwined with the merits of the case. It concluded that the question of jurisdiction should not be heard as a preliminary question. The NAFTA tribunal in the *Glamis Gold* arbitration considered a similar test when debating when to hear an objection to jurisdiction. The tribunal considered whether the objection was substantial, whether the costs and time involved in a preliminary hearing could be justified on the basis that such a hearing would reduce the costs and time involved at later stages of the proceedings, and whether bifurcation would be impractical given that the jurisdictional issue identified was heavily intertwined with the merits of the case.

---

27. UNCITRAL, *Report on Ninth Session* (1976), UN Doc A/31/17, para. 108, reprinted in (1976) VII UNCITRAL Ybk 66, 74.

[Further written statements]
Article 22

The arbitral tribunal shall decide which further written statements, in addition to the statement of claim and the statement of defence, shall be required from the parties or may be presented by them and shall fix the periods of time for communicating such statements.

1. Further written statements. Art. 22 grants an arbitral tribunal a discretion either to order or to authorise the submission of further written statements. These further statements may be required by a tribunal at its own initiative, or at the request of one or both of the parties. A tribunal is not obliged to order such statements, even following a unanimous request by the parties. However, a tribunal should normally acquiesce to a unanimous party request. Note that art. 22 deals with 'written statements' rather than documentary evidence, although it may be the case that a tribunal orders that both are to be submitted together.

2. Circumstances requiring further statements. Further written statements are often advisable given that under the Rules, both the statement of claim and the statement of defence may be concise in nature. The Rules' drafters envisaged provision in many arbitrations for a second round of written pleadings, consisting of a reply to the statement of defence and a rejoinder to this reply by the respondent.[28] This second round of pleadings may often be in the form of a second set of memorials and counter-memorials, combined with the submission of documentary evidence and expert reports. Further rounds of written pleadings may be added depending on the circumstances of the case. Situations including amendments to a claim or defence, requests for interim measures, the appointment of experts and jurisdictional issues or preliminary questions may also necessitate further written statements. The principle of equality set out in art. 15 may, in limited circumstances, necessitate the submission of post-hearing statements (see for example the Tribunal in the *American Bell* arbitration).

3. Time periods. A tribunal shall fix the periods of time for the communication of any further written statements. It is therefore in a tribunal's discretion as to whether such statements should be submitted simultaneously or successively. For further discussion of time limits, see the commentary to art. 23.

---

28. *Report of the Secretary-General on the Preliminary Draft Set of Arbitration Rules*, UNCITRAL, 8th Session, UN Doc A/CN.9/97 (1974), reprinted in (1975) VI UNCITRAL Ybk 163, 175 (Commentary on Draft Article 19).

[Periods of time]
Article 23

The periods of time fixed by the arbitral tribunal for the communication of written statements (including the statement of claim and statements of defence) should not exceed forty-five days. However, the arbitral tribunal may extend the time limits if it concludes that an extension is justified.

1. Forty-five days. Art. 23 states that the period of time fixed by a tribunal for communication of a written statement 'should not' exceed forty-five days. It is clear from the travaux préparatoires and from the wording of the article that the forty-five-day limit is 'intended to serve as a general guideline',[29] which may be adapted by a tribunal as necessary. The parties may also modify the forty-five-day rule by initial written agreement pursuant to art. 1(1).

2. Extensions. The article allows a tribunal to extend any time limit fixed by it if it concludes that such extension is 'justified'. The power of a tribunal to grant an extension is not limited by any given number of days, nor is a tribunal prohibited from increasing or renewing an extension once granted (see the further extensions granted by the Tribunal in Case No. A/33). The parties have no right to extend time limits without the approval of the tribunal.

3. Justified. The only limitation on a tribunal's power to extend time limits (other than the fact that it must have regard to the general principles set out in art. 15) is that any extension must be 'justified'. The burden of proof lies with the party requesting the extension. Further extensions may require the support of more compelling reasons than those required for an initial extension (see for example the *Texaco Iran* arbitration, in which the Tribunal rejected a request for a sixth extension with no supporting justification). A tribunal must balance the justification presented by a party in support of its request against the possible prejudice to the other party which the extension may cause. It can be inferred from *Texaco Iran* that an extension which will affect the orderly conduct of oral proceedings or cause such proceedings to be delayed should only be granted for exceptional reasons. A tribunal may ask a party to elaborate further on the reasons it has given for requesting an extension, as the Tribunal did in the *Thomas Earl Payne* arbitration.

4. Failure to meet time limits. Art. 28(1) sets out the consequence of failure to meet the time limit set for submission of a claim without showing sufficient cause for the delay: an order shall be issued for termination of

---

29. *Report of the Secretary-General on the Revised Draft Set of Arbitration Rules*, UNCITRAL, 9th Session, Addendum 1 (Commentary), UN Doc A/CN.9/112/Add.1 (1975), reprinted in (1976) VII UNCITRAL Ybk 166, 175 (Commentary on Draft Article 21).

proceedings. If a defendant fails to submit his statement of defence within the allotted time without showing sufficient cause, the tribunal shall order that proceedings continue regardless. Measures such as these are generally reserved for significant delays, and a delay of a few days should not normally lead to the rejection of a written statement.

[Evidence]
Article 24

(1) Each party shall have the burden of proving the facts relied on to support his claim or defence.

(2) The arbitral tribunal may, if it considers it appropriate, require a party to deliver to the tribunal and to the other party, within such a period of time as the arbitral tribunal shall decide, a summary of the documents and other evidence which that party intends to present in support of the facts in issue set out in his statement of claim or statement of defence.

(3) At any time during the arbitral proceedings the arbitral tribunal may require the parties to produce documents, exhibits or other evidence within such a period of time as the tribunal shall determine.

1. Burden of proof. Under art. 24(1) each party has the burden of proving the facts relied upon to support his claim or defence. By way of illustration, the Tribunal stated in the *Reza Said Malek* arbitration that the claimant would carry the initial burden of proving the facts on which he relied. A point would then be reached at which the claimant would be considered to have made a sufficient showing to shift the burden onto the respondent.

2. Standard of proof. Art. 24(1) does not address the standard of proof required of the parties. This is an issue normally determined by the applicable substantive law. Tribunal practice does not support the proposition that a claimant would have to prove its case beyond all reasonable doubt – the standard of proof varies according to the circumstances. In contested cases, it may be said that at least prima facie evidence will generally be required to satisfy the burden of proof, although this alone will often be held insufficient to discharge the burden. Art. 24(1) leaves intact any legal presumptions concerning fault or liability which exist under the applicable national law.

3. Summary of evidence. Under art. 24(2) a tribunal may require a party to produce an advance summary of the documents or other evidence upon which that party intends to rely in support of its case. Production of a summary is not obligatory unless required by the tribunal. A tribunal has a discretion as to when to request a summary and as to the time limit imposed upon the party to whom the request is made.

4. Power to require production of evidence. Under art. 24(3) a tribunal may order a party to produce evidence which that party has failed to submit voluntarily. Whilst the parties themselves do not have the power to require production of evidence, a tribunal may grant a party's request for the production of evidence by the other party. If a party's request is insufficiently specific it may not be granted. Art. 3 of the IBA Rules on the Taking of Evidence in International Commercial Arbitration allows parties to submit 'Requests to Produce' to the tribunal. These Requests may be for specific documents or for a narrow and specifically requested category of documents that are reasonably believed to exist.

5. Consequences of failure to produce evidence. The Rules are silent as to the consequences of a party's failure to produce evidence as requested under art. 24. However, if a party fails to give a satisfactory explanation for its failure, a tribunal may draw an adverse inference (see art. 9(4) and (5) of the IBA Rules on the Taking of Evidence in International Commercial Arbitration).

[Hearings]
Article 25

(1) In the event of an oral hearing, the arbitral tribunal shall give the parties adequate advance notice of the date, time and place thereof.

(2) If witnesses are to be heard, at least fifteen days before the hearing each party shall communicate to the arbitral tribunal and to the other party the names and addresses of the witnesses he intends to present, the subject upon and the languages in which such witnesses will give their testimony.

(3) The arbitral tribunal shall make arrangements for the translation of oral statements made at a hearing and for a record of the hearing if either is deemed necessary by the tribunal under the circumstances of the case, or if the parties have agreed thereto and have communicated such agreement to the tribunal at least fifteen days before the hearing.

(4) Hearings shall be held in camera unless the parties agree otherwise. The arbitral tribunal may require the retirement of any witness or witnesses during the testimony of other witnesses. The arbitral tribunal is free to determine the manner in which witnesses are examined.

(5) Evidence of witnesses may also be presented in the form of written statements signed by them.

(6) The arbitral tribunal shall determine the admissibility, relevance, materiality and weight of the evidence offered.

1. General. Art. 25 contains general provisions regarding the conduct of hearings (including both the hearing of witnesses and the hearing of oral argument).

2. Notice of hearing. Art. 25(1) requires that when an oral hearing is held, 'adequate' notice must be given to the parties of the date, time and place thereof. The adequacy of the notice will depend upon the nature of the case and the circumstances involved. According to the UNCITRAL Notes on Organizing Arbitral Proceedings, the notice should specify not only the time of the hearing but also its projected length. The rationale behind art. 25 is to give the parties some idea of the evidence to be presented and to enable the opposing party to prepare its response.[30]

3. Witnesses. Art. 25(2) deals with the preparations necessary for witness hearings. At least fifteen days prior to the hearing, the party presenting the witnesses must inform the other party and the tribunal of certain basic information, including the names and addresses of witnesses and the language in which they will testify. The party must also state the subject upon which the witnesses will testify. It is generally considered that the requirements of art. 25(2) apply to a party's principal witnesses, rather than to its 'rebuttal' witnesses (that is, those witnesses produced by a party in response to the witness notice produced by the other party). If a party fails to meet the requirements of art. 25(2) in respect of a witness, a tribunal may refuse to accept that witness (as in the *Frederica Lincoln Riahi* arbitration before the Tribunal).

4. Translations and records. If the tribunal deems it necessary in the light of the circumstances of the case, or if the parties have agreed upon it (and communicated their agreement to the tribunal at least fifteen days prior to the hearing), the tribunal shall make arrangements for the translation of oral statements made at the hearing, and for a record of the hearing. The record of the hearing (if required) need not be verbatim, although such possibility was not precluded by the drafters.

5. Conduct of hearing. Under art. 25(4) hearings will be not be held in public unless the parties agree otherwise. A tribunal retains the power to require sequestration of witnesses during the testimony of other witnesses. A tribunal is also free to determine the manner in which witnesses are examined; for example, it has complete freedom as to whether or not to allow cross-examination.

6. Confidentiality in general. Note that whilst art. 25(4) establishes a rule of privacy for the hearing, and art. 32(5) establishes the presumption that awards are confidential, the Rules do not contain a general rule of privacy or confidentiality regarding the arbitral process as a whole. This will be a matter for the applicable national law, including any contractual arrangements between the parties.

---

30. *Report of the Secretary-General on the Revised Draft Set of Arbitration Rules*, UNCITRAL, 9th Session, Addendum 1 (Commentary), UN Doc A/CN.9/112/Add. 1 (1975), 7 U.Y.B. 166, 175 (Commentary on Draft Article 22, para 2).

7. Written statements by witnesses. Art. 25(5) sets out a (possibly partial) alternative to the hearing of witnesses: the use of written statements. It was suggested during the drafting of the article that this alternative method could save time and money. A written statement by a witness need only be signed, not sworn.[31]

8. Evidence in general. Art. 25(6) states that the arbitral tribunal shall determine the 'admissibility, relevance, materiality and weight' of the evidence offered. The travaux préparatoires make clear that '[i]n making rulings on the evidence, arbitrators should enjoy the greatest possible freedom and they are therefore freed from having to observe the strict legal rules of evidence.'[32]

9. Admissibility of evidence. The Rules do not contain rules on admissibility. The applicable substantive and/or arbitration law will be relevant in this respect. Aside from very limited circumstances such as a significant delay in filing (or the exceptional case where a strict domestic evidentiary system must be applied), evidence should not be rejected on technical or formal grounds. An example of such an exceptional case is the exclusion of information concerning confidential settlement negotiations between the parties (see Case No. A/1 (Issues I, III and IV) before the Tribunal). In the NAFTA *Methanex* (Award) arbitration, documentation obtained by illegal means was deemed to be inadmissible.

10. Relevance, materiality and weight. The term 'weight' was added to the text of art. 25(6) at the final stage of drafting in order to emphasise the wide discretion the tribunal has when evaluating evidence.[33] A tribunal is likely to exercise common sense in its deliberations. For example, although the Rules contain no formal prohibition of hearsay evidence, a tribunal would be likely to accord it less weight than direct testimony.

---

31. *Report of the Secretary-General on the Preliminary Draft Set of Arbitration Rules*, UNCITRAL, 8th Session, UN Doc A/CN.9/97/Add. 2 (1975), 6 U.Y.B. 182, 184, paras. 17-18; *Report of the Secretary-General on the Revised Draft Set of Arbitration Rules*, UNCITRAL, 9th Session, Addendum 1 (Commentary), UN Doc A/CN.9/112/Add. 1 (1975), 7 U.Y.B. 166, 176 (Commentary on Draft Article 22, para 5).
32. *Report of the Secretary-General on the Preliminary Draft Set of Arbitration Rules*, UNCITRAL, 8th Session, UN Doc A/CN.9/97 (1974), reprinted in (1975) VI UNCITRAL Ybk 163, 176 (Commentary on Draft Article 21, para 5).
33. UNCITRAL, *Report on Ninth Session* (1976), UN Doc A/31/17, para 130, reprinted in (1976) VII UNCITRAL Ybk 66, 75 (Commentary on Draft Article 22, para 6).

[Interim measures of protection]
Article 26

(1) At the request of either party, the arbitral tribunal may take any interim measures it deems necessary in respect of the subject-matter of the dispute, including measures for the conservation of the goods forming the subject-matter in dispute, such as ordering their deposit with a third person or the sale of perishable goods.

(2) Such interim measures may be established in the form of an interim award. The arbitral tribunal shall be entitled to require security for the costs of such measures.

(3) A request for interim measures addressed by any party to a judicial authority shall not be deemed incompatible with the agreement to arbitrate, or as a waiver of that agreement.

1. Interim measures. Art. 26(1) states that interim measures may be granted by a tribunal at the request of either party. A tribunal may not order interim measures of its own initiative.[34]

2. Necessary in respect of the subject matter of the dispute. Any interim measure must be 'necessary in respect of the subject-matter of the dispute', and the Tribunal has stated in several cases that interim measures should only be sought in order to prevent irreparable harm to a party (see for example the *Behring* arbitration). Questions have arisen over whether a tribunal must satisfy itself that it has jurisdiction over the subject matter of the dispute before ordering an interim measure. The Tribunal has adopted 'the prima facie test' to resolve the issue of whether a tribunal should have positively ruled on jurisdiction. A prima facie showing of jurisdiction will suffice at the stage that interim measures are requested (see the discussion in *Bendone-Derossi International*).

3. Types of measure. Interim measures may include 'measures for the conservation of the goods forming the subject-matter in dispute, such as ordering their deposit with a third person or the sale of perishable goods.' However, these examples are not intended as an exhaustive list of the measures available; a tribunal may also order any other measure that it deems necessary, including a temporary interim measure. As a tribunal's jurisdiction will only cover the parties to the arbitration it may not direct interim measures at third parties (see the *Atlantic Richfield* arbitration). Interim measures involving a third party are likely to require the assistance of the relevant national courts.

---

34. *Report of the Secretary-General on the Revised Draft Set of Arbitration Rules*, UNCITRAL, 9th Session, Addendum 1 (Commentary), UN Doc A/CN.9/112/Add.1 (1975), reprinted in (1976) VII UNCITRAL Ybk 166, 176 (Commentary on Draft Article 23, paras 1 & 2); UNCITRAL, *Report on Eighth Session* (1975), UN Doc A/10017, para 164, reprinted in (1975) VI UNCITRAL Ybk 24, 40.

4. Form of interim measures. Art. 26(2) provides that an interim measure may be established 'in the form of an interim award', rather than in the form of an order. The purpose behind this provision is to ensure that any interim measure will be enforceable, as an interim award will generally be enforceable before the competent national court, subject to the provisions of the applicable national arbitration law. Before granting an interim measure, a tribunal should generally provide the party against whom such measures are sought with the opportunity to comment.

5. Security for costs. Art. 26(2) allows a tribunal to require security for the costs which an interim measure may cause. This protects the party who is subject to the measure should it turn out to have been wrong in light of the final award.

6. Relationship with national courts. Art. 26(3) addresses the respective roles of the tribunal and the relevant national courts in the consideration of interim measures. The law of the place of arbitration may restrict a tribunal's power to grant interim measures by reserving such powers to the national courts. More commonly, national laws will allow concurrent jurisdiction between the tribunal and the courts. Art. 26(3) envisages the possibility of co-operation between the courts and the tribunal, stating that 'a request for interim measures addressed by one party to a judicial authority shall not be deemed incompatible with the agreement to arbitrate, or as a waiver of that agreement.' Art. 26(3) therefore guarantees that a party requesting that the courts enact an interim measure will not be in violation of the arbitration agreement, either where the national law precludes the tribunal from granting such measures, or where the tribunal and the courts have concurrent jurisdiction but the party in question prefers to address the courts. Art. 26(3) allows the parties to approach courts in both the place of arbitration and elsewhere.

7. Conflict with national courts. Note that art. 26(3) only provides that a 'request' for an interim measure will not breach the arbitration agreement; it does not goes so far as prescribing that interim measures ordered by national courts necessarily prevail over conflicting measures ordered by a tribunal. Interim measures ordered by the courts of the place of arbitration and/or the courts contractually designated as the proper courts for issuing measures in support of the arbitration will almost certainly prevail over conflicting tribunal measures.

[Experts]
Article 27

(1) The arbitral tribunal may appoint one or more experts to report to it, in writing, on specific issues to be determined by the tribunal. A copy of the expert's terms of reference, established by the arbitral tribunal, shall be communicated to the parties.

(2) The parties shall give the expert any relevant information or produce for inspection any relevant documents or goods that he may require of them. Any dispute between a party and such expert as to the relevance of the required information or production shall be referred to the arbitral tribunal for decision.

(3) Upon receipt of the expert's report, the tribunal shall communicate a copy of the report to the parties who shall be given the opportunity to express, in writing, their opinion of the report. A party shall be entitled to examine any document on which the expert has relied in his report.

(4) At the request of either party the expert, after delivery of the report, may be heard at a hearing where the parties shall have the opportunity to be present and to interrogate the expert. At this hearing either party may present expert witnesses in order to testify on the points at issue. The provisions of article 25 shall be applicable to such proceedings.

1. Appointment. Art. 27(1) vests the power to appoint an expert with the arbitral tribunal. This power may be exercised spontaneously or in response to a party request. The tribunal should take into account the will of the parties when considering whether to appoint an expert, particularly where the parties are in agreement. The article does not provide guidance as to when it is appropriate for a tribunal to appoint an expert, although it has been suggested that two factors which should be considered are the complexity of the issue before the tribunal and the expediency of appointing an expert in all the circumstances of the case. In certain cases the Tribunal has ruled out the appointment of an expert on the basis that it would be too expensive or would create disproportionate delays given the circumstances of the case (see for example the *Gruen* arbitration).

2. Process of selection. Art. 27 is silent as to the process for selection of a expert. The article places responsibility for the drafting of the expert's terms of reference on the tribunal; a tribunal need only communicate a copy of the terms to the parties. However, a tribunal is not precluded from involving the parties in the drafting process. A tribunal will also be entitled to give any later interpretation of the terms of reference required – see for example *Richard D Harza*, in which the Tribunal was required to determine that the expert appointed had not exceeded his terms of reference. For an example of the appointment of an expert under art. 27 by an ad hoc tribunal, see the *Wintershall* (Partial) arbitration.

3. Provision of information. Art. 27(2) imposes an obligation on the parties to provide an expert with any 'relevant information', and more specifically 'any relevant documents or goods', that the expert may require. This obligation is broad enough to cover a wide range of information requests, including site inspections of relevant documents, goods or other information. The consequences of failure to meet an expert's request may include application by a tribunal of the default procedures set out in art.

28, or the drawing of adverse inferences against the party who has failed to provide the information requested. Art. 27(2) requires that a tribunal resolve any disputes between a party and an expert regarding the relevance of the required information or the need for production.

3. The report. Under art. 27(3), the parties are entitled to provide written comments on any expert report produced (these will be regarded as written statements under art. 22 and thus should in principle be filed within forty-five days). The parties will also be entitled to examine all documents upon which the report is based. It is for the tribunal to determine the weight to be given to an expert's report. In the *Starrett Housing* (Award) arbitration, the Tribunal held that the weight of an expert's opinion would depend on a number of factors, including the expert's qualifications; the procedure he had followed in developing his opinions (including his consideration of the parties' comments); the thoroughness with which he had verified information provided by the parties; and the thoroughness of the report, including citation to evidentiary support.

4. Expert hearings. Under art. 27(4), upon either party's request, a tribunal must hold a hearing at which both parties are given the opportunity to interrogate the expert. It is expressly provided that the parties may present expert witnesses at this hearing in order to challenge or corroborate the testimony of the tribunal-appointed expert. This reference to the presentation of expert witnesses is the only reference in the Rules to the use of party-appointed experts. However, the travaux préparatoires confirm that the drafters supported the use of party-appointed experts at any stage of proceedings.[35]

[Default]
Article 28

(1) If, within the period of time fixed by the arbitral tribunal, the claimant has failed to communicate his claim without showing sufficient cause for such failure, the arbitral tribunal shall issue an order for the termination of the arbitral proceedings. If, within the period of time fixed by the arbitral tribunal, the respondent has failed to communicate his statement of defence without showing sufficient cause for such failure, the arbitral tribunal shall order that the proceedings continue.

(2) If one of the parties, duly notified under these Rules, fails to appear at a hearing, without showing sufficient cause for such failure, the arbitral tribunal may proceed with the arbitration.

---

35. *Summary Record of the 9th Meeting of the Committee of the Whole (II)*, UNCITRAL, 9th Session, UN Doc A/CN.9/9/C.2/SR.9 at 7, paras 60-62 (1976); UNCITRAL, *Report on Ninth Session* (1976), UN Doc A/31/17, para 134, reprinted in (1976) VII UNCITRAL Ybk 66, 76 (1976).

UNCITRAL Arbitration Rules, art. 28

(3) If one of the parties, duly invited to produce documentary evidence, fails to do so within the established period of time, without showing sufficient cause for such failure, the arbitral tribunal may make the award on the evidence before it.

1. General. Art. 28 allows a tribunal to terminate proceedings in one situation (where the claimant does not submit a statement of claim), and to continue proceedings ex parte in three other situations where a party has failed to participate. These three situations comprise: where a respondent does not submit a statement of defence, where a party fails to appear for a hearing, and where a party fails to produce documentary evidence requested by a tribunal. The scope of a tribunal's powers to sanction a defaulting party under art. 28 is limited to the advancement of proceedings beyond the procedural step at issue. For example, if a party fails to attend a hearing, a tribunal may prevent that party from participating in the hearing phase of the arbitration, but may not prevent it from participating in subsequent phases of proceedings, such as post-hearing submissions. An application of art. 28 has no effect on the parties' evidentiary burdens.

2. Notice. A tribunal must give a party sufficient notice of its duties before invoking art. 28.

3. Sufficient cause. A tribunal may not invoke art. 28 if a party has shown 'sufficient cause' for his failure to participate in proceedings at issue. Whether a cause is sufficient to avert ex parte proceedings is determined at the discretion of the tribunal and will depend upon the circumstances of each particular case. The ad hoc *Himpurna* arbitrations addressed the meaning of 'sufficient cause'. In *Himpurna*, the tribunal held that the State of Indonesia had acted without sufficient cause in failing to submit its case-in-chief. The justification offered by Indonesia for its failure was that an injunction had been issued by the Indonesian courts ordering suspension of the arbitral proceedings. The tribunal rejected this justification as the injunction had been sought by Indonesia's state-run oil company, whose actions were controlled by the Indonesian state. It had therefore been within Indonesia's power to prevent the injunction.

4. Failure to file initial written submissions. Under art. 28(1), if a claimant fails to submit a statement of claim having communicated its wish for arbitration, the tribunal is required to terminate proceedings. This termination order will not prevent re-filing of the claim at a later date.[36] Conversely, if a defendant fails to submit its statement of defence, then the tribunal shall order that proceedings continue without the submission in question. Failure to submit a statement of defence does not amount to an admission of the allegations

---

36. UNCITRAL, *Report on Ninth Session* (1976), UN Doc A/31/17, para 136, reprinted in (1976) VII UNCITRAL Ybk 66, 76.

in the statement of claim (see art. 25(b) of the UNCITRAL Model Law). The respondent will not be prevented from addressing the claimant's allegations at a later stage, but his ability to raise a counter-claim may be prejudiced (see the Tribunal's Order of 22 February 1984 in *Amoco International Finance*).

5. Failure to appear at a hearing. Art. 28(2) allows a tribunal to move proceedings forward in the event that a party fails to appear at a hearing. For example, in the *Meyer* arbitration the respondent failed to attend the hearing scheduled and did not either prior to or on the date of the hearing inform the Tribunal of its inability to attend. The Tribunal denied the respondent's later request for a new hearing (although it did grant its request to submit a memorial into the arbitration record subsequent to the failure to attend, thus ensuring that the respondent could continue to participate in the proceedings). In the event that both parties fail to appear, the tribunal may call a second hearing or consider terminating proceedings.[37]

6. Failure to produce documentary evidence. If a party fails to produce documentary evidence as required by art. 24(3), the tribunal may 'make the award on the evidence before it'.

[Closure of hearings]

Article 29

(1) The arbitral tribunal may inquire of the parties if they have any further proof to offer or witnesses to be heard or submissions to make and, if there are none, it may declare the hearings closed.

(2) The arbitral tribunal may, if it considers it necessary owing to exceptional circumstances, decide, on its own motion or upon application of a party, to reopen the hearings at any time before the award is made.

1. Closure of hearings. Art. 29(1) sets out a simple mechanism by which a tribunal may, at its discretion, close the hearing phase of an arbitration. The aim behind the article is to avoid the delays to proceedings which the repeated requests for hearings and the taking of further evidence could cause.[38] A tribunal may enquire of the parties whether they have additional evidence, in either oral or written form, to submit. If a request for the submission of further evidence is made, the tribunal will consider whether there is a legitimate need to further develop a material aspect of the requesting party's case. If neither party has further evidence to submit, or if the tribunal chooses to deny a party's request for the submission of further evidence, the tribunal

---

37. UNCITRAL, *Report on Eighth Session* (1975), UN Doc A/10017, paras 171-72, reprinted in (1975) VI UNCITRAL Ybk 24, 40.
38. UNCITRAL, *Report on Ninth Session* (1976), UN Doc A/31/17, para 149, reprinted in (1976) VII UNCITRAL Ybk 66, 77.

may declare the hearings closed. For an example of a declaration of closure by an ad hoc tribunal, see *CME Czech Republic*.

2. Closure of proceedings. Although art. 29 only refers to the closure of the hearing phase of the arbitration, it is likely that it was intended to have the same effect at art. 22 of the ICC Rules of Arbitration, which provides a mechanism for the closure of the overall proceedings (rather than just the hearing phase).

3. Reopening hearings. Under art. 29(2) a tribunal has authority to reopen a hearing if it considers it necessary owing to 'exceptional circumstances'. The decision to reopen a hearing may be made by a tribunal of its own motion or upon the application of a party. *Dames & Moore* implies that the application of art. 29(2) is limited to the period prior to the issuing of the award.

4. Exceptional circumstances. The Rules are silent as to the meaning of 'exceptional circumstances'. Case law of the Tribunal underlines the extraordinary nature required for circumstances to justify reopening, certainly once deliberations have started (see *Dadras*, where the Tribunal was confronted with directly conflicting and irreconcilable statements from two alleged signatories to a contract, creating a need to decide which version of events was more accurate).

[Waiver of rules]
Article 30

A party who knows that any provision of, or requirement under, these Rules has not been complied with and yet proceeds with the arbitration without promptly stating his objection to such non-compliance, shall be deemed to have waived his right to object.

1. General. Art. 30 establishes a waiver of a party's right to object to non-compliance with the Rules in certain situations. If a party knows of an instance of non-compliance and yet continues with the arbitration without promptly stating an objection, that party will be barred from lodging a later objection, either during the proceedings themselves or arguably during any subsequent collateral court proceedings. The travaux préparatoires make clear that art. 30 was intended to apply to situations involving minor procedural violations,[39] and it is likely that the scope of its application in practice may depend upon the importance of the procedural right at stake.

2. Knowledge. Art. 30 requires that a party 'knows' of the procedural deviation in question for a waiver to take effect. Consideration was given to including a concept of constructive waiver in the article (that is to say that a

---

39. UNCITRAL, *Report on Ninth Session* (1976), UN Doc A/31/17, para 146, reprinted in (1976) VII UNCITRAL Ybk 66, 77.

waiver would also have been effected where a party should have known of the procedural deviation), but this idea was ultimately dismissed.

3. Prompt objection. An objection to a deviation from the Rules must be raised 'promptly'. For example, in the *Varo* arbitration the Tribunal ruled that the claimant had waived its right to object to the admission of the respondent's documentary submissions because it had not objected promptly to the Tribunal's order extending the time limit for submission of the respondent's rebuttal evidence. No time period is specified in art. 30, so it will be in a tribunal's discretion to determine whether an objection has been raised sufficiently quickly.

SECTION IV. THE AWARD
[Decisions]
Article 31

(1) When there are three arbitrators, any award or other decision of the arbitral tribunal shall be made by a majority of the arbitrators.

(2) In the case of questions of procedure, when there is no majority or when the arbitral tribunal so authorises, the presiding arbitrator may decide on his own, subject to revision, if any, by the arbitral tribunal.

1. Majority rule. Art. 31(1) states that where a tribunal is made up of three arbitrators, decisions shall be reached by majority rule. At least two of the three arbitrators must agree to an award or decision for it to bind the parties.

2. Inability to form a majority. After substantial debate as to the consequences of inability to form a majority, it was ultimately agreed that this would depend upon the type of issue which had resulted in the stalemate. With respect to certain procedural questions, art. 31(2) provides that the presiding arbitrator may act unilaterally. In all other situations, the arbitrators are required to continue to deliberate until a majority is formed, subject to any mandatory provisions of the governing arbitration law.[40]

3. Decision making on procedural questions. Art. 31(2) invests the presiding arbitrator with authority to end a stalemate in two circumstances. Firstly, where the tribunal is unable to form a majority on a procedural question and secondly, where the tribunal has authorised the presiding arbitrator to come to a unilateral decision on a procedural question. In both cases any decision by the presiding arbitrator is subject to revision by the tribunal.

---

40. *Report of the Secretary-General on the Revised Draft Set of Arbitration Rules*, UNCITRAL, 9th Session, Addendum 1 (Commentary), UN Doc A/CN.9/112/Add.1 (1975), reprinted in (1976) VII UNCITRAL Ybk 166, 178 (Commentary on Draft Article 27, para. 3).

4. Questions of procedure. The Rules are silent as to what constitutes a question of procedure and make no attempt to distinguish between procedural and substantive questions. It is generally accepted that substantive questions will involve the creation, definition and regulation of the rights of the parties to the dispute, while procedural questions will relate to the technical steps of the arbitral process. In practice, the distinction can be difficult to draw and a tribunal addressing a borderline case may wish to render its decision by majority rule under art. 31(1) if possible.

5. Revision. The travaux préparatoires are unclear as to whether the tribunal's power to revise a presiding arbitrator's decision constitutes a mere consultative power or whether it constitutes a broader power to overrule the presiding arbitrator's unilateral authority in the area of procedure.

[Form and effect of the award]

Article 32

(1) In addition to making a final award, the arbitral tribunal shall be entitled to make interim, interlocutory, or partial awards.

(2) The award shall be made in writing and shall be final and binding on the parties. The parties undertake to carry out the award without delay.

(3) The arbitral tribunal shall state the reasons upon which the award is based, unless the parties have agreed that no reasons are to be given.

(4) An award shall be signed by the arbitrators and it shall contain the date on which and the place where the award was made. Where there are three arbitrators and one of them fails to sign, the award shall state the reason for absence of the signature.

(5) The award may be made public only with the consent of both parties.

(6) Copies of the award signed by the arbitrators shall be communicated to the parties by the arbitral tribunal.

(7) If the arbitration law of the country where the award is made requires that the award be filed or registered by the arbitral tribunal, the tribunal shall comply with this requirement within the period of time required by law.

1. Types of award. Art. 32(1) empowers a tribunal to make interim, interlocutory and partial awards as well as final awards. These interim, interlocutory and partial awards may be made 'whenever justified under the circumstances of the particular dispute' and 'at any time during the arbitral proceedings'.[41] In the practice of the Tribunal, a 'partial award' is generally

---

41. *Report of the Secretary-General on the Revised Draft Set of Arbitration Rules*, UNCITRAL, 9th Session, Addendum 1 (Commentary), UN Doc A/CN.9/112/

an award which is final as to a distinct claim, whilst an 'interlocutory award' is a decision on a substantive or procedural issue bearing on the claim. However, regardless of how an award is labelled, the important point is that the inclusion of different types of award in art. 32(1) gives a tribunal freedom, within the boundaries of the applicable national arbitration law, to ensure maximum efficiency in case management.

2. Final and binding. Art. 32(2) states that a decision in the form of a valid award is 'final' and 'binding' on the parties. However, the article gives no guidance as to the meaning of these terms. 'Final' in the context of art. 32 is generally taken to mean that the award is no longer capable of revision by the tribunal, and that there is no appeal from or recourse against it before the presiding tribunal or any second-tier tribunal. In a broader context, final can also mean that the award is no longer capable of being overturned under the mandatory law of the arbitration. Whether an award is final in this broader sense will depend upon whether all available judicial recourse under that law has been exhausted. 'Binding' is generally taken to refer to the fact that an award will impose mandatory legal obligations on the parties. The criteria for a binding award will generally be determined by the mandatory law of the arbitration. In the *CME Czech Republic* and *Methanex* (Award) arbitrations both tribunals emphasised that partial awards granted were final and binding and that the Rules provided no mechanism for appeal, re-hearing or revision other than the provisions regarding interpretation or correction within a thirty-day time period.

3. Technical requirements. Under art. 32(2) and (4) an award must be in writing and include the date and place of the award's making. Furthermore, an award 'shall be signed by the arbitrators', that is be signed by all members of the arbitral tribunal. In the event that there are three arbitrators and one arbitrator fails to sign, the award must state the reason for this failure. In certain jurisdictions an award may not be binding unless signed by all the arbitrators.

4. Statement of reasons. Art. 32(3) states that the tribunal must include its reasons in the award, unless the parties have agreed that no reasons need be given. According to the travaux préparatoires, the parties' agreement on this point may be either express or implied.[42] The Rules provide no guidance as to the substance and form a statement of reasons should take. Equally, the question of whether dissenting opinions should be included with an award is left to the mandatory law of the arbitration.

Add.1 (1975), reprinted in (1976) VII UNCITRAL Ybk 166, 178 (Commentary on Draft Article 27, para. 1).
42. UNCITRAL, *Report on Ninth Session* (1976), UN Doc A/31/17, para. 157, reprinted in (1976) VII UNCITRAL Ybk 66, 77.

5. Publication. Art. 32(5) establishes the presumption that the award is confidential unless the parties agree to make it public. This presumption of confidentiality applies only to the award and not to any other aspect of the proceedings. such as the hearing or deliberations. The Rules do not contain a general rule of privacy or confidentiality regarding the arbitral process as a whole (see art. 25, note 6).

6. Copies. Art. 32(6) requires that the tribunal must transmit a final, signed copy of an award to the parties once it has been rendered. This communication of the award will notify the parties of their rights and obligations under it and will trigger the thirty-day period for requesting post-award proceedings under arts. 35, 36 and 37. It will also provide the parties with the documentation necessary to enforce the award before national courts. Although art. 32(6) is clearly designed so that the parties receive a copy of the award promptly, it contains no specific time limit for the award's communication.

7. Filing and registration. Art. 32(7) imposes a duty on a tribunal to file or register an award where the governing arbitration law requires such an action. For example, section 1058 of the Dutch Code of Civil Procedure requires a tribunal to file an original copy of its award with the courts as soon as possible after the award has been made.

[Applicable law, amiable compositeur]

Article 33

(1) The arbitral tribunal shall apply the law designated by the parties as applicable to the substance of the dispute. Failing such designation by the parties, the arbitral tribunal shall apply the law determined by the conflict of laws rules which it considers applicable.

(2) The arbitral tribunal shall decide as amiable compositeur or ex aequo et bono only if the parties have expressly authorised the arbitral tribunal to do so and if the law applicable to the arbitral procedure permits such arbitration.

(3) In all cases, the arbitral tribunal shall decide in accordance with the terms of the contract and shall take into account the usages of the trade applicable to the transaction.

1. Determination by the parties. The parties may designate the law that will apply to the substance of their dispute. However, as noted in the travaux préparatoires, their ability to choose may be limited by the mandatory law of the arbitration. For example, in some jurisdictions, parties may only choose as the law applicable to the substance of their dispute the law of a jurisdiction having some real connection with the transaction.[43]

---

43. *Report of the Secretary–General on the Revised Draft Set of Arbitration Rules,*

2. Determination by the arbitrators. Where the parties have failed to designate the applicable law, the tribunal shall apply the law determined by the conflict of laws rules 'which it considers applicable'. The applicable substantive law should therefore be determined by the arbitrators on the basis of conflict of laws rules, rather then by way of a direct determination (voie directe). However, a tribunal has considerable flexibility as to which conflict of laws rules to apply, and may refer to conflict of laws rules other than those of the place of arbitration where it is considered appropriate to do so.

3. Amiable compositeur and ex aequo et bono. A tribunal shall assume the role of amiable compositeur or decide ex aequo et bono if two conditions are fulfilled. Firstly, the parties must have expressly authorised the tribunal to assume such a role and, secondly, the law applicable to the proceedings must permit this. Both terms connote that a tribunal has a greater freedom to decide issues of evidence and/or (quantification of) damages than would otherwise be the case under the applicable arbitration law. The terms were retained as separate concepts on the grounds that they had different connotations in various national legal systems,[44] and their exact scope and meaning will depend on the applicable arbitration law. Note that jurisdictions adopting the UNCITRAL Model Law, according to art. 28(3) of that Law, recognise the power of a tribunal to decide ex aequo et bono or as amiable compositeur, subject to the authorisation of the parties.

4. Terms of the contract and trade usages. Art. 33(3) states that a tribunal shall decide 'in accordance with the terms of the contract and shall take into account the usages of the trade applicable to the transaction'. A tribunal should therefore apply the terms of the contract at issue both where an applicable law has been designated and where it has been authorised to act as amiable compositeur or ex aequo et bono. Art. 33(3) establishes the primacy of the terms of the contract over applicable trade usages; the latter have a supplementary role should the contract be unclear.

[Settlement or other grounds for termination]

Article 34

(1) If, before the award is made, the parties agree on a settlement of the dispute, the arbitral tribunal shall either issue an order for the termination of the arbitral proceedings or, if requested by both parties and accepted by the tribunal, record the settlement in the form of an

---

UNCITRAL, 9th Session, Addendum 1 (Commentary), UN Doc A/CN.9/112/Add.1 (1975), reprinted in (1976) VII UNCITRAL Ybk 166, 178 (Commentary on Draft Article 28, para. 1).

44. UNCITRAL, *Report on Ninth Session* (1976), UN Doc A/31/17, para. 175, reprinted in (1976) VII UNCITRAL Ybk 66, 78 (1976) (Commentary on Draft Article 28, para. 3).

arbitral award on agreed terms. The arbitral tribunal is not obliged to give reasons for such an award.

(2) If, before the award is made, the continuation of the arbitral proceedings becomes unnecessary or impossible for any reason not mentioned in paragraph 1, the arbitral tribunal shall inform the parties of its intention to issue an order for the termination of the proceedings. The arbitral tribunal shall have the power to issue such an order unless a party raises justifiable grounds for objection.

(3) Copies of the order for termination of the arbitral proceedings or of the arbitral award on agreed terms, signed by the arbitrators, shall be communicated by the arbitral tribunal to the parties. Where an arbitral award on agreed terms is made, the provisions of article 32, paragraphs 2 and 4 to 7, shall apply.

1. Termination order. Art. 34(1) sets out two scenarios for dealing with a settlement should one take place. Firstly, the tribunal may issue an order for the termination of proceedings. The parties' settlement agreement will then be rendered as a contract between them rather than as an award, enforceable to the extent that the governing contact law permits.

2. Award. Alternatively, the parties may have their settlement recorded as an award on the agreed terms. As an award, the recorded settlement will generally be enforceable both domestically and internationally. For an example of an award on agreed terms see the *Sun Company, Inc.* arbitration. Art. 34(1) implies that a tribunal has discretion as to whether to record a settlement, as the parties' decision to record their settlement as an award must be 'accepted by the tribunal'. However, it has been suggested that only a light standard of review is appropriate and that the types of situation in which a tribunal should refuse to record are where the settlement contains flagrant breaches of law or of public policy. In the unique context of the Tribunal, during Case No. A/1 (Issue II), it was held that 'although the Tribunal, when deciding on a request under Art. 34, should not attempt to review the reasonableness of the settlement in the place of the arbitrating parties, the Tribunal can refuse to record a settlement in the form of an award, provided that it does not act arbitrarily'. A tribunal may only record settlements that fall within its jurisdiction. Once the settlement is recorded as an award, the arbitration will come to an end. If a request for the recording of a settlement agreement is denied, the tribunal may issue an order terminating proceedings, unless the parties agree to continue with the arbitration.[45]

---

45. *Report of the Secretary-General on the Revised Draft Set of Arbitration Rules*, UNCITRAL, 9th Session, Addendum 1 (Commentary), UN Doc A/CN.9/112/Add.1 (1975), reprinted in (1976) VII UNCITRAL Ybk 166, 179 (Commentary on Draft Article 29, para. 1).

3. Other grounds for termination. Art. 34(2) states that, in all other circumstances where continuation of proceedings becomes 'unnecessary' or 'impossible', a tribunal shall inform the parties of its intention to terminate proceedings. The most typical instance of continuation becoming unnecessary or impossible would be where a claimant decides to withdraw his claim. Once a tribunal has notified the parties of its intention, it shall then have the power to issue an order terminating proceedings unless a party raises 'justifiable grounds' for objection. It can be inferred from the Tribunal's decision in the *Cherafat* case that withdrawal of a claim under duress would constitute a justifiable ground for an objection.

4. Technical requirements. Art. 34(3) states that an award on agreed terms must satisfy the technical requirements governing the form and effect of an award contained in art. 32(2) and (4) to (7) of the Rules. Art. 32(3) is inapplicable pursuant to art. 34(1), which provides that a tribunal need not give reasons. Finally, the tribunal is required to communicate to the parties copies of the award on agreed terms or the order for termination of the proceedings.

[Interpretation of the award]

Article 35

(1) Within thirty days after the receipt of the award, either party, with notice to the other party, may request that the arbitral tribunal give an interpretation of the award.

(2) The interpretation shall be given in writing within forty-five days after the receipt of the request. The interpretation shall form part of the award and the provisions of article 32, paragraphs 2 to 7, shall apply.

1. Interpretations. Art. 35(1) establishes a procedure by which a party may ask a tribunal to provide an interpretation of an award it has rendered. The interpretation process is intended to provide 'clarification of the award' by resolving any ambiguity and vagueness in its terms.[46] It is not intended to provide grounds for review when a party seeks to reargue the case or disagrees with a tribunal's conclusions, as was recognised by the Tribunal in *Parviz Karim-Panahi* (stating that likewise, there is no basis for review of an award because of objections to the conduct of the proceedings) and by the NAFTA tribunal during the *Methanex* (Letter) arbitration. The interpretation procedure is not intended to allow a party to raise new arguments or introduce new evidence, as has been confirmed by the Tribunal on numerous occasions.

---

46. *Report of the Secretary-General on the Revised Draft Set of Arbitration Rules*, UNCITRAL, 9th Session, Addendum 1 (Commentary), UN Doc A/CN.9/112/Add.1 (1975), reprinted in (1976) VII UNCITRAL Ybk 166, 180 (Commentary on Draft Article 30, para. 2).

2. Shall be given. Should a party request one, an interpretation 'shall be given'. However, provision of an interpretation shall only be mandatory if a party's request falls within the scope of art. 35 as determined by the arbitral tribunal. In the *Ford Aerospace* arbitration, the Tribunal rejected a request for an interpretation on the grounds that it could not identify any ambiguity in the award or other basis upon which an interpretation within the meaning of art. 35 could be based. It is good practice for a tribunal to set out its reasons for rejecting a request for an interpretation should it decide to do so.

3. Tribunal authority. Questions arose during the drafting of art. 35 as to how a tribunal could retain post-award authority to provide an interpretation (particularly in jurisdictions where interpretation was not expressly permitted). It was concluded that, through adoption of the Rules, the parties have concluded an express agreement to extend a tribunal's jurisdiction for the purposes of interpretation.[47]

4. Technical requirements. Art. 35(2) specifies that an interpretation shall 'form part of the award', and requires that an interpretation satisfy the technical requirements for an award set out in art. 32(2) to (7). Although art. 35 does not expressly require it, the majority vote rule in art. 31 should be deemed equally applicable.

5. Time limits. The parties have thirty days after receipt of an award to submit a request for interpretation. The requesting party must give notice to all other parties of its request. A tribunal must render an interpretation in writing within forty-five days of receiving a request by a party. A tribunal does not have authority to provide an interpretation of an award on its own motion.

6. Legal effect. The enforceability of an interpretation as part of an award is determined by the mandatory law of the arbitration. In the *Wintershall* arbitration, the governing Dutch law authorised the making of additional awards, but was silent as to interpretations. In order to ensure the enforceability of the interpretation it had given, the tribunal stated that the interpretation it had rendered could also constitute an additional award under art. 37.

[Correction of the award]

Article 36

(1) Within thirty days after the receipt of the award, either party, with notice to the other party, may request the arbitral tribunal to correct in the award any errors in computation, any clerical or typographical errors, or any errors of similar nature. The arbitral tribunal may within

---

[47]. *Report of the Secretary-General on the Revised Draft Set of Arbitration Rules*, UNCITRAL, 9th Session, Addendum 1 (Commentary), UN Doc A/CN.9/112/Add.1 (1975), reprinted in (1976) VII UNCITRAL Ybk 166, 180 (Commentary on Draft Article 30, para. 2).

thirty days after the communication of the award make such corrections on its own initiative.

(2) Such corrections shall be in writing, and the provisions of article 32, paragraphs 2 to 7, shall apply.

1. Correction. Art. 36(1) permits a tribunal to correct (unintentional) errors in an award, whether of a computational, clerical, typographical or other similar nature. For example, in the *American International Group* arbitration, the Tribunal appended a note to the award stating that, pursuant to art. 36, a typographical error in the final section text of the Award should be corrected from 'fifty' to 'forty'. The travaux préparatoires make clear that a tribunal has discretion as to whether it wishes to issue a correction.[48] A tribunal may therefore decide against correction of an error if that error has no impact upon an award's validity.

2. Limitations of the correction process. The correction process is limited to a restoration of the award's proper contents; it is not intended to be a means for revisiting an award in the sense of a change in the substantive holding (as stated by the Tribunal in *Harold Birnbaum*). The line between correction of an error and revision of a reasoned conclusion can be seen in the practice of the Tribunal. During the *Picker* arbitration the respondent sought correction of the wording used to describe the claimant. In *Petrolane*, correction was sought regarding the characterisation of an earlier decision as an award. In both cases, the Tribunal held the requests to be outside the scope of art. 36 as they did not involve an unintended calculation, mistake or typographical error.

3. Technical requirements and time limits. The requesting party must notify all other parties of its request for correction. The correction procedure is also subject to a time limit. Either the parties must request correction within thirty days of receiving the award, or the arbitrators must decide to correct the award within thirty days of its communication to the parties. Art. 36(2) states that a correction must be in writing and that it shall be subject to the technical requirements set out in art. 32(2) to (7).

[Additional award]

Article 37

(1) Within thirty days after the receipt of the award, either party, with notice to the other party, may request the arbitral tribunal to make an

---

48. *Report of the Secretary-General on the Revised Draft Set of Arbitration Rules*, UNCITRAL, 9th Session, Addendum 1 (Commentary), UN Doc A/CN.9/112/Add.1 (1975), reprinted in (1976) VII UNCITRAL Ybk 166, 180 (Commentary on Draft Article 31).

additional award as to claims presented in the arbitral proceedings but omitted from the award.

(2) If the arbitral tribunal considers the request for an additional award to be justified and considers that the omission can be rectified without any further hearings or evidence, it shall complete its award within sixty days after the receipt of the request.

(3) When an additional award is made, the provisions of article 32, paragraphs 2 to 7, shall apply.

1. Additional awards. Art. 37(1) authorises a tribunal to make an additional award where a claim or claims were presented during proceedings but have been omitted from the initial award. The article was deemed necessary as in most jurisdictions, an award which fails to address all the claims brought before a tribunal will not be recognised or enforced. The article thus averts the possibility of an arbitration being invalidated because a tribunal has failed to rule on every claim when making its award. As with arts. 35 and 36, the drafters intended art. 37 to serve as an express agreement by the parties to extend a tribunal's jurisdiction over the dispute, in order to enable it to make additional awards.

2. Justified. Under art. 37(2) a tribunal has a discretion to issue an additional award whenever it considers a party's request for such an award to be 'justified'. A tribunal may therefore reject a request that it considers unjustified, for example on grounds that there was no omission of claims from the award, that the award sufficiently addressed the supposed omissions (see *Harris International Telecommunications* (Decision)), or that the party's request generally falls outside the scope of art. 37 (see Case No. A/27).

3. Without further hearings or evidence. A tribunal may only issue an additional award if the omission from the initial award can be rectified 'without any further hearings or evidence'. In effect, a tribunal can only act on the basis of evidence already before it at the time that it issued the incomplete award.[49] A tribunal's power to issue an additional award is restricted to those issues that were formally presented during the arbitral proceedings.

4. Technical requirements. An additional award is an 'award' within the meaning of the Rules and under art. 37(3) shall be subject to the technical requirements set out in art. 32(2) to (7). Although art. 37 does not expressly require it, the majority vote rule in art. 31 should be deemed equally applicable.

5. Time limits. A party has thirty days after receipt of an award to submit a request for an additional award. A tribunal has no express authority to make

---

49. *Report of the Secretary-General on the Revised Draft Set of Arbitration Rules*, UNCITRAL, 9th Session, Addendum 1 (Commentary), UN Doc A/CN.9/112/Add.1 (1975), 7 U.Y.B. 166, 181 (Commentary on Draft Article 32 para. 2).

an additional award of its own accord where no request has been made. If a tribunal chooses to grant a party's request, it has sixty days from the date of receipt of the request to render the additional award.

6. Finality of awards in general. The Rules, like most arbitral rules, provide no explicit authority to a tribunal to reconsider its award. The initial practice of the Tribunal was to refuse requests for reconsideration (based on an alleged inherent power) that exceed the scope of review under arts. 35 to 37, on the basis that such requests fall outside the scope of arts. 35 to 37 (see *American Bell* (Decision)), and that the Tribunal does not have the power to entertain the requests. In later cases, all involving allegations of fraud, the Tribunal has suggested that it might have an inherent power to reopen a case outside the procedural rules (see *Harold Birnbaum*).

[Costs of the arbitration]
Article 38

The arbitral tribunal shall fix the costs of arbitration in its award. The term 'costs' includes only:
  (a) **The fees of the arbitral tribunal to be stated separately as to each arbitrator and to be fixed by the tribunal itself in accordance with article 39;**
  (b) **The travel and other expenses incurred by the arbitrators;**
  (c) **The costs of expert advice and of other assistance required by the arbitral tribunal;**
  (d) **The travel and other expenses of witnesses to the extent such expenses are approved by the arbitral tribunal;**
  (e) **The costs for legal representation and assistance of the successful party if such costs were claimed during the arbitral proceedings, and only to the extent that the arbitral tribunal determines that the amount of such costs is reasonable;**
  (f) **Any fees and expenses of the appointing authority as well as the expenses of the Secretary-General of the Permanent Court of Arbitration at The Hague.**

1. Duty to fix the costs. Art. 38 requires a tribunal to fix the costs of arbitration in its award (note that art. 40(3) contains a similar provision requiring a tribunal, when issuing an award on agreed terms or an order for the termination of proceedings, to fix the costs in the text of the award or order). Other than the arbitrators' fees, the costs may be stated as a lump sum figure.[50] Art. 38(a) requires the arbitrators' fees to be stated separately 'as to each arbitrator'.

---

50. *Report of the Secretary-General on the Revised Draft Set of Arbitration Rules*, UNCITRAL, 9th Session, Addendum 1 (Commentary), UN Doc A/CN.9/112/

2. Items constituting costs. The article sets out an exhaustive list of the items of expenditure incurred by either the parties or the tribunal that will be classified as the 'costs' of arbitration.

3. Arbitrators' fees and expenses. Arbitrators' fees, travel and other incidental expenses are classified as costs under art. 38(a) to (b).

4. Costs of expert advice. Under art. 38(c), the costs of 'expert advice' and 'other assistance required by the tribunal' will also be classified a costs. 'Expert advice' covers both the situation where a party hires an expert witness and the situation where a tribunal enlists a third party expert. 'Other assistance' may include expenditure for secretarial or stenographic support, or for language translation.

5. Witnesses' expenses. Witnesses' travel and other expenses will be classified as costs under art. 38(d) to the extent that such expenses are approved by the tribunal. The travaux préparatoires make it clear that a tribunal has the power both to approve and to apportion such expenses.

5. Costs of legal representation. Under art. 38(e), the expenses associated with the successful party's legal representation are included as costs subject to two qualifications. Such expenses must be 'claimed during the arbitral proceedings' and must also be determined by the tribunal to be 'reasonable', thus imposing an additional threshold for such costs.

6. Costs of the Secretary-General and appointing authority. Under art. 38(f) the fees and expenses of the appointing authority will be included in the costs of the arbitration, as will the expenses of the Secretary-General. Note, however, that the fees of the Secretary-General are not included.

7. Enforcement. In order to facilitate enforcement, a judgment as to costs should be stated in the form of an award rather than an order where possible.

[Arbitrators' fees]
Article 39

(1) The fees of the arbitral tribunal shall be reasonable in amount, taking into account the amount in dispute, the complexity of the subject-matter, the time spent by the arbitrators and any other relevant circumstances of the case.

(2) If an appointing authority has been agreed upon by the parties or designated by the Secretary-General of the Permanent Court of Arbitration at The Hague, and if that authority has issued a schedule

---

Add.1 (1975), reprinted in (1976) VII UNCITRAL Ybk 166, 181 (Commentary on Draft Article 33, para. 1).

of fees for arbitrators in international cases which it administers, the arbitral tribunal in fixing its fees shall take that schedule of fees into account to the extent that it considers appropriate in the circumstances of the case.

(3) If such appointing authority has not issued a schedule of fees for arbitrators in international cases, any party may at any time request the appointing authority to furnish a statement setting forth the basis for establishing fees which is customarily followed in international cases in which the authority appoints arbitrators. If the appointing authority consents to provide such a statement, the arbitral tribunal in fixing its fees shall take such information into account to the extent that it considers appropriate in the circumstances of the case.

(4) In cases referred to in paragraphs 2 and 3, when a party so requests and the appointing authority consents to perform the function, the arbitral tribunal shall fix its fees only after consultation with the appointing authority which may make any comment it deems appropriate to the arbitral tribunal concerning the fees.

1. Reasonable in amount. Art. 39 deals with the subject of arbitrators' fees. The purpose behind the article is to limit arbitrators' power to fix their own fees and thus avoid abuse. Art. 39(1) requires that a tribunal's fees be 'reasonable in amount'. The Rules do not establish or incorporate a schedule of fees, instead requiring that four factors be taken into consideration when setting the fees: the amount in dispute, the complexity of the subject matter, the time spent by the arbitrators, and any other relevant circumstances of the case. The parties may modify art. 39 in order that the arbitrators' fees are calculated by reference to either a bespoke fee schedule or one provided by an arbitral institution. For example, in the ad hoc *Glamis Gold* arbitration, art. 39 was modified to state that the arbitrators' fees would be determined in accordance with the ICSID Schedule of Fees.

2. Appointing authority's schedule of fees. Art. 39(2) states that the arbitrators shall take into account any schedule of fees issued by the appointing authority for use in international arbitrations administered by that authority when setting their fees. Any such schedule must be taken into account only 'to the extent that the tribunal considers necessary'.

3. Statement of customary practice. Art. 39(3) offers an alternative procedure for use where an appointing authority has not issued a schedule of fees. Any party may petition the appointing authority at any time to provide a statement setting out the way in which fees are usually established in the arbitrations for which that appointing authority appoints arbitrators. The parties will thus have a basis for comparison when assessing the fees set for their own arbitration. Again, the tribunal is bound to adhere to the appointing authority's statement of customary practice only to the extent that it considers appropriate in the circumstances of the case.

4. Consultation. Art. 39(4) establishes a party's right to request that the arbitrators consult the appointing authority regarding their proposed fees. Should the appointing authority agree to the consultation, it may make 'any comment it deems appropriate' to the arbitrators regarding their fees. However, the arbitrators are not required to heed the appointing authority's suggestions.

[Apportionment of costs]

Article 40

1. Except as provided in paragraph 2, the costs of arbitration shall in principle be borne by the unsuccessful party. However, the arbitral tribunal may apportion each of such costs between the parties if it determines that apportionment is reasonable, taking into account the circumstances of the case.

(2) With respect to the costs of legal representation and assistance referred to in article 38, paragraph (e), the arbitral tribunal, taking into account the circumstances of the case, shall be free to determine which party shall bear such costs or may apportion such costs between the parties if it determines that apportionment is reasonable.

(3) When the arbitral tribunal issues an order for the termination of the arbitral proceedings or makes an award on agreed terms, it shall fix the costs of arbitration referred to in article 38 and article 39, paragraph 1, in the text of that order or award.

(4) No additional fees may be charged by an arbitral tribunal for interpretation or correction or completion of its award under articles 35 to 37.

1. Non-legal costs. Art. 40(1) establishes the way in which the non-legal costs of the arbitration should be awarded. The article therefore deals with the items of expenditure set out in art. 38(a) to (d) and (f). The starting point is that 'in principle', the unsuccessful party shall bear all the costs of the arbitration except legal costs. However, art. 40(1) also provides that a tribunal may apportion each of the non-legal costs between the parties if it determines that apportionment is reasonable having regard to the circumstances of the case. In practice, a tribunal thus has a large amount of flexibility as to the award and apportionment of non-legal costs.

2. Legal costs. With regard to legal costs (that is, the items of expenditure set out in art. 30(e)), the drafters agreed that 'no principle of compensation should be laid down'.[51] Under art. 40(2), the costs of legal representation and

---

51. *Summary Reference of the 13th Meeting of the Committee of the Whole (II)*, UNCITRAL, 9th Session, UN Doc A/CN.9/9/C.2/SR.13, at 4, para. 20 (1976).

assistance are therefore excluded from the general principle in art. 40(1). A tribunal is free to determine which party should bear the legal costs, or to apportion the costs should it determine that apportionment is a reasonable option. As with non-legal costs, in reaching its decision on the award of legal costs, a tribunal must have regard to the circumstances of the case.

3. The circumstances of the case. Both the Rules and the travaux préparatoires are silent as to the meaning of the phrase 'circumstances of the case'. The practice of the Tribunal, along with that of other international tribunals, suggests that the factors forming part of the circumstances of the case include the parties' success, the parties' conduct, and the parties' nature.

[Deposit of costs]
Article 41

(1) The arbitral tribunal, on its establishment, may request each party to deposit an equal amount as an advance for the costs referred to in article 38, paragraphs (a), (b) and (c).

(2) During the course of the arbitral proceedings the arbitral tribunal may request supplementary deposits from the parties.

(3) If an appointing authority has been agreed upon by the parties or designated by the Secretary-General of the Permanent Court of Arbitration at The Hague, and when a party so requests and the appointing authority consents to perform the function, the arbitral tribunal shall fix the amounts of any deposits or supplementary deposits only after consultation with the appointing authority which may make any comments to the arbitral tribunal which it deems appropriate concerning the amount of such deposits and supplementary deposits.

(4) If the required deposits are not paid in full within thirty days after the receipt of the request, the arbitral tribunal shall so inform the parties in order that one or another of them may make the required payment. If such payment is not made, the arbitral tribunal may order the suspension or termination of the arbitral proceedings.

(5) After the award has been made, the arbitral tribunal shall render an accounting to the parties of the deposits received and return any unexpended balance to the parties.

1. Initial deposits. Art. 41(1) states that, at the outset of the arbitration, a tribunal may request monetary deposits in equal amounts from the parties, as advances against the items of expenditure set out in art. 38(a) to (c). The items listed at art. 38(a) to (c) comprise the reasonable fees of the arbitrators and their travel and other expenses, and the costs of expert advice and other assistance required by the tribunal.

2. Supplementary deposits. Art. 41(2) authorises a tribunal to require additional deposits to be placed during proceedings.

3. Division of deposits. In practice, a tribunal will typically order the parties to bear the financial burden of providing deposits equally, making proportional contributions based on the number of parties involved. For examples of equal division between the parties, see the Tribunal *Shahin Shaine Ebrahimi* arbitration and the NAFTA *SD Myers* and *Canfor Corp.* arbitrations. In certain instances, deposits may be divided differently. For example, in the *Behring International* arbitration, there was a disagreement as to whether an expert should be appointed, with the claimants opposed and the respondents in favour. The Tribunal appointed an expert, and required the respondents only to pay an advance deposit as to that expert's costs.

4. Consultation. Art. 41(3) states that the appointing authority may, at the request of a party, serve a consultative function regarding a tribunal's requests for deposits. If the appointing authority agrees to a party's request for consultation, then the tribunal must confer with the appointing authority before fixing the amount of the deposit. The appointing authority may provide the tribunal with any comments which it deems appropriate concerning the amount of any deposit or supplementary deposit.

5. Consequences of failure to pay a deposit. Art. 41(4) authorises a tribunal to suspend or terminate the arbitral proceedings in the case of the non-payment of a requested deposit. If one or both parties fail to make a deposit in full within thirty days of receipt of a formal request, the tribunal must inform the parties of the deficiency in order to allow one of the parties to satisfy the balance. If neither party wishes to cover the unpaid deposit, then the tribunal is empowered to suspend or terminate proceedings.

6. Return of deposits. Art. 41(5) requires the return of unexpended deposit monies to the parties 'after the award has been made'. The unexpended portions of the deposits must be returned to the parties in amounts proportionate to their relative contributions, plus interest. A tribunal is also required to render an accounting to the parties of all deposits received. This may include information on the amount of deposits obtained from a particular party, and how each portion of those deposits was spent, as well as any relevant account information and the applicable interest rates.

7. Administration. The degree to which a tribunal is involved in managing deposited funds may depend upon whether or not the arbitration is administered by an arbitral institution. The UNCITRAL Notes on Organizing Arbitral Proceedings caution at note 131, para. 30 that, in cases of unadministered arbitrations, the parties should ensure that 'matters such as the type and location of the account in which the money will be kept and how deposits will be managed' are clarified.

INTERNATIONAL CENTRE FOR SETTLEMENT OF INVESTMENT DISPUTES (ICSID) RULES OF PROCEDURE FOR ARBITRATION PROCEEDINGS (ARBITRATION RULES), 2006*

(As amended, effective 10 April 2006)

CHAPTER I. ESTABLISHMENT OF THE TRIBUNAL

[General obligations]

Arbitration Rule 1

(1) Upon notification of the registration of the request for arbitration, the parties shall, with all possible dispatch, proceed to constitute a Tribunal, with due regard to Section 2 of Chapter IV of the Convention.

(2) Unless such information is provided in the request, the parties shall communicate to the Secretary-General as soon as possible any provisions agreed by them regarding the number of arbitrators and the method of their appointment.

(3) The majority of the arbitrators shall be nationals of States other than the State party to the dispute and of the State whose national is a party to the dispute, unless the sole arbitrator or each individual member of the Tribunal is appointed by agreement of the parties. Where the Tribunal is to consist of three members, a national of either of these States may not be appointed as an arbitrator by a party without the agreement of the other party to the dispute. Where the Tribunal is to consist of five or more members, nationals of either of these States may not be appointed as arbitrators by a party if appointment by the other party of the same number of arbitrators of either of these nationalities would result in a majority of arbitrators of these nationalities.

(4) No person who had previously acted as a conciliator or arbitrator in any proceeding for the settlement of the dispute may be appointed as a member of the Tribunal.

1. General. Rule 1 assumes that the parties have agreed on the constitution of the tribunal (that is, the number of arbitrators and the method of their appointment) prior to the registration of the request for arbitration, whereas Rule 2 applies where there is no such agreement. Where the parties have

---

* Reproduced with permission of the International Centre for Settlement of Investment Disputes (ICSID). The text reproduced here is valid at the time of reproduction and covers developments through the summer of 2008. As amendments may from time to time be made to the text, please refer to the website <http://icsid.worldbank.org> for the latest version.

agreed on the constitution of the tribunal, Rule 1 applies immediately and regardless of whether the agreement is part of the clause that originally granted consent to the arbitration or is part of an ad hoc agreement.

2. With all possible dispatch. Rule 1 restates the obligation in art. 37(1) to constitute the tribunal as soon as possible.

3. Subject to Section 2 of Chapter IV of the Convention. The Convention provides the parties with substantial freedom with regard to the constitution of the tribunal. Certain obligations in Section 2 of Chapter IV of the Convention are, however, mandatory, regardless of any agreement to the contrary between the parties. First, the number of arbitrators must be uneven (art. 37(2)(a)). Secondly, the majority of the arbitrators must be nationals of States other than the Contracting State party to the dispute and the State of nationality of the other party (art. 39). Finally, arbitrators appointed from outside the Panel of Arbitrators (see Section 4 of Chapter I of the Convention) must possess the qualities required of those on the Panel (art. 40(2)).

4. Request for arbitration. The Institution Rules, and not the Arbitration Rules, govern the commencement of ICSID arbitration. Rules 1 and 2 of the Institution Rules set out the nature of the information which a request should contain. Rule 2 of the Institution Rules is a useful checklist to confirm that the Centre has jurisdiction over the dispute and provides as follows:

(1) The request shall:
  (a) designate precisely each party to the dispute and state the address of each;
  (b) state, if one of the parties is a constituent subdivision or agency of a Contracting State, that it has been designated to the Centre by that State pursuant to Art. 25(1) of the Convention;
  (c) indicate the date of consent and the instruments in which it is recorded, including, if one party is a constituent subdivision or agency of a Contracting State, similar data on the approval of such consent by that State unless it had notified the Centre that no such approval is required;
  (d) indicate with respect to the party that is a national of a Contracting State:
    (i) its nationality on the date of consent; and
    (ii) if the party is a natural person:
      (A) his nationality on the date of the request; and
      (B) that he did not have the nationality of the Contracting State party to the dispute either on the date of consent or on the date of the request; or
    (iii) if the party is a juridical person who on the date of consent had the nationality of the Contracting State party to the dispute, the parties may agree that he should be treated as a national of another Contracting State for the purposes of the Convention;

(e) contain information concerning the issues in dispute indicating that there is, between the parties, a legal dispute arising directly out of an investment; and
(f) state, if the requesting party is a juridical person, that it has taken all necessary internal actions to authorise the request.

Further official information on filing a request can be found on the ICSID website at: <icsid.worldbank.org/ICSID/ICSID/HowToFileReq.jsp#IC>. Rule 3 of the Institution Rules provides that the requesting party may inform the Secretary-General, in the request for arbitration, of the number of arbitrators and their method of appointment should this have been agreed by the parties in advance. In practice, the requesting party should do so. Indeed, Rule 7(c) of the Institution Rules requires the Secretary-General to invite the parties to provide this information if they have not already done so.

5. Agreement between the parties as to each arbitrator. Rule 1(3) will not apply where the parties have elected to agree between them the identity of each arbitrator, rather than merely the mechanism for their appointment. In order to take advantage of this exception, the parties must agree on every arbitrator – they may not oust the provision by agreeing on two arbitrators who together appoint a third.

6. Nationality of arbitrators. Rule 1(3) is designed to ensure the fair application of the art. 39 restriction on a majority of arbitrators being nationals of either State party to the dispute. It does so by preventing any national of a party being appointed to a three-person tribunal, unless the parties have appointed that arbitrator by agreement. This is to cure the otherwise inequitable consequence of art. 39 that the party acting first in the appointment of a three-member tribunal could appoint a national arbitrator and thereby preclude the other party from doing the same. Rule 1(3), therefore, prohibits any party from unilaterally appointing a national or co-national to a three-member tribunal. This prohibition can be excluded by agreement and has been so excluded in a number of cases. Although there have not been any five-member ICSID tribunals, in such a case, either party would be entitled to appoint a national candidate provided the majority of the tribunal was composed of non-nationals.

7. Impartiality of arbitrators. Rule 1(4) is based on the general principle that no person should act more than once in an investigation of the same dispute. This restriction only applies where the previous proceedings have actually taken place and may be waived by agreement. It is applicable whoever makes the appointment; whether the parties, the Chairman or other appointing authority. Similarly, Reg. 12 of the Administrative and Financial Regulations provides that the Secretary-General, the deputy Secretaries-General and ICSID staff members may not serve on any tribunal. See art. 52(3) for a similar restriction relating to the appointment of ad hoc annulment committees.

[Method of constituting the tribunal in the absence of previous agreement]

Arbitration Rule 2

(1) If the parties, at the time of the registration of the request for arbitration, have not agreed upon the number of arbitrators and the method of their appointment, they shall, unless they agree otherwise, follow the following procedure:
  (a) the requesting party shall, within 10 days after the registration of the request, propose to the other party the appointment of a sole arbitrator or of a specified uneven number of arbitrators and specify the method proposed for their appointment;
  (b) within 20 days after receipt of the proposals made by the requesting party, the other party shall:
     (i) accept such proposals; or
     (ii) make other proposals regarding the number of arbitrators and the method of their appointment;
  (c) within 20 days after receipt of the reply containing any such other proposals, the requesting party shall notify the other party whether it accepts or rejects such proposals.

(2) The communications provided for in paragraph (1) shall be made or promptly confirmed in writing and shall either be transmitted through the Secretary-General or directly between the parties with a copy to the Secretary-General. The parties shall promptly notify the Secretary-General of the contents of any agreement reached.

(3) At any time 60 days after the registration of the request, if no agreement on another procedure is reached, either party may inform the Secretary-General that it chooses the formula provided for in Article 37(2)(b) of the Convention. The Secretary-General shall thereupon promptly inform the other party that the Tribunal is to be constituted in accordance with that Article.

1. General. The purpose of Rule 2 is to provide a procedure for the parties to reach agreement on the constitution of a tribunal where they have not done so prior to the registration of a request for arbitration. Where they have previously agreed, Rule 1 applies. Rule 2 does not deal with the actual appointment of arbitrators, but merely prescribes a procedural framework within which the parties can agree, even after a dispute has commenced, upon the constitution of the tribunal and the method of appointment of arbitrators. A party cannot, however, prevent the appointment of an ICSID tribunal by being uncooperative. Rule 2(3) imposes the default rule in art. 37(2)(b) should the parties be unable to reach an agreement.

2. Time limits. The time limits set out in Rule 2 are intended to assist the parties in agreeing the constitution of the tribunal including appointment of arbitrators within sixty days of registration of the request for arbitration. In practice, the process will often take longer, as parties will extend the applicable time limits by agreement. Unless they are extended, the requesting party is required to take the initiative and make its first proposal within ten days. Rule 2(1)(b) gives the other party an opportunity to present any counter-proposals within twenty days. Thereafter, the requesting party has a further twenty days to respond.

3. Communication with the Secretary-General. The requirement in Rule 2(2) that all communications pursuant to Rule 2(1) be communicated through, or to, the Secretary-General is in accordance with the general obligation as to means of communication in Reg. 24(1) of the Administrative and Financial Regulations.

4. Failure to reach agreement. If no agreement concerning the number of arbitrators and the method of their appointment is reached after sixty days (or such other time period as has been agreed), Rule 2(3) provides that either party may abandon the procedure in Rule 2 and opt for the default rule in art. 37(2)(b).

[Appointment of arbitrators to a tribunal constituted in accordance with Convention art. 37(2)(b)]

Arbitration Rule 3

(1) If the Tribunal is to be constituted in accordance with Article 37(2)(b) of the Convention:

   (a) either party shall in a communication to the other party:
      (i) name two persons, identifying one of them, who shall not have the same nationality as nor be a national of either party, as the arbitrator appointed by it, and the other as the arbitrator proposed to be the President of the Tribunal; and
      (ii) invite the other party to concur in the appointment of the arbitrator proposed to be the President of the Tribunal and to appoint another arbitrator;
   (b) promptly upon receipt of this communication the other party shall, in its reply:
      (i) name a person as the arbitrator appointed by it, who shall not have the same nationality as nor be a national of either party; and
      (ii) concur in the appointment of the arbitrator proposed to be the President of the Tribunal or name another person as the arbitrator proposed to be President;
   (c) promptly upon receipt of the reply containing such a proposal, the initiating party shall notify the other party whether it concurs in the appointment of the arbitrator proposed by that party to be the President of the Tribunal.

ICSID Arbitration Rules, Rule 3

(2) The communications provided for in this Rule shall be made or promptly confirmed in writing and shall either be transmitted through the Secretary-General or directly between the parties with a copy to the Secretary-General.

1. General. Rule 3 applies whenever a tribunal is to be constituted by the parties in accordance with art. 37(2)(b), either because they have specifically agreed to adopt the procedure under art. 37(2)(b) or because they have failed to agree on the tribunal's constitution.

2. Art. 37(2)(b) default rule. Art. 37(2)(b) provides that, where the parties do not agree upon the number of arbitrators or the method of their appointment, the tribunal shall consist of three arbitrators; one arbitrator appointed by each party and the third, who shall be president of the tribunal, appointed by agreement of the parties.

3. Procedure. Pursuant to Rule 3(1), each party has the opportunity to appoint one arbitrator. Art. 40 provides that any such arbitrator need not be on the Panel of Arbitrators, but must possess the qualities stated in art. 14(1). Each party also has the opportunity to nominate a candidate to sit as the tribunal's president, subject to the other party's agreement. The purpose of art. 37(2)(b) and Rule 3 is, as with Rule 2, to facilitate the appointment of a tribunal through agreement of the parties. If the parties choose to appoint their own arbitrator and agree on the proposed identity of the tribunal's president then, unless the arbitrators do not have the qualifications required by art. 14(1), the Secretary-General (who must be informed pursuant to Rule 5(1)) will not intervene further, save to contact the proposed appointees to confirm that they are willing to accept appointment (see Rule 5(2)). Art. 37(2)(b) is a mandatory provision which the parties cannot modify or waive. It does not allow for two arbitrators to select the third, or for three arbitrators together to agree on which of them shall be the president of the tribunal.

4. Time limits. Rule 3 is designed to expedite the process of appointing arbitrators. The two steps – each party making their unilateral appointments and each party proposing a third arbitrator – happen simultaneously, thus minimising the number of communications between the parties. Whilst there are no time limits stipulated in Rule 3, art. 38 and Rule 4 provide that after ninety days following the registration of the request (or such other period as the parties may agree), either party may request that the Chairman intervene and appoint any arbitrators not yet appointed. Once this request is made, a party which has not yet appointed an arbitrator has no further right to do so (although in practice the party may be consulted by the Secretary-General or the ICSID Secretariat).

5. Nationality. The provisions in Rule 3 concerning the nationality of arbitrators are designed to take account of the nationality restrictions in art. 39. Art. 39 provides that the majority of arbitrators may not be nationals or co-nationals of the parties, unless the parties agree otherwise. The president of the tribunal appointed pursuant to the art. 37(2)(b) procedure may be a national or co-national, because this appointment is made by agreement.

6. Communications with the Secretary-General. As with Rule 2(2), the requirement in Rule 3(2) that all communications pursuant to Rule 3(1) be through or copied to the Secretary-General accords with the general direction in Reg. 24(1) of the Administrative and Financial Regulations.

[Appointment of arbitrators by the Chairman of the Administrative Council]

Arbitration Rule 4

(1) If the Tribunal is not constituted within 90 days after the dispatch by the Secretary-General of the notice of registration, or such other period as the parties may agree, either party may, through the Secretary-General, address to the Chairman of the Administrative Council a request in writing to appoint the arbitrator or arbitrators not yet appointed and to designate an arbitrator to be the President of the Tribunal.

(2) The provision of paragraph (1) shall apply mutatis mutandis in the event that the parties have agreed that the arbitrators shall elect the President of the Tribunal and they fail to do so.

(3) The Secretary-General shall forthwith send a copy of the request to the other party.

(4) The Chairman shall use his best efforts to comply with that request within 30 days after its receipt. Before he proceeds to make an appointment or designation, with due regard to Articles 38 and 40(1) of the Convention, he shall consult both parties as far as possible.

(5) The Secretary-General shall promptly notify the parties of any appointment or designation made by the Chairman.

1. General. If the parties fail to constitute a tribunal within the ninety day period specified under art. 38, Rule 4 allows each party to request the Chairman to intervene and appoint any arbitrators that have not yet been appointed. This process is not automatic. Unless a party invokes the art. 38 procedure, the parties may continue to seek to reach agreement under any other procedure that they have agreed upon or under the art. 37(2)(b) default procedure. The ninety-day time period may be – and often is – extended by agreement. In practice, the constitution of many ICSID tribunals frequently takes longer than ninety days.

2. Failure to constitute the tribunal. Rule 4(1) allows either party to request that the Chairman make all or any remaining appointments if the parties cannot agree to do so themselves within the ninety-day time limit under art. 38. Rule 4(2) allows either party to request that the Chairman intervene to designate the president of the tribunal if the parties have agreed that the arbitrators are to make such a designation and they have failed to do so.

3. Request to the Chairman. The request to the Chairman must be made through the Secretary-General in writing. The request can be made jointly, or by either party separately. In practice, the Secretary-General or the ICSID Secretariat will manage the process of appointing the arbitrators and, in doing so, will seek to consult with both parties. The request under art. 38 and Rule 4 should include details of any appointments already made and the agreement (if any) between the parties regarding the constitution of the tribunal.

4. Communications by the Secretary-General. A party's request to the Chairman to intervene will be communicated to the other party by the Secretary-General. Once an appointment has been made by the Chairman pursuant to Rule 4(2), the Secretary-General must promptly notify the parties. At the same time the Secretary-General must, pursuant to Rule 5(2), seek confirmation that the proposed arbitrator has accepted the appointment.

5. Thirty-day time limit. The Chairman must use his best efforts to make his appointments within thirty days of receipt of the request to intervene. Subject to the parties' agreement otherwise, the combined time limits of art. 38 and Rule 4(4) result in the constitution of the tribunal within 120 days from the registration of the request for arbitration.

6. Chairman's obligation to appoint. Under Rule 4(4), the Chairman does not have any discretion as to whether to appoint the remaining arbitrators: he must do so if requested. When a Chairman makes appointments under art. 38 and Arbitration Rule 4, the arbitrators must be appointed from the Panel of Arbitrators and may not share the nationality of either party. The failure to appoint an arbitrator by this stage may indicate a lack of relevant expertise within the Panel of Arbitrators. The ICSID Secretariat will therefore sometimes propose arbitrators from outside the Panel, but their appointment will not be effective without the consent of the parties.

7. Chairman's obligation to consult. Rule 4(4) requires that the Chairman consult the parties as far as possible regarding appointments and designations. Joint or separate consultations may be held, and they can be either oral or written. Thus, a party that has made its appointment within the ninety-day period will usually have an opportunity to comment on the proposed appointment of the arbitrator to be appointed in lieu of the other party's appointment. Although the Chairman has a duty to consult, this does not give a party the power to frustrate proceedings or to delay an appointment by being uncooperative, as the Chairman may eventually make any appointment he sees fit.

[Acceptance of appointments]

Arbitration Rule 5

(1) The party or parties concerned shall notify the Secretary-General of the appointment of each arbitrator and indicate the method of his appointment.

(2) As soon as the Secretary-General has been informed by a party or the Chairman of the Administrative Council of the appointment of an arbitrator, he shall seek an acceptance from the appointee.

(3) If an arbitrator fails to accept his appointment within 15 days, the Secretary-General shall promptly notify the parties, and if appropriate the Chairman, and invite them to proceed to the appointment of another arbitrator in accordance with the method followed for the previous appointment.

1. General. The purpose of Rule 5(1) is to ensure that the Centre is kept informed of appointments for which the parties are responsible.

2. Communications through the Secretary-General. The Secretary-General and the Secretariat closely monitor the constitution of ICSID tribunals. Any agreement and all communications leading up to the tribunal's constitution must be communicated to the Secretary-General in accordance with Reg. 24 of the Administrative and Financial Regulations. The duty under Rule 5(1) to notify the Secretary-General rests upon the appointing party where the appointment is unilateral and upon both parties in the case of an appointment by agreement. In turn, under Rule 5(3), the Secretary-General must inform the parties and, if necessary, the Chairman or other appointing authority, of an appointee's decision or refusal to accept accordance with Rule 6(1).

3. Arbitrator's failure to accept an appointment: notification of the failure. Rule 5(3) requires the Secretary-General promptly to notify the parties (and the Chairman, if appropriate) of an appointee's refusal to accept an appointment so that the party or appointing authority that made the original appointment has the opportunity to select another arbitrator. Rule 5(3) establishes a presumption that a person who does not respond to the Secretary-General's inquiry on behalf of a party or appointing authority within fifteen days has declined the appointment. This time limit may be extended by agreement of the parties. If an appointee does refuse (or is deemed to have refused), the Secretary-General will invite the relevant party to appoint another arbitrator.

4. Right of an arbitrator to refuse. An arbitrator is under no obligation to accept an appointment, even if he is a member of the Panel of Arbitrators. An arbitrator may refuse to accept an appointment in a specific case, although in practice a party or the appointing authority will first informally inquire whether a person under consideration is willing and available to serve as an arbitrator.

5. Form of acceptance. Neither the Convention nor the Arbitration Rules specify a particular form for the acceptance. It may be given orally, in writing or by fax, email or telephone. Rule 6(2) requires that an arbitrator sign a formal declaration, which can be done after the tribunal's constitution. Acceptance of an appointment may depend upon any agreement as to the arbitrators' fees in accordance with art. 60(2).

6. Loss of right to appoint an arbitrator. In general, the party or other authority that made the original appointment is given an opportunity to make a new appointment if the first appointee fails to accept. If in the meantime the time limit established under art. 38 has elapsed, either party can require the Chairman to make the new appointment in order to complete the constitution of the tribunal. In such a case, a party may lose its right to appoint an arbitrator even if it is willing to do so and has made every effort to make the appointment.

[Constitution of the tribunal]
Arbitration Rule 6

(1) The Tribunal shall be deemed to be constituted and the proceeding to have begun on the date the Secretary-General notifies the parties that all the arbitrators have accepted their appointment.

(2) Before or at the first session of the Tribunal, each arbitrator shall sign a declaration in the following form:

> **'To the best of my knowledge there is no reason why I should not serve on the Arbitral Tribunal constituted by the International Centre for Settlement of Investment Disputes with respect to a dispute between _____ and _____.**
>
> **'I shall keep confidential all information coming to my knowledge as a result of my participation in this proceeding, as well as the contents of any award made by the Tribunal.**
>
> **'I shall judge fairly as between the parties, according to the applicable law, and shall not accept any instruction or compensation with regard to the proceeding from any source except as provided in the Convention on the Settlement of Investment Disputes between States and Nationals of Other States and in the Regulations and Rules made pursuant thereto.**
>
> **'Attached is a statement of (a) my past and present professional, business and other relationships (if any) with the parties and (b) any other circumstance that might cause my reliability for**

independent judgment to be questioned by a party. I acknowledge that by signing this declaration, I assume a continuing obligation promptly to notify the Secretary-General of the Centre of any such relationship or circumstance that subsequently arises during this proceeding.'

Any arbitrator failing to sign a declaration by the end of the first session of the Tribunal shall be deemed to have resigned.

1. General. Rule 6 specifies the point at which a tribunal has been formally constituted and sets out the declaration that arbitrators must make either before or at the first session of the tribunal.

2. Constitution of the tribunal. Under Rule 6(1), the process of constituting the tribunal is completed when the parties are notified by the Secretary-General that every arbitrator has accepted their appointment. The conclusive date of constitution of the tribunal is the date written on the notice, as required by Reg. 29(1) of the Administrative and Finance Regulations. It appears, however, that, in practice, the date of constitution is sometimes treated as the date upon which all of the arbitrators accept their appointment (*SOABI* v *Senegal*).

3. Changing the composition of the tribunal. The significance of determining the tribunal's date of constitution is two-fold. First, this is when the proceedings, including the ability to obtain orders from the tribunal, formally commence. Secondly, after the tribunal's constitution, any change in the tribunal's composition has to take place in accordance with arts. 56 to 58. According to art. 56(1), the tribunal's composition shall remain unchanged once it is constituted and proceedings have begun.

4. Declaration. Rule 6(2) requires each arbitrator to file a declaration attesting to his or her impartiality and that he or she will only accept compensation with regard to the proceedings as provided for under the Convention. If an arbitrator fails to file the requested declaration on time, he or she shall be deemed to have resigned within the meaning of Rule 8(2), and he or she will have to be replaced in accordance with Rule 11. The Rule 6(2) declaration can be made after the tribunal has been constituted provided that it is made before or at the first session.

5. Impartiality: required disclosure. The disclosure and declaration of impartiality required by Rule 6 are intended to prevent the appointment of arbitrators with a conflict of interest. While Rule 6 does not say so specifically, a clear conflict of interest apparent from the declaration would preclude the appointment of the arbitrator on the basis that they lacked the quality of independent judgment required by art. 14(1). The circumstances to be disclosed by an appointee include any past or present professional or business relationships with the parties, as well as 'any circumstance that might cause [a prospective arbitrator's] reliability for independent judgment to be questioned by a party'. This latter requirement was added by the amendment to the Arbitration Rules in April 2006. Thus, a broad approach to disclosure by an appointee is warranted. The reforms also introduced the continuing obligation in order to ensure disclosure of conflicts of interest which developed after an arbitrator had made a declaration. The responsibility for disclosure lies with each arbitrator, and is encouraged by the Centre.

6. Impartiality: consequence of failure to disclose. Rule 6 does not expressly specify any consequence of either a failure to disclose a circumstance or for the existence of a conflict of interest. Art. 57 and Rule 9 provide, however, that a party may propose, by application to the tribunal, the disqualification of one of its members on the basis that such member manifestly lacks the qualities required by paragraph 14(1), which includes the quality of being able to be relied upon to exercise independent judgment. The tribunal (aside from the member who has been challenged) has the sole right to decide such an application, but if the remaining tribunal members are equally divided, the Chairman of the Council will decide.

7. Impartiality: disclosure and impartiality in international arbitration generally. The emerging principles on impartiality and independence of international arbitrators are not yet fully settled. In a general context they are addressed in the IBA Guidelines, which creates lists of circumstances which ought to be disclosed. Although these Guidelines have not received universal approval, they are a useful benchmark. To date, no ICSID tribunal member has been disqualified merely on account of his political convictions or legal orientations: indeed, these are often well-known. Thus, parties are free to appoint arbitrators whom they believe are sympathetic to their case and often do so.

8. Confidentiality. Rule 6(2) protects the privacy of the arbitration proceedings by requiring arbitrators to make a confidentiality declaration. There is no provision in the Arbitration Rules prohibiting the parties from unilaterally publishing their pleadings. The parties may, however, agree between themselves that their pleadings will remain confidential (see art. 47, note 8).

9. Prohibited appointments. Under Reg. 13 of the Administrative and Financial Regulations, the Secretary-General, the Deputy Secretary-General and ICSID members of staff cannot serve on the Panel and may not be appointed as arbitrators. This provision is not subject to waiver by the parties.

[Replacement of arbitrators]

Arbitration Rule 7

At any time before the Tribunal is constituted, each party may replace any arbitrator appointed by it and the parties may by common consent agree to replace any arbitrator. The procedure of such replacement shall be in accordance with Rules 1, 5 and 6.

1. General. A party may unilaterally replace an arbitrator it has unilaterally appointed at any time prior to the constitution of the tribunal. Before this time, the parties may also jointly agree to replace any other arbitrator appointed either by an external authority or the Chairman.

2. Any time before the tribunal is constituted. This requirement follows from art. 56(1), which states that the composition of a tribunal cannot be changed once it has been constituted and proceedings have begun. Pursuant to Rule 6(1), the tribunal is constituted and proceedings have begun when the Secretary-General notifies the parties that all the arbitrators have accepted their appointments. After this time, changes to the composition of the tribunal may only be made following the death, disability, resignation or disqualification of an arbitrator (see arts. 56 and 57 and Rules 6(2) and 8 to 11).

3. Replacement of arbitrators by agreement. Prior to the constitution of the tribunal, the parties may by mutual agreement replace any arbitrator regardless of whether he was appointed by the parties, an external appointing authority or the Chairman acting pursuant to art. 38 or otherwise. This rule underlines the parties' control over the proceedings, subject only to the mandatory provisions of the Convention.

4. In accordance with Rules 1, 5 and 6. Rule 7 stipulates that the procedure for replacing an arbitrator must be in accordance with the general obligations of the parties under Rule 1, the acceptance of appointments under Rule 5 and the requirements for the constitution of the tribunal under Rule 6.

[Incapacity or resignation of arbitrators]
Arbitration Rule 8

(1) If an arbitrator becomes incapacitated or unable to perform the duties of his office, the procedure in respect of the disqualification of arbitrators set forth in Rule 9 shall apply.

(2) An arbitrator may resign by submitting his resignation to the other members of the Tribunal and the Secretary-General. If the arbitrator was appointed by one of the parties, the Tribunal shall promptly consider the reasons for his resignation and decide whether it consents thereto. The Tribunal shall promptly notify the Secretary-General of its decision.

1. General. Rule 8 provides for the possibility of disqualifying an arbitrator if he becomes incapacitated or unable to perform his duties, according to the procedure set out in Rule 9. It also allows for the arbitrators' resignation subject to giving reasons. Neither the Convention nor the Arbitration Rules provides any guidance on legitimate grounds for resignation.

2. Disqualification of an arbitrator. The disqualification procedure is set out in detail in Rule 9. There must be a proposal from one of the parties.

There must also be a decision in this respect by the unchallenged members of the tribunal or by the Chairman (see Rule 9).

3. Resignation of an arbitrator. Given that acceptance of appointment entails an obligation to serve, any resignation must state serious reasons, which may be either professional or personal in nature. In case of a conflict of interest, there is an obligation to resign. In practice, resignation has occurred in several cases (there are about thirty such cases listed on the ICSID website). Resignation may occur in circumstances such as a supervening conflict of interest (*Holiday Inns* v *Morocco*) or disagreement with the tribunal's majority (*Tokios Tokeles* v *Ukraine* (DJ)).

4. Resignation procedure. An arbitrator who desires to resign must submit the resignation together with the reasons of resignation to the other members of the tribunal as well as to the Secretary-General. If the resigning member has been appointed by one of the parties, the tribunal must decide whether it consents to the resignation (see art. 56). In all other cases, the tribunal has no discretion.

[Disqualification of arbitrators]

Arbitration Rule 9

(1) A party proposing the disqualification of an arbitrator pursuant to Article 57 of the Convention shall promptly, and in any event before the proceeding is declared closed, file its proposal with the Secretary-General, stating its reasons therefor.

(2) The Secretary-General shall forthwith:
  (a) transmit the proposal to the members of the Tribunal and, if it relates to a sole arbitrator or to a majority of the members of the Tribunal, to the Chairman of the Administrative Council; and
  (b) notify the other party of the proposal.

(3) The arbitrator to whom the proposal relates may, without delay, furnish explanations to the Tribunal or the Chairman, as the case may be.

(4) Unless the proposal relates to a majority of the members of the Tribunal, the other members shall promptly consider and vote on the proposal in the absence of the arbitrator concerned. If those members are equally divided, they shall, through the Secretary-General, promptly notify the Chairman of the proposal, of any explanation furnished by the arbitrator concerned and of their failure to reach a decision.

(5) Whenever the Chairman has to decide on a proposal to disqualify an arbitrator, he shall use his best efforts to take that decision within 30 days after he has received the proposal.

(6) The proceeding shall be suspended until a decision has been taken on the proposal.

1. General. Rule 9 sets out the procedure that is to be followed in cases of disqualification of arbitrators. The initiative for disqualification must always come from a party to the dispute. Neither the tribunal nor the Centre may initiate the disqualification procedure (see art. 57).

2. Timing of the proposal to disqualify. Rule 9(1) provides that the proposal to disqualify must be made as soon as the concerned party learns of the grounds for a possible disqualification. A party that fails to object 'promptly' is deemed to have waived their right (see Rule 27, unless, of course, further grounds for disqualification come to light). Furthermore, the proposal must be made before the proceeding is declared closed. However, if a party learns of a ground for disqualification after the date of closure, the party may still request annulment of the award pursuant to art. 52. Similarly, where a proposal to disqualify does not succeed, the right to request annulment is technically still available.

3. Procedural steps. The decision on a proposal to disqualify a member of the tribunal is taken by the majority of the unchallenged members. These unchallenged members may look both to the timing of any challenge and to its substance (*Aguas Argentinas* v *Argentina*; see also arts. 57 and 58). If the remaining members do not agree or if the request for disqualification refers to the majority of the tribunal's members, the Chairman has to decide (see art. 58). According to Rule 9(3), the challenged arbitrator may furnish explanations (*Amco* v *Indonesia* (I) (DJ)). The proceedings in the case are suspended until a decision on the matter is rendered. If the request is rejected, the proceedings continue. If the proposal succeeds, the proceedings are suspended until a new arbitrator is appointed (see also Rule 10, note 1).

[Procedure during a vacancy on the tribunal]
Arbitration Rule 10

(1) The Secretary-General shall forthwith notify the parties and, if necessary, the Chairman of the Administrative Council of the disqualification, death, incapacity or resignation of an arbitrator and of the consent, if any, of the Tribunal to a resignation.

(2) Upon the notification by the Secretary-General of a vacancy on the Tribunal, the proceeding shall be or remain suspended until the vacancy has been filled.

1. General. Rule 10 deals with the question of vacancy on the tribunal and provides that in such cases proceedings must be suspended until the vacancy has been filled. Vacancies arise in cases of disqualification, death, incapacity or resignation of an arbitrator (see art. 56; Rules 8 and 9). In addition, a vacancy may result from the failure of an arbitrator to sign the declaration required under Rule 6(2).

[Filling vacancies on the tribunal]

Arbitration Rule 11

(1) Except as provided in paragraph (2), a vacancy resulting from the disqualification, death, incapacity or resignation of an arbitrator shall be promptly filled by the same method by which his appointment had been made.

(2) In addition to filling vacancies relating to arbitrators appointed by him, the Chairman of the Administrative Council shall appoint a person from the Panel of Arbitrators:
- **(a) to fill a vacancy caused by the resignation, without the consent of the Tribunal, of an arbitrator appointed by a party; or**
- **(b) at the request of either party, to fill any other vacancy, if no new appointment is made and accepted within 45 days of the notification of the vacancy by the Secretary-General.**

(3) The procedure for filling a vacancy shall be in accordance with Rules 1, 4(4), 4(5), 5 and, mutatis mutandis, 6(2).

1. General. Rule 11 provides for the procedure that must be followed in order to fill a vacancy on the tribunal. The general rule is that the new appointment shall follow the method that was used in the initial appointment. It follows that if the original appointment had been made by one of the parties, that party should make the new appointment. This general rule is subject to an exception. Rule 9(2) provides that the Centre will appoint a new arbitrator if the vacancy is caused by the resignation of a party-appointed arbitrator (without the consent of the tribunal), if there is a specific request to that effect by either party or if there is no new appointment within forty-five days of the notification of vacancy. The Rules referred to in Rule 11(3) deal with certain formalities which also apply in respect of the substitute appointment.

[Resumption of proceeding after filling a vacancy]

Arbitration Rule 12

As soon as a vacancy on the Tribunal has been filled, the proceeding shall continue from the point it had reached at the time the vacancy occurred. The newly appointed arbitrator may, however, require that the oral procedure be recommenced, if this had already been started.

1. General. Rule 12 provides that once the vacancy has been filled, the proceedings will resume. It also provides that prior proceedings need not be repeated. Nevertheless, the newly appointed arbitrator may require the repetition of the oral proceedings. The decision on the matter rests with that arbitrator alone.

CHAPTER II. WORKING OF THE TRIBUNAL
[Sessions of the tribunal]
Arbitration Rule 13

(1) The Tribunal shall hold its first session within 60 days after its constitution or such other period as the parties may agree. The dates of that session shall be fixed by the President of the Tribunal after consultation with its members and the Secretary-General. If upon its constitution the Tribunal has no President because the parties have agreed that the President shall be elected by its members, the Secretary-General shall fix the dates of that session. In both cases, the parties shall be consulted as far as possible.

(2) The dates of subsequent sessions shall be determined by the Tribunal, after consultation with the Secretary-General and with the parties as far as possible.

(3) The Tribunal shall meet at the seat of the Centre or at such other place as may have been agreed by the parties in accordance with Article 63 of the Convention. If the parties agree that the proceeding shall be held at a place other than the Centre or an institution with which the Centre has made the necessary arrangements, they shall consult with the Secretary-General and request the approval of the Tribunal. Failing such approval, the Tribunal shall meet at the seat of the Centre.

(4) The Secretary-General shall notify the members of the Tribunal and the parties of the dates and place of the sessions of the Tribunal in good time.

1. General. Arts. 41 to 47 and Rules 13 to 38 regulate the conduct of ICSID proceedings from the tribunal's constitution to the rendering of its award. Rule 13 regulates the planning of the sessions of the tribunal and the time and date of these sessions.

2. Definition of 'session'. A 'session' of the tribunal is one or more 'sittings' which are held without any extensive pauses and usually in the same place (see Notes to the Arbitration Rules, Rule 13, Note A). It is perhaps theoretically possible for a tribunal to dispose of a case in a single session, but in practice a number of sessions will generally be required.

3. Fixing of the dates of the initial and subsequent sessions. The date of the initial session is to be fixed by the president of the tribunal in accordance with Rule 13(1), in consultation with the other tribunal members, the Secretary-General and the parties, as far as possible. The initial session is typically the 'preliminary procedural consultation', described in Rule 20, at which the tribunal is required to consult the parties on questions of procedure. In accordance with Rule 13(2), the dates of any subsequent sessions are to be determined by the tribunal in consultation, to the extent possible, with the Secretary-General and the parties.

4. Where the tribunal has no president. If the parties agreed that the president of the tribunal is to be elected by the members of the tribunal themselves, the tribunal will not have a president at its first session. In this instance, Rule 13(1) requires the date of the first session to be fixed by the Secretary-General.

5. Sixty-day time limit. The sixty-day time limit in Rule 13(1) is designed to prevent undue delay. The parties may agree to alter this time limit. During this time, the president of the tribunal, if there is one, may undertake a preliminary consultation with the parties under Rule 20 regarding the procedural framework for the proceedings. Any subsequent time limit will be determined by the tribunal in its first procedural order, based on its assessment of the complexity of the facts and issues in dispute.

6. Meeting place of the tribunal: the seat of the Centre. Rule 13(3) requires that the tribunal meet at the seat of the Centre or any other place agreed by the parties under art. 63. The seat of the Centre is defined in art. 2 as the principal office of the International Bank for Reconstruction and Development, which is currently the World Bank headquarters in Washington, DC (see art. 2, note 2).

7. Meeting place of the tribunal: places other than the Centre. If the parties have agreed that the tribunal shall meet at a place other than the Centre, they must consult with the Secretary-General and request the approval of the tribunal under art. 63(b). If the tribunal does not approve, the tribunal shall meet at the seat of the Centre. Under Reg. 26(1) of the Administrative and Financial Regulations, the Secretary-General is responsible for making or supervising the necessary arrangements for the meeting of the tribunal at any other place agreed by the parties. ICSID has standing arrangements with other institutions in several cities, including The Hague, Cairo and Sydney. In the recent *Chevron* v *Bangladesh* case, the parties utilised the standing arrangement with the Permanent Court of Arbitration in The Hague.

8. Meeting place of the tribunal: legal effect. Because ICSID arbitration is regulated by the ICSID Convention and not by national laws, the choice of the location for an ICSID arbitration does not change the applicable procedural law or the law on the enforceability of any award. There may often be good reasons of convenience, cost and efficiency for the parties to agree to hold hearings outside of Washington, DC.

9. Notification to the parties and members of the tribunal. Rule 13(4) requires the Secretary-General to inform the parties and tribunal members of the dates and location of the sessions of the tribunal in 'good time'. This should be construed in relation to the geographical location of the parties and their means of communication. It is possible for the parties to agree during the procedural consultation under Rule 20 a certain notice period for subsequent notifications.

10. Failure of a party to attend a session. If one of the parties fails to cooperate and does not appear to present its case at a session, the provisions regarding default proceedings in art. 45 and Rule 42 may apply.

[Sittings of the tribunal]

Arbitration Rule 14

(1) The President of the Tribunal shall conduct its hearings and preside at its deliberations.

(2) Except as the parties otherwise agree, the presence of a majority of the members of the Tribunal shall be required at its sittings.

(3) The President of the Tribunal shall fix the date and hour of its sittings.

1. General. Rule 14 addresses the powers of the president of the tribunal in relation to the sittings of the tribunal and the requisite quorum. The sittings, which make up a session, consist either of 'hearings' (Rule 31) or of 'deliberations' (Rule 15).

2. Quorum for sittings. Rule 14(2) requires that a majority of the members of the tribunal must be in attendance for a sitting of the tribunal to be quorate. Therefore, a refusal by one of the members of the tribunal to attend a sitting does not affect the validity of such a sitting. Rule 20, providing for preliminary consultation with the parties on procedure, allows the president of the tribunal and the parties to agree a different number of members required for a sitting to be quorate. It should be noted, however, that art. 48(1) and Rule 16(1) provide that the decisions of the tribunal shall be taken by a majority of the votes of all its members and not just those present or voting.

3. Quorum for decisions by correspondence. The quorum requirement of Rule 14(2) applies to the tribunal's sittings, but does not apply to decisions by correspondence under Rule 16. The parties are free to agree that no decisions may be taken by correspondence or that such decisions may only be taken if all members participate.

4. Times and dates fixed by the president of the tribunal. As under Rule 13(2), Rule 14(3) requires the president of the tribunal to fix the date and time of each sitting. Rule 17 provides that one of the other members of the tribunal can perform the functions of the president where the president is unable to do so.

[Deliberations of the tribunal]

Arbitration Rule 15

(1) The deliberations of the Tribunal shall take place in private and remain secret.

(2) Only members of the Tribunal shall take part in its deliberations. No other person shall be admitted unless the Tribunal decides otherwise.

1. General. Rule 15 preserves the principle that arbitration proceedings are not public.

2. Deliberations of the tribunal are private. Rule 15(1) confirms and protects the privacy of the tribunal's deliberations and is intended to prevent the views of the arbitrators as expressed in deliberations from being made public. It also encourages a tribunal to work in a collegial fashion by ensuring that disagreements may be freely expressed without the risk of disclosure.

3. Attendance at deliberations of the tribunal. Rule 15(2) restricts attendance at the deliberations of the tribunal only to members of the tribunal in order to preserve the confidentiality of the deliberations. The Rule also empowers the tribunal to allow other persons to attend the deliberations should this be considered necessary. Permission will normally only be granted to administrative personnel such as the Secretary-General, a tribunal's secretary (if there is one), interpreters (if required), or clerical staff. Even if other persons are present with permission, only the tribunal members themselves should participate in the deliberations.

[Decisions of the tribunal]

Arbitration Rule 16

(1) Decisions of the Tribunal shall be taken by a majority of the votes of all its members. Abstention shall count as a negative vote.

(2) Except as otherwise provided by these Rules or decided by the Tribunal, it may take any decision by correspondence among its members, provided that all of them are consulted. Decisions so taken shall be certified by the President of the Tribunal.

1. General. There are two main elements to Rule 16: decisions of the tribunal must be taken by a majority of its members; and the tribunal may take decisions by correspondence.

2. Majority of votes of members. Rule 16(1) requires that decisions by a tribunal be taken by a majority vote of all its members. Similarly, art. 48(1) states that a tribunal must decide questions by a majority of the votes of all its members. Art. 48(1) applies to all decisions of the tribunal, whether they are procedural orders or substantive findings. Notably, Rule 16 does not require that all the arbitrators of a tribunal be present when a decision is taken, nor does it require that the president participate. The votes of absentees and other non-participants are counted as negative votes, however. It follows that it is not possible to delegate the power to make procedural decisions to the president of the tribunal alone. Finally, art. 48(2) and Rule 47(2) provide that an award need only be signed by the members of the tribunal who voted for it.

3. Decisions by correspondence. Decisions by correspondence allow the tribunal to avoid the expense and time of a physical meeting. Any decision of the tribunal can be made by correspondence, although this approach is more likely to be used for procedural matters. Every member of the tribunal must be consulted, but it is not necessary that every member respond in order to reach a decision. This rule can be altered by agreement of the parties or by a majority of the tribunal. Under one of the few exceptions to the Rule 16 and art. 48(1) requirement that the tribunal decide questions by majority, the tribunal may delegate to the president the power to fix time limits pursuant to Rule 26. Rule 16(2) does not change the rule in Rule 16(1) that decisions of the tribunal should be taken by a majority of the tribunal's members, regardless of the number of arbitrators actually participating in a decision.

[Incapacity of the president]
Arbitration Rule 17

If at any time the President of the Tribunal should be unable to act, his functions shall be performed by one of the other members of the Tribunal, acting in the order in which the Secretary-General had received the notice of their acceptance of their appointment to the Tribunal.

1. General. The Convention does not address the temporary inability of a member of a tribunal to participate in its work, but Rule 17 does deal with the temporary incapacity of the president of the tribunal. The Arbitration Rules assign a number of powers and functions expressly to the president (see Rules 13(1), 14(1) 20(1), 26(1) and 49(3)). Although this provision can be disapplied by consent of the parties, it is a useful rule that prevents the tribunal becoming gridlocked by the temporary inability of the president to act. Rule 17 was used, for example, in *Vacuum Salt* v *Ghana* where Judge Brower presided over oral hearings in the place of Sir Robert Jennings who could not preside because of his status as President of the International Court of Justice. It should be noted, however, that there is no recent practice of Rule 17 being applied.

2. Absence of the president of the tribunal. This rule applies only to the temporary incapacity of an incumbent president, and not in the event of a vacancy of the office. If the vacancy exists because no president has yet been elected, pursuant to Rule 13(1) the Secretary-General will fix the date and time of the tribunal's initial sitting. If a vacancy arises due to a president having been removed from the tribunal (for any of the reasons listed in Rule 10), the proceeding must be suspended pursuant to Rule 10(2) until a new president has been appointed.

4. Order of acceptance as received by the Secretary-General. The parties may agree to a different order of succession than that provided in Rule 17. In practice, as the remaining arbitrators will often have been party-appointed, such agreement will be rare.

[Representation of the parties]

Arbitration Rule 18

(1) Each party may be represented or assisted by agents, counsel or advocates whose names and authority shall be notified by that party to the Secretary-General, who shall promptly inform the Tribunal and the other party.

(2) For the purposes of these Rules, the expression 'party' includes, where the context so admits, an agent, counsel or advocate authorised to represent that party.

1. General. Under Rule 18, the parties are free to decide whether to be represented in proceedings and, if so, the identity of their representatives.

2. Each party may be represented or assisted. It is not mandatory under the Convention or Arbitration Rules that a party have a lawyer to act on its behalf, although in practice most parties will be assisted by or represented by legal counsel. It follows that it is not possible for a party to object to another party's legal representation on the grounds of lack of professional qualifications.

3. Agents, counsel or advocates: qualifications of the representatives. The terms 'agent', 'counsel' and 'advocate' do not imply any specific legal or other qualifications and may include attorneys, barristers, solicitors and other persons with legal knowledge, training and experience. Further, there is no requirement that a representative be admitted to practice in a particular jurisdiction.

4. Agents, counsel or advocates: background of the representatives. Generally in international litigation, State parties are represented by an 'agent', who is in charge of the general management and control of the case, and who is assisted by 'counsel'. In practice, parties have nearly always been represented by lawyers. State parties have been represented by government lawyers, lawyers in private practice or a combination of both. Investors are nearly always represented by lawyers in private practice or in-house counsel. Some international arbitral or administrative tribunals permit individuals and, in certain cases, even States or intergovernmental organisations (through their authorised representatives) to appear 'in person'. Counsel in ICSID arbitrations are normally either specialist practitioners in commercial law firms, academics or government lawyers.

5. Notification to the Secretary-General. In its notification to the Secretary-General under Rule 18(1), each party must indicate whether it is 'represented' or merely 'assisted' by an agent, counsel or advocate and what the scope of the authority of each such person is. Similarly, if a party prefers that all communications and notices in connection with the proceeding be sent to a particular individual, Rule 7(b) of the Institution Rules requires that it inform the Secretary-General accordingly. Normally, the request for arbitration under art. 36 will identify the agents, counsel and advocates of the parties. The identity of the representatives will be recorded in the award in accordance with Rule 47(1)(d).

CHAPTER III. GENERAL PROCEDURAL PROVISIONS

[Procedural orders]

Arbitration Rule 19

The Tribunal shall make the orders required for the conduct of the proceeding.

1. General. Rule 19 gives the tribunal the power to make the orders required for the conduct of the arbitration proceeding. Art. 44 confirms that, except as the parties otherwise agree, the tribunal is entitled to decide all questions of procedure in accordance with the Arbitration Rules and, if the Rules do not assist, in accordance with its own judgment.

2. Content of orders. The tribunal may make specific orders based on the Convention, Arbitration Rules, agreement of the parties or on its own initiative. In making its orders, the tribunal should be guided, in the first place, by information initially furnished by the parties (under Rule 3 of the Institution Rules) or as a result of the preliminary inquiry by its president (under Rule 20(1) of the Arbitration Rules).

3. Procedure. Rule 20 requires the president of the tribunal to consult with the parties as early as possible after the tribunal's constitution to ascertain their individual views with respect to procedural points and to garner initial agreement. However, procedural orders can be made at any time in the proceedings. Under Rule 3 of the Institution Rules, the parties can communicate any agreement they may have reached on procedural points at the early stages of the proceeding, although this will be very rare.

4. Legal effect of procedural orders. It is presumed that the tribunal's procedural orders under Rule 19 are to be legally binding, although this is nowhere expressly stated. The tribunal's procedural orders are made by a majority of the votes of all its members pursuant to arts. 44 and 48(1) and Rule 16(1).

[Preliminary procedural consultation]

Arbitration Rule 20

(1) As early as possible after the constitution of a Tribunal, its President shall endeavour to ascertain the views of the parties regarding questions

of procedure. For this purpose he may request the parties to meet him. He shall, in particular, seek their views on the following matters:
- (a) the number of members of the Tribunal required to constitute a quorum at its sittings;
- (b) the language or languages to be used in the proceeding;
- (c) the number and sequence of the pleadings and the time limits within which they are to be filed;
- (d) the number of copies desired by each party of instruments filed by the other;
- (e) dispensing with the written or the oral procedure;
- (f) the manner in which the cost of the proceeding is to be apportioned; and
- (g) the manner in which the record of the hearings shall be kept.

(2) In the conduct of the proceeding the Tribunal shall apply any agreement between the parties on procedural matters, except as otherwise provided in the Convention or the Administrative and Financial Regulations.

1. General. Rule 20 enables the tribunal, in close collaboration with the parties, and usually at the 'first session' contemplated by Rule 13(1), to create a procedural framework within which it can conduct proceedings and make Rule 19 orders. Art. 44 gives the parties a large degree of freedom to settle procedural questions by agreement. This first session can be crucial in setting the tone and the procedural framework for the ensuing proceedings.

2. As early as possible after the tribunal's constitution. Rule 20(1) requires that the president carry out the procedural consultation as soon as possible after the constitution of the tribunal. According to Rule 6(1), a tribunal is deemed to be constituted on the date the Secretary-General notifies the parties that all the arbitrators have accepted their appointments. If, upon its constitution, the tribunal has no president, the president must undertake the consultation upon his designation or election or the consultation must be undertaken by another member of the tribunal appointed under Rule 17.

3. President's duty to consult with parties. The president of the tribunal must seek cooperation with the parties, as well as between the parties, to avoid undue delay and procedural arguments.

4. Formalities of consultation: mode of consultation. The mode of consultation is determined by the president who may require the parties to express their views in writing and/or ask them or their representatives to attend a physical meeting with the tribunal. It is possible for the procedural consultations to be conducted through correspondence. However, the more common method is to settle questions of procedure by a physical meeting held at the tribunal's first session.

5. Formalities of consultation: non-participation of a party. If a party does not attend the first session and/or participate in the preliminary procedural consultation, the tribunal may still hold preliminary consultations on procedural matters with the cooperating party and is entitled to make appropriate procedural orders pursuant to Rule 19.

6. Formalities of consultation: record of proceedings. Agreements on the procedural framework are generally recorded in the minutes of the first session of the tribunal. The original 1968 Arbitration Rules contained detailed provisions on the keeping of minutes of all hearings, including a prohibition on their publication without the consent of the parties. However, the amended Rule 20(1)(g) now provides that the manner in which the record of the hearings shall be kept is to be settled at a preliminary procedural consultation. Amongst other matters, therefore, it is open to the parties to agree that the minutes evidencing their agreement to a procedural framework under Rule 20(1) be kept confidential.

7. Matters on which to consult. The matters expressly listed in Rule 20(1) have analogues with other Arbitration Rules, as follows:

(a)	Quorum requirement	Rule 14(2)
(b)	Procedural languages	Rule 22
(c)	Pleadings and time limits	Rules 31 and 26
(d)	Copies of instruments to be filed	Rules 23 and 24
(e)	Written and oral procedure	Rules 29 and 31-32
(f)	The apportionment of costs	Rule 28 (and art. 61(2))

In addition, the president may consult on any other relevant issues, including the arrangements for the taking of evidence, whether to bifurcate the proceedings, the channels of communication between the parties and the tribunal, the procedure for determining the admissibility of counterclaims and applications for provisional measures and confirming the location of the future proceedings.

8. Agreement of the parties. Under Rule 20(2), the tribunal must apply any agreement on procedural issues concluded between the parties to the extent that, in so doing, it does not modify mandatory provisions of the Convention and Arbitration Rules. In practice, such agreements are rare. Usually, it is the tribunal that establishes the steps of the proceedings and their time limits further to Rule 26.

[Pre-hearing conference]
Arbitration Rule 21

(1) At the request of the Secretary-General or at the discretion of the President of the Tribunal, a pre-hearing conference between the Tribunal and the parties may be held to arrange for an exchange of information and the stipulation of uncontested facts in order to expedite the proceeding.

(2) At the request of the parties, a pre-hearing conference between the Tribunal and the parties, duly represented by their authorised representatives, may be held to consider the issues in dispute with a view to reaching an amicable settlement.

1. General. There are two purposes underlying Rule 21: to establish uncontested facts; and to promote and facilitate an early settlement. This provision was introduced by the amendment to the Arbitration Rules in 1984 and gives the tribunal a procedural mechanism to seek to reduce the number of facts in dispute.

2. Rule 21(1) in practice. In practice, the pre-hearing session envisaged by Rule 21(1) is not always held, given the administrative burden and cost of convening the arbitrators, parties and counsel for a meeting prior to the hearing itself. Moreover, active cooperation from the parties is usually needed in order to narrow the facts and issues in dispute. Where it is held, this session is particularly suited to being conducted by telephone and video conference. This procedure was used successfully in *Mobil* v *NZ* and *Duke Energy Electroquil* v *Ecuador*.

3. Amicable settlement. Only the parties may request a pre-hearing conference under Rule 21(2). Rule 21(2) requires that the parties' authorised representatives be present at the pre-hearing conference to assist the parties in hearing each side's case in a formal forum, better understanding each other's position and possibly facilitating an amicable settlement.

[Procedural languages]

Arbitration Rule 22

(1) The parties may agree on the use of one or two languages to be used in the proceeding, provided, that, if they agree on any language that is not an official language of the Centre, the Tribunal, after consultation with the Secretary-General, gives its approval. If the parties do not agree on any such procedural language, each of them may select one of the official languages (i.e., English, French and Spanish) for this purpose.

(2) If two procedural languages are selected by the parties, any instrument may be filed in either language. Either language may be used at the hearings, subject, if the Tribunal so requires, to translation and interpretation. The orders and the award of the Tribunal shall be rendered and the record kept in both procedural languages, both versions being equally authentic.

1. General. This rule deals with the language regime for the settlement of a specific dispute. The choice of one of the official languages of the Centre under Rule 1(1) of the Institution Rules for the request for arbitration is without prejudice to the parties' choice of procedural language under Rule

22. The availability of translation and interpretation facilities is dealt with in Reg. 27 of the Administrative and Financial Regulations.

2. Freedom of the parties to choose. The parties have the freedom to choose the language of the proceedings. They may elect to choose a language each. They should, however, consider the extra time, administration and costs involved in having more than one procedural language.

3. Official languages. The official languages of the Centre are specified in Reg. 34(1) of the Administrative and Financial Regulations as English, French and Spanish. If the parties choose a language that is not one of the official languages of the Centre, they must seek the approval of the tribunal, which must in turn consult the Secretary-General.

4. Bilingual proceedings and translation: hearings, orders, awards and records. If the parties select two procedural languages, this means that the proceedings will be bilingual and written instruments and hearings may be in either or both languages. Orders and awards and the procedural records will be in both languages. Until 1996, all ICSID proceedings were conducted in English or French or both. Since 1996, Spanish is increasingly used.

5. Bilingual proceedings and translation: pleadings. The parties may submit pleadings and other documents in any of the chosen languages or together with a translation. Under Reg. 27(1) of the Administrative and Financial Regulations, the Centre undertakes to furnish any necessary interpretation and translation from one official language of the Centre into another. Even where there are two procedural languages, the tribunal may dispense with interpretation if the arbitrators and parties are sufficiently familiar with both languages. As shown, however, by a recent challenge to an arbitrator in an UNCITRAL BIT dispute, who expressed himself more imprecisely in Spanish than he would have done in his native English, there are risks to arbitrators dispensing with interpretation services (*National Grid v The Republic of Argentina*).

6. Bilingual proceedings and translation: supporting documents. Any supporting document which is not in a language approved for the proceeding in question must be accompanied by a certified translation. If the document is lengthy and relevant only in part, it is possible to submit a translation of the relevant parts only, although a fuller or more complete translation may be required by the tribunal at a later stage (Reg. 30(3) of the Administrative and Financial Regulations).

[Copies of instruments]

Arbitration Rule 23

Except as otherwise provided by the Tribunal after consultation with the parties and the Secretary-General, every request, pleading, applica-

tion, written observation, supporting documentation, if any, or other instrument shall be filed in the form of a signed original accompanied by the following number of additional copies:
  (a) before the number of members of the Tribunal has been determined: five;
  (b) after the number of members of the Tribunal has been determined: two more than the number of its members.

1. General. Rule 23 governs the number of copies a party must provide of any instrument submitted to the tribunal. This provision applies to every instrument filed in the proceedings other than the original request for arbitration, of which five additional copies must be provided (Rule 4(1) of the Institution Rules). The president may seek the views of the parties during the preliminary procedural consultation under Rule 20 as to the number of copies that are required of each instrument. Thus, this rule can be varied by agreement of the parties.

2. Original documents. Under Reg. 28(1)(a) of the Administrative and Financial Regulations, the original of every instrument filed in a proceeding is to be deposited in the archives of the Centre for permanent retention.

3. Supporting documents. The number of copies of supporting documents is regulated by Rule 23 and Reg. 30(2) of the Administrative and Financial Regulations, and is generally the same as the number of copies that have to be provided of the instrument to which they relate.

[Supporting documentation]

Arbitration Rule 24

Supporting documentation shall ordinarily be filed together with the instrument to which it relates, and in any case within the time limit fixed for the filing of such instrument.

1. General. Rule 24 provides that supporting documents should be filed together with the instrument to which they relate. Reg. 30 of the Administrative and Financial Regulations regulates the number of copies and translation of supporting documents.

2. Scope of supporting documentation. The term 'supporting documentation' is undefined. However, in practice, it may include witness statements and expert reports required by a tribunal's procedural order to be filed at the same time as a party's memorial or counter-memorial, as well as documentary exhibits.

3. Documents filed after time limit. If any document is filed after the expiration of the time limit indicated in Rule 24, it may be disregarded by the tribunal, subject to the tribunal exercising its discretion under Rule 26. Recent practice has been that tribunals will invariably use Rule 26 and not rely on Rule 24 to disregard late documentation.

[Correction of errors]

Arbitration Rule 25

An accidental error in any instrument or supporting document may, with the consent of the other party or by leave of the Tribunal, be corrected at any time before the award is rendered.

1. General. This rule relates only to accidental errors such as misprints, incorrect dates and typographical errors. Rule 25 should be considered alongside the duty of the Secretary-General to bring to the notice of the party filing an instrument or document any failure to conform to applicable requirements (Reg. 24(2) of the Administrative and Financial Regulations).

[Time limits]

Arbitration Rule 26

(1) Where required, time limits shall be fixed by the Tribunal by assigning dates for the completion of the various steps in the proceeding. The Tribunal may delegate this power to its President.

(2) The Tribunal may extend any time limit that it has fixed. If the Tribunal is not in session, this power shall be exercised by its President.

(3) Any step taken after expiration of the applicable time limit shall be disregarded unless the Tribunal, in special circumstances and after giving the other party an opportunity of stating its views, decides otherwise.

1. General. Rule 26 contains the general rules on time limits for the completion of procedural steps. ICSID arbitrations can be slow, averaging two to three years from the registration of the initial request to the rendering of the award. The arbitrators are usually not responsible for the protracted length of the arbitration – it is the written and oral procedures, not the drafting of the award, that are time consuming. It is not unusual for the parties themselves to request extensions of time and suspensions of proceedings.

2. Power of the tribunal to fix time limits. Rule 26(1) confers on the tribunal the power to fix time limits, where required. The time limits will be contained in orders made by the tribunal under Rule 19 and will be guided by any agreement between the parties made under Rule 20(2).

3. Delegation of power to fix time limits to president of tribunal. Since decisions relating to time limits frequently have to be made whilst a tribunal is not in session, Rule 26(1) and (2) provides that the tribunal may delegate to its president the power to fix and extend such limits. If the president is unwilling to act without the consent of his colleagues (or if the tribunal members do not decide to delegate this power), a decision can be taken by correspondence under Rule 16(2). Rule 26 is effectively a limited and expedient exception to the rule in art. 48(1) and Rule 16 that the tribunal must decide questions by a majority of the votes of its members.

4. Extension of time limits. Rule 26(2) grants the tribunal discretion to extend time limits.

5. Failure to comply with time limits. Any document filed after the expiration of the time limit may be disregarded by the tribunal unless the tribunal decides otherwise (Rule 26(3)). In exercising its discretion, a tribunal would be expected to consider the extent to which its acceptance of a late document prejudices the other party. Often a tribunal will accept a late document, but offer the other party an opportunity to make further submissions or comments.

6. Calculation of time limits. All time limits begin to run from the date on which the limit is announced to the parties or on which the Secretary-General dispatches the notification of the time limit (Reg. 29 of the Administrative and Financial Regulations). The day of the announcement or notification is excluded from the calculation.

7. Distinction from grace period under Rule 42(2)(a). Rule 42(2)(a) requires a tribunal to grant a period of grace in the case of a default. This period of grace, which is effectively a new time limit, can be distinguished from Rule 26 on the basis that it is not discretionary and is limited to a maximum of sixty days, unless the parties agree otherwise.

8. Time limits for rendering an award. ICSID tribunals have a period of 120 days from the closure of the proceedings within which to draft and issue the award (Rule 46). This time limit may be extended by a further sixty days. There is no provision, unlike in the ICC Arbitration Rules, for ICSID to scrutinise or otherwise review a draft award.

[Waiver]

Arbitration Rule 27

A party which knows or should have known that a provision of the Administrative and Financial Regulations, of these Rules, of any other rules or agreement applicable to the proceeding, or of an order of the Tribunal has not been complied with and which fails to state promptly its objections thereto, shall be deemed – subject to Article 45 of the Convention – to have waived its right to object.

1. General. Rule 27 requires objections to violations of rules and regulations to be raised promptly and states that failure to do so will mean that the party alleging breach is precluded from objecting later in the proceedings. This reflects a principle of civil procedure common to many jurisdictions.

2. Meaning of 'promptly'. Rule 27 requires that a party promptly submit its objections to non-compliance with a particular provision. What will constitute 'promptly' in any situation depends on the nature of the violation, the procedural framework agreed between the parties and the stage of the proceedings at which the issue arises.

3. Application for annulment. Rule 27 does not refer to annulment, but Rule 53 clarifies that the Arbitration Rules apply to annulment proceedings. Therefore, a party cannot make an application for the annulment of an award on the basis of a violation of the Arbitration Rules to which it did not object at an earlier point, if at that point it knew or should have known of the violation. The rule prevents a party from using ex post facto procedural challenges to invalidate an award with which it disagrees and means that parties with genuine grievances have to exhaust their remedies with regard to procedural challenges as the breaches occur.

4. Default proceedings. Rule 27 is limited by the rule in art. 45(1) and Rule 42 that the failure of a party to appear or to present its case is not to be deemed an admission of the other party's assertions. Therefore, a party that has failed to appear or present its case is not deemed to have waived its right to make objections under Rule 27.

[Cost of proceeding]
Arbitration Rule 28

(1) **Without prejudice to the final decision on the payment of the cost of the proceeding, the Tribunal may, unless otherwise agreed by the parties, decide:**
  (a) **at any stage of the proceeding, the portion which each party shall pay, pursuant to Administrative and Financial Regulation 14, of the fees and expenses of the Tribunal and the charges for the use of the facilities of the Centre;**
  (b) **with respect to any part of the proceeding, that the related costs (as determined by the Secretary-General) shall be borne entirely or in a particular share by one of the parties.**

(2) **Promptly after the closure of the proceeding, each party shall submit to the Tribunal a statement of costs reasonably incurred or borne by it in the proceeding and the Secretary-General shall submit to the Tribunal an account of all amounts paid by each party to the Centre and of all costs incurred by the Centre for the proceeding. The Tribunal may, before the award has been rendered, request the parties and the Secretary-General to provide additional information concerning the cost of the proceeding.**

1. General. Rule 28 addresses the question of costs in ICSID arbitral proceedings. It should be read in light of art. 61 regarding the apportionment of expenses. It provides that the question of costs may be addressed throughout the entire period of proceedings and that the tribunal has full discretion as to the apportionment of costs between the parties to the dispute.

2. Payment for part of the proceeding. Pursuant to Rule 9(1), the tribunal's decision on costs does not necessarily relate to the entire proceeding. Therefore, the tribunal is not restricted in apportioning the costs in the final award. The tribunal may charge one party the costs or the majority of such costs of a particular part of the proceedings. Furthermore, a party that requested a specific measure may have to bear the resulting costs (see art. 61, notes 3 and 4). As a matter of principle, each party shall advance half of the payments.

3. Final settlement of costs. All advance payments are provisional. It follows that the final award will decide the exact manner in which the costs of the entire proceedings will be divided between the parties. In order to do so, the parties and the Secretary-General will have to submit to the tribunal full statements and accounts of costs, which include the advance payments made by the parties.

CHAPTER IV. WRITTEN AND ORAL PROCEDURES

[Normal procedures]

Arbitration Rule 29

Except if the parties otherwise agree, the proceeding shall comprise two distinct phases: a written procedure followed by an oral one.

1. General. Chapter IV of the Convention divides the principal part of the proceeding into two distinct phases: the written procedure and the oral procedure.

2. Freedom of the parties. The parties are free under Rule 29 to determine whether to have both phases. In practice, ICSID arbitrations usually have both.

3. Two distinct phases. The written procedure comprises the request for arbitration and the pleadings. The oral procedure comprises the hearings. Rule 31 covers the written procedure and Rule 32 covers the oral procedure. In an ICSID arbitration, as with international arbitrations generally, the parties will usually carefully brief their case in detailed written submissions, with the result that the oral phase is comparatively shorter and focused on the giving of evidence (in contrast with some national court procedures which typically have shorter pleadings and longer oral opening and closing submissions). Rule 47(1)(f) stipulates that an award must contain a summary of the proceeding; accordingly, awards typically set out a comprehensive history of the written and oral procedures.

4. Jurisdictional objections. Many ICSID proceedings are divided into separate parts to consider first the tribunal's jurisdiction and then the merits of the claim (see art. 41 and Rule 41). Where this is the case, the tribunal will often apply the two-phase approach of written pleadings followed by an oral hearing to each part of the proceedings. The same approach can be taken to other incidental and subsidiary parts of the proceedings.

[Transmission of the request]

Arbitration Rule 30

As soon as the Tribunal is constituted, the Secretary-General shall transmit to each member a copy of the request by which the proceeding was initiated, of the supporting documentation, of the notice of registration and of any communication received from either party in response thereto.

1. General. Rule 30 provides for the transmission by the Secretary-General to each member of the tribunal of a copy of the request for arbitration and any supporting documentation, the notice of registration and any communication between the parties in that regard.

2. As soon as the tribunal is constituted. Under Rule 6(1), the tribunal is constituted upon the Secretary-General notifying the parties that all of the arbitrators have accepted their appointments.

3. Request for arbitration. The request for arbitration and the supporting documents form part of the written procedure in the dispute and may be needed by the tribunal when determining the Centre's jurisdiction or its own competence pursuant to art. 41. Under Rule 3 of the Institution Rules, the request may set forth any rules agreed by the parties, such as the number of arbitrators or the method of their appointment. The tribunal will need to be aware of such provisions when making orders under Rule 19 of the Arbitration Rules and conducting the preliminary procedural consultation under Rule 20(2).

[The written procedure]

Arbitration Rule 31

(1) In addition to the request for arbitration, the written procedure shall consist of the following pleadings, filed within time limits set by the Tribunal:
    (a) a memorial by the requesting party;
    (b) a counter-memorial by the other party;
and, if the parties so agree or the Tribunal deems it necessary:

(c) **a reply by the requesting party; and**
(d) **a rejoinder by the other party.**

(2) If the request was made jointly, each party shall, within the same time limit determined by the Tribunal, file its memorial and, if the parties so agree or the Tribunal deems it necessary, its reply; however, the parties may instead agree that one of them shall, for the purposes of paragraph (1), be considered as the requesting party.

(3) A memorial shall contain: a statement of the relevant facts; a statement of law; and the submissions. A counter-memorial, reply or rejoinder shall contain an admission or denial of the facts stated in the last previous pleading; any additional facts, if necessary; observations concerning the statement of law in the last previous pleading; a statement of law in answer thereto; and the submissions.

1. General. The written procedure consists of the request for arbitration and the pleadings (although the parties may agree to dispense with written pleadings under Rule 29). As with international arbitration generally, the written submissions in ICSID cases are often the most persuasive part of the proceedings.

2. Rounds of pleadings. ICSID arbitration revolves around two main pleadings: a 'memorial' filed by the claimant and a 'counter-memorial' filed by the respondent. Rule 31(1) allows the parties to agree or the tribunal to decide to permit further reply pleadings. Further pleadings are now common, particularly in complex cases. The tribunal also has the discretion to order post-hearing memorials in addition to, or as well as, closing oral submissions.

3. Formalities of pleadings. The formal requirements relating to pleadings are contained in Rules 22, 23 and 24. The tribunal has authority to fix time limits for the filing of pleadings pursuant to Rule 26. The parties' views on the number and sequence of the pleadings, the number of copies to be filed and the time limits for filing should be sought by the tribunal during the preliminary procedural consultation contemplated by Rule 20(1).

4. Order of pleadings. Rule 31(2) distinguishes between proceedings requested by one party and those requested jointly by the parties under Rule 1(2) of the Institution Rules. Filings are simultaneous in the rare cases where the request was made jointly. In addition, simultaneous pleadings may be appropriate where the facts are not disputed between the parties. A key disadvantage of simultaneous pleadings is that a party may not reveal the whole of its case or evidence until it has seen its opponent's submissions. The result can be delays and further rounds of pleadings. Consecutive pleading is the norm in commercial arbitration but, simultaneous filing is still used before ad hoc tribunals in intergovernmental arbitration. For the most part, pleadings in ICSID arbitrations are consecutive.

5. Time limits. The time limits for the filing of pleadings are determined by the tribunal under Rules 31(1) and 26(1). The parties are usually granted the same amount of time, although occasionally the requesting party is granted less time for filing its memorial to account for pre-request preparation. Time limits also apply to the filing of 'ancillary' claims. The respondent must file a counterclaim no later than in its counter-memorial; and a claimant must assert any additional or incidental claim no later than its reply (see art. 46 and Rule 40).

6. Contents of pleadings. Rule 31(3) sets out the required elements of the pleadings. A claimant's memorial must contain a statement of the relevant facts, a statement of law, the claimant's submissions (i.e. pleas) and a request for relief. The counter-memorial, reply and rejoinder must each contain a denial or admission of the facts in the prior pleading, any additional relevant facts, observations on the statement of law in the prior pleading and the party's submissions. In addition, evidence is often submitted along with the pleadings, most often witness statements and experts' reports. The provisions in Rule 31(3) are designed to prevent procedural arguments concerning the scope of the pleadings stemming from the different legal backgrounds of the parties. The parties can agree on a different content for the pleadings. In practice, the pleadings are important pieces of advocacy and are carefully crafted by the parties.

7. Filing pleadings. Unlike other forms of international commercial arbitration, the parties in an ICSID arbitration do not transmit their filings directly to the arbitrators. Until the tribunal is constituted, the parties are required by Reg. 24(2) of the Administrative and Financial Regulations and Rule 23 of the Arbitration Rules to file the original signed version of the pleadings, plus five copies, with the Secretary-General. Once the tribunal is constituted, the parties are required to file with the Secretariat a signed original, plus two copies more than the number of arbitrators in the tribunal.

8. Filing evidence. Pursuant to Rule 24, supporting documentation, witness statements and expert reports are ordinarily filed with the pleading to which they relate and, in any case, must be filed within the time limit for the relevant pleading. This issue will, however, be determined by the tribunal in its procedural order after consulting with the parties pursuant to Rule 20(1). See also Rule 33, which seeks to avoid surprise to the other party caused by the late filing of evidence.

[The oral procedure]
Arbitration Rule 32

(1) The oral procedure shall consist of the hearing by the Tribunal of the parties, their agents, counsel and advocates, and of witnesses and experts.

(2) Unless either party objects, the Tribunal, after consultation with the Secretary-General, may allow other persons, besides the parties, their agents, counsel and advocates, witnesses and experts during their

ICSID Arbitration Rules, Rule 32

testimony, and officers of the Tribunal, to attend or observe all or part of the hearings, subject to appropriate logistical arrangements. The Tribunal shall for such cases establish procedures for the protection of proprietary or privileged information.

(3) The members of the Tribunal may, during the hearings, put questions to the parties, their agents, counsel and advocates, and ask them for explanations.

1. General. The oral procedure consists of hearings which develop the arguments of the parties. The ICSID oral procedure is similar to that under other international arbitration rules. It may be dispensed with entirely under Rule 29.

2. Format of hearings: organisation. Hearings take place at 'sittings' of the tribunal, which constitute part of a 'session'. They are conducted under the control of the president of the tribunal (Rule 14(1)). The parties may appear in person or through their representatives (Rule 18). The language in which the hearings are to be conducted is governed by Rule 22. The Secretary-General will appoint a secretary to take notes of the hearings, unless the parties agree with the tribunal on another method for keeping a record of the hearings (Reg. 25(c) of the Administrative and Financial Regulations).

3. Format of hearings: length. There may be one or more hearings on jurisdiction and merits. Hearings are generally short, often lasting no longer than one or two weeks, which underscores the importance of the written procedure.

4. Format of hearings: statements. The requesting party or its representative normally makes an opening statement, followed by a statement by or on behalf of the other party. Sometimes, the tribunal may permit a short reply and rejoinder. Oral closing submissions may also be permitted, possibly at a separate sitting of the tribunal, together with or instead of written closing submissions. In practice, ICSID tribunals often prefer to receive written closing submissions.

5. Format of hearings: oral evidence. In addition to oral arguments, the parties may present fact witnesses and experts at the hearing. If oral evidence is submitted by a party, this will usually come after its first statement and be followed by an examination of its witnesses by their opponent's representatives. Rule 35 sets out the procedure governing the examination of witnesses and experts.

6. Secrecy of proceedings. The tribunal, with the consent of the parties, may permit the attendance of other persons at the hearing. As originally drafted, Rule 32 permitted the tribunal, with the consent of the parties, to control which persons, besides the parties, their authorised representatives and witnesses, could attend the oral hearing. During consultations prior to the April 2006 amendment of the ICSID Rules, it was proposed that the tribunal would retain the sole right to decide which other persons would be allowed to attend a hearing. Ultimately, however, it was decided that the parties' consent would remain necessary for the admission of other persons. The result is that ICSID hearings are not, without party consent, open to the public. Where the parties and the tribunal agree to permit third parties to attend, the tribunal may put in place appropriate procedures for the protection of proprietary or privileged information. The tribunal may require that any expert or witness leave the hearing when not giving testimony.

7. Right to put questions. Under Rule 32(3), each member of the tribunal has the right to put questions to the parties or their representatives. This is restated in Rule 35(1). The conduct of the proceeding and examination of witnesses by the parties is, however, under 'the control' of the president (see Rules 14(1) and 35(1)).

[Marshalling of evidence]

Arbitration Rule 33

Without prejudice to the rules concerning the production of documents, each party shall, within time limits fixed by the Tribunal, communicate to the Secretary-General, for transmission to the Tribunal and the other party, precise information regarding the evidence which it intends to produce and that which it intends to request the Tribunal to call for, together with an indication of the points to which such evidence will be directed.

1. General. Rule 33 requires each party to provide the Secretary-General with precise information regarding the evidence which it intends to produce. The rule relates to witness evidence, experts' reports and any proposed visits or local inquiries.

2. Purpose of marshalling evidence. This rule protects parties from being ambushed by unexpected evidence and facilitates the tribunal's organisation of the hearings. It was included in the Arbitration Rules to emphasise the parties' primary responsibility to produce relevant evidence, as opposed to placing the onus on the tribunal to seek to order the parties to produce such evidence.

3. What is 'precise' information? 'Precise' information regarding the evidence should include the names, addresses and expertise of witnesses and experts. The information should help the tribunal and the other party form a preliminary view as to admissibility and relevance.

[Evidence: general principles]

Arbitration Rule 34

(1) The Tribunal shall be the judge of the admissibility of any evidence adduced and of its probative value.

(2) The Tribunal may, if it deems it necessary at any stage of the proceeding:
- (a) call upon the parties to produce documents, witnesses and experts; and
- (b) visit any place connected with the dispute or conduct inquiries there.

(3) The parties shall cooperate with the Tribunal in the production of the evidence and in the other measures provided for in paragraph (2). The Tribunal shall take formal note of the failure of a party to comply with its obligations under this paragraph and of any reasons given for such failure.

(4) Expenses incurred in producing evidence and in taking other measures in accordance with paragraph (2) shall be deemed to constitute part of the expenses incurred by the parties within the meaning of Article 61(2) of the Convention.

1. General. It is long-standing international practice that a tribunal is the judge of the admissibility and the probative value of any evidence adduced by the parties. Each tribunal's approach to evidence will be different and may depend on the legal background of the arbitrators. Strict rules of evidence, such as those developed under national procedural codes, do not apply in ICSID arbitration proceedings and there is no extensive procedure for document production.

2. Power of the tribunal to determine the admissibility and probative value of evidence. Rule 34 confers on the tribunal the power to determine the admissibility, relevance and materiality of evidence. A tribunal will be expected to exercise its own judgment as to the probative value and/or prejudicial effect of evidence without regard to formal rules. The discretion of the tribunal under Rule 34 must be exercised subject to the principle of equal treatment of the parties.

3. Power of tribunal to call on parties to produce evidence. The emphasis of the ICSID procedure is on voluntary disclosure of evidence by the parties. Consequently, while the tribunal does have the power to request further evidence as the need arises (see Rule 34(2) and art. 43), it is generally expected to exercise this power sparingly. The tribunal does not have the power to subpoena any witness or expert.

4. Form of request to produce documents. Voluntary disclosure of documents is the default position in ICSID arbitration and large-scale discovery is unheard of. It is entirely up to the tribunal what level of document production to order beyond voluntary disclosure, and there is no specific form in which the tribunal may call upon the parties to produce documents. In practice, a party will usually have made a targeted request for production and the tribunal will usually only order the production of specific and narrow categories of documents, such as those mandated by art. 3 of the IBA Rules on the Taking of Evidence in International Commercial Arbitration.

5. Tribunal may visit any place connected with the dispute. Rule 34(2)(b) paraphrases art. 43 by authorising the tribunal to visit any place connected with the dispute or to conduct inquiries there. Rule 37 requires a separate procedural order by the tribunal for any visits and inquiries. If a particular visit or inquiry is undertaken upon a party's wish or insistence, they may be liable for any connected costs. This power of the tribunal to visit the scene cannot be denied by a Contracting State party to the Convention. Art. 21 grants arbitrators special immunities during site visits and art. 22 extends these privileges and immunities to witnesses, experts and the parties and their representatives.

6. Duty of parties to cooperate with the tribunal. Rule 34(3) imposes an obligation on the parties to cooperate with the tribunal with regard to the production of evidence and allows the tribunal to take 'formal note' of a party's failure to comply with this obligation. The Arbitration Rules do not contain any further express sanctions against an uncooperative party, but a tribunal may draw adverse inferences from that lack of cooperation. These may take the form of evidentiary findings and/or they may affect the allocation of costs. For example, in *SOABI* v *Senegal*, the tribunal accepted Senegal's demand that SOABI, who had failed to explain their financial calculations, have their accounts audited and bear the costs of the audit. If a party is not able to produce evidence for reasons outside its control, the tribunal must note the reasons given for the failure.

7. Expenses incurred in producing evidence. Art. 61(2) governs the position in relation to expenditure incurred by the parties in connection with producing evidence under Rule 34(2). Under Rule 28(1)(b), the tribunal may decide with respect to any part of the proceeding that the costs shall be borne entirely or in a particular proportion by one of the parties. This enables the tribunal to transfer the costs to the party that created the need for the measure. Such expenses must be assessed and attributed by the tribunal in its award.

[Examination of witnesses and experts]

Arbitration Rule 35

(1) Witnesses and experts shall be examined before the Tribunal by the parties under the control of its President. Questions may also be put to them by any member of the Tribunal.

(2) Each witness shall make the following declaration before giving his evidence: 'I solemnly declare upon my honour and conscience that I shall speak the truth, the whole truth and nothing but the truth.'

(3) Each expert shall make the following declaration before making his statement: 'I solemnly declare upon my honour and conscience that my statement will be in accordance with my sincere belief.'

1. General. The examination of witnesses and experts is governed by Rule 35.

2. Examination before the tribunal. It is normal for witnesses to present their evidence in person and to be cross-examined. It is open to the parties to agree departures from this rule, for example to allow witness evidence to be presented in writing (Rule 36). The examination is under the control of the president of the tribunal, in accordance with Rule 14(1), and any member of the tribunal may put questions to the witness or expert (see also Rule 32(3)).

3. Declarations. Rules 35(2) and (3) set out the declarations that witnesses and experts must make respectively. These statements would also typically appear in the witness statement or expert report filed prior to the evidentiary hearing.

4. Requesting an expert to give evidence. In ICSID proceedings, experts may be requested either by the parties or the tribunal to give evidence (see Rule 36(a)). In some cases, an expert may be appointed directly by a tribunal. Frequently, the experts that are appointed by the tribunal are financial experts qualified to assess the quantum of a party's loss.

[Witnesses and experts: special rules]

Arbitration Rule 36

Notwithstanding Rule 35 the Tribunal may:
  (a) admit evidence given by a witness or expert in a written deposition; and
  (b) with the consent of both parties, arrange for the examination of a witness or expert otherwise than before the Tribunal itself. The Tribunal shall define the subject of the examination, the time limit, the procedure to be followed and other particulars. The parties may participate in the examination.

1. General. Rule 35 provides that, in principle, evidence by witnesses and experts should be given before the tribunal. Rule 36 provides for two exceptions to this general rule, which accommodate the reality that an ICSID tribunal has no power to compel the presence of a witness or expert and recognise that an ICSID tribunal is not bound by strict rules of evidence.

Specifically, Rule 36 permits the tribunal to accept written evidence in lieu of live testimony or arrange for a witness or expert to be examined otherwise than before the tribunal itself.

2. Written evidence: source of tribunal's power to call for evidence. Rule 36(a) gives the tribunal the power to receive or call for evidence in the form of a written deposition by a witness or expert. In practice, witness statements and expert reports are almost always required as well as, and not instead of, live evidence. This rule has been identified by some commentators as a source of a tribunal's power to call for evidence, including to appoint experts to assist the tribunal.

3. Tribunal's discretion to admit written evidence only. Because neither the tribunal nor any party has the opportunity to question evidence presented only in writing, the probative value of such evidence is diminished. In *Tradex* v *Albania*, the tribunal found, upon the objection of Albania, that the claimant had not met its burden of proof by submitting the written statements of a single witness who was not available for questioning at the hearing. This decision accords with the approach of art. 4(8) of the IBA Rules on the Taking of Evidence in International Commercial Arbitration, which provides that the tribunal 'shall disregard' a witness statement if the witness does not appear at the hearing without a valid reason. Art. 36(a) does, however, permit an ICSID tribunal flexibility as to whether to accept a statement from a witness who does not appear. If evidence is submitted only in written form, it is advisable that it be notarised or attested in an appropriate manner.

4. Examination otherwise than before the tribunal. With the mutual consent of the parties, witnesses may be examined otherwise than before the tribunal, and both parties may participate. Where this is done, the tribunal may appoint a member to oversee the examination process. Modern technology, such as video-conferencing facilities, has made off-site examination easier and more prevalent.

[Visits and inquiries; submissions of non-disputing parties]
Arbitration Rule 37

(1) If the Tribunal considers it necessary to visit any place connected with the dispute or to conduct an inquiry there, it shall make an order to this effect. The order shall define the scope of the visit or the subject of the inquiry, the time limit, the procedure to be followed and other particulars. The parties may participate in any visit or inquiry.

(2) After consulting both parties, the Tribunal may allow a person or entity that is not a party to the dispute (in this Rule called the 'nondisputing party') to file a written submission with the Tribunal regarding a matter within the scope of the dispute. In determining whether to allow such a filing, the Tribunal shall consider, among other things, the extent to which:

(a) the non-disputing party submission would assist the Tribunal in the determination of a factual or legal issue related to the proceeding by bringing a perspective, particular knowledge or insight that is different from that of the disputing parties;
(b) the non-disputing party submission would address a matter within the scope of the dispute;
(c) the non-disputing party has a significant interest in the proceeding.

The Tribunal shall ensure that the non-disputing party submission does not disrupt the proceeding or unduly burden or unfairly prejudice either party, and that both parties are given an opportunity to present their observations on the non-disputing party submission.

1. General. Rule 37 elaborates on Rule 34(2)(b), which is based on art. 43(b), and authorises the tribunal to visit any place connected with the dispute or conduct inquiries there.

2. Discretion of the tribunal to visit a site. The tribunal has the discretion to determine whether it is necessary to visit a particular location connected with the dispute (Rule 37(1)).

3. The form of the order. This is one of the few rules which specifically requires the tribunal to make an order pursuant to Rule 19. In practice, ICSID tribunals will make numerous procedural orders in the conduct of the proceedings. The tribunal's procedural orders must be made by a majority of the votes of all its members pursuant to arts. 44 and 48(1) and Rule 16(1).

4. The content of the order. In the order, the tribunal must define the scope of the visit or the subject of the inquiry, fix a time limit pursuant to Rule 26, set out the procedure to be followed (referring to any procedural framework agreed between the parties either before the arbitration proceedings and provided to the Secretary-General under Rule 3 of the Institution Rules, or during consultations with the president of the tribunal under Rule 20 of the Arbitration Rules) and other particulars. The parties may participate in any visit or inquiry.

5. Arrangements for a site visit or inquiry. The language in Rule 37(1) is sufficiently broad to enable the tribunal to conduct an inquiry at any place connected with the dispute, or ask a third party to conduct the visit or inquiry on behalf of the tribunal. Reg. 26(2) of the Administrative and Financial Regulations provides that the Secretary-General is responsible for making the necessary arrangements for the tribunal's visit or inquiry. If a particular visit or inquiry is undertaken at the request of one of the parties, the associated costs arising from such a visit or inquiry may be charged to that party. See generally art. 7 of the IBA Rules on the Taking of Evidence in International Commercial Arbitration.

6. Submission by non-disputing party: the April 2006 amendments.
Rule 37(2) was introduced as an amendment to the Arbitration Rules in April 2006. The purpose of the amendment was to make it clear that ICSID tribunals may accept and consider written submissions from a non-disputing person or a State, after consulting the parties as far as possible. This amendment was passed to reflect the public interest in certain ICSID cases, particularly those that arise out of investment treaties. In fact, prior to the introduction of the new Rule 37(2), an ICSID tribunal had permitted the filing of an amicus curiae brief (see *Aguas Argentinas S.A., Suez & Ors* v *Argentine Republic* (2005), relying on art. 44), although another ICSID tribunal declined such a request (*Aguas del Tunari S.A.* v *Republic of Bolivia* (2003)). The right of non-parties to appear at a hearing is governed by Rule 32(2), and requires the consent of the parties. Thus, a party's consent is required for a non-party to attend a hearing, but not for the non-party to make written submissions or to file an amicus curiae brief. Amicus curiae briefs have, for some time, been a feature of NAFTA disputes conducted under the UNCITRAL Rules (see *Methanex* v *United States* (2001), *UPS* and *Glamis Gold* (Procedural Order)).

7. Applications under the new Rule 37(2). The new rule is limited in several ways, most significantly by the requirement that submissions are permitted only from third parties with a significant interest in the dispute. Although the rule is wide enough to encompass applications by private parties with an interest in the dispute, it is non-governmental organisations and lobbyists who are mostly likely to use the Rule 37(2) procedure, in order to intervene in cases on issues in the public interest. The leading case since the introduction of the new rule, *Biwater* v *Tanzania*, involved the tribunal accepting a joint amicus curiae submission from human rights and environmental groups. The tribunal clarified that Rule 37(2) allows the tribunal to accept a submission from a non-disputing party without the approval of one or both of the arbitrating parties. This third party right does not extend to the right to have such submissions accepted by the tribunal, or for them to form a basis for the final award if they are accepted. The *Biwater* tribunal did not, however, allow the petitioners access to documents filed in the case or the right to attend the hearing.

8. Considerations as to whether to allow a non-disputing party to file a submission. When determining whether to allow a filing by a non-disputing party, Rule 37(2) states that the tribunal must consider whether the non-disputing party's submission would: assist the tribunal to clarify or explain a factual or legal issue; address a matter sufficiently related to the dispute; and be from a non-disputing party who is sufficiently connected or has a significant enough interest in the proceeding to file such a submission. This is not an exhaustive list. The tribunal must also consider whether the submission would disrupt or frustrate proceedings by causing undue delay or would burden or unfairly prejudice either party. The tribunal must give both parties sufficient opportunity to present their views on and respond to the non-disputing party's submission. In the *Biwater* case, the parties were given the opportunity to comment on the amicus curiae submission.

[Closure of the proceeding]

Arbitration Rule 38

(1) When the presentation of the case by the parties is completed, the proceeding shall be declared closed.

(2) Exceptionally, the Tribunal may, before the award has been rendered, reopen the proceeding on the ground that new evidence is forthcoming of such a nature as to constitute a decisive factor, or that there is a vital need for clarification on certain specific points.

1. General. Rule 38 states that upon the completion of the presentation by the parties of their respective cases, the tribunal should declare the closure of the proceeding subject to any reopening on the ground that decisive new evidence has been discovered or further clarification is needed by the tribunal.

2. Closure of the proceeding. Closure of the proceeding triggers a time limit within which the tribunal must complete its award. Under Rule 46, the tribunal must draw up and sign its award, including the individual or dissenting opinions, within 120 days of the closure of the proceeding (or 180 days should the tribunal extend this deadline by sixty days, as permitted). The closure of the proceeding also marks the time limit before which any proposal under art. 57 and Rule 9(1) to disqualify an arbitrator must be submitted. If a party learns of a ground for the disqualification of an arbitrator after the closure of the proceeding, it may only request the annulment of the award in accordance with art. 52(1)(a). Even after an award has been rendered, the appearance of new evidence may lead to the award's revision under art. 51.

3. Reopening the proceeding. Rule 38 provides that, in exceptional circumstances, the tribunal may reopen the proceeding in order to take new evidence. The tribunal may reopen proceedings at the request of a party or on its own initiative. For example, in *Klöckner* v *Cameroon* (I), two days after the written and oral phases of the proceeding had finished and the tribunal had declared the proceeding to be at an end, the arbitrators met and decided under Rule 38(2) to ask the parties to respond to an additional question of fact.

4. Not closing the proceeding. It is unclear how much flexibility there is in determining when the 'presentation of the case' is completed under Rule 38(1). The tribunal could avoid the Rule 38(2) procedure of reopening proceedings by refusing to declare them closed. This occurred in the *SOABI* v *Senegal* case, where the tribunal indicated at the end of the hearing that the proceeding was not yet closed within the meaning of Rule 38 and that it reserved the right to request additional information.

ICSID Arbitration Rules, Rule 39

CHAPTER V. PARTICULAR PROCEDURES
[Provisional measures]
Arbitration Rule 39

(1) At any time after the institution of the proceeding, a party may request that provisional measures for the preservation of its rights be recommended by the Tribunal. The request shall specify the rights to be preserved, the measures the recommendation of which is requested, and the circumstances that require such measures.

(2) The Tribunal shall give priority to the consideration of a request made pursuant to paragraph (1).

(3) The Tribunal may also recommend provisional measures on its own initiative or recommend measures other than those specified in a request. It may at any time modify or revoke its recommendations.

(4) The Tribunal shall only recommend provisional measures, or modify or revoke its recommendations, after giving each party an opportunity of presenting its observations.

(5) If a party makes a request pursuant to paragraph (1) before the constitution of the Tribunal, the Secretary-General shall, on the application of either party, fix time limits for the parties to present observations on the request, so that the request and observations may be considered by the Tribunal promptly upon its constitution.

(6) Nothing in this Rule shall prevent the parties, provided that they have so stipulated in the agreement recording their consent, from requesting any judicial or other authority to order provisional measures, prior to or after the institution of the proceeding, for the preservation of their respective rights and interests.

1. General. Rule 39 provides the procedural framework within which the tribunal can make provisional measures under art. 47. The measures recommended must be 'provisional' in character and appropriate in nature, extent and duration to the rights that are to be protected.

2. Any time after the institution of proceeding. Under Rule 39(1), a party may request provisional measures at any time after the institution of the proceeding. According to Rule 6(2) of the Institution Rules the proceeding is deemed to have been instituted on the date of the registration of the request. Under Rule 6(1), the tribunal is deemed to be constituted on the date that the Secretary-General notifies the parties that all of the arbitrators have accepted their appointment. Many issues will still be unresolved at this early stage; in particular jurisdiction may still be disputed. The tribunal in *Occidental* v *Ecuador* (DPM) determined that whilst the absence of a complete examination of jurisdiction issues would not preclude the recommendation of provisional measures, the tribunal must establish that it has at least prima facie jurisdiction.

3. Request before constitution of the tribunal. Where a party requests provisional measures before a tribunal has been constituted, the Secretary-General will fix time limits for the parties to present observations on the request in order to facilitate the prompt consideration of the matter by the tribunal upon its constitution (Rule 39(5)). There is no mechanism for the Secretary-General to order provisional measures prior to the constitution of the tribunal. In practice, then, urgent relief required at the outset of proceedings would be sought from a court of competent jurisdiction, provided the parties have so agreed under Rule 39(6).

4. Discretion of the tribunal to recommend provisional measures. The tribunal must treat any request for provisional measures with priority (Rule 39(2)). The president of the tribunal may, if he considers the request to be urgent, propose to convene the tribunal for a special session or propose that a decision be taken by correspondence pursuant to Rule 16(2). The tribunal may at any time modify or revoke provisional measures if they are no longer required by the circumstances (Rule 39(3)). Whlst provisional measures motions are nearly always submitted by parties, a tribunal may also recommend provisional measures on its own initiative.

5. Meaning of 'recommend' provisional measures. Although art. 47 and Rule 39 are expressed in terms of the tribunal 'recommending' provisional measures, it is now settled that ICSID tribunals have the power to 'order' provisional measures and that a tribunal's order in this regard is legally binding. The binding nature of a provisional measures recommendation was first mooted in *Maffezini* v *Spain* and has been affirmed in several subsequent cases, including *Occidental* v *Ecuador* (DPM) and *Tokios Tokeles* v *Ukraine*. The binding nature of provisional measures stems from the obligation of all Contracting States to ensure that the object and purpose of the Convention are not frustrated. A party may also be obligated to comply with provisional measures by virtue of contractual obligations undertaken vis-à-vis the other party in its consent to ICSID jurisdiction. A recommendation for provisional measures does not, however, constitute an award and the rules as to the enforcement of arbitral awards do not apply. In practice, ICSID tribunals are hesitant to recommend provisional measures, particularly against State parties. It is, of course, open to the parties to agree that the tribunal will have more extensive provisional measures powers.

6. The existence of a right and the need for measures. Rule 39 refers to 'preservation of its rights', which the tribunal in *Maffezini* v *Spain* took to mean that provisional measures must relate to rights already in existence. The tribunal in *Occidental* v *Ecuador* (DPM) stated that when faced with a request for provisional measures, the tribunal will not determine if the right to which they relate exists in fact, but will merely make an assessment of whether the asserted right is of a nature that makes it amenable to protection by provisional measures. Provisional measures must always be exceptional; the tribunal in *Occidental* v *Ecuador* (DPM) found that there must be an urgent need to prevent irreparable harm to the pre-existing rights before a tribunal can recommend provisional measures. The tribunal in *City Oriente* v *Petroecuador* cast doubt on the requirement of irreparable harm, and instead found a test that the 'harm spared by the petitioner by such measures must be significant and that it exceed greatly the damaged caused to the party affected thereby'. Subsequent to *City Oriente* v *Petroecuador*, the tribunal in *Paushok* v *Mongolia* cited *Occidental* v *Ecuador* (DPM) and confirmed the application of the 'irreparable harm' test to arbitrations taking place under UNCITRAL Rules. It is unclear if the formulation in *City Oriente* v *Petroecuador* will be applied by future ICSID tribunals.

7. Content of request for provisional measures. All such requests should specify the rights to be preserved, the specific measures requested and the circumstances that have led to the request. Neither the Convention nor the Arbitration Rules specify what types of measures may be recommended by the tribunal. Examples and further discussion can be found in art. 47.

8. Effect of compliance with provisional measures on the final award. A tribunal can take into account the parties' conduct, including any non-compliance with any recommended provisional measures, when it makes the final award.

9. Right of the parties to be heard. Under Rule 39(4), a tribunal may only recommend, modify or revoke provisional measures after giving each party an opportunity to present its observations. Failure to do so may expose the final award to annulment on the grounds of a serious departure from a fundamental rule of procedure under art. 52(1)(d).

10. Requesting any judicial or other authority to order provisional measures. Rule 39(6) clarifies the effect of art. 26, which states that once the parties have consented to ICSID arbitration they may not resort to remedies outside the arbitration. Provisional measures by domestic courts are therefore permissible only if the parties have expressly agreed to them in the instrument recording their consent to arbitration. As investment treaties do not typically provide for seeking such relief, domestic provisional measures are effectively precluded in BIT arbitrations commenced under the ICSID Convention. This was recognised by the English Court of Appeal in *Ecuador* v *Occidental* (UK), and *ETI Telecom* v *Bolivia* (UK). The position is different for BIT arbitrations commenced under the UNCITRAL Rules (see Rule 26(3)). Investors anticipating the need for urgent interim measures from domestic courts should negotiate for such rights in their investment contracts.

11. The April 2006 amendments. Rule 39 was amended in April 2006 to clarify the position of parties who need to make requests for provisional measures at a very early stage in the proceeding. Rule 39(1) was amended to make clear that requests could be made after the proceeding has been instituted, even if the tribunal has not yet been constituted. Rule 39(5) was inserted to provided a clear procedure for the submission of requests for provisional measures before the tribunal has been constituted.

[Ancillary claims]

Arbitration Rule 40

(1) Except as the parties otherwise agree, a party may present an incidental or additional claim or counterclaim arising directly out of the subject-matter of the dispute, provided that such ancillary claim is within the scope of the consent of the parties and is otherwise within the jurisdiction of the Centre.

(2) An incidental or additional claim shall be presented not later than in the reply and a counterclaim no later than in the counter-memorial, unless the Tribunal, upon justification by the party presenting the ancillary claim and upon considering any objection of the other party, authorises the presentation of the claim at a later stage in the proceeding.

(3) The Tribunal shall fix a time limit within which the party against which an ancillary claim is presented may file its observations thereon.

1. General. Rule 40 sets out the procedural framework within which incidental and additional claims by the claimant, or counterclaims by the respondent, may be brought, as specified by art. 46.

2. Except as the parties may agree. The parties may vary or exclude the tribunal's power to deal with ancillary claims in their consent agreement or subsequently. The initiative for consideration of ancillary claims must come from one of the parties.

3. What is an ancillary claim? There is no legal distinction between incidental and additional claims and the difference between them was never clarified during the drafting of the Convention (*History*, Vol. II, p. 811). An incidental claim may be understood as a claim that arises as a consequence of the primary claim, whereas an additional claim is a later amendment to the original pleading. A counterclaim is a claim made by the respondent. 'Ancillary claims' is the term used to refer to all such claims collectively.

4. Preliminary conditions of ancillary claims. Ancillary claims are subject to three preliminary conditions stated in art. 46 and Rule 40: they must arise directly out of the subject matter of the dispute; in other words the factual connection between the original and the ancillary claim must be so close as to require the tribunal to determine the latter in order to achieve a final settlement of the dispute; ancillary claims must be within the jurisdiction of the Centre and within the scope of the consent of the parties as contained in the request for arbitration under Rule 2(1)(c) of the Institution Rules; and certain time limits apply as to when they may be filed.

5. Timing. Ancillary claims should be presented as early as possible. In the absence of specific justification, an ancillary claim should be presented in the course of the written proceedings. A claimant may present an incidental or additional claim in its memorial (its first pleading) but should do so no later than in its reply (its second pleading under Rule 30(1)). A respondent should present its counterclaim no later than in its counter-memorial (its first pleading).

6. Observations by the other party. Upon presentation of an ancillary claim by one party, Rule 40(3) requires that the parties be given an opportunity to file observations on ancillary claims by the other side, subject to time limits to be fixed by the tribunal. While there will usually only be one round of written procedure on an ancillary claim, the tribunal is free to decide otherwise. If a counterclaim is presented in the respondent's counter-memorial, the claimant can make its observations in its reply. If an incidental or additional claim is made in the claimant's reply, the respondent can make its observations in its rejoinder.

[Preliminary objections]

Arbitration Rule 41

(1) Any objection that the dispute or any ancillary claim is not within the jurisdiction of the Centre or, for other reasons, is not within the competence of the Tribunal shall be made as early as possible. A party shall file the objection with the Secretary-General no later than the expiration of the time limit fixed for the filing of the counter-memorial, or, if the objection relates to an ancillary claim, for the filing of the rejoinder – unless the facts on which the objection is based are unknown to the party at that time.

(2) The Tribunal may on its own initiative consider, at any stage of the proceeding, whether the dispute or any ancillary claim before it is within the jurisdiction of the Centre and within its own competence.

(3) Upon the formal raising of an objection relating to the dispute, the Tribunal may decide to suspend the proceeding on the merits. The President of the Tribunal, after consultation with its other members, shall fix a time limit within which the parties may file observations on the objection.

(4) The Tribunal shall decide whether or not the further procedures relating to the objection made pursuant to paragraph (1) shall be oral. It may deal with the objection as a preliminary question or join it to the merits of the dispute. If the Tribunal overrules the objection or joins it to the merits, it shall once more fix time limits for the further procedures.

(5) Unless the parties have agreed to another expedited procedure for making preliminary objections, a party may, no later than 30 days after the constitution of the Tribunal, and in any event before the first session

of the Tribunal, file an objection that a claim is manifestly without legal merit. The party shall specify as precisely as possible the basis for the objection. The Tribunal, after giving the parties the opportunity to present their observations on the objection, shall, at its first session or promptly thereafter, notify the parties of its decision on the objection. The decision of the Tribunal shall be without prejudice to the right of a party to file an objection pursuant to paragraph (1) or to object, in the course of the proceeding, that a claim lacks legal merit.

(6) If the Tribunal decides that the dispute is not within the jurisdiction of the Centre or not within its own competence, or that all claims are manifestly without legal merit, it shall render an award to that effect.

1. General. Art. 41 states the general principle that the tribunal has the power to rule on its own competence. Rule 41 supplements art. 41 and provides the rules which govern the 'jurisdictional phase' of ICSID proceedings. Rule 41 regulates an increasingly important area of ICSID arbitration. Objections to jurisdiction are now routine practice in ICSID arbitrations brought against State parties under investment treaties. Indeed, they have become so common that tribunals have resorted to setting time limits for jurisdictional challenges even before the respondent has indicated an intention to challenge the tribunal's jurisdiction (see *Occidental* v *Ecuador* (DJ) and *Duke Energy Electroquil* v *Ecuador*). Rule 41(5), introduced in 2006, now permits preliminary objections to claims on the basis that they are manifestly without merit, or frivolous, as well as objections on the Rule 41(1) basis that the claims fall outside the tribunal's jurisdiction.

2. Tribunal has power to determine its own competence and jurisdiction of the Centre. Under art. 41(1) and (2), the tribunal is the judge of its own competence and must also decide objections to the jurisdiction of the Centre. The tribunal is not bound to assume jurisdiction merely because the Secretary-General has, in the exercise of its screening power, decided that the dispute in question is not manifestly outside the jurisdiction of the Centre and therefore registered the request for arbitration under art. 36(3) and Rule 6(1) of the Institution Rules. The tribunal must make its own inquiry and satisfy itself of its jurisdiction to proceed.

3. Objections to jurisdiction should be made as early as possible: the earliest opportunity. Rule 41(1) requires that any objection to jurisdiction be made as early as possible. The earliest an objection can be made is immediately after notification the registration of the request for arbitration, which is when the proceedings commence (Rule 6(2) of the Institution Rules). Ordinarily an objection to jurisdiction will be addressed as the first order of business of a tribunal upon its constitution. In practice, given how important jurisdictional issues are in proceedings, tribunals will not be strict with delayed challenges to jurisdiction. When the respondent in one case introduced a new ground for objecting to jurisdiction nearly two years after its original jurisdictional objections had been dismissed, the tribunal found that it had not waived its right to object on the new ground as it was closely related to its original grounds of objection. The tribunal emphasised that there would be 'no drastic consequences' for late objections to jurisdiction (*Helnan Hotels* v *Egypt*).

4. Objections to jurisdiction should be made as early as possible: the latest opportunity. An objection to jurisdiction may be raised later in the proceeding, if the facts on which the objection is based were unknown to the party earlier. The latest this can be done is the deadline for the counter-memorial (Rule 41(1)). However, Rule 41(5) stipulates that unless the parties have agreed otherwise, a party may not file an objection that a claim is manifestly without merit any later than thirty days from the constitution of the tribunal.

5. Objection to jurisdiction may be made by a party or the tribunal. An objection to jurisdiction will generally be raised by one of the parties, although it may also be raised by the tribunal on its own motion under Rule 41(2). A tribunal will have to consider jurisdictional issues in the case of default proceedings under Rule 42(4). In either case, both parties must be given an opportunity to present their observations (Rule 41(3)).

6. Suspension and the right to file observations. Whether an objection to jurisdiction is raised by the parties or the tribunal itself, the tribunal may suspend the proceeding on the merits and both parties must be given an opportunity to file observations (Rule 43(3)). Prior to April 2006, it was mandatory for the tribunal to suspend the proceeding upon the filing of an objection. Such suspension would appear most appropriate if the objection relates to the dispute itself and not merely to an ancillary claim. Where the objection relates to an ancillary claim, the tribunal may elect simply to suspend consideration of the ancillary claim and continue to consider the merits of the principal claim until the parties have filed their observations. In terms of procedure, jurisdictional challenges increasingly follow the format of the merits element of the case, with both a written and an oral phase (see Rule 29). In *Occidental* v *Ecuador* (DJ), for example, the jurisdiction phase had a full 'objection, answer, reply and rejoinder' format, together with an oral hearing.

7. How the tribunal can proceed. Rule 41(4) states two ways in which the tribunal may proceed when considering an objection to jurisdiction. First, the tribunal may decide to deal with the objection as a preliminary question, in which case it is likely that separate written and oral stages will commence and the duration of the arbitration can be extended for a year or more; however, the tribunal may decide that more summary proceedings are more appropriate. The advantage of seeking a preliminary decision on jurisdiction is that the time and costs of the merits stage may be avoided completely if the tribunal finds it has no jurisdiction. Secondly, the tribunal may join the objection to the merits phase. This course may be appropriate where the facts upon which the objection is based are closely connected with the merits and a decision on the objection might prejudice the decision on the merits. Once an award on the merits has been rendered, the decision on jurisdiction becomes part of the final award for the purposes of annulment and recognition.

8. Requirement to render an award if lack of jurisdiction. If the tribunal finds that it does not have jurisdiction, the case comes to an end, and the tribunal will issue a final award dismissing the case for lack of jurisdiction (Rule 41(6)). Such an award should conform to the provisions of arts. 48 to 49 and the post-award remedies set out in arts. 49(2) and 50 to 52 apply.

9. Reasoned decision if objection to jurisdiction fails. If the tribunal ultimately finds that it has jurisdiction, it typically issues a reasoned decision (rather than an award) and proceeds to consider the merits of the principal claim. A finding that the tribunal has jurisdiction is not a formal award under art. 48(3) and is not therefore subject to the post-award proceedings available under the Convention, but it will form a part of the final award and may be challenged at that stage.

10. Format of objections. Objections to jurisdiction, as well as any observations filed by the parties, should conform to the requirements established for all instruments filed in the proceeding, in particular those specified in Rules 22 to 24 and in Regs. 24 and 30 of the Administrative and Financial Regulations.

11. Claims manifestly without merit: the amended Rule 41(5). In April 2006, Rule 41 was amended to introduce, in Rule 41(5), an expedited procedure for the dismissal of claims which manifestly lack merit. The Secretary-General's screening power (art. 36(3)) does not permit it to refuse to register requests on the merits of the case, or if jurisdiction is merely doubtful rather than manifestly lacking. The amended provision allows the parties, before the first session, and within thirty days of constitution, to submit an objection that the claim is manifestly without merit. The tribunal must give the parties an opportunity to present observations and then must deliver its decision at the first session or promptly thereafter.

12. Claims manifestly without merit: recent cases applying Rule 41(5). In the first case on this provision, *Trans-Global Petroleum*, the tribunal found that the object of the provision was to deal quickly with cases that presented points of law that were 'patently unmeritorious'. In assessing whether this is the case, the tribunal will assume that facts pleaded are true, but will not accept factual allegations that were 'manifestly incredible, frivolous, vexatious, inaccurate or made in bad faith'. The tribunal in *Ioan Micula* (DJ) emphasised that this rule requires a prima facie determination as to whether the facts can constitute a breach of the relevant legal provisions. In this way, it offers a form of summary judgment procedure for claims which clearly lack any merit. This new procedure is a useful development for ICSID proceedings and has the capacity to spare parties faced with frivolous claims the expense and inconvenience of contesting a full hearing on the merits, and potentially of having to produce evidence at all.

[Default]
Arbitration Rule 42

(1) If a party (in this Rule called the 'defaulting party') fails to appear or to present its case at any stage of the proceeding, the other party may, at any time prior to the discontinuance of the proceeding, request the Tribunal to deal with the questions submitted to it and to render an award.

(2) The Tribunal shall promptly notify the defaulting party of such a request. Unless it is satisfied that that party does not intend to appear or to present its case in the proceeding, it shall, at the same time, grant a period of grace and to this end:

    (a) if that party had failed to file a pleading or any other instrument within the time limit fixed therefor, fix a new time limit for its filing; or

    (b) if that party had failed to appear or present its case at a hearing, fix a new date for the hearing. The period of grace shall not, without the consent of the other party, exceed 60 days.

(3) After the expiration of the period of grace or when, in accordance with paragraph (2), no such period is granted, the Tribunal shall resume the consideration of the dispute. Failure of the defaulting party to appear or to present its case shall not be deemed an admission of the assertions made by the other party.

(4) The Tribunal shall examine the jurisdiction of the Centre and its own competence in the dispute and, if it is satisfied, decide whether the submissions made are well-founded in fact and in law. To this end, it may, at any stage of the proceeding, call on the party appearing to file observations, produce evidence or submit oral explanations.

1. General. Rule 42 provides a mechanism whereby an ICSID arbitration can proceed in the absence of one of the parties. The mechanism does not allow for a default judgment – the tribunal is required to determine whether the case is proven on the evidence presented and can still find in favour of the non-cooperating party.

2. Party may request tribunal to render an award. If a party fails to appear or present its case at any stage of the proceedings, the tribunal must continue to discharge its task and render its award, if requested to do so by the cooperating party. The consequent award will be binding upon both parties because of the mutual consent upon which the jurisdiction of the tribunal was based. It is open to both the respondent and the claimant to make a request under Rule 42(1). A request under Rule 42(1) can be made at any stage by a cooperating party.

3. What constitutes default? The Convention describes default as a failure by a party to appear or to present its case. It is possible that the cooperation of a party is so poor, whilst not entirely absent, that it may amount to default; for instance, if a party repeatedly fails to submit pleadings within the time limits fixed by the tribunal. Default may also be deemed to have arisen from a failure to make the advance payments under Reg. 14(3) of the Administrative and Financial Regulations.

4. Discretion of tribunal to determine whether default has occurred. Provided that there is a realistic chance that the defaulting party might co-operate, the Convention allows this defaulting party an opportunity to make amends. Therefore, the default procedure in Rule 45 is not an automatic sanction for procedural failings; it is a measure of last resort for the tribunal when it is clear that the non-cooperating party has no intention of ever cooperating. For minor infractions, a tribunal might elect to extend applicable time limits pursuant to Rule 26. The tribunal may end default proceedings if it becomes satisfied that a non-cooperating party is willing and able to cooperate, taking account of the prejudice caused to the cooperating party.

5. Grace period. An immediate consequence of a Rule 42(1) request is that the defaulting party must be placed on notice and granted a grace period (art. 45(2)). Rule 42(2) limits the grace period to sixty days, absent the consent of the cooperating party to a longer period of time. To give effect to the grace period, the tribunal will fix new time limits for all outstanding pleadings and hearings so that the non-cooperating party can re-engage in the proceedings within sixty days of the Rule 42(1) request. A grace period may not be granted where the tribunal is satisfied that the defaulting party has no intention ever to participate in the proceedings, for example, where the defaulting party has declared it has no such intention.

8. Examination of jurisdiction. In accordance with Rule 42(4), in default proceedings, the tribunal must, on its own initiative, examine the jurisdiction of the Centre and its own competence.

9. Examination of the merits. Once the tribunal has satisfied itself as to its jurisdiction, it must go on to consider the merits of the submissions of the cooperating party. As the arbitration now only has one party participating, the normal adversarial model has to be modified; the tribunal has to step forward and take on an examination role. Rule 42(2) allows the tribunal to call on the cooperating party to file observations, produce evidence or submit oral explanations of its case. The result will often be that the tribunal has to take a particularly sceptical approach to the cooperating party's case in order to discharge its examination duty effectively.

10. Obligation to appear and costs. As parties assume an obligation to participate in the ICSID procedure by ratifying the Convention and consenting to arbitrate, non-cooperating parties should expect adverse cost consequences.

[Settlement and discontinuance]
Arbitration Rule 43

(1) If, before the award is rendered, the parties agree on a settlement of the dispute or otherwise to discontinue the proceeding, the Tribunal, or the Secretary-General if the Tribunal has not yet been constituted, shall, at their written request, in an order take note of the discontinuance of the proceeding.

(2) If the parties file with the Secretary-General the full and signed text of their settlement and in writing request the Tribunal to embody such settlement in an award, the Tribunal may record the settlement in the form of its award.

1. General. Rule 43 allows the parties to discontinue proceedings if they settle their dispute or otherwise agree to discontinue proceedings, for example, to substitute a conciliation proceeding.

2. Order by tribunal or Secretary-General. The parties may discontinue proceedings without any award being rendered by the tribunal (Rule 43(1)). If the tribunal has already been constituted, it must issue an order noting the discontinuance. If the tribunal has not been constituted, the Secretary-General has the power to take note of the discontinuance of the proceeding and no tribunal will be constituted. The order, whether issued by the tribunal or the Secretary-General, is not an award, and therefore would not normally contain a decision on costs under art. 61(2) or be subject to the usual post-award remedies.

3. Settlement as part of the tribunal's award. If the parties have reached a settlement, they may, pursuant to Rule 43(2), request the tribunal to embody the terms agreed between them in an award. The tribunal has discretion whether to comply with such a request. In doing so, a tribunal would be expected to bear in mind the risk that consent awards may be used for improper purposes, such as to launder funds, and it should therefore satisfy itself that the parties have settled a genuine dispute. It may decide that it does not have jurisdiction or that it would be improper for it to sanction a particular settlement. If the tribunal does choose to make an award, the parties will benefit from the provisions on recognition and enforcement under the Convention. However, many of the post-award procedures are not appropriate to an award based on a settlement between the parties (for example, it is unclear how bias or a serious departure from fundamental rules could affect the settlement in such a way as to be the basis for annulment proceedings). Unlike discontinuance without an award, the Rule 43(2) procedure can only take place if the tribunal has been constituted because the Secretary-General does not have the power to make awards. The award should contain a decision on costs in accordance with art. 61(2), either as part of the agreed settlement or in addition to it.

[Discontinuance at request of a party]

Arbitration Rule 44

If a party requests the discontinuance of the proceeding, the Tribunal, or the Secretary-General if the Tribunal has not yet been constituted, shall in an order fix a time limit within which the other party may state whether it opposes the discontinuance. If no objection is made in writing within the time limit, the other party shall be deemed to have acquiesced in the discontinuance and the Tribunal, or if appropriate the Secretary-General, shall in an order take note of the discontinuance of the proceeding. If objection is made, the proceeding shall continue.

1. General. Rule 44 provides for the discontinuance of proceedings at the unilateral request of a party. The procedure requires the consent or deemed acquiescence of the other party. It is therefore similar to Rule 43(1), but applicable in cases where a claimant decides not to continue its claim further or a respondent decides to admit liability, and no particular settlement agreement is reached.

2. Request for discontinuance. Under the procedure, one party makes a request for discontinuance which will be effective unless the other party objects during a stipulated time period. If the request for arbitration has not yet been registered, the requesting party can withdraw its request without notifying the other party. If the request has been registered but the tribunal has not been constituted, the Secretary-General oversees the Rule 44 procedure. It would appear that there is no formal bar on a party discontinuing proceedings under Rule 44 from bringing a new claim at a later date. Accordingly, the other party would only be expected to agree to the discontinuance upon receipt of a binding assurance that the claim will not be reinstated. This would more naturally lend itself to the procedure specified in Rule 43.

4. Order to take note of discontinuance is not an award. An order discontinuing a proceeding under Rule 44, whether issued by the tribunal or the Secretary-General, is not an award, and therefore will not normally contain any provision regarding costs under art. 61(2) or be amenable to post-award remedies.

[Discontinuance for failure of parties to act]

Arbitration Rule 45

If the parties fail to take any steps in the proceeding during six consecutive months or such period as they may agree with the approval of

the Tribunal, or of the Secretary-General if the Tribunal has not yet been constituted, they shall be deemed to have discontinued the proceeding and the Tribunal, or if appropriate the Secretary-General, shall, after notice to the parties, in an order take note of the discontinuance.

1. General. If for six consecutive months no action is taken by the parties, they are deemed to have abandoned the proceeding and the proceeding must be discontinued by the tribunal or Secretary-General. Under Rule 45, the parties may agree, with the approval of the tribunal, on a different period for this rule. Rule 45 is conceptually useful in allowing the Secretary-General to put an end to abandoned proceedings, but, notably, there is no recent example of a discontinuance pursuant to Rule 45.

2. Relation to other rules. A tribunal may not continue proceedings on its own initiative in the case of default by both parties. If a party's default does not result in a request by the non-defaulting party to discontinue proceedings under Rule 44, a settlement and discontinuance under Rule 43, or a request that the tribunal continue default proceedings under Rule 42(1) – thus leading to complete stasis –Rule 45 provides that the proceeding must be discontinued for failure of the parties to act.

3. Procedure. Before ordering the discontinuance of the proceeding, the tribunal must give the parties notice of its intention to discontinue the proceeding. The parties and the tribunal may agree to extend the six-month period, for instance, if they are in the course of negotiating a settlement.

4. Order to take note of discontinuance is not an award. An order discontinuing a proceeding under Rule 45, whether issued by the tribunal or the Secretary-General, is not an award, and therefore would not normally contain any provision regarding costs in accordance with art. 61(2) or be amenable to post-award remedies.

5. Non-payment under the Administrative and Financial Regulations. If the inaction of the parties takes the form of non-payment of the advances and supplemental charges due to the Centre pursuant to Reg. 13(3)(a) of the Administrative and Financial Regulations, then the Secretary-General may move the tribunal to stay the proceeding before the funds previously received have been entirely exhausted. If a proceeding is stayed on this basis for more than six months, then the Secretary-General may, pursuant to Reg. 13(3)(d) of the Administrative and Financial Regulations, move that the tribunal discontinue the proceedings altogether.

CHAPTER VI. THE AWARD

[Preparation of the award]

Arbitration Rule 46

The award (including any individual or dissenting opinion) shall be drawn up and signed within 120 days after closure of the proceeding. The Tribunal may, however, extend this period by a further 60 days if it would otherwise be unable to draw up the award.

1. General. Rule 46 sets out the time limit within which the award must be drawn up and signed by the tribunal.

2. The closure of the proceedings. Under Rule 38, when the presentation of the case by the parties is completed, the proceedings shall be declared closed. The tribunal will issue a procedural order confirming this. When the proceedings are confirmed closed, the time limit within Rule 46 will commence.

3. Signature of the award. Each member of the tribunal must draw up and sign the award whether or not they voted in the majority or gave a separate opinion. The tribunal members need not sign the award at the same time nor must the tribunal members sign the award at a sitting (see art. 48, notes 3-4). It is only necessary that the award be signed by each member who voted for it, even if the decision of the tribunal was made by correspondence, or in the absence of one or more members of the tribunal.

4. The time limit in Rule 46. On 1 January 2003, Rule 46 was amended so that the time limits were extended from sixty days with a thirty-day extension to 120 days with a sixty-day extension. In cases preceding this amendment, tribunals had expressed criticism of the limited length of the time limits in Rule 46 (*Klöckner* v *Cameroon* (II)). However, Schreuer notes that tribunals have applied the pre-2003 time limits contained in Rules 38 and 46 in a flexible manner (Schreuer, *Commentary*, pp. 836-839, citing, e.g. *MINE* v *Guinea* (FA); *SPP* v *Egypt*; *Tradex* v *Albania*; *LETCO* v *Liberia*). In *SPP* v *Egypt* (FA), for example, the tribunal circumvented the provisions of Rule 46 by issuing its order closing proceedings five months after the last communications were received from the parties. The majority award was then signed forty-one days after the proceedings closed. As the new rule allows twice as much time for the tribunal to complete the preparation of the award, such measures may no longer be necessary.

[The award]

Rule 47

(1) The award shall be in writing and shall contain:
    (a) a precise designation of each party;

(b) **a statement that the Tribunal was established under the Convention, and a description of the method of its constitution;**
(c) **the name of each member of the Tribunal, and an identification of the appointing authority of each;**
(d) **the names of the agents, counsel and advocates of the parties;**
(e) **the dates and place of the sittings of the Tribunal;**
(f) **a summary of the proceeding;**
(g) **a statement of the facts as found by the Tribunal;**
(h) **the submissions of the parties;**
(i) **the decision of the Tribunal on every question submitted to it, together with the reasons upon which the decision is based; and**
(j) **any decision of the Tribunal regarding the cost of the proceeding.**

(2) The award shall be signed by the members of the Tribunal who voted for it; the date of each signature shall be indicated.

(3) Any member of the Tribunal may attach his individual opinion to the award, whether he dissents from the majority or not, or a statement of his dissent.

1. General. Rule 47 sets out the information that must be included in the award and allows for the inclusion of separate opinions.

2. The award shall be in writing and shall contain certain information. The provisions in Rule 47(1) provide further detail to those contained in art. 48(1) to (3) (see art. 48). Although the Convention fails to provide a definition of an 'award', Schreuer defines an award as a final decision of the tribunal by which it disposes of all questions before it (Schreuer, *Commentary*, p. 792). Under Rule 47 the award must clearly identify the parties; provide a statement from the tribunal regarding its constitution; provide the name of each tribunal member and the identification of their appointing authorities; provide the details of the agents, counsel and advocates of the parties; provide the dates and place of sitting of the tribunal; provide a summary of the proceedings; give a statement of the facts as found by the tribunal; outline the submissions of the parties; give the decision of the tribunal on every question submitted to it together with the reasons upon which that decision is based; and award costs in the proceedings. The requirement to give reasons is an important one as the failure to do so is a ground for annulment (see art. 52(1)(e)).

3. The award shall be signed and dated. The award need not be drawn up and signed at a sitting of the tribunal (see Rule 46). It is only necessary that each member who voted for the award should sign it: the decision of the tribunal may be made by correspondence (see Rule 16), or in the absence of one or more members of the tribunal. The requirement for each tribunal member to date the award upon his signature is due to the fact that the tribunal members will not necessarily be signing the award simultaneously. The date at which the last signature is added is the date relevant to the Secretary-General's duty to dispatch a certified copy of the award to the parties (art. 49(1) and Rule 48(1)). The date at which these copies are dispatched is the date of the award for the purposes of the time limits on requests for supplementation, rectification, revision and annulment.

4. Separate opinions. Rule 47(3) is based on art. 48(4), under which both concurring and dissenting opinions are allowed. The text of both provisions allows for a mere statement to be given in dissent, but requires an opinion if the tribunal member is in the majority. Concurring opinions are permitted to be brief and confined to a small number of points (see *SOABI* v *Senegal* (President's Declaration)). The requirements of art. 48(3) do not apply to dissenting opinions (Schreuer, *Commentary*, p. 817).

5. Future amendments to Rule 47. The Notes to the Arbitration Rules state that consideration was given to including a provision in Rule 47 to cover the contingency that a tribunal might be unable to reach a majority decision on an issue, in particular on the amount of damages to be awarded. However, it was concluded that with respect to most questions, only a positive or a negative answer is possible. Accordingly, no problem can arise under art. 48(1), since if a question fails to achieve a majority it is automatically decided negatively. This is especially so given that Rule 16(1) provides that an abstention shall be counted as a negative vote and art. 37(2) requires the tribunal to consist of an uneven number of arbitrators. If the question is not one that may only be answered in the positive or negative, a decision could be reached by a sequence of votes by which alternatives are successively eliminated. Accordingly, it was determined unnecessary and presumptuous to attempt to specify a precise voting procedure for the contingency that a tribunal might be unable to reach a majority decision on an issue (*Notes*, ICSID Reports, p. 108). Schreuer notes that the mandatory language of art. 48(1) suggests that the tribunal is under a duty to deliberate until a majority has been reached (Schreuer, *Commentary*, p. 789). In practice, a member may be required to vote in favour of a decision even though he has expressed a different opinion, purely with the aim of reaching a majority (*Guinea-Bissau* v *Senegal*).

[Rendering and publishing of the award]

Rule 48

(1) Upon signature by the last arbitrator to sign, the Secretary-General shall promptly:
- **(a) authenticate the original text of the award and deposit it in the archives of the Centre, together with any individual opinions and statements of dissent; and**

(b) **dispatch a certified copy of the award (including individual opinions and statements of dissent) to each party, indicating the date of dispatch on the original text and on all copies.**

(2) The award shall be deemed to have been rendered on the date on which the certified copies were dispatched.

(3) The Secretary-General shall, upon request, make available to a party additional certified copies of the award.

(4) The Centre shall not publish the award without the consent of the parties. The Centre shall, however, promptly include in its publications excerpts of the legal reasoning of the Tribunal.

1. General. Rule 48 provides the procedure by which an award is rendered.

2. Authentication and dispatch of awards. Rule 48 sets out in more detail the Secretary-General's duty under arts. 11 and 49 to transmit copies of the award to the parties. Under Rule 48, the Secretary-General must authenticate the original text of the award, along with any individual opinions and statements of dissent; note the date of dispatch on the original and all copies of the award; deposit the original in the Centre's archives; and dispatch certified copies of the award to the parties. A copy of the award is certified when the Secretary-General attaches a certificate that precisely identifies the case and states words to this effect: 'I hereby certify that the attached is a true copy of the original of the Award of the Arbitral Tribunal in the above case. The award is rendered in the English/French/Spanish language[s].' If there are separate opinions, these should be noted in the certificate before it is signed and dated by the Secretary-General. In order to avoid the inconvenience and additional expense that might be caused if the tribunal were required to reconvene merely to read the award to the parties, Rule 48 does not require that the award be delivered at a sitting of the tribunal and also does not require the award to be signed on the same date by all tribunal members. If the tribunal members fail to sign the award simultaneously, the Secretary-General's responsibility for prompt action under Rule 48(1) must be measured relative to the date on which the last required signature is added. Though not stated explicitly, that date should also mark the time limit within which individual opinions and statements of dissent should be filed with the Secretary-General in order to be attached to the award (*Notes*, p. 109).

3. Publishing the award. Art. 48(5) states that the Centre shall not publish the award without the consent of the parties. Rule 48(4) provides the additional requirement that the Centre shall promptly include in its publications excerpts of the legal reasoning of the tribunal. This is in contrast to Rule 48 before it was amended on 10 April 2006. The earlier version of Rule 48 stated that '[t]he Centre may ... include in its publications excerpts of the legal rules applied by the Tribunal'. Accordingly, the 2006 amendment makes the publication of excerpts of ICSID awards mandatory and expands publication from excerpts of the legal rules applied by the tribunal to excerpts of the legal reasoning of the tribunal. The amendment to Rule 48 is interesting in light of Schreuer's observation (made in 2001) that the power in (what was then) Rule 48(4) was only exercised with great prudence and the Secretariat rarely made use of the provision (Schreuer, *Commentary*, p. 820). The current version of Rule 48, as well as making excerpts of ICSID's awards and the reasons behind them more accessible to the public, also provides a body of case law that can be utilised by the parties, their representatives, and tribunals in future ICSID proceedings. While the decision of one ICSID tribunal is not binding on another, past decisions can be used as persuasive authority and guidance as to how a new tribunal should deal with the same or a similar issue. The award (or excerpts thereof) will be published in the ICSID Review – Foreign Investment Law Journal or on the Centre's website (<www.worldbank.org>). The provisions in art. 48 and Rule 48 only apply to the Centre. Accordingly, the parties are free to publish the award or release information regarding proceedings pending before a tribunal (*Amco v Indonesia* (I)), provided that in doing so they do not exacerbate the dispute (*CMS v Argentina*, (DPM)).

[Supplementary decisions and rectification]

Rule 49

(1) Within 45 days after the date on which the award was rendered, either party may request, pursuant to Article 49(2) of the Convention, a supplementary decision on, or the rectification of, the award. Such a request shall be addressed in writing to the Secretary-General. The request shall:
- **(a) identify the award to which it relates;**
- **(b) indicate the date of the request;**
- **(c) state in detail:**
  - **(i) any question which, in the opinion of the requesting party, the Tribunal omitted to decide in the award; and**
  - **(ii) any error in the award which the requesting party seeks to have rectified; and**
- **(d) be accompanied by a fee for lodging the request.**

(2) Upon receipt of the request and of the lodging fee, the Secretary-General shall forthwith:
- **(a) register the request;**
- **(b) notify the parties of the registration;**
- **(c) transmit to the other party a copy of the request and of any accompanying documentation; and**
- **(d) transmit to each member of the Tribunal a copy of the notice of registration, together with a copy of the request and of any accompanying documentation.**

(3) The President of the Tribunal shall consult the members on whether it is necessary for the Tribunal to meet in order to consider the request.

The Tribunal shall fix a time limit for the parties to file their observations on the request and shall determine the procedure for its consideration.

(4) Rules 46-48 shall apply, mutatis mutandis, to any decision of the Tribunal pursuant to this Rule.

(5) If a request is received by the Secretary-General more than 45 days after the award was rendered, he shall refuse to register the request and so inform forthwith the requesting party.

1. General. Rule 49 sets out the procedure by which applications for the supplementation and rectification of awards are made.

2. The request for supplementation and rectification. Rule 49 provides further detail to the power given to the tribunal in art. 49(2) to rectify or supplement its award. Under Rule 49, a request must identify the award to which it relates; indicate the date of the request; state in detail any question which, in the opinion of the requesting party, the tribunal omitted to decide in the award and any error in the award which the requesting party seeks to have rectified; and be accompanied by a fee for lodging the request. It is imperative that the request adequately identify the award to which it relates and state in detail the defects sought to be corrected. A request can be made for both the supplementation and rectification of an award simultaneously. However, any application for the interpretation, revision or annulment of the award must be made separately. At the time of writing, the fee for lodging a request for supplementation or rectification was USD 10,000 payable to the Centre by the party making the request. If the Secretary-General decides to register the request, the request can only be transmitted to the tribunal that rendered the original award. In this way, the procedure in art. 49(2) and Rule 49 differs from the procedures for the interpretation, revision or annulment of the award. If, for any reason, the original tribunal cannot be reconvened, the only remedy would be an application under Chapter VII of the Rules (that is, an application for the interpretation, revision or annulment of the award). Once the Secretary-General registers the request, the other party must be notified.

3. The decision as to whether the tribunal must meet to consider the request. Under Rule 49(3), the tribunal may determine the procedure it will use to consider and resolve the request. Under Rule 16(2), the tribunal may choose to make its decision by correspondence.

4. The application of Rules 46 to 48. Rule 49(4) provides that decisions made under it should in general conform to the requirements established for an award. Reg. 28(2) of the Administrative and Financial Regulations requires that any supplementary decision and rectification be recorded on all certified copies of an award issued by the Secretary-General. Art. 49(2) provides that for the purposes of an application to interpret, revise or annul an award, the time limits contained in Rules 46 to 48 will apply.

5. The Secretary-General's power of refusal. The Secretary-General's authority to refuse to register a request made pursuant to art. 48(2) is restricted to the case where the request is not made within the time limit prescribed by the Convention. Under Reg. 29 of the Administrative and Financial Regulations, a request for supplementation or rectification must be delivered at the seat of the Centre no later than the forty-fifth day after the certified copies of the award were dispatched to the parties. Thus, Schreuer notes, the Secretary-General may only refuse to register a request under art. 49(2) if the forty-five-day time limit has not been complied with. There is no scope for refusal of a request, e.g. that is manifestly lacking in merit or devoid of relevance (Schreuer, *Commentary*, p. 855).

CHAPTER VII. INTERPRETATION, REVISION AND ANNULMENT OF THE AWARD

[The application]

Rule 50

(1) An application for the interpretation, revision or annulment of an award shall be addressed in writing to the Secretary-General and shall:
  (a) **identify the award to which it relates;**
  (b) **indicate the date of the application;**
  (c) **state in detail:**
    (i) **in an application for interpretation, the precise points in dispute;**
    (ii) **in an application for revision, pursuant to Article 51(1) of the Convention, the change sought in the award, the discovery of some fact of such a nature as decisively to affect the award, and evidence that when the award was rendered that fact was unknown to the Tribunal and to the applicant, and that the applicant's ignorance of that fact was not due to negligence;**
    (iii) **in an application for annulment, pursuant to Article 52(1) of the Convention, the grounds on which it is based. These grounds are limited to the following:**
      – **that the Tribunal was not properly constituted;**
      – **that the Tribunal has manifestly exceeded its powers;**
      – **that there was corruption on the part of a member of the Tribunal;**
      – **that there has been a serious departure from a fundamental rule of procedure;**
      – **that the award has failed to state the reasons on which it is based;**

(d) be accompanied by the payment of a fee for lodging the application.

(2) Without prejudice to the provisions of paragraph (3), upon receiving an application and the lodging fee, the Secretary-General shall forthwith:
   (a) register the application;
   (b) notify the parties of the registration; and
   (c) transmit to the other party a copy of the application and of any accompanying documentation.

(3) The Secretary-General shall refuse to register an application for:
   (a) revision, if, in accordance with Article 51(2) of the Convention, it is not made within 90 days after the discovery of the new fact and in any event within three years after the date on which the award was rendered (or any subsequent decision or correction);
   (b) annulment, if, in accordance with Article 52(2) of the Convention, it is not made:
      (i) within 120 days after the date on which the award was rendered (or any subsequent decision or correction) if the application is based on any of the following grounds:
         – the Tribunal was not properly constituted;
         – the Tribunal has manifestly exceeded its powers;
         – there has been a serious departure from a fundamental rule of procedure;
         – the award has failed to state the reasons on which it is based;
      (ii) in the case of corruption on the part of a member of the Tribunal, within 120 days after discovery thereof, and in any event within three years after the date on which the award was rendered (or any subsequent decision or correction).

(4) If the Secretary-General refuses to register an application for revision, or annulment, he shall forthwith notify the requesting party of his refusal.

1. General. Rule 50 and the subsequent rules in Chapter VIII are designed to implement the various procedures provided for in arts. 50 to 52.

2. The request for interpretation, revision or annulment. Under Rule 50, an application for the interpretation, revision or annulment of an award must identify the award to which it relates; indicate the date of the application; and, depending on which type of request is being made, either: state in detail the precise points in dispute (for a request for interpretation), the change sought in the award and the evidence in support (for a request for revision) or the grounds upon which the request is based (for a request for annulment). Under art. 52, the grounds upon which an award may be annulled are: where the tribunal was not properly constituted; where the tribunal has manifestly exceeded its powers; where there was corruption on the part of a member of the tribunal; where there has been a serious departure from a fundamental rule of procedure; or where the award has failed to state the reasons on which it is based. Each request must be accompanied by the payment of a fee for lodging the application. At the time of writing, the fee for lodging a request was USD 10,000 payable to the Centre by the party making the request. In each case, it is imperative that the request state in detail the grounds upon which the particular remedy is sought. If the Secretary-General registers the application, he will notify the parties and will transmit a copy of the application and any supporting documentation to the non-requesting party. A request for each of the three types of remedies (interpretation, revision, annulment) must be made in a separate application. Thus, if a party is seeking more than one remedy, more than one application must be made. The Notes explain that this is necessary both because of the separate time limits provided for in the Convention, and also because of the difference in the procedures applying to each remedy. While interpretation or revision will (ordinarily) be considered by the original tribunal, annulment will be considered by a newly constituted ad hoc committee (*Notes*, p. 112). An application under Rule 50 must be made separately from a request under Rule 49.

3. The Secretary-General's power of refusal. The Secretary-General's authority to refuse to register an application made under arts. 51 or 52 is restricted to the case in which the application is made outside the absolute time limits prescribed by the Convention (i.e. three years after the date on which the award – or any supplement or rectification – was rendered in the case of a revision, and either ten days or three years after such date in the case of an annulment). The Convention also provides time limits specific to certain situations: art. 51(2) provides a ninety-day time limit 'after the discovery of [the] fact' on which the request for revision is based and art. 52(2) provides a 120-day time limit 'after discovery of the corruption'. However, as the Secretary-General may not be in a position to determine whether these limits have been complied with, his authority to refuse to register a request is restricted to situations where the non-compliance with the time limits is unambiguous (*Notes*, p. 112). The Secretary-General is also bound by Reg. 29(2) of the Administrative and Financial Regulations which states that a time limit shall be satisfied if the request is delivered to the seat of the Centre, or to the Secretary of the competent Commission, Tribunal or Committee that is meeting away from the seat of the Centre, before the close of business on the indicated date. The Secretary-General will accept an electronic filing, with a hard copy to follow, in satisfaction of this requirement. The Secretary-General may also elect to remind the requesting party that the registration of an application does not preclude the competent tribunal or committee from deciding that an application has been filed outside of the relevant time limit.

ICSID Arbitration Rules, Rule 51

[Interpretation or revision: further procedures]

Rule 51

(1) Upon registration of an application for the interpretation or revision of an award, the Secretary-General shall forthwith:
   (a) transmit to each member of the original Tribunal a copy of the notice of registration, together with a copy of the application and of any accompanying documentation; and
   (b) request each member of the Tribunal to inform him within a specified time limit whether that member is willing to take part in the consideration of the application.

(2) If all members of the Tribunal express their willingness to take part in the consideration of the application, the Secretary-General shall so notify the members of the Tribunal and the parties. Upon dispatch of these notices the Tribunal shall be deemed to be reconstituted.

(3) If the Tribunal cannot be reconstituted in accordance with paragraph (2), the Secretary-General shall so notify the parties and invite them to proceed, as soon as possible, to constitute a new Tribunal, including the same number of arbitrators, and appointed by the same method, as the original one.

1. General. Rule 51 details the further procedures that are necessary for the interpretation or revision of awards.

2. The constitution of the tribunal that will hear the application. Arts. 50(2) and 51(3) provide that a request for interpretation or revision shall, if possible, be submitted to the tribunal that rendered the award. It is only in the situation where this is not possible that a new tribunal shall be constituted to hear the application. Under Rule 51(1) and (2), the Secretary-General must attempt to reconstitute the original tribunal. The date of the reconstitution of the tribunal may be of particular significance in connection with the stay of enforcement of an award under Rule 54(2). In the event that the original tribunal cannot be reconstituted, the Secretary-General will invite the parties to proceed according to the same procedure that was used to constitute the original tribunal. The Secretary-General will also invite the parties to appoint the same number of arbitrators. The parties are not bound to follow the Secretary-General's recommendation. The Notes explain that in keeping the process identical to that utilised in the original proceedings, it is likely that the speed of constituting the new tribunal will be advanced (*Notes*, p. 113). Schreuer also notes that this procedure means that some of the original members may be employed in the new tribunal, so long as the requirement for an uneven number of arbitrators is met (art. 37(2)(a); Schreuer, *Commentary*, p. 865). Rule 2, which prescribes the procedure by which tribunals should be constituted, will not apply. Whichever tribunal members have agreed to make a decision on interpretation will be bound, under art. 49 and Rules 47 and 53, to make that decision and provide reasons for it.

[Annulment: further procedures]

Rule 52

(1) Upon registration of an application for the annulment of an award, the Secretary-General shall forthwith request the Chairman of the Administrative Council to appoint an ad hoc Committee in accordance with Article 52(3) of the Convention.

(2) The Committee shall be deemed to be constituted on the date the Secretary-General notifies the parties that all members have accepted their appointment. Before or at the first session of the Committee, each member shall sign a declaration conforming to that set forth in Rule 6(2).

1. General. Rule 52 details the further procedures that are necessary for the annulment of awards.

2. The constitution of the ad hoc committee that will hear the application. Requests for the annulment of awards differ from requests for the interpretation or revision of awards in that the body that hears the application (the ad hoc committee) is intended to be different to the body that heard the original dispute (the tribunal). The three members of the ad hoc committee will be appointed by the Chairman from the Panel of Arbitrators (for which, see art. 13). The procedure for this appointment is detailed in art. 52(3). Rules 1 to 12, which prescribe the procedures associated with tribunals, will accordingly be inapplicable to the constitution of ad hoc committees, with the exception that a declaration in a form analogous to that prescribed in Rule 6(2) must be signed by each member of the ad hoc committee (*Notes*, p. 113).

3. Deemed date of constitution. Rule 52(2) deems that the date of the constitution of the ad hoc committee will be the date on which the Secretary-General notifies the parties that all members have accepted their appointment. This mirrors Rule 6(1), which prescribes the deemed date of constitution for tribunals. This date may be of particular significance in connection with the stay of enforcement of an award pursuant to Rule 54(2).

[Rules of procedure]

Rule 53

The provisions of these Rules shall apply mutatis mutandis to any procedure relating to the interpretation, revision or annulment of an award and to the decision of the Tribunal or Committee.

1. General. Under Rule 53, the provisions of the Arbitration Rules which apply to original proceedings shall apply to decisions on interpretation, revision and annulment.

2. The application of Rule 53 in practice. Although decisions on interpretation, revision and annulment will be subject to the same considerations as those applicable to the original arbitration, the legal and factual issues will generally be fewer and more specific. Accordingly, the parties may be required to submit pleadings and a hearing may be (but will not always be) necessary so as to allow both parties to present their case. Whilst the tribunal retains a general power under Rule 19 to make orders required for the conduct of proceedings, the Notes explain that for the sake of simplicity the tribunal will rely on any procedural dispositions that the parties have already agreed to (e.g. the decision as to the language of the hearing or the number of copies of instruments to be filed). If the parties fail to indicate otherwise, the tribunal may assume that the representatives appointed under Rule 18 will remain in place for the secondary proceedings (*Notes*, p. 114).

3. Non-application of certain provisions. The provisions of the rules relating to provisional measures (Rule 39) and ancillary claims (Rule 40) are not applicable to the procedures specified in Rule 53.

[Stay of enforcement of the award]

Rule 54

(1) The party applying for the interpretation, revision or annulment of an award may in its application, and either party may at any time before the final disposition of the application, request a stay in the enforcement of part or all of the award to which the application relates. The Tribunal or Committee shall give priority to the consideration of such a request.

(2) If an application for the revision or annulment of an award contains a request for a stay of its enforcement, the Secretary-General shall, together with the notice of registration, inform both parties of the provisional stay of the award. As soon as the Tribunal or Committee is constituted it shall, if either party requests, rule within 30 days on whether such stay should be continued; unless it decides to continue the stay, it shall automatically be terminated.

(3) If a stay of enforcement has been granted pursuant to paragraph (1) or continued pursuant to paragraph (2), the Tribunal or Committee may at any time modify or terminate the stay at the request of either party. All stays shall automatically terminate on the date on which a final decision is rendered on the application, except that a Committee granting the partial annulment of an award may order the temporary stay of enforcement of the unannulled portion in order to give either party an opportunity to request any new Tribunal constituted pursuant to Article 52(6) of the Convention to grant a stay pursuant to Rule 55(3).

(4) A request pursuant to paragraph (1), (2) (second sentence) or (3) shall specify the circumstances that require the stay or its modification or termination. A request shall only be granted after the Tribunal or Committee has given each party an opportunity of presenting its observations.

(5) The Secretary-General shall promptly notify both parties of the stay of enforcement of any award and of the modification or termination of such a stay, which shall become effective on the date on which he dispatches such notification.

1. General. Rule 54 deals with the procedure for the application and grant of a stay of enforcement of the whole or part of an award. The Notes state that this rule is designed to implement arts. 50(2) (final sentence), 51(4) and 52(5).

2. The application for a stay of enforcement. A party submitting an application for interpretation, revision or annulment may request in that application a stay of the award's enforcement. The Secretary-General is bound to register this request automatically unless the application is made outside of the time limits contained in arts. 51(2) and 52(2). Until the tribunal or ad hoc committee has been constituted, only the party filing the application may request a stay of enforcement. Therefore, under Rule 54(2), this stay is both an automatic and provisional one which, if a party requests a continuance, shall be ruled upon by the tribunal or ad hoc committee within thirty days of being constituted. The tribunal or ad hoc committee shall give priority to the consideration of such a request and unless it decides to continue the stay, the stay will be automatically terminated. Once the tribunal or ad hoc committee has been constituted, either party may request a stay. At this time the granting of the stay is no longer automatic and the tribunal or ad hoc committee retains the discretion to grant the stay. It retains this direction until the time at which it issues its decision. The tribunal is not able to act of its own accord and impose a stay in the absence of a request by one of the parties. Whilst neither the Convention nor the Arbitration Rules provide an express power to the ad hoc committee to grant a stay, there is now what is considered to be a jurisprudence constante to the effect that a stay may be made conditional on the provision of security. Thus, a stay should be granted by an ad hoc committee unless that committee finds that there are very exceptional circumstances why this should not occur (*Enron* v *Argentina* (*Stay Decision*)).

3. Partial or total stays of enforcement. A tribunal or ad hoc committee may decide to stay the enforcement of part or all of the award, as the circumstances appear to justify. However, if a stay has been granted in accordance with art. 54(2), the stay can only relate to the entire award. Otherwise the moving party would be able to select the stay of only those portions of the award that are contrary to its interests (*Notes*, p. 115).

4. The termination of a stay of enforcement. Under Rule 54(3), if a stay has either been granted or continued, the tribunal or ad hoc committee may at any time modify or terminate the stay at the request of either party. Most stays will automatically terminate on the date on which a final decision is rendered on the application. The only exception occurs where an ad hoc committee has granted the partial annulment of an award. In this case, the ad hoc committee may order that the enforcement of the unannulled portion of the award be temporarily stayed. This will afford the parties the opportunity to have the annulled portion of their dispute resubmitted under art. 52(6). The ad hoc committee is likely to exercise this discretion where the enforcement of the unannulled portion might give one party an unfair advantage in light of the fact that the annulled portion might be considered and reinstated by a new tribunal (*Notes*, p. 115).

5. Notification of the stay of enforcement Under Reg. 28(2) of the Administrative and Financial Regulations, the Secretary-General must indicate any stay of enforcement which has been granted with respect to an award on each certified copy of such award issued while the stay is in effect.

[Resubmission of dispute after an annulment]

Rule 55

(1) If a Committee annuls part or all of an award, either party may request the resubmission of the dispute to a new Tribunal. Such a request shall be addressed in writing to the Secretary-General and shall:
   (a) identify the award to which it relates;
   (b) indicate the date of the request;
   (c) explain in detail what aspect of the dispute is to be submitted to the Tribunal; and
   (d) be accompanied by a fee for lodging the request.

(2) Upon receipt of the request and of the lodging fee, the Secretary-General shall forthwith:
   (a) register it in the Arbitration Register;
   (b) notify both parties of the registration;
   (c) transmit to the other party a copy of the request and of any accompanying documentation; and
   (d) invite the parties to proceed, as soon as possible, to constitute a new Tribunal, including the same number of arbitrators, and appointed by the same method, as the original one.

(3) If the original award had only been annulled in part, the new Tribunal shall not reconsider any portion of the award not so annulled. It may, however, in accordance with the procedures set forth in Rule 54, stay or continue to stay the enforcement of the unannulled portion of the award until the date its own award is rendered.

(4) Except as otherwise provided in paragraphs (1)-(3), these Rules shall apply to a proceeding on a resubmitted dispute in the same manner as if such dispute had been submitted pursuant to the Institution Rules.

1. General Rule 55 deals with the procedure for resubmitting a dispute following an annulment. This rule is designed to implement art. 52(6).

2. Filing a request for resubmission Once an ad hoc committee has annulled an award in whole or in part, either party may request that the dispute be resubmitted to a new tribunal. Art. 55(1) requires that any such request identify the award to which it relates; indicate the date of the request; explain in detail what aspect of the dispute is to be submitted to the new tribunal; and be accompanied by a fee for lodging the request. At the time of writing, the fee for resubmitting a dispute was USD 10,000 payable to the Centre by the party making the request. It is imperative that the request adequately identify the award to which it relates, and state in detail what aspects of the former dispute (the one to which the annulled award related) are to be considered by the new tribunal. The Secretary-General has no authority to refuse to register a request for resubmission. This is because art. 52(6) fails to designate a time limit or indicate any other limitations on the request. However, should the Secretary-General receive a request relating to an award that has not been annulled in whole or in part, he would logically be able to refuse registration (*Notes*, p. 116).

3. The constitution of the new tribunal. Under Rule 55(2)(d), the new tribunal is to be constituted by the same method as the original one. Accordingly, Rule 2 will be inapplicable. The Notes to Rule 55 explain that this provision is designed to simplify the procedure for constituting the new tribunal. However, the parties may agree to depart from the original procedure and may communicate this to the Secretary-General in accordance with Rule 1(2).

4. Resubmission of a partially annulled dispute. Under Rule 55(3), if the original award has only been annulled in part then the new tribunal is restricted to considering only the portion of the award that was subject to annulment. If the tribunal were to consider an unannulled section of the award, it would violate the principle contained in art. 53(1) that the award shall not be subject to appeal except as provided for in the Convention. Where the ad hoc committee has determined to only annul part of the award, the only remedy available to the parties is to request a revision under art. 51.

CHAPTER VIII. GENERAL PROVISIONS

[Final provisions]

Rule 56

(1) The texts of these Rules in each official language of the Centre shall be equally authentic.

(2) These Rules may be cited as the 'Arbitration Rules' of the Centre.

1. General. Rule 56 provides for the equal authenticity of the official languages of the Centre and explains how the Rules should be cited.

2. The official languages. Under Reg. 34(1) of the Administrative and Financial Regulations, the official languages of the Centre are English, French and Spanish. The original official languages of the Centre were English and French. However, when Ecuador became a party to the Convention in 1986, Spanish was added as an official language. This is because the Notes to Rule 56 of the Arbitration Rules provided for Spanish to be added as an official language as soon as a Spanish-speaking State became party to the Convention. The Notes to the Arbitration Rules also provided that whenever a new official language was added, the Secretary-General would prepare a text of these Rules in that language for the approval of the Council (*Notes*, p. 117).

INTERNATIONAL CHAMBER OF COMMERCE (ICC) RULES OF ARBITRATION, 1998*

(In force as from 1 January 1998)

[Introductory remarks]

History. The ICC International Court of Arbitration ('ICC Court') was established in 1923 as the dispute resolution body of the International Chamber of Commerce ('ICC'), which itself was established in 1919 with the objective of promoting international trade and investment. The ICC Court has pioneered international commercial arbitration as it is known today.

Features. The first edition of the ICC Rules of Arbitration (the 'ICC Rules') was published in 1922. They have been revised or amended nine times over the ICC Court's history, most recently in 1998 (the current version of the rules). While only the English and French versions of the ICC Rules are official, they have been translated into a number of other languages, including Arabic, Chinese, German, Brazilian Portuguese, Polish, Russian and Spanish. The ICC Court has administered over 15,000 arbitrations, involving parties and arbitrators from across the globe. While the ICC Court has its base in Paris, France, ICC arbitration is truly international. Members of the ICC Court come from some 86 countries. In 2009, the ICC Court received 817 Requests for Arbitration, involving 2,095 parties from 128 countries and independent territories. The places of arbitration were located in 53 countries throughout the world. In addition to arbitration under the ICC Rules, the ICC also acts as appointing authority in non-ICC arbitrations (but does not administer such cases) and provides other dispute resolution services such as ADR, expertise proceedings and a system for dispute boards. The standard ICC arbitration clause is:

All disputes arising out of or in connection with the present contract shall be finally settled under the Rules of Arbitration of the International Chamber of Commerce by one or more arbitrators appointed in accordance with the said Rules.

The ICC Court's website is <www.iccarbitration.org>.

---

*   Reproduced with permission of the International Chamber of Commerce (ICC). The text reproduced here is valid at the time of reproduction. As amendments may from time to time be made to the text, please refer to the website <http://www.iccarbitration.org> for the latest version.

INTRODUCTORY PROVISIONS

[International Court of Arbitration]

Article 1

(1) **The International Court of Arbitration (the 'Court') of the International Chamber of Commerce (the 'ICC') is the arbitration body attached to the ICC. The statutes of the Court are set forth in Appendix I. Members of the Court are appointed by the Council of the ICC. The function of the Court is to provide for the settlement by arbitration of business disputes of an international character in accordance with the Rules of Arbitration of the International Chamber of Commerce (the 'Rules'). If so empowered by an arbitration agreement, the Court shall also provide for the settlement by arbitration in accordance with these Rules of business disputes not of an international character.**

(2) **The Court does not itself settle disputes. It has the function of ensuring the application of these Rules. It draws up its own Internal Rules (Appendix II).**

(3) **The Chairman of the Court, or, in the Chairman's absence or otherwise at his request, one of its Vice-Chairmen shall have the power to take urgent decisions on behalf of the Court, provided that any such decision is reported to the Court at its next session.**

(4) **As provided for in its Internal Rules, the Court may delegate to one or more committees composed of its members the power to take certain decisions, provided that any such decision is be reported to the Court at its next session.**

(5) **The Secretariat of the Court (the 'Secretariat') under the direction of its Secretary General (the 'Secretary General') shall have its seat at the headquarters of the ICC.**

1. The ICC. Also known as the World Business Organization, the ICC is a private, non-profit organisation established in 1919 to 'serve world business by promoting trade and investment, open markets for goods and services, and the free flow of capital'. The ICC is involved in a wide spectrum of activities, the most significant being rule-setting, policy, and dispute resolution. The ICC is composed of National Committees or groups and independent members from more than 130 countries. Currently there are approximately 90 National Committees or groups akin to a National Committee. The supreme body is the ICC World Council, which is composed of delegates from all National Committees. The ICC World Council meets twice a year and nominates the members of the Executive Board (fifteen to twenty members) and the ICC's Chairman and Vice-Chairman. The Executive Board's main responsibility is to implement ICC policy. The ICC's administrative body is the International Secretariat based in Paris, directed by the ICC's Secretary General. However, the backbone of the ICC, in many ways, is its Commissions, composed of more than 500 business experts, who formulate ICC policy and elaborate ICC rules and guidelines. The Commissions also analyse proposed international and national government initiatives that affect their subject areas and prepare business positions for submission to international organisations and governments. The Commissions deal with a broad range of subject matters. For example, there are Commissions on anti-corruption, arbitration, commercial law and practice, economic policy, environment and energy.

2. The ICC Court. The ICC Court is part of the ICC and does not have its own legal personality. However, the ICC Court is autonomous from the ICC insofar as its handling of the cases before it is concerned. No one from the ICC who is not on the Court or a member of the Court's Secretariat has access to, or influence over, the ICC Court in the carrying out of its functions. The ICC Court has its own statutes and internal rules (Appendix I and II to the ICC Rules). Even though it is called the ICC 'Court', it is not a judicial body as such, as it does not settle the merits of the disputes brought before it; it only ensures the application of the ICC Rules (art. 1(2)) (the French Cour de Cassation confirmed the ICC Court's administrative role in the *Cubic* case).

3. The ICC Court's structure. The ICC Court consists of 'a Chairman, Vice-Chairmen and members and alternate members' (Appendix I, art. 2) appointed for three-year terms by the ICC World Council. The ICC Court holds monthly plenary sessions where all members are invited. In recent years, however, due to the increase in the Court's case load, only important issues such as the scrutiny of complex awards, awards involving state parties, the challenge and replacement of arbitrators and matters raising important new issues are decided in plenary sessions. All other matters are submitted to the ICC Court's committee sessions, constituted of three members, which meet weekly. If there is not unanimity among the three members on a particular matter at a committee session, it is sent to a plenary session. The ICC Court's permanent administrative body is the Secretariat (see notes 6 and 7).

4. The ICC Court's functions. As mentioned above (note 2) the ICC Court's mission is to ensure the correct application of the ICC Rules. While the ICC Court performs many procedural tasks during arbitration proceedings, its key functions are fixing the advances of costs, constituting the arbitral tribunal, scrutinising draft awards and fixing the costs of the arbitration.

5. Independence of the ICC Court. One of the most important characteristics of ICC arbitration is the independence of the ICC Court. Even though its members are generally appointed upon the proposal of the ICC National Committee of their country, they are independent from such ICC National Committees and are not remunerated for their services nor completely reimbursed for their expenses. Many of the ICC Court's members are prominent professionals in the field of international arbitration. Consequently, ICC Court members sometimes have a direct or indirect interest in certain matters (for example, a lawyer from their law firm is acting as counsel in a case). Hence, all members are obliged to excuse themselves during sessions when matters in which they may be involved are discussed. ICC Court members directly or indirectly involved in ICC cases do not have access to the materials concerning such cases that are placed before the Court.

6. The Secretariat. The Secretariat is the only link between the public (including parties, counsel and arbitrators) and the ICC Court. It is located at the ICC headquarters in Paris and composed of the Secretary General (head of the Secretariat), the Deputy Secretary General, the General Counsel and eight teams generally composed of a counsel, two or three assistant counsel and two administrative assistants. Since 2008, the ICC located one of the Secretariat's teams in Hong Kong. This team administers ICC cases involving the Asia-Pacific region. The counsel and assistant counsel are almost always qualified lawyers. The teams are divided roughly along geographical lines (for example, one of the teams deals predominantly with cases from Latin America or which involve Spanish or Portuguese). Members of the Secretariat speak numerous different languages and have various cultural and geographical backgrounds.

7. Functions of the Secretariat. The Secretariat handles the day-to-day administration of all ICC arbitrations and all communications with the parties and arbitrators. When a Request for Arbitration ('Request') reaches the ICC, the Secretary General will assign the matter to one of the Secretariat's teams, taking into consideration, among other things, the parties' nationalities, the place of arbitration, the language of arbitration, the applicable law and the teams' current case load. Whenever the ICC Court must make a decision in a case, the teams, under the supervision of the Secretary General, Deputy Secretary General and the General Counsel, prepare internal documents (referred to as agendas) for the ICC Court, which include a written summary of the factual and procedural history of the case, an analysis of the issues on which the ICC Court must decide and a discussion of any previous ICC Court decisions or policies relevant to the matter or the issues at hand. The recommendations of the Secretariat as to matters such as the place of arbitration, the number of arbitrators, the National Committee to which resort will be had for the nomination of arbitrators and the amount of the advance on costs are generally accepted by the Court, although this need not be case. The Secretariat does not, however, make recommendations for matters considered at one of the Court's plenary sessions.

8. Powers of the ICC Court's Chairman. Art. 1(3) gives the Chairman, or in his absence any of the Vice-Chairmen, the authority to take urgent decisions on behalf of the ICC Court. Thus, where the circumstances of a particular case call for an urgent decision of the ICC Court and it is not scheduled to meet in the time in which the decision must be taken, the Chairman will make the decision and notify it to the Court at its next session. The Chairman uses this prerogative only in urgent circumstances, such as the approval of awards for emergency interim relief or for 'fast track' arbitrations (arbitrations in which the parties agree to shortened time limits (see art. 32)). Art. 1(3) does not limit the scope of this power and it can thus apply to any type of decision.

9. Disputes arbitrable under the ICC Rules. Under art. 1(1), the Court can deal with both international business disputes and, if the parties so agree, domestic business disputes. The term 'business disputes' has been interpreted broadly by the ICC Court. It covers disputes that arise out of various types of contracts such as service contracts, joint-venture contracts, contracts for the sale of goods, investment contracts, but does not, for example, cover family law disputes or other areas of law that are not related to business.

10. Application of the ICC Rules. Art. 1 provides that disputes be settled in accordance with the ICC Rules. Occasionally, parties may wish to modify the Rules. Indeed, certain articles of the ICC Rules recognise expressly the possibility that the parties modify them or exclude their application (see, for example, arts. 6(1), 6(4), 7(6) and 23(1)). The ICC Court will generally respect any agreement of the parties to modify the Rules. However if the parties' agreement to modify the ICC Rules relates to elements that the ICC Court considers to be mandatory, such as the establishment of the Terms of Reference or scrutiny of draft awards, the Court will refuse to administer the arbitration.

[Definitions]
Article 2

In these Rules:
  (i) **'Arbitral Tribunal' includes one or more arbitrators.**
  (ii) **'Claimant' includes one or more claimants and 'Respondent' includes one or more respondents.**
  (iii) **'Award' includes, inter alia, an interim, partial or final Award.**

1. Defined terms in the ICC Rules. Art. 2 was included in the 1998 revision of the ICC Rules in order to clarify certain terms used in the rules that had given rise to problems under the previous versions.

2. 'Arbitral Tribunal'. Under the ICC Rules 'Arbitral Tribunal' should be understood as designating both a sole arbitrator and a larger arbitral tribunal.

3. 'Claimant' and 'Respondent'. The definition of Claimant and Respondent became necessary due to the insertion in the 1998 revision of the ICC Rules of an article regarding the constitution of the arbitral tribunal in multiparty arbitrations (see art. 10). Prior to this, arguments were occasionally advanced that the ICC Rules were only meant for arbitrations with a single

Claimant and a single Respondent. Therefore, it became necessary to clarify that the terms 'Claimant' and 'Respondent' were used without prejudice to the number of parties on each side.

4. 'Award'. The definition in art. 2 ensures that the term 'award' covers all types of awards. The term 'award' is not defined and the ICC Rules do not clarify which types of decisions should be considered 'awards'. Decisions on matters such as the arbitrators' jurisdiction, the applicable rules of law, the language of the arbitration, procedural issues such as the appointment of experts, preliminary questions, interim measures of protection and substantive claims in the arbitration, have given rise to various positions as to the form that they should take. There is still no agreed rule or guideline in this regard, notwithstanding the ICC Court's obligation to scrutinise all 'awards' (whereas it does not scrutinise decisions that are not 'awards') (see art. 27).

[Written notifications of communications; time limits]

Article 3

(1) **All pleadings and other written communications submitted by any party, as well as all documents annexed thereto, shall be supplied in a number of copies sufficient to provide one copy for each party, plus one for each arbitrator, and one for the Secretariat. A copy of any communication from the Arbitral Tribunal to the parties shall be sent to the Secretariat.**

(2) **All notifications or communications from the Secretariat and the Arbitral Tribunal shall be made to the last address of the party or its representative for whom the same are intended, as notified either by the party in question or by the other party. Such notification or communication may be made by delivery against receipt, registered post, courier, facsimile transmission, telex, telegram or any other means of telecommunication that provides a record of the sending thereof.**

(3) **A notification or communication shall be deemed to have been made on the day it was received by the party itself or by its representative, or would have been received if made in accordance with the preceding paragraph.**

(4) **Periods of time specified in, or fixed under the present Rules, shall start to run on the day following the date a notification or communication is deemed to have been made in accordance with the preceding paragraph. When the day next following such date is an official holiday or a non-business day in the country where the notification or communication is deemed to have been made, the period of time shall commence on the first following business day. Official holidays and non-business days are included in the calculation of the period of time. If the last day of the relevant period of time granted is an official holiday or a non-business day in the country where the notification or communication is**

deemed to have been made, the period of time shall expire at the end of the first following business day.

1. General. Art. 3 sets forth the basic provisions relating to communications. It is relevant at the beginning of the arbitration, before the Terms of Reference and the provisional timetable have been drafted (see art. 18) because such documents typically deal with how the parties and the arbitrators should communicate, as well as instructions made by the arbitral tribunal.

2. Importance of this provision in light of the New York Convention and national laws. Art. 3(2) only requires that notifications be made to 'the last address of the party or its representative'. The accuracy of the address is important because a national court may refuse to enforce an award should it consider that one of the parties was not given proper notice of the proceedings and was thus unable to present its case (see, for example, art. V(1)(b) New York Convention). So too, when notifying a party of any documents relevant to arbitral proceedings, the parties may wish to take into account any particular notification requirements set forth in the national law of the party being notified, as well as the law of the place of arbitration, in order to avoid the risk of a challenge to the award for failure to observe such provisions, whether or not such a challenge would be upheld.

3. Scope of 'written communications'. Art. 3(1) deals with 'all pleadings and other written communications'. It does not, however, specify which written communications fall within the scope of this article. The general practice is that this article applies to the Request, the Answer, the Reply to any counterclaim (if applicable) and all other subsequent pleadings (memorials, briefs, rebuttal, rejoinder, etc.), as well as any letters, faxes, emails sent by a party to the arbitral tribunal or the Secretariat. On the other hand, it is understood that documents exchanged between the parties as part of document production but not sent to the arbitral tribunal are not considered as 'written documents' that need to be provided to the Secretariat for the purposes of this article.

4. Copies of written communications. Art. 3(1) provides that the parties should send a copy of every communication to each party, each arbitrator and the Secretariat. When the parties have not agreed on the number of arbitrators, it is the general practice of the Secretariat to ask the parties to provide it with a sufficient number of copies for a three-member arbitral tribunal until the number of arbitrators is determined. There are certain communications that in practice are not copied to all players in the arbitration. This is the case, for example, for communications between the parties and their counsel with respect to settlement discussions, internal communications within the arbitral tribunal and communications between the arbitral tribunal and the Secretariat on administrative matters.

5. Address of notification. Art. 3(2) provides that all notifications from the Secretariat and the arbitral tribunal shall be made to the last address of the party as notified by the party itself or the other party. It is the Claimant that initially provides the Secretariat with the contact information for the Respondent. Thereafter, the Secretariat and the arbitral tribunal will use the Claimant's address as set out in the Request (see art. 4) and the Respondent's address as set out in the Answer (see art. 5), and all notifications and communications will be sent to such addresses, until otherwise informed by the parties. If documents notified by the Secretariat to the Respondent are returned, the Secretariat will usually request the Claimant to provide a new address for the Respondent in order for the Secretariat to proceed with the notification. If the Claimant does not provide another address, the Secretariat will usually invite it to consider whether it wishes to proceed with the arbitration. If the Claimant wishes to continue, the Secretariat will send correspondence to the Respondent at the address provided by the Claimant, even if it is returned. The parties' addresses will also be subsequently included in the Terms of Reference (see art. 18).

6. Effective date of notifications or communications. Art. 3(3) establishes that any notification or communication sent to the parties' last address by any of the provided methods (see notes 7 and 8) will be considered as being effected on the day it was received by the party or its representative, or would have been received by them if notified in accordance with art. 3(2). Therefore, even if a party does not actually receive a communication, the notification will be valid if the Secretariat or the arbitral tribunal sends it to the party's last address and have a record of the date of the delivery or attempted delivery.

7. Forms of communication in ICC arbitrations. Art. 3(2) establishes that notifications can be made 'by delivery against receipt, registered post, courier, facsimile transmission, telex, telegram or any other means of telecommunication that provides a record of the sending thereof'. Reference to 'delivery against receipt' in art. 3(2) contemplates any delivery method by which the recipient confirms having received the communication. However, art. 3(2) also permits 'any other means of telecommunication that provide a record of sending thereof'. This broadens the possible methods of transmittal so as to include the possibility of email. However, when there is a defaulting party, it is preferable to use a method of transmittal that provides a paper receipt and copy of what was sent. In ICC arbitration, the use of electronic means of communication is common. Certain documents, however, such as awards and the Request are almost never sent electronically.

8. NetCase. In November 2005, the ICC launched NetCase, an electronic arbitration platform which allows arbitration procedures to be conducted through a secure website. NetCase may only be used when the parties and the arbitrators explicitly agree to use it.

9. Language. Art. 3 does not deal with the language of notifications. The Secretariat is not bound by the arbitration agreement or by any subsequent agreement as to the language of the arbitration in terms of its own communications. Nevertheless, notifications by the Secretariat to the parties will be made, as appropriate, in any of the Secretariat's main working languages, which are currently English, French, Spanish and German. On the other hand, the parties may communicate with the Secretariat in the language of the arbitration and the Secretariat will, if necessary, translate the parties' communications for its own purposes. In such cases, the Secretariat will usually write to the parties in English.

10. Calculation of fixed deadlines. Art. 3(4) introduces the general rule of the 'next business day' for the calculation of any deadline fixed by the ICC Rules and by the arbitral tribunal. This rule establishes that any time period related to the arbitration begins to run on the next business day after receipt or deemed receipt. Therefore, if a notice is received on a holiday but the next day is a business day, the period of time shall begin on the next day. This paragraph distinguishes between a 'non-business day', an 'official holiday' and a 'business day' in the country where the notice is received or deemed to have been received.

COMMENCING THE ARBITRATION

[Request for arbitration]

Article 4

(1) A party wishing to have recourse to arbitration under these Rules shall submit its Request for Arbitration (the 'Request') to the Secretariat, which shall notify the Claimant and the Respondent of the receipt of the Request and the date of such receipt.

(2) The date on which the Request is received by the Secretariat shall, for all purposes, be deemed to be the date of the commencement of the arbitral proceedings.

(3) The Request shall, inter alia, contain the following information:
- **(a) the name in full, description and address of each of the parties;**
- **(b) a description of the nature and circumstances of the dispute giving rise to the claims;**
- **(c) a statement of the relief sought, including, to the extent possible, an indication of any amount(s) claimed;**
- **(d) the relevant agreements and, in particular, the arbitration agreement;**
- **(e) all relevant particulars concerning the number of arbitrators and their choice in accordance with the provisions of Articles 8, 9 and 10, and any nomination of an arbitrator required thereby; and**
- **(f) any comments as to the place of arbitration, the applicable rules of law and the language of the arbitration.**

(4) Together with the Request, the Claimant shall submit the number of copies thereof required by Article 3(1) and shall make the advance pay-

ment on administrative expenses required by Appendix III ('Arbitration Costs and Fees') in force on the date the Request is submitted. In the event that the Claimant fails to comply with either of these requirements, the Secretariat may fix a time limit within which the Claimant must comply, failing which the file shall be closed without prejudice to the right of the Claimant to submit the same claims at a later date in another Request.

(5) The Secretariat shall send a copy of the Request and the documents annexed thereto to the Respondent for its Answer to the Request once the Secretariat has sufficient copies of the Request and the required advance payment.

(6) When a party submits a Request in connection with a legal relationship in respect of which arbitration proceedings between the same parties are already pending under these Rules, the Court may, at the request of a party, decide to include the claims contained in the Request in the pending proceedings provided that the Terms of Reference have not been signed or approved by the Court. Once the Terms of Reference have been signed or approved by the Court, claims may only be included in the pending proceedings subject to the provisions of Article 19.

1. Commencement of the arbitral proceedings. Before a party considers initiating an arbitration under the ICC Rules, it may have to exhaust pre-arbitral procedures set forth in the arbitration agreement. However, the ICC Court will not take into account any such requirement in deciding whether or not a Request has been duly filed. This would be an issue for the arbitral tribunal to determine. Art. 4(2) establishes that the date of commencement of the arbitral proceedings is the date of reception by the Secretariat of the Request. The ICC Rules prefer this solution to that set out in many arbitration rules whereby the date of the commencement of the arbitration is the date of receipt of the Request by the Respondent. The ICC Rules avoid complications that may arise in locating the Respondent and in determining the actual date of receipt of the Request. Art. 4(2) only refers to the receipt by the Secretariat of the Request itself. If the Request is received without the required copies or the payment of the advance on administrative expenses, (as provided for in art. 4(4)) the date of commencement will still be the date of reception of the Request by the Secretariat, provided that the Claimant fulfils the requirements set forth in art. 4(4) within a reasonable time.

2. Contents of the Request. Unlike certain other arbitration rules, in ICC arbitration the Request is more than a simple notice of arbitration. Art. 4(3) sets out the basic information that should be included in the Request, which includes a description of the parties, a description of the dispute and the statement of relief, the relevant agreement(s), particularly the arbitration agreement, relevant information concerning the number of arbitrators and the nomination of an arbitrator (if applicable). Apart from these elements, the ICC Rules do not impose any minimum or maximum length or level of detail for the Request. The Claimant is therefore free to determine the level of detail included in the Request. It may be in the Claimant's interest to provide additional detail with respect to the parties, especially any information regarding the ownership and control of the counterparties, their activities and their origin. Such information will, among other things, assist prospective arbitrators in assessing their independence when invited to submit a statement of independence (see art. 7) and assist the Court when invited to examine whether to confirm arbitrators in accordance with art. 9. The Claimant must propose the number of arbitrators in the Request when the arbitration agreement does not specify the number. If the Claimant proposes a three-member arbitral tribunal, it must also nominate an arbitrator for confirmation (art. 8(4)). Art. 4(3)(f) invites, but does not oblige the Claimant to include comments regarding the place of arbitration, the applicable rules of law and the language of the arbitration. It is usually in the Claimant's interest to address these matters immediately in order to avoid, for example, the ICC Court deciding on the place of arbitration without the Claimant's input or deciding on the nationality of an arbitrator without input as to the applicable law. The Secretariat reviews Requests in order to ensure that they contain all the elements set out in art. 4(3). Should a Request not meet the necessary requirements, the Secretariat will invite the Claimant to provide the missing elements within a short time limit, not usually exceeding ten days. Unless the requested information is received, the Secretariat will consider that the Request was not filed in accordance with the ICC Rules and will not notify it to the Respondent. Such a decision may have implications in the event the statute of limitations expires without the Request being perfected.

3. Additional submissions. As discussed under note 2, the Claimant is not obliged to submit a detailed Request. When, because of time restrictions or for tactical reasons, the Claimant chooses to file a short Request, the ICC Rules do not prohibit the submission of supplemental documentation prior to the signature (or approval by the ICC Court) of the Terms of Reference.

4. Amended Request. Although not expressly provided in the ICC Rules, the Claimant may also amend its Request at any time before the constitution of the arbitral tribunal. Any subsequent submission filed by the Claimant, which modifies substantially the original Request, is considered as an amended Request. The ICC Court considers as substantial modifications, the addition or substitution of one or more parties, the introduction of new claims, and the amendment of the statement of relief. When the Claimant files an amended Request before the arbitral tribunal is constituted, the Secretariat will notify all parties and will invite the Respondent to file an Answer to the amended Request in accordance with art. 5. Once the arbitral tribunal is constituted, the Claimant cannot amend its Request to introduce new parties. However, if the arbitral tribunal has already been constituted, the Claimant may amend its relief sought, at least up to the point that the Terms of Reference are established (art. 18).

5. Filing of the Request. Art. 4 does not set forth any particular formalities that must be completed in the filing of the Request, except for the submission of the Request to the Secretariat and compliance with art. 3(1) as to the number of copies and the payment of the advance on administrative expenses (currently USD 2,500). Generally, the Request is sent to the Secretariat in hard copy only, but it can also be filed by fax or email, as long as a hard copy follows. In such cases, the Request will be deemed to have been received on the date the electronic copy was received, but it will not be notified to the Respondent until the hard copies have been received.

6. Language of the Request. When the language of the arbitration is determined in the arbitration agreement, the Request should be drafted in the agreed language. If the Request is not so drafted, the Secretariat will usually take note of the requirements of the arbitration agreement and draw the Claimant's attention to them. The Respondent may agree to use a language other than the one provided for in the arbitration agreement. However, if the Respondent objects to the use of such language, the matter will be finally resolved by the arbitral tribunal. Conversely, when the language of arbitration has not been determined, and until the arbitral tribunal has decided the matter (see art. 16), the parties and the Secretariat may use any language they wish for communications.

7. Notification of the Request. Once the Secretariat has the necessary copies of the Request and the advance on administrative expenses has been paid, the Secretariat will notify the Request to the Respondent. The Secretariat will also send the Respondent a copy of the ICC Rules and a letter informing it of its obligations under the Rules (the thirty-day time limit to submit the Answer and the information required to be included in the Answer, particularly regarding the constitution of the arbitral tribunal). Such notification is generally made by courier.

8. Consolidation. When two arbitrations are related, it may be in the interest of procedural and economic efficiency that the proceedings be joined and dealt with as a single arbitration. Under the ICC Rules, the ICC Court may consolidate arbitrations by agreement of all parties or at the request of one of the parties, provided certain conditions are met (see note 11).

9. Consolidation by agreement of the parties. The ICC Court will facilitate the consolidation of two or more arbitrations if all parties to such arbitrations agree. In such case, the ICC Court will take note of the parties' agreement to consolidate the arbitrations and will assign one reference to the consolidated case for administrative purposes. Art. 4(6), which deals expressly with consolidation, does not apply if all parties agree.

10. Consolidation of arbitral proceedings under art. 4(6). Art. 4(6) grants the ICC Court the power to consolidate ICC arbitrations and sets forth the conditions required for the ICC Court to do this. However, this provision does not oblige the parties to request consolidation, even if all of the conditions set out in art. 4(6) are met.

11. Conditions for consolidation under art. 4(6). In the absence of an agreement by all of the parties to each arbitration to consolidate the cases, art. 4(6) sets out four conditions that must be met before the ICC Court can consolidate two arbitrations. First, one of the parties must request the ICC Court to consolidate the arbitrations. The ICC Court will not apply this procedure on its own initiative. Second, the arbitral proceedings must both be under the ICC Rules and between the same parties. If the parties are not exactly the same, the ICC Court cannot consolidate two cases. Third, the arbitral proceedings to be consolidated must be in connection with the same legal relationship (or same economic transaction). It is not strictly necessary for both arbitrations to arise from the same underlying agreement. However, when the consolidation involves more than one agreement, the arbitration agreements must be consistent with each other. Consolidation would not be possible if, for example, the arbitration agreement in one contract provided for a sole arbitrator and the arbitration agreement in the other contract provided for a three-member arbitral tribunal. Finally, the Terms of Reference cannot have been signed or approved by the ICC Court. In addition to the conditions set forth in art. 4(6), the ICC Court will also take into consideration whether the arbitral tribunals in both arbitrations have already been constituted. When different arbitral tribunals have been constituted in the arbitrations, the ICC Court will not usually consolidate the arbitrations under art. 4(6).

[Answer to the Request; counterclaims]

Article 5

(1) Within 30 days from the receipt of the Request from the Secretariat, the Respondent shall file an Answer (the 'Answer') which shall, inter alia, contain the following information:
  (a) its name in full, description and address;
  (b) its comments as to the nature and circumstances of the dispute giving rise to the claim(s);
  (c) its response to the relief sought;
  (d) any comments concerning the number of arbitrators and their choice in light of the Claimant's proposals and in accordance with the provisions of Articles 8, 9 and 10, and any nomination of an arbitrator required thereby; and
  (e) any comments as to the place of arbitration, the applicable rules of law and the language of the arbitration.

(2) The Secretariat may grant the Respondent an extension of the time for filing the Answer, provided the application for such an extension contains the Respondent's comments concerning the number of arbitrators and their choice, and where required by Articles 8, 9 and 10, the

nomination of an arbitrator. If the Respondent fails to do so, the Court shall proceed in accordance with these Rules.

(3) The Answer shall be supplied to the Secretariat in the number of copies specified by Article 3(1).

(4) A copy of the Answer and the documents annexed thereto shall be communicated by the Secretariat to the Claimant.

(5) Any counterclaims made by the Respondent shall be filed with its Answer and shall provide:
   (a) a description of the nature and circumstances of the dispute giving rise to the counterclaim(s); and
   (b) a statement of the relief sought, including, to the extent possible, an indication of any amount(s) counterclaimed.

(6) The Claimant shall file a Reply to any counterclaim within 30 days from the date of receipt of the counterclaim(s) communicated by the Secretariat. The Secretariat may grant the Claimant an extension of time for filing the Reply.

1. General. The impact of art. 5 is that the Respondent must file its Answer before the constitution of the arbitral tribunal. This allows the ICC Court to obtain a better understanding of the issues at stake at an early stage of the arbitration, through the Request and the Answer. Among other things, this may assist the Court in the constitution of the arbitral tribunal and in assessing the total amount in dispute (particularly if there are counterclaims). It also allows the arbitral tribunal, once constituted, to obtain a more complete picture of the dispute early in the proceedings.

2. Time limit to submit the Answer. Pursuant to art. 5(1), the Respondent is to submit its Answer within thirty days from the receipt of the Request from the Secretariat. The thirty-day time limit commences on the business day after the date the Request was received or deemed to have been received by the Respondent at the address indicated in the Request by the Claimant (see art. 3, notes 5 and 6). This thirty-day time limit determines when the Respondent is to file its Answer, whether or not the Respondent has received a copy of the Request from the Claimant directly before the Secretariat notified it to the Respondent.

3. Filing of the Answer. In accordance with art. 5(3), the Respondent must submit its Answer in the number of copies specified in art. 3(1), that is, in a number sufficient to provide one copy for each party, one for each arbitrator, and one for the Secretariat. The Answer is deemed to be received by the Secretariat on the date it was sent by the Respondent (for example, by email) and not the date of the receipt of the hard copies of the Answer by the Secretariat. The Answer is notified by the Secretariat to the Claimant, in accordance with art. 5(4). The Respondent may also send a copy of its Answer to the Claimant directly and in practice this is often done. However, if the Answer contains counterclaims, the time limit for the Respondent's reply to such counterclaim does not start to run until the Respondent receives the Answer from the Secretariat (see note 11).

4. Contents of the Answer. Art. 5(1) sets out the basic requirements of the Answer. It essentially is the mirror image of what is called for in the Request. The Answer should contain the Respondent's name and address, the Respondent's comments as to the nature and circumstances of the dispute, its response to the relief sought and any comments on the number of arbitrators and the place of arbitration. The Respondent should also, pursuant to art. 5(1), provide its comments on the applicable law and the language of the arbitration. Apart from the elements in art. 5(1), the ICC Rules do not impose any minimum length or level of detail for the Answer. The Respondent may provide detailed arguments and defences, accompanied by supporting material and its version of the relevant facts, or it may simply deny the Claimant's allegations without substantiating its position and reserve its right to address them in future submissions. Usually, it is in the Respondent's interest to address certain issues in the Answer, such as the number of arbitrators and the place of arbitration. If not addressed in its Answer, the Respondent may not have a further opportunity to deal with them before the ICC Court takes certain decisions. (The ICC Court will, for example, usually determine the number of arbitrators and the place of arbitration shortly after the submission of the Respondent's Answer.) If the arbitration agreement provides for three arbitrators, the Respondent must also nominate its arbitrator in the Answer, in accordance with art. 8 (this is relevant only where the Respondent has not already nominated its arbitrator when requesting an extension to file its Answer, pursuant to art. 5(2)). As discussed below under note 6, the Respondent is not required to nominate its arbitrator in the Answer if the Claimant has failed to nominate its arbitrator or the Respondent has objected to the confirmation of the Claimant's nominee. In such cases, the Respondent may refrain from nominating an arbitrator as it is for the Claimant to nominate its arbitrator first. If the Respondent fails to nominate an arbitrator, after due notice, the ICC Court will appoint one on its behalf, in accordance with art. 8(4). Finally, if the Respondent considers that the arbitration agreement introduced by the Claimant is invalid or that it is not party to it, this should be raised in the Answer. In such case, the ICC Court will decide whether the arbitration will proceed pursuant to art. 6(2).

5. Late Answer or no Answer. If the Respondent submits its Answer after the thirty-day time limit expires, it does not forfeit its right to respond to the Request. Pursuant to art. 18(1), the parties can file further submissions before the Terms of Reference are established (see art. 18, note 3). If the Respondent decides to participate after the Terms of Reference have been approved by the ICC Court in accordance with art. 18(3), the arbitral tribunal will have to determine in what manner the Respondent should be allowed to participate. If the Respondent does not file its Answer and fails to participate in the proceedings, the ICC Court will take a decision as to whether the arbitration shall proceed, pursuant to art. 6(2), usually shortly after the thirty-day time limit for the Respondent to file its Answer expires.

6. Request for an extension to submit the Answer. Under art. 5(2), the Respondent may request an extension of the time limit to submit its Answer. Such request must be addressed to the Secretariat. The Secretariat can only grant an extension under art. 5(2) if the Respondent has provided its comments on the number of arbitrators and, where required by arts. 8, 9, and 10 to do so, nominated an arbitrator. In practice, Respondents frequently request an extension of time to submit the Answer. Respondents also sometimes request an extension of time to provide comments on the number of the arbitrators or their nomination. Such extensions are not granted by the Secretariat except where the Claimant has not nominated its arbitrator or the Respondent has raised objections to the confirmation of the Claimant's arbitrator (the ICC Court generally decides on such objections before the Respondent nominates its arbitrator). The Respondent may request an extension to file its Answer and reserve, at the same time, its right to raise jurisdictional objections in the Answer, even if it nominates an arbitrator when doing so.

7. Extension to submit the Answer. Requests for an extension of time to file the Answer are decided upon by the Secretariat and not by the ICC Court. The Secretariat checks that the conditions set out in art. 5(2) are satisfied. When the request is for an extension of thirty days or less, it will generally be granted. If the requested extension exceeds thirty days, the Secretariat usually grants the Respondent thirty days and invites the Claimant to provide its comments on the longer extension. If the Claimant does not agree, then the Secretariat decides, given the circumstances of the case, whether or not to grant the Respondent the longer extension or some of it. Extensions beyond sixty days are rare. If the conditions set out in art. 5(2) have not been satisfied, the Secretariat will not grant an extension.

8. Counterclaims. Art. 5(5) calls upon the Respondent to file a counterclaim against the Claimant at the same time as the Answer is filed. It does not, however, require that the Respondent do so. Such counterclaims may be raised at least until the Terms of the Reference are established. It is generally preferable for the Respondent to introduce its counterclaims in the Answer. The term 'counterclaim' has been interpreted as not including claims against third parties and referring only to claims that the Respondent may have against the Claimant. This interpretation, however, would not allow the Respondent to join third parties to the arbitration and has been the subject of criticism.

9. Joinder. The ICC Court's practice regarding the possibility for the Respondent to join third parties to the arbitration has developed over the recent years. As a general matter, a Respondent can only join a third party to the proceedings if both the Claimant and the third party consent. However, if the Respondent has a claim against a third party that is also a signatory to the agreement which contains the arbitration agreement on the basis of which the Request was filed, the ICC Court has accepted that this third party may be joined in the proceedings provided that three conditions are met: first, that the third party has signed the agreement on the basis of which the Request was filed; second, that the Respondent has introduced claims against the third party; and third, that the request for joinder of the third party is made before the arbitral tribunal is constituted. This last condition highlights the importance of introducing counterclaims or third party claims in the Answer.

10. Application of art. 4(6) to counterclaims. The Respondent may also wish to raise against the Claimant counterclaims that are based on a contract other than that which was the basis for the Request. The Claimant may consent to have such counterclaims dealt with in the same arbitration. If it does not consent, the Respondent could file a separate Request, introducing claims against the Claimant under a different contract between the parties and then request the consolidation of the two arbitrations under art. 4(6) (see art. 4, notes 9 and 10).

11. Claimant's reply. Art. 5(6) provides that the Claimant must file a reply to any counterclaim raised by the Respondent and provides the same time limit as for the Answer (thirty days) for doing so. The time limit runs from the date that the Respondent receives the counterclaim from the Secretariat. The Claimant may also apply to the Secretariat for an extension of this time limit. Such extension is usually granted for a reasonable period of time, on the same basis as an extension of time for the Answer (see notes 6 and 7). Such an extension does not generally affect the constitution of the arbitral tribunal. Indeed, it is common that the Claimant's reply is filed after the arbitral tribunal is constituted.

[Effect of the arbitration agreement]

Article 6

(1) Where the parties have agreed to submit to arbitration under the Rules, they shall be deemed to have submitted ipso facto to the Rules in effect on the date of commencement of the arbitration proceedings, unless they have agreed to submit to the Rules in effect on the date of their arbitration agreement.

(2) If the Respondent does not file an Answer, as provided by Article 5, or if any party raises one or more pleas concerning the existence, validity or scope of the arbitration agreement, the Court may decide, without prejudice to the admissibility or merits of the plea or pleas, that the arbitration shall proceed if it is prima facie satisfied that an arbitration agreement under the Rules may exist. In such a case, any decision as to the jurisdiction of the Arbitral Tribunal shall be taken by the Arbitral Tribunal itself. If the Court is not so satisfied, the parties shall be notified that the arbitration cannot proceed. In such a case, any party retains

the right to ask any court having jurisdiction whether or not there is a binding arbitration agreement.

(3) If any of the parties refuses or fails to take part in the arbitration or any stage thereof, the arbitration shall proceed notwithstanding such refusal or failure.

(4) Unless otherwise agreed, the Arbitral Tribunal shall not cease to have jurisdiction by reason of any claim that the contract is null and void or allegation that it is non-existent, provided that the Arbitral Tribunal upholds the validity of the arbitration agreement. The Arbitral Tribunal shall continue to have jurisdiction to determine the respective rights of the parties and to adjudicate their claims and pleas even though the contract itself may be non-existent or null and void.

1. General. Art. 6 deals mainly with issues relating to the validity and effect of arbitration agreements and sets out the basis on which the ICC Court and, subsequently, the arbitral tribunal decide jurisdictional questions.

2. Applicable version of the ICC Rules. Art. 6(1) explains which version of the rules applies in a given arbitration. It provides that the rules in force on the date of commencement of the arbitration shall apply, unless the parties have agreed that their dispute be submitted to the version of the rules in effect when the arbitration agreement was entered in to.

3. Objections regarding the arbitration agreement. Art. 6(2) applies when the Respondent does not submit an Answer or contests the ICC Court's jurisdiction by raising objections regarding the existence, validity or scope of the alleged arbitration agreement. A party may even decide to initiate an ICC arbitration in the absence of an ICC arbitration agreement. The Secretariat will then notify the Claimant's Request to the Respondent. If the Respondent files an Answer to the Request without raising jurisdictional objections, the Respondent is generally considered to have agreed to ICC arbitration. Should the Respondent contest the existence, validity or the scope of the arbitration agreement, but the Claimant wishes to proceed, the ICC Court will be invited to decide, in accordance with art. 6(2), whether it is 'prima facie' satisfied that an arbitration agreement under the ICC Rules may exist (see note 4). A decision pursuant to art. 6(2) is generally taken by the ICC Court before any other decision. For example, the ICC Court will normally take its art. 6(2) decision before fixing, if necessary, the place of arbitration or the advance on costs. Before the ICC Court takes a decision under art. 6(2), the Claimant is invited to provide its comments on the Respondent's jurisdictional objections. More rounds of comments may follow, in certain circumstances.

4. The prima facie test. Under art. 6(2) when a party raises jurisdiction objections, the ICC Court applies a prima facie test, in order to determine whether the arbitration will proceed in accordance with the ICC Rules. According to this test, the ICC Court must examine, first, whether an arbitration agreement may exist, second, whether the arbitration agreement makes reference to ICC arbitration, and third, to whom such an arbitration agreement applies. The ICC Court does not enter into a substantive examination of the evidence provided by the parties. In case of objections relating to the existence or validity of the arbitration agreement, the ICC Court will allow the matter to proceed if it finds that should the Claimant's allegations prove to be true, there may be a valid arbitration agreement. The Court will leave it to the arbitral tribunal to determine finally, on the basis of evidence and applicable law, whether there is indeed a valid arbitration agreement between the parties (see note 13). If the ICC Court decides that the matter shall not proceed with regard to one or more parties, any party may ask any court having jurisdiction whether or not there is a binding arbitration agreement (*Global Gold Mining* v *Robinson* (United States)).

5. Existence of the arbitration agreement. The most common objection to jurisdiction is that there is no arbitration agreement between the parties. When faced with objections regarding the existence of an arbitration agreement, the ICC Court adopts a liberal approach and will generally allow the arbitration to continue if the Claimant provides material demonstrating that an ICC arbitration agreement between the parties may exist. Almost any written evidence of the possible existence of an arbitration agreement will suffice (*Cekobank* v *ICC* (France)). The ICC Court rarely decides not to allow an arbitration to continue. It may, however, happen, for example, when the Claimant does not provide a copy of a contract between the parties containing an arbitration agreement or when the Claimant does not provide any cogent reasons to explain how the Respondent may be bound by an arbitration agreement.

6. Non-signatories. A jurisdictional objection that arises often is a claim that the party is not a signatory to the contract containing the arbitration agreement. Art. (6)2 does not require that all parties be signatories to the contract containing the arbitration agreement since there are a variety of situations whereby non-signatory parties can be bound by the arbitration agreement (alter ego, succession, group of companies, agency, assignment, etc.). The ICC Court will apply the prima facie test, in order to determine whether it may have been the parties' intention that the non-signatory be bound by the arbitration agreement, even if it has not signed it. The ICC Court will usually allow proceedings to continue against non-signatory parties if there are plausible arguments that indicate that the non-signatory might bound by the arbitration agreement. However, when the non-signatory party is a physical person or a state, the ICC Court will often be more conservative in the application of art. 6(2). In case of multiple Respondents, the ICC Court may decide that the arbitration will only proceed against some of the Respondents, if it is not prima facie satisfied that an arbitration agreement may exist between the Claimant and each of the Respondents.

7. Validity and scope of the arbitration agreement. When the validity or the scope of the arbitration agreement, rather than its existence, are called into question, the ICC Court is inclined to be prima facie satisfied that an arbitration agreement may exist between the parties. The ICC Court, therefore, generally leaves it to the arbitral tribunal to decide on the validity or the scope of the arbitration agreement, on the basis of the applicable law and the evidence provided by the parties.

8. Arbitration agreement does not refer to the ICC Rules. Respondents sometimes argue that the arbitration agreement does not designate the ICC (for example, when it designates 'the Chamber of Commerce of Paris', or 'the Arbitrage Court in Paris, France', or 'the Geneva Court of International Arbitration'). In such cases, the ICC Court tends to look beyond the literal wording of the arbitration agreement and to examine whether the parties might in fact have intended to submit their dispute to ICC arbitration. If, for example, the phrase 'international court of arbitration' is used and there is no such body in the city or country mentioned in the arbitration agreement, the ICC Court will normally assume, for the purposes of art. 6(2), that the intention was to submit the disputes to ICC arbitration.

9. Non-compliance with conditions precedent to arbitration. In some cases, the arbitration agreement may require the exhaustion of certain conditions prior to the commencement of ICC arbitration. When the Respondent objects to the arbitration on the grounds that the required pre-arbitral steps have not been complied with, the ICC Court will normally allow the arbitration to proceed under art. 6(2) and let the arbitral tribunal decide on the issue of the non-compliance with any conditions precedent.

10. Multiple contracts. Another problem that arises commonly is the question of whether a single arbitration can be set in motion in respect of a series of separate, but related, contracts between the same parties or possibly different parties. The ICC Court has permitted arbitrations to proceed even when there are different contracts and different arbitration agreements (*Eurodif* (France)), if the arbitration clauses are similar (*Westland* (Switzerland)). The ICC Court examines certain elements before deciding to allow a single arbitration to proceed in case of multiple contract cases. The following three criteria must be met in order for the ICC Court to allow such a matter to proceed: first, all contracts must have been signed by the same parties; second, they must relate to the same economic transaction; and third, the arbitration agreements must be compatible (for example, they must contain compatible provisions regarding the number of arbitrators and the constitution of the arbitral tribunal).

11. Defaulting parties. The ICC Court can set an arbitration in motion even when one of the parties fails or refuses to participate, as long as it is prima facie satisfied that an ICC arbitration agreement may exist between the parties. Art. 6(3) provides specifically the ICC Court and, subsequently, the arbitral tribunal with the authority to proceed with the arbitration even if any party (usually the Respondent) refuses to participate in the proceedings.

In such case, the ICC Court will examine the arbitration agreement on the basis of which the Request was filed to determine whether it is prima facie satisfied that an arbitration agreement between the parties (including the non-participating party) may exist. If the ICC Court is satisfied that this is the case, the arbitration will proceed. The Secretariat and, subsequently, the arbitral tribunal will continue notifying any documents and correspondence in the arbitration proceedings to the non-participating party. The ICC Court will also proceed, in case of a three-member arbitral tribunal, to appoint an arbitrator on behalf of such party, in accordance with arts. 8(4) and 9(6).

12. Objections raised by the Claimant. Objections to the existence, validity or scope of the arbitration agreement may also be raised by the Claimant, particularly, in cases where the Respondent attempts to join third parties to the proceedings (see art. 5, note 9).

13. Jurisdiction of the arbitral tribunal. Once the ICC Court has decided that an arbitration will proceed under art. 6(2), the arbitral tribunal, once constituted, will have to decide on its own jurisdiction. In practice, when transferring the file to the arbitral tribunal, the Secretariat will draw the arbitrators' attention to the ICC Court's decision pursuant to art. 6(2) and invite them to decide on their own jurisdiction. Art. 6(2) recognises the arbitral tribunal's authority to do so. The arbitral tribunal's decision on its own jurisdiction should take the form of an award, often an interim or partial award limited to this issue.

14. Autonomy of the arbitration agreement. Art. 6(4) establishes that the arbitration agreement is autonomous of the contract that contains it. This provision prevents a party from objecting to arbitration on the grounds of the nullity or non-existence of the contract containing the arbitration agreement. However, this does not mean that the arbitration agreement can never be found to be inexistent, null or void. The arbitral tribunal may ultimately determine that such is indeed the case. Even when such a decision is made, the arbitral tribunal is nevertheless entitled to award costs.

15. The ICC Court's decision. After the ICC Court has taken its decision as to the prima facie existence of an arbitration agreement under art. 6(2), the Secretariat will notify the parties of the Court's decision, without setting out its reasons. It has been confirmed in different national jurisdictions (*Apollo* v *Berg* (United States), *Cekobank* v *ICC* (France), *REDEC* (France), *Japan Time* v *Kienzle France & ICC* (France)) that the ICC Court's 'prima facie' determination is of an administrative character and thus not subject to judicial review. If the ICC Court decides that the matter shall not proceed with regard to one or more parties, a dissatisfied party must ask a national court having jurisdiction whether or not there is a binding arbitration agreement. Such party cannot compel the ICC allow the matter to proceed (*Global Gold Mining v Robinson* (United States)).

ICC Rules of Arbitration, art. 7

[General provisions]

Article 7

(1) Every arbitrator must be and remain independent of the parties involved in the arbitration.

(2) Before appointment or confirmation, a prospective arbitrator shall sign a statement of independence and disclose in writing to the Secretariat any facts or circumstances which might be of such a nature as to call into question the arbitrator's independence in the eyes of the parties. The Secretariat shall provide such information to the parties in writing and fix a time limit for any comments from them.

(3) An arbitrator shall immediately disclose in writing to the Secretariat and to the parties any facts or circumstances of a similar nature which may arise during the arbitration.

(4) The decisions of the Court as to the appointment, confirmation, challenge or replacement of an arbitrator shall be final and the reasons for such decisions shall not be communicated.

(5) By accepting to serve, every arbitrator undertakes to carry out his responsibilities in accordance with these Rules.

(6) Insofar as the parties have not provided otherwise, the Arbitral Tribunal shall be constituted in accordance with the provisions of Articles 8, 9 and 10.

1. General. One of the basic and most important features of ICC arbitration is the freedom the parties have in the selection of arbitrators. The ICC does not have a list of arbitrators from which the parties must choose. However, the ICC Rules do set out certain requirements that candidates must meet in order to be able to act as arbitrator. Art. 7 stipulates a series of principles of general application that concern an arbitrator's obligation of independence and duty to comply with the ICC Rules, and the parties' right to agree how the arbitral tribunal will be constituted.

2. Independence. Under the ICC Rules, all arbitrators, including party-nominated arbitrators, must be independent of each of the parties. Art. 7(1) provides that 'every arbitrator must be and remain independent'. Other rules and laws such as the LCIA Rules (art. 5(2)), the AAA-ICDR Rules (art. 7(1)) and the UNCITRAL Model Law (art. 12(2)) stipulate that arbitrators should not only be 'independent', but also 'impartial'. The ICC Rules are premised on the idea that 'independence' relates to the arbitrator's relationship with the parties and can be objectively analysed on the basis of elements such as a prior relationship between the arbitrator and one of the parties or its counsel (see note 3). The 'impartiality' of an arbitrator, however, is more difficult to determine given that it relates to the arbitrator's state of mind, which could be influenced by many factors such as nationality, religion or cultural and geographical background and may only be revealed during the course of the arbitration or through the writings of the person concerned. Objectively observed independence does not guarantee that an arbitrator will act impartially during the proceedings. Even though art. 7(1) does not mention impartiality, it is understood that the term 'independent' in art. 7(1) is broad enough to take into account impartiality. The ICC Court will not of its own initiative examine an arbitrator's independence (except in the rare circumstances when the ICC Court replaces an arbitrator under art. 12(2) based on a perceived lack of independence). It will analyse the matter only when one of the parties has objected to an arbitrator's confirmation in accordance with arts. 8 and 9 or challenged an arbitrator under art. 11.

3. Elements considered by the ICC Court when examining an arbitrator's independence. When examining an arbitrator's independence, the ICC Court does not follow any set of rules or particular guidelines. The ICC Court examines the prospective arbitrator's independence on a case by case basis considering the relevant circumstances. The ICC Court will take into account relationships, be they financial, professional, personal or of any other nature that could potentially affect the arbitrator's independence. The ICC Court will also take into account relationships between a party and the arbitrator's law firm, between the arbitrator and the party's counsel or even with third parties (such as direct competitors or business associates). The broad range of different challenges to arbitrators' independence can be illustrated by some examples. Arbitrators have been challenged because of prior appointments as arbitrator by the same party or by the same counsel. The ICC Court will generally not consider such appointments to affect an arbitrator's independence. However, there could be circumstances which evidence that this prior relationship has affected the arbitrator's independence (for example, the person has been nominated by the same law firm on numerous occasions). Arbitrators nominated by state parties or para-statal entities have been challenged because they are current or former government employees, or have done considerable work for the state or state-owned entities. In such circumstances, if objections are raised, the ICC Court will generally not confirm such nominees. However, this practice varies depending on the country in question, particularly because in some countries which have, or have had, heavily centralised governments, it is difficult for state parties to find a suitable candidate with no government connections. Arbitrators have also been challenged on the basis of their prior writings on legal or political issues.

4. Statement of independence. Art. 7(2) sets forth the obligation for arbitrators to submit a statement of independence. The contents of the statement of independence are not verified by the ICC Court. A statement of independence is considered 'qualified' when the arbitrator declares that he is independent of the parties, but discloses information regarding relationships or circumstances that could affect their independence in the eyes of the parties. A statement of independence is 'unqualified' when the arbitrator declares that he is independent of the parties and does not disclose any such information.

5. Information to be disclosed in the statement of independence. The ICC Rules do not contain guidelines as to the type of information that must be disclosed by arbitrators in their Statements of Independence. Arbitrators are expected to disclose any information that could be perceived as affecting their independence in the eyes of the parties. The statement of independence provides that, in deciding whether to disclose information, potential arbitrators should take into account, among other things, 'whether there exists any past or present relationship, direct or indirect, with any of the parties, their counsel, whether financial, professional or of another kind'. It also states that 'any doubt of whether it is necessary or not to disclose certain information should be resolved in favour of disclosure'. When inviting prospective arbitrators to submit a statement of independence, the Secretariat informs them of the parties' names, their counsel and the arbitrator nominated by the other side, or, in the case of the chairman, the co-arbitrators.

6. Comments of the parties. Art. 7(2) provides that the Secretariat must communicate prospective arbitrators' Statements of Independence to the parties. If the statement of independence is qualified, the parties are invited to submit any comments they may have, usually within fifteen days. If the parties do not comment within the time limit granted, it is generally considered that the parties have no objection to the facts disclosed. When objections are raised against the confirmation of an arbitrator, the Secretariat will forward them to all parties. It is not the general practice of the Secretariat to invite the nominee concerned to comment on the objections raised. If, however, one of the parties requests that the nominee be invited to comment, the Secretariat will inform the nominee of such request and allow them to comment on the objections or provide additional information. Parties may challenge an arbitrator later on in the arbitral proceedings on the basis of the disclosed information (see art. 11, note 4). The parties may also object to an arbitrator's confirmation on the basis of information not disclosed by the arbitrator, but obtained by other means.

7. Disclosure of new circumstances. Arbitrators are expected to remain independent during the arbitral proceedings and until the final award is rendered (see arts. 24 to 29). Art. 7(3) imposes on arbitrators the obligation to inform the Secretariat and the parties of any circumstances that arise during the arbitration that could affect their independence in the parties' eyes. Art. 7(3) establishes that such disclosure should be done immediately. Should an arbitrator inform the parties and the Secretariat of such new conditions, one of two things can happen: either the parties will consider that the new circumstances do not affect the arbitrator's independence or one or more parties may decide to challenge the arbitrator under art. 11.

8. Decisions of the ICC Court. Art. 7(4) provides that decisions by the ICC Court on the appointment, confirmation (or non-confirmation), challenge or replacement of arbitrators are final and thus not subject to appeal. It also provides that the reasons for such decisions shall not be communicated. The ICC Court's reluctance to communicate reasons for such decisions has been criticised for a lack of transparency. However, publishing reasons for not confirming an arbitrator or accepting a challenge may provide an additional means to attack an award or challenge an arbitrator in state court proceedings. Art. 7(4) does not prevent the parties from presenting their case before any competent national court of law. However, the ICC Court's decision is not jurisdictional in nature and therefore its decisions cannot be set aside (at least in France) (*Raffineries de petrol d'Homs et de Banias* v *Chambre de commerce international* (France)).

9. Arbitrators' obligations. When accepting an appointment in an ICC arbitration, arbitrators not only agree to settle the dispute, but also to comply with the ICC Rules. Arbitrators are expected to conduct the proceedings in accordance with the ICC Rules and to respect the ICC Court's decisions. The arbitrators may not usurp any of the functions of the ICC Court, nor decide upon any matters as to which the ICC Rules confer exclusive authority to the ICC Court. For examples, arbitrators cannot reach separate arrangements with the parties with regard to their fees.

10. Constitution of the arbitral tribunal. Art. 7(6) affirms the liberty of the parties as to the constitution of the arbitral tribunal. The provisions of the ICC Rules regarding the constitution of the arbitral tribunal will only apply when the parties have not agreed otherwise. The parties may, for example, agree on specific (quite often short) time limits for the appointment of the co-arbitrators or the chairman of the arbitral tribunal, or specify the qualities or specific skills (for example, language or technical skills) that the arbitrators should have. They may also agree that the parties themselves or the co-arbitrators nominate jointly the chairman, or that the co-arbitrators or the ICC Court provide a list of potential candidates to act as chairman to the parties to help them reach agreement on a candidate. As mentioned above, if the parties do not otherwise agree, the relevant provisions of the ICC Rules will apply (see arts. 8 and 9).

[Number of arbitrators]

Article 8

(1) The disputes shall be decided by a sole arbitrator or by three arbitrators.

(2) Where the parties have not agreed upon the number of arbitrators, the Court shall appoint a sole arbitrator, save where it appears to the Court that the dispute is such as to warrant the appointment of three arbitrators. In such case, the Claimant shall nominate an arbitrator within a period of 15 days from the receipt of the notification of the decision of the Court, and the Respondent shall nominate an arbitrator within a period of 15 days from the receipt of the notification of the nomination made by the Claimant.

(3) Where the parties have agreed that the dispute shall be settled by a sole arbitrator, they may, by agreement, nominate the sole arbitrator for confirmation. If the parties fail to nominate a sole arbitrator within 30 days from the date when the Claimant's Request for Arbitration has been received by the other party, or within such additional time as may be allowed by the Secretariat, the sole arbitrator shall be appointed by the Court.

(4) Where the dispute is to be referred to three arbitrators, each party shall nominate in the Request and the Answer, respectively, one arbitrator for confirmation by the Court. If a party fails to nominate an arbitrator, the appointment shall be made by the Court. The third arbitrator, who will act as chairman of the Arbitral Tribunal, shall be appointed by the Court, unless the parties have agreed upon another procedure for such appointment, in which case the nomination will be subject to confirmation pursuant to Article. 9. Should such procedure not result in a nomination within the time limit fixed by the parties or the Court, the third arbitrator shall be appointed by the Court.

1. General. While art. 8 is entitled 'Number of arbitrators', it deals with both the number of arbitrators and the default mechanism for the appointment of arbitrators. The ICC Rules generally respect and implement the parties' agreement as to the number of arbitrators. However, when the parties do not agree on the number of arbitrators, either in the arbitration agreement in the parties' contract or subsequently, the ICC Court will decide the number. Where the arbitration clause is silent as to the number of arbitrators and the amount in dispute is relatively small, the Secretariat informs the parties at the outset of the case of the financial consequences of having a three-member arbitral tribunal to encourage the parties to agree to a sole arbitrator.

2. Possible derogation from the general rule of a sole arbitrator or three arbitrators. Art. 8(1) provides that any dispute to be settled according to the ICC Rules shall be decided by a sole arbitrator or by a three-member arbitral tribunal. However, in cases where the parties expressly agree on a number of arbitrators other than one or three, the ICC Court will respect the parties' decision and proceed with the constitution of the arbitral tribunal in accordance with the parties' agreement. In certain cases, however, the Secretariat will inform the parties of the possible disadvantages of their choice.

3. Decision on the number of arbitrators by the ICC Court. When called upon to decide the number of arbitrators, the ICC Court will appoint a sole arbitrator save where it appears to the Court that the dispute is such as to warrant the appointment of three arbitrators (art. 8(2)). When exercising this power, the ICC Court will take into consideration various factors (see note 4). When the ICC Court decides to submit a case to a sole arbitrator, at the same Court session it will generally invite an ICC National Committee to propose an appropriate candidate (see art. 9(3)). On the other hand, when the ICC

Court decides that the dispute warrants the appointment of a three-member arbitral tribunal, the Secretariat will so notify the parties and invite them to nominate an arbitrator each for confirmation by the Court or the Secretary General, pursuant to art. 9(1) or 9(2). Art. 8(3) establishes that each party is entitled to a fifteen-day period in order to nominate an arbitrator. The fifteen-day period for the nomination of the Claimant's arbitrator commences the day after the receipt by the Claimant of the Secretariat's letter notifying the parties of the ICC Court's decision on the number of arbitrators. The fifteen-day period for the Respondent to nominate its arbitrator commences the day after the receipt of the Claimant's nomination. As a result, the Respondent can have up to thirty days to select an arbitrator. As the fifteen-day period is imposed by the ICC Rules, the Secretariat will not normally grant extensions to the parties for the nomination of their respective arbitrators, unless both parties agree to such an extension. Consequently, any nomination received by the Secretariat after the expiry of the fifteen-day period is not considered valid. However, the Secretariat will generally inform the ICC Court of a party's late nomination, and invite the Court to consider it, unless the Court has already appointed an arbitrator on that party's behalf (see art. 8(4)).

4. Criteria taken into account by the ICC Court in deciding the number of arbitrators. The ICC Court will take into consideration the specific circumstances of the case in deciding whether to submit a case to a sole arbitrator or three-member arbitral tribunal. These issues include the amount in dispute (for example, an amount in dispute higher than USD 5,000,000 would likely lead to the matter being submitted to a three-member arbitral tribunal), the nature of the parties (for example, if one of the parties is a state or state-owned company, the Court is inclined to submit the case to a three-member arbitral tribunal), the complexity of the legal and factual issues involved and the existence of multiple parties. While the amount in dispute is important, it is not the only factor taken into account. The ICC Court might decide, for example, to appoint a sole arbitrator in cases where the amount in dispute is relatively high, if the case appears to be factually or legally simple. On the other hand, the ICC Court might decide to submit a matter to a three-member arbitral tribunal even if the amount in dispute is relatively low where the dispute is particularly complex.

5. Nomination of the sole arbitrator. Art. 8(3) provides that in cases where the parties have agreed on the appointment of a sole arbitrator, they have thirty days from the reception by the Respondent of the Request to nominate jointly the sole arbitrator for confirmation by the ICC Court. The parties may jointly request the Secretariat to grant them an extension to do so. In such circumstances, the Secretariat will usually grant such an extension. If the parties fail to jointly nominate the sole arbitrator within the time limit, the ICC Court will appoint the sole arbitrator.

6. Constitution of a three-member arbitral tribunal. Art. 8(4) provides that, when the parties have agreed on a three-member arbitral tribunal, the nomination of the parties' co-arbitrators shall be made in the Request and the Answer, respectively, allowing the Respondent a thirty-day period from the receipt of the Request (see art. 5(1)) to nominate an arbitrator. When one of the parties does not nominate an arbitrator, the ICC Court will appoint one on its behalf (see arts. 8(4) and 9(6)). The third arbitrator, who shall act as chairman of the arbitral tribunal, will be appointed by the ICC Court, unless the parties agree otherwise. In practice, however, the ICC Court will only appoint the chairman when the parties have not agreed on a method for the nomination of the chairman, or when the method selected by the parties has failed to provide a nomination. The most common methods used by the parties for the nomination of the chairman are joint nomination by the parties themselves and joint nomination by the co-arbitrators. If the parties agree that the co-arbitrators nominate the chairman jointly, the parties' counsel and the co-arbitrators that they have nominated respectively will often consult informally with regard to the candidate for chairman. In cases where the parties do agree on a method for the appointment of the chairman, but such method fails to provide a nomination, the ICC Court will decide which ICC National Committee to invite to propose the chairman. In practice, when the parties notify the Secretariat that they have failed to nominate jointly the chairman, the Secretariat will usually, on the basis of the decision already taken by the ICC Court, invite the selected ICC National Committee to propose an appropriate candidate. As a result, the constitution of the arbitral tribunal is able to proceed without undue delay.

7. Time limit for nomination of the chairman. The parties are free to agree on any time limit they wish to nominate the chairman. Where the parties agree to nominate the chairman themselves or grant the co-arbitrators the power to nominate jointly the chairman, the Secretariat will always invite the parties first to agree on a time limit for such joint nomination. If the parties fail to do so, the ICC Court will fix a time limit at its discretion, which will usually be thirty days, with the possibility of an extension if the parties request it jointly. In case such a nomination is to be made by the co-arbitrators, the Secretariat will usually remind the parties that, unless they have expressly agreed otherwise, the relevant time limit will only commence the day after the notification to the parties of the confirmation of the Respondent's arbitrator by the ICC Court or by the Secretary General in accordance with art. 9(2).

[Appointment and confirmation of the arbitrators]

Article 9

(1) In confirming or appointing arbitrators, the Court shall consider the prospective arbitrator's nationality, residence and other relationships with the countries of which the parties or the other arbitrators are nationals and the prospective arbitrator's availability and ability to conduct the arbitration in accordance with these Rules. The same shall apply where the Secretary General confirms arbitrators pursuant to Article 9(2).

(2) **The Secretary General may confirm as co-arbitrators, sole arbitrators and chairmen of Arbitral Tribunals persons nominated by the parties or pursuant to their particular agreements, provided they have filed a statement of independence without qualification or a qualified statement of independence has not given rise to objections. Such confirmation shall be reported to the Court at its next session. If the Secretary General considers that a co-arbitrator, sole arbitrator or chairman of an Arbitral Tribunal should not be confirmed, the matter shall be submitted to the Court.**

(3) **Where the Court is to appoint a sole arbitrator or the chairman of an Arbitral Tribunal, it shall make the appointment upon a proposal of a National Committee of the ICC that it considers to be appropriate. If the Court does not accept the proposal made, or if the National Committee fails to make the proposal requested within the time limit fixed by the Court, the Court may repeat its request or may request a proposal from another National Committee that it considers to be appropriate.**

(4) **Where the Court considers that the circumstances so demand, it may choose the sole arbitrator or the chairman of the Arbitral Tribunal from a country where there is no National Committee, provided that neither of the parties objects within the time limit fixed by the Court.**

(5) **The sole arbitrator or the chairman of the Arbitral Tribunal shall be of a nationality other than those of the parties. However, in suitable circumstances and provided that neither of the parties objects within the time limit fixed by the Court, the sole arbitrator or the chairman of the Arbitral Tribunal may be chosen from a country of which any of the parties is a national.**

(6) **Where the Court is to appoint an arbitrator on behalf of a party which has failed to nominate one, it shall make the appointment upon a proposal of the National Committee of the country of which that party is a national. If the Court does not accept the proposal made, or if the National Committee fails to make the proposal requested within the time limit fixed by the Court, or if the country of which the said party is a national has no National Committee, the Court shall be at liberty to choose any person whom it regards as suitable. The Secretariat shall inform the National Committee, if one exists, of the country of which such person is a national.**

1. General. The ICC Court assists the parties in the constitution of the arbitral tribunal. This is one of the most important contributions of the ICC Court to the arbitration process. The ICC Court exercises two functions in the constitution process, depending on the parties' agreement: the appointment and the confirmation of arbitrators.

2. Distinction between confirmation and appointment. An arbitrator is 'confirmed' when a person is nominated to act as arbitrator by a party or parties, the co-arbitrators or any other person or entity and the ICC Court 'confirms' that person's nomination (they do not actually become an arbitrator until their nomination is 'confirmed'). An arbitrator is 'appointed' when the ICC Court itself (usually on the 'proposal' of an ICC National Committee) chooses ('appoints') the arbitrator.

3. Criteria taken into account by the ICC Court for the appointment of arbitrators. The ICC Court generally appoints arbitrators in three cases. First, it appoints the sole arbitrator, when the parties have themselves failed to nominate the sole arbitrator. Second, it appoints the chairman, when the parties have not agreed otherwise or have failed to do so themselves. Third, it appoints co-arbitrators on behalf of defaulting parties. When appointing arbitrators, the ICC Court will always take into account criteria set out in the arbitration agreement or a subsequent agreement between the parties. Subject to any such agreement, the ICC Court will take into consideration the parties' nationalities (see note 10), the language of arbitration, the place of arbitration, the subject matter of the arbitration, as well as the potential arbitrators' experience or expertise in the relevant field, familiarity with the applicable law, experience in, or knowledge of, the arbitral process (as arbitrator or counsel), and availability (that is, whether they have sufficient time to commit to the matter). In addition to the above mentioned criteria, the ICC Court will also examine the statement of independence that the candidate has completed pursuant to art. 7. The ICC Court generally does not appoint arbitrators who have filed a qualified statement of independence.

4. Criteria taken into account by the ICC Court in deciding whether to confirm arbitrators. In confirming arbitrators, the ICC Rules provide that the ICC Court should consider the elements mentioned in art. 9(1). However, in most cases, the ICC Court will confirm a nominated arbitrator irrespective of the criteria in art. 9(1) unless a party raises an objection. The ICC Court will not refuse to confirm an arbitrator in the absence of objections. The ICC Court may confirm an arbitrator even if objections are raised against his confirmation if it considers that the objections raised are not well-founded and do not affect the arbitrator's independence. The ICC Court does not follow any strict rules to determine the arbitrator's independence (see art. 11).

5. Confirmation by the Secretary General. The 1998 revision of the ICC Rules introduced a new procedure for the confirmation of arbitrators, aiming at expediting the constitution of the arbitral tribunal in cases where such constitution does not raise any particular problems. Thus, art. 9(2) enables the Secretary General, instead of the ICC Court, to confirm an arbitrator when no objections to the nomination are raised by the parties. Such confirmation is communicated to the ICC Court at one of its next sessions. When the Secretary General does not consider it appropriate to confirm an arbitrator, they will put the nomination before the ICC Court.

6. ICC National Committees. ICC National Committees represent the ICC in their respective countries. Each National Committee is an independent entity and, although they have a common general objective (promoting the global interests of international business), they may have different functions and organisational structures within their respective countries. National Committees play an important role in the constitution of the arbitral tribunal by assisting the ICC Court to appoint arbitrators. Most National Committees are well placed to know the arbitration specialists in their respective countries. As such, they are in a position to propose the best candidates to the ICC Court for any particular case.

7. Criteria for the determination of the ICC National Committee when appointing arbitrators. When the ICC Court is called upon to appoint a sole arbitrator or chairman, it will generally invite an ICC National Committee to propose a candidate (art. 9(3)). In order to determine which ICC National Committee should propose a candidate, the ICC Court will first determine the desired nationality of the prospective arbitrator by taking into account, among other things, the parties' and co-arbitrators' nationalities (in order to comply with art. 9(1) and (5)), the place of arbitration, the language of arbitration, the applicable law(s), and sometimes the nationalities of the parties' counsel. Conversely, when appointing a co-arbitrator on behalf of a defaulting party, the ICC Court does not generally have to chose an ICC National Committee, since art. 9(6) provides that the ICC Court must invite the ICC National Committee 'of the country of which that party is a national' (see note 9 for the situation where the relevant country has no ICC National Committee).

8. Proposals of arbitrators by ICC National Committees. For the appointment of a sole arbitrator or a chairman (art. 9(3)), the Secretariat requests the ICC National Committee selected by the ICC Court to propose a candidate for appointment by the ICC Court. The time limit granted to the ICC National Committee for such a proposal is usually ten to fifteen days. In its request, the Secretariat sets out the parties' details, their counsel, the co-arbitrators (when applicable), the amount in dispute, the applicable law and the place and language of the arbitration. Once the ICC National Committee proposes a candidate, the ICC Court will decide whether or not to appoint the proposed candidate. Should the ICC Court consider that the proposal submitted by the ICC National Committee is not appropriate, the Court will either invite the same National Committee to make another proposal, or invite another National Committee to propose a candidate. While rare, this does happen occasionally. When the ICC Court is called upon to appoint a co-arbitrator (art. 9(6)), the same procedural steps are generally followed.

9. Appointment of nationals of countries with no ICC National Committee. Art. 9(4) allows the ICC Court to appoint arbitrators from a country that does not have an ICC National Committee in certain circumstances. Art. 9(4) was inserted during the 1998 revision of the ICC Rules, in order to increase the diversity of the pool of prospective arbitrators that the ICC

Court might appoint. However, this provision has been resorted to less and less frequently over recent years due to the expansion of ICC National Committees worldwide (there are currently 92 National Committees). The ICC Court will consider the possibility of appointing a sole arbitrator or chairman from a country that does not have an ICC National Committee depending on the specific circumstances of the case. When the ICC Court considers it appropriate to use this provision, the Secretariat will request the parties' views on the matter before proceeding with the appointment. When a party fails to nominate a co-arbitrator and there is no ICC National Committee in that party's country, the ICC Court can appoint anyone it considers suitable, in accordance with art. 9(6).

10. Nationality. Art. 9(5) provides that the sole arbitrator or the chairman of the arbitral tribunal appointed by the ICC Court should be of a different nationality than either of the parties. However, this provision allows the ICC Court to appoint an arbitrator from a country of which one of the parties is a national in 'suitable circumstances' and provided that neither of the parties object. This might be appropriate, for example, when the parties and the co-arbitrators are of the same nationality. However, the application of art. 9(5) depends on the parties' non-objection 'within the time limit fixed by the Court', which is usually five days. When a party objects to the sole arbitrator or chairman having the same nationality as one of the parties, the ICC Court will invite an ICC National Committee of a different nationality to make a proposal. If there is a non-participating party, the ICC Court may be hesitant to apply art. 9(5).

[Multiple parties]

Article 10

(1) Where there are multiple parties, whether as Claimant or as Respondent, and where the dispute is to be referred to three arbitrators, the multiple Claimants, jointly, and the multiple Respondents, jointly, shall nominate an arbitrator for confirmation pursuant to Article 9.

(2) In the absence of such a joint nomination and where all parties are unable to agree to a method for the constitution of the Arbitral Tribunal, the Court may appoint each member of the Arbitral Tribunal and shall designate one of them to act as chairman. In such case, the Court shall be at liberty to choose any person whom it regards as suitable to act as arbitrator, applying Article 9 when it considers this appropriate.

1. Background. A long-running difficulty in international arbitration has been the constitution of the arbitral tribunal in cases where there are multiple Claimants and/or Respondents. The ICC Court's practice when presented with such cases had always been to invite the multiple Claimants and/or Respondents to nominate jointly an arbitrator. In 1992, the ICC Court's practice was brought into question by the *Dutco* case.

2. The *Dutco* case. In the *Dutco* case, there was one Claimant and two Respondents in an ICC arbitration. All three were parties to the same contract. The Claimant had appointed its arbitrator, and the ICC Court instructed the two Respondents to nominate jointly one arbitrator. Each Respondent claimed to be entitled to nominate an arbitrator, arguing that they had different interests. Ultimately, they proceeded to make the required single nomination, reserving their right to challenge the ICC Court's decision. The Respondents challenged the partial award upholding jurisdiction over the two Respondents before the French courts on the basis that the arbitral tribunal had been irregularly constituted. Ultimately, the French Cour de cassation, found that the ICC Court's requirement that the two Respondents nominate jointly an arbitrator was a violation of the 'right of equality of the parties in the constitution of the arbitral tribunal'. The court found that this right was a matter of public policy that could only be renounced by the parties after the dispute had arisen.

3. Current practice of the ICC Court under art. 10. The current, 1998 version of the ICC Rules has addressed the 'Dutco' issue in art. 10. This provision recognises the right of each party to nominate a member of the arbitral tribunal, but, where there are multiple Claimants and/or multiple Respondents, takes this right away and empowers the ICC Court to appoint the complete arbitral tribunal if the multiple Claimants or, most likely, multiple Respondents cannot jointly agree on an arbitrator to nominate and all of the parties cannot agree on how to constitute the arbitral tribunal. This solution has been widely accepted, and similar provisions have been included in other arbitral rules and laws (see, for example, art. 8(1), LCIA Rules).

4. The constitution of the arbitral tribunal under art. 10. Art. 10 applies only when there is a three-member arbitral tribunal. Under art. 10(1), multiple Claimants and/or multiple Respondents must nominate jointly an arbitrator. Where either the multiple Claimants or Respondents cannot reach an agreement as to the nomination of an arbitrator or where all parties cannot reach an agreement as to the method of constitution of the arbitral tribunal, art. 10(2) gives the ICC Court the power to appoint all three members of the arbitral tribunal.

5. Cases in which the ICC Court applies art. 10(2). The ICC Court does not automatically apply art. 10(2) when multiple parties (whether Claimant or Respondent) cannot agree on the joint nomination of an arbitrator. Art. 10(2) is drafted in broad terms so as to allow the ICC Court the possibility to decide when to apply it. For example, where either the multiple Claimants or Respondents are affiliated and their positions and interests are similar or identical, the ICC Court might not apply art. 10(2) if it appears that such parties do not have legitimate reasons for not agreeing on a nomination. However, the ICC Court will usually apply art. 10(2) when there is a possibility that not doing so would mean that the parties were not treated equally with regard to the constitution of the arbitral tribunal. The ICC Court applies art. 10(2) on a case-by-case basis, taking into consideration, among other things, the law of the place of arbitration and the possible place or places of enforcement of the award and the reasons why the Claimants or Respondents cannot agree on a joint nomination. It must be noted that art. 10(2) does not strictly meet the criterion set out in the *Dutco* decision that the agreement on the tribunal must take place after the dispute has arisen (i.e. not simply by agreeing to the ICC Rules in an arbitration clause when the contract is entered into). However, no problems in this regard have arisen before the ICC Court.

6. Appointment of arbitrators pursuant to art. 10(2). If applied, art. 10(2) allows the ICC Court to select anybody whom it regards suitable. The ICC Court may invite one or more National Committees to propose suitable candidates, but it is not required. The ICC Court usually directly appoints the three arbitrators that it considers to be most appropriate for each particular case. The Court's practice has been not to appoint any arbitrators nominated by the parties (thus, it will not appoint the arbitrator nominated by the Claimant in the Request).

[Challenge of arbitrators]

Article 11

(1) A challenge of an arbitrator, whether for an alleged lack of independence or otherwise, shall be made by the submission to the Secretariat of a written statement specifying the facts and circumstances on which the challenge is based.

(2) For a challenge to be admissible, it must be sent by a party either within 30 days from receipt by that party of the notification of the appointment or confirmation of the arbitrator, or within 30 days from the date when the party making the challenge was informed of the facts and circumstances on which the challenge is based if such date is subsequent to the receipt of such notification.

(3) The Court shall decide on the admissibility, and, at the same time, if necessary, on the merits of a challenge after the Secretariat has afforded an opportunity for the arbitrator concerned, the other party or parties and any other members of the Arbitral Tribunal, to comment in writing within a suitable period of time. Such comments shall be communicated to the parties and to the arbitrators.

1. General. Art. 11 provides the parties with the possibility of challenging an arbitrator after they have been appointed or confirmed by the ICC Court or confirmed by the Secretary General. This procedure is in addition to the possibility given to the parties to object to the confirmation of an arbitrator (see arts. 8 and 9). Notwithstanding that the grounds for making a challenge in accordance with art. 11 are very broad, the number of successful challenges is very low compared to the number of cases pending under the ICC Rules. For example, in 2007, 26 challenges were introduced in 22 cases and only one was accepted by the ICC Court (there were more than 1,200 cases pending at the end of 2007).

2. Basis for the challenge. Art. 11(1) provides that an arbitrator may be challenged 'for an alleged lack of independence or otherwise'. The 'otherwise' allows the parties the possibility to challenge an arbitrator for any reason they consider appropriate. Challenges are sometimes made on the basis of an alleged relationship between an arbitrator and one of the parties that is discovered after the arbitrator has been confirmed or appointed. For example, challenges have been made because, during the arbitration, one of the parties discovers that an arbitrator's law firm represents, or has represented, an affiliate of one of the parties. Challenges are sometimes introduced on the basis of procedural decisions taken by the arbitral tribunal, such as when an arbitral tribunal closed proceedings, allegedly in violation of due process. In another case, a party challenged the arbitral tribunal alleging that it had wrongfully refused to grant an application to correct or interpret an award. Challenges are sometimes introduced on the basis of decisions taken on the merits by an arbitral tribunal, such as an award on jurisdiction. Challenges succeed more often when they relate to a link between the arbitrator and a party (for example, that the arbitrator's law firm represents an affiliate of the party), rather than the arbitrator's conduct.

3. Procedure for submitting a challenge. Art. 11(1) provides that when a party wishes to challenge an arbitrator, it must submit a written statement to the Secretariat 'specifying the facts and circumstances on which the challenge is based'. Parties should specify the date on which they became aware of the facts and circumstances that support their allegations and submit any supporting documentation. This statement should be as detailed and complete as possible since the challenging party does not usually make further written submissions. The written statement is then notified to the parties and arbitrators.

4. Time limit for the admissibility of a challenge. Art. 11(2) provides that a challenge is admissible under the ICC Rules if the contesting party submits it 'within 30 days from the receipt of the party of the notification of the appointment or confirmation of the arbitrator'. Once the thirty-day period has expired, the parties can no longer challenge an arbitrator on the basis of information included in their statement of independence or known to them at or before the time of the notification of the arbitrator's appointment or confirmation. This does not preclude parties from later challenging an arbitrator if they become aware of new facts and circumstances after the arbitrator's confirmation or appointment. Art. 11(2) provides that for such a challenge to be admissible, it must be made 'within 30 days from the date when the party making the challenge was informed of the facts and circumstances on which the challenge is based'.

5. Determination of the date of discovery of the facts or circumstances on which the challenge is based. When the starting point of the thirty-day time limit established in art. 11(2) is the notification of the confirmation or appointment of the arbitrator, there is no difficulty in determining when the information was deemed to have been known or received. On the other hand, when a challenge is based on facts or circumstances discovered at a later stage in the arbitration, it may sometimes be difficult for the Court to determine the date of discovery of the information and decide if the challenge is admissible. In these cases, the ICC Court will usually accept the challenging party's assertion as to the date of discovery, except when there is evidence showing that the information was accessible to the party at an earlier date.

6. The parties' and arbitrators' comments on the challenge. When notifying the other party or parties and the arbitrators of the challenge submitted, the Secretariat also invites them to provide any comment they may have in writing on the challenge. The parties' and the arbitrators' written comments are then circulated by the Secretariat to the parties and other arbitrators. Art. 11(3) establishes that the other party or parties and the arbitrators will be given a 'suitable period of time' to submit their written comments. The Secretariat will usually grant a fifteen-day period. If so requested, the Secretariat may allow the parties or the arbitrators to submit further comments on the challenge.

7. Internal ICC Court procedure. The ICC Court decides on the admissibility and merits of a challenge during one of its monthly plenary sessions. The ICC Court will not only consider the ICC Rules when studying a challenge, but it will also take into consideration any mandatory provisions of relevant applicable laws. The ICC Court is reluctant to accept challenges on the basis of decisions which remain within the discretion of the arbitral tribunal, provided the arbitrator's conduct does not raise concerns as to due process or the arbitrator's independence. The ICC Court is also very conscious of the timing of challenges, particularly if they come towards the end of the procedure or at a time an award is about to be rendered. In making its decisions, the ICC Court does not take into account the IBA Guidelines on Conflict of Interest in International Arbitration (2004).

8. The ICC Court's decision. Once the Court's decision has been taken, the Secretariat notifies it to the parties and the arbitrators. As mentioned above, pursuant to art. 7(4), any decision of the ICC Court on a challenge 'shall be final' and reasons for such decision are not communicated. Nevertheless parties sometimes request that the ICC Court reconsider its decision on a challenge. The Court will not reconsider a decision unless new elements are brought to its attention. If the challenge is accepted, the arbitrator will be replaced in accordance with art. 12. If the challenge is not accepted, the arbitration will continue.

9. Suspension of the arbitral proceedings. The submission of a challenge to the ICC Court does not automatically suspend the arbitration. The ICC Court leaves the decision on this to the arbitral tribunal itself.

ICC Rules of Arbitration, art. 12

[Replacement of arbitrators]

Article 12

(1) An arbitrator shall be replaced upon his death, upon the acceptance by the Court of the arbitrator's resignation, upon acceptance by the Court of a challenge or upon the request of all the parties.

(2) An arbitrator shall also be replaced on the Court's own initiative when it decides that he is prevented de jure or de facto from fulfilling his functions, or that he is not fulfilling his functions in accordance with the Rules or within the prescribed time limits.

(3) When, on the basis of information that has come to its attention, the Court considers applying Article 12(2), it shall decide on the matter after the arbitrator concerned, the parties and any other members of the Arbitral Tribunal have had an opportunity to comment in writing within a suitable period of time. Such comments shall be communicated to the parties and to the arbitrators.

(4) When an arbitrator is to be replaced, the Court has discretion to decide whether or not to follow the original nominating process. Once reconstituted, and after having invited the parties to comment, the Arbitral Tribunal shall determine if and to what extent prior proceedings shall be repeated before the reconstituted Arbitral Tribunal.

(5) Subsequent to the closing of the proceedings, instead of replacing an arbitrator who has died or been removed by the Court pursuant to Articles 12(1) and 12(2), the Court may decide, when it considers it appropriate, that the remaining arbitrators shall continue the arbitration. In making such determination, the Court shall take into account the views of the remaining arbitrators and of the parties and such other matters that it considers appropriate in the circumstances.

1. General. Art. 12(1) sets forth the circumstances in which an arbitrator may be replaced. An arbitrator will be replaced when: he dies; he resigns and the resignation is accepted by the ICC Court; the parties jointly request that the arbitrator be replaced; or he is successfully challenged by one of the parties.

2. Death of an arbitrator. An arbitrator is automatically replaced under art. 12(1) if he dies.

3. Resignation of an arbitrator. Under the ICC Rules, an arbitrator may tender his resignation at any time, but such tender of resignation is not automatically effective. The ICC Court is invited to consider the reasons for such resignation and to decide whether or not to accept it. The ICC Rules do not provide a list of acceptable reasons for resignation and the ICC Court has broad discretion as to whether or not to accept a tender of resignation. The ICC Court will accept a tender of resignation if it is based on legitimate reasons, such as illness or a change in professional activity that does not permit the arbitrator to continue acting. The Court will also normally allow an arbitrator to resign when it discovers facts that could call into question his independence in the parties' eyes. The ICC Court might decide to not approve the resignation of an arbitrator if it considers that such resignation was tendered in order to delay the proceedings or when, for example, an arbitrator who does not agree with the content of an award resigns before the award is signed.

4. Removal of an arbitrator upon the request of all the parties. Should all the parties request that an arbitrator be removed, such arbitrator will be replaced. On the other hand, once appointed or confirmed, an arbitrator will not be removed simply because the removal request concerns the arbitrator nominated by the requesting party.

5. Removal of an arbitrator on the ICC Court's initiative. Art. 12(2) gives the ICC Court the power to replace an arbitrator at its own initiative when it considers that the arbitrator is not fulfilling his duties according to the ICC Rules or within the time limits set forth in the rules. The reference in art. 12(2) to an arbitrator's inability to perform his duties covers legal requirements that prevent an arbitrator from fulfilling his duties (for example, arbitrators may no longer be able to act because of an appointment as judge or other governmental official). The ICC Court is also vigilant regarding respect for the time limits set forth in the ICC Rules. The Secretariat will draw the Court's attention to cases where the arbitral tribunal is not proceeding in a diligent manner. The ICC Court will always take into consideration the particularities of each case when assessing these issues and is generally cautious when applying this provision. The Court takes into account that in some cases, although not all, removing a non-diligent arbitrator may lead to greater delays than allowing the already-constituted arbitral tribunal to continue.

6. Procedure for the removal of an arbitrator in accordance with art. 12(2). Art. 12(3) sets out the procedure that the ICC Court must follow when applying art. 12(2). In practice, the ICC Court, usually at a committee session, decides whether the information brought to its attention by the Secretariat justifies initiating replacement proceedings. If the ICC Court decides to initiate replacement proceedings, the Secretariat will notify the Court's decision to the arbitrator in question, the other members of the arbitral tribunal and the parties. The Secretariat invites the parties and arbitrators to submit to the ICC Court any written comments they might have on the matter. Once the arbitrators and the parties have had an opportunity to submit their comments on the replacement of the arbitrator, the ICC Court is invited to decide whether or not to replace the arbitrator in question, usually at one of the Court's plenary sessions.

7. Appointment of the new arbitrator. The first sentence of art. 12(4) gives the ICC Court broad discretion as to the method for replacing arbitrators. Prior to the 1998 revision of the ICC Rules, the ICC Court was obliged to follow the original nominating process. The ICC Court generally continues to follow this practice and, if the removed arbitrator was originally nominated by a party, it will request that party to nominate another arbitrator. If the removed arbitrator had been appointed by the ICC Court, then the Court will appoint a new arbitrator. In certain exceptional cases, such as in cases of abuse of the process (such as where the removed arbitrator acted partially and in agreement with the party that nominated him), or when the original nominating procedure does not produce a nomination, the ICC Court uses the power provided for in art. 12(4).

8. Prior proceedings. The second sentence of art. 12(4) deals with proceedings held before the originally constituted arbitral tribunal. Under the ICC Rules, it is for the newly constituted arbitral tribunal to decide which proceedings, if any, should be repeated. Art. 12(4) provides that the newly constituted arbitral tribunal must request the parties' comments on this issue. If the parties agree on the matter, the arbitral tribunal will usually follow such agreement. If the parties cannot agree, the arbitral tribunal will decide on its own. The ICC Rules do not set forth which proceedings should be repeated. However, issues that have been decided by interim or partial awards cannot be reopened. Arbitrators are often reticent to repeat hearings when written records of them exist due to the additional cost and inconvenience.

9. Remuneration of replaced arbitrators. The ICC Court has absolute discretion when fixing replaced arbitrators' fees (see art. 31, note 7).

10. 'Truncated' arbitral tribunals. In certain cases, the ICC Court may decide that it is in the best interests of the arbitration not to replace an arbitrator who has died, resigned or been removed by the Court pursuant to art. 12(1) or (2) and allow the arbitral tribunal to proceed with two members. Arbitral tribunals that fall within this description are commonly referred to as 'truncated' arbitral tribunals. Art. 12(5) only applies when the closing of the proceedings has been declared pursuant to art. 22. Unlike the ICC Rules, other arbitration rules, such as the LCIA Rules (art. 12), do not set such strict requirements and allow for similar provisions to apply at any time during the arbitration. The ICC Court is generally cautious when applying this provision and will always take into account the parties' and the remaining arbitrators' views, and be vigilant for any provisions of relevant laws that could adversely affect the award rendered by the truncated arbitral tribunal.

THE ARBITRAL PROCEEDINGS

[Transmission of the file to the arbitral tribunal]

Article 13

The Secretariat shall transmit the file to the Arbitral Tribunal as soon as it has been constituted, provided the advance on costs requested by the Secretariat at this stage has been paid.

Bond, Paralika and Secomb

ICC Rules of Arbitration, art. 13

1. General. Art. 13 provides that the Secretariat will transmit the file to the arbitral tribunal as soon as the arbitral tribunal is constituted and the advance on costs requested at that point has been paid.

2. Constitution of the arbitral tribunal. The arbitral tribunal is deemed to be constituted when the ICC Court (or the Secretary General under art. 9(2)) confirms or appoints the sole arbitrator or the chairman of the arbitral tribunal. The Secretariat generally transmits the file to the arbitral tribunal on the day that the above decision is taken and notified to the parties.

3. Contents of the file. The file consists of all the documents submitted by the parties (Request, Answer, Reply (if applicable) and any other submissions), as well as the correspondence received and sent by the Secretariat up to the date of the transmission of the file. The file is usually transmitted to all members of the arbitral tribunal at the same time. However, if the co-arbitrators are invited to nominate the chairman, the Secretariat normally sends them a copy of the Request and the Answer (if it has been received at that point), to assist them in making such nomination. When transmitting the file, the Secretariat informs the arbitral tribunal of the financial situation of the case. It also reminds the arbitral tribunal of its obligation to establish the Terms of Reference and, if the ICC Court has taken a decision pursuant to art. 6(2), to decide on its own jurisdiction. The Secretariat also draws the arbitral tribunal's attention to other administrative issues, such as the reimbursement of the arbitrators' expenses and the conditions for having a secretary to the arbitral tribunal.

4. Payment of the advance on costs. In order for the file to be transmitted, the advance on costs requested by the Secretariat at that stage has to have been paid fully. This is to ensure that there are sufficient funds to pay the arbitrators. The 'advance on costs requested by the Secretariat at this stage' is usually the provisional advance fixed by the Secretary General under art. 30(1) at the time the Request is notified to the Respondent. When a provisional advance is fixed, the Claimant is invited to pay the relevant amount within thirty days from notification of the Request to the Respondent. If the Claimant has not paid the provisional advance by the time the arbitral tribunal is constituted, the file is not transmitted and both the Claimant and the Respondent are invited to pay the requested amount. Either the Claimant or the Respondent can pay the provisional advance. If neither party pays the provisional advance within the time limit set by the Secretariat (usually fifteen days), the ICC Court reserves the right to apply art. 30(4) (see art. 30, notes 16 and 17). Art. 13 does not specifically mention the provisional advance. This leaves the Secretariat discretion to request the payment of additional amounts. The Secretariat may, for example, request the entire advance on costs in a 'fast track' case.

[Place of the arbitration]
Article 14

(1) The place of the arbitration shall be fixed by the Court, unless agreed upon by the parties.

(2) The Arbitral Tribunal may, after consultation with the parties, conduct hearings and meetings at any location it considers appropriate unless otherwise agreed by the parties.

(3) The Arbitral Tribunal may deliberate at any location it considers appropriate.

1. General. Art. 14 acknowledges the parties' right to chose the place of the arbitration. In the absence of such an agreement, the ICC Court will fix the place of the arbitration. The place of arbitration is important for various reasons, as the law of the situs determines the extent to which local courts can assist or hinder an arbitration, and the place of arbitration plays a critical role in the application (or non-application) of the New York Convention.

2. The parties' agreement on the place of arbitration. The ICC Rules allow the parties to determine freely the place of arbitration either in their initial agreement to arbitrate or subsequently. If the parties clearly agree on the place of arbitration, the ICC Court plays no role. However, sometimes it is not clear whether the parties have in fact agreed. The most common example is when an arbitration clause provides that any dispute 'shall be resolved under the Rules of the International Chamber of Commerce in Paris'. The question is whether the reference to 'Paris' is an agreement on the place of arbitration or simply a reference to the location of the ICC's headquarters. In such cases, the Secretariat inquires whether the parties intended to fix Paris as the place of arbitration. If at least one of the parties maintains that the reference to Paris reflects an agreement on the place of arbitration, the ICC Court will almost always fix Paris as the place of the arbitration. In cases where the arbitration agreement mentions 'ICC Geneva' or 'ICC London', the ICC Court will usually interpret this to indicate an agreement on the place of arbitration, unless the parties indicate otherwise.

3. The elements taken into account by the ICC Court when fixing the place of arbitration. When fixing the place of arbitration, the ICC Court takes into consideration the parties' comments. The ICC Court will not fix the place of arbitration in a country that is not a party to the New York Convention. It will also take into account any other legal instruments relating to the enforcement and recognition of awards and the legal regime for international arbitration in the relevant jurisdiction. Thereafter, the ICC Court will look at the neutrality of the prospective place, its convenience to the parties, the language of the arbitration, the availability of suitable arbitrators, the lex arbitri and the attitude and experience of the state courts with regard to international arbitration. The ICC Court will not generally fix the place of arbitration in either of the parties' countries or that of their counsel, so as not be seen to be favouring one of the parties.

4. Change of the place of the arbitration. It is quite rare that a place of arbitration is changed after it has been agreed by the parties or fixed by the ICC Court. However, such change is not prohibited by the ICC Rules, if agreed by the parties. The ICC Court does not have the power to change the place of the arbitration, however, even when it is the ICC Court that has fixed it.

5. Hearings and meetings. Art. 14(2) was introduced into the ICC Rules in the 1998 revision. It addresses situations whereby the parties and the arbitral tribunal wish to conduct part of the arbitral proceedings at a location other than the place of the arbitration. This is typically for such reasons as the convenience of witnesses, or political or health difficulties at the place of arbitration. Art. 14(2) requires the arbitral tribunal to consult with the parties before holding hearings and meetings at a location other than the place of arbitration. In one case, a chairman was challenged for having held the hearing outside of the place of arbitration. In the particular circumstances of that case, the challenge was rejected.

6. The arbitral tribunal's deliberations. Art. 14(3) allows the arbitral tribunal to deliberate at any location it chooses. In practice, arbitrators usually hold their deliberations in the place that is most convenient to them. These meetings are private and parties do not take part. Art. 14(3) does not oblige the arbitrators to meet physically in order to conduct their deliberations. Sometimes, depending on the complexity of the case, such deliberations may take place by correspondence or conference call.

[Rules governing the proceedings]

Article 15

(1) The proceedings before the Arbitral Tribunal shall be governed by these Rules, and, where these Rules are silent, any rules which the parties or, failing them, the Arbitral Tribunal may settle on, whether or not reference is thereby made to the rules of procedure of a national law to be applied to the arbitration.

(2) In all cases, the Arbitral Tribunal shall act fairly and impartially and ensure that each party has a reasonable opportunity to present its case.

1. General. Until the 1975 revision, the ICC Rules directed arbitral tribunals to apply the laws of the place of the arbitration with respect to procedural matters. The 1975 revision introduced a provision similar to the present art. 15, which grants arbitrators the power to decide on procedural issues without necessarily referring to national law. The procedural rules covered by art. 15 include, inter alia, those relating to the exchange of the parties' submissions, the production of documents, the appointment of experts and the conduct of hearings.

2. Rules governing the arbitral proceedings. Under art. 15(1), the ICC Rules apply to any proceedings initiated pursuant to the Rules. If the Rules are silent, the parties are free to agree on the procedural rules. If the parties do not reach agreement, the arbitral tribunal may decide the rules to be followed. In doing so, the arbitral tribunal does not have to apply the procedural rules of any national law, subject to any mandatory provisions of the place of arbitration. Most often, such mandatory provisions relate to due process aspects of an arbitration (see note 5). Art. 15(1) acknowledges the distinction between the rules of law governing the merits of the case and the rules governing the arbitral proceedings.

3. Rules agreed by the parties. The parties can agree virtually any rules they wish, either in their initial arbitration agreement or subsequently. Parties sometimes agree on procedural matters in the arbitration agreement in their contract. Such agreements will be binding on the parties and arbitral tribunal unless all parties agree to vary them. This can cause difficulties. For example, sometimes parties agree to unreasonably short time limits for a 'fast track' arbitration or time limits longer than the arbitral tribunal would wish. This gives rise to the question of 'whose arbitration is it?'. Under the ICC Rules, the answer is generally: 'the parties''.

4. Rules set by the arbitral tribunal. Subject to the ICC Rules and any agreements of the parties, arbitral tribunals have broad discretion in determining the procedure to be followed. In practice, arbitrators tend to develop procedures influenced by their different legal traditions, but consistent with broadly recognised practices for international arbitration. Experienced arbitrators do not normally adopt procedures directly from national courts. Usually procedural rules are set out in the Terms of Reference and the provisional timetable (see art. 18), which are established following a discussion between the parties and the arbitral tribunal. Thereafter, any additional rules are usually set out in procedural orders after due consultation with the parties.

5. Mandatory rules. Although art. 15(1) allows arbitral tribunals to disregard procedural rules of national law, it may be that 'mandatory' rules of law apply, in particular, 'mandatory' rules of the place of arbitration. These rules are referred to as 'mandatory' in part because their breach may justify the annulment of an award. In such cases, the arbitral tribunal should take into account these mandatory provisions, which generally relate to due process considerations.

6. Obligation of the arbitral tribunal to act fairly and impartially. Art. 15(2) sets out a general obligation for the arbitral tribunal to conduct the arbitral proceedings in a fair and impartial way and to allow each party a reasonable opportunity to present its case. Although art. 7 does not expressly require that arbitrators be impartial (at the appointment stage or subsequently), art. 15(2) imposes an obligation of impartiality upon arbitrators. Other arbitration rules contain a similar provision (art. 15, UNCITRAL Rules; art. 14(1), LCIA Rules), as do many national arbitration laws (art. 18 of the UNCITRAL Model Law provides: 'The parties shall be treated with equality and each party shall be given a full opportunity of presenting its case'). Under art. 15(2), where the parties cannot agree, the arbitral tribunal has the power to decide, for example, the extent to which the parties may be allowed to exchange further submissions or evidence. If one or more arbitrators do not act fairly and impartially, as provided for by art. 15(2), the parties can challenge the arbitrator(s), in accordance with art. 11.

[Language of the arbitration]

Article 16

In the absence of an agreement by the parties, the Arbitral Tribunal shall determine the language or languages of the arbitration, due regard being given to all relevant circumstances, including the language of the contract.

1. General. Under art. 16, the parties can determine the language or languages of the arbitration. The choice of language can be important, for example, to the choice of arbitrators. The language can also have a significant impact on the costs of the arbitration (translations, interpreters, etc.).

2. Agreement by the parties. The parties can determine the language or languages of the arbitration either in the arbitration agreement in their contract or subsequently. It is most common that the language agreed by the parties is the language of their contract. There are clear advantages in selecting the language of the arbitration before the proceedings are initiated. For example, the selection of arbitrators can be more efficient because the parties know in advance the language skills that the arbitrators must have. Under art. 16, the parties can agree to have two or more languages of arbitration. However, in such case, it is important to determine the exact nature of the parties' agreement. It should be clarified whether both languages must be used (that is, all documents must be in both languages) or either of the languages can be used (that is, documents need only be produced in one of the two languages). In addition, one language should be designated as the 'official' language for the award, as an award in two languages is likely to have disparities. Using two languages in an arbitration may have a significant impact on the length and cost of the arbitration. If all documents must be in two languages and all oral argument and testimony interpreted, the arbitration can be rendered significantly more expensive.

3. The role of the arbitral tribunal. If the parties fail to agree on the language of the arbitration, art. 16 provides that the language should be determined by the arbitral tribunal. In doing so, the arbitral tribunal is required by art. 16 to consider all relevant circumstances. Arbitral tribunals take into account, for example, the language or languages of the parties' contract, the applicable law and the languages of the parties and their counsel. Usually the arbitral tribunal will determine the language of the arbitration before drafting the Terms of Reference because such decision will determine the language of the Terms of Reference. Arbitrators normally decide the language of the arbitration by way of a procedural order.

4. The language used for correspondence with the Secretariat. As indicated above (art. 3, note 9), agreements and decisions as to the language of the arbitration do not bind the Secretariat and the ICC Court. The parties may correspond with the Secretariat in the language of the arbitration but the Secretariat has no obligation to correspond in a language other than English or French. However, if members of the Secretariat are fluent in the language of the arbitration, the Secretariat may correspond with the parties and the arbitral tribunal in such language. At present, the Secretariat corresponds in English, French, Spanish and German.

[Applicable rules of law]

Article 17

(1) The parties shall be free to agree upon the rules of law to be applied by the Arbitral Tribunal to the merits of the dispute. In the absence of any such agreement, the Arbitral Tribunal shall apply the rules of law which it determines to be appropriate.

(2) In all cases, the Arbitral Tribunal shall take account of the provisions of the contract and the relevant trade usages.

(3) The Arbitral Tribunal shall assume the powers of an amiable compositeur or decide ex aequo et bono only if the parties have agreed to give it such powers.

1. General. Art. 17 introduces the principle that the parties are free to agree upon the rules of law applicable to the merits of their dispute or to empower the arbitrators to decide as amiables compositeurs or ex aequo et bono. Should the parties not agree, the arbitral tribunal will determine the applicable rules of law.

2. Rules of law. Art. 17(1) makes reference to 'rules of law' rather than 'law'. The term 'rules of law' has a broader meaning than 'law' and has been widely used by other arbitral instruments such as the LCIA Rules (art. 22(3)), the AAA-ICDR Rules (art. 28 (1)) and the UNCITRAL Model Law (art. 28(1)). 'Rules of law' has been construed to include not only national laws and international instruments (conventions, treaties, etc.), but also the lex mercatoria or general principles of law. In 2007, in 79.3% of the Requests received, the contract specified a national law, in 0.6% of the Requests, the contract specified other rules (international conventions, lex mercatoria, general principles of law, etc.) and in 20.1%, the contract was silent on the applicable rule(s) of law. Although ICC arbitral tribunals overwhelmingly apply national law, the use of the lex mercatoria or general principles of law has increased marginally in recent years.

3. Parties' freedom to choose the applicable rules of law. Art. 17(1) acknowledges the parties' freedom to choose the rules of law that will be applied to their dispute. The only possible limit to such freedom may be 'mandatory' rules of law that may be relevant (for example, competition laws). Also, unless the parties decide otherwise, the law agreed by the parties to govern their contractual disputes may not necessarily be the law applicable to other issues, such as tortious claims, certain procedural elements or the arbitration clause.

4. Absence of an agreement. Prior to the 1998 revision, the ICC Rules directed the arbitral tribunal, in the absence of an agreement by the parties on the applicable law, to apply the law designated by the 'rule of conflict' that the arbitral tribunal considered appropriate. Art. 17 now allows the arbitral tribunal to choose directly the rules of law it considers appropriate, without first applying a choice of law rule. This development is consistent with a recent trend in international arbitration. For example, this approach has been adopted by other arbitration rules (art. 28(1), AAA-ICDR Rules; art. 22(3), LCIA Rules). However, the arbitral tribunal remains free to use conflicts of law rules if it considers such a method to be appropriate.

5. Deciding the applicable rules of law. If the parties have not agreed on the applicable rules of law in their contract, the Claimant will usually take a position on the issue in the Request and the Respondent will respond in its Answer. Unless there is an agreement on the applicable rules of law, this issue will be included as one of the issues to be determined in the Terms of Reference. The parties will ordinarily be able to make further submissions on the subject before the arbitral tribunal finally decides on the matter. The arbitral tribunal's decision on the applicable rules of law usually takes the form of a partial award.

6. Amiable compositeur and ex aequo et bono. The concepts of amiable compositeur and ex aequo et bono have been included in the ICC Rules since their inception. The concepts allow arbitrators to decide the parties' dispute without necessarily applying legal rules. Rather, the arbitrators can reach what they consider to be a fair and equitable resolution of the dispute. The precise meaning of these concepts and the difference between them has been the subject of much debate. In some countries, such as France, the concepts are considered identical (*Société Palanpina World Transports Holdings* v *Société Transco* (France)), whereas other legal systems use only one of the two terms, hence the inclusion of both concepts in the ICC Rules. Art. 17(3) allows arbitrators to act as amiables compositeurs or decide ex aequo et bono only when the parties have empowered them to do so. When using their powers as amiables compositeurs, arbitrators usually follow one of two approaches. The first is to compare the result that would arise from the strict application of the law with general principles, such as a presumption that parties intend their commercial relationship to result in quid pro quo, a presumption of intended equality of risk and good faith. The second approach is to find a solution that would be accepted by both parties, without affecting any potential future relationship. At the time of writing, a task force of the ICC Commission on Arbitration is preparing a paper on amiable composition and arbitrators acting ex aequo bono.

[Terms of reference; provisional timetable]

Article 18

(1) As soon as it has received the file from the Secretariat, the Arbitral Tribunal shall draw up, on the basis of documents or in the presence of the parties and in the light of their most recent submissions, a document defining its Terms of Reference. This document shall include the following particulars:

- **(a) the full names and descriptions of the parties;**
- **(b) the addresses of the parties to which notifications and communications arising in the course of the arbitration may be made;**
- **(c) a summary of the parties' respective claims and of the relief sought by each party with an indication to the extent possible of the amounts claimed or counterclaimed;**
- **(d) unless the Arbitral Tribunal considers it inappropriate, a list of issues to be determined;**
- **(e) the full names, descriptions and addresses of the arbitrators;**
- **(f) the place of the arbitration; and**
- **(g) particulars of the applicable procedural rules and, if such is the case, reference to the power conferred upon the Arbitral Tribunal to act as amiable compositeur or to decide ex aequo et bono.**

(2) The Terms of Reference shall be signed by the parties and the Arbitral Tribunal. Within two months of the date on which the file has been transmitted to it, the Arbitral Tribunal shall transmit to the Court the Terms of Reference signed by it and by the parties. The Court may extend this time limit pursuant to a reasoned request from the Arbitral Tribunal or on its own initiative if it decides it is necessary to do so.

(3) If any of the parties refuses to take part in the drawing up of the Terms of Reference or to sign the same, they shall be submitted to the Court for approval. When the Terms of Reference are signed in accordance with Article 18(2) or approved by the Court, the arbitration shall proceed.

ICC Rules of Arbitration, art. 18

(4) When drawing up the Terms of Reference, or as soon as possible thereafter, the Arbitral Tribunal, after having consulted the parties, shall establish in a separate document a provisional timetable that it intends to follow for the conduct of the arbitration and shall communicate it to the Court and the parties. Any subsequent modifications of the provisional timetable shall be communicated to the Court and the parties.

1. General. Terms of Reference are a unique feature of the ICC Rules, which have required them since the ICC Rules were first published in 1922 (even though the phrase 'Terms of Reference' was not used until the 1955 revision).

2. The role of the Terms of Reference. Terms of Reference are mandatory under the ICC Rules. They provide a framework for the arbitration and generally reflect the parties' agreement regarding its conduct. They allow the parties and the arbitral tribunal to identify early in the proceedings the substantive issues to be dealt with in the arbitration. The Terms of Reference also provide a useful tool to the arbitral tribunal by determining the scope of its mandate. They assist in avoiding awards that are either ultra petita or infra petita. They also constitute a reference used by the ICC Court for the scrutiny of awards and may be taken into consideration by national courts when deciding on various matters. When signed by all parties, the Terms of Reference may also be regarded as an arbitration agreement in cases where there are doubts as to the existence or validity of any earlier arbitration agreement. However, a party that signs the Terms of Reference whilst also raising jurisdictional objections in such Terms of Reference is not considered to have waived such objections.

3. The contents of the Terms of Reference. Art. 18(1) sets out the elements that should be included in the Terms of Reference. These include the parties' details and those of their counsel, arbitrators' details, a summary of the parties' positions, a list of issues to be determined, the place of the arbitration and particulars of any applicable procedural rules. Under art. 18(1), the arbitral tribunal must draft the Terms of Reference in the light of the parties' most recent submissions. In practice, the arbitral tribunal generally drafts the Terms of Reference on the basis of the Request, the Answer and the Reply (if any). However, as art. 18(1) does not define what is meant by 'most recent submissions', other submissions made by the parties before the establishment of the Terms of Reference are generally taken into consideration by the arbitral tribunal when drafting them.

4. The parties' claims. The Terms of Reference must contain a summary of the parties' positions and claims (art. 18(1)(c)). In order to properly reflect the parties' positions in the Terms of Reference, arbitral tribunals often ask the parties to draft a summary of their claims and positions for insertion into the Terms of Reference. It is important to set out clearly the relief sought by each party in the arbitration, as well as the amounts claimed or counterclaimed. Among other things, this facilitates the determination of the amount in dispute for the fixing of the advance on costs (see art. 30).

5. List of issues to be determined. The Terms of Reference should contain a list of issues to be determined (art. 18(1)(d)). This helps both parties and arbitrators to focus on key factual and legal issues and the questions that will need to be resolved in order to decide the parties' claims. However, such a list is not meant to be exhaustive or limitative. During the proceedings, the arbitral tribunal or the parties may realise that there are additional issues relevant to the case that must be dealt with. As such, the list of issues included in the Terms of Reference should not be considered as limiting the arbitrators' mandate to such issues only (*Société Farhat Trading Company* v *Société Daewoo* (France)). Prior to the 1998 revision, a list of issues to be determined had to be included in the Terms of Reference. The 1998 revision included a provision that arbitrators should include such a list 'unless the Arbitral Tribunal considers it inappropriate' (art. 18 (1)(d)). Some arbitrators, therefore, do not list the issues to be determined but rather use a general formula such as 'all the issues that arise from the parties' submissions'. However, such a formula should be the exception and not the rule.

6. Deadlines and extensions. Art. 18(2) provides that the arbitral tribunal shall transmit the Terms of Reference to the ICC Court signed by the arbitrators and the parties within two months from the transfer of the file to it. This time limit encourages the arbitral tribunal and the parties to move rapidly at this early stage of the arbitration. However, when it is not possible to respect this time limit, the ICC Court may extend it pursuant to art. 18(2) and does so periodically, either at the arbitral tribunal's request or on its own initiative. The ICC Court's practice is to grant two-month extensions. This process allows the ICC Court to be informed of any delays, especially those caused by arbitrators.

7. Signature of the Terms of Reference. The arbitral tribunal normally prepares a first draft of the Terms of Reference and sends it to the parties for comments. Arbitral tribunals sometimes also send a copy of the draft Terms of Reference to the Secretariat for its informal review. The Terms of Reference can be finalised by correspondence, although generally a meeting is held to sign them. At this meeting the provisional timetable is also usually determined (see note 9). The arbitral tribunal must send one original of the Terms of Reference to the Secretariat, so that it can be submitted to the ICC Court for its information. The time limit for the final award under art. 24(1) starts on the date of the signature of the Terms of Reference or, if a party fails to sign the Terms of Reference, the date of notification to the arbitral tribunal by the Secretariat of their approval by the ICC Court (see note 8). If an arbitrator refuses to sign the Terms of Reference, the ICC Court may initiate replacement proceedings against him in accordance with art. 12.

8. Approval of the Terms of Reference. If one or more parties do not participate or refuse to sign the Terms of Reference, art. 18(3) allows the arbitration to proceed by granting the ICC Court the power to approve the Terms of Reference. If a party is not participating in the arbitration, the arbitral tribunal should still make sure that such party has had an opportunity to sign the Terms of Reference. The arbitral tribunal should ensure that all drafts of the Terms of Reference are sent to the non-participating party. When approving the Terms of Reference, the ICC Court ensures that they do not include provisions that would require the agreement of the party that has not signed them, such as a determination of the applicable law (if the parties have not agreed such applicable law). If the Terms of Reference do contain such provisions, the ICC Court will not approve them and will invite the arbitral tribunal to revise the document. Arbitral tribunals usually send the Secretariat amended drafts of the Terms of Reference. This allows the Secretariat to review the document before it is finalised and to recommend to the arbitral tribunal appropriate changes. A revised Terms of Reference is subsequently submitted to the Court for its approval. Upon approval of the Terms of Reference by the ICC Court, the Secretariat sends another copy of the document to the party that did not sign, in a final attempt to obtain its signature. In these circumstances, the time limit for the rendering of the final award starts on the date that the Court's approval of the Terms of Reference is notified to the arbitral tribunal.

9. Provisional timetable. Under art. 18(4) the arbitral tribunal must issue a provisional timetable for the proceedings either when the Terms of Reference are signed or approved, or shortly thereafter. This provision encourages arbitrators and parties to plan the proceedings efficiently. The provisional timetable need not be very detailed. It also does not need to set out the steps for the entire arbitration. Indeed, sometimes it may be difficult for the parties and the arbitral tribunal to determine with precision the procedural steps they will need to follow to complete an arbitration (for example, the dates of steps that would follow a partial award). In any event, this timetable is provisional. In practice, arbitral tribunals normally amend or supplement the provisional timetable with further procedural orders. (This is why the provisional timetable should not be set out in the Terms of Reference, but in a separate procedural order.) Once the provisional timetable is issued, the arbitral tribunal must forward a copy to the Secretariat, which in turn submits it to the ICC Court for its information.

[New claims]

Article 19

After the Terms of Reference have been signed or approved by the Court, no party shall make new claims or counterclaims which fall outside the limits of the Terms of Reference unless it has been authorised

to do so by the Arbitral Tribunal, which shall consider the nature of such new claims or counterclaims, the stage of the arbitration and other relevant circumstances.

1. General. As mentioned under art. 18, the Terms of Reference allow the parties and the arbitral tribunal to agree a framework for the arbitration, including setting out what is to be decided during the arbitration. Art. 19 complements art. 18 by forbidding the parties from freely making new claims or counterclaims which fall outside the Terms of Reference. Art. 19 thus encourages parties to include all of their claims and counterclaims in the Terms of Reference. If new claims or counterclaims are raised after the Terms of Reference have been established, art. 19 grants the arbitral tribunal the exclusive power to decide whether they should be admitted in the arbitration.

2. Absence of definition of 'new claim'. Art. 19 does not define the term 'new claim'. Indeed, it is sometimes difficult to determine if a claim is new or not. It has been generally accepted that if the change leads to a modification of the relief requested, it is likely to be a 'new claim'. However, it is also generally accepted that a modification of the quantification of claims or counterclaims during the arbitration does not constitute a 'new claim'.

3. The relevant circumstances examined by the arbitral tribunal. When considering whether a new claim should be admitted, the arbitral tribunal takes into consideration such circumstances as whether the new claim has been introduced shortly after the signature of the Terms of Reference or much later in the proceedings, whether the party could have introduced the new claim earlier and whether the new claim is similar to an existing claim. The overriding principle is that a new claim submitted belatedly should not unduly interfere with the conduct of the original claims.

[Establishing the facts of the case]

Article 20

(1) The Arbitral Tribunal shall proceed within as short a time as possible to establish the facts of the case by all appropriate means.

(2) After studying the written submissions of the parties and all documents relied upon, the Arbitral Tribunal shall hear the parties together in person if any of them so requests or, failing such a request, it may of its own motion decide to hear them.

(3) The Arbitral Tribunal may decide to hear witnesses, experts appointed by the parties or any other person, in the presence of the parties, or in their absence provided they have been duly summoned.

(4) The Arbitral Tribunal, after having consulted the parties, may appoint one or more experts, define their terms of reference and receive their reports. At the request of a party, the parties shall be given the

opportunity to question at a hearing any such expert appointed by the Tribunal.

(5) At any time during the proceedings, the Arbitral Tribunal may summon any party to provide additional evidence.

(6) The Arbitral Tribunal may decide the case solely on the documents submitted by the parties unless any of the parties requests a hearing.

(7) The Arbitral Tribunal may take measures for protecting trade secrets and confidential information.

1. General. The ICC Rules provide considerable freedom to the parties and arbitrators regarding the conduct of the proceedings. Art. 20 deals with the manner in which the arbitral tribunal establishes the facts of the case, but does not provide detailed provisions regarding the procedure to be followed. Its purpose is to provide a general framework which can be completed by specific rules in each arbitration. Thus, the absence of detailed guidance in art. 20 guarantees the flexibility that the ICC Rules aim to achieve in the arbitral process.

2. Establishing the facts. Art. 20(1) grants the arbitral tribunal considerable liberty in establishing the facts of the case, allowing it to proceed 'by all appropriate means'. This provision confirms the procedural flexibility enjoyed under the ICC Rules. This flexibility is essential because arbitrators, parties and their counsel most often come from differing legal traditions and may be accustomed to differing procedural approaches. Of course, when establishing the facts of the case, the arbitral tribunal is subject to the provisions of the ICC Rules and, as a general rule, any agreement of the parties. Art. 20(1) provides that the arbitral tribunal must establish the facts of the case 'within as short a time as possible', thereby reinforcing another key objective of the ICC Rules: rapidity as appropriate to the circumstances of each case.

3. Hearings. Art. 20(2) grants the parties the right to request a hearing. In ICC arbitrations, it is usual to hold a hearing or hearings during which the parties have the opportunity to address, inter alia, the merits of the case, examine witnesses and make oral submissions. Art. 20(3) also grants the arbitral tribunal the power to convene a hearing at its own initiative. However, the parties' right to a hearing is not unlimited. While a hearing on the merits must be held if requested by a party, it is for the arbitral tribunal to decide when to hold the hearing and the extent to which it is necessary to hear witnesses, while acting in a fair and impartial way towards the parties. Art. 20(3) mentions a wide range of persons that may appear at a hearing, including witnesses, experts and 'any other person'. Art. 20(3), like art. 20(2) does not oblige the arbitral tribunal to hear witnesses, provided that this does not prevent a party from having a 'reasonable opportunity to present its case' (art. 15(2)). Refusing to hear oral testimony does not necessarily prevent a party from presenting its case if the requested testimony was not necessary in the circumstances

(*Dalmia Dairy Industries* v *National Bank of Pakistan* (England)). However, it is quite rare that an arbitral tribunal refuses to allow witness testimony or to hear particular witnesses that a party wishes to call. In ICC arbitrations, it has become common for parties to submit written witness statements before the witnesses are heard at a hearing. In such cases, witnesses are expected to appear at the hearing (primarily for cross examination).

4. Experts. Art. 20(4) grants the arbitral tribunal the power to appoint experts after consultation with the parties. Experts are typically appointed to assist the arbitral tribunal with matters of a technical or financial nature. The appointment of tribunal experts has become less common in ICC arbitration over recent years, due to the parties' increasing tendency to appoint their own independent experts. Art. 20(4) does not set out the exact role of the tribunal-appointed expert and allows the arbitral tribunal to determine the expert's functions. The use of an expert to advise the arbitral tribunal must be notified to the parties and the parties have the chance to question the expert at a hearing. Although arbitrators are not bound by appointed experts' reports, they often give them considerable weight.

5. Additional evidence. Art. 20(5) grants the arbitral tribunal the power to order a party to provide additional evidence. This happens most frequently in the context of document production procedures. While there is no sanction in the Rules for failing to comply with such an order, a refusal to provide evidence may lead the arbitral tribunal to draw an adverse inference.

6. Confidentiality. The ICC Rules do not contain express provisions providing confidentiality for various aspects of the arbitration, unlike other arbitration institutions, which have in recent years adopted such provisions (art. 30, LCIA Rules; arts. 73 to 76, WIPO Rules). Art. 20(7) does not specifically provide that ICC arbitrations shall be confidential. Rather, it grants the arbitral tribunal the power to take measures to protect 'trade secrets and confidential information'. Such measures can include, for example, an order that certain documents produced in the course of the arbitration shall remain confidential. The personnel of the ICC Court and the Secretariat are bound to maintain confidentiality (see art. 1, Appendix II).

[Hearings]

Article 21

(1) When a hearing is to be held, the Arbitral Tribunal, giving reasonable notice, shall summon the parties to appear before it on the day and at the place fixed by it.

(2) If any of the parties, although duly summoned, fails to appear without valid excuse, the Arbitral Tribunal shall have the power to proceed with the hearing.

(3) The Arbitral Tribunal shall be in full charge of the hearings, at which all the parties shall be entitled to be present. Save with the approval of the

ICC Rules of Arbitration, art. 22

Arbitral Tribunal and the parties, persons not involved in the proceedings shall not be admitted.

(4) The parties may appear in person or through duly authorised representatives. In addition, they may be assisted by advisers.

1. Holding a hearing. Art. 21 sets out the main elements relating to the conduct of hearings. Although art. 21(1) provides that the arbitral tribunal 'shall summon' the parties to appear at hearings, in practice, the arbitral tribunals consult with the parties and their counsel in order to agree on a date for hearings. If such agreement cannot be reached for various reasons, the arbitral tribunal has the power to summon the parties to hold the hearing on the day and at the place fixed by it. In doing so, the arbitral tribunal, pursuant to art. 14, may, after consultation with the parties, decide that the hearings will take place at any location that it considers appropriate. Further, art. 21(2) grants the arbitral tribunal the power to proceed with the hearing if a party does not appear without valid excuse. The requirement of a 'valid excuse' aims at ensuring that the parties will have a reasonable opportunity to be heard by the arbitral tribunal and that the hearing will not proceed if a party has a good reason for not being present. It is left to the arbitral tribunal to decide what constitutes a 'valid excuse'. For example, serious illness of a party's representative or impossibility to appear because of war or armed conflict might satisfy an arbitral tribunal's requirements for postponing a hearing.

2. Conduct of the hearings. Art. 21(3) grants the arbitral tribunal the power to determine how to conduct hearings. Generally, the arbitral tribunal will discuss with the parties' counsel the details regarding the organisation of a hearing. Art. 21(3) also protects the privacy of the hearings by forbidding persons not involved in the proceedings from being present. Art. 21(4) allows a party to appear at a hearing without being represented by a lawyer, even though this is unusual.

[Closing of the proceedings]

Article 22

(1) When it is satisfied that the parties have had a reasonable opportunity to present their cases, the Arbitral Tribunal shall declare the proceedings closed. Thereafter, no further submission or argument may be made, or evidence produced, unless requested or authorised by the Arbitral Tribunal.

(2) When the Arbitral Tribunal has declared the proceedings closed, it shall indicate to the Secretariat an approximate date by which the draft Award will be submitted to the Court for approval pursuant to Article 27. Any postponement of that date shall be communicated to the Secretariat by the Arbitral Tribunal.

1. General. Under art. 22 the arbitral tribunal must declare the proceedings closed when it is satisfied that the parties have had a reasonable opportunity to present their cases. Art. 22 ensures that it is clear when the proceedings are over and no further submissions can be made. In practice, the arbitral tribunal will inform the parties that the proceedings are declared closed pursuant to art. 22.

2. Reopening of the proceedings. In some cases, the arbitral tribunal may decide to reopen the proceedings. Although infrequent, this may happen where the arbitral tribunal realises, usually during its deliberations, that it requires further information from the parties in order to reach a decision. It is, however, unusual for an arbitral tribunal to reopen the proceedings at the request of a party.

3. Drafting of the award. After the closing of the proceedings, the arbitral tribunal will indicate to the Secretariat an approximate date for submission of the draft award for scrutiny by the ICC Court (see art. 27). When separate issues are to be decided at different stages of the arbitration by way of a partial or interim award (for example jurisdiction, liability, damages), the arbitral tribunal must declare the proceedings closed in accordance with art. 22 for each stage of the arbitration with respect to the issues that will be decided in that stage.

[Conservatory and interim measures]

Article 23

(1) **Unless the parties have otherwise agreed, as soon as the file has been transmitted to it, the Arbitral Tribunal may, at the request of a party, order any interim or conservatory measure it deems appropriate. The Arbitral Tribunal may make the granting of any such measure subject to appropriate security being furnished by the requesting party. Any such measure shall take the form of an order, giving reasons, or of an Award, as the Arbitral Tribunal considers appropriate.**

(2) **Before the file is transmitted to the Arbitral Tribunal, and in appropriate circumstances even thereafter, the parties may apply to any competent judicial authority for interim or conservatory measures. The application of a party to a judicial authority for such measures or for the implementation of any such measures ordered by an Arbitral Tribunal shall not be deemed to be an infringement or a waiver of the arbitration agreement and shall not affect the relevant powers reserved to the Arbitral Tribunal. Any such application and any measures taken by the judicial authority must be notified without delay to the Secretariat. The Secretariat shall inform the Arbitral Tribunal thereof.**

1. Background. Prior to the 1975 revision, the ICC Rules did not grant arbitrators the power to order interim or conservatory measures. They did, however, allow parties to apply to national courts for such measures in cases of 'urgency'. In the 1975 revision, the ICC Rules acknowledged arbitrators' power to grant interim or conservatory measures after the file was transmitted to them and limited the parties' rights to refer to the national courts for such measures to 'exceptional circumstances'.

2. Interim or conservatory measures. Art. 23(1) authorises the arbitral tribunal to order interim or conservatory measures that it considers appropriate. In addition, art. 23(1) allows the arbitral tribunal to order such measures 'as soon as the file has been transmitted to it'. Thus, such orders can be issued even before Terms of Reference are established. Art. 23(1) does not specify the kind of interim relief that parties may seek and arbitrators have broad discretion in this regard. The measures may be related to evidentiary matters (for example, disclosure of documents, preservation of evidence or access to witnesses) or standstill orders (for example, injunctions ordering a party to suspend legal proceedings before a state court). Although not mentioned specifically, art. 23(1) is broad enough to include applications for security for costs. Art. 23(1) does not specify what form the arbitral tribunal's decision should take. The arbitral tribunal is therefore free to decide whether its decision should take the form of an order or an award. If the decision takes the form of a partial award, a draft of the award must be submitted to the ICC Court for approval, pursuant to art. 27. Making the decision as an 'award' may increase the chances of its enforcement, although it is rare that a party does not voluntarily honour an order for provisional measures.

3. Applications to national courts. Art. 23(2) allows parties to apply to any competent judicial authority in order to obtain conservatory or interim relief. Under art. 23(2), a party may seek conservatory or interim relief from a national court either before the file is transferred to the arbitral tribunal or, in 'appropriate circumstances', after the file is transferred to the arbitral tribunal. Before the 1998 revision of the ICC Rules, art. 23(2) provided that the parties could apply to national courts for interim or conservatory measures only in 'exceptional' circumstances. In the 1998 revision 'exceptional' was replaced by 'appropriate', thereby allowing the parties greater flexibility to apply to national courts. It may be questioned whether not obtaining the requested relief from the arbitral tribunal should qualify as an 'appropriate' reason to seek such relief before a national court. In any event, even the term 'exceptional' did not seem to result in national courts refusing to consider applications for provisional measures. Art. 23(2) also requires a party making an application to a national court to send a copy of such a request to the Secretariat, which will then inform the arbitral tribunal. The absence of such notification does not generally have any consequences regarding the relief requested from the national courts. Art. 23(2) further specifies that a request to a national court for an interim award or conservatory relief shall not be deemed to constitute a waiver or infringement for the arbitration agreement, thereby allowing the

ICC Rules of Arbitration, art. 24

parties to seek interim or conservatory relief from national courts while pursuing the resolution of the overall dispute through arbitration.

AWARDS

[Time limit for the award]

Article 24

(1) The time limit within which the Arbitral Tribunal must render its final Award is six months. Such time limit shall start to run from the date of the last signature by the Arbitral Tribunal or of the parties of the Terms of Reference, or, in the case of application of Article 18(3), the date of the notification to the Arbitral Tribunal by the Secretariat of the approval of the Terms of Reference by the Court.

(2) The Court may extend this time limit pursuant to a reasoned request from the Arbitral Tribunal or on its own initiative if it decides it is necessary to do so.

1. General. A time limit for rendering the final award set out in art. 24(1) is unique amongst major arbitral rules. The AAA-ICDR, LCIA and UNCITRAL Rules, for example, do not contain such a time limit. The time limit for rendering the final award was initially included in the ICC Rules to satisfy the requirement in some national arbitration laws for such a time limit. However, today, the time limit is most commonly seen as encouraging arbitrators to proceed with the arbitration in the most expeditious manner possible and as a reference point for the review of the status of the arbitration by the ICC Court.

2. Start of the time limit. The six-month time limit commences on the date of the last signature of the Terms of Reference (if they are signed by all parties and arbitrators) or on the date of notification to the arbitral tribunal that the Terms of Reference have been approved by the ICC Court pursuant to art. 18(3). In practice, the Secretariat will notify the arbitrators of the date that the time limit started to run.

3. Shortening the time limit. The parties may agree to shorten the time limit for rendering the final award. Indeed, some arbitration clauses provide for a time limit of less than six months for rendering the final award. However, in practice, for a complex commercial arbitration, a period of less than six months (and even six months) may be unrealistically short. Thus, parties often agree to extend the period of time they initially included in their arbitration clause. Further, under art. 32(2), the ICC Court 'on its own initiative, may extend any time limit' set out in the rules that the parties have agreed to shorten (although see art. 32, note 6).

4. Extending the time limit. In practice, the final award is rarely rendered within the six-month time limit set out in art. 24(1) and the ICC Court usually extends the time limit. While arbitrators often request the ICC Court to extend the time limit, the Court will automatically extend the time limit even if not requested to do so. The extension normally granted for awards is three months, although the ICC Court may grant longer extensions if requested to do so by the arbitrators or parties or if the particular circumstances justify a longer extension. The ICC Court prefers not to grant long extensions so that it may assess the progress of arbitrations on a regular basis. The ICC Court's decision to extend a time limit is generally notified to the arbitrators only and not to the parties, although the arbitrators are requested to communicate the decision to the parties. The ICC Court will continue to grant extensions even if the arbitrators are not proceeding with the arbitration in a satisfactory manner so as not to put the validity of the arbitration in jeopardy. It has, however, on some occasions replaced under art. 12(2) the arbitrator or arbitrators responsible for the unacceptable delay.

5. Satisfying the time limit. The final award must be approved by the ICC Court under art. 27 and notified to the parties under art. 28(1) before the time limit expires. Thus, if the ICC Court has the draft final award before it for scrutiny, it will still extend the time limit under art. 24(2) so that there is sufficient time for it to be signed by the arbitrators and notified to the parties by the Secretariat before the time limit expires. The award that is rendered must be 'final' to satisfy art. 24(1), in the sense that it brings the arbitral proceedings to an end. Generally, the final award is either a final award on the merits or on costs, an award that the arbitrators do not have jurisdiction or an award by consent (see art. 26).

6. Expiry of the time limit. The ICC Court will not generally allow the time limit set out in art. 24(1) to expire. If it lapses, the arbitration is at an end and the arbitrators no longer have the power to render an award. There may be rare circumstances when the ICC Court allows the time limit to expire, such as when the parties have clearly lost all interest in the proceedings and the arbitrators request that the time limit be allowed to lapse so as to bring an end to the arbitration.

[Making of the award]

Article 25

(1) When the Arbitral Tribunal is composed of more than one arbitrator, an Award is given by a majority decision. If there be no majority, the Award shall be made by the chairman of the Arbitral Tribunal alone.

(2) The Award shall state the reasons upon which it is based.

(3) The Award shall be deemed to be made at the place of the arbitration and on the date stated therein.

1. General. Art. 25 deals with certain aspects of the making of awards. It applies to every type of award, whether interim, partial, final or otherwise.

Art. 25 does not describe what decisions must be made by award and what decisions may be made by procedural order (see art. 27, note 9), nor does it set out requirements as to the form or contents of awards (except that they must state the reasons upon which they are based (art. 25(2)). In practice, certain requirements as to the form and content of awards are imposed on arbitrators through the ICC Court's scrutiny process under art. 27.

2. Awards to be made by majority. The general rule set down in the first sentence of art. 25(1) is that awards are given by majority decision. Most awards are rendered unanimously, even if one or more of the arbitrators have reservations about aspects of the award. There are a number of reasons for this, including the perception that unanimous awards are more likely to be complied with voluntarily by the parties. The ICC Court does not, however, favour awards being unduly delayed due to efforts to achieve unanimity. Although not stated expressly in the ICC Rules, awards must be preceded by deliberations among the arbitrators. An absence of genuine deliberations (or at least the arbitrators having had the opportunity to take part in such deliberations) may justify an award being set aside or enforcement of the award being refused (*Intelcam* v *SA France Telecom* (France)).

3. In the absence of a majority, the chairman may make an award alone. If no majority can be reached, the chairman can make a decision alone. In practice, this is rare. In most cases, at least two of the three arbitrators are able to agree on an award. The power of the chairman to decide alone is thought to change the dynamics of the deliberations. Under rules that require a majority (such as the UNCITRAL Rules (art. 31(1)), the chairman must reach agreement with one of the two other arbitrators. This may force the chairman to make compromises that might not otherwise be acceptable in order to reach a majority decision. A chairman who has the power to decide alone may not feel that it is necessary to make such compromises.

4. Application to procedural orders. Although not stated expressly in the ICC Rules, it is generally considered that art. 25(1) applies by analogy to procedural orders. In any case, in many arbitrations the chairman will take more mundane procedural decisions without needing to consult the co-arbitrators. Indeed this power is often included in the Terms of Reference.

5. Dissenting opinions. The ICC Rules do not foresee expressly dissenting opinions. However, in a small number of cases, arbitrators prepare such opinions. Dissenting opinions do not form part of the award. They are not scrutinised or approved by the Court under art. 27, although they will be looked at by the ICC Court when it is considering the majority award. The Secretariat will generally send dissenting opinions to the parties when notifying the award under art. 28(1). However, a dissenting opinion will not be communicated to the parties by the Secretariat if the majority of the arbitral tribunal, having been invited by the Secretariat to consider the matter, believes that its communication is likely to jeopardise the enforceability of the award.

6. Absence of the signature of an arbitrator. One or more arbitrator may refuse to sign the award. Under the ICC Rules, the award will be valid if it is signed by the majority or the chairman alone if there is no majority. However, the arbitrator or arbitrators that do sign the award will generally note on the document the reason it is not signed by all arbitrators. Under the UNCITRAL Rules (art. 32(4)) and the LCIA Rules (art. 26(4)), arbitrators signing an award must note on the document the reason a signature is absent.

7. Awards must be reasoned. Art. 25(2) was added to the ICC Rules in the 1998 revision. It provides that awards must state the reasons on which they are based. However, even prior to 1998, the ICC Court required as part of the scrutiny process under art. 27 that awards be reasoned. Awards by consent do not have to include substantive reasons (see art. 26, note 4). Awards must be reasoned whether the arbitrators decide under a particular rule of law (art. 17(1)) or are empowered to act as amiable compositeur or decide ex aequo et bono (art. 17(2)).

8. Reasoning based on matters addressed. The award should be based on the matters put before the arbitrators by the parties and should not deal with claims or arguments that the parties did not have the opportunity to consider during the arbitration. In this respect, the Terms of Reference play an important role. During the scrutiny process (see art. 27), the ICC Court reviews the award in light of the Terms of Reference. The Terms of Reference may help the ICC Court to identify if the award is ultra petita or infra petita.

9. Award made at the place of arbitration. Art. 24(3) creates a presumption that the award is made at the place of arbitration. Art. 24(3) is useful in part because art. 14(2) allows hearings and meetings to take place somewhere other than the place of arbitration. Art. 24(3) also allows the arbitrators to physically sign the award at a place other than the place of arbitration. As part of the scrutiny process, the ICC Court requires that an award state: 'Place of arbitration:', followed by the place of arbitration (city and country) above the signature block on the final page of the award. To avoid confusion, the Court discourages arbitrators from setting down the actual place where the award was signed, particularly when it differs from the place of arbitration.

[Award by consent]

Article 26

If the parties reach a settlement after the file has been transmitted to the Arbitral Tribunal in accordance with Article 13, the settlement shall be recorded in the form of an Award made by consent of the parties if so requested by the parties and the Arbitral Tribunal agrees to do so.

1. General. Art. 26 allows the arbitrators to record a settlement agreement reached by the parties in an award by consent. The parties are not obliged to have their settlement agreement recorded in such an award. The principal reason that parties want an award by consent is so that their settlement agreement can be enforced as an award, if necessary. Awards by consent are generally considered to be enforceable under the New York Convention. Parties may also prefer not to have an award by consent because they deem it to be unnecessary (for example, the terms of the settlement agreement have been fully complied with) or for other reasons (for example, not to prolong the arbitration).

2. When an award by consent can be made. An award by consent cannot be made until the arbitral tribunal has been constituted and the file transmitted to it under art. 13. Generally, the ICC Court will not approve awards (even interim or partial awards) pursuant to art. 27 until after the Terms of Reference have been established. However, this rule does not apply to awards by consent: the ICC Court will approve them prior to the Terms of Reference being signed or approved, if the parties agree to dispense with the requirement of having Terms of Reference.

3. Agreement by the arbitrators. Art. 26 provides that the arbitrators may refuse to issue an award by consent when requested to render one. While in practice it is extremely rare that arbitrators refuse to do so, this provision is important because there are circumstances when such refusal is justified, such as when they believe that the aim of the award is to mislead third parties (for example, tax authorities) or is in the furtherance of money laundering.

4. Contents of an award by consent. Awards by consent generally reflect closely the terms of the settlement agreement reached by the parties. The arbitrators' role is thus limited to ensuring that the award by consent deals with all of the issues in dispute in the arbitration, including the allocation of the costs of the arbitration (see art. 31(3)). Awards by consent do not need to contain substantive reasoning for the decision given. The parties' consent is considered sufficient to justify the award (see art. 25(2)).

5. Drafting of an award by consent. Usually the arbitrators draft the award by consent and include the operative parts of the parties' settlement agreement in the awards dispositive section. Arbitrators often send the parties a draft of the award by consent for their comments. Sometimes the parties draft the award by consent and send it to the arbitrators. In that case, the arbitrators will still ensure that they are satisfied with the award in form and substance. Awards by consent must be approved by the ICC Court under art. 27 before they are rendered.

[Scrutiny of the award by the Court]

Article 27

Before signing any Award, the Arbitral Tribunal shall submit it in draft form to the Court. The Court may lay down modifications as to the

form of the Award and, without affecting the Arbitral Tribunal's liberty of decision, may also draw its attention to points of substance. No Award shall be rendered by the Arbitral Tribunal until it has been approved by the Court as to its form.

1. General. The scrutiny of awards pursuant to art. 27 is one of the most distinctive features of ICC arbitration. No other major arbitral institution has a similar process. Art. 27 has two goals. First, it seeks to ensure that ICC awards are of as high a quality as possible with respect to the form of the award. Ensuring the formal quality of awards increases the likelihood that the award will be enforced. Second, it seeks to ensure that the award is well-reasoned and persuasive so as to increase the likelihood that it is complied with voluntarily by the losing party and is less susceptible to being set aside or denied enforcement.

2. Timing of submission for scrutiny. The ICC Court will not approve an award under art. 27 (even if it is interim or partial) until the Terms of Reference have been signed or approved under art. 18. This rule, however, does not apply to awards by consent (see art. 26, note 2). Awards are only submitted to the Secretariat after deliberations amongst the arbitrators have taken place and the arbitrators agree unanimously on the text of the draft submitted or accept that they cannot reach such an agreement, in which case the draft is submitted by the majority or, if there is not majority, the chairman alone (see art. 25(1)).

3. Dissenting opinions. Sometimes a dissenting opinion is sent to the Secretariat along with the draft award (see art. 25, note 5). Dissenting opinions are not scrutinised or approved by the ICC Court. However, they are provided to the Court members who are present at the session when the award is considered. The ICC Court may draw to the majority's attention points from the dissenting opinion that it considers are not adequately dealt with in the draft award. In practice, the ICC Court expects that a majority opinion will have been finalised only after the majority has seen and considered the contents of a dissenting opinion. If the dissenting opinion is announced but not produced in a timely way, the majority may complete its draft award and send it to the ICC.

4. The scrutiny process. Awards are submitted in draft, unsigned, to the Secretariat. The counsel of the team that has been allocated the case will first review the draft award. The counsel may revert to the arbitral tribunal with comments on the document before submitting it to the ICC Court, if it contains substantial formal problems. This may be the case, for example, if the arbitrators who drafted the award have never previously drafted an ICC award. After the counsel's review, it is read by the Secretary General, Deputy Secretary General or the General Counsel, who then discusses the award with the counsel. The counsel then prepares a report on the award for submission to the ICC Court. If the award is in a language other than English or French (the ICC Court's working languages), it will be translated into one of those languages. Awards are generally considered by a committee session. However, if an award gives rise to particularly complex or novel issues, concerns a state party, involves a significant amount in dispute, or is accompanied by a dissenting opinion, it will generally be submitted to a plenary session. If the draft award is submitted to a plenary session, one of the court members will give a report on the award and whether or not it should be approved or sent back to the arbitral tribunal. If the draft award is in a language other than English or French, the Secretariat will normally ask a court member who is fluent in the language of the award to prepare the report. The ICC Court generally only has before it the draft award, the Terms of Reference and other awards previously rendered in the arbitration, along with the Secretariat's comments and the report of the Court members. Neither the ICC Court nor the Secretariat reviews the pleadings in the arbitration as part of the scrutiny process.

5. The ICC Court's decision on the award. After it has discussed the award, the ICC Court will generally take one of three decisions. First, it might approve the draft award exactly as it was presented. This is relatively rare because even the very best draft awards usually contain a small number of formal errors (typographical or mathematical errors, for example). Second, it might approve the draft award, subject to certain modifications. This is the most common decision taken by the ICC Court with regard to draft awards. This decision is generally taken when the modifications requested by the Court are self-explanatory. The ICC Court's decision is notified to the arbitral tribunal, which is invited to submit the signed award to the Secretariat after having taken into account the modifications requested. When the Secretariat receives the signed award, it is responsible for ensuring that the modifications requested by the ICC Court have been properly implemented. If the requested changes have not been done in a satisfactory manner, or the arbitrators have made other changes to the award, the Secretariat may return it to the Court for further review. Third, the ICC Court might decide not to approve the draft award and invite the arbitral tribunal to resubmit it after taking into account certain comments. The Court takes this decision when the draft award has more serious problems of form or substance. The arbitral tribunal then re-submits the award after having taken into account the ICC Court's comments and the scrutiny process is repeated.

6. Distinction between form and substance. Art. 27 draws a distinction between 'modifications as to the form of the Award' and 'points of substance'. The distinction between these two is significant with regard to the ICC Court's power. It can 'lay down modifications as to the form of the Award', but can only 'draw [the arbitrators'] attention to points of substance'. However, it is often difficult to distinguish between questions of 'form' and 'points of substance'. The ICC Court tends to err on the side of caution and, if in doubt, assume that matters are points of substance so as to ensure that it does not affect the arbitrators' liberty of decision.

7. Scrutiny as to form. Generally, the ICC Court's scrutiny as to form has two aspects. First, the award is reviewed for typographical and computational errors (which are frequent), and other errors relating to the quality of the award on its face. Second, the ICC Court will seek to ensure that the award contains certain formal elements. For example, the ICC Court will verify that the award sets out the parties' details, the procedural history, the constitution of the arbitral tribunal, any extensions of time granted for the rendering of the final award and the place of arbitration. Art. 6 of Appendix II provides that when 'the Court scrutinises draft Awards in accordance with Article 27 of the Rules, it considers, to the extent practicable, the requirements of mandatory law at the place of arbitration.' Thus, the ICC Court and its Secretariat may check if there are any mandatory form requirements for awards at the place of arbitration. This is often relevant when the place of arbitration is not a major arbitral venue. The ICC Court will also verify that all of the matters set out in the Terms of Reference have been dealt with, but that the arbitrators have not gone beyond the Terms of Reference by deciding points that were not at issue.

8. Scrutiny as to substance. The ICC Court does not act as an appellate court or verify that the legal and factual matters set out in the draft award are 'correct'. It can, however, draw the arbitrators' attention to points of substance, without affecting their liberty of decision. The ICC Court exercises this right sparingly. It does not want to be seen as interfering inappropriately in the arbitrators' deliberations. It will generally only raise questions with regard to points of substance when the award's reasoning is internally inconsistent, illogical or incomplete, or points made in a dissenting opinion are not dealt with in the draft majority award. Its goal is not to affect the outcome of the award, but to ensure that the reasoning is clear and persuasive.

9. Failure to submit an award for approval. Failure to submit for approval by the ICC Court a decision which constitutes an 'award', whether so labelled as such or not, will generally result in the decision being set aside or rendered unenforceable (*Brasoil* (France)). This problem can arise if the arbitral tribunal deems a decision to be a procedural order but it is subsequently decided by a national court to be in substance an award. That 'award' risks being set aside because it was not approved by the ICC Court pursuant to art. 27. The substance of the decision is what determines whether it is an award or a procedural order. However, there is no universally accepted rule that distinguishes an award from a procedural order. The qualification of 'award' certainly does not depend on the title used by the arbitrators (*Brasoil* (France)). Should an arbitral tribunal submit to the ICC Court a draft award which the Court may consider to be a procedural order, the Court will direct the Secretariat to discuss the issue with the arbitral tribunal, if the Secretariat had not already done so, even before submitting the draft to the Court.

[Notification, deposit and enforceability of the award]

Article 28

(1) Once an Award has been made, the Secretariat shall notify to the parties the text signed by the Arbitral Tribunal, provided always that the costs of the arbitration have been fully paid to the ICC by the parties or by one of them.

(2) Additional copies certified true by the Secretary General shall be made available on request and at any time to the parties, but to no one else.

(3) By virtue of the notification made in accordance with Paragraph 1 of this Article, the parties waive any other form of notification or deposit on the part of the Arbitral Tribunal.

(4) An original of each Award made in accordance with the present Rules shall be deposited with the Secretariat.

(5) The Arbitral Tribunal and the Secretariat shall assist the parties in complying with whatever further formalities may be necessary.

(6) Every Award shall be binding on the parties. By submitting the dispute to arbitration under these Rules, the parties undertake to carry out any Award without delay and shall be deemed to have waived their right to any form of recourse insofar as such waiver can validly be made.

1. General. Art. 28 deals with the mechanics of notifying awards, certain formalities with regard to awards after they are rendered and the legal effect of awards.

2. Notification of the award. After an award has been approved by the ICC Court pursuant to art. 27, the arbitrators are requested to sign and date originals of the document and send them to the Secretariat. The Secretariat must be provided with one original for each party and one for the Secretariat. Arbitrators typically retain one original themselves, although it is not a requirement under the ICC Rules that they do so. The advance on costs must be fully paid before the Secretariat will notify the award to the parties. This is rarely an issue because the ICC Court will not normally approve an award until the advance on costs has been fully paid. For notification purposes, the Secretariat uses the parties' addresses as determined under art. 3(2) or as set out in the Terms of Reference (see art. 18(1)(b)). The Secretariat generally sends the originals of the award to the parties by registered post or courier. If the parties are far apart (for example, one is in Europe and the other is in Latin America), one party may receive the award some time (even days) before the other. While the Secretariat will not do anything of its own initiative to deal with this problem, it may notify the award by different means if all parties agree. For example, the parties may agree that they will both collect the award from the ICC in person at the same time.

3. Additional certified copies. Pursuant to art. 28(4), the Secretariat retains an original of each award which is rendered. Upon request of a party, the Secretariat will provide, free of charge, certified copies of awards that have been rendered. The copies are certified as true by the Secretary General. Certified copies are generally provided for enforcement or set aside proceedings. For example, such certified copies are generally accepted for the purposes of art. IV(1) of the New York Convention as a 'duly certified copy' of the award. The Secretariat generally takes only a few days to provide certified copies.

4. Publication of awards. Art. 28(4) provides that certified copies of awards will be provided to the parties 'but to no one else'. Thus, third parties to the arbitration are not provided copies of awards without the express permission of the parties. While the ICC Rules do not deal expressly with the publication of awards, the ICC publishes awards regularly in a 'sanitised form' (that is, with the parties' names and other elements that would allow their identification removed). The ICC does not seek the parties' permission before publishing awards. However, it will not publish an award if requested by any party to the arbitration not to do so.

5. Waiver of other notification or deposit. Under art. 28(3) the parties waive any other form of notification or deposit provided for in any applicable law. Such waiver will only be effective to the extent that such requirements can validly be waived. There are, however, some jurisdictions which require that a copy of the award be deposited with a court or administrative body. This is the case, for example, in the Netherlands (see art. 1058(1)(b), Netherlands Arbitration Act). A party may also wish to deposit an award with a court or administrative body because, for example, such notification would start a limitation period running, within which a set aside action must be commenced (see, for example, art. 1505, French NCPC).

6. Assistance in enforcement proceedings. Under art. 28(5), the Secretariat has an obligation to assist the parties in complying with further formalities with regard to the award. This is a reference to assistance with regard to the formalities of enforcing awards. The Secretariat will arrange, for example, to obtain an apostille for an award under the Hague Convention or certified copies of documents other than the award (for example, documents relating to the notification of the Request or award). The ICC Court and Secretariat will not, however, become actively involved in enforcement or set aside proceedings. Art. 28(5) also applies to arbitrators. They may, for example, be requested to provide additional original copies of the award, if a national court requires an original signed copy.

7. Awards are binding. Art. 28(6) sets out the general principle that ICC awards are binding and the parties must comply with them without delay. The equivalent article in the rules prior to the 1998 revision used the term 'final' rather than 'binding'. This term was changed because not all ICC awards are necessarily 'final' (art. 2(ii) foresees expressly 'interim' awards). This change recognises that awards should be complied with whether or not they are final, as long as they are binding.

8. Waiver of recourse. Under art. 28(6), parties waive, to the extent possible, their right to any form of recourse against the award. This is an extension of the parties' general obligation to comply with awards without delay. The extent to which such waiver will be effective depends upon the law in each given jurisdiction and the exact circumstances of the case. In many jurisdictions, art. 28(6) would not be an effective waiver of the major accepted grounds of recourse against international awards: violations of due process, international public policy and the arbitrators lacking of jurisdiction.

[Correction and interpretation of the award]
Article 29

(1) On its own initiative, the Arbitral Tribunal may correct a clerical, computational or typographical error, or any errors of similar nature contained in an Award, provided such correction is submitted for approval to the Court within 30 days of the date of such Award.

(2) Any application of a party for the correction of an error of the kind referred to in Article 29(1), or for the interpretation of an Award, must be made to the Secretariat within 30 days of the receipt of the Award by such party, in a number of copies as stated in Article 3(1). After transmittal of the application to the Arbitral Tribunal, it shall grant the other party a short time limit, normally not exceeding 30 days, from the receipt of the application by that party to submit any comments thereon. If the Arbitral Tribunal decides to correct or interpret the Award, it shall submit its decision in draft form to the Court not later than 30 days following the expiration of the time limit for the receipt of any comments from the other party or within such other period as the Court may decide.

(3) The decision to correct or to interpret the Award shall take the form of an addendum and shall constitute part of the Award. The provisions of Articles 25, 27 and 28 shall apply mutatis mutandis.

1. General. Art. 29 was inserted in the ICC Rules in the 1998 revision. This change brought the ICC Rules in line with other major arbitral rules and laws, which allow arbitrators to correct awards after they have been rendered. Art. 29 applies to all awards, whether they be interim, partial, final or otherwise.

2. Correction of awards. Art. 29 allows arbitrators to correct 'a clerical, computational or typographical error, or any errors of similar nature'. Exactly what constitutes such an 'error' is not always clear. It is the arbitral tribunal itself that determines whether the application relates to an 'error' that is within the scope of art. 29.

3. Correction at the arbitrators' initiative. Under art. 29(1), the arbitrators may decide, on their own initiative, to correct 'a clerical, computational or typographical error, or any errors of similar nature'. In practice, such decisions are rare if only because arbitrators do not generally review awards after they have been rendered. However, art. 29(1) is sometimes used when a party brings an error to the arbitrators' attention without applying for correction of that error under art. 29(2). Art. 29(1) limits the arbitrators' power to the correction of errors and does not allow them to interpret the award on their own initiative. If the arbitrators wish to correct their award, they must submit such correction to the ICC Court for approval within thirty days of the date of the award.

4. Interpretation of awards. The issue of interpretation of awards is more contentious than that of their correction. Some rules, such as the UNCITRAL Rules (art. 35), allow interpretation of awards, whereas others, such as the LCIA Rules, do not. There is a concern that 'interpretation' is an unclear concept and that parties may use this provision to 'appeal' the underlying decision in the award. While in practice parties do sometimes make such applications, they are rarely successful, with the arbitrators finding generally that the application is not truly one for 'interpretation'.

5. Procedure when a party requests correction or interpretation. If a party wishes to apply to have an award corrected or interpreted under art. 29(2), it must make an application to the Secretariat within thirty days of receiving the award. The party must send the Secretariat one copy of the application for each party and arbitrator and one for the Secretariat (see art. 3(1)). The Secretariat sends the copies of the application to the arbitrators, who must grant the other party a time limit, normally not exceeding thirty days, to comment on it. While not stated in the ICC Rules, often the party applying for correction or interpretation is given a further chance to comment, and there may even been a further reply by the other party. The arbitrators then have thirty days from expiry of the time limit set for comments on the application (usually considered to be the last time limit fixed for such comments) to submit their decision on the application to the ICC Court. This time limit can be, and often is, extended by the Court.

6. Further advance on costs for correction or interpretation. The costs of the arbitration are fixed in the final award (see art. 31(3)). This means that before the final award is rendered, the ICC Court must determine how much to pay the arbitrators (see art. 31(1)). If a party submits an application for correction or interpretation of a final award, pursuant to art. 2(7) of Appendix III to the ICC Rules, the ICC Court can fix an advance to cover additional fees and expenses of the arbitrators for dealing with the application. In such a case, the transmission of the application by the Secretariat would be subject to the payment by the parties of the advance. In practice, the ICC Court rarely fixes such an advance. In the case of applications for correction, the Court considers that the parties should not have to pay extra to rectify an error in the award. It may, however, be more likely to consider a further advance in the case of a request for interpretation, particularly when the parties' submissions are extensive.

7. Addendum v decision. A decision by the arbitrators that corrects or interprets an award is referred to as an 'addendum'. By contrast, a determination by the arbitrators that an application for correction or interpretation is rejected, whether because of admissibility or on its merits, is referred to as a 'decision'. The important difference between an addendum and a decision is that, pursuant to art. 29(3), an addendum constitutes part of the award that it corrects or interprets, whereas a decision does not. Art. 29(3) states that arts. 25, 27 and 28 apply mutatis mutandis to addenda. This suggests that those provisions do not apply to decisions. However, in practice, the ICC Court and the Secretariat also apply those articles mutatis mutandis to decisions (see the ICC Court's note on 'Correction and Interpretation of Arbitral Awards' dated 1 October 1999 ('1999 Correction Note')).

8. Form and content of addenda and decisions. Addenda and decisions must be reasoned (see art. 25(2)). The arbitrators must decide on both the admissibility of the application (whether it was filed within the time limit set out in art. 29(2)) and its merits. In ruling on the merits, the arbitrators must first rule on whether the application properly falls within art. 29, that is, it is an application for correction of a clerical, computational, typographical or similar error or for interpretation. Many applications are rejected because they do not fall within art. 29, but rather are requests for reconsideration of the underlying decision in the award. If the arbitral tribunal decides that the application does fall within art. 29, it must then decide whether to correct or interpret the award. Addenda or decisions can be made by majority or, in the absence of a majority, by the chairman alone (see art. 25(1)), even if the original award was unanimous. Addenda and decisions must contain a decision as to costs (see art. 31(3)), however, parties often do not claim costs in relation to such applications. In such cases, it is usually sufficient that the arbitrators note in the addendum or decision that no costs were claimed.

9. No provision for additional award. Many other arbitral rules, including the LCIA Rules (art. 27(3)) and the UNCITRAL Rules (art. 37), allow arbitrators to render an additional award if claims or counterclaims presented in the arbitration were not dealt with in the award rendered. There is no such provision in the ICC Rules. However, if a relevant applicable law (usually the law at the place of arbitration) allows additional awards (for example, the English Arbitration Act (sect. 57(3)(b)) and the French NCPC (art. 1475)), the ICC Rules will not prevent the arbitrators from rendering such awards (see the 1999 Correction Note).

[Advance to cover the costs of the arbitration]
Article 30

(1) After receipt of the Request, the Secretary General may request the Claimant to pay a provisional advance in an amount intended to cover the costs of arbitration until the Terms of Reference have been drawn up.

(2) As soon as practicable, the Court shall fix the advance on costs in an amount likely to cover the fees and expenses of the arbitrators and the ICC administrative costs for the claims and counterclaims which have been referred to it by the parties. This amount may be subject to readjustment at any time during the arbitration. Where, apart from the claims, counterclaims are submitted, the Court may fix separate advances on costs for the claims and the counterclaims.

(3) The advance on costs fixed by the Court shall be payable in equal shares by the Claimant and the Respondent. Any provisional advance paid on the basis of Article 30(1) will be considered as a partial payment thereof. However, any party shall be free to pay the whole of the advance on costs in respect of the principal claim or the counterclaim should the other party fail to pay its share. When the Court has set separate advances on costs in accordance with Article 30(2), each of the parties shall pay the advance on costs corresponding to its claims.

(4) When a request for an advance on costs has not been complied with, and after consultation with the Arbitral Tribunal, the Secretary General may direct the Arbitral Tribunal to suspend its work and set a time limit, which must be not less than 15 days, on the expiry of which the relevant claims, or counterclaims, shall be considered as withdrawn. Should the party in question wish to object to this measure it must make a request within the aforementioned period for the matter to be decided by the Court. Such party shall not be prevented on the ground of such withdrawal from reintroducing the same claims or counterclaims at a later date in another proceeding.

(5) If one of the parties claims a right to a set-off with regard to either claims or counterclaims, such set-off shall be taken into account in determining the advance to cover the costs of arbitration in the same way as a separate claim insofar as it may require the Arbitral Tribunal to consider additional matters.

1. General. The manner with which costs are dealt is one of the most distinctive elements of ICC arbitration. Art. 30 deals with how funds are collected by the ICC from the parties for the arbitration. Requiring the parties to pay for arbitration services up front is not unique to ICC arbitration and, indeed, is natural in light of the services provided. Arbitrators are unlikely to have confidence that parties (particularly the losing party) will pay them after their services have been rendered (that is, the final award notified). Therefore, as with most systems of arbitration, if the parties fail to pay, the proceedings may be suspended and, if such non-payment continues, ultimately brought to an end (see notes 16 and 17). The money collected by the ICC under art. 30 is to cover three elements that will be determined at the end of the arbitration: the arbitrators' fees, the arbitrators' expenses, and the ICC administrative expenses. As set out below, the arbitrators' fees and the ICC administrative expenses are calculated by reference to the amount in dispute. Calculating the costs of the arbitration by reference to the amount in dispute is considered as having a number of advantages. First, the parties can, to a certain degree, predict in advance how much the arbitration will cost. Second, the costs of the arbitration are more likely to be appropriate to the commercial value of the claim. Third, such a system discourages excessive or frivolous claims, as over-inflated monetary claims will lead to an increase in the cost of the arbitration. Fourth, it avoids the possibility that arbitrators paid by the hour might inflate the number of hours worked.

2. Provisional advance. The concept of a 'provisional advance', as set out in art. 30(1), was introduced into the ICC Rules in the 1998 revision. The provisional advance is an amount paid by the Claimant alone. It is intended to cover the costs of the arbitration until the Terms of Reference have been drawn up and allows the file to be transmitted to the arbitrators under art. 13 before the full advance on costs has been fixed and paid. Prior to the introduction of this provision, transmission of the file to the arbitrators was often delayed due to the time necessary for the advance on costs to be fixed and paid. While the provisional advance is paid by the Claimant, such amount is credited to the Claimant for the purposes of the advance on costs ultimately fixed by the ICC Court (see art. 30(3)).

3. Fixing of the provisional advance. Art. 30(1) provides that the Secretary General 'may' fix a provisional advance. In practice, this is done in most cases. The Secretary General fixes the provisional advance when the Request is notified to the Respondent. The Claimant is normally requested to pay the provisional advance within 30 days. Art. 1(2) of Appendix III provides that the provisional advance 'shall normally not exceed' the ICC administrative expenses for the amount in dispute, along with the minimum fees for arbitrators for the amount in dispute plus 'the expected reimbursable expenses' of the arbitrators for the drafting of the Terms of Reference. The Secretary General normally fixes the provisional advance at half the ICC administrative expenses for the amount in dispute, along with half the minimum fees for arbitrators for the amount in dispute, and the arbitrators' estimated reimbursable expenses for the drafting of the Terms of Reference. The amount in dispute for the calculation of the provisional advance normally comes from the Request only and does not take into account any possible counterclaims. When the amount in dispute is not quantified, the Secretary General has broad discretion in fixing the provisional advance.

4. Number of arbitrators for calculation of the provisional advance. When the number of arbitrators is determined in the arbitration agreement, this is usually the number used for calculation of the provisional advance. When the number of arbitrators is not determined in the arbitration agreement, the Secretary Generally will generally base the provisional advance on the number of arbitrators that the Claimant proposes in the Request for the calculation of the provisional advance. Should the number of arbitrators used by the Secretary General for the calculation of the provisional advance turn out to be inappropriate, the provisional advance may be reconsidered.

5. When the provisional advance is not fixed. As noted above, the Secretary General normally fixes a provisional advance at the outset of the arbitration. There are, however, certain circumstances when the Secretary General will not do so. This may be the case, for example, when the parties' arbitration clause provides for 'fast track' arbitration (see art. 32, note 2). In those circumstances, the Secretariat sometimes invites the ICC Court to fix the full advance on costs at the outset of the arbitration and requests the parties to pay it within a relatively short deadline, so as to avoid the possibility that payment issues interfere with the 'fast track' procedure.

6. Advance on costs. The advance on costs is intended to cover the arbitrators' fees and expenses and the ICC administrative expenses until the end of the arbitration (art. 30(2)). Thus, the advance on costs requires the ICC Court to look to art. 31(1) and to the decision it will make when fixing the arbitrators' fees and expenses and the ICC administrative expenses at the end of the arbitration (see art. 1(4) of Appendix III). The advance on costs does not take into account the fees of any arbitrator-appointed experts (see art. 20(4) of the ICC Rules and art. 1(11) of Appendix III). Art. 30(2) requires the ICC Court to fix the advance on costs as 'soon as practicable'. In practice, the ICC Court generally fixes the advance on costs as soon as it has the necessary information to do so. In most arbitrations, this is after the Respondent has filed its Answer, or, at the latest, when the Terms of Reference are established.

7. Determination of the amount in dispute. As set out below, the primary determining factor for the advance on costs and, ultimately, the costs of the arbitration, is the amount in dispute. However, there are a number of elements that may render the calculation of the amount in dispute difficult. The ICC system for costs and expenses is calculated in US dollars. When claims are expressed in a currency other than US dollars, it is necessary to convert such amounts to US dollars for calculation purposes. The ICC Court uses the official exchange rate on the date the Request was received by the Secretariat. This exchange rate is used throughout the arbitration. If there are claims and counterclaims, both are added together to get the amount in dispute for calculation purposes (for set-off claims, see note 18). Although most parties claim interest on amounts claimed and costs, neither is generally taken into account for the purposes of calculation of the advance on costs.

ICC Rules of Arbitration, art. 30

8. Fixing of the advance on costs when claims are quantified. When the amount in dispute is quantified, it is possible to determine the minimum and maximum fees for the arbitrators from the scales in the rules. The scales change from time to time, the most recent version coming into effect on 1 January 2008. The ICC Court applies the scales that were in effect when the Request was received by the Secretariat. As the difference between the maximum and the minimum is significant, the ICC Court has broad discretion as to the fixing of the advance on costs. However, in practice, absent special factors, the ICC Court will fix the initial advance on costs based on the average arbitrators' fees provided in the scales (that is, the average between the minimum fee and the maximum fee). If not all of the claims for relief are quantified, the ICC Court will generally fix the advance on costs based on fees slightly higher than average for the quantified amount in dispute.

9. Fixing of the advance on costs when the claims are not quantified. When the amount in dispute is not quantified, the ICC Court can fix the advance on costs 'at its discretion' (art. 2(1) and (5) of Appendix III). While it enjoys broad discretion, the ICC Court's practice is generally to initially fix the advance on costs at USD 75,000 when a matter is to be decided by a sole arbitrator, and USD 160,000 when the matter is to be submitted to a three-member arbitral tribunal. In matters where the amount in dispute remains unquantified throughout the arbitration, the ICC Court reviews the matter from time to time to determine whether a reconsideration of the advance on costs is justified in light of the way in which the case is developing (see note 10).

10. Reconsideration of the advance on costs. While the advance on costs is fixed by the ICC Court early in the arbitration, it is 'subject to readjustment at any time during the arbitration.' (art. 30(2)). Art. 1(10) of Appendix III clarifies that such reconsideration may be 'to take into account fluctuations in the amount in dispute, changes in the amount of estimated expenses of the arbitrator, or the evolving difficulty or complexity of the arbitration proceedings'. While in theory changes to these elements could lead to an increase or decrease of the advance on costs, in practice, the advance on costs is rarely decreased. An exception may be if the amount in dispute is decreased significantly at an early stage of the arbitration. The ICC Court maintains this approach, at least partially, because excess funds available at the end of the case can always be reimbursed to the parties. By contrast, the ICC Court is generally reticent to increase the advance on costs at the end of the arbitration. The ICC Court generally prefers to increase the advance on costs as soon as possible after it receives information justifying such an increase. The Secretariat will often become aware of factors justifying a reconsideration of the advance on costs, such as an increase in the amount in dispute. However, arbitrators should not hesitate to draw the Secretariat's attention to such factors, particularly if they may not be evident from the correspondence exchanged in the arbitration. Before the Secretariat invites the ICC Court to reconsider the advance on costs, it normally notifies the parties that it will do so. Parties often object to an increase in the advance on costs, particularly if the arbitration is well advanced. The arbitrators would naturally prefer that the advance on costs be increased. It is the ICC Court's role to try to balance the parties' wish for a cost-efficient arbitration with the arbitrators' desire that they be properly remunerated.

11. Interest. The parties are not paid interest on sums held by the ICC.

12. Obligation to pay the advance on costs in equal shares. The general rule in ICC arbitration is that the Claimant and the Respondent must contribute to the advance on costs in equal shares (art. 30(3)). The Respondent is obliged to contribute equally to the advance on costs even if it has no counterclaims. The only exception to this rule is when separate advances on costs are fixed (see note 14). If there is more than one Claimant or Respondent, the Claimant or Claimants and the Respondent or Respondents must generally pay the advance on costs in equal shares (see art. 2(ii) and art. 30(3)). The ICC will not generally involve itself in determining what, if any, division of payment should be made among multiple Claimants or Respondents. (In the rare circumstances that there are three or more 'sides' in an arbitration, the ICC Court may be convinced to make special arrangements.) This rule does not prejudge who will ultimately bear the costs of the arbitration. That question will be determined by the arbitral tribunal in the final award (see art. 31(3)).

13. A party's failure to contribute to the advance on costs. Most parties, even Respondents, voluntarily contribute to the advance on costs in equal shares with the other party. However, some parties fail to pay their share. The defaulting party may continue to participate in the arbitration in order to assert its defences. However, it may pursue claims or counterclaims if, and only if, the non-defaulting party ultimately chooses to pay in substitution for the defaulting party so that the entire advance is satisfied. Art. 30(3) provides that 'any party shall be free to pay the whole of the advance on costs in respect of the principal claim or the counterclaim should the other party fail to pay its share'. Thus, the non-defaulting party is not obliged to pay in substitution, but rather is 'free' to do so. In practice, if there are no counterclaims, the non-defaulting party usually must pay in substitution for the defaulting party if it wishes the arbitration to continue and will generally do so. Where there are counterclaims, but the Respondent fails to pay its share of the total advance, the Claimant may request the ICC Court to fix separate advances on costs (see note 14).

14. Separate advances on costs. Art. 30(2) provides that where, 'apart from the claims, counterclaims are submitted, the Court may fix separate advances on costs for the claims and the counterclaims.' 'Separate advances on costs' are an often misunderstood part of the ICC Rules. Separate advances on costs are intended to deal with the situation where one party (usually the Respondent) introduces relatively large monetary claims (thus increasing the advance on costs), but refuses to pay half of the advance on costs based on both the claims and counterclaims. Separate advances on costs are the exception rather than the rule. The ICC Court prefers that the total advance on costs be paid by the parties. The ICC Court will generally only consider fixing separate advances if expressly invited by one of the parties to do so and both parties refuse to pay the outstanding balance of the total advance on costs. Usually the Claimant refuses to pay because the Respondent's relatively large counterclaim has (at least in the Claimant's opinion) artificially inflated the advance on costs. When the ICC Court fixes separate advances on costs, it applies the scales separately to the claims and counterclaims. Because of the steeply regressive nature of the scales (that is, the marginal increase in the arbitrators' fees becomes smaller as the amount in dispute increases), the total amount of separate advances will always be significantly more than a single 'global' advance on costs for both the claims and counterclaims. The Secretariat generally warns the parties of the financial consequences of fixing separate advances on costs before inviting the ICC Court to do so. Usually, the party that requested the fixing of separate advances on costs only wishes to proceed with such request where the other parties' claims are substantially larger than its own and it therefore is only prepared to pay an advance on costs calculated on its own claims only.

15. Payment by bank guarantee. The parties are usually obliged to pay their share of the advance on costs in cash. There are, however, certain circumstances when parties may post a bank guarantee to cover the relevant amount. If a party's share of the advance on costs exceeds an amount fixed from time to time by the ICC Court, the party may post a bank guarantee for the additional amount (art. 1(5), Appendix III). However, this provision is rarely, if ever, used. If a party has paid its share of the advance on costs, it may post a bank guarantee to cover the defaulting party's share (art. 1(6), Appendix III). Finally, if separate advances on costs are fixed, a party may post a bank guarantee to cover any amount requested of it that is in excess of one half of the total advance on costs (based on both claims and counterclaims) that was previously fixed (art. 1(8), Appendix III).

16. Deemed withdrawal for non-payment. The ICC Court has no way to compel parties to contribute to the advance on costs. The ultimate sanction that the ICC Court can impose in the case of non-payment is to apply art. 30(4), so that the claims or counterclaims are withdrawn. Art. 30(4) will only be applied if there has been significant delay in payment. There is a natural reluctance to apply art. 30(4) at an early stage if the amount of money held by the ICC would be more than sufficient to cover the arbitrators' fees and expenses and the ICC administrative expenses if the matter was to be withdrawn at that point. By contrast, the Secretary General may move quickly to apply the article if the ICC does not have sufficient funds to cover work that will soon be done.

17. Procedure for the application of art. 30(4). The first step under art. 30(4) is that the Secretariat will consult with the arbitrators with regard to the application of art. 30(4). Unless the arbitrators object, the Secretary General will direct the arbitrators to suspend their work. If separate advances on costs have been fixed, the arbitrators may be asked to suspend their work only with respect to the relevant claims or the counterclaims. At the same time as the arbitrators are asked to suspend their work, the Secretary General will grant the party or parties concerned a time limit for payment of the balance of the relevant advance on costs. Art. 30(4) provides that the time limit 'must be not less than 15 days', although, in practice the Secretary General usually grants fifteen days. If the time limit is not extended and it expires without the necessary payment being received or the relevant party objecting, the claims or counterclaims concerned 'shall be considered as withdrawn.' This means that the arbitration comes to an end or, if separate advances on costs have been fixed, comes to an end with respect to the claims or counterclaims that are considered as withdrawn. For these reasons, the non-defaulting party will sometimes pay the share of the defaulting party in order that the issues be decided once and for all. If a party wishes to avoid the claims or counterclaims being considered as withdrawn by paying the balance of the advance on costs requested, such payment must be received by the Secretariat before the time limit fixed by the Secretary General expires. It is not sufficient that payment is ordered or a cheque sent before the time limit expires. If a party wishes to object to the application of art. 30(4), it must also do so before the time limit granted by the Secretary General expires. Such objection suspends the time limit granted by the Secretary General. The ICC Court is then invited to consider whether to either reconsider the time limit by revoking or altering it, or refuse to reconsider the time limit. Usually, the ICC Court will refuse to reconsider the time limit granted. In such circumstances, the ICC Court will usually allow the relevant party at least the amount of time that it had left when the time limit was suspended due to its objection to pay the balance of the advance on costs. In practical terms, because it may take a week or more for the ICC Court to consider any objection, a party can effectively ensure itself an extension of time by objecting. Withdrawal under art. 30(4), does not prevent the party from reintroducing those claims or counterclaims in a subsequent arbitration.

18. Set-off claims. If a party claims a set-off with regard to claims or counterclaims, the amount of that set-off will be taken into account for the purposes of calculation of the advance on costs if such set-off may require the arbitrators to consider additional matters (art. 30(5)). Thus, counterclaims are always taken into account for the calculation of the advance on costs, whereas set-offs are only taken into account if they 'may require the Arbitral Tribunal to consider additional matters'. To determine whether a set-off claim may require additional work, the Secretariat usually consults with the arbitrators. In most cases, set-offs are considered to be likely to give rise to additional work for the arbitrators and are thus taken into account for the calculation of the advance on costs.

[Decision as to the costs of the arbitration]

Article 31

(1) The costs of the arbitration shall include the fees and expenses of the arbitrators and the ICC administrative costs fixed by the Court, in accordance with the scale in force at the time of the commencement of the arbitral proceedings, as well as the fees and expenses of any experts appointed by the Arbitral Tribunal and the reasonable legal and other costs incurred by the parties for the arbitration.

(2) The Court may fix the fees of the arbitrators at a figure higher or lower than that which would result from the application of the relevant scale should this be deemed necessary due to the exceptional circumstances of the case. Decisions on costs other than those fixed by the Court may be taken by the Arbitral Tribunal at any time during the proceedings.

(3) The final Award shall fix the costs of the arbitration and decide which of the parties shall bear them or in what proportion they shall be borne by the parties.

1. General. Art. 31 deals with the fixing of the various elements of the costs of the arbitration by the ICC Court and the arbitrators and the allocation of the costs of the arbitration between the parties by the arbitrators. Art. 31 provides that the costs of the arbitration include the arbitrators' fees and expenses, the ICC administrative expenses, the fees and expenses of any arbitrator-appointed experts and the parties' reasonable legal and other costs in relation to the arbitration. The ICC Rules set out an exclusive regime for the arbitrators' remuneration and the reimbursement of their expenses. Separate fee arrangements between the parties and arbitrators are not permitted (art. 2(4) of Appendix III) and would likely lead to the removal of the arbitrator in question, if discovered.

2. Arbitrators' fees. The arbitrators' fees are fixed by the ICC Court at the end of the arbitration, either when it approves the final award or after the matter has been withdrawn in the case of a settlement. The ICC Court generally sets the arbitrators' fees between the minimum and maximum fee provided in the scales for the amount in dispute (but see note 8) and not the amount ultimately awarded to one or another party. The minimum and maximum fees provided by the scales give the ICC Court quite broad discretion as to the amount to be paid to the arbitrators. In deciding the arbitrators' fees, the ICC Court takes into account the arbitrators' diligence, the time spent by the arbitrators on the matter, the rapidity of the proceedings and the complexity of the dispute (art. 2(2), Appendix III).

3. Diligence and rapidity. The ICC Court encourages arbitrators to proceed with arbitrations as expeditiously as possible. One way of doing this is by linking arbitrators' fees to their diligence and their ability to expedite arbitrations. That said, the ICC Court understands that some arbitrations are very complex, some parties are difficult and often the parties themselves agree upon an extended procedural calendar. If it perceives that the arbitrators are performing their functions efficiently and diligently in light of the circumstances of the case, it is likely to pay them more. However if it believes that the arbitrators are not handling the procedure well, it may pay them less. This is particularly the case when there is a significant delay between the final hearing or post-hearing submissions and the submission of an award.

4. The time spent by arbitrators. Before it invites the ICC Court to fix the arbitrators' fees, the Secretariat will invite the arbitrators to indicate the amount of time that they have spent on the matter. While the arbitrators are not paid at an hourly rate, the time spent by arbitrators is one factor that the ICC Court takes into account in determining the arbitrators' fees.

5. The complexity of the dispute. A number of factors can render an arbitration particularly complex. The matter could involve highly technical factual matters, as is often the case with construction, engineering or technology disputes. It could be that the parties' conduct makes the matter difficult from a procedural perspective (typically where one or more of the parties acts in an overly aggressive or dilatory manner). Novel or complex legal issues might also make a matter more complex. If arbitrators are faced with a particularly complicated arbitration, the ICC Court may be minded to pay them more.

6. Withdrawal prior to the final award. The minimum and maximum fees provided in the scales for the arbitrators' fees are for a completed arbitration, that is, one in which a final award is rendered. If the arbitration ends before the final award is rendered because, for example, the matter is settled, the ICC Court takes into account the stage attained in the arbitration (art. 2(6) of Appendix III), as well as any role that the arbitrators had in the parties' settlement. If a matter is withdrawn prior to the file being transmitted to the arbitrators under art. 13, the arbitrators will not normally be entitled to any fees or expenses.

7. Fees for replaced arbitrators. Arbitrators that are replaced because they die, resign, are replaced by the ICC Court under art. 12(2) or are the subject of a successful challenge, may or may not be entitled to fees. The ICC Court will determine a replaced arbitrator's fees based on the particular circumstances of the arbitration, including the reason that the arbitrator was replaced, the stage of the proceedings and the amount of work that must be repeated because of the arbitrator's replacement.

8. Exceptional circumstances. Art. 31(2) provides that the ICC Court can pay the arbitrators less than the minimum fee or more than the maximum fee provided for in the scale in 'exceptional circumstances', which term is not elaborated upon in the ICC Rules. The ICC Court is extremely reticent to fix fees under the minimum or over the maximum. It will generally only do so when remaining within the scales would lead to a manifestly inappropriate result, with the arbitrators being either massively over-paid or under-paid. In practice, the ICC Court almost never pays fees under the minimum. By contrast, it does from time to time pay arbitrators over the maximum due to the extraordinary circumstances of a matter.

9. Division of fees among a three-member arbitral tribunal. While not set out in the ICC Rules, it is the ICC Court's long-standing practice that when there is a three-member arbitral tribunal, the chairman receives 40% of the total fees and each co-arbitrator receives 30%. This is notified to prospective arbitrators in the documents sent by the ICC to any person nominated or appointed as arbitrator. Chairmen generally receive a greater share because they normally take on a greater burden of work (for example, the chairman normally drafts the majority of procedural correspondence and takes primary responsibility for drafting awards). However, the ICC Court will respect any agreement reached between the arbitrators as to the allocation of the arbitral tribunal's fees as agreement to divide the fees and a division of 50:25:25 is not unknown. Also, in very rare circumstances the ICC Court will of its own initiative depart from the 40:30:30 division.

10. VAT. The arbitrators' fees fixed by the ICC Court do not include value added taxes ('VAT'). The ICC Rules provide that the parties must pay any VAT or similar taxes and charges incurred by arbitrators (art. 2(9), Appendix III). However, they do not deal with the allocation of such amounts between the parties, nor do they set out a mechanism for their payment. Indeed, the ICC Rules provide that the recovery by the arbitrators of VAT 'is a matter solely between the arbitrator and the parties'. In practice, arbitrators often include the parties' obligation to pay VAT in the Terms of Reference. Some arbitrators also go as far as to request the parties to pay a deposit to cover the VAT that they expect to incur. Such deposit may be paid to the ICC. In such a case, the Secretariat will pay the amount corresponding to VAT to the arbitrators when paying their fees.

11. Advances on fees. The general principle in ICC arbitration is that the arbitrators are only paid at the end of the arbitration, so as to encourage the arbitrators to proceed as quickly and as efficiently as possible with the arbitration. The ICC Court will, however, pay the arbitrators certain relatively modest 'advances' on the fees that they will ultimately receive upon certain milestones in the arbitration being achieved, such as the signing of the Terms of Reference or a partial award.

ICC Rules of Arbitration, art. 31

12. Reimbursement of expenses. The ICC Court does not 'fix' the arbitrators' expenses. Rather, the arbitrators submit their expenses to the Secretariat for reimbursement, usually on an on-going basis. The Secretariat verifies if the expenses incurred are reasonable and justified and, if so, reimburses the arbitrator. To guide arbitrators and the Secretariat, the ICC Court issued a 'Revised Notice to the Arbitrators, Personal and Arbitral Tribunal Expenses' dated 1 January 2005 ('2005 Expenses Note'). The 2005 Expenses Note sets out certain guidelines as to expenses that will be reimbursed, including certain 'per diem' rates to simplify the claiming of expenses. Generally all requests for reimbursement must be received before the session at which the ICC Court approves the final award. At that session, the ICC Court will generally allocate the entire advance on costs. Therefore, the Secretariat may not be able to reimburse expenses which come to its attention after the session.

13. Administrative secretaries. Arbitrators often wish to appoint an administrative secretary to help them with certain tasks. Arbitrators may do so if none of the parties object. However, unless the parties expressly agree otherwise, the administrative secretary's fees must be paid out of the arbitrators' fees (see the ICC Court's 'Note Concerning the Appointment of Administrative Secretaries by Arbitral Tribunals' dated 1 October 1995). The administrative secretary's expenses, as opposed to fees, will be reimbursed out of the advance on costs.

14. ICC administrative expenses. If the amount in dispute is quantified, the ICC administrative expenses are calculated mathematically according to the scale in the rules (art. 2(5), Appendix III). The amount is fixed and the ICC Court does not exercise any discretion. The ICC Court may depart from the scale in 'exceptional circumstances' (art. 2(5), Appendix III), but in practice almost never does so. If the amount in dispute is not quantified, the ICC Court has broad discretion to determine the ICC administrative expenses. If the arbitration ends before the final award, the ICC administrative expenses will usually be reduced by the ICC Court, taking into account the stage attained in the arbitration and the work undertaken by it and the Secretariat. The administrative fees are capped, so that at the time of writing they may not exceed USD 88,800 regardless of the amount in dispute.

15. Fixing of the costs of the arbitration by the ICC Court. When the ICC Court approves the final award it also fixes the arbitrators' fees and the ICC administrative expenses. While, as noted above, the ICC Court does not 'fix' the arbitrators' expenses, it crystallises such expenses by including them in its decision on the costs of the arbitration. When the arbitrators are notified of the ICC Court's approval of their award, they are also informed of the decisions with regard to their fees, the ICC administrative expenses and the expenses. The Secretariat invites the arbitral tribunal to include such decisions in the final award.

16. Fixing of the costs of the arbitration in the final award. While the ICC Court fixes the arbitrators' fees, their expenses (in effect) and the ICC administrative expense, the arbitrators must fix the other elements of the costs of the arbitration, namely, the fees and expenses of any experts appointed by them and the parties' 'reasonable legal and other costs'. The parties normally make submissions with regards to their costs at the end of the procedure. If they do not do so, the arbitrators should solicit the parties' comments on the costs of the arbitration, even if just to confirm that they have no comments.

17. Fees and expenses of arbitrator-appointed experts. If the arbitrators appoint an expert, they normally consult with the parties as to the expert's remuneration. Further, they should ensure either that the expert is paid by the parties directly or that the Secretariat holds a sufficient advance on costs to cover the expert's fees and expenses (see art. 1(11), Appendix III).

18. The parties' reasonable legal and other costs. Parties typically claim the fees and expenses of legal counsel, along with the fees and expenses of experts. Other costs may include costs associated with witnesses, transcripts, interpreters and translators. Parties also sometimes claim amounts for in-house counsel.

19. Decision as to the allocation of the costs of the arbitration. In the final award, the arbitrators must decide which party or parties should bear the costs of the arbitration or in which proportion they must be born by the parties (art. 31(3)). Unlike certain other rules, such as the UNCITRAL Rules (art. 40(1)) and the LCIA Rules (art. 28(4)), there is no assumption in the ICC Rules that cost will be allocated in a certain manner (typically that 'costs follow the event'). Thus, arbitrators have broad discretion as to the allocation of costs, although, they must provide reasons for their decision (see art. 25(2)). Typical costs decisions are: that the parties bear their own costs; that the 'loser' must pay the 'winner's' costs; and that the costs are split according to the percentage by which each party was 'successful' with its claims.

20. Reimbursement to the parties. If money is to be reimbursed to the parties (that is, the costs of the arbitration as fixed by the ICC Court did not exhaust the entire advance on costs), the remaining sum will be reimbursed to the parties in proportion to the amount that they paid. The ICC will not take into account the terms of the final award. The ICC takes this approach because it does not want to be seen as being involved inappropriately in the enforcement of the award.

MISCELLANEOUS

[Modified time limits]

Article 32

(1) The parties may agree to shorten the various time limits set out in these Rules. Any such agreement entered into subsequent to the constitution of an Arbitral Tribunal shall become effective only upon the approval of the Arbitral Tribunal.

(2) The Court, on its own initiative, may extend any time limit which has been modified pursuant to Article 32(1) if it decides that it is necessary to do so in order that the Arbitral Tribunal or the Court may fulfil their responsibilities in accordance with these Rules.

1. Background. Prior to 1998, the ICC Court was faced with a number of cases in which the parties had agreed to shorten time limits that are specifically provided for in the ICC Rules (so-called 'fast track' cases). Art. 32 was included in the 1998 revision of the ICC Rules in order to deal explicitly with such cases. It provides that the parties can shorten time limits contained in the ICC Rules, but that the ICC Court can extend these shortened time limits if necessary. Art. 32 is one of the few articles in the ICC Rules that foresees expressly the parties derogating from them (see also arts. 6(1), 6(4), 7(6) and 23(1)).

2. 'Fast track' arbitration. The concept of 'fast track' arbitration arose in response to concerns in the business community that international arbitration was not always dealing with disputes, or certain types of disputes, in a timely manner. Certain types of contracts or issues were deemed particularly suitable for resolution by fast track arbitration (for example, disputes arising out of a price adjustment clause in an on-going contract). Fast track arbitration is generally considered to be most useful when ongoing commercial relationships are concerned. While, in principle, any dispute can be resolved by fast track arbitration, it can be impractical for complex disputes. Indeed, frequently parties underestimate the time or difficulty in complying with certain steps in an arbitration when fast track clauses are drafted and both arbitrators and parties generally recognise that in such case fast track cases result in 'rough justice'.

3. Time limits that may be modified. Art. 32 allows the parties to modify all of the time limits set out in the ICC Rules. For example, the parties may modify the thirty-day period for the Respondent to file the Answer (art. 5(1)), the fifteen- or thirty-day period for the nomination of an arbitrator (art. 8(3) and (4)) and the six-month period for the arbitral tribunal to render the award (art. 24(1)). However, the parties may not impose time limits on the ICC Court or the Secretariat. For example, the parties could not agree on a time limit for the ICC Court to scrutinise the award under art. 27. However, in 'fast track' cases, the Secretariat and the ICC Court endeavour, insofar as possible, to undertake scrutiny on an expedited basis (usually pursuant to art. 1(3)).

4. Agreement of the parties. Art. 32 applies only if all parties agree to shorten the relevant time limit. This may be done in the arbitration agreement, in the parties' contract, or by way of a subsequent agreement. The parties implement fast track arbitration by either setting a time limit for the award (usually the final award) to be rendered, by shortening various procedural time limits during the course of the arbitration, or both.

5. Agreement of the arbitral tribunal. When the parties have agreed to fast track arbitration before the arbitral tribunal is constituted, prospective arbitrators must take this into consideration when deciding whether to accept their nomination. Nominees not convinced that they can comply with the shortened time limits should decline the nomination. If the parties decide on fast track arbitration after the arbitral tribunal has been constituted, they must seek the arbitral tribunal's approval. The parties' agreement to modify time limits will only become effective if it is approved by the arbitral tribunal.

6. Power of the ICC Court under art. 32(2). The parties, the arbitral tribunal, the ICC Court and the Secretariat will do everything possible to comply with time limits agreed by the parties. However, even with the best intentions, there are cases where compliance with such time limits becomes impossible. Therefore, art. 32(2) grants the ICC Court the power to extend such time limits to the extent it considers necessary. The ICC Court may extend time limits when requested by the arbitral tribunal or by one of the parties to do so, or on its own initiative. The ICC Court strongly encourages parties and arbitrators to comply with any time limits agreed by the parties and is reticent to extend such time limits. It will, however, extend such time limits if it is necessary to do so (that is, the time limit would expire if it were not to do so). The parties may agree to modify any time limit they have previously fixed.

[Waiver]

Article 33

A party which proceeds with the arbitration without raising its objection to a failure to comply with any provisions of these Rules, or any other rules applicable to the proceedings, any direction given by the Arbitral Tribunal, or any requirement under the arbitration agreement relating to the constitution of the Arbitral Tribunal, or to the conduct of the proceedings, shall be deemed to have waived its right to object.

1. Background. Art. 33 was added in the 1998 revision of the ICC Rules. Similar provisions had already been included in a number of major arbitration rules (see, for example, art. 25, AAA-ICDR Rules; art. 30, UNCITRAL Rules). This article prevents parties from raising objections late in the proceedings, or after the arbitration has been completed, with regard to allegedly irregular conduct which took place long before the objection is made. Art.

33 implements the widely accepted principle of waiver (also referred to as estoppel or related to the broader concept of good faith). Waiver prevents a party from asserting or denying something when to do so would contradict its prior behaviour. Thus, under art. 33, when a party knowingly does not object to an irregularity in the arbitral proceedings, and continues to participate in the arbitration without showing its disproval, it will waive its right to object subsequently (*Hunt* v *Mobile Corporation* (United States)).

2. What constitutes a waiver under art. 33. A waiver is the voluntary relinquishment or surrender of a right. While a waiver is often in writing, under the ICC Rules it is more often the lack of action that constitutes the waiver. Under art. 33, a party generally waives a right by proceeding with the arbitration without raising an objection to a procedural irregularity. However, a party can only waive a right to object to a procedural irregularity about which it knows. Moreover, in order for a waiver to be effective, it must be permitted under the applicable law (see note 4).

3. The scope of art. 33. Art. 33 does not limit the possible procedural irregularities that may be subject to a waiver. Indeed, art. 33 is phrased in a very broad manner ('failure to comply with any provision of these Rules, or any other rules applicable to the proceedings, any direction given by the Arbitral Tribunal', etc.). Thus, for example, under art. 33, the parties can waive their right to object where the conduct of the proceedings by the arbitral tribunal is concerned (subject to limits set out in note 4).

4. Limits to waiver under art. 33. Rights can only be waived to the extent permitted by the relevant applicable law. Thus, art. 33 is limited by the relevant applicable law. Most laws do not allow the waiver of rights if such waiver would infringe public policy. For example, laws will generally not allow the parties to waive their fundamental procedural rights or the compliance with the basic due process. In practice, the two most relevant laws to determine the effectiveness of any waiver would be the law at the place of arbitration and the law of the possible place or places of enforcement of the award.

5. Time limit to raise an objection. Art. 33 is silent as to the time limit within which a party must raise an objection. It just states that the party's right to object is waived if it 'proceeds with the arbitration' without objecting. Thus, the party must object in a timely fashion (*Société Nihon Plast* v *Takata-Petri* (France)). It is possible to use the time limit set forth in art. 11(2) for the challenge of an arbitrator (thirty days) by analogy, although this is by no means universally accepted. Parties should raise objections as soon as they become aware of the circumstances that give rise to them. In any case, any objections should be raised before the closing of the proceedings (art. 22).

6. Art. 33 and the enforcement of awards. Art. 33 is most relevant to applications to have awards set aside or objections to their enforcement. Indeed, the waiver concept under art. 33 is generally applied after the arbitration has finished. Art. 33 gives a party seeking to have an award enforced or defending an application to have an award set aside a basis to argue that the award should be enforced or the setting-aside application refused if the party making the challenge had the opportunity to raise the relevant procedural point during the arbitration, but did not do so (see, for example, *ISEC* v *Bridas* (United States)).

[Exclusion of liability]
Article 34

Neither the arbitrators, nor the Court and its members, nor the ICC and its employees, nor the ICC National Committees shall be liable to any person for any act or omission in connection with the arbitration.

1. Background. State-court judges are generally granted immunity from claims by parties to proceedings before them. As arbitrators exercise what is, in effect, a judicial function, it was considered that they should also be protected from potential claims by parties. Thus, art. 34 was introduced in the 1998 revision of the rules in order to protect arbitrators, as well as the ICC, from liability in connection with arbitrations.

2. Scope of application. Art. 34 was drafted to provide total immunity to arbitrators and the ICC. This is in contrast to certain other arbitration rules, which provide that the exclusion of liability does not apply in the case of conscious and deliberate wrongdoing or gross negligence (see, for example, art. 31(1), LCIA Rules). The effectiveness of art. 34 may be limited by mandatory provisions of applicable law, which vary from jurisdiction to jurisdiction. Some laws may not allow such an exclusion. Art. 34 was not intended to exclude or limit any recourse the parties may have under the applicable law to request the annulment of an award, to object to an award's enforcement or to challenge an arbitrator. Parties may, based on the arbitrators' or the ICC's conduct or decisions, request the annulment or the refusal of enforcement of an award, even if they cannot sue the arbitrators or the ICC for such actions or decisions (*Bompard* (France)).

3. Act or omission. Art. 34 provides that neither the arbitrators nor the ICC is liable for 'any act or omission in connection with the arbitration' and covers both contractual and tortious claims if they relate to an 'act or omission in connection with the arbitration'.

4. Parties covered by art. 34. Art. 34 covers the arbitrators and the ICC. It expressly extends to the ICC, the ICC Court (even though, as set out in art. 1, note 2, the ICC Court does not have its own legal personality) and its members, including the Chairman. Art. 34 also covers the ICC's employees and ICC National Committees. Art. 34 does not exclude liability only from actions by the parties to the arbitration but rather extends to 'any person'.

However, it is questionable whether art. 34 would apply to a party that had not agreed to the ICC Rules.

[General rule]

Article 35

In all matters not expressly provided for in these Rules, the Court and the Arbitral Tribunal shall act in the spirit of these Rules and shall make every effort to make sure that the Award is enforceable at law.

1. General. Art. 35 provides the arbitral tribunal and the ICC Court with guidance when considering matters that are not specifically dealt with by the ICC Rules. It also provides both arbitrators and the ICC Court with the authority to act in such circumstances. Art. 35 provides that in the absence of express provisions that deal with a particular issue, the arbitral tribunal and the ICC Court shall 'act in the spirit of these rules'. The 'spirit' of the rules is considered to include elements such as the autonomy of the parties, the independence of arbitrators and the fairness and transparency of the proceedings.

2. The limited nature of art. 35. Art. 35 applies only to matters not dealt with expressly in the ICC Rules. Art. 35 does not place a general obligation on arbitrators and the ICC Court to ensure that awards are enforceable. If a matter is dealt with by the ICC Rules, art. 35 does not apply. Further, Art. 35 only requires the arbitral tribunal and the ICC Court to 'make every effort to make sure that the Award is enforceable at law.' Neither the arbitral tribunal nor the ICC Court guarantee that awards will be enforceable. Moreover, arbitrators are not obliged to take art. 35 into account in reaching their decision on the merits of the parties' dispute.

3. The law at the place of arbitration. The law at the place of arbitration is the primary law that arbitrators and the ICC look to when applying art. 35. As noted above (see art. 27, note 7), art. 6 of Appendix II requires the ICC Court, 'to the extent practicable' to take into account 'the requirements of mandatory law at the place of arbitration' when scrutinising awards. While art. 35 should not affect the arbitrators' decision on the merits, usually the arbitrators and the ICC endeavour to take mandatory law at the place of arbitration into account to the extent possible.

4. The law(s) of possible place(s) of enforcement of the award. Arbitrators and the ICC may also look to the law of the possible place or places of enforcement when applying art. 35 (ICC Case No. 6474). However, this is not always possible as it may be, for example, impossible to predict the jurisdiction or jurisdictions in which an effort will be made to enforce the award.

APPENDIX I
STATUTES OF THE INTERNATIONAL COURT OF ARBITRATION

[Function]

Article 1

(1) The function of the International Court of Arbitration of the International Chamber of Commerce (the 'Court') is to ensure the application of the Rules of Arbitration of the International Chamber of Commerce, and it has all the necessary powers for that purpose.

(2) As an autonomous body, it carries out these functions in complete independence from the ICC and its organs.

(3) Its members are independent from the ICC National Committees.

[Composition of the Court]

Article 2

The Court shall consist of a Chairman, Vice-Chairmen, and members and alternate members (collectively designated as members). In its work it is assisted by its Secretariat (Secretariat of the Court).

[Appointment]

Article 3

(1) The Chairman is elected by the ICC World Council upon the recommendation of the Executive Board of the ICC.

(2) The ICC World Council appoints the Vice-Chairmen of the Court from among the members of the Court or otherwise.

(3) Its members are appointed by the ICC World Council on the proposal of National Committees, one member for each Committee.

(4) On the proposal of the Chairman of the Court, the World Council may appoint alternate members.

(5) The term of office of all members is three years. If a member is no longer in a position to exercise his functions, his successor is appointed by the World Council for the remainder of the term.

[Plenary session of the Court]

Article 4

The Plenary Sessions of the Court are presided over by the Chairman or, in his absence, by one of the Vice-Chairmen designated by him. The deliberations shall be valid when at least six members are present. Decisions are taken by a majority vote, the Chairman having a casting vote in the event of a tie.

[Committees]

Article 5

The Court may set up one or more Committees and establish the functions and organisation of such Committees.

[Confidentiality]

Article 6

The work of the Court is of a confidential nature which must be respected by everyone who participates in that work in whatever capacity. The Court lays down the rules regarding the persons who can attend the meetings of the Court and its Committees and who are entitled to have access to the materials submitted to the Court and its Secretariat.

[Modification of the Rules of Arbitration]

Article 7

Any proposal of the Court for a modification of the Rules is laid before the Commission on Arbitration before submission to the Executive Board and the World Council of the ICC for approval.

APPENDIX II
INTERNAL RULES OF THE INTERNATIONAL COURT OF ARBITRATION

[Confidential character of the work of the International Court of Arbitration]

Article 1

(1) The sessions of the Court, whether plenary or those of a Committee of the Court, are open only to its members and to the Secretariat.

(2) However, in exceptional circumstances, the Chairman of the Court may invite other persons to attend. Such persons must respect the confidential nature of the work of the Court.

(3) The documents submitted to the Court, or drawn up by it in the course of its proceedings, are communicated only to the members of the Court and to the Secretariat and to persons authorised by the Chairman to attend Court sessions.

(4) The Chairman or the Secretary General of the Court may authorise researchers undertaking work of a scientific nature on international trade law to acquaint themselves with Awards and other documents of general interest, with the exception of memoranda, notes, statements and documents remitted by the parties within the framework of arbitration proceedings.

(5) Such authorisation shall not be given unless the beneficiary has undertaken to respect the confidential character of the documents made available and to refrain from any publication in their respect without having previously submitted the text for approval to the Secretary General of the Court.

(6) The Secretariat will in each case submitted to arbitration under the Rules retain in the archives of the Court all Awards, Terms of Reference and decisions of the Court, as well as copies of the pertinent correspondence of the Secretariat.

(7) Any documents, communications or correspondence submitted by the parties or the arbitrators may be destroyed unless a party or an arbitrator requests in writing within a period fixed by the Secretariat the return of such documents. All related costs and expenses for the return of those documents shall be paid by such party or arbitrator.

[Participation of members of the International Court of Arbitration in ICC arbitration]

Article 2

(1) The Chairman and the members of the Secretariat of the Court may not act as arbitrators or as counsel in cases submitted to ICC arbitration.

(2) The Court shall not appoint Vice-Chairmen or members of the Court as arbitrators. They may, however, be proposed for such duties by one or more of the parties, or pursuant to any other procedure agreed upon by the parties, subject to confirmation.

(3) When the Chairman, a Vice-Chairman or a member of the Court or of the Secretariat is involved in any capacity whatsoever in proceedings pending before the Court, such person must inform the Secretary General of the Court upon becoming aware of such involvement.

(4) Such person must refrain from participating in the discussions or in the decisions of the Court concerning the proceedings and must be absent from the courtroom whenever the matter is considered.

(5) Such person will not receive any material documentation or information pertaining to such proceedings.

[Relations between the members of the Court and the ICC National Committees]

Article 3

(1) By virtue of their capacity, the members of the Court are independent of the ICC National Committees which proposed them for appointment by the ICC World Council.

(2) Furthermore, they must regard as confidential, vis-à-vis the said National Committees, any information concerning individual cases with which they have become acquainted in their capacity as members of the Court, except when they have been requested by the Chairman of the Court or by its Secretary General to communicate specific information to their respective National Committees.

[Committee of the Court]

Article 4

(1) In accordance with the provisions of Article 1(4) of the Rules and Article 5 of its Statutes (Appendix I), the Court hereby establishes a Committee of the Court.

(2) The members of the Committee consist of a Chairman and at least two other members. The Chairman of the Court acts as the Chairman of the Committee. If absent, the Chairman may designate a Vice-Chairman of the Court or, in exceptional circumstances, another member of the Court as Chairman of the Committee.

(3) The other two members of the Committee are appointed by the Court from among the Vice-Chairmen or the other members of the Court. At each Plenary Session the Court appoints the members who are to attend the meetings of the Committee to be held before the next Plenary Session.

(4) The Committee meets when convened by its Chairman. Two members constitute a quorum.

(5)
- (a) The Court shall determine the decisions that may be taken by the Committee.
- (b) The decisions of the Committee are taken unanimously.
- (c) When the Committee cannot reach a decision or deems it preferable to abstain, it transfers the case to the next Plenary Session, making any suggestions it deems appropriate.
- (d) The Committee's decisions are brought to the notice of the Court at its next Plenary Session.

[Court Secretariat]

Article 5

(1) In case of absence, the Secretary General may delegate to the General Counsel and Deputy Secretary General the authority to confirm arbitrators, to certify true copies of Awards and to request the payment of a provisional advance, respectively provided for in Articles 9(2), 28(2) and 30(1) of the Rules.

(2) The Secretariat may, with the approval of the Court, issue notes and other documents for the information of the parties and the arbitrators, or as necessary for the proper conduct of the arbitral proceedings.

[Scrutiny of arbitral Awards]

Article 6

When the Court scrutinises draft Awards in accordance with Article 27 of the Rules, it considers, to the extent practicable, the requirements of mandatory law at the place of arbitration.

APPENDIX III

ARBITRATION COSTS AND FEES

[Advance on costs]

Article 1

(1) Each request to commence an arbitration pursuant to the Rules must be accompanied by an advance payment of US$ 2,500 on the administrative expenses. Such payment is non-refundable, and shall be credited to the Claimant's portion of the advance on costs.

(2) The provisional advance fixed by the Secretary General according to Article 30(1) of the Rules shall normally not exceed the amount obtained by adding together the administrative expenses, the minimum of the fees (as set out in the scale hereinafter) based upon the amount of the claim and the expected reimbursable expenses of the Arbitral Tribunal incurred with respect to the drafting of the Terms of Reference. If such amount is not quantified, the provisional advance shall be fixed at the discretion of the Secretary General. Payment by the Claimant shall be credited to its share of the advance on costs fixed by the Court.

(3) In general, after the Terms of Reference have been signed or approved by the Court and the provisional timetable has been established, the Arbitral Tribunal shall, in accordance with Article 30(4) of the Rules, proceed only with respect to those claims or counterclaims with regard to which the whole of the advance on costs has been paid.

(4) The advance on costs fixed by the Court according to Article 30(2) of the Rules comprises the fees of the arbitrator or arbitrators (hereinafter referred to as 'arbitrator'), any arbitration-related expenses of the arbitrator and the administrative expenses.

(5) Each party shall pay in cash its share of the total advance on costs. However, if its share exceeds an amount fixed from time to time by the Court, a party may post a bank guarantee for this additional amount.

(6) A party that has already paid in full its share of the advance on costs fixed by the Court may, in accordance with Article 30(3) of the Rules, pay the unpaid portion of the advance owed by the defaulting party by posting a bank guarantee.

(7) When the Court has fixed separate advances on costs pursuant to Article 30(2) of the Rules, the Secretariat shall invite each party to pay the amount of the advance corresponding to its respective claim(s).

(8) When, as a result of the fixing of separate advances on costs, the separate advance fixed for the claim of either party exceeds one half of such global advance as was previously fixed (in respect of the same claims and counterclaims that are the subject of separate advances), a bank guarantee may be posted to cover any such excess amount. In the event that the amount of the separate advance is subsequently increased, at least one half of the increase shall be paid in cash.

ICC Rules of Arbitration, Appendix III

(9) The Secretariat shall establish the terms governing all bank guarantees which the parties may post pursuant to the above provisions.

(10) As provided in Article 30(2) of the Rules, the advance on costs may be subject to readjustment at any time during the arbitration, in particular to take into account fluctuations in the amount in dispute, changes in the amount of the estimated expenses of the arbitrator, or the evolving difficulty or complexity of arbitration proceedings.

(11) Before any expertise ordered by the Arbitral Tribunal can be commenced, the parties, or one of them, shall pay an advance on costs fixed by the Arbitral Tribunal sufficient to cover the expected fees and expenses of the expert as determined by the Arbitral Tribunal. The Arbitral Tribunal shall be responsible for ensuring the payment by the parties of such fees and expenses.

[Costs and fees]

Article 2

(1) Subject to Article 31(2) of the Rules, the Court shall fix the fees of the arbitrator in accordance with the scale hereinafter set out or, where the sum in dispute is not stated, at its discretion.

(2) In setting the arbitrator's fees, the Court shall take into consideration the diligence of the arbitrator, the time spent, the rapidity of the proceedings, and the complexity of the dispute, so as to arrive at a figure within the limits specified or, in exceptional circumstances (Article 31(2) of the Rules), at a figure higher or lower than those limits.

(3) When a case is submitted to more than one arbitrator, the Court, at its discretion, shall have the right to increase the total fees up to a maximum which shall normally not exceed three times the fees of one arbitrator.

(4) The arbitrator's fees and expenses shall be fixed exclusively by the Court as required by the Rules. Separate fee arrangements between the parties and the arbitrator are contrary to the Rules.

(5) The Court shall fix the administrative expenses of each arbitration in accordance with the scale hereinafter set out or, where the sum in dispute is not stated, at its discretion. In exceptional circumstances, the Court may fix the administrative expenses at a lower or higher figure than that which would result from the application of such scale, provided that such expenses shall normally not exceed the maximum amount of the scale. Further, the Court may require the payment of administrative expenses in addition to those provided in the scale of administrative expenses as a condition to holding an arbitration in abeyance at the request of the parties or of one of them with the acquiescence of the other.

(6) If an arbitration terminates before the rendering of a final Award, the Court shall fix the costs of the arbitration at its discretion, taking

into account the stage attained by the arbitral proceedings and any other relevant circumstances.

(7) In the case of an application under Article 29(2) of the Rules, the Court may fix an advance to cover additional fees and expenses of the Arbitral Tribunal and may make the transmission of such application to the Arbitral Tribunal subject to the prior cash payment in full to the ICC of such advance. The Court shall fix at its discretion any possible fees of the arbitrator when approving the decision of the Arbitral Tribunal.

(8) When an arbitration is preceded by an attempt at amicable resolution pursuant to the ICC ADR Rules, one half of the administrative expenses paid for such ADR proceedings shall be credited to the administrative expenses of the arbitration.

(9) Amounts paid to the arbitrator do not include any possible value added taxes (VAT) or other taxes or charges and imposts applicable to the arbitrator's fees. Parties have a duty to pay any such taxes or charges; however, the recovery of any such charges or taxes is a matter solely between the arbitrator and the parties.

[ICC as appointing authority]

Article 3

Any request received for an authority of the ICC to act as appointing authority will be treated in accordance with the Rules of ICC as Appointing Authority in UNCITRAL or Other Ad Hoc Arbitration Proceedings and shall be accompanied by a non-refundable sum of US$ 2,500. No request shall be processed unless accompanied by the said sum. For additional services, ICC may at its discretion fix administrative expenses, which shall be commensurate with the services provided and shall not exceed the maximum sum of US$ 10,000.

[Scales of administrative expenses and arbitrator's fees]

Article 4

(1) The Scales of Administrative Expenses and Arbitrator's Fees set forth below shall be effective as of 1 January 2008 in respect of all arbitrations commenced on or after such date, irrespective of the version of the Rules applying to such arbitrations.

(2) To calculate the administrative expenses and the arbitrator's fees, the amounts calculated for each successive slice of the sum in dispute must be added together, except that where the sum in dispute is over US$ 80 million, a flat amount of US$ 88,800 shall constitute the entirety of the administrative expenses.

A. ADMINISTRATIVE EXPENSES

Sum in dispute (in US Dollars)	Administrative expenses
up to 50,000	$ 2,500
from 50,001 to 100,000	4.30%
from 100,001 to 200,000	2.30%
from 200,001 to 500,000	1.90%
from 500,001 to 1,000,000	1.37%
from 1,000,001 to 2,000,000	0.86%
from 2,000,001 to 5,000,000	0.41%
from 5,000,001 to 10,000,000	0.22%
from 10,000,001 to 30,000,000	0.09%
from 30,000,001 to 50,000,000	0.08%
from 50,000,001 to 80,000,000	0.01%
over 80,000,000	$ 88,800

B. ARBITRATOR'S FEES

	Fees	
Sum in dispute (in US Dollars)	minimum	maximum
up to 50,000	$ 2,500	17.00%
from 50,001 to 100,000	2.50%	12.80%
from 100,001 to 200,000	1.35%	7.25%
from 200,001 to 500,000	1.29%	6.45%
from 500,001 to 1,000,000	0.90%	3.80%
from 1,000,001 to 2,000,000	0.65%	3.40%
from 2,000,001 to 5,000,000	0.35%	1.30%
from 5,000,001 to 10,000,000	0.12%	0.85%
from 10,000,001 to 30,000,000	0.06%	0.225%
from 30,000,001 to 50,000,000	0.056%	0.215%
from 50,000,001 to 80,000,000	0.031%	0.152%
from 80,000,001 to 100,000,000	0.02%	0.112%
over 100,000,000	0.01%	0.056%

LONDON COURT OF INTERNATIONAL ARBITRATION (LCIA) ARBITRATION RULES, 1998*

(Adopted to take effect for arbitrations commencing on or after 1 January 1998)

[Introductory remarks]

History. The LCIA is one of the oldest arbitral institutions in the world, dating back to 1892, when it was founded by the City of London as the 'London Chamber of Arbitration'. The name of the institution was changed in 1903 to 'London Court of Arbitration' and in 1975 to 'London Court of International Arbitration'. In 1998 this was abbreviated to 'LCIA'. From 1975 to 1986 the LCIA was run by a Joint Management Committee consisting of representatives of the Chartered Institute of Arbitrators, the City of London and the London Chamber of Commerce and Industry. The committee was replaced in 1985 by the LCIA Court (see art. 3, note 3), and the following year the LCIA was incorporated as a 'company limited by guarantee'. Since that time the LCIA has been autonomous. The LCIA's arbitration rules have been revised repeatedly over the years, most recently in 1985 and in 1998. (Not all editions of the rules survive.) The current edition of the rules, which is adapted to the provisions of 1996 English Arbitration Act, is available in a number of languages, including Arabic, Chinese, French, German, Russian and Spanish.

Distinguishing features. The LCIA rules distinguish themselves from those of other international arbitral institutions chiefly by the emphasis they place on party autonomy (arts. 14 and 15(1)) and the confidentiality of the proceedings (art. 30); by requiring arbitrators to charge for their services by the hour rather than by reference to the sum in dispute (art. 5(3) and art. 4 Schedule of Arbitration Fees and Costs); by allowing third parties to be joined to the arbitration without the consent of all the existing parties (art. 22(1)(h)); by making the tribunal's awards 'final and binding' so that they cannot be reviewed by a state court save to the extent permitted by any mandatory provisions of the applicable law (art. 26(9)); and by granting to the tribunal (unless the parties agree otherwise) some specific powers, e.g. to order the disclosure of whole classes of documents within a party's 'possession, custody or power' (art. 22(1)(e)) or security for a party's legal and other costs (art. 25(2)). In addition to conducting arbitrations in accordance with its own rules, the LCIA acts as the appointing authority and administrator in UNCITRAL rules cases and as fundholder for deposits filed on account of costs in otherwise ad hoc proceedings. It also provides services in relation to other forms of dispute resolution (mediation,

---

* Reproduced with permission of the London Court of International Arbitration (LCIA). The text reproduced here is valid at the time of reproduction. As amendments may from time to time be made to the text, please refer to the website <http://www.lcia-arbitration.com> for the latest version.

expert determination and adjudication). For further information regarding these services and the LCIA generally, see <www.lcia.arbitration.com>.

[Preamble]

Where any agreement, submission or reference provides in writing and in whatsoever manner for arbitration under the rules of the LCIA or by the Court of the LCIA ('the LCIA Court'), the parties shall be taken to have agreed in writing that the arbitration shall be conducted in accordance with the following rules ('the Rules') or such amended rules as the LCIA may have adopted hereafter to take effect before the commencement of the arbitration. The Rules include the Schedule of Costs in effect at the commencement of the arbitration, as separately amended from time to time by the LCIA Court.

[The request for arbitration]

Article 1

(1) Any party wishing to commence an arbitration under these Rules ('the Claimant') shall send to the Registrar of the LCIA Court ('the Registrar') a written request for arbitration ('the Request'), containing or accompanied by:

    (a) the names, addresses, telephone, facsimile, telex and e-mail numbers (if known) of the parties to the arbitration and of their legal representatives;

    (b) a copy of the written arbitration clause or separate written arbitration agreement invoked by the Claimant ('the Arbitration Agreement'), together with a copy of the contractual documentation in which the arbitration clause is contained or in respect of which the arbitration arises;

    (c) a brief statement describing the nature and circumstances of the dispute, and specifying the claims advanced by the Claimant against another party to the arbitration ('the Respondent');

    (d) a statement of any matters (such as the seat or language(s) of the arbitration, or the number of arbitrators, or their qualifications or identities) on which the parties have already agreed in writing for the arbitration or in respect of which the Claimant wishes to make a proposal;

    (e) if the Arbitration Agreement calls for party nomination of arbitrators, the name, address, telephone, facsimile, telex and e-mail numbers (if known) of the Claimant's nominee;

    (f) the fee prescribed in the Schedule of Costs (without which the Request shall be treated as not having been received by the Registrar and the arbitration as not having been commenced); and

    (g) confirmation to the Registrar that copies of the Request (including all accompanying documents) have been or are being served

simultaneously on all other parties to the arbitration by one or more means of service to be identified in such confirmation.

(2) The date of receipt by the Registrar of the Request shall be treated as the date on which the arbitration has commenced for all purposes. The Request (including all accompanying documents) should be submitted to the Registrar in two copies where a sole arbitrator should be appointed, or, if the parties have agreed or the Claimant considers that three arbitrators should be appointed, in four copies.

1. Request is not a pleading. The Claimant's written request for arbitration (the 'Request') does not normally function as a pleading ('Written Statement'). It will only do so if the Claimant serves a notice saying that it elects to treat the Request as its Statement of Case (art. 15, notes 3 and 4) and any such election will not take effect until the tribunal has been appointed. With this exception, Written Statements are served after the tribunal has been appointed, unless the parties have agreed otherwise in accordance with art. 14(1) (see art. 15(1) and (3)).

2. Limitation. Art. 1(1)(f) and (2) provide that receipt by the Registrar of the Request and the accompanying registration fee marks the beginning of the arbitration for limitation and other purposes. The effectiveness of these provisions depends on whether or not the procedural law applicable to the arbitration (which will usually be the law of the seat of the arbitration) allows the parties to determine the effective commencement of their arbitration. Section 14 English Arbitration Act does allow this. (See also art. 1, note 5 regarding incomplete Requests.)

3. Content of Request. Art. 1(1) contains a list of items that must be contained in (or should accompany) the Claimant's Request. These include, among other things, a copy of the arbitration clause or agreement (art. 1(1)(b)), a 'brief statement describing the nature and circumstances of the dispute, and specifying the claims advanced by the Claimant against the [Respondent]' (art. 1(1)(c)), details of the Claimant's nominee arbitrator if a nomination is called for by the arbitration clause/agreement (art. 1(1)(e) and art. 7), and the non-refundable registration fee: currently GBP 1,500 (art. 1(1)(f) and art. 1(a) Schedule of Arbitration Fees and Costs). Whether or not the Claimant wishes to limit himself to a 'brief statement' in respect of his claim will depend in part on practical and tactical considerations. In theory a Request that sets out a claim in full obviates the need for a separate Statement of Case later in the proceedings (see art. 1, note 1 and art. 15, notes 3 and 4; see also art. 15.6 for the 'essential documents' which must accompany a Statement of Case). It also gives the LCIA Court more information on which to base its choice of arbitrator(s). However, where a limitation period is coming to an end it may well be more practical for a Claimant to provide only a bare outline of the dispute and his claim at this stage. Equally, it may be appropriate for tactical reasons only to set out one's case in brief at this stage.

4. Copies. Two copies of the Request and all accompanying documentation should be submitted to the Registrar (or four copies if a three-member tribunal is anticipated) (art. 1(2)). At the same time, the Claimant should serve a further copy of all of the documents on each of the other parties and confirm in its covering letter to the Registrar that it has done or is doing this, specifying the method of service used (arts. 1(1)(g) and 13(3)). (See art. 4, note 3 re permitted methods of service.) A wise Claimant will also provide proof of service, in the form of a courier delivery receipt, fax receipt, etc. This will help to pre-empt any delay or notice disputes, which are common with Respondents who choose the avenue of being non-responsive as their defence.

5. Incomplete Request. Art. 5(4) allows the LCIA Court to proceed with the appointment of the tribunal even where the Request and accompanying documentation is incomplete. (It will not, however, do so in the absence of the registration fee.)

6. Arbitration agreement. The arbitration agreement may be free-standing or part of a larger agreement. The very broad wording in the preamble to the Rules ('provides in writing and in whatsoever manner for arbitration under the rules of the LCIA…') is consistent with modern arbitral practice in not requiring that the agreement be signed by the parties. The LCIA recommends two arbitration clauses, the first for use in relation to future disputes, the second in relation to a dispute which has already arisen:

Clause 1 (Future disputes):

'Any dispute arising out of or in connection with this contract, including any question regarding its existence, validity or termination, shall be referred to and finally resolved by arbitration under the LCIA Rules, which Rules are deemed to be incorporated by reference into this clause.

'The number of arbitrators shall be [one/three].

'The seat, or legal place, of arbitration shall be [City and/or Country].

'The language to be used in the arbitral proceedings shall be [ ].

'The governing law of the contract shall be the substantive law of [ ].'

Clause 2 (Existing disputes):

'A dispute having arisen between the parties concerning [ ], the parties hereby agree that the dispute shall be referred to and finally resolved by arbitration under the LCIA Rules.

'The number of arbitrators shall be [one/three].

'The seat, or legal place, of arbitration shall be [City and/or Country].

'The language to be used in the arbitral proceedings shall be [ ].

'The governing law of the contract [is/shall be] the substantive law of [ ].'

The wording of the two clauses may be modified if, for example, the parties wish to restrict the powers of the tribunal under arts. 22 and 23; to modify the provisions in art. 28 governing costs; to exclude the possibility of a third party being joined to the arbitration (art. 22(1)(h)); to give themselves the right to nominate an arbitrator (art. 7); or to ensure that a tribunal consists of three members (art. 5(4)). It is generally wise to keep modifications to a minimum. Major changes may have unintended consequences or even result in the arbitration agreement being declared 'inoperative or incapable of being performed' (art. II(3) New York Convention). The LCIA is willing to discuss any modifications to its recommended clauses and there is no charge for this service.

[The response]

Article 2

(1) Within 30 days of service of the Request on the Respondent, (or such lesser period fixed by the LCIA Court), the Respondent shall send to the Registrar a written response to the Request ('the Response'), containing or accompanied by:
   (a) confirmation or denial of all or part of the claims advanced by the Claimant in the Request;
   (b) a brief statement describing the nature and circumstances of any counterclaims advanced by the Respondent against the Claimant;
   (c) comment in response to any statements contained in the Request, as called for under Article 1.1(d), on matters relating to the conduct of the arbitration;
   (d) if the Arbitration Agreement calls for party nomination of arbitrators, the name, address, telephone, facsimile, telex and e-mail numbers (if known) of the Respondent's nominee; and
   (e) confirmation to the Registrar that copies of the Response (including all accompanying documents) have been or are being served simultaneously on all other parties to the arbitration by one or more means of service to be identified in such confirmation.

(2) The Response (including all accompanying documents) should be submitted to the Registrar in two copies, or if the parties have agreed or the Respondent considers that three arbitrators should be appointed, in four copies.

(3) Failure to send a Response shall not preclude the Respondent from denying any claim or from advancing a counterclaim in the arbitration. However, if the Arbitration Agreement calls for party nomination of arbitrators, failure to send a Response or to nominate an arbitrator within time or at all shall constitute an irrevocable waiver of that party's opportunity to nominate an arbitrator.

1. Response is not a pleading. The Response is not a pleading (Written Statement) and, unlike the Request, cannot be made to serve as one by issuing a notice (see art. 1, note 1 and art. 15, notes 3 and 4). The Respondent's case is normally set out in full in its Statement of Defence, which is due after the tribunal has been appointed (and the Claimant has submitted its Statement of Case), unless the parties have agreed otherwise in accordance with art. 14(1) (see art. 15(1) and (3)).

2. Timing of Response and default. The Response is generally required within 30 days of service of the Request on the Respondent (see art. 4, note 5 re the computation of time under the LCIA rules.) However, the Response may be required earlier if the Claimant can convince the LCIA Court to use the expedited procedure for appointing a tribunal contained in art. 9. Where a Respondent fails to submit his Response on time or at all, this does not prevent him from participating in the arbitration and defending and making claims of his own at some later stage (see also art. 14(2) and Section 34 English Arbitration Act). However, if the arbitration agreement gives him the right to nominate an arbitrator, he will lose this right as a result of his default (arts. 2(3) and 7(2)). The LCIA Court may accept a late nomination, depending upon how late it is, although this is entirely discretionary.

3. Content of Response. Art. 2(1) contains a list of items to be contained in (or which should accompany) the Response. These include, among other things, confirmation or denial of all or part of the claims advanced by the Claimant in its Request (art. 2(1)(a)), a 'brief statement describing the nature and circumstances of any counterclaim advanced by the Respondent against the Claimant' (art. 2(1)(b)), and details of the Respondent's nominee arbitrator if a nomination is called for by the arbitration clause/agreement (art. 2(1)(d) and art. 7). No fee is payable by the Respondent at this stage. Although art. 2(1)(b) refers to counterclaims, it appears from art. 15(3) ('Any counterclaims shall be submitted with the Statement of Defence in the same manner as claims are to be set out in the Statement of Case') that a Respondent may be able to wait until it submits its Statement of Defence before filing a counterclaim. It is good practice for the Respondent to raise any jurisdictional defences in the Response, although these can also be raised in the Statement of Defence.

4. Copies. Two copies of the Response and all accompanying documentation should be submitted to the Registrar (or four copies if a three-member tribunal is anticipated) (art. 2(2)). At the same time, the Respondent should serve a further copy of all of the documents on each of the other parties and confirm in its covering letter to the Registrar that it has done or is doing this, specifying the method of service used (arts. 2(1)(e) and 13(3)). (See art. 4, note 3 regarding permitted methods of service.)

[The LCIA Court and Registrar]

Article 3

(1) The functions of the LCIA Court under these Rules shall be performed in its name by the President or a Vice President of the LCIA Court or by a division of three or five members of the LCIA Court

appointed by the President or a Vice President of the LCIA Court, as determined by the President.

(2) The functions of the Registrar under these Rules shall be performed by the Registrar or any deputy Registrar of the LCIA Court under the supervision of the LCIA Court.

(3) All communications from any party or arbitrator to the LCIA Court shall be addressed to the Registrar.

1. Structure of the LCIA. The LCIA has a three-tier structure comprising the Company, the Court and the Secretariat. The last-mentioned is headed by the Registrar.

2. Functions of the LCIA Court and Registrar. The LCIA Court is the final authority for the proper application of the LCIA rules. Its principal functions are the appointment of tribunals, the determination of challenges to arbitrators, and the control of costs. In contrast to the ICC Court under the ICC rules, the LCIA Court may not involve itself in questions such as the joinder of a third party to the arbitration or the quality of awards. The same is true of the Registrar, who performs a purely administrative role. The tribunal is therefore given considerable freedom to run the arbitration as it wishes, subject only to the agreed instructions of the parties, the tribunal's general duties, and the law applicable to the arbitration (see art. 14). The Registrar will however conduct a preliminary review of all Requests received to ensure that there is, at least on its face, a valid reference to LCIA arbitration by the Claimant, which conforms to the requirements of the preamble to the rules. If there is room for doubt but the Registrar considers that, on balance, there is the appearance of a valid reference, then in practice the Registrar will seek the view of the Court. If the Court agrees, the Registrar will then write to the parties accepting the reference but highlighting that the reference to LCIA arbitration is the Claimant's interpretation. The Registrar generally seeks to interpret references to LCIA arbitration broadly. For example, a reference to the 'London Court of Arbitration' will be accepted as this was a former name of the LCIA. Equally, a reference to 'the International Court of Arbitration in London' will usually be construed as a valid reference to LCIA arbitration. Also, bye-law 6.01 of the London Chamber of Commerce and Industry provides that disputes referred to the Chamber for arbitration, or for the appointment of arbitrators, are deemed to be references to the LCIA. In such cases, therefore, the LCIA acts as appointing authority and/or the arbitration is commenced and conducted in accordance with the LCIA Rules.

3. Who acts for the LCIA Court. Art. 3(1) provides that where the rules say that the Court will perform a particular function, that function will in practice be performed by either the President or one of the Vice Presidents of the Court. Alternatively, the function may be delegated to a division of three or five members of the Court. (The Court is made up of up to thirty-five members, including the President and Vice Presidents.) These divisions are appointed by the President or, if the President so wishes, by a Vice President. The Registrar is entitled to act for the Court in directing the parties to make interim or final payments and in authorising the payment of monies to the arbitrators, tribunal-appointed experts, and the LCIA itself (see art. 8 Schedule of Arbitration Fees and Costs).

4. Who acts for the Registrar. Art. 3(2) allows the functions of the Registrar under the rules to be performed by a deputy Registrar under the supervision of the Court.

5. Communications to another party, an arbitrator or the LCIA Court. Art. 3(3) requires all communications to the LCIA Court, whether from a party or an arbitrator, to be made through (and addressed to) the Registrar. (See art. 13(3) for provisions governing the copying of correspondence between a party and the Registrar.)

[Notices and periods of time]

Article 4

(1) Any notice or other communication that may be or is required to be given by a party under these Rules shall be in writing and shall be delivered by registered postal or courier service or transmitted by facsimile, telex, e-mail or any other means of telecommunication that provide a record of its transmission.

(2) A party's last-known residence or place of business during the arbitration shall be a valid address for the purpose of any notice or other communication in the absence of any notification of a change to such address by that party to the other parties, the Arbitral Tribunal and the Registrar.

(3) For the purpose of determining the date of commencement of a time limit, a notice or other communication shall be treated as having been received on the day it is delivered or, in the case of telecommunications, transmitted in accordance with Articles 4.1 and 4.2.

(4) For the purpose of determining compliance with a time limit, a notice or other communication shall be treated as having been sent, made or transmitted if it is dispatched in accordance with Articles 4.1 and 4.2 prior to or on the date of the expiration of the time limit.

(5) Notwithstanding the above, any notice or communication by one party may be addressed to another party in the manner agreed in writing between them or, failing such agreement, according to the practice followed in the course of their previous dealings or in whatever manner ordered by the Arbitral Tribunal.

(6) For the purpose of calculating a period of time under these Rules, such period shall begin to run on the day following the day when a notice or other communication is received. If the last day of such period is an official holiday or a non-business day at the residence or place of busi-

ness of the addressee, the period is extended until the first business day which follows. Official holidays or non-business days occurring during the running of the period of time are included in calculating that period.

(7) The Arbitral Tribunal may at any time extend (even where the period of time has expired) or abridge any period of time prescribed under these Rules or under the Arbitration Agreement for the conduct of the arbitration, including any notice or communication to be served by one party on any other party.

1. General. Art. 4 was introduced in the 1998 edition of the LCIA rules. It governs the manner and timing of the service of communications whenever these are required by the rules, ordered by the tribunal, or agreed between the parties.

2. Meaning of 'communication'. Wherever the LCIA rules refer to a 'communication', art. 4(1) makes clear that the communication must take a written form. (The issue is confused somewhat by art. 13's use of the term 'written communication', as if other communications may be made orally. That is not the case.) The term 'communication' encompasses 'notice', notwithstanding the wording of art. 4(5) and (7), which suggests otherwise. (See for example art. 4(1), which refers to 'any notice or other communication'.)

3. Permitted methods of service. Art. 4(1) permits two traditional methods of service (registered post and courier) and three electronic methods (fax, telex and email). In addition, it allows 'any other means of telecommunication that provide a record of [the communication's] transmission'. This leaves the door open to new means of electronic communication that may be developed in future. (It does not, however, cover the communication of information, e.g. by giving access to virtual data rooms or secure websites. In such cases the necessary record of transmission is lacking.)

4. Address for service. Initially, it is the responsibility of the Claimant to provide the LCIA with the names, addresses, telephone, fax and telex numbers and email addresses of all the parties to the arbitration and of their legal representatives (art. 1(1)(a)), and a Claimant risks a delay in the proceedings if the Respondent's contact details are inaccurate or out-of-date. Thereafter, it is expected that a party will notify the Registrar, the tribunal and the other parties of any change of address. Failing this, it is sufficient for communications to be sent to the party's last-known residence or place of business during the arbitration (art. 4(2)). Where a party has notified the LCIA of its chosen legal counsel after the initiation of the arbitral proceedings, the Registrar confirms with the party and its legal representative that all future communications shall then only be sent to the legal representative, unless otherwise requested by the party.

5. Calculating periods of time. In general, time periods specified by the rules or an order of the tribunal start on the day after the relevant communication has been delivered (art. 4(3) and (6)). (With faxes, telexes, emails and other telecommunications the rule is slightly different. Here the time period starts on the day after the communication is sent. In practice as telecommunications are (usually) instantaneous in their effect, the distinction is rarely of any significance.) A party complies with a time limit if it sends the relevant communication on the last day of the period in question. It is irrelevant when on a particular day the communication is sent, and on what day the communication actually arrives, provided that the party uses one of the means of service permitted by art. 4(1). If the last day of the time period falls on an official holiday, the communication may be sent on the next working day. (The same applies where the last day of a time period falls on a non-business day at the residence or place of business of the addressee.) Otherwise, an official holiday (or non-business day) counts as a normal day (art. 4(3)).

6. Exception for party/party communications. Art. 4(5) makes an exception for party/party communications. These may be addressed to the other party in any manner agreed between the parties, notwithstanding the provisions of art. 4(1) to (4), provided the agreement is in writing or can be inferred (in effect) from their previous dealings. Where there is no written agreement, the tribunal also has the power to vary the manner in which communications may be addressed by one party to another.

7. Tribunal's powers. In addition to its powers under art. 4(5), the tribunal has the power either to shorten or to lengthen any period of time set by the LCIA rules or the arbitration agreement in relation to the conduct of the arbitration (art. 4(7)). This may be done retrospectively, after the time period has expired. The power covers, among other things, extending time limits for the service of a communication by one party on another party. Taken together with art. 22(1) (b), this power can also arguably be used by the Tribunal to extend the time limits for the correction of an award set out in art. 27. (For the power of the LCIA Court, rather than the tribunal, to shorten time periods in the interests of appointing a tribunal quickly, see art. 9.) (Art. 4(7) appears to be subject to any contrary agreement reached by the parties and recorded by them in writing – see art. 22(1).)

[Formation of the arbitral tribunal]

Article 5

(1) The expression 'the Arbitral Tribunal' in these Rules includes a sole arbitrator or all the arbitrators where more than one. All references to an arbitrator shall include the masculine and feminine. (References to the President, Vice President and members of the LCIA Court, the Registrar or deputy Registrar, expert, witness, party and legal representative shall be similarly understood).

(2) All arbitrators conducting an arbitration under these Rules shall be and remain at all times impartial and independent of the parties; and

none shall act in the arbitration as advocates for any party. No arbitrator, whether before or after appointment, shall advise any party on the merits or outcome of the dispute.

(3) Before appointment by the LCIA Court, each arbitrator shall furnish to the Registrar a written résumé of his past and present professional positions; he shall agree in writing upon fee rates conforming to the Schedule of Costs; and he shall sign a declaration to the effect that there are no circumstances known to him likely to give rise to any justified doubts as to his impartiality or independence, other than any circumstances disclosed by him in the declaration. Each arbitrator shall thereby also assume a continuing duty forthwith to disclose any such circumstances to the LCIA Court, to any other members of the Arbitral Tribunal and to all the parties if such circumstances should arise after the date of such declaration and before the arbitration is concluded.

(4) The LCIA Court shall appoint the Arbitral Tribunal as soon as practicable after receipt by the Registrar of the Response or after the expiry of 30 days following service of the Request upon the Respondent if no Response is received by the Registrar (or such lesser period fixed by the LCIA Court). The LCIA Court may proceed with the formation of the Arbitral Tribunal notwithstanding that the Request is incomplete or the Response is missing, late or incomplete. A sole arbitrator shall be appointed unless the parties have agreed in writing otherwise, or unless the LCIA Court determines that in view of all the circumstances of the case a three-member tribunal is appropriate.

(5) The LCIA Court alone is empowered to appoint arbitrators. The LCIA Court will appoint arbitrators with due regard for any particular method or criteria of selection agreed in writing by the parties. In selecting arbitrators consideration will be given to the nature of the transaction, the nature and circumstances of the dispute, the nationality, location and languages of the parties and (if more than two) the number of parties.

(6) In the case of a three-member Arbitral Tribunal, the chairman (who will not be a party-nominated arbitrator) shall be appointed by the LCIA Court.

1. Overview. Art. 5 is a key provision of the LCIA rules. It gives the power to appoint arbitrators exclusively to the LCIA Court, as well as providing a mechanism aimed at ensuring each arbitrator's independence and impartiality. In addition, it determines the size of the tribunal and the timing of appointments, and obliges the arbitrator to be bound at the outset by the provisions of the Schedule of Arbitration Fees and Costs currently in force (presently as of 1 January 2010).

2. Independence and impartiality. Art. 5(2) and (3) provide that an arbitrator should be independent (an objective test) and impartial (a subjective test). Not all arbitration rules make this double demand at the outset. (See for example the ICC rules, where no mention is made of impartiality in the context of the appointment of an arbitrator, although arbitrators can be challenged at a later stage for 'lack of independence or otherwise' (art. 7(1) ICC rules) and there is a general duty to conduct the arbitration 'fairly and impartially' (art. 15(2)) ICC rules.) Guidance may be sought in the IBA's 2004 Guidelines on Conflicts of Interest in International Arbitration. These contain four lists of factors which should be considered when determining whether a potential arbitrator meets the IBA's 'General Standards Regarding Independence, Impartiality and Disclosure'. The question of independence is closely linked to that of the nationality of an arbitrator (see art. 6). A party may challenge an arbitrator under art. 10 if there are circumstances which give rise to justifiable doubts as to his impartiality or independence.

3. Advice on the merits or outcome of the dispute. The requirement in art. 5(2) that an arbitrator should not advise a party as to the merits or outcome of the dispute was introduced in the current (1998) edition of the LCIA rules. An explicit requirement of this kind is unusual but not unique, corresponding to art. 5(1) IBA's Ethics for International Arbitrators 1987 and art. 4(5)(1) Guidelines on Conflicts of Interest in International Arbitration. Although the restriction applies at all times, it is aimed principally at the period immediately before the nomination and appointment of arbitrators to a three person tribunal. At that stage there is a particular danger that potential arbitrators, when being 'vetted' by the parties, may be asked for an opinion – formal or more likely informal – on the subject matter of the arbitration. This may undermine a candidate's independence and impartiality if he is subsequently nominated and appointed. See also art. 13(1), which expressly forbids direct correspondence between a future arbitrator and any of the parties until such time as the tribunal has been formed. Up to that point, such correspondence must pass through the Registrar. (This is the general rule also after the tribunal has been formed (art. 13(2), until such time as the tribunal directs otherwise.) If (as is quite often the case) party-nominated arbitrators wish to consult with their nominating parties on appointment of the chairman, this should first be agreed with the LCIA in writing.

4. Arbitrator's résumé. Art. 5(3) requires a potential arbitrator to supply the Registrar with a written résumé of his past and present professional positions. In many cases, of course, the LCIA will already have the arbitrator's resumé on file.

5. Arbitrator's fees. Art. 5(3) also requires a potential arbitrator to agree in writing to fee rates conforming with those set out in the Schedule of Arbitrator's Fees and Costs currently in force (in practice, this is usually achieved by the Registrar informing the arbitrator in writing that, in accepting the appointment, the arbitrator is taken to have agreed to the fee-rates set out in the Schedule). The Schedule determines the way in which an arbitrator charges for his services (by the hour, rather than by reference to the sum in dispute), as well as setting the normal upper and lower limits to his hourly rate. (For the procedure regarding rates outside these limits, see art. 28, note 2.)

6. Declaration. The disclosure of relevant circumstances demanded by art. 5(3) is an almost universal requirement of arbitration rules. In practice, the Registrar provides a candidate with a standard form inviting him to sign one, and strike out the other, of the following two declarations:

Statement A:

'I am impartial, and independent of each of the parties, and I intend to remain so, and there are no circumstances known to me likely to give rise to any justified doubts as to my impartiality or independence'.

Statement B:

'I am impartial, and independent of each of the parties, and I intend to remain so, but I wish to disclose certain circumstances for the consideration of the LCIA Court prior to my appointment, whether or not any such circumstances is likely to give rise to any justified doubts as to my impartiality or independence. Other than such circumstances here disclosed by me, there are no circumstances known to me likely to give rise to any justified doubts as to my impartiality or independence.'

Art. 5(3) makes it clear that the duty to inform the LCIA Court of relevant circumstances is ongoing and continues to the end of the arbitration. When such circumstances are disclosed, whether at the outset or during the course of proceedings, the LCIA Court has to consider whether they do in fact impact on the arbitrator's independence and impartiality. In borderline cases the parties will be consulted before a decision is made. They will be informed of the disclosure in any event.

7. Timing of the appointment of the tribunal. Under art. 5(4), the tribunal is generally appointed 'as soon as practicable' after the Response is received by the Registrar. If the Response is late or simply fails to appear, the LCIA Court will proceed with the appointment after 30 days have elapsed following service of the Request on the Respondent. (If the Request and/or the Response is incomplete, this has no effect on the timing of the appointment.) In cases of exceptional urgency, the appointment procedure may be accelerated pursuant to art. 9 and, in particular circumstances, by agreement of the parties. This is usually done by cutting the 30 days down to 25, 20 or even 15 days. (See art. 4, note 5 regarding the computation of time under the LCIA rules.)

8. Number of arbitrators. Art. 5(4) raises a presumption that only one arbitrator will be appointed. (This provision dates back at least 90 years – see art. 9(a) of the 1915 edition of the rules.) However, three arbitrators will be appointed if the parties have agreed this in writing or if the LCIA Court thinks it appropriate. In the latter case, the Court reaches its decision by looking at 'all the circumstances of the case'. Relevant circumstances may include the sum in dispute, the legal or factual complexity of the case; and whether one of the parties is a state (in which case a three-member tribunal may be appropriate). Note that this provision is not affected by art. 9, which gives the LCIA Court the power in cases of exceptional urgency to shorten the timeframe within which a tribunal is appointed, but not to appoint a sole arbitrator where the parties have agreed the opposite in writing. This contrasts, for example, with the position under the WIPO Expedited Arbitration Rules (art. 14), which provide for the appointment of a sole arbitrator in urgent cases.

9. Appointment by the LCIA Court. There is an important distinction between 'nomination' and 'appointment'. Under the LCIA rules, parties may nominate an arbitrator, provided there is an express agreement between the parties to that effect (see art. 7), failing which all members of the tribunal will be chosen by the LCIA (note that the standard LCIA arbitration clause does not provide for party nominations). However, in contrast to some arbitration rules, the LCIA rules do not allow a party to appoint an arbitrator or, as is sometimes the case with three-member tribunals, allow two nominated arbitrators to elect the chairman of a tribunal (see art. 7(1) UNCITRAL rules). Art. 5(5) provides that the arbitral tribunal is appointed by the LCIA Court alone. The principle is confirmed in art. 7(1) of the LCIA rules, which makes it clear that the LCIA Court's approval of a party's nominee is not a mere formality (see art. 7, note 2). (The LCIA's insistence that it alone is empowered to appoint an arbitrator, rejecting where appropriate the nominations of the parties, goes back at least as far as the 1915 edition of the LCIA rules. Before that, the parties were free to decide who should try their case, provided they could agree on a name (or names) selected from an 'approved list' – see art. 11(a) of the rules as published by William Heinemann in 1893, the year after the institution's foundation, in 'The Arbitrator's Manual under the London Chamber of Arbitration' by Joseph Seymour Salaman.) To soften the basic rule, art. 5(5) requires the Court to have 'due regard' to any particular method or criteria of selection the parties have agreed upon, provided their agreement is in writing. Art. 5(5) also supplies a short list of further factors which the Court is obliged to take into consideration: the nature of the transaction; the nature and circumstances of the dispute; the nationality, location and languages of the parties; and (if more than two) the number of parties. (The reference to nationality reflects the provisions of art. 6, which deals specifically with this issue.) In practice, the LCIA Court will consider first the individuals (if any) nominated by the parties, and then the approximately 800 names on its database of arbitrators. This allows the LCIA to search (using specific fields) for suitable candidates by reference to their legal and other qualifications, language abilities, practical experience and expertise in specific areas, and knowledge of the legal systems and commercial and cultural practices of countries other than their own, taking into account factors such as the governing law of any contract at the heart of the dispute, the sum in issue and the speed with which the arbitration is intended to progress. In appropriate cases, the LCIA will also confer with other arbitral institutions to obtain additional names. The LCIA

Court's choice of arbitrator(s) is conclusive and binding, and need not be supported by any reasons (art. 29(1)).

10. Appointment of the chairman. In a three-member tribunal, the chairman may not be a candidate nominated by any of the parties (art. 5(6)), although in practice it is open to the parties to agree that the chairman may be nominated by all parties by agreement; or that the party-nominated arbitrators shall nominate the chairman. (See also art. 6(1), which precludes the chairman being of the same nationality as any of the parties, unless they agree the opposite in writing.)

11. Appointment of LCIA Court President and Vice-Presidents. Note that, under the Constitution of the LCIA Court, Section F: Appointment of Arbitrators and Mediators, sub-clause 2, certain restrictions are placed on the appointment of the President and Vice-Presidents of the LCIA Court as arbitrators. Furthermore, 'The President or Vice President so nominated shall take no part in the appointment of an arbitral tribunal to which they have been nominated or in any other function of the Court relating to such an arbitration'.

[Nationality of arbitrators]
Article 6

(1) Where the parties are of different nationalities, a sole arbitrator or chairman of the Arbitral Tribunal shall not have the same nationality as any party unless the parties who are not of the same nationality as the proposed appointee all agree in writing otherwise.

(2) The nationality of parties shall be understood to include that of controlling shareholders or interests.

(3) For the purpose of this Article, a person who is a citizen of two or more states shall be treated as a national of each state; and citizens of the European Union shall be treated as nationals of its different Member States and shall not be treated as having the same nationality.

1. General rule. It is important not only that arbitrators are fair and impartial in their dealings with the parties (see art. 5, note 2), but that they are perceived to be so. For this reason the LCIA rules, like those of some other international arbitral institutions, make it a general principle that, where the parties are of different nationalities, a sole arbitrator or chairman of an arbitral tribunal should not be of the same nationality as any party. Art. 6, which sets out this principle, is echoed in art. 5(5). This provides that, when appointing arbitrators, consideration will be given by the LCIA Court to (among other things) the 'nationality, location and languages of the parties'.

2. Exception to general rule. Where the LCIA rules differ from other rules is in the exception they make to this principle. Unlike the ICC rules, for example, which require there to be 'suitable circumstances' as well as the tacit consent of the parties if the principle is to be breached (art. 9.5 ICC rules), the LCIA rules provide that the general principle will always prevail unless the parties who are not of the same nationality as the proposed appointee 'all agree in writing otherwise' (art. 6(1)).

3. Meaning of 'nationality'. Art. 6 is also exceptional in stating that citizenship of the European Union is irrelevant in this context: an arbitrator will not be considered to be of the same 'nationality' as a party simply because they are both citizens of the EU (art. 6(3)). However, 'nationality' is in other respects interpreted widely, taking into account not only the place of incorporation of a company, but also the nationality of its controlling shareholders or interests (art. 6(2)); and when writing to the parties at the outset of an arbitration, the Registrar will usually seek clarification of the nationalities of controlling shareholders of corporate entities. Also, while the LCIA rules do not specifically address the question of how to treat parties from a colony or dependant territory, the LCIA's practice is to err on the side of caution and avoid appointing an arbitrator who is a citizen of the 'mother' country.

[Party and other nominations]

Article 7

(1) If the parties have agreed that any arbitrator is to be appointed by one or more of them or by any third person, that agreement shall be treated as an agreement to nominate an arbitrator for all purposes. Such nominee may only be appointed by the LCIA Court as arbitrator subject to his prior compliance with Article 5.3. The LCIA Court may refuse to appoint any such nominee if it determines that he is not suitable or independent or impartial.

(2) Where the parties have howsoever agreed that the Respondent or any third person is to nominate an arbitrator and such nomination is not made within time or at all, the LCIA Court may appoint an arbitrator notwithstanding the absence of the nomination and without regard to any late nomination. Likewise, if the Request for Arbitration does not contain a nomination by the Claimant where the parties have howsoever agreed that the Claimant or a third person is to nominate an arbitrator, the LCIA Court may appoint an arbitrator notwithstanding the absence of the nomination and without regard to any late nomination.

1. No automatic right to nominate an arbitrator. Under the LCIA rules, a party has a right to nominate an arbitrator only if the parties have agreed this between themselves. (This contrasts with the ICC rules, which automatically grant each party the right to nominate one member of a three-member tribunal (art. 8 ICC rules).) Moreover, the LCIA Court is not bound to follow any nomination procedure agreed between the parties where it thinks that a nominee is not independent or impartial, or that he is unsuitable for some other reason (art. 11(1)). (Although the model arbitration clauses recommended by the LCIA do not refer to the nomination of arbitrators, typically, some 60% of arbitrators appointed by the LCIA Court have been nominated by the parties.)

2. Parties cannot appoint an arbitrator. Art. 7(1) provides that where the parties purport to agree that an arbitrator may be appointed by one of them, or by a third party, their agreement will not be taken at face value. Instead, the power to appoint will be understood as a power merely to nominate an arbitrator. This is a logical consequence of art. 5(5), which says that the LCIA Court alone has the power to make an appointment. Art. 7(1) makes it clear that the appointment of a party's nominee is not a mere formality: the Court can reject a nominee if it thinks that he is not independent and impartial, or that he is unsuitable for some other reason. (See art. 5, note 9 for the history of this rule.) In practice, when this happens the LCIA usually asks the party in question to put forward a second nominee, whether or not the agreement between the parties provides for this. If a second nomination is not forthcoming within 15 days (or any shorter period fixed by the Court), the Court may proceed to appoint an arbitrator without further delay, regardless of the wording of the agreement (art. 11(2)). (See art. 4, note 5 regarding the computation of time under the LCIA rules.)

3. Compliance with art. 5(3). As with any other candidate, a nominee must comply with the provisions of art. 5(3) before his appointment can take place. Art. 5(3) requires him to supply the Registrar with a written résumé of his past and present professional positions; to agree in writing upon fee rates conforming to the Schedule of Costs; and to sign a declaration to the effect that there are no circumstances known to him likely to give rise to any justified doubts as to his impartiality or independence, other than any circumstances disclosed by him in the declaration.

4. Delay in nominating an arbitrator. If the Respondent (or a third party) is late in nominating an arbitrator, or neglects to do so at all, art. 7(2) empowers the LCIA Court to proceed with the appointment of the tribunal without delay. A late nomination may be disregarded by the Court altogether.

5. Joint nomination. It is possible for Claimant and Respondent to put forward a joint nomination for a sole arbitrator or the chairman of a three-member tribunal, although the LCIA rules do not explicitly provide for this. In such a case, the LCIA Court will generally appoint the joint nominee, provided it does not think him unsuitable and subject to the requirement of art. 5(3).

[Three or more parties]

Article 8

(1) Where the Arbitration Agreement entitles each party howsoever to nominate an arbitrator, the parties to the dispute number more than two

and such parties have not all agreed in writing that the disputant parties represent two separate sides for the formation of the Arbitral Tribunal as Claimant and Respondent respectively, the LCIA Court shall appoint the Arbitral Tribunal without regard to any party's nomination.

(2) In such circumstances, the Arbitration Agreement shall be treated for all purposes as a written agreement by the parties for the appointment of the Arbitral Tribunal by the LCIA Court.

1. Court's veto where parties cannot agree. Since the LCIA rules (like those of most arbitral institutions) envisage a tribunal consisting of no more than three arbitrators, a problem naturally arises in multi-party arbitration if the parties have agreed that each of them has the right to nominate an arbitrator. In such cases art. 8(1) offers two solutions to the problem: either the parties agree in writing to group themselves for these purposes into two 'sides' so that each side can nominate a single arbitrator and the LCIA Court can appoint the chairman of the tribunal or, if there is no such agreement, the Court simply appoints all three arbitrators itself. Art. 8(2) follows the point through by stating that in such circumstances the arbitration agreement will be treated for all purposes as if it were a written agreement by the parties specifically authorising the LCIA Court to appoint the arbitral tribunal. It is possible in theory (although unlikely in practice) for parties to agree to divide into two sides, but for one of the sides to fail to agree a nomination. In such a case art. 8 would not apply; however, the LCIA Court still has discretion to proceed as per art. 8(2) by virtue of the powers conferred on it by art. 5(5).

2. Background to rule. Art. 8 was introduced in the 1998 edition of the LCIA rules. Art. 8(2) in particular is designed to deal with the kind of problem that arose in the *Dutco* case in France, which concerned an ICC arbitration involving one Claimant and two Respondents. In that case the Claimant made its nomination, and the ICC Court called upon the Respondents to make a joint nomination. The Respondents complied, whilst at the same time reserving their rights. After the tribunal had been constituted, and had rendered an interim award, the Respondents challenged the award before the Paris Cour d'appel. That challenge was unsuccessful, but the Paris Cour de cassation overruled the lower court and annulled the interim award.

[Expedited formation]

Article 9

(1) In exceptional urgency, on or after the commencement of the arbitration, any party may apply to the LCIA Court for the expedited formation of the Arbitral Tribunal, including the appointment of any replacement arbitrator under Articles 10 and 11 of these Rules.

(2) Such an application shall be made in writing to the LCIA Court, copied to all other parties to the arbitration; and it shall set out the

specific grounds for exceptional urgency in the formation of the Arbitral Tribunal.

(3) The LCIA Court may, in its complete discretion, abridge or curtail any time limit under these Rules for the formation of the Arbitral Tribunal, including service of the Response and of any matters or documents adjudged to be missing from the Request. The LCIA Court shall not be entitled to abridge or curtail any other time limit.

1. General. This article was introduced in the 1998 edition of the LCIA rules, and is one of their distinguishing features. It allows the LCIA Court, where necessary, to shorten radically the time normally taken to appoint the arbitral tribunal or, once proceedings are under way, to replace an individual arbitrator (see arts. 2, 5 and 11 for the usual time limits involved in these procedures). This in turn makes it possible for a party to obtain interim relief within days of referring a dispute to arbitration, and in very urgent cases within 24 hours.

2. History of the rule. This article is not without precedent in the history of the LCIA rules. Art. 9 of the 1935 edition of the rules made similar provision for urgent action, though by different means. It allowed the predecessor to the LCIA Court to take swift action in relation to a reference without necessarily requiring the parties to wait for the tribunal to be formed. A similar provision was proposed in a draft of the present rules, but was rejected in favour of the current art. 9, which keeps the LCIA Court at arm's length from the conduct of the arbitration.

3. Procedure. Applications must be in writing, giving specific reasons why the arbitral tribunal should be appointed with exceptional urgency, and should be copied to all other parties to the arbitration (art. 2(2)). No guidance is given as to when the LCIA Court might agree to expedite the appointment procedure (e.g. by shortening the time limit for service of the Response under art. 2), this being left to the Court's 'complete discretion' (art. 9(3)). In practice, slightly more than 50% of applications under this rule are successful.

4. No need for prior written agreement. Art. 9 is not dependent on the consent of the parties. This contrasts with the ICC's Pre-Arbitral Procedure, for example, which allows for the appointment of a person empowered to make certain orders before the tribunal itself has been formed, but only where the parties have agreed in writing that the Procedure is applicable: a simple agreement to be bound by the ICC rules is not sufficient for these purposes (see ICC rules: Standard Clause for an ICC Pre-Arbitral Referee Procedure and ICC Arbitration). Art. 37 of the AAA-ICDR rules, introduced in March 2008, adopts a compromise position, allowing for the appointment of a single emergency arbitrator 'unless the parties agree otherwise', so that interim measures can be ordered pending the formation of the tribunal proper.

5. Use in practice. Art. 9 is clearly meant to be used only rarely. However, it fulfils an important function, giving a party (usually, but not always, the Claimant) the freedom to obtain at the earliest opportunity interim remedies similar to those available from a court. Most frequently, the article is used to apply for the kind of 'conservatory measures' covered by art. 25 which are intended to prevent a party shifting its assets; but can also be used in cases where a decision on the merits is urgently needed, for example where the period for exercise of an option is about to expire, or relief is needed in the context of the holding of an important (e.g. sporting) event. Naturally, it is easier for a party to take advantage of art. 9 when the arbitration agreement does not give the parties the right to nominate an arbitrator and where it provides for a sole arbitrator rather than a full arbitral panel (unlike the WIPO rules, the LCIA's art. 9 does not provide for the appointment of a sole arbitrator in all expedited cases). Where only one arbitrator needs to be appointed, the LCIA has done this on occasion within 24 hours. In other cases, the deadline for the Response has been shortened by 5, 10 or 15 days. Note that in contrast to some other arbitration rules, e.g. art. 14 of the WIPO expedited rules, art. 5(4) does not allow the LCIA Court to reduce the size of a tribunal from three to one in cases of exceptional urgency. If the parties have agreed on a three-member tribunal, this agreement will be honoured (see art. 5(4)).

[Revocation of arbitrator's appointment]

Article 10

(1) If either (a) any arbitrator gives written notice of his desire to resign as arbitrator to the LCIA Court, to be copied to the parties and the other arbitrators (if any) or (b) any arbitrator dies, falls seriously ill, refuses, or becomes unable or unfit to act, either upon challenge by a party or at the request of the remaining arbitrators, the LCIA Court may revoke that arbitrator's appointment and appoint another arbitrator. The LCIA Court shall decide upon the amount of fees and expenses to be paid for the former arbitrator's services (if any) as it may consider appropriate in all the circumstances.

(2) If any arbitrator acts in deliberate violation of the Arbitration Agreement (including these Rules) or does not act fairly and impartially as between the parties or does not conduct or participate in the arbitration proceedings with reasonable diligence, avoiding unnecessary delay or expense, that arbitrator may be considered unfit in the opinion of the LCIA Court.

(3) An arbitrator may also be challenged by any party if circumstances exist that give rise to justifiable doubts as to his impartiality or independence. A party may challenge an arbitrator it has nominated, or in whose appointment it has participated, only for reasons of which it becomes aware after the appointment has been made.

(4) A party who intends to challenge an arbitrator shall, within 15 days of the formation of the Arbitral Tribunal or (if later) after becoming aware of any circumstances referred to in Article 10.1, 10.2 or 10.3, send a written statement of the reasons for its challenge to the LCIA Court, the Arbitral Tribunal and all other parties. Unless the challenged arbitrator withdraws or all other parties agree to the challenge within 15 days of receipt of the written statement, the LCIA Court shall decide on the challenge.

1. Overview. Art. 10 sets out the circumstances in which an arbitrator's appointment may be revoked, as well as the mechanism for achieving this. It also gives the LCIA Court complete discretion when deciding how much should be paid to an outgoing arbitrator for his fees and expenses (art. 10(1)). Where English procedural law applies to the arbitration process, art. 10 does not exclude a party's statutory right to challenge an arbitrator under Section 24 English Arbitration Act. However, the Section 24 right is exercisable only after the art. 10 procedure has been exhausted.

2. Resignation of arbitrator. If an arbitrator wishes to resign from the tribunal, art. 10(1) requires him to give notice to the LCIA Court in writing, at the same time copying the notice to the parties and the other arbitrators (if any). His appointment is then revoked by the LCIA Court and a new arbitrator appointed in accordance with art. 11. In practice, a resigning arbitrator is required to provide a reason for his resignation, although, this is not specifically set out in the Rules.

3. Arbitrator unable or unfit to act, or lacking independence or impartiality. Art. 10 provides for the revocation of an appointment where the arbitrator dies, falls seriously ill, refuses to act, or becomes either unable or unfit to act (art. 10(1)); alternatively where circumstances exist which give rise to 'justifiable doubts' as to his impartiality or independence, irrespective of the way he has actually conducted himself in the arbitration (art. 10(3)). In these cases one or more of the parties or other arbitrators (if any) are expected to take the initiative and challenge the appointment or (in the case of the other arbitrators) 'request' the LCIA Court to revoke it (art. 10(1)). A party can challenge an arbitrator it has itself nominated, but where the challenge is based on 'justifiable doubts' it may do so only if the circumstances in question have arisen (or the party has become aware of the circumstances) after the appointment was made. The same applies where a party wishes to challenge an arbitrator in whose appointment it has participated (art. 10(3)).

4. Meaning of 'unfit to act'. Whether or not the LCIA Court decides to revoke an appointment on the ground that the arbitrator is 'unfit to act' in accordance with art. 10(1) will depend on whether he meets one or more of the three criteria set out in art. 10(2). This provides that an arbitrator is 'unfit' for these purposes if he (a) acts in deliberate violation of the arbitration agreement or the LCIA rules; (b) does not act fairly or impartially as between the parties; or (c) does not conduct or participate in the arbitration proceedings with reasonable diligence. Acting with 'reasonable diligence' includes avoiding unnecessary delay or expense. Art. 10(2) is broader in scope than the equivalent provisions in art. 3(6) of the previous (1985) edition of the LCIA rules. It now reflects, in part, the wording of Section 33 English Arbitration Act regarding the general duties of the tribunal (this is replicated almost word for word in art. 14).

5. Procedure. It is possible to challenge an arbitrator immediately after the appointment of the tribunal or later on in the proceedings. In the former case, the challenge has to be made within 15 days of the formation of the tribunal. In the latter case, the challenger has 15 days from the date he became aware of the circumstances which are the basis of his challenge. The challenge is made by sending a Written Statement to the LCIA Court, the tribunal and the other parties, setting out the reasons for the challenge. There then follows a further period of 15 days in which the arbitrator has the opportunity to resign and the other parties have the opportunity to express their agreement with the challenge. If neither of these things happens, the Court makes its decision, which is final and binding (art. 29(1)). Although the Court is not obliged to give its reasons, in the context of a challenge decision it will always do so (art. 29(1)). (In May 2006, it was decided that the LCIA Court's decisions on challenges to arbitrators would be published, in the form of abstracts.) The time limits imposed by art. 10(4) are strict (see by way of contrast art. 11(2) of the ICC rules, which gives a party 30 days to make a challenge). However, they serve the purpose of limiting the opportunities for abuse of the procedure by a party who wishes simply to gain a tactical advantage or to buy time. They also make it difficult for a party to challenge an arbitrator once the arbitration appears to be going against it. (See art. 32(1) regarding the parties' general duty to object 'promptly' to any non-compliance with any provision of the LCIA rules or the arbitration agreement; and art. 4, note 5 regarding the computation of time under the LCIA rules.) Decisions of the LCIA Court relating to all matters in the arbitration, including challenge decisions, are conclusive and binding on the parties and, to the extent permitted by the law of the seat of the arbitration, the parties shall be taken to have waived any right of appeal or review of such decision by the LCIA Court by any state court or other judicial authority. (See art. 29(1) and (2)).

6. Statutory right to challenge an arbitrator if seat of arbitration is in England. Art. 10 does not exclude a party's statutory right to challenge an arbitrator under Section 24 English Arbitration Act where English law applies. However, Section 24(2) provides that a state court will not exercise its power to remove an arbitrator unless it is satisfied that the applicant has first exhausted 'any available recourse' to the relevant institution or person, i.e. in an LCIA arbitration, the art. 10(4) procedure. The grounds on which a party may challenge an arbitrator under Section 24 are slightly different from those set out in art. 10(1) and (2). They are: that circumstances exist that give rise to justifiable doubts as to the arbitrator's impartiality; that he does not possess the qualifications required by the arbitration agreement; that he is physically or mentally incapable of conducting the proceedings or there are justifiable doubts as to his capacity to do so; or that he has refused or failed (i) properly to conduct the proceedings, or (ii) to use all reasonable despatch in conducting the proceedings or making an award. In addition, the state court must be satisfied that substantial injustice has been or will be caused to the applicant (Section 24(1)).

[Nomination and replacement of arbitrators]

Article 11

(1) In the event that the LCIA Court determines that any nominee is not suitable or independent or impartial or if an appointed arbitrator is to be replaced for any reason, the LCIA Court shall have a complete discretion to decide whether or not to follow the original nominating process.

(2) If the LCIA Court should so decide, any opportunity given to a party to make a re-nomination shall be waived if not exercised within 15 days (or such lesser time as the LCIA Court may fix), after which the LCIA Court shall appoint the replacement arbitrator.

1. LCIA Court's power to override agreed nomination procedure. In general, the LCIA Court will respect any nomination procedure agreed between the parties. (No such procedure is included in the arbitration clauses recommended by the LCIA, although the LCIA Secretariat is always pleased to discuss 'modifications to recommended clauses'.) However, where a party's initial nominee proves unacceptable, whether because he is lacking in impartiality or independence or because he is unsuitable in some other way, art. 11(1) gives the LCIA Court the freedom to reject the nominee and appoint an arbitrator of its own choosing, regardless of the wording of the parties' agreement. The Court has a similar freedom to override the parties' agreement and appoint a replacement arbitrator of its choosing where one of the original arbitrators has been removed for any reason. (In practice, the Court is likely to give the party concerned the opportunity to put forward a second nominee – see art. 11, note 3.)

2. Purpose of rule. Art. 11 is intended to ensure that the arbitration can proceed with minimal delay where the Court believes this to be the overriding priority. In practice the Court is most likely to use its powers under the article where a party acts in bad faith by deliberately putting forward unacceptable nominees in an attempt to delay the formation of the tribunal or the progress of an arbitration that is already under way. Art. 11 also serves to dissuade an arbitrator from resigning simply so as to buy time or gain some other tactical advantage for the party that appointed him (see also arts. 13 and 26(2) and (4)). (Art. 11 now has its counterpart in the ICC rules, art. 12(4), which was inspired by art. 11's predecessor, art. 3(5) in the previous (1985) edition of the LCIA rules. However, art. 12(4) ICC rules applies only to the replacement of arbitrators, not their initial appointment.)

3. Deadline for second nomination. Where the LCIA Court allows a party to make a nomination for a second time, art. 11(2) requires this to be done within 15 days. (The Court has the power to set an earlier deadline if it wishes.) (See art. 4(1) and (3) for details of how this time period should be calculated.) Again, art. 11(2) prevails over any contrary provisions in the arbitration agreement.

[Majority power to continue proceedings]
Article 12

(1) If any arbitrator on a three-member Arbitral Tribunal refuses or persistently fails to participate in its deliberations, the two other arbitrators shall have the power, upon their written notice of such refusal or failure to the LCIA Court, the parties and the third arbitrator, to continue the arbitration (including the making of any decision, ruling or award), notwithstanding the absence of the third arbitrator.

(2) In determining whether to continue the arbitration, the two other arbitrators shall take into account the stage of the arbitration, any explanation made by the third arbitrator for his non-participation and such other matters as they consider appropriate in the circumstances of the case. The reasons for such determination shall be stated in any award, order or other decision made by the two arbitrators without the participation of the third arbitrator.

(3) In the event that the two other arbitrators determine at any time not to continue the arbitration without the participation of the third arbitrator missing from their deliberations, the two arbitrators shall notify in writing the parties and the LCIA Court of such determination; and in that event, the two arbitrators or any party may refer the matter to the LCIA Court for the revocation of that third arbitrator's appointment and his replacement under Article 10.

1. Overview. Arts. 10 and 11 allow the LCIA Court (among other things) to remove and replace an arbitrator who fails to conduct or participate in an arbitration with 'reasonable diligence'. However, in arbitrations conducted by a three-member tribunal, art. 12 provides another solution to the problem. Instead of going through the lengthy and expensive procedure of arranging a change of arbitrator, the other two arbitrators may proceed with the arbitration on their own, making decisions, rulings and awards as necessary, provided the behaviour of the third arbitrator amounts to a refusal to act or at least a persistent failure to participate in the tribunal's deliberations. Before they do this, art. 12(1) requires the remaining two arbitrators (generally known as the 'truncated tribunal') to issue a notice of refusal or failure to the Court, the parties and the third arbitrator. (For the tribunal's freedom to make an award notwithstanding the dissent or non-cooperation of one of its members, see art. 26(2) to (4).)

2. Arbitrators' decision. When considering whether to continue as a truncated tribunal or to request the removal and replacement of their colleague, the two arbitrators are obliged to take into account the three factors listed in art. 12(2), namely the stage reached in the arbitration, any explanation which the third arbitrator has given for his non-participation, and 'such other matters as [the two arbitrators] consider appropriate in the circumstances of the case'. The reasons for their decision have to be set out in every award, order or other decision which they subsequently make (art. 12(2)). If the two arbitrators discuss the issue between themselves, but decide not to proceed as a truncated tribunal, they are obliged to notify the Court, the parties and the third arbitrator of their decision (art. 12(3)). They are then free to request the removal of the arbitrator under art. 10 if they believe that to be the appropriate course of action.

3. History and purpose of rule. Provisions similar to those of art. 12 appeared in the c. 1926 edition of the LCIA rules. However, in its present form the article follows loosely art. 35 WIPO rules, which in turn is based on art. 11(1) AAA-ICDR rules. Art. 12, like art. 11, is meant to deter an arbitrator from indulging in obstructive tactics intended to benefit the party that nominated him; however, it may also be used where an arbitrator falls ill or dies. It is particularly useful as an alternative to art. 11 (i.e. to the removal and replacement of an arbitrator) where the arbitration has reached an advanced stage and the disruption and expense involved in appointing a new arbitrator would be disproportionate to the advantages of proceeding with a complete tribunal. (See also art. 26(2) to (4) regarding the making of an award where one of the three arbitrators dissents or defaults in any way.)

[Communications between parties and the Arbitral Tribunal]

Article 13

(1) Until the Arbitral Tribunal is formed, all communications between parties and arbitrators shall be made through the Registrar.

(2) Thereafter, unless and until the Arbitral Tribunal directs that communications shall take place directly between the Arbitral Tribunal and the parties (with simultaneous copies to the Registrar), all written communications between the parties and the Arbitral Tribunal shall continue to be made through the Registrar.

(3) Where the Registrar sends any written communication to one party on behalf of the Arbitral Tribunal, he shall send a copy to each of

the other parties. Where any party sends to the Registrar any communication (including Written Statements and Documents under Article 15), it shall include a copy for each arbitrator; and it shall also send copies direct to all other parties and confirm to the Registrar in writing that it has done or is doing so.

1. Communications between parties and arbitrators. Art. 13 requires the parties to communicate with the arbitrators (and vice versa) through the Registrar, at least until the tribunal is formed (art. 13(1)). From then on, the tribunal will usually direct that such communications may be made directly. However, the Registrar must continue to be copied simultaneously on all communications between the parties and the tribunal (art. 13(2)). This is an important consideration to be upheld throughout the whole of the arbitration.

2. Copying communications. Art. 13(3) governs written communications passing between a party and the Registrar. (These include, but are not limited to, Written Statements and Documents under art. 15.) It provides that, where the Registrar sends a written communication to a party on behalf of the tribunal, it will also send copies to the other parties. Similarly, where a party sends a communication to the Registrar it must copy in the other parties; confirm in writing to the Registrar that it has done, or is doing, this; and (where the communication in question is a Request or Response) inform the Registrar of the method of service used (arts. 1(1)(g) and 2(1)(e)). It is also required to supply the Registrar with one further copy of the communication for each member of the tribunal.

3. Communications with the LCIA Court. Since all communications from a party to the LCIA Court pass through (and are addressed to) the Registrar (art. 3(3)), these communications are also covered by the provisions of art. 13(3).

[Conduct of the proceedings]

Article 14

(1) The parties may agree on the conduct of their arbitral proceedings and they are encouraged to do so, consistent with the Arbitral Tribunal's general duties at all times:
- **(i) to act fairly and impartially as between all parties, giving each a reasonable opportunity of putting its case and dealing with that of its opponent; and**
- **(ii) to adopt procedures suitable to the circumstances of the arbitration, avoiding unnecessary delay or expense, so as to provide a fair and efficient means for the final resolution of the parties' dispute.**

Such agreements shall be made by the parties in writing or recorded in writing by the Arbitral Tribunal at the request of and with the authority of the parties

(2) Unless otherwise agreed by the parties under Article 14.1, the Arbitral Tribunal shall have the widest discretion to discharge its duties allowed under such law(s) or rules of law as the Arbitral Tribunal may determine to be applicable; and at all times the parties shall do everything necessary for the fair, efficient and expeditious conduct of the arbitration.

(3) In the case of a three-member Arbitral Tribunal the chairman may, with the prior consent of the other two arbitrators, make procedural rulings alone.

1. Overview. Art. 14 governs the overall conduct of the arbitration. It gives considerable freedom both to the parties and to the tribunal, within the bounds set by Section 33 English Arbitration Act. (The provisions of that section are 'mandatory' where English law governs the arbitration (Section 4 and Schedule 1 English Arbitration Act).) The article is based on art. 5 of the 1985 edition of the LCIA rules (then an innovation), and corresponds to Art. 19 UNCITRAL model law.

2. Parties' freedom and duty. Art. 14 not only permits, but actively encourages the parties to agree as to how the arbitration should be run. However, any such agreement must be consistent with the tribunal's general duties under art. 14(1) (see note 3). The agreement should also be committed to writing, both by the parties and (with the authority and at the request of the parties) by the tribunal. The parties have an overriding duty (corresponding to that of the tribunal) to ensure the 'fair, efficient and expeditious' conduct of the arbitration (art. 14(2)).

3. Tribunal's general duties and discretion. The tribunal's general duties are set out in art. 14(1). They are to act fairly and impartially as between the parties, in particular giving each party a reasonable opportunity to put its case and to deal with that of its opponent. In addition, the tribunal must adopt procedures suitable to the circumstances of the arbitration. This includes avoiding unnecessary delay and expense, and providing 'a fair and efficient means for the resolution of the parties' dispute'. (The wording of this part of art. 14 is closely modelled on that of Section 33 English Arbitration Act.) Provided the arbitrators follow any agreement reached by the parties regarding the conduct of the arbitration and comply with the law(s) or rules of law which they decide are applicable, art. 14(2) gives the tribunal the 'widest discretion' in discharging its duties.

4. Chairman's power. Art. 14(3) gives the chairman of a tribunal the power to act alone on the tribunal's behalf, provided his fellow arbitrators agree to this in advance. However, the power extends only to procedural rulings, not to the making of an award. Note that it is not necessary to seek the parties' prior agreement. This power may be useful where it would be cumbersome or time-consuming to bring the entire tribunal together to deal with relatively minor procedural issues.

[Submission of written statements and documents]

Article 15

(1) Unless the parties have agreed otherwise under Article 14.1 or the Arbitral Tribunal should determine differently, the written stage of the proceedings shall be as set out below.

(2) Within 30 days of receipt of written notification from the Registrar of the formation of the Arbitral Tribunal, the Claimant shall send to the Registrar a Statement of Case setting out in sufficient detail the facts and any contentions of law on which it relies, together with the relief claimed against all other parties, save and insofar as such matters have not been set out in its Request.

(3) Within 30 days of receipt of the Statement of Case or written notice from the Claimant that it elects to treat the Request as its Statement of Case, the Respondent shall send to the Registrar a Statement of Defence setting out in sufficient detail which of the facts and contentions of law in the Statement of Case or Request (as the case may be) it admits or denies, on what grounds and on what other facts and contentions of law it relies. Any counterclaims shall be submitted with the Statement of Defence in the same manner as claims are to be set out in the Statement of Case.

(4) Within 30 days of receipt of the Statement of Defence, the Claimant shall send to the Registrar a Statement of Reply which, where there are any counterclaims, shall include a Defence to Counterclaim in the same manner as a defence is to be set out in the Statement of Defence.

(5) If the Statement of Reply contains a Defence to Counterclaim, within 30 days of its receipt the Respondent shall send to the Registrar a Statement of Reply to Counterclaim.

(6) All Statements referred to in this Article shall be accompanied by copies (or, if they are especially voluminous, lists) of all essential documents on which the party concerned relies and which have not previously been submitted by any party, and (where appropriate) by any relevant samples and exhibits.

(7) As soon as practicable following receipt of the Statements specified in this Article, the Arbitral Tribunal shall proceed in such manner as has been agreed in writing by the parties or pursuant to its authority under these Rules.

(8) If the Respondent fails to submit a Statement of Defence or the Claimant a Statement of Defence to Counterclaim, or if at any point any party fails to avail itself of the opportunity to present its case in the

manner determined by Article 15.2 to 15.6 or directed by the Arbitral Tribunal, the Arbitral Tribunal may nevertheless proceed with the arbitration and make an award.

1. Overview of timetable. Art. 15 sets out the procedural timetable for the submission of Written Statements (pleadings) and key documentary evidence. Essentially, the Written Statements succeed each other at 30-day intervals until the Respondent has served his Statement of Reply to Counterclaim (if any – note that, strictly speaking, this should be termed 'Statement of Reply to Defence to Counterclaim'). The timetable is not set in stone: the tribunal may vary it, as may the parties. (See art. 4, note 5 regarding the computation of time under the LCIA rules.)

2. Background to rule. The timetable set out in art. 15 is slightly tighter than that provided by the 1985 edition of the LCIA rules. (These allowed the Respondent 40 days to draw up his Statement of Defence (art. 6(3).) The inclusion of a Statement of Reply (art. 15(4)) reflects court procedure in Common Law jurisdictions. On the other hand, the requirement that the parties submit copies (or a list) of key documents with their Written Statements (art. 15(6)) is more characteristic of Civil Law systems. It is also common in international arbitration rules (see for example the similar, though not identical, wording of art. 18(2) of the UNCITRAL rules). In contrast to the ICC rules, art. 15 provides for no 'terms of reference' summarising the parties' claims.

3. Timing of Claimant's Statement of Case (particulars of claim). The Claimant's Statement of Case (particulars of claim) is due 30 days after receipt of written notification from the Registrar that the tribunal has been formed. If a Statement of Case is not necessary, the claim having been set out in full in its Request, the Claimant must send the Registrar a notice in lieu of the Statement. The notice should state that the Claimant elects to treat the Request as his Statement of Case (art. 15(2) and (3)), which election will take effect upon appointment of the tribunal.

4. Timing of Respondent's Defence. The Respondent's Statement of Defence is due 30 days after receipt of the Claimant's Statement of Case (or notice in lieu). Art. 15(3) does not say this, but the LCIA has indicated that if the Statement of Case or notice in lieu is submitted very early, before the parties are notified by the Registrar that the tribunal has been formed, the 30-day period for preparation of the Statement of Defence will run from receipt of such notification, and not from receipt of the Claimant's Statement of Case or notice in lieu. It is expected that the LCIA will clarify this point in the next edition of its rules.

5. Contents of Written Statements. In principle, the Statement of Case must contain a detailed account of the facts and any contentions of law on which the Claimant relies, together with the relief claimed against all other parties. The Statement of Defence must give details of which of the facts and contentions of law in the Statement of Case (or Request) the Respondent admits or denies, and explain the grounds on which it does this. It should also set out any other facts and contentions of law on which the Respondent wishes to rely. These rules apply equally to the Respondent's Counterclaim (if any) and the Claimant's Defence to Counterclaim, which must be included in the Statement of Defence and Statement of Reply respectively. Apart from this, art. 15 says nothing about the contents of the Claimant's Statement of Reply or the Respondent's Statement of Reply to Defence to Counterclaim (if any) (art. 15(2) to (5)).

6. Documents, samples and exhibits. As a rule, each Written Statement should be accompanied by copies of the essential documents on which the party relies, as well as any samples and exhibits which are relevant. However, where the documents in question are 'especially voluminous', a list of documents will suffice. Also, no document needs to be enclosed with a Written Statement twice, so if it has already been submitted in the proceedings, it need not be submitted again (art. 15(6)).

7. Party's default. Art. 15(8) makes clear that where a party fails to submit one of its Written Statements in accordance with the provisions of art. 15(2) to (6) or as directed by the tribunal, this will not prevent the tribunal from proceeding with the arbitration and making an award (see also art. 14(2), which gives the tribunal the widest discretion to discharge its duties under the applicable law and requires it to 'do everything necessary for the fair, efficient and expeditious conduct of the arbitration').

8. Agreement to amend timetable. Where the parties agree to amend the timetable set out in art. 15, they must comply with the formalities set out in art. 14 (see art. 14, note 2).

9. Communicating through the Registrar. Unless the tribunal has decided otherwise, all Written Statements must be submitted to the tribunal through the Registrar. (The Registrar must receive copies in any event.) (Art. 13(1) and (2))

10. Amendments to Written Statements. Once submitted, the parties may be able to amend their Written Statements, but only with the permission of the tribunal (art. 22(1)(a)).

[Seat of arbitration and place of hearings]

Article 16

(1) The parties may agree in writing the seat (or legal place) of their arbitration. Failing such a choice, the seat of arbitration shall be London, unless and until the LCIA Court determines in view of all the circumstances, and after having given the parties an opportunity to make written comment, that another seat is more appropriate.

(2) The Arbitral Tribunal may hold hearings, meetings and deliberations at any convenient geographical place in its discretion; and if elsewhere than the seat of the arbitration, the arbitration shall be treated as an arbitration conducted at the seat of the arbitration and any award as an award made at the seat of the arbitration for all purposes.

(3) The law applicable to the arbitration (if any) shall be the arbitration law of the seat of arbitration, unless and to the extent that the parties have expressly agreed in writing on the application of another arbitration law and such agreement is not prohibited by the law of the arbitral seat.

1. Terminology. Art. 16 follows common practice and treats the terms 'seat' and 'legal place' as synonymous. The physical location of individual hearings, meetings and deliberations may well be different from the seat/legal place of the arbitration as a whole. To make the distinction clear, art. 16 refers to the physical location of hearings, etc., as their 'geographical place'.

2. Scope of rule. Art. 16, which was introduced in the 1998 edition of the LCIA rules, deals with three related issues: the seat (or legal place) of the arbitration (art. 16(1)), the physical location of hearings, meetings and deliberations (art. 16(2)), and the law applicable to the arbitration. With the first and third of these (seat/legal place and applicable arbitral law), the principle of party autonomy applies, although the default position is that the seat of the arbitration is London and that, therefore, English arbitral law is applicable. The physical location of hearings, etc., is determined by the tribunal alone.

3. Seat (or legal place) of arbitration. Art. 16(1) governs the seat (or legal place) of the arbitration. The general rule is that the parties decide what the legal seat of the arbitration should be. This decision is important, since it determines the legal background against which the arbitration takes place, including the support (or lack of it) available from local courts. Ultimately, the seat of an arbitration also determines the nationality of any award and therefore the extent to which it is enforceable. (If the seat of the arbitration is in a country which is a party to the New York Convention, then it will be widely enforceable internationally.) Unusually, art. 16(1) provides that where the parties do not agree on the seat of the arbitration, this will generally be London. This compares with the ICC rules, art. 14(1) of which simply provides for the International Court of Arbitration to make the choice in the absence of agreement between the parties. (Art. 16(1) allows the LCIA Court to choose a seat other than London, but only if the alternative is 'more appropriate' given 'all the circumstances' and the parties have been given the opportunity to make representations in writing.)

4. Geographical place of hearings etc. Art. 16(2) gives the tribunal the freedom to hold hearings and meetings (and to make their deliberations) in any geographical place of their choosing. There is no requirement that most, or indeed any, of the hearings, etc., should be held in the legal seat of the arbitration, so (in theory at least) an LCIA arbitration can be conducted in its entirety at a location or locations wholly unrelated to its seat/legal place. The freedom art. 16(2) confers is not uncommon: similar or identical provisions can be found in many other international arbitration rules (see, for example, art. 16(2) of the UNCITRAL rules and art. 14(2) of the ICC rules). To avoid complications, art. 16(2) provides that the arbitration will be 'treated' as having been conducted at the seat of the arbitration, and the award will be 'treated' as having been made there. This wording was introduced in the 1998 edition of the LCIA rules and reflects the wording of Section 53 English Arbitration Act. It is intended to ensure, for example, that an award may be signed in any country and still be enforceable internationally under the New York Convention if the seat of the arbitration is in a Convention state. (See art. I New York Convention, which talks of an award being 'made in the territory of a State' etc.; also *Hiscox* v *Outhwaite* (House of Lords), which was decided before the English Arbitration Act was introduced. In that case it was held (controversially) that the place in which awards were signed was the place in which they were 'made' for the purposes of the Convention.) Naturally, where hearings, etc., are held in a country other than that of the seat of the arbitration, the law of that country should be respected, e.g. regarding the taking of evidence. Practitioners should also be aware of the danger that the arbitral law of the jurisdiction in which a hearing physically takes place may not recognise the possibility of the seat of the arbitration being elsewhere. In such a case, there is a risk that the arbitration may be held to have two legal seats, not one.

5. Applicable procedural law. Art. 16(3) provides that, as a general rule, the procedural law applicable to the arbitration (if any) is that of the seat of the arbitration (see art. 16(1)). However, the parties are free to agree otherwise, provided their agreement is recorded in writing. In theory, then, it is possible for an LCIA arbitration to be governed by the arbitral law of country A, to have its seat in country B, but to be conducted exclusively in country C. Art. 16(3) does however recognise that the law of the seat may not permit an arbitration to be governed by foreign procedural law, in which case the law of the arbitration will be that of the seat.

[Language of arbitration]

Article 17

(1) The initial language of the arbitration shall be the language of the Arbitration Agreement, unless the parties have agreed in writing otherwise and providing always that a non-participating or defaulting party shall have no cause for complaint if communications to and from the Registrar and the arbitration proceedings are conducted in English.

(2) In the event that the Arbitration Agreement is written in more than one language, the LCIA Court may, unless the Arbitration Agreement provides that the arbitration proceedings shall be conducted in more

than one language, decide which of those languages shall be the initial language of the arbitration.

(3) Upon the formation of the Arbitral Tribunal and unless the parties have agreed upon the language or languages of the arbitration, the Arbitration Tribunal shall decide upon the language(s) of the arbitration, after giving the parties an opportunity to make written comment and taking into account the initial language of the arbitration and any other matter it may consider appropriate in all the circumstances of the case.

(4) If any document is expressed in a language other than the language(s) of the arbitration and no translation of such document is submitted by the party relying upon the document, the Arbitral Tribunal or (if the Arbitral Tribunal has not been formed) the LCIA Court may order that party to submit a translation in a form to be determined by the Arbitral Tribunal or the LCIA Court, as the case may be.

1. Basic rule. Art. 17 allows the parties to choose the language of the arbitration. If they do not do this, either in the arbitration agreement or subsequently in writing, the arbitration is conducted in the language of the arbitration agreement unless and until the tribunal decides otherwise (see art. 17, rule 2) (art. 17(1)). Where the arbitration agreement is written in two languages, the LCIA Court will decide between them (art. 17(2)).

2. Tribunal's power. The tribunal will not change the language of the arbitration without first consulting the parties, giving each of them the opportunity to submit its comments in writing. The tribunal will also take into account the initial language of the arbitration (i.e. the disruption that would be caused by switching languages) and any other matters which it considers appropriate given 'all the circumstances of the case' (art. 17(3)). The tribunal's power to determine the language of the arbitration, absent any agreement by the parties, was introduced in the 1998 edition of the LCIA rules and brings them closer to the position, e.g. under the ICC rules. (The latter provide that the language of the arbitration shall be decided by the tribunal if not agreed between the parties. The language of the contract is simply one factor among others for the tribunal to take into account (art. 16 ICC rules).) Art. 17 is more flexible than its predecessor, art. 8(1) of the 1985 edition of the LCIA rules, which provided that an arbitration must be conducted in the language of the document(s) containing the arbitration agreement if the parties could not agree on any other. This frequently led to the parties incurring unnecessary costs in the form of translators' and interpreters' fees.

3. Use of English. Art. 17(1) is intended to prevent a recalcitrant party from challenging the validity of the arbitration or any award made on the basis that communications to and from the Registrar and the arbitration proceedings were conducted in English.

4. Translations. Where a document is submitted in a language other than that of the arbitration, it is advisable for the party submitting the document to provide a translation. However, it is not obliged to do so unless the tribunal makes an order to that effect. (Alternatively, the Court may make the order if the tribunal has yet to be formed.) (Art. 17(4))

[Party representation]

Article 18

(1) Any party may be represented by legal practitioners or any other representatives.

(2) At any time the Arbitral Tribunal may require from any party proof of authority granted to its representative(s) in such form as the Arbitral Tribunal may determine.

1. Freedom to choose representatives. Art. 18(1) reflects the wording of Section 36 English Arbitration Act: 'Unless otherwise agreed by the parties, a party to arbitral proceedings may be represented in the proceedings by a lawyer or other person chosen by him'. Art. 18(1) is unusual in expressly providing for the representation of a party by non-lawyers; however, most other rules allow this implicitly (see, for example, art. 21(4) of the ICC rules and art. 4 of the UNCITRAL rules). Under the LCIA rules, a party may also choose to represent himself, although art. 18 does not spell this out. (Art. 21(4) ICC rules is clearer in this respect.) When considering who should represent it in the arbitration, a party should not forget to consider the law of the arbitration's seat, which may preclude, e.g. representation by lawyers from another jurisdiction. (Such restrictions are increasingly uncommon, however.) In England, a party to an arbitration of any size will commonly be represented by a firm of solicitors. Solicitors may, in turn, instruct a barrister to deal with certain aspects of the case – although the larger firms with specialist arbitration practices will often handle arbitrations without any barrister assistance. It remains challenging for a lay client to instruct a barrister directly: although, since 2004, a self-employed barrister has been allowed to take instructions directly from a client, he is still forbidden by the relevant Code of Conduct (paragraph 401(b)) from generally managing a case, including corresponding with the other parties, instructing expert witnesses, collecting evidence for use in court, etc. (See art. 20, note 7 regarding the LCIA rules regarding contact between a witness and a party or its representatives generally.)

2. Proof of authority. Art. 18(2) gives the tribunal the power to request proof from a party that it has given its representative the necessary authority. In practice the tribunal is unlikely to ask for this unless requested to do so by another party to the arbitration.

[Hearings]

Article 19

(1) Any party which expresses a desire to that effect has the right to be heard orally before the Arbitral Tribunal on the merits of the dispute, unless the parties have agreed in writing on documents-only arbitration.

(2) The Arbitral Tribunal shall fix the date, time and physical place of any meetings and hearings in the arbitration, and shall give the parties reasonable notice thereof.

(3) The Arbitral Tribunal may in advance of any hearing submit to the parties a list of questions which it wishes them to answer with special attention.

(4) All meetings and hearings shall be in private unless the parties agree otherwise in writing or the Arbitral Tribunal directs otherwise.

(5) The Arbitral Tribunal shall have the fullest authority to establish time limits for meetings and hearings, or for any parts thereof.

1. Right to be heard. Art. 10(1) of the previous (1985) edition of the LCIA rules provided simply that a party had the right to be heard before the Tribunal unless the parties had agreed to a documents-only arbitration. This had the disadvantage that a tribunal was obliged to convene a hearing if one or more of the parties refused to participate in the arbitration, even where the active participants were happy to have the dispute dealt with on a documents-only basis. The present rule (art. 19(1)) solves this problem by allowing a party the right to demand a hearing only where it intends to exercise that right by making oral submissions in relation to the merits of the dispute. (As before, the right is subject to the parties' agreement to conduct the arbitration on a documents-only basis. Under the current rules, an agreement of this kind must be recorded by them in writing.) Art. 19(1) is similar in effect to art. 20(2) and (6) of the ICC rules and art. 15(2) of the UNCITRAL rules and, in combination with art. 20(4) regarding the right to cross-examine other parties' witnesses (see art. 20, note 5), is sufficient to prevent a party claiming after the event that it has been denied the opportunity of a hearing and thus of a fair arbitration. Further, despite the reference in Art. 19(1) to 'merits', in practice a tribunal will usually convene an oral hearing to deal with important interim matters, such as jurisdiction challenges or interim measures, unless all parties agree to dispense with a hearing.

2. Costs. Parties should beware of calling for a hearing which might need to be postponed or cancelled at short notice. Arbitrators are entitled to charge for time set aside for such a hearing, provided the LCIA Court agrees (see paragraph 4(c) Schedule of Arbitration Fees and Costs).

3. Timing and location of hearings. The tribunal alone decides when and where meetings and hearings take place (art. 19(2)) and how long they should last (art. 19(5)) (though this is subject to the Art. 16(2) requirement that the geographical location chosen must be 'convenient').

4. List of questions. Before a hearing, the tribunal has the power to present the parties with a list of questions which it wishes them to answer 'with special attention' (art. 19(3)).

5. Hearings in private. In general, hearings are held in private. However, this is subject to the parties agreeing differently in writing, and to any order of the tribunal (art. 19(4)). (For the participation of third parties in an arbitration, see art. 22(1)(h).)

[Witnesses]
Article 20

(1) Before any hearing, the Arbitral Tribunal may require any party to give notice of the identity of each witness that party wishes to call (including rebuttal witnesses), as well as the subject matter of that witness's testimony, its content and its relevance to the issues in the arbitration.

(2) The Arbitral Tribunal may also determine the time, manner and form in which such materials should be exchanged between the parties and presented to the Arbitral Tribunal; and it has a discretion to allow, refuse, or limit the appearance of witnesses (whether witness of fact or expert witness).

(3) Subject to any order otherwise by the Arbitral Tribunal, the testimony of a witness may be presented by a party in written form, either as a signed statement or as a sworn affidavit.

(4) Subject to Article 14.1 and 14.2, any party may request that a witness, on whose testimony another party seeks to rely, should attend for oral questioning at a hearing before the Arbitral Tribunal. If the Arbitral Tribunal orders that other party to produce the witness and the witness fails to attend the oral hearing without good cause, the Arbitral Tribunal may place such weight on the written testimony (or exclude the same altogether) as it considers appropriate in the circumstances of the case.

(5) Any witness who gives oral evidence at a hearing before the Arbitral Tribunal may be questioned by each of the parties under the control of the Arbitral Tribunal. The Arbitral Tribunal may put forth questions at any stage of his evidence.

(6) Subject to the mandatory provisions of any applicable law, it shall not be improper for any party or its legal representatives to interview any witness or potential witness for the purpose of presenting his testimony in written form or producing him as an oral witness.

(7) Any individual intending to testify to the Arbitral Tribunal on any issue of fact or expertise shall be treated as a witness under these Rules notwithstanding that the individual is a party to the arbitration or was or is an officer, employee or shareholder of any party.

LCIA Arbitration Rules, art. 20

1. Overview. Art. 20 governs the use of witnesses of fact and expertise in an LCIA arbitration. (Tribunal-appointed experts are dealt with in art. 21.) It allows for flexibility in the way in which a witness's evidence is presented to the tribunal, but makes it clear that some form of written record of each witness's evidence is generally required in advance of the hearing at which the witness is to appear (art. 20(1) and (2)). A witness on whose evidence one party seeks to rely should generally be made available for cross-examination where this is requested by another party (art. 20(4) and (5)). The LCIA rules are unusual in giving such detailed guidance regarding witness evidence. (See, by way of contrast, art. 20(3) of the ICC rules. For rules similar to the LCIA's art. 20, see art. 4 of the IBA Rules on the Taking of Evidence.).

2. Notice of witness evidence. Art. 20(1) allows the tribunal to order a party to give notice of the identity of each witness it intends to call (including rebuttal witnesses). The notice should include details of the subject matter of the witness's testimony, its content, and its relevance to the issues in dispute. Notices are generally exchanged by the parties in accordance with the relevant order of the tribunal (art. 20(2)).

3. Form of witness evidence. Art. 20(3) provides that the evidence of a witness, whether of fact or expertise, should generally be presented in the form of a signed witness statement or a sworn affidavit. However, the tribunal is free to order that another form of written testimony should be used (e.g. a witness summary). In some cases, the notice required under art. 20(1) may be sufficient. (Art. 20(2) and (3)).

4. Tribunal's power to exclude witnesses and limit testimony. Art. 20(2) expressly empowers the tribunal to forbid a witness to give evidence, or to limit a witness's appearance at a hearing. This applies whether the witness is one of fact or expertise.

5. Questioning of witnesses. Art. 20(4) allows a party to request the opportunity to cross-examine a witness on whose evidence another party seeks to rely. This is subject to any contrary agreement reached by the parties regarding the conduct of the arbitration, and to the other rights and obligations of the parties and the tribunal set out in art. 14(1) and (2) (see art. 14, notes 2 and 3). A party has the right to question (under the supervision of the tribunal) every witness who gives oral evidence in an arbitration, regardless of who called the witness and who seeks to rely on his evidence. At the same time, the tribunal may itself ask questions of the witness (art. 20(5)) or, indeed, propose a particular process such as witness conferencing (where opposing witnesses are typically questioned side-by-side).

6. Non-appearance of witnesses. Where a witness fails to appear at the hearing at which he is due to give evidence, and there is no good reason for this, the tribunal is free to deal with the written evidence of that witness as it wishes. It may place full or relatively little weight on it, or even exclude it altogether, depending on what the tribunal judges to be appropriate in the circumstances (art. 20(4); see also art. 22(1)(f), which gives the tribunal the power to decide whether or not to apply any strict rules of evidence (or any other rules) as to the admissibility, relevance or weight of any material submitted by a party).

7. Preparation of witness evidence. Art. 20(6) acknowledges that, in some jurisdictions, a party or party's representative may not be allowed to prepare a witness's written testimony, or even interview a witness before trial. However, unless an applicable law imposes a limitation of this sort, art. 20(6) allows a party or any of its representatives to interview a witness or potential witness with a view to presenting his written testimony or preparing him to give evidence in court. This reflects the position under, for example, the IBA Rules on the Taking of Evidence (art. 4(3)) and accords with international arbitration practice generally.

8. Who can give evidence. Art. 20(7) allows a party to give factual or expert evidence on its own behalf, i.e. to act as a witness in its own arbitration. Officers, employees and shareholders of a party may also appear as witnesses. This reflects the Common Law position, but not that of some Civil Law systems (see for, example, para. 445ff of the German Zivilprozessordnung (Civil Procedural Code)).

[Experts to the Arbitral Tribunal]

Article 21

(1) Unless otherwise agreed by the parties in writing, the Arbitral Tribunal:
- **(a) may appoint one or more experts to report to the Arbitral Tribunal on specific issues, who shall be and remain impartial and independent of the parties throughout the arbitration proceedings; and**
- **(b) may require a party to give any such expert any relevant information or to provide access to any relevant documents, goods, samples, property or site for inspection by the expert.**

(2) Unless otherwise agreed by the parties in writing, if a party so requests or if the Arbitral Tribunal considers it necessary, the expert shall, after delivery of his written or oral report to the Arbitral Tribunal and the parties, participate in one or more hearings at which the parties shall have the opportunity to question the expert on his report and to present expert witnesses in order to testify on the points at issue.

(3) The fees and expenses of any expert appointed by the Arbitral Tribunal under this Article shall be paid out of the deposits payable by the parties under Article 24 and shall form part of the costs of the arbitration.

1. Tribunal's power to appoint experts. Art. 21 regulates the appointment, evidence and fees of the tribunal's experts. (The parties' expert witnesses are covered by art. 20, which deals with witnesses generally.) The power of the tribunal in an LCIA arbitration to appoint one or more experts, independent of the parties' own expert witnesses, is by no means unusual – see, for example, art. 27(1) of the UNCITRAL rules and art. 22 of the AAA-ICDR rules. However, art. 21 is exceptional in allowing the parties a veto over this power. The veto can prove useful, for example, where the parties wish to limit the costs of the arbitration and believe their own witnesses to possess sufficient expertise to assist the tribunal in reaching its decision. (For a rule which gives the parties some influence over the tribunal's power, but not the right of veto, see art. 20(4) ICC rules. This obliges the tribunal to consult with the parties before making an appointment.)

2. Impartiality and independence of the tribunal's expert. Art. 21(1) provides that the tribunal's experts shall be impartial and independent throughout the arbitration (see art. 5(3) regarding the meaning of these terms).

3. Parties' duty to provide information and documents, etc. Art. 21(1)(b) requires parties to cooperate with the tribunal's expert(s), giving him such information and access to documents as the tribunal orders. The tribunal may also order a party to allow a tribunal-appointed expert to inspect goods, samples, property or a site.

4. Questioning the tribunal's expert. Art. 21(2) envisages that a party will be allowed to question a tribunal-appointed expert on his report once this has been delivered in writing or orally to the parties and the tribunal. However, the questioning will only happen if the party requests it or the tribunal thinks it necessary, and is subject to any agreement to the contrary reached by the parties and recorded by them in writing.

5. Oral evidence of parties' expert witnesses. Art. 21(2) also provides that, where the tribunal's expert is to be questioned at a hearing about the content of his report, the parties will have the opportunity to call their own expert witnesses to give oral evidence at the same hearing (or series of hearings) in relation to the points at issue. Again, this provision is subject to any agreement to the contrary reached by the parties and recorded by them in writing.

6. Fees of the tribunal's expert. Art. 21(3) provides for the fees and expenses of the tribunal's expert(s) to be paid initially out of the parties' deposits (see arts. 24 and 7(a) Schedule of Arbitration Fees and Costs). Unless the parties have agreed otherwise in writing, the tribunal generally decides who is responsible for the expert's fees and expenses when it allocates the costs of the arbitration as a whole at the same time as making its award (see art. 28(2)).

[Additional powers of the Arbitral Tribunal]
Article 22

(1) Unless the parties at any time agree otherwise in writing, the Arbitral Tribunal shall have the power, on the application of any party or of its own motion, but in either case only after giving the parties a reasonable opportunity to state their views:

    (a) to allow any party, upon such terms (as to costs and otherwise) as it shall determine, to amend any claim, counterclaim, defence and reply;

    (b) to extend or abbreviate any time limit provided by the Arbitration Agreement or these Rules for the conduct of the arbitration or by the Arbitral Tribunal's own orders;

    (c) to conduct such enquiries as may appear to the Arbitral Tribunal to be necessary or expedient, including whether and to what extent the Arbitral Tribunal should itself take the initiative in identifying the issues and ascertaining the relevant facts and the law(s) or rules of law applicable to the arbitration, the merits of the parties' dispute and the Arbitration Agreement;

    (d) to order any party to make any property, site or thing under its control and relating to the subject matter of the arbitration available for inspection by the Arbitral Tribunal, any other party, its expert or any expert to the Arbitral Tribunal;

    (e) to order any party to produce to the Arbitral Tribunal, and to the other parties for inspection, and to supply copies of, any documents or classes of documents in their possession, custody or power which the Arbitral Tribunal determines to be relevant;

    (f) to decide whether or not to apply any strict rules of evidence (or any other rules) as to the admissibility, relevance or weight of any material tendered by a party on any matter of fact or expert opinion; and to determine the time, manner and form in which such material should be exchanged between the parties and presented to the Arbitral Tribunal;

    (g) to order the correction of any contract between the parties or the Arbitration Agreement, but only to the extent required to rectify any mistake which the Arbitral Tribunal determines to be common to the parties and then only if and to the extent to which the law(s) or rules of law applicable to the contract or Arbitration Agreement permit such correction; and

    (h) to allow, only upon the application of a party, one or more third persons to be joined in the arbitration as a party provided any such third person and the applicant party have consented thereto in writing, and thereafter to make a single final award, or separate awards, in respect of all parties so implicated in the arbitration.

(2) By agreeing to arbitration under these Rules, the parties shall be treated as having agreed not to apply to any state court or other judicial authority for any order available from the Arbitral Tribunal under Article 22.1, except with the agreement in writing of all parties.

(3) The Arbitral Tribunal shall decide the parties' dispute in accordance with the law(s) or rules of law chosen by the parties as applicable to the merits of their dispute. If and to the extent that the Arbitral Tribunal determines that the parties have made no such choice, the Arbitral Tribunal shall apply the law(s) or rules of law which it considers appropriate.

(4) The Arbitral Tribunal shall only apply to the merits of the dispute principles deriving from 'ex aequo et bono', 'amiable composition' or 'honourable engagement' where the parties have so agreed expressly in writing.

1. Overview. Importantly, art. 22 gives the tribunal a number of powers in addition to those granted by specific provisions of the LCIA rules. The article is somewhat broader in scope (and more detailed) than its predecessor, art. 13 of the 1985 edition of the LCIA rules. It now gives the tribunal the power, for example, to decide whether or not to apply any strict rules of evidence as to the admissibility, relevance or weight of any material tendered by a party on any matter of fact or expert opinion (art. 22(1)(f)). (This reflects Section 34(2)(f) English Arbitration Act.) Other arbitration rules may give a tribunal similar powers, but these are generally not spelt out in such detail (see, for example, arts. 15 and 20 of the ICC rules, and arts. 15 and 24 of the UNCITRAL rules). The powers given to the tribunal under art. 22(1) are subject to any contrary agreement reached by the parties and recorded by them in writing. With the exception of the power to join third parties to the proceedings (art. 22(1)(h)), the powers may be exercised either on the tribunal's own initiative or at the request of one or more of the parties. In all cases the parties will be given a reasonable opportunity to make their views known before the tribunal takes action.

2. Permission to amend Written Statements. Art. 22(1)(a) allows the parties to amend their Written Statements after they have been submitted. However, this may only be done with the permission of the tribunal. This follows Common Law practice, which allows the parties to refine and correct their cases, where necessary and with appropriate permission, as the proceedings unfold. The power is not intended to allow parties to add new claims and, in practice, there is often a debate about whether the proposed amendment amounts in substance to a new claim. It is likely that the next edition of the rules will seek to address this.

3. Power to amend time limits. Art. 22(1)(b) gives the tribunal the power to amend any time limit, whether this is imposed by the rules, by the arbitration agreement, or by the tribunal itself. The period of time may be made shorter or longer than originally envisaged. (See also art. 4(7).)

4. Tribunal's enquiries. It may be appropriate for the tribunal to take the initiative in identifying the issues in dispute, ascertaining the relevant facts, and finding out which law(s) is applicable to the arbitration, the merits of the parties' dispute and the arbitration agreement. However, before it decides whether or not to do this, the tribunal may have to make preliminary enquiries. Art. 22(1)(c) allows it to do this (unless the parties agree otherwise), and also to make enquiries for other purposes, where these appear to the tribunal to be 'necessary' or 'expedient'. Art. 22(1)(c) is considerably more detailed than its predecessor, art. 13(1)(f) in the 1985 edition of the LCIA rules, although the thrust of the two articles is the same. The more recent wording underlines the freedom which the tribunal has in comparison to a judge in Common Law jurisdictions.

5. Inspection of property, etc. Art. 22(1)(d) gives the tribunal the power to order a party to make any relevant property, site, etc., available for inspection. The inspection can be carried out by another party, by the tribunal itself, or by the tribunal's or a party's expert(s). The property, etc., need not belong to the party ordered to allow inspection: it is sufficient if it is under that party's control.

6. Disclosure of documents. Art. 22(1)(e) reflects the Common Law practice of ordering 'discovery' or 'disclosure' of a party's documents. In Common Law litigation, such orders can be wide ranging, but in arbitration they must generally be much more specific and targeted, concentrated on either specific documents or narrowly defined classes of documents. Art. 22(1)(e) reflects this practice. As with art. 22(1)(d), such orders are not limited to documents belonging to a party: it is sufficient in this case if the documents are in a party's 'possession, custody or power'. In practice, 'document production' is a key stage of most arbitrations and will usually be provided for by the tribunal in the procedural timetable, often (with the parties' agreement) adopting the IBA Rules on the Taking of Evidence, either as a binding code or as 'guidelines'.

7. Rules of evidence. Under art. 22(1)(f), the tribunal may decide what strict rules of evidence (if any) should apply to the arbitration in respect of the admissibility, relevance or weight of any material submitted by a party, whether that material relates to fact or to expert opinion. For example, as a matter of English law, the general rule is that evidence of parties' pre-contractual negotiations (e.g. drafts of an agreement) is not admissible as a guide to interpretation; art. 22(1)(f) allows a tribunal to disregard this rule. The tribunal has a similar discretion in relation to any other rules it might wish to apply to such material, and is free to lay down rules as to when it should be exchanged between the parties and presented to the tribunal, as well as in what manner this should be done and in what form.

8. Correction of mistakes. Art. 22(1)(g) allows the tribunal to order the correction of a mistake in the arbitration agreement or any other contract between the parties, provided the mistake is common to the parties. However, the tribunal may not authorise corrections which are forbidden by the law(s) or other rules applicable to the agreement or contract in question.

9. Joinder of third party. Under art. 22(1)(h) a party may apply to the tribunal for a third party (or third parties) to be joined to the arbitration. The tribunal can comply with the request only if the applicant party and the third party agree to the joinder in writing. The other parties to the arbitration are given a reasonable opportunity to make their views known, but their agreement is not required. The tribunal itself may not take the initiative in joining a third party to the arbitration. When the arbitration is complete, the tribunal may make a single award (alternatively several separate awards) dealing with all the parties to the arbitration. Art. 22(1)(h) is one of the more controversial provisions of the LCIA rules. It is not clear that it is entirely compatible with the parties' undertaking of confidentiality (art. 30); nor is it clear what relationship exists between the non-applicant parties and the third party once the latter is joined to the arbitration. (They cannot logically be said to be parties to the same arbitration agreement.) Moreover, it is arguably unsatisfactory that the party joined to the arbitration has no opportunity to influence the composition of the tribunal where the initial parties had the right to nominate an arbitrator (see art. 5, note 9; art. 7, note 2; and art. 11, note 1) – although, as the third party must consent to joinder, presumably he would not do so unless he were content to submit to the jurisdiction of the existing tribunal. Art. 22(1)(h) is an expanded version of art. 13(1)(c) of the 1985 edition of the LCIA rules, and also echoes provisions in art. 41 of the c. 1931 edition of the rules regarding chains of contracts of sale. It differs from most other arbitration rules and laws, including Section 35 English Arbitration Act, which require the consent of all the parties before a third party can be joined to the arbitration. As at the end of 2008, approximately twelve applications had been made under art. 22(1)(h), of which five were granted and one case was settled before a decision had been made. (No figures are available in relation to art. 13(1)(c) in the 1985 edition of the LCIA rules.)

10. No right to apply to state court for order. Art. 22(2) precludes a party from applying to a state court (or other judicial authority) for an order available from the tribunal under art. 22(1). This is subject to any contrary written agreement between the parties. Where English law applies, this provision has the effect of preventing a party from seeking a ruling from a state court on a preliminary point of law.

11. Choice of law. Art. 22(3) recognises that it is primarily for the parties to choose the law(s) applicable to the merits of their dispute. Only where they have failed to agree on this will the tribunal choose the law or laws it decides is appropriate. This pragmatic approach ('voie directe') eschews national conflict of laws principles and is reflected, for example, in art. 17(1) ICC rules and art. 28(1) AAA-ICDR rules. All three rules use the term 'appropriate', though without explaining what this means. A tribunal may choose the law most closely associated with the subject matter of the dispute, but it is free to base its decision on other criteria.

12. Amiable composition, etc. It is possible for a tribunal to apply principles of 'amiable composition', i.e. their own, non-legal sense of what is right and fair in the circumstances, when deciding a dispute. However, art. 22(4) allows the tribunal to apply these principles only when expressly authorised by the parties to do so – usually in a so-called 'equity clause' in the arbitration agreement. (The other terms used in art. 22(4), 'ex aequo et bono' and 'honourable engagement', refer to the same concept as 'amiable composition'.) Equity clauses are favoured, for example, by parties who want a dispute to be decided by market rather than legal principles, or who prefer a tribunal not to be constrained by legal precedent. The effectiveness of art. 22(4) depends in practice on the law applicable to the arbitration. (Section 46 English Arbitration Act allows the use of 'amiable composition' principles (with the parties' agreement), though it does not use the term.) For provisions similar to those of art. 22(4), see for example art. 17(3) ICC rules and art. 33(2) UNCITRAL rules.

[Jurisdiction of the Arbitral Tribunal]

Article 23

(1) The Arbitral Tribunal shall have the power to rule on its own jurisdiction, including any objection to the initial or continuing existence, validity or effectiveness of the Arbitration Agreement. For that purpose, an arbitration clause which forms or was intended to form part of another agreement shall be treated as an arbitration agreement independent of that other agreement. A decision by the Arbitral Tribunal that such other agreement is non-existent, invalid or ineffective shall not entail ipso jure the non-existence, invalidity or ineffectiveness of the arbitration clause.

(2) A plea by a Respondent that the Arbitral Tribunal does not have jurisdiction shall be treated as having been irrevocably waived unless it is raised not later than the Statement of Defence; and a like plea by a Respondent to Counterclaim shall be similarly treated unless it is raised no later than the Statement of Defence to Counterclaim. A plea that the Arbitral Tribunal is exceeding the scope of its authority shall be raised promptly after the Arbitral Tribunal has indicated its intention to decide on the matter alleged by any party to be beyond the scope of its authority, failing which such plea shall also be treated as having been

LCIA Arbitration Rules, art. 23

waived irrevocably. In any case, the Arbitral Tribunal may nevertheless admit an untimely plea if it considers the delay justified in the particular circumstances.

(3) The Arbitral Tribunal may determine the plea to its jurisdiction or authority in an award as to jurisdiction or later in an award on the merits, as it considers appropriate in the circumstances.

(4) By agreeing to arbitration under these Rules, the parties shall be treated as having agreed not to apply to any state court or other judicial authority for any relief regarding the Arbitral Tribunal's jurisdiction or authority, except with the agreement in writing of all parties to the arbitration or the prior authorisation of the Arbitral Tribunal or following the latter's award ruling on the objection to its jurisdiction or authority.

1. Origin of rule. Art. 23(1) and (2) are based on art. 14 of the 1985 edition of the LCIA rules. Art. 23(3) and (4) were introduced in the 1998 edition of the rules.

2. Kompetenz-Kompetenz. Art. 23(1) gives the tribunal the power to rule on its own jurisdiction (so-called 'Kompetenz-Kompetenz'). This includes the power to decide on the (initial and continuing) existence and validity of the arbitration agreement, as well as its effect. Whether the arbitration agreement is free-standing or forms part of a larger agreement (or was intended to do so), it is regarded for these purposes as an independent agreement. This has the important consequence, spelt out in art. 23(1), that the tribunal can decide that the larger agreement is less than fully valid or effective without undermining the arbitration agreement or the tribunal's own authority. (For similar provisions in other arbitration rules, see for example art. 6(4) ICC rules, art. 15(2) AAA-ICDR rules, and art. 21(2) UNCITRAL rules.)

3. Timing of pleas. Art. 23(2) requires a party who wishes to challenge the jurisdiction of the tribunal to do so in its Statement of Defence or (if it is the Claimant) in its Statement of Defence to Counterclaim. (Where English law applies, it is arguable that an earlier time limit applies by virtue of Section 31(1) English Arbitration Act. This requires 'an objection that the arbitral tribunal lacks substantive jurisdiction at the outset of the proceedings [to] be raised by a party not later than the time he takes the first step in the proceedings to contest the merits of any matter in relation to which he challenges the tribunal's jurisdiction'. Nominating an arbitrator would not be a 'first step' for these purposes, but submitting a Response in accordance with art. 2(1) might be, given the requirement for the Response to contain 'confirmation or denial of all or part of the claims advanced by the Claimant in the Request' (art. 2(1)(a)). (However, see also art. 15(3), which makes it clear that the first full statement of the Respondent's position is made in its Statement of Defence.) Where the tribunal has said that it will decide a particular matter which is outside the scope of its authority, a party must object to this

Nesbitt

'promptly' after the tribunal has indicated its intentions. (Where English law applies, Section 31(2) English Arbitration Act – a mandatory provision of the Act – requires the objection to be made 'as soon as possible' after the matter is raised.) The tribunal has the discretion to accept late pleas if there are extenuating circumstances. Otherwise the party concerned is deemed to have waived its right to object to the alleged irregularity.

4. Timing of tribunal's decision. The tribunal is not obliged to decide a challenge to its jurisdiction or authority straightaway. It may do so either in a separate award, or later in its award on the merits of the dispute (art. 23(3)). Which course it chooses is likely to depend on matters of convenience: for example, the degree of overlap between issues relevant to jurisdiction and the merits. If the overlap is significant, the tribunal may be more likely to decide jurisdiction and the merits in a single award.

5. Application to a state court, etc. Art. 23(4) forbids a party from taking its objection to a state court or judicial authority until the tribunal has made its decision. This rule is subject to any written agreement between the parties, and may be relaxed by the tribunal.

[Deposits]
Article 24

(1) The LCIA Court may direct the parties, in such proportions as it thinks appropriate, to make one or several interim or final payments on account of the costs of the arbitration. Such deposits shall be made to and held by the LCIA and from time to time may be released by the LCIA Court to the arbitrator(s), any expert appointed by the Arbitral Tribunal and the LCIA itself as the arbitration progresses.

(2) The Arbitral Tribunal shall not proceed with the arbitration without ascertaining at all times from the Registrar or any deputy Registrar that the LCIA is in requisite funds.

(3) In the event that a party fails or refuses to provide any deposit as directed by the LCIA Court, the LCIA Court may direct the other party or parties to effect a substitute payment to allow the arbitration to proceed (subject to any award on costs). In such circumstances, the party paying the substitute payment shall be entitled to recover that amount as a debt immediately due from the defaulting party.

(4) Failure by a claimant or counterclaiming party to provide promptly and in full the required deposit may be treated by the LCIA Court and the Arbitral Tribunal as a withdrawal of the claim or counterclaim respectively.

1. Interim and final payments. Art. 24(1) allows the LCIA Court to direct parties to make whatever interim and final payments ('deposits on account of costs') are required to fund the arbitration. The Court decides how much should be paid by each party, and is free to use the money to pay the arbitrators, any tribunal-appointed experts, and itself, as it sees fit (see also art. 7 Schedule of Arbitration Fees and Costs). (This represents a significant strengthening of the Court's role: in the 1985 edition of the LCIA rules these functions were exercised by the tribunal (art. 15(1)).) The Court's decisions are conclusive and binding, and need not be supported by reasons (art. 29(1)).

2. Consequences of default. Where a party fails to make a payment as directed, this has two possible consequences. First, the Court may direct the other party (or parties) to fill the gap in the Court's finances. When this happens, the sum in question becomes a debt due directly from the defaulting party to the paying party, and the latter may take immediate steps to recover the monies owing (arts. 24(3) and 28(2)). Second, where the defaulting party is the Claimant or Counterclaimant, the Court and tribunal may treat the default as a withdrawal of the claim or counterclaim respectively. (This sanction may be imposed even if the payment is merely delayed (art. 24(4).)

3. Tribunal's duty. The tribunal must satisfy itself that all necessary deposits have been paid. If the Court is out of funds, it may not proceed with the arbitration (art. 24(2)).

4. Account where monies are held. Art. 5(e) Schedule of Arbitration Fees and Costs requires payments made by the parties on account of the fees and expenses of the tribunal and of the LCIA to be held on trust in a designated client bank account managed by the LCIA. If any money is left in the account at the end of the arbitration, this is returned to the parties (with interest) in the same proportions as the deposits were made by the parties to the LCIA, unless the parties have agreed otherwise (see art. 28(5) and arts. 5(e) and 6 Schedule of Arbitration Fees and Costs).

5. Security for costs and costs generally. For the tribunal's power to order a claiming or counterclaiming party to give security for another party's costs, see art. 25(2). For the tribunal's power to award costs generally, see art. 28.

6. Registrar's authority. The Registrar may act for the Court in ordering the parties to make interim, final or substitute payments, and in releasing monies from the relevant client account to the arbitrators, the arbitrators' experts (if any), and the LCIA itself. However, the Court, not the Registrar, decides any dispute which arises regarding the administration costs or the fees and expenses of the tribunal (art. 8 Schedule of Arbitration Fees and Costs).

[Interim and conservatory measures]
Article 25

(1) The Arbitral Tribunal shall have the power, unless otherwise agreed by the parties in writing, on the application of any party:

(a) to order any respondent party to a claim or counterclaim to provide security for all or part of the amount in dispute, by way of deposit or bank guarantee or in any other manner and upon such terms as the Arbitral Tribunal considers appropriate. Such terms may include the provision by the claiming or counterclaiming party of a cross-indemnity, itself secured in such manner as the Arbitral Tribunal considers appropriate, for any costs or losses incurred by such respondent in providing security. The amount of any costs and losses payable under such cross-indemnity may be determined by the Arbitral Tribunal in one or more awards;
(b) to order the preservation, storage, sale or other disposal of any property or thing under the control of any party and relating to the subject matter of the arbitration; and
(c) to order on a provisional basis, subject to final determination in an award, any relief which the Arbitral Tribunal would have power to grant in an award, including a provisional order for the payment of money or the disposition of property as between any parties.

(2) The Arbitral Tribunal shall have the power, upon the application of a party, to order any claiming or counterclaiming party to provide security for the legal or other costs of any other party by way of deposit or bank guarantee or in any other manner and upon such terms as the Arbitral Tribunal considers appropriate. Such terms may include the provision by that other party of a cross-indemnity, itself secured in such manner as the Arbitral Tribunal considers appropriate, for any costs and losses incurred by such claimant or counterclaimant in providing security. The amount of any costs and losses payable under such cross-indemnity may be determined by the Arbitral Tribunal in one or more awards. In the event that a claiming or counterclaiming party does not comply with any order to provide security, the Arbitral Tribunal may stay that party's claims or counterclaims or dismiss them in an award.

(3) The power of the Arbitral Tribunal under Article 25.1 shall not prejudice howsoever any party's right to apply to any state court or other judicial authority for interim or conservatory measures before the formation of the Arbitral Tribunal and, in exceptional cases, thereafter. Any application and any order for such measures after the formation of the Arbitral Tribunal shall be promptly communicated by the applicant to the Arbitral Tribunal and all other parties. However, by agreeing to arbitration under these Rules, the parties shall be taken to have agreed not to apply to any state court or other judicial authority for any order for security for its legal or other costs available from the Arbitral Tribunal under Article 25.2.

1. Overview. Art. 25 allows the tribunal (among other things) to order a party to provide security and to preserve or dispose of property relating to the subject matter of the arbitration. The article is divided into three parts. The first explains what the Respondent might be ordered to do (or refrain from doing); the second covers similar ground in respect of the Claimant; and the third regulates each party's freedom to seek similar orders from a state court or other judicial authority. Art. 25 is rather more detailed than similar provisions in other arbitration rules (e.g. art. 23(1) ICC rules and art. 26 UNCITRAL rules). This is because, where English law applies, Section 38 English Arbitration Act gives the tribunal only limited powers to make orders in respect of security and the preservation, etc., of property and evidence. Any further powers of this nature have to be granted explicitly by the parties to the tribunal (Section 39 English Arbitration Act). The tribunal will only exercise its powers under art. 25 on the application of a party (art. 25(1) and (2)).

2. Orders for security. Art. 25(2) gives the tribunal the power to order the Claimant to provide security in respect of the Respondent's legal and other costs in the arbitration ('security for costs'). If the parties have not agreed the contrary in writing, art. 25(1)(a) also gives the tribunal the power to order the Respondent to provide security, not for the Claimant's costs, but for all or part of the amount in dispute. (The same rules apply to the counterclaiming and respondent parties respectively in any counterclaim brought in the proceedings.) Security may be given in the form of a payment to the LCIA (held ring-fenced in an LCIA account) or a bank guarantee, or in some other form, depending on the precise terms of the tribunal's order. Where a claiming or counterclaiming party fails to provide the security ordered, the tribunal is empowered to stay the relevant claim or counterclaim or to dismiss it in an award. Where English law applies, the power to order security for costs may not be exercised on the ground that the Claimant or Counter-Claimant is (essentially) a non-UK individual or company (Section 38(3) English Arbitration Act). In practice, such orders are most often made where there are grounds to suspect that the Claimant may be seeking to insulate itself from liability for costs, for example where the Claimant is a shell company with few or no assets.

3. Cross-indemnities. Whether it is the Claimant or the Respondent who is ordered to give security, the tribunal may order the other party to give a cross-indemnity to cover the costs or losses incurred in providing the security. (The precise extent of these costs or losses is determined by the tribunal in one or more of its awards.) The tribunal may order that the cross-indemnity should itself be secured in some way (art. 25(1)(a) and (2)).

4. Orders to preserve property, etc. Unless the parties agree the contrary in writing, art. 25(1)(b) gives the tribunal the power to order the Respondent to preserve or store (or alternatively sell or dispose of in some other way) any property relating to the subject matter of the arbitration. The property in question must be in the control of the relevant party, but does not have to

5. Interim measures generally. Unless the parties agree the contrary in writing, the tribunal is empowered by art. 25(1)(c) to grant any relief on an interim basis which it would be entitled to grant in an award. This power extends (but is not limited) to ordering a party to make a payment or transfer other property to another party, or to prevent the dissipation of assets by a party.

6. Freedom to apply to state court, etc. By agreeing to arbitration under the LCIA rules, the parties agree not to apply to a state court or other judicial authority for an order that the Claimant (or a Counterclaimant) give security for costs. In other respects, the provisions of art. 25 do not prevent a party from seeking orders for interim or conservatory measures from a state court or other judicial authority before the tribunal is formed. It is even possible for a party to do this after the tribunal is formed, provided there are 'exceptional circumstances' and the application to the court/authority in question (and any resulting order) is copied 'promptly' to the tribunal and the other parties (art. 25(3)). This broadly reflects the position under Section 44 English Arbitration Act, which will generally apply where the seat of the arbitration is in England (art. 16(3)). Under Section 44(3) an English court will only intervene without the prior approval of the tribunal or the agreement of all the parties if 'the case is one of urgency', and then only to the extent 'necessary for the purpose of preserving evidence or assets'.

7. Enforcement of tribunal orders. If the law applicable to the arbitration process is English law, Section 42(1) and (2) English Arbitration Act allow a party to use court procedures to enforce orders made by the tribunal. However, this option is only open where procedures have been exhausted in the arbitration itself and the other party is late in complying with any order which the tribunal has made (Section 42(3) and (4)). It may also be excluded by agreement between the parties (Section 42(1)).

[The award]

Article 26

(1) The Arbitral Tribunal shall make its award in writing and, unless all parties agree in writing otherwise, shall state the reasons upon which its award is based. The award shall also state the date when the award is made and the seat of the arbitration; and it shall be signed by the Arbitral Tribunal or those of its members assenting to it.

(2) If any arbitrator fails to comply with the mandatory provisions of any applicable law relating to the making of the award, having been given a reasonable opportunity to do so, the remaining arbitrators may proceed in his absence and state in their award the circumstances of the other arbitrator's failure to participate in the making of the award.

(3) Where there are three arbitrators and the Arbitral Tribunal fails to agree on any issue, the arbitrators shall decide that issue by a majority. Failing a majority decision on any issue, the chairman of the Arbitral Tribunal shall decide that issue.

(4) If any arbitrator refuses or fails to sign the award, the signatures of the majority or (failing a majority) of the chairman shall be sufficient, provided that the reason for the omitted signature is stated in the award by the majority or chairman.

(5) The sole arbitrator or chairman shall be responsible for delivering the award to the LCIA Court, which shall transmit certified copies to the parties provided that the costs of arbitration have been paid to the LCIA in accordance with Article 28.

(6) An award may be expressed in any currency. The Arbitral Tribunal may order that simple or compound interest shall be paid by any party on any sum awarded at such rates as the Arbitral Tribunal determines to be appropriate, without being bound by legal rates of interest imposed by any state court, in respect of any period which the Arbitral Tribunal determines to be appropriate ending not later than the date upon which the award is complied with.

(7) The Arbitral Tribunal may make separate awards on different issues at different times. Such awards shall have the same status and effect as any other award made by the Arbitral Tribunal.

(8) In the event of a settlement of the parties' dispute, the Arbitral Tribunal may render an award recording the settlement if the parties so request in writing (a 'Consent Award'), provided always that such award contains an express statement that it is an award made by the parties' consent. A Consent Award need not contain reasons. If the parties do not require a consent award, then on written confirmation by the parties to the LCIA Court that a settlement has been reached, the Arbitral Tribunal shall be discharged and the arbitration proceedings concluded, subject to payment by the parties of any outstanding costs of the arbitration under Article 28.

(9) All awards shall be final and binding on the parties. By agreeing to arbitration under these Rules, the parties undertake to carry out any award immediately and without any delay (subject only to Article 27); and the parties also waive irrevocably their right to any form of appeal, review or recourse to any state court or other judicial authority, insofar as such waiver may be validly made.

1. Overview. Art. 26 deals with the tribunal's interim, final and additional awards. (These are equal in status and effect (arts. 26(7) and art. 27(3)).) It is mainly concerned with formalities, but includes important provisions allowing the tribunal to make an award notwithstanding the dissent or non-cooperation of one of its members (art. 26(2) to (4)); governing interest on awards (art. 26(8)); and precluding where legally possible a party's right to appeal (art. 26(9)).

2. Written award and reasons. Art. 26(1) obliges the tribunal to record its award(s) in writing. In general, the tribunal must explain the reasoning behind the award, although this is not required where the parties have agreed it is unnecessary or where the award merely records a settlement (art. 26(8)). An award should be signed by each of the arbitrators (or at least by those who assent to it), and should record the date on which it is made and the seat of the arbitration. (The seat determines where the award is made, which need not be the same as the geographical place at which it is signed – see art. 16(2), note 4.) Art. 26(1) reflects the wording of Section 52 English Arbitration Act.

3. No need for unanimity. It is not necessary for the members of a tribunal to come to unanimous decisions: issues can be decided by a majority of the arbitrators. Where there is no majority (e.g. because a truncated tribunal is operating – see art. 12, note 1), the chairman may decide any issue for the tribunal as a whole (art. 26(3)). Similarly, where an arbitrator refuses or fails to sign an award, or does so without complying with mandatory provisions of any applicable law, it is sufficient for the other arbitrators to sign the award or (in the absence of a majority) for the chairman alone to do this. However, in these circumstances the award must record the reason why the defaulting arbitrator has failed to sign the award or to comply with the relevant law, as the case may be (art. 26(2) and (4)).

4. Issuing an award. Awards are issued by the LCIA Court, not the tribunal. The procedure is for the tribunal chairman (or sole arbitrator) to deliver the award to the LCIA Court via the Registrar. The Registrar then transmits certified copies to the parties. The Registrar will only do this, however, after the Court has received sufficient funds to cover the entire costs of the arbitration (art. 26(5) and art. 9(b) Schedule of Arbitration Fees and Costs). (See art. 24, note 4 regarding the distribution of any excess monies held by the Court after a final award is made.)

5. Currency and interest. There is no need for an award to be expressed in a currency relating to the seat of the arbitration or its applicable law: any currency is permissible. In addition, the tribunal has complete discretion with regards to the interest which should accrue on any award made, provided that interest stops accruing as soon as the award is complied with. (This provision pre-empts arguments based on laws governing the interest payable on court judgments.) Interest may be simple or compound, and set at any rate which the tribunal thinks appropriate (art. 26(6)).

6. Settlement. When parties settle their dispute, the LCIA rules give them two choices. They may either request a consent award, or simply allow the tribunal to be discharged and the arbitration terminated. Either way, the parties need to write to the LCIA and to the tribunal saying that the case has been settled (and requesting a consent award if this is required). They also need to ensure that the LCIA Court has received sufficient money to cover the entire costs of the arbitration. Until these two things happen, the LCIA will not bring the arbitration to a close. Where a consent award is issued, it will describe itself as such and need not give any reasons (art. 26(8)).

7. No appeal allowed. Where English procedural law applies to the arbitration process, art. 26(9) and Section 69 English Arbitration Act combine to preclude any appeal to a state court on a point of fact or law. Parties who wish to reserve the right to appeal under Section 69 of the Arbitration Act should make express provision for this in their arbitration agreement. Simple errors or omissions may be remedied by the tribunal in accordance with art. 27, and awards can be challenged in the courts on jurisdictional grounds or because of serious irregularity under Sections 67 and 68 English Arbitration Act respectively, but otherwise an award once issued is final and binding. The House of Lords made clear in the Lesotho case that Section 68 cannot be used to challenge a mere error of law. In that case, the parties had agreed to arbitrate under the ICC Rules, which also exclude any right of appeal. An application was made under Section 68(2)(b), complaining of an erroneous exercise of a power conferred on the tribunal. However, the House of Lords held that this would not amount to an excess of power under Section 68(2)(b). Awards must be complied with promptly, 'immediately and without any delay', except to the extent that art. 27 applies (art. 26(9)).

[Correction of awards and additional awards]
Article 27

(1) Within 30 days of receipt of any award, or such lesser period as may be agreed in writing by the parties, a party may by written notice to the Registrar (copied to all other parties) request the Arbitral Tribunal to correct in the award any errors in computation, clerical or typographical errors or any errors of a similar nature. If the Arbitral Tribunal considers the request to be justified, it shall make the corrections within 30 days of receipt of the request. Any correction shall take the form of separate memorandum dated and signed by the Arbitral Tribunal or (if three arbitrators) those of its members assenting to it; and such memorandum shall become part of the award for all purposes.

(2) The Arbitral Tribunal may likewise correct any error of the nature described in Article 27.1 on its own initiative within 30 days of the date of the award, to the same effect.

(3) Within 30 days of receipt of the final award, a party may by written notice to the Registrar (copied to all other parties), request the Arbitral Tribunal to make an additional award as to claims or counterclaims presented in the arbitration but not determined in any award. If the Arbitral Tribunal considers the request to be justified, it shall

make the additional award within 60 days of receipt of the request. The provisions of Article 26 shall apply to any additional award.

1. Overview. Art. 27 allows for the correction of errors in an award, either at the request of a party (art. 27(1)) or on the tribunal's own initiative (art. 27(2)). It also allows the tribunal to make an additional award where the existing awards fail to deal with all claims and counterclaims presented in the arbitration. The tribunal may do this only at the request of one of the parties (art. 27(3)). (Additional awards are permitted by some, but by no means all, international arbitration rules. Compare, for example, art. 37 UNCITRAL rules, which is very similar to the LCIA's art. 27(1), to the ICC rules, which are silent on the subject.)

2. Errors which may be corrected. Art. 27(1) and (2) are drafted narrowly, allowing for the correction only of errors in computation, clerical or typographical errors, and 'errors of a similar nature'.

3. Procedure and time limits: correction of awards. Unless the parties agree in writing that an earlier deadline should apply, requests for the correction of errors must be submitted in writing to the Registrar, and copied to the other parties, within 30 days of the receipt of any award. The tribunal then has 30 days (counting from the day it received the request) to make the corrections requested, assuming it thinks the request justified. Where the tribunal corrects an award on its own initiative, it must do so within 30 days of the date the award is made (art. 27(1) and (2)). (See art. 4, note 5 regarding the computation of time under the LCIA rules; and art. 4, note 7 regarding the extension of time limits.)

4. Procedure and time limits: additional awards. If a party believes that an additional award is needed, this should be requested from the tribunal within 30 days of the receipt of the final award. (Copies of the request should be sent simultaneously to the other parties.) The tribunal then has 60 days (counting from the day it received the request) to make an additional award, if it believes the request to be justified. (Again, see art. 4, note 5 regarding the computation of time under the LCIA rules; and art. 4, note 7 regarding the extension of time limits.)

5. Form of correction. When it agrees to correct an award, the tribunal does not interfere directly with the original document, or produce a revised version of it. Instead, it issues a memorandum describing the errors that need to be corrected, and signed and dated by all the arbitrators (or at least by those who agree to it). From that point on, the memorandum forms part of the award for all purposes and should state on its face that it does so (art. 27(1)).

[Arbitration and legal costs]

Article 28

(1) The costs of the arbitration (other than the legal or other costs incurred by the parties themselves) shall be determined by the LCIA Court in accordance with the Schedule of Costs. The parties shall be jointly and severally liable to the Arbitral Tribunal and the LCIA for such arbitration costs.

(2) The Arbitral Tribunal shall specify in the award the total amount of the costs of the arbitration as determined by the LCIA Court. Unless the parties agree otherwise in writing, the Arbitral Tribunal shall determine the proportions in which the parties shall bear all or part of such arbitration costs. If the Arbitral Tribunal has determined that all or any part of the arbitration costs shall be borne by a party other than a party which has already paid them to the LCIA, the latter party shall have the right to recover the appropriate amount from the former party.

(3) The Arbitral Tribunal shall also have the power to order in its award that all or part of the legal or other costs incurred by a party be paid by another party, unless the parties agree otherwise in writing. The Arbitral Tribunal shall determine and fix the amount of each item comprising such costs on such reasonable basis as it thinks fit.

(4) Unless the parties otherwise agree in writing, the Arbitral Tribunal shall make its orders on both arbitration and legal costs on the general principle that costs should reflect the parties' relative success and failure in the award or arbitration, except where it appears to the Arbitral Tribunal that in the particular circumstances this general approach is inappropriate. Any order for costs shall be made with reasons in the award containing such order.

(5) If the arbitration is abandoned, suspended or concluded, by agreement or otherwise, before the final award is made, the parties shall remain jointly and severally liable to pay to the LCIA and the Arbitral Tribunal the costs of the arbitration as determined by the LCIA Court in accordance with the Schedule of Costs. In the event that such arbitration costs are less than the deposits made by the parties, there shall be a refund by the LCIA in such proportion as the parties may agree in writing, or failing such agreement, in the same proportions as the deposits were made by the parties to the LCIA.

ANNEX I. SCHEDULE OF ARBITRATION COSTS

(Effective 1 January 2010)

For all arbitrations in which the LCIA provides services, whether as administrator, or as appointing authority only, and whether under the LCIA Rules, UNCITRAL Rules or other, *ad hoc*, rules or procedures agreed by the parties to the arbitration.

LCIA Arbitration Rules, art. 28

(1) **Administrative charges under LCIA Rules, UNCITRAL Rules, or other, *ad hoc*, rules or procedures***
   (a) Registration Fee (payable in advance with Request for Arbitration non-refundable).   £1,500
   (b) Time spent** by the Secretariat of the LCIA in the administration of the arbitration.***
   Registrar / Deputy Registrar / Counsel   £200 per hour
   Other Secretariat personnel   £100 per hour
   (c) Time spent by members of the LCIA Court in carrying out their functions in deciding any challenge brought under the applicable rules.***   at hourly rates advised by members of the LCIA Court
   (d) A sum equivalent to 5% of the fees of the Tribunal (excluding expenses) in respect of the LCIA's general overhead.***
   (e) Expenses incurred by the Secretariat and by members of the LCIA Court, in connection with the arbitration (such as postage, telephone, facsimile, travel etc.), and additional arbitration support services, whether provided by the Secretariat or the members of the LCIA Court from their own resources or otherwise.***   at applicable hourly rates or at cost
   (f) The LCIA's fees and expenses will be invoiced in sterling, but may be paid in other convertible currencies, at rates prevailing at the time of payment, provided that any transfer and/or currency exchange charges shall be borne by the payer.
(2) **Request to act as Appointing Authority only***
   (a) Appointment Fee (payable in advance with request – non-refundable).   £1,000
   (b) As for 1(b) and 1(e), above.
(3) **Request to act in deciding challenges to arbitrators in non-LCIA arbitrations***
   (a) As for 2(a) and 2(b), above; plus
   (b) Time spent by members of the LCIA Court in carrying out their functions in deciding the challenges.   at hourly rates advised by members of the LCIA Court
(4) **Fees and expenses of the Tribunal***
   (a) The Tribunal's fees will be calculated by reference to work done by its members in connection with the arbitration and will be charged at rates appropriate to the particular circumstances of the case, including its complexity and the special qualifications of the arbitrators. The Tribunal shall agree in writing upon fee rates conforming to this Schedule of Arbitration Costs prior to its appointment by

the LCIA Court. The rates will be advised by the Registrar to the parties at the time of the appointment of the Tribunal, but may be reviewed annually if the duration of the arbitration requires.

Fees shall be at hourly rates not exceeding £400.

However, in exceptional cases, the rate may be higher or lower, provided that, in such cases, (a) the fees of the Tribunal shall be fixed by the LCIA Court on the recommendation of the Registrar, following consultations with the arbitrator(s), and (b) the fees shall be agreed expressly by all parties.

(b) The Tribunal's fees may include a charge for time spent travelling.

(c) The Tribunal's fees may also include a charge for time reserved but not used as a result of late postponement or cancellation, provided that the basis for such charge shall be advised in writing to, and approved by, the LCIA Court.

(d) The Tribunal may also recover such expenses as are reasonably incurred in connection with the arbitration, and as are in a reasonable amount, provided that claims for expenses should be supported by invoices or receipts.

(e) The Tribunal's fees may be invoiced either in the currency of account between the Tribunal and the parties, or in sterling. The Tribunal's expenses may be invoiced in the currency in which they were incurred, or in sterling.

(f) In the event of the revocation of the appointment of any arbitrator, pursuant to the provisions of Article 10 of the LCIA Rules, the LCIA Court shall decide upon the amount of fees and expenses to be paid for the former arbitrator's services (if any) as it may consider appropriate in all the circumstances.

(5) Deposits

(a) The LCIA Court may direct the parties, in such proportions as it thinks appropriate, to make one or several interim or final payments on account of the costs of the arbitration. The LCIA Court may limit such payments to a sum sufficient to cover fees, expenses and costs for the next stage of the arbitration.

(b) The Tribunal shall not proceed with the arbitration without ascertaining at all times from the Registrar or any deputy Registrar that the LCIA is in requisite funds.

(c) In the event that a party fails or refuses to provide any deposit as directed by the LCIA Court, the LCIA Court may direct the other party or parties to effect a substitute

payment to allow the arbitration to proceed (subject to any award on costs). In such circumstances, the party paying the substitute payment shall be entitled to recover that amount as a debt immediately due from the defaulting party.
- (d) Failure by a claimant or counterclaiming party to provide promptly and in full the required deposit may be treated by the LCIA Court and the Arbitral Tribunal as a withdrawal of the claim or counterclaim, respectively.
- (e) Funds lodged by the parties on account of the fees and expenses of the Tribunal and of the LCIA are held on trust in client bank accounts which are controlled by reference to each individual case and are disbursed by the LCIA, in accordance with the LCIA Rules and with this Schedule of Arbitration Fees and Costs. In the event that funds lodged by the parties exceed the costs of the arbitration at the conclusion of the arbitration, surplus monies will be returned to the parties as the ultimate default beneficiaries under the trust.

(6) **Interest on deposits**

Interest on sums deposited shall be credited to the account of each party depositing them, at the rate applicable to an amount equal to the amount so credited.

(7) **Interim payments**
- (a) When interim payments are required to cover the LCIA's administrative costs, or the fees or expenses of members of the LCIA Court, or the Tribunal's fees or expenses, including the fees or expenses of any expert appointed by the Tribunal, such payments may be made out of deposits held, upon the approval of the LCIA Court.
- (b) The LCIA may, in any event, submit interim invoices in respect of all current arbitrations, in March, June, September and December of each year, for payment direct by the parties or from funds held on deposit.

(8) **Registrar's authority**
- (a) For the purposes of sections 5(a) and 5(c) above, and of Articles 24.1 and 24.3 of the LCIA Rules, the Registrar has the authority of the LCIA Court to make the directions referred to, under the supervision of the Court.
- (b) For the purposes of section 7(a) above, and of Article 24.1 of the LCIA Rules, the Registrar has the authority of the LCIA Court to approve the payments referred to.
- (c) Any request by an arbitrator for payment on account of his fees shall be supported by a fee note, which shall include, or be accompanied by, details of the time spent

at the rates that have been advised to the parties by the LCIA.
(d) Any dispute regarding administration costs or the fees and expenses of the Tribunal shall be determined by the LCIA Court.

(9) **Arbitration costs**
(a) The parties shall be jointly and severally liable to the Arbitral Tribunal and the LCIA for the arbitration costs (other than the legal or other costs incurred by the parties themselves).
(b) The Tribunal's Award(s) shall be transmitted to the parties by the LCIA Court provided that the costs of the arbitration have been paid in accordance with Article 28 of the LCIA Rules.

* Charges may be subject to Value Added Tax at the prevailing rate.
** Minimum unit of time in all cases: 15 minutes.
*** Items 1(b), 1(c), 1(d) and 1(e) above, are payable on interim invoice; with the award, or as directed by the LCIA Court under Article 24.1 of the Rules.

1. Basic rule. Art. 28 regulates both the costs of the LCIA and the tribunal ('arbitration costs') and the legal and other costs incurred by the parties when preparing and presenting their cases. Arbitration costs consist of the fees and expenses of the arbitrators and tribunal-appointed experts (if any), as well as administrative charges levied by the LCIA itself (see the Schedule of Arbitration Fees and Costs, which are incorporated into the LCIA rules by virtue of their introductory wording). The basic principle is that the LCIA Court determines the costs of the arbitration, but the tribunal decides who should pay them (art. 28(1) and (2)). The tribunal also decides which party (if any) should pay its opponent's legal and other costs. The tribunal's costs orders will generally reflect the parties' relative success or failure in the award or arbitration, unless the parties have agreed otherwise or 'particular circumstances' make this approach appear 'inappropriate' (art. 28(3) and (4)). (Note that, where English procedural law applies, any agreement reached by the parties to the effect that one party must pay the whole or part of the costs of the arbitration in any event is only valid if made after the dispute in question has arisen (Section 60 English Arbitration Act).) In determining the relative success or failure of a party, the tribunal may adopt the approach of looking to the sums actually awarded to the parties. Alternatively it may adopt the approach (characteristic of the English courts) of looking also at the effectiveness of specific steps taken (e.g. the commissioning of an expert witness's report) in furthering a party's case, and the general conduct of the successful party.

2. Arbitration costs in LCIA arbitrations. The Court determines the arbitration costs by reference to the Schedule of Arbitration Fees and Costs currently in force (art. 28(1)). Art. 4 of the Schedule restricts, among other things, the way in which an arbitrator is allowed to charge for his services (by the hour, rather than by reference to the sum in dispute) and his expenses. It also sets out normal upper limit to his fee rate: currently GBP 400/hour. An arbitrator is deemed to agree to fee rates conforming with the Schedule when he accepts appointment to the tribunal (art. 5(3)). However, the Schedule does provide for exceptional cases where an arbitrator's rates might be outside the specified range, e.g. if the value or complexity of the arbitration mean that a higher fee is appropriate. In such cases the Registrar recommends a suitable rate to the Court, which fixes the rate after consulting with the parties. All the parties must then expressly agree to the rate fixed by the Court. In other cases, the Registrar simply informs the parties of the fee rate agreed with the arbitrator. If the arbitration runs for many months, these may be revised on a yearly basis (art. 4 Schedule of Arbitration Fees and Costs). The other component of arbitration costs is the administrative charges levied by the LCIA itself. These comprise an initial registration fee of GBP 1,500, a sum equivalent to 5% on the fees of the tribunal, charges for time spent by the Registrar (or the Deputy Registrar or Counsel) and the Secretariat (GBP 200/hour and GBP 100/hour respectively), and various types of expenses (art. 1 Schedule of Arbitration Fees and Costs). The arbitration costs, once determined by the LCIA Court, are set out by the tribunal in its award (art. 28(2)).

3. Arbitration costs in non-LCIA arbitrations. The LCIA's charges are the same whether the arbitration is governed by the LCIA or the UNCITRAL rules. Where the LCIA acts as an appointing authority only, or is called upon to decide challenges to arbitrators in non-LCIA arbitrations, the initial fee is GBP 1,000, and no commission is charged on arbitrators' fees. Otherwise the Registrar's and Secretariat's fees are the same as those charged in an LCIA arbitration. (When deciding challenges to arbitrators, the Court also charges for its time at a rate of its choosing.) (Schedule of Arbitration Fees and Costs, arts. 2 to 4)

4. Parties' legal and other costs. When assessing a party's legal and other costs, the tribunal is free to adopt any approach it thinks fit, providing it is 'reasonable' and involves considering each element of the costs on an item by item basis. Note that, in accordance with the so-called indemnity principle, the tribunal will only assess costs which have been 'incurred'. In practice, this means that the party concerned must have already paid the costs or at least be legally liable for them (art. 28(3)).

5. Joint and several liability. However the tribunal chooses to allocate the costs of the arbitration, the parties remain jointly and severally liable to the LCIA and the tribunal for these until they are paid in full (art. 28(1) and art. 9(b) Schedule of Arbitration Fees and Costs; see also art. 24, note 2).

This is the case whether the arbitration is concluded in the regular way or is abandoned or suspended (by agreement or otherwise) before a final award is made (art. 28(5)). (The joint and several liability of the parties for arbitration costs was introduced in the 1998 edition of the LCIA rules.)

6. Deposits, interest and the distribution of excess monies. See art. 24, notes 1, 2, 4 and 6.

[Decisions by the LCIA Court]
Article 29

(1) The decisions of the LCIA Court with respect to all matters relating to the arbitration shall be conclusive and binding upon the parties and the Arbitral Tribunal. Such decisions are to be treated as administrative in nature and the LCIA Court shall not be required to give any reasons.

(2) To the extent permitted by the law of the seat of the arbitration, the parties shall be taken to have waived any right of appeal or review in respect of any such decisions of the LCIA Court to any state court or other judicial authority. If such appeals or review remain possible due to mandatory provisions of any applicable law, the LCIA Court shall, subject to the provisions of that applicable law, decide whether the arbitral proceedings are to continue, notwithstanding an appeal or review.

1. LCIA Court's decisions conclusive and binding. Under the LCIA rules, the LCIA Court's role is chiefly to appoint arbitrators (art. 5(5)) and, where necessary, remove and replace them (art. 10(1)); to order the parties to make final, interim and substitute payments (art. 24(1) and (3)); to determine arbitration costs (art. 28(1)); and to resolve any disputes regarding administration costs or the fees and expenses of the tribunal (art. 8(d) Schedule of Arbitration Fees and Costs). Art. 29(1) provides that the Court's decisions are final and binding, subject only to any right of appeal or review given by the mandatory provisions of the law(s) applicable to the arbitration. To limit the possibility of such an appeal or review, the Court's decisions are characterised as administrative in nature.

2. Reasons. The Court is not obliged to give reasons for any of its decisions (art. 29(1)). However, it always does so in the interests of transparency when rejecting a party's nomination of an arbitrator, when removing and replacing an arbitrator, as a result of a challenge. It will rarely do so when resolving disputes regarding administration costs or the fees and expenses of the tribunal.

3. Court's right to suspend the arbitration. Where a party chooses to appeal (or seek a review of) a decision of the Court, and the applicable law allows this, the Court has the option of suspending the arbitration, provided this is not forbidden by the applicable law (art. 29(2)).

[Confidentiality]

Article 30

(1) Unless the parties expressly agree in writing to the contrary, the parties undertake as a general principle to keep confidential all awards in their arbitration, together with all materials in the proceedings created for the purpose of the arbitration and all other documents produced by another party in the proceedings not otherwise in the public domain – save and to the extent that disclosure may be required of a party by legal duty, to protect or pursue a legal right or to enforce or challenge an award in bona fide legal proceedings before a state court or other judicial authority.

(2) The deliberations of the Arbitral Tribunal are likewise confidential to its members, save and to the extent that disclosure of an arbitrator's refusal to participate in the arbitration is required of the other members of the Arbitral Tribunal under Articles 10, 12 and 26.

(3) The LCIA Court does not publish any award or any part of an award without the prior written consent of all parties and the Arbitral Tribunal.

1. General. The LCIA rules are unusual in regulating explicitly and in detail the confidentiality of an arbitration (the WIPO rules also do this: see arts. 52 and 73 to 76). Art. 30, which contains the relevant provisions, was introduced in the 1998 edition of the LCIA rules. The effectiveness of the article depends largely on the laws which govern the production of documents in litigation, and in particular the case law which has developed in this area in Common Law jurisdictions (see, for example, the Australian *Cockatoo Dockyard* case, which confirmed the 'public interest' exception to the confidentiality of documents and other materials disclosed in court and arbitral proceedings). The article is in any case more effective during the course of the arbitration, when the tribunal can take measures to prevent or respond to any breach of confidentiality, than after the arbitration has ended.

2. Extent of confidentiality. Art. 30 protects the confidentiality of an arbitration in three ways. First, no part of an award may be published by the LCIA without the parties' prior written consent (art. 30(3)). The parties are similarly bound not to release the whole or part of an award to third parties (art. 30(1)). (In practice, the LCIA never publishes an award on its own initiative. When awards are published or released by the parties, these tend to relate to arbitrations conducted under the UNCITRAL rules, with the LCIA acting only as the appointing authority, and in particular where the arbitration concerns an investment dispute – see, e.g., *Occidental Exploration* v *Ecuador*.) Second, a party must keep confidential all materials created for the purposes of the arbitration and all documents disclosed by another party in the arbitration, except to the extent that the latter are already in the public domain. Art. 30(1) explicitly recognises that this second kind of confidentiality is subject to the legal duty of a party to disclose documents in litigation and when enforcing or challenging an award in a state court, etc. Third, the tribunal must keep its deliberations secret, not only from third parties, but also from the LCIA and the parties themselves. The only exception to this is when an arbitrator discloses to the LCIA Court the refusal of another member of the tribunal to participate in the arbitration (arts. 10, 12, 26 and 30(2)). See also art. 31(2), regarding the parties' contractual agreement not to require statements from arbitrators or the LCIA, or to call them as witnesses, once an arbitration has ended.

3. Confidentiality where English law applies. In *Emmott* v *Wilson*, the Court of Appeal confirmed that the general duty of confidentiality owed by the parties to arbitration may be waived in circumstances where to do so is in the legitimate interests of one of the parties, and/or it is in the public interest do so. The question of confidentiality was raised in the English Court of Appeal case of *City of Moscow* v *Bankers Trust*. Here the issue was the confidentiality not of arbitration proceedings as such, but of an application to a state court challenging an arbitration award on the ground of serious irregularity (Section 68 English Arbitration Act). The Court of Appeal accepted that an application of this kind would normally be heard in private. However, it ruled that the court decision resulting from such an application should generally be published, provided this could be done without disclosing confidential information. In deciding whether or not to allow publication of its judgment, the court should consider first and foremost the interests of the parties (and of parties to other pending or imminent proceedings) and not the interests or concerns of other parties such as the business community as a whole. As was noted by the English Court of Appeal in *Emmott* v *Michael Wilson & Partners Ltd*, there will be cases where the details of an arbitral dispute become public, e.g. where a court deals with a challenge to an award for serious irregularity or an appeal on a point of law (e.g. *Lesotho Highlands Development Authority* v *Impregilo SpA*) or where enforcement of an award is resisted on grounds of public policy (e.g. *Westacre* v *Jugo-Import-SPDR*).

[Exclusion of liability]

Article 31

(1) None of the LCIA, the LCIA Court (including its President, Vice Presidents and individual members), the Registrar, any deputy Registrar, any arbitrator and any expert to the Arbitral Tribunal shall be liable to any party howsoever for any act or omission in connection with any arbitration conducted by reference to these Rules, save where the act or omission is shown by that party to constitute conscious and deliberate wrongdoing committed by the body or person alleged to be liable to that party.

(2) After the award has been made and the possibilities of correction and additional awards referred to in Article 27 have lapsed or been exhausted, neither the LCIA, the LCIA Court (including its President, Vice Presidents and individual members), the Registrar, any deputy Registrar, any arbitrator or expert to the Arbitral Tribunal shall be under any legal obligation to make any statement to any person about any matter concerning the arbitration, nor shall any party seek to make any of these persons a witness in any legal or other proceedings arising out of the arbitration.

1. Scope of exclusion. The LCIA rules, like those of a number of other institutions (e.g. the ICC), seek to exclude liability for the institution's own acts and omissions and those of the arbitrators it appoints. However, unlike art. 34 ICC rules, art. 31(1) limits the exclusion so that it applies only to acts or omissions that do not amount to conscious and deliberate wrongdoing on the part of the body or individual concerned. Art. 31(1) needs to be read in the context of the law applicable to the contract between the relevant parties. Contractual relations between the parties and the LCIA are governed by English law (as a result of art. 4(2) Rome Convention) and are therefore subject to Section 74 English Arbitration Act. This limits the liability of an arbitral institution (including its employees and agents) to such of its acts and omissions as can be shown to have been made in 'bad faith'. (An institution is not liable for any of the acts or omissions of an arbitrator simply by virtue of having appointed or nominated him.) The governing law of contractual relations between the parties and the arbitrators is uncertain, but may generally be assumed to be that of the seat of the arbitration.

2. Agreement re: confidentiality. In order to preserve the confidentiality of the arbitration, as well as to protect the LCIA and its arbitrators, art. 31(2) provides that the LCIA shall not be under a legal obligation to make a statement concerning an arbitration once it has finished. An arbitration is finished for these purposes when a final award has been made and the procedures set out in art. 27 (regarding correcting and supplementing awards) have run their course or are time-barred. Art. 31(2) applies not only to the LCIA as an institution, but also to officers of the LCIA, the LCIA Court and its members, the arbitrators, and any expert appointed by the tribunal. In addition, none of these individuals may be asked by the parties to act as a witness in any legal (or other) proceedings arising out of the arbitration.

[General rules]

Article 32

(1) A party who knows that any provision of the Arbitration Agreement (including these Rules) has not been complied with and yet proceeds with the arbitration without promptly stating its objection to

such non-compliance, shall be treated as having irrevocably waived its right to object.

(2) In all matters not expressly provided for in these Rules, the LCIA Court, the Arbitral Tribunal and the parties shall act in the spirit of these Rules and shall make every reasonable effort to ensure that an award is legally enforceable.

1. Overview. Art. 32 contains general provisions aimed at smoothing the conduct of the arbitration. Art. 32(1) in effect forbids a party from raising a late objection (e.g. regarding an arbitrator's independence or impartiality – see also art. 10) to any breach of the provisions of the LCIA rules or the arbitration agreement. Art. 32(2) is similar to art. 35 ICC rules in requiring the parties, the tribunal and the LCIA Court to abide by the spirit as well as the letter of the rules. Unlike the ICC rules, which require 'every effort' to be made to ensure that an award is legally enforceable, the LCIA rules ask only that 'every reasonable effort' be made to this end.

AMERICAN ARBITRATION ASSOCIATION (AAA) INTERNATIONAL CENTRE FOR DISPUTE RESOLUTION (ICDR) INTERNATIONAL ARBITRATION RULES, 2009*

(Amended and effective 1 June 2009)

[Applicability of the International Arbitration Rules]

Article 1

(1) Where parties have agreed in writing to arbitrate disputes under these International Arbitration Rules or have provided for arbitration of an international dispute by the International Centre for Dispute Resolution or the American Arbitration Association without designating particular Rules, the arbitration shall take place in accordance with these Rules, as in effect at the date of commencement of the arbitration, subject to whatever modifications the parties may adopt in writing.

(2) These Rules govern the arbitration, except that, where any such rule is in conflict with any provision of the law applicable to the arbitration from which the parties cannot derogate, that provision shall prevail.

(3) These Rules specify the duties and responsibilities of the administrator, the International Centre for Dispute Resolution, a division of the American Arbitration Association. The administrator may provide services through its Centre, located in New York, or through the facilities of arbitral institutions with which it has agreements of cooperation.

1. Introduction to the AAA's International Rules and the ICDR. The American Arbitration Association ('AAA') has various different arbitration rules. These include, among others, the Commercial Arbitration Rules, the Construction Industry Arbitration Rules, as well as the International Arbitration Rules. These are available on the AAA's website (see <www.adr.org>). This commentary deals only with the International Arbitration Rules and will say little where a rule or part of a rule is self-explanatory. The International Centre for Dispute Resolution ('ICDR') was established in 1996 as the division of the AAA responsible for the administration of international disputes. The ICDR administers international disputes submitted to arbitration under any of the AAA Rules, including, therefore, the International Arbitration Rules (the 'Rules' or the 'International Arbitration Rules'). Its website is <www.icdr.org>. The addresses of the ICDR offices are given in Appendix A.

---

* Reproduced with permission of the American Arbitration Association (AAA) and the International Centre for Dispute Resolution (ICDR). The text reproduced here is valid at the time of reproduction. As amendments may from time to time be made to the text, please refer to the website <http://www.adr.org/icdr> for the latest version.

2. General. Art. 1 of the International Arbitration Rules describes the circumstances in which those Rules apply to an arbitration (art. 1(1)), limitations on their application (art. 1(2)), and the role of the administrator, the ICDR (art. 1(3)).

3. When the International Rules apply. In some cases, the parties to an arbitration agreement may agree that a case is to be arbitrated under the rules of the AAA, without specifying which of the particular AAA rules they have in mind. Given that there is no such thing as 'the AAA Rules' per se, a question arises as to which of the various AAA rules would apply when the parties simply designate the rules of the AAA, without specifying which ones. Art. 1(1) addresses this question and provides that where the parties have provided for arbitration of an 'international dispute' by the ICDR or the AAA under the AAA rules generically, without specifying which of the particular rules they want to have govern, the International Arbitration Rules shall apply. This raises the question of what is an 'international dispute' for the purposes of the Rules and who decides it. The ICDR relies on the criteria set forth in art. 1(3) of the UNCITRAL Model Law in determining whether a dispute is international. (See art. 1 of the UNCITRAL Model Law.) The paradigm example of an 'international dispute' for the purposes of art. 1 of UNCITRAL Model Law, and therefore of art. 1 of the International Arbitration Rules, is a dispute arising out of an agreement between parties from different countries. The ICDR will determine whether a case involves an 'international dispute' for the purpose of art. 1(1) based on the Notice of Arbitration (see art. 2). (See Michael Hoellering, 'Administering International Arbitration Proceedings: Explanation of How the AAA's Program Works', 53-WTR Disp. Resol. J. 64, 66 (1998).) The requirement that international disputes specifying the AAA rules generically will be arbitrated under the International Arbitration Rules changes a presumption under the previous version of the International Arbitration Rules that those Rules applied only when the parties explicitly chose them. Under the previous version of the Rules, the AAA's Commercial Rules were applied, even in international contexts, unless the parties explicitly designated the International Arbitration Rules. (See Michael Hoellering, 'Administering International Arbitration Proceedings: Explanation of How the AAA's Program Works', 53-WTR Disp. Resol. J. 64, 66 (1998).) (Now, if parties 'have provided for arbitration of an international dispute by … the American Arbitration Association without designating particular Rules', the ICDR Rules apply. In some cases, if only the AAA has been specified, parties may have access to different procedures depending on whether their dispute is characterised as international or domestic.)

4. Some differences between the International Rules and other AAA arbitration rules. It matters which of the various AAA rules apply to a dispute because there are some differences between the various rules (although parties can override the content of particular rules in their arbitration agreement). First, the International Arbitration Rules allow arbitrators to award attorneys' fees to the prevailing party, while the Commercial Rules do not explicitly authorise such an award (compare art. 31(d) International Arbitration Rules, with Rule 43(d)(ii) AAA Commercial Rules). Secondly, parties arbitrating under the International Arbitration Rules also 'expressly waive and forego any right to punitive, exemplary or similar damages unless a statute requires that compensatory damages be increased in a specified manner'. The AAA Commercial Rules have no such provision (see art. 28(5) International Arbitration Rules). Finally, the International Arbitration Rules incorporate the ICDR Guidelines for Arbitrators Concerning Exchanges of Information for cases convened after 31 May 2008, which suggest limitations on the scope of discovery (see art. 19(3), note 4 and Appendix B). The AAA Commercial Rules have no such limitations.

5. Application of International Rules in effect as of the date of the commencement of the arbitration. Art. 1(1) also provides that 'arbitration shall take place in accordance with these Rules, as in effect at the date of commencement of the arbitration', unless the parties have agreed otherwise. In other words, if the Rules were amended between the date of the agreement out of which the dispute arises and the date the arbitration was commenced, the Rules in effect at the date of the commencement of the arbitration, rather than those in effect on the date the agreement was entered into, will apply, unless the parties have agreed otherwise, for example, in their arbitration clause. Other arbitration rules have a similar provision (see, e.g., art. 6.1 ICC Arbitration Rules).

6. Mandatory rules. Art. 1(2) makes clear that the Rules cannot override mandatory rules of law, that is, such rules of law that apply irrespective of the agreement of the parties. As one commentator has noted, 'Mandatory rules limit the parties' autonomy', because parties may not avoid them through contract (Christoph Liebscher, 'European Public Policy After Eco Swiss', 10 Am. Rev. Int'l Arb. 81, 85 (1999)). Nathalie Voser suggests that mandatory rules are important for two reasons: 'First, since the traditional requirement of a connection between the contract and the chosen law (or at least the reasonableness of a specific choice) has been given up, mandatory rules of law have become the modern tool to restrict the parties' autonomy regarding choice of law. Second, the development of the notion of the Social State ("Sozialstaat") and its goal to regulate more and more purely private legal relationships to pursue economic and social public interests of the community has led to an increase in "Interventionist Rules" in the form of mandatory rules. Thus, very often the determination of which party wins may depend on the application or non-application of a mandatory rule.' (Nathalie Voser, 'Mandatory Rules of Law as a Limitation on the Law Applicable in International Commercial Arbitration', 7 Am. Rev. Int'l Arb. 319, 321 (1996).)

7. Role of ICDR. Art. 1(3) provides that the International Arbitration Rules specify the duties and responsibilities of the administrator, the ICDR. (See also art. 36 (the tribunal shall interpret Rules relating to its powers and duties and the ICDR shall interpret all others).)

CHAPTER 1. COMMENCING THE ARBITRATION

[Notice of Arbitration and Statement of Claim]

Article 2

(1) The party initiating arbitration ('claimant') shall give written notice of arbitration to the administrator and at the same time to the party against whom a claim is being made ('respondent').

(2) Arbitral proceedings shall be deemed to commence on the date on which the administrator receives the notice of arbitration.

(3) The notice of arbitration shall contain a statement of claim including the following:
- **(a) a demand that the dispute be referred to arbitration;**
- **(b) the names, addresses and telephone numbers of the parties;**
- **(c) a reference to the arbitration clause or agreement that is invoked;**
- **(d) a reference to any contract out of or in relation to which the dispute arises;**
- **(e) a description of the claim and an indication of the facts supporting it;**
- **(f) the relief or remedy sought and the amount claimed; and**
- **(g) may include proposals as to the means of designating and the number of arbitrators, the place of arbitration and the language(s) of the arbitration.**

(4) Upon receipt of the notice of arbitration, the administrator shall communicate with all parties with respect to the arbitration and shall acknowledge the commencement of the arbitration.

1. General. Art. 2 describes how to commence a claim under the International Arbitration Rules by the filing of a Notice of Arbitration (art. 2(1)), when that claim is deemed to have commenced (art. 2(2)), the contents of the Statement of Claim that is central to the Notice of Arbitration (art. 2(3)), and the ICDR's duties upon receipt of a Notice of Arbitration (art. 2(4)).

2. Commencement of arbitration by submission of Notice of Arbitration. Art. 2(1) provides that a claim is initiated by the submission of a Notice of Arbitration to the ICDR 'and at the same time' to the respondent. In serving a Notice of Arbitration on the respondent, the claimant must comply with art. 18(1), which sets forth how notices and other written communications are to be served on a party unless the parties have agreed on a different method, for example, in the agreement out of which the dispute arises. The ICDR requires that an initial fee be paid by a filing party when a claim, counterclaim or additional claim is filed, based on the amount of the claim. The current schedule, as of 31 December 2008, is set forth as Appendix C. For an updated schedule, please check the ICDR website, <www.icdr.org>, before filing. A sample Notice of Arbitration form is available at <www.adr.

org/si.asp?id=3849>. Claims can be filed electronically at <www.adr.org/fileacase>. When hard copies are used for filing, two copies of the Notice of Arbitration as well as the arbitration agreement itself, and the filing fee, should be submitted to the ICDR at its New York office (see Appendix A for the address.) While it is possible to file at ICDR's other offices, it is more efficient to submit hard copies directly to the ICDR's New York office, because all hard copies will ultimately be forwarded to the New York office if they are filed at another office of the ICDR.

3. Date of commencement of arbitration. It is important to note, for statute of limitations purposes, that, under art. 2(2), a proceeding is deemed to commence on the date of receipt of the Notice of Arbitration by the ICDR. Thus, if the Notice is mailed, the proceeding commences on the date of receipt by the ICDR, not on the date of mailing.

4. The Statement of Claim. Although art. 2(3) specifies in subparagraphs (a) to (g) the minimum contents of the Statement of Claim that forms part of the Notice of Arbitration, it can, in some cases, be prudent to go beyond this bare minimum when submitting a claim. Unlike in litigation, where notice pleading is the norm because pleadings are not seen by the jury and rarely read by a judge, in arbitration, the tribunal will almost certainly read the Notice of Arbitration so as to understand the case they have been selected to arbitrate. As a result, it is advantageous for a party to treat the submission of the Notice of Arbitration as an opportunity to advocate its case, rather than simply to lay out the bare elements of its claim. Thus, when providing the information required under art. 2(3)(e) – 'a description of the claim and the facts supporting it' – it is useful to provide some detail and to attach supporting documents.

5. Claimant's proposal regarding arbitrators. In art. 2(3)(g), the Rules provide that the Statement of Claim 'may include proposals as to the means of designating and the number of arbitrators, the place of arbitration and the language(s) of the arbitration'. It is worth noting in this context that the ICDR recommends that the parties address the number of arbitrators, the place of arbitration and the language of the arbitration in their arbitration clause. (See ICDR: Guide To Drafting Dispute Resolution Clauses, at <www.adr.org/si.asp?id=4945>.) The ICDR recommends the following model clauses: '"Any controversy or claim arising out of or relating to this contract, or the breach thereof, shall be determined by arbitration administered by the International Centre for Dispute Resolution in accordance with its International Arbitration Rules" or "Any controversy or claim arising out of or relating to this contract, or the breach thereof, shall be determined by arbitration administered by the American Arbitration Association in accordance with its International Arbitration Rules". The parties may wish to consider adding: (a) "The number of arbitrators shall be (one or three)"; (b) "The place of arbitration shall be (city and/or country)"; or (c) "The language(s) of the arbitration shall be_____".'

Fellas

[Statement of Defence and Counterclaim]

Article 3

(1) Within 30 days after the commencement of the arbitration, a respondent shall submit a written statement of defense, responding to the issues raised in the notice of arbitration, to the claimant and any other parties, and to the administrator.

(2) At the time a respondent submits its statement of defense, a respondent may make counterclaims or assert setoffs as to any claim covered by the agreement to arbitrate, as to which the claimant shall within 30 days submit a written statement of defense to the respondent and any other parties and to the administrator.

(3) A respondent shall respond to the administrator and the other parties within 30 days after the commencement of the arbitration as to any proposals the claimant may have made as to the number of arbitrators, the place of the arbitration or the language(s) of the arbitration, except to the extent that the parties have previously agreed as to these matters.

(4) The arbitral tribunal, or the administrator if the arbitral tribunal has not yet been formed, may extend any of the time limits established in this article if it considers such an extension justified.

1. General. Art. 3 describes how a respondent, having received the Notice of Arbitration, is to respond.

2. Submission of Statement of Defence. Art. 3(1) provides that the respondent 'shall' submit a Statement of Defence, together with any counterclaim or setoff defence (art. 3(2)), to the claimant, any other parties and to the ICDR within thirty days of the commencement of the arbitration. Again, art. 18(1) specifies how the statements are to be served on the other party. In complying with the thirty-day time limit and any other time limits in the Rules, it is important to consult art. 18(2) which specifies how time periods are to be calculated under the Rules. The same considerations in favour of a party treating the Notice of Arbitration as an opportunity to advocate its position apply equally to the Statement of Defence or Statement of Defence and Counterclaim. Art. 3(2) also provides that a claimant 'shall' submit a Statement of Defence to any counterclaim within thirty days. It is worth noting in this context that, under art. 15(3), a party is required to lodge any objection it may have to the tribunal's jurisdiction or to the arbitrability of a claim or counterclaim 'no later than the filing of the Statement of Defense, as provided in art. 3, to the claim or counterclaim that gives rise to the objection'.

3. Respondent's response to claimant's proposal regarding arbitrators. Under art. 3(3), the respondent is also required to provide, within thirty days after the commencement of the arbitration, its response to the claimant's proposal (made in the Statement of Claim in accordance with art. 2(3)(g)) as to the number of arbitrators, and the place or language(s) of the arbitration, unless the parties have agreed otherwise. This response is typically made in the Statement of Defence.

4. Extension of time limit to submit Statement of Defence. Art. 3(4) allows a party to make a request for an extension to the time limits set forth in art. 3 either to the tribunal, or to the ICDR if the tribunal has not yet been constituted. A request for an extension of time under art. 3 is likely to be made to the ICDR in the first instance because the tribunal is unlikely to be in place before a Statement of Defence to a claim or counterclaim is submitted. In practice, the ICDR will encourage the parties to agree amongst themselves regarding extensions of time, and will generally respect agreements to reasonable extensions. In the absence of an agreement among the parties, the ICDR does not, as a general matter, follow a liberal approach to the granting of extensions of the time limits but will consider a party's reasons for requesting an extension of time. It is worth noting in the context of discussing the Statement of Defence that art. 23(1) provides that '[i]f a party fails to file a statement of defence within the time established by the tribunal without showing sufficient cause for such failure, as determined by the tribunal, the tribunal may proceed with the arbitration'. The rationale for this is discussed in art. 23, notes 1-3.

[Amendments to claims]

Article 4

During the arbitral proceedings, any party may amend or supplement its claim, counterclaim or defense, unless the tribunal considers it inappropriate to allow such amendment or supplement because of the party's delay in making it, prejudice to the other parties or any other circumstances. A party may not amend or supplement a claim or counterclaim if the amendment or supplement would fall outside the scope of the agreement to arbitrate.

1. General. Art. 4 provides that a party may amend or supplement its claim, counterclaim, or defence, unless the tribunal does not consider it appropriate because of that party's delay, any prejudice to the other parties, or any other circumstances. Art. 4 also makes clear that no amendments may go beyond the scope of the original agreement to arbitrate. In other words, a party may not seek to include by amendment a claim that is not properly arbitrable.

CHAPTER 2. THE TRIBUNAL

[Number of arbitrators]

Article 5

If the parties have not agreed on the number of arbitrators, one arbitrator shall be appointed unless the administrator determines in its

discretion that three arbitrators are appropriate because of the large size, complexity or other circumstances of the case.

1. Number of arbitrators where clause is silent. Art. 5 addresses the number of arbitrators. As noted in art. 2, note 5, the ICDR recommends that the parties specify the number of arbitrators in their arbitration clause. Typically parties choose to have their dispute arbitrated either by one arbitrator or by three arbitrators. Art. 5 addresses the situation when the parties fail to agree on the number of arbitrators either in their arbitration clause or after a dispute has arisen. It provides that one arbitrator shall be appointed, unless the ICDR determines 'in its discretion that three arbitrators are appropriate because of the large size, complexity or other circumstances of the case'. In making its determination, the ICDR will typically consult with the parties regarding their respective views on the number of arbitrators in the event the parties do not agree on this.

2. Criteria used by ICDR to decide on number of arbitrators where clause is silent. While there is no absolute rule, once the amount in issue exceeds USD 500,000, the ICDR will begin to consider having three arbitrators, although this alone is not decisive. The ICDR will also consider the complexity of the case regardless of the amount in issue, and 'other circumstances', such as the need for expertise in different fields. For example, in a construction dispute, it may be helpful to appoint an engineer in addition to a lawyer.

[Appointment of arbitrators]

Article 6

(1) The parties may mutually agree upon any procedure for appointing arbitrators and shall inform the administrator as to such procedure.

(2) The parties may mutually designate arbitrators, with or without the assistance of the administrator. When such designations are made, the parties shall notify the administrator so that notice of the appointment can be communicated to the arbitrators, together with a copy of these Rules.

(3) If within 45 days after the commencement of the arbitration, all of the parties have not mutually agreed on a procedure for appointing the arbitrator(s) or have not mutually agreed on the designation of the arbitrator(s), the administrator shall, at the written request of any party, appoint the arbitrator(s) and designate the presiding arbitrator. If all of the parties have mutually agreed upon a procedure for appointing the arbitrator(s), but all appointments have not been made within the time limits provided in that procedure, the administrator shall, at the written request of any party, perform all functions provided for in that procedure that remain to be performed.

(4) In making such appointments, the administrator, after inviting consultation with the parties, shall endeavor to select suitable arbitrators. At

the request of any party or on its own initiative, the administrator may appoint nationals of a country other than that of any of the parties.

(5) Unless the parties have agreed otherwise no later than 45 days after the commencement of the arbitration, if the notice of arbitration names two or more claimants or two or more respondents, the administrator shall appoint all the arbitrators.

1. General. Art. 6 addresses the method of appointment of arbitrators. Art. 6(1) makes it clear that the parties can choose the method by which arbitrators are appointed either in their arbitration agreement or after a dispute has arisen, and requires that they inform the ICDR of such method. The ICDR advises parties to get in touch with the ICDR before the submission of a Notice of Arbitration to discuss the method of selecting arbitrators: 'Parties are encouraged, when writing their contracts or when a dispute arises, to request a conference, in person or by telephone, with the ICDR, to discuss an appropriate method for selection of arbitrators or any other matter that might facilitate efficient arbitration of the dispute. Under these rules, the parties are free to adopt any mutually agreeable procedure for appointing arbitrators, or may designate arbitrators upon whom they agree. Parties can reach agreements concerning appointing arbitrators either when writing their contracts or after a dispute has arisen. This flexible procedure permits parties to utilise whatever method they consider best suits their needs. For example, parties may choose to have a sole arbitrator or a tribunal of three or more. They may agree that arbitrators shall be appointed by the ICDR, or that each side shall designate one arbitrator and those two shall name a third, with the ICDR making appointments if the tribunal is not promptly formed by that procedure. Parties may mutually request the ICDR to submit to them a list of arbitrators from which each can delete names not acceptable to it, or the parties may instruct the ICDR to appoint arbitrators without the submission of lists, or may leave that matter to the sole discretion of the ICDR. Parties also may agree on a variety of other methods for establishing the tribunal. In any event, if parties are unable to agree on a procedure for appointing arbitrators or on the designation of arbitrators, the ICDR, after inviting consultation by the parties, will appoint the arbitrators. The rules thus provide for the fullest exercise of party autonomy, while assuring that the ICDR is available to act if the parties cannot reach mutual agreement. By providing for arbitration under these rules, parties can avoid the uncertainty of having to petition a local court to resolve procedural impasses. These rules, as administered by the ICDR, are intended to provide prompt, effective and economical arbitration services to the global business community.'

2. Parties' right to agree on arbitrators or method of their selection. Art. 6(2) provides that the parties may jointly agree on the arbitrator(s) or a method of selecting the arbitrators(s), with or without the assistance of the ICDR. This can be done even after a dispute arises.

3. Time limit for agreement on arbitrators or method of their selection. Art. 6(3) provides that if, forty-five days after the commencement of the arbitration, the parties have not jointly agreed on the arbitrator(s) or a method of selecting the arbitrator(s), the ICDR 'shall' appoint the arbitrators at the written request of 'any party'. One purpose of this forty-five-day time limit is to prevent delay. The fact that 'any party' can ask the ICDR to appoint the arbitrator(s) within forty-five days of the commencement of the arbitration ensures that one party cannot delay the arbitration by engaging in dilatory tactics in the appointment process.

4. The ICDR's authority to select the arbitrators where parties fail to agree. If the parties have not agreed upon either the arbitrator(s) or a method of selection, the ICDR has the authority under art. 6(4) to 'select suitable arbitrators', 'after inviting consultation with the parties'. The ICDR typically uses the 'list procedure' to do so, although use of such a procedure is not mandatory. Under the list procedure, the ICDR prepares a list of prospective arbitrators with experience in the subject matter of the arbitration and who otherwise meet any qualifications in the arbitration agreement, by consulting its roster of arbitrators. The ICDR reviews its roster of arbitrators regularly for the purpose of ensuring the quality of the arbitrators. Once a list is prepared, it is submitted to each party, which may delete some or all of the proposed arbitrators and rank others in order of preference. The administrator will then choose the most mutually acceptable arbitrator(s). (See Michael Hoellering, 'Managing International Commercial Arbitration: The Institution's Role', 49-Jun Disp. Resol. J. 12, 15 (1994).) Although, in principle, a party may delete all the proposed names on a list and seek a new list from the ICDR, the forty-five-day time limit in art. 6(3) operates to discourage a party from engaging in dilatory tactics in the appointment process, because, as noted, after the expiration of forty-five days, 'any party' may request that the ICDR appoint the arbitrator(s). Art. 6(4) also specifically provides that '[a]t the request of any party or on its own initiative' the ICDR may appoint arbitrators who are not nationals of the country of any party.

5. Selection of arbitrators in cases with more than two parties. Art. 6(5) addresses the situation where there are multiple parties to an arbitration. In such cases, the inability of co-claimants or co-respondents to agree on an arbitrator can result in a delay. As a result, art. 6(5) provides that, in such circumstances, the ICDR 'shall' appoint all the arbitrators, '[u]nless the parties agree otherwise no later than 45 days after the commencement of the arbitration'.

[Impartiality and independence of arbitrators]

Article 7

(1) Arbitrators acting under these Rules shall be impartial and independent. Prior to accepting appointment, a prospective arbitrator shall disclose to the administrator any circumstance likely to give rise

to justifiable doubts as to the arbitrator's impartiality or independence. If, at any stage during the arbitration, new circumstances arise that may give rise to such doubts, an arbitrator shall promptly disclose such circumstances to the parties and to the administrator. Upon receipt of such information from an arbitrator or a party, the administrator shall communicate it to the other parties and to the tribunal.

(2) No party or anyone acting on its behalf shall have any ex parte communication relating to the case with any arbitrator, or with any candidate for appointment as party-appointed arbitrator except to advise the candidate of the general nature of the controversy and of the anticipated proceedings and to discuss the candidate's qualifications, availability or independence in relation to the parties, or to discuss the suitability of candidates for selection as a third arbitrator where the parties or party designated arbitrators are to participate in that selection. No party or anyone acting on its behalf shall have any ex parte communication relating to the case with any candidate for presiding arbitrator.

1. The requirement of impartiality and independence. Art. 7 expresses the principle – central to international arbitration – that an arbitrator acting under the Rules shall be impartial and independent and that, before accepting an appointment, a prospective arbitrator shall disclose any circumstance likely to give justifiable doubts as to his impartiality or independence. This principle is critical because a failure by an arbitrator to respect it can form a basis for a challenge to an ultimate arbitral award. Thus, one of the few ways to challenge an arbitral award in the United States is to assert that it is the product of 'evident partiality' on the part of an arbitrator (9 U.S.C.A. §10(a)(2)). This has been construed by a plurality opinion of the United States Supreme Court to require 'that arbitrators disclose to the parties any dealings that might create an impression of possible bias' (*Commonwealth Coatings* v *Continental Casualty*). It is also worth noting, however, that courts in the United States have not vacated awards where an arbitrator has failed to disclose 'a trivial or insubstantial prior relationship between the arbitrator and the parties to the proceeding' (*Positive Software Solutions* v *New Century Mortgage*).

2. The notice of appointment. To ensure the impartiality and independence of its arbitrators and to assist them in fulfilling their disclosure obligations, the ICDR sends a prospective arbitrator a notice of appointment. This states that '[a]ny doubts should be resolved in favor of disclosure', and contains a questionnaire. The questions are given in Appendix D. A prospective arbitrator, accepting an invitation to serve, must also sign an Arbitrator's Oath, which is also set forth in Appendix D.

3. Ex parte communications. Art. 7(2) expresses the general rule prohibiting ex parte communications between any party and an arbitrator as well as a narrow exception (see note 4). United States courts have acknowledged the importance of this prohibition, noting that, 'Ex parte evidence to an arbitration panel that disadvantages any of the parties in their rights to submit and rebut evidence violates the parties' rights and is grounds for vacation of an arbitration award' under the Federal Arbitration Act, at 9 U.S.C. § 10. (See *Totem Marine* v *North American Towing* ('The ex parte receipt of evidence bearing on this matter constituted misbehavior by the arbitrators prejudicial to [the party's] rights'). See also *Pacific Reinsurance* v *Ohio Reinsurance*, in which the Ninth Circuit refused to overturn an award because the ex parte communication did not prejudice the opposing party.)

4. Scope of interview with prospective party-appointed arbitration. Although the general rule is that a party may not engage in ex parte communications with an arbitrator, there is a recognised, narrow exception also set forth in art. 7(2). Parties may communicate with 'a candidate for appointment as a party-appointed arbitrator' about the 'general nature of the controversy, to discuss the candidate's qualifications, availability or independence', or 'the suitability of candidates for selection as a third arbitrator where the parties or party-designated arbitrator are to participate in that selection'. This rule explicitly permits a common phenomenon in international arbitration – the interview with a candidate for appointment as a party-arbitrator before he is appointed. Although parties may not discuss the details of the case with the candidate, they can discuss his qualifications, availability and independence as well as potential candidates for presiding arbitrator (or chair) of the panel without violating art. 7. But art. 7 also provides that parties may not have 'any ex parte communication relating to the case with any candidate for presiding arbitrator'. The fact that art. 7 permits ex parte communications on narrow subjects only with a 'candidate for appointment' makes it clear that once the tribunal is constituted, there can be no further ex parte communications. (See also art. 16(4), prohibiting ex parte communications with the tribunal by providing that documents submitted to the tribunal must be submitted to the other party or parties at the same time.)

[Challenge of arbitrators]

Article 8

(1) A party may challenge any arbitrator whenever circumstances exist that give rise to justifiable doubts as to the arbitrator's impartiality or independence. A party wishing to challenge an arbitrator shall send notice of the challenge to the administrator within 15 days after being notified of the appointment of the arbitrator or within 15 days after the circumstances giving rise to the challenge become known to that party.

(2) The challenge shall state in writing the reasons for the challenge.

(3) Upon receipt of such a challenge, the administrator shall notify the other parties of the challenge. When an arbitrator has been challenged by one party, the other party or parties may agree to the acceptance of the challenge and, if there is agreement, the arbitrator shall withdraw.

The challenged arbitrator may also withdraw from office in the absence of such agreement. In neither case does withdrawal imply acceptance of the validity of the grounds for the challenge.

1. General. While art. 7 discusses an arbitrator's obligations prior to appointment, arts. 8 and 9 address the basis to challenge and method of challenging an arbitrator after he has been appointed.

2. Grounds to challenge an arbitrator. Under art. 8(1), a party may challenge an arbitrator 'whenever circumstances exist that give rise to justifiable doubts as to the arbitrator's impartiality or independence'. Article 8(1) provides that a party must challenge an arbitrator within fifteen days of being notified of his appointment or learning of the circumstances giving rise to the challenge. This is designed to prevent a party from adopting a wait-and-see approach to the arbitration by learning of a basis to challenge an arbitrator but waiting to see how the case turns out before deciding whether to assert it. It is important to note that the challenge must be made in writing, stating the reasons for the challenge (art. 8(2)), and that it be made to the ICDR, not to the tribunal. Challenges to arbitrators are relatively infrequent; recently, there have been about thirty challenges per year out of the approximately 600 cases per year administered by the ICDR.

3. Withdrawal of challenged arbitrator. Art. 8(3) provides that the ICDR must notify the other parties of the challenge. The Rules distinguish three situations in the event of the challenge. Two are addressed in art. 8(3). First, if all parties, having been notified of the challenge, accept it, the arbitrator must withdraw. Secondly, if, having been notified, not all parties accept the challenge, the arbitrator may withdraw, but is not required to. Art. 8(3) makes it clear that in neither situation does withdrawal by an arbitrator imply that there is any legitimacy to the challenge. Art. 9 addresses the third situation: not all the parties accept the challenge and the arbitrator does not withdraw (see art. 9).

[Administrator's authority to decide on challenges to arbitrators]

Article 9

If the other party or parties do not agree to the challenge or the challenged arbitrator does not withdraw, the administrator in its sole discretion shall make the decision on the challenge.

1. The ICDR's discretion to decide on a challenge. Art. 9 provides that when the parties do not all agree to a challenge and the arbitrator does not withdraw, the ICDR will decide on whether the challenge is valid. The ICDR typically invites the parties to submit their views.

2. The IBA Guidelines on Conflicts of Interests in International Arbitration. It is common knowledge that the International Bar Association has issued Guidelines on Conflict of Interests in International Arbitration. The ICDR does not consider itself to be bound by those Guidelines, although it may take them into account if the parties refer to them in their submissions in support of, or against, a challenge to an arbitrator.

[Replacement of an arbitrator]

Article 10

If an arbitrator withdraws after a challenge, or the administrator sustains the challenge, or the administrator determines that there are sufficient reasons to accept the resignation of an arbitrator, or an arbitrator dies, a substitute arbitrator shall be appointed pursuant to the provisions of Article 6, unless the parties otherwise agree.

1. Circumstances in which a substitute arbitrator is appointed. Art. 10 provides that, unless the parties agree otherwise, a substitute arbitrator shall be appointed pursuant to the provisions of art. 6 in the following circumstances: an arbitrator withdraws after a challenge (pursuant to art. 8); an arbitrator is removed by the ICDR after a challenge (pursuant to art. 9); the ICDR accepts the resignation of an arbitrator; or an arbitrator dies.

[Authority of two arbitrators on a three-person tribunal to continue arbitration without the third]

Article 11

(1) If an arbitrator on a three-person tribunal fails to participate in the arbitration for reasons other than those identified in Article 10, the two other arbitrators shall have the power in their sole discretion to continue the arbitration and to make any decision, ruling or award, notwithstanding the failure of the third arbitrator to participate. In determining whether to continue the arbitration or to render any decision, ruling or award without the participation of an arbitrator, the two other arbitrators shall take into account the stage of the arbitration, the reason, if any, expressed by the third arbitrator for such nonparticipation and such other matters as they consider appropriate in the circumstances of the case. In the event that the two other arbitrators determine not to continue the arbitration without the participation of the third arbitrator, the administrator on proof satisfactory to it shall declare the office vacant, and a substitute arbitrator shall be appointed pursuant to the provisions of Article 6, unless the parties otherwise agree.

(2) If a substitute arbitrator is appointed under either Article 10 or Article 11, the tribunal shall determine at its sole discretion whether all or part of any prior hearings shall be repeated.

1. Authority of majority of a three-person panel to continue arbitration without the third. Art. 11 applies only to a three-person tribunal and empowers two of the three arbitrators on the tribunal to continue an arbitration and render an award in the event that the other arbitrator fails to participate in the arbitration in circumstances other than those set forth in art. 10. By empowering the remaining arbitrators to proceed without the third, this provision prevents one arbitrator on a three-person tribunal from derailing an arbitration by refusing to participate. In making a decision about whether to continue without a third arbitrator, the remaining arbitrators must consider, inter alia, the stage of the arbitration and the reason, if any, the third arbitrator offers for refusing to participate. If the remaining arbitrators decide not to continue without a third arbitrator, the ICDR will declare that office vacant and, unless the parties agree otherwise, a third arbitrator will be appointed under art. 6.

2. Authority of tribunal to decide whether to repeat prior hearings if substitute arbitrator is appointed. Art. 11(2) provides that if a substitute arbitrator is appointed under arts. 10 or 11, the tribunal shall decide whether all or part of any prior hearings need to be repeated.

CHAPTER 3. GENERAL CONDITIONS

[Representation]

Article 12

Any party may be represented in the arbitration. The names, addresses and telephone numbers of representatives shall be communicated in writing to the other parties and to the administrator. Once the tribunal has been established, the parties or their representatives may communicate in writing directly with the tribunal.

1. General. Art. 12 makes it clear that any party may be represented in the arbitration. Typically this representation is by a lawyer. It also provides that, once the tribunal is constituted, the parties or their representatives may communicate directly with the tribunal, rather than through the ICDR.

[Place of arbitration]

Article 13

(1) If the parties disagree as to the place of arbitration, the administrator may initially determine the place of arbitration, subject to the power of the tribunal to determine finally the place of arbitration within 60 days after its constitution. All such determinations shall be made having regard for the contentions of the parties and the circumstances of the arbitration.

(2) The tribunal may hold conferences or hear witnesses or inspect property or documents at any place it deems appropriate. The parties shall be given sufficient written notice to enable them to be present at any such proceedings.

1. Place of arbitration where clause is silent. Art. 13 addresses the place – or legal seat – of the arbitration. As noted in art. 2, note 5, the ICDR advises the parties to designate the place of arbitration in their arbitration clause. Art. 13 addresses the situation when the parties have not done so and have been unable, after the dispute has arisen, to agree on the place of arbitration. Art. 13(1) makes it clear that the ICDR 'may initially determine the place of arbitration', but that the tribunal shall have the final say within sixty days after it is constituted. In making a determination as to the place of the arbitration, the ICDR will typically invite the comments of the parties. The selection of the place of arbitration is significant, as it will determine the lex arbitri, that is the procedural arbitration law that will apply.

2. No requirement that hearings held at place of arbitration. Art. 13(2) provides that the tribunal does not have to hold hearings at the legal seat of arbitration. Rather, it may hold hearings or conferences, or inspect property and documents, 'at any place it deems appropriate', provided that the parties are given sufficient written notice so that they can attend the proceedings.

[Language]

Article 14

If the parties have not agreed otherwise, the language(s) of the arbitration shall be that of the documents containing the arbitration agreement, subject to the power of the tribunal to determine otherwise based upon the contentions of the parties and the circumstances of the arbitration. The tribunal may order that any documents delivered in another language shall be accompanied by a translation into the language(s) of the arbitration.

1. Language of arbitration where clause is silent. Art. 14 addresses the language of the arbitration. As noted in art. 2, note 5, the ICDR recommends that the parties choose the language of the arbitration in their arbitration clause. Art. 14 addresses the situation when the parties have failed to do so and are otherwise unable to agree on the language. The language of the arbitration will affect the language in which documents such as memorials, briefs, witness statements and documentary evidence are submitted, and thus whether documentary evidence will need to be translated into the language of the arbitration, as well as whether an interpreter is needed to translate testimony into the language of the arbitration at any hearings.

2. Presumption that language of arbitration is that of contract. There is a presumption in art. 14 that, where the parties have failed to agree, the language of the arbitration shall be the language of the arbitration agreement. However, if the tribunal determines that circumstances make another language more appropriate, they may select another language.

[Pleas as to jurisdiction]

Article 15

(1) The tribunal shall have the power to rule on its own jurisdiction, including any objections with respect to the existence, scope or validity of the arbitration agreement.

(2) The tribunal shall have the power to determine the existence or validity of a contract of which an arbitration clause forms a part. Such an arbitration clause shall be treated as an agreement independent of the other terms of the contract. A decision by the tribunal that the contract is null and void shall not for that reason alone render invalid the arbitration clause.

(3) A party must object to the jurisdiction of the tribunal or to the arbitrability of a claim or counterclaim no later than the filing of the statement of defense, as provided in Article 3, to the claim or counterclaim that gives rise to the objection. The tribunal may rule on such objections as a preliminary matter or as part of the final award.

1. General. Art. 15 addresses the jurisdiction of the tribunal, with art. 15(1) addressing the doctrine of competence-competence, and art. 15(2) the doctrine of separability.

2. Tribunal's authority to rule on its jurisdiction. Art. 15(1) provides that an arbitral tribunal 'has the power to rule on its own jurisdiction'. Thus, if there is a disagreement between the parties as to whether a particular dispute should be resolved by arbitration, art. 15 provides that the arbitrators have jurisdiction to decide whether that dispute is arbitrable. It is important to be clear that, under United States law, the general rule is that a court – rather than an arbitration tribunal – is authorised to decide whether a particular dispute is arbitrable 'unless there is clear and unmistakable evidence' that the parties agreed to submit that dispute to an arbitrator (*First Options of Chicago* v *Kaplan*). At least two Courts of Appeals have held that an agreement to the language in art. 15(1) constitutes just such 'clear and unmistakable evidence' (*Qualcomm* v *Nokia*, accord. *Contec* v *Remote Solution*, interpreting art. 15 of the AAA Commercial Arbitration Rules, which, for relevant purposes, is identical to art. 15 of the International Arbitration Rules). Thus, there is solid authority for the proposition that where parties have agreed to arbitrate in the United States under the International Arbitration Rules, a tribunal has the authority to rule on its own jurisdiction.

3. Separability of arbitration clause from the contract. Art. 15(2) provides that 'an arbitration clause shall be treated as an agreement independent of the other terms of the contract', embodying the notion of separability. Thus, if there is an allegation that a contract is invalid or void then that allegation cannot form the basis of an attack on the tribunal's jurisdiction on the theory that, if the contract is invalid, then so is the arbitration clause contained within it. Art. 15(2) makes it clear that a finding that a contract is null and void does not render the arbitration clause contained within that contract invalid because that clause is treated as an independent agreement.

4. Deadline for raising jurisdictional objections. Art. 15(3) provides that a party must raise a jurisdictional objection no later than the Statement of Defence to a claim or counterclaim, submitted in accordance with art. 3. Art. 15(3) also makes it clear that the tribunal may address jurisdictional objections prior to the merits. This promotes the efficiency of the proceedings, because if the tribunal determines that it does not have jurisdiction, it will never have to decide on the merits.

[Conduct of the arbitration]

Article 16

(1) Subject to these Rules, the tribunal may conduct the arbitration in whatever manner it considers appropriate, provided that the parties are treated with equality and that each party has the right to be heard and is given a fair opportunity to present its case.

(2) The tribunal, exercising its discretion, shall conduct the proceedings with a view to expediting the resolution of the dispute. It may conduct a preparatory conference with the parties for the purpose of organizing, scheduling and agreeing to procedures to expedite the subsequent proceedings.

(3) The tribunal may in its discretion direct the order of proof, bifurcate proceedings, exclude cumulative or irrelevant testimony or other evidence and direct the parties to focus their presentations on issues the decision of which could dispose of all or part of the case.

(4) Documents or information supplied to the tribunal by one party shall at the same time be communicated by that party to the other party or parties.

1. Discretion of the tribunal regarding conduct of arbitration. Art. 16 addresses the conduct of the arbitration. Art. 16(1) provides that the conduct of the arbitration rests on the discretion of the tribunal subject only to the following limitations: 'the parties are treated with equality' and 'each party has the right to be heard and is given a fair opportunity to present its case'. It is worth stressing that, like other arbitration rules, the International Arbitration Rules do not set forth specific procedures for the conduct of an arbitration

– as would be set forth in the procedural rules governing civil litigation in national courts (such as the Federal Rules of Civil Procedure and state law counterparts in the United States). Thus, for example, there is no right for a party to conduct discovery or to submit dispositive motions as there is under the Federal Rules of Civil Procedure. This is up to the tribunal. It is also worth noting that the opportunity to be heard is limited to a 'fair opportunity'. The UNCITRAL Arbitration Rules, by contrast, provide in art. 15 that each party must be given 'a full opportunity' to present its case.

2. Tribunal's responsibility to expedite resolution of dispute. Art. 16(2) provides that the tribunal 'shall' conduct the proceeding with a view to 'expediting the resolution of the dispute'. This puts a premium on speed and makes it clear that the tribunal has an obligation, in establishing the procedures for the case, to get it resolved quickly within the constraints established by art. 16(1) of 'equality' and 'fair opportunity'. A tribunal typically holds a preparatory conference shortly after being constituted for the purpose of determining and scheduling the procedures for the conduct of the case.

3. Authority of tribunal to bifurcate case, direct order of proof and exclude evidence. Art. 16(3) contemplates that a tribunal may bifurcate a case, addressing, for example, the merits before damages, that it may exclude cumulative or irrelevant evidence and may direct the parties to focus their presentation on issues that would dispose of the entire case. Again, this promotes efficiency.

4. Submission of documents to tribunal and simultaneously to other party. Art. 16(4), providing that documents or information submitted by one party to the tribunal must be supplied to the other party or parties at the same time, is consistent with the prohibition on ex parte communications that applies once the tribunal is constituted as set forth in art. 7(2).

[Further written statements]

Article 17

(1) The tribunal may decide whether the parties shall present any written statements in addition to statements of claims and counterclaims and statements of defense, and it shall fix the periods of time for submitting any such statements.

(2) The periods of time fixed by the tribunal for the communication of such written statements should not exceed 45 days. However, the tribunal may extend such time limits if it considers such an extension justified.

1. General. Art. 17 addresses the submission of written statements in addition to the Statement of Claim and the Statement of Defence. Other written statements include pre-hearing briefs or memorials, witness statements and post-hearing briefs.

2. The tribunal's discretion regarding written statements. Art. 17(1) provides that the tribunal has the authority to determine whether any such written statements are to be submitted and, if so, the timetable for their submission.

3. Time limits for submission. Art. 17(2) provides that the time limit for the submission of such statements should be no more than forty-five days, subject to the tribunal's authority to grant extensions.

[Notices]

Article 18

(1) Unless otherwise agreed by the parties or ordered by the tribunal, all notices, statements and written communications may be served on a party by air mail, air courier, facsimile transmission, telex, telegram or other written forms of electronic communication addressed to the party or its representative at its last known address or by personal service.

(2) For the purpose of calculating a period of time under these Rules, such period shall begin to run on the day following the day when a notice, statement or written communication is received. If the last day of such period is an official holiday at the place received, the period is extended until the first business day which follows. Official holidays occurring during the running of the period of time are included in calculating the period.

1. General. Art. 18 addresses how notices, statements and written communications are to be served on a party and how time periods in the Rules are to be calculated.

2. Methods of service. Art. 18(1) provides that, unless the parties agree or the tribunal orders otherwise, notices, statements and written communications may be served by a variety of different methods, including e-mail.

[Evidence]

Article 19

(1) Each party shall have the burden of proving the facts relied on to support its claim or defense.

(2) The tribunal may order a party to deliver to the tribunal and to the other parties a summary of the documents and other evidence which that party intends to present in support of its claim, counterclaim or defense.

(3) At any time during the proceedings, the tribunal may order parties to produce other documents, exhibits or other evidence it deems necessary or appropriate.

1. General. Art. 19 addresses the burden of proof and the submission of evidence in the arbitration.

2. Burden of proof. Art. 19(1) specifies that each party has the burden of proving the facts on which it bases its claim or defence.

3. Summary of documents and evidence. Art. 19(2) gives the tribunal the discretion to order a party to provide to the tribunal and to the other party a summary of the documents and other evidence that party intends to present in support of its case.

4. ICDR Guidelines Concerning Exchanges of Information. As noted in art. 16, note 2, there is no right per se to disclosure under the International Arbitration Rules. This is left to the discretion of the tribunal. Art. 19(3) makes clear that the tribunal does have the discretion to order a party to produce 'documents, exhibits or other evidence it deems necessary or appropriate'. The ICDR recently issued the ICDR Guidelines for Arbitrators Concerning Exchanges of Information. The purpose is to promote 'the goal of providing a simpler, less expensive and more expeditious process'. Unless the parties agree otherwise in writing, the Guidelines apply to all international cases administered by the ICDR convened after 31 May 2008, 'and may be adopted by the tribunal in pending cases'. The ICDR has also made clear that the Guidelines 'will be reflected in amendments incorporated into the next revision of the ICDR Rules'. The Guidelines are contained in Appendix B.

[Hearings]

Article 20

(1) The tribunal shall give the parties at least 30 days advance notice of the date, time and place of the initial oral hearing. The tribunal shall give reasonable notice of subsequent hearings.

(2) At least 15 days before the hearings, each party shall give the tribunal and the other parties the names and addresses of any witnesses it intends to present, the subject of their testimony and the languages in which such witnesses will give their testimony.

(3) At the request of the tribunal or pursuant to mutual agreement of the parties, the administrator shall make arrangements for the interpretation of oral testimony or for a record of the hearing.

(4) Hearings are private unless the parties agree otherwise or the law provides to the contrary. The tribunal may require any witness or witnesses to retire during the testimony of other witnesses. The tribunal may determine the manner in which witnesses are examined.

(5) Evidence of witnesses may also be presented in the form of written statements signed by them.

(6) The tribunal shall determine the admissibility, relevance, materiality and weight of the evidence offered by any party. The tribunal shall take into account applicable principles of legal privilege, such as those

involving the confidentiality of communications between a lawyer and client.

1. Notice of hearings. Art. 20 addresses hearings. Art. 20(1) provides that the tribunal shall give the parties at least thirty days' advance notice of the date of the initial hearing and reasonable notice of subsequent hearings.

2. Notice of witnesses. Art. 20(2) provides that each party shall give at least fifteen days' notice to the tribunal and the other party of the witnesses it intends to present at the hearings, providing their names, addresses, subject of their testimony and the language in which they will testify. Notwithstanding this, the Rules also make it clear in art. 20(5) that the evidence of a witness may be presented in the form of a written witness statement – a common method of presenting the direct testimony of a witness in international arbitration. However, in such cases, the witness is typically required to appear at the hearings for cross-examination.

3. Privacy of hearings. Unlike litigation in the United States, where court proceedings are, as a general matter, open to the public, art. 20(4) provides that arbitral hearings are private. See also arts. 27 and 34. Art. 20(4) also authorises the tribunal to exclude a witness from hearings during the testimony of another witness, and to 'determine the manner in which witnesses are examined'.

4. Tribunal's discretion regarding evidence. Unlike litigation, where strict and detailed rules govern the admissibility, relevance, materiality and weight of evidence, such as the Federal Rules of Evidence and state law counterparts in the United States, art. 20(6) makes it clear that these issues are left entirely to the discretion of the tribunal.

[Interim measures of protection]

Article 21

(1) At the request of any party, the tribunal may take whatever interim measures it deems necessary, including injunctive relief and measures for the protection or conservation of property.

(2) Such interim measures may take the form of an interim award, and the tribunal may require security for the costs of such measures.

(3) A request for interim measures addressed by a party to a judicial authority shall not be deemed incompatible with the agreement to arbitrate or a waiver of the right to arbitrate.

(4) The tribunal may in its discretion apportion costs associated with applications for interim relief in any interim award or in the final award.

1. General. Interim relief is dealt with in both arts. 21 and 37. Art. 21 contains the rules governing the right to seek interim relief from the tribunal after it is constituted. Art. 37, a relatively new rule, sets forth the right to seek interim relief, on an expedited emergency basis, before the tribunal is constituted. Art. 37 was enacted to deal with a gap in the Rules, where a party might need interim relief prior to the constitution of the tribunal.

2. Tribunal's discretion regarding the issuance of interim relief. Art. 21(1) does not set forth any standards for the issuance of interim relief, providing only that 'the tribunal may take whatever interim measures it deems necessary'. Art. 21 also makes it clear that the tribunal may issue interim relief in the form of an interim award, that it may require security for the costs of such interim measures (art. 21(2)), and that it may, within its discretion, apportion the costs associated with an application for interim relief (art. 21(4)). Costs are addressed more generally in art. 31.

3. Application for interim relief not a waiver of the right to arbitrate. Art. 21(3) provides that an application to a judicial authority for interim protection is not a waiver of the right to arbitrate. However, it is not entirely settled in the United States whether federal courts have the authority to hear an application for interim relief under the Federal Arbitration Act. (See *In Re S & R Co. of Kingston v Latona Trucking, Inc.*: parties may seek interim relief from courts without waiving the right to arbitrate as long as they do not 'engage in litigation pertaining to substantial issues going to the merits'. But see, e.g, *James Associates* v *Anhui Machinery & Equipment*: 'Whether preliminary injunctive relief is available in actions governed by the Arbitration Act is not a completely settled area of federal law, but the majority of courts now hold that a grant of preliminary injunctive relief is not inconsistent with the Act, provided the court properly exercises its discretion in issuing the relief.')

[Experts]

Article 22

(1) The tribunal may appoint one or more independent experts to report to it, in writing, on specific issues designated by the tribunal and communicated to the parties.

(2) The parties shall provide such an expert with any relevant information or produce for inspection any relevant documents or goods that the expert may require. Any dispute between a party and the expert as to the relevance of the requested information or goods shall be referred to the tribunal for decision.

(3) Upon receipt of an expert's report, the tribunal shall send a copy of the report to all parties and shall give the parties an opportunity to express, in writing, their opinion on the report. A party may examine any document on which the expert has relied in such a report.

(4) At the request of any party, the tribunal shall give the parties an opportunity to question the expert at a hearing. At this hearing, parties may present expert witnesses to testify on the points at issue.

1. General. Art. 22 addresses experts. While the norm in United States litigation is for each party to retain its own expert, art. 22 provides that the tribunal may appoint one or more independent experts. Art. 22 contains certain requirements in the event that the tribunal appoints an expert: the parties 'shall' provide the expert with relevant information or produce for inspection any relevant documents or goods required by the expert (art. 22(2)); the parties 'shall' have an opportunity to express a written opinion on the expert's report and 'may' examine any documents relied upon by the expert in his or her report (art. 22(3)); any party 'shall' have the opportunity to question the expert at the hearing if it so requests (art. 22(4)); and the parties 'may' present expert witnesses at the hearing to testify on the points at issue (art. 22(4)).

[Default]

Article 23

(1) If a party fails to file a statement of defense within the time established by the tribunal without showing sufficient cause for such failure, as determined by the tribunal, the tribunal may proceed with the arbitration.

(2) If a party, duly notified under these Rules, fails to appear at a hearing without showing sufficient cause for such failure, as determined by the tribunal, the tribunal may proceed with the arbitration.

(3) If a party, duly invited to produce evidence or take any other steps in the proceedings, fails to do so within the time established by the tribunal without showing sufficient cause for such failure, as determined by the tribunal, the tribunal may make the award on the evidence before it.

1. Tribunal authority to proceed with arbitration. Art. 23 addresses default by a party. It is designed to ensure that one party cannot derail the arbitration process by refusing to participate. Thus art. 23(1) prevents a party from using its failure to file a Statement of Defence as a tactic to delay the arbitration, by providing that the tribunal may proceed with the arbitration notwithstanding this failure.

2. Failure of a party to appear at hearing. Similarly, art. 23(2) makes clear that a party cannot derail the process by failing to appear at a hearing. It provides that if a party, with due notice of hearing (see art. 20(1)), fails to appear without sufficient cause, the tribunal may proceed with the arbitration.

3. Failure of a party to produce evidence or take other steps. Similarly, art. 23(3) prevents a party undermining the process by failing, without sufficient cause, to produce evidence or take any other steps in the proceedings. It provides that in such circumstances the tribunal may nonetheless make an award based on the evidence before it.

4. Entry of default judgment not authorised. It is clear from art. 23 that entry of a default judgment by a tribunal is not authorised in an arbitration under the International Arbitration Rules, as it is in United States litigation where a court may issue a judgment in favour of one party simply as a result of the failure of the other to appear or participate. Under the Rules, the tribunal must, before rendering any award, still proceed with the arbitration, and consider the evidence before rendering an award, even if a party fails to appear or participate.

[Closure of hearing]

Article 24

(1) After asking the parties if they have any further testimony or evidentiary submissions and upon receiving negative replies or if satisfied that the record is complete, the tribunal may declare the hearings closed.

(2) The tribunal in its discretion, on its own motion or upon application of a party, may reopen the hearings at any time before the award is made.

1. General. Art. 24 addresses the closure of the hearing. The decision to close the hearing is made by the tribunal. The effect of this closure is that no further evidence may be submitted. Art. 24 provides that the hearings may be closed by the tribunal in two situations: first, if the parties, after being asked by the tribunal, affirm that they do not wish to submit any additional evidence, or secondly, if the tribunal is satisfied that the record is complete. Art. 24(2) also provides that the tribunal has the discretion to reopen the hearing after it has been closed 'at any time before the award is made'.

[Waiver of Rules]

Article 25

A party who knows that any provision of the Rules or requirement under the Rules has not been complied with, but proceeds with the arbitration without promptly stating an objection in writing thereto, shall be deemed to have waived the right to object.

1. General. Art. 25 provides that a party shall be deemed to waive any objection it may have to the fact that any International Arbitration Rule has not been complied with if it knows of such non-compliance but proceeds with the arbitration 'without promptly stating an objection in writing thereto'.

[Awards, decisions and rulings]

Article 26

(1) When there is more than one arbitrator, any award, decision or ruling of the arbitral tribunal shall be made by a majority of the

arbitrators. If any arbitrator fails to sign the award, it shall be accompanied by a statement of the reason for the absence of such signature.

(2) When the parties or the tribunal so authorize, the presiding arbitrator may make decisions or rulings on questions of procedure, subject to revision by the tribunal.

1. Majority of tribunal may render an award. Art. 26 addresses awards, decisions and rulings by the tribunal. Art. 26(1) provides that, where there is more than one arbitrator, a majority of the tribunal has authority to render an award. It also authorises the issuance of a dissenting opinion in the event that the arbitrators are not unanimous, providing that 'if any arbitrator fails to sign the award, it shall be accompanied by a statement of the reason for the absence of such signature'.

2. Tribunal's authority to permit chair to decide procedural issues alone. One of the disadvantages of a three-person tribunal is that it takes longer for three arbitrators to decide an issue than it does a sole arbitrator. One reason for this is that the schedule of three people is harder to coordinate than that of just one. Art. 26(2) permits the tribunal or the parties to authorise the chair alone to decide procedural issues, such as disputes about disclosure, without having to consult with all the arbitrators. Art. 26 does provide, however, that such rulings are 'subject to revision by the tribunal'.

[Form and effect of the award]

Article 27

(1) Awards shall be made in writing, promptly by the tribunal, and shall be final and binding on the parties. The parties undertake to carry out any such award without delay.

(2) The tribunal shall state the reasons upon which the award is based, unless the parties have agreed that no reasons need be given.

(3) The award shall contain the date and the place where the award was made, which shall be the place designated pursuant to Article 13.

(4) An award may be made public only with the consent of all parties or as required by law.

(5) Copies of the award shall be communicated to the parties by the administrator.

(6) If the arbitration law of the country where the award is made requires the award to be filed or registered, the tribunal shall comply with such requirement.

(7) In addition to making a final award, the tribunal may make interim, interlocutory or partial orders and awards.

(8) Unless otherwise agreed by the parties, the administrator may publish or otherwise make publicly available selected awards, decisions and rulings that have been edited to conceal the names of the parties and

other identifying details or that have been made publicly available in the course of enforcement or otherwise.

1. Form of award. Art. 27 addresses the form and effect of an award. It provides, among other things, that the award must be made in writing, that it is final and binding on the parties, and that it must be a reasoned award unless the parties have agreed otherwise.

2. Publication of award. Art. 27(4) provides that the award may be made public only with the consent of all parties or as required by law. Art. 27(8) provides that the ICDR may, unless the parties agree otherwise, publish awards, decisions or rulings after editing them to remove any identifying details. Art. 27(8) does, however, permit the ICDR to publish awards in full if they have been made public.

[Applicable laws and remedies]

Article 28

(1) The tribunal shall apply the substantive law(s) or rules of law designated by the parties as applicable to the dispute. Failing such a designation by the parties, the tribunal shall apply such law(s) or rules of law as it determines to be appropriate.

(2) In arbitrations involving the application of contracts, the tribunal shall decide in accordance with the terms of the contract and shall take into account usages of the trade applicable to the contract.

(3) The tribunal shall not decide as amiable compositeur or ex aequo et bono unless the parties have expressly authorized it to do so.

(4) A monetary award shall be in the currency or currencies of the contract unless the tribunal considers another currency more appropriate, and the tribunal may award such pre-award and post-award interest, simple or compound, as it considers appropriate, taking into consideration the contract and applicable law.

(5) Unless the parties agree otherwise, the parties expressly waive and forego any right to punitive, exemplary or similar damages unless a statute requires that compensatory damages be increased in a specified manner. This provision shall not apply to any award of arbitration costs to a party to compensate for dilatory or bad faith conduct in the arbitration.

1. Applicable law. Art. 28 addresses applicable law and remedies. Art. 28(1) provides that the tribunal shall apply the law designated by the parties to be applicable to the dispute. This, for example, would include the law designated by a choice of law clause in the underlying agreement out of which the dispute arises. It also provides that if the parties have not designated the applicable law, then the tribunal shall apply the law 'it determines to be appropriate'.

2. Interpretation of contracts. Art. 28(2) provides that, in interpreting contracts, the tribunal shall 'decide in accordance with the terms of the contract and shall take into account usages of the trade applicable to the contract'.

3. Tribunal not authorised to decide case ex aequo et bono. Art. 28(3) makes clear that although parties may expressly authorise the tribunal to decide as amiable compositeur or ex aequo et bono – that is, to dispense with the law and decide only on the basis of what it considers to be fair and equitable in the particular case – a tribunal shall not decide on that basis unless so authorised.

4. Currency of award. Art. 28(4) provides that the tribunal shall render a monetary award in the currency or currencies of the contract unless it considers another currency 'more appropriate' and that it may award pre-award and post-award interest.

5. Punitive and multiple damages. In the United States, punitive damages may be awarded in many different circumstances under the law of various states, and there are certain statutes in the United States providing that compensatory damages may be doubled or trebled. Art. 28(5) prohibits the tribunal from awarding punitive damages, but it does not prohibit it from applying statutes that permit multiple damages unless the parties agree otherwise. (See, e.g., Chapter 93A of Massachusetts General Laws, which prohibits deceptive and unfair business practices, and provides that damages may be multiplied.)

[Settlement or other reasons for termination]

Article 29

(1) If the parties settle the dispute before an award is made, the tribunal shall terminate the arbitration and, if requested by all parties, may record the settlement in the form of an award on agreed terms. The tribunal is not obliged to give reasons for such an award.

(2) If the continuation of the proceedings becomes unnecessary or impossible for any other reason, the tribunal shall inform the parties of its intention to terminate the proceedings. The tribunal shall thereafter issue an order terminating the arbitration, unless a party raises justifiable grounds for objection.

1. Recording of settlement in the form of an award. Art. 29 addresses the settlement or termination of an arbitration. If the parties reach a settlement agreement before an arbitral award is made, the tribunal is required to terminate the proceedings. The parties together may request that the tribunal record their settlement agreement as an arbitral award. The tribunal does not have to give reasons for such an award. This is advantageous to the parties, because if a settlement agreement is embodied in an arbitral award, it can be enforced pursuant to the provisions of New York Convention.

2. Refund by ICDR in event of settlement. In the case of settlement, the ICDR will refund any unused deposits received from the parties as an advance on costs and in some cases a portion of the initial filing fee (see art. 33(4), note 4).

[Interpretation or correction of the award]

Article 30

(1) Within 30 days after the receipt of an award, any party, with notice to the other parties, may request the tribunal to interpret the award or correct any clerical, typographical or computation errors or make an additional award as to claims presented but omitted from the award.

(2) If the tribunal considers such a request justified, after considering the contentions of the parties, it shall comply with such a request within 30 days after the request.

1. Limited scope for correction or intepretation of award. Art. 30 addresses the interpretation or correction of an award. Art. 30(1) both limits the time in which a party can ask the tribunal to take any action after an award is rendered to '30 days after the receipt of the award', and limits the bases on which a party may seek further consideration to 'interpret[ation of] the award or correct[ion of] any clerical, typographical or computation errors' or to a request that the arbitrators consider 'claims presented but omitted from the award'. This is designed to promote the finality of the arbitration process by prohibiting the parties from asking the tribunal to reconsider the merits of a case after an award has been rendered.

2. Time limit. Art. 30(2) provides that if the tribunal considers a request under Art. 30(1) to be justified, the tribunal shall comply with such request within thirty days after it is made.

[Costs]

Article 31

The tribunal shall fix the costs of arbitration in its award. The tribunal may apportion such costs among the parties if it determines that such apportionment is reasonable, taking into account the circumstances of the case.

Such costs may include:

  (a) the fees and expenses of the arbitrators;

(b) **the costs of assistance required by the tribunal, including its experts;**
(c) **the fees and expenses of the administrator;**
(d) **the reasonable costs for legal representation of a successful party; and**
(e) **any such costs incurred in connection with an application for interim or emergency relief pursuant to Article 21.**

1. Tribunal's authority to fix costs under the International Rules. Art. 31 provides that the tribunal shall fix the costs of the arbitration. These costs include the items set forth in art. 31(a) to (g). Art. 31(d) refers to 'the reasonable costs for legal representation of a successful party'. The authority of the tribunal to award attorneys' fees to the prevailing party stands in contrast to the practice in United States litigation where, except in some discrete cases, there is no cost-shifting based on the outcome of a lawsuit.

2. Contrast to AAA Commercial Rules. The AAA's Commercial Rules, in contrast to the International Arbitration Rules, allow cost-shifting only if 'all parties have requested such an award or it is authorized by law or by their arbitration agreement' (Rule 43(d)(ii) Commercial Rules).

[Compensation of arbitrators]

Article 32

Arbitrators shall be compensated based upon their amount of service, taking into account their stated rate of compensation and the size and complexity of the case. The administrator shall arrange an appropriate daily or hourly rate, based on such considerations, with the parties and with each of the arbitrators as soon as practicable after the commencement of the arbitration. If the parties fail to agree on the terms of compensation, the administrator shall establish an appropriate rate and communicate it in writing to the parties.

1. Basis of compensation of arbitrators. Art. 32 addresses the compensation of the arbitrators. Under the International Arbitration Rules, arbitrators are compensated based on 'a daily or hourly rate' taking into account their stated rate of compensation and the size and complexity of the case. The ICC, by contrast, fixes an arbitrator's compensation based on the amount in dispute (see art. 31(a) ICC). The ICC provides a scale, setting forth the appropriate range of fees for an arbitrator (see art. 2 of Appendix III of ICC Rules (Arbitration Costs and Fees)).

2. Payment by ICDR. The arbitrators submit a bill for their fees to the ICDR, and, after scrutinising the bill for reasonableness, the ICDR pays the arbitrators from the funds that have been deposited by the parties pursuant to art. 33.

[Deposit of costs]
Article 33
(1) When a party files claims, the administrator may request the filing party to deposit appropriate amounts as an advance for the costs referred to in Article 31, paragraphs (a.), (b.) and (c.).
(2) During the course of the arbitral proceedings, the tribunal may request supplementary deposits from the parties.
(3) If the deposits requested are not paid in full within 30 days after the receipt of the request, the administrator shall so inform the parties, in order that one or the other of them may make the required payment. If such payments are not made, the tribunal may order the suspension or termination of the proceedings.
(4) After the award has been made, the administrator shall render an accounting to the parties of the deposits received and return any unexpended balance to the parties.

1. General. Art. 33 addresses the deposits by the parties as an advance on the following costs set forth in art. 31(a), (b) and (c): the fees and expenses of the arbitrators; the costs of assistance required by the tribunal, including its experts; and the fees and expenses of the ICDR.

2. Deposits by parties as an advance on costs. Art. 33(1) provides that the ICDR may request a party filing a claim or a counterclaim to deposit 'appropriate amounts as an advance' for such costs, and art. 33(2) provides that supplementary deposits may be requested. While art. 33(2) refers to 'the tribunal' requesting supplementary deposits, in practice the ICDR, rather than the tribunal, communicates with the parties directly about funds.

3. Time limit for payment of deposits. Art. 33(3) provides that if the deposits are not paid in full within thirty days of being requested, the ICDR shall inform the parties, 'in order that one or the other of them may make the required payment'. This is designed to prevent one party derailing an arbitration by failing to make a requested payment, because the other party may make that payment, knowing that the tribunal has the authority under art. 31 to apportion costs between the parties. If the requested payments are not made, the tribunal may suspend or terminate the proceedings.

4. Refund of unused deposits. Art. 33(4) provides that the ICDR shall refund any unused part of the deposits to the parties 'after the award has been made'. While art. 33(4) refers to refunds 'after the award has been made', in practice the ICDR refunds any unused portion of the deposits in the event of a settlement or other termination prior to the rendering of any award. The ICDR also has a schedule for the refund of the initial filing fee in the event of a settlement (see Appendix E).

[Confidentiality]

Article 34

Confidential information disclosed during the proceedings by the parties or by witnesses shall not be divulged by an arbitrator or by the administrator. Except as provided in Article 27, unless otherwise agreed by the parties, or required by applicable law, the members of the tribunal and the administrator shall keep confidential all matters relating to the arbitration or the award.

1. Confidentiality contrasted to privacy. Art. 34 addresses confidentiality. This concept is distinct from that of privacy, which is addressed in art. 20(4). Privacy relates to who can attend hearings; confidentiality relates to whether any participant in the arbitration can disclose any materials exchanged between the parties or submitted to the arbitrators in connection with the arbitration.

2. Confidentiality obligation. Art. 34 contains a relatively modest confidentiality obligation: only the 'members of the tribunal and the administrator' are prohibited from disclosing confidential information, not the parties. However, the parties may agree and/or request that the tribunal enter an order providing for the confidentiality of submissions, testimony and other material. Similarly, they may agree on an appropriate confidentiality obligation in their arbitration clause.

[Exclusion of liability]

Article 35

The members of the tribunal and the administrator shall not be liable to any party for any act or omission in connection with any arbitration conducted under these Rules, except that they may be liable for the consequences of conscious and deliberate wrongdoing.

1. Exclusion of liability. Art. 35 provides that the tribunal and the ICDR shall not be liable to any party except 'for the consequences of conscious and deliberate wrongdoing'.

[Interpretation of rules]

Article 36

The tribunal shall interpret and apply these Rules insofar as they relate to its powers and duties. The administrator shall interpret and apply all other Rules.

1. Allocation of responsibility for interpretation of rules between ICDR and tribunal. Art. 36 provides that the tribunal has the authority to interpret and apply 'these Rules insofar as they relate to its powers and duties', while the administrator 'shall interpret and apply all other Rules'.

[Emergency measures of protection]

Article 37

(1) Unless the parties agree otherwise, the provisions of this art. 37 shall apply to arbitrations conducted under arbitration clauses or agreements entered on or after May 1, 2006.

(2) A party in need of emergency relief prior to the constitution of the tribunal shall notify the administrator and all other parties in writing of the nature of the relief sought and the reasons why such relief is required on an emergency basis. The application shall also set forth the reasons why the party is entitled to such relief. Such notice may be given by e-mail, facsimile transmission or other reliable means, but must include a statement certifying that all other parties have been notified or an explanation of the steps taken in good faith to notify other parties.

(3) Within one business day of receipt of notice as provided in paragraph 2, the administrator shall appoint a single emergency arbitrator from a special panel of emergency arbitrators designated to rule on emergency applications. Prior to accepting appointment, a prospective emergency arbitrator shall disclose to the administrator any circumstance likely to give rise to justifiable doubts to the arbitrator's impartiality or independence. Any challenge to the appointment of the emergency arbitrator must be made within one business day of the communication by the administrator to the parties of the appointment of the emergency arbitrator and the circumstances disclosed.

(4) The emergency arbitrator shall as soon as possible, but in any event within two business days of appointment, establish a schedule for consideration of the application for emergency relief. Such schedule shall provide a reasonable opportunity to all parties to be heard, but may provide for proceedings by telephone conference or on written submissions as alternatives to a formal hearing. The emergency arbitrator shall have the authority vested in the tribunal under Article 15, including the authority to rule on her/his own jurisdiction, and shall resolve any disputes over the applicability of this Article 37.

(5) The emergency arbitrator shall have the power to order or award any interim or conservancy measure the emergency arbitrator deems necessary, including injunctive relief and measures for the protection or conservation of property. Any such measure may take the form of an interim award or of an order. The emergency arbitrator shall give reasons in either case. The emergency arbitrator may modify or vacate the interim award or order for good cause shown.

(6) The emergency arbitrator shall have no further power to act after the tribunal is constituted. Once the tribunal has been constituted, the tribunal may reconsider, modify or vacate the interim award or order of emergency relief issued by the emergency arbitrator. The emergency arbitrator may not serve as a member of the tribunal unless the parties agree otherwise.

(7) Any interim award or order of emergency relief may be conditioned on provision by the party seeking such relief of appropriate security.

(8) A request for interim measures addressed by a party to a judicial authority shall not be deemed incompatible with this Article 37 or with the agreement to arbitrate or a waiver of the right to arbitrate. If the administrator is directed by a judicial authority to nominate a special master to consider and report on an application for emergency relief, the administrator shall proceed as in paragraph 2 of this article and the references to the emergency arbitrator shall be read to mean the special master, except that the special master shall issue a report rather than an interim award.

(9) The costs associated with applications for emergency relief shall initially be apportioned by the emergency arbitrator or special master, subject to the power of the tribunal to determine finally the apportionment of such costs.

1. Effective date of application of article 37. Art. 37, like art. 21, deals with the interim relief. Art. 37 sets forth procedures for a party to obtain emergency preliminary relief before the tribunal is constituted. It applies only to 'arbitrations conducted under arbitration clauses or agreements entered on or after May 1, 2006'.

2. Appointment of single emergency arbitrator. Art. 37 is somewhat self-explanatory. It authorises the ICDR to appoint a single emergency panel at short notice to deal solely with an emergency request for preliminary relief. The emergency arbitrator is in turn required to act expeditiously to address any application.

3. Emergency arbitrator may issue any interim relief deemed necessary. Art. 37 contains no explicit standards but simply authorises the emergency arbitrator to order any interim measure he 'deems necessary'. The emergency arbitrator shall have no further authority to act after the tribunal is constituted, and the tribunal is authorised to reconsider, modify or vacate any interim relief granted by the emergency arbitrator.

APPENDIX A

The ICDR has offices at the following addresses:

INTERNATIONAL CASE MANAGEMENT CENTER
International Centre for Dispute Resolution®
Thomas Ventrone
Vice President
1633 Broadway, 10th Floor
New York, New York 10019-6708
Tel: +1-212-484-4115
Fax: +1-212-246-7274
Email: VentroneT@adr.org

EUROPE, MIDDLE EAST, AFRICA
International Centre for Dispute Resolution®
Mark Appel
Senior Vice President
1633 Broadway, 10th Floor
New York, New York 10019-6708
Mobile: +353-868 201 054
Email: AppelM@adr.org

Mandy Sawier
Regional Manager – EMEA
International Centre for Dispute Resolution®
225 N. Michigan Ave. Suite 1840
Chicago, Illinois 60601-7601
Tel: 312-616-6560
Email: SawierM@adr.org

International Centre for Dispute Resolution® – Bahrain
BCDR-AAA
Tom Simotas
Case Management Advisor
Suite 401 Park Plaza
Building 247 Road 1704
Diplomatic Area
PO Box 20006
Manama
Kingdom of Bahrain
Tel: +973 17 511 321
Email: TSimotas@bcdr-aaa.org

AAA-ICDR International Arbitration Rules, Appendix A

ASIA
International Centre for Dispute Resolution® – Singapore
Michael Lee
Director
Maxwell Chambers
32 Maxwell Road
069115
Singapore
Tel: +65-6227-2879
Mobile: +65 9171 2240
Fax: +65-6227-3942
Email: LeeM@adr.org

CENTRAL/SOUTH AMERICA and NE USA
International Centre for Dispute Resolution®
Luis Martinez
Vice President
1633 Broadway, 10th Floor
New York, New York 10019
Tel: +1-212-716-5833
Fax: +1-212-716-5904
Email: MartinezL@adr.org

USA – MEXICO – CANADA
International Centre for Dispute Resolution®
Steve Andersen
Vice President
1108 E. South Union Avenue
Midvale, UT 84047
Tel: +1-801-569-4618
Fax: +1-801-984-8170
Email: AndersenS@adr.org

ICDR MANAGEMENT & GENERAL INFORMATION
International Centre for Dispute Resolution®

Richard Naimark, Senior Vice President
1633 Broadway, 10th Floor
New York, New York 10019
Tel: +1-212-716-5800
Fax: +1-212-716-590

Bryan Branon
Regional Liaison
1633 Broadway, 10th Floor

New York, New York 10019
Tel: +1-212-484-3207
Fax: +1-212-716-5904
Email: BranonB@adr.org

APPENDIX B

ICDR GUIDELINES FOR ARBITRATORS CONCERNING EXCHANGES OF INFORMATION

Introduction

The American Arbitration Association (AAA) and its international arm, the International Centre for Dispute Resolution® (ICDR) are committed to the principle that commercial arbitration, and particularly international commercial arbitration, should provide a simpler, less expensive and more expeditious form of dispute resolution than resort to national courts.

While arbitration must be a fair process, care must also be taken to prevent the importation of procedural measures and devices from different court systems, which may be considered conducive to fairness within those systems, but which are not appropriate to the conduct of arbitrations in an international context and which are inconsistent with an alternative form of dispute resolution that is simpler, less expensive and more expeditious. One of the factors contributing to complexity, expense and delay in recent years has been the migration from court systems into arbitration of procedural devices that allow one party to a court proceeding access to information in the possession of the other, without full consideration of the differences between arbitration and litigation.

The purpose of these guidelines is to make it clear to arbitrators that they have the authority, the responsibility and, in certain jurisdictions, the mandatory duty to manage arbitration proceedings so as to achieve the goal of providing a simpler, less expensive, and more expeditious process. Unless the parties agree otherwise in writing, these guidelines will become effective in all international cases administered by the ICDR commenced after May 31, 2008, and may be adopted at the discretion of the tribunal in pending cases. They will be reflected in amendments incorporated into the next revision of the International Arbitration Rules. They may be adopted in arbitration clauses or by agreement at any time in any other arbitration administered by the AAA.

1. In General

a. The tribunal shall manage the exchange of information among the parties in advance of the hearings with a view to maintaining efficiency and economy. The tribunal and the parties should endeavor to avoid unnecessary delay and expense while at the same time balancing the goals of avoiding surprise, promoting equality of treatment, and safeguarding each party's opportunity to present its claims and defenses fairly.

b. The parties may provide the tribunal with their views on the appropriate level of information exchange for each case, but the tribunal retains final authority to apply the above standard. To the extent that the Parties wish to depart from this standard, they may do so only on the basis of an express agreement among all of them in writing and in consultation with the tribunal.

2. Documents on which a Party Relies

Parties shall exchange, in advance of the hearing, all documents upon which each intends to rely.

3. Documents in the Possession of Another Party

a. In addition to any disclosure pursuant to paragraph 2, the tribunal may, upon application, require one party to make available to another party documents in the party's possession, not otherwise available to the party seeking the documents, that are reasonably believed to exist and to be relevant and material to the outcome of the case. Requests for documents shall contain a description of specific documents or classes of documents, along with an explanation of their relevance and materiality to the outcome of the case.

b. The tribunal may condition any exchange of documents subject to claims of commercial or technical confidentiality on appropriate measures to protect such confidentiality.

4. Electronic Documents

When documents to be exchanged are maintained in electronic form, the party in possession of such documents may make them available in the form (which may be paper copies) most convenient and economical for it, unless the Tribunal determines, on application and for good cause, that there is a compelling need for access to the documents in a different form. Requests for documents maintained in electronic form should be narrowly focused and structured to make searching for them as economical as possible. The Tribunal may direct testing or other means of focusing and limiting any search.

5. Inspections

The tribunal may, on application and for good cause, require a party to permit inspection on reasonable notice of relevant premises or objects.

6. Other Procedures

a. Arbitrators should be receptive to creative solutions for achieving exchanges of information in ways that avoid costs and delay, consistent with the principles of due process expressed in these Guidelines.

b. Depositions, interrogatories, and requests to admit, as developed in American court procedures, are generally not appropriate procedures for obtaining information in international arbitration.

7. Privileges and Professional Ethics

The tribunal should respect applicable rules of privilege or professional ethics and other legal impediments. When the parties, their counsel or their documents would be subject under applicable law to different rules, the tribunal should to the extent possible apply the same rule to both sides, giving preference to the rule that provides the highest level of protection.

8. Costs and Compliance

a. In resolving any dispute about pre-hearing exchanges of information, the tribunal shall require a requesting party to justify the time and expense that its request may involve, and may condition granting such a request on the payment of part or all of the cost by the party seeking the information. The tribunal may also allocate the costs of providing information among the parties, either in an interim order or in an award.

b. In the event any party fails to comply with an order for information exchange, the tribunal may draw adverse inferences and may take such failure into account in allocating costs.

APPENDIX C

ICDR INITIAL FILING FEES (EFFECTIVE JANUARY 1, 2010)

An Initial Filing Fee is payable in full by a filing party when a claim, counterclaim or additional claim is filed. A Case Service Fee will be incurred for all cases that proceed to their first hearing. This fee will be payable in advance at the time that the first hearing is scheduled. This fee will be refunded at the conclusion of the case if no hearings have occurred.

However, if the administrator is not notified at least 24 hours before the time of the scheduled hearing, the Case Service Fee will remain due and will not be refunded.

All fees for the Standard Fee Schedule, effective January 1, 2010, will be billed in accordance with the schedule below:

Amount of Claim	*Initial Filing Fee*	*Case Service Fee*
Above $0 to $10,000	$775	$200
Above $10,000 to $75,000	$975	$300
Above $75,000 to $150,000	$1,850	$750
Above $150,000 to $300,000	$2,800	$1,250
Above $300,000 to $500,000	$4,350	$1,750
Above $500,000 to $1,000,000	$6,200	$2,500
Above $1,000,000 to $5,000,000	$8,200	$3,250
Above $5,000,000 to $10,000,000	$10,200	$4,000
Above $10,000,000	Base fee of $12,800 plus .01% of the amount of claim above $10 million	$6,000
Nonmonetary Claims*	$3,350	$1,250
	Filing fees capped at $65,000	

* This fee is applicable only when a claim or counterclaim is not for a monetary amount. Where a monetary claim amount is not known, parties will be required to state a range of claims or be subject to a filing fee of $10,200.

Fees are subject to increase if the amount of a claim or counterclaim is modified after the initial filing date. Fees are subject to decrease if the amount of a claim or counterclaim is modified before the first hearing.

The minimum fees for any case having three or more arbitrators are $2,800 for the filing fee, plus a $1,250 case service fee.

Parties on cases held in abeyance for one year by agreement, will be assessed an annual abeyance fee of $300. If a party refuses to pay the assessed fee, the other party or parties may pay the entire fee on behalf of all parties, otherwise the matter will be administratively closed.

APPENDIX D

The notice of appointment questionnaire asks:

1. Do you or your law firm presently represent any person in a proceeding involving any party to the arbitration?

2. Have you represented any person against any party to the arbitration?

3. Have you had any professional or social relationship with counsel for any party in this proceeding or the firms for which they work?

4. Have you had any professional or social relationship with any parties or witnesses identified to date in this proceeding or the entities for which they work?

5. Have you had any professional or social relationship of which you are aware with any relative of any of the parties to this proceeding, or any relative of counsel to this proceeding, or any of the witnesses identified to date in the proceeding?

6. Have you, any member of your family, or any close social or business associate ever served as an arbitrator in a proceeding in which any of the identified witnesses or named individual parties gave testimony?

7. Have you, any member of your family, or any close social or business associate been involved in the last five years in a dispute involving the subject matter contained in the case, which you are assigned?

8. Have you ever served as an expert witness or consultant to any party, attorney, witness or other arbitrator identified in this case?

9. Have any of the party representatives, law firms or parties appeared before you in past arbitration cases?

10. Are you a member of any organization that is not listed on your panel biography that may be relevant to this arbitration?

11. Have you ever sued or been sued by either party or its representative?

12. Do you or your spouse own stock in any of the companies involved in this arbitration?

13. If there is more than one arbitrator appointed to this case, have you had any professional or social relationships with any of the other arbitrators?

14. Are there any connections, direct or indirect, with any of the case participants that have not been covered by the above questions?

Should the answer to any question be 'Yes', or if you are aware of any other information that may lead to a justifiable doubt as to your impartiality or independence or create an appearance of partiality, then describe the nature of potential conflict(s) …

* * *

A prospective arbitrator, accepting an invitation to serve, must also sign an Arbitrator's Oath which states:

'I attest that I have reviewed the panel biography which the American Arbitration Association provided to the parties on this case and confirm it is current, accurate and complete.

'I attest that I have diligently conducted a conflicts check, including a thorough review of the information provided to me about this case to date, and that I have performed my obligations and duties to disclose in accordance with the Rules of the American Arbitration Association, Code of Ethics for Commercial Arbitrators and/or all applicable statutes pertaining to arbitrator disclosures.

'I understand that my obligation to check for conflicts and make disclosures is ongoing for the length of my service as an arbitrator in this matter, and that failing to make appropriate and timely disclosures may result in my removal from the AAA's Roster of Neutrals.

'The Arbitrator being duly sworn, hereby accepts this appointment, and will faithfully and fairly hear and decide the matters in controversy between the parties in accordance with their arbitration agreement, the Code of Ethics, and the rules of the American Arbitration Association will make an Award according to the best of the arbitrator's understanding.'

APPENDIX E

ICDR REFUND SCHEDULE (EFFECTIVE MARCH 1, 2000)

The ICDR offers a refund schedule on filing fees. For cases with claims up to $75,000, a minimum filing fee of $350 will not be refunded. For all other cases, a minimum fee of $600 will not be refunded. Subject to the minimum fee requirements, refunds will be calculated as follows:

- 100% of the filing fee, above the minimum fee, will be refunded if the case is settled or withdrawn within five calendar days of filing.
- 50% of the filing fee will be refunded if the case is settled or withdrawn between six and 30 calendar days of filing.
- 25% of the filing fee will be refunded if the case is settled or withdrawn between 31 and 60 calendar days of filing. No refund will be made once an arbitrator has been appointed (this includes one arbitrator on a three-arbitrator panel).
- No refunds [of the initial filing fee] will be granted on awarded cases.

Note: the date of receipt of the demand for arbitration with the ICDR will be used to calculate refunds of filing fees for both claims and counterclaims.

CHINA INTERNATIONAL ECONOMIC AND TRADE ARBITRATION COMMISSION (CIETAC) ARBITRATION RULES, 2005

(Adopted at the Ninth Meeting of the Standing Committee of the Eighth National People's Congress on 31 August 1994, promulgated by Order No. 31 of the President of the People's Republic of China on 31 August 1994 and effective as of 1 September 1995)

CHAPTER I. GENERAL PROVISIONS

[The rules]

Article 1

These Rules are formulated in accordance with the Arbitration Law of the People's Republic of China and the provisions of other relevant laws, as well as the 'Decision' of the former Administration Council of the Central People's Government and the 'Notice' and the 'Official Reply' of the State Council.

1. Introductory remarks. Originally, arbitration commissions which were allowed to handle foreign-related cases were established under the auspices of the China Council for the Promotion of International Trade ('CCPIT'), a governmental body operating under the writ of the then Ministry of Foreign Trade. However, gradually, its legal status was transformed from a government institution into a non-governmental organisation aimed at promoting international trade and foreign economic co-operation, and generally enhancing the understanding and friendship between Chinese and foreigners. Commencing in 1988, CCPIT began to simultaneously use the name 'China Chamber of International Commerce' or its abbreviation 'CCOIC'. In that regard, it generally functions as a chamber of commerce in the same way as its counterparts overseas.

2. Source of the rules. In its 'Decision Concerning the Establishment of a Foreign Trade Arbitration Commission of 6 May 1954' ('Decision 1954'), the Government Administration Council authorised the CCPIT to establish the Foreign Trade Arbitration Commission ('FTAC'), and detailed the provisions relating to such establishment, including provisions pertaining to its jurisdiction, organisation, arbitration tribunal formation, the effectiveness of an award and award enforcement procedures. On 31 March 1956, CCPIT promulgated the 'Provisional Rules of Arbitral Procedure of the Foreign Trade Arbitration Commission'. In February 1980, FTAC was renamed the Foreign Economic and Trade Arbitration Commission ('FETAC') of CCPIT in accordance with the 'Notice Concerning the Conversion of the FTAC into the FETAC' ('Notice 1980'). In June 1988, FETAC amended its name to the China International Economic and Trade Arbitration Commission ('CIETAC') pursuant to the 'Official Reply Concerning the Renaming of the FETAC as CIETAC' ('Official Reply 1988'). Significantly, CCPIT was also authorised to adopt and revise the CIETAC arbitration rules of its own accord, i.e. without having to submit proposed amendments to the State Council for prior approval. In September 1988, CCPIT adopted the (first) CIETAC Arbitration Rules of 1988. Since then the CIETAC arbitration rules have been revised several times. In 1994 and 1995 revisions were made to adapt the CIETAC Rules to the Arbitration Law of 1995. Further revisions to adapt the rules to international standards were made in 1998, 2000 and 2005.

[Name and structure]

Article 2

(1) The China International Economic and Trade Arbitration Commission (originally named the Foreign Trade Arbitration Commission of the China Council for the Promotion of International Trade, later renamed the Foreign Economic and Trade Arbitration Commission of the China Council for the Promotion of International Trade, and currently called the China International Economic and Trade Arbitration Commission, hereinafter referred to as the 'CIETAC') independently and impartially resolves, by means of arbitration, disputes arising from economic and trade transactions of a contractual or non-contractual nature.

(2) The CIETAC concurrently uses the 'Court of Arbitration of the China Chamber of International Commerce' as its name.

(3) Where an arbitration agreement or an arbitration clause contained in a contract provides for arbitration by the CIETAC, one of its Sub-Commissions, or by the CIETAC using one of its prior names, the parties shall be deemed to have unanimously agreed that the arbitration shall be administered by the CIETAC or by one of its Sub-Commissions.

(4) Where an arbitration agreement or an arbitration clause contained in a contract provides for arbitration by the China Council for the Promotion of International Trade/China Chamber of International Commerce or by the Arbitration Commission or the Court of Arbitration of the China Council for the Promotion of International Trade/China Chamber of International Commerce, the parties shall be deemed to have unanimously agreed that the arbitration shall be administered by the CIETAC.

(5) The Chairman of the CIETAC shall perform the functions and duties vested in him by these Rules while a Vice-Chairman may perform the Chairman's functions and duties with the Chairman's authorisation.

(6) The CIETAC has a Secretariat, which handles its day-to-day work under the direction of its Secretary-General.

(7) The CIETAC is based in Beijing, and has a South China Sub-Commission (formerly known as the Shenzhen Sub-Commission) in the

Shenzhen Special Economic Zone and a Shanghai Sub-Commission in Shanghai. These Sub-Commissions are integral parts of the CIETAC. The Sub-Commissions have their respective secretariats, which handle their day-to-day work under the direction of the Secretaries-General of the respective Sub-Commissions.

(8) The parties may agree to have their disputes arbitrated by the CIETAC in Beijing, the South China Sub-Commission in Shenzhen, or the Shanghai Sub-Commission in Shanghai. In the absence of such an agreement, the Claimant shall have the option to submit the case for arbitration to the CIETAC in Beijing, the South China Sub-Commission in Shenzhen, or the Shanghai Sub-Commission in Shanghai. When such option is exercised, the first choice by the party shall prevail. In case of any dispute, the final decision shall be made by the CIETAC.

(9) The CIETAC may, at its discretion, establish arbitration centres for specific business sectors and issue arbitration rules therefor.

(10) The CIETAC shall establish a Panel of Arbitrators, and may, in its discretion, establish Panels of Arbitrators for specific business sectors.

1. Various names. As mentioned before (see art. 1, note 2) and reflected in art. 2(1) and (2), CIETAC was first called the Foreign Trade Arbitration Commission, then the Foreign Economic and Trade Arbitration Commission, and since 1988 the China International Economic and Trade Arbitration Commission. Simultaneously CIETAC has started to use the name 'the Court of Arbitration of the China Chamber of International Commerce', since it is under the administration of the CCOIC (see art. 1, note 1). Despite several changes in name and the use of different names, the FTAC, FETAC, CIETAC, and the Court of Arbitration of the CCOIC are regarded as one and the same arbitration institution.

2. Reference to an outdated name of CIETAC. According to art. 16 Arbitration Law in combination with art. 18 Arbitration Law, if the designation of an arbitration institution in the arbitration agreement is unclear, the arbitration agreement will be considered invalid, unless the parties reach a supplementary agreement (see art. 16 Arbitration Law, notes 10 et seq. and art. 18 Arbitration Law, notes 9 et seq.). Thus the question arises as to what will happen if an arbitration agreement refers to a inaccurate name of CIETAC. Art. 2(3) and (4) deals with this problem and establishes the principle that any former name of CIETAC or any reference to one of the names mentioned in art. 2(4) will be interpreted as a clear designation of CIETAC (see, for example, *China Nonferrous* v *Xinquan Trade*).

3. Structure. CIETAC's headquarters are located in Beijing with two Sub-Commissions in Shanghai and Shenzhen, respectively known as the CIETAC Shanghai Sub-Commission and the CIETAC South China Sub-Commission. In order to meet the increasing demand for arbitration, CIETAC has successively established nineteen liaison offices in different regions and specific business sectors (see note 5). According to art. 2(8), the parties can choose CIETAC or one of its Sub-Commissions in any of the three cities Beijing, Shanghai or Shenzhen. If they fail to agree thereon in their arbitration agreement, the claimant may choose before which CIETAC (sub-)commission it wants to initiate arbitration. Disputes concerning the competence of any of the CIETAC (sub-)commissions will be decided by the headquarters of CIETAC.

4. Internal organisation. According to art. 12 Arbitration Law and art. 66 Arbitration Law (see art. 12 Arbitration Law, note 2 and art. 66 Arbitration Law, note 2), art. 2(5) provides that CIETAC has a Chairman, several Vice-Chairmen, and a Secretariat headed by a Secretary-General. Concerning the Sub-Commissions, there is a Vice-Chairman, assisted by a Secretariat and a Secretary-General (see art. 4).

5. Sector-specific arbitration. In accordance with art. 2(9), which entitles CIETAC to establish arbitration centres and issue arbitration rules for specific business sectors, CIETAC promulgated in 2003 a new set of rules for resolving disputes arising in connection with financial transactions: the CIETAC Financial Arbitration Rules. In 2000, the CIETAC Domain Name Dispute Resolution Centre was established and is devoted to providing alternative dispute resolution services in the areas of intellectual property and information technology. Further, the CIETAC Grain Sectors Arbitration Centre was founded in 2003 to resolve disputes involving grain trade.

6. Panel of arbitrators. Art. 2(10) implements arts. 13 and 67 Arbitration Law (see arts. 13 and 67 Arbitration Law notes 1 et seq.), according to which each arbitration commission shall appoint a Panel of Arbitrators. CIETAC has prepared a 'List of Arbitrators on Domestic Cases' and a 'List of Arbitrators on International Cases', and several other lists concerning specific business sectors such as financial transactions, construction and land and building transactions. A comparison between the two major CIETAC Panel lists reveals that the List of Arbitrators on Domestic Cases actually contains the same Chinese arbitrators as those in the List of Arbitrators on International Cases, but does not contain any foreign arbitrators. The very establishment of CIETAC, and more particularly the composition of its Panel of Arbitrators with a large contingent of foreign experts, were designed to enhance confidence in the Chinese dispute resolution process amongst foreign investors in China. Certainly, it is a generally held view amongst foreign investors, that arbitration before a domestic arbitral commission is considerably less attractive than arbitration before CIETAC – the latter generally being regarded as better suited to foreign-related arbitration, partly because of its long experience and expertise in arbitration, but primarily due to its conceptual links to Western legal thinking exercised through its diverse Panel of Arbitrators.

[Jurisdiction]

Article 3

The CIETAC accepts cases involving:
(a) international or foreign-related disputes;
(b) disputes related to the Hong Kong Special Administrative Region or the Macao Special Administrative Region or the Taiwan region; and
(c) domestic disputes.

1. Historical development of CIETAC's jurisdiction. Originally, CIETAC's (at that time FTAC) jurisdiction was confined to disputes arising from international trade transactions between foreign economic entities and Chinese economic entities. Notice 1980 broadened CIETAC's (at that time FETAC) jurisdiction to include disputes arising not only from foreign trade, but also from foreign economic co-operation, i.e. disputes pertaining to foreign investment in China and particularly disputes relating to Sino-foreign joint ventures. Based on the Official Reply 1988, CIETAC's jurisdiction was further extended to all disputes arising from international economic and trade transactions. However, disputes involving parties from Hong Kong, Macao or Taiwan were not considered to be 'foreign' or 'international' until the late 1980s, when the State Council promulgated in 1988 the 'Regulations for the Encouragement of Investment by Taiwanese Compatriots' and in 1990 the 'Regulations Concerning the Encouragement of Investment by Overseas Chinese and Hong Kong and Macao Compatriots' permitting the parties concerned to submit such disputes for arbitration to a PRC arbitration commission, including CIETAC. Under the CIETAC Rules of 1994, CIETAC's jurisdiction encompassed disputes arising from international or foreign-related, contractual or non-contractual economic and trade transactions between: foreign legal persons and/or natural persons and Chinese legal persons and/or natural persons (i.e. 'foreign-related' disputes); foreign legal persons and/or natural persons (i.e. 'international' disputes); and between Chinese legal persons and/or natural persons where the disputed subject matter is located in a foreign country, or where the events that gave rise to the facts of the case occurred overseas (i.e. 'foreign-related' dispute). The CIETAC Rules of 1995 further permitted CIETAC to accept cases based on a special authorisation provided in relevant Chinese laws and administrative regulations. One problem during all these years was that Foreign Invested Enterprises ('FIEs') were considered to be Chinese legal entities. As a consequence thereof, disputes involving a Chinese entity and an FIE were deemed to be purely domestic and thus outside the scope of CIETAC's jurisdiction. Under the CIETAC Rules of 1998, CIETAC's jurisdiction was expanded to specifically include disputes involving FIEs. In 2000, CIETAC further expanded its jurisdiction over domestic arbitral cases.

2. CIETAC's jurisdiction under the CIETAC Rules of 2005. In 2005, CIETAC adopted a series of major revisions. At this time, CIETAC consolidated its jurisdiction regrouping it into three categories: international or foreign-related disputes (as defined in note 1); disputes related to Hong Kong, Macao, or Taiwan; and domestic disputes exclusively involving Chinese domestic entities and where the dispute happened in China only. This amendment, although of a formal nature, reaffirms CIETAC's wide jurisdiction in domestic, foreign-related, and/or international disputes. By allowing CIETAC to hear purely domestic cases, the CIETAC Rules of 2000 placed CIETAC firmly in direct competition with domestic arbitral institutions. The 2005 revision of the rules opens the door for the handling of purely foreign disputes, putting CIETAC – in theory – in direct competition with foreign arbitration institutions.

[Scope of application]

Article 4

(1) These Rules uniformly apply to the CIETAC and its Sub-Commissions. When arbitration proceedings are administered by a Sub-Commission, the functions and duties under these Rules allocated to the Chairman, the secretariat and the Secretary-General of the CIETAC shall be performed, respectively, by a Vice-Chairman authorised by the Chairman, a secretariat and a Secretary-General of the relevant Sub-Commission except for the power to make decisions on challenges to arbitrators.

(2) The parties shall be deemed to have agreed to arbitrate in accordance with these Rules whenever they have provided for arbitration by the CIETAC. Where the parties have agreed on the application of other arbitration rules, or any modification of these Rules, the parties' agreement shall prevail except where such agreement is inoperative or in conflict with a mandatory provision of the law of the place of arbitration.

(3) Where the parties agree to refer their disputes to arbitration under these Rules without providing the name of an arbitration institution, they shall be deemed to have agreed to refer the dispute to arbitration by the CIETAC.

(4) Where the parties agree to refer their dispute to arbitration under the CIETAC's arbitration rules for a specific business sector or profession and the dispute falls within the scope of such rules, the parties' agreement shall prevail; otherwise, these Rules shall apply.

1. Uniform application among CIETAC commissions and Sub-Commissions. CIETAC in Beijing, as well as its Sub-Commissions, uniformly apply the CIETAC Rules (art. 4(1)). For this purpose, if a Sub-Commission of CIETAC is entrusted with an arbitration, the functions and duties of the

Chairman of CIETAC described in the Rules will be assumed by the Vice-Chairman of the Sub-Commission. However, the power to decide on the challenge of arbitrators always remains with the Chairman of CIETAC in Beijing, even though a Sub-Commission is handling the arbitration (see art. 26, note 7).

2. Subsidiary application of the CIETAC Rules. Where, in their arbitration agreement, the parties merely refer to CIETAC without specifying any arbitration rules, the CIETAC Rules as in force at the time of the initiation of the arbitration proceedings shall apply (art. 4(2)). Also, if the parties have referred to a set of CIETAC's arbitration rules for a specific business sector, these rules shall only apply if the dispute falls within their scope, otherwise the general CIETAC Rules will be applied by default (art. 4(4)).

3. Possibility of choosing other arbitration rules. Prior to 1998, all disputes submitted to CIETAC for arbitration were automatically conducted under the CIETAC Rules. In 1998, the Rules were revised allowing the parties to agree on the application of other rules, subject to CIETAC's consent. Undoubtedly, the requirement that CIETAC's consent had first to be obtained substantially limited the autonomy of the parties and effectively permitted CIETAC to deny the use of other rules without having to furnish any reasons for its decision. The revision of the CIETAC Rules in 2000 failed to correct this iniquity, but this issue was finally addressed by art. 4(2) of the CIETAC Rules of 2005. According to art. 4(2) of the current Rules, the agreement of the parties as to the applicable arbitration rules shall prevail, unless such choice is inoperative or in violation of mandatory law, i.e. the Arbitration Law or the Civil Procedure Law

4. Application of the rules chosen by parties. The application of the rules chosen by the parties no longer depends on CIETAC's consent, which has lost its discretionary power in this respect. Full effect is given to the parties' chosen arbitration rules, except where such an agreement is inoperative or in conflict with the lex arbitri.

5. Mere reference to the CIETAC Rules in the arbitration agreement. According to art. 4(3), where the parties merely refer to the CIETAC Rules in their arbitration agreement, such reference is interpreted as a designation of CIETAC as the competent arbitration commission. This provision appears to play a major role. It was for a long time questionable whether a mere reference to the arbitration rules, without an express mention of the arbitration commission, would comply with arts. 16 and 18 Arbitration Law, which require an express and clear designation of the arbitration commission (see art. 16 Arbitration Law, notes 10 et seq. and art. 18 Arbitration Law, notes 4 et seq.). Case law in this respect has been very diverse and partly contradictory. Eventually, the Supreme People's Court ('SPC') issued the SPC Judicial Interpretations of 8 September 2006, in which it established in art. 4 the following principle: a mere reference to arbitration rules is, in principle, not sufficient to comply with the requirement of an express designation of the arbitration commission, unless the arbitration rules mentioned allow the determination of the competent arbitration commission simply on the basis of referring the case to that arbitration commission's rules. Thus, based on art. 4(3), an arbitration agreement which refers to the CIETAC Rules but does not designate an arbitration commission, should in the future be considered as designating CIETAC as the competent arbitration commission and should therefore be valid. The same is not true for the ICC Rules, since they do not contain any similar provision to art. 4(3). The risk therefore persists that arbitration agreements which merely refer to the ICC Rules, but do not expressly designate the ICC Court of Arbitration as the competent arbitration commission, may be considered invalid by the Chinese courts. This happened in the *Zueblin* case, in which the Supreme People's Court decided in 2004 that the arbitration clause providing 'Arbitration: ICC Rules, Shanghai shall apply' was invalid, since no provision of the ICC Rules provided that the choice of the ICC Rules also implied that the ICC International Court of Arbitration would be the competent arbitration institution and that it could not be excluded that another arbitration institution may apply the ICC Rules (see also art. 18 Arbitration Law, note 6).

[Arbitration agreement]

Article 5

(1) The CIETAC shall, upon the written application of a party, accept a case in accordance with an arbitration agreement concluded between the parties, either before or after the occurrence of the dispute, in which it is provided that disputes are to be referred to arbitration by the CIETAC.

(2) An arbitration agreement means an arbitration clause in a contract concluded between the parties or any other form of written agreement providing for the settlement of disputes by arbitration.

(3) The arbitration agreement shall be in writing. An arbitration agreement is in writing if it is contained in a tangible form of a document such as a contract, letter, telegram, telex, facsimile, EDI or email. A written arbitration agreement shall be deemed to exist where its existence is asserted by one party and not denied by the other during the exchange of the Request for Arbitration and the Statement of Defence.

(4) An arbitration clause contained in a contract shall be treated as a clause independent and separate from all other clauses of the contract, and an arbitration agreement attached to a contract shall also be treated as independent and separate from all other clauses of the contract. The validity of an arbitration clause or an arbitration agreement shall not be affected by any modification, rescission, termination, transfer, expiry, invalidity, ineffectiveness, revocation or non-existence of the contract.

1. Arbitration agreement as a basis for CIETAC's jurisdiction. Art. 5(1) implements the principle contemplated by art. 4 Arbitration Law and provides that an agreement of the parties to submit their dispute under the auspices of CIETAC is sufficient to found CIETAC's competence.

2. Types of arbitration agreement. Art. 5(2) implements the principle contemplated by art. 16(1) Arbitration Law (note 3), according to which an arbitration agreement can take the form of an arbitration clause incorporated in the contract, or of a subsequent submission agreement.

3. Written form. Art. 5(3) ab initio reconfirms the requirement of written form contemplated by art. 16(1) Arbitration Law. The definition of written form is identical to the definition provided for in art. 11 Contract Law, and encompasses any form capable of tangible representation of its content, such as written instruments, letters and electrically or electronically transmitted documents including telegrams, telexes, facsimiles, electronic data interchange and email (see art. 16 Arbitration Law, note 3). Further, an arbitration agreement will be considered concluded if one party initiates arbitration and the other does not contest the arbitral jurisdiction during the exchange of written submissions. However, this only applies where CIETAC has already accepted an arbitration case following a prima facie check for the existence of an arbitral agreement (see art. 6, notes 1 et seq.). In other words, the lack of objection of the defendant may cure the invalidity of an existing arbitration agreement, but may not replace the non-existence of an arbitration agreement, since CIETAC will not accept a case if there is no evidence whatsoever of an arbitration agreement.

4. Severability of the arbitration agreement. Art. 5(4) reconfirms the principle of severability of the arbitration agreement contemplated by art. 19 Arbitration Law (see note 2). The doctrine of severability provides that, even if the main contract ceases to exist or is ab initio invalid, this does not affect the arbitration agreement which continues to produce all its effects. Thereby, the principle of severability ensures the continued exercise of jurisdiction by an arbitration institution over a case where one party objects to such jurisdiction on the grounds that the main contract was terminated or is invalid. The principle of severability was first introduced in 1995 into the CIETAC Rules as a consequence of art. 19 of the Arbitration Law. In judicial practice, prior to the Arbitration Law, the People's Courts felt that if a contract was found to be void ab initio due to fraud, then the arbitration clause was also void (see *CNTIC* v *Swiss Industrial Resources*). The principle of severability of the arbitration clause has since then been tested on numerous occasions before the Chinese courts and is now widely acknowledged. In a well-known case, a Chinese company and a Hong Kong company concluded an equity joint venture contract that included a CIETAC arbitration clause. Before the administrative authorities approved the contract, a dispute occurred and the Chinese party submitted the dispute to the Intermediate People's Court in Huizhou, Guangdong Province. The Hong Kong company challenged the jurisdiction of the court on the grounds of the existence of an arbitration clause contained in the contract. The Intermediate People's Court held that the contract had not come into force as the relevant State approval authority had not furnished its approval of the contract as required by law and therefore held the arbitration clause to be invalid. However, this decision was overruled by the Higher People's Court of Guangdong Province, which held that notwithstanding the invalidity of the underlying contract, a written arbitration agreement existed and that it was not subject to the approval of an administrative authority. In consequence, the Court further ruled that the courts had no jurisdiction over any dispute falling within the scope of the arbitration agreement.

[Objection to an arbitration agreement and/or jurisdiction]
Article 6

(1) The CIETAC shall have the power to determine the existence and validity of an arbitration agreement and its jurisdiction over an arbitration case. The CIETAC may, if necessary, delegate such power to the arbitral tribunal.

(2) Where the CIETAC is satisfied by prima facie evidence that an arbitration agreement providing for arbitration by the CIETAC exists, it may make a decision based on such evidence that it has jurisdiction over the arbitration case, and the arbitration shall proceed. Such a decision shall not prevent the CIETAC from making a new decision on jurisdiction based on facts and/or evidence found by the arbitral tribunal during the arbitration proceedings that are inconsistent with the prima facie evidence.

(3) An objection to an arbitration agreement and/or jurisdiction over an arbitration case shall be raised in writing before the first oral hearing is held by the arbitral tribunal. Where a case is to be decided on the basis of documents only, such an objection shall be raised before the submission of the first substantive defence.

(4) The arbitration shall proceed notwithstanding an objection to the arbitration agreement and/or jurisdiction over the arbitration case.

(5) The aforesaid objections to and/or decisions on jurisdiction by the CIETAC shall include objections to and/or decisions on a party's qualification to participate in the arbitration.

1. Decision on jurisdiction to be taken by CIETAC. According to art. 20(1) Arbitration Law, the power to decide on the arbitral jurisdiction firstly belongs to the arbitration commission. This principle is implemented in art. 6(1) CIETAC Rules, according to which CIETAC (and not the arbitral tribunal) shall determine the existence and validity of the arbitration agreement. Where the facts relating to the jurisdiction issue and the law are clear, and where the legal questions raised are not complicated, CIETAC will – after inviting the parties to submit written comments – decide on the jurisdiction issue. If the questions related to the jurisdiction are complicated, and/or require the analysis of substantive issues, CIETAC will decide based on prima facie evidence and render a preliminary decision. The final decision will be rendered after the arbitral tribunal has analysed the substantive issues at stake. Where CIETAC is of the opinion that the jurisdiction issues are complicated, and if the arbitral tribunal is already constituted, CIETAC will consult with the arbitral tribunal before taking a decision.

2. Possibility to delegate such competence to the arbitral tribunal. According to art. 6(1), CIETAC may also delegate the competence to decide on jurisdiction to the arbitral tribunal itself. This is quite a daring provision, given the express wording of art. 20(1) Arbitration Law which does not provide for such an option. Actually, this provision was not created by CIETAC, but by the Beijing Arbitration Commission ('BAC') in 2001 (art. 10 of BAC Rules 2001). It was then reconfirmed in 2004 by art. 6 of the revised BAC Rules, which provides that: 'The BAC or, if authorised by the BAC, the Arbitral Tribunal, shall have the power to rule on jurisdictional objections and objections to the validity of an arbitration agreement'. CIETAC took over this provision when revising its Rules in 2005. In practice, CIETAC will often delegate such competence when the question of jurisdiction is related to substantive issues of the case. The main reason is to avoid CIETAC deciding on such substantive issues, which it is not allowed to do.

3. Conflict of jurisdiction with the People's Court. Although art. 6(1) states that CIETAC, or the arbitral tribunal, has the power to determine the existence and validity of an arbitration agreement, this is only true within the limits set by art. 20(1) Arbitration Law. According to art. 20(1) Arbitration Law, if the jurisdiction of an arbitral tribunal is in dispute, such dispute can be decided either on the one hand by the arbitration institution or the arbitral tribunal itself, or, on the other hand, by a relevant court, whereby if one of the parties submits the dispute to a court and the other relies on the arbitral tribunal, the court's decision should prevail. In such circumstances, although in contradiction to the international principle of Kompetenz-Kompetenz, the court may even advise the arbitration commission to suspend or even terminate the arbitral proceedings relating to the same case until it reaches a decision on the jurisdiction issue. Thus, in fact, CIETAC only has the authority to decide on its own jurisdiction, if none of the parties applies for a ruling before the courts (see art. 20 Arbitration Law, note 1).

4. Time limit for raising an objection to arbitration. Art. 6(3) implements the principle contemplated by art. 20(2) Arbitration Law, according to which a party's challenge of the validity of the arbitration agreement should be raised prior to the arbitration tribunal's first hearing. Art. 6(3) further defines the moment of the 'first hearing', in cases where the procedure is conducted on the basis of documents only. In such cases, the first hearing is deemed to be the moment of submission of the first substantive defence, generally the so-called 'Statement of Defence'. Moreover, art. 6(3) is broader than art. 20(2) Arbitration Law and applies to all kind of objections to the arbitral jurisdiction, including objections to a party's qualification to participate to the arbitration (see art. 6(4) CIETAC Rules), and not only to objections concerning the validity of the arbitration agreement.

[Bona fide cooperation]
Article 7

The parties shall proceed with the arbitration in bona fide cooperation.

1. General principle of good faith. Art. 7 implements what art. 6 Contract Law states for contractual relationships in general in the field of arbitration, i.e. that parties should observe the principle of good faith in exercising their rights and fulfilling their obligations. Since an arbitration agreement is also a contract, the parties have to follow the principle of good faith and cooperate in order to allow the arbitration to take place and proceed smoothly.

2. Consequences of a violation of the principle of good faith. Unfortunately, there is no express provision on the consequence of a violation of the principle of good faith. In practice, the arbitral tribunal will take the conduct of the parties into consideration at least when allocating the arbitration costs and extra expenses.

[Waiver of the right to object]
Article 8

A party shall be deemed to have waived its right to object where it knows or should have known that any provision of, or requirement under, these Rules has not been complied with and yet participates in or proceeds with the arbitration proceedings without promptly and explicitly submitting its objection in writing to such non-compliance.

1. Obligation to raise objections in good time. Art. 8 derives from the principle of good faith, that if a party has an objection to raise as regards any aspect of the arbitration procedure, it should to do without delay. If it fails to do so, it is not allowed to raise the objection at a later stage and will be deemed to have waived its right to object. A similar solution is provided for in various other arbitration rules, such as art. 30 UNCITRAL Arbitration Rules, art. 29 SCC Arbitration Rules, art. 33 ICC Rules and art. 30 Swiss Rules.

CHAPTER II. ARBITRAL PROCEEDINGS

Section 1. Request for Arbitration, Defence and Counterclaim

[Commencement of the arbitration proceedings]

Article 9

The arbitral proceedings shall commence on the date on which the CIETAC or one of its Sub-Commissions receives a Request for Arbitration.

1. Moment of commencement. In accordance with other arbitration rules (see, for example, art. 4(2) ICC Rules, art. 8 SCC Rules and art. 3(2) Swiss Rules), the arbitration proceedings start from the moment of receipt by CIETAC of the Request for Arbitration, and not from the moment of acceptance of the case.

[Request for Arbitration]

Article 10

A party applying for arbitration under these Rules shall:
- **(a) Submit a Request for Arbitration in writing signed by and/or affixed with the seal of the Claimant and/or its authorised representative(s), which shall, inter alia, include:**
  - **(i) the names and addresses of the Claimant and the Respondent, including the zip code, telephone, telex, fax and telegraph numbers, email addresses or any other means of electronic telecommunications;**
  - **(ii) a reference to the arbitration agreement that is invoked;**
  - **(iii) the facts of the case and the main issues in dispute;**
  - **(iv) the claim of the Claimant; and**
  - **(v) the facts and grounds on which the claim is based.**
- **(b) Attach to the Request for Arbitration the relevant evidence supporting the facts on which the Claimant's claim is based.**
- **(c) Make payment of the arbitration fees in advance to the CIETAC according to its Arbitration Fee Schedule.**

1. Written form. According to art. 10(a), and in accordance with art. 23 Arbitration Law, a Request for Arbitration has to be submitted in written form and must be signed by a duly authorised person.

2. Content. Art. 10(a) implements, in greater detail, art. 23 Arbitration Law and provides that a Request for Arbitration should include detailed personal contact data of the parties, the claims, the relevant facts, and the grounds on which the claims are based. In practice, requests for arbitration are structured in three parts, the first mentioning the claims, the second the relevant facts, and the third explaining the legal basis of the claim, i.e. the grounds.

3. Evidence. As does art. 23 Arbitration Law (see note 4), art. 10(b) CIETAC Rules requires a party to attach all the relevant evidence to its Request for Arbitration. This requirement is, however, not very strict, and it is admitted that evidence can also be submitted at a later stage. Usually, the arbitral tribunal will set a time period for the submission of evidence (see art. 36, note 2).

4. Payment of the fee. CIETAC will only accept the case if the claimant fully pays the advance of arbitration fees according to the Arbitration Fee Schedule. For foreign-related arbitration, the fees are as follows:

Amount of claim	Amount of fee
CNY 1,000,000 or less	3.5% of the claimed amount, minimum CNY 10,000
Between CNY 1,000,000 and 5,000,000	CNY 35,000 plus 2.5% of the amount above CNY 1,000,000
Between CNY 5,000,000 and 10,000,000	CNY 135,000 plus 1.5% of the amount above CNY 5,000,000
Between CNY 10,000,000 and 50,000,000	CNY 210,000 plus 1% of the amount above CNY 10,000,000
Above CNY 50,000,000	CNY 610,000 plus 0.5% of the amount above CNY 50,000,000

Each case, when being accepted, will be charged an additional amount of CNY 10,000 as a registration fee, which includes the expenses for examining the Request for Arbitration, initiating the arbitration proceedings, computerising management and filing the documents. Apart from charging arbitration fees according to the above schedule, CIETAC may collect other extra, reasonable and actual expenses pursuant to art. 69 (see art. 69, note 1).

5. Modification of claims. The claimant can at a later stage still modify his claim, provided that it will not affect the smooth process of the arbitral proceedings (see art. 14, notes 1 et seq.).

6. Comparison with international practice. In practice, the Request for Arbitration is usually already a detailed and substantiated submission. In this respect it is closer to a 'Statement of Claim' than to a 'Request for Arbitration' under an ICC arbitration, for example. However, although the Request for Arbitration under CIETAC arbitration may (and often will) cover complicated substantive issues together with a mass of evidence, it is still permitted to submit supplementary documents within a time limit fixed by the arbitral tribunal. A party could thus submit a very short Request for Arbitration and wait for the next round of submissions before substantiating its case in detail. Theoretically, if the arbitral tribunal does not fix a specific time limit, it should accept any submission, even after the oral hearing.

[Acceptance of a case]

Article 11

(1) Upon receipt of the Request for Arbitration and its attachments, if, after examination, the CIETAC finds the formalities required for an arbitration application to be incomplete, it may request the Claimant to complete them. Where the formalities are found to be complete, the CIETAC shall send a Notice of Arbitration to both parties together with one copy each of the CIETAC Arbitration Rules, the Panel of Arbitrators, and the Arbitration Fee Schedule. The Request for Arbitration and its attachments submitted by the Claimant shall be sent to the Respondent under the same cover.

(2) The CIETAC or its Sub-Commission shall, after accepting a case, appoint a staff member of its secretariat to assist the arbitral tribunal in the procedural administration of the case.

1. Notice of Arbitration. Art. 11 implements art. 25 Arbitration Law (see art. 25 Arbitration Law, note 1), according to which the arbitration institution should – after its acceptance of the case – issue a Notice of Arbitration to the parties. CIETAC will join the Request for Arbitration and all annexes thereto with the Notice of Arbitration, the CIETAC Rules, the list of arbitrators and the Arbitration Fee Schedule.

2. Incomplete Request for Arbitration. Where an application for arbitration is found to be incomplete or defective, the Secretariat of CIETAC will offer the claimant an opportunity to amend or supplement the application within a specified time limit. If the claimant fails to comply with CIETAC's request, CIETAC will reject the application until the claimant submits a complete file.

3. Preservation of evidence and/or property. If when initiating arbitration, the claimant also requests measures for property and/or evidence preservation, he will have to fulfil supplementary requirements. (See in this respect art. 15, note 2.)

[Statement of Defence]

Article 12

(1) Within forty-five (45) days from the date of receipt of the Notice of Arbitration, the Respondent shall file a Statement of Defence in writing with the Secretariat of the CIETAC or its Sub-Commission. The arbitral tribunal may extend that time period if it believes that there are justified reasons. The Statement of Defence shall be signed by and/or affixed with the seal of the Respondent and/or its authorised representative(s), and shall, inter alia, include:

(a) **the names and addresses of the Respondent, including the zip code, telephone, telex, fax and telegraph numbers, email addresses or any other means of electronic telecommunications;**
(b) **the defence to the Request for Arbitration setting forth the facts and grounds on which the defence is based; and**
(c) **the relevant evidence supporting the defence.**

(2) The arbitral tribunal has the power to decide whether to accept a Statement of Defence submitted after expiration of the above time limit.

(3) Failure of the Respondent to file a Statement of Defence shall not operate to affect the arbitral proceedings.

1. Contents of the Statement of Defence. The Answer to the Request for Arbitration is called Statement of Defence and is – as is the Request for Arbitration (see art. 10, note 2) – supposed to contain all the main elements of the dispute, including the defence case, as well as the facts, the grounds and the evidence the defence is based upon.

2. Time limit. The respondent has to submit his Statement of Defence within forty-five days of receipt of the Notice of Arbitration (see art. 11, note 1). A late submission may be rejected by the arbitral tribunal, but it will in practice mainly depend on the reasons for the delay. Indeed, the arbitral tribunal should take all the circumstances into consideration before deciding not to accept the Statement of Defence, otherwise the respondent may argue that there has been a violation of its right to be heard.

3. Evidence. According to art. 12(1)(c), the supportive evidence shall be submitted with the Statement of Defence. However, this rule is not very strict and it is admitted that further evidence may be submitted during the arbitration proceedings, within the time limit fixed by the arbitral tribunal (see art. 36, notes 2 et seq.).

4. Failure to submit the Statement of Defence. A failure by the respondent to submit its Statement of Defence will not stop the arbitration from proceeding, provided the Notice of Arbitration has been duly served on the respondent. The arbitral tribunal will then be entitled to render a default award.

5. Other rounds of written submissions? Contrary to the practice of international arbitration institutions, there is no predominant practice in China as to the number of rounds of exchange of written submissions. Under the ICC, the procedure will start with the 'Request for Arbitration', followed by the 'Answer to the Request for Arbitration'. These documents are often very short. Once the arbitral tribunal is constituted, the parties will start exchanging more substantive briefs: exchange of the 'Statement of Claim' and 'Statement of Defence', usually followed by the exchange of a 'Replic' and 'Duplic'. In very complex cases, a third round of exchange may be provided for. After the exchange of the written submissions, the arbitral tribunal will usually set up one or several hearings, after which the parties will be invited to submit post-hearing briefs commenting on the evidence presented at the hearing. In CIETAC arbitration, there is no uniform practice as to the number of rounds of written submissions. The arbitration starts with the exchange of the 'Request for Arbitration' and the 'Statement of Defence', which are already relatively detailed submissions. It is up to the arbitral tribunal to decide, whether it considers it useful to provide for another round of exchange before or even after the first hearing. It should, however, be mentioned that in practice it is quite common that parties submit – on their own initiative – supplementary documents (such as 'Counsel's Opinions' or new evidence) to the arbitral tribunal. The other party will then be given the opportunity to respond to each of these submissions. The further submission of documents will usually be possible until the last hearing, unless the arbitral tribunal decides otherwise (see art. 14, note 2). After the last hearing, the arbitral tribunal will usually fix a time limit for the parties to submit their post-hearing briefs. This is the last opportunity for the parties to file a submission; after expiry of the time limit, no more submissions will be accepted by the arbitral tribunal.

[Counterclaim]

Article 13

(1) Within forty-five (45) days from the date of receipt of the Notice of Arbitration, the Respondent shall file with the CIETAC its counterclaim in writing, if any. The arbitral tribunal may extend that time period if it believes that there are justified reasons.

(2) When filing a counterclaim, the Respondent shall specify its counterclaim in its written Statement of Counterclaim and state the facts and grounds upon which its counterclaim is based with relevant evidence attached thereto.

(3) When filing a counterclaim, the Respondent shall pay an arbitration fee in advance according to the Arbitration Fee Schedule of the CIETAC within a specified time period.

(4) Where the formalities required for filing a counterclaim are found to be complete, the CIETAC shall send the Statement of Counterclaim and its attachments to the Claimant. The Claimant shall, within thirty (30) days from the date of receipt of the Statement of Counterclaim and the attachment, submit in writing its Statement of Defence to the Respondent's counterclaim.

(5) The arbitral tribunal has the power to decide whether to accept a counterclaim submitted after expiration of the above time limit.

(6) Failure of the Claimant to file a Statement of Defence to the Respondent's counterclaim shall not operate to affect the arbitral proceedings.

1. Submission of the counterclaim. When submitting its Statement of Defence according to art. 12 (see art. 12, notes 1 et seq.), the respondent is also given the opportunity to raise – in written form – a counterclaim. The period for submitting such counterclaim is the same as the period for submitting a Statement of Defence, i.e. forty-five days, and it can be extended if the respondent has good reason for not complying with the deadline.

2. Content of the counterclaim. A counterclaim is actually a claim raised by the respondent against the claimant. As a consequence thereof, the same principles which apply to the Request for Arbitration (see art. 10, notes 2 et seq.) also apply to the counterclaim: the 'Statement of Counterclaim' should contain the counterclaims, as well as the grounds and the facts on which the counterclaims are based, and any relevant evidence.

3. Arbitration fee. If the respondent raises a counterclaim, it has to pay the corresponding arbitration fees according to the Arbitration Fee Schedule (see art. 10, note 4). If the respondent fails to pay such fees, its counterclaim will be dismissed.

4. Statement of Defence to the Respondent's Counterclaim. If the Statement of Counterclaim fulfils all requirements as to form and content, it is forwarded to the claimant, who will be invited to submit its defence, i.e. 'Statement of Defence to the Respondent's Counterclaim', within thirty days of receipt of the Statement of Counterclaim. The same rules as applicable to the Statement of Defence also apply to the Statement of Defence to Respondent's Counterclaim, in particular as regards the failure to submit such statement within the fixed deadline (see art. 12, note 2).

[Amendments to claim or counterclaim]

Article 14

The Claimant may amend its claim and the Respondent may amend its counterclaim. However, the arbitral tribunal may not permit any such amendment if it considers that the amendment is too late and may delay the arbitral proceedings.

1. The principles. Art. 14 states that the parties may amend their respective (counter-)claim(s). It gives, however, no indication of a specific time limit, but gives the arbitral tribunal the authority to decide when an amendment is unreasonably late.

2. Tolerant practice. It is widely admitted that a party may amend its claim or counterclaim at any stage during the proceedings, generally until the last hearing. It is quite common in practice to have parties submit all kinds of documents at different stages of the procedure (see art. 10, note 6).

3. Power of the arbitral tribunal. Based on the authority conferred to it in art. 14, the arbitral tribunal is entitled to issue procedural orders fixing time limits for the amendment of the claim or counterclaim and to decide on the consequences of a delayed submission. The practice is here again quite flexible and an arbitral tribunal will usually admit late submissions, unless it would affect the proper proceeding of the arbitration (see also art. 10, note 1).

4. Withdrawal of the claim or counterclaim. The withdrawal of a claim or counterclaim is not considered an amendment in the sense of art. 14, but is subject to a different provision, i.e. to art. 41 (art. 41, notes 1 et seq.). However, this is only true where the withdrawal is total; where a party withdraws only part of its claim or counterclaim, such partial withdrawal is considered an amendment in the sense of art. 14 (see art. 41, note 2).

[Copies of submissions]
Article 15

When submitting the Request for Arbitration, the Statement of Defence, the Statement of Counterclaim, evidence and other documents, the parties shall make the submissions in quintuplicate. Where there are more than two parties, additional copies shall be provided accordingly. Where the arbitral tribunal is composed of a sole arbitrator, the number of copies submitted may be reduced by two. Where the preservation of property or protection of evidence is applied for, the party shall forward one additional copy accordingly.

1. Number of copies of written submissions. In the ordinary case of a two-party arbitration before an arbitral tribunal composed of three arbitrators, the parties should file all their submissions in quintuplicate, i.e. one for each arbitrator, one for the CIETAC Secretariat and one for the other party. If there are more parties, there should be one supplementary copy for each supplementary party. If the arbitration is handled by a sole arbitrator, three copies will suffice, i.e. one for the sole arbitrator, one for CIETAC Secretariat and one for the other party.

2. Preservation of evidence and/or property. According to arts. 28 and 46 Arbitration Law, neither the arbitral tribunal nor the arbitration commission has the competence to issue interim measures of property and/or evidence preservation (see art. 28 Arbitration Law, notes 1 et seq. and art. 46 Arbitration Law notes 1 et seq.). A request for such measures will be passed on by the arbitration commission to the competent court (see art. 17, notes 2 et seq. and art. 18, notes 1 et seq.). As a consequence, one additional copy of the request for such measures should be provided for the court. Moreover, a Chinese translation of all main documents and a notarisation of all evidence that has been issued and/or collected outside of the PRC should be prepared and handed to the court together with the request for evidence and/or property preservation. This is because the courts are much stricter and less flexible regarding evidentiary procedure than an arbitral tribunal.

[Representation]

Article 16

(1) A party may be represented by its authorised representative(s) in handling matters relating to the arbitration. In such a case, a Power of Attorney shall be forwarded to the CIETAC by the party or its authorised representative(s).

(2) Either Chinese or foreign citizens may be authorised by a party to act as its representative(s).

1. Freedom of agency. Art. 16 implements the principle contemplated by art. 29 Arbitration Law (see art. 29 Arbitration Law, note 1), according to which each party may chose a lawyer or other agent to represent it during the arbitration proceedings.

2. Power of attorney. Counsel must present to the arbitration institution an original power of attorney detailing their defined scope of authorisation. Unlike in litigation, the power of attorney need not be certified or notarised. Counsel need not necessarily be lawyers.

3. Chinese nationals and foreigners? Art. 16(2) confirms that the agent may be either a Chinese or a foreign national. Indeed, unlike in litigation, foreign lawyers are permitted to represent their clients in arbitration proceedings and it is quite common for a Foreign Invested Enterprise ('FIE') to be represented at an arbitration by both a foreign lawyer and a local Chinese lawyer. This was not always the case and foreigners were even temporarily forbidden to act as counsel in arbitration proceedings (for more details see art. 29 Arbitration Law, note 2).

[Preservation of property]

Article 17

When any party applies for the preservation of property, the CIETAC shall forward the party's application for a ruling to the competent court at the place where the domicile of the party against whom the preservation of property is sought is located or where the property of the said party is located.

1. No jurisdiction of CIETAC. Art. 17 implements the principle of art. 28 Arbitration Law, according to which neither CIETAC nor the arbitral tribunal itself is empowered to determine applications for property preservation. CIETAC will forward such a request to the competent court (see art. 28 Arbitration Law, note 1).

2. Transfer of the request to the People's Court. A party filing a request for measures of property preservation will file such a request with CIETAC,

CIETAC Arbitration Rules, art. 18

and CIETAC will then forward this request to the competent court, i.e. the court at the place where the property is located or where the party against whom the preservation is sought is located.

3. Application of the Civil Procedure Law. The Civil Procedure Law details the procedure applicable to the submission of applications for property preservation in arts. 92 et seq. and 249 et seq., providing that a party may file an application for property preservation with the court in circumstances where that party believes: that the execution of a judgment may become difficult or impossible because of the actions of the other party or for other reasons; or that in the absence of an immediate property preservation order its legitimate rights and interests would suffer irreparable damage. In hearing the property preservation application of a party, the court may require the applicant to provide monetary security, in default of which, the court will reject the application. In urgent cases, the court will determine an application within forty-eight hours. Once issued, a property preservation order takes effect immediately. If the People's Court subsequently determines that an application for property preservation was wrongfully made, the applicant will be required to compensate the person against whom the property preservation order was made.

4. No preservation of property before the arbitration proceedings. Because of the requirement to go through CIETAC to apply for preservation of property, such an application may only be filed once CIETAC has been entrusted with the case, i.e. once an application for arbitration has been filed. Thus, as long as CIETAC has not been entrusted with a case, no preservation measures can be requested, which means that under Chinese arbitration law and practice, no pre-arbitration preservation measures are available (for more details see art. 46 Arbitration Law, note 2).

[Preservation of evidence]
Article 18

When a party applies for the preservation of evidence, the CIETAC shall forward the party's application for a ruling to the competent court at the place where the evidence is located.

1. No jurisdiction of CIETAC. Art. 18 implements the principle contemplated by art. 46 Arbitration Law (see note 1), according to which requests for preservation of evidence are of the exclusive competence of the courts. Although the request has to be filed with CIETAC, CIETAC will then forward it to the competent court at the place where the evidence is located.

2. No preservation of evidence before the arbitration proceedings. Because of the requirement to pass through CIETAC to apply for preservation of evidence, such an application may only be filed once CIETAC has been entrusted with the case. Thus, under the Chinese arbitration system, a party may not request pre-arbitration preservation measures (see art. 17, note 4; for more details see art. 46 Arbitration Law, note 2).

Section 2. The Arbitral Tribunal

[Duties of the arbitrator(s)]

Article 19

An arbitrator shall not represent either party and shall remain independent of the parties and treat them equally.

1. Duty of independence. Each arbitrator, whether appointed by a party or by the Chairman of CIETAC, is and should remain independent at all times during the procedure and should treat the parties equally.

2. Duty of impartiality? Although art. 19 only mentions the term of 'independence', it is widely admitted that an arbitrator also has to be 'impartial'. This can firstly be deduced from the requirement to treat both parties equally, and also from the following art. 25 on disclosure (see art. 25, notes 1 et seq.) and art. 26 on the challenge of an arbitrator (see art. 26, notes 1 et seq.).

3. Ethical rules for arbitrators. In 1993, CIETAC and CMAC issued the so-called 'Ethical Rules for Arbitrators', amended in 1994. These rules provide details regarding the conduct and behaviour expected of an arbitrator in undertaking an arbitration. The Ethical Rules for Arbitrators reiterate the duty of an arbitrator to remain independent and impartial in conducting the arbitration, to thoroughly and meticulously examine all the evidence, and to be both fair and reasonable in assessing and determining the merits of the arguments furnished by the disputing parties.

4. Duty of disclosure. In order to ensure their independence and impartiality, each arbitrator has the duty to submit a 'Declaration of Independence' (see art. 25, notes 1 et seq.). This duty is also contemplated by the Ethical Rules for Arbitrators.

5. Consequences of a violation of the duty of independence and impartiality. If an arbitrator violates his duty of independence or any other duty as provided for in the Ethical Rules for Arbitrators, he is obliged to withdraw from the arbitration proceedings, or he may be challenged according to art. 26 (see art. 26, notes 1 et seq.) or revoked by CIETAC according to art. 27 (see art. 27, notes 1 et seq.)

[Number of arbitrators]

Article 20

(1) The arbitral tribunal shall be composed of one or three arbitrators.

(2) Unless otherwise agreed by the parties or provided by these Rules, the arbitral tribunal shall be composed of three arbitrators.

1. One or three arbitrators. Art. 20 merely repeats the principle contemplated by art. 30 Arbitration Law, according to which parties may chose between one or three arbitrators (see art. 30 Arbitration Law).

2. Three arbitrators as the most common solution. Contrary to the ICC Rules, which provide that where the parties have not agreed on the number of arbitrators, the case shall be handled by a sole arbitrator unless the complexity of the case or other circumstances justify a panel of three arbitrators (see art. 8(2) ICC Rules), the CIETAC Rules provide for the opposite solution: unless otherwise provided by the parties, there will be a panel of three arbitrators. Under CIETAC, this solution is not really problematic, since the fees of arbitrators are substantially lower than under ICC arbitration.

[Panel of arbitrators]
Article 21

(1) The parties shall appoint arbitrators from the Panel of Arbitrators provided by the CIETAC.
(2) Where the parties have agreed to appoint arbitrators from outside of the CIETAC's Panel of Arbitrators, the arbitrators so appointed by the parties or nominated according to the agreement of the parties may act as co-arbitrator, presiding arbitrator or sole arbitrator after the appointment has been confirmed by the Chairman of the CIETAC in accordance with the law.

1. Internal list of arbitrators. Art. 21 implements the principle set forth in art. 13 and art. 67 Arbitration Law and according to which each arbitration commission shall establish a Panel of Arbitrators, whereby it is entitled to also appoint foreign arbitrators.

2. CIETAC Panel of Arbitrators. The CIETAC Panel of Arbitrators is presently composed of a total of over 1000 arbitrators, among whom approximately 270 arbitrators are foreign nationals drawn from over thirty countries and regions.

3. Qualification as arbitrator. Art. 13 Arbitration Law sets forth minimum requirements for Chinese arbitrators (see art. 13 Arbitration Law, notes 2 et seq.), whereas art. 67 Arbitration Law merely mentions that foreign arbitrators shall have a special knowledge in the field of law, economy and trade, science and technology, etc. (see art. 67 Arbitration Law note 3). To complement these minimum requirements set by the Arbitration Law, CIETAC has issued the Stipulations for the Appointment of Arbitrators, which provide for different requirements for the appointment of Chinese arbitrators and foreign arbitrators or arbitrators from Hong Kong, Macao or Taiwan. Those requirements are less restrictive than those applicable to Chinese arbitrators (compare with art. 13 Arbitration Law, note 2). For Hong Kong, Macao or Taiwan and foreign nationals, the Stipulations require that a prospective arbitrator: has a keen interest in arbitration, and can uphold the principle of independence and impartiality in handling cases; has acquired professional knowledge of law, economy and trade, science and technology or maritime affairs, and has working experience; is willing to observe the arbitration rules of the Arbitration Commission, the Ethical Rules for Arbitrators and other relevant regulations; and has a good grasp of English and some knowledge of Chinese. However, the requirements can be relaxed for well-known individuals in the field of international arbitration.

4. Free choice of the parties. In forming arbitral tribunals, the parties to an intended CIETAC arbitration and the Chairman of the arbitration commission were traditionally obliged to select arbitrators from the appropriate Panel lists, although CIETAC granted some exceptions in the past. Based on the new article 21(2), introduced in 2005, the choice of an arbitrator outside the list of CIETAC should now be much easier. Although such appointment still needs to be confirmed by CIETAC, such confirmation is more of a formal nature and should not allow CIETAC to refuse the appointment of a foreign arbitrators without good reason.

[Three arbitrators]
Article 22

(1) Within fifteen (15) days from the date of receipt of the Notice of Arbitration, the Claimant and the Respondent shall each appoint one arbitrator or entrust the Chairman of the CIETAC to make such appointment. Where a party fails to appoint or to entrust the Chairman of the CIETAC to appoint an arbitrator within the specified time period, the arbitrator shall be appointed by the Chairman of the CIETAC.

(2) Within fifteen (15) days from the date of the Respondent's receipt of the Notice of Arbitration, the presiding arbitrator shall be jointly appointed by the parties or appointed by the Chairman of the CIETAC upon the parties' joint authorisation.

(3) The parties may each recommend one to three arbitrators as candidates for the presiding arbitrator and shall submit the list of recommended candidates to the CIETAC within the time period specified in paragraph 2. Where there is only one common candidate in the lists, such candidate shall be the presiding arbitrator jointly appointed by the parties. Where there are more than one common candidate in the lists, the Chairman of the CIETAC shall choose a presiding arbitrator from among the common candidates based on the specific nature and circumstances of the case, who shall act as the presiding arbitrator jointly appointed by the parties. Where there is no common candidate in the

lists, the presiding arbitrator shall be appointed by the Chairman of the CIETAC from outside of the lists of recommended candidates.

(4) Where the parties have failed to jointly appoint the presiding arbitrator according to the above provisions, the presiding arbitrator shall be appointed by the Chairman of the CIETAC.

1. Priority of party autonomy. Art. 22, which implements art. 31 Arbitration Law, largely reflects international practice and gives the parties the autonomy to decide on the mechanism of constitution of the arbitral tribunal. Art. 22(3) further contains an unusual and quite innovative rule concerning the appointment of the presiding arbitrator.

2. Appointment of party arbitrators. Art. 22(1) provides that each party shall appoint one arbitrator within fifteen days upon receipt of the 'Notice of Arbitration', or shall entrust the Chairman of CIETAC to make such appointment. If a party fails to appoint an arbitrator, the arbitrator will be appointed by the Chairman of CIETAC. Thus, where the parties do not specifically specify the mechanism for the constitution of the arbitral tribunal, they will have the choice between appointing an arbitrator themselves or referring this task to the Chairman.

3. Appointment of the presiding arbitrator. Art. 22(2) states that the parties must jointly appoint the presiding arbitrator. By 'jointly appoint', art. 22(2) actually refers to the mechanism provided for in art. 22(3). According to this peculiar mechanism, each party must suggest three arbitrators. If there is one common candidate on both lists, such person shall be appointed presiding arbitrator. If there is more than one common candidate on both lists, the Chairman of CIETAC will decide on the most appropriate one based on the circumstances of the dispute. If there is no common candidate, the Chairman of CIETAC will rule out all the candidates mentioned on the lists and appoint a different presiding arbitrator. The parties are, however, free to provide for another mechanism of appointment of the presiding arbitrator, as for example its nomination by the two party-appointed arbitrators.

4. Important role of the Chairman of CIETAC. The Chairman of CIETAC plays an important role in the appointment of arbitrators, since he is responsible for appointing arbitrators whenever the parties fail to constitute the arbitral tribunal using the applicable mechanism, or whenever they expressly entrust the Chairman with the task.

[Sole arbitrator]

Article 23

Where the arbitral tribunal is composed of one arbitrator, the sole arbitrator shall be appointed pursuant to the procedure stipulated in paragraphs 2, 3 and 4 of Article 22.

1. List system. Art. 23 refers to the mechanism of appointment of the presiding arbitrator provided for in art. 22(2), (3) and (4). Each party will thus have to suggest three arbitrators, and the sole arbitrator will be appointed by the Chairman of CIETAC either among the common recommendations of the parties, or failing such common recommendation, outside of the lists of recommended candidates. Here again, the parties may provide for a different mechanism in their arbitration agreement.

[Multi-party]

Article 24

(1) Where there are two or more Claimants and/or Respondents in an arbitration case, the Claimant side and/or the Respondent side each shall, through consultation, jointly appoint or jointly entrust the Chairman of the CIETAC to appoint one arbitrator from the CIETAC's Panel of Arbitrators.

(2) Where the Claimant side and/or the Respondent side fail to jointly appoint or jointly entrust the Chairman of the CIETAC to appoint one arbitrator within fifteen (15) days from the date of receipt of the Notice of Arbitration, the arbitrator shall be appointed by the Chairman of the CIETAC.

(3) The presiding arbitrator or the sole arbitrator shall be appointed in accordance with the procedure stipulated in paragraphs 2, 3 and 4 of Article 22. When appointing the presiding arbitrator or the sole arbitrator pursuant to paragraph 3 of Article 22, the Claimant side and/or the Respondent side each shall, through consultation, submit a list of their jointly agreed candidates to the CIETAC.

1. Multi-party. Art. 25 refers to the case where there are more than two parties to the arbitration, in particular where there are two or more claimants and/or two or more respondents.

2. Appointment of the party arbitrators. For the appointment of the party arbitrators, the parties are separated into two groups, i.e. claimants and respondents, and each group must either jointly designate one arbitrator or entrust the Chairman of CIETAC to do so.

3. Appointment of the presiding arbitrator. The presiding arbitrator will be determined according to the mechanism described in art. 22(3). Each group of claimants and respondents must recommend three candidates, and the presiding arbitrator will be appointed from both groups' common candidates. If there is no common candidate, the presiding arbitrator will be appointed by the Chairman of CIETAC outside the two lists of recommended candidates (see art. 22, note 3).

4. Joinder of proceedings/third party intervention. Sometimes, when there are more than two parties involved in a dispute, it may happen that each of them has a claim against the other and that they cannot be separated into two groups of claimants and respondents, or that although the dispute affects several parties, the arbitration is only initiated against some of them. The question then arises whether these disputes between the different parties can be joined into one arbitration procedure, or whether it is necessary to initiate separate arbitration proceedings. The Arbitration Law and the CIETAC Rules are silent concerning these questions. In practice and contrary to other arbitration institutions, CIETAC is very reluctant to join different proceedings, although it is not excluded that, based on a well-drafted arbitration agreement providing for an appropriate mechanism, a joinder of proceedings or third party intervention may be possible and admitted by CIETAC. With the development of international arbitration practice in this respect, it is only a matter of time until CIETAC adopts a more flexible approach. It remains, however, uncertain how local courts will react when faced with a request for cancellation or non-enforcement of an arbitral award based on such joinder of proceedings or third party intervention.

[Disclosure]
Article 25

(1) An arbitrator appointed by the parties or by the Chairman of the CIETAC shall sign a Declaration and disclose to the CIETAC in writing any facts or circumstances likely to give rise to justifiable doubts as to his impartiality or independence.

(2) If circumstances that need to be disclosed arise during the arbitral proceedings, the arbitrator shall promptly disclose such circumstances in writing to the CIETAC.

(3) The CIETAC shall communicate the Declaration and/or the disclosure of the arbitrator to the parties.

1. Declaration of Independence. As with most international arbitration institutions, in order to ensure the independence and impartiality of the arbitrator, the arbitrator must disclose to CIETAC any circumstances that may give rise to 'justifiable doubts' as to his impartiality or independence. He does so by filling out a 'Declaration of Independence' within three to five days of his appointment. The Declaration of Independence will then be forwarded to the parties, each of them being able to raise objections as to the appointment of such arbitrator (see art. 26, notes 1 et seq.). If no objection is raised, CIETAC will confirm the appointment of the arbitrator.

2. Form of the Declaration of Independence. The Declaration of Independence is very similar to the ICC Arbitrator's Declaration of Acceptance and Statement of Independence. In the first part of the document, the arbitrator accepts the case and undertakes to respect all applicable laws and rules; in the second part of the document, the arbitrator confirms being independent and is invited to disclose circumstances that may give rise to any doubts as to his impartiality or independence.

3. Disclosure during the proceedings. If any circumstances giving rise to justifiable doubts as to an arbitrator's impartiality and independence arise during the arbitration proceedings, the arbitrator shall 'promptly' inform CIETAC in writing and disclose such circumstances. According to the circumstances, the arbitrator may be obliged to withdraw, or the parties may have the right to request his challenge according to art. 26 (see art. 26, notes 3 et seq.).

4. Justifiable doubts as to his independence or impartiality. In this respect, see art. 26, note 4.

[Challenge]

Article 26

(1) Upon receipt of the Declaration and/or written disclosure of an arbitrator communicated by the CIETAC, a party who intends to challenge the arbitrator on the grounds of the facts or circumstances disclosed by the arbitrator shall forward the challenge in writing to the CIETAC within ten (10) days from the date of such receipt. If a party fails to file a challenge within the above time limit, it shall not challenge an arbitrator later on the basis of matters disclosed by the arbitrator.

(2) A party who has justifiable doubts as to the impartiality or independence of an appointed arbitrator may make a request in writing to the CIETAC for that arbitrator's withdrawal. In the request, the facts and reasons on which the request is based shall be stated with supporting evidence.

(3) A party may challenge an arbitrator in writing within fifteen (15) days from the date of its receipt of the Notice of Formation of the Arbitral Tribunal. Where a party becomes aware of the reasons for a challenge after the said receipt, the party may challenge the arbitrator in writing within fifteen (15) days after such reasons become known, but no later than the conclusion of the last oral hearing.

(4) The CIETAC shall promptly communicate the challenge to the other party, the arbitrator being challenged and the other members of the arbitral tribunal.

(5) Where an arbitrator is challenged by one party and the other party agrees to the challenge, or the arbitrator being challenged withdraws from his office, such arbitrator shall no longer be on the arbitral tribunal. Neither case implies that the challenge made by the party is sustainable.

(6) In circumstances other than those specified in paragraph 5, the Chairman of the CIETAC shall make a final decision on the challenge with or without stating the reasons therefor.

(7) An arbitrator who has been challenged shall continue to fulfil the functions of arbitrator until a decision on the challenge has been made by the Chairman of the CIETAC.

1. Challenge based on the content of the Declaration of Independence. According to art. 26(1), upon receipt by the parties of the Declaration of Independence, they are given ten days to request in writing the challenge of an arbitrator based on the facts or circumstances described in his Declaration. If the parties fail to raise such a request within those ten days, they will be precluded from doing so in the future based on a matter already disclosed in the Declaration.

2. Challenge based on facts revealed after the receipt of the Declaration of Independence but before the constitution of the arbitral tribunal. Art. 26(2) entitles the parties to challenge an arbitrator within fifteen days after receipt of the Notice of Formation of the arbitral tribunal. The parties may, however, only challenge the arbitrator for reasons that were not disclosed in the Declaration of Independence and that came to light in the meantime, i.e. between the receipt of the Declaration of Independence and the receipt of the Notice of Formation of the arbitral tribunal.

3. Challenge based on facts revealed at a later stage. Where a party becomes aware of grounds to challenge an arbitrator (which were not disclosed in the Declaration of Independence), it has to do so within fifteen days of such grounds becoming known. In any case, however, the challenge must be submitted before the end of the last hearing. However, it should be mentioned that if a party is informed – after the last hearing or even after the rendering of the award – of circumstances that create doubts as to the arbitrator's impartiality and independence, the party concerned may request to set aside the award or may object to its enforcement based on arts. 70 and 71 Arbitration Law in connection with art. 258(3) Civil Procedure Law (see art. 70 Arbitration Law, notes 1 et seq.).

4. Justifiable doubts. The reasons for challenge are listed in art. 34 Arbitration Law and apply to situations: where the arbitrator is a party to the arbitral proceedings, or is related to any party or their respective attorneys in the arbitral proceedings; where the case is one in which the arbitrator has a personal interest; where the arbitrator has a relationship with a disputing party or any attorneys involved in the case that may prejudice the rendering of a fair and impartial arbitral award; or where the arbitrator has met in private with any party to the arbitration or their respective attorneys, or has accepted gifts or hospitality from any of the parties or their respective attorneys. This list is further complemented by the CIETAC Ethical Rules for Arbitrators, which provides for a list of further circumstances: the arbitrator has discussed the case with a party or counsel, or has given advice or opinions concerning the merits of the case to a party or his counsel; the arbitrator has a relationship with a party or his counsel that involves debt or credit, or concerns business cooperation or competition; the arbitrator is an advisor to or has previously provided advice to a party or to the counsel of a party; the arbitrator has the same employer as a party or the counsel of a party; the arbitrator was previously engaged as a conciliator in a separate conciliation process that failed to resolve the dispute, and all the parties to the arbitration object to the arbitrator serving as an arbitrator in the subsequent arbitral proceedings; or the arbitrator has a relationship with a party or his counsel, such as teacher, student, neighbour or friend, to such an extent that it may possibly affect the impartiality of the arbitrator. The IBA Guidelines on Conflicts of Interest in International Arbitration have not been adopted by CIETAC, although they are well known in arbitration circles in China and serve as guidelines for the arbitrators. As a consequence, a violation of the principles stated in the IBA Guidelines on Conflicts of Interest in International Arbitration will usually not constitute a sufficient basis to challenge an arbitrator, unless the violation of such principle simultaneously violates a rule already contained in the CIETAC Rules or in the Ethical Rules for Arbitrators.

5. Consequences of the request for challenge. Where a party raises a request for challenge to an arbitrator, the consequences of such request differ according to whether: the other party agrees, the arbitrator agrees to withdraw, or neither the other party nor the concerned arbitrator agrees with the request. In the first two cases, the arbitrator will no longer be a member of the arbitral tribunal, and no further decision is necessary. In the case where neither the other party nor the concerned arbitrator agrees with the request for his challenge, CIETAC shall take a final decision on the challenge. Until such decision is taken, the concerned arbitrator shall continue to exercise his duties as arbitrator.

6. Decision by the Chairman of CIETAC. Requests for challenge of an arbitrator have to be addressed to CIETAC, and not to the arbitral tribunal. Such request has to be made in writing and should explain the facts and reasons giving rise to justifiable doubts as to the impartiality or independence of the arbitrators. The Chairman of CIETAC will decide upon the challenge, unless he is himself a member of the concerned arbitral tribunal, in which case the decision will be made collectively by CIETAC (see art. 36 Arbitration Law). If the arbitration is handled by a Sub-Commission of CIETAC, the decision on the challenge of an arbitrator will still be taken by the Chairman of CIETAC at CIETAC's headquarters, and not by the Vice-Chairman of the Sub-Commission (see art. 4(1), note 1).

[Replacement of arbitrator]

Article 27

(1) In the event that an arbitrator is prevented de jure or de facto from fulfilling his functions, or it fails to fulfil his functions in accordance with the requirements of these Rules or within the time period specified

in these Rules, the Chairman of the CIETAC shall have the power to decide whether the arbitrator shall be replaced. The arbitrator may also withdraw from his office.

(2) In the event that an arbitrator is unable to fulfil his functions owing to his demise, removal from the CIETAC's Panel of Arbitrators, withdrawal, resignation or any other reasons, a substitute arbitrator shall be appointed within a time period specified by the CIETAC pursuant to the procedure applied to the appointment of the arbitrator being replaced.

(3) After the replacement of the arbitrator, the arbitral tribunal shall decide whether the whole or a part of the previous proceedings of the case shall be repeated.

(4) The Chairman of the CIETAC shall make a final decision on whether an arbitrator should be replaced or not with or without stating the reasons therefor.

1. Grounds for replacement. According to art. 27, the Chairman of CIETAC has the power to revoke and replace an arbitrator, when that arbitrator is unable to fulfil his functions in accordance with the Rules. The phrase 'unable to fulfil his functions' may refer to different kinds of situations, including but not limited to the case where there are grounds for challenge or withdrawal of the arbitrator, where the arbitrator is removed from the CIETAC's Panel of Arbitrators, where he has resigned, or where he simply no longer fulfils the minimum requirements for arbitrators (see art. 13, note 2). Thus, although art. 27 follows art. 26 concerning the challenge/withdrawal of an arbitrator, its scope of application is much wider and is not only limited to cases where an arbitrator is challenged due to a lack of impartiality or independence. Art. 27 applies to all cases where an arbitrator is unable – for whatever reasons – to fulfil his obligations.

2. Removal from CIETAC's Panel of Arbitrators. In certain serious cases of a violation of his duties, an arbitrator may be removed from CIETAC's Panel of Arbitrators. This is the case when an arbitrator violates his duties under arts. 34(4) and 58(6) Arbitration Law (see art. 38 Arbitration Law, note 1), i.e. when he has privately met with a party or when he has committed embezzlement, accepted bribes or engaged in malpractice for personal benefit, or perverted the law in the arbitration of the case. In those cases, it is evident that such arbitrator will also be replaced in any pending arbitration proceedings he may act in. Actually, the CIETAC Rules only stipulate certain circumstances under which an arbitrator shall be replaced, but there is no exhaustive list of such circumstances, nor is there any provision as to when and how to remove such arbitrator from the CIETAC Panel. Besides the abovementioned circumstances, CIETAC has in practice removed arbitrators from its Panel where the arbitrator was charged of a crime, or where he had seriously delayed the procedure or unjustifiably influenced other arbitrators. CIETAC has a wide discretion in this respect.

3. Resignation of an arbitrator. Art. 27 also mentions the case in which an arbitrator resigns from the arbitral tribunal. The term resignation applies to situations where an arbitrator steps out of the arbitration, not because of any lack of independence or impartiality, but for other reasons mainly unrelated to the arbitration case. The CIETAC Rules do not address the question of when an arbitrator is allowed to resign from the arbitral tribunal. Art. 7 of the Ethical Rules for Arbitration sets forth that '[f]ollowing acceptance of appointment to an arbitral tribunal, an arbitrator must guarantee the availability of sufficient time for conducting any arbitral hearing, and sitting in private session for effecting deliberations on the case. In no circumstances may an arbitrator impede the handling of a case'. The resignation of an arbitrator strongly affects the arbitration proceedings, as it causes delays and supplementary costs in the case of a replacement. Based thereon, it can be deduced that an arbitrator may not resign from an arbitral tribunal as he wishes, but can only do so where there exist justifiable reasons that impede him from fulfilling his task as an arbitrator. In practice, it is rare that arbitrators resign, and where they do, their request needs to be approved by the Chairman of CIETAC, who will usually grant such request.

4. Replacement procedure. According to art. 27(2) in fine, the new arbitrator must be appointed according to the same procedure applied to the appointment of the replaced arbitrator (i.e. art. 22 et seq.).

5. Recommencement of proceedings? According to art. 27(3), in case an arbitrator is replaced, the newly constituted arbitral tribunal (and not CIETAC itself) should decide whether it is necessary to repeat the whole or part of the previous proceedings (see also art. 37(2) Arbitration Law). In practice, it is extremely rare to repeat the whole proceedings. However, it is common to repeat a hearing, if the new arbitrator joined after that hearing. This is to make sure that all the arbitrators make a decision based on the same information. If the replacement takes place before the oral hearing, there is usually no reason to repeat the proceedings, since the new arbitrator can gain a view of the case based on the written submissions.

6. Discretionary power of CIETAC. Arising out of art. 27(4), CIETAC has a certain discretionary power when deciding on 'whether an arbitrator should be replaced'. This discretionary power applies to the removal of an arbitrator and to his subsequent replacement, and means that CIETAC will have the final word (see further art. 28, note 1).

[Majority to continue arbitration]

Article 28

In the event that, after the conclusion of the last oral hearing, an arbitrator on a three-member arbitral tribunal is unable to participate in the deliberation and/or render the award owing to his demise or removal from the CIETAC's Panel of Arbitrators, the other two arbitrators may

request the Chairman of the CIETAC to replace the arbitrator pursuant to Article 27. After consulting with the parties and upon the approval of the Chairman of the CIETAC, the other two arbitrators may continue the arbitration and make decisions, rulings or the award. The Secretariat of the CIETAC shall notify the parties of the above circumstances.

1. Avoidable replacement of an arbitrator if his removal occurs after the conclusion of the last oral hearing. Art. 28 sets out the principle that, if an arbitrator is removed (for whatever reasons) from the arbitration proceedings after the conclusion of the last oral hearing, this does not necessarily trigger his replacement. The main purpose of this article is to avoid extra delay. The concerned arbitrator will only be replaced if the two other arbitrators make an according request with the Chairman of CIETAC or if CIETAC otherwise deems it necessary. In any case, the Chairman of CIETAC will consult with the parties. CIETAC may then allow the two arbitrators to continue the proceedings and render an award. It should be noted that this provision, which is largely inspired by art. 12(5) ICC Rules, is not totally in compliance with art. 37(1) Arbitration Law, which provides that '[i]f an arbitrator cannot perform his duties due to his withdrawal or for other reasons, a substitute arbitrator shall be selected or appointed in accordance with this Law'. Although the Arbitration Law does seem to impose a replacement and does not seem to leave any space for discretionary power of the arbitration commission, CIETAC holds its position giving priority to the parties' autonomy. Actually, this discrepancy is not very important in practice, since art. 28 has – to our knowledge – never been applied.

Section 3. Hearing

[Conduct of hearing]

Article 29

(1) The arbitral tribunal shall examine the case in any way that it deems appropriate unless otherwise agreed by the parties. Under any circumstance, the arbitral tribunal shall act impartially and fairly and shall afford reasonable opportunities to all parties for presentations and debates.

(2) The arbitral tribunal shall hold oral hearings when examining the case. However, oral hearings may be omitted and the case shall be examined on the basis of documents only if the parties so request or agree and the arbitral tribunal also deems that oral hearings are unnecessary.

(3) Unless otherwise agreed by the parties, the arbitral tribunal may adopt an inquisitorial or adversarial approach when examining the case, having regard to the circumstances of the case.

(4) The arbitral tribunal may hold deliberation at any place or in any manner that it considers appropriate.

(5) The arbitral tribunal may, if it considers it necessary, issue procedural directions and lists of questions, hold pre-hearing meetings and preliminary hearings, and produce terms of reference, etc., unless otherwise agreed by the parties.

1. Oral hearing not compulsory. Art. 29(2) implements the principle set forth in art. 39 Arbitration Law (see art. 39 Arbitration Law, note 1), according to which the arbitral tribunal may omit to conduct oral hearings based on a corresponding agreement of the parties. However, the arbitral tribunal may still insist on the conduct of oral hearing if it deems such hearings necessary. In practice, it is extremely rare that an arbitral tribunal will decide to render an award based on written applications only.

2. Hearings: inquisitorial or adversarial? According to art. 29(3), the arbitral tribunal may adopt either an inquisitorial or an adversarial approach when examining the case. The term 'inquisitorial' refers to the role of the judge in civil law systems, and means that the arbitrators will be taking the lead in the proceedings, especially as regards the evidentiary proceedings. The term 'adversarial' refers to the common law approach and means that the parties' counsel will be given the lead in the proceedings. Although art. 29(3) keeps both doors open, in practice, arbitral tribunals composed of a majority of Chinese arbitrators will adopt a more inquisitorial than adversarial approach. This is also due to the fact that there is a lack of detailed rules on evidentiary proceedings, and that arbitrators will therefore often refer to statutory procedural rules (as for example the SPC Provisions on Evidence), which are heavily influenced by an inquisitorial system.

3. Place of deliberation. According to art. 29(4), the arbitral tribunal can hold deliberations at any given place (see also art. 32(1), note 1). This provision applies to 'deliberations', i.e. internal meetings of the arbitral tribunal. The place of the hearing is determined in accordance with art. 32.

4. Procedural orders. Art. 29(5) expressly gives the arbitral tribunal the authority to issue procedural orders and other documents in order to efficiently organise the proceedings. The arbitral tribunal is also free to decide on the number, place and time of hearings. By doing so, the arbitral tribunal has nevertheless the duty to respect the procedural rights of the parties, and shall also comply with any existing agreement of the parties as regards procedural issues.

[Notice of oral hearing]

Article 30

(1) The date of the first oral hearing shall be fixed by the arbitral tribunal and notified to the parties by the Secretariat of the CIETAC at least twenty (20) days in advance of the oral hearing date. A party

having justified reasons may request a postponement of the oral hearing. However, such request must be communicated to the arbitral tribunal at least ten (10) days in advance of the oral hearing date. The arbitral tribunal shall decide whether to postpone the oral hearing or not.

(2) A notice of oral hearing subsequent to the first oral hearing and a notice of a postponed oral hearing shall not be subject to the twenty (20)-day time limit provided for in the foregoing paragraph.

1. Short time limit. When deciding to hold an oral hearing, the arbitral tribunal has to notify the parties and their counsel. Compared with the CIETAC Rules of 2000, the time limit for notice for an oral hearing has been shortened from thirty days to twenty days. This aims to accelerate the proceedings, although in practice it is common for the parties to request postponement of the hearing.

[Place of arbitration]

Article 31

(1) Where the parties have agreed on the place of arbitration in writing, the parties' agreement shall prevail.

(2) Where the parties have not agreed on the place of arbitration, the place of arbitration shall be the domicile of the CIETAC or its Sub-Commission.

(3) The arbitral award shall be deemed as being made at the place of arbitration.

1. Free choice of arbitration venue. The CIETAC Rules (2000) did not mention the 'place of arbitration' (more commonly known as the 'seat' or the 'venue' of arbitration), but only contained a provision on the 'place of hearing' (i.e. the venue of the hearing). Under these Rules, the parties can only choose Beijing, Shenzhen, or Shanghai as the place of the hearing. Based on this, and given the absence of a provision on the place of arbitration, general confusion arose among arbitration practitioners as to the distinction between the place of hearing and the place of arbitration. The CIETAC Rules of 2005 now clearly make a distinction between the place of arbitration (art. 31) and the place of oral hearing (art. 32). With the introduction of art. 31(1) in 2005, the parties are free to chose the place of arbitration. Further, this freedom is not limited to places in China: the parties can chose a place abroad. This is a big step forward for Chinese arbitration, as it opens the way for CIETAC to conduct foreign arbitration proceedings. It is the first time that CIETAC arbitrators may handle arbitration proceedings subject to foreign arbitration laws.

2. Limitation of free choice. While the parties may freely choose any venue within the PRC, they may only choose an arbitration venue abroad if admissible under Chinese Law. According to art. 128 Contract Law, parties to an arbitration agreement may choose a place of arbitration abroad if their dispute is 'foreign-related'. If the dispute is purely domestic, the parties may not choose an arbitration venue abroad, and if they do they will face problems when trying to enforce any award in China.

3. Written form. In order to prevail, the parties' agreement concerning the place of arbitration must be in writing, i.e. in any form capable of tangible representation of its content, such as written instruments, letters and electrically or electronically transmitted documents including telegrams, telexes, facsimiles, electronic data interchange and email (see art. 5, note 3 and also art. 11 Contract Law).

4. Subsidiary place of arbitration. If the parties fail to provide for a place of arbitration, the place of arbitration will be deemed to be the place where CIETAC, or its Sub-Commission is located (see also art. 2(8), note 3 in fine).

5. Importance of the place where the award was rendered. The place where the award was rendered will determine the nationality of the award. This question is crucial from the perspective of enforcement, as according to the nationality of the award its enforcement may be subject to a different set of rules. The Arbitration Law is silent as regards the place were the arbitral award is deemed to be made. Traditionally, an award is considered to be made at the seat of the arbitration commission. This solution may have made sense when Chinese arbitration commissions were only entitled to handle Chinese (domestic and foreign-related) arbitration cases. However, since CIETAC has been given the authority to handle foreign arbitration cases, i.e. cases having their arbitration venue abroad, sticking to the competent arbitration commission as relevant criteria would be inappropriate. Accordingly, art. 31(3) provides that the award is deemed to be made at the place of arbitration. It is thus the place of arbitration that will determine the nationality of the award. This new provision is finally in accordance with international practice. However, parties should be aware that if they fail to provide for a place of arbitration, the place of arbitration will be deemed to be at the domicile of the relevant CIETAC Commission or Sub-Commission (see note 4), which will make the award a 'Chinese' award. Enforcement procedures of the award will thus be subject to the Arbitration Law (see art. 70 Arbitration Law, note 1), and not to the New York Convention or other relevant international treaties.

[Place of oral hearing]

Article 32

(1) Where the parties have agreed on the place of oral hearings, the case shall be heard at that agreed place except for circumstances stipulated in paragraph 3 of Article 69 of these Rules.

CIETAC Arbitration Rules, art. 33

(2) Unless the parties agree otherwise, a case accepted by the CIETAC shall be heard in Beijing, or if the arbitral tribunal considers it necessary, at other places with the approval of the Secretary-General of the CIETAC. A case accepted by a Sub-Commission of the CIETAC shall be heard at the place where the Sub-Commission is located, or if the arbitral tribunal considers it necessary, at other places with the approval of the Secretary-General of the Sub-Commission.

1. Party's autonomy as to the place of hearing. In general, hearings may be held at: the place agreed upon between the parties; the place where the arbitration commission is located; or any place designated by the arbitral tribunal, upon approval by the Secretary-General of CIETAC. Art. 32 contemplates the priority of the party's autonomy. However, it should be mentioned that if the parties chose a place different from the domicile of the competent CIETAC Commission or Sub-Commission, CIETAC may charge the parties for the supplementary costs incurred. If the parties fail to pay those additional costs, the hearings will take place at the domicile of CIETAC (see art. 69, note 3).

2. Distinction as to the place of arbitration. Again, it should be stressed that the place of hearing is different from the place of arbitration. Whereas the place of arbitration determines the law applicable to the arbitration and the nationality of the award, the place of the hearing is simply the place where oral hearings will take place and have no further influence on the arbitration proceedings (see art. 31, note 1 et seq.).

[Confidentiality]

Article 33

(1) Hearings shall be held in camera. Where both parties request an open hearing, the arbitral tribunal shall make a decision.

(2) For cases heard in camera, the parties, their representatives, witnesses, interpreters, arbitrators, experts consulted by the arbitral tribunal and appraisers appointed by the arbitral tribunal and the relevant staff members of the Secretariat of the CIETAC shall not disclose to any outsiders any substantive or procedural matters of the case.

1. Confidentiality of hearings. Art. 33(1) is identical to art. 40(1) Arbitration Law, and provides that hearings should not be public, but held in camera, unless both parties agree otherwise.

2. General duty of confidentiality? Art. 33 is located in between provisions concerning arbitral hearings, and art. 33(1) expressly refers to the term 'hearings'. There is no express mention of a general duty of confidentiality. The same is true as regards the Arbitration Law, which also only mentions the privacy of hearings but makes no statement as to a general duty of confidentiality (see art. 40 Arbitration Law, note 2). However, it is widely admitted among arbitration practitioners that the duty of confidentiality has a much wider scope and encompasses not only information exchanged during the 'hearings', but applies to the entire arbitration proceedings, including their existence. This is confirmed by art. 33(2), which prohibits any participant to the arbitration to disclose 'any substantive or procedural matters of the case'.

3. Reinforced duty of confidentiality of the arbitrator. According to art. 13 of the Ethical Rules for Arbitrators, an arbitrator must strictly maintain the confidentiality of all information revealed during the case and may not disclose this information to third parties, including substantive and procedural information relating to the arbitration – this includes details of the dispute, the process of conducting the hearings or information relating to private sittings of the arbitral tribunal. In particular, arbitrators may not reveal their personal opinions regarding the case or any information concerning the private sittings of the arbitral tribunal to any party.

4. Consequences of a violation of the duty of confidentiality. The consequences of a violation of the duty of confidentiality will depend on the perpetrator of the violation. If an arbitrator violates his duty, so as to compromise his independence or impartiality, he may be challenged by a party or his appointment may be revoked by CIETAC. In case of serious violation, he may also be removed from CIETAC's Panel of Arbitrators (see art. 27, notes 2 et seq.). If a party violates its duty of confidentiality, it is uncertain how an arbitral tribunal will react. It will firstly depend on whether the arbitral tribunal considers the duty of confidentiality to be a substantive (i.e. contractual) or a procedural duty. In the case of a substantive obligation, the arbitral tribunal may decide on the violation of the duty of confidentiality and may condemn the violating party to compensate the other for any damages incurred therefrom. However, if the arbitral tribunal considers that the duty of confidentiality is of a purely procedural nature, it is unlikely that it will decide thereon in the award. It may, at the utmost, compel the party concerned to respect its obligation of confidentiality and take any violation thereof into account when allocating the arbitration costs.

[Default]

Article 34

(1) If the Claimant fails to appear at an oral hearing without showing sufficient cause for such failure, or withdraws from an ongoing oral hearing without the permission of the arbitral tribunal, the Claimant may be deemed to have withdrawn its Request for Arbitration. In such a case, if the Respondent has filed a counterclaim, the arbitral tribunal shall proceed with the hearing of the counterclaim and make a default award.

(2) If the Respondent fails to appear at an oral hearing without showing sufficient cause for such failure, or withdraws from an ongoing oral hearing without the permission of the arbitral tribunal, the arbitral tribunal may proceed with the arbitration and make a default award. In such a case, if the Respondent has filed a counterclaim, the Respondent may be deemed to have withdrawn its counterclaim.

1. Failure to appear at a hearing. Art. 34 resembles art. 42 Arbitration Law. Where a claimant fails to appear at the hearing without good reason, or leaves the hearing without the permission of the arbitral tribunal, then such claimant will be deemed to have withdrawn his claim. The same applies to the respondent as regards its counterclaim. Further, if the respondent fails to appear at a scheduled hearing without good reason, or leaves the hearing without the permission of the arbitral tribunal, then the arbitral tribunal may proceed to render an award in default.

[Record of oral hearing]

Article 35

(1) During the oral hearing, the arbitral tribunal may arrange a stenographic and/or audio-visual record. The arbitral tribunal may, when it considers it necessary, take minutes stating the main points of the oral hearing and request the parties and/or their representatives, witnesses and/or other persons involved to sign and/or affix their seals to the minutes.

(2) The stenographic and/or audio-visual record of the oral hearing shall be available for the use and reference by the arbitral tribunal.

1. Optional recording in writing of oral hearings. In accordance with art. 69 Arbitration Law, whilst it is mandatory for a domestic arbitration tribunal to retain a written record of the hearing (see art. 64, note 1 and art. 48 Arbitration Law, note 1), CIETAC may, in a foreign-related arbitration, free the arbitral tribunal from such obligation. The main difference lies in whether the minutes need to be signed by the parties. In domestic arbitration, such signature is necessary, whereas in foreign-related arbitration the signature of the parties is not necessary.

2. Commonly used means of recording. In the recent practice of CIETAC, the secretary of CIETAC in charge of the case will usually make a transcript of the hearing. Moreover, if the oral hearing is held in the hearing rooms of CIETAC or its Sub-Commissions, an audio-visual recording of the hearing will be made. Also, if the arbitral tribunal considers it useful, it may arrange for written minutes and have all participants sign the minutes.

3. Access to the records. The records are freely accessible only by the arbitrators, whereas the parties will not be granted such access. Nevertheless, this does not prevent the parties from recording the hearings themselves. Such recording may, however, only be done in writing (other means of recording are prohibited) and will have no official value.

[Evidence]

Article 36

(1) Each party shall have the burden of proving the facts relied on to support its claim, defence or counterclaim.

(2) The arbitral tribunal may specify a time period for the parties to produce evidence and the parties shall produce evidence within the specified time period. The arbitral tribunal may refuse to admit any evidence produced beyond the period. If a party has difficulties to produce evidence within the specified time period, it may apply for an extension before the expiration of the period. The arbitral tribunal shall decide whether or not to extend the time period.

(3) If a party having the burden of proof fails to produce evidence within the specified time period, or the produced evidence is not sufficient to support its claim or counterclaim, it shall bear the consequences thereof.

1. Burden of proof. Art. 36 resembles art. 43 Arbitration Law and is the corollary in arbitration of the general principle contemplated by art. 64(1) Civil Procedure Law, according to which each party has to bear the burden of proving the facts it relies on. The arbitral tribunal may, either of its own accord, or at the request of a party to the arbitration, require the party bearing the burden of proof to provide supporting evidence. Failure to present evidence will lead to the rejection of the claim by the arbitral tribunal.

2. Production of evidence. Based on the wording of art. 36(2), the arbitral tribunal is entitled to order the parties to submit certain evidence. Thus, an arbitral tribunal established under the CIETAC Rules in principle has the power to order the production of evidence, in particular of documents. In fact, historically, arbitral tribunals proceeding under the CIETAC Rules have had ample powers in terms of the discovery of evidence, according to the strong inquisitorial tradition of the Chinese legal system. The arbitral tribunal will fix a time limit for the submission of all relevant evidence. Although practice is quite flexible in this respect, it is generally admitted that all relevant evidence has to be submitted at the latest before the end of the last hearing.

3. Types of evidence. Neither the Arbitration Law nor the CIETAC Rules contain detailed provisions as to which kind of evidence is admissible. Arbitral tribunals in China will therefore often refer to art. 63 Civil Procedure Law, which classifies evidence into seven types: documentary evidence, physical evidence, audio-visual materials, witness testimonies, statements of interested parties, including the disputing parties, expert conclusions, and records of inquests. However, arbitrators usually handle evidence with much more flexibility than courts.

4. Evidentiary procedure. Neither the Arbitration Law nor the CIETAC Rules provide for a detailed mechanism of evidence production. Here again, the arbitral tribunal will often refer to the rules applicable before courts. In December 2001, the SPC promulgated its Provisions on Evidence which comprehensively outline the rules of evidence to be used in civil lawsuits before the People's Courts. Whilst these Provisions on Evidence do not directly apply to arbitration in China, it is widely expected that they will ultimately be formally incorporated into the next revision of the Chinese Arbitration Law. Therefore, it is to be expected that the same principles of evidence-gathering will apply mutatis mutandis to Chinese arbitration. As regards the IBA Rules on Evidence, they do not apply automatically, but only if the parties have provided for their applicability. In practice, it is rare that parties reach an agreement regarding the application of the IBA Rules on Evidence in their arbitration agreement. Nevertheless, the Chinese arbitration community has begun to refer to the IBA Rules of Evidence when dealing with matters of evidence in the arbitral proceedings, especially when international practitioners are involved in the arbitration. In order to encourage the use of the IBA Rules on Evidence, CIETAC has provided a Chinese translation.

[Investigation by the arbitral tribunal]
Article 37

(1) The arbitral tribunal may, on its own initiative, undertake investigations and collect evidence as it considers necessary.

(2) When investigating and collecting evidence by itself, the arbitral tribunal shall promptly notify the parties to be present at such investigation if it considers it necessary. In the event that one or both parties fail to be present, the investigation and collection shall proceed without being affected.

(3) The arbitral tribunal shall, through the Secretariat of the CIETAC, transmit the evidence collected by itself to the parties and afford them an opportunity to comment.

1. Inquisitorial power of the arbitral tribunal. Contrary to the principle stated in art. 36(1), the arbitral tribunal may in certain circumstances also collect evidence on its own. This is namely the case when the parties and their representatives cannot collect the evidence because of objective reasons or simply when the arbitral tribunal deems it necessary for the hearing (see also art. 64(2) Civil Procedure Law and art. 43 in fine Arbitration Law).

2. Notification of the parties. The arbitral tribunal has the duty to inform the parties of any investigations it is conducting on its own initiative and must give the parties the opportunity to be present when collecting evidence.

However, the absence of a party will not prevent the arbitral tribunal from collecting evidence, provided that such absence is unjustified and/or unexcused.

3. Examination of evidence. After the collection of the evidence by the arbitral tribunal, the parties must be given the opportunity to comment on it.

[Expert's report and appraiser's report]

Article 38

(1) The arbitral tribunal may consult or appoint experts and appraisers for clarification on specific issues of a case. Such an expert or appraiser may either be a Chinese or foreign organisation or citizen.

(2) The arbitral tribunal has the power to request the parties to deliver or produce to the expert or appraiser any relevant materials, documents, or property and goods for checking, inspection and/or appraisal. The parties shall be obliged to comply.

(3) Copies of the expert's report and the appraiser's report shall be communicated to the parties, who shall be given an opportunity to comment on the report. At the request of either party and with the approval of the arbitral tribunal, the expert and appraiser may be heard at an oral hearing where, if considered necessary and appropriate by the arbitral tribunal, they may give explanations on their reports.

1. Appointment of an expert. The arbitral tribunal may, on its own initiative or on request of one party or both parties, appoint an appraiser or expert for clarification of specific, usually technical, issues.

2. Production of evidence. The arbitral tribunal has the right to order the parties to deliver to the expert/appraisal any relevant material, documents or other property (see also art. 36(2), note 2).

3. Examination of the report. After rendering the report by the expert or appraiser, each party must be given the opportunity to comment on the results. A violation of this provision could lead to the setting aside or the non-enforcement of the arbitral award (see art. 70 Arbitration Law in connection with art. 258(2) Civil Procedure Law). In 1993, the Hong Kong High Court refused to enforce a CIETAC award on the grounds that one party had been deprived of its right to comment on a report by the tribunal-appointed experts (*Paklito* v *Klockner*).

[Examination of evidence]

Article 39

(1) All evidence submitted by a party shall be filed with the Secretariat of the CIETAC for transmission to the other party.

CIETAC Arbitration Rules, art. 40

(2) Where a case is examined by way of an oral hearing, the evidence shall be exhibited at the hearing and examined by the parties.

(3) In the event that evidence is submitted after the hearing and the arbitral tribunal decides to admit the evidence without holding further hearings, the arbitral tribunal may require the parties to submit their opinions thereon in writing within a specified time period.

1. Right to examination of evidence by the parties. The title of art. 39 is somewhat confusing, since it gives the impression that art. 39 relates to the examination of the evidence by the arbitral tribunal. However, art. 39 actually concerns the right of each party to have access to the collected evidence and to comment thereon.

2. Access to evidence. All evidence filed during the arbitration, be it by the arbitral tribunal itself or by one of the parties, must be submitted to the CIETAC Secretariat, which will in turn transmit it to the parties and – if applicable – the arbitral tribunal.

3. Right to comment on the evidence. If oral hearings are held, all the evidence collected to that point must be exhibited during the hearing and each party must be given the opportunity to comment on it. If evidence is submitted after the hearing, or if there is no oral hearing, each party must be given the opportunity to comment on the evidence in writing within a specific period of time.

4. Violation of the parties' rights. In case the arbitral tribunal does not notify the parties of its collection of evidence (art. 37(2), note 2), and/or fails to give the parties the opportunity to comment on the evidence collected, or if the parties were not given access to all the evidence, this may – according to the circumstances – constitute a ground for challenge of the award (see art. 70 Arbitration Law, note 3).

[Combination of conciliation with arbitration]

Article 40

(1) Where the parties have reached a settlement agreement by themselves through negotiation or conciliation without involving the CIETAC, either party may, based on an arbitration agreement concluded between them that provides for arbitration by the CIETAC and the settlement agreement, request the CIETAC to constitute an arbitral tribunal to render an arbitral award in accordance with the terms of the settlement agreement. Unless the parties agree otherwise, the Chairman of the CIETAC shall appoint a sole arbitrator to form such arbitral tribunal, which shall examine the case in the procedure it considers appropriate and render an award in due course. The specific procedure and the time

limit for rendering the award shall not be subject to other provisions of these Rules.

(2) Where both parties have the desire for conciliation or one party so desires and the other party agrees when approached by the arbitral tribunal, the arbitral tribunal may conciliate the case during the course of the arbitration proceedings.

(3) The arbitral tribunal may conciliate the case in the manner it considers appropriate.

(4) The arbitral tribunal shall terminate the conciliation and continue the arbitration proceedings if one of the parties requests a termination of the conciliation or if the arbitral tribunal believes that further efforts to conciliate will be useless.

(5) A settlement agreement reached between the parties during the course of conciliation by the arbitral tribunal but without the involvement of the arbitral tribunal shall be deemed as one reached through the conciliation by the arbitral tribunal.

(6) Where settlement is reached through conciliation by the arbitral tribunal, the parties shall sign a written settlement agreement. Unless otherwise agreed by the parties, the arbitral tribunal will close the case and render an arbitral award in accordance with the terms of the settlement agreement.

(7) Where conciliation fails, the arbitral tribunal shall proceed with the arbitration and render an arbitral award.

(8) Where conciliation fails, any opinion, view or statement and any proposal or proposition expressing acceptance or opposition by either party or by the arbitral tribunal in the process of conciliation shall not be invoked as grounds for any claim, defence or counterclaim in the subsequent arbitration proceedings, judicial proceedings or any other proceedings.

1. Historical background. In China, mediation and conciliation have been widely used for centuries as an effective means of dispute resolution, and havenow become embedded as an integral part of both the litigation and arbitral processes. Traditionally, the Chinese believe that parties to a dispute, particularly a domestic dispute, have an obligation to engage in negotiations with a view to determining an acceptable compromise that enables the parties to avoid conflict and loss of face, thereby promoting social harmony. Today, in drafting arbitration clauses, it is common practice to require the parties to first attempt to resolve their dispute via consultation or mediation prior to arbitration. Moreover, the practice of conciliation and/or mediation before and during arbitration proceedings is not only permitted, but actively encouraged (see art. 49 Arbitration Law, note 1).

2. Conciliation prior to arbitration proceedings. Art. 40(1) applies to cases where the parties have, prior to initiating arbitration proceedings, successfully settled their dispute by conciliation. In such cases, if the contract between the parties provided for a CIETAC arbitration clause, each party can initiate arbitration before CIETAC and request the arbitral tribunal to render an award implementing the terms of the settlement agreement, i.e. a 'Consent Award'. The Chairman of CIETAC will usually appoint a sole arbitrator to render such award. The examination of the case and the time limit for rendering the award are at the discretion of the sole arbitrator, and are not subject to the remaining provisions of the CIETAC Rules.

3. Conciliation during arbitration proceedings. Art. 40(2) to (8) applies to cases where the parties conduct conciliation during the arbitration proceedings, with or without the involvement of the arbitral tribunal.

4. Conciliation by the arbitral tribunal. Art. 40(3) to (4) applies to conciliation conducted by the arbitral tribunal itself. In order to conduct such conciliation, the express agreement of both parties is necessary. The agreement of the parties is the basic requirement for any conciliation conducted by the arbitral tribunal, and the conciliation will be terminated whenever one of the parties refuses to continue. The conciliation may also be terminated if the arbitral tribunal deems that it has no chance of success. Where conciliation is initiated, the arbitration proceedings will be suspended for as long as the conciliation proceeds (see art. 51 Arbitration Law, note 2).

5. Conciliation without the arbitral tribunal. According to art. 40(5), the parties are also entitled to conduct conciliation talks without the involvement of the arbitral tribunal. Such conciliation talks will not automatically suspend the arbitration proceedings, unless otherwise requested by all parties. Moreover, even if such talks are conducted outside the arbitration proceeding, a settlement agreement reached between the parties during the arbitration proceeding will be deemed 'reached through the conciliation by the arbitral tribunal', and will be subject to the same rules as if the settlement had been reached with the involvement of the arbitral tribunal.

5. Successful conciliation. If the conciliation conducted during the arbitration proceedings is successful, the parties will sign a written 'Conciliation Settlement' and the arbitral tribunal will render an award (i.e. a 'Consent Award') corresponding to the terms of such settlement. However, the parties may also decide to terminate the arbitration, i.e. dismiss the case without the rendering of an award (see art. 50 Arbitration Law, note 1).

6. Failed conciliation. If the conciliation conducted during the arbitration fails, the arbitral tribunal will resume or continue, as the case may be, the arbitration proceedings and render an award. Any information exchanged during conciliation proceedings is strictly confidential and may not be used by any party or any arbitrator in subsequent arbitration, court or other proceedings.

CIETAC Arbitration Rules, art. 41

[Withdrawal and dismissal]

Article 41

(1) A party may file a request with the CIETAC to withdraw its claim or counterclaim in its entirety. In the event that the Claimant withdraws its claim in its entirety, the arbitral tribunal shall proceed with its examination of the counterclaim and render an arbitral award thereon. In the event that the Respondent withdraws its counterclaim in its entirety, the arbitral tribunal shall proceed with the examination of the claim and render an arbitral award thereon.

(2) Where a case is to be dismissed before the formation of the arbitral tribunal, the decision shall be made by the Secretary-General of the CIETAC. Where the case is to be dismissed after the formation of the arbitral tribunal, the decision shall be made by the arbitral tribunal.

(3) Where a party files with the CIETAC a Request for Arbitration for a claim which has been withdrawn, the CIETAC shall decide whether or not to accept the request anew.

1. Withdrawal of claim. Art. 41 implements art. 27 Arbitration Law, according to which a party may withdraw or alter its claim or counterclaim. Thus, art. 41 CIETAC Rules sets forth that a claimant may at any time withdraw its claim. The same is true for the respondent as regards its counterclaim.

2. Partial withdrawal. If a party withdraws only part of its claim or counterclaim, such partial withdrawal is considered an amendment and is subject to art. 14 (see art. 14, notes 1 et seq.)

3. Dismissal. Where there is a claim and a counterclaim, and one is withdrawn, the arbitral tribunal will decide on the claim or counterclaim not withdrawn and render an award. Where respondent did not raise any counterclaim, and claimant withdraws its claim, the case will be dismissed. The power to dismiss a case belongs to the arbitral tribunal, or to CIETAC where the arbitral tribunal has not yet been constituted. The case will also be dismissed where CIETAC holds that it has no jurisdiction to hear the case, for example where there is no valid arbitration agreement.

4. Cost consequences. Whether or not a party will be entitled to claim back part of the arbitration costs depends on when the withdrawal occurs, i.e. on how far the arbitration proceedings have proceeded. In practice, half of the arbitration fees will be refunded to the party if the arbitral tribunal has not been constituted, or the first oral hearing has not been concluded. For all other cases, there is no standard practice, but CIETAC (i.e. the Secretary-General) will decide on the refund based on all the circumstances of the case.

5. Re-arbitration? According to art. 41(3), if a party has withdrawn its claim or counterclaim, but subsequently decides to re-initiate arbitration, the decision whether or not to accept such request lies with CIETAC. Art. 41(3) encompasses different situations: a party who has withdrawn its claim resubmits the exact same claim; a party who has withdrawn its claim reinitiates arbitration based on a new claim; a party who has withdrawn its claim reinitiates arbitration based partly on the original claim and partly on a new claim. In such situations, CIETAC will first of all have to verify whether the arbitration clause is still valid. Indeed, a re-arbitration may only take place, if the case was dismissed based on the withdrawal (see note 3; see also art. 50 Arbitration Law, note 1). If the arbitration proceeded despite the withdrawal, i.e. because the other party raised a claim/counterclaim which was not withdrawn, and resulted in an arbitration award, the question arises as to whether the arbitration clause is still in force. In principle, the rendering of an award will extinguish the arbitration agreement, and a party may not reinitiate an arbitration based on the same arbitration clause. This derives from the principle of res judicata, according to which the same matter between the same parties may not be re-adjudicated. Thus, if a party withdraws its claim/counterclaim, but the arbitration proceeds because the other party raised a claim/counterclaim which is not withdrawn and results in the rendering of an arbitration award, the former party will be precluded from re-submitting its claim/counterclaim, unless it reserved the right to do so and such reservation is acceptable under the applicable procedural law.

CHAPTER III. ARBITRAL AWARD

[Time limits]

Article 42

(1) The arbitral tribunal shall render an arbitral award within six (6) months as from the date on which the arbitral tribunal is formed.

(2) Upon the request of the arbitral tribunal, the Chairman of the CIETAC may extend said time period if he considers it truly necessary and the reasons for the extension are truly justified.

1. Six months. Whereas the CIETAC Rules of 2000 provided for a nine-month time limit to render an award, the CIETAC Rules of 2005 have cut this limit to six months. The time limit starts to run from the date of constitution of the arbitral tribunal. The time limit can be extended by the Chairman of CIETAC on request of the arbitral tribunal, but good reason must be shown.

2. In practice. In practice, more than 50% of the cases handled by CIETAC are completed within the six-month time limit. However, for complicated cases, involving objections to the arbitral jurisdiction or intervention of experts, the time limit will usually be extended for as long as necessary.

[Rendering the award]

Article 43

(1) The arbitral tribunal shall independently and impartially make its arbitral award on the basis of the facts, in accordance with the law and the terms of the contracts, with reference to international practices, and in compliance with the principle of fairness and reasonableness.

(2) The arbitral tribunal shall state in the award the claims, the facts of the dispute, the reasons on which the award is based, the result of the award, the allocation of the arbitration costs, and the date on which and the place at which the award is made. The facts of the dispute and the reasons on which the award is based may not be stated in the award if the parties have agreed so, or if the award is made in accordance with the terms of a settlement agreement between the parties. The arbitral tribunal has the power to determine in the arbitral award the specific time period for the parties to execute the award, and the liabilities to be borne by a party failing to execute the award within the specified time.

(3) The CIETAC's stamp shall be affixed to the award.

(4) Where a case is examined by an arbitral tribunal composed of three arbitrators, the award shall be rendered by all three arbitrators or a majority of the arbitrators. A written dissenting opinion shall be docketed into the file and may be attached to the award, but it shall not form a part of the award.

(5) Where the arbitral tribunal cannot reach a majority opinion, the award shall be rendered in accordance with the presiding arbitrator's opinion. The written opinion of other arbitrators shall be docketed into the file and may be attached to the award, but it shall not form a part of the award.

(6) Unless the award is made in accordance with the opinion of the presiding arbitrator or the sole arbitrator, the arbitral award shall be signed by a majority of arbitrators. An arbitrator who has a dissenting opinion may or may not sign his name on the award.

(7) The date on which the award is made shall be the date on which the award comes into legal effect.

(8) The arbitral award is final and binding upon both parties. Neither party may bring a suit before a law court or make a request to any other organisation for revising the award.

1. Basis for the award. The arbitral tribunal will render an award based on: the facts, the law and the relevant terms of the contract, international practice and the principle of fairness and reasonableness. If not provided for otherwise by Chinese law, the parties to a 'foreign-related' dispute may submit their dispute to a law other than Chinese law (see art. 7 Arbitration Law, notes 3 et seq.). The applicable law and the contract between the parties will then form the core legal frame for the arbitrators' decision. However, the CIETAC Rules also recommend that the arbitrators to take into consideration international practice. In this respect, such practice will only be considered if not contrary to the applicable law. As regards reference to the principle of fairness and reasonableness, it is just a reminder of a general principle under Chinese law that motives of equity should always be taken into consideration (as regards the arbitral tribunal's power to decide ex aequo et bono, see art. 7 Arbitration Law, note 2).

2. Content of the award. Art. 43(2) implements the principle contemplated by art. 54 Arbitration Law, according to which an award should include: the relevant facts of the dispute, the claims and counterclaims, the grounds on which the award is based, the result of the award and the allocation of the arbitration costs, as well as the date and the place at which the award was made. However, when the award is based on a conciliation settlement (see art. 40, notes 5 et seq.) or where the parties so agree, the facts of the dispute and the grounds on which the award is based may be omitted. Further, according to art. 43(2), the arbitral award may fix a time limit for the parties to perform their obligations under the award and the sanctions they may face if they fail to do so. However, the power of the arbitral tribunal towards non-complying parties is very limited. In most cases, the arbitral tribunal will merely provide that a party who does not execute the payment due under the award will have to pay interest for delay. When enforcement of the award is sought, the enforcement will also apply to this interest. Where the obligation of a party is not of a monetary nature, the situation is more delicate. Arbitral tribunals in China have no jurisdiction to issue 'astreintes' or other penalties for non-compliance with the award. The concerned party will have no other choice than to request the enforcement of the award before the competent courts.

3. Majority decision. According to art. 53 Arbitration Law (note 1), decisions of the arbitral tribunal should be taken based on a majority vote, and if no majority consensus can be reached, the award will be rendered in accordance with the opinion of the presiding arbitrator.

4. Dissenting opinion. Dissenting opinions are allowed under Chinese law (see art. 53 Arbitration Law, note 2). Based on the request of the dissenting arbitrator, such opinions may be 'attached to the award', although they do not form part of the award itself. The dissenting opinion will be sent to the parties together with the award. If the dissenting arbitrator does not request that his dissenting opinion be attached to the award, such opinion will only be filed in CIETAC's records, and will not to be submitted to the parties.

5. Signature of the award. The award needs to be signed by either: the sole arbitrator, the majority of the arbitrators in case of a majority decision, or the presiding arbitrator if no majority consensus could be reached. The signatures of dissenting arbitrators are not necessary, but can be added.

6. Effect of the award. The award becomes effective on the day it is made, i.e. on the date mentioned on the award, provided that the award has been duly signed by the relevant arbitrators and stamped by CIETAC.

7. Finality of the award. Art. 43(8) is a reminder of the internationally recognised principle of finality of the arbitral award, which has finally also been contemplated by art. 9 Arbitration Law. Once the parties have opted for arbitration and have obtained an award, the award is final and binding, meaning that the parties may not submit the same case to a court, arbitration commission or other organisation to re-decide on the matter (see art. 9 Arbitration Law, note 4).

[Interlocutory award and partial award]
Article 44

An interlocutory arbitral award or partial award may be made by the arbitral tribunal on any issue of the case, at any time during the arbitration before the final award is made if considered necessary by the arbitral tribunal, or if the parties request and the arbitral tribunal accepts. Either party's failure to perform the interlocutory award will not affect the continuation of the arbitration proceedings, nor will it prevent the arbitral tribunal from making a final award.

1. Power of the arbitral tribunal to render an interlocutory or partial award. In accordance with art. 55 Arbitration Law, art. 44 gives the arbitral tribunal the power to render 'interlocutory' and 'partial' awards, whenever it considers it useful. Whereas art. 55 Arbitration Law only mentions 'partial awards' (see note 2), it is admitted that these terms also encompass 'interlocutory awards', which is expressly confirmed by art. 44 CIETAC Rules. The arbitral tribunal may render such awards on its own initiative or when so requested by a party, where the arbitral tribunal deems it useful.

2. Distinction between interlocutory and partial award. Although art. 44 mentions both 'interlocutory' and 'partial' awards, it fails to draw a distinction between the two. According to international practice, arbitral awards are categorised into three types, i.e. interim awards, partial awards, and final awards. Whereas a final award puts an end to the entire dispute by deciding on all remaining legal and factual questions, interim and the partial awards only address part of the case. In a 'partial award' the arbitral tribunal decides on a quantitative part of the dispute, for example on the claims based on contract and not on the claims based on tort. In an 'interim award' the arbitral tribunal decides on a qualitative part of the dispute, meaning that the arbitral tribunal does not decide on specific claims but deals with preliminary material or procedural questions, such as the question of the validity of the main contract. In the CIETAC Arbitration Rules, the term 'interlocutory award' refers to 'interim award' as defined above, whereas the term 'partial award' has the same meaning as described above.

3. Procedural orders. It is sometimes difficult to draw a line between a so-called 'procedural order' and an 'interim award', namely when the matter decided upon is of a procedural nature. In such cases, the distinctive criteria should be the object of the decision: when the validity of the arbitration proceedings is at stake, whether in its entirety or only regarding some of its aspects, such decision should take the form of an 'interim' award; when the decision concerns the conduct of the arbitration procedure, without questioning the arbitration itself, the decision should take the form of a 'procedural order'. Thus, questions relating to either the jurisdiction of the arbitral tribunal or to the qualification of the parties both relate to the validity of the arbitration proceedings, and should therefore be addressed in an interim award. Questions relating to the time and date of hearings, to the admissibility of evidence, and to deadlines for written submissions all relate to the conduct of the arbitration procedure, and should be addressed in a procedural order. Although the CIETAC Rules are silent on procedural orders, it is widely admitted that the arbitral tribunal has the power to issue any such orders it deems necessary.

4. Enforcement of interlocutory/partial awards. Although interlocutory and partial awards only rule on part of the dispute, they are final and binding for the parties and the arbitral tribunal, in the sense that the matter ruled on in such an award cannot be re-adjudicated at a later stage. Insofar as cancellation or enforcement issues are concerned (see art. 70 Arbitration Law, notes 1 et seq., and art. 71 Arbitration Law, notes 1 et seq.), interlocutory and partial awards are equal to final awards and subject to the same regime. On the contrary, procedural orders are neither enforceable, nor can they be cancelled. However, the arbitral tribunal may reconsider a procedural order at any time.

[Scrutiny of draft award]

Article 45

The arbitral tribunal shall submit its draft award to the CIETAC for scrutiny before signing the award. The CIETAC may remind the arbitral tribunal of issues in the award on condition that the arbitral tribunal's independence in rendering the award is not affected.

1. Scrutiny by CIETAC. As with ICC Arbitration, an award rendered by the arbitral tribunal has to be submitted to CIETAC for its 'scrutiny', i.e. review. Although CIETAC has no power to instruct the arbitral tribunal to modify its award, it may draw the arbitral tribunal's attention to certain problems or inconsistencies. The arbitral tribunal may then decide whether or not to amend the award. After scrutiny, and amendment of the award by the arbitral tribunal if necessary, CIETAC will stamp the award (see art. 43(3)).

2. CIETAC's influence. If CIETAC disagrees with the award prepared by the arbitral tribunal, it may – in serious cases – postpone the approval of the award and submit it to the advisory committee in order to collect the advisors' opinions. Although CIETAC's influence, and in particular the influence of the advisory board is not to be underestimated, the last say on the award belongs to the arbitral tribunal.

[Fees]

Article 46

(1) The arbitral tribunal has the power to determine in the arbitral award the arbitration fee and other expenses to be paid by the parties to the CIETAC.

(2) The arbitral tribunal has the power to decide in the award, according to the specific circumstances of the case, that the losing party shall compensate the winning party for the expenses reasonably incurred by it in pursuing its case. In deciding whether the winning party's expenses incurred in pursuing its case are reasonable, the arbitral tribunal shall consider such factors as the outcome and complexity of the case, the workload of the winning party and/or its representative(s), and the amount in dispute, etc.

1. Arbitration fees and other expenses. According to art. 43(2) (art. 43, note 2), the allocation of the arbitration costs has to be mentioned in the award. The arbitration costs will be calculated by CIETAC according to the Arbitration Fee Schedule, and the arbitral tribunal will insert the corresponding amount in the award.

2. Allocation of the costs. When allocating the costs, the arbitral tribunal will generally order that the losing party pay the costs of the proceedings and all related expenses of the winning party. However, if it is justified in the specific circumstances of the case, the arbitral tribunal may decide on a different allocation of costs. Moreover, the expenses incurred by the winning party, which the losing party will have to pay, need to be reasonable. In this respect, it is not rare that an arbitral tribunal reduces the lawyers' fees to be reimbursed by the losing party. This is especially the case when the legal costs of the winning party are substantially higher than the costs of the losing party, due, for example, to the involvement of foreign lawyers.

[Correction of the Award]

Article 47

Within thirty (30) days from its receipt of the arbitral award, either party may request in writing for a correction of any clerical, typographical, or calculation errors or any errors of a similar nature contained in the award; if such an error does exist in the award, the arbitral tribunal shall make a correction in writing within thirty (30) days from the date

of receipt of the written request for the correction. The arbitral tribunal may likewise correct any such errors in writing on its own initiative within a reasonable time after the award is issued. Such correction in writing shall form a part of the arbitral award.**

1. Correction of clerical, typographical, calculation errors, etc. Art. 47 implements art. 56 Arbitration Law and allows the arbitral tribunal to correct an award that contains clerical, typographical or calculation errors or any errors of a similar nature, i.e. non-substantive errors that are visible based on the award itself and without any further investigation. The arbitral tribunal cannot correct mistakes in the logical or legal reasoning of the award.

2. On request of a party. A correction of the award can be done based on the request of a party. Such request has to be filed within thirty days from the receipt of the arbitral award. If the arbitral tribunal concludes that an error exists, it must correct it within thirty days of receipt of the request for correction. If the arbitral tribunal concludes that no error exists, it will simply reject the request.

3. On the initiative of the arbitral tribunal. The arbitral tribunal may also correct errors on its own initiative, within a reasonable time after the award is issued. Here, the arbitral tribunal is not formally bound to the thirty-day time limit.

4. Corrections form an integral part of the award. Any correction effected by the arbitral tribunal will form an integral part of the original award. Time limits for enforcement and/or setting aside of the award will however run from the date of issuance of the original award.

[Additional award]

Article 48

Within thirty (30) days from the date on which the arbitral award is received, either party may request the arbitral tribunal in writing for an additional award on any claim or counterclaim which was advanced in the arbitration proceedings, but was omitted from the award. If such omission does exist, the arbitral tribunal shall make an additional award within thirty (30) days from the date of receipt of the written request. The arbitral tribunal may also make an additional award on its own initiative within a reasonable period of time after the arbitral award is issued. Such additional award shall form a part of the arbitral award previously rendered.

1. Supplementation of the award. Whereas art. 47 applies to the case where an award contains an error, art. 48 applies to the case where the award is incomplete, i.e. where it fails to decide on all the claims and counterclaims raised during the arbitration proceedings. The omission mentioned concerns claims, counterclaims or parts thereof. Other kinds of omission (facts, grounds, legal arguments, etc.) may in principle not be remedied by the way of an additional award.

2. On a party's request or on the arbitral tribunal's own initiative. As for the correction of the award (see art. 47, notes 1 et seq.), a supplementation can be either requested by a party within thirty days from the date of receipt of the award or done on the arbitral tribunal's own initiative within a reasonable period of time.

3. Integral part of the award. The additional award will form an integral part of the arbitral award previously rendered, and – although there is no specific provision in this regard – it should, in principle, be assumed that the time limit for requesting the cancellation or the enforcement of the award will, in principle, start anew upon the award of the additional award. However, if a party requests cancellation of the award based on grounds that relate to the original award, it is highly recommended that it considers the day the original award was rendered as the starting point for the relevant time limits.

[Execution of the award]

Article 49

(1) The parties must automatically execute the arbitral award within the time period specified in the award. If no time limit is specified in the award, the parties shall execute the arbitral award immediately.

(2) Where one party fails to execute the award, the other party may apply to a competent Chinese court for enforcement of the award pursuant to Chinese laws, or apply to a competent court for enforcement of the award according to the 1958 United Nations Convention on Recognition and Enforcement of Foreign Arbitral Awards or other international treaties that China has concluded or acceded to.

1. General principle. Art. 49(1) contemplates the basic principle that parties are bound to the award and are thus obligated to comply with it, i.e. to perform it, without prior notice or intervention of any judicial enforcement body. If no specific time limit is mentioned in the award, it is deemed that each party should execute the award immediately.

2. Judicial enforcement. Art. 49(2) repeats the basic principle contemplated by art. 62 Arbitration Law (see note 1), which provides that if a party refuses to comply with an arbitral award, the other party may require the courts to enforce it. According to the nationality of the award, different rules will apply: the enforcement of foreign awards is subject to relevant international treaties, in particular the New York Convention (see art. 267 Civil Procedure Law), whereas the enforcement of Chinese foreign-related awards is subject to art. 258 Civil Procedure Law (see art. 71 Arbitration Law, notes 1 et seq.).

CHAPTER IV. SUMMARY PROCEDURE

[Application]

Article 50

(1) Unless otherwise agreed by the parties, this Summary Procedure shall apply to any case where the amount in dispute does not exceeded CNY 500,000, or to any case where the amount in dispute exceeds CNY 500,000, yet one party applies for arbitration under this Summary Procedure and the other party agrees in writing.

(2) Where no monetary claim is specified or the amount in dispute is not clear, the CIETAC shall determine whether or not to apply the Summary Procedure after a full consideration of such factors as the complexity of the case and the interests involved, etc.

1. General. Many arbitration commissions have provided for a simplified procedure, called Summary Procedure. The aim of such Summary Procedure is to deal with low-value and/or simple cases in a quick and cost efficient way. The Summary Procedure of the CIETAC Rules differs from the ordinary procedure insofar as it provides for simplified rules with respect to: the applicable time limits, the conduct of hearings, and the number of arbitrators, etc.

2. Scope of application. The Summary Procedure is a simplified procedure meant to apply in cases where: the amount in dispute does not exceed CNY 500,000 (approx USD 65,000), the parties agree to submit their dispute to the Summary Procedure, irrespective of the amount in dispute, or there is no monetary claim or the amount in dispute cannot be clearly determined, if CIETAC deems that the Summary Procedure is more appropriate.

[Notice of Arbitration]

Article 51

Where a Request for Arbitration is submitted to the CIETAC and is found to be acceptable for arbitration under the Summary Procedure, the Secretariat of the CIETAC or its Sub-Commission shall send a Notice of Arbitration to the parties.

1. Initiation of Summary Procedure. When receiving a Request for Arbitration, CIETAC will automatically check whether the case falls within the scope of application of the Summary Procedure (see art. 50, note 2). Thus, it is not necessary for a party to expressly request the application of the Summary Procedure. However, where the amount in dispute exceeds CNY 500,000, the Summary Procedure may only apply if a party so requests, and if the other agrees in writing. If the claim raised by claimant is not monetary, it may be useful to specify in the Request for Arbitration whether the party wishes the Summary Procedure to apply, although the final decision will lie with CIETAC.

2. Notice of Arbitration. After acceptance of the case, CIETAC will send to the parties a Notice of Arbitration (see art. 11, notes 1 et seq.), specifying that the case is subject to the Summary Procedure.

[Formation of the arbitral tribunal]

Article 52

An arbitral tribunal of a sole arbitrator shall be formed in accordance with Article 23 of these Rules to hear a case under the Summary Procedure.

1. Sole arbitrator. Whereas in ordinary proceedings, the arbitral tribunal is usually composed of three arbitrators (unless otherwise provided for by the parties, see art. 20, notes 1 et seq.), in the Summary Procedure the case is heard by a sole arbitrator.

2. Appointment procedure. As regards the appointment mechanism of the sole arbitrator, art. 52 refers to art. 23, which in turns refers to art. 22(2) to (4) concerning the nomination of the presiding arbitrator. Thus, each party should submit the names of three candidates, and the sole arbitrator will be designated by the Chairman of CIETAC from the common candidates. If there are no common candidates, the Chairman of CIETAC will choose a sole arbitrator outside the parties' lists (for more details see art. 22, note 3).

[Statement of Defence and counterclaim]

Article 53

(1) Within twenty (20) days from the date of receipt of the Notice of Arbitration, the Respondent shall submit its Statement of Defence and relevant evidence to the Secretariat of the CIETAC; counterclaims, if any, shall also be filed with supporting evidence within the said time period. The arbitral tribunal may extend this time period if it considers it justified.

(2) Within twenty (20) days from the date of receipt of the counterclaim and its attachments, the Claimant shall file its Statement of Defence to the Respondent's counterclaim.

1. Time limit: twenty days. Art. 53 sets forth the applicable time limit for the respondent to submit his defence and any counterclaim, as well as the time limit for the claimant to respond to a counterclaim, if necessary. Whereas in the ordinary procedure, the respondent has forty-five days upon receipt of the Notice of Arbitration, in the Summary Procedure this time limit is shortened to twenty days. The same deadline applies to any counterclaim that respondent wants to submit and to any response by claimant to such counterclaim.

2. Extension. As is the case in the ordinary procedure, the arbitral tribunal may extend this time limit. The practice is relatively flexible. The system, however, contains one small inconsistency: if one compares the time necessary to constitute the arbitral tribunal (see art. 52 in connection with art. 22, note 2) with the time limit set to file the Statement of Defence (twenty days upon receipt of the Notice of Arbitration), one notices that the time limit for the submission of the Statement of Defence will expire before the arbitral tribunal is fully constituted. In such cases CIETAC has been very forthcoming in granting extensions of the time limit to submit the Statement of Defence.

[Conduct of hearing]
Article 54

The arbitral tribunal may examine the case in the manner it considers appropriate. The arbitral tribunal may in its full discretion decide to examine the case only on the basis of the written materials and evidence submitted by the parties or to hold oral hearings.

1. Power of examination. In the Summary Procedure, as well as in the ordinary procedure, the arbitral tribunal (i.e. the sole arbitrator) has the power to examine the case in any manner it considers appropriate. Art. 29(1) applicable to the ordinary procedure further mentions that the arbitral tribunal should act impartially and must give reasonable opportunity to all parties to present their case. Although this is not mentioned in art. 54, it is undisputed that the arbitral tribunal has the same duties in the Summary Procedure.

2. Written procedure as principle. Whereas in the ordinary procedure, the holding of oral hearings is the rule and purely written proceedings the exception, the situation is different in the Summary Procedure. The sole arbitrator may freely (i.e. 'in its full discretion') decide whether to hold oral hearings or to conduct the arbitration based on written submissions only. The practice is quite different from the theoretical rule: as it is the case in the ordinary procedure, it is also common practice in the Summary Procedure that the sole arbitrator holds an oral hearing. It is extremely rare to conduct an arbitration – even in Summary Procedure – based on written submissions only.

[Oral hearing]

Article 55

(1) For a case examined by way of an oral hearing, the Secretariat of the CIETAC shall, after the arbitral tribunal has fixed a date for the oral hearing, notify the parties of the date at least fifteen (15) days in advance of the oral hearing date. A party having justified reasons may request the arbitral tribunal for a postponement of the oral hearing. However, such request must be communicated to the arbitral tribunal at least seven (7) days in advance of the oral hearing date. The arbitral tribunal shall decide whether to postpone the oral hearing or not.

(2) Where the arbitral tribunal decides to hear the case orally, only one oral hearing shall be held unless it is otherwise truly necessary.

(3) A notice of oral hearing subsequent to the first oral hearing and a notice of a postponed oral hearing shall not be subject to the fifteen (15)-day time limit provided for in the foregoing paragraph 1.

1. Limited number of oral hearings. If the sole arbitrator decides to hold an oral hearing, there will usually be only one hearing. Subsequent oral hearings may also be arranged if 'truly necessary'.

2. Shortened time limits. Besides the number of hearings, the main difference with the ordinary procedure lies in the time limits. If the sole arbitrator decides to hold an oral hearing, the parties will be notified fifteen days in advance, compared with twenty days under the ordinary procedure (see art. 30, note 1). A party may request to postpone such hearing for 'justifiable reasons', given that the request is filed at least seven days before the scheduled hearing (in comparison to ten days under the ordinary procedure). In the rare case where there will be more than one hearing, notices of hearings are no longer subject to the fifteen-day time limit, but it will be left to the arbitrator to set a reasonable time limit according to the circumstances.

[Time limits for rendering award]

Article 56

(1) The arbitral tribunal shall render an arbitral award within three (3) months from the date on which the arbitral tribunal is formed.

(2) Upon the request of the arbitral tribunal, the Chairman of the CIETAC may extend the time period if he considers it truly necessary and the reasons for the extension truly justified.

1. Three months. Whereas under the ordinary procedure the arbitral tribunal has six months to render an award, this deadline is shortened to three months for the Summary Procedure. An extension of this deadline is possible.

2. In practice. In practice, most of the cases handled under the Summary Procedure will be completed within the three-month deadline. Only cases involving complicated issues, such as jurisdiction issues or the collection of evidence, will usually require an extension.

[Change of procedure]
Article 57

The application of the Summary Procedure shall not be affected by any amendment to the claim or by the filing of a counterclaim. Where the amount in dispute of the amended claim or that of the counterclaim exceeds CNY 500,000, the procedure of the case shall be changed from the Summary Procedure to the general procedure unless the parties have agreed to the continuous application of the Summary Procedure.

1. Change from Summary Procedure to ordinary procedure. If, by amending a claim and/or counterclaim, the amount in dispute exceeds CNY 500,000, the Summary Procedure will automatically be changed to the ordinary procedure. However, in accordance with art. 50(1) (see art. 50, note 2), the parties may agree to continue the application of the Summary Procedure.

2. No change from ordinary procedure to Summary Procedure. If, based on the amount in dispute, a case is submitted to the ordinary procedure, it will remain under such procedure for the whole duration of the arbitration, even if a party withdraws whole or part of its claims thereby reducing the amount in dispute to less than CNY 500,000.

[Context reference]
Article 58

As to matters not covered in this Chapter, the relevant provisions in the other Chapters of these Rules shall apply.

1. Reference to ordinary procedure. Arts. 50 to 58 mainly deal with questions of time limits, composition of the arbitral tribunal, and the conduct of hearings. For other matters not dealt with in this Chapter, such as examination of evidence, appointment of an expert or appraisal, the rules applicable to the ordinary procedure shall apply.

CHAPTER V. SPECIAL PROVISIONS FOR DOMESTIC ARBITRATION

[Application]

Article 59

(1) The provisions of this Chapter shall apply to domestic arbitration cases accepted by the CIETAC.

(2) The provisions of the Summary Procedure of Chapter IV shall apply if a domestic arbitration case falls within the scope of Article 50 of these Rules.

1. Introductory remarks. Arts. 59 to 66 exclusively apply to domestic arbitration cases, i.e. cases that do not involve any relevant foreign element. These provisions are a hangover of the strict separation between foreign-related and domestic arbitration, though during the several revisions of the CIETAC Rules the two systems have been largely harmonised (see art. 1, notes 1 et seq.). The main differences between the two regimes actually concerns time limits for submissions, for hearings and for the rendering of the award.

2. Summary Procedure. As regards the Summary Procedure, no distinction is made between a domestic and a foreign-related arbitration. Both regimes are subject to the same provisions, i.e. art. 50 et seq. (see art. 50, notes 1 et seq.).

[Acceptance]

Article 60

(1) Where a Request for Arbitration is found to meet the formality requirements specified in Article 10 of these Rules, the CIETAC shall accept the Request and notify the parties accordingly within five (5) days from its receipt of the Request or immediately upon its receipt of the Request. Where a Request for Arbitration is found not in conformity with the formality requirements, the CIETAC shall notify the party in writing of its refusal of the Request with reasons stated.

(2) Upon receipt of a Request for Arbitration, the CIETAC may request the party to make corrections within a specified time period if it finds the Request is not in conformity with the provisions of Article 10 of these Rules.

1. Notice of Arbitration. Art. 60 is very similar to art. 11 (see art. 11, notes 1 et seq.) and applies to the acceptance of the case by CIETAC. The major difference with art. 11 lies in the time limit: in a domestic arbitration, CIETAC has to take a decision on the acceptance of the case within five days to comply with art. 24 Arbitration Law, whereas no specific time limit is stipulated in art.

11 as regards foreign-related arbitration, since no relevant provision governing foreign related arbitration is provided for in the Arbitration Law.

[Formation of arbitral tribunal]

Article 61

The arbitral tribunal shall be formed in accordance with the provisions of Articles 21, 22, 23 and 24 of these Rules.

1. Same principle. Art. 61 merely refers to arts. 21 to 24 concerning the constitution of the arbitral tribunal. There is thus no difference in the constitution mechanism of the arbitral tribunal in domestic and foreign-related arbitrations.

2. Arbitrators. However, there is one substantial difference between the two regimes: according to CIETAC practice, in a domestic arbitration, the arbitrators may only be Chinese nationals (this is actually not totally justified since there is no such limitation of nationality of arbitrators provided for in the Arbitration Law), and will usually (but not necessarily) be chosen from CIETAC's List of Arbitrators on Domestic Cases.

[Statement of Defence and counterclaim]

Article 62

(1) Within twenty (20) days from the date of receipt of the Notice of Arbitration, the Respondent shall submit its Statement of Defence and relevant evidence to the CIETAC; counterclaims, if any, shall also be filed with supporting evidence within the said time period. The arbitral tribunal may extend this time period if it considers it justified.

(2) Within twenty (20) days from the date of receipt of the counterclaim and its attachments, the Claimant shall file its Statement of Defence to the Respondent's counterclaim.

1. Same principle, different time limits. Art. 62 is very similar to arts. 12 and 13 (see art. 12, notes 1 et seq., and art. 13, notes 1 et seq.). The only difference lies in the time limits: whereas according to arts. 12 and 13 the time limit for submission of a Statement of Defence and counterclaim is forty-five days upon receipt of the Notice of Arbitration, such time limit is shortened to twenty days in a domestic arbitration.

[Notice of oral hearing]

Article 63

(1) For a case examined by way of an oral hearing, the Secretariat of the CIETAC or its Sub-Commission shall notify the parties of the

date of oral hearing at least fifteen (15) days in advance of the oral hearing date. The arbitral tribunal may hold the oral hearing ahead of the schedule with consent from both parties. A party having justified reasons may request the arbitral tribunal for a postponement of the oral hearing. However, such request must be communicated to the arbitral tribunal seven (7) days in advance of the oral hearing date. The arbitral tribunal shall decide whether to postpone the oral hearing or not.

(2) A notice of oral hearing subsequent to the first oral hearing and a notice of a postponed oral hearing shall not be subject to the fifteen (15)-day time limit provided in the foregoing paragraph 1.

1. Same principle, different time limits. Art. 63 is very similar to art. 30 (see art. 30, note 1) and provides that in the case of an oral hearing, the arbitral tribunal needs to notify the parties in advance. The main difference between the two articles lies in the time limits: whereas art. 30 provides that such notice shall be given twenty days in advance and that a party may ask for postponement of such hearing by submitting a request at least ten days prior to the scheduled hearing, these time limits are shortened to fifteen and seven days respectively as regards domestic arbitration.

2. Hearing ahead of schedule. Art. 63 provides that the arbitral tribunal may, with the consent of the parties, hold the hearing ahead of schedule. This possibility is not expressly mentioned in art. 30, but the same principle applies – if both parties give their consent, there is no reason to prevent the arbitral tribunal from holding the hearing ahead of schedule.

[Record of oral hearing]
Article 64

(1) The arbitral tribunal shall make a brief written record of the oral hearing. Any party or participant in the arbitration may apply for a correction of the record if any omission or mistake is found in the record regarding its own statement. If the application is refused by the arbitral tribunal, it shall nevertheless be recorded into the file.

(2) The written record shall be signed or sealed by the arbitrator(s), the recorder, the parties and other participants in the arbitration, if any.

1. Mandatory written records. In compliance with art. 48 Arbitration Law (see note 1), the arbitral tribunal has to arrange for written records of the oral hearing(s) held in a domestic arbitration case (compare with art. 35, note 1). Such record has to be signed by all the participants to the arbitration, but does not necessarily need to be sealed by CIETAC.

[Time limits for rendering award]

Article 65

(1) **The arbitral tribunal shall render an award within four (4) months from the date on which the arbitral tribunal is formed.**

(2) **Upon the request of the arbitral tribunal, the Chairman of the CIETAC may extend this time period if he considers it truly necessary and the reasons are truly justified.**

1. Shorter time limit. Whereas in a foreign-related arbitration case the arbitral tribunal should render an arbitral award within six months from the date on which the arbitral tribunal was formed, the time limit is shortened to four months for domestic arbitrations.

2. In practice. Here again, in practice most of the cases handled under the Summary Procedure will be completed within the deadline. Only cases involving complicated issues, such as jurisdiction issues or the collection of evidence will require an extension.

[Context reference]

Article 66

As to matters not covered in this Chapter, the relevant provisions in the other Chapters of these Rules shall apply.

1. Reference to ordinary procedure. Any aspect of the arbitration not ruled by arts. 59 to 65 is subject to the ordinary procedure.

CHAPTER VI. SUPPLEMENTARY PROVISIONS

[Language]

Article 67

(1) **Where the parties have agreed on the arbitration language, their agreement shall prevail. Absent such agreement, the Chinese language shall be the official language to be used in the arbitration proceedings.**

(2) **At an oral hearing, if a party or its representative(s) or witness requires language interpretation, the Secretariat of the CIETAC or its Sub-Commission may provide an interpreter, or the party may bring its own interpreter.**

(3) **The arbitral tribunal and/or the Secretariat of the CIETAC or its Sub-Commission may, if it considers necessary, request the parties to submit a corresponding version of the documents and evidence by the parties in Chinese or in other languages.**

1. Free choice of language. In principle, the parties are free to choose any language of their choice and it is recommended that they include such choice in the arbitration clause. Failing such agreement on the language of the arbitration, the Chinese language will be used. However, the choice of language is in practice limited to the languages spoken by the available arbitrators. Although the parties are now allowed to choose an arbitrator outside the CIETAC List of Arbitrators and may thus be able to find suitable arbitrators with mastery of the chosen language, choosing an exotic language will render the constitution of the arbitral tribunal substantially more difficult and time consuming.

2. Interpreter. If one of the people involved in the arbitration, be it as party, counsel or witness cannot speak the language of the arbitration, CIETAC may be asked to arrange for adequate interpretation. The party concerned may also bring its own interpreter, which is very common in practice.

3. Translation at CIETAC's request. Since CIETAC does not have the sufficient manpower to handle arbitration in any language, if an arbitration is conducted in a language not commonly used in China, art. 67(3) gives CIETAC the right to request a party to submit a translation of relevant material in Chinese or in other languages.

[Service of documents]

Article 68

(1) All documents, notices and written materials in relation to the arbitration may be sent to the parties and/or their representatives in person, or by registered mail or express mail, facsimile, telex, telegraph, or by any other means considered proper by the Secretariat of the CIETAC or its Sub-Commission.

(2) Any written correspondence to a party and/or its representative(s) shall be deemed to have been properly served on the party if delivered to the addressee or delivered at his place of business, registration, domicile, habitual residence or mailing address, or where, after reasonable inquiries by the other party, none of the aforesaid addresses can be found, the written correspondence is sent by the Secretariat of the CIETAC or its Sub-Commission to the addressee's last known place of business, registered address, domicile, habitual residence or mailing address by registered mail or by any other means that provides a record of the attempt of delivery.

1. Methods of service. Art. 68(1) sets forth the different admissible ways to serve judicial documents on one of the parties and/or its representatives. Art. 68(1) encompasses a wide range of service methods including delivery in person, by registered or express mail and by fax or similar transmission means. This list is not exhaustive and CIETAC may consider any other way of transmission. It should be noted that as regards important notices and submissions, such as the Request of Arbitration, the Notice of Arbitration, the Statement of Defence, the Notice of Constitution of the Arbitral Tribunal, the Notice of Oral Hearing and the Arbitral Award, email is not considered an admissible means of service.

2. Places of service. Art. 68(2) determines the places where judicial documents need to be served. The principle is that documents should be served to the addressee in person or at his current place of registration or domicile, at his place of business or habitual residence, or at any other mailing address. Once counsel have been appointed, CIETAC will address all relevant judicial documents to the counsel. If none of the relevant addresses of the respondent can be established and if the respondent has not appointed counsel, the documents may legitimately be served at the last known of these places by registered mail or any other means that provides a record of the attempt of delivery. In summary, a document will be deemed served if the serving party or CIETAC make reasonable efforts to establish any of the addressee's addresses, and provided that the method of service provides a record of attempt of delivery. In practice, if the respondent cannot be located despite extensive research by claimant and the claimant has communicated the respondent's last known address to CIETAC, CIETAC will entrust a specific law firm to receive all judicial documents in the name of respondent and such documents will be deemed duly served.

[Arbitration fees and actual expenses]

Article 69

(1) Apart from charging arbitration fees to the parties according to the Fee Schedule of the CIETAC, the CIETAC may collect from the parties other extra, reasonable and actual expenses including arbitrators special remuneration and their travel and accommodation expenses incurred in dealing with the case, as well as the costs and expenses of experts, appraisers and interpreters appointed by the arbitral tribunal, etc.

(2) Where a party has appointed an arbitrator who will incur extra expenses, such as travel and accommodation expenses, and fails to pay in advance as a deposit within a time period specified by the CIETAC, the party shall be deemed not to have appointed the arbitrator. In such event, the Chairman of the CIETAC may appoint an arbitrator for the party pursuant to Article 22 or Article 23 of these Rules.

(3) Where the parties have agreed to hold an oral hearing at a place other than the CIETAC's domicile, extra expenses including travel and accommodation expenses incurred thereby shall be paid in advance as a deposit by the parties. In the event that the parties fail to do so, the oral hearing shall be held at the domicile of the CIETAC.

1. Extra costs. In addition to the arbitration fees charged in accordance with the Arbitration Fee Schedule, CIETAC is allowed to request payments of additional expenses (see art. 10, note 4). These expenses are mainly of two kinds: an 'arbitrator's special remuneration', and costs related to the holding of hearings or meetings.

2. Arbitrator's special remuneration. The term 'arbitrator's special remuneration' may sound somewhat suspicious, but actually only refers to the supplementary fees charged by CIETAC for foreign arbitrators. The fee for a foreign arbitrator is usually higher than for a Chinese arbitrator. This is linked to the low arbitration fees charged by CIETAC, in comparison to other international arbitration institutions such as ICC or AAA. Many foreign arbitrators refuse to participate in CIETAC arbitration proceedings, due the unattractive compensation for arbitrators and CIETAC has therefore introduced the concept of 'special remuneration'.

3. Costs related to the holding of hearings and meetings. These expenses include the travel expenses of arbitrators (especially when they come from abroad) and CIETAC's support staff (especially if the hearing is held somewhere else than in CIETAC's premises), accommodation (especially for arbitrators from another country or city), and other costs relating to the intervention of third parties such as experts, appraisers and interpreters. If the parties fail to pay these costs, the hearings will take place at CIETAC's domicile (see art. 32, note 1).

4. Payment in advance. As a matter of principle, the parties have to make advance payments to cover those costs. Where a party appointed an arbitrator with 'special remuneration' and fails to pay for the additional costs caused by his participation to the arbitration, the appointment will be considered invalid and the Chairman of CIETAC will appoint another arbitrator (without special remuneration) pursuant to arts. 22 and 23 (see art. 22 notes 1 et seq., and art. 23 notes 1 et seq.).

[Interpretation]

Article 70

(1) The headings of the articles in these Rules shall not serve as interpretations of the contents of the provisions contained herein.
(2) These Rules shall be interpreted by the CIETAC.

1. Interpretation by CIETAC. In case there is a doubt on how to interpret a specific provision in these rules, the authority to interpret such provision is exclusively reserved by CIETAC and does not fall to the arbitral tribunal itself.

[Coming into force]

Article 71

These Rules shall be effective as from 1 May 2005. For cases accepted by the CIETAC or by its Sub-Commissions before these Rules become effective, the Arbitration Rules effective at the time of acceptance shall apply, or these Rules shall apply where both parties agree.

1. Transitional provision. The CIETAC Rules of 2005 came into force on 1 May 2005. Art. 71 provides that these rules shall only apply to cases accepted by CIETAC after 1 May 2005, or otherwise where both parties agree.

UNITED NATIONS COMMISSION ON INTERNATIONAL TRADE LAW (UNCITRAL) MODEL LAW ON INTERNATIONAL COMMERCIAL ARBITRATION, 1985/2006*

(As adopted by the United Nations Commission on International Trade Law on 21 June 1985, and as amended by the United Nations Commission on International Trade Law on 7 July 2006)

[Introductory remarks]

General. With impressive foresight, the United Nations General Assembly recognised in December 1985 that the Model Law on International Commercial Arbitration adopted by the United Nations Commission on International Trade Law on 21 June 1985 ('Model Law')[1] would become one of three pillars of the modern era of international dispute resolution:

'Convinced that the Model Law, together with the Convention on the Recognition and Enforcement of Foreign Arbitral Awards and the Arbitration Rules of the United Nations Commission on International Trade Law recommended by the General Assembly in its resolution 31/98 of 15 December 1976, significantly contributes to the establishment of a unified legal framework for the fair and efficient settlement of disputes arising in international commercial relations, ... [emphasis in the original; footnotes omitted].'

The Model Law as adopted in 1985 has served as the basis for the national arbitration acts of more than sixty jurisdictions. As amended in 2006,[2] the

---

* Reproduced with permission of the United Nations Commission on International Trade Law (UNCITRAL). The text reproduced here is valid at the time of reproduction. As amendments may from time to time be made to the text, please refer to the website <http://www.uncitral.org> for the latest version.
1. Official Records of the General Assembly, Fortieth Session, Supplement No. 17 (A/40/17), annex I; Official Records of the General Assembly, Sixty-first Session, Supplement No. 17 (A/61/17) (together, United Nations Documents A/40/17, annex I and A/61/17, annex I). As discussed below, amendments were made to the Model Law in 2006, so when this chapter refers to the Model Law it should be assumed that the amendments are included, unless the text of the chapter indicates otherwise. Those interested in crucial background information on the Model Law should consult the UNCITRAL website: <www.uncitral.org/uncitral/en/uncitral_texts/arbitration/1985Model_arbitration.html>. The website contains, inter alia, the 1985 and current (2006) texts of the Model Law with an 'Explanatory Note' prepared by the UNCITRAL Secretariat ('for informational purposes only'; the Explanatory Note is expressly stated not to be an 'official commentary'); relevant General Assembly resolutions; the status of the Model Law (i.e. the jurisdictions that have based national arbitration acts on the Model Law); travaux preparatoires; and a useful bibliography on arbitration issues.
2. The General Assembly's Resolution of 18 December 2006, in recommending that States give 'favourable consideration to the enactment of the revised articles

Model Law has become the foundation for the national acts of another five jurisdictions (Ireland (2008), Mauritius (2008), New Zealand (2007), Peru (2008) and Slovenia (2008)). There are, however, several crucially important arbitration jurisdictions that are not model law jurisdictions (i.e. based on the Model Law) – Switzerland, France, England, the United States, Sweden and the Netherlands, to name a few. Moreover, model law jurisdictions themselves are not identical to each other; yet the Model Law's goals of standardising international commercial arbitration procedure and serving as a useful legislative guide may be achieved even if national arbitration acts are not identical. Still, the first question that is often raised when researching a State's approach to international arbitration – i.e. 'is it a model law jurisdiction?' – speaks volumes about the Model Law's lasting significance. Once you have the answer to that question, you are well on the road towards formulating a research plan. The Model Law was drafted with both the 1958 New York Convention and the 1976 UNCITRAL Arbitration Rules in mind; e.g. the enforcement of award provisions of the Model Law (Chapter 8) are drawn from the 1958 New York Convention, and a number of other provisions of the Model Law rely on provisions set out in the UNCITRAL Arbitration Rules. The latter reliance is necessary because the Model Law, in providing guidance for national legislators, had to take into account the fallback possibility that rules for the conduct of proceedings will be needed if the parties do not identify rules (whether institutional or ad hoc or otherwise specified) in their arbitration clause. For such fallback rules, the Model Law naturally looks to the UNCITRAL Arbitration Rules. Thus, if the UNCITRAL Arbitration Rules undergo significant revision, national legislatures that have based their arbitration acts on the Model Law may well wish to modify certain sections of said national acts, and UNCITRAL may wish to consider certain sections of the Model Law when incorporating changes in the Arbitration Rules. Note here that the 2006 amendments to the Model Law have already addressed certain key developments in arbitration practice in advance of the revision of the UNCITRAL Arbitration Rules.

CHAPTER I. GENERAL PROVISIONS

[Scope of application]*

Article 1

(1) This Law applies to international commercial** arbitration, subject to any agreement in force between this State and any other State or States.

---

of the Model law', expressed 'the need for provisions in the Model law to conform to current practices in international trade and modern means of contracting with regard to the form of the arbitration agreement and the granting of interim measures'.

(2) The provisions of this Law, except articles 8, 9, 17 H, 17 I, 17 J, 35 and 36, apply only if the place of arbitration is in the territory of this State.

(3) An arbitration is international if:
   (a) the parties to an arbitration agreement have, at the time of the conclusion of that agreement, their places of business in different States; or
   (b) one of the following places is situated outside the State in which the parties have their places of business:
      (i) the place of arbitration if determined in, or pursuant to, the arbitration agreement;
      (ii) any place where a substantial part of the obligations of the commercial relationship is to be performed or the place with which the subject-matter of the dispute is most closely connected; or
   (c) the parties have expressly agreed that the subject-matter of the arbitration agreement relates to more than one country.

(4) For the purposes of paragraph (3) of this article:
   (a) if a party has more than one place of business, the place of business is that which has the closest relationship to the arbitration agreement;
   (b) if a party does not have a place of business, reference is to be made to his habitual residence.

(5) This Law shall not affect any other law of this State by virtue of which certain disputes may not be submitted to arbitration or may be submitted to arbitration only according to provisions other than those of this Law.

* Article headings are for reference purposes only and are not to be used for purposes of interpretation.

** The term 'commercial' should be given a wide interpretation so as to cover matters arising from all relationships of a commercial nature, whether contractual or not. Relationships of a commercial nature include, but are not limited to, the following transactions: any trade transaction for the supply or exchange of goods or services; distribution agreement; commercial representation or agency; factoring; leasing; construction of works; consulting; engineering; licensing; investment; financing; banking; insurance; exploitation agreement or concession; joint venture and other forms of industrial or business co-operation; carriage of goods or passengers by air, sea, rail or road.

1. General. The UNCITRAL Model Law on International Commercial Arbitration was adopted on 21 June 1985 as a prototype arbitration law which could be adopted as is by national legislators or which can at least provide the essential basis for the drafting of a national domestic or international arbitration law (e.g. Hong Kong, Australia, Canada), or a law for both international and domestic arbitrations (see, e.g., Germany, Spain). The law has been adopted verbatim by a large number of countries, including Hong Kong, Australia and Canada and has been modified to some extent by other jurisdictions (e.g. Germany, Spain).

2. Model Law as a flexible model framework. A model law is designed to serve as a model, or at least a framework, for a national arbitration act rather than one that articulates every definition and detail, and thus it should not require frequent alteration. The comments contained in the travaux preparatoires of Francois Knoepfler (Observer for Switzerland) and Sir Michael (now Lord) Mustill of the United Kingdom at the 306th Meeting of the Model Law Working Group (3 June 1985), are notable in this regard. Knoepfler commented that 'in drafting a Model Law it was possible to accept a more flexible approach. If the form of a convention was adopted, a precise definition [of the term 'commercial'] in the body of the text would have a restrictive effect'. For the Model Law, he favoured the system which had been used (a footnote containing interpretive guidance). Mustill took a slightly different approach, disfavouring a footnote and preferring either a 'general expression in the text' or an explanation in a commentary outside the text, but concluded with the same understanding as Knoepfler about flexibility: 'It would be open to individual States to define the term, if required; that would not be a departure from the spirit of the Model Law.' Moreover, the matter of flexibility within the Model Law and the possibility and reality of national variations in implementing the Model Law are crucial to an understanding of the Model Law's benefits and limits. It is also crucial to understanding its expression of the tension in international commercial arbitration between the goal of uniformity across borders while taking into account the reality that: (i) an arbitration has to take place somewhere; (ii) national acts are still the preserve of individual States; (iii) individual States delegate authority to arbitral tribunals to conduct arbitrations in different ways; and (iv) the absence of a convention on this delegation means that individual variations based on the designation of an arbitral seat are unlikely to vanish anytime soon and therefore should be acknowledged and, while perhaps not celebrated, also not denigrated.[3] The Model Law certainly derives its meaning and usefulness from 'the entirety of the legal systems', but the Model Law

---

3. For a different perspective on the question of the significance of the arbitral seat, see Emmanuel Gaillard, 'Aspects Philosophiques de L'Arbitrage International', 329 *Recueil des cours* 49 (2008). As he expressed it in a summary article, 'The Representations of International Arbitration', 238 *New York Law Journal* 67 (4 October 2007), Gaillard's view is that international arbitration is 'an autonomous process where the arbitrators derive their powers from the sum of all legal systems that recognize, under certain conditions, the legal force of the arbitration agreement and the resulting award'.

also recognises the reality that the national legal system of the seat of the arbitration is the ultimate source of the arbitrator's power to sit as an arbitrator and issue an award that is in most instances more readily enforceable in other countries than a national court judgment issued at the seat. Indeed, the UN General Assembly's December 1985 Resolution quoted at the outset of this chapter indicated the tension between flexibility and uniformity in referring to the Model Law's contribution to the establishment of a 'unified legal framework'. That is, it was intended that a single framework of rules and procedures be adopted by States, which was needed, as the resolution continued to state, in view of the desirability of uniformity of the law of arbitral procedures and the specific needs of international commercial arbitration practice. A legislative 'framework' or standard, however, was also intended to recognise the individual State's power to legislate within the framework as it deemed appropriate. At a subsequent Working Group session, the 308th Meeting (4 June 1985), the French delegate, Roehrich, helpfully expanded on the meaning and implications of a 'model law' and the role of national legislatures: 'a Model Law should deal with basic principles. It should not go into too many details, which could give rise to difficulties with national legislations on procedure.' Roehrich thus recognised that international arbitration still had a territorial element that could not be overlooked, and a State would be willing to delegate much but not all adjudicatory authority to an arbitral tribunal. This was also the understanding of the Working Group Chairman, Loewe (Austria), who at the same (308th) meeting observed that 'the Model law would be used according to the requirements of the country concerned. States which did not have rules on international arbitration might take the Model law as it stood; others would modify it in conformity with their general rules of law.' As the above-quoted comments in the travaux preparatoires indicate, the Model Law was designed, above all, to enhance party autonomy in the conduct of an international arbitration and to limit national court intervention to that of a supporting role, and its provisions 'give substance to and implement' these concepts (Lucio, *UNCITRAL Model Law*). In doing so, the Model Law's drafters effected an often seamless compromise between several different legal systems. One commentator posited soon after the Model Law's promulgation that '[a]ssuming near-universal adoption of some variant of the Model Law, international businessman will find greater tolerance among foreign courts in recognizing and enforcing international arbitral awards' (Lucio, *UNCITRAL Model Law*). This is a well-stated and carefully balanced prediction, and, as it turns out, an accurate one. The Model Law, to be useful, had to be adopted in some form by many States. It did not need to be adopted in the same form because, as explained above, the Model Law is a framework that had flexibility built into its provisions. Adoption of the framework principles would contribute to the creation and recognition of a sufficiently unified arbitral procedure such that the element that underpins all of international arbitration – effective enforcement under the New York Convention – would be strengthened. That is, adoption of the Model Law in some variant by many States would raise the confidence level of national courts in supporting international arbitration because it would be understood that most States have, as expressed in their national arbitration acts, a broadly similar understanding of the international arbitral process. This is precisely what has happened, and it is hard to see that anything more could reasonably be asked of the Model Law.

3. The meaning of 'international commercial arbitration'. Art. 1 was the subject of much discussion in the Working Group in 1985, as reported in the travaux preparatoires, and art. 1(2) was amended by UNCITRAL at its thirty-ninth session, in 2006. The first step for the Model Law was to address its applicability: how should a national legislature define 'international commercial arbitration' in its national arbitration act, and what would be the territorial scope of application – i.e. which international commercial arbitrations would come within the purview of the provisions of the national arbitration act. Does the Model Law, or should the Model Law, seek to define the three key words: international, commercial and arbitration? The Working Group found this to be an extremely difficult issue, and discussed it at some length: at the 306th Meeting (3 June 1985), the Chairman (Loewe of Austria) 'invited the Commission to consider whether it wished the Model law to be applied to international commercial arbitration and, if so, how were international arbitration and commercial arbitration to be defined'. Some delegates favoured defining 'commercial' in the text instead of a footnote, and numerous possible definitions of 'commercial' were considered, including the possibility of not defining the term. In determining a suitable definition, due consideration was given to the need to accommodate different legal systems. Moreover, there was even a proposal (Magnusson of Sweden) to omit the words 'international commercial,' as they were not needed to modify 'arbitration'. The Chairman summed up the discussion on art. 1(1) as follows: 'the majority of speakers had favored that paragraph being confined to the commercial field but some had wanted a slight expansion in the text of the definition of "commercial".' An equal number had not favoured that proposal because they feared that it would lead to problems with domestic legislation, in which the term 'commercial' was used in many other contexts; they had therefore supported the retention of the footnote. He therefore suggested, as a preliminary for further work, that the possibility should be considered of making art. 1(1) more explicit but retaining a footnote with the examples of the activities which the Commission had had in mind: '… [i]t should also be drafted clearly to show that it was not intended to infringe State immunity'. This was the path ultimately taken: the key concept expressed by the term 'international commercial arbitration' is retained; 'international' is defined in art. 1(3) and given a very broad scope, 'commercial' is not defined and is instead described in a footnote that calls for a 'wide interpretation' and gives a non-exhaustive list of commercial relationships. (It should be noted that several States have moved the footnote on 'commercial' into the text of their national arbitration act, and Professor

Sanders has pointed out that several other States omitted 'commercial'. Indeed, he also observes that a number of States have adopted the Model Law for both domestic and international arbitration, such as Germany.) The Analytical Commentary contained in the Report of the Secretary General (the 'Commentary') indicates that the Commissioners drafting the Model Law anticipated that the word 'commercial' would be given a broad interpretation so as to embrace matters arising from all relationships of a commercial nature, and that the broad interpretation for the term 'commercial' would mean inclusion of commercial relationships, irrespective of whether the parties are 'commercial parties' or 'merchants' under any given national law. Aligned with this interpretative suggestion, State courts have held, for example, that the sale and purchase of a home was considered a commercial transaction, as it was done in a business-like way, notwithstanding the fact that the sale was unconnected to the regular business activity of either party (CLOUT Case No. 390, Ontario Court, Canada, 1 February 1996). However, a contract that created a master and servant relationship was held not to be a commercial relationship under art. 1(1) (cf. also CLOUT Case No. 111, Alberta Court of Queen's Bench, Canada, 12 August 1994). Similarly, State courts tend to construe the term 'international' widely. Thus, in an FOB case where the parties had their places of business in Singapore, Singapore law was the governing law of the contract and the payment and nomination obligations were performed in Singapore, the courts of Singapore held, by reference to art. 1(3)(b), that the arbitration was held to be 'international' because many other parts of the contract (such as the obligation to provide the cargo, the tendering of notice of readiness, the transfer of risks and the loading operations) were performed in Korea (CLOUT Case No. 209, High Court of Singapore, 27 May 1996). Furthermore, according to the court, it was crucial that the demurrage claim in question was alleged to have been incurred at the loading port in Yosu, Korea). In the same vein, the High Court of Hong Kong found that an arbitration in relation to a dispute between two parties from Hong Kong was nevertheless an 'international arbitration' in the meaning of art. 1(3)(b)(ii), since the subject matter of the dispute was most closely connected to China. More specifically, the dispute related to the architectural design and supervision of a construction project in Dongshan Island, China (CLOUT Case No. 108, High Court of Hong Kong, 4 May 1995). State courts will also look into the most characteristic performance of the contract (even if this is not the subject matter of the dispute before them) to decide whether to classify an arbitration as 'international' or not. For example, an arbitration was held to be 'international' in a case where the High Court of Hong Kong was asked to appoint a second arbitrator in an arbitration between two Hong Kong companies arising out of a contract for the sale of soya beans. While the subject matter before the High Court of Hong Kong was the appointment of an arbitrator, the crucial factor that the court looked into in order to hold that the arbitration was international was the fact that delivery, which constitutes a substantial part of the obligations of the commercial relationship, was to take place in China, i.e. outside Hong Kong (CLOUT Case No. 20, High Court of Hong Kong, 29 October 1991).

4. Model Law and the 'territorial principle'. Art. 1(2) expresses the territorial principle that 'the Model Law as enacted in a given State applies only if the place of arbitration is in the territory of that State' (Explanatory Note, para. 13). However, as the Secretariat observed, there are exceptions to this territorial principle, and the 2006 amendment recognises that the number of exceptions have been increasing. Thus, the territorial principle does not apply in (a) the context of arbitration agreements and court actions, (b) the context of the 2006 amendments regarding interim measures, and (c) the context of recognition and enforcement of arbitral awards. Still, the territorial principle is one of the foundations of a plausible national arbitration act, and, despite the presence of many devotees of international arbitration in UNCITRAL, the Model Law's provisions are consistent with the reality that the place of arbitration determines the applicability of national law (see Explanatory Note, para. 4, where there is an admonition to States in the 2006 amendment not to lose sight of the international nature of international arbitration). In general, State courts have abided by the territorial principle. Thus, German courts rejected an application to grant interim relief in support of an arbitration in Geneva under Swiss law (OLG, Nuremberg, 30 November 2005, IPRax 468 (2006)), and Canadian courts refused to wait for a tribunal to render its decision on jurisdiction, on the basis that neither art. 5 (rule of minimum court intervention) nor art. 16 (the principle of Kompetenz-Kompetenz) were applicable to a case where the seat of arbitration was outside Canada (CLOUT Case No. 13, Ontario District Court, Canada 27 October 1988; Case 383, Ontario District Court, 27 October 1989). In one case, however, national courts of Canada deviated from the territorial principle and applied art. 1(3), in order to determine whether the agreement in question – which eventually was found to be void – was an 'international arbitration agreement' within the meaning of the Model Law, despite the fact that seat of the arbitration was in Geneva and Swiss law was applicable (CLOUT Case No. 28, Saskatchewan Court of Queen's Bench, Canada, 19 March 1993).

5. Arbitrability. Art. 1(5) effectively invites individual States to 'fill in' the arbitrability provision. For example, it has been argued that art. 1(5) of the Model Law, in leaving matters of arbitrability to the individual State, fails to promote uniformity or predictability, and several model law jurisdictions have taken steps to address arbitrability 'more extensively' than art. 1(5), leaning 'toward the adoption of a wide conception of arbitrability' (Mantilla-Serrano/Adam, *UNCITRAL Model Law*). However, contrary to these critics, it is difficult to see this development on arbitrability as anything other than the Model Law working properly in practice, functioning in precisely the manner that was intended by the original and subsequent Working Groups. States do take different views on arbitrability, and the revisions that certain model law States have made to art. 1(5) are themselves hardly models of clarity that would necessarily attract wide approval (one reason, perhaps, that the Model Law drafters did not seek to define arbitrability). The Model Law, it could be said, has at least not stood in the way of (and has quite possibly encouraged) the widening of the conception of arbitrability, and attempts to 'reduce uncertainty' by inserting a more precise provision on arbitrability in the Model Law would achieve very little. When certain arbitration practitioners argue that the 'current Model Law formulation [on arbitrability] is simply too broad and, if directly adopted in national statutes, affords far too much leeway for domestic courts and legislators to exclude from the ambit of arbitration (at their whim and leisure) matters which, in the reasonable expectations of international arbitration users and practitioners, are properly arbitrable matters' (Mantilla-Serrano/Adam, *UNCITRAL Model Law*), they are according themselves far too much authority to speak for 'international arbitration users and practitioners'. These critics are essentially proposing that an unidentified narrow group of allegedly like-minded lawyers should legislate for all States, based on their untested knowledge of what is actually an 'arbitrable matter'. Such confidence in this narrow group's omniscience and unity,[4] and in an abstract notion of international arbitration may be appealing in some respects, but it would not lead to the ability to disregard national laws – in point of fact, it might require the application of a competing set of national laws (if one does not rely on the rules of law regarding arbitrability at the seat of arbitration), and thereby foster even greater uncertainty and confusion. Moreover, it does not seem wholly unreasonable for the learned body of international arbitration practitioners to know the provisions of national law relating to arbitration at the seat of arbitration;[5] neither does it seem too demanding to expect that users of international arbitration would seek to have some understanding, from their external counsel, of the arbitration laws at the seat of the arbitration.

---

4. Pieter Sanders, 'UNCITRAL's Model Law on International and Commercial Arbitration: Present Situation and Future', 21 Arbitration International 4, LCIA 2005, p. 443, at pp. 475-76, questions the existence of the arbitration community's unity on this issue and the usefulness of creating a list of three or four non-arbitrable issues (as the UNCITRAL Secretariat had earlier suggested: 'I doubt whether this list idea and a worldwide discussion on arbitrability is to be recommended. The topic of arbitrability could, in my opinion, better be left to national arbitration laws.').

5. See Fernando Mantilla-Serrano and John Adam, 'UNCITRAL Model Law: Missed Opportunities for Enhanced Uniformity', 31 *UNSW Law Journal* (2008) 309, at 314: 'international arbitration practitioners are not always familiar with the intricate aspects of the arbitration law of the country of the seat of the arbitration'. While this is undoubtedly a true statement, it is not a particularly compelling ground for overriding sovereignty.

[Definitions and rules of interpretation]

Article 2

For the purposes of this Law:
  (a) 'arbitration' means any arbitration whether or not administered by a permanent arbitral institution;
  (b) 'arbitral tribunal' means a sole arbitrator or a panel of arbitrators;
  (c) 'court' means a body or organ of the judicial system of a State;
  (d) where a provision of this Law, except article 28, leaves the parties free to determine a certain issue, such freedom includes the right of the parties to authorise a third party, including an institution, to make that determination;
  (e) where a provision of this Law refers to the fact that the parties have agreed or that they may agree or in any other way refers to an agreement of the parties, such agreement includes any arbitration rules referred to in that agreement;
  (f) where a provision of this Law, other than in articles 25(a) and 32(2)(a), refers to a claim, it also applies to a counter-claim, and where it refers to a defence, it also applies to a defence to such counter-claim.

1. Meaning of 'arbitration'. The term 'arbitration' is here given a wide scope, which includes both ad hoc and institutional arbitration. However, the term does not cover any form of compulsory (i.e. non-voluntary) arbitration or any other type of non-binding dispute resolution mechanism (see Commentary, art. 1 para. 15; Holtzmann/Neuhaus, Article 1, pp. 151-152). It should be noted though, that where the parties have agreed on a multi-tier dispute resolution agreement, which provides for a non-binding mechanism, such as expert determination, as a pre-arbitration step, parties cannot dispute the existence of an arbitration agreement altogether (*Westco Airconditioning* v *Sui Chong Construction & Engineering*).

2. Meaning of 'arbitral tribunal' and 'court'. The definitions of the terms 'arbitral tribunals' and 'court' are in fact self-evident (as the Commentary itself also notes, art. 2 para. 1); however, it was considered necessary to include these definitions in order to prevent any terminological misunderstanding, which can arise in some languages (the Commentary makes reference to French and Spanish, see art. 2 para. 1).

3. Determination of an issue by a third party. This provisions provides for the ability of the parties to authorise a third party to make a determination in relation to certain issues (with the exception of art. 28, the applicable substantive law, as the arbitral tribunal's authority cannot be substituted for by a third party entity on this point). Issues that the parties may refer to a third party to determine include the number of arbitrators, the place of arbitration and other procedural points (Commentary, art. 2 para. 3).

4. Incorporation of arbitration rules by reference. This provision codifies the already general practice among commercial parties to incorporate arbitration rules by reference in their arbitration agreements. These rules are thus part of the arbitration agreement itself, as is intended throughout the Model Law.

5. Claim and counter-claim. The provision effectively establishes the rule of equal treatment of a claim and counter-claim, which is provided nowhere else in the Model Law (see Holtzmann/Neuhaus, Article 2, p. 153).

[International origin and general principles]

Article 2 A

(1) In the interpretation of this Law, regard is to be had to its international origin and to the need to promote uniformity in its application and the observance of good faith.

(2) Questions concerning matters governed by this Law which are not expressly settled in it are to be settled in conformity with the general principles on which this Law is based.

1. General. Art. 2 A is a 2006 amendment. As noted above, it seeks to balance the enduring significance of the seat in international commercial arbitration, given territorial realities, with the direction to States to recognise that the Model Law on which they are basing their national arbitration act is a compromise between a number of legal systems, and an 'internationalist' perspective should therefore guide the national understanding and implementation of the Model Law's provisions. This amendment is little more than hortatory, but manifests the continuing efforts of UNCITRAL to provide a 'unified legal framework' to States.

[Receipt of written communications]

Article 3

(1) Unless otherwise agreed by the parties:
  (a) any written communication is deemed to have been received if it is delivered to the addressee personally or if it is delivered at his place of business, habitual residence or mailing address; if none of these can be found after making a reasonable inquiry, a written communication is deemed to have been received if it is sent to the addressee's last-known place of business, habitual residence or mailing address by registered letter or any other means which provides a record of the attempt to deliver it;

(b) the communication is deemed to have been received on the day it is so delivered.

(2) The provisions of this article do not apply to communications in court proceedings.

1. General. Professor Sanders notes that when 'the [Model Law] was drafted in the 1980s it could not take into account the influence of electronic communication' (Sanders, *UNCITRAL's Model Law*, at p. 446). The new art. 7, amended in 2006, does take this into account. Art. 3 is unlikely to provide ongoing difficulties because of the qualification in art. 3(1) – 'unless otherwise agreed by the parties'. The aim of the provision is twofold: first, to ensure that standards of due process are met; second, to prevent recalcitrant parties from denying receipt of arbitration documents that have actually been received. This provision is mainly relevant at the commencement stage of the arbitration proceedings with regard to documents initiating arbitral proceedings.

2. 'Unless otherwise agreed by the parties'. This would usually be the case where the parties have referred to a set of arbitration rules. For example, if the parties have agreed on the ICC Arbitration Rules, ICC art. 3 would be applicable.

3. 'Written communications'. Written communication in the meaning of art. 3 includes both communications between the parties (CLOUT Case No. 20, High Court of Hong Kong, 29 October 1991) and communications by the tribunal to the parties (CLOUT Case No. 29, Ontario Court of Justice, Canada, 30 January 1992).

4. Meaning of 'reasonable inquiry'. In a case where the claimant sent out a notice to the defendant at all three addresses of the defendant known to the claimant, it was held that the claimant had met the conditions set out in art. 3 (CLOUT Case No. 384, Ontario Court of Justice, Canada, 26 April 1991). However, in another case the arbitral tribunal failed to ask for evidence that the respondent had actually received the notice of request for arbitration, and no further effort was made to allocate the actual address of the respondent at the time (CLOUT Case No. 402, Highest Regional Court of Bavaria, Germany, 16 March 2000). Accordingly, it was held that the respondent was not duly served.

5. Written communications regarding court proceedings in relation to arbitration. Art. 3 does not apply to written communications regarding court proceedings in relation to arbitration. These will be governed by the relevant provisions about written communications in court proceedings, such as, for example, the Hague Convention on Service Abroad of Judicial and Extra-Judicial Documents in Civil and Commercial Matters (cf. Holtzmann/Neuhaus, Article 3, p. 185).

[Waiver of right to object]
Article 4

A party who knows that any provision of this Law from which the parties may derogate or any requirement under the arbitration agreement has not been complied with and yet proceeds with the arbitration without stating his objection to such non-compliance without undue delay or, if a time-limit is provided therefor, within such period of time, shall be deemed to have waived his right to object.

1. General. Art. 4 recognises that although it would be impractical to include the detail of time limits, which will vary by State, the important uniform principle is that a party cannot 'hedge its bets' and save its objections to a procedural defect. Art. 4 originates from the well-established principles of estoppel, found in common law, and venire contra factum proprium, found in civil law (Commentary art. 4 para. 1). This provision applies only to derogation from contractual arrangements between the parties (including, of course, arbitration rules) or any default rule of the Model Law, as waiver of right to object cannot be accepted as regards mandatory rules. Moreover, it applies only to derogation from procedural rather than substantive requirements of the arbitration, such as the invalidity of the arbitration agreement (Commentary, art. 4 para. 2).

2. Conditions of waiver and time limits. For art. 4 to apply, a party must know or ought to have known of the derogation. According to the Commentary, this condition should be given a restrictive interpretation, which would exclude any negligent ignorance (Commentary, art. 4 para. 3). This restrictive interpretation is justified by the exceptional character of this provision. No specific time limits for the waiver of the right to object are set out in this provision. It has been held that the condition of 'without undue delay' requires a party to object either at the next scheduled oral hearing or raise the issue in its next written submission to the tribunal (Oberlandesgericht Haumburg, Germany, 10 Sch 08/01, 21 February 2002, available at <www.dis-arb.de>). When a party is deemed to have waived his right to object, it will be not only precluded from raising this right before the tribunal at any subsequent phase of the arbitration proceedings, but also before a national court in order to challenge or refuse the enforcement of the ensuing award (Commentary, art. 4 para. 6).

[Extent of court intervention]
Article 5

In matters governed by this Law, no court shall intervene except where so provided in this Law.

UNCITRAL Model Law, art. 6

1. General. Art. 5 reiterates a bedrock principle of the Model Law: State court intervention is tightly restricted. Both art. 5 and art. 6 are in essence conflict of jurisdictions rules regulating the relationships between national courts and arbitral tribunals. In accordance with this provision, national courts must intervene only in exceptional circumstances, which are exhaustively provided in the Model Law. It follows that art. 5 establishes a presumption against the intervention of national courts. Accordingly, model law State courts have, by reference to art. 5, adopted a non-interventionist role towards arbitrations taking place in their territory. For example, in arbitral proceedings between the International Civil Aviation Organization (ICAO) and a contractor for the ICAO regarding a dispute that arose out of the contraction and installation of an airport in Vietnam, ICAO raised its immunity to the context of the jurisdiction of the arbitral tribunal. At the same time ICAO applied to the Superior Court of Quebec to declare that it enjoyed absolute immunity. The Superior Court, by reference to art. 5, refused to determine the issue, noting that it should refrain from intervening in ongoing arbitral proceedings (CLOUT Case No. 182, Superior Court of Quebec, 9 September 1994, Canada).

2. Limitations of the rule of 'non-intervention'. The rule of 'non-intervention' aims to safeguard arbitration from the unnecessary disruption of the arbitral proceedings. It follows that when the intervention of national courts is necessary, it should be allowed. Indeed, the intervention of national courts is permitted for the purposes of supporting the arbitration process and the work of the arbitral tribunal. Thus, for example, in arts. 13 to 16 and 27, the court has a possible role in relation to challenges to arbitrators, appointment of substitute arbitrators, ruling on jurisdiction after the arbitral tribunal has found that it has jurisdiction, and assisting in the taking of evidence – but only at the request of (or approval by) the arbitral tribunal. It should be noted that the scope of art. 5 is narrower than the purview of the Model Law itself, namely to 'international commercial arbitration' (Commentary, art. 5 para. 4). Thus art. 5 will not apply, and therefore not exclude court intervention, in any matter not covered by the Model Law, or when the seat of the arbitration is outside the geographical boundaries of a model law State (CLOUT Case No. 13, Ontario District Court Canada, 27 October 1989, where seat of the arbitration was outside Canada, and accordingly Canadian courts refused to stay its proceedings to determine the validity and the scope of the arbitration agreement at hand).

[Court or other authority for certain functions of arbitration assistance and supervision]

Article 6

The functions referred to in articles 11(3), 11(4), 13(3), 14, 16(3) and 34(2) shall be performed by ... [Each State enacting this model law

specifies the court, courts or, where referred to therein, other authority competent to perform these functions.]

1. Courts specifically designated for arbitration related proceedings. The aim of art. 6 is to concentrate all arbitration related proceedings into specifically designated national courts. The rationale behind this provision is that arbitration cases that are to be determined by national courts are expected to have the necessary specialisation in the area of international commercial arbitration. Furthermore, concentration of arbitration related disputes into specifically designed national courts will increase predictability with regard to exactly which court would be competent to address an arbitration issue, and thus it would be easier for foreign parties to locate that court (cf. Commentary, art. 6 para. 2).

CHAPTER II. ARBITRATION AGREEMENT

[Definition and form of arbitration agreement]

Article 7

(1) 'Arbitration agreement' is an agreement by the parties to submit to arbitration all or certain disputes which have arisen or which may arise between them in respect of a defined legal relationship, whether contractual or not. An arbitration agreement may be in the form of an arbitration clause in a contract or in the form of a separate agreement.

(2) The arbitration agreement shall be in writing. An agreement is in writing if it is contained in a document signed by the parties or in an exchange of letters, telex, telegrams or other means of telecommunication which provide a record of the agreement, or in an exchange of statements of claim and defence in which the existence of an agreement is alleged by one party and not denied by another. The reference in a contract to a document containing an arbitration clause constitutes an arbitration agreement provided that the contract is in writing and the reference is such as to make that clause part of the contract.

1. Meaning of 'arbitration agreement'. Arbitration agreements are defined along the lines of New York Convention art. II(1). The term 'arbitration agreement' includes an agreement in relation to both present and future disputes; an agreement in the form of a clause included in the main substantive contract; an agreement which is separate from the main contract; and an agreement in relation to contractual or non-contractual (e.g. pre-contractual or tortious) disputes. With regard to the last point, courts have held that arbitration agreements should be given a wide interpretation to include the whole spectrum of disputes arising out of a specific relationship between two parties (cf. Commentary, art. 7 para. 4). It has been pertinently held that an agreement that contains both an arbitration clause and a clause providing for a right to sue will qualify as an 'arbitration agreement' according to art. 7 (CLOUT Case No. 32, Ontario Court, Canada, 30 April 1992). The basic difference with the definition of the term arbitration agreement provided in the New York Convention art. II(1) and that in art. 7 is that the latter does not include the wording 'concerning a subject matter capable of settlement by arbitration'. However, as the Commentary notes, this does not mean that an arbitration agreement concerning a subject matter that is inarbitrable will be upheld under the Model Law (Commentary, art. 7 para. 5).

2. Formal requirements of an arbitration agreement. Art. 7 provides for formal requirements of arbitration agreements in line with the basic conditions provided in New York Convention art. II(2). The purpose of the formal requirements is to provide apparent proof of consent to the arbitration agreement. Thus, if the specified formal conditions in art. 7 are not met, consent to arbitrate will usually be very unlikely to be proven. Conversely, if the formal conditions of art. 7 are met, consent will be unlikely to be challenged. Having said that, the German Supreme Court held that a member of an association who signed the articles of association before an arbitration clause was added thereto, was not bound by that arbitration clause. This was especially the case since the particular member had later dissented to the introduction of the arbitration clause, which was upheld by the majority of the members of the association (CLOUT Case No. 406, Bundesgerichtshof, Germany, II ZR 373/98, 3 April 2000). The provision adheres to the writing requirement which can be met in two ways: first, when an arbitration clause or agreement is contained in a single document which is signed by all the relevant parties; secondly, when an arbitration clause or agreement is contained in an exchange of documents (which includes letters, telex, telegrams or other means of telecommunication which provide a record of the agreement, or statements of claim and defence) in which case no signature of the parties is required. The strict formal requirements provided for in the art. 7(2) have been heavily criticised (see the discussion in detail in Lew/Mistelis/Kroll, *Comparative and International Commercial Arbitration*, para. 7-7 et seq.). Accordingly, some national courts have attempted to relax the writing requirement, adopting a less strict approach to the signature in particular. For example, the Courts of Hong Kong upheld an arbitration agreement included in a charter-party, despite the fact that it was not signed by both parties (CLOUT Case No. 40, High Court of Hong Kong, 30 July 1992; the same was held in Case 63, High Court of Hong Kong, 2 February 1994. Contrary, CLOUT Case No. 64, High Court of Hong Kong, 13 May 1994). Taking into account the factual circumstances of the case (pre-voyage communications), the court found that the parties had consented to the charter-party and the arbitration clause included therein, and concluded that the writing requirement of art. 7 was met. In the same vein, a court in Canada found that the writing requirement was met in the following case (CLOUT Case No. 365, Saskatchewan Court of Queen's Bench, Canada, 1 October 1996): a buyer sent a written offer to purchase, which included an arbitration clause; the seller never returned a signed copy of the offer, however it submitted a sample of the goods and promised delivery. The courts held that the seller was bound by the arbitration agreement as a result of its conduct (i.e. submission of sample and promise to deliver). The Court noted that art. 7 should be construed broadly, allowing the conclusion that arbitration agreements exist even when the signature of one party was missing. Moreover, national courts have given priority to arbitration agreements over jurisdiction agreements, in cases where parties have wrongfully referred to conflicting dispute resolution clauses. For example, in one case, a bill of lading contained both a clause providing for arbitration in China and an exclusive jurisdiction clause for Chinese courts. In addition, the bill of lading was not signed by both parties. One of the parties brought a claim before the courts of Hong Kong (at the time Hong Kong was not part of China). The defendant applied for a stay. The High Court of Hong Kong granted a stay holding first that, despite the lack of signature of both parties, the arbitration agreement was formally valid, by reference to the conduct of the parties after the conclusion of the bill of lading. More crucially though, the High Court of Hong Kong held that, despite the fact that the parties were referring to both an arbitration agreement and an exclusive jurisdiction agreement, the arbitration agreement should be the one to prevail. As the court noted, the clause was offering a choice to the claimant between arbitration and litigation in China. As the claimant wrongfully opted for litigation in Hong Kong, it was open to the defendants to exercise that choice. By applying for a stay of proceedings pursuant to art. 8, the defendants opted for arbitration in China. As already mentioned, art. 7(2) is modelled upon New York Convention art. II(2). Nevertheless, art. 7(2) contains three additions: first, it contains an open-ended clause on the means of telecommunication, the exchange of which may meet the writing requirement, as opposed to the exhaustive list of such means provided in New York Convention art. II(2) ('exchange of letters or telegrams'). The wording 'or other means of telecommunication which provide a record of the agreement' is open enough to include any new means of telecommunication that will be developed in the future, which provides a record of an agreement, and certainly this seems enough to include email. Still, any agreement not recorded, such as oral agreements or agreements over phone, will not be covered by art. 7(2) (see Holtzmann/Neuhaus, Article 7, p. 263). Secondly, it makes reference to the exchange of statements of claim and defence as a means that constitutes an arbitration agreement in writing. Here, even the failure of one of the parties to deny the existence of the arbitration agreement will be enough for the writing requirement to be met.[6] Thirdly, it attempts to clarify

---

6. Cf. a case where the claimant in the arbitration proceedings made an informal claim on 'contractual loss and expenses', in which the existence of an arbitration agreement was alleged and not denied by the respondent. The High Court of Hong Kong court held that this claim constituted an arbitration agreement in the sense

the complicated issue of conclusion of an arbitration agreement by reference. Very often in practice, parties refer to a separate document which contains an arbitration agreement. Here the main problem that arises is whether a general reference to the document, which otherwise meets the writing requirement, would be enough for a formally valid arbitration agreement. Here, the Model Law takes a liberal approach to this issue as well: according to art. 7(2), it is enough for the parties to make a general reference to the document only, rather than to the arbitration clause specifically (cf. the report of the Working Group A/CN.9/246, para. 19).

3. Conflict of laws issues arising under the provision. Art. 7 deals only with the formal requirements of an arbitration agreement. Issues pertaining to substantive validity of an arbitration agreement, such as capacity of the parties or consent, were consciously left outside the harmonisation scope of the Model Law (Commentary, art. 7 para. 5). These are issues that will be determined by reference to the general requirements that national legislation provides for any other ordinary substantive contract. Therefore, it is important to identify the law applicable to the substantive validity of an arbitration agreement. Here, art. 34(2)(a)(i) provides useful guidelines that could be taken into account by national courts when examining the substantive validity of an arbitration agreement at a pre-award stage: issues relating to substantive validity (other than capacity for which no reference to law is provided) will be determined by the law agreed by the parties or, failing that, by the law of the courts examining the issue (i.e. lex fori).

Option I

[Definition and form of arbitration agreement]

Article 7

(As adopted by the Commission at its thirty-ninth session, in 2006)

(1) 'Arbitration agreement' is an agreement by the parties to submit to arbitration all or certain disputes which have arisen or which may arise between them in respect of a defined legal relationship, whether contractual or not. An arbitration agreement may be in the form of an arbitration clause in a contract or in the form of a separate agreement.

(2) The arbitration agreement shall be in writing.

(3) An arbitration agreement is in writing if its content is recorded in any form, whether or not the arbitration agreement or contract has been concluded orally, by conduct, or by other means.

---

of art. 7, reasoning that the phrase 'statements of claim and defence' in art. 7(2) was not defined in the Model Law, and thus it found no reason why it should be interpreted as referring 'only to pleadings in the formal sense once an arbitration has commenced'; CLOUT Case No. 87, High Court of Hong Kong, 17 November 1994.

(4) The requirement that an arbitration agreement be in writing is met by an electronic communication if the information contained therein is accessible so as to be useable for subsequent reference; 'electronic communication' means any communication that the parties make by means of data messages; 'data message' means information generated, sent, received or stored by electronic, magnetic, optical or similar means, including, but not limited to, electronic data interchange (EDI), electronic mail, telegram, telex or telecopy.

(5) Furthermore, an arbitration agreement is in writing if it is contained in an exchange of statements of claim and defence in which the existence of an agreement is alleged by one party and not denied by the other.

(6) The reference in a contract to any document containing an arbitration clause constitutes an arbitration agreement in writing, provided that the reference is such as to make that clause part of the contract.

Option II

[Definition of arbitration agreement]

Article 7

(As adopted by the Commission at its thirty-ninth session, in 2006)

'Arbitration agreement' is an agreement by the parties to submit to arbitration all or certain disputes which have arisen or which may arise between them in respect of a defined legal relationship, whether contractual or not.

1. The 2006 amendments. The amendment of the 'arbitration agreement' provisions in the Model Law was one of the two major revisions accomplished in 2006 (the other being the amendment of art. 17, interim measures). The 1985 version of art. 7 relied heavily on art. II(2) of the 1958 New York Convention, and favoured a conservative approach requiring an agreement in writing. Roerich's delegation, 'based on the need for written agreement', preferred such an approach 'to the way in which the Model Law should deal with the question of proof of the existence of an arbitration agreement' (311th Meeting, 6 June 1985). The concern, as Moeller (Observer for Finland) explained at the same meeting, was that 'if the notion of an agreement in writing was broadened, situations might arise in which an award could not be enforced under the New York Convention'. International contract practices, according to the UNCITRAL Secretariat (Explanatory Note at para. 19), led to the need to amend art. 7. However, because the issue remained controversial, the amendment actually contains two options.

2. The first option. The first option expresses a definition of 'arbitration agreement' and then supplies a comprehensive statement of how the various forms of this arbitration agreement would satisfy an 'in writing' requirement. The first option does not actually mention the 1958 New York Convention, but it is clear that art. II(2) of the Convention is the standard that art. 7 seeks to satisfy. The existence of electronic communication is expressly recognised and taken into account. In specifying the acceptable forms of an 'arbitration agreement', the first option tracks national court decisions interpreting the 'in writing' requirement of the New York Convention.

3. The second option. The second option offers a much simpler approach: it provides the definition of 'arbitration agreement' but nothing else; there is no mention of various forms of such an agreement and there is no reference to the 'in writing' requirement. Again, though it is unstated, the intention is to satisfy the section on enforceable arbitration agreements in the 1958 New York Convention.

4. Evaluation of the two options. Although UNCITRAL has not indicated a preferred option, this is an instance where, perhaps in the interest of enhancing uniformity and predictability and in strengthening the enforcement arm of the 1958 New York Convention, the Commission might have recommended that model law jurisdictions adopt the first option. At the same time that it promulgated the 2006 amendments to the Model Law, UNCITRAL issued a 'Recommendation regarding the interpretation of article II, paragraph 2, and article VII, paragraph 1, of the Convention on the Recognition and Enforcement of Foreign Arbitral Awards, done in New York, 10 June 1958, adopted by the United Nations Commission on International Trade Law on 7 July 2006 at its thirty-ninth session.'[7] Uniformity in the interpretation of a convention is, as discussed above, a matter of necessity and substantially different to interpretation in a model law context. But where there is a clear and compelling intersection between a Model Law provision and a provision in the 1958 New York Convention, uniformity should be overlapping and clear. UNCITRAL's Recommendation in relation to two New York Convention articles recognises this point. Specifically, in relation to art. II(2) of the New York Convention, UNCITRAL recommends that it 'be applied recognizing

---

7. This 'Recommendation' was embraced by the United Nations General Assembly in the same Resolution (Official Records of the General Assembly, Sixty-first Session, Supplement No. 17 (A/61/17), at the 4 December 2006, 64th plenary meeting), in which it accepted the revised articles of the Model Law. The relevant paragraphs of the Resolution referring to the New York Convention are as follows: 'Believing that, in connection with the modernization of articles of the Model law, the promotion of a uniform interpretation and application of the Convention on the Recognitions and Enforcement of Foreign Arbitral Awards, …, is particularly timely, … Also expressed its appreciation to the [UNCITRAL] for formulating and adopting the recommendation regarding the interpretation of article II, paragraph 2, and article VIII, paragraph 1, of the Convention …, the text of which is contained in annex II to the report of [UNCITRAL] on the work of its thirty-ninth session.'

that the circumstances described therein are not exhaustive'. In relation to art. VII(1) of the New York Convention,[8] UNCITRAL recommends that it 'should be applied to allow any interested party to avail itself of rights it may have, under the law or treaties of the country where an arbitration agreement is sought to be relied upon, to seek recognition of the validity of such an arbitration agreement.' The first option for the amended art. 7 attempts to give meaning to the 'non-exhaustive' interpretation of art. II(2)'s 'in writing' requirement, and has the virtue of providing substantive guidance to national legislatures in conjunction with an effort to maintain the viability of the New York Convention. UNCITRAL's recommendation regarding art. VII(1) of the New York Convention seeks to clarify that an arbitration agreement should enjoy the benefits of the 'most favoured law' approach contained in art. VII(1) (see Explanatory note at para. 20). Although the first option of art. 7 would not appear to advance this particular New York Convention interpretation any further than option 2, it would still seem to be potentially more effective to rely on a more comprehensive characterisation of 'arbitration agreement' in order to lay the ground work for persuading States to give the widest possible scope to find that such an agreement is valid and should be enforced.

[Arbitration agreement and substantive claim before court]
Article 8

(1) A court before which an action is brought in a matter which is the subject of an arbitration agreement shall, if a party so requests not later than when submitting his first statement on the substance of the dispute, refer the parties to arbitration unless it finds that the agreement is null and void, inoperative or incapable of being performed.

(2) Where an action referred to in paragraph (1) of this article has been brought, arbitral proceedings may nevertheless be commenced or continued, and an award may be made, while the issue is pending before the court.

1. Allocation of jurisdiction between national courts and tribunals as regards the existence and validity of an arbitration agreement: which forum should decide first. Art. 8, alongside the following art. 9, seeks to

---

8. Art. VII(1) of the 1958 New York Convention provides as follows: 'The provisions of the present Convention shall not affect the validity of multilateral or bilateral agreements concerning the recognition and enforcement of arbitral awards entered into by the Contracting States nor deprive any interested party of any right he may have to avail himself of an arbitral award in the manner and to the extent allowed by the law or the treaties of the country where such award is sought to be relied upon.'

delimit national court intervention in the arbitral process so that the courts will be a servant of the arbitration process. However, art. 8 arguably leaves too much room for national legislatures to confuse the issue of who decides first in terms of the validity of a purported arbitration clause, thereby permitting the courts to ride in the saddle while tribunals trudge behind on foot. It need not be this way, but as Professor Sanders observed, the question raised by art. 8(1) is whether, 'in case a party invokes that no valid or operative agreement to arbitrate exists, the court should immediately decide this issue' ('UNCITRAL's Model Law', at p. 447). That is, assume an action is brought in a national court and the defendant pleads an arbitration clause, but the plaintiff bringing the court case argues that the arbitration clause is invalid or somehow inoperative. In these circumstances, who should first decide the whether arbitration clause is valid: the court or the arbitral tribunal that would be constituted pursuant to the alleged arbitration clause? The Model Law unfortunately provides no direct guidance on this difficult issue, which arises not infrequently in national court practice.[9] Professor Sanders answered this question with a rhetorical question: 'Would it not be more in line with the priority generally given to arbitration, to refer this issue first of all to the arbitrators?' ('UNCITRAL's Model Law', at p. 447). Unfortunately, the Model Law declined to indicate this priority, which, in this context, may well have been extremely useful in leading to compromise uniformity on a procedural step that many national courts have struggled with. Thus, art. 8 might have provided, in effect, that if the respondent challenges the alleged arbitration agreement and the court makes a prima facie determination that there is any potential basis for validity, an arbitral tribunal shall be constituted pursuant to the alleged agreement to make the first decision on this issue.[10] As Professor Sanders notes, giving priority to the decision of the arbitral tribunal is consistent with art. 16 (see Explanatory Note, para. 25; this is the Model Law's 'Kompetenz-Kompetenz' provision).[11] Despite the non-instructive wording of art. 8(1), there have been national courts that

---

9. The intricacies of this procedural issue may be divined from a reading of the judgments in, e.g., *Premium Nafta Products* v *Fili Shipping Co.* [2007] All ER 951; and *Will-Drill Resources, Inc.* v *Samson Resources Co.*, 352 F 3d 211 (5th Cir 2003).

10. 'UNCITRAL's Model Law', at 448: Professor Sanders's suggestion for revision is that 'when the defendant not later than when submitting his first statement on the substance of the dispute, requests a reference to arbitration, the court shall do so "on a prima facie evidence that parties agreed to arbitrate the dispute".'

11. Id. at 449. Professor Sanders explains that in 'this way, the normal course under the ML [Model Law] for a decision on the jurisdiction issue will be restored. First of all, the arbitral tribunal rules on its jurisdiction … with the possibility of a quick decision on the jurisdiction issue [under art. 16]. In any case the court has the last word on the jurisdiction issue. Article 8 (1) deviates from the normal course by stating that, when the jurisdiction issue arises, the court decides this issue.'

have given priority to the arbitral tribunal to decide the issue of existence or substantive validity of an arbitration agreement, holding that evidence that an arbitration agreement existed prima facie only would be enough for the courts to refer the issue to arbitration for final determination (CLOUT Case No. 31, British Columbia Court of Appeal, Canada, 10 March 2002; CLOUT Case No. 367, Ontario Superior Court of Justice, Canada, 29 July 1999; CLOUT Case No. 179, British Columbia Court of Appeal, Canada, 4 July 1995; *Nanhai West Shipping Co.* v *Hong Kong United Dockyards*). On the other hand, there have been court decisions requiring a more detailed review of the substantive validity of the arbitration agreement in question (CLOUT Case No. 178, British Columbia Supreme Court, Canada, 31 January 1996; Bayerisches Oberstes Landesgericht, Germany, 4 Z SchH 03/99, 9 September 1999, available at <www.dis-arb.de>). In any case when it comes to the examination of formal validity, it seems that national courts will perform a full review of the arbitration agreement in question (CLOUT Case No. 43, High Court of Hong Kong, 8 September 1992; CLOUT Case No. 44, High Court of Hong Kong, 17 February 1993; CLOUT Case No. 78, High Court of Hong Kong, 18 August 1994; CLOUT Case No. 87, High Court of Hong Kong, 17 November 1994).

2. Global scope of art. 8. It should be also noted that the scope of art. 8 is not limited to arbitration agreements providing for arbitration in the State the courts of which are examining the arbitration agreement (See art. 1(2). Cf. Commentary, art. 8 para. 2; Holtzmann/Neuhaus, Article 8, p. 304). National courts will have to refer the parties to arbitration even if the arbitration is to take place in a different State. Thus art. 8 has a 'global application', which promotes uniformity and strengthens the legal framework for the enforceability of arbitration agreements.

3. Conditions of application of art. 8. First, the arbitration agreement must be invoked by one of the parties within the time limits. Art. 8 is consistent with the provision found in New York Convention art. II(3), in that both provisions require that for a court to refer the parties to arbitration, one of the parties has to invoke and rely on a valid arbitration agreement. Ex officio reference of national courts to arbitration is not provided for (CLOUT Case No. 508, *United Laboratories, Inc*. v *Abraham*, Ontario Superior Court of Justice, Canada, 8 October 2002). Their basic difference is that art. 8, as opposed to New York Convention art. II(3), sets out a clear deadline for the party relying on the arbitration agreement to request a reference to arbitration 'not later than when submitting his first statement on the substance of the dispute'. Failure of that party to invoke the arbitration agreement in time would prevent that party from relying on it at the subsequent stages of the court proceedings, but not necessarily from other (for example, arbitration) proceedings (Commentary, art. 8 para. 4). In other words, failure to invoke the arbitration agreement in the context of art. 8 does not automatically mean that the arbitration agreement is revoked. Secondly, the arbitration agreement must not be null, void, inoperative or incapable of being performed. There are many decisions of national courts in relation to the meaning of the phrase 'null, void, inoperative or incapable of being performed'. For instance, it was held that an arbitration agreement providing that one of the parties to the arbitration agreement would also act as an arbitrator in case a dispute would arise was held to be inoperative (CLOUT Case No. 66, Superior Court of Quebec, Canada, 14 March 1989). On the other hand, the use of permissive language by the parties will not always render an arbitration agreement inoperative. For example, it has been held that an arbitration agreement providing that the 'matter may be submitted for arbitration' is valid and establishes a duty for the parties to arbitrate (CLOUT Case No. 23, High Court of Hong Kong, 2 March 1991). In another case, a court held that for an arbitration agreement to be held inoperative on the basis that the parties revoked it and agreed to proceed to courts, there must be clear evidence of that decision of the parties. Where parties have agreed on an arbitration clause, the court 'should not be astute in trying to reduce the ambit of the arbitration clause' (CLOUT Case No. 370, High Court of Zimbabwe, 24 and 31 May 2000). National courts will often attempt to save the validity and enforceability of an arbitration agreement that contains a wrong reference to an arbitration institution, or reference to a non-existing institution. For example, Canadian Courts enforced an arbitration agreement that referred to 'the College of Arbitrators (Arbitration Court) at the Polish Chamber of Foreign Trade in Warsaw' which, due to legislative changes made by the Polish government in 1989, had ceased to exist (*Dalimpex* v *Janicki*; see also the decision of the Ontario Court of Appeal, 30 May 2003, available at <www.kluwerarbitration.com>, that upheld the decision of the first instance). A similar approach was taken by the Courts of Hong Kong with regard to an arbitration agreement that provided for arbitration in a '3rd country, under the rule of the 3rd country and in accordance with the rules of procedure of the International Commercial Arbitration Association' (CLOUT Case No. 57, High Court of Hong Kong, 5 May 1993). Moreover, national courts have on many occasions held that the fact that an arbitration agreement does not bind all of the several parties which are involved in the pending dispute, is no reason to render the arbitration agreement inoperative or incapable of being performed (CLOUT Case No. 354, British Columbia Court of Appeal, Canada, 11 December 1998; CLOUT Case No. 381, Federal Court of Canada, 24 May 2000; *City of Prince George* v *A.L. Sims & Sons*). However, in disputes involving more than two parties, only parties to the arbitration agreement may rely upon art. 8. Thus, third or non-signatory parties, allegedly bound by an arbitration agreement, cannot request the national courts to refer the issue to arbitration. As it was held, under art. 8, a party to an arbitration agreement did not include a person claiming through or under a party bound by the arbitration agreement (CLOUT Case No. 119, Ontario Court of Justice, Canada, 23 December 1994). Finally, it has been held that when a party has become insolvent due to the acts or omissions of the other party and is thus financially incapable of commencing arbitral proceedings, the arbitration agreement is incapable of being performed (CLOUT Case No. 404, Federal Supreme Court, Germany, 14 September 2000).

4. Arbitration proceedings may continue pending court proceedings. This provision is also an addition to the text of New York Convention art. II(3), giving power to the tribunal to continue with the arbitration proceedings. Although it may increase the risk of conflicting determinations between tribunals and courts, the provision is justified on the basis that it reduces the effect of dilatory tactics of recalcitrant parties, and thus it diminishes their incentive to bring an action before national courts on an issue covered by an arbitration agreement (cf. Commentary, art. 8 para. 5).

[Arbitration agreement and interim measures by court]

Article 9

It is not incompatible with an arbitration agreement for a party to request, before or during arbitral proceedings, from a court an interim measure of protection and for a court to grant such measure.

1. General. Art. 9 contains the crucial statement that an application for interim measures to a national court before or during arbitration, and a court's granting of such an application, does not affect the arbitration clause. (See also art. 17 for the 2006 amendment regarding interim measures, which is largely designed to obviate the need for a party to seek interim measures from a court once the arbitral tribunal has been constituted.)

2. Jurisdiction of national courts to grant interim measures. As already mentioned above (see arts. 5 and 6), courts have jurisdiction to assist arbitration proceedings, and should exercise it. One of the clear cases where they can and should assist tribunals is by granting interim relief for one of the parties to arbitration proceedings. Under art. 9, national courts will have the power to grant interim relief in relation to an arbitration even if the seat of the arbitration proceedings is not yet determined, or is outside their State territory (cf. art. 1(2)).[12]

---

12. See CLOUT Case No. 354, British Columbia Court of Appeal, Canada, 11 December 1998, where the court found that it had jurisdiction to order interim measures in relation to foreign arbitrations; cf., however, CLOUT Case No. 42, High Court of Hong Kong, 2 March 1992 where the court held that, pursuant to s. 14(6) of the Arbitration Ordinance, Hong Kong courts had no jurisdiction to grant interim relief, in cases where there was a valid arbitration agreement providing for arbitration elsewhere than in Hong Kong.

3. Relationship between art. 9 and art. 17. Although both arts. 9 and 17 refer to interim measures in relation to arbitration, they take a different perspective. Art. 9 refers to the jurisdiction of national courts to grant interim measures, whereas art. 17 provides for the power of arbitral tribunals to grant such measures. Therefore, under the Model Law, both a national court and an arbitral tribunal will have jurisdiction to grant interim relief with regard to the same arbitration. Thus, a question arises as to whether the two fora, namely a national court and an arbitral tribunal, will have concurrent jurisdiction to grant the same interim measures, or whether either forum should be given priority over the other. A national court may be able to issue interim measures before a tribunal is constituted. It has been argued, however, that once the tribunal has been constituted, national courts would only have subsidiary jurisdiction to grant interim measures; their power to assist an arbitration would arise only in cases where the tribunal is not able to do so itself.[13] However, the wording of art. 9 ('before or during arbitral proceedings') seems to indicate that no priority should be given to arbitral tribunals. National courts and tribunal will have concurrent jurisdiction to grant interim relief, under the Model Law. This view is also supported by case law.[14]

CHAPTER III. COMPOSITION OF ARBITRAL TRIBUNAL

[Number of arbitrators]

Article 10

(1) The parties are free to determine the number of arbitrators.
(2) Failing such determination, the number of arbitrators shall be three.

1. Power of the parties to determine the number of arbitrators. The provision, in line with the principle of party autonomy which is widely accepted in procedural issues, provides parties with the freedom to determine the number of arbitrators. Parties will usually make such determination in their arbitration agreement; this determination is independent of the arbitration agreement and its validity will be examined separately. Thus, the invalidity of the parties' agreement with regard to the number of the arbitrators will not entail the invalidity of the arbitration agreement itself. This was

---

13. Cf., for example, CLOUT Case No. 386, Ontario Court of Justice, Canada, 8 June 1995], held that the tribunals should be the right forum to grant interim measures by virtue of art. 17 and that these would then be enforceable by national courts under art. 9.
14. See for example, CLOUT Case No. 353, Supreme Court of British Columbia, Canada. See also CLOUT Case No. 71, British Columbia Supreme Court, Canada, 25 February 1994.

held by the Supreme Court of India, where the parties agreement to provide for two arbitrators and an umpire was held to be invalid, being in conflict with the new 1996 Arbitration and Conciliation Act (adapted from art. 10) which provide that parties are free to determine the number of arbitrators, provided that such number shall not be an even number (CLOUT Case No. 177, Supreme Court of India, 18 November 1996).

2. Fall-back determination of the number of arbitrators. This is a fall-back provision determining that, failing such determination by the parties, the number of arbitrators will be three. This provision is aligned with the equivalent provision in the UNCITRAL Arbitration Rules, art. 5. This is a typical type of fall-back provision extensively found in the model law scheme, which adopts a 'two-level system': at first it gives parties the freedom and the initiative to determine their procedural relationships as they see fit; failing such determination by the parties, model law provides for fall-back solutions (cf. Commentary, art. 10 para. 1).

[Appointment of arbitrators]

Article 11

(1) No person shall be precluded by reason of his nationality from acting as an arbitrator, unless otherwise agreed by the parties.

(2) The parties are free to agree on a procedure of appointing the arbitrator or arbitrators, subject to the provisions of paragraphs (4) and (5) of this article.

(3) Failing such agreement,
- **(a) in an arbitration with three arbitrators, each party shall appoint one arbitrator, and the two arbitrators thus appointed shall appoint the third arbitrator; if a party fails to appoint the arbitrator within thirty days of receipt of a request to do so from the other party, or if the two arbitrators fail to agree on the third arbitrator within thirty days of their appointment, the appointment shall be made, upon request of a party, by the court or other authority specified in article 6;**
- **(b) in an arbitration with a sole arbitrator, if the parties are unable to agree on the arbitrator, he shall be appointed, upon request of a party, by the court or other authority specified in article 6.**

(4) Where, under an appointment procedure agreed upon by the parties,
- **(a) a party fails to act as required under such procedure, or**
- **(b) the parties, or two arbitrators, are unable to reach an agreement expected of them under such procedure, or**
- **(c) a third party, including an institution, fails to perform any function entrusted to it under such procedure,**

any party may request the court or other authority specified in article 6 to take the necessary measure, unless the agreement on the appointment procedure provides other means for securing the appointment.

(5) A decision on a matter entrusted by paragraph (3) or (4) of this article to the court or other authority specified in article 6 shall be subject to no appeal. The court or other authority, in appointing an arbitrator, shall have due regard to any qualifications required of the arbitrator by the agreement of the parties and to such considerations as are likely to secure the appointment of an independent and impartial arbitrator and, in the case of a sole or third arbitrator, shall take into account as well the advisability of appointing an arbitrator of a nationality other than those of the parties.

1. Nationality of an arbitrator. Art. (11)1 ensures that nationality is not a valid reason to preclude a person from acting as an arbitrator, unless both parties have expressly agreed otherwise. According to the Commentary, this provision was inserted in order to override national laws precluding foreigners from acting as arbitrators, even in international cases (Commentary, art. 11 para. 1).

2. Parties' agreement on the procedure for the appointment of the tribunal. Parties are free to determine the procedure for the appointment of the arbitral panel. However, in their agreement, the parties cannot waive their right to resort to national courts to appoint the arbitrators when the conditions provided for in art. 11(3) are met (Commentary, art. 11 para. 3). Also, the parties are not free to agree on an appointment procedure which would not meet the required standards of independence and impartiality. Any compromise in terms of due process agreement of the parties would be invalid (Holtzmann/Neuhaus, Article 11, pp. 359-360).

3. Fall-back procedure for the appointment of the tribunal. Art. 11(3) provides for a fall-back procedure for the appointment of arbitrators, when the parties or the arbitrators fail or unduly delay to appoint or agree on an arbitrator in accordance with their original agreement. In one case, national courts found that a party that was refusing to take part in arbitration and in the appointment of the panel was eventually bound by the arbitration agreement, and thus the court appointed an arbitrator on behalf of the party. The decision was appealed by that party, and the Court of Appeal of Hong Kong held that the decision of the first instance on this issue was subject to appeal, despite art. 11(5) (which prohibits the appeal of a decision of a court on matters entrusted to it by art. 11(3)-(4)) (CLOUT Case No. 109, Court of Appeal, Hong Kong, 7 July 1995). The Court of Appeal reasoned that the decision of the first instance was not made under art. 11(3), which applies to cases where the failure to agree on the appointment of an arbitrator was due to the parties' failure to agree on the arbitrators' appointment procedure rather than due to the parties disagreement as to whether there should be an arbitration at all, or on whether the arbitration should involve a particular party, as in the present case.

4. Assistance by national courts or other appointing authorities. The aim of art. 11(4) is to provide for solutions to any stalemate that might occur in the appointment procedures. Here, the role of national courts is crucial, and their assistance may be needed even if the parties have designated an appointing authority (cf. art. 11(4)(c)) (Cf. Commentary art. 11 para. 4). It has been rightly held that the party failing to appoint its own arbitrator would be liable to pay the cost for the court proceedings appointing its arbitrator (CLOUT Case No. 59, High Court of Hong Kong, 28 September 1993).

5. Decision regarding the appointment of arbitrators. Art. 11(5) sets out the rule of finality of the court's decision on the appointment of arbitrators. This rule is justified by the need to have the tribunal constituted as soon as possible (Commentary, art. 11 para. 7). The provision also calls for national courts to take into account any of the arbitrators' qualifications required by the agreement of the parties, which would of course include the requirement of independence and impartiality.

[Grounds for challenge]

Article 12

(1) When a person is approached in connection with his possible appointment as an arbitrator, he shall disclose any circumstances likely to give rise to justifiable doubts as to his impartiality or independence. An arbitrator, from the time of his appointment and throughout the arbitral proceedings, shall without delay disclose any such circumstances to the parties unless they have already been informed of them by him.

(2) An arbitrator may be challenged only if circumstances exist that give rise to justifiable doubts as to his impartiality or independence, or if he does not possess qualifications agreed to by the parties. A party may challenge an arbitrator appointed by him, or in whose appointment he has participated, only for reasons of which he becomes aware after the appointment has been made.

1. Duty of disclosure. Art. 12(1) establishes the duty of the arbitrator to disclose any circumstances that may give rise to justifiable doubts as to his impartiality or independence. The duty of disclosure is placed upon both an arbitrator who is appointed by a party and an arbitrator who is appointed by the other arbitrators, an appointing authority or a court (Commentary, art. 12 para. 2). Also, an arbitrator continues to be bound by the duty of disclosure during the whole course of arbitration proceedings in relation to any circumstances that may arise after his appointment (cf. art. 12(1) 'throughout the arbitral proceedings'). However, the Supreme Court of Germany held that failure of an arbitrator to comply with the duty of disclosure did not constitute a valid reason for the annulment of an award (Bundesgerichtshof, Germany, III ZR 72/98, 4 March 1999, available at <www.dis-arb.de>).

2. Grounds for challenge. Art. 12(2) sets out the grounds upon which an arbitrator can be challenged. There are two different grounds provided for in art. 12(2): first, circumstances that give rise to justifiable doubts as to his impartiality or independence; secondly, lack of qualifications agreed by the parties. The question here is whether the above two grounds are exhaustive or not. In particular, an issue may arise as to whether failure of an arbitrator to comply with his duty to disclose circumstances that otherwise could have been waivable under art. 12(2) constitutes an autonomous ground for challenge, additional to those provided under art. 12(2). The Commentary states that the word 'only' found in art. 12(2) means that there could be no other grounds for challenge (Commentary, art. 12 para. 4). However, the title of art. 12 ('Grounds for challenge') seems to apply equally to both paragraphs, and will of course include the failure of an arbitrator to comply with the duty of disclosure set out in art. 12(1). Another pertinent issue relates to the standards required for the successful challenge of an arbitrator for lack of independence or impartiality. Here the first sentence of art. 12(2) is instructive 'An arbitrator may be challenged only if circumstances exist that give rise to justifiable doubts as to his impartiality or independence, or if he does not possess qualifications agreed to by the parties.' The Model Law thus posits a 'justifiable doubts' standard for challenging arbitrators, meaning that an objective basis for any alleged lack of impartiality or independence must be demonstrated. This view is supported by national case law (see for example, Oberlandesgericht Naumburg, Germany, 10 SchH 03/01, 19 December 2001, available at <www.dis-arb.de>). This standard has been widely influential in imposing an appropriately stern test for a party's challenge application, thereby diminishing the opportunities for a recalcitrant party to disrupt the arbitral process.

3. Challenge of an arbitrator by the party that appointed him. Art. 12(2) prevents a party from challenging the arbitrator that the party itself appointed, unless it is for a ground that arose after the appointment or for a ground that existed before the appointment, which the party only became aware of after the appointment.

[Challenge procedure]

Article 13

(1) The parties are free to agree on a procedure for challenging an arbitrator, subject to the provisions of paragraph (3) of this article.

(2) Failing such agreement, a party who intends to challenge an arbitrator shall, within fifteen days after becoming aware of the constitution of the arbitral tribunal or after becoming aware of any circumstance referred to in article 12(2), send a written statement of the reasons for the challenge to the arbitral tribunal. Unless the challenged arbitrator

withdraws from his office or the other party agrees to the challenge, the arbitral tribunal shall decide on the challenge.

(3) If a challenge under any procedure agreed upon by the parties or under the procedure of paragraph (2) of this article is not successful, the challenging party may request, within thirty days after having received notice of the decision rejecting the challenge, the court or other authority specified in article 6 to decide on the challenge, which decision shall be subject to no appeal; while such a request is pending, the arbitral tribunal, including the challenged arbitrator, may continue the arbitral proceedings and make an award.

1. Parties' agreement on the procedure for the challenge of an arbitrator. The parties are given the freedom to set out their own procedure for challenging an arbitrator. This agreement will, of course, include any institutional rules that the parties have referred to in their arbitration agreement. However, the parties are not free to exclude the power of the national courts to review the decision that rejects the challenge 'subject to the provisions of paragraph (3) of this article' (cf. Commentary art. 13 para. 2).

2. Fall-back procedure for the challenge of an arbitrator. Art. 13(2) sets out a fall-back procedure for the challenge of an arbitrator. The tribunal itself is designated as the appropriate forum to decide upon the challenge of a member of its panel. The challenged arbitrator will also take part in the deliberations and decision (Commission Report, art. 13 para. 128). The Commentary states that to have the tribunal itself deciding upon the challenge is justified on the basis of saving time and expenses (art. 13(4)); in addition, national courts, which would act as the last resort, will ensure (or at least will be expected to ensure) that all standards of due process are met.

3. Challenge of an arbitrator before national courts. National courts are designated as the last forum that will review the decision of any previous decision on the challenge of an arbitrator. However, the jurisdiction of the national courts will not be triggered unless the parties have first exhausted any previous forum available to the parties for a challenge (tribunal, institution or appointing authority). When all previous means have been exhausted, a party need not wait until the arbitral award has been handed down in order to resort to national courts in accordance with art. 13(3). Short time limits for challenge and exclusion of appeal on the decision of the courts are provided to ensure that time is saved and dilatory tactics are prevented.

[Failure or impossibility to act]

Article 14

(1) If an arbitrator becomes *de jure* or *de facto* unable to perform his functions or for other reasons fails to act without undue delay, his mandate terminates if he withdraws from his office or if the parties agree

on the termination. Otherwise, if a controversy remains concerning any of these grounds, any party may request the court or other authority specified in article 6 to decide on the termination of the mandate, which decision shall be subject to no appeal.

(2) If, under this article or article 13(2), an arbitrator withdraws from his office or a party agrees to the termination of the mandate of an arbitrator, this does not imply acceptance of the validity of any ground referred to in this article or article 12(2).

1. Termination of an arbitrator's mandate. Art. 14(1) provides for two grounds for the termination of an arbitrator's mandate: when an arbitrator becomes unable to perform his duties or fails to act without undue delay. These grounds should be distinguished from the grounds for challenge provided in art. 12. Art. 14(1) provides that the arbitrator in question will not be challenged by one of the parties before the tribunal or the institution; rather, both the parties will agree to terminate his mandate or one party will directly request a national court or the appointing authority to terminate his mandate. As the Commentary states, the standards for the determination of the termination of an arbitrator's mandate are subjective: the issue will be determined by reference to what was expected by the arbitrator in the light of the arbitration agreement and the specific procedural circumstances (art. 14(4)). Failure of an arbitrator to act without undue delay may, in addition, provide parties with a cause to sue him for any damages linked with the acts or omissions of this arbitrator.

2. Withdrawal of an arbitration does not mean acceptance of his liability. According to art. 14(2), the fact that an arbitrator withdraws does not mean that he accepts that the grounds for his challenge were valid. It follows that his withdrawal cannot be used as evidence for his liability if one of the parties sues him for damages for any act or omission as an arbitrator. In this sense, the provision was introduced to facilitate the withdrawal of an arbitrator.

[Appointment of substitute arbitrator]

Article 15

Where the mandate of an arbitrator terminates under article 13 or 14 or because of his withdrawal from office for any other reason or because of the revocation of his mandate by agreement of the parties or in any other case of termination of his mandate, a substitute arbitrator shall be appointed according to the rules that were applicable to the appointment of the arbitrator being replaced.

1. General. The procedure for the replacement of an arbitrator should follow the same procedure used for the appointment of the replaced arbitrator.

Thus, for example, the same party, institution or appointing authority that appointed the replaced arbitrator must appoint his replacement, too. If the replaced arbitrator has been appointed by a national court (in accordance with art. 11(3), for example, because a party failed to appoint him), it will be for the party, which failed to appoint the replaced arbitrator, to appoint the new arbitrator rather than the national court. The latter will come into play only if the party fails again to make the appointment (Holtzmann/Neuhaus, Article 15, p. 465).

CHAPTER IV. JURISDICTION OF ARBITRAL TRIBUNAL

[Competence of arbitral tribunal to rule on its jurisdiction]

Article 16

(1) The arbitral tribunal may rule on its own jurisdiction, including any objections with respect to the existence or validity of the arbitration agreement. For that purpose, an arbitration clause which forms part of a contract shall be treated as an agreement independent of the other terms of the contract. A decision by the arbitral tribunal that the contract is null and void shall not entail *ipso jure* the invalidity of the arbitration clause.

(2) A plea that the arbitral tribunal does not have jurisdiction shall be raised not later than the submission of the statement of defence. A party is not precluded from raising such a plea by the fact that he has appointed, or participated in the appointment of, an arbitrator. A plea that the arbitral tribunal is exceeding the scope of its authority shall be raised as soon as the matter alleged to be beyond the scope of its authority is raised during the arbitral proceedings. The arbitral tribunal may, in either case, admit a later plea if it considers the delay justified.

(3) The arbitral tribunal may rule on a plea referred to in paragraph (2) of this article either as a preliminary question or in an award on the merits. If the arbitral tribunal rules as a preliminary question that it has jurisdiction, any party may request, within thirty days after having received notice of that ruling, the court specified in article 6 to decide the matter, which decision shall be subject to no appeal; while such a request is pending, the arbitral tribunal may continue the arbitral proceedings and make an award.

1. The doctrines of Kompetenz-Kompetenz and separability. Arguably, art. 16 has had a highly significant influence on the acceptance by large numbers of national legislatures of two crucial arbitration doctrines: (i) Kompetenz-Kompetenz, and (ii) separability. Even in non-model law jurisdictions, it is apparent that the Model Law's endorsement of these doctrines has been instrumental in achieving their recognition. Under art. 16(1), the arbitral tribunal may rule on its own jurisdiction, and for this purpose an arbitration clause 'shall be treated as an agreement independent of the other terms of the contract'. For example, an arbitral tribunal may determine whether an arbitration clause covers the particular dispute referred to arbitration, or may determine that, even though the underlying contract is void, the arbitration clause is valid (see CLOUT Case No. 349, British Columbia Supreme Court, 13 September 1991). Jurisdiction is ultimately under the control of the court, but art. 16(1) keeps the arbitral tribunal as the adjudicator of first resort on the matter of jurisdict

2. Deadline for objection against the tribunal's jurisdiction. Art. 16(2) sets the time limits for an objection against the jurisdiction of a tribunal. Thus, the respondent will have to object no later than the submission of the statement of defence. The provision does not expressly refer to the case of the counter-claim, however, it is accepted that art. 16(2) applies by analogy to this case too, so that the claimant must bring a jurisdictional objection no later than the time that he submits his reply to the counter-claim (Commentary, art. 16 para. 5). In any case, the objecting party needs to make clear in his statement of defence that he objects to the jurisdiction of the tribunal, rather than to just state the facts upon which an objection can be based. Thus, in one case, the respondent had mentioned in its statement of defence that it was not the legal successor to the party of the contract which had given rise to the claim and could not be a defendant in the action in question. However, the plaintiff failed to make an express objection to the jurisdiction of the arbitral tribunal either in its statement of defence or in the subsequent correspondence with the arbitral tribunal, and had not raised any plea regarding the jurisdiction of the arbitral tribunal during the hearing of the case. The court that reviewed the jurisdictional ruling of the tribunal rejected the argument of the defendant that by submitting before the arbitral tribunal that it was not the legal successor to the party of the contract, the defendant had actually objected against the jurisdiction of the arbitral tribunal. The court found that those references related exclusively to the legal succession in respect of a disputed legal relationships and to the validity of claims brought by the plaintiff, rather than the jurisdiction of the tribunal (CLOUT Case No. 148, Russian Federation, Moscow City Court, 10 February 1995). Another important issue that arises here is what would be the effect of the failure of a party to object (or object in time) to the jurisdiction of the tribunal. The Working Group (A/CN.9/246 para. 51), with which the Commentary agrees (art. 16(8)-(9); the same was held in CLOUT Case No. 148, Moscow City Court, Russian Federation, 10 February 1995. Contra Hanseatisches Oberlandesgericht Hamburg, Germany, 6 Sch 04/01, 8 November 2001, available at <www.dis-arb.de>), states that the party that failed to object under art. 16(2) should be precluded from bringing an objection, not only at a later stage of the arbitral proceedings, but also at any other context of court proceedings (e.g. under art. 34 or art. 36), subject only to objections that relate to public policy, which would include any arbitrability objection.

3. Form of the tribunal's decision on jurisdiction and appeal against this decision. Art. 16(3) provides that an arbitral tribunal may rule on an objection to jurisdiction 'either as a preliminary question or in an award on the merits'. If the arbitral tribunal rules as a preliminary question that it has jurisdiction, the objecting party may ask the court at the seat to finally decide the matter. There are a couple of points of continuing interest here. First, and perhaps unavoidably, the Model Law makes it clear that an arbitral tribunal facing a jurisdictional objection may delay ruling on the objection by joining the issue of jurisdiction to the merits. In so doing, this provision does not encourage bold decision-making on the part of arbitral tribunals, for whom the safest course is usually to delay any potential court review. Professor Sanders also observes that art. 16(3) does not deal with the possibility of a negative ruling of the arbitral tribunal on the matter of jurisdiction (i.e. a ruling that the tribunal does not have jurisdiction over the claim in arbitration). He has proposed that the Model Law should 'extend the possibility for a quick decision of the court on the ruling of the arbitral tribunal that it has jurisdiction, to the ruling of the arbitral tribunal that is has no jurisdiction. Why should this negative ruling not be submitted to the court? ... The court will always have the final word on the jurisdiction of the arbitral tribunal' ('UNCITRAL's Model Law', at pp. 452-453). Indeed, England, a non-model law jurisdiction, has included negative rulings in its provision on court review of jurisdictional rulings by arbitral tribunals (see s. 32, Arbitration Act 1996). However, as a practical matter, the omission of negative rulings cannot be considered a serious flaw in art. 16. Indeed, it was held that since art. 16(3) failed to expressly refer to a review of a negative jurisdictional ruling of a tribunal, courts may only review this negative ruling at the stage of the challenge of the award.[15] The form of the jurisdictional ruling of the tribunal will be crucial as to whether art. 16(3) will be applicable. Thus, it was held that if the jurisdictional ruling takes the form of an award, then this award would have to be reviewed by national courts at separate annulment proceedings under art. 34, rather than under art. 16(3) (*Christian Mutual Insurance, Central United Life Insurance, Connecticut Reassurance* v *Ace Bermuda Insurance*). However, if a tribunal decides not to rule on a plea that it lacks jurisdiction, this omission cannot be subject to review under art. 16(3); the respondent will have to wait to challenge the final award (CLOUT Case No. 441, Oberlandesgericht Köln, Germany, 20

---

15. Bundesgerichtshof, Germany, III ZB 44/01, 6 June 2002, available at <www.dis-arb.de>. See also the decision of the National Court of Moscow which first confirmed the right of an arbitral tribunal under art. 16(1) to rule on its own jurisdiction; and secondly, reviewed and upheld the ruling of the tribunal that it had not had jurisdiction (the tribunal held that that at the time of the conclusion of the arbitration agreement the person signed the contract on behalf of the defendant had not have the necessary powers to do so), CLOUT Case No. 147, Russian Federation, Moscow City Court, 13 December 1994.

July 2000). Finally, it should be noted that State courts will have the power to review the jurisdictional ruling of a tribunal only if the arbitration takes place within the State of the court (CLOUT Case No. 392, Supreme Court of Quebec, 15 February 2000). Art. 16(3), thus, has a limited territorial scope of application (cf. also art. 1(2) that does not include art. 16).

CHAPTER IV.A. INTERIM MEASURES AND PRELIMINARY ORDERS

[Power of arbitral tribunal to order interim measures]

Article 17

Unless otherwise agreed by the parties, the arbitral tribunal may, at the request of a party, order any party to take such interim measure of protection as the arbitral tribunal may consider necessary in respect of the subject-matter of the dispute. The arbitral tribunal may require any party to provide appropriate security in connection with such measure.

1. General. Art. 17 gives tribunals default (unless otherwise agreed by the parties) power to order interim measures of protection as the tribunal may consider necessary. This power would include, for example, any measure for the preservation of goods that are the subject matter of the dispute, but also any measure for the stabilisation of the relationship between the disputed parties (such as the order for continuation of works in a construction project) or an order to secure evidence that is crucial for the determination of the dispute (Commentary, art. 18 para. 2). Here, the general restrictions arising out of the contractual nature of arbitration will also limit the power of a tribunal with regard to interim measures of protection. In particular, a tribunal has no power to enforce its orders. Interim measures will need to be enforced by a State court (see CLOUT Case No. 385, Ontario Court of Justice, Canada, 8 June 1995; cf. Commentary, art. 18 para. 4). This will usually, but not exclusively, be the national court of the seat of the arbitration. Equally, a tribunal has no power to issue an order that would go beyond the subject matter of the dispute, submitted to the tribunal, or affecting a third party. In this respect the wording of the provision itself: 'measure...in respect of the subject matter of the dispute' and 'order any party' (rather than 'anyone', which would include third parties), does not actually restrict the authority of the tribunal any further.

2. Conditions of application. For a tribunal to grant interim measures of protection, the following conditions must be satisfied. First, the tribunal has jurisdiction over both the dispute and the parties before it. Thus, it should be accepted that when one of the parties has objected to the jurisdiction of the tribunal and the tribunal has not yet decided on the issue, the tribunal would have no power to order interim measures of protection. Secondly, the interim measure has been requested by one of the parties. The tribunal has no power to grant interim relief ex officio. Thirdly, the tribunal is satisfied that there is a risk that the party applying for interim relief may suffer an irreparable or substantial harm if the measure is not granted. This requirement is not expressly provided by the provision itself, which merely refers to any measure that the tribunal may consider 'necessary'. Nevertheless, this is a condition that is usually required in practice, and which is consonant to the rationale of the interim relief, as an urgent measure to prevent a situation that would undermine the effectiveness of the final award. Fourthly, the requested interim measure does not pre-empt the dispute. This caveat results from the interim nature of the measure, which is a means to preserve and stabilise the dispute rather than finally resolve it. Finally, the tribunal may even order measures of protection that are not available to the State courts of the seat of the arbitration (this follows from the wording of the provision 'any measure'). However, the granted measure cannot conflict with the mandatory rules or the public policy of the seat of the arbitration (this would be the case, for example, with a measure ordering the physical arrest of one of the parties).

(As adopted by the Commission at its thirty-ninth session, in 2006)

Section 1. Interim measures

[Power of arbitral tribunal to order interim measures]

Article 17

(1) Unless otherwise agreed by the parties, the arbitral tribunal may, at the request of a party, grant interim measures.

(2) An interim measure is any temporary measure, whether in the form of an award or in another form, by which, at any time prior to the issuance of the award by which the dispute is finally decided, the arbitral tribunal orders a party to:
- **(a) Maintain or restore the status quo pending determination of the dispute;**
- **(b) Take action that would prevent, or refrain from taking action that is likely to cause, current or imminent harm or prejudice to the arbitral process itself;**
- **(c) Provide a means of preserving assets out of which a subsequent award may be satisfied; or**
- **(d) Preserve evidence that may be relevant and material to the resolution of the dispute.**

[Conditions for granting interim measure]

Article 17 A

(1) The party requesting an interim measure under article 17(2)(a), (b) and (c) shall satisfy the arbitral tribunal that:

(a) Harm not adequately reparable by an award of damages is likely to result if the measure is not ordered, and such harm substantially outweighs the harm that is likely to result to the party against whom the measure is directed if the measure is granted; and
(b) There is a reasonable possibility that the requesting party will succeed on the merits of the claim. The determination on this possibility shall not affect the discretion of the arbitral tribunal in making any subsequent determination.

(2) With regard to a request for an interim measure under article 17(2)(d), the requirements in paragraphs (1)(a) and (b) of this article shall apply only to the extent the arbitral tribunal considers appropriate.

Section 2. Preliminary orders

[Applications for preliminary orders and conditions for granting preliminary orders]

Article 17 B

(1) Unless otherwise agreed by the parties, a party may, without notice to any other party, make a request for an interim measure together with an application for a preliminary order directing a party not to frustrate the purpose of the interim measure requested.

(2) The arbitral tribunal may grant a preliminary order provided it considers that prior disclosure of the request for the interim measure to the party against whom it is directed risks frustrating the purpose of the measure.

(3) The conditions defined under article 17 A apply to any preliminary order, provided that the harm to be assessed under article 17 A(1)(a), is the harm likely to result from the order being granted or not.

[Specific regime for preliminary orders]

Article 17 C

(1) Immediately after the arbitral tribunal has made a determination in respect of an application for a preliminary order, the arbitral tribunal shall give notice to all parties of the request for the interim measure, the application for the preliminary order, the preliminary order, if any, and all other communications, including by indicating the content of any oral communication, between any party and the arbitral tribunal in relation thereto.

(2) At the same time, the arbitral tribunal shall give an opportunity to any party against whom a preliminary order is directed to present its case at the earliest practicable time.

(3) The arbitral tribunal shall decide promptly on any objection to the preliminary order.

(4) A preliminary order shall expire after twenty days from the date on which it was issued by the arbitral tribunal. However, the arbitral tribunal may issue an interim measure adopting or modifying the preliminary order, after the party against whom the preliminary order is directed has been given notice and an opportunity to present its case.

(5) A preliminary order shall be binding on the parties but shall not be subject to enforcement by a court. Such a preliminary order does not constitute an award.

Section 3. Provisions applicable to interim measures and preliminary orders

[Modification, suspension, termination]

Article 17 D

The arbitral tribunal may modify, suspend or terminate an interim measure or a preliminary order it has granted, upon application of any party or, in exceptional circumstances and upon prior notice to the parties, on the arbitral tribunal's own initiative.

[Provision of security]

Article 17 E

(1) The arbitral tribunal may require the party requesting an interim measure to provide appropriate security in connection with the measure.

(2) The arbitral tribunal shall require the party applying for a preliminary order to provide security in connection with the order unless the arbitral tribunal considers it inappropriate or unnecessary to do so.

[Disclosure]

Article 17 F

(1) The arbitral tribunal may require any party promptly to disclose any material change in the circumstances on the basis of which the measure was requested or granted.

(2) The party applying for a preliminary order shall disclose to the arbitral tribunal all circumstances that are likely to be relevant to the arbitral tribunal's determination whether to grant or maintain the order, and such obligation shall continue until the party against whom the order has been requested has had an opportunity to present its case. Thereafter, paragraph (1) of this article shall apply.

[Costs and damages]

Article 17 G

The party requesting an interim measure or applying for a preliminary order shall be liable for any costs and damages caused by the measure or the order to any party if the arbitral tribunal later determines that, in the circumstances, the measure or the order should not have been granted. The arbitral tribunal may award such costs and damages at any point during the proceedings.

Section 4. Recognition and enforcement of interim measures

[Recognition and enforcement]

Article 17 H

(1) An interim measure issued by an arbitral tribunal shall be recognised as binding and, unless otherwise provided by the arbitral tribunal, enforced upon application to the competent court, irrespective of the country in which it was issued, subject to the provisions of article 17 I.

(2) The party who is seeking or has obtained recognition or enforcement of an interim measure shall promptly inform the court of any termination, suspension or modification of that interim measure.

(3) The court of the State where recognition or enforcement is sought may, if it considers it proper, order the requesting party to provide appropriate security if the arbitral tribunal has not already made a determination with respect to security or where such a decision is necessary to protect the rights of third parties.

[Grounds for refusing recognition or enforcement][16]

Article 17 I

(1) Recognition or enforcement of an interim measure may be refused only:
    (a) At the request of the party against whom it is invoked if the court is satisfied that:
        (i) Such refusal is warranted on the grounds set forth in article 36(1)(a)(i), (ii), (iii) or (iv); or

---

16. Footnote to art. 17 I appearing in the official 2006 version of the Model Law as issued by UNCITRAL: 'The conditions set forth in article 17 I are intended to limit the number of circumstances in which the court may refuse to enforce an interim measure. It would not be contrary to the level of harmonization sought to be achieved by these model provisions if a State were to adopt fewer circumstances in which enforcement may be refused.'

(ii) The arbitral tribunal's decision with respect to the provision of security in connection with the interim measure issued by the arbitral tribunal has not been complied with; or

(iii) The interim measure has been terminated or suspended by the arbitral tribunal or, where so empowered, by the court of the State in which the arbitration takes place or under the law of which that interim measure was granted; or

(b) If the court finds that:
  (i) The interim measure is incompatible with the powers conferred upon the court unless the court decides to reformulate the interim measure to the extent necessary to adapt it to its own powers and procedures for the purposes of enforcing that interim measure and without modifying its substance; or
  (ii) Any of the grounds set forth in article 36(1)(b)(i) or (ii), apply to the recognition and enforcement of the interim measure.

(2) Any determination made by the court on any ground in paragraph (1) of this article shall be effective only for the purposes of the application to recognise and enforce the interim measure. The court where recognition or enforcement is sought shall not, in making that determination, undertake a review of the substance of the interim measure.

Section 5. Court-ordered interim measures

[Court-ordered interim measures]

Article 17 J

A court shall have the same power of issuing an interim measure in relation to arbitration proceedings, irrespective of whether their place is in the territory of this State, as it has in relation to proceedings in courts. The court shall exercise such power in accordance with its own procedures in consideration of the specific features of international arbitration.

1. Purpose of the 2006 amendments. Chapter IV A contains the most extensive – and most controversial – amendments to the Model Law, regarding interim measures issued by an arbitral tribunal (an entirely new art. 17). We therefore need to consider the amendment regarding the arbitral tribunal's power to order interim measures, a topic that had long caused concern in international arbitral circles. It was felt by many that the 1985 Model Law art. 17 was inadequate on several grounds, and an interim measures provision without 'teeth' would render international commercial arbitral tribunals unfit to deal with the complex nature of modern disputes. In particular, the concerns were, inter alia, that the term 'interim measures' was undefined; there was no established test for assessing an interim measures application; there was no basis for arbitral tribunals to entertain ex parte applications, which on occasion are central to an applicant's obtaining emergency relief and thereby preserving the validity of its position in the arbitration; and enforcement of interim measures orders and awards was problematic. Accordingly, the revisers of the Model Law focused on these points in fashioning a new interim measures regime. Whether this new regime was truly needed, and in any event whether it will be successful (in the sense that model law jurisdictions will adopt it and it will influence the approaches taken in non-model law jurisdictions), may still be debated, but the mere fact that agreement could be achieved by the Working Group on the text of a lengthy and elaborate new rule at least indicates that there was a high degree of motivation to give teeth to interim measures granted by arbitral tribunals and a high degree of consensus on how such a new regime should function.

2. The new provisions in particular. The new art. 17 states that the arbitral tribunal may grant interim measures ('in the form of an award or another form'), and defines the term principally by identifying its purpose to preserve the status quo in some manner, by, e.g., preserving assets or evidence or requiring a party to act or refrain from acting to ensure that the arbitral process itself will not be harmed. Art. 17 A then provides the test for obtaining interim relief: irreparable harm (though the word 'irreparable' is not used in the article) outweighing the harm to the party against whom the measure is directed; and 'reasonable possibility' of success on the merits. US lawyers will recognise this as largely representing the test in US courts for obtaining a preliminary injunction.

3. Ex parte interim measures. Art. 17 B and art. 17 C set out what is undoubtedly the most controversial aspect of the new regime: the possibility of making an ex parte interim measures application. This application may be granted in the form of a 'preliminary order' if it determines that prior disclosure of the request would risk frustrating the purpose of the measure, and if the art. 17 A test is met.

4. Preliminary orders. Art. 17 C provides a 'specific regime for preliminary orders', which entails disclosure of all communications relating to the preliminary order, including the preliminary order itself (if granted), to the counterparty, and inter partes consideration of any objection to the preliminary order, which expires in twenty days (though the tribunal may extend this after the counterparty has been heard). Again, this procedure will be familiar to US lawyers, as it is a variant of the 'temporary restraining order' (TRO) followed by the 'preliminary injunction' process that is used in many US courts. Preliminary orders cannot be enforced by courts and are not awards. The applicants for preliminary orders and interim measures may be required to provide security in connection with the relief sought (such security is more likely to be required in the case of a preliminary order), and the applicant remains liable in any event for costs and damages caused by the interim measure.

5. Enforcement of interim measures. As for enforcement, an interim measure is to be enforced by the courts of the State where enforcement is sought, unless the counterparty can make what is essentially an art. V New York Convention showing. Art. 17 I also contains a 'saving' provision. Art. 17 J provides that court-ordered interim measures may be obtained either at the seat or outside the seat of the arbitration.

6. Concluding remarks on the amendments. The amended art. 17 is intended to effect a compromise between, on the one hand, practitioners who thought that ex parte applications were not problematic in international arbitration and were needed to retain the usefulness of arbitration for business people, and, on the other hand, practitioners who deemed it to be a violation of the consensual foundation of arbitration and the right of a party to be heard. The narrowly confined 'preliminary order' process was determined to walk this fine line – though it is hard to see how practitioners in the latter camp will reconcile themselves to a fine line that would appear to stamp out the consensual principle – even if it is for a short period of time (twenty days). The remainder of the amended rule is needed to put the preliminary order process in place, or is designed to strengthen the enforcement aspect of the interim measures process. However, absent an amendment to the 1958 New York Convention, aspects of the amended art. 17 would still seem to raise some knotty enforcement issues. For example, art. 17(2) refers to a temporary measure in the form of an award or another form – but 'another form' will not be cognisable under the New York Convention. Enforcement in the New York Convention sense still depends on an 'award', and the failure of a tribunal to grant relief in the form of an award will be viewed by an enforcing court as strange, unless it enacts art. 17 H and art. 17 I, and there may well be a paucity of such enactments. In sum, the remarkable achievement of promulgating an amended art. 17 does not mean that uniformity on this issue will actually be achieved where it really matters – in national arbitration acts – and that does not mean that practitioners will be able to avoid the need to obtain interim measures from a State court that can immediately preserve the status quo without reference to another State court.

CHAPTER V. CONDUCT OF ARBITRAL PROCEEDINGS

[Equal treatment of parties]

Article 18

The parties shall be treated with equality and each party shall be given a full opportunity of presenting his case.

UNCITRAL Model Law, art. 18

1. General. This provision is a reflection of international procedural public policy (i.e. due process), and alongside with the following art. 19 it has been labelled by the Commentary as the 'Magna Carta of arbitral procedure' and as the 'most important provision[s] of the Model Law' (Commentary, art. 19 para. 1). Art. 18, which is of course a mandatory provision, sets out the limitations of procedural party autonomy: parties and arbitrators are given a wide discretion as to what procedural rules will apply to arbitration (cf. art. 19) as long as due process is not violated. Otherwise the award will be set aside (under art. 34) and refused enforcement (under art. 36). Particular expressions of the principle of due process established here can also be found in other provisions of the Model Law, such as arts. 24(3)-(4) and 26(2) (see Commentary, art. 19 para. 8).

2. The meaning of due process. The principles of 'equality of the parties' and of the 'right of each party to be given a full opportunity of presenting his case' are by nature abstract guidelines of due process. Therefore, whether due process has been violated would depend on the specific factual circumstances of a case. It could be argued, though, that the principle of 'equality of the parties' would not necessarily be determined on a simple quantitative basis: for example, the fact that a party was not given exactly the same amount of time as the other party, but was nevertheless given enough time to present its case, it would not mean that the principle of equality has been violated. Similarly, 'full opportunity of a party to present his case' cannot be abused to result to dilatory tactics (cf. Commentary, art. 19 para. 8). It has been held that the fact that a tribunal dismissed a claim, despite the fact that this claim had been partially acknowledged by the respondent, did not amount to a violation of the principle due process (CLOUT Case No. 146, Russian Federation, Moscow City Court, 10 November 1994). The court noted that a tribunal is not bound by the acknowledgment of the claim by a respondent. In another case, one of the parties challenged the award on the basis, inter alia, that the tribunal violated due process as it failed to compel a witness to testify (CLOUT Case No. 391, Superior Court of Justice, Canada, 22 September 1999). The court rejected the challenge holding that the arbitral tribunal had no power under art. 27 to compel witnesses to testify. The court noted that the applicant should have had resorted to national courts to compel testimony; failure of the applicant to seek judicial assistance cannot be imputed to the tribunal, as the purpose of art. 18 is to protect a party from egregious and injudicious conduct by an arbitral tribunal, rather than to protect a party from its own failures or strategic choices.

[Determination of rules of procedure]

Article 19

(1) **Subject to the provisions of this Law, the parties are free to agree on the procedure to be followed by the arbitral tribunal in conducting the proceedings.**

(2) **Failing such agreement, the arbitral tribunal may, subject to the provisions of this Law, conduct the arbitration in such manner as it considers appropriate. The power conferred upon the arbitral tribunal includes the power to determine the admissibility, relevance, materiality and weight of any evidence.**

1. Party autonomy and rules of procedure. At the 305th Meeting (3 June 1985), Mustill stated that 'the theoretical foundation of the Model law should not be emphasised at the expense of its practical function, which was to promote the efficient conduct of international commercial arbitration. The Commission should bear in mind the need for parties to a commercial dispute to be free to solve it in the manner which suited them best.' Indeed, art. 19 is a triumph of procedural party autonomy. It provides both the parties with considerable freedom to set out the procedural rules of their arbitration (art. 19(1)) and the tribunal with wide discretion as to how to conduct the proceedings (art. 19(2)). Thus, art. 19 provides the legal framework for the fundamental purpose of arbitration to materialise, namely to allow the parties to tailor the proceedings in accordance with their commercial needs. Parties are thus free to lay down one-off procedural rules, or agree on pre-existing arbitration rules (institutional or non-institutional, such as the UNCITRAL Arbitration Rules). Parties may even agree that the provisions of another national law will apply to their arbitration in a model law country. However, in this case, the agreed applicable national law will have contractual power only (cf. Commentary, art. 19 para. 2) (as part of the arbitration agreement of the parties) and it will thus yield to any contrary mandatory provision of the Model Law.

2. Limitations of procedural party autonomy. As mentioned above under art. 18, procedural party autonomy is only limited by due process. A question that is pertinent here is whether the parties may go as far as to contractually exclude review of the arbitral award by national courts under art. 34. Canadian courts answered this question in the affirmative, holding that art. 34 is not a mandatory provision (*Noble China* v *Lei Kat Cheong*). While party autonomy is limited only by due process, arbitrators are additionally limited by the agreement of the parties, including any arbitration rules agreed therein. Thus, arbitrators cannot adopt any procedure (even one that is generally applied in arbitration practice) that deviates from the wishes of the parties, or the award will be set aside by virtue of art. 34(2)(a)(iv).

Brekoulakis and Shore

[Place of arbitration]

Article 20

(1) The parties are free to agree on the place of arbitration. Failing such agreement, the place of arbitration shall be determined by the arbitral tribunal having regard to the circumstances of the case, including the convenience of the parties.

(2) Notwithstanding the provisions of paragraph (1) of this article, the arbitral tribunal may, unless otherwise agreed by the parties, meet at any place it considers appropriate for consultation among its members, for hearing witnesses, experts or the parties, or for inspection of goods, other property or documents.

1. 'Legal place'. In line with the typical 'two-level' system adopted by the Model Law, art. 20 (and a number of the following provisions dealing with procedural issues, such as language, statements of claim and defence, hearings) first gives priority to the parties to determine the place of the arbitration, and then, if the parties fail to make such determination, the baton is passed to the tribunal. Art. 20 should be read in light of art. 1(2) and the 'territorial principle' established therein. As was commended under art. 1(2), the Model Law rejected the idea or theory of delocalisation, espoused by many scholars and some tribunals in international arbitration. Under the legislative framework of the Model Law, arbitration needs to take place somewhere, in the sense that it needs to be attached to a national legal system. Consequently, the place of the arbitration referred to in art. 20(1) should be considered as the link between an arbitration and the legal system of a particular State (the 'legal place'). Therefore, the determination of the place under art. 20(1) carries specific legal consequences (Commentary, art. 20 para. 2). For example, the nationality of the award will be determined by reference to the place of the arbitration, which will in turn be relevant to the determination of the national court that has jurisdiction to hear an action to set aside the award. In an interesting case relevant to the meaning of the legal seat, two parties agreed on a binding determination of the value of a partnership share by a sole arbitrator, although no formal agreement was ever signed (CLOUT Case No. 374, Oberlandesgericht Düsseldorf, Germany, 23 March 2000). Then, there was initially an unsuccessful attempt for settlement in Düsseldorf, after which the arbitrator started working through an audit of the partnership in Zurich, Switzerland (where the partnership was located). Finally, the arbitrator rendered an arbitral award at his home in Düsseldorf which stated his address. The respondent applied before the German courts to have the award set aside. The German courts, however, refused to determine the validity of the award, on the basis that the award was not a German one. The court noted that the place of the arbitration was neither agreed upon by the parties, nor determined by the arbitrator. Thus, the Court noted that the place of the arbitration was the place where the arbitrator actually performed its duties, i.e. Zurich. Other legal consequences linked with the choice of the place of arbitration include the characterisation of the award as 'international' for the purposes of art. 1(3)(b), or as 'foreign' for the purposes of the application of the New York Convention on Recognition and Enforcement of Foreign Arbitral Awards.

2. 'Physical place' or 'venue of hearings'. Notwithstanding the choice of the 'legal place' by the parties or the tribunal, there may be good reasons for the arbitral hearings or meetings to take place elsewhere. This, for example, may be necessary if the arbitrators want to perform on-site inspections of premises located elsewhere; or it may just be convenient to hold some hearings close to the witnesses (cf. Commentary, art. 20 paras. 3-4). Thus, art. 20(2) gives the tribunal the power to have actual hearings in a place different from the legal place. This, however, would not alter the choice of the legal place, determined by reference to art. 20(1), even in the case where no actual hearing or meeting ever occurred in the legal place.

[Commencement of arbitral proceedings]

Article 21

Unless otherwise agreed by the parties, the arbitral proceedings in respect of a particular dispute commence on the date on which a request for that dispute to be referred to arbitration is received by the respondent.

1. Relevance of the provision. Determination of the point of time at which the arbitral proceedings commence may have important legal consequences. For example, it is relevant in order to determine the cessation or interruption of limitation periods (Commentary, art. 21 para. 1. See also Holtzmann/Neuhaus, Article 21, p. 610).

2. Determination of point of commencement. The relevant point for the commencement of the proceedings is, according to the provision, the date on which the claimant's request to refer the dispute to arbitration will be received by the respondent. However, this is merely a default provision, which the parties are free to contract out of. This is usually the case when the parties refer their dispute to institutional arbitration rules, which often provide for a different time for commencement of the arbitration proceedings.[17] The exact time that the above request is received by the claimant will be determined by art. 3. However, the Model Law does not define the required content of this request to commence arbitral proceedings. It has been held that a letter which

---

17. For example, art. 4(2) ICC Rules provides that the date on which the request is received by the ICC Secretariat, rather than the tribunal, is the date of the commencement of the arbitral proceedings.

the claimant sent to the respondent to inform him that his (the claimant's) arbitrator has been appointed, and to invite him (the respondent) to appoint his arbitrator, would qualify as a 'request' under art. 21 (CLOUT Case No. 20, High Court of Hong Kong, 29 October 1991).

[Language]

Article 22

(1) The parties are free to agree on the language or languages to be used in the arbitral proceedings. Failing such agreement, the arbitral tribunal shall determine the language or languages to be used in the proceedings. This agreement or determination, unless otherwise specified therein, shall apply to any written statement by a party, any hearing and any award, decision or other communication by the arbitral tribunal.

(2) The arbitral tribunal may order that any documentary evidence shall be accompanied by a translation into the language or languages agreed upon by the parties or determined by the arbitral tribunal.

1. General. Parties often fail to make any arrangements in their arbitration agreement concerning the language of the arbitration proceedings. Nevertheless, the issue of the determination of the language can be of considerable practical importance, in particular, in the context of international arbitration, where parties usually come from different countries speaking different languages. Depending on which language will be used, the cost of the arbitration proceedings might be unnecessarily increased. In typical model law fashion, the provision first grants the power to the parties to determine the language or the languages of the proceedings (the omnipresent principle of party autonomy), and if the parties fail to agree on this, the issue is then passed to the tribunal to decide.

2. Determination of the language of proceedings. It is worth noting that the provision establishes no presumption in favour of, for example, the language of the seat of the arbitration or the language of the contract or the language of the arbitrators. Thus, arbitrators are, in principle, free to determine the language of the proceedings. However, it seems that the arbitrators should make the decision regarding the language on the basis of the factual circumstances of the case (Commentary, art. 22 para. 3). Any arbitrary decision of the arbitrators to opt for the language of one of the parties might violate the principle of equal treatment of the parties or even curtail the right of the other party to present its case, which will raise due process concerns (Commentary, art. 22 para. 3; see also the Commission Report, art. 22, para. 189). However, this does not necessarily mean that the tribunal should avoid choosing the language of any of the parties. If the circumstances of the case point to the language of one of the parties, the tribunal could and should adopt that language for the proceedings. Relevant circumstances that arbitrators should look into to determine the language would be, for example, the language of the contract or the correspondence between the parties, or the language of any previous dealings between the same parties (Commentary, art. 22 para. 4).

3. Language of the initial statements. A question might arise as to which language each party should rely on in their initial statements, when the parties have failed to agree on a language for the proceedings and at a stage before the tribunal has made any relevant determination. It could be argued here that each party would be free to choose the language for its own initial statements.

[Statements of claim and defence]
Article 23

(1) Within the period of time agreed by the parties or determined by the arbitral tribunal, the claimant shall state the facts supporting his claim, the points at issue and the relief or remedy sought, and the respondent shall state his defence in respect of these particulars, unless the parties have otherwise agreed as to the required elements of such statements. The parties may submit with their statements all documents they consider to be relevant or may add a reference to the documents or other evidence they will submit.

(2) Unless otherwise agreed by the parties, either party may amend or supplement his claim or defence during the course of the arbitral proceedings, unless the arbitral tribunal considers it inappropriate to allow such amendment having regard to the delay in making it.

1. Required content of statements of claim and defence. Art. 23 sets out the essential content requirements of a statement of claim and defence, namely the facts supporting the claim, the issues at stake and the relief or remedy sought (cf. also CLOUT Case No. 118, Ontario Court of Justice, Canada 21 December 1994). It should be noted, however, that this provision is not considered mandatory; indeed, some model law countries have deviated from it somewhat. In Germany, for example, the equivalent provision (German ZOP s. 1046(1)) required the parties only to refer to the claim and the facts supporting the claim. Thus, the issues at stake or the relief or remedy sought are not considered essential content of the statement of claim and defence (a similar position is taken in Greece, see 2735/1999 Act, art. 23).

2. Evidence supporting claim and defence. The parties do not have to submit the evidence supporting the claim at the same time as the initial statement. Depending on their procedural strategy, parties may choose to submit documents or other evidence at a later stage. However, the parties do not have absolute freedom to determine the time for submitting the relevant documents or evidence. The tribunal will usually have the power by reference to art. 19(2) to set out a time frame for the parties to submit their evidence (cf. also art. 25(c); see Commentary, art. 23 para. 3).

3. Amendment or supplement of the claim and defence. Art 23(2) allows a party to 'amend or supplement his claim or defence'. The language 'claim or defence' suggests that a party can amend the claims themselves, but not the facts underlying them. Any amendment must be based on the facts already submitted in the statement of claim and defence. Furthermore, the right of a party to amend or supplement his claim or defence is naturally constrained by the contractual character of arbitration: any amendment or supplement cannot exceed the scope of the arbitration agreement (Commentary, art. 23 para. 5). In any case, amending or supplementing the claim of defence depends on the discretion of the tribunal, which will normally not allow it if the amendment would cause procedural prejudice to the other party or unduly delay and disrupt the process of the arbitration.

4. Counter-claim and set-off. Art. 23 applies by analogy to counter-claims and set-offs. This is not expressly mentioned in the provision itself but it is generally accepted (see Commentary, art. 23 paras. 7-8; see also Sachs/Lörcher, § 1046 in Böckstiegel/Kröll/Nacimiento, *Arbitration in Germany*, para. 10 et seq.). In some model law countries this is expressly mentioned in their national legislation (see, for example, in Germany, s. 1046(3) (equivalent of art. 23) 'subsections 1 and 2 apply mutatis mutandis to counter-claims').

[Hearings and written proceedings]

Article 24

(1) Subject to any contrary agreement by the parties, the arbitral tribunal shall decide whether to hold oral hearings for the presentation of evidence or for oral argument, or whether the proceedings shall be conducted on the basis of documents and other materials. However, unless the parties have agreed that no hearings shall be held, the arbitral tribunal shall hold such hearings at an appropriate stage of the proceedings, if so requested by a party.

(2) The parties shall be given sufficient advance notice of any hearing and of any meeting of the arbitral tribunal for the purposes of inspection of goods, other property or documents.

(3) All statements, documents or other information supplied to the arbitral tribunal by one party shall be communicated to the other party. Also any expert report or evidentiary document on which the arbitral tribunal may rely in making its decision shall be communicated to the parties.

1. Oral hearings. Art. 24, in line with art. 19, gives wide discretion to the arbitral tribunal with regard to whether oral hearings will be held. However, any relevant agreement by the parties would be binding on the tribunal, especially if the parties have agreed that oral hearings will be held. The Commission, however, was split as to whether an agreement by the parties that no oral hearings would be held should be equally binding on the tribunal. According to one view, parties should never be deprived of the right to have oral presentation of their case, so that a party that previously agreed that no hearings would be held should still have the right at a later stage to request that the tribunal hold oral hearings (Commission Report, art. 24 para. 205). In the end, a compromise was accepted: as the provision now stands, each party will have the right to request the tribunal to hold oral hearings, which will be binding upon the tribunal.[18] However, this right will be available to each party only if the parties have previously failed to make arrangements on oral hearings. Otherwise, an agreement of the parties that no oral hearings will be held will be binding upon them, and preclude them from requesting oral hearings at a later stage.

2. Advance notice of hearings and written communication of documents. Art. 24 (2) to (3) reflect due process considerations. The right of each party to have advance notice and to have knowledge of all the documents supplied to the tribunal, irrespective of their nature, directly relates to the principle of the right of each party to be heard. The duties set out here originate from art. 18 and are thus mandatory for the tribunal. As national courts have observed, any violation of art. 24(2) and (3) will most likely lead to the annulment of the award or the refusal of its enforcement (See CLOUT Case No. 402, Highest Regional Court of Bavaria, Germany, 16 March 2000). Whether the notice has been given sufficiently in 'advance' will be determined on the basis of the specific factual circumstances of the case and in particular on whether the party actually had enough time to prepare its case. As already mentioned, art. 24(2) and (3) are of mandatory nature. Thus, any agreement of the parties setting out notice time frames which prove to be unduly short for one of the parties will be invalid (See Commentary, art. 24, para. 7).

[Default of a party]

Article 25

Unless otherwise agreed by the parties, if, without showing sufficient cause,
> **(a) the claimant fails to communicate his statement of claim in accordance with article 23(1), the arbitral tribunal shall terminate the proceedings;**

---

18. See Oberlandesgericht Naumburg, Germany, 1 21 February 2002, available at <www.dis-arb.de>, that held that a tribunal that did not accept the request of one of the parties to hold oral hearings violated art. 34(2)(a)(iv).

(b) **the respondent fails to communicate his statement of defence in accordance with article 23(1), the arbitral tribunal shall continue the proceedings without treating such failure in itself as an admission of the claimant's allegations;**

(c) **any party fails to appear at a hearing or to produce documentary evidence, the arbitral tribunal may continue the proceedings and make the award on the evidence before it.**

1. Without 'sufficient cause'. The default sanctions provided in art. 25 will apply only if a party fails to submit its statement without a 'sufficient cause'. A question that arises here is whether the tribunal, after the claimant fails to submit its statement within the deadline, should take the initiative and inquire whether the claimant was prevented by a 'sufficient cause' to submit its statement before it terminates the proceedings. It is, of course, not within the duties of the tribunal to assume the role of the 'counsel' of the claimant and, ex officio, perform a detailed investigation of why the claimant failed to submit his statement. Nevertheless, it would be advisable for the tribunal to attempt to contact the claimant to find out whether there has been a sufficient cause that has prevented him from submitting his statement, and letting the tribunal know in advance. Otherwise, the tribunal might, as soon as the deadline passes, terminate the proceedings only to receive sufficient justification for the claimant's default afterwards, in which case the tribunal might not have the mandate to reopen the arbitral proceedings (cf. art. 32). Of course, the tribunal should only make a minimum and brief effort to inquire about the claimant's failure to submit his statement; otherwise, it would risk violating the principle of impartiality or equal treatment of the parties. In any case, failure of one of the parties to submit its statement without sufficient reason would prevent the other party from challenging the award at a later stage (CLOUT Case No. 391, Superior Court of Justice, Canada, 22 September 1999).

2. Default of the claimant. It is not uncommon for the claimant to submit a full statement of claim when requesting the commencement of the arbitration, in which case there will be no scope for art. 25(a) to apply. However, the claimant will often initially submit a brief request only, in which case he will then need to submit a full statement of claim in accordance with art. 23. Otherwise, the claimant will be in default and the proceedings will be terminated by virtue of art. 25(a). In any case, when in doubt, tribunals should seek clarification of whether the initial document submitted by the claimant is a request for arbitration or a statement of claim. It is not clear, and certainly it is not provided for in art. 25(a), whether the tribunal should issue an award with res judicata covering the substantive part of the dispute when a claimant is in default. It would seem, however, too harsh for a default claimant to lose his right to bring the issue again at a later stage, especially when the claimant's initial request is too brief to allow for an arbitral award on the merits.

3. Default of the respondent. In contrast with the case where the claimant defaults, if the respondent defaults, the tribunal must continue the arbitral proceedings and eventually issue an award on the basis of the evidence before it. However, the absence of the respondent's statement should not necessarily be taken by the tribunal as an admission of the claimant's allegations. Tribunals should independently examine the merits of the dispute (see Commentary, art. 25 para. 4), especially looking into issues such as the arbitrability of the dispute or any public policy implications of it, which tribunals have the right to invoke ex officio. In all cases though, tribunals should avoid assuming the role of the respondent's counsel. Again, as in the case of the default of the claimant, the question will arise as to whether the tribunal should take the initiative and inquire whether there was sufficient cause for the respondent's failure to submit a statement of defence, before the tribunal issues a final award. It seems that the best approach would be for the tribunal to ensure at least that the respondent was indeed served with a request for arbitration and to ensure that his right to present his case has not been violated.

[Expert appointed by arbitral tribunal]

Article 26

(1) **Unless otherwise agreed by the parties, the arbitral tribunal**
  (a) **may appoint one or more experts to report to it on specific issues to be determined by the arbitral tribunal;**
  (b) **may require a party to give the expert any relevant information or to produce, or to provide access to, any relevant documents, goods or other property for his inspection.**

(2) **Unless otherwise agreed by the parties, if a party so requests or if the arbitral tribunal considers it necessary, the expert shall, after delivery of his written or oral report, participate in a hearing where the parties have the opportunity to put questions to him and to present expert witnesses in order to testify on the points at issue.**

1. General. This provision is the product of a compromise between the civil law model of a neutral expert appointed by the tribunal and the common law model of party-appointed experts. Thus, the Model Law at first provides in art. 26(1) that experts may be appointed by the tribunal; however, art. 26(2) provides that the tribunal-appointed experts will be examined by the parties, which additionally can bring into the proceedings their own experts as witnesses to counter the opinion of the tribunal-appointed expert (Commission Report, para. 219).

2. The role of the parties in the appointment of experts. The tribunal should try to consult with the parties before deciding whether experts will be appointed. The parties, which eventually will incur the costs of the arbitration, have the right to refuse the appointment of experts (Commission

Report, para. 219). Similarly, the tribunal should involve the parties in the selection of persons that will act as experts. This will eventually increase the confidence of the parties in the final opinion of the experts.

3. Impartiality standards of experts. Although not expressly provided in art. 26, it must be accepted that the party-appointed experts meet the necessary standards of impartiality and independence. Nevertheless, it is not clear whether the parties will have the right to challenge an expert by analogous application of arts. 12 and 13, in case there are justifiable doubts as to the expert's independence and impartiality. The right view would be not to allow parties to challenge them, especially in view of the opportunity afforded to parties to question the experts and also bring their own expert witnesses, which would mitigate or even overturn any partial opinion expressed by the party-appointed expert. Having said that, it is worth noting that some model law countries, such as Germany, expressly provide for the possibility of a challenge of the party-appointed arbitrators by reference to the provisions for the challenge of the arbitrators (ZPO s. 1049(3)).

[Court assistance in taking evidence]

Article 27

The arbitral tribunal or a party with the approval of the arbitral tribunal may request from a competent court of this State assistance in taking evidence. The court may execute the request within its competence and according to its rules on taking evidence.

1. General. Art. 27 provides for 'court assistance in taking evidence', which may have interesting implications if a State opens itself to the possibility of assisting an arbitral tribunal seated in another State; the Model Law is not clear on this point. It is at least arguable that art. 27 could function in a manner similar (albeit with a narrower scope) to a US statute that has received substantial attention of late because of its applicability, as deemed by various federal district courts, to foreign arbitral tribunals: 28 U.S.C. Section 1782.[19] From the Commission Report though it seems that the prevailing view of the Commission was that the scope of application of the article should be limited territorially (Commission Report, para. 223). This was also the position adopted by the courts of Canada (CLOUT Case No. 391, Superior Court of Justice, Canada, 22 September 1999). In any case, the assistance does not have to be granted by the competent court designated in art. 6; another court of the same country may be closer to the location of the evidence and thus be in a better place to provide assistance (Commentary, art. 27 para. 5).

---

19. I am indebted to Professor Hilmar Raeschke-Kessler for this observation, which he made at a recent ICC Institute seminar (Paris, 24 November 2008), in relation to a paper that I presented on 28 U.S.C. Section 1782.

2. Request for court assistance by a party. It was held that the tribunal has no obligation to compel a witness to testify even if this is requested by one of the parties (CLOUT Case No. 391, Superior Court of Justice, Canada, 22 September 1999). In such a case, the party should then request a national court to compel the testimony of the witness; if the party fails to seek the assistance of the court, then it does not have a valid ground to challenge the award at a later stage on the basis that its right to present its case was violated. Failure of one of the parties to request judicial assistance cannot be imputed to the tribunal. Also, the court is not obliged to provide assistance to the requesting party. This is especially the case when the court has valid reasons to believe that the request of the party is part of a strategy to delay arbitration proceedings (CLOUT Case No. 68, Federal Court of Canada, 3 December 1993). In one case, a court rejected the request of a party to assist in the production of relevant documents, on the grounds that this request was untimely. This is because it related to earlier arbitration proceedings, which were 'months, if not years away' from the current stage of the arbitration proceedings (CLOUT Case No. 77, High Court of Hong Kong, 15 August 1994).

CHAPTER VI. MAKING OF AWARD AND TERMINATION OF PROCEEDINGS

[Rules applicable to substance of dispute]

Article 28

(1) The arbitral tribunal shall decide the dispute in accordance with such rules of law as are chosen by the parties as applicable to the substance of the dispute. Any designation of the law or legal system of a given State shall be construed, unless otherwise expressed, as directly referring to the substantive law of that State and not to its conflict of laws rules.

(2) Failing any designation by the parties, the arbitral tribunal shall apply the law determined by the conflict of laws rules which it considers applicable.

(3) The arbitral tribunal shall decide *ex aequo et bono* or as *amiable compositeur* only if the parties have expressly authorised it to do so.

(4) In all cases, the arbitral tribunal shall decide in accordance with the terms of the contract and shall take into account the usages of the trade applicable to the transaction.

1. Determination of the rules applicable to the substance of dispute by the parties. Parties not only have the freedom to determine the procedural rules that will apply to their arbitration; art. 28(1) also gives them the power to choose the substantive rules that will govern their substantive rights and duties. The principle of party autonomy is, thus, given a full meaning. This is even more so, since art. 28(1) provides parties with the right to contract out of from the constraints of national laws and opt for non-national substantive rules (cf. the wording 'such rules of law' rather than 'law') (cf. Commentary, art. 28 para. 4). These anational substantive rules will include rules coming from various sources such as the lex mercatoria, general principles of law, customary trade rules, the UNIDROIT principles of international commercial contracts, or other uniform substantive rules codified in soft law documents, such as the ICC UCP or the INCOTERMS. In addition, the parties are free to choose a law or a set of rules that is not connected with the dispute or the parties in any way (for example, the law of the nationality of either party, or the law of the place where the contract was concluded or performed) (cf. Commentary, art. 28 para. 3). The choice of the parties is binding upon the tribunal. If the tribunal does not apply the law or rules of law suggested by the parties, the award will be open to challenge. However, national courts will only review whether the tribunal applied the agreed rules or law rather than examine whether the agreed rules or law were correctly applied by the tribunal (CLOUT Case No. 375, Bayerisches Oberstes Landesgericht, Germany, 15 December 1999). The latter would require a review by national courts of the merits of the case, which, in principle, is not allowed. A pertinent issue here would be whether the parties enjoy unfettered freedom to choose the law or rules applicable to their contract or whether their choice can be limited by the application of the mandatory laws of any country, and if so, which country that would be. Here, it is generally accepted in many model law countries that the substantive mandatory rules of the seat of the arbitration will apply and may restrict the application of the law or rules agreed upon by the parties (see, for example, in Germany, Fredrich, § 1051 in Böckstiegel/Kröll/Nacimiento, *Arbitration in Germany*, para. 29 et seq.; in Greece, see Kousoulis, *Arbitration*, art. 28 para. 2, p. 246 [in Greek]). As regards the mandatory rules of a country other than the seat of the arbitration, the discussion usually focuses on whether arbitrators should take into account the mandatory rules of a country that is most closely connected with the dispute, by analogous application of art. 3(3-4) of the Regulation (EC) No. 593/2008 of the European Parliament and of the Council of 17 June 2008 on the Law Applicable to Contractual Obligations (Rome I), which, of course, does directly apply to arbitration (art. 1(2)(e) Rome I). This is an ongoing discussion in arbitration, which goes beyond art. 28(1) and beyond the purpose of this commentary (see in general Am. Rev. Int'l Arb. 18(1-2)). Furthermore, it is questionable as to whether national courts, in the context of reviewing the validity of an arbitration agreement under art. 8, may review the scope of the parties' choice of applicable law on the basis that this choice would violate the mandatory rules of the State of the reviewing court. In Germany, for example, the Higher Regional Court of Munich held that an arbitration agreement that provided for arbitration in California under US law was considered invalid in Germany, as the application of US law may result in the circumvention of the mandatory compensation claim provided in German law (art. 34 EGBGB) (OLG München 17 May 2006, IPRax 322 (2007) cited by Fredrich, § 1051 in Böckstiegel/Kröll/Nacimiento, *Arbitration in Germany*, para. 10).

2. Determination of the rules applicable to the substance of the dispute by the tribunal. If the parties fail to agree on the law or rules that will apply to determine their dispute, it is the tribunal that must identify and apply the substantive applicable law. However, in contrast to the wide freedom accorded to the parties, the tribunal is limited by specific guidelines as to how it will determine the law applicable to the merits of the dispute. According to art. 28(2) the tribunal needs to apply the conflict of laws rules which it considers applicable. This in effect means that the tribunal may not apply non-national rules of law, as the application of conflict of laws or rules will necessarily lead to the application of the national law of a specific country. This discrepancy between the freedom enjoyed by the parties to directly agree on the application of rules of laws and the obligation of the tribunal to follow the conflict of laws rules may seem questionable. Once the drafters of the Model Law accepted in art. 28(1) the principle that a dispute may be determined by non-national rules in arbitration (a progressive step away from the equivalent art. 33(1) of the older UNCITRAL Arbitration Rules which provides for application of 'law' only) there is no obvious reason why non-national rules could not also be relied upon by the arbitrators in a dispute that has a truly international character.[20] It would be for the national legislation to eliminate this discrepancy (see, for example, German ZPO, s. 1051). However, the Commentary here mentions that the parties would be free to expand the scope of the tribunal's power to determine the applicable substantive law, and provide, for example, that the tribunal may identify the applicable law directly rather than via conflict of laws rules (Commentary, art. 28 para. 6). One imagines, though, that it would be unlikely for the parties, who failed to foresee the need to provide for a substantive applicable law in accordance with art. 28(1), to insert an express provision in their agreement expanding the tribunal's power to identify the applicable law under art. 28(2).

3. Ex aequo et bono and amiable compositeur. Arbitrators may even apply non-legal rules to determine the dispute, deciding ex aequo et bono or as amiable compositeur, but only if the parties have expressly provided them with this power. There is no general acceptance as to the exact meaning of the terms ex aequo et bono and amiable compositeur, or even as to whether these terms have the same meaning at all. It is most likely because

---

20. Professor Sanders also agrees with that view, stating that the distinction between rules of law and law should 'disappear': 'in case there is no designation by the parties, the arbitral tribunal should apply the rules of law', 'UNCITRAL's Model Law', at p. 460.

of this uncertainty that the Model Law first makes reference to both of these terms, and secondly makes no attempt to define either of them. However, it can be safely argued that under either term, the tribunal is instructed to decide based on general considerations of fairness and equity, rather than on specific legal rules (national or non-national). It has been held that a reference to an 'honourable agreement' in the arbitration agreement was an express request for the arbitrators to decide the dispute ex aequo et bono (*Liberty Reinsurance Canada* v *QBE Insurance and Reinsurance*).

4. Contractual terms and trade usages. Art. 28(4) expressly calls for the arbitrators first to apply the contractual terms agreed to by the parties, and to take into account the trade usages applicable to the transaction. As regards the application of the contractual terms in the context of a national law or rules of law (art. 23(2) to (3)), this seems to be a self-evident call: as is generally accepted in law, the contractual terms of the parties will in any case prevail over any default national provision, but will yield to any mandatory national provision. Art. 28(4) does not suggest otherwise or add anything in this regard. It seems that art. 28(4) makes more sense with regard to the application of the contractual terms in the context of art. 28(3), i.e. when arbitrators are instructed to decide ex aequo et bono or as amiable compositeur. Thus, arbitrators will have to decide on the basis of equity and fairness. However, they cannot make any determination that is contrary to contractual terms of the parties. As regards the trade usages applicable to the transaction, the operative language here is 'take into account', as opposed to 'decide in accordance with' as used for the contractual terms. Thus, this provision should not be understood as giving the power to the tribunal to apply lex mercatoria (part of which are trade customs and usages), unless of course the parties have expressly provided for it under art. 28(1).

[Decision making by panel of arbitrators]

Article 29

In arbitral proceedings with more than one arbitrator, any decision of the arbitral tribunal shall be made, unless otherwise agreed by the parties, by a majority of all its members. However, questions of procedure may be decided by a presiding arbitrator, if so authorised by the parties or all members of the arbitral tribunal.

1. Principle of majority. Art. 29 establishes the principle of majority with regard to the decision among the members of the tribunal, when the panel consists of more than one arbitrator. The principle of majority was preferred over the principle of unanimity, because it makes it easier for a decision to be reached (Commentary, art. 29, paras. 1-2). The provision is however non-mandatory ('unless otherwise agreed by the parties'), and thus the parties are free to agree on the principle of unanimity.

2. Exceptions from the majority principle. In any case, it should be noted that the principle of majority does not mean that it is not necessary for all arbitrators to take part in the deliberations or at least be given the chance to take part therein (Commentary, art. 29 paras. 1-2). By contrast to a decision on the merits of the dispute, procedural decisions may only be taken by the presiding arbitrator. This is justified on the basis of expediency and efficiency.

[Settlement]

Article 30

(1) If, during arbitral proceedings, the parties settle the dispute, the arbitral tribunal shall terminate the proceedings and, if requested by the parties and not objected to by the arbitral tribunal, record the settlement in the form of an arbitral award on agreed terms.

(2) An award on agreed terms shall be made in accordance with the provisions of article 31 and shall state that it is an award. Such an award has the same status and effect as any other award on the merits of the case.

Award on agreed terms. The purpose for recording the settlement in the form of an arbitral award on agreed terms is to enhance the effectiveness of the settlement. A settlement alone would have contractual, i.e. limited, enforceability, whereas an award obtains the force of res judicata and is enforceable under the 1958 New York Convention. The insertion of the caveat 'not objected to by the arbitral tribunal' serves obvious public policy purposes to prevent colluding parties from obtaining an enforceable title (i.e. award) for illegal purposes (for example, money laundering). It would be for the arbitrators to examine such a contingent ex officio. Furthermore, arbitrators should object to an award on agreed terms if the dispute is inarbitrable.

Form and effect of an award on agreed terms. An award on agreed terms will have the same characteristics and legal consequences as any other award made after determination of the merits. It is questionable as to whether one of the parties to the proceedings may at a later stage challenge the award issued on agreed terms. The Commentary offers nothing to clarify this issue. It seems, however, that an award on agreed terms should be open to challenge by either party on grounds that pertain to public policy, which parties cannot waive.[21]

---

21. Cf. also CLOUT Case No. 407, Bundesgerichtshof, Germany, 2 November 2000, that indirectly supports this view. According to the decision, an award on agreed terms tainted by fraud is not automatically void; it needs to be set aside under art. 34.

UNCITRAL Model Law, art. 31

[**Form and contents of award**]

Article 31

(1) The award shall be made in writing and shall be signed by the arbitrator or arbitrators. In arbitral proceedings with more than one arbitrator, the signatures of the majority of all members of the arbitral tribunal shall suffice, provided that the reason for any omitted signature is stated.

(2) The award shall state the reasons upon which it is based, unless the parties have agreed that no reasons are to be given or the award is an award on agreed terms under article 30.

(3) The award shall state its date and the place of arbitration as determined in accordance with article 20(1). The award shall be deemed to have been made at that place.

(4) After the award is made, a copy signed by the arbitrators in accordance with paragraph (1) of this article shall be delivered to each party.

1. The writing requirement. The writing form and signature of an award are required for reasons of certainty. However, it is also provided that only the majority of the arbitrators need to sign the award in arbitrations with more than one arbitrator, provided that the reason for omission of the signature is stated in the award. It seems that omission of signature should be condoned only for serious reasons. For example, the Commentary refers to the example of an arbitrator that dies or becomes physically unable to sign the award (Commentary, art. 31 para. 2). Thus, according to the same source, it might not be a good enough reason for an arbitrator to refuse to sign it, simply because he disagrees with the majority of the arbitrators (Commentary, art. 31 para. 2). It is arguable whether this view taken by the Commentary is correct for the following reasons. First, the provision, at least on the face of it, does not require good or serious reasons for an arbitrator to refuse to sign the award. Secondly, and more importantly, if omission of signature would be condoned only for serious reasons, recalcitrant arbitrators would then have the power to block the issuance of an award by refusing to sign it for no serious reason. In any case, dissenting opinions are not prohibited by the Model Law, and indeed they do occur in practice. In one case, Canadian courts refused to set an award aside, despite the fact that one of the arbitrators had not signed it, and no reason for the omission of the signature was stated in the award itself. The court held that it was enough that the president of the tribunal gave the reason for the arbitrator's lack of signature in court, at the annulment proceedings (CLOUT Case No. 12, Federal Court of Canada, 7 April 1988).

2. Reasoning of an award. Reasoning is part of the required form of an award. However, the reasoning of an award should not be considered a public policy requirement. As the Commentary states, the reasoning of an award may well be waived by the parties (Commentary, art. 31 para. 3). It is important that the reasoning indicates that arbitrators have identified and examined all relevant facts and legal points raised by the parties. Also, the reasoning should not be conflicting. If the reasoning lacks substance and it is clearly inconsistent, the award can be annulled (Oberlandesgericht Frankfurt, 6 September 2001, available at <www.dis-arb.de>). However, the reasoning does not need to be expressed in strict legal terms. In an interesting case, the arbitrators, who were not lawyers, supported their views in business rather than legal terms. One of the parties challenged the award on the basis that it lacked coherent and comprehensible reasoning. The court refused to set the award aside, stating that the reasons were adequate and that the arbitrators cannot be criticised for expressing themselves as businessmen rather than lawyers. To determine whether reasoning was sufficient or not, the court in this case looked into both what was expressly stated and what was implied in the award (CLOUT Case No. 1, Superior Court of Quebec, 16 April 1987).

3. Date and place of the award. The award must state the date and the place of arbitration. Both requirements have practical relevance. The date stated in the award will be the crucial date for the commencement of the deadline for the challenge of the award, or the calculation of the award interest. The place stated in the award is equally, if not more, significant, as this will be the 'place where the award shall be deemed to have been made', which, as already explained in detail under art. 20, has important legal consequences. The arbitrators have no discretion to state any other place than the one determined in accordance with art. 20(1), i.e. the 'legal seat'. The place where the actual hearings took place or the place where the arbitrators were when signing the award is irrelevant. However, failure of the arbitrators to state the date or the place of the award will not necessarily render the award null or challengeable, at least if it is possible for the lacking date or place to be ascertained by other means (Oberlandesgericht Stuttgart, 1 Sch 22/01, 4 June 2002, available at <www.dis-arb.de>).

4. Delivery of the award to each party. A signed copy of the award by the arbitrators is required to be delivered to each party for obvious reasons of due process. Whether the award was duly delivered and submitted will be determined by reference to art. 3, rather than domestic law (CLOUT Case No. 29, Ontario Court, General division, Canada, 30 January 1992). No additional administrative requirements, such as registration or deposit of the award with a national authority, are imposed by the Model Law (Commentary, art. 31 para. 5).

[Termination of proceedings]

Article 32

(1) The arbitral proceedings are terminated by the final award or by an order of the arbitral tribunal in accordance with paragraph (2) of this article.

(2) The arbitral tribunal shall issue an order for the termination of the arbitral proceedings when:
- (a) the claimant withdraws his claim, unless the respondent objects thereto and the arbitral tribunal recognises a legitimate interest on his part in obtaining a final settlement of the dispute;
- (b) the parties agree on the termination of the proceedings;
- (c) the arbitral tribunal finds that the continuation of the proceedings has for any other reason become unnecessary or impossible.

(3) The mandate of the arbitral tribunal terminates with the termination of the arbitral proceedings, subject to the provisions of articles 33 and 34(4).

1. Termination of the proceedings. Arbitral proceedings are terminated when the final award is granted (art. 32(1)) or when the tribunal issues an order for the termination of the proceedings (for the reasons stated in art. 32(2)). A final award is one that addresses and settles all substantive issues, including costs, between the parties to the proceedings (see also *Tang Boon Jek Jeffrey* v *Tan Poh Leng Stanley*). However, until they issue a final award, arbitrators cannot become functus officio (Commentary, art. 32 para. 2).

[Correction and interpretation of award; additional award]

Article 33

(1) Within thirty days of receipt of the award, unless another period of time has been agreed upon by the parties:
- (a) a party, with notice to the other party, may request the arbitral tribunal to correct in the award any errors in computation, any clerical or typographical errors or any errors of similar nature;
- (b) if so agreed by the parties, a party, with notice to the other party, may request the arbitral tribunal to give an interpretation of a specific point or part of the award.

If the arbitral tribunal considers the request to be justified, it shall make the correction or give the interpretation within thirty days of receipt of the request. The interpretation shall form part of the award.

(2) The arbitral tribunal may correct any error of the type referred to in paragraph (1)(a) of this article on its own initiative within thirty days of the date of the award.

(3) Unless otherwise agreed by the parties, a party, with notice to the other party, may request, within thirty days of receipt of the award, the arbitral tribunal to make an additional award as to claims presented in the arbitral proceedings but omitted from the award. If the arbitral tribunal considers the request to be justified, it shall make the additional award within sixty days.

(4) The arbitral tribunal may extend, if necessary, the period of time within which it shall make a correction, interpretation or an additional award under paragraph (1) or (3) of this article.

(5) The provisions of article 31 shall apply to a correction or interpretation of the award or to an additional award.

1. General. A tribunal retains a very limited authority on the award for a period of thirty days after the award is issued. Thus, a tribunal may revisit the award for one of the following purposes provided exclusively in art. 33.

2. Correction of error in computation, or of clerical/typographical error. Correction of the error must not result in amendment of the content of the award. The tribunal would lack the jurisdiction to go beyond correction (Oberlandesgericht Stuttgart, 20 December 2001, 1 Sch 13/01, cited by Lew/Mistelis/Kroll, *Comparative and International Commercial Arbitration*, para. 24-92). In any case, error in computation cannot amount to the annulment of the award (CLOUT Case No. 267, Harare High Court, 29 March and 9 December 1998).

3. Interpretation. It is not usual for a national law to provide that arbitrators may revisit the award to provide interpretation. Indeed, the issue was debated among the Model Law drafters (Holtzmann/Neuhaus, *A Guide to the UNCITRAL Model Law*, pp. 890-891). In the end it was decided to include a provision for interpretation, although it must be underlined that this provision should be construed restrictively: interpretation must be allowed only in relation to a specific point or part of the award. Interpretation cannot amount to a rewriting of the award.

4. Additional award. A tribunal may issue an additional award to cover a claim that was omitted from the award, only if this claim has initially been presented in the proceedings. Additional awards are sometimes granted in relation to a requested interest which was inadvertently not awarded (cf. Commentary, art. 33 para. 1). It should be noted that additional awards are autonomous and therefore they can be challenged or enforced independently from the main award.

CHAPTER VII. RECOURSE AGAINST AWARD

[Application for setting aside as exclusive recourse against arbitral award]

Article 34

(1) Recourse to a court against an arbitral award may be made only by an application for setting aside in accordance with paragraphs (2) and (3) of this article.

(2) An arbitral award may be set aside by the court specified in article 6 only if:

- (a) the party making the application furnishes proof that:
    - (i) a party to the arbitration agreement referred to in article 7 was under some incapacity; or the said agreement is not valid under the law to which the parties have subjected it or, failing any indication thereon, under the law of this State; or
    - (ii) the party making the application was not given proper notice of the appointment of an arbitrator or of the arbitral proceedings or was otherwise unable to present his case; or
    - (iii) the award deals with a dispute not contemplated by or not falling within the terms of the submission to arbitration, or contains decisions on matters beyond the scope of the submission to arbitration, provided that, if the decisions on matters submitted to arbitration can be separated from those not so submitted, only that part of the award which contains decisions on matters not submitted to arbitration may be set aside; or
    - (iv) the composition of the arbitral tribunal or the arbitral procedure was not in accordance with the agreement of the parties, unless such agreement was in conflict with a provision of this Law from which the parties cannot derogate, or, failing such agreement, was not in accordance with this Law; or
- (b) the court finds that:
    - (i) the subject-matter of the dispute is not capable of settlement by arbitration under the law of this State; or
    - (ii) the award is in conflict with the public policy of this State.

(3) An application for setting aside may not be made after three months have elapsed from the date on which the party making that application had received the award or, if a request had been made under article 33, from the date on which that request had been disposed of by the arbitral tribunal.

UNCITRAL Model Law, art. 34

(4) The court, when asked to set aside an award, may, where appropriate and so requested by a party, suspend the setting aside proceedings for a period of time determined by it in order to give the arbitral tribunal an opportunity to resume the arbitral proceedings or to take such other action as in the arbitral tribunal's opinion will eliminate the grounds for setting aside.

1. General. The penultimate chapter of the Model Law concerns recourse against an award, art. 34, and is lengthy and intricate. The UNCITRAL Secretariat has observed that this is an area in which harmonising national arbitration legislation is extremely difficult. The Secretariat has asserted that this 'situation' has been 'greatly improved by the Model Law, which provides uniform grounds upon which (and clear time periods within which) recourse against an arbitral award may be made' (Explanatory Note at para. 44). Setting aside an award is the sole recourse; the grounds mirror those in art. V of the 1958 New York Convention, and there is a three-month time limit for applications. However, the Secretariat has pointed out that there is a distinction between art. 34(2) and art. 36(1) (regarding enforcement): an application for setting aside 'may only be made to a court in the State where the award was rendered whereas an application for enforcement might be made in a court in any State. For this reason the grounds relating to public policy and non-arbitrability may vary in substance with the law applied by the court (in the State of setting aside or in the State of enforcement)' (Explanatory Note at para. 48). Harmonisation can also be undermined by the fact that national laws are free to provide for additional actions or remedies against an arbitral award (see, for example, Germany, ZPO s. 1065 providing for the possibility of a party to attack an arbitral award on 'a point of law') or to provide for a decision on whether a national court on annulment will be open to appeal (this is the case in Zimbabwe for example; see, CLOUT Case 323 Zimbabwe Supreme Court, 21 October and 21 December 1999). It should be noted that for art. 34 to apply, a decision taken by a tribunal must qualify as an arbitral award in the first place. This will include not only final and global awards, but also separate awards on jurisdiction or costs, or awards on agreed terms.[22] Some courts have focused on the substance of an arbitral decision, holding that an award is a decision if it provides for a determination on the merits of the case (CLOUT Case No. 455, Hanseatisches Oberlandesgericht Hamburg, Germany, 4 September 1998). Some other courts put more emphasis on the formal characteristics of an arbitral decision, holding that an award is a decision that meets the formal requirements set out in art. 31 (CLOUT Case No. 441, Oberlandesgericht Köln, Germany, 20 July 2000). The party challenging the arbitral award must prove that one of the grounds listed in art. 34 ex-

---

22. Although the Working Group initially had decided to include a definition of an award in Model Law, in the end failed to do so, due to lack of time, see A/CN.9/246, paras. 129, 192-194.

Brekoulakis and Shore

UNCITRAL Model Law, art. 34

ists, and that therefore the award must be set aside (CLOUT Case No. 391, Superior Court of Justice, Canada, 22 September 1999). Also, it is rightly accepted that art. 34 provides for an exhaustive list of grounds and that it should be narrowly construed, in accordance with the wide trend for restricting the scope of judicial intervention into commercial arbitration (CLOUT Case No. 16, British Columbia Court of Appeal, 24 October 1990; see also CLOUT Case 391, Superior Court of Justice, Canada, 22 September 1999). There are six grounds for setting an award aside provided in art. 34, none of which allows for a review of the merits of the dispute. Thus, under no circumstances may national courts examine whether the tribunal has properly assessed the evidence or applied the law correctly, or applied the correct law. Art. 34 is a mandatory provision which the parties cannot contract out of. Thus, any provision found in arbitration rules, agreed to by the parties, purporting to exclude the right to recourse against an arbitral award, such as art. 28(6) ICC, would be inapplicable in relation to art. 34 (CLOUT Case No. 403, Oberlandesgericht, 15 December 1999).

2. Grounds for annulment of an award. In particular, the grounds upon which an award can be set aside are given below.

3. Incapacity, invalidity of the arbitration agreement. As regards incapacity, it should be noted that the Model Law does not provide for the law applicable to determine the issue, as opposed to the New York Convention (art. V(1)a) which expressly refers to 'the law applicable to the parties'. This is a conscious omission as it was decided that the reference to 'the law applicable to the parties' was in fact an 'incomplete' conflict of law provision, as it does not point to a specific connecting factor such as nationality or domicile (see Holtzmann/Neuhaus, *A Guide to the UNCITRAL Model Law*, p. 916). As regards invalidity of an arbitration agreement, the provision refers to the law agreed to by the parties, or, failing that, to the law of the seat of arbitration. In practice, arbitration agreements have been found to be invalid when they have been contrary to the mandatory provisions of a specific national law. For example, in Germany, a dispute resolution agreement which was included in general terms and conditions, and which exclusively gave one party the right to choose between different types of dispute resolution, was held to be invalid (see BGH, 24 September 1998, NJW 282 (1999) (cited in Kröll/Kraft, § 1059 at para. 54, note 94, in Böckstiegel/Kröll/Nacimiento, *Arbitration in Germany*).

4. Violation of due process. This ground includes both procedural and substantive fairness, and thus it overlaps with the public policy ground in art. 34(2)(b)(ii) (CLOUT Case No. 391, Superior Court of Justice, Canada, 22 September 1999). For example, it has been held that the fact that an applicant failed to seek judicial assistance from a national court to compel the testimony of a witness, which the tribunal refused to compel, cannot be imputed to the tribunal as a violation of due process (CLOUT Case No. 391, Superior Court of Justice, Canada, 22 September 1999). Similarly, it was held that the fact that a tribunal dismissed a claim, although this had been partially acknowledged by the respondent, did not amount to a violation of the principle of equality and due process (CLOUT Case No. 146, Russian Federation, Moscow City Court, 10 November 1994). The court noted that a tribunal is not bound by the acknowledgment of the claim by the respondent. However, it was held that a tribunal had violated procedural due process when it deliberately concealed documents from a party or it obtained evidence on its own initiative, on which it relied, but it failed to disclose the relevant evidence to the parties (CLOUT Case No. 391, Superior Court of Justice, Canada, 22 September 1999).

5. Tribunal exceeded its jurisdiction. This ground is infrequently invoked, and it is even less frequently accepted by national courts to set an award aside. Indeed, it has been characteristically noted that this ground should be construed narrowly and that a strong presumption should exist that a tribunal acts within its mandate (CLOUT Case No. 16, British Columbia Court of Appeal, Canada, 24 October 1990).

6. Irregularity in the constitution of an arbitral tribunal; deviation from the procedure agreed to by the parties. Constitution of a tribunal, and proceedings in general, must follow the procedure agreed upon by the parties, which would include the arbitration rules referred to in an arbitration agreement. In one case (CLOUT Case No. 436, Bayerisches Oberstes Landesgericht, Germany, 24 February 1999), the claimant, a farmer, nominated two potential arbitrators from his industry; both were challenged by the defendant, a trader, who successfully convinced the rest of the tribunal that the arbitration rules required that all nominees come from a pre-set list of potential arbitrators (the claimant's appointee did not). Instead, the rest of the tribunal assigned the claimant an arbitrator from the defendant's industry. The claimant challenged this forced appointment, but the appellate tribunal rejected his complaint, and then dismissed his claim. A German court set aside the appellate award, citing procedural errors including the misguided belief that the arbitration rules required that all nominees come from a certain list. Other examples of violations of agreed-upon procedure include cases where a tribunal refused to hold an oral hearing where requested by a party (CLOUT Case No. 371, OLG, Bremen, Germany, 30 September 1999 (although the objection eventually was rejected as it was not timely brought forward)) or where the tribunal decided ex aequo et bono without the express agreement of the parties (see BGH, 24 September 1998, NJW 282 (1999) cited in Kröll/Kraft, § 1059 at para. 54, note 94, in Böckstiegel/Kröll/ Nacimiento, *Arbitration in Germany*).

7. Inarbitrability. Inarbitrability is provided under art. 34 as an ex officio ground of annulment of an arbitral award. However, the Model Law does not provide for a definition of the scope of arbitrability, leaving this matter to the national legislators. Indeed, model law countries set out different standards of arbitrability;[23] accordingly, case law on this matter would depend on the national standards on arbitrability.

8. Public policy. The public policy point is one that, in a slightly different context, has caught the attention of Professor Sanders: 'In countries where the arbitration law also contains the remedy of requete civil (revocation), the time limit of three months for instituting this action [i.e. setting aside] only starts upon discovery of the fraud, bribery or corruption. In my opinion it is a gap in the [Model Law] not to contain a provision in which violation of rules of public policy has been discovered later than three months after receipt of the award' (Sanders, *UNCITRAL's Model Law*, at 465). This may be a gap, but the Model Law's drafters probably were right to highlight the possibility, and thereby encourage misguided respondents that a time frame may, depending on an individual State's law, be opened up by alleged discovery of fraud. Professor Sanders further notes that the Model Law does not deal with the situation where the award has been set aside – is the arbitration agreement still operative (id. at 467)? Here, Sanders undoubtedly makes a very useful point, given the goals of enhancing uniformity and reducing uncertainty, though his preference of reviving the jurisdiction of the court (unless otherwise agreed by the parties) is somewhat surprising and disappointing. Germany's 1998 national act provides that the arbitration agreement becomes operative again after the award has been set aside. This is clearly the option to be favoured, and the Model Law might have provided very useful guidance in this regard, but fails to do so. Annulment grounds related to public policy should be construed narrowly, and only in exceptional circumstances when the award violates basic notions of morality and justice, such as corruption, bribery or fraud (CLOUT Case No. 391, Superior Court of Justice, Canada, 22 September 1999; similar in CLOUT Case No. 267, Harare High Court of Zimbabwe, 29 March and 9 December 1998). However, what does constitute violation of the basic notion of morality and justice is entirely open to be decided by the national courts of each country, which, of course, leaves a lot of room for divergence. For example, in one case, a tribunal based its decision that suspension of an employee was unlawful due to a mistake in the calculation of a deadline. The Supreme Court of Zimbabwe held that this was such a fundamental error on which the tribunal based its decision, that it constituted a palpable inequity which was so far-reaching and outrageous in its defiance of logic or accepted moral standards that a sensible and fair minded person would consider that the conception of justice in Zimbabwe would be intolerably hurt by the award. Thus, according to the Supreme Court of Zimbabwe, the award was contrary to public policy, and it was thus set aside (CLOUT Case No. 323, Zimbabwe Supreme Court, 21 October and 21 December 1999). On the other hand, Russian Courts

---

23. See for example, Greek Code of Civil Procedure art. 867, providing that 'disputes can be submitted to arbitration if the parties have the power to freely dispose of the subject matter of the dispute'; whereas German ZPO s. 1030 provides 'Any claim involving an economic interest can be the subject of an arbitration agreement'.

have held that an award ordering the respondent to pay the claimant in foreign currency, even though the respondent did not have a foreign currency account, was not against the public policy of Russia (CLOUT Case No. 149, Russian Federation, Moscow City Court, 18 September 1995).

9. Remission. Art. 34(4) provides that a court, instead of setting an award aside, may remit it back to the tribunal to eliminate the reasons for which the award can be set aside. However, it was held that the court cannot draw authority from art. 34(4) to refer the matter back to the arbitral tribunal and request that it consider the question of the applicable rate of interest where that question had not been originally considered by the arbitrators (CLOUT Case No. 12, Federal Court of Canada, 7 April 1988). Similarly, a remission will not be ordered so that the tribunal take fresh evidence on the merits of the case (CLOUT Case No. 391, Superior Court of Justice, Canada, 22 September 1999).

CHAPTER VIII. RECOGNITION AND ENFORCEMENT OF AWARDS

[Recognition and enforcement]

Article 35

(1) **An arbitral award, irrespective of the country in which it was made, shall be recognised as binding and, upon application in writing to the competent court, shall be enforced subject to the provisions of this article and of article 36.**

(2) **The party relying on an award or applying for its enforcement shall supply the duly authenticated original award or a duly certified copy thereof, and the original arbitration agreement referred to in article 7 or a duly certified copy thereof. If the award or agreement is not made in an official language of this State, the party shall supply a duly certified translation thereof into such language.*****

New article 35(2)

The party relying on an award or applying for its enforcement shall supply the original award or a copy thereof. If the award is not made in an official language of this State, the court may request the party to supply a translation thereof into such language.

1. The principle of automatic recognition. The purpose of art. 35, in line with the spirit of the 1958 New York Convention, was to facilitate the automatic recognition of arbitral awards. Thus, an award, as long as it meets the formal requirements of art. 31, will be automatically recognised and thus be binding upon the parties to the proceedings. There is no need for an award to be previously confirmed or otherwise made binding in the seat of the arbitration (CLOUT Case No. 117, Ontario Court of Justice, 19 December 1994, where the court rejected the argument of the resisting party that for the award to be enforced in Canada, had to first been confirmed by a New York court). In any case, when the award is confirmed by a national judgment it is not merged with the judgment confirming the award (CLOUT Case No. 30, Ontario Court, Canada, 13 February 1992).

2. Effects of recognition of an arbitral award. Recognised arbitral awards have all the legal consequences of a domestic court judgment. Therefore, the boundaries of the res judicata effect will be determined in accordance with the country of recognition, rather than the country of the seat of the arbitration.

3. The new provision in art. 35(2). As the Secretariat has explained, art. 35(2) was amended in 2006 'to liberalize formal requirements and reflect the amendment made to art. 7 on the form of the arbitration agreement. Presentation of a copy of the arbitration agreement is no longer required under article 35(2)' (Explanatory Note at para. 53). This is an understated description of an amendment that arbitration practitioners will recognise as extremely useful as a matter of practice. Under the New York Convention, originals or *duly certified* copies of the award and the arbitration agreement are required. The meaning of 'duly certified' can vary across jurisdictions, and the issue can become quite important. Many parties do not safely maintain original contracts containing the original arbitration agreements (such contracts have often been executed a number of years earlier). The question of certification of the original arbitration agreement then looms large, and it is not an easy question. Art. 35(2) eliminates the arbitration agreement requirement – which is an unnecessary requirement in view of the existence of the arbitration award – and it also eliminates the 'duly certified' copy requirement in the case of an award, an original or a 'copy' will suffice. Again, this seemingly small change is potentially very helpful, although the original of an arbitration award is generally more readily available than the original of the contract (mostly because of the recent delivery of the award), a party may only receive one original and may well need to enforce an award in more than one jurisdiction. A copy, as opposed to a duly certified copy, thus makes the enforcement process less bureaucratic and potentially less expensive and burdensome. What seems like a small change is, then, quite useful as a matter of arbitral practice, and it is hoped that national legislatures will rapidly adopt this amended provision of the Model Law.

[Grounds for refusing recognition or enforcement]

Article 36

(1) Recognition or enforcement of an arbitral award, irrespective of the country in which it was made, may be refused only:

(a) at the request of the party against whom it is invoked, if that party furnishes to the competent court where recognition or enforcement is sought proof that:
  (i) a party to the arbitration agreement referred to in article 7 was under some incapacity; or the said agreement is not valid under the law to which the parties have subjected it or, failing any indication thereon, under the law of the country where the award was made; or
  (ii) the party against whom the award is invoked was not given proper notice of the appointment of an arbitrator or of the arbitral proceedings or was otherwise unable to present his case; or
  (iii) the award deals with a dispute not contemplated by or not falling within the terms of the submission to arbitration, or it contains decisions on matters beyond the scope of the submission to arbitration, provided that, if the decisions on matters submitted to arbitration can be separated from those not so submitted, that part of the award which contains decisions on matters submitted to arbitration may be recognised and enforced; or
  (iv) the composition of the arbitral tribunal or the arbitral procedure was not in accordance with the agreement of the parties or, failing such agreement, was not in accordance with the law of the country where the arbitration took place; or
  (v) the award has not yet become binding on the parties or has been set aside or suspended by a court of the country in which, or under the law of which, that award was made; or
(b) if the court finds that:
  (i) the subject-matter of the dispute is not capable of settlement by arbitration under the law of this State; or
  (ii) the recognition or enforcement of the award would be contrary to the public policy of this State.

(2) If an application for setting aside or suspension of an award has been made to a court referred to in paragraph (1)(a)(v) of this article, the court where recognition or enforcement is sought may, if it considers it proper, adjourn its decision and may also, on the application of the party claiming recognition or enforcement of the award, order the other party to provide appropriate security.

1. General. As with art. 35, art. 36 is based on the 1958 New York Convention. However, as many commentators have observed, the Model Law is broader than the New York Convention in that the Convention applies to foreign arbitral awards or awards not considered as domestic awards in the

State where recognition and enforcement are sought, whereas recognition and enforcement of the award under the Model Law applies 'irrespective of the country in which it was made' (art. 36(1)). One of the Model Law's goals, in the context of enforcement, is to limit the importance of the seat of the arbitration and to avoid the traditional distinction between 'foreign' and 'domestic' awards, relying instead on an 'international' versus 'non-international' distinction (see the UNCITRAL Secretariat's Explanatory Note at para. 50). As is generally accepted, the grounds for refusing enforcement are exhaustively listed in art. 36 and they should be construed narrowly (CLOUT Case No. 391, Superior Court of Justice, Canada, 22 September 1999). There are two different groups of grounds in art. 36. Art. 36(1)(a) contains all those grounds that must be invoked by the party resisting the award whereas art. 36(1)(b) contains those grounds that national courts may invoke ex officio. This distinction, however, does not affect the burden of proof, which stays with the party resisting the enforcement in all cases (cf. S. Kröll, § 1061 in Böckstiegel/Kröll/Nacimiento, *Arbitration in Germany*, para. 108). Thus, Canadian courts were wrong to hold that under art. 36(1)(b) there was no burden of proof on the respondent (CLOUT Case No. 30, Ontario Court, General Division, Canada, 13 February 1992). In any case, review of the merits of the award is not allowed. Any ground relating to the merits of the award must be raised during the arbitral proceedings, rather than during the enforcement stage before national courts (*Phesco* v *Canac*).

2. Grounds requiring an application by a party. In particular, the grounds requiring an application by a party are given below.

3. Incapacity of the parties or invalidity of the arbitration agreement. Here, according to the prevailing view, the party relying on the award has the burden to prove the conclusion of the arbitration agreement (cf. art. V(1)(a) New York Convention '… to the agreement referred to in Article II'). Once the conclusion of the arbitration agreement is proved, the burden is shifted to the party resisting the enforcement to prove that the concluded agreement is in fact invalid (see OLG Celle, Germany, 4 September 2003, XXX Yearbook 528 (2005)). However, it is questionable as to whether this view is the correct one, especially in view of the new art. 35(2) which does not require the party seeking enforcement to provide an arbitration agreement for the recognition and enforcement. In addition, art. 36(1)(a)(i) makes no reference to art. 7 (on validity of arbitration agreements). Thus, it should be accepted that the resisting party must bear the burden to prove both that an agreement was never concluded and that an agreement is invalid.

4. Due process. The required standards of due process should be determined by reference to art. 18, which provides that parties shall be treated equally and that each party shall be given a full opportunity of presenting its case. For example, German courts have held that the fact that the tribunal had denied a motion to take evidence did not violate the right of a party to present its case. As the court noted, it was not possible to determine whether the evidence could have caused the case to be decided differently (CLOUT Case No. 371, Hanseatisches Oberlandesgericht Bremen, Germany, 30 September 1999). A tribunal is required only to give the opportunity to each party to present its case. Whether the party actually makes use of its opportunity or not will not affect the enforceability of the award (CLOUT Case No. 88, High Court of Hong Kong, 16 December 1994).

5. Tribunal exceeded its mandate. The jurisdictional remit of a tribunal is defined by the arbitration agreement of the parties. Thus, any decision taken by the tribunal in relation to issues that are excluded by the arbitration agreement will not be enforced. For example, it was held that an award that determined the right of a party to terminate a franchise agreement was unenforceable, since the arbitration agreement contained a provision excluding arbitration from matters relating to termination (CLOUT Case No. 67, Saskatchewan Court of Appeal, Canada, 17 September 1991).

6. Irregularity in the constitution of the arbitral tribunal; deviation from the procedure agreed upon by the parties. Here, national courts must examine both the applicable arbitration rules and any agreement among the parties regarding the constitution of the tribunal and the arbitration proceedings. Examples falling under this provision include situations where a tribunal proceeded in bifurcated proceedings, contrary to the applicable arbitration rules, or where a sole arbitrator decided the case, instead of an agreed three-member tribunal (BGH, 1 February 2001, XXIX Yearbook 700 (2004)). However, the defendant needs to object to the irregular constitution of the tribunal during the arbitral proceedings, or otherwise it risks waiving its right to resist enforcement of the award (CLOUT Case No. 76, High Court of Hong Kong, 13 July 1994).

7. An award is not binding or it has been suspended or set aside. This provision has generated considerable debate in the context of 1958 New York Convention (art. V(1)(e)) as to whether national courts have a discretion to enforce an award that has been set aside in the country of origin (cf. for example the cases *Chromalloy*, holding that courts do have a discretion only to enforce annulled awards; contra *Baker Marine* v *Chevron*; and the more recent *Karaha Bodas* v *Perusahaan Pertambangan Minyak Dan Gus Bumi Negara* and *Termorio* v *Electranta*). It seems that, in the context of the Model Law, this issue is not debated. While there have been some courts holding, as a matter of principle, that courts have a discretion to enforce the award even if one of the grounds listed under art. 36 applies, the prevailing view (CLOUT Case No. 88, High Court of Hong Kong, 16 December 1994), at least with regard to art. 36 (1)(a)(v), in particular is that national courts are obliged to reject the enforcement of an annulled award in the country of origin. German courts, for example, were adamant on this issue, rejecting that application of enforcement of an award set aside in Russia (the country of origin) could be enforced in Germany (CLOUT Case No. 372, Oberlandesgericht Rostock, Germany, 1 Sch 3/99, 28 October 1999).

8. Grounds examined ex officio by the tribunal. In particular, the grounds examined ex officio by the tribunal are given below

9. Inarbitrability. The law that will apply to determine the issue of arbitrability is the law of the courts of the enforcement State. This is expressly stated in this provision, in line with art. V(2)(a) of the New York Convention. Thus, the scope of art. 36 (1)(b)(i)) will be determined by the scope of the arbitrability provisions of each model law country, which, as mentioned above, vary.

10. Public Policy. A few points need to be made with regard to the notion of public policy here. First, only if the enforcement of an award violates the most basic principles of morality and justice of the enforcement State, may a court refuse to enforce the award on public policy grounds (CLOUT Case No. 37, Ontario Court, Canada, 12 March 1993). Secondly, public policy objections may relate to both procedural and substantive issues (CLOUT Case No. 391, Superior Court of Justice, Canada, 22 September 1999). In an example of violation of procedural public policy,[24] German courts refused to enforce an award that was fictitiously served to the respondent. As it was held, fictitious service violated German public policy, notwithstanding the fact that it was considered legal in accordance with the law of the country of origin (Russia) of the award (CLOUT Case No. 402, Highest Regional Court of Bavaria, Germany, 16 March 2000). Violation of substantive public policy may occur, for example, where the tribunal has misapplied the law of limitation (CLOUT Case No. 371, Hanseatisches Oberlandesgericht Bremen, Germany, (2) Sch 4/99, 30 September 1999). In one case, the resisting party argued that the recognition and enforcement of an award in Zimbabwe would be against public policy since the amount of the interest due for the amount of damages awarded by the tribunal contravened the in dublum common law rule, according to which interest stops running when it equals the capital sum owing (CLOUT Case No. 342, Harare High Court, Zimbabwe 1 March and 5 April 2000, although in this case it was found that the tribunal had not actually misapplied the law on limitation). The High Court held that enforcement of the award was allowed but subject to the in dublum rule. Thus, the Court held that the maximum amount (including the interest) that could be enforced would be double the capital. Finally, in an interesting case, the claimant was awarded a sum of money for port services which the claimant had incurred and paid while the respondent's ship was moored in Bilbao. The amount of money was in fact greater than the usual port services, apparently because the claimant had to pay ransom to the port authority in Bilbao to allow the respondent's ship to leave the port. The respondent argued that the enforcement of this award would be contrary to the public policy of Canada, but this

---

24. Here, examples of violation of procedural public policy will necessarily overlap to some extent with violation of the right of 'a party to be heard' under art. 36(1)(a)(ii).

argument was rejected by the Canadian Court of Appeal, who distinguished between bribery and ransom: while the former constitutes an immoral action for both the offeror and the receiver, the latter involves immorality only on the part of the blackmailer. Therefore, the Court concluded that the reimbursement of the sum paid as ransom to the claimant did not violate the public policy of Canada. It should be noted that the principle of prohibition of review by national courts of the merits of the case applies under this provision as well as, of course, under art. 36. Nevertheless, it is possible, and indeed not rare, for national courts to examine the substance of the dispute when examining the violation of substantive public policy (CLOUT Case No. 371, Hanseatisches Oberlandesgericht Bremen, Germany, (2) Sch 4/99, 30 September 1999).

ARBITRATION LAW OF THE
PEOPLE'S REPUBLIC OF CHINA, 1994

(Adopted at the Ninth Meeting of the Standing Committee of the Eighth National People's Congress on 31 August 1994, promulgated by Order No. 31 of the President of the People's Republic of China on 31 August 1994 and effective as of 1 September 1995)

CHAPTER I. GENERAL PROVISIONS

[Aim of the law]

Article 1

This Law is formulated in order to ensure the impartial and prompt arbitration of economic disputes, to protect the legitimate rights and interests of the parties, and to safeguard the sound development of the socialist market economy.

1. Historical background. China's arbitration system has its origins in the early 1950s. During that period, the government of the People's Republic of China ('PRC') actively promoted arbitration and conciliation as the preferred means for resolving domestic economic disputes. Subsequently, beginning in the early 1960s, various regulations were put into effect that effectively denied party autonomy by providing for the mandatory arbitration of economic contract disputes by economic commissions at various levels. As a result of these regulations, China developed a domestic administrative arbitration system separate from its system of foreign-related arbitration.

2. Domestic arbitration. Dismantled during the chaos of the Cultural Revolution (1966–1976), the domestic arbitration system was revived in the 1970s in a manner that saw the restoration of many of the key elements of the pre-Cultural Revolution domestic arbitration system. Prior to the enactment of the Arbitration Law, China's domestic arbitration system consisted of a number of distinct arbitration institutions, whose jurisdiction was limited to disputes arising exclusively between domestic Chinese legal and natural persons, whereby foreign invested enterprises established in China partially or wholly by foreign capital were deemed to constitute Chinese legal persons under Chinese law. The main features of China's domestic arbitration system prior to the promulgation of the Arbitration Law may be summarised as follows: (i) a lack of independence of the arbitration commissions, which where affiliated to governmental administrative authorities; (ii) the lack of party autonomy, the parties being very limited in their choice on whether to arbitrate and of a specific arbitration commission; (iii) the lack of binding force of the arbitral award.

3. Foreign-related arbitration. Foreign-related arbitration started to develop in the 1950s. The real impetus for the development of foreign-related arbitration was the commencement, in the late 1970s, of the 'open door' policy. In July 1979, China adopted the Sino-Foreign Equity Joint Venture Law, which provides for arbitration concerning disputes between foreign investors and local parties. Foreign-related arbitration was then addressed in a specific chapter in the Civil Procedure Law (Trial Implementation) of 1982 and then in the final Civil Procedure Law of 1991 and its latest revision of 2007. Contrary to the situation in domestic arbitration, the Civil Procedure Law implemented international principles, such as party autonomy and the finality of the award.

4. Adoption of the arbitration law. The adoption in August 1994 of the Arbitration Law was a milestone in the history of China's arbitral development. The law applies to both domestic and foreign-related arbitration, but contains provisions dedicated to foreign-related arbitration. The Arbitration Law aims to provide a unified and organised framework for an arbitration system able to further promote the development of the Chinese economy, in compliance with international standards and protecting the legitimate interests of the parties involved.

5. International standards. The implementation of the Arbitration Law in 1995 substantially changed the face of arbitration in China, which finally adopted some of the most important internationally recognised principles of arbitration, such as the doctrine of severability, party autonomy, the independence of arbitration institutions, and the binding force of the award.

[Definition of arbitrable disputes]

Article 2

Contractual disputes and other disputes over rights and interests in property between citizens, legal persons and other organisations that are equal subjects may be arbitrated.

1. Introductory remarks. Prior to the Arbitration Law, the arbitration of disputes was effectively confined to labour-related disputes and disputes arising from specific economic relationships. With art. 2, the Arbitration Law created for the first time a general basis for determining the arbitrability of disputes. Art. 2 gives a general definition of arbitrable disputes, which encompasses any contractual disputes and other disputes over rights and interests in property.

2. Scope of arbitrability. In order to be arbitrable, disputes must be of a contractual or non-contractual nature and must relate to rights and interests in property between equal civil subjects. Disputes between parties not on an equal footing may not be referred to arbitration. The Arbitration Law permits the arbitral resolution of all disputes of a commercial nature, including disputes relating to intellectual property rights and disputes relating to securities.

3. General capacity requirement of the parties. Indirectly, art. 2 also establishes that natural persons, legal persons and other organisations, as equal subjects before the law, may be parties to an arbitration agreement. This question will be further discussed in relation to art. 17 (see art. 17, note 3).

4. Definitions. In China, the term 'legal person' refers to an organisation that has civil capacity and independently enjoys civil rights and bears civil obligations, i.e. joint stock companies (see art. 36 General Principles of the Civil Law). The term 'other organisations' means lawfully established organisations that own properties, but do not possess the status of a legal person, e.g. partnerships and local branches of commercial banks (see art. 40 Supreme People's Court ('SPC') Several Opinions Concerning the Implementation of the Civil Procedure Law).

[Definition of non-arbitrable disputes]
Article 3

The following disputes may not be arbitrated:
  (i) Marital, adoption, guardianship, support and succession disputes;
  (ii) Administrative disputes that shall be handled by administrative organs as prescribed by law.

1. General. Art. 2 provides a definition of arbitrable disputes. This definition is complemented by art. 3, which enumerates non-arbitrable disputes.

2. Non-arbitrable disputes. According to art. 3 the following types of dispute may not be submitted for arbitration: (i) disputes concerning personal rights, i.e. disputes pertaining to marriage, adoption, guardianship, child maintenance and inheritance, and (ii) administrative disputes, i.e. disputes arising from administrative management by the government, between governmental organs themselves, or between the governmental organs and other social organisations or individuals.

3. Disputes concerning personal rights. The Arbitration Law prohibits the arbitration of disputes relating to marriage, adoption, guardianship, support or succession. Where a contract dealing with any of the foregoing matters, such as a pre-marriage contract, contains an arbitration clause, such arbitration clause is invalid.

4. Administrative disputes. It is important to distinguish two categories of dispute: disputes arising from contract, and disputes between persons or organisations and the administrative authorities. Whilst disputes under the first category may be resolved by arbitration, those arising under the second category may not. The Administrative Procedure Law gives the People's Courts exclusive jurisdiction over a series of disputes, such as in cases of administrative sanctions, compulsory administrative measures, infringement of managerial decision-making powers by an administrative organ, refusal by an administrative organ to issue a permit or licence, etc. In the area of intellectual property, for example, under art. 2 of the Trademark Law, the Trademark Office is the administrative body charged with responsibility for undertaking the registration and administration of trademarks in China. However, the same clause also provides for the establishment of a separate and independent body, i.e. the Trademark Review and Adjudication Board, for the purpose of handling trademark disputes. If any party refuses to accept the decision of the Trademark Review and Adjudication Board, it may, within thirty days from the receipt of notice of the decision, file a suit with the People's Court. In no instance may any of the foregoing disputes be resolved by arbitration. However, disputes arising from contracts for the assignment of intellectual property rights, whether they are of a domestic or international nature, may be resolved by arbitration.

5. Labour and agricultural projects. Actually, there is another category of non-arbitrable disputes not mentioned in art. 3, but referred to in art. 77 (see art. 77, note 1): labour disputes and agricultural projects.

[Arbitration agreement as basis for arbitral jurisdiction]

Article 4

The parties' submission to arbitration to resolve their dispute shall be on the basis of both parties' free will and an arbitration agreement reached between them. If a party applies for arbitration in the absence of an arbitration agreement, the arbitration commission shall not accept the case.

1. Historical background/general. Prior to the Arbitration Law, the jurisdiction of arbitral commissions in domestic matters was limited to the cases specifically provided for in the various applicable laws and regulations. Although some legislation started to allow arbitration on the basis of an arbitration agreement reached by the disputing parties, this principle was not generalised. With art. 4, the Arbitration Law finally and firmly established the arbitration agreement as the sole and exclusive basis for the jurisdiction of an arbitral tribunal.

2. Effect of the arbitration agreement. The conclusion of an arbitration agreement produces two main effects: first, it establishes the jurisdiction of an arbitration institution; second, it excludes the jurisdiction of the courts. Art. 4 indirectly contemplates the first principle: through a valid agreement to arbitrate, the parties establish the jurisdiction of an arbitration commission.

3. Necessity of a valid arbitration agreement. In any arbitral proceedings, the jurisdiction of the relevant arbitration institution is based upon the existence of a valid arbitration agreement. If there is a valid agreement between the parties to arbitrate, such agreement is sufficient to establish the jurisdiction of an arbitration commission. If there is no valid arbitration agreement (concerning the conditions for validity, see art. 16, note 1 et seq.), the arbitration institution shall not accept the case, otherwise the award may be cancelled (see art. 58, note 1 et seq.).

4. Free will of the parties. Art. 4 provides that the agreement to arbitrate must be concluded on the basis of the parties' free will. In other words, their intent to arbitrate must be true, i.e. given both freely and fairly, in the absence of duress, fraud or coercion (see also art. 17, note 4).

[Arbitration agreement as effective inhibition of court jurisdiction]

Article 5

If the parties have concluded an arbitration agreement and one party institutes an action in a People's Court, the People's Court shall not accept the case, unless the arbitration agreement is null and void.

1. Exclusion of the People's Court's jurisdiction. This provision is the counterpart of art. 4 and expresses the principle that a valid arbitration agreement excludes the jurisdiction of the court (see art. 4, note 2). Only where the arbitration agreement is invalid may a court accept its competence (see art. 16 concerning the question of validity of an arbitration agreement). However, the exclusion of court jurisdiction is more partial than absolute (see art. 20, note 1 et seq.).

2. No application to interim protection measures. Notwithstanding the wording of art. 5, a request for interim protection measures addressed by any party to a People's Court will not be deemed as incompatible with the arbitration agreement or as a waiver of the arbitration agreement (see in this respect art. 28, note 1 and art. 46, note 2).

[Parties' autonomy as to the choice of competent arbitration institution]

Article 6

(1) The arbitration commission shall be selected by the parties through agreement.

(2) In arbitration, there shall be no jurisdiction by level and no territorial jurisdiction.

1. General. Art. 6 is meant to illustrate the difference between: (i) an arbitration system, where the jurisdiction of the arbitration institution is exclusively based on the arbitration agreement concluded between the parties (see art. 4, note 2), and (ii) a court system, where the jurisdiction of the court is pre-determined by the applicable procedural rules.

2. No jurisdiction by level and no territorial jurisdiction. When initiating court proceedings, the first step is always to determine the competent court based on the applicable procedural rules. The competent court will usually be determined based on three types of jurisdictions: (i) the material jurisdiction (rationae materiae), which depends on the legal nature of the dispute and/or the claim (e.g. civil, penal, administrative, etc); (ii) the territorial jurisdiction (rationae loci), which determines which court is geographically competent, and (iii) the jurisdiction by level, which determines whether a lower or a higher court has jurisdiction to hear the case. In arbitration, only the first type of jurisdiction is relevant and concerns the question as to whether the disputes at stake may be heard by an arbitration commission, i.e. whether the dispute is arbitrable (see art. 2, note 2 et seq.), and whether it falls within the scope of the arbitration agreement (see art. 16, note 9). As to the two other types of jurisdiction, they do not apply to the arbitration: there is no hierarchy order among arbitration commissions (i.e. no jurisdiction by level), and the territorial jurisdiction is left to the choice of the parties.

3. Parties' autonomy as to the choice of the arbitration institution. Art. 6 establishes the principle that, contrary to the jurisdiction of courts, the jurisdiction of an arbitration institution is based on the arbitration agreement and is therefore determined by the parties themselves. This is a big change compared to the situation prior to the Arbitration Law, when parties would often be forced to refer their dispute to arbitration under the auspices of pre-determined arbitration commissions.

4. Limited freedom. However, the parties' autonomy as to the choice of the arbitration commission is not unlimited. First of all, the choice of the parties is obviously limited to a pre-existing arbitration commission; ad hoc arbitration is not permissible under the Arbitration Law. Secondly, some commissions are established to handle only specific kinds of disputes (e.g. the China Maritime Arbitration Commission, 'CMAC'), and will therefore not accept cases which fall outside the scope as described in their rules. Finally, there is controversy over whether parties to a dispute may choose to submit their arbitration to an international arbitration commission such as the ICC International Court of Arbitration, in China.

5. Compulsory choice. If, as mentioned before (see art. 6, note 3), art. 6 gives the parties the autonomy to choose an arbitration commission, it simultaneously forces them to make use of this autonomy. The parties can, but also must designate an arbitration commission in their arbitration agreement (see art. 16, note 10).

[General principles as to the applicable law]

Article 7

In arbitration, disputes shall be resolved based on true facts and relative laws to yield a fair and reasonable settlement for the parties concerned.

1. General. Art. 7 is just a reminder of a general principle under Chinese law. In fact, equitable principles will automatically be followed by operation of law. In that respect, many fundamental Chinese statutes expressly provide for the application of equitable principles. Arts. 5 and 6 of the Contract Law, for example, provide that the parties shall observe the principle of fairness in defining their respective rights and obligations, and shall observe the principles of good faith in exercising their rights and performing their obligations. Further, art. 54 of the Contract Law states that a party has the right to request a People's Court or an arbitration body, as the case may be, to alter or nullify a contract that was clearly unfair at the time it was concluded.

2. Decision ex aequo et bono. In many countries, arbitral legislation permits the disputing parties to direct the arbitral tribunal to act as amiable compositeur or ex aequo et bono, and to adopt equitable principles in determining arbitral cases. If so authorised, it is well established that the arbitral tribunal will only invoke equitable principles rather than strictly apply the relevant law in circumstances where, in the opinion of the tribunal, such application would clearly yield a fairer outcome in the case. In China, the Arbitration Law does not contain dedicated provisions expressly permitting the parties to instruct the arbitral tribunal to determine their dispute ex aequo et bono. Art. 7, however, provides that arbitration 'shall be rendered based on true facts and relative laws to yield a fair and reasonable settlement for the parties concerned'. These concepts of fairness and reasonableness are echoed in the arbitration rules of the China International Economic Trade Arbitration Commission ('CIETAC', see art. 43 CIETAC Rules). In consequence, Chinese arbitration commissions are empowered to render their determination based on the principle of ex aequo et bono. In fact, it is impossible for the disputing parties to instruct the arbitral tribunal to disregard the principle of ex aequo et bono and determine the dispute via a strict application of the relevant laws. Of course, as the applicable law and the principles of equity are occasionally mutually exclusive, a question then arises as to which has priority and is to be applied in determining a dispute. The well-established position in China is that the law as selected by the parties and recorded in their arbitration agreement will be applied without equivocation. The arbitration commission may not render a decision exclusively on the basis of ex aequo et bono, totally ignoring the applicable law. However, where the selected law is silent on a particular point, the arbitral tribunal will apply international practice and the principles of equity.

3. Choice of law. Neither art. 7 nor any other provision of the Arbitration Law provides any specific guidelines regarding the law applicable to the dispute itself or to the arbitration agreement. However, the principle of free choice of law by the parties to a foreign-related dispute is recognised, unless otherwise expressly provided for by a specific law.

4. Law applicable to the arbitration (lex arbitri). While the question of the law applicable to the arbitration was left unresolved for a long time, and practices as to how to determine such law substantially diverged, the SPC has in its last Judicial Interpretations of 8 September 2006 finally provided for a clear solution. According to art. 16 of such Interpretations, the law as agreed by the parties shall apply to the examination over the validity of the foreign-related arbitration agreement; where the parties concerned have not agreed on the applicable law but have agreed on the place of arbitration, the law of the place of arbitration shall apply; and where neither the applicable laws nor the place of arbitration is agreed or the agreement on the place of arbitration is not clear, the laws of the place where the court is located, i.e. Chinese law, shall apply. In fact, this provision mirrors the solution contemplated by art. V(1) lit. a of the New York Convention. As far as domestic arbitration is concerned, the law applicable to the arbitration, i.e. to the arbitration agreement, is always Chinese Law.

5. The law applicable to the substance of the case. According to art. 126 of the Contract Law, the parties to a contract with a foreign element are entitled to select the law applicable to the handling of any disputes that may arise between them, unless otherwise expressly provided by law. One example of a law which limits this right is the Sino-Foreign Equity Joint Venture Law, which provides that Chinese law shall govern any disputes arising from a sino-foreign equity joint venture contract. Where the contract is silent with respect to the applicable substantive law, the contract will be governed in accordance with the law of the country having the closest connection to the contract, i.e. the law of the country most closely associated or connected with the performance of the contract. This conforms to Article 28 of the UNCITRAL Model Law.

[Independence of arbitration]

Article 8

Arbitration shall be carried out independently according to law and shall be free from interference of administrative organs, public organisations or individuals.

1. Independence of arbitration. The Arbitration Law has been a catalyst relieving domestic arbitration commissions from government interference (see art. 1, note 1 et seq.) and local protectionism, and thus furthering the independence of arbitration in China. The legislator's intention was to have arbitration commissions hierarchically separated from any governmental bodies. Art. 8 implements such principle and states that arbitration shall be conducted independently in accordance with the law and shall not be subject to interference by any administrative organs, social organisations or individuals. The same principle is valid for arbitration institutions (see art. 14, note 1).

Arbitration Law of the PRC, art. 9

[Finality of arbitral award]

Article 9

(1) A system of single and final awards shall be practised for arbitration. If a party applies for arbitration to an arbitration commission or institutes an action in a People's Court regarding the same dispute after an arbitral award has been made, the arbitration commission or the People's Court shall not accept the case.

(2) If an arbitral award is set aside or its enforcement is disallowed by the People's Court in accordance with the law, a party may apply for arbitration on the basis of a new arbitration agreement reached between the parties, or institute an action in the People's Court, regarding the same dispute.

1. Historical background/general. Prior to the introduction of the Arbitration Law, most domestic arbitral commissions fell under the remit of administrative organs and were not based on an arbitration agreement of the disputing parties (see art. 1, note 2). Awards rendered by those commissions were not final. A party against whom an award was made could effectively block enforcement proceedings by filing a lawsuit with the People's Court. Although the situation was different for foreign-related arbitration (based namely on the adoption by China in 1987 of the New York Convention), art. 9 provided the general legislative basis for the establishment of a system of a single and final award.

2. Finality of the award. Art. 9(1) expresses the principle of finality of the award: by choosing arbitration, the parties exclude the jurisdiction of the courts (see art. 5, note 1) and simultaneously waive any rights that may derive from local procedural laws, in particular the right to appeal against a decision. The arbitral tribunal will judge the case as first and last instance; the arbitral award will be final and binding upon both parties, and neither party may bring a suit before a People's Court or make a request to any other organisation (including the arbitration institution itself) in order to re-judge the case.

3. Two exceptions: setting-aside and non-enforcement of the arbitral award. The principle of finality of the award is, however, not absolute. In certain specific cases, the parties can file a request for the setting aside or for the non-enforcement of the award (see art. 58 et seq. and art. 62 et seq.). If the award is set aside or its enforcement refused by the court, the award loses its final character and the parties are allowed to re-arbitrate the matter or to go before the courts regarding the same dispute.

4. New arbitration agreement required. Although it is an internationally recognised principle that through its cancellation, the award loses its final character, the solution provided for in art. 9 is somewhat unique. In fact, according to the wording of art. 9, in order for the parties to re-arbitrate the matter, it is necessary for them to conclude a new arbitration agreement. This means that the cancellation of the award does not only cancel the award itself, but also the arbitration agreement. Thus, unless the parties conclude a new arbitration agreement, the courts will have jurisdiction to re-judge the matter. Depending on the reasons for cancellation of the award, this solution is not always justified. If an award is cancelled based on the invalidity of the arbitration agreement, the parties can obviously not re-arbitrate the matter based on the same arbitration agreement, and the courts are competent to hear the case. However, if an award is cancelled for reasons not related to the arbitration agreement itself, such as a violation of relevant procedural rules or a violation of the ordre public (see art. 70, note 3), the original arbitration agreement should remain valid and the parties should, based thereon, be able to re-arbitrate the matter.

CHAPTER II. ARBITRATION COMMISSIONS AND THE ARBITRATION ASSOCIATION

[Geographical organisation of arbitration commissions]

Article 10

(1) Arbitration commissions may be established in municipalities directly under the Central Government and in cities that are the seats of the People's Governments of provinces or autonomous regions. They may also be established in other cities divided into districts, according to the need. Arbitration commissions shall not be established at each level of the administrative divisions.

(2) The People's Governments of the cities referred to in the preceding paragraph shall arrange for the relevant departments and chambers of commerce to organise arbitration commissions in a unified manner.

(3) The establishment of an arbitration commission shall be registered with the administrative department of justice of the relevant province, autonomous region or municipality directly under the Central Government.

1. Introductory remarks. Arts. 10 to 15 concern the establishment of arbitration commissions and their internal organisation. In order to validly handle arbitration cases, arbitration commissions need to fulfil the requirements set out in Chapter II. Art. 10 aims to keep control over the growth of such commissions.

2. Controlled establishment. According to art. 10, arbitration commissions should be firstly established in municipalities and major cities, and only if needed will further commissions be established in districts (i.e. parts of a city). The establishment of arbitration commissions is organised by the relevant departments of the People's government unit in charge in the municipality, city or district, or by the chambers of commerce. The Ministry of Justice is the ultimate authority in charge of the registration of arbitration commissions.

[Minimum requirements for arbitration commissions]

Article 11

(1) An arbitration commission shall meet the conditions set forth below:
  (i) To have its own name, domicile and charter;
  (ii) To have the necessary property;
  (iii) To have the personnel that are to form the commission; and
  (iv) To have appointed arbitrators.

(2) The charter of an arbitration commission shall be formulated in accordance with this Law.

1. Minimum requirements. Art. 11 sets a list of minimum requirements that an arbitration commission has to fulfil in order to be functioning. An arbitration commission should have its own name, a domicile (i.e. duly registered according to art. 10(3)) and its own byelaws. It should further dispose over the necessary property of premises, personnel and arbitrators allowing it to fulfil its tasks.

[Key personnel of the arbitration commission]

Article 12

(1) An arbitration commission shall be composed of one chairman, two to four vice chairmen and seven to eleven members.

(2) The offices of chairman, vice chairman and members of an arbitration commission shall be held by experts in the field of law, economy and trade and persons with practical working experience. Experts in the field of law, economy and trade shall account for at least two thirds of the people forming an arbitration commission.

1. Directorship. Art. 12(1) defines the directorship structure of the arbitration commission, setting forth a minimum and maximum number for its composition.

2. Minimum qualification. Art. 12(2) then sets minimum qualifications to be met by key personnel of the arbitration commissions. The chairman, vice chairmen and members shall be experts in the field of law, economy and/or trade and persons with practical experience in those fields. This requirement further applies to the two thirds of all the employees of the arbitration commission.

3. Aim. Art. 12 aims at ensuring a minimum level of structure and efficiency in the work of the arbitration commission, although rigidity is not necessarily the best way to promote efficiency.

[Minimum requirements for arbitrators]
Article 13

(1) An arbitration commission shall appoint its arbitrators from among righteous and upright persons.

(2) An arbitrator shall meet one of the conditions set forth below:
  (i) To have been engaged in arbitration work for at least eight years;
  (ii) To have worked as a lawyer for at least eight years;
  (iii) To have served as a judge for at least eight years;
  (iv) To have been engaged in legal research or legal education, possessing a senior professional title; or
  (v) To have acquired the knowledge of law, engaged in the professional work in the field of economy and trade, etc., possessing a senior professional title or having an equivalent professional level.

(3) An arbitration commission shall have a register of arbitrators in different specialisations.

1. Scope of applicability limited to domestic arbitration. Art. 13 details the qualifications necessary to be appointed to the panel of arbitrators of any arbitration commission in China, excluding international arbitration panels. Chapter 7, which addresses foreign-related arbitration, contains a dedicated provision treating the appointment of foreign specialists to foreign-related arbitration panels (see art. 67, note 1). However, the duty set forth in art. 13(1) to establish a panel of arbitrators is valid for domestic and foreign-related arbitration.

2. Minimum requirements. In addition to the statutory requirement that a candidate must be 'righteous' and 'upright', it further provides that a person may not be appointed as an arbitrator unless he can satisfy at least one of the five following requirements: a senior title in the legal research or legal education field; at least eight years' experience working as a lawyer; experience as a judge for at least eight years; a senior title in the legal research or legal education field; or knowledge of the law and senior title or equivalent professional level in fields such as economic relations and trade.

3. Supplementary requirements of specific arbitration commissions. CIETAC and CMAC jointly promulgated in 1995 the Stipulations for the

Appointment of Arbitrators and later amended them in 2000, listing different criteria for Chinese arbitrators, foreign arbitrators, and Hong Kong and Macao Arbitrators (see art. 67, note 1 et seq.). CIETAC and CMAC have also issued Ethical Rules for Arbitrators, which regulate the conduct of arbitrators. In this respect see art. 20 CIETAC Rules (see art. 20).

4. List of arbitrators. Art. 13(3) encourages arbitration commissions to set up a list of potential arbitrators specialising in different areas. Most arbitration commissions have established such a list. CIETAC has prepared a List of Arbitrators on Domestic Cases and a List of Arbitrators on International Cases. However, according to latest practice and the 2005 revision of the CIETAC Rules, parties are now allowed to choose arbitrators outside the list of arbitrators of the arbitration commission (see art. 21 CIETAC Rules).

[Independence of arbitration commissions]

Article 14

Arbitration commissions shall be independent from administrative organs and there shall be no subordinate relationships between arbitration commissions and administrative organs. There shall also be no subordinate relationships between arbitration commissions.

1. Aim. The Communist Party and the Government used to interfere in institutional bodies' affairs (NGOs or other associations, etc.). The concept of hierarchy has very deep roots in China and forms part of the ancient traditions of Chinese administration. Art. 14 aims to stop this trend and guarantee the independence of arbitration commissions by prohibiting subordinated relationships between arbitration commissions and administrative authorities, or between different arbitration commissions. Art. 14 is the corollary to art. 8, which guarantees the independence of arbitration proceedings in general (see art. 8, note 1). Indeed, the independence of arbitration proceedings can only be guaranteed if the arbitration commissions in charge of the cases are themselves independent from any third party intervention.

[China Arbitration Association]

Article 15

(1) The China Arbitration Association is a social organisation with the status of a legal person. Arbitration commissions are members of the China Arbitration Association. The charter of the China Arbitration Association shall be formulated by its national congress of members.

(2) The China Arbitration Association is a self-disciplined organisation of arbitration commissions. It shall, in accordance with its charter, supervise arbitration commissions, their members, and arbitrators as to whether or not they breach discipline.

(3) The China Arbitration Association shall formulate rules of arbitration in accordance with this Law and the relevant provisions of the Civil Procedure Law.

1. Non-existence of the China Arbitration Association. Whilst art. 15 provides for the founding of the China Arbitration Association ('CAA'), the organisation remains, as yet, unestablished.

2. Future functions of the CAA. The CAA is to be a self-regulated organisation, possessing the status of a legal person, although it is believed that the State Council has yet to determine its exact nature and status. One of its main functions will be the supervision of the arbitration commissions, its members and their arbitrators. Another main function of the CAA will be the formulation of unified arbitration rules for domestic arbitration commissions in accordance with the Arbitration Law and the Civil Procedure Law. Before the establishment of the CAA, this function is being exercised by the Legal Affairs Bureau of the State Council. In accordance with the Arbitration Law, all domestic arbitration commissions are all required to be members of the CAA.

CHAPTER III. ARBITRATION AGREEMENT

[Validity requirements of the arbitration agreement]

Article 16

(1) An arbitration agreement shall include arbitration clauses stipulated in the contract and agreements of submission to arbitration that are concluded in other written forms before or after disputes arise.

(2) An arbitration agreement shall contain the following particulars:
  (i) **An expression of intention to apply for arbitration;**
  (ii) **Matters for arbitration; and**
  (iii) **A designated arbitration commission.**

1. General. Art. 16(1) sets the formal requirement of validity of the arbitration agreement, i.e. the written form, while art. 16(2) concerns substantive requirements, i.e. requirements as to the content of the arbitration agreement.

2. Written form requirement. Art. 16(1) explicitly requires an arbitration agreement to be in written form or as a separate agreement, but does not provide such an explicit requirement on the form of an arbitration clause 'provided in the contract'. However, a brief examination of the background information shows that the writing requirement also applies to such an arbitration clause. In this regard, it is both important and interesting to note that whilst Contract Law recognises oral contracts, any arbitration clause or agreement still must be recorded in writing. This is consistent with the prevailing rule in international arbitration.

3. Definition of written form. As for what constitutes a written form, the Arbitration Law does not provide direct answers, but Contract Law fills the vacuum. In accordance with art. 11 of the Contract Law, 'written form' includes any form capable of tangible representation of its content, such as written instruments, letters and electrically or electronically transmitted documents including telegrams, telexes, facsimiles, electronic data interchange and email. A very similar provision is also contemplated by art. 5 CIETAC Arbitration Rules (see art. 5 CIETAC Rules) and echoes art. 7(2) of the UNCITRAL Model Law (see art. 7(2) UNCITRAL Model Law).

4. Signature. As for the issue of signature, whilst the generally accepted view is that a 'signature' is not necessary – in any event, it is not a statutory requirement in China – it is interesting to note that the New York Convention has defined 'writing' as follows: 'the term "agreement in writing" shall include an arbitral clause in a contract or an arbitration agreement, signed by the parties or contained in an exchange of letters or telegrams' (see art. II New York Convention).

5. Types of arbitration agreement. Whilst the Arbitration Law requires that an arbitration agreement must be in writing, that agreement may appear as an arbitration clause within the contract, as an independent 'Arbitration Agreement' contained in a separate document, in a written submission agreement concluded after a dispute has arisen, or an agreement adopted by the parties via reference to a provision for arbitration detailed in a third party document.

6. Incorporation by reference. Arbitration agreements incorporated by reference to another contractual document containing such arbitration agreement are also valid under Chinese law, as confirmed by the SPC in its Reply on the Manner of Determining Jurisdiction of 14 December 1996.

7. Substantive requirements. Art. 16(2) provides that, in order for an arbitration agreement to be valid it must at a minimum contain the following elements: the expression of the parties' intention to apply for arbitration, the matters to be arbitrated, the arbitration institution selected by the parties.

8. The parties' true and clear intent to arbitrate. As parties are free to select arbitration as a means of dispute resolution, it is therefore paramount that an arbitration agreement clearly records the intention of the parties to submit disputes relating to specified subject matter to arbitration. The arbitration agreement must record the true (see art. 17, note 4), clear and unambiguous intention of the parties to refer specific disputes arising between them to arbitration. An arbitration agreement designating both arbitration and litigation, as being concurrently available to the parties as a dispute resolution means, would be considered now in China as invalid due to a lack of clear and unambiguous intent to arbitrate (see art. 7 SPC Judicial Interpretations of 8 September 2006).

9. A clear description of the matters to be arbitrated. In order to successfully reach an arbitration agreement, it is necessary that such agreement contain a precise and definitive statement of all disputes that the parties wish to submit to arbitration. Sometimes a minor discrepancy in the specification of the subject matter may create jurisdictional difficulties for arbitration. In this respect, the SPC reaffirmed in art. 2 of its latest Judicial Interpretations of 8 September 2006 that where the parties concerned summarise the matters agreed upon for arbitration as 'contractual disputes', this should include disputes arising on the basis of the formation, validity, change, transfer, performance, liability for breach, interpretation, cancellation, etc., of the contract. In the *Mikeda* case of 2006, the SPC went even further. In this case, the parties had concluded a Manufacturing Agreement containing an arbitration clause which referred 'all disputes related to this Agreement' to arbitration. The parties then signed a Repayment Agreement, which did not contain any arbitration clause, but which was related to payments due under the Manufacturing Agreement. *Mikeda* initiated arbitration proceedings under the Repayment Agreement, although it contained no arbitration clause. The other party contested the jurisdiction of the arbitral tribunal based on the absence of an arbitration clause in the Repayment Agreement. The Supreme People's Court admitted the competence of the arbitral tribunal based on the argument that a dispute arising out of the Repayment Agreement was actually also a dispute related to the Manufacturing Agreement, and therefore fell under the scope of application of the arbitration clause contained in the Manufacturing Agreement.

10. The clear designation of an arbitration commission. Whereas the two previous requirements are common and can be found in most arbitration laws and rules, the requirement of the designation of an arbitration commission is peculiar to the Chinese Arbitration Law. Art. 16(3) strictly requires that the parties to an arbitration agreement expressly designate the arbitration commission, which will be competent to handle a future arbitration procedure. The non-compliance with this requirement can have fatal consequences and lead to the invalidity of the arbitration clause (see art. 18, note 2).

11. 'Arbitration commission'. The term 'arbitration commission' refers to the commonly used term 'arbitration institution'. However, there is controversy as to whether this term only refers to Chinese arbitration institutions or also encompasses foreign arbitration institutions. Part of the doctrine is of the opinion that any arbitration institution should be considered as an 'arbitration commission'. However, based on the wording and content of art. 10 (see art. 10, note 1 et seq.), which governs the establishment of arbitration commissions and only refers to arbitration commissions to be established in China, some authors fear that art. 16 will be interpreted as requiring the designation of a Chinese arbitration commission in the sense of art. 10 of the Arbitration Law. The SPC has yet to decide on this matter and the controversy therefore remains open.

[Invalidity of an arbitration agreement]

Article 17

An arbitration agreement shall be null and void under one of the following circumstances:
  (i) **The agreed matters for arbitration exceed the range of arbitrable matters as specified by law;**
  (ii) **One party that concluded the arbitration agreement has no civil capacity or has limited civil capacity; or**
  (iii) **One party coerced the other party into concluding the arbitration agreement.**

1. General. Whereas art. 16 set positive conditions for the validity of an arbitration agreement, art. 17 lists circumstances in which an arbitration agreement will be deemed invalid.

2. Arbitrability. Art. 17(i) refers to art. 2 and 3 and reminds us that only arbitrable matters as defined therein may be subject to arbitration (see art. 2, note 1 et seq. and art. 3, note 1 et seq.).

3. Capacity of the parties. Art. 2 already (indirectly) establishes that natural persons, legal persons and other organisations as equal subjects before the law may be party to an arbitration agreement (see art. 2, note 3). Art. 17(ii) further requires that individuals seeking to bind themselves to an arbitration agreement must have the full legal capacity to conclude an agreement. Determination of such capacity depends on the provisions of the national law to which such party is subject. According to the General Principles of the Civil Law, a Chinese citizen over 18 years of age has full capacity for civil acts; a Chinese citizen over 16 years of age but less than 18 years of age who primarily lives on earnings from his or her own labour may also be deemed a person with full capacity for civil acts. However, Chinese citizens under 16 years of age or citizens affected by insanity are considered to be without or with a limited capacity for conducting civil acts. Persons falling within the two last-mentioned categories are deemed legally incapable of entering into an arbitration agreement. As to 'legal persons' and 'other organisations' as referred to in art. 2, they have per definition civil capacity (see art. 2, note 4).

4. Free will of the parties. Art. 16(2)(i) required that parties to an arbitration agreement expressly mention their intent to arbitrate (see art. 16, note 8). Art. 17(iii) further provides that such intent must be true, i.e. based on the parties' free will (see also art. 4, note 4). Art. 17(iii) governs the consequences of a lack of free will, providing that, if by means of duress, one party forces another party to execute an arbitration agreement or an agreement incorporating an arbitration clause, then such arbitration agreement will be held invalid.

[Lack of clear designation of an arbitration commission]

Article 18

If an arbitration agreement contains no or unclear provisions concerning the matters for arbitration or the arbitration commission, the parties may reach a supplementary agreement. If no such supplementary agreement can be reached, the arbitration agreement shall be null and void.

1. General. Art. 18 is to be read in connection with art. 16(2)(iii). Whereas art. 16(2)(iii) requires the parties to expressly designate an arbitration commission in their arbitration agreement, art. 18 rules the consequences of the non-compliance with such requirement.

2. Invalidity of the arbitration agreement. According to art. 18, if the parties fail to designate an arbitration institution in the arbitration agreement in accordance with art. 16(2)(iii), or if such designation is unclear, the arbitration agreement will be considered invalid, unless the parties reach a supplementary agreement. This principle has two main implications: no ad hoc arbitration in China and restrictive interpretation of pathological arbitration clauses.

3. No ad hoc arbitration. An arbitration agreement which shows a clear intent of the parties to arbitrate, but does not designate an arbitration commission is – according to international practice – usually considered to be opting for ad hoc arbitration. Under art. 18, such an agreement is invalid, which means that there is no ad hoc arbitration in China. (However, an award rendered following ad hoc arbitration proceedings abroad will be recognised in China based on the New York Convention.)

4. Pathological arbitration clauses. Due to art. 18's strict requirement of clarity, pathologies relating to the designation of the arbitration commission will often lead to the invalidity of the arbitration agreement. What art. 18 does not state is how far the lack of clarity of the arbitration clause may be bridged by interpretation, or whether any ambiguity whatsoever justifies its annulment. In its latest Judicial Interpretations dated 8 September 2006, the SPC established a series of interpretation principles as concerns ambiguities in the designation of the arbitration commission.

5. Inaccurate name. Where the name of the arbitration institution as agreed in the arbitration agreement is not accurate, but the specific arbitration institution can nevertheless be determined, it shall be deemed that the arbitration institution has been designated (art. 3 of the SPC Judicial Interpretations of 8 September 2006). This interpretation confirms a long-lasting practice of the SPC, which has been fairly generous when interpreting erroneous designations of arbitration institutions, especially when the mistake was due to the fact that the arbitration clause refers to a former name of CIETAC.

6. Reference only to the rules. Where the arbitration agreement only agrees upon the applicable arbitration rules, it shall be deemed that no arbitration institution has been agreed upon, except where the parties concerned have reached a supplementary agreement, or where the arbitration institution can be determined according to the arbitration rules that have been agreed on (art. 4 of the SPC Judicial Interpretations of 8 September 2006). In the famous *Züblin* case, which took place in 2004, the parties concluded an arbitration clause stating 'Arbitration: ICC Rules, Shanghai shall apply'. In this case the SPC instructed the lower court from Jiangsu Province to refuse to enforce such an arbitration clause, since it did not designate an arbitration commission clearly enough. Indeed, although it is widely recognised that if parties choose the ICC Rules as the relevant arbitration rules, they thereby implicitly designate the ICC International Court for Arbitration as the competent arbitration institution, the SPC found that since there is no express provision in the ICC Rules stating that by choosing the ICC Rules the parties also choose to submit their dispute to the ICC International Court for Arbitration, the arbitration clause at stake did not designate clearly enough the arbitration institution.

7. Two or more arbitration commissions. Where two or more arbitration institutions have been agreed upon in the arbitration agreement, the parties concerned may choose by agreement to apply to one of the specified arbitration institutions for arbitration; if the parties concerned fail to reach an agreement on the arbitration institution, the arbitration agreement shall be deemed invalid (art. 5 of the SPC Judicial Interpretations of 8 September 2006). In *Zhongchen International Project Contracting Co. Ltd.* v *Beijing Jiangong Group LLC* from 2001, the parties had provided for an arbitration agreement referring to the 'Beijing Municipal Arbitral Institution'. Although the name was inaccurate, the Beijing Intermediate People's Court concluded that the parties had chosen institutional arbitration in Beijing, that Beijing had only two arbitration commissions (the CIETAC and the Beijing Arbitration Commission ('BAC')), and that this case should thus be treated as if the parties had provided for two alternative arbitration institutions. The Beijing Intermediate People's Court then gave the parties the choice between either one of the arbitration institutions. Based on art. 5 of the SPC Judicial Interpretations of 8 September 2006, such choice would now need to be done in the form of a supplementary arbitration agreement, and could no longer simply be exercised by either party by initiating arbitration proceedings before any of the two arbitration commissions.

8. Reference only to a place. Where the arbitration agreement specifies that the arbitration shall be handled by the arbitration institution at a certain place, and there is only one arbitration institution at that place, that arbitration institution shall be deemed to be the arbitration institution agreed upon by the parties. Where there are two or more arbitration institutions at that place, the parties may choose by agreement one of the arbitration institutions to apply for arbitration; and where the parties fail to reach an agreement on the arbitration institution, the arbitration agreement shall be deemed invalid (art. 6 of the SPC Judicial Interpretations of 8 September 2006).

9. Practical impact of art. 18. Art. 18 provides that an unclear designation of an arbitration commission will lead (failing a supplementary agreement between the parties) to the invalidity of the arbitration agreement. However, art. 18 fails to give further guidance on when and how to interpret ambiguous arbitration agreements. As to the guidelines issued by the SPC and the local high courts in this respect, they are all based on the same scheme. In principle, an ambiguity in the arbitration agreement will lead to its invalidity, unless the parties remedy such ambiguity by a supplementary agreement. Exceptionally, the ambiguity in the arbitration agreement can in specific cases be bridged by interpretation, despite the absence of a supplementary arbitration agreement. This approach widely diverges from international practice, where the principle of effective interpretation applies and suggests that in doubt, one should prefer the interpretation that gives the words meaning, rather than makes them useless or absurd. As it stands today, the principle of effective interpretation is not recognised in China with regard to the interpretation of arbitration agreements.

[Severability of the arbitration agreement]

Article 19

(1) An arbitration agreement shall exist independently. The amendment, rescission, termination or invalidity of a contract shall not affect the validity of the arbitration agreement.

(2) The arbitral tribunal shall have the power to affirm the validity of a contract.

1. Historical background. In judicial practice, prior to the Arbitration Law, the People's Courts felt that if a contract was found to be void ab initio due to fraud, then the arbitration clause was also void (see *CNTIC* v *Swiss Industrial Resources Company Incorporated*). With art. 19 the Arbitration Law introduced the concept of severability of the arbitration agreement in accordance with international standards (see for example art. 16 UNCITRAL Model Law).

2. Severability of the arbitration agreement. Art. 17 contemplates the doctrine of severability, which provides that even if the main contract ceases to exist or is ab initio invalid, this does not affect the arbitration agreement which continues to be effective. Thereby, the principle of severability ensures the continued exercise of jurisdiction by an arbitration institution over a case where one party objects to such jurisdiction on the grounds that the main contract was terminated or is invalid. Unusually, the issue of the validity of the arbitration clause contained within a contract is treated separately from the issue of the validity of the contract itself. For example, whilst a case may be accepted on the basis of a valid arbitration clause subsumed within a contract, the arbitral tribunal may subsequently render an award that declares the contract itself to be invalid.

[Priority of Court Jurisdiction]
Article 20

(1) If a party challenges the validity of the arbitration agreement, he may request the arbitration commission to make a decision or apply to the People's Court for a ruling. If one party requests the arbitration commission to make a decision and the other party applies to the People's Court for a ruling, the People's Court shall give a ruling.

(2) A party's challenge of the validity of the arbitration agreement shall be raised prior to the arbitral tribunal's first hearing.

1. No recognition of the principle of Kompetenz-Kompetenz. According to art. 20(1), if the jurisdiction of an arbitral tribunal is in dispute, the dispute can be decided by either the arbitral tribunal itself or a relevant court. Article 20(1) goes even further and contemplates that if one of the parties submits the dispute to a court and the other relies on the arbitral tribunal, the court's decision should prevail. Thus, whilst the decision of an arbitration commission is pending, it is open to any of the disputing parties to file a similar application with the court. In such circumstances, the court may advise the arbitration commission to suspend or even terminate the arbitral proceedings pertaining to the same application. Thereby the Arbitration Law rejects the internationally recognised principle of Kompetenz-Kompetenz, according to which the arbitral tribunal has the authority to decide on its own jurisdiction (see also art. 16(1) UNCITRAL Model Law). In China, the arbitral institution or tribunal has only the authority to decide on its own jurisdiction, if none of the parties applies for a ruling before the courts. Nevertheless, where an arbitration commission has already rendered a decision regarding the validity of an arbitration agreement, a court may not subsequently accept the same application (see art. 13 par. 2 of the SPC Judicial Interpretations of 8 September 2006).

2. The prior reporting system in foreign-related arbitration. Where, based on art. 20(1), a lower court determines that an arbitration agreement is invalid, it will have to go through the so called 'Prior Reporting System' and report such decision to higher courts for approval. (See art. 70, note 5 et seq.).

3. Preclusion. According to art. 20(2), if a party intends to object to the validity of the arbitration agreement and thereby to the jurisdiction of the arbitral tribunal, it has to do so before the first hearing. If it fails to raise the objection in a timely manner, the party is deemed to have accepted arbitration and is precluded from invoking the invalidity of the arbitration agreement at a later stage. According to art. 27 of the SPC Judicial Interpretations of 8 September 2006, where a party has not raised an objection as to the validity of the arbitration agreement during the arbitration proceedings, but tries – once an award has been rendered – to cancel it or raises a plea of non-enforcement based on the alleged invalidity of the arbitration agreement, the People's Court shall reject such claim or plea.

CHAPTER IV. ARBITRATION PROCEDURE

Section 1. Application and Acceptance

[Request for arbitration]

Article 21

A party's application for arbitration shall meet the following requirements:
   (i) **There is an arbitration agreement;**
   (ii) **There is a specific arbitration claim, based on specific facts and grounds; and**
   (iii) **The application is within the scope of the arbitration commission's competence.**

1. Introductory remarks. In this chapter, arts. 21 to 23 set forth the prerequisites as concerns the form of the application for arbitration, its content and other documents to be submitted with the application. Arts. 24 to 26 deal with the conditions and consequences of acceptance and/or rejection by the arbitration commission of the arbitration application. Arts. 27 to 29 deal with specific procedural questions.

2. Prerequisites for a request for arbitration. Art. 21 lists three prerequisites that a request for arbitration must satisfy, i.e. (i) the existence of a valid arbitration agreement concluded by the disputing parties (see art. 16, note 7 et seq.), (ii) there is a specific claim with facts and arguments on which such claim is based, and (iii) the dispute must fall within the jurisdictional remit of the selected arbitration commission.

[Requirement of a written application]

Article 22

To apply for arbitration, a party shall submit to the arbitration commission the written arbitration agreement and a written application for arbitration together with copies thereof.

1. Written form. A party pursuing arbitration must formally submit to the arbitration commission a written application accompanied by the underlying arbitration agreement and duplicate copies thereof.

[Content of the request for arbitration]
Article 23

A written request for arbitration shall specify the following particulars:
   (i) The name, sex, age, occupation, work unit and domicile of each party, or the name and domicile of legal persons or other organisations and the names and positions of their legal representatives or chief responsible persons;
   (ii) The arbitration claim and the facts and reasons on which it is based; and
   (iii) The evidence, the source of the evidence, and the names and domiciles of witnesses.

1. Content. Art. 23 provides guidelines as to the content of a request for arbitration, such as the personal data of the claimant and respondent, the legal and factual arguments, as well as all evidence on which the claimant bases its claim. Where the application is found to be incomplete or defective by the Secretariat of the arbitration commission, the claimant is usually afforded an opportunity to amend or supplement the application within a specified time limit.

2. Particulars of claimant and respondent. It is necessary to specify all the personal particulars of claimant and respondent, so that he/she can be sufficiently identified and served with legal documents.

3. Argument. The application for arbitration must contain at least a summary of the dispute, the legal argument and the financial or other claims raised by claimant.

4. Evidence. Although art. 23 seems to foresee that evidence will be submitted with the application for arbitration, it is also admitted that such evidence can be provided at a later stage, according to the applicable arbitration rules or the relating instructions of the arbitral tribunal.

5. Signature and payment of fees. The application for arbitration must be signed and/or stamped by the claimant and/or the attorney duly authorised by the claimant, and filed together with payment of the arbitration fee in accordance with the arbitration fee schedule.

[Decision of acceptance by the arbitration commission]
Article 24

When an arbitration commission receives a written application for arbitration and considers that the application complies with the conditions for acceptance, it shall accept the application and notify the party within five days from the date of receipt. If the arbitration commission considers that the application does not comply with the conditions for acceptance, it shall inform the party in writing of its rejection of the application and explain the reasons for rejection within five days from the date of receipt.

1. Examination of the application. Upon receipt of the application and its attachments, the arbitration commission conducts a thorough examination of the documentation to ensure that it satisfies the statutory application filing requirements as set forth in arts. 21 to 24.

2. Notice of acceptance/rejection. Within five days from the date of receipt of the application for arbitration, the arbitration commission will issue a notice to the parties notifying them of its acceptance, or otherwise, of its rejection. In the latter case, the arbitration commission must provide the parties concerned with reasons for its rejection.

3. Consequences of a rejection. If the arbitration commission rejects its competence, the possibilities left to the parties mainly depend on the reasons for the rejection. If the rejection is justified by the lack of a valid arbitration agreement, the parties will have to bring the dispute before the competent courts. If the rejection is based on non-compliance with the formal requirements as to the form or content of the application for arbitration, the claimant will usually be given an opportunity to amend it within a specific time limit. If he fails to do so, his application will definitely be rejected. If the arbitration commission designated in the arbitration clause rejects its competence, the parties will have no other choice than to submit their dispute to the courts, since no other arbitration commission than the one designated in the arbitration agreement may hear the case and ad hoc arbitration is not permissible.

[Notice of arbitration]

Article 25

(1) After an arbitration commission accepts an application for arbitration, it shall, within the time limit specified in the rules of arbitration, deliver a copy of the rules of arbitration and the register of arbitrators to the claimant, and serve one copy of the application for arbitration together with the rules of arbitration and the register of arbitrators on the respondent.

(2) After receiving the copy of the request for arbitration, the respondent shall submit a written defence to the arbitration commission within the time limit specified in the rules of arbitration. After receiving the written defence, the arbitration commission shall serve a copy thereof on the claimant within the time limit specified in the rules of arbitration. Failure on the part of the respondent to submit a written defence shall not affect the progress of the arbitration proceedings.

Arbitration Law of the PRC, art. 26

1. Notice of arbitration. Art. 25 imposes an obligation on the arbitration commission, to, within the time frame specified in the arbitration rules of the commission, issue a Notice of Arbitration and serve a copy of the arbitration rules and the list of the arbitrators to the parties. A copy of the arbitration application must also be served to the respondent.

2. Notification of a defence. A copy of any defence filed by the respondent must be served to the applicant within the time frame specified in the relevant arbitration rules. Any failure on the part of the respondent to file a defence will not affect the progress of the arbitral proceedings.

3. Reference to arbitration rules. Art. 25 is not very detailed, but merely sets forth the principle that each of the parties must have been duly notified of the other party's submissions and must be aware of the applicable rules. As concerns the detailed time limit for submission, art. 25 refers to the applicable arbitration rules.

[Primary jurisdiction of the courts]
Article 26

If the parties have concluded an arbitration agreement and one party has instituted an action in the People's Court without declaring the existence of the arbitration agreement and, after the People's Court has accepted the case, the other party submits the arbitration agreement prior to the first hearing, the People's Court shall dismiss the case unless the arbitration agreement is null and void. If, prior to the first hearing, the other party has not raised an objection to the People's Court's acceptance of the case, he shall be deemed to have renounced the arbitration agreement and the People's Court shall continue to try the case.

1. General. At first sight, art. 26 does not state anything different to or newer than arts. 5 and 20 (see art. 5, note 1 and art. 20, note 3): the courts have jurisdiction only if the arbitration agreement is null and void. However to exclude the court's jurisdiction it is necessary that one of the parties invokes such arbitration clause before the first hearing. Art. 26 focuses on the last requirement.

2. The necessity to raise an objection to the court's jurisdiction. Art. 26 states that where a People's Court commences court proceedings unaware of the existence of an arbitration agreement, that arbitration agreement will not bar or in any way negate the court proceedings unless the party relying on the agreement submits a copy of the same and files a Motion to Revoke Jurisdiction prior to the convening of the first hearing.

3. Waiver of the arbitration agreement. Failure to raise an objection to the court's jurisdiction in a timely manner is regarded as a waiver of the arbitration agreement and, where proceedings have commenced, the court may continue to hear the case (see also art. 20, note 3).

[Alteration of claim and right to counterclaim]
Article 27
The claimant may renounce or alter its arbitration claim. The respondent may accept or refuse an arbitration claim and shall have the right to make a counter-claim.

1. Right to modify the claim. According to art. 27, the claimant has the right to modify or waive the claim submitted in his application for arbitration. The specific implementation of and limit to this right will largely depend on the applicable arbitration rules.

2. Right to counterclaim. Every time the claimant modifies his claim, the respondent shall be given the opportunity to comment and – if necessary – to raise a counterclaim.

[Interim measures for property preservation]
Article 28
(1) A party may apply for property preservation if it may become impossible or difficult for the party to execute the award due to an act of the other party or other causes.

(2) If a party applies for property preservation, the arbitration commission shall submit the party's application to the People's Court in accordance with the relevant provisions of the Civil Procedure Law.

(3) If an application for property preservation has been wrongfully made, the applicant shall compensate the person against whom the application has been made for any loss incurred from property preservation.

1. No jurisdiction of the arbitral tribunal for property preservation. Contrary to the impression given by the wording of art. 28(1), an arbitration commission and/or arbitral tribunal are not empowered to determine applications for property preservation, a matter that is the sole preserve of the courts. While a party to an arbitration may submit a property preservation application to the arbitral tribunal, the arbitral tribunal must submit that application to the People's Court for determination (see for example art. 17 CIETAC Rules).

2. Application of the Civil Procedure Law. The Civil Procedure Law details the procedure applicable to the submission of applications for property preservation in arts. 92 et seq. and 249 et seq. These articles provide that a party may file an application for property preservation with the People's Court in circumstances where that party believes (a) that the execution of a judgment may become impossible or difficult because of the actions of the other party or for other reasons, or (b) that in the absence of an immediate property preservation order, his legitimate rights and interests would suffer irretrievable damage. In hearing the property preservation application of a party, the People's Court may require the applicant to provide monetary security to the court, in default of which, the court will reject the application. In urgent cases, the People's Court will determine an application within 48 hours. Once issued, a property preservation order takes effect immediately. If the applicant fails to initiate civil litigation within 15 days after the issuing of property preservation order, the People's Court will cancel the property preservation order. If the People's Court subsequently determines that an application for property preservation was wrongfully made, the applicant will be required to compensate the person against whom the property preservation order was made.

[Power of attorney]
Article 29

A party or statutory agent may appoint a lawyer or other agent to carry out arbitration activities. To appoint a lawyer or other agent to carry out arbitration activities, a power of attorney shall be submitted to the arbitration commission.

1. Freedom of agency. According to art. 29, parties to an arbitration are allowed to be represented by counsel in the arbitral proceedings. Counsel must present to the arbitration institution an original Power of Attorney detailing their defined scope of authorisation. Unlike in litigation, the Power of Attorney need not be certified or notarised. Counsel need not necessarily be lawyers and may be either Chinese or foreign nationals. Indeed, over the years, unlike in litigation, foreign lawyers have been permitted to represent their clients in arbitration proceedings and it has been quite common for a Foreign Invested Enterprise ('FIE') to be represented at an arbitration by both a foreign lawyer and a local Chinese lawyer.

2. Limitation for foreign lawyers. However, the situation changed in 2002. In January 2002, the State Council issued new Regulations on the Administration of the Operation of Offices of Foreign Law Firms in China. The regulations limit the scope of legal activities that may be undertaken by foreign law firms and expressly deny such firms the right to provide advice in relation to 'Chinese legal matters', the latter being the sole preserve of Chinese law firms. In July 2002, the Ministry of Justice issued Implementation Rules of 25 June 2002 pertaining to the implementation of the above-mentioned regulations – effective from 1 September 2002. These rules provided a wide definition of the term 'Chinese legal matters', further denying foreign lawyers the right to act as lawyers before the courts or to provide opinions in relation to Chinese law, and even denying foreign lawyers the right to act as counsel in arbitration proceedings where the subject-matter of the dispute is subject to Chinese law. Following broad criticism from part of CIETAC and the foreign legal community, the Ministry of Justice eventually officially clarified the situation and stated in its Clarification of January 2003 addressed to CIETAC that foreign lawyers can serve as agents for the parties in arbitration in China.

Section 2. Formation of the Arbitral Tribunal

[Number of arbitrators]

Article 30

An arbitral tribunal may be composed of either three arbitrators or one arbitrator. An arbitral tribunal composed of three arbitrators shall have a presiding arbitrator.

1. One or three. According to art. 30, the parties to an arbitration can choose between a sole arbitrator or an arbitral tribunal composed of three arbitrators, in which one of them will assume the role of chairman. In practice, an arbitral tribunal composed of three arbitrators is the most common (see art. 20(2) CIETAC Rules).

[Appointment of arbitrators]

Article 31

(1) If the parties agree that the arbitral tribunal shall be composed of three arbitrators, they shall each appoint or entrust the chairman of the arbitration commission to appoint one arbitrator. The parties shall jointly select or jointly entrust the chairman of the arbitration commission to appoint the third arbitrator who shall be the presiding arbitrator.

(2) If the parties agree that the arbitral tribunal shall be composed of one arbitrator, they shall jointly appoint or jointly entrust the chairman of the arbitration commission to appoint the arbitrator.

1. General. Art. 31 reflects international practice and gives the parties a certain autonomy in appointing the arbitrators. Although this is not mentioned in art. 31, in practice the parties will often have to choose one arbitrator from the list of arbitrators established by the competent arbitration commission (see art. 13, note 4). This practice has, nevertheless, been loosened. Certain arbitration rules now allow the parties to choose arbitrators outside their panel of arbitrators (see art. 21(2) CIETAC Rules).

2. Three arbitrators. If the parties select a three-member arbitral tribunal, the applicant and respondent must each appoint one arbitrator (drawn from the then pertaining panel of arbitrators), whilst the third presiding arbitrator is jointly selected by agreement between the parties. Although this is not expressly mentioned in art. 31, the arbitrator does not need to be directly selected by the parties, rather it is sufficient if they jointly agree on a 'method of formation' of the arbitral tribunal (see art. 32, note 1). For example, it is common that the parties agree to entrust the party-arbitrators to jointly appoint a chairman. Alternatively, the parties may also jointly or separately entrust the chairman of the arbitration commission to select the arbitrators, and/or the presiding arbitrator.

3. One Arbitrator. The parties are free to jointly agree on the person of the sole arbitrator, or to delegate such competence to the chairman of the arbitration commission.

4. Consequences of Non-Compliance with art. 31. See art. 32, note 2.

[Subsidiary appointing authority]
Article 32

If the parties fail to agree on the mechanism of formation of the arbitral tribunal or to select the arbitrators within the time limit specified in the rules of arbitration, the arbitrators shall be appointed by the chairman of the arbitration commission.

1. Appointing authority. Where the parties fail to appoint their respective arbitrators within the time frame set forth in the applicable arbitration rules and have not provided for another mechanism of composition of the tribunal, the chairman of the arbitration commission is obliged to make the appointments. Thus, a failure by one party to nominate an arbitrator will not hinder the arbitration proceedings.

2. Non-compliance as grounds for challenge of the award. Art. 31 and 32 are of primordial importance, since a non-compliance with these articles and/or with the mechanism of formation provided for by the parties can be a ground for challenge of the award (cf. art. 58, note 2 and art. 70, note 3).

[Notification of constitution of the arbitral tribunal]
Article 33

After the arbitral tribunal has been formed, the arbitration commission shall notify the parties in writing of the tribunal's formation.

1. Written notification. Once each arbitrator has been appointed and confirmed by the arbitration commission, the arbitration commission will send to the parties a notice that the arbitral tribunal has been constituted.

[Challenge and/or withdrawal of an arbitrator]

Article 34

In one of the following circumstances, the arbitrator must withdraw, and the parties shall also have the right to challenge the arbitrator:
  (i) **The arbitrator is a party in the case or a close relative of a party or of an agent in the case;**
  (ii) **The arbitrator has a personal interest in the case;**
  (iii) **The arbitrator has another relationship with a party or his agent in the case which may affect the impartiality of arbitration; or**
  (iv) **The arbitrator has privately met with a party or agent or accepted an invitation to entertainment or gift from a party or agent.**

1. Four main reasons for withdrawal/challenge of an arbitrator. Art. 34 sets forth four main circumstances in which an arbitrator may be challenged by the disputing parties or/and must withdraw from the arbitral tribunal. The aim of this provision is to guarantee the independence and impartiality of the arbitrators.

2. Ethical rules for arbitrators. However, an analysis of Chinese arbitration practice, together with an examination of the Ethical Rules for Arbitrators, reveal that there exist additional circumstances which may be considered to constitute grounds for disqualification under art. 34: (i) the arbitrator has discussed the case with a party or counsel, or has given advice or opinions concerning the merits of the case to a party or his counsel; (ii) the arbitrator has a relationship with a party or his counsel that involves debt or credit, or concerns business co-operation or competition; (iii) the arbitrator is an advisor to or has previously provided advice to a party or to the counsel of a party; (iv) the arbitrator has the same employer as a party or the counsel of a party; (v) The arbitrator was previously engaged as a conciliator in a separate conciliation process that failed to resolve the dispute, and all the parties to the arbitration object to the arbitrator serving as an arbitrator in the subsequent arbitral proceedings; (vi) the arbitrator has a relationship with a party or his counsel, such as teacher, student, neighbour, friend, etc., to such an extent that may possibly affect the impartiality of the arbitrator. Other arbitration institutions also have similar rules, such as the Ethical Standards for Arbitrators of the Beijing Arbitration Commission, which further lists a series of circumstances in which the arbitration commission can revoke an arbitrator.

3. Objective or subjective reasons. Compared with the rules of some international arbitration institutions, such as the ICC, art. 34 bases the criteria for disqualification of an arbitrator on objective circumstances (i.e. on questions of apparent independence) rather than on the more subjective and generalised criteria of 'impartiality'. However, such a difference should not be a substantial problem in practice, since the relevant rules of these international institutions usually take both subjective and objective criteria into consideration, and it is widely admitted in China that an arbitrator should be impartial and treat the parties equally (see our comments at art. 20 CIETAC Rules).

4. Duty of disclosure. Although it is not expressly mentioned in art. 34, in order to ensure the arbitrators' independence and impartiality, each of them has to disclose any potential conflict of interest or other circumstances that may create doubts as to his/her independence and impartiality. This will usually be done in the form of a Declaration of Independence (see, for example, art. 26 CIETAC Rules).

5. Revocation of an arbitrator. In some cases, it is necessary to revoke the appointment of an arbitrator, not because he lacks impartiality or independence, but because he is not in a position to fulfil his duties anymore (see art. 37, note 1).

6. Legal liability of the arbitrator. In certain cases, namely in the circumstances provided for in art. 34(iv), an arbitrator may be held legally liable (see art. 38, note 1 et seq.).

[Withdrawal procedure]
Article 35

If a party challenges an arbitrator, he shall submit his challenge, with a statement of the reasons, prior to the first hearing. If the matter giving rise to the challenge becomes known after the first hearing, the challenge may be made before the conclusion of the final hearing of the case.

1. Procedure. A request for withdrawal must be submitted to the arbitration commission prior to the first hearing. If, following the commencement of a hearing, a party to the arbitration becomes aware of facts or circumstances, which, in the opinion of that party, affect the independence or impartiality of any arbitrator, then such party may still submit a written request for the withdrawal of the relevant arbitrator. In this situation, the challenge must be submitted prior to the conclusion of the final hearing of the case.

2. After the rendering of the award. If reasons for challenge only become known after the rendering of the award, the situation is very delicate. On the one hand, the reasons listed in art. 34 for challenging an arbitrator do not per se constitute ground for a challenge of the arbitral award based on arts. 58 and 70 (in connection with art. 258 Civil Procedure Law). However, where the arbitrator has intentionally withheld the relevant information or prevented such information from being known before the rendering of the award, a challenge of the arbitral award should be considered on the grounds of art. 58(1)(vi) for domestic arbitration (see art. 58, note 1 et seq.) and art. 70 in connection with art. 258 Civil Procedure Law (see art. 70, note 1 et seq.).

[Competent authority]

Article 36

The decision as to whether or not the arbitrator should withdraw shall be made by the chairman of the arbitration commission. If the chairman of the arbitration commission serves as an arbitrator, the decision shall be made collectively by the arbitration commission.

1. Chairman of the arbitration commission. Art. 36 empowers the chairman of an arbitration commission to determine applications for the withdrawal of an arbitrator. However, where the chairman serves as an arbitrator on the arbitral tribunal, it is the arbitration commission that will render the decision on the withdrawal of an arbitrator.

[Replacement of an arbitrator]

Article 37

(1) If an arbitrator cannot perform his duties due to his withdrawal or for other reasons, a substitute arbitrator shall be selected or appointed in accordance with this Law.

(2) After a substitute arbitrator has been selected or appointed on account of an arbitrator's withdrawal, a party may request that the arbitration proceedings already carried out should be carried out anew. The decision as to whether to approve it or not shall be made by the arbitral tribunal. The arbitral tribunal may also make a decision of its own motion as to whether or not the arbitration proceedings already carried out should be carried out anew.

1. Withdrawal or revocation of an arbitrator. Art. 37 applies to cases where an arbitrator cannot perform his duties due to 'his withdrawal or for other reasons'. So, art. 37 firstly refers to the cases of withdrawal, respectively of challenge of arbitrators foreseen in art. 34 (see art. 34, note 1 et seq.). However, art. 37 further explicitly states that an arbitrator can be replaced if he cannot perform his duties 'for other reasons'. Indeed, in some cases it will be necessary to revoke the appointment of an arbitrator, not because he lacks impartiality or independence, but because he is no longer in a position to fulfil his duties. Although this case is not expressly dealt with in the law, it is admitted – based on art. 37 – that the arbitration commission can revoke arbitrators who fail to comply with their duties. Most arbitration rules or other ethical rules for arbitrators contain provisions on the revocation of an arbitrator by the arbitration commission (art. 27 CIETAC Rules et seq.).

2. Replacement. If the challenged arbitrator is successfully withdrawn, a substitute arbitrator must be selected in accordance with the usual appointment procedures. However, according to the CIETAC Rules, under special circumstances the arbitration institution may decide not to replace the removed arbitrator and continue the arbitration proceedings with the remaining arbitrators (art. 27(4) CIETAC Rules).

3. Recommencement of the arbitral procedure. Once a substitute arbitrator has been appointed, either party may request, or the tribunal may itself direct, the re-commencement, in whole or in part, of the arbitral proceedings. The final decision on whether or not to recommence the arbitration rests with the newly constituted arbitral tribunal.

[Liability of arbitrators in serious cases]

Article 38

If an arbitrator is involved in the circumstances described in item (iv) of Article 34 of this Law and the circumstances are serious or involved in the circumstances described in item (vi) of Article 58 of this Law, he shall assume legal liability according to law and the arbitration commission shall remove his name from the register of arbitrators.

1. Removal of the arbitrator from the panel list in serious cases. Art. 38 directs that an arbitration commission shall not only revoke an arbitrator from an arbitration proceeding, but shall remove his name from its panel of arbitrators if: (i) there is a serious violation of art. 34(iv), i.e. the arbitrator is found to have met privately with any party to the arbitration or their respective attorneys, or to have accepted any gift or hospitality from any of the disputing parties or their respective attorneys (see art. 34, note 1 et seq.), or (ii) while arbitrating the case, the arbitrator has committed embezzlement, accepted bribes, resorted to deception for personal gain or made an award that has perverted the law (see art. 58, note 2).

2. Legal liability. In circumstances falling within art. 38, the arbitrator will bear legal responsibility in accordance with applicable laws. In fact, according to the latest amendment of the Criminal Law (see art. 399 thereof), an arbitrator who intentionally violates the law and misrepresents the facts when rendering a judgment may face up to three years of imprisonment.

Section 3. Hearing and Award

[Oral hearings as a principle]

Article 39

Arbitration shall be conducted by means of oral hearings. If the parties agree to arbitration without oral hearings, the arbitral tribunal may render an arbitral award on the basis of the written application for arbitration, the written defence and other material.

1. Oral hearings are not compulsory in theory. Art. 39 provides that the arbitral tribunal will hold oral hearings for the case unless the parties otherwise agree to dispense with hearings and permit a determination of their dispute based upon the arbitral pleadings and 'other material' filed with the arbitral tribunal.

2. Always oral hearings in practice. In practice, it is however extremely rare that the arbitral tribunal will decide the case based only on the written application and without oral hearings. This is mainly due to the influence of Chinese court proceedings in Chinese arbitration proceedings, and in particular to the influence of the SPC Provisions on Evidence (in this respect see art. 43, note 3).

[Private hearings]

Article 40

Arbitration shall be conducted in camera. If the parties agree to public arbitration, the arbitration may be public unless State secrets are involved.

1. Private hearings. Hearings are held in private session unless otherwise agreed by the parties.

2. Confidentiality of arbitration. Apart from the privacy of hearings, there is no general principle of confidentiality in arbitration practice or judicial interpretation in China. Nevertheless, doctrine and most of the arbitration rules of arbitration commissions in China acknowledge the confidential nature of arbitration (see art. 33 CIETAC).

[Administration by the arbitration commission]

Article 41

The arbitration commission shall notify the parties of the date of the hearing within the time limit specified in the rules of arbitration. A party may, within the time limit specified in the rules of arbitra-

tion, request a postponement of the hearing if he has good reason to so request. The arbitral tribunal shall decide whether or not to postpone the hearing.

1. Schedule of hearings. The arbitration commission determines all hearing dates. It is open to any party, with good reason, to request a postponement of a scheduled hearing date.

2. Typical schedule. According to the CIETAC Rules, the arbitral tribunal should give 20 days advanced notice of a hearing, and any party may – at least 10 days in advance of the scheduled hearing date – request the postponement of such hearing (see art. 30 CIETAC Rules).

[Default of one party]

Article 42

(1) If the claimant fails to appear before the arbitral tribunal without good reason after having been notified in writing or leaves the hearing prior to its conclusion without the permission of the arbitral tribunal, he may be deemed to have withdrawn his application for arbitration.

(2) If the respondent fails to appear before the arbitral tribunal without good reason after having been notified in writing or leaves the hearing prior to its conclusion without the permission of the arbitral tribunal, a default award may be made.

1. Failure of claimant: deemed withdrawal. Where a claimant fails to appear at the hearing without good reason then he will be deemed to have withdrawn his claim.

2. Failure of defendant: default award. Where the respondent fails to appear at a scheduled hearing without good reason, then the arbitral tribunal may proceed to render an award in default.

3. Discretion of the arbitral tribunal. It is up to the arbitral tribunal to decide on the reasonableness and/or justifiability of a party's absence.

[Evidence]

Article 43

Parties shall provide evidence in support of their own arguments. The arbitral tribunal may, as it considers necessary, collect evidence on its own.

1. Burden of proof. Art. 43 is the corollary in arbitration of the general principle contemplated in art. 64(1) of the Civil Procedure Law, according to which each party has to bear the burden of proving the facts it relies on. The arbitral tribunal may, either of its own accord, or at the request of a party to the arbitration, require the party bearing the burden of proof to provide supporting evidence. Failure to present evidence will lead to the rejection of the claim by the arbitral tribunal. However, according to art. 64(2) of the Civil Procedure Law and to art. 43 in fine of the Arbitration Law, it is also admitted that, in certain circumstances, the arbitral tribunal may collect evidence on its own. This is namely the case when the parties and their representatives cannot collect the evidence because of objective reasons or simply when the court deems it necessary for the hearing.

2. Types of evidence. Art. 43 is silent as regards the type of evidence admitted before an arbitral tribunal. Arbitral Tribunals in China will therefore often refer to art. 63 Civil Procedure Law, which classifies evidence into seven types: (i) documentary evidence, (ii) physical evidence, (iii) audio-visual materials, (iv) testimony of witnesses, (v) statements of interested parties, including the disputing parties, (vi) expert conclusions, and (vii) records of inquests.

3. The SPC Provisions on Evidence. Obviously, art. 43 et seq. do not provide for a detailed mechanism of evidence production. In December 2001, the Supreme People's Court promulgated its SPC Provisions on Evidence which comprehensively outline the rules of evidence to be used in civil lawsuits before the People's Court. Whilst these SPC Provisions on Evidence do not directly apply to arbitration in China, it is widely expected that they will ultimately be formally incorporated into the next revision of the Chinese Arbitration Law. Therefore, it is to be expected that the same principles of evidence-gathering, will apply mutis mutandis to Chinese arbitration.

4. IBA Rules. As to the IBA Rules, they do not apply automatically, but only if the parties have provided for their applicability. In practice, it is rare that the parties reach an agreement regarding the application of the IBA Rules in their arbitration agreement. Nevertheless, the Chinese arbitration community has begun to refer to the IBA Rules when dealing with matters of evidence in the arbitral proceedings, especially when international practitioners are involved in Chinese arbitration.

[Appraisal]

Article 44

(1) If the arbitral tribunal considers that a special issue requires appraisal, it may refer the issue for appraisal to an appraisal department agreed on by the parties or to an appraisal department designated by the arbitral tribunal.

(2) If requested by a party or required by the arbitral tribunal, the appraisal department shall send its appraiser to attend the hearing. Sub-

ject to the permission of the arbitral tribunal, the parties may question the appraiser.

1. Appointment of an appraiser on the arbitral tribunal's own initiative. Although it rarely occurs, the arbitral tribunal may, if it considers it necessary, freely consult with experts and appoint appraisers of its own choice (i.e. other than party-nominated experts) for the purpose of clarifying any specific issue relating to the matters at stake. These issues will normally relate to technical, mechanical or scientific issues, and may include the undertaking of in-depth consultations, investigations and inspections.

2. A party's request for appraisal. Actually both the arbitral tribunal and the disputing parties are entitled to call upon experts from the selected qualified appraisal institutions to attend a hearing to give evidence. The experts will be drawn from qualified appraisal institutions agreed upon by the parties, or selected by the arbitral tribunal itself. Following presentation of the evidence and completion of questioning, the disputing parties are entitled to debate the arguments put forward during the arbitral procedure and to submit closing statements.

3. Duty of cooperation of the parties. When investigating and collecting evidence through qualified appraisal institutions, the arbitral tribunal is required to promptly inform the parties to be present. Should a party fail to appear, the investigation and the collection of evidence will not be affected. At the request of a disputing party, such third party experts and appraisers may, upon the consent of the tribunal, attend an oral hearing. However, a third party expert or appraiser may only give oral explanations of their reports if the tribunal considers it both necessary and appropriate to do so. The tribunal may also, for the purposes of inspection, direct the disputing parties to deliver to such experts or appraisers all materials, records or documentation in their possession as the tribunal deems necessary (see art. 38 CIETAC Rules).

[Cross-examination]

Article 45

The evidence shall be presented during the hearings and may be examined by the parties.

1. General. This provision is very general and does not provide many guidelines for the parties and the arbitrators. It merely states that evidence needs to be presented during the hearing and that the other party must be given the opportunity to comment on the evidence submitted by the other party, the arbitral tribunal or an appraiser. Thus, in theory, art. 45 gives large flexibility to the arbitral tribunal and the parties as concerns the handling of evidence.

2. Cross-examination. At the hearing, each party may examine and challenge the evidence of its opponent. However, cross-examination of witnesses rarely occurs in China. Rather it is more common for the arbitral tribunal to directly question witnesses either of its own initiative or at the request of one of the disputing parties. Cross-examination of third party experts may only be undertaken with the consent of the arbitral tribunal.

[Preservation of evidence]

Article 46

Under circumstances where the evidence may be destroyed or lost or difficult to obtain at a later time, a party may apply for preservation of the evidence. If a party applies for preservation of the evidence, the arbitration commission shall submit his application to the Basic People's Court in the place where the evidence is located.

1. No jurisdiction of the arbitral tribunal for evidence preservation. If circumstances exist that may result in the destruction or loss of evidence or if evidence may be difficult to collect at a later date, then a party relying on such evidence may apply to the arbitral tribunal for a preservation order. In turn, the arbitral tribunal will, via the arbitration commission, submit the application for determination to the Basic People's Court at the place where the evidence is located. As for the preservation of property (see art. 28, note 1 et seq.), neither the arbitral tribunal, nor the arbitration commission may directly issue such an order.

2. No preservation of evidence before the arbitration proceedings. Because of the requirement to pass through the arbitration commission to apply for preservation of evidence, such an application may only be filed once an arbitration commission has been entrusted with the case, i.e. once an application for arbitration has been filed. A contrario, this means that if there is no arbitration commission, the parties may not file any application for preservation of evidence. The only exception applies under Chapter V of the Maritime Procedure Law, according to which the evidence preservation in a maritime arbitration can be sought prior to the commencement of arbitration proceedings by submitting the application directly to the maritime court at the place where the evidence to be preserved is situated.

[Right to debate]

Article 47

The parties shall have the right to debate in the course of arbitration. At the end of the debate, the presiding arbitrator or the sole arbitrator shall solicit final opinions from the parties.

1. Right to debate. Following presentation of the evidence and completion of questioning, the disputing parties are entitled to debate the arguments put forward during the arbitral procedure and to submit closing statements.

[Compulsory recording of hearings in domestic arbitration proceedings]

Article 48

(1) The arbitral tribunal shall make records of the hearings in writing. The parties and other participants in the arbitration shall have the right to apply for supplementation or correction of the record of their own statements if they consider that such record contains omissions or errors. If no supplementation or corrections are to be made, their application therefore shall be recorded.

(2) The record shall be signed or sealed by the arbitrators, the recording person, the parties and other participants in the arbitration.

1. Compulsory recording. Art. 48 only applies to domestic arbitration and sets forth an obligation for any domestic arbitral tribunal to retain a written record of the hearing. The situation is different in international arbitration, where the arbitration commission may dispense with this requirement upon the arbitral tribunal (see art. 69, note 1).

2. Signature of the final records. The final records shall be signed by all intervening parties in the arbitration, including witnesses and experts as concerns their statements. If one party disagrees with the content of the record, it may file an application for correction or supplementation. Although the request may be denied, the request itself will remain with the records of the proceedings.

[Mediation, conciliation, and consent awards]

Article 49

After an application for arbitration has been made, the parties may settle their dispute on their own. If the parties have reached a settlement agreement, they may request the arbitral tribunal to make an arbitral award in accordance with the settlement agreement. Alternatively, they may withdraw their application for arbitration.

1. Conciliation during the arbitration proceedings. Arts. 49 to 52 provide for the possibility of conciliation during the arbitration proceedings, and do not refer to conciliation which may take place before the arbitration proceedings. In fact, the Arbitration Law permits and actively encourages the practice of conciliation and/or mediation during arbitration proceedings.

2. Conciliation settlement. Art. 49 provides that, following an application for arbitration, the parties may, of their own initiative, reach a conciliation settlement agreement. If successful, the parties may request the arbitral tribunal to render an award in accordance with the terms of the conciliation settlement, or require the withdrawal of the case (see art. 51, note 1 et seq.).

[Repudiation of a conciliation settlement after the dismissal of the case]

Article 50

If a party repudiates the settlement agreement after the application for arbitration has been withdrawn, he may apply for arbitration again in accordance with the arbitration agreement.

1. Dismissal of the Case. Art. 50 refers to the case in which the parties reach a settlement and request the arbitration commission to dismiss the arbitration case without rendering an award endorsing the settlement agreement.

2. Re-Arbitration. Art. 50 provides that, in case the terms of the settlement are not met after the Secretary-General of the arbitral commission has granted a dismissal, the parties may re-apply for arbitration according to the original arbitration agreement.

[Conciliation procedure and result]

Article 51

(1) The arbitral tribunal may carry out conciliation prior to giving an arbitral award. The arbitral tribunal shall conduct conciliation if both parties voluntarily seek conciliation. If conciliation is unsuccessful, an arbitral award shall be made promptly.

(2) If conciliation leads to a settlement agreement, the arbitral tribunal shall make a written conciliation statement or make an arbitral award in accordance with the result of the settlement agreement. A written conciliation statement and an arbitral award shall have equal legal effect.

1. Conciliation on the initiative of the arbitral tribunal. Whereas art. 49 (see art. 49, note 1) provides that the parties may settle the dispute on their own, they can also do so with the support of the arbitral tribunal. Indeed, art. 51 enables the arbitral tribunal, upon the prior consent of the disputing parties, to initiate conciliation proceedings prior to rendering an arbitral award. In such case, it is the arbitral tribunal itself that will conduct the conciliation process. Indeed, the arbitral tribunal can carry out conciliation at any time prior to the rendering of an arbitral award if so requested or agreed upon by the disputing parties. In undertaking such conciliation, the arbitral tribunal may adopt whatever means it considers appropriate, but may only conciliate a dispute in respect of which that arbitral tribunal was specifically formed.

2. Suspension of arbitration proceedings. Once both parties have agreed to conciliation, the presiding arbitrator must announce the suspension of arbitration proceedings and all formal record keeping related to arbitration must cease. However, the conciliation process may be terminated and arbitration proceedings recommenced at the request of a party or alternatively where the arbitral tribunal considers that it is impossible for the parties to reach a settlement agreement through the conciliation process.

3. Unsuccessful conciliation. According to art. 51(1), if the conciliation efforts are unsuccessful, the arbitration proceedings will be resumed and the arbitral tribunal will decide on the dispute by rendering an arbitral award.

4. Successful conciliation: conciliation statement or consent award. If the conciliation proceedings are successful, the parties will agree to a conciliation settlement. The arbitral tribunal may then decide whether to incorporate this settlement into a written 'conciliation statement' or an 'arbitral award' (so-called 'Consent Award'). A conciliation statement has the same legal effect as an arbitral award. However, this is only valid as far as the conciliation statement was rendered after the commencement of the arbitration proceedings and either involved the arbitral tribunal or was later endorsed by the arbitral tribunal at the parties' request (see in this respect art. 40 of the CIETAC Rules). A conciliation statement of a conciliation institution rendered prior to the commencement of arbitration proceedings or independently thereof does not have the same legal effect as an arbitral award, and does not fall within the remit of the New York Convention.

5. Enforcement particularity. According to art. 28 of the SPC Judicial Interpretations of 8 September 2006, where a party applies for non-enforcement of an arbitral award which has been rendered on the basis of the settlement agreement between the parties, the People's Court will not support such application.

[Content and binding effect of a conciliation statement]

Article 52

(1) A written conciliation statement shall specify the arbitration claim and the results of the settlement agreed upon between the parties. The written conciliation statement shall be signed by the arbitrators, sealed by the arbitration commission and then served on both parties.

(2) The written conciliation statement shall become legally effective immediately after both parties have signed for receipt thereof.

(3) If the written conciliation statement is repudiated by a party before he signs for receipt thereof, the arbitral tribunal shall promptly make an arbitral award.

1. Content of the conciliation statement. A conciliation statement must recite the arbitration claim and counter-claim of the parties and the terms of agreement reached by the parties.

2. Binding effect of the conciliation statement. The disputing parties and the arbitrators must each execute the conciliation statement, which is then stamped by the arbitration commission, and served upon all parties. The conciliation statement takes legal effect once signed by the parties. A conciliation statement signed by the parties and the arbitral tribunal and stamped by the arbitration commission has the same legal effect as an award.

3. Repudiation of the conciliation settlement. If a party repudiates the conciliation settlement prior to the execution of the conciliation statement, the arbitral tribunal will resume the arbitration proceedings and render an arbitral award.

[Decision making]

Article 53

The arbitral award shall be made in accordance with the opinion of the majority of the arbitrators. The opinion of the minority of the arbitrators may be entered in the record. If the arbitral tribunal is unable to form a majority opinion, the arbitral award shall be made in accordance with the opinion of the presiding arbitrator.

1. Majority vote. An arbitral award must be rendered on the basis of a majority decision of the arbitral tribunal. If, however, a majority consensus cannot be reached, the vote of the presiding arbitrator shall be determinant.

2. Dissenting opinion. A dissenting opinion of an arbitrator may be included in the record, but does not form part of the award. This means that the parties will not have access to the Dissenting Opinion, which will only be submitted to the arbitration commission.

[Content and form of the arbitral award]

Article 54

An arbitral award shall specify the arbitration claim, the facts of the dispute, the reasons for the decision, the results of the award, the allocation of arbitration fees and the date of the award. If the parties agree that they do not wish the facts of the dispute and the reasons for the decision to be specified in the arbitral award, the same may be omitted.

The arbitral award shall be signed by the arbitrators and sealed by the arbitration commission. An arbitrator with dissenting opinions as to the arbitral award may sign the award or choose not to sign it.

1. Content of the award. In principle, the arbitral award should record the arbitration claim (and counter-claim if applicable), the relevant facts, the reasoning of the arbitral tribunal and the result of the award, including the allocation of interests and arbitration fees. The date on which and the place at which the arbitral award is made should also be mentioned, since these elements will be crucial in further enforcement and/or cancellation procedures. Art. 54 is in accordance with international practice. Nevertheless, the facts of the dispute and the reasoning of the arbitral tribunal may be omitted if the parties have so agreed in advance, or if the award is made in accordance with an agreement reached through amicable settlement by the parties (see art. 52, note 1).

2. Signature of the award by the arbitrators and the arbitration commission. For the arbitral award to become effective, it has to be signed by the majority of the arbitrators and stamped by the arbitration commission.

[Partial award]

Article 55

In arbitration proceedings, if a part of the facts involved has already become clear, the arbitral tribunal may first make an award in respect of such part of the facts.

1. Definitions. According to international practice, arbitral awards are categorised into three types, i.e. (i) interim awards, (ii) partial awards, and (iii) final awards. Whereas a final award puts an end to the entire dispute by deciding on all remaining legal and factual questions, interim and partial awards only address part of the case. In a 'partial award' the arbitral tribunal decides on a quantitative part of the dispute, for example on claims based on contract and not on claims based on tort. In an 'interim award' the arbitral tribunal decides on a qualitative part of the dispute, meaning that the arbitral tribunal does not decide on specific claims, but deals with preliminary material or procedural questions, such as the question of the validity of the main contract. Although art. 55 expressly refers to 'partial awards', i.e. awards in which the arbitral tribunal puts an end to a quantitative part of the dispute, the term 'partial award' also covers 'interim awards' (see art. 44 CIETAC Rules).

2. Partial award. Art. 55 expressly refers to partial awards only, i.e. awards that address a quantitative part of the dispute ('part of the facts'), and does not address the question of interim awards. In practice however, it is widely recognised that arbitral tribunals also have the competence to render interim awards.

[Correction and supplementation of the arbitral award]

Article 56

If there are literal or calculation errors in the arbitral award, or if the matters which have been decided by the arbitral tribunal are omitted in the arbitral award, the arbitral tribunal shall make due corrections on supplementation. The parties may, within 30 days from the date of receipt of the award, request the arbitral tribunal to make such corrections or supplementation.

1. Correction and supplementation. In accordance with international practice, art. 56 allows and obliges the arbitral tribunal to correct the award, where such award contains typographical or calculation errors, or to supplement it, where relevant matters were omitted in the arbitral award.

2. On the Parties' Request. The parties may, within 30 days from the date of receipt of the award, request the arbitral tribunal to make such corrections or issue a supplementary award. In the event that the arbitral tribunal agrees with the submission, the arbitral tribunal must make a written correction to the award, or issue a supplemental award, as the case may be.

3. On the Arbitral Tribunal's Own Initiative. The arbitral tribunal itself shall, on its own initiative: (i) make written corrections of any errors that it discovers in the award, and (ii) issue a supplemental award in respect of any claim or counter-claim discovered to have been unaddressed in the original award. Any such written corrections and any supplemental awards will constitute an integral part of the arbitral award.

[Binding legal effect of the arbitral award]

Article 57

The arbitral award shall be legally effective as of the date on which it is made.

1. Legally effective. From the moment it is made, an arbitral award becomes legally effective. This means that it produces all legal effects attached to it by law, i.e. that it is final and binding upon the parties, enforceable under the applicable rules, etc.

2. Date of rendering of the award. In China, an arbitral award is considered 'made' on the date which appears in the award or next to the arbitrators' signature (see art. 54, note 2).

CHAPTER V. APPLICATION FOR SETTING ASIDE ARBITRAL AWARD

[Grounds for setting aside a domestic award]

Article 58

(1) A party may apply for setting aside an arbitral award to the Intermediate People's Court in the place where the arbitration commission is located, if he can produce evidence which proves that the arbitral award involves one of the following circumstances:
  (i) There is no arbitration agreement;
  (ii) The matters decided in the award exceed the scope of the arbitration agreement or are beyond the arbitral authority of the arbitration commission;
  (iii) The formation of the arbitral tribunal or the arbitration procedure was not in conformity with the legal procedure;
  (iv) The evidence on which the award is based is forged;
  (v) The other party has withheld the evidence which is sufficient to affect the impartiality of the arbitration; or
  (vi) An arbitrator has committed embezzlement, accepted bribes or engaged in malpractice for personal benefit or perverted the law in the arbitration of the case.

(2) The People's Court shall rule to set aside the arbitral award if a collegial panel formed by the People's Court verifies upon examination that the award involves one of the circumstances set forth in the preceding paragraph.

(3) If the People's Court determines that the arbitral award violates the social and public interest, it shall rule to set aside the award.

1. Scope of application. Art. 58 sets forth the conditions under which a domestic arbitral award may be cancelled. This article exclusively applies to domestic arbitration, whereas the cancellation of a foreign-related award is subject to art. 70 (see note 1 et seq.).

2. Grounds for cancellation. Art. 58 exhaustively enumerates a list of circumstances under which a party is entitled to request the setting aside of the arbitral award. There are seven grounds, concerning both procedural as well as substantive matters, which may justify the cancellation of the award: (i) the lack of an arbitration agreement, whereby an invalid arbitration clause is considered as non-existent; (ii) the matters determined in the award exceed the scope of the arbitration agreement or are beyond the arbitral authority of the arbitration commission (in this case, only the part of the award exceeding the scope of arbitration will be cancelled, unless it is inseparable from the other matters, in which case the whole award will be cancelled); (iii) the formation of the arbitral tribunal or the arbitration procedures was in violation of the procedural rules, i.e. of the Arbitration

Law, the Civil Procedure Law or the applicable arbitration rules; (iv) the evidence on which the arbitral award is based was forged; (v) the other party has withheld evidence sufficient to affect the impartiality of the arbitration; (vi) while arbitrating the case, the arbitrator has committed embezzlement, accepted bribes, resorted to deception for personal gain or rendered an award that perverts the law (in this case an arbitrator may even face legal liability, see art. 38, note 2); and (vii) the award proves to be contrary to social and public interest.

3. Difference with foreign-related arbitral awards. The grounds listed under art. 58 are much wider than the grounds admitted for cancellation of a foreign-related arbitral award (see art. 70, note 3). Only the grounds listed under art. 58(1)(i), (ii), (iii) and the ground relating to the violation of public interest are also valid grounds for cancellation of foreign-related arbitral awards. As for art. 58(1)(iv) and (v), these grounds relate to the evidence submitted and actually allow the court to review the merits of the case, while art. 58(1)(vi) is meant to sanction the improper behaviour of the arbitrators. These last three grounds may only be taken into consideration when deciding on the cancellation of domestic awards.

4. Competent court. The competent court to decide on an application for cancellation of a domestic arbitral award is the Intermediate People's Court in the place where the arbitration commission is located. Contrary to the cancellation procedure for foreign-related awards (see art. 70, note 5 et seq.), the Intermediate People's Court will decide autonomously on the cancellation of the domestic award, without needing to further consult with a higher courts.

5. Collegiate bench. The competent Intermediate People's Court will decide on the cancellation in a collegial panel of three judges and will interrogate the parties before rendering its decision (see art. 24 of the SPC Judicial Interpretations of 8 September 2006).

[Period of limitation]

Article 59

A party that wishes to apply for setting aside the arbitral award shall submit such application within six months from the date of receipt of the award.

1. Time limit. Any request for cancellation of an arbitral award based on any of the grounds mentioned in art. 58 has to be filed within six months from the date of receipt by the requesting party of the award.

2. Foreign-related arbitration. The six-month time limit provided for in art. 59 is also applicable to the cancellation of foreign-related arbitral awards.

This time frame can seem very short, if one considers the need to collect, translate and authenticate evidence.

3. Preclusion of the right to ask for cancellation of the award. It should be remembered that if a party bases its request for cancellation of the award on the lack of a valid arbitration agreement, but has failed to raise an appropriate objection during the arbitration proceedings, i.e. before the first hearing, the People's Court hearing such request for cancellation should not accept the case (see art. 20, note 3).

[Time frame for deciding on the request for cancellation]
Article 60

The People's Court shall, within two months from the date of accepting an application for setting aside an arbitral award, rule to set aside the award or to reject the application.

1. Two months. The People's Court seized with a request for cancellation of the arbitral award has to render a decision within two months from the date of accepting the application.

2. Result. If the People's Court admits the existence of grounds for cancellation, it will render a decision cancelling the award. The award loses any legal binding effect. If the People's Court rejects the request for cancellation, the award will keep its binding effect. If a party refuses to comply with it, the other may file a request for enforcement (see art. 62 et seq., note 1 et seq.).

[Re-arbitration as an alternative to cancellation]
Article 61

If, after accepting an application for setting aside an arbitral award, the People's Court considers that the case may be re-arbitrated by the arbitral tribunal, it shall notify the tribunal that it shall re-arbitrate the case within a certain time limit and shall rule to stay the setting-aside procedure. If the arbitral tribunal refuses to re-arbitrate the case, the People's Court shall rule to resume the setting-aside procedure.

1. Re-arbitration instead of cancellation. As provided for by art. 9 (see note 4), if an award is cancelled, the cancellation does not only concern the award itself, but also the arbitration agreement. As a consequence thereof, if an award is cancelled, the parties may only refer their dispute to the courts. However, art. 61 provides that before cancelling an award, the People's Court may advise the arbitral tribunal to re-arbitrate the case. This provision is only applicable to domestic arbitration. Re-arbitration is, in particular, encouraged when a domestic award is cancelled because the evidence on which it is based is forged (art. 58(1)(iv)), or when a party has concealed substantial evidence (art. 58(1)(v)) (see art. 21 of the SPC Judicial Interpretations of 8 September 2006).

2. Successful re-arbitration. If the arbitral tribunal accepts to re-arbitrate the case, it will render a new award. The new award will replace the first award, the first award losing any legal effect.

3. Refusal to re-arbitrate. According to art. 61 in fine, the arbitral tribunal may refuse to re-arbitrate. If so, the People's Court will resume the cancellation procedure and will eventually cancel the award. The parties will then have no other choice than to refer their dispute to the People's Court. The parties themselves cannot directly oppose the Court's decision or the arbitral tribunal's acceptance to re-arbitrate. They will, however, be allowed to apply for the cancellation of the new award according to art. 58 (see art. 23 of the SPC Judicial Interpretations of 8 September 2006).

CHAPTER VI. ENFORCEMENT

[Right to enforce the award]

Article 62

The parties shall perform the arbitral award. If a party fails to perform the arbitral award, the other party may apply to the People's Court for enforcement in accordance with the relevant provisions of the Civil Procedure Law. The People's Court to which the application has been made shall enforce the award.

1. General. Art. 62 establishes the basic principle for both domestic and foreign-related arbitration, which provides that if a party refuses to comply with an arbitral award, the other party may require the court to enforce said award. This reflects the legislation and prevailing practices of most of other countries: firstly, the parties are generally obliged to perform the binding arbitral award; secondly, the parties enjoy the right to seek enforcement by the courts. Courts enforce arbitral awards on the basis of an application submitted by a party rather than ex officio.

2. Application of the Civil Procedural Law. The procedures and measures for the enforcement of an award mirror those that apply to the enforcement of civil judgments, and art. 62 actually expressly refers to relevant provisions of the Civil Procedural Law. The Enforcement Regulations issued by the SPC in 1998 should also be considered.

3. Time limit. Art. 215 of the Civil Procedure Law sets forth a unified time limit for the initiation of enforcement proceedings regardless of the nature of the award for which enforcement is sought. The Civil Procedure Law of

2007 provides that the time limit for the submission of an application for enforcement shall be two years. The time runs from the final date upon which, pursuant to the award, the losing party is obliged to comply with its terms.

4. Competent court. Finally, the parties must apply to the competent court for enforcement. Requests for enforcement of a foreign-related award shall be addressed to the Intermediate People's Court of the place where the party subjected to enforcement has his domicile or where his property is located (see art. 257 of the Civil Procedure Law). As concerns the enforcement of a domestic award, there was, until recently, no unified provision in either the Arbitration Law or the Civil Procedure Law regarding the level of the competent courts. Rather, the competent court was determined based on the regulations of the relevant Higher People's Court, which is entitled to make proposals on the jurisdiction. Jurisdiction concerning the enforcement of domestic awards lay – depending where – with either the Intermediate People's Courts or the Basic People's Courts. For example, both the Shanghai and Beijing Higher People's Courts have respectively authorised the Basic People's Court in each city respectively to exercise such jurisdiction (see the Circular of the Beijing Higher People's Court of 10 March 2000 and the Opinions of the Shanghai Higher Peoples' Court of 1 February 2001). However, art. 29 of the SPC Judicial Interpretations of 8 September 2006 finally provides for a unified legal basis, setting forth that where a party applies for the enforcement of the arbitral award, the Intermediate People's Court at the domicile of the defendant to the enforcement or at the place where the property to be enforced is located shall have jurisdiction.

[Grounds for non-enforcement]

Article 63

If the party against whom the enforcement is sought presents evidence which proves that the arbitral award involves one of the circumstances set forth in the second paragraph of Article 217 [new art. 213] of the Civil Procedure Law, the People's Court shall, after examination and verification by a collegial panel formed by the People's Court, rule to disallow the award.

1. General. Whereas art. 62 sets forth the principle that an award has to be executed by the parties, otherwise it may be enforced by the courts, art. 63, in relation with art. 213 of the Civil Procedure Law, provides for a series of exceptions to that principle, i.e. circumstances in which a People's Court will refuse to enforce an arbitral award.

2. Application only to domestic awards. Arts. 63 and 213 of the Civil Procedural Law exclusively apply to the enforcement of domestic arbitral awards, and not to foreign-related awards, which are subject to art. 70 (see art. 70, note 1 et seq.).

3. Grounds for non-enforcement. Art. 213 Civil Procedure Law empowers the competent People's Court to rule to refuse enforcement of a domestic award when one of the following circumstances are involved: (i) the lack of an arbitration agreement, whereby an invalid or challenged arbitration clause is assimilated to a non-existent one; (ii) the matters decided in the award exceed the scope of the arbitration agreement or are beyond the remit of the arbitration commissions authority (in this case, only the part of the award exceeding the scope of arbitration will be cancelled, unless it is inseparable from the other matters, in which case the whole award will be cancelled); (iii) the formation of the arbitral tribunal or the arbitration procedures were in violation of the procedural rules, i.e. of the Arbitration Law and/or the applicable arbitration rules; (iv) the main evidence for ascertaining the facts was insufficient; (v) the application of the law was incorrect; vi) while arbitrating the case, one or several arbitrators committed embezzlement, accepted bribes, practised favouritism or perverted the law.

4. Comparison with Grounds for Setting Aside the Award. The grounds for the setting aside of a domestic arbitral award under art. 58 (see art. 58, note 2) are similar to those pertaining to the denial of enforcement set forth in art. 213 of the Civil Procedure Law. In addition to the grounds set forth in art. 213(i), (ii), (iii) and (vi), art. 58 also directs that a domestic arbitral award will be set aside where the evidence on which the award is based was forged; or where the other party withheld evidence of sufficient importance so as to affect the impartiality of the arbitration. The grounds set forth in art. 213(iv) and (v) relate directly to the substantive grounds or the merits of the award, and may only justify the non-enforcement of the award, not its cancellation.

[Priority of the cancellation procedure over an enforcement procedure]

Article 64

(1) If one party applies for enforcement of the arbitral award and the other party applies for setting aside the arbitral award, the People's Court shall rule to suspend the procedure of enforcement.

(2) If the People's Court rules to set aside the arbitral award, it shall rule to terminate the enforcement procedure. If the People's Court rules to reject the application for setting aside the arbitral award, it shall rule to resume the enforcement procedure.

1. Priority of the cancellation procedure. Under art. 64, an application to set aside an arbitral award will result in the suspension of any enforcement proceedings pertaining to the award. If the People's Court rules to set aside the award, then the court hearing the application for enforcement is obliged to terminate the enforcement procedure. If the application for setting aside is rejected, the enforcement procedure will then resume.

2. Major system deficiency. Whilst it is the Intermediate People's Court situated in the jurisdiction of the arbitration commission that handles applications for the setting aside of an arbitral award (see art. 58, note 4), applications for enforcement are determined by different courts (see art. 62, note 4). In consequence, an award that may have been affirmed by the Intermediate People's Court in the jurisdiction where the arbitration commission is located, might subsequently be denied enforcement by the court situated in the jurisdiction where the non-compliant party is domiciled or where his property and/or assets are located. This anomaly is undoubtedly a major deficiency of the present judicial system.

3. New guidelines from the SPC. In order to clarify the situation and avoid conflicts between the courts handling requests for cancellation and courts handling requests for (non-)enforcement, the SPC has issued a series of guidelines. In art. 26 of the SPC Judicial Interpretations of 8 September 2006, the SPC has established the following principle: Where, after a party's application to the People's Court for the cancellation of an arbitral award has been rejected, that party raises a plea of the non-enforcement on the basis of the same cause, the People's Court shall not support such a plea. This principle should facilitate the enforcement of awards, which have been subject of a cancellation procedure and whose validity was confirmed by the court.

CHAPTER VII. SPECIAL PROVISIONS FOR ARBITRATION INVOLVING FOREIGN ELEMENTS

[Special provisions for foreign-related arbitration]

Article 65

The provisions of this Chapter shall apply to the arbitration of disputes arising from economic, trade, transportation and maritime activities involving a foreign element. For matters not covered in this Chapter, the other relevant provisions of this Law shall apply.

1. Introductory remarks. Arts. 65 to 73 only apply to 'arbitration involving foreign elements', i.e. to so called foreign-related arbitrations. For matters not covered by arts. 65 to 73, the other relevant provisions of the Arbitration Law apply.

2. Foreign-related arbitration. An arbitration is considered 'foreign-related' if one of the following circumstances is met: (i) where either or both parties are of foreign nationality or stateless, or a company or organisation is located in a foreign country; (ii) where the legal facts that establish, alter or terminate the civil legal relationship between the parties occur in a foreign country; or (iii) where the subject matter in dispute is situated in a foreign country.

[Organisation of foreign-related arbitration commissions]
Article 66
(1) Foreign-related arbitration commissions may be organised and established by the China Chamber of International Commerce.
(2) A foreign-related arbitration commission shall be composed of one chairman, a certain number of vice chairmen and members.
(3) The chairman, vice chairmen and members of a foreign-related arbitration commission may be appointed by the China Chamber of International Commerce.

1. Supervising authority. Originally, arbitration commissions which were allowed to handle foreign-related cases were established under the auspices of the China Council for the Promotion of International Trade ('CCPIT'), a governmental body operating under the writ of the then Ministry of Foreign Trade. However, gradually, its legal status was transformed from a government institution into a non-governmental organisation aimed at promoting international trade and foreign economic co-operation. Commencing in 1988, CCPIT began to simultaneously use the name 'China Chamber of International Commerce' or its abbreviation 'CCOIC'. In that regard, it generally functions as a chamber of commerce in the same way as its counterparts overseas. In accordance with art. 66, the CCOIC is in charge of organising and establishing foreign-related arbitration commissions (i.e. mainly CIETAC and CMAC) and for the formulation of arbitration rules for such foreign-related arbitration commissions (see art. 73, note 1).

2. Structure of the arbitration commissions. Each foreign-related arbitration commission shall be composed of one chairman, a certain number of vice chairmen and members. The chairman, vice chairmen and members shall be appointed by the CCOIC.

3. Lack of independence of the arbitration commissions. There exists a close relationship between CCOIC and CIETAC/CMAC, and one can say that CIETAC/CMAC are controlled by CCPIT. In trying to keep with international practice and in an effort to publicly promote its relationship with the CCOIC, CIETAC formally adopted on 1 October 2000 the name 'Court of Arbitration of China Chamber of International Commerce' ('CCOIC Court of Arbitration').

[Panel of arbitrators]
Article 67
A foreign-related arbitration commission may appoint arbitrators from among foreign nationals with special knowledge in the fields of law, economy and trade, science and technology, etc.

1. Panel of foreign arbitrators. Art. 67 provides that a foreign-related arbitration commission (i.e. CIETAC and CMAC) may select and appoint to their international panel of arbitrators foreign nationals possessing specialised knowledge of law, economics, trade, science and technology. Domestic arbitration commissions are now also allowed to conduct foreign-related arbitrations, provided that the disputing parties thereto voluntarily agree to submit the case to it for arbitration (see Notice of the General Office of the State Council of 8 June 1996). Thus, domestic arbitration commissions may now also draw from the same pool of international expertise when compiling their panels of arbitrators for foreign-related arbitration.

2. CIETAC panel of arbitrators. CIETAC international panel of arbitrators is presently comprised of some 1000 arbitrators, among whom approximately 270 arbitrators are foreign nationals drawn from over thirty countries and regions (see arts. 2(10) and 21, CIETAC Rules).

3. Lower requirements for foreign arbitrators. The Stipulations for the Appointment of Arbitrators provide for different requirements for the appointment of Chinese arbitrators and foreign arbitrators or arbitrators from Hong Kong or Macao. Those requirements are less restrictive than those applicable to Chinese arbitrators (compare with art. 13, note 3). For Hong Kong, Macao and foreign nationals, the Stipulations require that a prospective arbitrator: (i) has a keen interest in arbitration, and can uphold the principle of independence and impartiality in handling cases; (ii) has acquired professional knowledge of law, economy and trade, science and technology or maritime affairs, and has working experience; (iii) is willing to observe the arbitration rules of the arbitration commission, the Ethical Rules for Arbitrators and other relevant regulations; (iv) has a good grasp of English and some knowledge of Chinese. However, the terms can be lessened appropriately for certain well-known individuals in the field of international arbitration.

4. Nationality of the sole or presiding arbitrator. Under Chinese law, there is no particular requirement as to the nationality of the sole or presiding arbitrator. In order to guarantee a minimum level of independence and impartiality, it is always prudent to expressly provide in the arbitration agreement that the presiding or sole arbitrator should be of a different nationality than the parties involved.

[Preservation of evidence]

Article 68

If a party to a foreign-related arbitration applies for the preservation of evidence, the foreign-related arbitration commission shall submit his application to the Intermediate People's Court in the place where the evidence is located.

1. Reminder of art. 46. Art. 68 repeats the principle set forth in art. 46, according to which, only courts may order measures for evidence preservation (see art. 46, note 1). Here again, a request for evidence preservation will be addressed by the parties to the arbitral tribunal, who will in turn, via the arbitration commission, submit the application for determination to the competent court.

2. Competent court. Contrary to domestic arbitration, the competent court to rule on an application for evidence preservation is the Intermediate People's Court in the place where the evidence is located, and not the Basic People's Court (see art. 46, note 1).

[Records of hearings]
Article 69

A foreign-related arbitral tribunal may enter the details of the hearings in written records or make written minutes thereof. The written minutes may be signed or sealed by the parties and other participants in the arbitration.

1. Optional recording in writing of hearings. Whereas the recording in writing of the hearings is compulsory in domestic arbitration (see art. 48, note 1), the arbitration commission may relieve the arbitral tribunal from this obligation in a foreign-related arbitration.

[Procedure for setting aside a foreign-related award]
Article 70

If a party presents evidence which proves that a foreign-related arbitral award involves one of the circumstances set forth in the first paragraph of Article 260 [new art. 258] of the Civil Procedure Law, the People's Court shall, after examination and verification by a collegial panel formed by the People's Court, rule to set aside the award.

1. Art. 258 of the Civil Procedure Law. Pursuant to art. 70, where a party files a motion for the setting-aside of a foreign-related arbitral award and produces evidence to substantiate one of the circumstances set forth at art. 258 Civil Procedure Law, then the People's Court must form a collegiate bench to verify and confirm the facts. If so verified and confirmed, the People's Court is obliged to order the setting aside of the foreign-related arbitral award.

2. Competent court. As for requests for cancellation of domestic awards under art. 58 (see art. 58, note 4), the competent court is the Intermediary People's Court at the place where the arbitration commission is located.

3. Grounds for setting aside a foreign-related award. Unlike for domestic arbitral awards (see art. 58, note 2 et seq.), the Intermediate People's Courts may only review a limited number of procedural matters when deciding on an application for cancellation of a foreign-related arbitral award. In that regard, the court will set aside an arbitral award under following circumstances listed exhaustively in art. 258 of the Civil Procedure Law: (i) the lack of an arbitration agreement, whereby an invalid or challenged arbitration clause is considered non-existent; (ii) the party requesting cancellation of the award was not notified to appoint an arbitrator or to take part in the arbitration proceedings, or was unable to state his opinions due to reasons for which he is not responsible; (iii) the formation of the arbitral tribunal or the arbitration procedures were not in conformity with the applicable procedural rules, i.e. of the Arbitration Law and/or the applicable arbitration rules; (iv) the matters decided in the award exceed the scope of the arbitration agreement or are beyond the arbitration authority of the arbitration commission (in this case, only the part of the award exceeding the scope of arbitration will be cancelled, unless it is inseparable from the other matters, in which case the whole award will be cancelled). Furthermore, as in the case of domestic awards, the People's Court is obliged to cancel a foreign-related arbitral award ex officio if it concludes that the execution of the award would be contrary to the ordre public. Except as concerns the violation of the ordre public, the grounds for setting aside a foreign-related award are of procedural nature only, the court may not review the award based on material grounds. In *China Leasing* v *Shenzhen Zhongji*, the Shenzhen Intermediate People's Court rejected an argument that the compensation awarded was unreasonable, and confirmed that it was not empowered to review any substantive issues pertaining to the case.

4. Major challenges. Under the Chinese supervision mechanism, the possibility to apply for cancellation of an arbitral award can serve to hinder or delay the enforcement of awards, since an application to set aside an arbitral award will result in the suspension of any enforcement proceedings (see art. 64, note 1). Further, efficient implementation of the Arbitration Law depends on the correct understanding and the proper handling of cases by judicial personnel. In practice, however, the Intermediate People's Court has, in the past, erroneously set aside or denied enforcement of foreign-related arbitral awards, raising questions of the competency of China's judiciary to effectively implement the Arbitration Law and international conventions such as the New York Convention. To check these developments, the Supreme People's Court has implemented a system, the so-called 'Prior Reporting System', requiring that any judicial decision to set aside a foreign-related arbitral award be examined and confirmed by a higher court.

5. Prior reporting system – background. In August 1995, the SPC issued its Notice on Prior Reporting System of 28 August 1995, establishing the 'Prior Reporting System', a centralised report and review system covering all cases where an Intermediate People's Court refuses enforcement of a foreign-related arbitral award, or refuses recognition and enforcement of a foreign arbitral award. According to this Prior Reporting System, if the Intermediate People's Court determines that a foreign-related arbitral award ought not to be enforced, it must within 30 days from the date of acceptance of the relevant application, refer the matter to the Higher People's Court for a determination. Should the latter concur with the decision of the lower level court, it must, within 15 days from the date of receipt of the report from the Intermediate People's Court, submit an Approval Advice to the SPC and may not render any decision until the SPC has replied to the Approval Advice. In April 1998, the SPC issued a second SPC Notice on Prior Reporting System of 23 April 1998, further extending this Prior Reporting System to any decision of the Intermediate or Higher People's Courts to cancel a foreign-related arbitral award. This mechanism effectively serves to ensure that the enforcement of a foreign-related arbitral award, or the issuing of an order to an arbitration commission to re-arbitrate the dispute, may not occur without the prior examination and confirmation of the SPC.

6. Prior reporting system – scope of applicability. The Prior Reporting System, with respect to both enforcement and cancellation, does not apply to domestic arbitral awards. Furthermore, the prior reporting requirement only applies where the People's Court determines that enforcement of the foreign-related arbitral award or the recognition and/or enforcement of a foreign award should be denied, or where the court determines that a foreign-related arbitral award should be cancelled. There is no requirement to report decisions to enforce a foreign-related arbitral award, or decisions dismissing applications for the cancellation of a foreign-related arbitral award.

[Non-enforcement of foreign-related arbitral awards]

Article 71

If the party against whom the enforcement is sought presents evidence which proves that the foreign-related arbitral award involves one of the circumstances set forth in the first paragraph of Article 258 of the Civil Procedure Law, the People's Court shall, after examination and verification by a collegial panel formed by the People's Court, rule to disallow the enforcement.

1. Grounds for non-enforcement identical to grounds for cancellation of the award. Art. 71 provides that the People's Court must refuse the enforcement of a foreign-related award, where one of the circumstances listed in art. 258 Civil Procedure Law is given. The grounds for non-enforcement are thus identical to the grounds for cancellation of a foreign-related award (see art. 70, note 3).

2. Prior reporting system. The Prior Reporting System which has been described in relation to the cancellation of a foreign-related award applies mutatis mutandis to the non-enforcement of such award. In fact, the Prior Reporting System was first established to supervise the enforcement of the lower People's Courts of foreign-related awards and was only later on extended to decisions of lower courts to set aside a foreign-related award (see art. 70, note 5 et seq.).

3. Competent court. The court competent to decide over the enforcement of a foreign-related award is the Intermediate People's Court in the place where the person against whom the application is made has his domicile or where the property of the said person is located (art. 257 Civil Procedure Law).

[Lack of jurisdiction rationae loci of the People's Courts]

Article 72

If a party applies for enforcement of a legally effective arbitral award made by a foreign-related arbitration commission and if the party against whom the enforcement is sought or such party's property is not within the territory of the People's Republic of China, he shall directly apply to a competent foreign court for recognition and enforcement of the award.

1. Lack of jurisdiction of the Chinese courts. According to art. 257 of the Civil Procedure Law, requests for enforcement of a foreign-related award shall be addressed to the Intermediate People's Court of the place where the party subjected to enforcement has his domicile or where his property is located (see art. 62, note 4). Thus, if the party against which the award is to be enforced is not domiciled in China or does not have any property within Chinese territory, the People's Court will lack jurisdiction rationae loci to enforce the award.

[Competence of the CCOIC to formulate arbitration rules]

Article 73

Foreign-related arbitration rules may be formulated by the China Chamber of International Commerce in accordance with this Law and the relevant provisions of the Civil Procedure Law.

1. Reminder of art. 66. Art. 73 is similar to art. 66, which provides that the CCOIC is the authority in charge of organising and establishing the arbitration commissions. Under art. 73, CCOIC has additional authority to issue arbitration rules.

Arbitration Law of the PRC, art. 74

CHAPTER VII. SUPPLEMENTARY PROVISIONS

[Period of limitation]

Article 74

If prescription for arbitration is provided by law, such provisions shall apply. In the absence of such provisions, the prescription for litigation shall apply to arbitration.

1. General. Art. 74 provides that where an applicable law provides for a time frame within which arbitration of the dispute must be completed, then such requirements must be met. Where no such time constraints apply, the general litigation time limits will apply.

2. General period of limitation. Arts. 135-137 of the General Principles of the Civil Law provide that, except as otherwise stipulated by law, the time limitation for the initiation of a suit for the protection of a civil right is two years. However, a limitation period of one year will apply in certain cases, such as: (i) claims for compensation for bodily injuries; (ii) the sale of substandard goods without proper notice to that effect; (iii) delays in paying rent or refusal to pay rent; and (iv) loss of or damage to property left in the care of another person. There are further exceptions to the general rule of the two year prescription period provided for in specific laws, such as, for example, in art. 129 of the Contract Law, which imposes a four-year time limit for the filing of a lawsuit or the submission of an application for arbitration in relation to a dispute arising from an international contract for the sale of goods or a contract for the import and export of technology. The statutory time limitations are calculated from the date when the person knew or ought to have known of the infringement of his rights.

3. Absolute period of limitation. In any case, the People's Court will not protect the right to file suit if twenty years have passed since the alleged infringement.

[Formulation of arbitration rules by the China Arbitration Association]

Article 75

Pending the formulation of rules of arbitration by the China Arbitration Association, arbitration commissions may formulate provisional rules of arbitration in accordance with this Law and the relevant provisions of the Civil Procedure Law.

1. General. Pending the establishment of the CAA (see art. 15, note 2), the law specifically permits arbitration commissions to formulate their own interim rules for arbitration. Furthermore, in the absence of the CAA, the General Office of the State Council, issued on 28 July 1995 the model

Provisional Rules for Domestic Arbitration Commissions aimed at standardising the rules for domestic arbitration commissions.

[Arbitration fees]

Article 76

(1) Parties shall pay arbitration fees according to regulations.
(2) Measures for charging arbitration fees shall be submitted to the price control authorities for examination and approval.

1. Arbitration fees. According to art. 76, the parties have the obligation to pay arbitration fees. However, the amount of the fees is not provided in the Arbitration Law itself, but it is left open to the arbitration commission to determine.

2. Different fee rates for domestic arbitration and foreign-related arbitration. Arbitration commissions in China all have different fee rates for domestic and foreign-related arbitration. Domestic arbitration commissions have set their respective fee structures in accordance with the Notice on Measures Regarding Arbitration Fees issued by the General Office of the State Council. For foreign-related arbitration, there are no fixed fees. The arbitration commissions are in theory free to fix those fees, but due to the competition of other arbitration commissions and of domestic arbitration, the fees for foreign-related arbitration are similar to the fees for domestic arbitration.

3. Different types of fees. Arbitration commissions in China mainly apply two types of fees: (i) an acceptation or registration fee, and (ii) a handling fee. In addition to the collection of arbitration fees, the arbitration commissions may, according to the relevant arbitration rules, collect other additional actual expenses.

[No application of the Arbitration Law to labour and agricultural disputes]

Article 77

Regulations concerning arbitration of labour disputes and agricultural contractor's contract disputes arising within the agricultural collective economic organisations shall be formulated separately.

1. No application to labour and agricultural disputes. The Arbitration Law does not apply to labour disputes and disputes over contracts for the undertaking of agricultural projects within agricultural collective economic organisations. Thus, these disputes are in a certain way not arbitrable (see art. 3, note 2). However, this is only correct in the sense that such disputes are not arbitrable under the Arbitration Law, they may be subject to other special arbitration procedures. In that regard, art. 79 of the Labour Law provides that labour disputes must be submitted to a dedicated arbitration commission for the resolution of labour disputes and established by the government authorities responsible for labour issues. Moreover, the awards rendered by such arbitration commissions are eligible for appeal before a local People's Court. Disputes relating to the undertaking of agricultural projects within agricultural collective economic organisations are primarily resolved by the relevant local government departments or via litigation.

[Priority of the Arbitration Law on previous legislation]

Article 78

If regulations governing arbitration promulgated prior to the implementation of this Law contravene the provisions of this Law, the provisions of this Law shall prevail.

1. General. Art. 78 is a common transitional provision, according to which existing regulations of an inferior or equal level of the Arbitration Law, which are contrary to the Arbitration Law will not be applied anymore ('lex posterior derogat legi priori').

[Reorganisation of arbitration commissions]

Article 79

(1) Arbitration institutions established prior to the implementation of this Law in the municipalities directly under the Central Government, in the cities that are the seats of the people's governments of provinces or autonomous regions and in other cities divided into districts shall be reorganised in accordance with this Law. Arbitration institutions that have not been reorganised shall terminate upon the end of one year from the date of the implementation of this Law.

(2) Other arbitration institutions established prior to the implementation of this Law that do not comply with the provisions of this Law shall terminate on the date of the implementation of this Law.

1. Compulsory reorganisation. Art. 79 requires the reorganisation of all arbitration commissions existing before the enactment of the Arbitration Law in district cities and all cities in which municipal, provincial or autonomous regional governments are located. Art. 79 also provides for the automatic termination, within one year of the date of effectiveness of the Law, of any arbitration institution established prior to the Law's date of effectiveness, that subsequently fails to conform to the reorganisation requirements set forth in the Arbitration Law. This led to the automatic dissolution per 1 September 1996 of number of arbitration commissions established within administrative organs of local government, such as the SAIC, the State Construction

Commission, the State Science and Technology Commission, etc. Indeed these commissions no longer fulfilled the requirement of independence of art. 14 (see art. 14, note 1).

[Effectiveness of the law]
Article 80
This Law shall come into force as of 1 September 1995.

1. Effectiveness. Because of art. 79, which required a substantial reorganisation throughout the country, the Arbitration Law is one of few laws which took one year from the date of promulgation to its effectiveness, i.e. from 31 August 1994 to 1 September 1995.

ENGLISH ARBITRATION ACT 1996 (CHAPTER 23), 1996 – ARBITRATION LAW IN ENGLAND, WALES AND NORTHERN IRELAND

(In force as from 31 January 1997)

[Introduction]

Sources of arbitration law. The arbitration law of England, Wales and Northern Ireland can be found principally in the Arbitration Act 1996 (c. 23). The 1996 Act is not a comprehensive code and therefore some aspects of English arbitration law are still prescribed by the common law (i.e. decisions of the courts). In addition, it is necessary to look to case law for rulings on the interpretation and application of many provisions of the 1996 Act. The procedure for making arbitration claims to the court is set out in Civil Procedure Rules, Part 62, and Practice Direction 62. The 1996 and 1997 DAC Reports (see below) and several commentaries provide a very useful aid to the understanding of English arbitration law.

Territorial scope. The Arbitration Act 1996 applies in England, Wales and Northern Ireland (but not in Scotland, except for Sections 89 to 91: see the Arbitration (Scotland) Act 2010). However, as an abbreviation, this commentary refers to 'England' and 'English', unless otherwise stated, with apologies to those in Wales and Northern Ireland.

Applicable laws. When reading the 1996 Act, it is important to bear in mind that a number of different laws may apply or be relevant to any arbitration, including: (a) the governing (or proper) law of the underlying agreement; (b) the governing (or proper) law of the arbitration agreement; (c) the law of the domicile/nationality/incorporation of the parties; (d) the procedural (or curial or adjectival) law(s) of the arbitration; and (e) the laws in jurisdictions other than the seat of the arbitration which give certain powers to the courts in those jurisdictions to support foreign arbitrations (e.g. to order injunctive relief or to enforce an award). The Act is concerned principally with (d) – the procedural laws applicable to an arbitration taking place in England. The parties may agree different procedural rules (e.g. by submitting their dispute to the rules of an arbitral institution), with the exception of any mandatory provisions of the Act (see Section 4(1) and Schedule 1). The English courts have also indicated that, absent an express agreement by the parties to the contrary, where the seat or the arbitration is England, the governing law of the arbitration agreement (that is, (b) above) will probably be English law, even where the governing law of the underlying agreement (that is, (a) above) is not English law (see *C* v *D*). The Act also contains provisions aimed at supporting foreign arbitrations.

History of arbitration in England. The private resolution of disputes by experts familiar with the relevant industry, particularly in the construction, insurance, and maritime and commodity sectors, has long been favoured in England as an alternative to determination by the courts. In addition, the fact that London is one of the major centres of international commerce, together with the prevalence of English language contracts, the influence of English law, and the reputation of the English legal system and legal profession, means that many international agreements provide for arbitration in London. Accordingly, English arbitration law and its application are of major significance, both domestically and internationally. English legislation relating to arbitration dates back to the Arbitration Act 1698. Modern English arbitration law was created in the 19th century with the Civil Procedure Act 1833, the Common Law Procedure Act 1854 (c. 125) and the Arbitration Act 1889 (c. 49) (by which the courts were given powers to enforce arbitration agreements and to support the arbitral process). The earlier legislation was consolidated in the Arbitration Act 1950 (c. 27) and that remained the principal arbitration statute until the 1996 Act. There was, in addition: the Arbitration Act 1975 (c. 3), which gave effect to the 1958 New York Convention; the Arbitration (Internal Investments Disputes) Act 1966 (c. 41), which enacted the 1965 Washington Convention (i.e. the ICSID Convention); and the Arbitration Act 1979 (c. 42), which abolished the special case procedure and reduced the supervisory powers of the English courts over commercial arbitrations. The 1996 Act was intended to restate in clearer terms the previous legislation on arbitration, codify principles established by case law and generally to improve the law, particularly in order to increase the attractiveness and efficacy of arbitration as a method of dispute resolution and the attractiveness of London as a venue for international arbitration. The Act implemented most of the recommendations of the Departmental Advisory Committee (DAC) chaired by Lord Saville. It was intended to reflect as far as possible the format and language of the UNCITRAL Model Law, although the Act is significantly more detailed. The DAC published a detailed Report on the proposed new legislation in February 1996 (which included recommendations on the text of the Bill introduced in Parliament in December 1995 and supplementary recommendations based on the second reading of the Bill in the House of Lords and on comments made by domestic and international practitioners), and a Supplementary Report on the Arbitration Act 1996 (in January 1997). The DAC's Reports have often been referred to by courts when construing the Act's provisions. After public consultation and parliamentary debate, the 1996 Act was enacted on 17 June 1996 and came into force on 31 January 1997 (save for Sections 85 to 87): see Arbitration Act 1996 (Commencement No. 1) Order 1996 (S.I. 1996 No. 3146 (c. 96). A report of the parliamentary debates in the House of Commons and House of Lords concerning the Act can be found in *Hansard*.

Philosophy of the 1996 Act. The Act is intended to be a comprehensive statute (but not an exhaustive code) that – through its logical structure and non-technical language – will more easily enable the lay arbitrator or foreign lawyer to find out how an arbitration under English law should be conducted.

The Act is notable in particular for its statements of general principle, which is unusual in English legislation. Section 1 states that Part I of the Act is founded on certain general principles and shall be construed accordingly. Thus, the object of arbitration is explicitly stated to be 'to obtain the fair resolution of disputes by an impartial tribunal without unnecessary delay or expense'. In addition, party autonomy is acknowledged and direction is given to the courts not to interfere with the arbitral process unless absolutely necessary. Later in the Act, general duties of the tribunal and parties are set out (Sections 33 and 40, respectively). These are aimed at ensuring that arbitrations are conducted fairly, economically and expeditiously. One of the main purposes of the Act is to define clearly an arbitrator's powers in the common situations which might arise, such as a challenge to his jurisdiction. In addition to the statements of general principle, many sections of the Act reinforce the policy considerations that party autonomy and the supremacy of the arbitration agreement are paramount. In addition, the Act redefines the relationship between the courts and the arbitral process in favour of the arbitrator(s): the role of the court is limited to those occasions when it is obvious either that the arbitral process needs assistance or that there has been or is likely to be a clear denial of justice. There is no distinction made between domestic and international arbitration. Two notable aspects of arbitration law not addressed in the 1996 Act, but found in some other countries' legislation are: privacy and confidentiality; and joinder and consolidation.

Privacy and Confidentiality. Two basic tenets of English arbitration law that have not been addressed by the Act are those of privacy and confidentiality. These are often cited as two of the main advantages of arbitration over court proceedings. However, the DAC concluded that 'given [the] exceptions and qualifications, the formulation of any statutory principles would be likely to create new impediments to the practice of English arbitration and, in particular, to add to English litigation on the issue' (DAC Report, para. 17). The privacy and confidentiality of arbitration has been upheld in strong and unequivocal terms by the English courts (e.g. in *Ali Shipping Corporation* v *'Shipyard Trogir'*; *AEG Insurance Services Ltd* v *European Reinsurance Co. of Zurich*; *Michael Wilson & Partners Ltd* v *Emmott*). The courts have, however, recognised a limited number of exceptions, namely where there is: express or implied consent; an appropriate order or other leave granted by a court; a necessity to protect the legitimate interests of one party to the arbitration in subsequent legal proceedings; and, in the interests of justice. The CPR provides that the court has a discretion, but generally proceedings relating to arbitration should remain private, except for applications concerning a point of law (CPR Part 62, Rule 62.10). However, the courts have held that the presumption should be that any judgment should be made public, but redacted if necessary to protect sensitive information (*City of Moscow* v *Bankers Trust*).

Joinder and Consolidation. The Act provides that the parties may agree that two or more arbitral proceedings shall be consolidated or that concurrent hearings shall be held (Section 35). It is, of course, open for a third party to be joined as a party to an arbitration, if all parties agree. The DAC was not prepared to recommend that parties should be forced to arbitrate with others with whom they had not agreed to do so, particularly in light of the overriding principle of party autonomy (DAC Report, para. 180). This is a controversial and difficult area, but one which some commentators have suggested might have benefited from legislation giving a discretion to the courts to make appropriate orders.

European Convention on Human Rights. The English courts have confirmed that arbitration generally and the 1996 Act in particular satisfy art. 6 of the ECHR, so long as the agreement to arbitrate is freely entered into and due process is adhered to (see, e.g., *Stretford* v *Football Association*; *Sumukan* v *Commonwealth Secretariat*).

New start. The 1996 Act was intended to create a new arbitration regime in England and to encourage a supportive approach from the courts. It has succeeded in these aims. Since its enactment, the courts have often said that the Act marked a new start and they have regularly expressed a pro-arbitration attitude. See, for example, the discussion of the novel aspects of the Act by the House of Lords in *Lesotho Highlands Development Authority* v *Impregilo SpA* and the positive reception of the House of Lords' decision in *Fiona Trust* v *Privalov*, which concerned the separability and scope of the arbitration agreement.

PART I. ARBITRATION PURSUANT TO AN ARBITRATION AGREEMENT

INTRODUCTORY

[General principles]

Section 1

The provisions of this Part are founded on the following principles, and shall be construed accordingly –
- (a) **the object of arbitration is to obtain the fair resolution of disputes by an impartial tribunal without unnecessary delay or expense;**
- (b) **the parties should be free to agree how their disputes are resolved, subject only to such safeguards as are necessary in the public interest;**
- (c) **in matters governed by this Part the court should not intervene except as provided by this Part.**

1. General. Section 1 sets out the three fundamental principles underlying Part I of the Act (i.e. paras. 1-84). Part I is to be construed in accordance with these principles. Although it is non-mandatory (see Section 4(2)), it is unlikely that the English courts would accept that Section 1 can be affected by contrary agreement of the parties. A statement of general principles is unusual in English legislation and is to be welcomed. Parallels can be drawn between this provision and CPR Rule 1.1, which sets out the 'overriding objective enabling the court to deal with cases justly'. Section 1 and its three general principles have been referred to and approved in many cases. See DAC Report paras. 18-22.

2. The object of arbitration. Section 1(a) describes the object of arbitration by reference to principles of procedural fairness and efficiency. The DAC Report stated the Committee's intention was that 'all the provisions of the Bill must be read with this object of arbitration in mind' (para. 18). This objective is expanded upon later in the Act (see Sections 33 and 40, which provide further corresponding general duties of the tribunal and the parties). The requirement of impartiality is reinforced in Section 24(1)(a) of the Act (power of court to remove an arbitrator).

3. Party autonomy. Section 1(b) affirms the consensual nature of the arbitral process and the principle of party autonomy and reflects art. 19(1) of the Model Law. Absent overriding public interest concerns (as prescribed in the mandatory provisions of the Act, see Section 4(1), and principles of public policy), this has two consequences. First, parties are to be held to their agreements to arbitrate. Secondly, parties are given considerable freedom to customise their arbitration and to opt-in or opt-out of the non-mandatory provisions of the Act (see Section 4(2)); however, any agreement of the parties must be in writing (see Section 5). Agreeing the procedural rules of an arbitral institution or UNCITRAL constitutes such an agreement (and such rules also often recognise the principle of party autonomy, e.g. LCIA art. 14.1). Failure by a tribunal to conduct the proceedings in accordance with the procedure agreed by the parties is a ground for challenging any subsequent award (see Section 68(2)(c)).

4. Limitations on court intervention. Section 1(c) reflects art. 5 of the Model Law (although it uses permissive language) and by giving strong guidance to the courts it seeks to address the criticism that was often made that the English court intervened excessively in international arbitrations. (See also Section 44(5).) The English courts have respected this important principle. Section 1 applies only to Part I of the Act and therefore it does not apply in respect of consumer arbitrations under Sections 89 to 91 of the Act.

[Scope of application of provisions]

Section 2

(1) The provisions of this Part apply where the seat of the arbitration is in England and Wales or Northern Ireland.

(2) The following sections apply even if the seat of the arbitration is outside England and Wales or Northern Ireland or no seat has been designated or determined –
    (a) sections 9 to 11 (stay of legal proceedings, &c.), and
    (b) section 66 (enforcement of arbitral awards).

(3) The powers conferred by the following sections apply even if the seat of the arbitration is outside England and Wales or Northern Ireland or no seat has been designated or determined –
    (a) section 43 (securing the attendance of witnesses), and
    (b) section 44 (court powers exercisable in support of arbitral proceedings);
but the court may refuse to exercise any such power if, in the opinion of the court, the fact that the seat of the arbitration is outside England and Wales or Northern Ireland, or that when designated or determined the seat is likely to be outside England and Wales or Northern Ireland, makes it inappropriate to do so.

(4) The court may exercise a power conferred by any provision of this Part not mentioned in subsection (2) or (3) for the purpose of supporting the arbitral process where –
    (a) no seat of the arbitration has been designated or determined, and
    (b) by reason of a connection with England and Wales or Northern Ireland the court is satisfied that it is appropriate to do so.

(5) Section 7 (separability of arbitration agreement) and section 8 (death of a party) apply where the law applicable to the arbitration agreement is the law of England and Wales or Northern Ireland even if the seat of the arbitration is outside England and Wales or Northern Ireland or has not been designated or determined.

1. General. Section 2 sets out the scope of application of Part I of the Act. While it is not a mandatory provision (see Section 4(1)), the courts are unlikely to accept that its meaning and application can be affected by contrary agreement of the parties. It reflects art. 1(2) of the Model Law. See DAC Report paras. 23-25 and DAC Suppl. paras. 6-19.

2. Seat. Part I of the Act applies where the seat is in England and Wales or in Northern Ireland. Scotland is a separate jurisdiction for these purposes, with a different arbitration law (Arbitration (Scotland) Act 2010). Concerning the determination of the seat of the arbitration, see Section 3. The simplicity of Section 2(1) was intended to mask the complexity of the rules of conflict of laws as they apply to arbitration, upon which there was no consensus. Section 2(2) to (5) are exceptions to the basic rule in Section 2(1). It remains possible for the parties to choose a foreign law as the applicable law in respect of any matter which is not governed by a mandatory provision (Section 4(5)), although this is not recommended.

3. Application of Part I notwithstanding foreign or no designated seat. Under Section 2(2), certain provisions of Part I are stated to apply even if the seat of the arbitration is outside of England and Wales or Northern Ireland or where no seat has been designated. These relate to: (a) the stay of legal proceedings (Sections 9 to 11), because of the UK's obligations under the 1958 New York Convention to stay legal proceedings brought in contravention of a valid arbitration agreement, wherever that arbitration is to take place; and (b) the enforcement of arbitral awards (Section 66), which applies to all awards wherever made. (See *A* v *B*.)

4. Arbitral powers notwithstanding foreign or no designated seat. Under Section 2(3), the English court may exercise certain powers even if the seat of the arbitration is outside of England and Wales or Northern Ireland or where no seat has been designated. This provision is intended to overcome the common law position that the English court cannot exercise its powers in support of a foreign arbitration. The court's powers relate to securing the attendance of witnesses (Section 43) and the court's general powers in support of arbitral proceedings (Section 44), including the granting of freezing and search orders. However, as the proviso indicates, the court retains a broad discretion to refuse to exercise such powers where there is little or no connection with England (see *Commerce & Industry Insurance Co. of Canada* v *Lloyd's Underwriters*; and *Mobil Cerro Negro Ltd* v *Petroleos De Venezuela SA*).

5. Exercise of powers by a court. Under Section 2(4), the court may exercise any additional powers conferred by any provision in Part I where the seat of the arbitration has not yet been determined, but the court must be satisfied that the connection with England is sufficient to make it appropriate to do so.

6. Sections of the Act that have substantive effect. Under Section 2(5), the English courts are able to make orders in respect of Sections 7 (separability of arbitration agreement) and 8 (death of a party) where the governing law of the arbitration agreement is English law, notwithstanding that the seat of the arbitration is foreign or not yet determined.

[The seat of the arbitration]

Section 3

In this Part 'the seat of the arbitration' means the juridical seat of the arbitration designated –
  (a) by the parties to the arbitration agreement, or
  (b) by any arbitral or other institution or person vested by the parties with powers in that regard, or
  (c) by the arbitral tribunal if so authorised by the parties,
or determined, in the absence of any such designation, having regard to the parties' agreement and all the relevant circumstances.

1. General. Section 3 concerns the juridical seat of the arbitration. While it is not a mandatory provision (see Section 4(1)), the courts are unlikely to accept that its meaning and application can be affected by contrary agreement of the parties. It reflects art. 20(1) of the Model Law (which uses the phrase 'place of arbitration', but the two phrases have the same meaning). The concept of a seat or place of arbitration is not new to English law, having been developed by the courts. The seat is of considerable significance in determining the application of the Act, the powers of the court to review the award, and for enforcement purposes (see below). See DAC Report paras. 26 and 27.

2. Identified by seat or country. The seat of the arbitration is the legal jurisdiction in which the arbitration is said to be rooted. It must be a State or territory associated with a recognisable and distinct system of law. Accordingly, the seat could be England and Wales or Northern Ireland; but not the United Kingdom, because Scotland has a different arbitration regime: see *Braes of Doune Wind Farm (Scotland) Ltd* v *Alfred McAlpine*. (However, a reference to the laws of or the seat being the United Kingdom is often construed as a reference to England and Wales.) Parties often prescribe a particular city rather than State or territory, but a reference to, for example, London implies that the juridical seat is England and Wales.

3. Determining the seat. If the seat is not prescribed by the parties in writing (see Section 5(2)), it may be determined by any applicable arbitral institution with powers in that regard (e.g. see LCIA art. 16.1) or by the arbitral tribunal once constituted if so authorised by the parties. In the absence of any such designation, the court may have to determine the seat if an arbitration application is made by a party. The court (and also by implication any arbitral institution or tribunal) will have regard to the parties' agreement and all the relevant circumstances. The courts have held that the circumstances they will consider are limited to those which existed before the issue of proceedings (*Dubai Islamic Bank PJSC* v *Paymentech Merchant Services*). Relevant factors include the nationality of the parties, the location of performance of any obligations, the language of the agreement, the substantive governing law (if expressly chosen by the parties) and any reference to national courts (see *Sumitomo Heavy Industries* v *Oil and Natural Gas Commission*). Unlike certain other jurisdictions, the Act does not allow for the possibility under English law for an arbitration that has no seat (sometimes referred to as a 'floating' or 'delocalised' arbitration). Statutory arbitrations are deemed to have their seat in England and Wales or Northern Ireland (as appropriate) (see Section 95(2)).

4. Venue. Where the seat of the arbitration is England and Wales, hearings may take place anywhere (typically referred to as the 'venue' of the arbitration or 'place of hearings'), see Section 34(2)(a). This is often confirmed expressly in arbitral procedural rules (e.g. LCIA art. 16.2; UNCITRAL art. 16.2).

5. Legal consequences. The seat of the arbitration determines the curial or procedural law of the arbitration (see *ABB Lummus Global Ltd* v *Keppel Fels Ltd*). Accordingly, an arbitration with its seat in England is governed by the Act, and the parties may only opt out of its non-mandatory provisions (see Section 4(2)). The seat determines the scope of application of the Act (see Section 2), with most provisions in Part I only applying where the seat is in England and Wales or Northern Ireland. In addition, unless the parties agree otherwise, the seat is the place in which the arbitration award shall be deemed to have been made (see Sections 53). The seat is also significant in relation to the enforcement of awards under international conventions, e.g. 1958 New York Convention, art. I (and see Section 100(2)(b)). The choice or determination of England to be the seat of the arbitration may also mean that, absent an agreement by the parties to the contrary, the governing law of the agreement to arbitrate is English law (see *C* v *D*).

[Mandatory and non-mandatory provisions]

Section 4

(1) The mandatory provisions of this Part are listed in Schedule 1 and have effect notwithstanding any agreement to the contrary.

(2) The other provisions of this Part (the 'non-mandatory provisions') allow the parties to make their own arrangements by agreement but provide rules which apply in the absence of such agreement.

(3) The parties may make such arrangements by agreeing to the application of institutional rules or providing any other means by which a matter may be decided.

(4) It is immaterial whether or not the law applicable to the parties' agreement is the law of England and Wales or, as the case may be, Northern Ireland.

(5) The choice of a law other than the law of England and Wales or Northern Ireland as the applicable law in respect of a matter provided for by a non-mandatory provision of this Part is equivalent to an agreement making provision about that matter.

For this purpose an applicable law determined in accordance with the parties' agreement, or which is objectively determined in the absence of any express or implied choice, shall be treated as chosen by the parties.

1. General. Section 4 explains that some provisions of the Act are mandatory (Section 4(1)), whilst others are not (Section 4(2)). Although it is not stated to be mandatory itself, it is unlikely that the English courts would accept that Section 4 can be affected by contrary agreement of the parties. It is not based on any previous provision in English law or the Model Law. See DAC Report paras. 28 to 30.

2. Mandatory provisions. Section 4(1) provides that those provisions listed in Schedule 1 of the Act cannot be overridden by agreement between the parties. In addition to those provisions listed in Schedule 1, it is likely that the court would consider that the parties could not derogate from Sections 1 to 6 of the Act. However, all such mandatory provisions only apply to an arbitration where the seat is in England and Wales or Northern Ireland (see Section 2); they do not apply to an arbitration where the seat is elsewhere even if the governing substantive law is English law.

3. Non-mandatory provisions. Most of the provisions in the Act are non-mandatory, but they apply in the absence of agreement to the contrary, i.e. the parties need to opt out. Such provisions usually include the phrase 'unless otherwise agreed by the parties'. Certain other provisions need to be opted into, and have the phrase 'the parties are free to agree that ...' or similar wording. Any agreement to opt in or opt out of a non-mandatory provision must be in writing (see Section 5).

4. Importing other arbitral rules. Section 4(3) allows the parties to displace non-mandatory provisions of the Act by agreeing to the use of institutional or ad-hoc rules (for instance, those of the LCIA, ICC, WIPO or UNCITRAL). Where the chosen rules are silent, the default provisions in the Act will still apply (unless the chosen rules purport to be a complete code).

5. Importing arbitral laws from another jurisdiction. Section 4(5) allows the parties to displace non-mandatory provisions of the Act by agreeing to the application of a foreign procedural law. However, in practice, such an agreement may raise substantial practical difficulties and even prove unworkable (see *ABB Lummus Global Ltd* v *Keppel Fels Ltd*). In no circumstances can foreign provisions override the mandatory provisions of the Act.

[Agreements to be in writing]

Section 5

(1) The provisions of this Part apply only where the arbitration agreement is in writing, and any other agreement between the parties as to any matter is effective for the purposes of this Part only if in writing.

The expressions 'agreement', 'agree' and 'agreed' shall be construed accordingly.

(2) There is an agreement in writing –
  (a) if the agreement is made in writing (whether or not it is signed by the parties),
  (b) if the agreement is made by exchange of communications in writing, or
  (c) if the agreement is evidenced in writing.

(3) Where parties agree otherwise than in writing by reference to terms which are in writing, they make an agreement in writing.

(4) An agreement is evidenced in writing if an agreement made otherwise than in writing is recorded by one of the parties, or by a third party, with the authority of the parties to the agreement.

(5) An exchange of written submissions in arbitral or legal proceedings in which the existence of an agreement otherwise than in writing is alleged by one party against another party and not denied by the other party in his response constitutes as between those parties an agreement in writing to the effect alleged.

(6) References in this Part to anything being written or in writing include its being recorded by any means.

1. General. Section 5 concerns the writing requirement for any arbitration agreement or matter affecting that agreement. Although it is not stated to be mandatory (see Section 4(1)), it is unlikely that the English courts would accept that it can be affected by contrary agreement of the parties. It derives from art. 7(2) of the Model Law. See DAC Report paras. 31-40. For the definition of an arbitration agreement, see Section 6.

2. Application of Part I. Section 5(1) provides that Part I of the Act only applies to an agreement in writing. In addition, any ancillary matter affecting the arbitration agreement, such as an agreement to opt out of a non-mandatory provision of the Act, must also be in writing. However, an agreement to abandon or terminate arbitration proceedings does not have to be in writing in order to be effective (see Section 23(4)).

3. Agreement in writing. Section 5(2) defines 'agreement in writing' very widely, with the reference in para. (c) to agreements 'evidenced in writing' intended to be a 'catch-all' provision. Such definition is wider than that in the Model Law and art. III.2 of the 1958 New York Convention. There is no need for there to be a signed agreement: it is sufficient, for instance, for there to be an exchange of correspondence. In addition, it is sufficient for one party or a third party to record the agreement if so authorised (Section 5(4)). Further, an arbitration agreement will be held to exist if such agreement is alleged and is not denied in the exchange of written submissions in arbitral or legal proceedings (Section 5(5)).

4. Oral agreement. An arbitration agreement that is not in writing may still be enforced. The common law rules concerning the effect of an oral agreement are expressly saved by Section 81(1)(b). In addition, Section 5(3) provides that Part I of the Act nevertheless applies to oral agreements that refer to terms that are in writing (such as is common in salvage operations, e.g. Lloyd's Open Form) or by making reference to written arbitration rules. It would also be sufficient for there to be an oral agreement referring to the Act.

5. Recorded by any means. Section 5(6) provides that agreements in writing may be recorded by any means. This is more extensive than the definition of 'writing' in Schedule 1 of the Interpretation Act 1978, which provides that 'writing' includes 'modes of representing or reproducing words in visible form'.

THE ARBITRATION AGREEMENT

[Definition of arbitration agreement]

Section 6

(1) In this Part an 'arbitration agreement' means an agreement to submit to arbitration present or future disputes (whether they are contractual or not).

(2) The reference in an agreement to a written form of arbitration clause or to a document containing an arbitration clause constitutes an arbitration agreement if the reference is such as to make that clause part of the agreement.

1. General. Section 6 provides a definition of 'arbitration agreement'. Although it is not stated to be mandatory (see Section 4(1)), it is unlikely that the English courts would accept that it can be affected by contrary agreement of the parties. It reflects art. 7(1) of the Model Law and re-enacts with minor differences Section 32 of the 1950 Act. See DAC Report paras. 41 and 42. A party may challenge the substantive jurisdiction of the tribunal on grounds that there is no valid arbitration agreement (Section 30(a)).

2. Agreement. The usual common law rules apply for determining whether or not the parties have made a concluded contract (see *Birse Construction* v *St David Ltd*). Accordingly, a party may, for instance, evidence its agreement by conduct (see *Oceanografia SA de CV* v *DSND Subsea AS*). For statutory arbitrations, the relevant enactment is treated as the arbitration agreement (Section 95(1)(a)).

3. Arbitration. The agreement must be to refer a dispute to arbitration, but 'arbitration' is not defined. Its essential characteristics may be identified by reference to the Act, including Section 1(a) (i.e. the fair resolution of disputes by an impartial tribunal). In addition, it entails a procedure aimed at determining legal rights and obligations, by way of a binding decision enforceable in law (see *Walkinshaw* v *Diniz*).

4. Dispute. A dispute includes 'any difference' (see definition in Section 82(1)) and should be construed broadly. It is not necessary for there to exist an arguable defence to an allegation in order for a dispute to be said to exist (see *Halki Shipping Corp.* v *Sopex*; and *Amec Civil Engineering Ltd* v *Secretary of State for Transport*).

5. Existing and future disputes. Most arbitration agreements concern future disputes, but existing disputes may also be referred to arbitration (pursuant to what is sometimes called a submission agreement).

6. Contractual disputes or not. The reference to non-contractual disputes is merely a restatement of the common law, whereby tortious and restitutionary disputes may be referred to arbitration. However, the scope of the matters that are referred to arbitration depends upon the wording of the specific agreement.

7. Scope of agreement. The parties may limit the type of disputes that may be referred to arbitration (with all other disputes subject to another specified dispute resolution procedure or the default jurisdiction of national courts). A typical formulation which is intended to be as wide as possible is: 'any disputes arising out of or in connection with this contract' (i.e. the LCIA recommended clause). The House of Lords, in *Fiona Trust* v *Privalov*, held in a forceful and influential decision that it was time to draw a line under the authorities that made fine semantic distinctions (e.g. between 'disputes arising under' and 'disputes arising out of' an agreement) and that the construction of an arbitration clause had to start from the assumption that the parties, as rational businessmen, were likely to have intended any dispute arising out of the relationship into which they had entered, or purported to have entered, to be decided by the same tribunal, unless the language of an arbitration clause made it clear that certain questions were intended to be excluded from the arbitrator's jurisdiction. (See also Section 7, separability of the arbitration agreement.)

8. Arbitrability. The common law rules relating to arbitrability are saved by Section 81(1)(a).

9. Incorporation by reference. Consistent with the wide definition of 'agreement in writing' in Section 5(3), Section 6(2) allows for the parties to incorporate an arbitration clause by reference in an agreement to another written form of arbitration clause or to another document containing an arbitration clause. This is common in the construction industry where a bespoke agreement may refer to an industry standard form (e.g. one of the FIDIC forms of contract) or a subcontractor agreement may refer to the terms of the main agreement between contractor and employer. It is also common in the shipping industry where bills of lading often incorporate the terms of a charterparty. However, it was not intended that Section 6(2) should resolve the then conflict of authorities as to whether a mere reference to another document containing an arbitration clause is sufficient or whether a specific reference to the arbitration clause must also be made. The DAC Report preferred the former approach. While the trend is towards accepting a general reference as being sufficient, the issue has not been finally settled (see *Sea Trade Marine Corp.* v *Hellenic Mutual War Risks Association (Bermuda) Ltd ('The Athena')*). Ultimately, the question is one of construction of the relevant incorporating clause.

10. Parties to the agreement. The Act does not prescribe how to determine the proper parties to the arbitration agreement, save that Section 82(2) provides that references in Part I of the Act to a party to an arbitration agreement include any person claiming under or through a party to the agreement. Accordingly, the usual common law rules of privity of contract apply in determining whether or not a person is party to an arbitration agreement, including the rules relating to agency and estoppel. However, English law does not include a 'group of companies' doctrine (see *Peterson Farms Inc.* v *M Farming Ltd*). Absent a specific prohibition on assignment, an assignee of the underlying contract becomes a party to any arbitration agreement contained therein (see *Through Transport* v *New India Assurance*). While not a party to the original agreement, a third party seeking to enforce any benefit bestowed upon it pursuant to the Contracts (Rights of Third Parties) Act 1999 must do so in accordance with any agreement between the contracting parties to refer disputes to arbitration.

[Separability of arbitration agreement]

Section 7

Unless otherwise agreed by the parties, an arbitration agreement which forms or was intended to form part of another agreement (whether or not in writing) shall not be regarded as invalid, non-existent or ineffective because that other agreement is invalid, or did not come into existence or has become ineffective, and it shall for that purpose be treated as a distinct agreement.

1. General. Section 7 confirms the common law position that an arbitration clause is effective even in circumstances where the contract that forms the subject matter of the dispute is invalid, lapsed or otherwise ineffective. This Section is non-mandatory (see Section 4(2)), but will apply to the extent that there is no written agreement to the contrary. It reflects art. 16(1) of the Model Law. See DAC Report paras. 43 to 47 and DAC Suppl. para. 20.

2. Survivorship. Under English law and that of many jurisdictions, the arbitration agreement is severable from the main contractual obligations. This is the position whether or not the agreement to arbitrate forms part of a contract or is contained in separate documentation. Accordingly, the arbitration agreement survives the termination of the underlying contract.

3. Jurisdiction. A further application of the doctrine of separability is that an arbitral tribunal has jurisdiction to determine disputes between the parties even when it is alleged that the substantive contract is illegal or induced by fraud or misrepresentation or duress. It is only when it is alleged that the arbitration agreement itself is impeached that the tribunal may have to defer jurisdiction over that issue to the courts (*Fiona Trust* v *Privalov*).

4. Governing law. Because the arbitration agreement is regarded as a separate agreement, it has its own governing law. The English courts have indicated that, absent agreement to the contrary, where the seat is England, the governing law of the arbitration agreement will probably be English law, even if the underlying contract has a different governing law (see *C* v *D*).

5. Assignment. Although it is deemed to be a separate agreement, the common law position is that an assignment of the underlying contract will carry with it the agreement to arbitrate (absent a specific prohibition on assignment).

[Whether agreement discharged by death of a party]
Section 8

(1) Unless otherwise agreed by the parties, an arbitration agreement is not discharged by the death of a party and may be enforced by or against the personal representatives of that party.

(2) Subsection (1) does not affect the operation of any enactment or rule of law by virtue of which a substantive right or obligation is extinguished by death.

1. General. Section 8 concerns the effect of the death of a party on the agreement to arbitrate. It is non-mandatory (see Section 4(2)) and largely recreates the position under Section 2 of the 1950 Act (that provision did not, however, allow the parties any discretion to agree otherwise). This Section does not apply to statutory arbitrations (Section 97(a)). See DAC Report paras. 48 and 49. Whilst the death of an individual is addressed in the Act, provisions relating to the effect of bankruptcy of an individual or the dissolution or liquidation of a company are found in other legislation (see below).

2. Effect of death of a party. The death of a party does not discharge the arbitration agreement, unless the parties have agreed otherwise. However, Section 8(2) limits the application of this rule of survivability so that it does not affect the operation of any other legal provision (either statutory or at common law) which operates to extinguish legal rights upon death. Accordingly, Section 8 cannot operate to sustain a cause of action that would otherwise fall away upon the death of a party (e.g. specific performance). Concerning the effect of the death of a party on the authority of the arbitrator appointed by that party, see Section 26(b).

3. Bankruptcy. For the effect on arbitration of bankruptcy of an individual, see Section 349A of the Insolvency Act 1986, as inserted by para. 46 of Schedule 3 of the Act. The enforceability of an arbitration agreement to which that individual is a party depends upon whether or not the Trustee in Bankruptcy adopts the contract or not. If he does, then it is enforceable by or against him. If he does not, then nevertheless he (subject to the consent of the creditors' committee) or the other party to the arbitration agreement can apply to the court with bankruptcy jurisdiction for an order referring a dispute under the agreement to arbitration.

4. Dissolution of a company. Where a corporate entity ceases to exist, any arbitration agreement to which it is a party cannot be enforced and any arbitration in which it was involved lapses completely and cannot be revived. There may be exceptions to this rule where a company is temporarily struck off the register only to be reinstated (*Union Trans-Pacific Co. Ltd* v *Orient Shipping Rotterdam BV*) or where a company merges with another and is then dissolved, i.e. corporate succession (*Eurosteel Ltd* v *Stinnes AG*).

5. Insolvency of a company. For the effect on arbitration of the appointment of an administrator or administrative receiver over a company, see Sections 11(3)(d), 14(1)(b) and 42(1) and Schedule 1 of the Insolvency Act 1986. For the effect of the appointment of a liquidator, see Sections 126, 130(2) and (3), 165(3) and 167 (1)(a) and Schedule 4 of the Insolvency Act 1986. The court will allow a claim to proceed only if it had a real prospect of success (*Enron Metals* v *HIH Casualty*). Where insolvency proceedings have been opened in another EU Member State, it is English law that determines the effect of that insolvency on any arbitration seated in England and may allow the arbitration to proceed (*Syska* v *Vivendi*).

STAY OF LEGAL PROCEEDINGS

[Stay of legal proceedings]

Section 9

(1) A party to an arbitration agreement against whom legal proceedings are brought (whether by way of claim or counterclaim) in respect of a matter which under the agreement is to be referred to arbitration may (upon notice to the other parties to the proceedings) apply to the court in which the proceedings have been brought to stay the proceedings so far as they concern that matter.

(2) An application may be made notwithstanding that the matter is to be referred to arbitration only after the exhaustion of other dispute resolution procedures.

(3) An application may not be made by a person before taking the appropriate procedural step (if any) to acknowledge the legal proceedings against him or after he has taken any step in those proceedings to answer the substantive claim.

(4) On an application under this section the court shall grant a stay unless satisfied that the arbitration agreement is null and void, inoperative, or incapable of being performed.

(5) If the court refuses to stay the legal proceedings, any provision that an award is a condition precedent to the bringing of legal proceedings in respect of any matter is of no effect in relation to those proceedings.

English Arbitration Act (Chapter 23), Section 9

1. General. Section 9 concerns the stay of litigation in favour of arbitration. It is mandatory (see Section 4(1)) and applies even if the seat of the arbitration is outside England and Wales or Northern Ireland or has not been determined (see Section 2(2)). Section 9 largely re-enacts Section 4 of the 1950 Act and Section 1 of the 1975 Act; however, the court no longer has any discretion if the conditions of a stay are met, so as to comply with the UK's obligations under the 1958 New York Convention (art. II). See DAC Report paras. 50-57.

2. Legal proceedings. Legal proceedings is defined to mean civil proceedings in the High Court or county court (Section 82(1)), i.e. essentially any civil litigation.

3. Party. Only a defendant to a claim or counterclaim can apply to have the legal proceedings stayed. A party includes any person claiming under or through a party to the agreement, e.g. an insurer or assignee (Section 82(2)). It does not permit another party to the putative arbitration agreement to apply if it is not a defendant in the legal proceedings (which is a change from the 1950 Act).

4. Arbitration agreement. Any application must be based upon the existence of an arbitration agreement, as defined in Section 6. Where the party resisting the stay calls into question the existence of an arbitration agreement, the court may either decide that issue itself or refer the matter to arbitration for the tribunal to rule on its substantive jurisdiction (pursuant to Section 30, with the right of that party to object and ultimately challenge any award under Sections 31 to 32 and 67). The trend is in favour of granting a stay and referring the issue to the arbitral tribunal in the first instance, which reflects the doctrine of 'Kompetenz-Kompetenz' (see *Birse Construction Ltd* v *St David Ltd*). Nevertheless, before granting the stay, the court should be satisfied that there is prima facie evidence of the existence of an arbitration agreement and the matters in dispute falls within it. An allegation that the underlying agreement (including any arbitration agreement) is illegal or induced by fraud, duress or misrepresentation does not prevent the court granting a stay and referring that issue to the arbitral tribunal, unless the arbitration agreement itself is impeached (*Fiona Trust* v *Privalov*).

5. Application and notice. Any application for a stay must be made pursuant to CPR Part 62.8. Notice must be given to the other parties to the proceedings (see Section 80).

6. Discretion. A stay will be granted only if a party makes an application. Even if a valid arbitration agreement exists, a party may prefer to have the dispute determined by the courts and will waive its right to insist on arbitration. The court cannot grant a stay of its own motion. Once the conditions of a stay are satisfied, the court does not have any discretion as to whether or not to grant a stay (as it did under the previous law). The DAC intended for the court to retain a discretion in respect of domestic arbitrations (see Section

86), but this was not brought into effect because it was inconsistent with the United Kingdom's obligations under the 1958 New York Convention and EC law.

7. Counterclaim and/or part of proceedings. Section 9(1) removes the doubt that existed under the previous law concerning the possibility of a stay of proceedings in respect of a counterclaim as well as a claim. In addition, the Section now makes clear that a stay can be in respect of a part of the claim as well as the whole. Nevertheless, this can give rise to complications where all the claims arise from the same underlying facts and either the arbitral tribunal or the courts may, as part of their case management powers, suspend their proceedings until after the outcome of the other.

8. Pre-condition to arbitration. Section 9(2) allows for a stay to be granted even though the matter cannot be referred to arbitration until certain pre-conditions (such as satisfying other dispute resolution procedures) have been met.

9. Taking a step in the legal proceedings. Under Section 9(3), a party is precluded from applying for a stay once it has taken any steps in the substantive proceedings beyond acknowledging the proceedings and objecting to the jurisdiction of the court. Applying to set aside a default judgment does not constitute a 'step' in the proceedings (see *Patel* v *Patel*).

10. Null and void, inoperative or incapable of being performed. A stay must be granted by a court presented with evidence of a prima facie applicable arbitration agreement unless the opposing party can establish that the arbitration agreement falls within one of the exceptions in Section 9(4), namely that it is null and void, inoperative or incapable or being performed. This repeats almost word for word art. II(3) of the 1958 New York Convention. 'Null and void' refers to a situation in which there is no effective agreement. 'Inoperative' relates to the scope of the arbitration clause, the arbitrability of the subject matter, the termination or cancellation of the arbitration clause and the identities of the parties to the arbitration clause (see Section 6). The phrase 'incapable of being performed' covers the case in which one of the parties is prevented by some external cause from performing its obligations. The relevant date for the court to assess the validity or the arbitration clause is upon commencement of the judicial proceedings. If a clause is invalid on that date, the stay must be granted. Following *Fiona Trust* v *Privalov*, it is likely to be more difficult to resist applications for a stay because arbitration clauses are now to be interpreted as widely as possible by the courts. Following that case, it is also more likely that a court will defer to the arbitral tribunal to determine jurisdiction rather than, for example, decide on the basis of affidavit evidence that there is an arbitration agreement, decide that the issue will be tried under CPR Rule 62(8), or decide that there is neither an agreement to arbitrate nor does the claim fall within the scope of the arbitration clause.

11. No dispute. A previous supplemental ground in the 1975 Act which allowed for stay applications to be resisted on the ground that there was no dispute between the parties has not been retained in the 1996 Act. Nonetheless, it remains a sine qua non of the granting of a stay that a dispute must have arisen between the parties; this will be a factual determination to be made on a case-by-case basis. As noted under Section 7, an allegation that the underlying contract is void ab initio on grounds that it is illegal or was induced by fraud or duress or misrepresentation is not sufficient to resist an application for stay, unless the arbitration agreement itself is impeached.

12. *Scott* v *Avery* clauses. Section 9(5) is a new provision designed to address *Scott* v *Avery* clauses. Under such a clause, the parties agree that arbitration is a condition precedent to court proceedings, such that court proceedings can only be brought to enforce the tribunal's award. The Act provides that where the arbitration agreement is found to be null and void, inoperative or incapable of being performed, it no longer operates as a condition precedent to legal proceedings.

13. Right of appeal against decision under Section 9. Although the Act prescribes no express right of appeal of a decision under Section 9, the House of Lords has held that a right of appeal exists (*Inco Europe Ltd* v *First Choice Distribution*).

14. Consumer contracts. Pursuant to Sections 89 to 91 of the Act, the Unfair Terms in Consumer Contracts Regulations 1999 are extended to arbitration agreements and any agreement which is found to be unfair may not be enforced, thus justifying a refusal to grant a stay under Section 9.

15. Anti-suit injunctions. To ensure that the parties abide by their agreement to arbitrate, the English courts may, pursuant to their inherent jurisdiction, issue an injunction to restrain proceedings brought in a non-EU foreign jurisdiction in breach of an arbitration agreement (see *Aggeliki Charis Compania* v *Pagnan SA ('The Angelic Grace')* and the many cases in which injunctions have been granted; but see the recent decision of the ECJ curtailing this power where legal proceedings are brought in a country which is party to EU Council Regulation 44/2001, *Allianz SpA* v *West Tankers*). Also pursuant to its inherent jurisdiction, as preserved in Section 49(3) of the Supreme Court Act 1981, the court may exceptionally stay court proceedings in England and Wales or Northern Ireland pending the outcome of related arbitration proceedings taking place abroad (see *Reichhold Norway ASA* v *Goldman Sachs International*).

[Reference of interpleader issue to arbitration]

Section 10

(1) Where in legal proceedings relief by way of interpleader is granted and any issue between the claimants is one in respect of which there is an

arbitration agreement between them, the court granting the relief shall direct that the issue be determined in accordance with the agreement unless the circumstances are such that proceedings brought by a claimant in respect of the matter would not be stayed.

(2) Where subsection (1) applies but the court does not direct that the issue be determined in accordance with the arbitration agreement, any provision that an award is a condition precedent to the bringing of legal proceedings in respect of any matter shall not affect the determination of that issue by the court.

1. General. Section 10 concerns the effect of an arbitration agreement on an interpleader application in court proceedings. It is mandatory (see Section 4(1)) and applies even if the seat of the arbitration is outside England and Wales or Northern Ireland or has not been determined (see Section 2(2)). Consistent with Section 9, the court will order a stay of court proceedings where there is an applicable and valid arbitration agreement. Section 10 is based on Section 5 of the 1950 Act, but the opportunity was taken to make the stay mandatory in order to comply with the UK's obligations under the 1958 New York Convention. See DAC Report paras. 58 and 59.

2. Interpleader proceedings. Interpleading is an equitable court proceeding brought by a third party in order for the court to determine the ownership rights of a debt or money or property that is held by that third party and over which two rival claimants assert rights (see CPR Schedule 1, RSC Ord. 17). The relief granted by the court will normally be in the form of an order that the competing claims be withdrawn or set off, allowing the third party effectively to step away from the dispute.

3. Interpleader and arbitration. Where the two claimants that assert rights in the asset have agreed to refer disputes between them to arbitration, then the court must direct that the issue be determined in accordance with that agreement, unless the circumstances (i.e. those specified in Section 9(4)) are such that had they started court proceedings a stay to arbitration would not have been granted.

4. *Scott* v *Avery* clauses. Section 10(2) is a new provision which reflects Section 9(5) and allows the effect of a *Scott* v *Avery* clause to be denied where the court deals with the matter itself. This Section does not apply to statutory arbitrations (see Section 97(c)).

[Retention of security where Admiralty proceedings stayed]

Section 11

(1) Where Admiralty proceedings are stayed on the ground that the dispute in question should be submitted to arbitration, the court granting the stay may, if in those proceedings property has been arrested or

bail or other security has been given to prevent or obtain release from arrest –
- (a) order that the property arrested be retained as security for the satisfaction of any award given in the arbitration in respect of that dispute, or
- (b) order that the stay of those proceedings be conditional on the provision of equivalent security for the satisfaction of any such award.

(2) Subject to any provision made by rules of court and to any necessary modifications, the same law and practice shall apply in relation to property retained in pursuance of an order as would apply if it were held for the purposes of proceedings in the court making the order.

1. General. Section 11 concerns the provision of security in Admiralty proceedings. It is mandatory (see Section 4(1)) and applies even if the seat of the arbitration is outside England and Wales or Northern Ireland or has not been determined (see Section 2(2)). Subject to minor differences, this clause has re-enacted Section 26 of the Civil Jurisdiction and Judgments Act 1982. See DAC Report paras. 60 and 61.

2. Security. Where Admiralty proceedings (see CPR Part 61) are stayed under Section 9 in order for the dispute to be submitted to arbitration, the court may order the retention of any vessel that has been arrested or the provision of equivalent security as a means of ensuring the satisfaction of any arbitral award. For more general powers of the courts to grant injunctive relief in support of arbitral proceedings, see Section 44(2)(e).

COMMENCEMENT OF ARBITRAL PROCEEDINGS

[Power of court to extend time for beginning arbitral proceedings, &c]

Section 12

(1) Where an arbitration agreement to refer future disputes to arbitration provides that a claim shall be barred, or the claimant's right extinguished, unless the claimant takes within a time fixed by the agreement some step –
- (a) to begin arbitral proceedings, or
- (b) to begin other dispute resolution procedures which must be exhausted before arbitral proceedings can be begun,

the court may by order extend the time for taking that step.

(2) Any party to the arbitration agreement may apply for such an order (upon notice to the other parties), but only after a claim has arisen and after exhausting any available arbitral process for obtaining an extension of time.

(3) The court shall make an order only if satisfied –

Sheppard

(a) that the circumstances are such as were outside the reasonable contemplation of the parties when they agreed the provision in question, and that it would be just to extend the time, or
(b) that the conduct of one party makes it unjust to hold the other party to the strict terms of the provision in question.

(4) The court may extend the time for such period and on such terms as it thinks fit, and may do so whether or not the time previously fixed (by agreement or by a previous order) has expired.

(5) An order under this section does not affect the operation of the Limitation Acts (see section 13).

(6) The leave of the court is required for any appeal from a decision of the court under this section.

1. General. Section 12 is concerned with protecting parties from the unforeseen effects of contractual time limitations. It is mandatory (Section 4(1)). A similar power is found in Section 27 of the 1950 Act. See DAC Report paras. 62 to 75.

2. Future disputes. Section 12 only applies to proceedings commenced pursuant to an agreement to refer future disputes to arbitration. There should not be any need for a similar provision in respect of an agreement to refer existing disputes to arbitration, because a submission agreement implies that the parties agree that the commencement of arbitration is within time (or any objection is waived).

3. Claim barred or right extinguished. Section 12 applies where the contractual provision provides that the claim shall be barred or the claimant's rights extinguished. Under English law, a statutory limitation period acts to bar the right of a claimant to bring a claim or seek a remedy, but it does not extinguish the parties' substantive rights in respective thereof (accordingly, for example, the party may still rely on such rights as a defence to a claim by the other party). However, the parties in their agreement may agree that rights are extinguished.

4. Beginning arbitral proceedings. Concerning the time when arbitral proceedings are to be regarded as commenced for purposes of limitation, see Section 14.

5. Preceding dispute resolution conditions. The court also has the power to extend time limits placed on the commencement of 'other dispute resolution procedures' (such as mediation) which the parties have agreed must precede arbitration (Section 12(1)(b)), reflecting the increasing use of tiered dispute resolution provisions.

6. Exhaustion of available arbitral remedies. A party applying to the court for an extension of time must first exhaust any available arbitral processes, e.g. an application to the relevant arbitral institution or to the tribunal (Section 12(2)). The DAC Report notes that if the tribunal has refused to extend time, it will be almost impossible to persuade the court to do otherwise (DAC Report, para. 74(ii)). In practice, this provision will limit the number of applications that are made.

7. Application and notice. Any application for an extension of time must be made pursuant to CPR Part 62 Rule 4(3). This Rule states that the claim form may include in the alternative an application for a declaration that the time for commencing an arbitration has not expired, although this may overlap with the jurisdiction of the arbitral tribunal (see *Grimaldi Compagnia di Navigazione* v *Sekihyo Lines*). Notice must be given to the other parties to the proceedings (see Section 80).

8. Exercise of discretion. The court may only extend time if the conditions in Section 12(3)(a) or (b) are met. A prevailing theme is what would be just; however, the circumstances relied on by the applicant must not have been foreseen. The cases show that the courts are taking a strict approach. For example, failure properly to have read or applied the contractual provision does not justify extending time limits (*Harbour and General Works Ltd* v *The Environment Agency*). If satisfied, the court may extend time for such period and on such terms as it thinks fit (Section 12(4)).

9. Statutory time limits. Section 12 does not give the court power to extend statutory time limits (Section 12(4) and Section 13).

10. Extending other time limits. Concerning the power of the court to extend time limits relating to later stages of the arbitral proceedings, see Sections 79 and 80.

[Application of Limitation Acts]

Section 13

(1) The Limitation Acts apply to arbitral proceedings as they apply to legal proceedings.

(2) The court may order that in computing the time prescribed by the Limitation Acts for the commencement of proceedings (including arbitral proceedings) in respect of a dispute which was the subject matter –
  (a) **of an award which the court orders to be set aside or declares to be of no effect, or**
  (b) **of the affected part of an award which the court orders to be set aside in part, or declares to be in part of no effect,**

the period between the commencement of the arbitration and the date of the order referred to in paragraph (a) or (b) shall be excluded.

(3) In determining for the purposes of the Limitation Acts when a cause of action accrued, any provision that an award is a condition precedent to the bringing of legal proceedings in respect of a matter to which an arbitration agreement applies shall be disregarded.

(4) In this Part 'the Limitation Acts' means –

(a) in England and Wales, the [1980 c. 58.] Limitation Act 1980, the [1984 c. 16.] Foreign Limitation Periods Act 1984 and any other enactment (whenever passed) relating to the limitation of actions;
(b) in Northern Ireland, the [S.I. 1989/1339 (N.I. 11).] Limitation (Northern Ireland) Order 1989, the [S.I. 1985/754 (N.I. 5).] Foreign Limitation Periods (Northern Ireland) Order 1985 and any other enactment (whenever passed) relating to the limitation of actions.

1. General. Section 13 concerns the application of statutory limitation periods to arbitral proceedings. It is mandatory (see Section 4(1)). This Section reflects art. 21 of the Model Law and derives from Section 34 of the Limitation Act 1980. See DAC Report paras. 76 and 77.

2. Application to arbitral proceedings. Section 13(1) confirms that, in England and Wales, the Limitation Act 1980, the Foreign Limitation Act 1984 and any other applicable enactments apply to arbitral proceedings in the same way as they apply to legal proceedings (i.e. civil court proceedings, see Section 82(1)).

3. Applicable limitation period. For most contractual and tortious disputes governed by English law, the applicable limitation period is six years from when the cause of action arose, i.e. the date of breach for contract claims (see Limitation Act 1980, Section 5) or the date when damage occurred for tort claims (see Limitation Act 1980, Section 2). Some claims have specific limitation periods (see, e.g., Carriage of Goods by Sea Act 1971). An English law statutory limitation period may be shortened by agreement of the parties. The court has the power under the Act to extend contractual limitation periods in limited circumstances (Section 12), but not statutory limitation periods.

4. Foreign limitation periods. Limitation is characterised as a substantive issue and therefore claims governed by a foreign law will be subject to the limitation period prescribed by that law.

5. Commencement of proceedings. Concerning the time when arbitral proceedings are to be regarded as commenced for purposes of limitation, see Section 14.

6. New claims. Section 35 of the Limitation Act 1980, which allows new claims to be added to an action as of the date of commencement of the original action, cannot apply to arbitral proceedings where the new claim would not otherwise fall within the jurisdiction of the tribunal (*Kenya Railways* v *Antares Pte Ltd*).

7. Enforcement of award. The limitation period for enforcing an award is also six years (Limitation Act 1980, Section 7), running from the date on which the award ought to have been implemented according to its terms. Time does not start running immediately, because a party is entitled to a reasonable time from the date of the award to honour it (see *International Bulk Shipping* v *Minmetals Trading*).

8. Awards which have been set aside, nullified or changed by the court. Where an award or part of an award has been set aside or declared to be of no effect, the court has power to order that the period of time between the commencement of the original proceedings and the date of the court's order be excluded, so that new proceedings can be commenced relating to that dispute and not be time barred (Section 13(2)).

9. *Scott* v *Avery* clauses. Section 13(3) addresses the difficulties caused by *Scott* v *Avery* clauses, which make arbitration a condition precedent to legal proceedings (see Section 9, note 12). This Section permits the court to disregard such a clause when computing time.

[Commencement of arbitral proceedings]

Section 14

(1) The parties are free to agree when arbitral proceedings are to be regarded as commenced for the purposes of this Part and for the purposes of the Limitation Acts.

(2) If there is no such agreement the following provisions apply.

(3) Where the arbitrator is named or designated in the arbitration agreement, arbitral proceedings are commenced in respect of a matter when one party serves on the other party or parties a notice in writing requiring him or them to submit that matter to the person so named or designated.

(4) Where the arbitrator or arbitrators are to be appointed by the parties, arbitral proceedings are commenced in respect of a matter when one party serves on the other party or parties notice in writing requiring him or them to appoint an arbitrator or to agree to the appointment of an arbitrator in respect of that matter.

(5) Where the arbitrator or arbitrators are to be appointed by a person other than a party to the proceedings, arbitral proceedings are commenced in respect of a matter when one party gives notice in writing to that person requesting him to make the appointment in respect of that matter.

1. General. Section 14 sets out when arbitral proceedings are to be regarded as commenced. It is not mandatory (see Section 4(2)), but it will apply in the absence of written agreement to the contrary. This Section re-enacts Section 34(3) of the Limitation Act 1980 and reflects art. 21 of the Model Law. See DAC Report para. 77 and DAC Suppl. para. 21. The date of commencement of the arbitral proceedings is important principally for purposes of statutory and contractual limitation periods (see Sections 12 and 13).

2. Parties' agreement. The parties are free to agree when arbitral proceedings are to be regarded as commenced (Section 14(1)). Where institutional rules have been agreed, the date of commencement is generally the date of receipt by the institution of the prescribed request or notice of arbitration (see, e.g., LCIA art. 1.2; ICC art. 4.2).

3. Default provision. Where there has been no agreement on when proceedings are to commence, Sections 14(3) to (5) apply. Generally, arbitration is commenced when one party serves on the other party a notice in writing requiring it to submit the matter to a previously designated arbitrator or to agree to the appointment of an arbitrator(s). The request may be implied rather than express (see *Allianz Versicherungs AG* v *Fortuna ('The Baltic Universal')*). It must, however, identify the dispute to which it relates with sufficient particularity and it must also make clear that the dispute is being referred to arbitration and there is not merely a threat to do so (*Atlanska Plovidba* v *Consignaciones Asturianas SA*). Where the tribunal is to be appointed by a third party, arbitration is commenced when a notice in writing is given to that person requesting him to make the appointment. For the requirements of service of notices, see Section 76.

THE ARBITRAL TRIBUNAL

[The arbitral tribunal]

Section 15

(1) The parties are free to agree on the number of arbitrators to form the tribunal and whether there is to be a chairman or umpire.

(2) Unless otherwise agreed by the parties, an agreement that the number of arbitrators shall be two or any other even number shall be understood as requiring the appointment of an additional arbitrator as chairman of the tribunal.

(3) If there is no agreement as to the number of arbitrators, the tribunal shall consist of a sole arbitrator.

1. General. Section 15 concerns the number of arbitrators in an arbitral tribunal. It is non-mandatory (see Section 4(2)), but Sections 15(2) and (3) apply in the absence of written agreement to the contrary (see Section 5). This Section is similar to art. 10 of the Model Law and derives from Sections 6 to 10 of the 1950 Act. See DAC Report paras. 78 and 79.

2. Uneven number. The usual number of arbitrators is one or three. Unless otherwise agreed, an agreement that there is to be an even number of arbitrators is now to be understood as requiring the appointment of an additional arbitrator as chairman (whereas Section 8(1) of the 1950 Act had provided the arbitrators with the power to appoint an umpire). For the role of a chairman, see Section 20, and for the role of an umpire, see Section 21.

3. Default number. Where there is no agreement, the default number of arbitrators is one (which was also the previous rule under Section 6 of the 1950 Act) rather than three (as in the Model Law, art. 10(2)). Any arbitration rules chosen by the parties may prescribe a different default number and this would override the Act (e.g. the UNCITRAL Rules prescribe three as the default; but the LCIA and ICC Rules prescribe one unless the institution determines that three would be more appropriate in view of all the circumstances).

4. Appointment. Concerning the appointment of the tribunal, see Sections 16 to 19.

[Procedure for appointment of arbitrators]
Section 16

(1) The parties are free to agree on the procedure for appointing the arbitrator or arbitrators, including the procedure for appointing any chairman or umpire.

(2) If or to the extent that there is no such agreement, the following provisions apply.

(3) If the tribunal is to consist of a sole arbitrator, the parties shall jointly appoint the arbitrator not later than 28 days after service of a request in writing by either party to do so.

(4) If the tribunal is to consist of two arbitrators, each party shall appoint one arbitrator not later than 14 days after service of a request in writing by either party to do so.

(5) If the tribunal is to consist of three arbitrators –
  (a) each party shall appoint one arbitrator not later than 14 days after service of a request in writing by either party to do so, and
  (b) the two so appointed shall forthwith appoint a third arbitrator as the chairman of the tribunal.

(6) If the tribunal is to consist of two arbitrators and an umpire –
  (a) each party shall appoint one arbitrator not later than 14 days after service of a request in writing by either party to do so, and
  (b) the two so appointed may appoint an umpire at any time after they themselves are appointed and shall do so before any substantive hearing or forthwith if they cannot agree on a matter relating to the arbitration.

(7) In any other case (in particular, if there are more than two parties) section 18 applies as in the case of a failure of the agreed appointment procedure.

1. General. Section 16 concerns the formation of the tribunal. It is non-mandatory (see Section 4(2)), but Sections 16(3) to (7) apply to the extent that there is no written agreement to the contrary (see Section 5). This Section is based upon art. 11 of the Model Law. See DAC Report paras. 80 to 82 and 360 and DAC Suppl. para. 22. Any arbitration rules chosen by the parties are likely to prescribe a procedure and time limits for appointing the tribunal, which would override the Act (e.g. LCIA Rules arts. 5-9, ICC Rules arts. 9-10, UNCITRAL Rules arts. 6-8).

2. Procedure. The default procedure for appointing a sole arbitrator is set out in Section 16(3); for appointing two arbitrators in Section 16(4) (see also Section 15(2)); for appointing three arbitrators in Section 16(5); for appointing two arbitrators and an umpire in Section 16(6) (see also Section 21); and any other case (in particular, where there are more than two parties) in Section 16(7), in which case Section 18 also applies. Section 16 applies equally to the filling of a vacancy as it does to an original appointment (Section 27(3)). In the event of failure of the statutory appointment procedure, see Sections 17 and 18.

3. Time limits. The time limits prescribed in this Section may be varied by agreement (Section 16(1)) and, in exceptional circumstances, extended by order of the court (Section 79). For reckoning periods of time, see Section 78.

4. Completion of appointment. An appointment is not complete until accepted by the nominated arbitrator (see *Tradax Export SA* v *Volkswagenwerk AG*).

5. Determination of a properly constituted tribunal. Unless otherwise agreed by the parties, the arbitrators themselves are empowered to determine whether the tribunal has been properly constituted (see Section 30(1)(b)).

[Power in case of default to appoint sole arbitrator]

Section 17

(1) Unless the parties otherwise agree, where each of two parties to an arbitration agreement is to appoint an arbitrator and one party ('the party in default') refuses to do so, or fails to do so within the time specified, the other party, having duly appointed his arbitrator, may give notice in writing to the party in default that he proposes to appoint his arbitrator to act as sole arbitrator.

(2) If the party in default does not within 7 clear days of that notice being given –
   (a) make the required appointment, and
   (b) notify the other party that he has done so,
the other party may appoint his arbitrator as sole arbitrator whose award shall be binding on both parties as if he had been so appointed by agreement.

(3) Where a sole arbitrator has been appointed under subsection (2), the party in default may (upon notice to the appointing party) apply to the court which may set aside the appointment.

(4) The leave of the court is required for any appeal from a decision of the court under this section.

1. General. Section 17 concerns the situation where a respondent fails to appoint an arbitrator. It is non-mandatory (see Section 4(2)), but it applies in the absence of written agreement to the contrary (see Section 5). This Section replaces (with some changes) Section 7(b) of the 1950 Act. There is no corresponding provision in the Model Law. See DAC Report paras. 83 to 86. The appointment of the claimant's chosen arbitrator as sole arbitrator constitutes a significant deterrent to a respondent contemplating the dilatory tactic of not appointing an arbitrator. This contrasts with the approach taken by many arbitration rules, which instead make provision for an arbitrator to be appointed on behalf of the defaulting party (e.g. LCIA art. 7.2, ICC art. 8(4), UNCITRAL art. 7(2)).

2. Refusal or failure to appoint an arbitrator. By the wording of Section 17(1), this Section only applies to a two-party arbitration in which a three-person tribunal is envisaged and where one party (save in exceptional cases – the respondent) 'refuses' or 'fails' to appoint an arbitrator 'within the time specified' (as required under the agreed procedure or pursuant to Section 16(4) to (6)). Where the defaulting party 'refuses' to make an appointment, as opposed to 'fails' to do so, the non-defaulting party need not wait until the expiry of the 'time specified' before proceeding under Section 17(2). For the giving of notices, see Section 80. In the case of a multi-party arbitration, the parties may, in the absence of an agreed procedure, apply to the court for an appropriate order under Section 18.

3. Seven clear days. For the reckoning of the '7 clear days', see Section 78(4). The party in default may apply to the court for this time limit to be extended, see Section 79.

4. Setting aside appointment. The party in default may, nevertheless, apply to the court to have the appointment of the sole arbitrator set aside. Any such application should be made very promptly. For applications to the court, see Section 80 and CPR Part 62.

[Failure of appointment procedure]
Section 18

(1) The parties are free to agree what is to happen in the event of a failure of the procedure for the appointment of the arbitral tribunal.

Sheppard

There is no failure if an appointment is duly made under section 17 (power in case of default to appoint sole arbitrator), unless that appointment is set aside.

(2) If or to the extent that there is no such agreement any party to the arbitration agreement may (upon notice to the other parties) apply to the court to exercise its powers under this section.

(3) Those powers are –
  (a) to give directions as to the making of any necessary appointments;
  (b) to direct that the tribunal shall be constituted by such appointments (or any one or more of them) as have been made;
  (c) to revoke any appointments already made;
  (d) to make any necessary appointments itself.

(4) An appointment made by the court under this section has effect as if made with the agreement of the parties.

(5) The leave of the court is required for any appeal from a decision of the court under this section.

1. General. Section 18 sets out what is to happen when the procedure for appointing an arbitrator fails. It is non-mandatory (see Section 4(2)), but Sections 18(2) to (5) apply to the extent that there is no written agreement to the contrary (see Section 5). This Section is based upon art. 11(4) of the Model Law and replaces Section 10 of the 1950 Act. See DAC Report paras. 87 to 89. Many arbitration rules, if chosen by the parties, make provision as to how the tribunal should be appointed where there is failure of the appointment procedure (e.g. LCIA arts. 5, 7 and 8, ICC art. 8, UNCITRAL art. 7).

2. Application. This Section applies where there is a failure of the procedure agreed by the parties or the procedure prescribed in Section 16. It does not apply in situations where Section 17 operates, unless such appointment has been set aside. Section 18 applies more usually where the parties cannot agree on a sole arbitrator or in a multi-party situation. This Section applies to the filling of a vacancy as it does to an original appointment (Section 27(3)).

3. Powers of the court. The court has powers beyond simply making the appointment(s) itself and may, for example, revoke a previous appointment which it considers unfair in the circumstances. Guidance as to the exercise of the court's discretion was given in *Atlanska Plovidba* v *Consignaciones Asturianas SA*. The court's power under Section 18(4)(c) is not affected by any agreement between the parties as to the circumstances in which they may revoke the authority of an arbitrator (see Section 23(5)(a)). For applications to the court, see Section 80 and CPR Part 62.

4. Whether arbitration agreement exists. When asked to make orders under this Section, the court may also have to consider whether a binding arbitration agreement exists entitling the claimant to constitute a tribunal (see *Sinochem International Oil* v *Fortune Oil*).

[Court to have regard to agreed qualifications]
Section 19

In deciding whether to exercise, and in considering how to exercise, any of its powers under section 16 (procedure for appointment of arbitrators) or section 18 (failure of appointment procedure), the court shall have due regard to any agreement of the parties as to the qualifications required of the arbitrators.

1. General. Section 19 requires the court to have regard to any qualifications that the parties may have prescribed. It is non-mandatory (see Section 4(2)), but it applies in the absence of written agreement to the contrary (see Section 5). This Section is based upon art. 11(5) of the Model Law. See DAC Report para. 90.

2. Agreed qualifications. The parties may stipulate in their arbitration agreement (or agree subsequently) that an arbitrator should have certain qualifications or experience (e.g. that he/she should be a civil engineer or lawyer or engaged in the shipping industry and/or be a member of a specified professional body and/or have been so for a certain number of years). Problems sometimes arise when the stipulated qualifications yield too few suitable candidates although, in relation to this Section, the court need only have 'due regard' to the parties' stipulations.

3. Application to the appointment of arbitrators. The reference to the court's powers under Section 16 (procedure for appointment of arbitrators) is curious: that Section does not provide for the exercise of any powers by the court save in Section 16(7), in which case Section 18 applies, to which separate reference is made in any event.

[Chairman]
Section 20

(1) Where the parties have agreed that there is to be a chairman, they are free to agree what the functions of the chairman are to be in relation to the making of decisions, orders and awards.

(2) If or to the extent that there is no such agreement, the following provisions apply.

(3) Decisions, orders and awards shall be made by all or a majority of the arbitrators (including the chairman).

(4) The view of the chairman shall prevail in relation to a decision, order or award in respect of which there is neither unanimity nor a majority under subsection (3).

1. General. Section 20 concerns the functions of the chairman of the tribunal. It is non-mandatory (see Section 4(2)), but it applies where the parties have agreed in writing (see Section 5) that there is to be a chairman of the arbitral tribunal or where Section 15(2) (i.e. reference to an even number of arbitrators shall require appointment of a chairman) applies. Where this Section applies, Sections 20(3) and (4) apply to the extent that the parties have not agreed in writing as to the functions of the chairman in relation to the making of decisions, orders and awards. This Section is derived from Section 9 of the 1950 Act and art. 29 of the Model Law (both of which also provide for majority awards, but do not provide for the office of chairman). See DAC Report paras. 91 to 94.

2. Terminology. Some agreements to arbitrate and institutional rules refer to the presiding arbitrator. There is no significance in the difference in wording.

3. Matters dealt with by the chairman alone. The parties may agree that, in order to save time and costs, specified matters (e.g. questions of procedure, Section 34) may be dealt with by the chairman alone. The arbitrators themselves cannot come to such an agreement. In all situations, the tribunal must decide unanimously or by majority (Section 20(3)).

4. Chairman's casting vote. The view of the chairman will prevail in situations where the other arbitrators hold different views such that no majority decision can be reached. For example, there is no majority if one arbitrator dissents and the other two agree on liability but disagree on the relief – damages or specific performance – to be awarded. In that case, the chairman's decision on the appropriate relief will prevail. However, where each arbitrator agrees that damages should be awarded, but has a different view as to the quantum, it is arguable that there is a majority in favour of the lowest figure (under art. 29 of the Model Law, this situation could create a potential deadlock).

5. Award. The award need not state that members of the tribunal hold different views, but it may do so, see Section 52(4). Concerning whom should sign the award when there is disagreement, see Section 52(3). There are no similar provisions in the Act concerning orders and directions, but generally they are signed by (or on behalf of) all the members of the tribunal (unless the chairman alone has been entrusted with interlocutory matters), even when there are different views.

6. No chairman. For decision-making where there is no chairman, see Section 22.

[Umpire]

Section 21

(1) Where the parties have agreed that there is to be an umpire, they are free to agree what the functions of the umpire are to be, and in particular –
  (a) whether he is to attend the proceedings, and
  (b) when he is to replace the other arbitrators as the tribunal with power to make decisions, orders and awards.

(2) If or to the extent that there is no such agreement, the following provisions apply.

(3) The umpire shall attend the proceedings and be supplied with the same documents and other materials as are supplied to the other arbitrators.

(4) Decisions, orders and awards shall be made by the other arbitrators unless and until they cannot agree on a matter relating to the arbitration.

In that event they shall forthwith give notice in writing to the parties and the umpire, whereupon the umpire shall replace them as the tribunal with power to make decisions, orders and awards as if he were sole arbitrator.

(5) If the arbitrators cannot agree but fail to give notice of that fact, or if any of them fails to join in the giving of notice, any party to the arbitral proceedings may (upon notice to the other parties and to the tribunal) apply to the court which may order that the umpire shall replace the other arbitrators as the tribunal with power to make decisions, orders and awards as if he were sole arbitrator.

(6) The leave of the court is required for any appeal from a decision of the court under this section.

1. General. Section 21 concerns the functions of an umpire. It is non-mandatory (see Section 4(2)), but it applies where the parties have agreed in writing (see Section 5) that there is to be an umpire, in which case Sections 21(3) to (6) apply to the extent that there is no written agreement to the contrary as to the umpire's functions. This Section derives in part from Section 8(2) and (3) of the 1950 Act. See DAC Report paras. 91 to 94 and 360 and DAC Suppl. para. 22.

2. Distinction between an umpire and a chairman. The role of an umpire, as distinct from a chairman, is a 'peculiarly English concept' (DAC Report, para. 94) and sometimes causes confusion. (In the United States, the term 'umpire' is often used to describe the presiding arbitrator, who is referred to as 'chairman' in the Act.) A chairman is appointed at the commencement of the proceedings and acts throughout as one of the arbitrators: receiving correspondence, pleadings and submissions; attending hearings; and casting his vote in connection with all decisions which have to be made by the tribunal. (He will also, most probably, be responsible for convening hearings, and may have additional powers given to him by agreement or under the Act (see Section 20).) An umpire only has a role if the two arbitrators cannot agree, whereupon the umpire makes the decision instead of the arbitrators. Often, the two arbitrators will then act as advocates in front of the umpire on behalf of the parties that appointed them. Under the previous law, the umpire was not required to attend any hearings or be supplied with any documents until his services were required. In practice, the appointment of an umpire is uncommon.

3. Appointment of umpire. By Section 16(1), the parties are free to agree upon the procedure for appointing the umpire but, to the extent that there is no such agreement, Section 16(6)(b) requires the two arbitrators to appoint the umpire before any substantive hearing or forthwith if they cannot agree on a matter relating to the arbitration.

4. Replacement of arbitrators. The umpire replaces the two arbitrators as soon as they cannot agree on a matter relating to the arbitration and appropriate notice has been given (Section 21(4)). His powers include procedural and evidential matters (see Section 34). He then proceeds to act for the rest of the arbitration as if he was a sole arbitrator. The parties can agree in writing that the umpire should not replace the tribunal, but only decide those matters upon which the two arbitrators disagree (Section 21(1)(b)). In certain circumstances, any party may apply to the court for an order that the umpire shall replace the arbitrators. For applications to the court, see Section 80 and CPR Part 62.

5. Attendance at proceedings. In the absence of agreement to the contrary, the umpire shall attend the proceedings and be supplied with the same documents and other materials as the arbitrators (Section 21(3)). But if the umpire does attend any part of the proceedings, he should not take an active part until he is called upon to perform his role (although it may be useful for him to listen in on the arbitrators' deliberations). If an umpire intends to charge the parties for his time for attending the proceedings before he formally assumes his role, it would be sensible for him to get the agreement of the parties first.

6. No umpire. For decision-making where there is no umpire, see Section 22.

[Decision-making where no chairman or umpire]

Section 22

(1) Where the parties agree that there shall be two or more arbitrators with no chairman or umpire, the parties are free to agree how the tribunal is to make decisions, orders and awards.

(2) If there is no such agreement, decisions, orders and awards shall be made by all or a majority of the arbitrators.

1. General. Section 22 concerns decision-making where the parties have agreed on two or more arbitrators, but no chairman or umpire. It is non-mandatory (see Section 4(2)), but Section 22(2) applies in the absence of written agreement to the contrary (see Section 5). (If the parties simply provide that there should be an even number of arbitrators, under Section 15(2) an additional arbitrator should be appointed as chairman.) This Section applies the same principle as is found in art. 29 of the Model Law (see also Section 20(3) of the Act). It fills the decision-making gap left by Section 20(3) and (4) (which apply if there is a chairman) and Section 21(4) (which applies if there is an umpire). See DAC Report para. 95.

2. Majority decisions. In the absence of agreement to the contrary, decisions, orders and awards shall be made by all or a majority of the arbitrators. If the arbitrators cannot reach a unanimous or majority view, there is a deadlock and the arbitration agreement cannot continue to operate (as opposed to the situation where there is a chairman, who has a casting vote, Section 20(4)).

[Revocation of arbitrator's authority]

Section 23

(1) The parties are free to agree in what circumstances the authority of an arbitrator may be revoked.

(2) If or to the extent that there is no such agreement the following provisions apply.

(3) The authority of an arbitrator may not be revoked except –
  (a) by the parties acting jointly, or
  (b) by an arbitral or other institution or person vested by the parties with powers in that regard.

(4) Revocation of the authority of an arbitrator by the parties acting jointly must be agreed in writing unless the parties also agree (whether or not in writing) to terminate the arbitration agreement.

(5) Nothing in this section affects the power of the court –
  (a) to revoke an appointment under section 18 (powers exercisable in case of failure of appointment procedure), or
  (b) to remove an arbitrator on the grounds specified in section 24.

1. General. Section 23 concerns the limits on the power of a party to revoke an arbitrator's authority. It is non-mandatory (see Section 4(2)), but Sections 23(3) and (4) apply to the extent that there is no written agreement to the contrary (see Section 5). This Section derives from Section 1 of the 1950 Act. The comparable provision in the Model Law is art. 14. See DAC Report paras. 96 to 99.

2. Terminology. The difference in terms such as 'remove' and 'revocation of authority' is not intended to be of any legal significance (DAC Report, para. 98).

3. Revocation of authority. Section 23(3) retains the long-established rule that the appointment of an arbitrator cannot be unilaterally revoked by a party (including the party which appointed him). However, under Section 23(4), the parties acting jointly may agree to revoke the appointment for any reason (unlike art. 14 of the Model Law which requires that the arbitrator be unable to perform his functions or has failed to act without undue delay) and they need not obtain the leave of the court. Section 23(4), to the extent that it addresses termination of the arbitration agreement, provides an exception to the general rule that all agreements affecting the arbitration must be in writing (see Section 5). A party, which is dissatisfied with an arbitrator, but cannot reach agreement with the other party(ies) as to his revocation, may apply to the institution or person vested with powers in that regard (Section 23(3)(b)) and/or to the court for his removal on various grounds (Section 24).

4. Fees and expenses. An arbitrator whose authority is revoked under this Section is entitled to his reasonable fees and expenses (subject to any application to the court for the amount to be adjusted) (see Section 28).

5. Immunity. An arbitrator whose authority is revoked under this Section would enjoy immunity (save for acts or omissions shown to have been in bad faith) (see Section 29).

6. Termination of authority. An arbitrator's authority ends automatically upon the issue of a valid final award (whereupon he becomes functus officio, see Section 58) or upon earlier termination of the arbitration by the parties (Section 23(4)).

7. Removal and replacement of arbitrators. For replacement of arbitrators by an umpire, see Section 21; removal of an arbitrator by the court, see Sections 17, 18 and 24; resignation of an arbitrator, see Section 25; death of an arbitrator, see Section 26; and filling a vacancy and other consequential matters, see Section 27.

[Power of court to remove arbitrator]

Section 24

(1) A party to arbitral proceedings may (upon notice to the other parties, to the arbitrator concerned and to any other arbitrator) apply to the court to remove an arbitrator on any of the following grounds –
- **(a) that circumstances exist that give rise to justifiable doubts as to his impartiality;**
- **(b) that he does not possess the qualifications required by the arbitration agreement;**
- **(c) that he is physically or mentally incapable of conducting the proceedings or there are justifiable doubts as to his capacity to do so;**
- **(d) that he has refused or failed –**

English Arbitration Act (Chapter 23), Section 24

    (i) **properly to conduct the proceedings, or**
    (ii) **to use all reasonable despatch in conducting the proceedings or making an award,**
and that substantial injustice has been or will be caused to the applicant.

(2) If there is an arbitral or other institution or person vested by the parties with power to remove an arbitrator, the court shall not exercise its power of removal unless satisfied that the applicant has first exhausted any available recourse to that institution or person.

(3) The arbitral tribunal may continue the arbitral proceedings and make an award while an application to the court under this section is pending.

(4) Where the court removes an arbitrator, it may make such order as it thinks fit with respect to his entitlement (if any) to fees or expenses, or the repayment of any fees or expenses already paid.

(5) The arbitrator concerned is entitled to appear and be heard by the court before it makes any order under this section.

(6) The leave of the court is required for any appeal from a decision of the court under this section.

1. General. Section 24 sets out the situations where the court may remove an arbitrator. It is mandatory (see Section 4(1) and Schedule 1). The grounds for removal are narrower than under the old law (Sections 13(3), 23(1) and 24(1) of the 1950 Act). The corresponding provisions of the Model Law are arts. 12 to 14. See DAC Report paras. 100 to 110 and 361 and 362 and DAC Suppl. paras. 23 to 25.

2. Impartiality. An arbitrator may be removed where there are justifiable doubts as to his impartiality (Section 24(1)(a), see also Sections 1(a) and 33(1)(a) as to the requirement of impartiality). Unlike much arbitration legislation around the world, the Model Law (art. 12) and the 1950 European Convention on Human Rights (art. 6(1)), the Act does not require an arbitrator to be both impartial and independent. The DAC concluded that 'lack of independence, unless it gives rise to justifiable doubts about the impartiality of the arbitrator, is of no significance' (Report, para. 101) and that 'the inclusion of independence would give rise to endless arguments, as it has, for example, in the United States, where almost any connection (however remote) has been put forward to challenge the 'independence' of an arbitrator' (Report, para. 102). However, arbitration rules adopted by the parties may require an arbitrator to be independent as well as impartial (e.g. LCIA art. 5.2). Impartiality calls for a state of mind which is free from any influences extraneous to the merits of the particular case, which is capable of dispassionate inquiry and an objective judgment, and which is not turned aside by any motivation to favour one side as against the other (see *Roylance* v *General Medical Council*). The test for bias is the same for arbitrators as it is for judges (see *Locabail (UK) Ltd* v *Bayfield Properties Ltd*). The relevant test is 'whether the fair-minded and informed observer, having considered the facts, would conclude that there was a real possibility that the tribunal was biased' (*Porter* v *Magill*). In formulating the test in that way, the court has sought to be consistent with the jurisprudence of the Strasbourg court in its application of the ECHR. For examples of where an arbitrator has been removed because of prior dealings or inappropriate contact with a witness or party, see *Sphere Drake Insurance* v *American Reliable Insurance*, *ASM Shipping Ltd* v *TTMI Ltd*, *Norbrook Laboratories* v *A Tank* and *Rompetrol Group NV* v *Romania*. For the position of a counsel and arbitrator from the same barristers' chambers, see *Lawal* v *Northern Spirit Ltd*, *Smith* v *Kvaerner Cementation Foundations Ltd*, and *Hrvatska Elektroprivreda* v *The Republic of Slovenia*. In addition to apparent or unconscious bias, evidence of actual bias will, of course, justify removal of an arbitrator (see *Andrews* v *Bradshaw*). Also a pecuniary or proprietary interest in the subject matter of the dispute or if the arbitrator promotes the same cause in the same organisation as a party to the arbitration (where that cause is relevant to the issues in dispute) (see *R* v *Bow Street Metropolitan Stipendiary Magistrate, ex parte Pinochet (No. 2)*). A de minimis exception will apply if any financial interest is insignificant. The fundamental principle is that a person may not be a judge in his own cause. Unlike art. 12 of the Model Law, the Act does not require an arbitrator to disclose circumstances likely to give rise to justifiable doubts as to his impartiality. It is doubtful that the common law recognises any such obligation the breach of which, in the absence of impartiality, has legal consequences (see *AT & T Corp.* v *Saudi Cable Co.*). An award made by a tribunal that is not impartial may be challenged on grounds of serious irregularity (see Section 68(2)(a)). However, where a party knows of, or could have reasonably discovered, circumstances likely to give rise to doubts as to an arbitrator's impartiality, and does not object promptly, he may lose the right to object at a later stage (see Section 73).

3. Required qualifications. The parties may stipulate in their arbitration agreement (or agree subsequently) that an arbitrator must have certain qualifications or experience (Section 19). An arbitrator who does not meet such requirements may be removed (Section 24(1)(b)). An award made by a tribunal which does not possess the qualifications required by the arbitration agreement may be challenged on grounds that the tribunal lacked substantive jurisdiction, i.e. the tribunal was not properly constituted (see Sections 30(1)(b) and 67(1)).

4. Physically or mentally incapable. An arbitrator must not be physically or mentally incapable of conducting the proceedings (Section 24(1)(c)). Justifiable doubts will suffice to have an arbitrator removed.

5. Conduct of proceedings. An arbitrator must not refuse or fail properly to conduct the proceedings or to use all reasonable dispatch (Section 24(1)(d)). Such obligation includes a failure to comply with the arbitrator's duties

English Arbitration Act (Chapter 23), Section 24

under Section 33(1) (to act fairly and impartially as between the parties, giving each party a reasonable opportunity of putting its case and dealing with that of his opponent, and to adopt procedures suitable to the circumstances of the particular case, avoiding unnecessary delay or expense) and Section 68(2) (serious irregularity affecting the proceedings justifying the award being challenged), see *Benaim (UK) Ltd* v *Davies Middleton & Davies Ltd (No. 2)*. To justify removal under this ground, the court must be satisfied that substantial injustice has been or will be caused to the applicant. This is intended to dissuade parties from making applications intended to delay or disrupt the arbitration proceedings. Section 68(2) (challenging an award on grounds of serious irregularity) has a similar requirement, see also Sections 50(3) (order for extending time for making an award) and 79(3((b) (extending a time limit in relation to the arbitral proceedings).

6. Court application. For applications to the court, see Section 80 and CPR Part 62. An application under this Section must name each arbitrator as a defendant (CPR PD 62.6).

7. Prompt application. An application to the court under this Section should be made promptly: participation in the arbitration without objection after a party knows of grounds on which an arbitrator may be removed may lose that party the right to object (see Section 73, but also see Section 24(2)), and see *Wicketts* v *Brine Builders*.

8. Exhaustion of available recourse. Section 24(2) requires that a party seeking to remove an arbitrator first exhaust any available recourse to a relevant arbitral institution or person (for example, the chosen appointing authority). Many institutional rules make provision for the removal of an arbitrator on various grounds (e.g. LCIA art. 10, ICC arts. 11 and 12, UNCITRAL arts. 9-12). However, a decision by any such institution not to remove an arbitrator is not finally determinative of the issue and an application may then be made to the court.

9. Continuance of arbitral proceedings. The tribunal may continue with the arbitration while an application is pending (Section 24(3)), but the tribunal should consider carefully whether it would be more prudent to stay the arbitral proceedings, especially a substantive hearing.

10. Fees and expenses. The court may make an order concerning the entitlement (if any) of an arbitrator who has been removed to his fees or expenses (Section 24(4)).

11. Immunity. Contrary to the recommendation of the DAC Report (para. 361), an arbitrator removed pursuant to this Section will be immune from liability save where bad faith is shown (see Section 29) (whereas an arbitrator who resigns will not enjoy immunity, Section 25).

12. Right to appear and be heard. As a matter of justice, the arbitrator concerned is entitled to appear and be heard by the court (Section 24(5)), although this might expose him to cross-examination and/or costs. The safer course may be for the arbitrator to write to the parties and to allow them to submit such correspondence in evidence.

13. Parties' agreement. The court's power under this Section is not affected by any agreement between the parties as to the circumstances in which they may revoke the authority of an arbitrator (see Section 23(5)(b)).

14. Other circumstances. For other circumstances where an arbitrator may be removed by the court, see Sections 17 and 18. For replacement of arbitrators by an umpire, see Section 21; revocation of an arbitrator's authority by the parties, see Section 23; resignation of an arbitrator, see Section 25; and death of an arbitrator, see Section 26.

15. Filling a vacancy. For filling a vacancy and other consequential matters, see Section 27.

16. Challenge to award. For challenging an award on grounds of serious irregularity affecting the tribunal, the proceedings or the award, see Section 68.

[Resignation of arbitrator]

Section 25

(1) The parties are free to agree with an arbitrator as to the consequences of his resignation as regards –
- **(a) his entitlement (if any) to fees or expenses, and**
- **(b) any liability thereby incurred by him.**

(2) If or to the extent that there is no such agreement the following provisions apply.

(3) An arbitrator who resigns his appointment may (upon notice to the parties) apply to the court –
- **(a) to grant him relief from any liability thereby incurred by him, and**
- **(b) to make such order as it thinks fit with respect to his entitlement (if any) to fees or expenses or the repayment of any fees or expenses already paid.**

(4) If the court is satisfied that in all the circumstances it was reasonable for the arbitrator to resign, it may grant such relief as is mentioned in subsection (3)(a) on such terms as it thinks fit.

(5) The leave of the court is required for any appeal from a decision of the court under this section.

1. General. Section 25 concerns the financial consequences for the arbitrator should he resign. It is non-mandatory (see Section 4(2)), but Sections 25(3) to (5) apply to the extent that there is no written agreement to the contrary (see Section 5). This Section derives from art. 14 of the Model Law. See DAC Report paras. 111 to 115 and 363 and DAC Suppl. para. 26.

2. Breach of contract. By resigning without good cause, an arbitrator will most likely be in breach of his contract with the parties. In the absence of any agreement to the contrary, the arbitrator may no longer be entitled to any fees and/or expenses and may be liable for any wasted costs incurred by the parties. In such circumstances, an arbitrator does not enjoy any immunity (Section 29(3)). Institutional arbitration rules, if chosen by the parties, often prescribe the financial consequences of an arbitrator resigning (e.g. LCIA art. 10.1, but not the UNCITRAL Rules).

3. Application to court for relief. Section 25(3) provides relief for arbitrators who have good reason to resign. The DAC Report (para. 115) gives as possible examples, where the arbitrator reasonably perceives a conflict between his duties under Section 33 and the requirements of the parties, and where the parties' actions have made the arbitration an unfair burden on the arbitrator. For applications to the court, see Section 80 and CPR Part 62.

4. Filling a vacancy. For filling a vacancy and other consequential matters (such as whether the previous proceedings should stand), see Section 27.

[Death of arbitrator or person appointing him]
Section 26

(1) The authority of an arbitrator is personal and ceases on his death.
(2) Unless otherwise agreed by the parties, the death of the person by whom an arbitrator was appointed does not revoke the arbitrator's authority.

1. General. Section 26 concerns the death of the arbitrator or the person by whom he was appointed. Section 26(1) is mandatory (see Section 4(1) and Schedule 1). Section 26(2) is non-mandatory (see Section 4(2)), but it will apply in the absence of a written agreement to the contrary (see Section 5). Similar provisions were implicit in the 1950 Act. There is no comparable provision in the Model Law. See DAC Report para. 116. Whether an arbitration agreement is discharged by the death of a party, see Section 8.

2. Death of an arbitrator. Section 26(1) is a new provision, but its effect was implicit in Sections 7 and 10 of the 1950 Act, which provided for the replacement of an arbitrator who had died (rather than his personal representative(s) having any continuing role). For filling a vacancy and other consequential matters (such as whether the previous proceedings should stand), see Section 27.

3. Death of appointer. Section 26(2) widens Section 2(2) of the 1950 Act by referring to the death of the 'person' who made the appointment rather than the 'party', making it clear that, subject to the parties agreeing to the contrary, where an arbitrator has been appointed by a third party, the death of that third party does not terminate the arbitrator's appointment. Where

Sheppard

[Filling of vacancy, &c]

Section 27

(1) Where an arbitrator ceases to hold office, the parties are free to agree –
  (a) whether and if so how the vacancy is to be filled,
  (b) whether and if so to what extent the previous proceedings should stand, and
  (c) what effect (if any) his ceasing to hold office has on any appointment made by him (alone or jointly).

(2) If or to the extent that there is no such agreement, the following provisions apply.

(3) The provisions of sections 16 (procedure for appointment of arbitrators) and 18 (failure of appointment procedure) apply in relation to the filling of the vacancy as in relation to an original appointment.

(4) The tribunal (when reconstituted) shall determine whether and if so to what extent the previous proceedings should stand.

This does not affect any right of a party to challenge those proceedings on any ground which had arisen before the arbitrator ceased to hold office.

(5) His ceasing to hold office does not affect any appointment by him (alone or jointly) of another arbitrator, in particular any appointment of a chairman or umpire.

1. General. Section 27 concerns the filling of a vacancy on the tribunal. It is non-mandatory (Section 4(2)), but Sections 27(3) to (5) apply to the extent that there is no written agreement to the contrary (see Section 5). Section 27 replaces Sections 7(a), 10 and 25 of the 1950 Act. This Section also derives from art. 15 of the Model Law. See DAC Report paras. 117 to 119.

2. Causes. A vacancy on the tribunal may exist as a result of revocation of an arbitrator's authority (Section 23), removal by the court (Section 24), resignation (Section 25) or death (Section 26).

3. Filling of vacancy. Where the parties have not agreed upon an appointment procedure for the replacement arbitrator, Section 16 (procedure for appointment of arbitrators) and Section 18 (failure of appointment procedure) will apply. Even if there is no express provision in the contract on how to fill a vacancy, the same procedure and time limits prescribed for making the original appointment will generally apply (see *Federal Insurance Co.* v *Transamerica Occidental Life Insurance Co.*). The court has not retained a power to make a direct appointment (as was the case under Section 25 of the 1950 Act). Where the parties have chosen arbitration rules, those rules will usually provide how a vacancy should be filled (e.g. LCIA art. 11, ICC art. 12(4), UNCITRAL art. 13).

4. Standing of previous proceedings. In the absence of an agreement to the contrary, the tribunal once reconstituted shall determine the standing of the prior proceedings. If appropriate, it may determine that prior oral evidence/submissions should be reheard. For decision-making by the tribunal, see Sections 20 and 22. Any institutional rules chosen by the parties may prescribe whether and to what extent prior proceedings should be repeated before the reconstituted tribunal (e.g. ICC art. 12(4) and UNCITRAL art. 14; but not LCIA).

5. Appointments. In the absence of an agreement to the contrary, any appointments in which the former arbitrator participated, such as appointment of the chairman or umpire and/or an expert to assist the tribunal, are not affected. Section 27(5) overlaps with Section 26(2) (death of the person who appointed a chairman or umpire).

[Joint and several liability of parties to arbitrators for fees and expenses]

Section 28

(1) The parties are jointly and severally liable to pay to the arbitrators such reasonable fees and expenses (if any) as are appropriate in the circumstances.

(2) Any party may apply to the court (upon notice to the other parties and to the arbitrators) which may order that the amount of the arbitrators' fees and expenses shall be considered and adjusted by such means and upon such terms as it may direct.

(3) If the application is made after any amount has been paid to the arbitrators by way of fees or expenses, the court may order the repayment of such amount (if any) as is shown to be excessive, but shall not do so unless it is shown that it is reasonable in the circumstances to order repayment.

(4) The above provisions have effect subject to any order of the court under section 24(4) or 25(3)(b) (order as to entitlement to fees or expenses in case of removal or resignation of arbitrator).

(5) Nothing in this section affects any liability of a party to any other party to pay all or any of the costs of the arbitration (see sections 59 to 65) or any contractual right of an arbitrator to payment of his fees and expenses.

(6) In this section references to arbitrators include an arbitrator who has ceased to act and an umpire who has not replaced the other arbitrators.

1. General. Section 28 concerns the liability of the parties to pay the tribunal's fees. It is mandatory (see Section 4(1) and Schedule 1). There is no comparable provision in the Model Law nor the previous legislation. See DAC Report paras. 120 to 130.

2. Joint and several liability. Section 28(1) confirms what was generally regarded to be the position at common law, namely that all parties are jointly and severally liable for the reasonable fees and expenses of the arbitrator(s), meaning that the tribunal may seek payment of all such fees and expenses from just one or some or all of the parties. There is some doubt as to whether a respondent who successfully challenges jurisdiction was ever a 'party' and therefore liable for the arbitrator's fees. In this author's opinion, to the extent that such respondent participates in the proceedings, it should be regarded as a 'party' pursuant to an ad hoc submission on the question of jurisdiction, and that in the normal course it should pay its share of the fees, but the reasonable costs of a successful challenge should be reimbursed by the other side.

3. Reasonable fees and expenses. The parties' liability is to pay such reasonable fees and expenses of the arbitrators as are appropriate in the circumstances, which may be determined by the court if necessary. The court will likely have regard to the usual fees of the arbitrator, the time spent, the complexity of the matter, and whether the tribunal adopted procedures suitable to the circumstances of the case (Section 33(1)(b)). Expenses include the fees and expenses of any expert, legal adviser or assessor appointed by the tribunal for which the arbitrator is liable (Section 37(2)). The court may even review the determination by an arbitral institution as to the fees to which an arbitrator is entitled (see *Hussmann (Europe) Ltd* v *Al Ameen Development & Trade*). The amount properly payable for the purposes of obtaining delivery of the award (Section 56(3)) is the amount a party is liable to pay the tribunal pursuant to Section 28.

4. Court application. For applications to the court, see Section 80 and CPR Part 62. An application under this Section must name each arbitrator as a defendant (CPR PD 62.6).

5. Repayment. Where fees or expenses have already been paid to an arbitrator, a party will only be able to obtain repayment if it shows the court both that the amount was excessive and that it is reasonable to order repayment (Section 28(3)), but the court may excuse even a lengthy delay (see *United Tyre Company* v *Born*).

6. Removal/resignation. Section 28 must be read in conjunction with the court's powers under Section 24(4) (removal of an arbitrator) and Section 25(3)(b) (resignation of an arbitrator) to make such order as it thinks fit with respect to the arbitrator's entitlement to fees and expenses (Section 28(4)).

7. Agreement on fees and expenses. Where an arbitrator has agreed his fees and expenses with the parties, the arbitrator's contractual rights to payment of that amount will be upheld (Section 28(5)). However, where one party, but not the other, has agreed the fees of an arbitrator and these are later held to be unreasonable, the other party is only liable on a joint and several basis for the amount determined by the court to be reasonable, but the first party may be contractually liable to pay the balance.

8. Liability as to costs. For the liability of one party to any other party to pay all or any of the latter's costs of the arbitration, see Sections 59 to 65 (Section 28(5)).

[Immunity of arbitrator]
Section 29

(1) An arbitrator is not liable for anything done or omitted in the discharge or purported discharge of his functions as arbitrator unless the act or omission is shown to have been in bad faith.

(2) Subsection (1) applies to an employee or agent of an arbitrator as it applies to the arbitrator himself.

(3) This section does not affect any liability incurred by an arbitrator by reason of his resigning (but see section 25).

1. General. Section 29 concerns the immunity of arbitrators from suit. It is mandatory (see Section 4(1) and Schedule 1). There is no comparable provision in the Model Law nor in the previous legislation. It resolves the previous uncertainty at English common law as to the degree of immunity enjoyed by arbitrators (and their employees or agents) in favour of immunity save where bad faith is shown. See DAC Report paras. 131 to 136 and 361 to 362. For the immunity of arbitral institutions and appointing bodies, see Section 74.

2. Functions as arbitrator. An arbitrator enjoys immunity in respect of anything done or omitted in the discharge or purported discharge of his functions as arbitrator. Anything outside the scope of such functions (e.g. defamatory comments not connected to the proceedings) would not be protected. It is unlikely that an arbitrator would enjoy immunity in respect of any criminal conduct.

3. Bad faith. There are a number of English cases in which the meaning of the expression 'bad faith' has been considered (e.g. *Melton Medes Ltd* v *Securities and Investment Board*). It has been defined as malice (in the sense of personal spite or desire to injure for improper reason) or it describes a situation where a decision is made when the arbitrator knew that he had no power to make it.

4. Effect of resignation. An arbitrator who resigns (Section 25) does not enjoy immunity from liability; although, curiously, if an arbitrator is removed from office by the court (Section 24(1)) he does (contrary to the recommendation of the DAC Report para. 361).

5. Party to court proceedings. An arbitrator may have to become a party to court proceedings, for example, as a defendant where an application is made to remove him (Section 24, and CPR PD 62.6), or in respect of his fees and expenses (Sections 28 and 56, and CPR PD 62.6) or as an applicant under the Act (such as to enforce a peremptory order, see Section 42(2)(a)).

JURISDICTION OF THE ARBITRAL TRIBUNAL

[Competence of tribunal to rule on its own jurisdiction]

Section 30

(1) Unless otherwise agreed by the parties, the arbitral tribunal may rule on its own substantive jurisdiction, that is, as to –
  (a) whether there is a valid arbitration agreement,
  (b) whether the tribunal is properly constituted, and
  (c) what matters have been submitted to arbitration in accordance with the arbitration agreement.

(2) Any such ruling may be challenged by any available arbitral process of appeal or review or in accordance with the provisions of this Part.

1. General. Section 30 provides that the arbitral tribunal may decide its own jurisdiction and enacts the internationally recognised doctrine of 'Kompetenz/Kompetenz'. This Section is non-mandatory (see Section 4(2)), but it applies unless the parties agree in writing to the contrary (see Section 5). It is based upon art. 16.1 of the Model Law and reflects the position as it was at common law. It should be read together with Section 31. See DAC Report paras. 137 to 139. The arbitral rules chosen by the parties may also provide that the tribunal shall have the power to rule on its own jurisdiction (e.g. LCIA art. 23.1, ICC art. 8). For the related principle of separability of the arbitration agreement, see Section 7.

2. Ruling. A tribunal may make a ruling on jurisdiction, but it may be challenged in the courts (see note 4 below). The tribunal may do so without being requested or it may accede to a request by the claimant (in the event, for example, that the respondent is not participating in the arbitration, but is expected to raise an objection at a later stage) and must do so if an objection is raised by the respondent (or by a claimant concerning a counterclaim) (see Section 31). The tribunal may choose to make a separate award as to jurisdiction or deal with the matter in its award on the merits, unless the parties agree in writing which course it should take (see Section 31(4)). For the court's powers to make a ruling at the outset of proceedings that the tribunal lacks substantive jurisdiction, see Section 32. For the relationship between Sections 30, 31 and 32, see *Azov Shipping Co.* v *Baltic Shipping Co*. For the relationship between these provisions and an application for a stay of litigation, see Section 9 and, e.g., *Law Debenture Trust Corporation* v *Elektrim Finance*, which held that the court need not necessarily stay proceedings to let the tribunal first decide issues of jurisdiction, but contrast *Fiona Trust* v *Privalov*, which appears to favour letting the tribunal decide in the first instance.

3. Substantive jurisdiction. Section 30(1) defines what is meant by 'substantive jurisdiction' (see also Section 82(1)). Concerning Section 30(1)(a), 'arbitration agreement' is defined in Section 6. For arbitration agreements which are null and void, inoperative or incapable of being performed, see also Section 9(4) (stay of legal proceedings). In relation to statutory arbitration, the reference to 'whether there is a valid arbitration agreement' should be construed as a reference to 'whether the enactment applies to the dispute or difference in question' (see Section 96(2)). Section 30(1)(b) concerns the appointment of the tribunal (see Section 16). It would also include an issue as to whether an arbitrator possessed the qualifications required by the arbitration agreement (see Sections 19 and 24(1)(b)). Section 30(1)(c) concerns the scope of the arbitration agreement (see Section 6(1)). Since the House of Lords' decision in *Fiona Trust* v *Privalov*, general wording is likely to be given a broad interpretation. The common law rules relating to what matters are capable of settlement by arbitration have been retained (see Section 81(1)(a)).

4. Challenge. The arbitration rules chosen by the parties may provide a mechanism for appealing or reviewing the tribunal's ruling on substantive jurisdiction (e.g. GAFTA Rule 8.1). In any event, a dissatisfied party may challenge the tribunal's ruling in the courts: see Section 66(3) (refusing leave to enforce the award); Section 67 (challenging the award on grounds that the tribunal lacked substantive jurisdiction); and Section 72 (saving for rights of person who takes no part in proceedings). The right to object to a lack of substantive jurisdiction may be lost, see Section 73.

5. Foreign awards. For refusing enforcement of a foreign award on grounds that the tribunal lacked jurisdiction, see Sections 99 (and Section 37 of the 1950 Act), 103 and 104 (and 66(3)).

[Objection to substantive jurisdiction of tribunal]

Section 31

(1) An objection that the arbitral tribunal lacks substantive jurisdiction at the outset of the proceedings must be raised by a party not later than the time he takes the first step in the proceedings to contest the merits of any matter in relation to which he challenges the tribunal's jurisdiction.

A party is not precluded from raising such an objection by the fact that he has appointed or participated in the appointment of an arbitrator.

(2) Any objection during the course of the arbitral proceedings that the arbitral tribunal is exceeding its substantive jurisdiction must be made as soon as possible after the matter alleged to be beyond its jurisdiction is raised.

English Arbitration Act (Chapter 23), Section 31

(3) The arbitral tribunal may admit an objection later than the time specified in subsection (1) or (2) if it considers the delay justified.

(4) Where an objection is duly taken to the tribunal's substantive jurisdiction and the tribunal has power to rule on its own jurisdiction, it may –

    (a) rule on the matter in an award as to jurisdiction, or

    (b) deal with the objection in its award on the merits.

If the parties agree which of these courses the tribunal should take, the tribunal shall proceed accordingly.

(5) The tribunal may in any case, and shall if the parties so agree, stay proceedings whilst an application is made to the court under section 32 (determination of preliminary point of jurisdiction).

1. General. Section 31 sets out various procedural issues relating to an application to the tribunal to determine its substantive jurisdiction. This Section is mandatory (see Section 4(1) and Schedule 1), but it is relevant only if the tribunal has power to rule upon its own jurisdiction pursuant to Section 30 (which is subject to any written agreement of the parties to the contrary). This Section is based upon arts. 16(2) and (3) of the Model Law. See DAC Report paras. 140 to 146. For applications to the court (instead of the tribunal) to determine a preliminary point of jurisdiction, see Section 32. For the rights of a party which does not take part in an arbitration commenced against it to challenge the jurisdiction of the tribunal, see Section 72.

2. First step in the proceedings. The expression 'first step in the proceedings to contest the merits' in Section 31(1) is analogous to the time restriction for challenging the jurisdiction of the High Court pursuant to CPR Rule 11.1(4)(a). It is generally understood to mean some formal step. The first step in the proceedings to contest the merits will often be the submission of a statement of defence (see art. 16(2) of the Model Law and CPR Rule 11.1(4)(b)), although it may be as early as the written response to a request for arbitration (e.g. ICC art. 5). See also Section 9(3) (stay of legal proceedings), which contains a similar phrase.

3. Exceeding substantive jurisdiction. A party may also object during the course of the arbitration that the tribunal is exceeding its substantive jurisdiction (Section 31(2)). The phrase 'as soon as possible' is likely to be subject to an implied level of reasonableness (see for example *Wicketts* v *Brine Builders*, where under Section 73 'forthwith' was held to mean something equivalent to 'promptly' or 'without unnecessary delay'). However, the right to object may also be lost pursuant to Section 73 if the objection is not made 'forthwith'.

4. Form of objection. The Act does not prescribe the form which any objection should take. It would usually be made in writing and supported at the time or subsequently by reasons and evidence (if any) and, if there has been any delay, an explanation as to why the objection was not made earlier. Objections to jurisdiction are usually made by a respondent, but they could be made by a claimant (in relation to a counterclaim) or a claimant could request the tribunal to make a preliminary ruling under Section 30 confirming its jurisdiction.

5. Ruling. Whether to rule on jurisdiction as a preliminary issue or together with the merits is for the discretion of the tribunal (see *AOOT Kalmneft* v *Glenmore International*), unless the parties agree and direct the tribunal (Section 31(4)). (See also Section 47, awards on different issues.) Concerning the form and effect of any award, see Sections 46 to 52.

6. Challenge. As noted in relation to Section 30, the tribunal's ruling may be appealed/reviewed pursuant to any mechanism prescribed by the arbitration rules chosen by the parties (if any) (see Section 30(2)) and/or challenged in the courts (see Sections 66(3), 67 and 70).

7. Stay. A tribunal should consider staying the arbitration whilst an application is made to the court under Section 32, and, in any event, must do so if unanimously directed to do so by the parties (see Section 31(5)).

[Determination of preliminary point of jurisdiction]

Section 32

(1) The court may, on the application of a party to arbitral proceedings (upon notice to the other parties), determine any question as to the substantive jurisdiction of the tribunal.

A party may lose the right to object (see section 73).

(2) An application under this section shall not be considered unless –
  (a) it is made with the agreement in writing of all the other parties to the proceedings, or
  (b) it is made with the permission of the tribunal and the court is satisfied –
   (i) that the determination of the question is likely to produce substantial savings in costs,
   (ii) that the application was made without delay, and
   (iii) that there is good reason why the matter should be decided by the court.

(3) An application under this section, unless made with the agreement of all the other parties to the proceedings, shall state the grounds on which it is said that the matter should be decided by the court.

(4) Unless otherwise agreed by the parties, the arbitral tribunal may continue the arbitral proceedings and make an award while an application to the court under this section is pending.

(5) Unless the court gives leave, no appeal lies from a decision of the court whether the conditions specified in subsection (2) are met.

(6) The decision of the court on the question of jurisdiction shall be treated as a judgment of the court for the purposes of an appeal.

But no appeal lies without the leave of the court which shall not be given unless the court considers that the question involves a point of law which is one of general importance or is one which for some other special reason should be considered by the Court of Appeal.

1. General. Section 32 sets out the power of the court to determine the tribunal's substantive jurisdiction. This Section is mandatory (see Section 4(1) and Schedule 1). There is no comparable provision in the Model Law (but see art. 16(3) which provides for appealing the tribunal's ruling on jurisdiction to the court) nor in the previous legislation. See DAC Report paras. 147 to 149 and DAC Suppl. para. 27. For applications to the tribunal (instead of the court) to determine a preliminary point of jurisdiction, see Sections 30 and 31.

2. Conditions. Section 32(2) sets out a number of conditions to the making of an application to the court. It must be with the agreement of all the parties or with the permission of the tribunal. It must be made without delay (contrast 'prior to taking the first step in the proceedings' and 'as soon as possible' in Section 31, and 'forthwith' in Section 73). It must be likely to produce a substantial saving in costs and there must be good reason why the matter should be decided by the court. The strong implication is that a party should apply to the tribunal. The DAC Report noted that Section 32 is only intended to be relied upon in exceptional cases (para. 147).

3. Application. For applications to the court, see Section 80 and CPR Part 49 and PD 49G para. 19.

4. Stay. Unless the parties all agree in writing that the arbitration should be stayed, the tribunal has a discretion as to whether or not to continue the arbitral proceedings while the court application is pending (Section 32(4), see also Section 31(5)). It may be prudent to stay the arbitration, in order to avoid possible wasted costs.

5. Other provisions. For additional powers of the court in relation to the tribunal's jurisdiction, see Sections 66(3) (refusing leave to enforce the award) and 67 (challenging the award). For the rights of a party which does not take part in an arbitration commenced against it to challenge the jurisdiction of the tribunal, see Section 72. For refusing enforcement of a foreign award on grounds that the tribunal lacked jurisdiction, see Sections 66(3), 99 (and 37 of the 1950 Act), 103 and 104.

6. Declaration of validity. Following the decision of the ECJ in *West Tankers* that the English courts cannot issue an anti-suit injunction in connection with court proceedings commenced in another EU Member State in purported breach of an agreement to arbitrate, a party may not apply for a declaration that such arbitration agreement is valid and binding (see Section 6), see *National Navigation* v *Endesa*.

THE ARBITRAL PROCEEDINGS
[General duty of the tribunal]
Section 33

(1) The tribunal shall –
   (a) act fairly and impartially as between the parties, giving each party a reasonable opportunity of putting his case and dealing with that of his opponent, and
   (b) adopt procedures suitable to the circumstances of the particular case, avoiding unnecessary delay or expense, so as to provide a fair means for the resolution of the matters falling to be determined.

(2) The tribunal shall comply with that general duty in conducting the arbitral proceedings, in its decisions on matters of procedure and evidence and in the exercise of all other powers conferred on it.

1. General. Section 33 sets out the general duty of the tribunal. This Section is mandatory (see Section 4(1) and Schedule 1) and it is one of the most important provisions in the Act. This Section is based on arts. 18 and 19(2) of the Model Law. There is no comparable provision in the previous law. See DAC Report paras. 150 to 165. Section 33 complements Section 1 (general principles) and Section 40 (general duty of parties).

2. Positive duty. This Section imposes a positive duty upon the tribunal to fulfil the object of arbitration set out in Section 1(a) (i.e. 'to obtain the fair resolution of disputes by an impartial tribunal without unnecessary delay or expense'). The tribunal must comply with this duty in the exercise of all its powers (Section 33(2)). Sections 34, 35, 37, 38 and 39 set out the tribunal's powers and each must be read in the context of the tribunal's general duty contained in this Section 33.

3. Acting fairly and impartially. The tribunal must act fairly and impartially (Section 33(1)(a)). For the test of impartiality, see Section 24(1)(a). An arbitrator whose partiality is reasonably in doubt may be removed under Section 23 or 24. The phrase 'reasonable opportunity' (of putting its case) was chosen instead of 'full opportunity' as used in the Model Law in order to deter a party from arguing that it is entitled to as much time as its likes and to encourage the tribunal to impose reasonable time limits. Its Section 33 duty is not incompatible with Section 41(4), which gives the tribunal power to proceed in the event of non-participation of a party. However, it may be a breach of this Section for an arbitrator to rely upon any argument in making an order or award which had not been advanced by either party without giving the affected party an opportunity to deal with it (see *Gbangbola* v *Smith & Sherriff Ltd*; and *Vee Networks Ltd* v *Econet Wireless International Ltd*).

4. Suitable procedures. The tribunal must adopt suitable procedures. The relevant 'circumstances of the particular case' might include the complexity of the issues, the amount in dispute, the importance of the outcome to the parties, the type and extent of the evidence, the financial status of the parties, and the approach of the respondent. The tribunal may achieve the objective of this provision by making appropriate procedural and/or evidential decisions (Section 34) and/or exercising the powers given to it in case of a party's default (Section 41) and/or by dividing up the matters to be determined (Section 47) and/or limiting recoverable costs (Section 65) and/or otherwise. The procedures adopted need not reflect court procedures, but must be concerned principally with avoiding unnecessary delay and expense. It has been endorsed by the courts that it is unnecessary for an arbitrator to follow 'court' procedures slavishly or at all (see *Margauld Ltd* v *Exide Technologies*, where it was held that an arbitrator had acted correctly in refusing to allow the claimant the last word).

5. Non-compliance. An arbitrator who does not comply with his duty under this Section may be removed by the parties (Section 23) or the relevant arbitral institution (e.g. LCIA art. 10.2) or the court (Section 24(1)(a) and (d)) or his award may be challenged on grounds of serious irregularity (Section 68(2)(a)). However, unmeritorious applications, relying upon the general language of this Section (due to the difficulty in legislating for the wide range of arbitrations to which it applies) are likely to be given short shrift (see DAC Report para. 151).

6. Conflict. Should an arbitrator consider that his obligation to respect the principle of party autonomy (see Section 1(b) and proviso to Section 34(1)) gives rise to a conflict with his duty under this Section, he may either proceed as directed by the parties (in which event there would be a good defence to any subsequent claim under Sections 24 or 68(2)(a) that he had failed properly to conduct the proceedings) or resign (and seek the discretionary relief of the court pursuant to Section 25).

[Procedural and evidential matters]

Section 34

(1) It shall be for the tribunal to decide all procedural and evidential matters, subject to the right of the parties to agree any matter.
(2) Procedural and evidential matters include –
- **(a) when and where any part of the proceedings is to be held;**
- **(b) the language or languages to be used in the proceedings and whether translations of any relevant documents are to be supplied;**

(c) whether any and if so what form of written statements of claim and defence are to be used, when these should be supplied and the extent to which such statements can be later amended;
(d) whether any and if so which documents or classes of documents should be disclosed between and produced by the parties and at what stage;
(e) whether any and if so what questions should be put to and answered by the respective parties and when and in what form this should be done;
(f) whether to apply strict rules of evidence (or any other rules) as to the admissibility, relevance or weight of any material (oral, written or other) sought to be tendered on any matters of fact or opinion, and the time, manner and form in which such material should be exchanged and presented;
(g) whether and to what extent the tribunal should itself take the initiative in ascertaining the facts and the law;
(h) whether and to what extent there should be oral or written evidence or submissions.

(3) The tribunal may fix the time within which any directions given by it are to be complied with, and may if it thinks fit extend the time so fixed (whether or not it has expired).

1. General. Section 34 sets out the very wide powers of the tribunal to deal with procedural and evidential matters. This Section is non-mandatory (see Section 4(2)). It applies to the extent that there is no written agreement to the contrary (see Section 5). This Section is drawn partly from arts. 9, 20 and 22 to 24 of the Model Law and replaces Sections 12(1) to (3) of the 1950 Act. See DAC Report paras. 166 to 176.

2. Discretion of tribunal. The tribunal has a broad discretion to conduct the arbitration as it thinks appropriate, subject to party autonomy. It is sometimes said that the tribunal is master of its own procedure. Certainly, the tribunal may depart from court procedures. However, in all cases (not just those listed in Section 34(2)), the tribunal must exercise its powers in accordance with its mandatory duty under Section 33 (which includes adopting 'procedures suitable to the circumstances of the particular case'). Additional powers of the tribunal are set out in Section 38. Section 40(2) (general duty of parties) provides that the parties shall comply 'without delay with any determination of the tribunal as to procedural or evidential matters'. For the powers of the tribunal in case of a party's default, see Section 41; and for the support powers of the court, see Sections 42 to 44.

3. When and where. Pursuant to Section 34(2)(a), the tribunal may fix the timetable. It may also decide where any meetings, hearings, etc. are to be held. The venue of hearings need not be at the seat of the arbitration (see Section 3). For example, in some cases, a site visit may be appropriate or to have the hearing at a venue where witnesses can obtain visas more easily.

4. Language. Pursuant to Section 34(2)(b), the tribunal may determine the language of the arbitration. This will often be the language of the contract, but not necessarily if the majority of the relevant communications are in a different language. Usually, the party relying on a document must provide a translation. A witness may provide a statement in his own language, but must provide a translation and have an interpreter at any oral hearing.

5. Form of pleadings. Pursuant to Section 34(2)(c), the tribunal can direct the timing and style of the parties' written pleadings, including statements of claim, defence (and counterclaim), and reply (and defence to counterclaim), and rejoinder. For example, the tribunal may order that the statements must be accompanied by all documents relied upon and/or include reference to which witnesses will prove a particular allegation and/or include any submissions on the law. The arbitrators even have the power, albeit rarely used in practice, to order that no written pleadings be submitted.

6. Document production. Pursuant to Section 34(2)(d), the tribunal has power over the production of documents. The tribunal may order full disclosure of all documents in the possession, custody or power of a party relating to matters in question in the action (e.g. the Peruvian Guano test – named after the case of that name (1881) QBD 55, CA); or 'standard disclosure' (being documents relied on together with documents which adversely affect that party's case, adversely affect another party's case or support another party's case: see CPR Rule 31.6); or disclosure on a more limited basis. It is increasingly common in international arbitration for the tribunal to apply the test prescribed in the International Bar Association Rules on the Taking of Evidence in International Commercial Arbitration (art. 3), namely for the parties to be ordered to produce only those documents that are requested in sufficient detail and that are relevant and material to the outcome of the case. Although it may have the power to do so, a tribunal should not generally order the disclosure of documents which are privileged (see also Section 43(4)). In court proceedings in England, that includes: (i) documents protected by legal professional or litigation privilege; (ii) documents tending to incriminate or expose to a penalty the party who would produce them; and (iii) documents privileged on the ground of public policy (e.g. 'without prejudice' correspondence). Where any of the parties and/or their legal advisers and/or the substantive law is not English, different principles may apply. For the power of the court to order third parties to attend before the tribunal to produce documents, see Section 43.

7. Examination of parties. Pursuant to Section 34(2)(e), the tribunal may direct how (if at all) the parties' witnesses and/or experts may be questioned. A tribunal which orders that there should be no oral cross-examination may be criticised for not allowing a party a reasonable opportunity of dealing with his opponent's case and the award may be challenged if a risk of substantial injustice can be demonstrated (see Sections 33(1)(a) and 68(2)(a)); however, the tribunal should be less reluctant to place a reasonable time limit on cross-examination and/or stop questioning which it considers irrelevant. This provision would allow the tribunal to order interrogatories (i.e. written questions), although such an order is uncommon.

8. Rules of evidence. Pursuant to Section 34(2)(f), the tribunal may direct the time, manner and form of the presentation of witness, expert, documentary and physical evidence. It may decide whether to apply strict (or other) rules of evidence to the material tendered (e.g. whether to require compliance with the 'hearsay rule' and/or whether every document relied on must be proved by its author/recipient). In practice, most arbitrators will admit all relevant evidence and invite submissions as to the weight to be given to it.

9. Taking the initiative. Pursuant to Section 34(2)(g), the tribunal may adopt an inquisitorial (as opposed to adversarial) and/or proactive approach (e.g. asking questions of the witnesses and/or directing that evidence on certain matters be produced). Again, it must have regard to its duty under Section 33(1)(a) and should not rely on any material upon which the parties have not been given an opportunity to comment. In this regard, see *Norbrook Laboratories Ltd* v *A Tank* where direct and unilateral contact by the arbitrator with witnesses was held to be objectionable and justified his removal under Section 24.

10. Oral proceedings. Pursuant to Section 34(2)(h), the tribunal may direct that it will determine some or all issues on the basis of documents only (which may be substantially quicker and cheaper than holding a hearing with oral examination). By way of contrast, under art. 24(1) of the Model Law, unless otherwise agreed by the parties, any party can insist on a hearing. Again, the tribunal must have regard to its duty under Section 33(1)(a) and ensure that the parties are given a reasonable opportunity of putting their respective cases and dealing with that of their opponent. Where the amount in dispute is substantial, it is generally prudent to have a hearing.

11. Time limits. Pursuant to Section 34(3), the tribunal may fix and amend time limits for any directions which it gives. For reckoning periods of time, see Section 78. Where the parties have fixed a time limit by agreement between themselves, this Section would appear not to apply. For the duty of the parties to do all things necessary for the proper and expeditious conduct of the arbitral proceedings, see Section 40(2)(a). For the powers of the tribunal in case of a party's default, including the issue of peremptory orders, see Section 41.

[Consolidation of proceedings and concurrent hearings]

Section 35

(1) The parties are free to agree –
  (a) that the arbitral proceedings shall be consolidated with other arbitral proceedings, or
  (b) that concurrent hearings shall be held,
on such terms as may be agreed.

(2) Unless the parties agree to confer such power on the tribunal, the tribunal has no power to order consolidation of proceedings or concurrent hearings.

1. General. Section 35 sets out that the power to order consolidated or concurrent proceedings. It is non-mandatory (see Section 4(2)). There is no comparable provision in the Model Law or in the previous legislation. See DAC Report paras. 177 to 182. For the tribunal to have the power to make a provisional order under this Section, the parties must have agreed in writing (see Section 5).

2. Consolidation/concurrent. 'Consolidation' is combining two or more arbitrations into one proceeding. 'Concurrent hearings' means holding a hearing at which the matters heard (including evidence) may be relevant to the issues in two or more arbitrations. Consolidation or concurrent hearings is often sought when one party is common to two or more arbitrations which arise out of the same project or event. Consolidation and/or concurrent hearings can save duplication of proceedings (and costs) and reduce the potential for inconsistent awards.

3. Procedural considerations. Because of the contractual nature of arbitration, and the importance of privacy and confidentiality (see the Introduction to this Commentary above), and of party autonomy (see Section 1(b)), all the parties to all of the proceedings must agree to consolidation and/or concurrent hearings or have agreed that all the relevant tribunals have power to make such an order. This will avoid parties who have agreed a procedure for the private resolution of their own disputes finding themselves part of someone else's arbitration. Consolidation will usually require the tribunal in one of the proceedings (if already appointed) to stop acting (by having its authority revoked, see Section 23; or by resigning, see Section 25). The parties may agree that a completely new tribunal be appointed. In such circumstances, any arbitrator who becomes redundant should be entitled to his fees and expenses (see Sections 23(3) and 25(3)). Concurrent hearings may be held by a tribunal of identical constitution which has been appointed in two or more related arbitrations, or by two different tribunals sitting together. If the procedures in the original arbitrations conflict (e.g. pursuant to different rules, or different timetables), the parties may need to agree new procedures.

4. No court powers. Unlike some jurisdictions, the court has not been given the power to order consolidation or concurrent arbitration hearings upon the application of a party, albeit where one or more other parties object. This omission has been criticised, especially by the construction industry.

5. Statutory arbitration. In relation to statutory arbitration, this Section applies only so as to authorise consolidation or concurrent hearings under the same enactment (see Section 96(3)).

6. Joinder. The Act does not refer to the 'joinder' of one or more third parties into the arbitration as a party. However, like consolidation, this can be achieved if the original parties to the arbitration and the proposed third party(ies) all consent. In such circumstances, the tribunal should respect party autonomy and not oppose the joinder of the additional party(ies) even though it might lead to delay and/or additional expense. Unlike the Act, some arbitration rules provide that the tribunal has power to order joinder of a consenting third party upon the application of just one of the original parties (e.g. LCIA art. 22.1(h)). By agreeing to the application of such rules, the other party(ies) consent to such joinder in advance. Such agreement is also often found in project documents, where there are several related agreements.

[Legal or other representation]
Section 36

Unless otherwise agreed by the parties, a party to arbitral proceedings may be represented in the proceedings by a lawyer or other person chosen by him.

1. General. Section 36 confirms that a party need not be represented by a lawyer in arbitration proceedings. It is non-mandatory (see Section 4(2)), but it applies subject to written agreement to the contrary (see Section 5). There is no comparable provision in the Model Law nor in the previous legislation. See DAC Report paras. 183 to 186.

2. Lawyer or other person. A 'lawyer' includes non-English qualified lawyers. 'Other person' refers to non-lawyers; however, legal professional privilege cannot be claimed in respect of communications with non-lawyers. A party is entitled to represent himself.

3. Not an absolute right. This Section does not establish an absolute right and it would be inconsistent with the obligation to avoid delay (see Sections 1(a) (general principles), 33(1)(b) (general duty of the tribunal) and 40(1) (general duty of parties)) for a party to insist on being represented by a person who is unavailable, e.g. to attend a hearing, for an unreasonably long time. In some limited circumstances, a tribunal may be able to order that a party not be represented by its counsel of choice, e.g. if counsel is appointed late in proceedings and this would create a conflict of interest (see *Hrvatska Elektroprivreda* v *The Republic of Slovenia*). Some arbitral rules provide that the parties shall not be represented by lawyers save by agreement (e.g. GAFTA).

4. Award of costs. For recovery of legal or other costs from the losing party, see Sections 59 to 65.

5. Court proceeding. Rights of audience in respect of arbitration applications to the court (pursuant to CPR Part 49 and PD 49G) are governed by the Courts and Legal Services Act 1990 (c. 41) (Section 27).

[Power to appoint experts, legal advisers or assessors]

Section 37

(1) Unless otherwise agreed by the parties –
  (a) the tribunal may –
   (i) appoint experts or legal advisers to report to it and the parties, or
   (ii) appoint assessors to assist it on technical matters,
   and may allow any such expert, legal adviser or assessor to attend the proceedings; and
  (b) the parties shall be given a reasonable opportunity to comment on any information, opinion or advice offered by any such person.
(2) The fees and expenses of an expert, legal adviser or assessor appointed by the tribunal for which the arbitrators are liable are expenses of the arbitrators for the purposes of this Part.

1. General. Section 37 sets out the power of the tribunal to appoint experts to assist it. Section 37(1) is non-mandatory (see Section 4(2)), but it applies subject to written agreement to the contrary (see Section 5). Section 37(2) is mandatory in the event that the tribunal appoints an expert, legal adviser and/or assessor (see Section 4(1) and Schedule 1). This Section is based on art. 26 of the Model Law. A tribunal had a similar power at common law. See DAC Report paras. 187 and 188. The arbitral rules chosen by the parties may also expressly allow the tribunal to appoint an expert to assist it (e.g. LCIA art. 12, ICC art. 14(2)).

2. Experts, legal advisers and assessors. The category of third parties that may be appointed is widely phrased. This power is available so that tribunals can obtain an independent opinion on matters on which they consider they do not have the necessary expertise or understanding. The appointment of legal advisors is common in maritime and trade arbitrations where the tribunal does include a lawyer. However, it is a fundamental principle that the tribunal must not delegate decision-making or responsibility for the substance of the award to an expert, etc.

3. Procedural considerations. It is prudent for a tribunal to discuss with the parties the appointment of an expert, etc., before doing so, having regard to the general duty to adopt suitable procedures and to avoid unnecessary delay and expense (Section 33). The Act does not expressly require the expert, etc., to be impartial, but it would be inconsistent with its duty under Section 33 (i.e. to act fairly and impartially as between the parties) for the tribunal to retain an expert, etc., where circumstances existed that gave rise to justifiable doubts as to his impartiality (see Section 24(1)(a) and contrast CPR PD35 para. 6.2). The tribunal can direct that the parties provide information to the expert and to give him access to property (under Sections 34 and 38(4); see also the parties' general duty under Section 40(1)). The parties must be given a 'reasonable opportunity' (see Section 33(1)(a)) to comment upon any information, opinion or advice offered by the expert, etc., but need not necessarily be allowed to put questions to him or to cross-examine him (contrast art. 26(2) of the Model Law). The tribunal ought not to discuss the report with its expert, etc., in the absence of the parties (see *Hussmann (Europe) Ltd* v *Al Ameen Development & Trade*).

4. Fees and expenses. The reasonable fees and expenses of the expert, etc., may be recovered as 'expenses of the arbitrators' (see Sections 28 and 59 to 65), but the choice of expert and his fees must be proportionate (see *Agrimex Ltd* v *Tradigrain SA*).

[General powers exercisable by the tribunal]

Section 38

(1) The parties are free to agree on the powers exercisable by the arbitral tribunal for the purposes of and in relation to the proceedings.

(2) Unless otherwise agreed by the parties the tribunal has the following powers.

(3) The tribunal may order a claimant to provide security for the costs of the arbitration.

This power shall not be exercised on the ground that the claimant is –
   (a) an individual ordinarily resident outside the United Kingdom, or
   (b) a corporation or association incorporated or formed under the law of a country outside the United Kingdom, or whose central management and control is exercised outside the United Kingdom.

(4) The tribunal may give directions in relation to any property which is the subject of the proceedings or as to which any question arises in the proceedings, and which is owned by or is in the possession of a party to the proceedings –
   (a) for the inspection, photographing, preservation, custody or detention of the property by the tribunal, an expert or a party, or

(b) **ordering that samples be taken from, or any observation be made of or experiment conducted upon, the property.**

(5) The tribunal may direct that a party or witness shall be examined on oath or affirmation, and may for that purpose administer any necessary oath or take any necessary affirmation.

(6) The tribunal may give directions to a party for the preservation for the purposes of the proceedings of any evidence in his custody or control.

1. General. Section 38 sets out the broad powers of the tribunal and is intended to avoid unnecessary applications to the courts. This Section is nonmandatory (see Section 4(2)). Sections 38(3) to (6) apply to the extent that there is no written agreement to the contrary (see Section 5). This provision is based in part on art. 17 of the Model Law and Section 12(1) of the 1950 Act. See DAC Report paras. 189 to 199 and 364 to 370 and DAC Suppl. paras. 28 and 29. Arbitral rules often prescribe the powers exercisable by the tribunal (e.g. LCIA art. 22). For the tribunal's power to determine procedural and evidential matters, see Section 34. For powers of the tribunal in case of a party's default, see Section 41. For the powers of the court exercisable in support of arbitral proceedings, see Section 44.

2. Security for costs. Pursuant to Section 38(3), the tribunal may order a party (claimant or counter-claimant) to provide security for costs. Unlike the position prior to the Act, a party should not apply to the court (see Section 44(5)). In exercising its discretion, the tribunal should have regard to its general duty under Section 33. It might also find it helpful to consider the principles applied by the court in relation to applications for security for costs in court proceedings pursuant to CPR Schedule 1 R23.A1, where the test is stated to be: 'if, having regard to all the circumstances of the case, the court thinks it just to do so ...'. In practice, attention is likely to focus upon financial information regarding the claimant and upon the location of its assets, i.e. whether it has sufficient assets, and whether those assets are readily available, to meet any award for costs (see *Azov Shipping Co.* v *Baltic Shipping Co.*). However, to avoid any appearance of prejudice to foreign parties (and to comply with the Treaty of Rome as far as European Union claimants are concerned), security for costs is not to be ordered on the ground that the claimant's residence or domicile is outside the UK. Foreign sovereign States and their instrumentalities are not mentioned: an application for security for costs against such an entity is only likely to be made in exceptional circumstances, and may raise issues of State immunity. 'Costs of the arbitration' for the purposes of security are defined in Section 59. They are not restricted to the legal costs of the parties. Thus, under this provision, security may also be required for the arbitrators' fees and expenses (if not collected in advance by an arbitral institution, e.g. ICC), the fees and expenses of any arbitral institution concerned and the costs (in addition to legal fees) of the parties. For the tribunal's power in relation to making an award of costs, see Sections

59 to 65. If a party fails to comply with a peremptory order of the tribunal to provide security for costs, the tribunal may make an award dismissing its claim (see Section 41(6)). For the power of the court to order security for costs in relation to an application or appeal, see Section 70(6). For the tribunal's power to make a provisional order that a party make an interim payment on account of the costs of the arbitration, see Section 39(2)(b). The tribunal does not, however, have power to issue a freezing order against assets of a party, as security for any substantive award.

3. Property. Pursuant to Section 38(4), unlike the position prior to the Act, the tribunal may now make an order relating to any property which is owned by or in the possession of a party to the proceedings. For the power of the court to make such orders in support of the arbitral proceedings, see Section 44(2)(c).

4. Oath/affirmation. Section 38(5) derives from Section 12(1) to (3) of the 1950 Act and gives the tribunal power to direct that a party or witness be examined under oath or affirmation. An order may be made upon the application of a party or by the tribunal of its own motion. A witness or expert may take the oath on the holy book of his religion or affirm (i.e. promise) to tell 'the truth, the whole truth and nothing but the truth'. In practice, tribunals usually tell the witness to tell the truth and do not administer an oath/affirmation.

5. Preservation of evidence. Pursuant to Section 38(6), unlike the position prior to the Act, the tribunal may now make an order for the preservation of evidence. Unlike art. 17 of the Model Law, the tribunal is not empowered to require an applicant party to provide appropriate security. For the power of the court to make such orders in support of the arbitral proceedings, see Section 44(2)(b).

[Power to make provisional awards]
Section 39

(1) The parties are free to agree that the tribunal shall have power to order on a provisional basis any relief which it would have power to grant in a final award.

(2) This includes, for instance, making –
  (a) a provisional order for the payment of money or the disposition of property as between the parties, or
  (b) an order to make an interim payment on account of the costs of the arbitration.

(3) Any such order shall be subject to the tribunal's final adjudication; and the tribunal's final award, on the merits or as to costs, shall take account of any such order.

(4) Unless the parties agree to confer such power on the tribunal, the tribunal has no such power.

This does not affect its powers under section 47 (awards on different issues, &c.).

1. General. Section 39 gives the tribunal power to make provisional orders. It is non-mandatory (see Section 4(2)). For the tribunal to have the power to make a provisional order under this Section, the parties must have agreed in writing (see Section 5). In practice, this is uncommon. There is no comparable provision in the Model Law or in the previous legislation. See DAC Report paras. 200 to 203.

2. Provisional order. Whilst the heading refers to 'awards', the DAC made clear that this Section concerns provisional 'orders' (Report paras. 202 and 203). A provisional order should not be confused with a partial award (see Sections 39(4) and 47). The former may be amended or reversed in a subsequent partial or final award (Section 39(3)), whereas a partial or final award is (unless otherwise agreed by the parties) final and binding and the tribunal is functus officio in relation thereto (Section 58). A provisional order need not comply with any form (although, no doubt, it would be in writing), whereas a partial award must (unless otherwise agreed by the parties), inter alia, give reasons (Section 52). A provisional order cannot be challenged or appealed, whereas a partial award is immediately subject to challenge (Section 68) and may be subject to appeal on a question of law (Section 69). A provisional order may be enforced if it becomes a peremptory order of the tribunal (Sections 41 and 42), whereas a partial award can be enforced within the jurisdiction as a judgment of the court (Section 66) or overseas pursuant to the 1958 New York Convention. The parties must positively agree to confer upon the tribunal the power to make provisional orders, whereas the tribunal has power to make partial awards unless agreed otherwise by the parties.

3. Relief. The tribunal may only order such relief as it would have power to grant in a final award, examples of which are given in Section 39(2). For the remedies which a tribunal may order in a final award, see Section 48. For the general powers exercisable by the tribunal, see Section 38, including the power to order security for costs. It is disputed whether Sections 38 and 39 allow the tribunal to make a freezing order (see *Kastner* v *Jason*).

4. Discretion. In exercising its discretion, the tribunal should have regard to its general duty under Section 33. It might also find it helpful to consider the principles applied by the courts in relation to applications for interim remedies in court proceedings pursuant to CPR Part 25 and PD 25.

5. Final adjudication. Any provisional order should be made final or reversed or otherwise taken into account in the relief granted in the tribunal's final award (see Section 39(3)).

[General duty of parties]

Section 40

(1) The parties shall do all things necessary for the proper and expeditious conduct of the arbitral proceedings.

(2) This includes –
   (a) complying without delay with any determination of the tribunal as to procedural or evidential matters, or with any order or directions of the tribunal, and
   (b) where appropriate, taking without delay any necessary steps to obtain a decision of the court on a preliminary question of jurisdiction or law (see sections 32 and 45).

1. General. Section 40 sets out the overriding duties of the parties. This Section is mandatory (see Section 4(1) and Schedule 1). This Section is based, in part, upon Section 12(1) of the 1950 Act. There is no comparable provision in the Model Law. See DAC Report paras. 204 and 205. Section 40 complements Section 1 (general principles) and Section 33 (general duty of the tribunal).

2. Conduct required. Whilst the obligation to do 'all things necessary' is very wide, examples of what is required are set out in Section 40(2). First, the parties must comply with any determination of the tribunal without delay. Where a party fails to do so, the tribunal may order it to do so, prescribing a time limit for compliance (Section 41(5)). Secondly, the parties must take any necessary steps to obtain a decision of the court on a preliminary question of jurisdiction or law without delay. The scope of the obligation may also be derived from Section 41 (powers of tribunal in case of party's default).

3. Non-compliance. The sanctions for non-compliance lie elsewhere; for example, Sections 41 (powers of tribunal in case of a party's default), 42 (enforcement of peremptory orders of tribunal) and 73 (loss of right to object).

[Powers of tribunal in case of party's default]

Section 41

(1) The parties are free to agree on the powers of the tribunal in case of a party's failure to do something necessary for the proper and expeditious conduct of the arbitration.

(2) Unless otherwise agreed by the parties, the following provisions apply.

(3) If the tribunal is satisfied that there has been inordinate and inexcusable delay on the part of the claimant in pursuing his claim and that the delay –
   (a) gives rise, or is likely to give rise, to a substantial risk that it is not possible to have a fair resolution of the issues in that claim, or

(b) has caused, or is likely to cause, serious prejudice to the respondent,

the tribunal may make an award dismissing the claim.

(4) If without showing sufficient cause a party –
  (a) fails to attend or be represented at an oral hearing of which due notice was given, or
  (b) where matters are to be dealt with in writing, fails after due notice to submit written evidence or make written submissions,

the tribunal may continue the proceedings in the absence of that party or, as the case may be, without any written evidence or submissions on his behalf, and may make an award on the basis of the evidence before it.

(5) If without showing sufficient cause a party fails to comply with any order or directions of the tribunal, the tribunal may make a peremptory order to the same effect, prescribing such time for compliance with it as the tribunal considers appropriate.

(6) If a claimant fails to comply with a peremptory order of the tribunal to provide security for costs, the tribunal may make an award dismissing his claim.

(7) If a party fails to comply with any other kind of peremptory order, then, without prejudice to section 42 (enforcement by court of tribunal's peremptory orders), the tribunal may do any of the following –
  (a) direct that the party in default shall not be entitled to rely upon any allegation or material which was the subject matter of the order;
  (b) draw such adverse inferences from the act of non-compliance as the circumstances justify;
  (c) proceed to an award on the basis of such materials as have been properly provided to it;
  (d) make such order as it thinks fit as to the payment of costs of the arbitration incurred in consequence of the non-compliance.

1. General. Section 41 sets out the powers of the tribunal in the event that a party is in default of the tribunal's previous orders. This Section is non-mandatory (see Section 4(2)). Sections 41 (3) to (7) apply to the extent that there is no written agreement to the contrary (see Section 5). This Section derives from Section 13A of the 1950 Act, Section 5 of the 1979 Act and art. 25 of the Model Law. See DAC Report paras. 206 to 211. For the tribunal's powers to decide procedural and evidential matters, see Section 34; and for the general powers exercisable by the tribunal, see Section 38.

2. Proper and expeditious conduct. For the general duty of the parties to do all things necessary for the proper and expeditious conduct of the arbitral proceedings, see Section 40.

3. Inordinate and inexcusable delay. Section 41(3) retains the tribunal's power to strike out a claim for want of prosecution (see Section 13A of the

1950 Act and the cases decided under that Section, e.g. *James Lazenby & Co.* v *McNicholas Construction Co.*). 'Inordinate delay' means significantly longer than what would normally be regarded as acceptable. 'Inexcusable delay' means not excused by such objective factors as illness, accident or the conduct of the respondent. Both these two requirements must be met. In addition, either of the circumstances in paras. (a) and (b) must be satisfied. A claim should not normally be struck out during its limitation period.

4. Non-participation. Section 41(4) provides that the tribunal may proceed in the absence of a defaulting party, provided always that such party was given due notice (e.g. by issuing a peremptory order under Section 41(5)). Failure to give due notice may constitute a breach by the tribunal of Section 33(1)(a) (i.e. its duty to give each party a reasonable opportunity of putting his case and dealing with that of his opponent) and be a ground for challenging any subsequent award (Section 68(2)(a)) or resisting enforcement (Section 66 and art. V.1(b) of the 1958 New York Convention). It would be prudent for a tribunal acting under this provision to take all reasonable steps to ensure that the party received due notice (e.g. by using several means of communication) and by sending a follow-up notice if circumstances allow.

5. Peremptory order. Sections 41(5) to (7) set out a scheme in respect of peremptory orders, which must be 'to the same effect' as the preceding orders (see also *Wicketts* v *Brine Builders*), but which add a time limit for compliance with the order and make it clear that if there is a failure to comply within that time limit, certain consequences will follow. In addition, they set out the powers available to the tribunal for non-compliance with such orders within the time prescribed. If a party fails to comply with a peremptory order to provide security for costs (see Section 38(3)), the tribunal may dismiss the claim altogether (Section 41(6)). In other cases, the tribunal may exercise the powers in Section 41(7). For costs of the arbitration, see Sections 59 to 65. It would be prudent for a tribunal expressly to identify any such order as 'peremptory' and that it is made pursuant to this provision.

6. Support power of the courts. Additional powers available to the court to enforce peremptory orders are set out in Section 42.

POWER OF COURT IN RELATION TO ARBITRAL PROCEEDINGS

[Enforcement of peremptory orders of tribunal]

Section 42

(1) Unless otherwise agreed by the parties, the court may make an order requiring a party to comply with a peremptory order made by the tribunal.

(2) An application for an order under this section may be made –
  (a) by the tribunal (upon notice to the parties),
  (b) by a party to the arbitral proceedings with the permission of the tribunal (and upon notice to the other parties), or
  (c) where the parties have agreed that the powers of the court under this section shall be available.

(3) The court shall not act unless it is satisfied that the applicant has exhausted any available arbitral process in respect of failure to comply with the tribunal's order.

(4) No order shall be made under this section unless the court is satisfied that the person to whom the tribunal's order was directed has failed to comply with it within the time prescribed in the order or, if no time was prescribed, within a reasonable time.

(5) The leave of the court is required for any appeal from a decision of the court under this section.

1. General. Section 42 permits the court to supplement the powers available to the tribunal by applying those sanctions that are available to the court for breach of a court order on a non-performing party. It is non-mandatory (see Section 4(2)), but it applies in the absence of written agreement to the contrary (see Section 5). This Section derives from Section 5 of the 1979 Act. There is no comparable provision in the Model Law. See DAC Report para. 212.

2. Tribunal's powers. For the tribunal's power to make peremptory orders, see Section 41(5), and for the sanctions that the tribunal may impose for failing to comply with such orders, see Section 41(6) and (7).

3. Application to court. An application may be made by the tribunal or a party with the permission of the tribunal or the prior agreement of all other parties (Section 42(2)), but only after exhausting any available arbitral process (Section 42(3)). Resort to Section 42 is very rare. For applications to the court, see Section 80 and CPR Part 62.

4. Court's discretion. Where the tribunal has reached a clear, firm and reasoned view, it is not necessary nor appropriate for the court to review the tribunal's prior determination. However, it is not appropriate to order compliance with a tribunal's peremptory order where such an order is not required in the interests of justice to assist the proper functioning of the arbitral process (see *Emmot* v *Michael Wilson & Partners*).

5. Court sanction. Failure to comply with a court order constitutes contempt, and the court may then impose a fine and/or imprison the defaulting party (see CPR Schedule 1 RSC Order 52).

[Securing the attendance of witnesses]
Section 43

(1) A party to arbitral proceedings may use the same court procedures as are available in relation to legal proceedings to secure the attendance before the tribunal of a witness in order to give oral testimony or to produce documents or other material evidence.

(2) This may only be done with the permission of the tribunal or the agreement of the other parties.

(3) The court procedures may only be used if –
  (a) the witness is in the United Kingdom, and
  (b) the arbitral proceedings are being conducted in England and Wales or, as the case may be, Northern Ireland.

(4) A person shall not be compelled by virtue of this section to produce any document or other material evidence which he could not be compelled to produce in legal proceedings.

1. General. Section 43 entitles a party to apply to the court to secure evidence from a witness. This Section is mandatory (see Section 4(1)). It derives from Section 12(4) and (5) of the 1950 Act and reflects, in part, art. 27 of the Model Law. See DAC Report para. 213.

2. Purpose and scope. This Section should not be allowed to be used to undermine a decision by the tribunal under Section 34 to have limited or no oral evidence. In addition, it cannot be used to disguise an application for 'document hunting' and the documents to be produced must be specifically identified (see *Tajik Aluminium Plant* v *Hydro Aluminium Plant*).

3. Application to court. An application must be made by a party, but only with the permission of the tribunal or the prior agreement of all other parties (Section 43(2). For applications to the court, see Section 80 and CPR Part 62.

4. Court procedures. The procedure available in High Court litigation for securing the attendance of witnesses in order to give oral testimony or to produce documents (or other material evidence) is by 'witness summons', see CPR Part 34 Rules 1-7 (formerly writs of subpoena ad testificandum and subpoena duces tecum). Failure to comply with a witness summons is a contempt of court and is punishable by the court (see CPR Schedule 1 R52).

5. Foreign arbitrations. This Section applies even if the seat of the arbitration is outside England and Wales or Northern Ireland or has not been designated or determined (see Section 2(3)(a)), although the court must have regard to whether such circumstances would make the exercise of any of its powers under this Section inappropriate. In any event, first, the witness must be in the UK and, secondly, the arbitral proceedings which he is to attend must be being conducted in England and Wales or Northern Ireland (Section 43(3)(a)). 'In' the UK is not defined – it probably requires the witness to be resident in the UK, rather than simply present in the UK at the time of service of the witness summons. To satisfy the second requirement, the tribunal may decide (if it has the power) to hold one or more evidential hearings within the jurisdiction. Section 43 overcomes the difficulties in using the Hague Convention on the Taking of Evidence Abroad in Civil or Commercial Matters 1970, the Evidence (Proceedings in Other Jurisdictions) Act 1975, or Council Regulation (EC) No. 1206/2001, to acquire evidence in support of a foreign arbitration (see CPR Part 34 Rules 16-24).

6. Privilege. Section 43(4) confirms that privileged documents and evidence remain protected from disclosure (see CPR Part 31 Rules 3(1)(b) and 19), which would include legal advice privilege, litigation privilege and without prejudice communications (see, e.g., *Three Rivers District Council v Bank of England*).

7. Other powers. For the court's powers in relation to the taking of the evidence of witnesses, the preservation of evidence, and making orders relating to property that is the subject of the proceedings, including in support of foreign arbitrations, see Section 44.

[Court powers exercisable in support of arbitral proceedings]

Section 44

(1) Unless otherwise agreed by the parties, the court has for the purposes of and in relation to arbitral proceedings the same power of making orders about the matters listed below as it has for the purposes of and in relation to legal proceedings.

(2) Those matters are –
  (a) the taking of the evidence of witnesses;
  (b) the preservation of evidence;
  (c) making orders relating to property which is the subject of the proceedings or as to which any question arises in the proceedings –
  (d) for the inspection, photographing, preservation, custody or detention of the property, or
  (e) ordering that samples be taken from, or any observation be made of or experiment conducted upon, the property;
  (f) and for that purpose authorising any person to enter any premises in the possession or control of a party to the arbitration;
  (g) the sale of any goods the subject of the proceedings;
  (h) the granting of an interim injunction or the appointment of a receiver.

(3) If the case is one of urgency, the court may, on the application of a party or proposed party to the arbitral proceedings, make such orders as it thinks necessary for the purpose of preserving evidence or assets.

(4) If the case is not one of urgency, the court shall act only on the application of a party to the arbitral proceedings (upon notice to the other parties and to the tribunal) made with the permission of the tribunal or the agreement in writing of the other parties.

(5) In any case the court shall act only if or to the extent that the arbitral tribunal, and any arbitral or other institution or person vested by the parties with power in that regard, has no power or is unable for the time being to act effectively.

(6) If the court so orders, an order made by it under this section shall cease to have effect in whole or in part on the order of the tribunal or of any such arbitral or other institution or person having power to act in relation to the subject-matter of the order.

(7) The leave of the court is required for any appeal from a decision of the court under this section.

1. General. Section 44 provides the court with powers to support the arbitration process to the extent that the tribunal (or relevant arbitral institution or other person) is unable to act effectively, e.g. where an order is needed urgently or an order against a third party is required. It is non-mandatory (see Section 4(2)), but applies subject to written agreement to the contrary (see Section 5). The Section is derived from (but is more limited in scope than) Section 12(6) of the 1950 Act and corresponds, in part, to arts. 9 and 27 of the Model Law. See DAC paras. 214-216. For the general powers exercisable by the tribunal, see Section 38.

2. Powers of the court. Section 44(2) sets out an exhaustive list of powers exercisable by the court. (The court no longer has power to order security for costs in respect of the arbitral proceedings, which is now a matter for the tribunal alone (see Section 38(3)). The parties may limit or exclude such powers, but they cannot vary or supplement them. An agreement that the arbitral tribunal does not have power to grant certain remedies does not deprive the court of such power (see *Vertex Data Science Ltd* v *Powergen Retail Ltd*). An agreement that any dispute shall be referred to the 'exclusive jurisdiction' of an arbitral tribunal does not exclude the court's powers under Section 44. Nor does an application under Section 44 constitute a waiver of the arbitration agreement. For applications to the court, see Section 80 and CPR Part 2.

3. Taking of evidence of witnesses (Section 44(2)(a)). For the powers of the tribunal in relation to procedural and evidential matters, see Section 34, and to administer any necessary oath or affirmation, see Section 38(5). For the power of the court to secure the attendance of witnesses where the witness is in the UK and the arbitral proceedings are being conducted in England and Wales or Northern Ireland, see Section 43. The court may exercise its powers under this Section when the seat is abroad (see *Commerce and Industry Insurance Co. of Canada* v *Lloyd's Underwriters*). For the court's powers where a witness is abroad, see CPR Part 34.

4. Preservation of evidence (Section 44(2)(b)). A party to arbitral proceedings may apply for a Search Order (formerly an 'Anton Pillar' Order) which allows admission to another party's premises for the purpose of preserving evidence (see CPR Part 25 Rule 1(1)(h) and PD 25). Section 44 does not include the power to order a non-party to disclose documents relevant to an issue in the arbitration (although see Section 43); however, the preservation of the contents of certain documents highly likely to contain directly relevant evidence for the purpose of resolving the issues in the arbitration has been held to justify the exercise of the court's jurisdiction under Section 44 (see *Assimina Maritime Ltd* v *Pakistan Shipping Corporation*; and *Edo Corporation* v *Ultra Electronics Ltd*).

5. Preservation of property (Section 44(2)(c)). For the power of the tribunal to give directions in relation to any property which is the subject matter of the proceedings or as to which any question arises in the proceedings, see Section 38(4). Unlike the tribunal's power, the court's power is not limited to property owned by or in the possession of parties to the proceedings (see CPR Part 25 Rule 1(1)(i) and (j)). In addition, the court can authorise 'any person to enter any premises in the possession or control of a party', whereas a tribunal may only authorise itself, an expert or a party to inspect, etc. 'Premises' is defined in Section 81(2) to 'include land, buildings, moveable structures, vehicles, vessels, aircraft and hovercraft'.

6. Sale of goods (Section 44(2)(d)). The court may order the sale of perishable goods (see CPR Part 25 Rule 1(1)(c)(v)).

7. Interim injunction/receiver (Section 44(2)(e)). A party to arbitral proceedings may apply for a freezing order (formerly a 'Mareva' Injunction) which restrains another party from removing its assets from the jurisdiction or dealing with its assets wherever located (see CPR Part 25 Rule 1(1)(f) and PD 25). A party may seek such an order because it asserts a proprietary claim over the property or in order to ensure that there are assets against which a monetary award in its favour can be enforced. A freezing order, like the other powers in this Section, may be made in support of foreign arbitration proceedings; however, the court is more likely to favour the granting of relief if the defendant is domiciled in England or carries on business there and the court at the situs of the proceedings could not make an effective order (see *Credit Suisse Fides Trust SA* v *Cuoghi*, albeit not a case under the Act). 'Assets' has been held to encompass choses in action, so contractual rights can be enforced by interim injunction (see *Cetelem SA* v *Roust Holdings Ltd*; and *Permasteelisa Japan UK* v *Bouygesstroi*). A party may also apply for a mandatory injunction which requires another party to do a positive act to repair some omission or to restore the prior position by undoing some wrongful act (see CPR Part 25 Rule 1(1)(a) and PD 25). Section 44(2)(e) also permits the court to grant a temporary anti-suit injunction, preventing a party from commencing or pursuing legal proceedings elsewhere in breach of the arbitration agreement. A permanent injunction can only be granted under

Section 37 of the Supreme Court Act 1981. However, an anti-suit injunction cannot be granted where the offending legal proceedings are taking place in another Member State of EU (see decision of the ECJ in *West Tankers*, and also *National Navigation Co.* v *Endessa Generacion SA*). The appointment of a receiver occurs mainly in partnership disputes where an impartial third party is required to deal with assets in dispute (see CPR Part 69).

8. Availability. Unless the case is one of urgency, the applicant must have the permission of the tribunal or the agreement in writing of all the other parties, and in any event only where the arbitral institution is unable to act effectively (Sections 44(3) to (5)). An application for a search and/or freezing order is often made urgently before an arbitration has commenced or at least before the tribunal has been constituted and 'ex parte' (i.e. without notice to the other party). In such circumstances, it is unlikely that any arbitral institution or other person would have the power to make such orders or be able to act effectively (e.g. make an order which third parties within the jurisdiction on notice must obey, as is the case with court orders) (see *Dolphin Tankers SRL* v *China Shipbuilding Trading Co.*; and *Belair LLC* v *Basel LLC*).

9. Tribunal assuming control. The tribunal may be given power by the court to determine when an order of the court made under this Section shall cease to have effect in whole or in part (Section 44(6)). The tribunal may not otherwise vary the court's order.

10. Foreign arbitrations. Section 44 applies even if the seat of the arbitration is outside England and Wales or Northern Ireland or has not been designated or determined (Section 2(3)(b)), although the court must have regard to whether such circumstances would make the exercise of any of its powers under this Section inappropriate (see *Mobil Cerro Negro Ltd* v *Petroleos de Venezuela SA*).

[Determination of preliminary point of law]
Section 45

(1) Unless otherwise agreed by the parties, the court may on the application of a party to arbitral proceedings (upon notice to the other parties) determine any question of law arising in the course of the proceedings which the court is satisfied substantially affects the rights of one or more of the parties.

An agreement to dispense with reasons for the tribunal's award shall be considered an agreement to exclude the court's jurisdiction under this section.

(2) An application under this section shall not be considered unless –
  (a) it is made with the agreement of all the other parties to the proceedings, or
  (b) it is made with the permission of the tribunal and the court is satisfied –

(i) that the determination of the question is likely to produce substantial savings in costs, and
(ii) that the application was made without delay.

(3) The application shall identify the question of law to be determined and, unless made with the agreement of all the other parties to the proceedings, shall state the grounds on which it is said that the question should be decided by the court.

(4) Unless otherwise agreed by the parties, the arbitral tribunal may continue the arbitral proceedings and make an award while an application to the court under this section is pending.

(5) Unless the court gives leave, no appeal lies from a decision of the court whether the conditions specified in subsection (2) are met.

(6) The decision of the court on the question of law shall be treated as a judgment of the court for the purposes of an appeal.

But no appeal lies without the leave of the court which shall not be given unless the court considers that the question is one of general importance, or is one which for some other special reason should be considered by the Court of Appeal.

1. General. Section 45 preserves a form of the old Consultative Case procedure by allowing, in very limited circumstances, the court to make a preliminary determination of a point of law that has arisen in the course of arbitral proceedings. It is non-mandatory (see Section 4(2), but it applies in the absence of written agreement to the contrary (see Section 5). It is based on Section 2 of the 1979 Act. There is no comparable provision in the Model Law. See DAC Report paras. 217-221. For appeals to the court on a question of law arising out of an award made in the proceedings, see Section 69.

2. Question of law. The 'question of law' must be: for a court in England and Wales, one of English and Welsh law; or for a court in Northern Ireland, one of Northern Irish law (see Section 82(1)). It does not include any question relating to any other law. No question of law would arise if the tribunal had been empowered to decide the dispute other than in accordance with rules of law, e.g. as amiable compositeurs or ex aequo et bono (see Section 46(1)(b)), or if the parties agree to dispense with reasons for the tribunal's award (see Section 52(4)).

3. Discretion. The question of law must substantially affect the rights of one of the parties (Section 45(1)), meaning that it must be of practical importance and not be an academic or minor point. Even if this requirement is met, the court retains a discretion as to whether or not to consider the matter (see *Taylor Woodrow Holdings Ltd* v *Barnes & Elliot*).

4. Application to court. The parties must all agree to the application being made. If not, the applicant will need to obtain the tribunal's permission and satisfy the court that the determination is likely to produce substantial cost savings and that the application was made without delay (Section 45(2), see also Section 40(2)(b)). For applications to the court, see Section 80 and CPR Part 62.

5. Continuing the arbitration. Unless the parties all agree that the arbitration should be stayed, the tribunal has a discretion as to whether or not to continue the arbitral proceedings whilst the court application is pending (Section 45(4)). However, a tribunal should seriously consider staying the arbitration; unless, for example, other aspects of the dispute may conveniently be dealt with.

6. Appeals. Leave to appeal the decision of the court as to whether the conditions specified in Section 45(2) have been met or from the decision of the court on the question of law is rarely given (Sections 45(5) and (6)).

7. Jurisdictional issues. For determination of a preliminary point of jurisdiction (which may raise questions of law), see Section 32. For challenging an award on grounds that the tribunal lacked substantive jurisdiction (which likewise may raise questions of law), see Section 67.

THE AWARD
[Rules applicable to substance of dispute]
Section 46
(1) The arbitral tribunal shall decide the dispute –
  (a) in accordance with the law chosen by the parties as applicable to the substance of the dispute, or
  (b) if the parties so agree, in accordance with such other considerations as are agreed by them or determined by the tribunal.
(2) For this purpose the choice of the laws of a country shall be understood to refer to the substantive laws of that country and not its conflict of laws rules.
(3) If or to the extent that there is no such choice or agreement, the tribunal shall apply the law determined by the conflict of laws rules which it considers applicable.

1. General. Section 46 concerns the governing substantive law that the tribunal should apply to determine the dispute; that is, the law applicable to the parties' relationship and not that applicable to the arbitration agreement or to the arbitral procedure. It is non-mandatory (see Section 4(2)), but it is written in mandatory language and applies in the absence of written agreement to the contrary (see Section 5). It corresponds to art. 28 of the Model Law. However, unlike the Model Law, it does not direct the tribunal to 'take into account the usages of the trade applicable to the transaction'. There is no comparable provision in the previous legislation. See DAC Report para. 46 and DAC Suppl. para. 30.

English Arbitration Act (Chapter 23), Section 46

2. Freedom of choice. The parties are generally free to choose, expressly or by implication, which substantive law shall apply. English law does not require the governing law to have any connection with the underlying subject matter or the parties. The parties' choice is subject to any applicable mandatory laws (see note 4 below). In addition, para. (b) does not apply to statutory arbitrations (Section 96(4)). Further, it only applies to arbitration agreements entered into on or after 31 January 1997, by virtue of Schedule 2, para. 4 of the Arbitration Act 1996 (Commencement No. 1) Order 1996 (S.I. 1996 No. 3146 (c. 96)). Choice of a national law does not include its conflict of laws rules, which avoids the application of concepts such as renvoi (i.e. a conflict of laws rule in the applicable legal system which directs that another legal system's substantive law should apply to the dispute).

3. Non-national rules. Under Section 46(1)(b), the parties are not limited to choosing a national legal system, and may choose, for example: lex mercatoria; or the UNIDROIT Principles of International Commercial Contracts; or 'internationally accepted principles of law governing contractual relations' (see *DST* v *RAK National Oil*); or Jewish law (see *Soleimany* v *Soleimany*; *Halpern* v *Halpern*); or Shari'a law (see *Musawi* v *RE International (UK) Ltd*). Such choice will be respected by the English courts, so long as it does not contravene English public policy (see *Soleimany* v *Soleimany*). The parties may also empower the tribunal to decide 'in accordance with equity', or in accordance with 'honourable engagement', or ex aequo et bono, or as amiable compositeurs, etc. However, in agreeing that a dispute should be resolved other than in accordance with English law, the parties will not be able to apply to the court for determination of a preliminary point of law (Section 45) or to appeal on a point of law (Section 69), there being no 'question of [English] law' at issue (see Section 82(1)).

4. Mandatory rules. Mandatory rules are those imperative rules of law that cannot be excluded by agreement of the parties. They might be found in the law of the seat, the governing substantive law, the law governing the arbitration agreement, the law of the parties' domicile or incorporation or place of business, the law of the place of performance, the law of a supranational legal system, and international law. For example, the parties cannot avoid the application of mandatory EC law, e.g. art. 81 EC on competition, by choosing a non-EC national law as the governing law (see *Eco Swiss China Time* v *Benetton*) or EC Commercial Agents Regulation (see *Accentuate Ltd* v *Asigra*). In England, mandatory rules might also be found in employment legislation or legislation to protect consumers (referred to as 'overriding legislation'), see also Sections 89 to 91 concerning consumer arbitration agreements.

5. Determination by the tribunal. Where there is no such choice or agreement, the tribunal will have to determine the governing law, applying such conflict of laws rules as it considers applicable. Some arbitral rules prescribe that the tribunal may select whichever law(s) or rules of law that it considers appropriate, i.e. the voie directe method, without having to go through a conflict of laws analysis (e.g. LCIA art. 22.3) (although in practice a tribunal is likely to conduct some sort of analysis). In the absence of such direction and discretion, a tribunal seated in England is likely to follow the Contracts (Applicable Law) Act 1990 (c. 36), which gives effect in English law to the EC Convention on the Law Applicable to Contractual Obligations 1980 (often referred to as the 'Rome I Convention', which was superseded by Regulation (EC) 593/2008 of 17 June 2008, applicable to contracts concluded after 17 December 2009) or Regulation (EC) 864/2007 on the Law Applicable to Non-contractual Obligations of 11 July 2007 ('Rome II', applicable from 11 January 2009).

6. Arbitration agreement. The English courts have also indicated that, absent an express agreement by the parties to the contrary, where the seat of the arbitration is England, the governing law of the arbitration agreement will probably be English law, even where the governing law of the underlying agreement is not English law (see *C* v *D*).

[Awards on different issues, &c]

Section 47

(1) Unless otherwise agreed by the parties, the tribunal may make more than one award at different times on different aspects of the matters to be determined.

(2) The tribunal may, in particular, make an award relating –
  (a) to an issue affecting the whole claim, or
  (b) to a part only of the claims or cross-claims submitted to it for decision.

(3) If the tribunal does so, it shall specify in its award the issue, or the claim or part of a claim, which is the subject matter of the award.

1. General. Section 47 allows the parties and/or the tribunal to select some issues for early and/or separate determination with a view to saving time and costs or for purposes of sensible case management. It is non-mandatory (see Section 4(2)), but it applies in the absence of written agreement to the contrary (see Section 5). It is derived from Section 14 of the 1950 Act. The Model Law has no comparable provision, but it does not prohibit the tribunal making more than one award. See DAC Report paras. 226 to 233. This provision complements the tribunal's duty under Section 33(1)(b) to 'adopt procedures suitable to the circumstances of the particular case' and the DAC hoped that tribunals would make much use of this provision. The arbitration rules chosen by the parties may also provide for awards on separate issues (e.g. LCIA art. 26.7, ICC art. 2).

2. Separate awards. Separate awards are sometimes made in respect of one or more of: jurisdiction (as envisaged in Section 31(4)(a)); liability;

quantum; and/or costs. In some cases, it is appropriate to make a separate award in respect of certain preliminary legal issues, or to make separate awards in respect of claims and counterclaims. See *Sea Trade Marine Corp.* v *Hellenic Mutual War Risks Association (Bermuda) Ltd ('The Athena')*.

3. Partial award. Whilst often referred to as 'interim awards' (because they are made part way through the arbitration, and such was the wording used in the 1950 Act), such wording may be misleading because awards made pursuant to this Section are final in respect of the issues they determine (Section 58(1)). They are also immediately subject to challenge (Sections 67 and 68) and any right to appeal on a question of law (Section 69, if applicable). An interim/partial award must comply with any requirements as to the form of awards, e.g. including reasons (Section 52). A partial award is different to a 'provisional' award/order (Section 39), which may be subsequently altered. Where a final award is set aside by the court, the parties may also lose the right to rely on any preceding partial award (see *Kazakhstan* v *Istill Group*).

[Remedies]

Section 48

(1) The parties are free to agree on the powers exercisable by the arbitral tribunal as regards remedies.

(2) Unless otherwise agreed by the parties, the tribunal has the following powers.

(3) The tribunal may make a declaration as to any matter to be determined in the proceedings.

(4) The tribunal may order the payment of a sum of money, in any currency.

(5) The tribunal has the same powers as the court –
  (a) to order a party to do or refrain from doing anything;
  (b) to order specific performance of a contract (other than a contract relating to land);
  (c) to order the rectification, setting aside or cancellation of a deed or other document.

1. General. Section 48 prescribes the remedies (or relief) that a tribunal may grant. It is non-mandatory (see Section 4(2)), but Sections 48(3) to (5) will apply in the absence of written agreement to the contrary (see Section 5). This Section derives in part from Section 15 of the 1950 Act. There is no comparable provision in the Model Law, which leaves the question of remedies to be determined according to the applicable substantive law. See DAC Report para. 234. For the types of relief which a tribunal may grant in a provisional order, see Section 39(2). The common law rules relating to matters not capable of settlement by arbitration are preserved by Section

81(1)(a); accordingly, a tribunal could not make an enforceable declaration concerning, for example, the status of a marriage.

2. Declaration. A tribunal may make a declaration concerning the parties' rights and obligations, for example under a disputed contract (Section 48(3)).

3. Payment of money, in any currency. An award for the payment of money is the remedy most often sought (Section 48(4)). While the tribunal has the power to make an award in any currency, this provision does not empower arbitrators to disregard the contract and/or the substantive law in relation to foreign currency obligations (see *Lesotho Highlands Development Authority* v *Impreglilo SpA*).

4. Injunction. Section 48(5)(a) concerns the power of the tribunal to make a mandatory (i.e. positive) or prohibitory (i.e. negative) order in a final award (see *Kastner* v *Jason*). Concerning the tribunal's power to make interim orders, see Section 38. Unlike the courts, an arbitral tribunal cannot issue a freezing order that is binding on third parties immediately upon notice thereof. A tribunal may issue an anti-suit injunction, which may become an important power following the ECJ's decision in *West Tankers* proscribing the ability of the English court from issuing such an order where the offending proceedings are taking place in the courts of another EU Member State (but the tribunal may also be constrained in such circumstances, see *National Navgation Co.* v *Endessa Generacion SA*). For the court's power to grant an interim injunction in support of arbitral proceedings, see Section 44(2)(e). An agreement that the arbitral tribunal does not have power to grant certain remedies does not deprive the court of such power (see *Vertex Data Science Ltd* v *Powergen Retail Ltd*).

5. Specific performance. The tribunal may also make an award that a party perform its obligations (Section 48(5)(b)). However, because such an award is difficult to enforce and can only be awarded in particular circumstances, this remedy is not frequently ordered. It does not apply to contracts for the creation or transfer of an interest in land (see *Tilia Sonera Ab* v *Hilcourt Docklands Ltd*).

6. Other orders. An order that the underlying agreement should be set aside or cancelled (Section 48(5)(c)) is not inconsistent with the tribunal having jurisdiction to make that determination (see Section 7, separability of arbitration agreement).

7. Interest and costs. For the power to award interest and costs to a successful party, see Sections 49 and 61.

8. Additional remedies. It is an implied term of a reference to arbitration that the tribunal has the same power to grant remedies as would a court of law having jurisdiction to decide the same subject matter, therefore it may grant remedies not mentioned in Section 48, e.g. apportionment under the Civil Liability (Contribution) Act 1978 (see *Wealands* v *CLC Contractors*

Ltd). The parties are free to empower the tribunal to grant remedies that are not available to the English court (e.g. punitive damages). This can be done expressly or it may result from choosing the substantive law of a foreign legal system (see Section 4(5)). However, the remedy must not violate the public policy of England (see Sections 68(2)(g) and 81(c)) or of the place of enforcement if it is to be enforceable.

9. Excess of power. It may be an excess of power and a serious irregularity justifying a challenge to the award (Section 68(2)(b)), if the tribunal grants a remedy that has not been requested by the successful party. Accordingly, the parties should be asked to specify the relief sought, at the latest immediately before the award is finalised.

[Interest]

Section 49

(1) The parties are free to agree on the powers of the tribunal as regards the award of interest.

(2) Unless otherwise agreed by the parties the following provisions apply.

(3) The tribunal may award simple or compound interest from such dates, at such rates and with such rests as it considers meets the justice of the case –
- **(a) on the whole or part of any amount awarded by the tribunal, in respect of any period up to the date of the award;**
- **(b) on the whole or part of any amount claimed in the arbitration and outstanding at the commencement of the arbitral proceedings but paid before the award was made, in respect of any period up to the date of payment.**

(4) The tribunal may award simple or compound interest from the date of the award (or any later date) until payment, at such rates and with such rests as it considers meets the justice of the case, on the outstanding amount of any award (including any award of interest under subsection (3) and any award as to costs).

(5) References in this section to an amount awarded by the tribunal include an amount payable in consequence of a declaratory award by the tribunal.

(6) The above provisions do not affect any other power of the tribunal to award interest.

1. General. Section 49 concerns the tribunal's power to award interest. It is non-mandatory (see Section 4(2)), but Sections 49(2) to (6) apply in the absence of written agreement to the contrary (see Section 5). This Section replaces Section 19A and Section 20 of the 1950 Act, and Section 3 of the Private International Law (Miscellaneous Provisions) Act 1995, and clarifies the common law. There is no comparable provision in the Model Law. See DAC Report paras. 235 to 238. Under English law, there is no power to award interest as general damages in the absence of a statutory provision. This Section is notable not only in giving such power to arbitral tribunals, but also in allowing simple or compound interest before and after the award.

2. Parties' choice. The parties are free to agree upon the tribunal's power to award interest different from that in Sections 49(3) to (6). This can be done expressly or it may result from the choice of particular arbitration rules (see Section 4(3)) or the choice of substantive law of a foreign legal system (see Section 4(5)). However, choice of a governing law that does not allow for the award of compound interest is not an agreement in writing sufficient to satisfy Section 5 and therefore would not prevent an arbitral tribunal awarding compound interest (see *Lesotho Highlands Development Authority* v *Impregilo SpA*). In addition, the parties must request the award of interest in their claim, otherwise the tribunal will not have jurisdiction to make such an award (see *Westland Helicopters Ltd* v *Sheikh Salah Al-Hejailan*, and *Pirtek (UK) Ltd* v *Deanswood Ltd*).

3. Interest up to the award. The tribunal may award interest on both (i) any part of the amount awarded, which remains unpaid, up to the date of the award, and (ii) any sums claimed but paid before the award, up to the date of payment.

4. Interest after the award. The outstanding amount of the award, together with interest up to the date of the award, and costs, may all be the subject of an award of interest from the date of the award (or a later date) until payment. Some tribunals will allow the unsuccessful party a grace period in which to make payment, during which interest does not accrue. Interest no longer automatically accrues on a monetary award, as it did under Section 20 of the 1950 Act, so it is important that tribunals remember expressly to provide for post-award interest (if justified). Where an applicant seeks to enforce an award of interest under Section 66 and the whole or part of it relates to a period after the date of the award, it must file a statement giving particulars of how the interest is calculated (CPR Part 62 Rule 19). Unlike the award itself, a judgment enforcing an award does carry interest at the rate prescribed in the Judgments Act 1838, which from 1 April 1993 has been 8% (see Judgment Debts (Rate of Interest) Order 1993 (S.I. 1993 No. 564) and CPR Part 40 Rule 8) (see *Gater Assets Ltd* v *NAK Naftogaz Ukrainiy*).

5. Simple or compound interest. Where the underlying contract between the parties includes provisions concerning interest to be paid on overdue sums, the tribunal must give effect to that agreement (see *Lesotho Highlands Development Authority* v *Impregilo SpA*). Absent such agreement by the parties, the tribunal has a discretion to determine the rate of interest, and if compound also the applicable rests. Such interest should be awarded on a compensatory and not a punitive basis.

English Arbitration Act (Chapter 23), Section 50

[Extension of time for making award]

Section 50

(1) Where the time for making an award is limited by or in pursuance of the arbitration agreement, then, unless otherwise agreed by the parties, the court may in accordance with the following provisions by order extend that time.

(2) An application for an order under this section may be made –
  (a) by the tribunal (upon notice to the parties), or
  (b) by any party to the proceedings (upon notice to the tribunal and the other parties),

but only after exhausting any available arbitral process for obtaining an extension of time.

(3) The court shall only make an order if satisfied that a substantial injustice would otherwise be done.

(4) The court may extend the time for such period and on such terms as it thinks fit, and may do so whether or not the time previously fixed (by or under the agreement or by a previous order) has expired.

(5) The leave of the court is required for any appeal from a decision of the court under this section.

1. General. Section 50 concerns the ability of the tribunal to apply for an extension of time to make its award, where the arbitration agreement or institutional rules chosen by the parties prescribe a time limit for making an award which cannot be met. This Section is non-mandatory (see Section 4(2)), but Sections 50(2) to (5) apply in the absence of written agreement to the contrary (see Section 5). Section 50 derives from Section 13(2) of the 1950 Act. There is no comparable provision in the Model Law. See DAC Report para. 239. For the general power of the court to extend time limits relating to the arbitral proceedings, see Section 79.

2. Application to arbitral institution. The relevant arbitral institution will usually have power to extend any time limit prescribed in its rules and that process must be exhausted before applying to the court (Section 50(2)).

3. Application to court. An application under this Section may be made by the tribunal or any party (without agreement of the other parties). An application must be made pursuant to Section 80 and CPR Part 62.

4. Substantial injustice. The court has a wide discretion, including extending time after the period has expired, but the court must be satisfied that a substantial injustice would be done if time were not extended. An award not made within the prescribed time (including any extended time) would be a nullity and unenforceable, on the basis that the tribunal lacked the appropriate jurisdiction. It would then fall to be decided under the applicable law whether or not a claimant could commence new arbitration proceedings or, alternatively, court proceedings in respect of the same claim. It would most likely constitute a substantial injustice if time was not extended when the delay was due to no fault of the claimant and the claimant was unable to pursue its claim in other proceedings.

[Settlement]

Section 51

(1) If during arbitral proceedings the parties settle the dispute, the following provisions apply unless otherwise agreed by the parties.

(2) The tribunal shall terminate the substantive proceedings and, if so requested by the parties and not objected to by the tribunal, shall record the settlement in the form of an agreed award.

(3) An agreed award shall state that it is an award of the tribunal and shall have the same status and effect as any other award on the merits of the case.

(4) The following provisions of this Part relating to awards (sections 52 to 58) apply to an agreed award.

(5) Unless the parties have also settled the matter of the payment of the costs of the arbitration, the provisions of this Part relating to costs (sections 59 to 65) continue to apply.

1. General. Section 51 concerns agreed (or 'consent') awards. It is non-mandatory (see Section 4(2)), but Sections 51(2) to (5) apply in the absence of written agreement to the contrary (see Section 5). This Section corresponds to art. 30 of the Model Law. There is no comparable provision in the previous legislation. See DAC Report paras. 240 to 244. Many arbitral rules make provision for agreed awards, e.g. LCIA art. 26.8, ICC art. 26, UNCITRAL art. 34.1.

2. Advantages. The advantage of an agreed award is that it should be honoured voluntarily, but in any event it should be more readily enforceable through the mechanisms for enforcement of arbitral awards than a mere settlement agreement. It can also be registered pursuant to the 1958 New York Convention and thus act as a shield to further claims. However, an agreed award can only be made if a tribunal has been constituted.

3. Tribunal's right to object. The tribunal may object to making an award on agreed terms if, for example, it is concerned that the settlement agreement has been structured to mislead third parties (e.g. the tax authorities) or deals with matters not arbitrable under the applicable law (see Section 81(1)(a)) or is contrary to law or public policy (e.g. contrary to art. 81 EC concerning competition).

4. Form. An agreed award must be in the proper form if it is to be enforced as an award (see Section 66). But the award need not (but may) contain reasons (see Section 52(4)). Further, the award need not (but may) state on its face that it is agreed. However, where the applicant applies to enforce an agreed award under Section 66, the claim form must state that the award is an agreed award and any order made by the court must also contain such a statement (CPR Part 62 Rule 18(5)). If no provision is made for the costs of the tribunal, Sections 59 to 65 continue to apply.

[Form of award]

Section 52

(1) The parties are free to agree on the form of an award.

(2) If or to the extent that there is no such agreement, the following provisions apply.

(3) The award shall be in writing signed by all the arbitrators or all those assenting to the award.

(4) The award shall contain the reasons for the award unless it is an agreed award or the parties have agreed to dispense with reasons.

(5) The award shall state the seat of the arbitration and the date when the award is made.

1. General. Section 52 sets out the formal requirements of an award. It is non-mandatory (see Section 4(2)), but Sections 52(3) to (5) apply in the absence of written agreement to the contrary (see Section 5). This Section corresponds to art. 31 of the Model Law (although for consistency with the Act it refers to 'seat' rather than 'place of the arbitration'). There is no comparable provision in the previous legislation. See DAC Report paras. 245 to 252.

2. Parties' agreement. Arbitral rules chosen by the parties often make provision for the form of the award, e.g. LCIA art. 26, ICC art. 25, UNCITRAL art. 32, which may differ from Section 52. Some institutions – such as the ICC, but not the LCIA – will scrutinise an award in draft before it is notified to the parties to ensure that it complies with any requirements of that institution as to form.

3. Writing. The requirement that (at least) the assenting arbitrators sign the award probably means that an original hard copy rather than an electronic copy of the award must exist (in contrast to the possible forms of an arbitration agreement, see Section 5(6)). There is no requirement that a dissenting arbitrator sign the award or write a separate opinion (see also Section 22), but an arbitrator might also choose to sign the award even if he disagrees with the majority.

4. Own award. It is the duty of the arbitrators to draft their own award, albeit a draftsman may be employed to assist, see *Agrimex Ltd* v *Tradigrain SA*.

5. Reasons. Under the previous law, reasons were not required unless requested. The DAC considered it a basic rule of justice that those charged with making a binding decision affecting the rights and obligations of others should (unless those others agree) explain the reasons for making that decision (DAC Report para. 247). For the function and contents of a reasoned award generally, see *Transcatalana de Commercio SA* v *Incobrasa Industrial e Commercial Brazileira SA*. An agreed award need not contain reasons (see Section 51). And the parties may agree that reasons are not required (see *Bay Hotel and Resort Ltd* v *Cavailier Construction Co. Ltd*). An agreement to dispense with reasons shall be considered an agreement to exclude the court's jurisdiction to consider a preliminary point of law (Section 45(1)) or an appeal from the award on a point of law (Section 69(1)).

6. Seat and date. For the meaning of the seat of the arbitration, see Section 3. The seat is significant for determining (in the absence of contrary agreement) the place where the award is made (see Section 53) and where the award may be challenged (see Sections 67 to 69). To avoid confusion, the arbitrator(s) should not also state on the award where it was signed. The tribunal may decide what is to be taken to be the date on which the award was made (see Section 54), unless otherwise agreed by the parties. The date is commonly the date that the last arbitrator signs the award, but it need not be that date.

7. Failure of form. A failure to comply with the requirements as to the form of the award may entitle a party to challenge the award on grounds of serious irregularity (Section 68(2)(h)). An award may also be challenged under Section 68(2) if the tribunal fails to deal with all the issues put to it (para. (d)) or if there is uncertainty or ambiguity as to the effect of the award (para. (f)). In all such cases, the court must consider that the failure has or will cause substantial injustice to the applicant. If, on an application or appeal under Sections 67, 68 or 69, it appears to the court that the award does not contain the tribunal's reasons or that they are in insufficient detail, the court may order the tribunal to state the reasons for its award in sufficient detail (Section 70(4), see *Petroships Pte Ltd* v *Petec Trading*). Tribunals do not have to deal with every argument made by the parties, nor explain why they attach more weight to some evidence than to other evidence (see *World Trade Corporation* v *C Czarnikow Sugar Ltd*, in the context of Section 57). A ruling may still constitute an award notwithstanding that it fails to comply with the requirements of this Section, if the document would have been understood by its recipients as intended to be the arbitrator's decision on the disputed issue(s).

8. Other matters. For awards on different issues, see Section 47. For correction of an award or making an additional award, see Section 57.

[Place where award treated as made]

Section 53

Unless otherwise agreed by the parties, where the seat of the arbitration is in England and Wales or Northern Ireland, any award in the

proceedings shall be treated as made there, regardless of where it was signed, despatched or delivered to any of the parties.

1. General. Section 53 concerns the place where the award is deemed to have been made. It is non-mandatory (see Section 4(2)), but it applies in the absence of written agreement to the contrary (see Section 5). It derives from art. 31(3) of the Model Law. There is no comparable provision in the previous legislation. See DAC Report para. 253.

2. Made in England. Unless otherwise agreed, an award in an arbitration seated in England is deemed to be made in England. This allows an award to be signed in or sent from a different jurisdiction without having any impact on its enforceability or otherwise. (This Section was enacted to negate the House of Lords' decision in *Hiscox* v *Outhwaite* that an award is made where it is signed.) The arbitrator(s) must state on the award the seat of the arbitration (Section 52(5)). To avoid confusion, the arbitrator(s) should not also state on the award where they signed it. For a corresponding provision concerning 1958 New York Convention awards, see Section 100(2)(b).

[Date of award]

Section 54

(1) Unless otherwise agreed by the parties, the tribunal may decide what is to be taken to be the date on which the award was made.

(2) In the absence of any such decision, the date of the award shall be taken to be the date on which it is signed by the arbitrator or, where more than one arbitrator signs the award, by the last of them.

1. General. Section 54 concerns the deemed date of the award. It is non-mandatory (see Section 4(2)), but it applies in the absence of written agreement to the contrary (see Section 5). There is no comparable provision in the Model Law or the previous legislation. See DAC Report, para. 254.

2. Discretion. The tribunal must state on the award the date on which it was made (Section 52(5)), but the tribunal has a discretion to decide the date of the award (absent agreement of the parties to the contrary), and therefore it need not be the date on which the last arbitrator signed the award. For example, where the award is withheld awaiting payment (Section 56), it may be appropriate to date the award on the day it is released.

3. Significance of date. The date of the award is significant for purposes of: determining whether the award has been made within any time limit fixed by the parties (for the power of the court to extend the time for making an award, see Section 50); calculating when interest starts to accrue (see Section 49(4)); determining the commencement of the time limit for correcting the award (Section 57(4)); and challenging or appealing the award (see Sections

English Arbitration Act (Chapter 23), Section 55

67 to 69 and 70(3)). It may also be relevant in some jurisdictions for determining the commencement of the limitation period for enforcing the award (albeit in England time runs from the date on which the award should have been paid).

[Notification of award]

Section 55

(1) The parties are free to agree on the requirements as to notification of the award to the parties.

(2) If there is no such agreement, the award shall be notified to the parties by service on them of copies of the award, which shall be done without delay after the award is made.

(3) Nothing in this section affects section 56 (power to withhold award in case of non-payment).

1. General. Section 55 allows the parties to agree on the requirements as to notification of the award. It is non-mandatory (see Section 4(2)), but Section 55(2) applies in the absence of written agreement to the contrary (see Section 5). There is no comparable provision in the Model Law or in the previous legislation. See DAC Report paras. 255 to 256.

2. Service. In the absence of any agreement to the contrary, the tribunal must serve copies of the award on the parties. An award may be served by any effective means (see Section 76), including pre-paid post to a person's principal residence or last known principal business address or to a corporate's registered or principal office. Some arbitral institutions take responsibility for notifying the award to the parties (e.g. LCIA and ICC).

3. Without delay. Prompt notification of an award is important because the time limits for correcting the award (Section 57) and challenging or appealing the award (see Sections 67 to 69 and 70(3)) run from the date of the award (Section 54). However, the court has power to extend such time limits (Sections 79 and 80(5)) if, for example, the tribunal has withheld the award because of non-payment of the fees and expenses of the arbitrators (Section 56). In such circumstances, the tribunal should notify the parties of the availability of the award and provide them with copies 'without delay' thereafter.

4. Original award. Sections 52 and 53 appear to envisage there being only one original award and it being retained by the tribunal with 'copies' served on the parties. Art. IV.1(a) of the 1958 New York Convention requires a 'duly authenticated original award or a duly certified copy thereof' to obtain enforcement. Unless it is an institutional arbitration and the institution keeps an original, it is considered good practice to send to each of the parties a signed original.

[Power to withhold award in case of non-payment]

Section 56

(1) The tribunal may refuse to deliver an award to the parties except upon full payment of the fees and expenses of the arbitrators.

(2) If the tribunal refuses on that ground to deliver an award, a party to the arbitral proceedings may (upon notice to the other parties and the tribunal) apply to the court, which may order that –
- **(a) the tribunal shall deliver the award on the payment into court by the applicant of the fees and expenses demanded, or such lesser amount as the court may specify,**
- **(b) the amount of the fees and expenses properly payable shall be determined by such means and upon such terms as the court may direct, and**
- **(c) out of the money paid into court there shall be paid out such fees and expenses as may be found to be properly payable and the balance of the money (if any) shall be paid out to the applicant.**

(3) For this purpose the amount of fees and expenses properly payable is the amount the applicant is liable to pay under section 28 or any agreement relating to the payment of the arbitrators.

(4) No application to the court may be made where there is any available arbitral process for appeal or review of the amount of the fees or expenses demanded.

(5) References in this section to arbitrators include an arbitrator who has ceased to act and an umpire who has not replaced the other arbitrators.

(6) The above provisions of this section also apply in relation to any arbitral or other institution or person vested by the parties with powers in relation to the delivery of the tribunal's award.

As they so apply, the references to the fees and expenses of the arbitrators shall be construed as including the fees and expenses of that institution or person.

(7) The leave of the court is required for any appeal from a decision of the court under this section.

(8) Nothing in this section shall be construed as excluding an application under section 28 where payment has been made to the arbitrators in order to obtain the award.

1. General. Section 56 recognises the tribunal's right to withhold the award pending payment of its full fees and expenses. It is mandatory (see Section 4(1)). It is based on Section 19 of the 1950 Act. There is no comparable provision in the Model Law. See DAC Report paras. 257 to 260.

2. Lien. The Section recognises the tribunal's right to exercise a lien over its work product – the award – until it has been paid. It has the effect of suspending the tribunal's duty, under Section 55, to provide the parties with copies of the award without delay. For the joint and several liability of the parties for the tribunal's fees and expenses, see Section 28. For costs of the arbitration, see Sections 59 to 65.

3. Recourse to the court. In the absence of any recourse through the arbitral machinery (e.g. to the relevant institution, Section 56(4)), in order to have the award released, a party may apply to the court and pay into court such fees and expenses as the court may specify. The court shall then decide how the fees and expenses 'properly payable' shall be determined having regard to the factors prescribed in Section 28, including any contractual right of the tribunal to payment of their fees. The court will probably refer the matter to a costs judge or court appointed expert. Any amount shown to be excessive will be repaid to the applicant (contrast Section 28(3) in which repayment must be shown to be reasonable in the circumstances) and the balance paid to the tribunal. For applications to the court, see Section 80 and CPR Part 62.

4. Others withholding the award. This Section also applies to institutions or other persons who are entitled to withhold the award (and includes their fees and expenses) (Section 56(6)). Most institutional rules make provision for the tribunal or the institution to withhold the award pending payment (e.g. LCIA Schedule of Fees and Costs, para. 8(c); ICC art. 28.1).

5. Later adjustment of fees. A decision by a party to pay any disputed fees and expenses to the tribunal in order to have the award released, rather than make an application under this Section, does not prevent and is without prejudice to an application to the court under Section 28 for it to consider the reasonableness of such fees and expenses and to order repayment if appropriate (Section 56(8)).

[Correction of award or additional award]

Section 57

(1) The parties are free to agree on the powers of the tribunal to correct an award or make an additional award.

(2) If or to the extent there is no such agreement, the following provisions apply.

(3) The tribunal may on its own initiative or on the application of a party –
- **(a) correct an award so as to remove any clerical mistake or error arising from an accidental slip or omission or clarify or remove any ambiguity in the award, or**
- **(b) make an additional award in respect of any claim (including a claim for interest or costs) which was presented to the tribunal but was not dealt with in the award.**

These powers shall not be exercised without first affording the other parties a reasonable opportunity to make representations to the tribunal.

(4) Any application for the exercise of those powers must be made within 28 days of the date of the award or such longer period as the parties may agree.

(5) Any correction of an award shall be made within 28 days of the date the application was received by the tribunal or, where the correction is made by the tribunal on its own initiative, within 28 days of the date of the award or, in either case, such longer period as the parties may agree.

(6) Any additional award shall be made within 56 days of the date of the original award or such longer period as the parties may agree.

(7) Any correction of an award shall form part of the award.

1. General. Section 57 concerns the ability of the tribunal either to correct an award or to make an additional award. It is non-mandatory (see Section 4(2)), but Sections 57(3) to (7) apply to the extent that there is no written agreement to the contrary (see Section 5). This Section is based on Sections 17 and 18(4) of the 1950 Act and corresponds to art. 33 of the Model Law. See DAC Report para. 261 and DAC Suppl. para. 31. Some arbitral rules give similar and additional powers to tribunals, e.g. LCIA art. 27 (correction and additional award), ICC art. 26 (correction and interpretation), UNCITRAL arts. 35 to 37 (correction, interpretation and additional award). The Act does not give a power to the tribunal to interpret its award, nor does it exclude such power.

2. Notice. The tribunal may act under this Section on its own initiative or on the application of a party, but it must afford the parties a reasonable opportunity to make representations. That opportunity will be restricted in practice by the time limits in Sections 57(5) and (6).

3. Clerical mistake or error arising from an accidental slip or omission. This provision allows for errors in computation and typographical errors to be corrected (see *Gannet Shipping Ltd* v *Eastrade Commodities Inc.*).

4. Remove ambiguity. The power to clarify or remove an ambiguity in an award is new. Uncertainty or ambiguity as to the effect of the award are grounds for challenging the award for serious irregularity (Section 68(2)(f)), but the challenging party must first make an application under this Section (Sections 68(1) and 70(2)) (see *Torch Offshore LLC* v *Cable Shipping Inc.*). If it appears to the court that the flaw goes further than mere ambiguity and the award does not contain the tribunal's reasons or that they are in insufficient detail, the court may order the tribunal to state the reasons for its award in sufficient detail (Section 70(4), see *Petroships Pte Ltd* v *Petec Trading*).

5. Additional award. The tribunal also has the power to make an additional award in respect of any claim which was presented to the tribunal, but was not dealt with. Failure by the tribunal to deal with all the issues put to it is a ground for challenging the award for serious irregularity (Section 68(2)(d)).

The court may remit the award to the tribunal to state its reasons in sufficient detail (Section 70(4)). However, tribunals do not have to deal with every argument made by the parties, nor explain why they attach more weight to some evidence than to other evidence (see *World Trade Corporation* v *C Czarnikow Sugar Ltd*). The power to make an additional award cannot be used by the tribunal to overturn its earlier decision (see *The Dredging and Construction Co. Ltd* v *Delta Civil Engineering Co. Ltd*).

6. Time limits. The time limit for correction of an award (i.e. 28 days from the date of the award) corresponds with the limit imposed by Section 70(3) for challenges or appeals under Sections 67 to 69. However, the time for making an additional award is 56 days (see *Pirtek (UK) Ltd* v *Deanswood Ltd*). For determining the date of the award, see Section 54. For reckoning periods of time, see Section 78, and for the power of the court to extend time limits relating to arbitral proceedings, see Section 79 (for an extension of the time limit in Section 57, see *Gold Coast Ltd* v *Nava Gijon SA*).

7. Fees. The Act does not stipulate whether the tribunal can charge additional fees for work done pursuant to Section 57. If a corrected or additional award is needed because of the tribunal's oversight, it would seem inappropriate for it to seek additional payment.

[Effect of award]

Section 58

(1) Unless otherwise agreed by the parties, an award made by the tribunal pursuant to an arbitration agreement is final and binding both on the parties and on any persons claiming through or under them.

(2) This does not affect the right of a person to challenge the award by any available arbitral process of appeal or review or in accordance with the provisions of this Part.

1. General. Section 58 explains the final and binding effect of an award. It is non-mandatory (see Section 4(2)), but it applies in the absence of written agreement to the contrary (see Section 5). This Section restates Section 16 of the 1950 Act and reflects art. 35 of the Model Law. See DAC Report paras. 262 to 264.

2. Other parties. References to a party to an arbitration agreement include any person claiming under or through a party to that agreement (see Section 82(2)). This might include assignees. It would also include insurers.

3. Tribunal functus officio. An arbitrator's authority ends automatically upon the issue of a valid final award, whereupon he becomes functus officio (see *Carter* v *Harold Simpson Associates Ltd*). After issuing a partial award (see Section 47), the arbitrator becomes functus officio in relation to the subject matter of that award, but he has continuing authority in respect of any other issues not yet determined. However, the tribunal may be entitled to correct the award or make an additional award (see Section 57). Further, following a challenge or appeal, the court may order the tribunal to state the reasons for its award in greater detail (see Section 70(4)) and/or the award may be remitted to the tribunal, in whole or in part, for reconsideration (see Sections 68(3)(a), 69(7)(c) and 71(3)) (see *Glencore International Ag* v *Beogradska Plovidba*). The setting aside of an award or a declaration that it is of no effect means that the arbitrator is no longer functus in respect of the issues dealt with in that award (see *Hussmann (Europe) Ltd* v *Pharaon*).

4. Challenge. Notwithstanding that an award is final and binding, it may still be challenged or appealed (Section 58(2)). Similarly, the use of the terms 'final, conclusive and binding' in an arbitration clause in an agreement could not be read as excluding the jurisdiction of the court to entertain an appeal on a point of law under Section 69, and if such is intended, clearer words have to be used (see *Shell Egypt* v *Dana Gas*). An award with its seat in England may only be challenged in the English courts, even if the underlying agreement is governed by another law (see *C* v *D*). A party may, of course, resist enforcement wherever enforcement is sought. Where a final award is set aside by the court, the parties may also lose the right to rely on any preceding partial award (see *Kazakhstan* v *Istill Group*).

5. Enforcement. The effect of the award being final and binding is that either party may proceed to enforcement of the award (subject to any rights of challenge or appeal, see Sections 66 to 69).

6. Res judicata. In addition, the parties cannot in other proceedings re-open or re-try an issue which has been finally determined (i.e. the matter is res judicata and/or may give rise to issue estoppel) (see *Sun Life Assurance Co. of Canada* v *Lincoln National Life Insurance Co.*).

COSTS OF THE ARBITRATION

[Costs of the arbitration]

Section 59

(1) References in this Part to the costs of the arbitration are to –
  (a) the arbitrators' fees and expenses,
  (b) the fees and expenses of any arbitral institution concerned, and
  (c) the legal or other costs of the parties.
(2) Any such reference includes the costs of or incidental to any proceedings to determine the amount of the recoverable costs of the arbitration (see section 63).

1. General. Section 59 explains what is meant by 'costs of the arbitration', as referred to in Sections 60 to 65. It is non-mandatory (see Section 4(2)), but it is unlikely that the parties would or could change such definition (whereas they may seek to amend the subsequent provisions concerning the award of costs). There is no comparable provision in the prior legislation nor in the Model Law, although the recovery of costs was allowed under the common law. See DAC Report paras. 265 and 266.

2. Costs of the arbitration. Section 59 does away with the distinction sometimes made between the 'costs of the reference' and the 'costs of the award'. For the award of the costs of the arbitration, see Sections 60 to 65. Any arbitral rules chosen by the parties may also define costs (e.g. ICC art. 31 and UNCITRAL art. 38, but not LCIA).

3. Arbitrators' fees and expenses. This term includes not only the fees and expenses of the arbitrators themselves, but also any fees and expenses of experts, legal advisors or assessors appointed by the tribunal for which the tribunal is liable (see Section 37(2)) and any tribunal secretary appointed with the agreement of the parties. The arbitrators' fees and expenses must be reasonable and appropriate in the circumstances and may be challenged by a party (see Sections 28, 56 and 64).

4. Arbitral institution's fees and expenses. Arbitral institutions typically charge a filing fee, together with a fee for administering the arbitration based on hourly rates and/or a percentage of the tribunal's fees (e.g. LCIA) or a percentage of the amount in dispute (e.g. ICC). It may also have printing and courier expenses, and it may also pay for the hearing room and transcription services, etc.

5. Legal or other costs of the parties. Legal costs would include the fees and expenses of a party's external lawyers. (The costs of in-house counsel are rarely allowed.) Other costs would include the fees and expenses of witnesses of fact and expert witnesses, and any necessary additional advisers (e.g. lawyers in other relevant jurisdictions), the legitimate costs incurred in lay representation (as allowed by Section 36), and costs such as hiring the hearing room, translation services, etc. (A party's management costs related to a dispute are rarely allowed, unless it can be shown that they would not otherwise have been incurred.) It is possible that an uplift in a conditional fee arrangement may also be included, if the applicable rules for their application are complied with (see *Protech Projects Construction* v *Al-Kharafi & Sons*).

6. Relevant proceedings. Section 59 applies to the costs of the arbitration proceedings themselves, and not the cost of ancillary proceedings (e.g. applications to the English court in support of the arbitration, which are subject to their own costs regime, see CPR Parts 43-48). The costs of defending proceedings brought abroad in breach of the arbitration agreement may be able to be claimed as damages (see *Union Discount Co. Ltd* v *Zoller*; and *National Westminster Bank plc* v *Rabobank Nederland*). Section 59(2) confirms that this Section applies to proceedings in which the recoverable costs themselves are determined (see Sections 63 and 64).

7. Agreed awards. Where there is an agreed award (Section 51), but it does not include an allocation of costs, Sections 59 to 65 continue to apply.

[Agreement to pay costs in any event]
Section 60

An agreement which has the effect that a party is to pay the whole or part of the costs of the arbitration in any event is only valid if made after the dispute in question has arisen.

1. General. Section 60 concerns agreements relating to the allocation of costs made before the dispute has arisen. It is mandatory (see Section 4(1)). It derives from Section 18(3) of the 1950 Act. See DAC Report para. 267.

2. Prior agreement not valid. Any agreement entered into before a dispute has arisen in which a party agrees to pay the whole or part of the costs irrespective of the outcome of the arbitration is not valid. Such restriction on party autonomy is justified on grounds of public policy, i.e. not to encourage speculative claims and also to protect consumers. However, an agreement which provides that the 'losing' party will pay the costs of the arbitration should be valid given that it is consistent with Section 61(2) (general principle that costs follow the event).

[Award of costs]
Section 61

(1) The tribunal may make an award allocating the costs of the arbitration as between the parties, subject to any agreement of the parties.

(2) Unless the parties otherwise agree, the tribunal shall award costs on the general principle that costs should follow the event except where it appears to the tribunal that in the circumstances this is not appropriate in relation to the whole or part of the costs.

1. General. Section 61 permits the tribunal to allocate the costs of the arbitration between the parties. It is non-mandatory (see Section 4(2)), but it applies in the absence of written agreement to the contrary (see Section 5). It derives from Section 18(1) of the 1950 Act. See DAC paras. 265 to 272. For a definition of costs of the arbitration, see Section 59. For the determination of recoverable costs, see Sections 62 and 63.

2. Agreement of the parties. Section 61 emphasises more than many other Sections that it is subject to any agreement of the parties. The parties may agree once a dispute has arisen (see Section 60) how recoverable costs are to be allocated, or more likely that there should be no award of costs irrespective of the outcome (i.e. each side bears its own costs). Any arbitral rules chosen by the parties may include provisions relating to the award of costs (e.g. LCIA art. 28, ICC art. 31 and UNCITRAL art. 40).

3. Costs follow the event. Absent agreement to the contrary, the tribunal should allocate costs on the basis of costs follow the event, i.e. the costs of the successful party should be paid by the unsuccessful party. The 'event' may be the ultimate outcome of the dispute or each significant issue or the outcome of various stages of the arbitration (e.g. separate awards of costs in connection with any interlocutory applications).

4. Discretion. Circumstances justifying departure from the general principle include: if the successful party caused unnecessary delay and expense in the proceedings; or if the claimant, although successful on the merits, was only awarded a small sum by way of damages relative to the amount claimed. But the tribunal must be careful to exercise its discretion fairly and impartially (see Section 33). The tribunal must act in a 'judicial manner' and must not base its decision on grounds that had not been argued by or put to the parties (see *Gbangbola* v *Smith & Sherriff Ltd*). It has been held that the practice of the courts and Costs Officers in allocating the costs of court proceedings (see CPR Parts 43-48) is irrelevant to arbitration (see *Fence Gate Ltd* v *NEL Construction Ltd*), although many English arbitrators are nevertheless likely to find the factors referred to in CPR Part 44 Rule 3 to be equally apposite to arbitrations.

5. Award. The allocation of costs must be made in an award in order to be enforceable (see Section 52).The tribunal must give reasons (unless the parties agree otherwise). The tribunal may make more than one award of costs (e.g. if it issues two or more partial awards) and may do so as part of an award on the merits or separately (although, if separately, care must be taken by the tribunal to avoid becoming functus officio as a result of issuing the first award, see *Algahanim Industries* v *Skandia*).

6. Settlement offers. The tribunal should have regard to any offers to settle the dispute (which are often referred to by English practitioners as 'Calderbank letters'). Such offers are typically made 'without prejudice save as to costs' and include terms relating to the allocation of costs up to the time of the offer. If the settlement offer is rejected, but the claimant ultimately is awarded less than the settlement offer, the offeror will usually inform the tribunal of its offer. The tribunal may in its discretion order that the offeree is not entitled to its costs after the date of the offer or that the offeree must pay the offeror's costs from the date of the offer to the end of the proceedings, because it unreasonably rejected the settlement proposal (see CPR Part 36, in respect of sealed offers). So as to be able to compare the settlement offer with the ultimate outcome, in order to determine whether the tribunal's decision is more or less favourable than the offer, it is important that the offer clearly distinguishes between the principal claims, interest and costs.

7. Interest. A tribunal may award interest to accrue on an award of costs (see Section 49).

8. Third party funders. The court may, exceptionally, order third party funders to pay the costs of the successful party. An arbitral tribunal would have no such power.

[Effect of agreement or award about costs]
Section 62

Unless the parties otherwise agree, any obligation under an agreement between them as to how the costs of the arbitration are to be borne, or under an award allocating the costs of the arbitration, extends only to such costs as are recoverable.

1. General. Section 62 introduces the concept of recoverable costs. It is not mandatory (see Section 4(2)), but it applies in the absence of written agreement to the contrary (see Section 5). There is no comparable provision in the previous legislation nor in the Model Law. See DAC Report paras. 268 and 269.

2. Recoverable costs. Absent agreement to the contrary, a party is only entitled to receive its recoverable costs as determined in accordance with Sections 63 to 65.

[The recoverable costs of the arbitration]
Section 63

(1) The parties are free to agree what costs of the arbitration are recoverable.

(2) If or to the extent there is no such agreement, the following provisions apply.

(3) The tribunal may determine by award the recoverable costs of the arbitration on such basis as it thinks fit.

If it does so, it shall specify –
  - **(a) the basis on which it has acted, and**
  - **(b) the items of recoverable costs and the amount referable to each.**

(4) If the tribunal does not determine the recoverable costs of the arbitration, any party to the arbitral proceedings may apply to the court (upon notice to the other parties) which may –
  - **(a) determine the recoverable costs of the arbitration on such basis as it thinks fit, or**
  - **(b) order that they shall be determined by such means and upon such terms as it may specify.**

(5) Unless the tribunal or the court determines otherwise –
  (a) the recoverable costs of the arbitration shall be determined on the basis that there shall be allowed a reasonable amount in respect of all costs reasonably incurred, and
  (b) any doubt as to whether costs were reasonably incurred or were reasonable in amount shall be resolved in favour of the paying party.
(6) The above provisions have effect subject to section 64 (recoverable fees and expenses of arbitrators).
(7) Nothing in this section affects any right of the arbitrators, any expert, legal adviser or assessor appointed by the tribunal, or any arbitral institution, to payment of their fees and expenses.

1. General. Section 63 sets out the basis for assessing recoverable costs. It is non-mandatory (see Section 4(2)), but it applies in the absence of written agreement to the contrary (see Section 5). It derives from Sections 18(1) and (2) of the 1950 Act. See DAC Report para. 270. For the award of recoverable costs, see Sections 59 to 65.

2. Party agreement. English parties that are familiar with the 'costs follow the event' principle (see Section 61) and typical fees for various types of proceedings are often able to agree on what would be a reasonable amount of costs to be recovered by the successful party. However, if the parties are unable to agree or only agree on certain of the costs, the tribunal (Section 63(2)) or the court (Section 3) may decide.

3. Determination by the tribunal. The tribunal must issue an award (see Section 52), specifying the basis on which it has acted and the items of recoverable costs and their quantum. Failure to do so would give grounds to challenge the award (see Section 68(2)(h)).

4. Determination by the court. The court may determine the recoverable costs on any basis it deems appropriate, or it may order that the costs shall be determined by such means and upon such terms as it may specify, e.g. referring the matter to a Costs Officer (see CPR Parts 43-48). For applications to court, see Section 80 and CPR Part 62.

5. Basis for determination. Unless otherwise determined, the tribunal or court shall allow a reasonable amount in respect of all costs reasonably incurred and any doubt shall be resolved in favour of the paying party (Section 63(5)). This is similar to the 'standard basis' applied in English court proceedings (see CPR Part 44 Rule 4(2)), with proportionality being an important principle. The alternative approach, which is justified in certain circumstances, e.g. where a party has deliberately or unnecessarily caused wasted costs or exaggerated its claim, is the 'indemnity basis' (see CPR Part 44 Rule 4(3)), in which any doubts should be resolved in favour of the receiving party. In either case, CPR Part 44 Rule 5(3) refers to a number of factors that the court must take into account, which an arbitral tribunal might also find helpful when assessing costs: (a) the conduct of all the parties, including in particular – (i) conduct before, as well as during, the proceedings; and (ii) the efforts made, if any, before and during the proceedings in order to try to resolve the dispute; (b) the amount or value of any money or property involved; (c) the importance of the matter to all the parties; (d) the particular complexity of the matter or the difficulty or novelty of the questions raised; (e) the skill, effort, specialised knowledge and responsibility involved; (f) the time spent on the case; and (g) the place where and the circumstances in which work or any part of it was done. In international arbitrations, tribunals often make no reference to either the standard or the indemnity basis and provide only brief reasoning justifying their assessment of costs. Some tribunals will allow all the costs claimed unless patently unjustified and some will reduce the claims as a matter of principle because of assumed inefficiencies or duplication of work by the legal team. Some tribunals consider the overall outcome and others take an issue-by-issue approach.

6. Evidence. The tribunal or court must be satisfied on the balance of probabilities that the costs have actually been incurred. In court proceedings, a claiming party must submit a Bill of Costs, in a prescribed format (see CPR PD 43, Section 4). However, the practice in arbitration varies, with some tribunals asking for a Bill of Costs, some asking just for copies of all law firm and experts' fee notes, etc., whereas some tribunals will accept merely a summary schedule. Some tribunals require express affirmation from the law firm representing the claiming party that the fee notes have been paid (or at least are due and payable) whilst others do not. The other party must be given an opportunity to comment before the tribunal makes its decision.

7. Right to payment from parties. Section 63, which concerns the allocation of recoverable costs as between the parties, does not affect the right of the arbitrator (see Section 28) or experts, etc., or arbitral institutions, to be paid their fees by the parties.

[Recoverable fees and expenses of arbitrators]

Section 64

(1) Unless otherwise agreed by the parties, the recoverable costs of the arbitration shall include in respect of the fees and expenses of the arbitrators only such reasonable fees and expenses as are appropriate in the circumstances.

(2) If there is any question as to what reasonable fees and expenses are appropriate in the circumstances, and the matter is not already before the court on an application under section 63(4), the court may on the application of any party (upon notice to the other parties) –

   (a) determine the matter, or

(b) order that it be determined by such means and upon such terms as the court may specify.

(3) Subsection (1) has effect subject to any order of the court under section 24(4) or 25(3)(b) (order as to entitlement to fees or expenses in case of removal or resignation of arbitrator).

(4) Nothing in this section affects any right of the arbitrator to payment of his fees and expenses.

1. General. Section 64 sets out the fees and expenses of the tribunal that may be recovered from another party. It is non-mandatory (see Section 4(2)), but it applies in the absence of written agreement to the contrary (see Section 5). It derives from Section 19 of the 1950 Act. See DAC Report paras. 270 and 271. For the award of recoverable costs, see Sections 59 to 65.

2. Reasonable fees and expenses. Only such reasonable fees and expenses as are appropriate in the circumstances are recoverable (Section 64(1)). This would include the expenses of experts, legal advisers and assessors for which the arbitrators are liable (see Section 37(3)), so long as such fees are proportionate (see *Agrimex Ltd* v *Tradigrain SA*). No guidance is provided as to what factors are relevant to determining reasonableness, but they might include the usual fees of the arbitrator for other professional work, the complexity of the matter and quantum of the claims, the time spent and whether the tribunal adopted procedures suitable to the circumstances of the case (see Section 33(1)(b)).

3. Determination by the court. Any dispute shall be determined by the court (Section 64(2)), because it would be inappropriate to have the arbitral tribunal responsible for determining whether its own fees and expenses were reasonable. The court may order the determination to be carried out by such means and upon such terms as it may specify, e.g. having the matter decided by a Costs Officer (see CPR Parts 43-48). The recoverable costs are also subject to any orders of the court relating to fees and expenses following the removal or resignation of an arbitrator (see Sections 24(4) and 25(3)(b)). The court may even review the determination by an arbitral institution as to the fees to which an arbitrator is entitled (see *Hussmann (Europe) Ltd* v *Al Ameen Development & Trade*). For applications to court, see Section 80 and CPR Part 62.

4. Right to payment from parties. Section 64, which concerns the allocation of recoverable costs as between the parties, does not affect an arbitrator's right to receive payment for his fees and expenses from the parties (see Sections 28 and 63(7)); however, the parties may also challenge the fees and expenses that they pay on grounds that they are not reasonable (see Section 28(2)). An arbitrator may withhold the award in case of non-payment (see Section 56).

[Power to limit recoverable costs]

Section 65

(1) Unless otherwise agreed by the parties, the tribunal may direct that the recoverable costs of the arbitration, or of any part of the arbitral proceedings, shall be limited to a specified amount.

(2) Any direction may be made or varied at any stage, but this must be done sufficiently in advance of the incurring of costs to which it relates, or the taking of any steps in the proceedings which may be affected by it, for the limit to be taken into account.

1. General. Section 65 permits the tribunal to limit the amount of recoverable costs before any such costs are incurred. It is non-mandatory (see Section 4(2)), but it applies in the absence of written agreement to the contrary (see Section 5). There is no comparable provision in the prior legislation nor in the Model Law. See DAC Report para. 272. For the award of recoverable costs, see Sections 59–64.

2. Purpose. This is a new power given to tribunals and was intended to discourage those who wish to use their financial muscle to intimidate their opponents into giving up because of the fear that in going on they might be subject to a costs order which they could not sustain. However, this power is very rarely exercised.

3. Discretion. A limit may be imposed on the tribunal's own initiative, without any application from a party. In exercising its discretion, the tribunal must act fairly and impartially as between the parties (see Section 33(a)) and must allow he parties the opportunity to present submissions on any proposed limit (see *Home of Homes Ltd* v *Hammersmith and Fulham LBC*). It must be imposed sufficiently in advance of the relevant costs being incurred. The limit may be varied or even lifted altogether. A limit may be imposed on total recoverable costs, or the costs of certain phases of the arbitration, or some discrete aspect of the arbitration (e.g. expert reports). Such an order does not prevent a party from incurring costs above the limit, but such excess costs cannot be recovered from the other party.

POWERS OF THE COURT IN RELATION TO AWARD

[Enforcement of the award]

Section 66

(1) An award made by the tribunal pursuant to an arbitration agreement may, by leave of the court, be enforced in the same manner as a judgment or order of the court to the same effect.

English Arbitration Act (Chapter 23), Section 66

(2) Where leave is so given, judgment may be entered in terms of the award.

(3) Leave to enforce an award shall not be given where, or to the extent that, the person against whom it is sought to be enforced shows that the tribunal lacked substantive jurisdiction to make the award.

The right to raise such an objection may have been lost (see section 73).

(4) Nothing in this section affects the recognition or enforcement of an award under any other enactment or rule of law, in particular under Part II of the [1950 c. 27.] Arbitration Act 1950 (enforcement of awards under Geneva Convention) or the provisions of Part III of this Act relating to the recognition and enforcement of awards under the New York Convention or by an action on the award.

1. General. Section 66 deals with the enforcement of an award by the court. It is mandatory (see Section 4(1)). It replaces Section 26(l) of the 1950 Act. It also reflects art. 35 of the Model Law. See the DAC Report paras. 273 to 274 and DAC Suppl. paras. 32 to 34.

2. Options available for enforcement. Section 66 provides one of several procedures for enforcement of arbitral awards. It applies to awards made in England and abroad. For awards enforced pursuant to the: (a) 1927 Geneva Convention, see Section 99 of this Act and Part II of the 1950 Act; (b) 1958 New York Convention, see Sections 100 to 104 of this Act; (c) 1965 Washington (ICSID) Convention, see the Arbitration (Internal Investments Disputes) Act 1966; and (d) Part I of the Foreign Judgments (Reciprocal Enforcement) Act 1933, see CPR Part 62 Rule 20. Awards may also be enforced under the common law as an 'action on the award', i.e. for breach of an implied term in the submission to arbitration that any award made would be fulfilled (see Section 104).

3. Enforced and/or entered as a judgment. This Section provides an option to an award creditor to have the award enforced in the same manner as a judgment (Section 66(1)) or to take the further step and have judgment entered in terms of the award (Section 66(2)). There is little practical difference, save that a judgment may be able to be exported to other jurisdictions (see *ASM Shipping Ltd* v *TTMI Ltd*). Once judgment is entered, the judgment creditor may apply to register and/or enforce that judgment abroad (rather than seek to register and enforce the award, should that be less advantageous). For an award to be enforceable, it must be capable of being copied effectively word-for-word into a judgment. The court must not enter judgment in different terms to those of the award, e.g. the court cannot award interest if it is not provided for in the award (see *Walker* v *Rowe*).

4. Limitation. The limitation period of six years under Section 7 of the Limitation Act 1980 applies, with time starting to run from the date that the award should have been honoured (see *National Ability SA* v *Tinna Oils & Chemicals Ltd*).

5. Application. For applications to court to enforce an award, see Section 80 and CPR Part 62 Rules 18 and 19. An application may be made with or without notice to the award debtor. The applicant must support its application with written evidence, attaching the arbitration agreement and the award (either an original or a copy of it) and state the extent (if any) to which the award has been complied with as of the date of the application. Details of any post-award interest must be provided. The enforcement order itself must be served on the award debtor. If necessary, service may be effected outside of England & Wales with the court's permission. The courts will not be overly formalistic if asked to set aside an application for procedural failings (see *Colliers International Property Consultants* v *Colliers Jordan Lee Jafaar Sdn Bhd*).

6. Challenge. The award debtor then has 14 days (or longer if outside the jurisdiction) in which to challenge the order. If he does so, a hearing will be held and the award may not be enforced until his application is finally disposed of (see CPR Part 62 Rule 18(9)). The hearing is held in private (see CPR Part 62 Rule 10), but the presumption is that any judgment should be made public, but redacted if necessary to protect sensitive information (*City of Moscow* v *Bankers Trust*).

7. Lack of substantive jurisdiction. The court must refuse enforcement if it can be shown that the tribunal lacked substantive jurisdiction. As to the meaning of that phrase, see Sections 30 to 32 and 67, i.e. (a) no valid arbitration agreement; (b) the tribunal was not properly constituted; and (c) the matters submitted to arbitration do not fall within the scope of the arbitration agreement. Issues of substantive jurisdiction cannot be raised at the enforcement stage if they have been raised and resolved by the court via a preliminary ruling (see Section 32). A party may lose the right to challenge enforcement if it has participated in the arbitration proceedings without registering an objection to jurisdiction (see Section 73).

8. Other grounds for refusing enforcement. Although not expressly referred to, the court may also refuse enforcement on other grounds, such as the same grounds as those for challenging an award, i.e. serious irregularity (see Section 68), non-arbitrability (see Section 81(1)(a)) and public policy (see Section 81(1)(c)). Although the court's power to enforce an award is discretionary, this discretion is normally exercised in favour of enforcement except where there is real doubt that the award is valid. For additional commentary on the grounds for refusing enforcement and the pro-arbitration approach of the English courts, see Section 103.

9. Previous challenge. Where an award has been challenged under Sections 67 to 69 and that challenge has failed, the award debtor cannot raise the same issues to resist enforcement under Section 66. However, the fact that a foreign court has rejected a challenge application or refused enforcement does not prevent the award debtor raising the same arguments if enforcement is sought in England (except for facts and points of law that have become res judicata (see *Good Challenger Nevegante SA* v *Metalimportexport SA*).

10. Execution. Once judgment is entered, the award may be executed in the same way as a judgment, e.g. the interception of a debt due to the respondent (i.e. a third party debt order, previously known as a garnishee order, see CPR Part 72); and the charging and sale of the debtor's property (see CPR Part 73). If the award/judgment requires action to be taken or stopped, failure to do so would be a contempt of court and punishable by a fine or even imprisonment. Pending actual execution, the award creditor may apply for a freezing order preventing the award debtor from disposing of its assets (see *Tsavliris Salvage* v *The Grain Board of Iraq*). Execution may be stayed whilst the enforcement order is challenged, e.g. if there are outstanding proceedings involving a counterclaim or a challenge to an award, but the award debtor may be ordered to provide security (see *Socadec SA* v *Pan Africa Impex Co. Ltd*; and *Hillcourt (Docklands) Ltd* v *Telia Sonera AB*).

11. State immunity. State immunity does not prevent an application for leave to enforce an arbitral award being made, but it may prevent execution against non-commercial assets pursuant to the State Immunity Act 1978 (see *Svenska Petroleum Exploration AB* v *Lithuania*).

[Challenging the award: substantive jurisdiction]

Section 67

(1) A party to arbitral proceedings may (upon notice to the other parties and to the tribunal) apply to the court –
  (a) challenging any award of the arbitral tribunal as to its substantive jurisdiction; or
  (b) for an order declaring an award made by the tribunal on the merits to be of no effect, in whole or in part, because the tribunal did not have substantive jurisdiction.

A party may lose the right to object (see section 73) and the right to apply is subject to the restrictions in section 70(2) and (3).

(2) The arbitral tribunal may continue the arbitral proceedings and make a further award while an application to the court under this section is pending in relation to an award as to jurisdiction.

(3) On an application under this section challenging an award of the arbitral tribunal as to its substantive jurisdiction, the court may by order –
  (a) confirm the award,
  (b) vary the award, or
  (c) set aside the award in whole or in part.

English Arbitration Act (Chapter 23), Section 67

(4) The leave of the court is required for any appeal from a decision of the court under this section.

1. General. Section 67 entitles a party to challenge an award on grounds that the tribunal lacked substantive jurisdiction. It is mandatory (see Section 4(l)). It reflects arts. 16 and 34 of the Model Law. See DAC Report paras. 275 to 277.

2. Substantive jurisdiction. This phrase is defined in Sections 30 and 82(1) to mean: (a) there is no valid arbitration agreement; (b) the tribunal was not properly constituted; and (c) the matters submitted to arbitration do not fall within the scope of the arbitration agreement.

3. Other proceedings. For determination by the tribunal of its own jurisdiction, see Sections 30 and 31. (Section 67 cannot be used to challenge a decision by the tribunal to take this course, see *AOOT Kalmneft* v *Glencore International.*) For determination by the court as a preliminary point, see Section 32. As a ground for resisting enforcement, see Section 66(3). As a ground for resisting enforcement of 1958 New York Convention awards, see Section 103(2)(b).

4. Loss of right. A party cannot reopen the issue of substantive jurisdiction if it had already been determined by the court under Section 32. It may also lose the right if it has taken part in the proceedings without raising an objection (Section 73(1)(a)) or does not challenge the award within time (Sections 73(2) and 70, usually 28 days) (see *Broda Agro Trade Cyprus* v *Alfred C Toepfer*). If the challenging party has participated in the arbitration, the grounds for challenge must have previously been raised before the arbitral tribunal (see *Zestafoni G Nikoladze Ferroalloy Plant* v *Ronly Holdings*). For the right of a party who has taken no part in the proceedings to question whether there is a valid arbitration agreement, see Section 72(1)(a). The doctrine of non-justiciability does not prevent the English courts from hearing an application under this Section to review the jurisdiction of an arbitral tribunal appointed under a bilateral investment treaty (see *Ecuador* v *Occidental Exploration*).

5. Application. An application may be made in respect of a separate award on jurisdiction or an award dealing with both jurisdiction and the merits. For applications to court, see Section 80 and CPR Part 62.

6. Security. Leave to appeal may be made subject to providing security for costs (see Section 70(6)), the payment into court of any money payable under the award or otherwise secured (see Section 70(7)), or any other condition (Section 70(8)).

7. Rehearing. The question that the court will ask itself is whether the tribunal was correct in its decision on jurisdiction and not whether the tribunal was entitled to reach the decision that it did (see *Czech Republic* v *European Media Ventures*). This may result in a full rehearing (see *Tajik Aluminium Plant* v *Hydro Aluminium SA*). There are limits on introducing new evidence (see *Primetrade AG* v *Ythan Ltd*).

8. Remedies. The court may confirm, vary or set aside an award in whole or in part (Sections 67(1) and (3)). Setting aside an award is the same as declaring it to be of no effect (see *Hussmann* v *Ahmed Pharaon*). The court may order the tribunal to state the reasons for the award in sufficient detail (see Section 70(4)).

9. Appeals. The court's discretion in Section 67(4) has been held to be compliant with the European Convention on Human Rights (see *Kazakhstan* v *Istil Group*). The Court of Appeal may not give leave to appeal where leave has been refused by the High Court (see *Athletic Union of Constantinople* v *National Basketball Association*); however, the Court of Appeal can grant permission if the judge acted outside of his jurisdiction (see *Cetelem SA* v *Roust Holdings Ltd*) or exceptionally if the Court of Appeal considers the refusal to give permission to be unfair (see *CGU International Insurance plc* v *Astra Zeneca Insurance*).

[Challenging the award: serious irregularity]

Section 68

(1) A party to arbitral proceedings may (upon notice to the other parties and to the tribunal) apply to the court challenging an award in the proceedings on the ground of serious irregularity affecting the tribunal, the proceedings or the award.

A party may lose the right to object (see section 73) and the right to apply is subject to the restrictions in section 70(2) and (3).

(2) Serious irregularity means an irregularity of one or more of the following kinds which the court considers has caused or will cause substantial injustice to the applicant—

- **(a) failure by the tribunal to comply with section 33 (general duty of tribunal);**
- **(b) the tribunal exceeding its powers (otherwise than by exceeding its substantive jurisdiction: see section 67);**
- **(c) failure by the tribunal to conduct the proceedings in accordance with the procedure agreed by the parties;**
- **(d) failure by the tribunal to deal with all the issues that were put to it;**
- **(e) any arbitral or other institution or person vested by the parties with powers in relation to the proceedings or the award exceeding its powers;**
- **(f) uncertainty or ambiguity as to the effect of the award;**
- **(g) the award being obtained by fraud or the award or the way in which it was procured being contrary to public policy;**
- **(h) failure to comply with the requirements as to the form of the award; or**

(i) any irregularity in the conduct of the proceedings or in the award which is admitted by the tribunal or by any arbitral or other institution or person vested by the parties with powers in relation to the proceedings or the award.

(3) If there is shown to be serious irregularity affecting the tribunal, the proceedings or the award, the court may —
- (a) remit the award to the tribunal, in whole or in part, for reconsideration,
- (b) set the award aside in whole or in part, or
- (c) declare the award to be of no effect, in whole or in part.

The court shall not exercise its power to set aside or to declare an award to be of no effect, in whole or in part, unless it is satisfied that it would be inappropriate to remit the matters in question to the tribunal for reconsideration.

(4) The leave of the court is required for any appeal from a decision of the court under this section.

1. General. Section 68 entitles a party to challenge an award on the grounds of serious irregularity affecting the arbitral tribunal, the proceedings or the award. It is mandatory (see Section 4(1)). It is based on Section 22(1) of the Arbitration Act 1950 and art. 34 of the Model Law. See DAC Report paras. 278 to 283 and DAC Suppl. para. 35.

2. Serious irregularity. This phrase is defined in Section 68(2) by reference to the kinds of irregularity that the court considers have caused or will cause substantial injustice to the applicant. The serious irregularity may affect the tribunal, the proceedings or the award. Section 68(2) is a closed list and cannot be added to by the courts (see *Petroships Pte Ltd* v *Petec Trading*; and DAC Report para. 282). An award made in England can only be challenged in England (see *C* v *D*). The courts view this Section as a longstop and only rarely conclude that there has been a serious irregularity (see *Warborough Investments Ltd* v *S Robinson & Sons (Holdings) Ltd*).

3. Substantial injustice. The courts have addressed this question in a variety of ways depending upon the conduct complained of. In some cases, the court has seen that the wrong decision has been reached, this evidencing irregularity (see *Newfield Construction* v *Tomlinson*). In others, the courts have asked whether but for the irregularity the arbitrator may have reached a different conclusion, which conclusion is reasonably arguable (see *Cameroon Airlines* v *Transnet Ltd*; and *Vee Networks Ltd* v *Econet Wireless International Ltd*). However, the court should not infer that an irregularity has occurred simply because it would have done things differently. It is not necessary to show substantial injustice where the applicant has established lack of impartiality.

4. Failure to comply with general duty (Section 68(2)(a)). For the general duty on the arbitral tribunal, see Section 33. The violation must be sufficiently serious (see *Hussmann (Europe) Ltd* v *A1 Ameen Development & Trade*). For example, an arbitrator is permitted not to hold an oral hearing or follow traditional English court practice; but it may be a violation if the arbitral tribunal created unnecessary delay and expense as a consequence of its own conduct. The tribunal is entitled to limit the amount of evidence put to it on particular issues, assess the evidence before it without further unnecessary submissions and, provided the parties are given an opportunity to comment on the evidence, take account of its own expertise in analysing the evidence. But the tribunal's decision should not be based on matters which the parties never had the chance to deal with. The tribunal must not have direct contact with witnesses outside the arbitration or delegate its decision-making. A failure to act impartially is a breach of the general duty of fairness and would amount to a serious irregularity under Section 68(2)(a). The test for setting aside the award is the same as that for the removal of an arbitrator pursuant to Section 24 (see *Rustal Trading Ltd* v *Gill & Duffis SA*).

5. Excess of powers by the tribunal (Section 68(2)(b)). There is a distinction between a tribunal purporting to exercise a power which it did not have (which might amount to a serious irregularity) and erroneously exercising a power that it did have (which would not) (see *Lesotho Highlands Development Authority* v *Impregilo SpA*). An example of excess of powers is where the tribunal awards compound interest where the arbitration agreement prescribed simple interest. It does not include a wrong conclusion on a matter of fact or law. For exceeding its substantive jurisdiction, see Sections 30 to 32 and 67. For excess of powers by the arbitral institution, see Section 68(2)(e).

6. Breach of agreed procedure (Section 68(2)(c)). The tribunal must conduct the proceedings in accordance with the procedure agreed by the parties (see Section 34). Where the parties have agreed that a hearing should take place, the arbitral tribunal cannot conclude that documents alone are sufficient. Where the agreed procedure for the appointment of the president of the tribunal had not been complied with, his participation in the arbitration was unlawful and any award a nullity (see *Sumukan Ltd* v *The Commonwealth Secretariat*).

7. Failure to deal with all the issues (Section 68(2)(d)). This provision is designed to cover those issues the determination of which is essential to a decision on the claims or specific defences raised in the course of the reference, and it does not protect against errors in weighing or evaluating the evidence (see *World Trade Corp.* v *Czarnikow Sugar Ltd*). The issue must be an important or fundamental one and it must have been put to the tribunal (see *Fidelity Management SA* v *Myriad International Holdings BV*). It is not a ground for intervention that the court may have done things differently, or that the tribunal's reasoning is compressed, confusing or unsatisfactory (see *ABB AG* v *Hoctief Airport GmbH*).

8. Excess of powers by the arbitral institution (Section 68(2)(e)). The arbitral rules or procedures chosen by the parties may result in the involvement of an arbitral or other institution to a greater or lesser extent (e.g. LCIA, ICC, PCA for UNCITRAL arbitrations, any appointing authority). Any such institution must not exceed its powers. For excess of powers by the tribunal, see Section 68(2)(b).

9. Uncertainty or ambiguity as to the effect of an award (Section 68(2) (f)). This provision enshrines the common law doctrine that an award is only valid if it is clear and capable of performance and enforcement. Before making an application under this paragraph, the applicant must pursue any recourse under Section 57 (correction of an award for clerical errors or errors arising from an accidental slip or omission).

10. Fraud or contrary to public policy (Section 68(2)(g)). Unsurprisingly, an award may be challenged if obtained by fraud or if the way in which it was procured was contrary to public policy. Deliberate concealment of relevant evidence would amount to serious irregularity, but not a genuine oversight (see *Profilati Italia Srt* v *Painewebber Inc.*) or inadvertently misleading the other party (see *Cuflet Chartering* v *Caroussel Shipping*) or fraud by a non-party (*Elektrim* v *Vivendi*). The Court of Appeal has held that considerations of public policy could not be exhaustively defined and should be approached with extreme caution. It has to be shown that there is some element of illegality or that enforcement of the award would be clearly injurious to the public good or, possibly, that enforcement would be wholly offensive to the ordinary reasonable and fully informed member of the public on whose behalf the powers of the State are exercised (see *DST* v *R'AS al-Khaimah*; *Soleimany* v *Soleimany*; and for a recent review of the authorities, see *R* v *V*).

11. Failure to comply with formal requirements (Section 68(2)(h)). Absent an agreement between the parties to the contrary, an award must comply with its formal requirements (Section 52), such that failure to give reasons on costs constituted an irregularity as to form within the terms of this provision (see *Norbrook Labratories Ltd* v *A Tank*). But the applicant must pursue any recourse under Section 57 (correction of award or additional award) before making an application under this Section.

12. Admitted irregularity (Section 68(2)(i)). Any serious irregularity in the conduct of the proceedings or in the award admitted by the tribunal or arbitral institution is a ground for challenging the award. This provision allows the tribunal to seek to correct mistakes that cannot be corrected under Section 57 (see *Kasakhstan* v *Istil Group*).

13. Loss of right. A party may lose the right if it has taken part in the proceedings without raising an objection (Section 73(1)(a)) or does not challenge the award within time (Sections 73(2) and 70, usually 28 days). If the challenging party has participated in the arbitration, the grounds for challenge must have been raised previously before the arbitral tribunal (see

Zestafoni G Nikoladze Ferroalloy Plant v *Ronly Holdings*). For the right of a party who has taken no part in the proceedings to question whether there is a valid arbitration agreement, see Section 72(1)(a). An agreement between the parties that an award would be final and binding does not exclude a party's rights under Section 68 (see *Shell Egypt* v *Dana Gas*).

14. Application. An application may be made in respect of a provisional, partial or final award. For applications to court, see Section 80 and CPR Part 62. An applicant is obliged to exhaust all available arbitral procedures and recourse before making an application under Section 68 (Section 70(2)).

15. Security. The application may be allowed subject to providing security for costs (see Section 70(6)), the payment into court of any money payable under the award or otherwise secured (see Section 70(7)) or any other condition (Section 70(8)).

16. Remedies. The court may remit the award to tribunal, set aside the award or declare the award to be of no effect, in whole or in part (Section 68(3)). Remission is the preferred option, unless it is inappropriate, e.g. it is necessary to carry out a rehearing (see *Pacol Ltd* v *Joint Stock Co. Rossakhar*). Setting aside an award has been held to be the same as declaring it to be of no effect (see *Hussmann* v *Ahmed Pharaon*). An order made under this Subsection may apply to part of an award only (*Petroships Pte Ltd* v *Petec Trading*).

17. Appeals. The Court of Appeal may not give leave to appeal where leave has been refused by the High Court (see *Athletic Union of Constantinople* v *National Basketball Association*); however, the Court of Appeal can grant permission if the judge acted outside of his jurisdiction (see *Cetelem SA* v *Roust Holdings Ltd*) or exceptionally if the Court of Appeal considers the refusal to give permission to be unfair (see *CGU International Insurance plc* v *Astra Zeneca Insurance*).

[Appeal on point of law]
Section 69

(1) Unless otherwise agreed by the parties, a party to arbitral proceedings may (upon notice to the other parties and to the tribunal) appeal to the court on a question of law arising out of an award made in the proceedings.

An agreement to dispense with reasons for the tribunal's award shall be considered an agreement to exclude the court's jurisdiction under this section.

(2) An appeal shall not be brought under this section except –
   (a) with the agreement of all the other parties to the proceedings, or
   (b) with the leave of the court.

The right to appeal is also subject to the restrictions in section 70(2) and (3).

(3) Leave to appeal shall be given only if the court is satisfied –
  (a) that the determination of the question will substantially affect the rights of one or more of the parties,
  (b) that the question is one which the tribunal was asked to determine,
  (c) that, on the basis of the findings of fact in the award –
    (i) the decision of the tribunal on the question is obviously wrong, or
    (ii) the question is one of general public importance and the decision of the tribunal is at least open to serious doubt, and
  (d) that, despite the agreement of the parties to resolve the matter by arbitration, it is just and proper in all the circumstances for the court to determine the question.

(4) An application for leave to appeal under this section shall identify the question of law to be determined and state the grounds on which it is alleged that leave to appeal should be granted.

(5) The court shall determine an application for leave to appeal under this section without a hearing unless it appears to the court that a hearing is required.

(6) The leave of the court is required for any appeal from a decision of the court under this section to grant or refuse leave to appeal.

(7) On an appeal under this section the court may by order –
  (a) confirm the award,
  (b) vary the award,
  (c) remit the award to the tribunal, in whole or in part, for reconsideration in the light of the court's determination, or
  (d) set aside the award in whole or in part.

The court shall not exercise its power to set aside an award, in whole or in part, unless it is satisfied that it would be inappropriate to remit the matters in question to the tribunal for reconsideration.

(8) The decision of the court on an appeal under this section shall be treated as a judgment of the court for the purposes of a further appeal.

But no such appeal lies without the leave of the court which shall not be given unless the court considers that the question is one of general importance or is one which for some other special reason should be considered by the Court of Appeal.

1. General. Section 69 entitles a party to appeal an award on a point of English law. It is non-mandatory (see Section 4(2)), but it applies in the absence of written agreement to the contrary. It derives from Sections 1 and 3 of the 1979 Act. There is no comparable provision in the Model Law. See DAC Report paras. 284 to 292. For determination of a preliminary point of law during the course of the arbitration, see Section 45.

2. Question of law. The 'question of law' must be: for a court in England and Wales, one of English and Welsh law; or for a court in Northern Ireland, one of Northern Irish law (see Section 82(1). It does not include any question relating to any other law. No question of law would arise if the tribunal had been empowered to decide the dispute other than in accordance with rules of law, e.g. as amiable compositeurs or ex aequo et bono (see Section 46(1)(b)), or if the parties agree to dispense with reasons for the tribunal's award (see Section 52(4)). A question of law would include the scope or meaning of a contract, or the meaning of an award (*Sun Life Assurance Co. of Canada* v *Lincoln National Life Insurance Co.*). But issues relating to a performance do not (*Cadmus Investment* v *Amec Building Ltd*). An argument that there was no basis whatsoever in the evidence for a finding or inference of fact would not amount to an error of law (see *Newfield Construction* v *Tomlinson*).

3. Unless otherwise agreed. Any international arbitration rules chosen by the parties may include a provision that the parties shall not appeal an award (e.g. LCIA art. 26.9 and ICC art. 24, but notably not the UNCITRAL Rules) (see *Sanghi Polyesters* v *The International Investor*). However, where such rules are incorporated by reference, any waiver of a right of appeal is not effective due to art. 6 European Convention on Human Rights (see *Sumukan* v *Commonwealth Secretariat*). Wording in an arbitration agreement that the award would be 'final, conclusive and binding' has been held not to exclude rights of appeal under Section 69 (see *Shell Egypt* v *Dana Gas*).

4. Requirements for application. This Section applies to all awards, whether provisional or partial or final, as long as the error of law 'arises out of the award' (Section 69(1)). The applicant must first have exhausted any available arbitral process of appeal or review, or recourse under Section 57 (correction of award). He must also obtain the agreement in writing of all the parties or the leave of the court (Section 69(3)). The appeal must be brought within 28 days of the date of the award (or notification to the appellant of the result of any arbitral process of appeal or review)(Section 70(3)), unless extended by the court pursuant to Section 80(5). Only the arbitral award and the witness statement accompanying the application should be put before the court, and no pleadings or other evidence. The application is generally decided without a hearing (Section 69(5)), but a hearing may be ordered where it is necessary to elucidate the issues (see *HOK Sport* v *Aintree Racecourse*). Reasons should be given if permission to appeal is refused (see *North Range Shipping Ltd* v *Seatrans Shipping Corporation*). For applications to the court, see Section 80 and CPR Part 62.

5. Substantially affect rights (Section 69(3)(a). Under Section 69(3), for leave to appeal a point of law to be given by the court, the point of law must substantially affect the rights of one or more of the parties, such that it affects the outcome of the arbitration and not just a small part of the award (see *Taylor Woodrow Holdings Ltd* v *Barnes & Elliot*).

6. Tribunal was asked to determine (Section 69(3)(b)). In addition, the point of law must have been raised in the proceedings (see *Marklands* v *Virgin Retail*).

7. Obviously wrong/serious doubt (Section 69(3)(c)). Furthermore, the tribunals's decision on the point of law must be obviously wrong (subparagraph (i)); or the question must be one of general importance and the decision at least open to serious doubt (subparagraph (ii)). A point of law may be of general importance if it concerns the interpretation of a standard form contract or where the issue had been subject to differing opinions in previous decisions (*The Northern Pioneer*). However, where the contract is individually negotiated or based on a unique scenario, the fact that the court would have reached a different conclusion to that of the tribunal does not render an award open to serious doubt.

8. Just and proper (Section 69(3)(d)). In addition, the court has an overriding discretion to refuse leave if it would not be just and proper; for example, subjecting the respondent to considerable injustice (see *Braes of Doune Wind Farm (Scotland) Ltd* v *Alfred McAlpine*).

9. Security. Leave to appeal may be made subject to providing security for costs (see Section 70(6)), the payment into court of any money payable under the award or otherwise secured (see Section 70(7)), or any other condition (Section 70(8)).

10. Remedies. After hearing the appeal itself, the court may confirm, vary, remit or set aside the award in whole or in part (Section 69(7)), although remission is preferred over setting aside (see *Vrinera Marine Co. Ltd* v *Eastern Rich Operations Inc.*).

11. Further appeals. The High Court may allow a further appeal, but only where it considers that the question is one of general importance or is one which for some other reason should be considered (Section 69(8)). The Court of Appeal may not give leave to appeal where leave has been refused by the High Court (see *Athletic Union of Constantinople* v *National Basketball Association*); however, the Court of Appeal can grant permission if the judge acted outside of his jurisdiction (see *Cetelem SA* v *Roust Holdings Ltd*) or exceptionally if the Court of Appeal considers the refusal to give permission to be unfair (see *CGU International Insurance plc* v *Astra Zeneca Insurance*).

[Challenge or appeal: supplementary provisions]

Section 70

(1) The following provisions apply to an application or appeal under section 67, 68 or 69.

(2) An application or appeal may not be brought if the applicant or appellant has not first exhausted –

(a) any available arbitral process of appeal or review, and
(b) any available recourse under section 57 (correction of award or additional award).

(3) Any application or appeal must be brought within 28 days of the date of the award or, if there has been any arbitral process of appeal or review, of the date when the applicant or appellant was notified of the result of that process.

(4) If on an application or appeal it appears to the court that the award –
(a) does not contain the tribunal's reasons, or
(b) does not set out the tribunal's reasons in sufficient detail to enable the court properly to consider the application or appeal,

the court may order the tribunal to state the reasons for its award in sufficient detail for that purpose.

(5) Where the court makes an order under subsection (4), it may make such further order as it thinks fit with respect to any additional costs of the arbitration resulting from its order.

(6) The court may order the applicant or appellant to provide security for the costs of the application or appeal, and may direct that the application or appeal be dismissed if the order is not complied with.

The power to order security for costs shall not be exercised on the ground that the applicant or appellant is –
(a) an individual ordinarily resident outside the United Kingdom, or
(b) a corporation or association incorporated or formed under the law of a country outside the United Kingdom, or whose central management and control is exercised outside the United Kingdom.

(7) The court may order that any money payable under the award shall be brought into court or otherwise secured pending the determination of the application or appeal, and may direct that the application or appeal be dismissed if the order is not complied with.

(8) The court may grant leave to appeal subject to conditions to the same or similar effect as an order under subsection (6) or (7).

This does not affect the general discretion of the court to grant leave subject to conditions.

1. General. Section 70 contains a number of supplementary provisions that apply to all applications made under Sections 67, 68 and 69. It is mandatory (see Section 4(1)). It derives from Section 23(3) of the 1950 Act and Section 1(5) and (6) of the 1979 Act. See DAC Suppl. para. 35.

2. Exhausting arbitral procedure. Section 70(2) requires that an applicant/appellant first exhaust all available arbitral procedures and any available recourse under Section 57 of the Act (see *Torch Offshore LLC* v

Cable Shipping Inc.) even if the party thinks that the award is incapable of clarification (see *Sinclair* v *Woods of Winchester Ltd*). Satisfaction of this requirement should be stated on the arbitration claim form (see CPR Part 62 Rule 4). This requirement does not apply to a party contesting jurisdiction who elects not to participate in the proceedings (see Section 72(2)).

3. Time limit. Any application/appeal (i.e. filing the application claim form with the witness statements in support) must be brought within 28 days of the date of the award (see Section 54), or correction (see Section 57, and *Gbangbola* v *Smith & Sherriff Ltd*, and *Al Hadha Trading* v *Tradigrain SA*), or the date of notification of the result of any arbitral process of appeal or review (see Section 70(2)). Time starts running even if the arbitral tribunal refuses to deliver an award pending payment of its fees and expenses (see Section 56). However, the 28 days may be extended by the court (see Section 79, and *L Brown and Sons Ltd* v *Crosby Homes (North West) Ltd*).

4. Reasons. For the requirement of a reasoned award, see Section 52(4)). If the reasons are not sufficiently detailed, Section 70(4) permits the court to order the tribunal to remedy this. It may do so, exceptionally, even if reasons were not required (see *Petroships* v *Petec Trading*; and *Tame Shipping Ltd* v *Easy Navigation Ltd*). This power cannot be used to remedy a failure by the tribunal to deal with an issue (see *Van der Giessen-De Noord Shipbuilding Division BV* v *Imtech Marine & Offshore BV*). Where the court makes an order requiring sufficient reasons, it may also make an order relating to costs (Section 70(5)), e.g. that the arbitrators are not entitled to any further fees.

5. Security for costs. Under Section 70(6), the court may order security for the costs of any challenge/appeal (which overrides the power prescribed in CPR Part 25 Rule 13). For the power of the tribunal to award security for costs in connection with the arbitral proceedings, see Section 38(3). Similarly, the court may not discriminate against non-UK parties. Such power is an effective deterrent against frivolous or time-wasting applications/appeals (see *Gater Assets Ltd* v *Nak Naftogaz Ukrainiy*; *Azou Shipping* v *Baltic Shipping (No. 2)*; and *Kazakhstan* v *Istil Group*).

6. Securing award. As a further deterrent and to protect the award creditor from possible dissipation of the debtor's assets, the court is also empowered to order the applicant/appellant that money payable under the award be paid into court (and held in escrow) or otherwise secured (Section 70(7)). However, some judges have held that the power should be exercised only when the application/appeal appears weak (see *Peterson Farms* v *C&M Farming Ltd*; and *Danco International BVIO* v *Faucon Investment Co.*).

7. Further appeal. The court may grant leave to appeal a decision made under Section 67, 68 or 69 subject to similar conditions relating to security for costs or payment into court (Section 70(8)).

[Challenge or appeal: effect of order of court]

Section 71

(1) The following provisions have effect where the court makes an order under section 67, 68 or 69 with respect to an award.

(2) Where the award is varied, the variation has effect as part of the tribunal's award.

(3) Where the award is remitted to the tribunal, in whole or in part, for reconsideration, the tribunal shall make a fresh award in respect of the matters remitted within three months of the date of the order for remission or such longer or shorter period as the court may direct.

(4) Where the award is set aside or declared to be of no effect, in whole or in part, the court may also order that any provision that an award is a condition precedent to the bringing of legal proceedings in respect of a matter to which the arbitration agreement applies, is of no effect as regards the subject matter of the award or, as the case may be, the relevant part of the award.

1. General. Section 71 concerns the effect of a court order relating to a challenge or appeal of an award under Sections 67, 68 and 69. It is mandatory (see Section 4(1)). It derives from Section 22(2) of the 1950 Act and Section 1(8) of the 1979 Act. There is no comparable provision in the Model Law. See DAC Report paras. 293 and 294 and DAC Suppl. paras. 36 and 37.

2. Variation of award. For the power of the court to order a variation of an award, see Section 67(3)(b) (challenge on grounds of substantive jurisdiction) and Section 69(7)(b) (appeal on point of law). Any variation forms part of the award.

3. Remittance. For the power of the court to order remittance of an award, in whole or in part, to the tribunal, see Section 68(3)(a) (challenge on grounds of serious irregularity) and Section 69(7)(c) (appeal on point of law). The tribunal should make a fresh award in respect of the matters remitted and only those matters (see *Carter* v *Harold Simpson Associates*), within three months or such other time as ordered by the court (Section 79; for reckoning periods of time, see Section 78). Once a new award is issued, the relevant parts of the old award become null and void (see *Huyton* v *Jakil*). Remittance to the tribunal is an exception to the principle that an arbitrator's authority ends automatically upon the issue of a valid final award, whereupon he becomes functus officio (see Section 58). For the scope of an arbitrator's jurisdiction after making an award and having the case remitted back to him, see *Glencore International Ag* v *Beogradska Plovidba*. The court may also order the tribunal to state the reasons for its award in greater detail (Section 70(4)). For the power of the tribunal to correct an award or make an additional award, see Section 57.

4. *Scott* v *Avery* clauses. Section 71(4) allows the court to deny effect to *Scott* v *Avery* type clauses, whereby the parties agree that arbitration is a condition precedent to judicial proceedings (see also Sections 9(5), 10(2) and 13(3)). This provision does not apply in relation to statutory arbitrations (Section 97(c)).

MISCELLANEOUS

[Saving for rights of person who takes no part in proceedings]

Section 72

(1) A person alleged to be a party to arbitral proceedings but who takes no part in the proceedings may question –
  (a) whether there is a valid arbitration agreement,
  (b) whether the tribunal is properly constituted, or
  (c) what matters have been submitted to arbitration in accordance with the arbitration agreement,

by proceedings in the court for a declaration or injunction or other appropriate relief.

(2) He also has the same right as a party to the arbitral proceedings to challenge an award –
  (a) by an application under section 67 on the ground of lack of substantive jurisdiction in relation to him, or
  (b) by an application under section 68 on the ground of serious irregularity (within the meaning of that section) affecting him;

and section 70(2) (duty to exhaust arbitral procedures) does not apply in his case.

1. General. Section 72 sets out the rights of a party that takes no part in the arbitration nevertheless to challenge jurisdiction and/or any award. It is mandatory (see Section 4(1)). There is no comparable provision in the prior legislation nor in the Model Law, although such rights did exist under the common law. See DAC Report paras. 295 and 296.

2. Challenge to arbitral proceedings. A party who does not take part in the arbitral proceedings, but who seeks to challenge substantive jurisdiction, can do so by questioning the validity of the arbitration agreement, the constitution of the tribunal or matters which have been submitted for arbitration (Section 72(1)). (For an application to restrain the continuation of arbitration proceedings, see *Zaporozhye Shareholders Society* v *Ashly Ltd*; for an application to restrain publication of an award, see *Arab National Bank* v *El-Abdali*.) An objecting party may seek a declaration, injunction or other form of relief from the court. For the right of a participating party to raise such issues before the tribunal or the court as a preliminary issue, see Sections 30 to 32 (for relationship between Sections 32 and 72, see *British Telecommunications plc* v *SAE Group Inc.*). If a non-participating party starts court proceedings in respect of the same matter, the party who commenced arbitration will very likely seek a stay of the litigation under Section 9. The Court of Appeal has held that the application for a stay is the primary matter to be decided, rather than the application under Section 72, on the basis that the arbitral tribunal should, in general, be the first forum to consider whether there is a valid arbitration agreement and whether the arbitrators have jurisdiction to determine the dispute (see *Fiona Trust* v *Privalov*). This is a strong endorsement of the concept of 'Kompetenz-Kompetenz' (see Section 30). Where a challenge is unsuccessful, it is up to the tribunal as to whether that party can then participate in the arbitration (see *Hackwood* v *Areen Design Services*).

3. Challenge to award. Instead of challenging the arbitral proceedings, an objecting party can wait and challenge any award on grounds of lack of substantive jurisdiction or serious irregularity (Section 72(2)). Such grounds are the same as those available to a participating party under Sections 67 and 68 respectively. The 28-day time limit applies (see Section 70(3)).

4. Challenge to enforcement. If enforcement of an award is sought in England, a non-participating party may resist it on grounds that the tribunal lacked substantive jurisdiction (Section 66(3)). If enforcement is sought abroad, the non-participating party can also raise lack of substantive jurisdiction, most likely under art. V(1)(a) or (c) of the 1958 New York Convention.

5. Taking no part. A party may lose any rights under Section 72 if it takes a substantive step in the proceedings (e.g. serves a defence or asks the tribunal to determine its jurisdiction), but not if it merely writes to the arbitral institution objecting to jurisdiction (see *Broda Agro Trade Cyprus* v *Alfred C Toepfer*).

6. Duty to exhaust arbitral procedures. The general duty to exhaust any available arbitral procedures in respect of jurisdiction or serious irregularity prescribed in Section 70(2) does not apply to a party availing itself of Section 72, because the objecting party is not participating in the arbitral process.

7. Court application. For applications to the court, see Section 80 and CPR Part 62.

[Loss of right to object]

Section 73

(1) If a party to arbitral proceedings takes part, or continues to take part, in the proceedings without making, either forthwith or within such time as is allowed by the arbitration agreement or the tribunal or by any provision of this Part, any objection –
  (a) that the tribunal lacks substantive jurisdiction,
  (b) that the proceedings have been improperly conducted,
  (c) that there has been a failure to comply with the arbitration agreement or with any provision of this Part, or

(d) that there has been any other irregularity affecting the tribunal or the proceedings,

he may not raise that objection later, before the tribunal or the court, unless he shows that, at the time he took part or continued to take part in the proceedings, he did not know and could not with reasonable diligence have discovered the grounds for the objection.

(2) Where the arbitral tribunal rules that it has substantive jurisdiction and a party to arbitral proceedings who could have questioned that ruling –

(a) by any available arbitral process of appeal or review, or

(b) by challenging the award,

does not do so, or does not do so within the time allowed by the arbitration agreement or any provision of this Part, he may not object later to the tribunal's substantive jurisdiction on any ground which was the subject of that ruling.

1. General. Section 73 sets out the circumstances in which a party may lose the right to object to jurisdiction or a procedural irregularity if it does not object promptly. It is mandatory (see Section 4(1)). It is derived from art. 4 of the Model Law. See DAC Report paras. 297 and 298. Some arbitration rules also include waiver provisions (see LCIA art. 32, ICC art. 33 and UNCITRAL art. 30).

2. Grounds for objection. Section 73(1) refers to four grounds of objection, that: the tribunal lacks substantive jurisdiction (see Sections 31 and 67); the proceedings have been improperly conducted (see Section 68 and Section 24, application to remove arbitrator); there has been a failure to comply with the arbitration agreement or with any provision of Part I of the Act (see Section 68); or there has been any other irregularity affecting the tribunal or the proceedings (see Section 68). The objection must have been separate and free standing (see *Athletic Union of Constantinople* v *National Basketball Association*).

3. Forthwith or within such time as allowed. Unless otherwise allowed, the objection must be made forthwith. That means promptly or without unnecessary delay (see *Wicketts* v *Brine Builders*). The purpose of this Section is to prevent a party from abusing the arbitral process by saving up objections in the hope of a favourable arbitral outcome, only to raise an objection if the result is not favourable (see *Rustal Trading Ltd* v *Gill & Duffus SA*; and *ASM Shipping Ltd* v *Harris*).

4. Did not or could not know grounds for objection. It is for the applicant to discharge the burden of showing that it did not know or could not, with reasonable diligence, have discovered the grounds for its objection earlier (see *Sumukan Ltd* v *Commonwealth Secretariat*). The Model Law, by contrast, requires actual knowledge (see also the arbitral rules referred to above).

5. Continues to take part. The Section does not require a party to take positive steps in relation to the proceedings to be considered to have continued to take part. For example, if after the hearing, but before the final award, a party discovers an objection, but fails to withdraw from the proceedings, it will be taken to have continued to participate in the proceedings, even though it is simply waiting for the award (see *Margulead Ltd* v *Exide Technologies*; and *Sinclair* v *Woods of Winchester Ltd*).

6. Objecting to substantive jurisdiction. Section 30 permits the tribunal to rule on its own jurisdiction. If the objecting party fails to question the tribunal's ruling by way of appeal or review or challenge, or fails to do so within any specified time limit, it may not subsequently object to the tribunal's ruling on any ground which was the subject of that ruling. Section 73(2) forces an objecting party to challenge any award on substantive jurisdiction pursuant to Section 67 promptly.

[Immunity of arbitral institutions, &c]

Section 74

(1) An arbitral or other institution or person designated or requested by the parties to appoint or nominate an arbitrator is not liable for anything done or omitted in the discharge or purported discharge of that function unless the act or omission is shown to have been in bad faith.

(2) An arbitral or other institution or person by whom an arbitrator is appointed or nominated is not liable, by reason of having appointed or nominated him, for anything done or omitted by the arbitrator (or his employees or agents) in the discharge or purported discharge of his functions as arbitrator.

(3) The above provisions apply to an employee or agent of an arbitral or other institution or person as they apply to the institution or person himself.

1. General. Section 74 extends immunity to arbitral institutions and appointing authorities. It is mandatory (see Section 4(1)). There is no comparable provision in the prior legislation nor in the Model Law. See DAC Report paras. 299 to 301. For the immunity of arbitrators, see Section 29.

2. Discharge of function. Immunity applies to anything done (or omitted) in the discharge or purported discharge of the function of an arbitral institution or appointing authority in appointing or nominating an arbitrator (only), except in cases of bad faith. Thus, an arbitral institution cannot be liable for the act or consequences of such appointment, including anything done (or omitted) by the arbitrator. Section 74 does not, however, grant immunity for breaches of contract related to the administration of an arbitration or in respect of criminal conduct.

3. Bad faith. There are a number of English cases in which the meaning of the expression 'bad faith' has been considered (e.g. *Melton Medes Ltd* v *Securities and Investments Board*). It has been defined as malice (in the sense of personal spite or desire to injure for improper reason) or it describes a situation in which a decision is made when the arbitrator knew that he had no power to make it.

4. Employee or agent. Immunity under Section 74 extends to employees and agents of arbitral institutions and appointing authorities (Section 74(3)).

[Charge to secure payment of solicitors' costs]

Section 75

The powers of the court to make declarations and orders under section 73 of the Solicitors Act 1974 or Article 71H of the Solicitors (Northern Ireland) Order 1976 (power to charge property recovered in the proceedings with the payment of solicitors' costs) may be exercised in relation to arbitral proceedings as if those proceedings were proceedings in the court.

1. General. Section 75 enables solicitors to obtain a charge over property as security for unpaid fees. It is mandatory (see Section 4(1)). It is derived from Section 18(5) of the 1950 Act. See DAC Report para. 302.

2. Charge on property. The legislation referred to empowers a court to declare a charge on property which has been recovered or preserved in court proceedings by a solicitor to secure payment of that solicitor's taxed costs (i.e. cost that have been assessed and approved by a Taxing Master, now called a Costs Officer, see CPR Part 47). Section 75 extends that power in respect of recoverable costs of the arbitration as assessed and approved by the tribunal (see Section 63).

SUPPLEMENTARY

[Service of notices, &c]

Section 76

(1) The parties are free to agree on the manner of service of any notice or other document required or authorised to be given or served in pursuance of the arbitration agreement or for the purposes of the arbitral proceedings.

(2) If or to the extent that there is no such agreement the following provisions apply.

(3) A notice or other document may be served on a person by any effective means.

(4) If a notice or other document is addressed, pre-paid and delivered by post –
  (a) to the addressee's last known principal residence or, if he is or has been carrying on a trade, profession or business, his last known principal business address, or
  (b) where the addressee is a body corporate, to the body's registered or principal office,
it shall be treated as effectively served.
(5) This section does not apply to the service of documents for the purposes of legal proceedings, for which provision is made by rules of court.
(6) References in this Part to a notice or other document include any form of communication in writing and references to giving or serving a notice or other document shall be construed accordingly.

1. General. Section 76 concerns service of notices and other documents within the arbitral proceedings. It is non-mandatory (see Section 4(2)), but Sections 76(3) and (4) apply in the absence of written agreement to the contrary (see Section 5). This provision reflects art. 3 of the Model Law. See DAC Report paras. 303 to 305 and DAC Suppl. para. 39.

2. Application. This Section is especially relevant to the notice that commences arbitration (typically a 'Request for Arbitration' or 'Notice of Arbitration'), after which the parties usually notify each other of the respective addresses to which documents should be sent. For commencement of arbitral proceedings, see Section 14. This Section will remain relevant where the respondent does not reply, in particular having regard to art. V(1)(b) of the New York Convention, which provides that enforcement may be resisted on grounds that the party against whom the award is invoked was not given proper notice of the appointment of the arbitrator or of the arbitration proceedings.

3. Parties' agreement. Contracts often provide the address to which contractual notices and other documents must be sent. This would satisfy Section 76(1). Any arbitration rules chosen by the parties may prescribe additional rules, such as requiring that the Request for Arbitration must be filed with the institution and served on the respondent by it (e.g. ICC) or that any notice may be addressed according to the practice followed in the course of their previous dealings or in whatever manner ordered by the tribunal (e.g. LCIA art. 4.5).

4. Any effective means. Any means of service which will bring the notice or document successfully to the attention of the other party should satisfy Section 76(3). In most cases, a party will know to whom notice should be sent, be it someone at the contractual counterpart itself or its lawyers. Service by courier and/or fax and/or email are regarded as being effective because receipt can be demonstrated (see *Bernuth Lines Ltd* v *High Seas Shipping Ltd*).

5. Default position. Section 76(4) sets out a default procedure for effecting service, namely sending a notice or document to the last known principal residence or business address or registered or principal office.

6. Service not practicable. Where service of a document on a person in the manner agreed by the parties, or in accordance with Sections 76(3) and (4), is not reasonably practicable, see Section 77 for powers of the court.

7. Notice of award. For notification of an award, see Section 55. The Court of Appeal had held obiter that for purposes of Section 76, clarification of an award (Section 57) can be given directly or indirectly and notification by letter from solicitors acting for the opponent party may be effective notice (see *Zwiebel* v *Konig*).

8. Court proceedings. Section 76 does not apply to any court proceedings instigated under the Act, for which the prescribed rules of service for court documents will apply: CPR Part 6 and PDs 6 and 6b and Part 62 Rule 16 (for service of arbitration claims outside of the jurisdiction). Service of court documents by electronic means is permitted in certain circumstances.

[Powers of court in relation to service of documents]

Section 77

(1) This section applies where service of a document on a person in the manner agreed by the parties, or in accordance with provisions of section 76 having effect in default of agreement, is not reasonably practicable.

(2) Unless otherwise agreed by the parties, the court may make such order as it thinks fit –
    (a) for service in such manner as the court may direct, or
    (b) dispensing with service of the document.

(3) Any party to the arbitration agreement may apply for an order, but only after exhausting any available arbitral process for resolving the matter.

(4) The leave of the court is required for any appeal from a decision of the court under this section.

1. General. Section 77 concerns the powers of the court to order alternative service or to dispense with service altogether. It is non-mandatory (see Section 4(2)), but it applies in the absence of written agreement to the contrary (see Section 5). There is no comparable provision in the prior legislation nor in the Model Law. See DAC Report para. 306 and DAC Suppl. para. 40.

2. Application. This Section applies where service pursuant to Section 76 (i.e. in the manner agreed by the parties or in accordance with Sections 76(3) and (4)) is not reasonably practicable and in the absence of agreement to the contrary and only after exhausting any available arbitral process for resolving the matter. This situation might arise when a party is actively evading service or where a party's (most likely an individual's) whereabouts is unknown. Before seeking the assistance of the court, a party should try all available methods of service such as courier, fax and email and be able to demonstrate that they have been unsuccessful.

3. Powers of the court. The court has power to order alternative means of effecting service, which might bring the notice or document to the attention of the respondent (e.g. service on a lawyer known to have recently represented a party) or to dispense with service altogether.

4. Enforcement. Where resort is had to Section 77, because service cannot be effected on the respondent, difficulties might still arise at the enforcement stage under art. V(2)(b) 1958 New York Convention, which provides that enforcement may be resisted on grounds that the party against whom the award is invoked was not given proper notice of the appointment of the arbitrator or of the arbitration proceedings.

5. Court application. For applications to the court, see Section 80 and CPR Part 62.

[Reckoning periods of time]

Section 78

(1) The parties are free to agree on the method of reckoning periods of time for the purposes of any provision agreed by them or any provision of this Part having effect in default of such agreement.

(2) If or to the extent there is no such agreement, periods of time shall be reckoned in accordance with the following provisions.

(3) Where the act is required to be done within a specified period after or from a specified date, the period begins immediately after that date.

(4) Where the act is required to be done a specified number of clear days after a specified date, at least that number of days must intervene between the day on which the act is done and that date.

(5) Where the period is a period of seven days or less which would include a Saturday, Sunday or a public holiday in the place where anything which has to be done within the period falls to be done, that day shall be excluded.

In relation to England and Wales or Northern Ireland, a 'public holiday' means Christmas Day, Good Friday or a day which under the Banking and Financial Dealings Act 1971 is a bank holiday.

1. General. Section 78 sets out how time should be counted for the purpose of the Act. It is non-mandatory (see Section 4(2)), but it applies in the absence of written agreement to the contrary. There is no comparable provision in the prior legislation nor in the Model Law. See DAC Report para. 307.

2. Application. This Section applies to arbitration proceedings. For time periods for applications or appeals to court, time must be reckoned in accordance with the relevant rules of court (see Section 80(5)). The principal provisions in the Act with time limits are: Section 16 (appointment of arbitrators); Section 17 (power in case of default to appoint sole arbitrator); Section 57 (correction of award or additional award); and Section 70 (challenge or appeal). Any arbitration rules chosen by the parties may prescribe how time periods in their rules are to be calculated (LCIA art. 4.6; ICC art. 3.4; UNCITRAL art. 2.2).

3. Clear days. Where the Act refers to a period of clear days (e.g. Section 17(2)), neither the day after which time starts running nor the date when the act must have occurred should be included in the reckoning of the period.

4. Weekends and public holidays. Unless otherwise stated, or unless the stipulated period is seven days or less, periods include weekends and public holidays. The latter is defined as being a public holiday in the place where anything which has to be done within the period falls to be done. Although it is ambiguous, this would include public holidays at the place(s) where a party is conducting the arbitration (e.g. where its lawyers and/or general counsel and/or witnesses are based).

[Power of court to extend time limits relating to arbitral proceedings]

Section 79

(1) Unless the parties otherwise agree, the court may by order extend any time limit agreed by them in relation to any matter relating to the arbitral proceedings or specified in any provision of this Part having effect in default of such agreement.

This section does not apply to a time limit to which section 12 applies (power of court to extend time for beginning arbitral proceedings, &c.).

(2) An application for an order may be made –
  (a) by any party to the arbitral proceedings (upon notice to the other parties and to the tribunal), or
  (b) by the arbitral tribunal (upon notice to the parties).

(3) The court shall not exercise its power to extend a time limit unless it is satisfied –
  (a) that any available recourse to the tribunal, or to any arbitral or other institution or person vested by the parties with power in that regard, has first been exhausted, and
  (b) that a substantial injustice would otherwise be done.

(4) The court's power under this section may be exercised whether or not the time has already expired.

(5) An order under this section may be made on such terms as the court thinks fit.

(6) The leave of the court is required for any appeal from a decision of the court under this section.

1. General. Section 79 gives the court power to extend time limits in certain circumstances. It is non-mandatory (see Section 4(2)), but it applies in the absence of written agreement to the contrary (see Section 5). There is no comparable provision in the prior legislation nor in the Model Law. See DAC Report paras. 308 and 309 and 382 and DAC Suppl. para. 41.

2. Scope. Unless the parties agree otherwise, the court may extend time limits agreed by the parties or prescribed in Part I of the Act in respect of arbitration proceedings. The court has separate powers under Section 12 (extension of time for beginning arbitral proceedings) and Section 50 (extension of time for making award). In addition, this Section does not apply to Section 70(3) (time period for bringing application to challenge or appeal award), but Section 80(5) acknowledges that the court may extend time.

3. Applicant. An application may be made either by the parties or the arbitral tribunal, as appropriate (Section 79(2)). For example, a tribunal may wish to apply to court in order to extend the time to correct an award. An application to court may be made before or after the time has expired (Section 79(4)).

4. Court's discretion. The court's power to extend time is discretionary, but the court must be satisfied that the applicant has exhausted all means available to it (i.e. recourse to the tribunal or arbitral institution) and that a substantial injustice would otherwise be done (Section 79(3)). 'Substantial injustice' is not defined, but it echoes the language of Section 50(3) (extension of time for making an award). The court has held that a potential loss of interest of USD 83,000 if the time to apply for correction of an award was not granted, where the applicant had strong arguments for such correction, would be a substantial injustice (see *Gold Coast Ltd* v *Naval Gijon SA*, but see *Minermet SpA Milan* v *Luckyfield Shipping Corp.* for a decision to the opposite effect). An application should be brought promptly once it is known that an extension is required (see *Equatorial Traders Ltd* v *Louis Dreyfus Trading Ltd*).

5. Court application. For applications to the court, see Section 80 and CPR Part 62.

[Notice and other requirements in connection with legal proceedings]

Section 80

(1) References in this Part to an application, appeal or other step in relation to legal proceedings being taken 'upon notice' to the other parties

to the arbitral proceedings, or to the tribunal, are to such notice of the originating process as is required by rules of court and do not impose any separate requirement.

(2) Rules of court shall be made –
  (a) requiring such notice to be given as indicated by any provision of this Part, and
  (b) as to the manner, form and content of any such notice.

(3) Subject to any provision made by rules of court, a requirement to give notice to the tribunal of legal proceedings shall be construed –
  (a) if there is more than one arbitrator, as a requirement to give notice to each of them; and
  (b) if the tribunal is not fully constituted, as a requirement to give notice to any arbitrator who has been appointed.

(4) References in this Part to making an application or appeal to the court within a specified period are to the issue within that period of the appropriate originating process in accordance with rules of court.

(5) Where any provision of this Part requires an application or appeal to be made to the court within a specified time, the rules of court relating to the reckoning of periods, the extending or abridging of periods, and the consequences of not taking a step within the period prescribed by the rules, apply in relation to that requirement.

(6) Provision may be made by rules of court amending the provisions of this Part –
  (a) with respect to the time within which any application or appeal to the court must be made,
  (b) so as to keep any provision made by this Part in relation to arbitral proceedings in step with the corresponding provision of rules of court applying in relation to proceedings in the court, or
  (c) so as to keep any provision made by this Part in relation to legal proceedings in step with the corresponding provision of rules of court applying generally in relation to proceedings in the court.

(7) Nothing in this section affects the generality of the power to make rules of court.

1. General. Section 80 concerns legal proceedings commenced under the Act. It is non-mandatory (see Section 4(2)), but it is unlikely that parties could deviate from its terms. There is no comparable provision in the prior legislation nor in the Model Law. See DAC Report para. 310 and DAC Suppl. paras. 42 and 43.

2. Precedence of court rules. The rules of court relating to arbitration claims are set out at CPR Part 62 and PD 62. These rules of court take priority over the Act concerning all aspects of procedure, including service, notice and time periods. For example, CPR Part 62 Rule 6 requires that an application to remove an arbitrator (under Section 24) must make each arbitrator a defendant, whereas there is no such requirement in the Act.

3. Originating process. CPR Part 62 prescribes rules and time periods for the service of originating process (see Rule 15).

4. Notice. Under the Act, an application to court by one party without the consent of the other requires notice to be given to that other party and to the tribunal. CPR Rule 62.6 provides that where notice must be given to an arbitrator or any other person, it may be given by sending him a copy of the arbitration claim form and any written evidence filed in support of it.

5. Application to extend time. An application to extend any time limit for court proceedings must be made under Section 80(5), including the time limit for challenging or appealing an award pursuant to Section 70(3) (see *RC Pillar & Sons* v *Edwards*). The primary factors to be considered are: the length of the delay; whether, in permitting the time limit to expire and the subsequent delay to occur, the applicant had acted reasonably in all the circumstances; whether the applicant or the arbitrator had caused or contributed to the delay; and whether the other party would suffer irremediable prejudice if the application were permitted to proceed (see *ASM Shipping Ltd* v *TTMI Ltd*; *Nagusina Naviera* v *Allied Maritime Inc.*; and *People's Insurance Company of China* v *Vysanthi Shipping Co. Ltd*). Unlike Section 79(3) (the power of the court to extend time limits relating to arbitral proceedings), the applicant does not need to establish that substantial injustice would otherwise result if the time limit were not extended.

[Saving for certain matters governed by common law]
Section 81

(1) Nothing in this Part shall be construed as excluding the operation of any rule of law consistent with the provisions of this Part, in particular, any rule of law as to –
- **(a) matters which are not capable of settlement by arbitration;**
- **(b) the effect of an oral arbitration agreement; or**
- **(c) the refusal of recognition or enforcement of an arbitral award on grounds of public policy.**

(2) Nothing in this Act shall be construed as reviving any jurisdiction of the court to set aside or remit an award on the ground of errors of fact or law on the face of the award.

1. General. Section 81 confirms that any common law rules relating to arbitration that are not inconsistent with the Act are retained. It is non-mandatory (see Section 4(2)), but it is unlikely that parties would or could deviate from its terms. There is no comparable provision in the prior legislation nor in the Model Law. See DAC Report paras. 311 to 313 and 383 to 386 and DAC Suppl. para. 44.

2. Any rule of law. The DAC considered it to be impractical to enact an exhaustive code relating to all aspects of arbitration law and therefore other rules of law may be applicable, including in particular English common law rules relating to arbitration.

3. Not capable of settlement by arbitration. The common law continues to determine issues of arbitrability. There are very few matters that are thought of as not capable of settlement by arbitration. One example might be custody of children. In addition, private parties cannot resolve matters by arbitration that are determined by third parties, especially the State, such as criminal responsibility, taxation or intellectual property rights. Some aspects of insolvency may not be arbitrable (see *Exeter City AFC Ltd* v *Football Conference Ltd*; but contrast *Syska* v *Vivendi*). Some issues relating to a foreign friendly State, such as compliance with its treaty obligations, may not be justiciable (which may be an issue of admissibility rather than arbitrability) (see *Azov Shipping Co.* v *Baltic Shipping Co.*; *Occidental* v *Ecuador*; and *Serbia* v *Imagesat*). However, arbitration of family disputes by religious or community tribunals is permitted, subject to the award not being contrary to public policy (see *Soleimany* v *Soleimany*; and *Kohn* v *Wagschal*; also see Section 46, the rules applicable to the substance of the dispute). The House of Lords has confirmed that claims of fraud are arbitrable unless the fraud relates to the arbitration agreement specifically (*Fiona Trust* v *Privalov*). Competition law issues are arbitrable (see *ET Plus SA* v *Welter*).

4. Oral arbitration agreement. The Act applies only to written arbitration agreements (see Sections 5 and 6). Oral arbitration agreements may still be valid and enforceable under the common law, subject to satisfactory proof.

5. Public policy. The recognition and enforcement of arbitral awards may be refused on grounds of public policy, as determined by the common law. The Act expressly provides that enforcement of 1958 New York Convention awards may be refused on grounds of public policy (Section 103(3)), but public policy is also a relevant bar to enforcement under Section 66 (enforcement of awards), Section 99 (Geneva Convention awards) and by an action on the award. It is also a ground for challenging an award for serious irregularity (Section 68(2)(g)). The Court of Appeal has held that considerations of public policy could not be exhaustively defined and should be approached with extreme caution. It has to be shown that there is some element of illegality or that enforcement of the award would be clearly injurious to the public good or, possibly, that enforcement would be wholly offensive to the ordinary reasonable and fully informed member of the public on whose behalf the powers of the State are exercised (see *DST* v *R'AS al-Khaimah*; and for a recent review of the authorities, see *R* v *V*). For the application of English public policy as a ground for resisting enforcement of foreign awards, see Section 103, note 10 below. For the application of public policy as a ground for challenging an award made in England, see Section 68, note 10 above.

6. Privacy and confidentiality. Although not mentioned in Section 81, the privacy and confidentiality of arbitration is determined by the English common law (see *Emmott* v *Michael Wilson & Partners Ltd*). As noted in the Introduction to the Act (above), the DAC concluded that 'given [the] exceptions and qualifications, the formulation of any statutory principles would be likely to create new impediments to the practice of English arbitration and, in particular, to add to English litigation on the issue' (DAC Report, para. 17).

7. Error of fact or law. Section 81(2) is a technical provision which confirms that repeal of the Arbitration Act 1979 does not revive the power of the court to set aside or remit an award on the grounds of an error of fact or law on the face of the award.

[Minor definitions]

Section 82

(1) In this Part –

'arbitrator', unless the context otherwise requires, includes an umpire;

'available arbitral process', in relation to any matter, includes any process of appeal to or review by an arbitral or other institution or person vested by the parties with powers in relation to that matter;

'claimant', unless the context otherwise requires, includes a counter-claimant, and related expressions shall be construed accordingly;

'dispute' includes any difference;

'enactment' includes an enactment contained in Northern Ireland legislation;

'legal proceedings' means civil proceedings in the High Court or a county court;

'peremptory order' means an order made under section 41(5) or made in exercise of any corresponding power conferred by the parties;

'premises' includes land, buildings, moveable structures, vehicles, vessels, aircraft and hovercraft;

'question of law' means –
  (a) for a court in England and Wales, a question of the law of England and Wales, and
  (b) for a court in Northern Ireland, a question of the law of Northern Ireland;

'substantive jurisdiction', in relation to an arbitral tribunal, refers to the matters specified in section 30(1)(a) to (c), and references to the tribunal exceeding its substantive jurisdiction shall be construed accordingly.

(2) References in this Part to a party to an arbitration agreement include any person claiming under or through a party to the agreement.

1. General. Section 82 contains definitions of various terms used in the Act. It is non-mandatory (see Section 4(2)), but it is unlikely that any parties would want to deviate from its terms (and to the extent that any of these terms are found in mandatory provisions – see Section 4(1) – deviation may not be possible). There is no comparable provision in the prior legislation nor in the Model Law. See DAC Report paras. 387 and 388. For an index of defined expressions, see Section 83.

2. Claimant. The definition of 'claimant' means that a party making a counterclaim might be required to provide security for costs pursuant to Section 38(3) (powers exercisable by the tribunal).

3. Dispute. The definition of 'dispute' as including 'any difference' gives it the broadest meaning possible (see *Amec Civil Engineering Ltd* v *Secretary of State for Transport*; see also Section 6). A dispute may exist even where it is clear that one party is right and the other wrong (see *Halki Shipping Corp.* v *Sopex*) or where liability is admitted (see *Glencore Grain Ltd* v *Agros Trading Co.*).

4. Legal proceedings. The definition of 'legal proceedings' does not include service of a statutory demand such as to justify a stay in favour of arbitration (see Section 9, *Shalson* v *DF Keane Ltd*).

5. Question of law. The definition of a 'question of law' means that Sections 45 (determination of a preliminary point of law) and 69 (appeal on a point of law) only apply to questions of law of England and Wales, or Northern Ireland. Even if it accepted that the principles of foreign law are the same as English law, Sections 45 and 69 do not apply (see *Reliance Industries Ltd* v *Enron Oil & Gas India Ltd*).

6. Claiming under or through a party. The effect of Section 82(2) is that various persons who were not a party to the original arbitration agreement may enforce that agreement and exercise rights prescribed in the Act. This provision should be given a wide interpretation (see *West Tankers* v *Ras Riunione*), and includes a permitted assignee (see *Bawejem Ltd* v *MC Fabrications Ltd*) or insurer (see *Through Transport* v *New India Assurance*) or liquidator or new entity resulting from a corporate merger (see *SEB Trygg Holding* v *Manches*) or statutory novation (see *Astra SA* v *Yasuda*). However, English law does not recognise the group of companies doctrine (see *Peterson Farms Inc.* v *M Farming Ltd*). Under the Contracts (Rights of Third Parties) Act 1999, where a third party is enforcing its right under a contract that contains a written agreement to arbitrate, the third party will be treated as a party to that arbitration agreement (see Section 8(1) of that Act) (see *Nisshin Shipping* v *Cleaves*).

[Index of defined expressions: Part I]

Section 83

In this Part the expressions listed below are defined or otherwise explained by the provisions indicated –

agreement, agree and agreed	section 5(1)
agreement in writing	section 5(2) to (5)
arbitration agreement	sections 6 and 5(1)
arbitrator	section 82(1)
available arbitral process	section 82(1)
claimant	section 82(1)
commencement (in relation to arbitral proceedings)	section 14
costs of the arbitration	section 59
the court	section 105
dispute	section 82(1)
enactment	section 82(1)
legal proceedings	section 82(1)
Limitation Acts	section 13(4)
notice (or other document)	section 76(6)
party –	
– in relation to an arbitration agreement	section 82(2)
– where section 106(2) or (3) applies	section 106(4)
peremptory order	section 82(1) (and see section 41(5))
premises	section 82(1)
question of law	section 82(1)
recoverable costs	sections 63 and 64
seat of the arbitration	section 3
serve and service (of notice or other document)	section 76(6)
substantive jurisdiction (in relation to an arbitral tribunal)	section 82(1) (and see section 30(1)(a) to (c))
upon notice (to the parties or the tribunal)	section 80
written and in writing	section 5(6)

1. General. Section 83 lists various expressions used in Part I of the Act and cross-refers those to the Section where its definition or explanation may be found. It is non-mandatory (see Section 4(2)), but it is unlikely that any parties would or could deviate from its terms. There is no comparable provision in the prior legislation nor in the Model Law. See DAC Report para. 314.

[Transitional provisions]

Section 84

(1) The provisions of this Part do not apply to arbitral proceedings commenced before the date on which this Part comes into force.

(2) They apply to arbitral proceedings commenced on or after that date under an arbitration agreement whenever made.

(3) The above provisions have effect subject to any transitional provision made by an order under section 109(2) (power to include transitional provisions in commencement order).

1. General. Section 84 concerns the start date for the application of Part I of the Act. It is non-mandatory (see Section 4(2)), but it is unlikely that any parties would want to deviate from its terms. It corresponds to Section 33 of the 1950 Act. See DAC Report paras. 315 and 316.

2. Coming into force. Part I of the Act came into force on 31 January 1997 pursuant to the Arbitration Act (Commencement No. 1) Order 1996 (S.I. 1996 No. 3146). For the coming into force of the remainder of the Act, see Section 109.

3. Commencement of arbitral proceedings. Concerning the date on which arbitral proceedings are commenced, see Section 14. The Act also clearly applies to agreements to arbitrate entered into prior to the coming into force of the Act or even its enactment.

4. Transitional provisions. Various transitional provisions were set out in Schedule 2 to the Commencement Order. Among others, it provided that the old law (meaning the enactments specified in Section 107 as they stood before their amendment or repeal by the Act) would continue to apply to: (a) arbitral proceedings commenced before 31 January 1997; (b) arbitration applications commenced or made before that date; and (c) arbitration applications commenced or made on or after that date relating to arbitral proceedings commenced before that date.

PART II. OTHER PROVISIONS RELATING TO ARBITRATION

DOMESTIC ARBITRATION AGREEMENTS

[Modification of Part I in relation to domestic arbitration agreement]

Section 85

(1) In the case of a domestic arbitration agreement the provisions of Part I are modified in accordance with the following sections.

(2) For this purpose a 'domestic arbitration agreement' means an arbitration agreement to which none of the parties is –

(a) an individual who is a national of, or habitually resident in, a state other than the United Kingdom, or
(b) a body corporate which is incorporated in, or whose central control and management is exercised in, a state other than the United Kingdom,

and under which the seat of the arbitration (if the seat has been designated or determined) is in the United Kingdom.

(3) In subsection (2) 'arbitration agreement' and 'seat of the arbitration' have the same meaning as in Part I (see sections 3, 5(1) and 6).

1. General. Sections 85 to 87 set out special provisions for domestic arbitrations (as defined in Section 85(2)), but they never came onto force (see the express exception in Section 3 of the Arbitration Act 1996 (Commencement No. 1) Order 1996 (S.I. 1996 No. 3146)). These Sections were concerned with the staying of legal proceedings (Section 86, reflecting Section 4 of the 1950 Act) and the effectiveness of an agreement to exclude the court's jurisdiction in relation to points of law (Section 87, reflecting Section 3 of the 1979 Act). The DAC took the view that the same regime for all arbitrations, both domestic and international, was more appropriate and that drawing any distinction on the basis of nationality could be contrary to EC law concerning equal treatment of European nationals (see *Philip Alexander Securities and Futures Ltd* v *Bamberger*). See DAC Report, paras. 317 to 331 and para. 389 and DAC Suppl., paras. 47 to 52. For the power to repeal or amend Sections 85 to 87, see Section 88, but this would now be unnecessary.

[Staying of legal proceedings]

Section 86

(1) In section 9 (stay of legal proceedings), subsection (4) (stay unless the arbitration agreement is null and void, inoperative, or incapable of being performed) does not apply to a domestic arbitration agreement.

(2) On an application under that section in relation to a domestic arbitration agreement the court shall grant a stay unless satisfied –
  (a) that the arbitration agreement is null and void, inoperative, or incapable of being performed, or
  (b) that there are other sufficient grounds for not requiring the parties to abide by the arbitration agreement.

(3) The court may treat as a sufficient ground under subsection (2)(b) the fact that the applicant is or was at any material time not ready and willing to do all things necessary for the proper conduct of the arbitration or of any other dispute resolution procedures required to be exhausted before resorting to arbitration.

(4) For the purposes of this section the question whether an arbitration agreement is a domestic arbitration agreement shall be determined by reference to the facts at the time the legal proceedings are commenced.

1. General. Section 86 sets out special provisions for domestic arbitrations (as defined in Section 85(2)) in connection with the staying of legal proceedings (see Section 9). However, this Section never came into force (see Section 85, note 1).

[Effectiveness of agreement to exclude court's jurisdiction]

Section 87

(1) In the case of a domestic arbitration agreement any agreement to exclude the jurisdiction of the court under –
  (a) section 45 (determination of preliminary point of law), or
  (b) section 69 (challenging the award: appeal on point of law),
is not effective unless entered into after the commencement of the arbitral proceedings in which the question arises or the award is made.

(2) For this purpose the commencement of the arbitral proceedings has the same meaning as in Part I (see section 14).

(3) For the purposes of this section the question whether an arbitration agreement is a domestic arbitration agreement shall be determined by reference to the facts at the time the agreement is entered into.

1. General. Section 87 sets out special provisions for domestic arbitrations (as defined in Section 85(2)) in connection with the effectiveness of an agreement to exclude the court's jurisdiction to determine a point of law (see Sections 45 and 69). However, this Section never came into force (see Section 85, note 1).

[Power to repeal or amend sections 85 to 87]

Section 88

(1) The Secretary of State may by order repeal or amend the provisions of sections 85 to 87.

(2) An order under this section may contain such supplementary, incidental and transitional provisions as appear to the Secretary of State to be appropriate.

(3) An order under this section shall be made by statutory instrument and no such order shall be made unless a draft of it has been laid before and approved by a resolution of each House of Parliament.

1. General. Section 88 concerns the repeal or amendment of Sections 85 to 87. However, those Sections have not come into force (see Section 85, note 1), therefore the power in Section 88 is unlikely to be needed.

CONSUMER ARBITRATION AGREEMENTS

[Application of unfair terms regulations to consumer arbitration agreements]

Section 89

(1) The following sections extend the application of the [S.I. 1994/3159] Unfair Terms in Consumer Contracts Regulations 1994 in relation to a term which constitutes an arbitration agreement.

For this purpose 'arbitration agreement' means an agreement to submit to arbitration present or future disputes or differences (whether or not contractual).

(2) In those sections 'the Regulations' means those regulations and includes any regulations amending or replacing those regulations.

(3) Those sections apply whatever the law applicable to the arbitration agreement.

1. General. Sections 89 to 91 deal with the regulation of consumer arbitration agreements. They replace the Consumer Arbitration Agreements Act 1988. Section 89 confirms the application of the Unfair Terms in Consumer Contracts Regulations 1994 (S.I. 1994 No. 3159), which implemented the Unfair Terms in Consumer Contracts Directive (93/13/EC). The 1994 Regulation was replaced by the Unfair Terms in Consumer Contracts Regulations 1999 (S.I. 1999 No. 2083). See DAC Report paras. 332 to 337 and DAC Suppl. para. 54.

2. Consumer. The 1999 Regulations define 'consumer' as a natural person who, in the contracts covered by the Regulations, is acting for purposes outside his trade, business or profession (Regulation 3(1)). This definition is extended to legal persons by Section 90 of the Act.

3. Arbitration agreements. Whilst the main focus of the Regulations is exclusion clauses (i.e. contract provisions that exclude or limit liability), Schedule 2 includes as an express example of a term which may be regarded as unfair, any contractual term that has the object or effect of excluding or hindering a consumer's right to legal redress, particularly by requiring the consumer to take disputes exclusively to arbitration not covered by legal provisions (para. 1(q)). Accordingly, any term providing exclusively for arbitration, to the exclusion of the courts may be unfair, except where it is under a special statutory regime implemented with the intention of assisting consumers. 'Arbitration agreement' is defined in Section 89(1), because the definition in Section 6 is confined to Part I of the Act.

4. Unfair. Regulation 5(1)) provides that a contract term shall be regarded as unfair and therefore unenforceable, if the term: (i) was not individually negotiated, e.g. it forms part of a standard term contract (see *Heifer International Inc.* v *Helge Christiansen*); (ii) contrary to the requirement of good faith; and (iii) causes a significant imbalance in the rights and obligations of the parties to the detriment of the consumer (see *Zealander* v *Laing Homes*; and *Mylcrist Builders Ltd* v *Buck*). An assessment as to whether a contractual term is unfair must be made taking into account the nature of the goods and services for which the contract was concluded and referring, as at the time of the conclusion of the contract, to all the circumstances attending the conclusion of the contract and to all other terms of the contract or of another contract on which it is dependant (see Regulation 6). Factors relevant to the fairness of arbitration agreements also include: (i) whether the costs of the arbitration are disproportionate to the sum in dispute; (ii) whether the claimant has failed to draw sufficient attention to the arbitration clause; and (iii) whether the defendant would have objected to the arbitration agreement had they been made aware of its likely effect. Where the claim is less than a prescribed amount (GBP 5,000 for arbitrations seated in England), the underlying arbitration agreement is automatically considered to be unfair (see Section 91).

5. Effect. Should the arbitration agreement be deemed to be unfair, it will not be binding on the consumer. The remainder of the contract will remain in force if it is capable of continuing in existence without the unfair term, but would need to be enforced in court proceedings (see Regulation 8).

6. Foreign law. Sections 89 to 91 apply irrespective of the governing law of the arbitration agreement (Section 89(3)), but the 1999 Regulations apply only where the contract has a close connection with the territory of an EC Member State (see Regulation 9).

7. Scope of application. Whereas most of the provisions of the Act apply only where the seat of the arbitration is in England, Wales or Northern Ireland (see Section 2), Sections 89 to 91 also apply where the seat is in Scotland (see Section 108(3)).

[Regulations apply where consumer is a legal person]
Section 90

The Regulations apply where the consumer is a legal person as they apply where the consumer is a natural person.

1. General. Section 90 confirms that the 1999 Regulations apply equally where the consumer is a legal person (e.g. a company or partnership). However, the legal or natural person must be acting for purposes which are outside his trade, business or profession (see Regulation 3(1)) (see *Heifer*

International Inc. v *Christiansen*). See DAC Report paras. 332 to 337 and DAC Suppl. para. 54.

[Arbitration agreement unfair where modest amount sought]

Section 91

(1) A term which constitutes an arbitration agreement is unfair for the purposes of the Regulations so far as it relates to a claim for a pecuniary remedy which does not exceed the amount specified by order for the purposes of this section.

(2) Orders under this section may make different provision for different cases and for different purposes.

(3) The power to make orders under this section is exercisable –
  (a) for England and Wales, by the Secretary of State with the concurrence of the Lord Chancellor,
  (b) for Scotland, by the Secretary of State with the concurrence of the Lord Advocate, and
  (c) for Northern Ireland, by the Department of Economic Development for Northern Ireland with the concurrence of the Lord Chancellor.

(4) Any such order for England and Wales or Scotland shall be made by statutory instrument which shall be subject to annulment in pursuance of a resolution of either House of Parliament.

(5) Any such order for Northern Ireland shall be a statutory rule for the purposes of the [S.I. 1979/1573 (N.I. 12).] Statutory Rules (Northern Ireland) Order 1979 and shall be subject to negative resolution, within the meaning of section 41(6) of the [1954 c. 33 (N.I.).] Interpretation Act (Northern Ireland) 1954.

1. General. Section 91 provides that where a monetary claim is below a certain amount, the underlying arbitration agreement will be deemed to be unfair. Where the claim is above the prescribed amount, the onus is on the consumer to demonstrate that the arbitration agreement is unfair by reference to the criteria in the 1999 Regulations. There is no comparable provision in the previous legislation. See DAC Report paras. 332 to 337 and DAC Suppl. para. 54.

2. England, Wales and Scotland. The prescribed amount for arbitrations seated in England and Wales and Scotland is currently GBP 5,000 (see Unfair Arbitration Agreements (Specified Amount) Order 1999 (S.I. 1999 No. 2167), which increased it from GBP 3,000).

3. Northern Ireland. The prescribed amount for arbitrations seated in Northern Ireland is currently GBP 3,000 (see Unfair Arbitration Agreements (Specified Amount) Order (Northern Ireland) 1996 (S.I. 1996 No. 598).

4. Amendment. Section 91(3)(b) was amended by the Transfer of Functions (Lord Advocate and Secretary of State) Order 1999 (No. 678) to delete the words 'with the concurrence of the Lord Advocate'.

SMALL CLAIMS ARBITRATION IN THE COUNTY COURT

[Exclusion of Part I in relation to small claims arbitration in the county court]

Section 92

Nothing in Part I of this Act applies to arbitration under section 64 of the [1984 c. 28.] County Courts Act 1984.

1. General. Section 93 makes clear that the Act was not intended to affect the entirely separate regime applying to arbitration of small claims in the County Court. It derives from Section 7(3) of the 1979 Act. See DAC Report paras. 338 and 339.

2. Small claims track. The County Court arbitration regime has now been replaced by the small claims track (see CPR Part 27). Accordingly, Section 92 is redundant in England and Wales.

3. Scope. Section 92 does not apply to Northern Ireland (see Section 108(2)).

APPOINTMENT OF JUDGES AS ARBITRATORS

[Appointment of judges as arbitrators]

Section 93

(1) A judge of the Commercial Court or an official referee may, if in all the circumstances he thinks fit, accept appointment as a sole arbitrator or as umpire by or by virtue of an arbitration agreement.

(2) A judge of the Commercial Court shall not do so unless the Lord Chief Justice has informed him that, having regard to the state of business in the High Court and the Crown Court, he can be made available.

(3) An official referee shall not do so unless the Lord Chief Justice has informed him that, having regard to the state of official referees' business, he can be made available.

(4) The fees payable for the services of a judge of the Commercial Court or official referee as arbitrator or umpire shall be taken in the High Court.

(5) In this section –

'arbitration agreement' has the same meaning as in Part I; and

'official referee' means a person nominated under section 68(1)(a) of the [1981 c. 54.] Supreme Court Act 1981 to deal with official referees' business.

(6) The provisions of Part I of this Act apply to arbitration before a person appointed under this section with the modifications specified in Schedule 2.

1. General. Section 93 allows a judge of the Commercial Court or official referee (now a judge of the Technology and Construction Court) to be appointed as a sole arbitrator or an umpire. It derives from Section 4 and Schedule 3 to the Administration of Justice Act 1970. See DAC Report paras. 340 to 343 and 390 and DAC Suppl. para. 55. Parties rarely appoint sitting judges as sole arbitrator, principally because a number of recently retired judges are available for appointment.

2. Consequential amendments to the Act. The appointment of a judge as arbitrator requires various modifications to Part I of the Act, which are set out in Schedule 2. These recognise that the powers given to the parties to apply to the courts in certain circumstances are unnecessary where a judge already possessing such powers has been appointed as arbitrator. In addition, references to a 'court' in Part I are to be read as references to the Court of Appeal, so that any appeal or challenge would be to the Court of Appeal (see *Henry Boot Ltd* v *Alstom Combined Cycles*).

3. Scope. Section 93 and Schedule 2 do not apply to Northern Ireland (see Section 108(2)).

STATUTORY ARBITRATIONS

[Application of Part I to statutory arbitrations]

Section 94

(1) The provisions of Part I apply to every arbitration under an enactment (a 'statutory arbitration'), whether the enactment was passed or made before or after the commencement of this Act, subject to the adaptations and exclusions specified in sections 95 to 98.

(2) The provisions of Part I do not apply to a statutory arbitration if or to the extent that their application –
- **(a) is inconsistent with the provisions of the enactment concerned, with any rules or procedure authorised or recognised by it, or**
- **(b) is excluded by any other enactment.**

(3) In this section and the following provisions of this Part 'enactment' –
- **(a) in England and Wales, includes an enactment contained in subordinate legislation within the meaning of the [1978 c. 30.] Interpretation Act 1978;**
- **(b) in Northern Ireland, means a statutory provision within the meaning of section 1(f) of the [1954 c. 33 (N.I.).] Interpretation Act (Northern Ireland) 1954.**

1. General. Sections 94 to 98 adapt Part I of the Act for statutory arbitrations. They re-enact Section 31 of the 1950 Act. See DAC Report paras. 344 and 391 and DAC Suppl. paras. 56 and 57.

2. Statutory arbitration. Various statutes and subordinate legislation require certain types of disputes to be referred to arbitration (e.g. Agricultural Tenancies Act 1995, Section 28(1)). The statutory scheme overrides Part I of the 1996 Act, if inconsistent (see *Durham County Council* v *Darlington Borough Council*).

[General adaptation of provisions in relation to statutory arbitrations]

Section 95

(1) The provisions of Part I apply to a statutory arbitration –
   (a) as if the arbitration were pursuant to an arbitration agreement and as if the enactment were that agreement, and
   (b) as if the persons by and against whom a claim subject to arbitration in pursuance of the enactment may be or has been made were parties to that agreement.

(2) Every statutory arbitration shall be taken to have its seat in England and Wales or, as the case may be, in Northern Ireland.

1. General. Section 95 is a deeming provision so as to enable Part I of the Act to apply effectively to statutory arbitrations (see Section 94). The given enactment is deemed to be an arbitration agreement and the parties to the dispute are deemed to be parties to such agreement. In addition, the seat is deemed to be England and Wales or Northern Ireland. See DAC Report paras. 344 and 391 and DAC Suppl. paras. 56 and 57.

[Specific adaptations of provisions in relation to statutory arbitrations]

Section 96

(1) The following provisions of Part I apply to a statutory arbitration with the following adaptations.

(2) In section 30(1) (competence of tribunal to rule on its own jurisdiction), the reference in paragraph (a) to whether there is a valid arbitration agreement shall be construed as a reference to whether the enactment applies to the dispute or difference in question.

(3) Section 35 (consolidation of proceedings and concurrent hearings) applies only so as to authorise the consolidation of proceedings, or concurrent hearings in proceedings, under the same enactment.

(4) Section 46 (rules applicable to substance of dispute) applies with the omission of subsection (1)(b) (determination in accordance with considerations agreed by parties).

1. General. Section 96 sets out the specific adaptations to Part I that are necessary to make the relevant provisions apply effectively to statutory arbitrations (see Section 94). For excluded provisions, see Section 97. See DAC Report paras. 344 and 391 and DAC Suppl. paras. 56 and 57.

2. Jurisdiction. It would not be acceptable to have a tribunal ruling on its own jurisdiction in a way that impugned the validity of the enactment in question (see Section 30(1)) and therefore the tribunal is confined to ruling on whether the dispute or difference falls within the terms of the enactment (Section 96(2), see *Road Management Services (A13) plc* v *London Power Networks plc*).

3. Consolidation. Consolidation of statutory arbitrations or holding concurrent hearings (see Section 35) is only permitted where both or all arbitrations arise under the same enactment (Section 96(3)).

4. Governing substantive law. The arbitral tribunal may only determine the rules applicable to the substance of the dispute (see Section 46) in accordance with the law chosen by the parties (Section 96(4)). The parties may not agree that 'other considerations' should apply (e.g. deciding ex aequo et bono).

[Provisions excluded from applying to statutory arbitrations]

Section 97

The following provisions of Part I do not apply in relation to a statutory arbitration –
   (a) section 8 (whether agreement discharged by death of a party);
   (b) section 12 (power of court to extend agreed time limits);
   (c) sections 9(5), 10(2) and 71(4) (restrictions on effect of provision that award condition precedent to right to bring legal proceedings).

1. General. Section 97 sets out the specific provisions in Part I that do not apply to statutory arbitrations (see Section 94). For adapted provisions, see Section 96. See DAC Report paras. 344 and 391 and DAC Suppl. paras. 56 and 57.

2. Death of a party. Because there is no actual arbitration agreement, there could be no question of it being discharged by the death of a party (see Section 8).

3. Extension of time. Because the enactment will provide when arbitration is to be commenced, it was not thought appropriate for the court to have power to extend that time (see Section 12).

4. *Scott* v *Avery* clause. Because there is no actual arbitration agreement, restrictions on the application of *Scott* v *Avery* clauses (which require completion of arbitration proceedings before referring a dispute to court) were considered to be inapplicable (see Sections 9(5), 10(2) and 71(4)).

[Power to make further provision by regulations]
Section 98

(1) The Secretary of State may make provision by regulations for adapting or excluding any provision of Part I in relation to statutory arbitrations in general or statutory arbitrations of any particular description.

(2) The power is exercisable whether the enactment concerned is passed or made before or after the commencement of this Act.

(3) Regulations under this section shall be made by statutory instrument which shall be subject to annulment in pursuance of a resolution of either House of Parliament.

1. General. Section 98 allows the Secretary of State, by statutory instrument, to make additional adaptations or exclusions in respect of Part I as it applies to statutory arbitrations (see Section 94). No statutory instruments have yet been issued. See DAC Report paras. 344 and 391 and DAC Suppl. paras. 56 and 57.

2. Scope. This Section does not extend to Scotland (see Section 108(1)).

PART III. RECOGNITION AND ENFORCEMENT OF CERTAIN FOREIGN AWARDS
ENFORCEMENT OF GENEVA CONVENTION AWARDS
[Continuation of Part II of the Arbitration Act 1950]
Section 99

Part II of the [1950 c. 27.] Arbitration Act 1950 (enforcement of certain foreign awards) continues to apply in relation to foreign awards within the meaning of that Part which are not also New York Convention awards.

1. General. Section 99 provides that Geneva Convention awards may continue to be enforced pursuant to Part II of the 1950 Act. See DAC Report paras. 345 to 354.

2. Geneva Convention awards. Part II of the 1950 Act applies only to those awards made in the territory of a State which: (i) has been recognised by Order in Council as a party to the Protocol on Arbitration Clauses signed at a Meeting of the Assembly of the League of Nations held on 24 September 1923; and (ii) is a party to the Convention on the Execution of Foreign Arbitral Awards made in Geneva on 26 September 1927 (see Section 35 of

1950 Act). In addition, Section 99 requires that the State where the award was made is not a party to the 1958 New York Convention. There are very few countries that meet these criteria, e.g. Anguilla, Belize, British Virgin Islands, Falkland Islands, Grenada, Guyana, Montserrat, Saint Christopher and Nevis, Saint Lucia, Turks and Caicos Islands, and Samoa. For recognition and enforcement of 1958 New York Convention awards, see Sections 100 to 104.

3. Procedure. An application for enforcement should be made pursuant to CPR Part 62 Rule 18.

RECOGNITION AND ENFORCEMENT OF NEW YORK CONVENTION AWARDS

[New York Convention awards]

Section 100

(1) In this Part a 'New York Convention award' means an award made, in pursuance of an arbitration agreement, in the territory of a state (other than the United Kingdom) which is a party to the New York Convention.

(2) For the purposes of subsection (1) and of the provisions of this Part relating to such awards –
- **(a) 'arbitration agreement' means an arbitration agreement in writing, and**
- **(b) an award shall be treated as made at the seat of the arbitration, regardless of where it was signed, despatched or delivered to any of the parties.**

In this subsection 'agreement in writing' and 'seat of the arbitration' have the same meaning as in Part I.

(3) If Her Majesty by Order in Council declares that a state specified in the Order is a party to the New York Convention, or is a party in respect of any territory so specified, the Order shall, while in force, be conclusive evidence of that fact.

(4) In this section 'the New York Convention' means the Convention on the Recognition and Enforcement of Foreign Arbitral Awards adopted by the United Nations Conference on International Commercial Arbitration on 10th June 1958.

1. General. Sections 100 to 104 provide for the recognition and enforcement of 1958 New York Convention awards. They re-enact, with minor modifications, the 1975 Act. See DAC Report paras. 345 to 354 and 392 and DAC Suppl. para. 58.

2. Ratification by UK. The UK did not ratify the 1958 New York Convention until 23 September 1975 (the thirty-eighth country to do so). It came into force on 23 December 1975, with the enactment of the 1975 Act. Since its incorporation into English law, the 1958 New York Convention has received favourable judicial endorsement. No less an English arbitration jurist than Lord Mustill has declared that the Convention is 'rightly acclaimed as one of the most successful international statutes in the entire history of commercial law' (see Mustill/Boyd, *Commercial Arbitration Companion*, at 82). Lord Steyn has described the Convention as 'the great success story of international commercial arbitration' (see *Rosseel NV v Oriental Commercial & Shipping Co. (UK) Ltd*).

3. NY Convention award. These Sections apply to those awards made in the territory of a State which is a party to the 1958 New York Convention. Recognition as a party to the 1958 New York Convention in an Order in Council is conclusive evidence (Section 100(3)). Not all parties to the 1958 New York Convention have been recognised by an Order in Council, but the court will accept other evidence. The list of parties to the 1958 New York Convention are listed on the UNCITRAL website: <www.uncitral.org/uncitral/en/uncitral_texts/arbitration/NYConvention_status.html>. There are currently 144. The relevant date at which the State must be a party to the 1958 New York Convention is the date of enforcement and it does not matter if it was not a party either at the date of the award or the date of the arbitration agreement (see *Minister of Public Works of the Kuwait State Government v Sir Frederick Snow & Partners*).

4. Arbitration agreement. The award must be made in pursuance of an arbitration agreement which must be in writing. An invalid arbitration agreement is a ground for refusing enforcement (see Section 103(2)(b)). Much has been written internationally about the writing requirement in the 1958 New York Convention. The Act provides that for purposes of enforcement in England, it has the same meaning as the expansive definition in Section 5.

5. Where made. An award is taken to have been made at the place of the seat of arbitration (Section 100(2)(b), see also Section 3 for definition of seat and Section 53 for where English awards are treated as made), which reverses the House of Lords' decision in *Hiscox v Outhwaite*, which held that an award was signed at the place of signature.

[Recognition and enforcement of awards]

Section 101

(1) A New York Convention award shall be recognised as binding on the persons as between whom it was made, and may accordingly be relied on by those persons by way of defence, set-off or otherwise in any legal proceedings in England and Wales or Northern Ireland.

(2) A New York Convention award may, by leave of the court, be enforced in the same manner as a judgment or order of the court to the same effect.

As to the meaning of 'the court' see section 105.

English Arbitration Act (Chapter 23), Section 101

(3) Where leave is so given, judgment may be entered in terms of the award.

1. General. Section 101 notes that a party may apply to have a 1958 New York Convention award recognised and/or enforced. It derives from Section 3 of the 1975 Act. See DAC Report paras. 345 to 354 and 392 and DAC Suppl. para. 60.

2. Recognition. Recognition of an award is typically used as a shield when the court is asked by another party to grant a remedy that is inconsistent with the outcome of previous arbitral proceedings. Through recognition of the prior award, the court accepts that it is final and binding (see also Section 58), and consequently the matters decided therein are res judicata and/or give rise to issue estoppel and may be relied upon as a defence or set-off. Questions of recognition may arise independently of enforcement.

3. Legal proceedings. This term is not defined, but given the context it must be intended to have a broader meaning than in Part I of the Act and/or the definition at Section 82(1), which includes only High Court or County Court civil proceedings.

4. Set-off. A set-off is a monetary cross-claim which is raised as a defence. It operates to cancel part or all of the claim being made. Instead of raising a cross-claim, if a party seeks to recover a net positive amount, it needs to apply to enforce its award.

5. Enforcement. Sections 100(2) and (3) mirror the procedure for enforcing a domestic award (see Section 66). The award may be enforced in the same manner as a judgment (or order of the court to the same effect) or judgment may be entered in terms of the award. There is little practical difference, save that a judgment may be able to be exported to other jurisdictions (see *ASM Shipping Ltd* v *TTMI Ltd*). The court must not enter judgment in terms different to those of the award, albeit clerical errors may be corrected (see *Norsk Hydro ASA* v *State Property Fund of Ukraine*). An award creditor may seek to enforce part of an award only (see *IPCO (Nigeria) Ltd* v *Nigerian National Petroleum Corporation*). Where an award is entered as a judgment, interest is payable in respect of the judgment under the Judgments Act 1838, Section 17, at the rate of 8 per cent per annum (see *Gater Assets Ltd* v *Nak Naftogaz Ukrainy*).

6. Court. Proceedings to enforce an award may be brought in the High Court or the County Court (see Section 105 and the High Court and County Courts (Allocation of Arbitration Proceedings) Order 1996 (S.I. No. 3215) and the courts listed in CPR PD 62 para. 2.3).

7. Limitation. The limitation period of six years under Section 7 of the Limitation Act 1980 applies, with time starting to run from the date that the award should have been honoured (see *National Ability SA* v *Tinna Oils & Chemicals Ltd*).

8. Application. The procedure for applying to enforce an award is set out in the CPR Part 62 Rule 18 and is the same as that for Section 66. An application may be made with or without notice to the award debtor. The applicant must support its application with written evidence, attaching the arbitration agreement and the award (see Section 108) and stating the extent (if any) to which the award has been complied with as of the date of the application. Details of any post-award interest must be provided. The enforcement order itself must be served on the award debtor. If necessary, service may be effected outside of England and Wales with the court's permission.

9. Challenge. The award debtor then has 14 days (or longer if outside the jurisdiction) in which to challenge the order. If it does so, a hearing will be held and the award may not be enforced until its application is finally disposed of (see CPR Part 62 Rule 18(9)). The hearing is held in private (see CPR Part 62 Rule 10), but the presumption is that any judgment should be made public, but redacted if necessary to protect sensitive information (see *City of Moscow* v *Bankers Trust*).

10. Refusing recognition or enforcement. The grounds on which the court may refuse recognition or enforcement are set out in Section 103.

11. Execution. Once judgment is finally entered, the award may be executed in the same way as a judgment: the interception of a debt due to the respondent (i.e. a third party debt order, previously known as a garnishee order, see CPR Part 72); and/or the charging and sale of the debtor's property (see CPR Part 73). If the award/judgment requires action to be taken or stopped, failure to do so would be a contempt of court and punishable by a fine or even imprisonment. Pending actual execution, the award creditor may apply for a freezing order preventing the award debtor from disposing of its assets (see *Tsavliris Salvage* v *The Grain Board of Iraq*).

12. State immunity. State immunity does not prevent an application for leave to enforce an arbitral award being made, but it may prevent execution against non-commercial assets pursuant to the State Immunity Act 1978 (see *Svenska Petroleum Exploration AB* v *Lithuania*).

[Evidence to be produced by party seeking recognition or enforcement]

Section 102

(1) A party seeking the recognition or enforcement of a New York Convention award must produce –
  (a) the duly authenticated original award or a duly certified copy of it, and
  (b) the original arbitration agreement or a duly certified copy of it.

(2) If the award or agreement is in a foreign language, the party must also produce a translation of it certified by an official or sworn translator or by a diplomatic or consular agent.

English Arbitration Act (Chapter 23), Section 103

1. General. Section 102 sets out the evidence to be produced by a party seeking recognition or enforcement. It re-enacts Section 4 of the 1975 Act and largely reflects art. IV of the 1958 New York Convention and art. 35(2) of the Model Law. See DAC Report paras. 345 to 354 and 392 and DAC Suppl. para. 60.

2. Duly authenticated or duly certified. These terms repeat the requirements in the 1958 New York Convention (art. IV), but they are unfamiliar in an English court context. However, it is sufficient if the documents are exhibited to a witness statement deposing to their authenticity, accuracy as a copy, or truth as a translation, as the case may be (see CPR Part 62 Rule 18). Once such documents have been produced, the onus is on the award debtor to prove that the documents are not authentic and to raise any of the grounds in Section 103 justifying refusal of enforcement (see *Dardana Ltd v Yukos Oil*; and *Svenska Petroleum Exploration AB v Lithuania*).

[Refusal of recognition or enforcement]

Section 103

(1) Recognition or enforcement of a New York Convention award shall not be refused except in the following cases.

(2) Recognition or enforcement of the award may be refused if the person against whom it is invoked proves –
  (a) that a party to the arbitration agreement was (under the law applicable to him) under some incapacity;
  (b) that the arbitration agreement was not valid under the law to which the parties subjected it or, failing any indication thereon, under the law of the country where the award was made;
  (c) that he was not given proper notice of the appointment of the arbitrator or of the arbitration proceedings or was otherwise unable to present his case;
  (d) that the award deals with a difference not contemplated by or not falling within the terms of the submission to arbitration or contains decisions on matters beyond the scope of the submission to arbitration (but see subsection (4));
  (e) that the composition of the arbitral tribunal or the arbitral procedure was not in accordance with the agreement of the parties or, failing such agreement, with the law of the country in which the arbitration took place;
  (f) that the award has not yet become binding on the parties, or has been set aside or suspended by a competent authority of the country in which, or under the law of which, it was made.

(3) Recognition or enforcement of the award may also be refused if the award is in respect of a matter which is not capable of settlement by arbitration, or if it would be contrary to public policy to recognise or enforce the award.

(4) An award which contains decisions on matters not submitted to arbitration may be recognised or enforced to the extent that it contains decisions on matters submitted to arbitration which can be separated from those on matters not so submitted.

(5) Where an application for the setting aside or suspension of the award has been made to such a competent authority as is mentioned in subsection (2)(f), the court before which the award is sought to be relied upon may, if it considers it proper, adjourn the decision on the recognition or enforcement of the award.

It may also on the application of the party claiming recognition or enforcement of the award order the other party to give suitable security.

1. General. Section 103 sets out the grounds on which the court may refuse recognition or enforcement of a 1958 New York Convention award. It re-enacts Section 5 of the 1975 Act and largely reflects arts. V and VI of the 1958 New York Convention and art. 36 of the Model Law. See DAC Report paras. 345 to 354 and 392 and DAC Suppl. para. 60.

2. Court's approach to enforcement. The English courts have a strong pro-enforcement attitude. For example, Mr Justice Steyn, as he then was, said: 'the burden rests squarely on a respondent, who resists enforcement, to prove the existence of the grounds of refusal … That burden must be discharged on a balance of probabilities. … This Court ought to be astute to avoid making an order which will derogate from the efficacy of the New York Convention system and our treaty obligations …' (see *Rosseel NV* v *Oriental Commercial & Shipping Co. (UK) Ltd*). The effective and speedy enforcement of international arbitral awards has been held to be a matter of public policy. There are very few reported cases where enforcement has been refused (but see *Dallah* v *Pakistan*, currently on appeal to the Supreme Court).

3. Incapacity. For determining incapacity (Section 103(2)(a)), the relevant law is the law applicable to the party, which is likely to be the law of that party's domicile. It is rare that enforcement is refused on grounds of incapacity. An exceptional example is where a party is unable to instruct counsel or solicitors on account of a serious illness (see *Kanoria* v *Guinness*).

4. Invalidity of arbitration agreement. This ground is akin to lack of substantive jurisdiction (see Sections 30(a) and 66(3)). For determining invalidity (Section 103(2)(b)), the relevant law is the law to which the parties subjected the arbitration agreement or the law of the country where the award was made. An example of invalidity is where the award debtor is not a party to the arbitration agreement (see *Yukos Oil* v *Dardana*; and *Dallah* v *Pakistan*).

5. Not given proper notice or unable to present case. For determining lack of due process (Section 103(2)(c)), the relevant standard is that at the seat of the arbitration. However, the English courts will have regard to general notions of fairness, often referring to principles of natural justice. An example of an inability to present its case is where a party is not given the opportunity to review all of the evidence and arguments made before the tribunal (see *Kanoria* v *Guinness*). A party may not complain if it was given a reasonable opportunity to make submissions but did not do so or where the party subsequently took part in proceedings without complaint (e.g. *Minmetal Germany GmbH* v *Ferco Steel Ltd*, see also *Irvani* v *Irvani*).

6. Beyond scope of the submission. For determining the scope of the submission (Section 103(2)(d)), the relevant law is the law of the arbitration agreement and/or other submission agreement (e.g. ICC Terms of Reference). An example of a decision concerning the scope of the submission is where it was argued that the investment treaty excluded determination of certain tax disputes (see *Ecuador* v *Occidental Exploration*). Where an award contains decisions on matters that are beyond the scope of the submission together with decisions that are within its scope, the latter may be enforced (Section 103(4), and see *IPCO (Nigeria) Ltd* v *Nigerian National Petroleum Corp.*).

7. Deviation from agreement of the parties. For determining the agreement of the parties concerning the composition of the arbitral tribunal or the arbitral procedure (Section 103(2)(e)), the relevant law is the law of the arbitration agreement and any additional agreements on such matters and also, in some cases, the curial law at the seat of the arbitration. The deviation must not be insignificant or deemed to be waived by the lack of a timely objection (see *Minmetals German GmbH* v *Ferco Steel Ltd*; *Tongyuan (USA) International Trading Group* v *Uni-Clan Ltd*; and *Ommium de Traitement et de Valorisation SA* v *Hilmartion Ltd*).

8. Award not yet binding or set aside. For determining whether the award is not yet binding or has been set aside or suspended (Section 103(2)(f)), the relevant law is the law of the country in which or under which it was made. Where an application for setting aside or suspension has been made but not yet decided, the English court may adjourn the enforcement proceedings (Section 103(5), see *Minmetals German GmbH* v *Ferco Steel Ltd*). When deciding to adjourn or not, the court may take into account the conduct of the parties and the risk of assets leaving the jurisdiction, and may order that security be provided by the award debtor (see *IPCO (Nigeria) Ltd* v *Nigerian National Petroleum Corp.*; and *Dardana* v *Yukos Oil*).

9. Arbitrability. For determining whether the award is in respect of a matter not capable of settlement by arbitration (Section 103(3)), the relevant law is English law. There are very few matters that are thought of as not capable of settlement by arbitration (see Section 81(a)).

10. Public policy. For determining whether the award is contrary to public policy (Section 103(3)), the relevant test is English international public policy (see also Sections 81(c) and 68(2)(g)). The Court of Appeal has held that considerations of public policy could not be exhaustively defined and should be approached with extreme caution. It has to be shown that there is some element of illegality or that enforcement of the award would be clearly injurious to the public good or, possibly, that enforcement would be wholly offensive to the ordinary reasonable and fully informed member of the public on whose behalf the powers of the State are exercised (see *DST* v *R'AS al-Khaimah*). It has also been held that public policy goes to maintaining the fair and orderly administration of justice in England (see *IPCO (Nigeria) Ltd* v *Nigerian National Petroleum Corp.*; and for a recent review of the authorities, see *R* v *V*). Examples of public policy arguments that have been made include: the award has been obtained by perjury or fraud (*Westacre Investments Inc.* v *Jugoimport-SDPR Holding Co. Ltd*); the award is tainted by illegality (see *Soinco SACI* v *Novokuznetsk Aluminium Plant*; *Omunium de Traitement et de Valorisation SA* v *Hilmarton Ltd*); the award was obtained in breach of the rules of natural justice (*Minmetals Germany GmbH* v *Ferco Steel Ltd*); and the award is incapable of performance due to lack of clarity and events subsequent to the making of the award might make the award unfair (see *Tonguyan (USA) International Trading Corp.* v *Uni-Clan Ltd*). On the basis of the facts of each of these cases, the public policy challenge was unsuccessful.

11. Burden of proof. The burden rests on the resisting party to 'prove' that one of the grounds set out in Section 103(2) has been satisfied, on the balance of probabilities (see *Dallah* v *Pakistan*; *Gater Assets Ltd* v *Nak Naftogaz Ukrainiy*). Section 103(3) does not refer to the resisting party having to prove its case, because arbitrability and public policy may be raised by the court, but nevertheless the burden is likely to fall on the award debtor.

12. Role of supervisory court. The English court may give weight to whether the resisting party has invoked the remedial jurisdiction of the supervisory court at the seat of the arbitration and what reason that court had given for not annulling the award (see *Minmetals Germany GmbH* v *Ferco Steel Ltd*, and *Westacre Investments Inc.* v *Jugoimport-SDPR Holding Co. Ltd*), but there is no obligation to challenge the award at the seat (see *Dallah* v *Pakistan*).

13. Court's discretion. Even where one of the grounds in Section 103 is made out, the court is not required to refuse enforcement and may exercise its discretion to allow enforcement in any event. However, the English court has held that the grounds for refusing enforcement in Sections 103(2) and (3) relate to the structural integrity of the arbitration proceedings and, if such structural integrity is fundamentally unsound in respect of a particular award, then the court is unlikely to make a discretionary decision in favour of enforcement (see *Dallah* v *Pakistan*).

[Saving for other bases of recognition or enforcement]

Section 104

Nothing in the preceding provisions of this Part affects any right to rely upon or enforce a New York Convention award at common law or under section 66.

1. General. Section 104 confirms that a party is not limited to enforcing a 1958 New York Convention award only under Sections 100 to 103 of the Act. It re-enacts Section 6 of the 1975 Act. See DAC Report para. 392 and DAC Suppl. para. 61.

2. Common law. Any arbitral award may be enforced at common law by way of an 'action' or 'claim' on the award, i.e. for breach of an implied term in the submission to arbitration that any award made would be fulfilled (see *SC Rolinay Sea Star SRL* v *Petromin SA*). An award creditor can pursue this course instead of applying under Sections 66 or 101 or even if it is unsuccessful in obtaining leave to enforce under those provisions. The grounds at common law for refusing enforcement include lack of jurisdiction, violation of due process, non-arbitrability (see Section 81(1)(a)) and public policy (see Section 81(1)(c)). The court has a wider discretion to refuse enforcement than permitted by Section 103.

3. Section 66. Any arbitral award may be enforced under Section 66 in the same manner as a judgment (Section 104(1)) or by having judgment entered in terms of the award (Section 104(2)). CPR Part 62 Rule 18 sets out the application procedure. Section 66 expressly refers to lack of substantive jurisdiction as a ground for resisting enforcement, but the court may also refuse enforcement on other common law grounds.

4. Geneva Convention awards. Although this Section only refers to 1958 New York Convention awards, Geneva Convention awards (see Section 99) should also be able to be enforced at common law or pursuant to Section 66.

PART IV. GENERAL PROVISIONS

[Meaning of 'the court': jurisdiction of High Court and county court]

Section 105

(1) In this Act 'the court' means the High Court or a county court, subject to the following provisions.
  (2) The Lord Chancellor may by order make provision –
   (a) allocating proceedings under this Act to the High Court or to county courts; or
   (b) specifying proceedings under this Act which may be commenced or taken only in the High Court or in a county court.

(3) The Lord Chancellor may by order make provision requiring proceedings of any specified description under this Act in relation to which a county court has jurisdiction to be commenced or taken in one or more specified county courts.

Any jurisdiction so exercisable by a specified county court is exercisable throughout England and Wales or, as the case may be, Northern Ireland.

(4) An order under this section –
  (a) may differentiate between categories of proceedings by reference to such criteria as the Lord Chancellor sees fit to specify, and
  (b) may make such incidental or transitional provision as the Lord Chancellor considers necessary or expedient.

(5) An order under this section for England and Wales shall be made by statutory instrument which shall be subject to annulment in pursuance of a resolution of either House of Parliament.

(6) An order under this section for Northern Ireland shall be a statutory rule for the purposes of the [S.I. 1979/1573 (N.I. 12).] Statutory Rules (Northern Ireland) Order 1979 which shall be subject to annulment in pursuance of a resolution of either House of Parliament in like manner as a statutory instrument and section 5 of the [1946 c. 36.] Statutory Instruments Act 1946 shall apply accordingly.

1. General. Section 105 defines the 'court' for the purposes of the entire Act (see Section 83) to mean the High Court or a county court and entitles the Lord Chancellor to allocate proceedings between the two. See DAC Suppl. para. 62.

2. Allocation. For the allocation of proceedings, see the High Court and County Courts (Allocation of Arbitration Proceedings) Order 1996 (S.I. 1996 No. 3215), as amended by SIs 1999/1010 and 2002/439. The CPR further allocates proceedings amongst divisions of the High Court, e.g. Chancery, Queens Bench Division, Admiralty and Commercial Court, Technology and Construction Court, Mercantile Court. For example, for issuing a claim form, see CPR PD 62, para. 2.3.

3. Judge-arbitrators. Where a judge has been appointed as sole arbitrator, references to the 'court' may be a reference to the Court of Appeal (see Section 93(6) and Schedule 2).

[Crown application]
Section 106

(1) Part I of this Act applies to any arbitration agreement to which Her Majesty, either in right of the Crown or of the Duchy of Lancaster or otherwise, or the Duke of Cornwall, is a party.

(2) Where Her Majesty is party to an arbitration agreement otherwise than in right of the Crown, Her Majesty shall be represented for the purposes of any arbitral proceedings –
   (a) where the agreement was entered into by Her Majesty in right of the Duchy of Lancaster, by the Chancellor of the Duchy or such person as he may appoint, and
   (b) in any other case, by such person as Her Majesty may appoint in writing under the Royal Sign Manual.
(3) Where the Duke of Cornwall is party to an arbitration agreement, he shall be represented for the purposes of any arbitral proceedings by such person as he may appoint.
(4) References in Part I to a party or the parties to the arbitration agreement or to arbitral proceedings shall be construed, where subsection (2) or (3) applies, as references to the person representing Her Majesty or the Duke of Cornwall.

1. General. Section 106 confirms that Part I of the Act applies to the Crown. This provision is necessary because Acts of Parliament bind the Crown only to the extent expressly stated in the Act. It re-enacts Section 30 of the 1950 Act and Section 7(1)(c) of the 1979 Act. It is not referred to in the DAC Report.

2. In right of the Crown. This phrase refers to HM The Queen acting through her government, in which case any arbitration proceedings would be commenced by or against the relevant ministry or government department. 'Otherwise than in right of the Crown' refers to matters conducted in her private capacity.

3. Personal representatives. HM The Queen and the Duke of Cornwall shall be represented in any arbitration proceedings by such person as they may appoint (see also the extended definition of 'party' in Section 83).

[Consequential amendments and repeals]

Section 107

(1) The enactments specified in Schedule 3 are amended in accordance with that Schedule, the amendments being consequential on the provisions of this Act.

(2) The enactments specified in Schedule 4 are repealed to the extent specified.

1. General. Section 107 gives effect to Schedules 3 and 4 of the Act, which set out the consequential amendments and repeals brought about by the Act. See DAC Report para. 393 and DAC Suppl. para. 61.

2. Amendments. Schedule 3 sets out the consequential amendments needed to various enactments. Some of these legislative Acts have subsequently been repealed.

3. Repeals. Schedule 4 sets out the repeals that were necessary. Most of the previous arbitration legislation was repealed, namely; the 1950 Act (save for Part II which concerns the Geneva Convention, see Section 99 of this Act); the 1975 Act; the 1979 Act; the Consumer Arbitration Agreements Act 1988 (replaced by Sections 89 to 91 of this Act); and the Arbitration Act (Northern Ireland) 1937. The Arbitration (International Investment Disputes) Act 1966, implementing the 1965 Washington Convention, was not repealed.

4. Rights of appeal. Section 18(1) of the Supreme Court Act 1981, which deals with restrictions on appeals to the Court of Appeal, was amended to read that there is to be no appeal 'except as provided by Part I of the Arbitration Act 1996, from any decision of the High Court under that Part' (Schedule 3, para. 37). This appeared to remove any right of appeal unless it was expressly referred to in the relevant Section. This view was rejected by the House of Lords on the basis that it cannot have been Parliament's intention to effect such a substantial change to the rights of appeal by way of consequential amendment (*Inco Europe Ltd* v *First Choice Distribution*). Accordingly, a right of appeal to the Court of Appeal does exist in respect of Sections 9, 10, 13, 28, 64 and 72.

5. Scope. Schedules 3 and 4 extend to Scotland so far as they relate to enactments that apply there (see Section 108(3)). The 1975 Act, which implements the NY Convention, was repealed only as it applies in England and Wales and Northern Ireland (see Section 108(4)).

[Extent]

Section 108

(1) The provisions of this Act extend to England and Wales and, except as mentioned below, to Northern Ireland.

(2) The following provisions of Part II do not extend to Northern Ireland –

section 92 (exclusion of Part I in relation to small claims arbitration in the county court), and

section 93 and Schedule 2 (appointment of judges as arbitrators).

(3) Sections 89, 90 and 91 (consumer arbitration agreements) extend to Scotland and the provisions of Schedules 3 and 4 (consequential amendments and repeals) extend to Scotland so far as they relate to enactments which so extend, subject as follows.

(4) The repeal of the [1975 c. 3.] Arbitration Act 1975 extends only to England and Wales and Northern Ireland.

English Arbitration Act (Chapter 23), Section 110

1. General. Section 108 sets out the territorial application of the Act within the UK. It is a partial re-enactment of Section 34 of the 1950 Act, Section 8(4) of the 1975 Act, and Section 8(4) of the 1979 Act. The DAC Report does not refer to this provision.

2. England and Wales. The entire Act applies in England and Wales.

3. Northern Ireland. Almost the entire Act applies in Northern Ireland, with the exception of Section 92 (small claims arbitration in the County Court), and Section 93 and Schedule 2 (appointment of judges as arbitrators).

4. Scotland. The Act does not apply in Scotland, except for Sections 89, 90 and 91 (unfair terms regulations) and Schedules 3 and 4 (consequential amendments or repeals to UK legislation). Scotland is a separate jurisdiction for arbitration purposes, having adopted the Model Law (see Section 2 of the Act and Section 66(2) of the Law Reform (Miscellaneous Provisions) (Scotland) Act 1990); replaced by the Arbitration (Scotland) Act 2010. In addition, the provisions relating to the recognition and enforcement of foreign arbitral awards under the 1927 Geneva Convention and the 1958 New York Convention continued to apply in Scotland rather than being replaced by Sections 99 to 103 of the Act (see Section 41 of the 1950 Act and the 1975 Act).

[Commencement]

Section 109

(1) The provisions of this Act come into force on such day as the Secretary of State may appoint by order made by statutory instrument, and different days may be appointed for different purposes.

(2) An order under subsection (1) may contain such transitional provisions as appear to the Secretary of State to be appropriate.

1. General. Section 109 concerns the commencement date of the Act. There is no comparable provision in the Model Law nor the previous legislation. The DAC Report does not refer to this Section.

2. Into force. Pursuant to S.I. 1996 No. 3146 (c. 96) the Arbitration Act 1996 (Commencement No. 1) Order 1996: (i) Sections 91 (in part), 105, 107(1) and (2), and 108 to 110 came into force on 17 December 1996; and (ii) the remainder of the Act (except Sections 85 to 87) came into force on 31 January 1997. Sections 85 to 87 did not come into force (see Section 85, note 1). Certain transitional provisions are contained in Schedule 2 to the Order.

[Short title]

Section 110

This Act may be cited as the Arbitration Act 1996.

English Arbitration Act (Chapter 23), Section 110

1. General. Section 110 sets out the short title of the Act. It is dated 1996 because it was enacted that year, albeit that most of its provisions did not come into force until 1997 (see Section 109). The Act may also be identified as 'Chapter 23' or 'c. 23' of 1996, which indicates that it is the 23rd statute enacted in that calendar year. The DAC Report does not refer to this Section.

FRENCH CODE OF CIVIL PROCEDURE
(BOOK IV: ARBITRATION), 1981

(In force as from 14 May 1981)

[Introductory remarks]

1. International as distinguished from domestic arbitration. Provisions of French arbitration law are divided between those applicable to international arbitration in arts. 1492 to 1507 of the French 'Code of Civil Procedure' (CPC, Book IV, Title V-VI), and those applicable to domestic arbitration in arts. 2059 to 2061 of the French Civil Code and in arts. 1442 to 1491 of the CPC (Book IV, Title I-IV). The provisions applicable to French domestic arbitration are generally not applicable to international arbitration. There are three exceptions to this general rule, however. First, French international arbitration provisions sometimes expressly provide that certain French domestic arbitration provisions also apply to international arbitrations (see arts. 1493, 1500 and 1507). Second, French courts have held certain provisions of French domestic arbitration to be applicable to international arbitration (see arts. 1458 and 1466). Third, although rare in practice, parties to an international arbitration may expressly agree that some or all of the French domestic arbitration provisions shall apply to their dispute (see art. 1495). The following article-by-article commentary will only address the international arbitration provisions contained in arts. 1492 to 1507 of the CPC, and those domestic arbitration provisions that are applicable to international arbitration because either the international arbitration provisions themselves, or the French courts, say they are.

2. CPC provisions and French case law on international arbitration. Pursuant to the French international private law tradition, issues which are not specifically addressed in the CPC provisions are most often addressed in French court decisions, which are most commonly rendered by the Court of Appeal of Paris or by the French Supreme Court (Cour de cassation). As a consequence, the CPC provisions on international arbitration should always be read in conjunction with applicable case law. In very few cases, French court decisions made in the context of domestic arbitration may also be considered applicable to international arbitration. The following commentary will generally only refer to case law made in the context of international arbitrations, with the exception of domestic arbitration cases that may also be relevant in the context of international arbitration.

3. CPC provisions and international conventions on international arbitration. France is a party to the following international conventions related to international arbitration: the New York Convention of 1958 on the Recognition and Enforcement of Foreign Arbitral Awards, the Geneva Protocol on the Enforcement of Arbitration Clauses of 1923, the Geneva Convention of 21 April 1961 on International Arbitration, the Washington Convention of

1965 on the Settlement of Investment Disputes between States and Nationals of Other States, as well as various bilateral and multilateral international conventions relating or referring to arbitration. These conventions provide minimum standards ratifying countries must observe in supporting international arbitration through the recognition and enforcement of arbitration agreements and awards. The French provisions on international arbitration set forth in the CPC are more favourable to arbitration than the international conventions to which France is a party. As a consequence, in reaching their decisions, French courts rely upon the relevant provisions of the CPC rather than upon the provisions set forth in these conventions.

4. Scope of French international arbitration law. French international arbitration law applies to international arbitrations with their seat in France. It also applies to the recognition of international arbitration agreements and to the recognition and enforcement of international awards. Under French international arbitration law, there are two types of international arbitration awards: foreign awards (awards rendered in arbitrations where the seat of arbitration is outside France), and international awards rendered in France (awards rendered in international arbitrations – as defined below in art. 1492 – where the seat of arbitration is in France). Although both international awards rendered in France and foreign awards are 'international awards', French law draws certain distinctions between the two with respect to their enforcement. The similarities and differences in the enforcement regimes applicable to foreign awards and to international awards rendered in France are detailed below in the section concerning the enforcement of awards (see arts. 1498 to 1507).

[Definition of international arbitration]
Article 1492

An international arbitration is one that involves the interests of international trade.

1. Definition of arbitration. There is no definition of the word 'arbitration' in French law. However, French authors generally agree that arbitration is a process whereby one or more individuals are entrusted by parties with the power to decide their dispute by way of one or more binding and final decisions. Arbitration is distinguished from expert determination, conciliation or mediation in that the arbitral tribunal's mission involves deciding on one or more issues of law and the tribunal's decision is binding upon the parties.

2. Definition of international arbitration and international arbitration awards. Under French law, an arbitration is international if the subject matter of the dispute is commercially connected with more than one country at the time the arbitration is commenced. Therefore, an arbitration is international even if the seat of arbitration is in France as long as the parties' dispute is commercially connected with more than one country. The intent of the parties to make, or not to make, the arbitration international is irrelevant (Cour de cassation, 13 March 2007, *Chefaro*). In particular, the nationality of the parties and the law applicable to the merits of the dispute or to the arbitration procedure do not in and of themselves, determine whether the arbitration is international (Cour d'appel Paris, 29 March 2001, *Carthago Films*). By way of example, arbitrations concerning the transfer of shares of a French company among shareholders of different nationalities are international arbitrations. Likewise, arbitrations among French companies concerning a dispute that involves deliveries or payments abroad are also international arbitrations under French law. Moreover, as noted above (see Introductory remarks, note 4), both foreign awards and international awards rendered in France are considered international arbitration awards under French law. Foreign awards will be treated as international awards under French law even if they resolve a dispute that involves the economy of only one country (Cour de cassation, 17 October 2000, *Asecna*).

[Applicability of French provisions on domestic arbitration to international arbitration]

Article 1495

Where international arbitration is governed by French law, the provisions of titles I, II and III of this Book shall only apply in the absence of a specific agreement, and subject to articles 1493 and 1494.

1. Application. Art. 1495 has a limited impact from a practical standpoint. As a preliminary matter, it concerns only those rare cases where parties to an international arbitration agree that French domestic arbitration law shall apply. In such a case, art. 1495 provides that all French domestic arbitration provisions shall apply. Having said this, art. 1495 also provides that, in such a case, the parties may still expressly agree to deviate from these provisions. For example, the parties may agree that the French domestic arbitration law shall apply to their arbitration, but also agree to the UNCITRAL Arbitration Rules. In such a case, pursuant to art. 1495, the UNCITRAL Arbitration Rules would displace the French domestic arbitration law with respect to those issues addressed by the UNCITRAL Rules. In practice, parties to an international arbitration seldom opt for the application of the French domestic arbitration law, and such an election is not recommended.

[Constitution of the arbitral tribunal]

Article 1493

The arbitration agreement may, directly or by reference to arbitration rules, appoint the arbitrator or arbitrators or provide for the terms and conditions of their appointment.

French Code of Civil Procedure (Book IV), art. 1493

Where an issue affecting the constitution of the arbitral tribunal arises in arbitrations having their seat in France, or in arbitrations governed by French procedural law pursuant to the parties' agreement, and in the absence of an agreement to the contrary, the most diligent party may apply to the President of the First Instance Court (Tribunal de Grande Instance) of Paris pursuant to the terms and conditions of article 1457.

1. General. Pursuant to art. 1493, the parties may agree on the procedure for determining the constitution of the tribunal. If parties have agreed on a specific procedure for the constitution of the tribunal and the agreed on procedure is not followed, the ensuing award may not be enforceable in France (see art. 1502, notes 4 and 14). Art. 1493 further provides that unless the parties agree otherwise, the President of the Paris First Instance Court (Tribunal de grande instance) has exclusive jurisdiction over issues affecting the constitution of arbitral tribunals in international arbitrations where either the seat of the arbitration is in France or where French arbitration law has been chosen by the parties to apply to the arbitration. Of note, there is no requirement under French international arbitration law that the tribunal comprise an odd number of arbitrators. However, as deadlock may easily arise in even-numbered tribunals, such tribunals are rare and are not recommended.

2. Jurisdiction of the President of the Paris First Instance Court. According to art. 1493, the President of the Paris First Instance Court only has jurisdiction to rule upon issues affecting the constitution of the tribunal where an international arbitration has its seat in France and the parties have not agreed on another procedure. However, where the seat of arbitration is outside France, the President may also have jurisdiction, as long as the arbitration is connected with France and the parties would otherwise suffer a 'denial of justice' if the French courts did not act (Cour de cassation, 1 February 2005, *NIOC*). The President of the Paris First Instance Court may delegate his powers to another judge within the same court. The President's jurisdiction is neither mandatory nor exclusive, since parties may agree to designate any entity or person, such as an arbitral institution or another judge, to decide upon all matters that would otherwise fall to the President under this article. In such a case, the parties' choice will prevail and only the failure of an entity or person agreed upon by the parties to act, will give rise to the exclusive jurisdiction of the President of the Paris First Instance Court under art. 1493 (Cour d'appel Paris, 5 June 2003, *Rose*).

3. Effect of the reference to arbitration rules in the parties' arbitration agreement. The reference in the parties' arbitration agreement to a set of rules that grants certain or all of the powers of the President of the Paris First Instance Court under this article to a person or to an arbitral institution deprives the President of these powers (TGI Paris, 18 January 1991, *Chérifienne des Pétroles*). Should the parties' agreement only grant certain tasks to that person or arbitral institution, such as, for instance, the appointment of arbitrators, then the President of the Paris First Instance Court will still have exclusive jurisdiction with regard to any other issues affecting the constitution of the arbitral tribunal, such as challenges or replacement of arbitrators (TGI, Paris 29 October 1996, *GECI*).

4. The 'most diligent party'. Art. 1493 provides that the 'most diligent party' may apply to the President of the Paris First Instance Court to resolve issues affecting the constitution of the arbitral tribunal. The 'most diligent party' is any party to the case that first applies to the President. In addition, the 'most diligent party' may also be an arbitrator on the arbitral tribunal, who applies to the President in the absence of any party taking the initiative to do so. In this regard, art. 1457 referred to in art. 1493 (see art. 1457), contemplates that requests to the President of the Paris First Instance Court may be made by the parties or the 'arbitral tribunal'. The French courts have interpreted this language to allow individual arbitrators to seek action from the President of the Paris First Instance Court (TGI Paris, 29 November 1989, *République de Guinée*). In practice, however, it is the parties, not the arbitrators, who usually apply to the President of the Paris First Instance Court to resolve issues affecting the constitution of the arbitral tribunal.

5. Issues affecting the constitution of the arbitral tribunal. Issues affecting the constitution of the arbitral tribunal most obviously include issues regarding the appointment of arbitrators. Issues that fall within the scope of this article include: an objection to the appointment of an arbitrator (Cour d'appel Paris, 1 March 2007, *AGRR*); a request for an order against an arbitrator to disclose how many times he was appointed by the same party (Cour de cassation, 20 June 2006, *Nigioni*); issues arising from or relating to the appointment of an arbitrator, such as challenges and replacements (TGI Paris, 28 October 1988, 14 and 29 June 1989, 15 July 1989, *Philipp Brothers*); and cases where the arbitration clause is either vague or internally inconsistent with respect to how the arbitral tribunal is to be constituted (Cour de cassation, 20 February 2007, *UOP*). Issues that do not relate to the constitution or the composition of the tribunal, such as, for instance, the extension of the time limit for the rendering of an award, are not subject to the President of the Paris First Instance Court's jurisdiction under art. 1493 (Cour de cassation, 7 March 2000, *Adidas-Salomon*).

6. The arbitrators' duty to disclose. In order to establish and maintain trust among the parties and the arbitrators, arbitrators have a duty to disclose (Cour d'appel Paris, 1 February 2005, *Mytileneos Holdings*) facts and circumstances that may affect their judgment and create, in the mind of the parties, a reasonable doubt as to their independence or impartiality (Cour d'appel Paris, 2 April 2003, *Fremarc*, and Cour de cassation, 16 March 1999, *Creighton*). The arbitrators' disclosure duty applies from the time of their appointment until the end of the arbitration (Cour d'appel Paris, 12 February 2009, *J&P Avax*). A breach of an arbitrator's duty to disclose at any time during the arbitration proceedings may justify a challenge to that arbitrator, or prevent enforcement of the award (see art. 1502, notes 4 and 14, and art. 1504), and also may give rise to the personal liability of that arbitrator for damages (Cour d'appel Paris, 9 April 1992, *L'Oréal*).

7. Objections and challenges to arbitrators. Should an arbitrator disclose upon his appointment, any fact or circumstance that may affect his judgment and create, in the mind of the parties, a reasonable doubt as to his independence or impartiality, any party may object to the appointment of that arbitrator before the President of the First Instance Court or any other person or organisation designated under the parties' agreement to resolve issues relating to the constitution of the tribunal. Similarly, if the arbitrator discloses, in the course of the proceedings, a fact or circumstance that may affect that arbitrator's independence or impartiality, any party may challenge that arbitrator. By way of example, the repetitive and frequent appointment of the same arbitrator by the same party in similar disputes may create a reasonable doubt as to the independence of that arbitrator (Trib. Com Paris, 6 July 2004, *Chomat*). An arbitrator who sits in two parallel arbitrations involving similar issues also runs a risk of challenge. Any decision the arbitrator renders in one of the cases may be seen as a prejudgment of any similar issues still awaiting decision in the other case. Such prejudgment may be considered to affect that arbitrator's independence and impartiality and justify the challenge of that arbitrator (Cour d'appel Paris, 2 April 1998, *Asmidal*). If a party discovers, after an arbitrator is appointed, that the arbitrator breached his duty to disclose, that party may challenge the arbitrator before the President of the First Instance Court or any other person or organisation designated under the parties' agreement to resolve issues relating to the constitution of the tribunal. In evaluating a challenge based on an arbitrator's alleged breach of the duty of disclosure, the President will take into account whether the information at issue was publically known and whether it would have affected the arbitrator's judgment (Cour d'appel Paris, 28 June 1991, *KFTCIC*). In both cases of challenge or of objection to the appointment of an arbitrator, it will be for the President of the First Instance Court or any other person or organisation designated under the parties' agreement to decide whether the disclosing arbitrator may stay on the tribunal. If a decision is made that the arbitrator may stay on the arbitral tribunal, the enforceability of the ensuing award may still be in jeopardy before the French courts pursuant to art. 1502(2) or (5), unless that decision has become final during the time the Court of Appeal is deciding on the setting aside of the award on the ground provided under art. 1502(2) or (5) (see art. 1502, notes 14 and 21).

8. Procedure for making an application pursuant to art. 1493. As mentioned in the last sentence of art. 1493, applications made on the basis of that provision are to be filed before the President of the First Instance Court of Paris, pursuant to the terms and conditions of art. 1457. In this respect, see arts. 1457 and 1444, para. 3, notes 1-4.

[Procedure for making an application pursuant to art. 1493]

Article 1457

[…], the President of the court shall decide upon the request of a party or of the arbitral tribunal, as in expedited proceedings (référé) by way of an order against which no recourse is available.

However, appeal is available against this order, if the President has declined to make an appointment for any grounds foreseen under article 1444 (para. 3). The appeal is filed, heard, and decided in the same manner as an appeal against a jurisdictional decision.

[…]

Article 1444, para. 3

Where the arbitration clause is either manifestly void or insufficient to allow for the constitution of the arbitration tribunal, the President shall so state and declare that there can be no such appointment.

1. Decision 'as in expedited proceedings'. Pursuant to art. 1457, the President of the Paris First Instance Court shall decide upon a request regarding issues affecting the constitution of the tribunal 'as in expedited proceedings'. According to that provision, requests to the President for action under 1493 should be made pursuant to procedures applicable to expedited proceedings in France (référé) for parties seeking provisional measures. Having said that, parties seeking action under art. 1493 do not have to satisfy any of the criteria that a French judge would normally require to retain jurisdiction over a request for provisional measures through expedited proceedings, such as, for example, urgency or likelihood of success on the merits (Cour de cassation, 14 November 2007, *Vinexpo*). Rather, the only requirement for the President of the Paris First Instance Court to have jurisdiction under art. 1493 is that the request made before him relates to an issue affecting the constitution of the tribunal as described in art. 1493, note 5. In addition, unlike decisions on provisional measures taken through expedited proceedings, the decision of the President of the Paris First Instance Court under art. 1493 will be issued in the form of a judgment with full res judicata effect.

2. Arbitration clause 'manifestly void'. Pursuant to art. 1444, para. 3, the President of the Paris First Instance Court shall decline to appoint an arbitrator where the arbitration clause is either manifestly void or insufficient to allow for the constitution of the arbitral tribunal (Cour de cassation, 14 November 2007, *Vinexpo*). For a discussion of what is meant by 'manifestly void', see arts. 1458 and 1466, notes 3-5.

3. Arbitration clause 'insufficient'. Pursuant to art. 1444, para. 3, the President shall also reject requests based on art. 1493 where the arbitration clause is insufficient to allow for the constitution of the arbitration tribunal.

In practice, this will seldom arise in international arbitration. While the validity of an arbitration agreement may be subject to specific requirements in domestic arbitrations, such requirements do not apply in international arbitration (see art. 1458, notes 3 and 5). Therefore, where a dispute involves international trade, a clause which provides for 'arbitration Paris' and nothing more will be sufficient to allow for the constitution of an arbitral tribunal with its seat in Paris (Cour d'appel Paris, 23 October 2008, *Limak*).

4. Recourse against the decision of the President of the Paris First Instance Court. In general, the President's decisions on issues affecting the constitution of the tribunal cannot be appealed. However, art. 1444, para. 3 referred to in art. 1457, allows a party to appeal a decision not to appoint arbitrators to the tribunal. Having said this, action against other decisions on issues affecting the constitution of the arbitral tribunal may nevertheless be available where the President's decision is grossly affected by a violation of a fundamental principle of procedure or a violation of public policy, including a violation of due process (Cour d'appel Paris, 19 December 1995, *GECI II*), or if the President has exceeded his powers. For example, an excess of powers would occur if the President were to appoint a replacement arbitrator without first offering the party who had appointed the departing arbitrator an opportunity to propose another arbitrator (Cour d'appel Paris, 1 March 2007, *AGRR*, 10 October 2002, *Gastrolouvre* and Cour de cassation, 16 March 2000, *Sechet*).

[Kompetenz-Kompetenz]

Article 1458

Where a dispute submitted to an arbitral tribunal pursuant to an arbitration agreement is filed before a French court, the latter shall decline jurisdiction.

Where the dispute has not yet been submitted to an arbitral tribunal, the court shall also decline jurisdiction unless the arbitration agreement is manifestly void.

In both cases, the court may not decline jurisdiction on its own motion.

Article 1466

If a party challenges the principle or scope of the arbitrator's jurisdiction before the arbitrator, the arbitrator shall decide upon the validity or scope of his or her jurisdiction.

1. General. Arts. 1458 and 1466 were originally drafted for French domestic arbitration. However, the French courts have expressly stated that these provisions also apply to international arbitration (Cour de cassation, 28 June 1989, *Eurodiff* and 7 June 1989, *Anhydro*). Together, arts. 1458 and 1466 set forth the principle of Kompetenz-Kompetenz under French law. Art. 1458 is aimed at the French courts, and specifically provides that, when asked by a party to do so, French courts must decline jurisdiction over disputes already submitted to an arbitral tribunal. Further, even where a dispute has not yet been submitted to an arbitral tribunal, the French court must still decline jurisdiction if asked by a party to do so, unless the arbitration agreement is manifestly void or manifestly inapplicable. This is true wherever the seat of the existing or as-yet unfiled arbitration may be. The French court may not decline jurisdiction on its own motion; rather, it is up to the parties to raise any objection they may have with regard to the French court's jurisdiction. Where a party participates in a French court action and pleads on the merits of the dispute without first raising an objection to that court's jurisdiction, that party will be considered to have renounced the arbitration agreement and waived its right to arbitrate the dispute (Cour de cassation, 23 January 2007, *Alix*). Art. 1466 is aimed at the arbitral tribunal. Pursuant to this provision, arbitrators have the power to decide on their own jurisdiction when jurisdictional objections are raised in the arbitration. Having said this, an arbitral tribunal that decides on its own jurisdiction does not have the final say on the matter. This is because the French Court of Appeal may consider the issue de novo in the context of enforcement proceedings with respect to the tribunal's award (see art. 1502, notes 6, 8 and 18, and art. 1504, notes 1-2).

2. Dispute already submitted to an arbitral tribunal. Pursuant to art. 1458, a French court faced with an objection to jurisdiction based on the existence of an arbitration agreement must decline jurisdiction over the dispute already submitted to an arbitral tribunal. A dispute is considered submitted to an arbitral tribunal under French arbitration law once the tribunal is fully constituted, that is to say once all members of the tribunal have accepted to act as arbitrators over that dispute (Cour de cassation, 7 March 2002, *Royal Mougins*, 26 April 2006, *Chays Frères* and 6 February 2007, *Painchaud*). There is no requirement that the arbitrators must have signed terms of reference for the tribunal to be considered constituted under French law.

3. Dispute not yet submitted to an arbitral tribunal: 'manifestly void'.
Pursuant to art. 1458, a French court will also decline jurisdiction where the dispute has not yet been submitted to the arbitral tribunal, unless the arbitration agreement is 'manifestly void'. When applying art. 1458 and determining whether or not the alleged agreement to arbitrate is 'manifestly void', the French court is barred from carrying out a substantive, in-depth examination of the arbitration agreement (Cour de cassation, 7 June 2006, *Jules Vernes*). A clause that is 'manifestly void' is, as those words suggest, void on its face. In other words, under art. 1458, the French court will review the arbitration clause on a prima facie basis (Cour d'appel Paris, 15 June 2006, *Fincantieri*). Where there are any doubts, the French court should decline jurisdiction and the arbitral tribunal should, once constituted, rule on its own jurisdiction pursuant to art. 1466 (see note 7). In practice, cases where an arbitration clause

could be found to be manifestly void are those where the issue in dispute is not arbitrable due to mandatory rules of French law or French international public policy. This may be the case, for instance, in a labour dispute where the employee first files his claim before a French labour court with jurisdiction (Cour de cassation, 9 October 2001, *Lopez-Alberdi*).

4. Dispute not yet submitted to an arbitral tribunal: 'manifestly inapplicable'. As discussed in note 1, art. 1458 provides that a French court must also decline jurisdiction where the dispute has not yet been submitted to an arbitral tribunal, unless the arbitration agreement at issue is 'manifestly void'. French case law has extended this principle to allow French courts to retain jurisdiction over cases where the arbitration clause at issue is 'manifestly inapplicable' to the dispute at hand (Cour de cassation, 16 October 2001, *Quatro Children's Book*). In practice, however, manifest inapplicability rarely provides a basis for the French courts to retain jurisdiction (Cour de cassation, 1 July 2009, *Encore*). This is principally because of the prima facie nature of the French court's inquiry under art. 1458 (see notes 3 and 5).

5. Dispute not yet submitted to an arbitral tribunal: burden on the party asking the French court to retain jurisdiction. The burden to show that an arbitration clause is manifestly void or manifestly inapplicable is on the party asking the French court to retain jurisdiction. Cases finding a clause manifestly void or manifestly inapplicable in international arbitration are rare, for several reasons. First, the French courts examine arbitration agreements on a prima facie basis when deciding whether they are 'manifestly void' under art. 1458, and it is rare that an arbitration clause is found by the French courts to be void on its face (see note 3). The reason it is particularly rare for an arbitration agreement to be void on its face is because, under French international arbitration law, it is rare for an arbitration agreement to be void at all. This is because French international arbitration law takes a liberal approach to finding arbitration agreements enforceable. To that end, French law considers arbitration agreements to be separable from the main contract in which they are contained (Cour de cassation, 7 May 1963, *Gosset*). That is to say, the enforceability of an arbitration agreement is evaluated independently of the enforceability of the main contract, and the unenforceability of the main contract does not necessarily impair the enforceability of the arbitration agreement (Cour de cassation, 6 December 1988, *Navimpex*). Moreover, French international arbitration law has no formal requirements for an agreement to arbitrate to be valid. Indeed, arbitration agreements do not have to be signed or even in writing at all. Rather, under French international arbitration law, an agreement to arbitrate may exist whenever there is a 'common intent of the parties' to arbitrate their disputes (Cour de cassation, 20 December 2000, *FMT Productions*; see also art. 1502(1), note 12). Indeed, the existence, validity and scope of an arbitration agreement is only determined based on the 'common intent of the parties' (subject to mandatory rules of French law and international public policy) without reference to any national law (Cour de cassation 20 December 1993, *Dalico*, and 5 January 1999, *Zanzi*) (see art. 1502(1), notes 11 and 12). Similarly, it is also rare for an arbitration agreement to be found manifestly inapplicable pursuant to art. 1458, because French arbitration law requires that any doubts regarding the scope of that agreement be first resolved by the arbitral tribunal (Cour de cassation, 7 June 2006, *Jules Vernes*).

6. Provisional measures. Even where a French court should decline jurisdiction over the dispute in favour of arbitration on the basis of art. 1458, a French court may nevertheless order provisional measures until the arbitral tribunal is constituted. These measures might include an order for the preservation or production of evidence, or an order requiring expertise (Cour de cassation, 25 April 2006, *Chays Frères*). A request for provisional payment in expedited proceedings (référé) before the French courts may also be available pending the constitution of a tribunal, as long as evidence is submitted that there is an urgent need justifying the order for payment (Cour d'appel Paris, 8 November 2006, *Thales International*). Of note, the participation of a party in expedited proceedings (référé) regarding provisional measures does not amount to a waiver of the arbitration agreement on the part of that party (Cour d'appel Paris, 25 October 2006, *Nuovo Pignone*). Moreover, attachment of assets, which may not be ordered by arbitral tribunals, may be requested from the French courts even after a dispute has been submitted to an arbitral tribunal.

7. Priority of the arbitral tribunal to decide on its own jurisdiction. Arts. 1458 and 1466 embody the Kompetenz-Kompetenz principle and empower arbitral tribunals to rule on their jurisdiction (see note 1). This does not mean, however, that the arbitral tribunal's decision on its jurisdiction is the last word on the matter. The French Court of Appeal has the power to later deny enforcement of an award if it concludes that, in fact, the arbitral tribunal erred on the issue of jurisdiction. Accordingly, the Kompetenz-Kompetenz principle under French law gives the arbitral tribunal a priority to decide on its own jurisdiction. However, if a party resists enforcement of the award in France on the grounds that the tribunal erred on the issue of jurisdiction, that question will be examined de novo by the Court of Appeal when deciding whether or not the award should be enforced in France (Cour de cassation 11 July 2006, *Generali France*) (see art. 1502, note 4, art. 1502(1), notes 8-13 and art. 1504).

[Procedural rules applicable during the arbitration proceedings]

Article 1494

The arbitration agreement may, directly or by reference to arbitration rules, determine the procedure to be followed in the course of the arbitration proceedings; this agreement may also determine a procedural law to be applied to the proceedings.

French Code of Civil Procedure (Book IV), art. 1496

Where the agreement is silent, the arbitrator shall determine the procedure to the extent necessary, either directly or by reference to a law or to arbitration rules.

1. General. Art. 1494 addresses the issue of the procedure to be followed in the arbitration proceedings. This includes the procedure to be followed from and including the constitution of the arbitral tribunal until the rendering of its final award, including correction and interpretation of that award. This provision does not concern the issue of the law applicable to the merits of the parties' dispute (see art. 1496, note 1). Pursuant to art. 1494, parties are free to agree on the procedure to be followed during the arbitration, whether or not by reference to a pre-existing set of rules, such as the UNCITRAL Arbitration Rules or the International Chamber of Commerce Rules of Arbitration. Should the parties designate an arbitral institution in their arbitration agreement, such designation will be considered as an agreement that that institution's rules govern the conduct of the arbitration (Cour d'appel Paris, 15 May 1985, *Raffineries de Pétrole D'homs et de Banias*). Where the parties agree upon rules to govern the arbitral proceedings, the arbitral tribunal must conduct the proceedings in accordance with those rules. In all cases, the parties' agreement will bind the tribunal, so long as that agreement is express and sufficiently specific (Cour de cassation, 8 March 1988, *Sofidif*). If the arbitrators breach the parties' procedural agreement, the award may be denied enforcement in France for failure of the tribunal to comply with its mission (see art. 1502(3), note 15 and art. 1504). Failing an express and specific agreement of the parties on any part of the procedure, the tribunal may freely establish procedural rules without reference to any national procedural law or pre-existing set of arbitration rules. That discretion also applies to any procedural issue that may arise in the course of the arbitration procedure, such as the production and admissibility of evidence, procedural calendars, the sequence or form of written or oral pleadings, hearing of witnesses and experts (as well as expert appointments), and the taking and notification of procedural decisions. In any event, all procedural decisions made by the tribunal must be made in conformity with French procedural international public policy, such as the principles of due process (see art. 1502(3), (4) and (5), notes 17 and 19-21 and art. 1504).

[Law applicable to the merits]

Article 1496

The arbitrator shall decide upon the dispute in accordance with the rules of law chosen by the parties; in the absence of such a choice, in accordance with rules of law he or she considers appropriate.

In all cases, he or she shall take trade usages into account.

French Code of Civil Procedure (Book IV), art. 1496

1. General. Art. 1496 concerns the determination of the law applicable to the merits of a dispute submitted to arbitration. This provision does not address the issue of the law applicable to the arbitration agreement itself. Nor does this provision address that of the law applicable to the arbitration procedure (see art. 1494, note 1), unless this has been expressly stated by the parties (Cour de cassation, 10 May 1988, *Wasteels*).

2. Party autonomy in international arbitration. Art. 1496 confirms that parties are free to choose the rules of law applicable to the merits of their dispute. That means they are free to agree upon the rules of law that the tribunal is to apply to settle their dispute, whether or not those rules are connected to the parties' relationship. The parties' choice of law may be express or implicit. Where the parties have agreed on rules of law to govern the merits of their dispute, the arbitral tribunal must apply those rules of law in its awards (see art. 1502(3), note 15 and art. 1504). In the absence of an agreement by the parties on the rules of law applicable to the merits of their dispute, the tribunal has complete discretion to determine which rules of law shall apply. The tribunal does not need to refer to any conflict of laws rules in order to determine the applicable rules of law. Thus, to satisfy the requirements of art. 1496, in practice, the arbitral tribunal needs merely to state in the award that the rules of law selected and applied by the tribunal are appropriate in the circumstances. Should the arbitral tribunal consider that it may be appropriate to apply rules of law that have not been suggested by any party, the tribunal must first request the parties' comments on such rules of law before taking a decision, in order to comply with the requirements of due process (see art. 1502(4), note 19 and art. 1504).

3. Parties and tribunals may select 'rules of law' rather than national laws. The wording 'rules of law' used in art. 1496 includes, but is not limited to, national law. Indeed, in exercising their autonomy, the parties and arbitrators are not bound to choose a national law to govern the merits of the parties' dispute. 'Rules of law' include, among other things, 'a-national' or transnational rules of law, as well as general principles of law (UNIDROIT principles, for instance). Thus, an award which relies upon 'rules of international commerce determined by practice recognised in national court case law' was held to have been made in accordance with 'rules of law' (Cour de cassation, 22 October 1991, *Compania Valencia de Cementos Portland*).

4. Tribunals must take into account trade usages. According to art. 1496, the tribunal must in all cases take trade usages into account. Despite the use of the words 'shall' and 'in all cases' in art. 1496, there is no French case law annulling an award on the basis that a tribunal failed to take trade usages into account. Trade usages are generally defined as the 'usual practices observed in the parties' area of business' and include the parties' past practices in dealing with each other.

Bensaude

[Amiable composition]
Article 1497
The arbitrator shall decide as amiable compositeur if so empowered by the parties' agreement.

1. General. An arbitral tribunal may only decide as amiable compositeur when empowered to do so by the parties' agreement. In such cases, the arbitral tribunal cannot limit its reasoning only to the strict application of the law or that of the parties' contract terms, but must also take fairness into account. Failing an agreement from the parties to vest the arbitral tribunal with the power of amiable compositeur (which is also sometimes referred to as the power to decide ex aequo et bono or in an 'equitable manner' (équité)), the tribunal would fail to comply with its mission if it expressly relied upon these concepts in reaching the decisions in its award (see art. 1502(3), note 15 and art. 1504). In all cases, an arbitral tribunal vested with powers of amiable compositeur must abide by due process and other fundamental rules of procedural international public policy (Cour d'appel Paris, 28 November 1996, *Minhal*) (see art. 1502(5), note 21).

2. Definition of amiable composition. An arbitrator is empowered to rule as amiable compositeur when vested with the powers to decide the parties' dispute either in amiable composition, ex aequo et bono or in an equitable manner. French courts generally understand these concepts to have similar meanings in the context of international arbitration. Under French arbitration law, such powers amount to a waiver of the effects and benefits of the rule of law, whereby arbitrators are granted the power to moderate the consequences of the contractual provisions, where required, by fairness or the common interest of the parties, and the parties lose their right to expect a strict application of the rule of law (Cour d'appel Paris, 28 November 1996, *Minhal*). Although the tribunal may moderate the effects of the parties' contractual agreement, such power is not without limit. The arbitral tribunal cannot go so far as to create a new contract that was not envisaged by the parties (Cour d'appel Paris, 4 November 1997, *Taurus Films*).

3. Powers and duties of a tribunal deciding as amiable compositeur. A tribunal sitting in France that is entrusted with the powers of amiable compositeur must indicate in the award, either expressly or implicitly, that the solution reached in the award complies with the tribunal's own sense of fairness. The mere absence of a reference to the powers of amiable compositeur in an award rendered by an amiable compositeur is not, in and of itself, a ground for annulment of the award (Cour de cassation, 28 November 2007, *C* et al.). On the other hand, the strict application of the contractual terms or legal provisions, with no reference to the powers of amiable compositeur and no consideration of fairness, could jeopardise the enforcement of the award in France (Cour d'appel Paris, 3 July 2007, *Bachelier*). A tribunal vested with such powers may refer to rules of law and adopt such rules if the tribunal considers these

French Code of Civil Procedure (Book IV), art. 1498

rules to provide a fair solution. The tribunal's reasoning should not be limited only to the strict application of rules of law, but should also indicate that the decision reached by the tribunal complies with that tribunal's own sense of fairness (Cour d'appel Paris, 15 March 1984, *Soubaigne*).

4. Amiable composition and choice of law. In rare cases, parties agree that certain rules of law shall apply to the merits of their dispute, and vest the tribunal with the powers of amiable compositeur. In such cases, the tribunal should first apply the rules of law chosen by the parties to the dispute and thereafter compare the solution reached at law with fairness, and decide in accordance with its own sense fairness (Cour de cassation, 15 February 2001, *Hanin*, and Cour d'appel Paris, 4 December 2003, *Gutzwiller*, see also Cour d'appel Paris, 15 January 2004, *Vanoverbeke*).

[Recognition and enforcement in France of international awards]
Article 1498

Arbitral awards shall be recognised in France if their existence is proven by the party relying upon the award and if said recognition is not manifestly contrary to international public policy.

Under the same conditions, such awards shall be declared enforceable in France by the enforcement judge.

1. General. Art. 1498 sets forth the conditions for recognition and enforcement in France of both international arbitration awards rendered in France and foreign awards (see notes 2-4). Recognition and enforcement is only subject to the verification that the award exists and that, prima facie, recognition or enforcement of the award is not contrary to French international public policy. In practice, a party that wishes to have an international award executed in France initiates an ex parte procedure by submitting the text of the award, together with that of the arbitration clause pursuant to which the award was rendered, before the President of the Court of First Instance with jurisdiction (see art. 1477, notes 1-5). After verifying that on its face enforcement of the award does not appear to violate French international public policy, the judge will stamp the award with an 'enforcement order' which mandates the French authorities to assist with execution of the award in France (see note 3 and 6).

2. International awards rendered in France and foreign awards. In considering issues of enforceability of international awards in France, it is important to always bear in mind that there are two types of international awards under French law: foreign awards (that is, awards rendered in arbitrations where the seat of arbitration is outside France), and international awards rendered in France (that is, awards rendered in international arbitrations where the seat of arbitration is in France) (see Introductory remarks, note 4 and art. 1492, note 2). Although both foreign awards and international awards rendered in France are 'international awards' under French international

Bensaude

arbitration law, French law draws certain distinctions between the two with respect to enforcement. The similarities and differences in the enforcement regimes applicable to foreign awards, on the one hand, and international awards rendered in France, on the other hand, are detailed hereafter.

3. Recognition, enforcement and execution: three different concepts. Requests for recognition of an international award may be made before any French court where the award is submitted as evidence or before which a party merely intends to benefit from the res judicata effects of that award (see art. 1476). Recognition takes place when a French court takes note of the award's existence and takes note that the award does not blatantly violate French international public policy (see note 6 and 7). Enforcement is the process pursuant to which a party obtains an enforcement order stamped on the award from the President of the First Instance Court with jurisdiction (see notes 1-7 and art. 1477). Once an enforcement order is stamped in France on an international award, the award bearing that order becomes part of the French legal order and is considered a French court decision for the purpose of execution. Execution of an award is the process pursuant to which a party actually proceeds with the seizure of assets in France or otherwise goes about getting what it was awarded against a party to the award (see art. 1477, notes 1-5 and art. 1506, note 1).

4. Definition of an award under French arbitration law. Under French international arbitration law, an award is any decision rendered by an arbitral tribunal which finally settles all or part of the parties' dispute submitted to it, and which addresses either jurisdiction, the merits of the dispute, or a procedural issue that terminates the procedure (Cour d'appel Paris, 25 March 1994, *Sardisud*). Only decisions of arbitral tribunals that satisfy this definition may be recognised, stamped with an enforcement order, and set aside or executed in France. It is not for the arbitral tribunal or for the parties to say whether a decision is or is not an award. The agreement of the parties to name a decision an award is not binding on the French courts. It is always for the French judge to decide for himself whether the document before him is or is not an award (Cour d'appel Paris, 1 July 1999, *Brasoil*). The French law definition of an award encompasses partial, interim and final awards. Arbitral tribunals' decisions on provisional measures that finally settle all or part of the parties' dispute may also constitute awards under French law (Cour d'appel Paris, 7 October 2004, *Otor*). Arbitral tribunals' decisions that are not considered awards under French law include procedural decisions of the arbitral tribunal during the course of the proceedings which do not terminate the procedure (Cour d'appel Paris, 29 November 2007, *Crédirente*), and decisions that refuse to order a provisional payment before the parties have fully argued the matter (Cour d'appel Paris, 11 April 2002, *ABCI*). Decisions of arbitral institutions (Cour d'appel Paris, 5 January 1985, *Opinter*) and decisions rendered in the course of an ICC pre-arbitral referee procedure (Cour d'appel Paris, 29 April 2003, *SNPC*) are not awards.

French Code of Civil Procedure (Book IV), art. 1498

Moreover, dissenting opinions are generally not considered to form part of the award to which they relate.

5. A request for recognition and enforcement of an award is filed ex parte. In principle, a request for recognition and enforcement of an international award is to be filed ex parte. In order to be valid, the request for enforcement of an award must be filed before the President of the First Instance Court with jurisdiction by way of an ex parte submission (Cour de cassation, 9 December 2003, *Noga*). The procedure for recognition and enforcement is also followed ex parte. However, in practice, if the President of the First Instance Court in charge of recognition or enforcement of an award considers that there may be international public policy reasons not to recognise or enforce the award at stake, that President may request other parties named in the award to present observations on this issue.

6. French international public policy. Under art. 1498, an international award shall not be recognised or enforced in France if recognition or enforcement would be contrary to international public policy. French courts apply their own definition of international public policy. French international public policy is defined as the set of rules and values that the French legal order cannot accept to be disregarded, even in situations having an international character (Cour d'appel Paris, 27 October 1994, *LTDC*). That set of rules and values is not clearly determined and may vary with time. Those rules may generally be found in fundamental principles of procedure as well as in certain stock exchange regulations, currency control regulations, bankruptcy rules, criminal law, and European consumer protection regulation and competition law provisions. For concrete examples of French international public policy, including procedural public policy (see art. 1502(5), notes 21-22).

7. French international public policy versus French domestic public policy. French courts distinguish between French international public policy and French domestic public policy. French domestic public policy is considerably broader than French international public policy. As a consequence, breach of French domestic public policy does not necessarily entail breach of French international public policy (Cour d'appel Paris, 12 March 1985, *Intrafor*). Moreover, French international public policy is applied less rigorously than French domestic public policy (Cour de cassation, 15 March 1988, *Grands Moulins de Strasbourg*, and 19 November 1991, *Grands Moulins de Strasbourg II*).

8. 'Manifestly contrary' and the extent of the judge's review under art. 1498. In deciding whether or not to recognise or order enforcement of an international award in France in accordance with art. 1498, the President of the First instance Court with jurisdiction may only verify that the award exists and that recognition and enforcement of the award is not manifestly contrary to French international public policy (Cour de cassation, 15 March 1988, *Grands Moulins de Strasbourg*). As the word 'manifestly' suggests, in determining whether recognition or enforcement of an international award would be manifestly contrary to French public policy, the President of the First Instance Court carries out a prima facie review. Moreover, and as mentioned in note 5, that review is usually carried out in ex parte proceedings where the party against whom enforcement is sought is not present. As a result, decisions that refuse to recognise or enforce an international award under art. 1498 on the basis that the award manifestly violates French international public policy are rare. Furthermore, under art. 1498, the President of the First Instance Court with jurisdiction may only grant or refuse recognition or enforcement, and may not add to the award or otherwise alter its content in any way (Cour de cassation, 14 December 1983, *Convert*). Having said this, the judge may recognise or grant an order enforcing only part of an award if, for instance, part of the award is separable from other parts that the judge finds would be manifestly contrary to French international public policy to recognise or enforce in France. Of note, awards that bear an enforcement order are considered French court's decisions for the purpose of execution. As a consequence, where an arbitral tribunal did not decide in its award on the issue of post-award interest on damages and that this issue may no longer be submitted to that same tribunal, the award of damages will nevertheless bear interest for the purpose of execution of the award in France, at the French legal rate, from the date of the award (Cour de cassation, 30 June 2004, *BAII*). The Court of Appeal deciding on the setting aside of an international award rendered in France or against the enforcement order of a foreign award may not order payment of such interest (Cour d'appel Paris, 15 May 2003, *Central Timber Business*). It is for the First Instance Court, sitting with a single judge to do so (Cour d'appel Paris, 18 January 2001, *BAII*).

9. Review under art. 1498 should not be confused with review under art. 1502. Under art. 1498, the President of the First Instance Court with jurisdiction will not examine whether the international award at issue may be unenforceable on any of the grounds set forth art. 1502(1) to (4) (lack of jurisdiction of the tribunal, irregular composition of the tribunal, failure of the tribunal to fulfil its mission, denial of due process) (see art. 1502, notes 8-21). Moreover, although art. 1498 and art. 1502(5) both provide that an award may be denied enforcement on grounds of breach of French international public policy, these provisions apply differently. Specifically, a President of a First Instance Court with jurisdiction examining whether enforcement of an international award would be manifestly contrary to French international public policy under art. 1498, may look no further than the face of the award at issue. The Court of Appeal examining whether enforcement of an international award may be contrary to French international public policy under 1502(5), may in fact look further than that (see art. 1502(5), notes 20-22). Moreover, whereas the President of the First Instance Court acting under art. 1498 makes his decision based on ex parte proceedings where the party against whom enforcement is sought is not present, the Court of Appeal acting under art. 1502(5) makes its decision after hearing both sides.

[Evidence of the existence of an award; translation]
Article 1499

The existence of an arbitral award is established by submission of an original thereof together with the arbitration agreement, or of copies of such documents satisfying the conditions required to ascertain their authenticity.

If such documents are not in the French language, the party shall produce a certified translation by a translator registered on the list of experts.

1. Evidence of the existence of an international award. In order to obtain recognition and enforcement of an international award in France – be it an international award rendered in France or a foreign award – the requesting party must file an original or a certified copy of the award, together with a copy of the arbitration clause pursuant to which the award was rendered, with the President of the First Instance Court with jurisdiction. There is no express requirement under French international arbitration law that an award be made or rendered in writing. However, pursuant to art. 1498, the party requesting recognition and enforcement of an award bears the burden of proving the existence of the award, and art. 1499 provides that proving the existence of an award is established by the production of an original or certified copy of the award. In practice, the Paris Court generally requires that both an original and a certified copy of the award be filed with the Court. What constitutes a certified copy acceptable under art. 1499 will vary depending on the seat of arbitration where the award was rendered. France has bilateral treaties with different countries around the world and there is no uniform format for the conditions a document must satisfy in order for French courts to accept their authenticity.

2. Official translation requirement. The translation requirement under art. 1499 varies somewhat depending on whether the international award at issue is one rendered in France or a foreign award. An international award rendered in France must be translated by a translator registered on the list of experts at the court where recognition or enforcement is sought. Pursuant to art. IV(2) of the New York Convention, a foreign award should be translated either by a sworn translator or by a diplomatic or consular agent. In practice, the French courts admit that the translation of foreign awards be made by a sworn translator registered at the seat of arbitration (Cour d'appel Paris, 18 March 2004, *Synergie*).

[Res judicata effects of awards; formalities for execution of awards; form of the enforcement order; provisional execution of awards]
Article 1500

The provisions of articles 1476 to 1479 are applicable.

French Code of Civil Procedure (Book IV), art. 1476

1. General. Arts. 1476 to 1479 were originally drafted for domestic arbitration and subsequently made applicable to international arbitration by art. 1500.

[Res judicata effects of awards]

Article 1476

From the time it is rendered, the arbitral award is res judicata in respect of the dispute it resolves.

1. General. Pursuant to art. 1476, referred to in art. 1500, an international award – be it a foreign award or an international award rendered in France – has res judicata effects as soon as it is rendered, without further formalities. Accordingly, once rendered, an international award may be raised in a French litigation against another party to the award to prevent re-litigation of the same matters in France. Specifically, for the award to have res judicata effects in France, there is no need to obtain an enforcement order in France. The fact that an award may be, or is, actually challenged at the seat of arbitration does not deprive the award of res judicata effects in France. Of note, French law has yet to define when an international award is 'rendered'.

[Formalities for execution of awards in France]

Article 1477

The arbitral award may only be executed pursuant to an enforcement order (exequatur) issued by the First Instance Court (Tribunal de Grande Instance) with jurisdiction at the place where the award was rendered.

1. General. Art. 1477 addresses the formalities necessary in order to execute an international award in France, be it a foreign award or an international award rendered in France (see art. 1498, notes 2 and 3). Specifically, to be enforceable in France, an international award must be stamped with an enforcement order (exequatur) by the President of the First Instance Court (Tribunal de Grande Instance) with jurisdiction (see art. 1498, notes 1-5). The President may delegate this power to another judge within his court.

2. Jurisdiction for enforcement of international awards rendered in France. In the case of international awards rendered in France (see art. 1498, notes 1-3), the President with jurisdiction is that of the First Instance Court with territorial jurisdiction over the place in France where the award was rendered. Of note, pursuant to art. 1504 (see art. 1504, notes 1-2), the filing of an action to set aside an international award rendered in France before the Court of Appeal terminates that President's jurisdiction. That is to say that, if a request to set aside an international award rendered in France is filed in France pending a French judge's decision on either recognition and enforcement or provisional execution, the award may not be recognised or enforced, or executed in France until the decision of the Court of Appeal on the setting aside application has been rendered, unless the award has been granted provisional execution (see art. 1506, note 1 and art. 1479, notes 1-2).

3. Jurisdiction for enforcement of foreign awards. In the case of foreign awards, the President with jurisdiction is that of the First Instance Court of Paris or that of the First Instance Court with territorial jurisdiction over the place where the assets that are the target of execution of the award are located (Cour d'appel Paris, *Société ivoirienne de Raffinage*).

4. Execution of international awards. An international award may only be executed in France once the award is stamped in France with an enforcement order and after one month has elapsed from the date when the award bearing the enforcement order has been served on the party against whom the award is to be executed (see arts. 1503, notes 1-3, art. 1504, notes 1-2, art. 1505, note 1 and art. 1506, note 1). Having said this, as soon as the award is rendered, it is a legal title with res judicata effects in France, pursuant to which, conservatory attachment may be obtained in France (Cour de cassation, *Motokov*, Cour d'appel Paris, 9 July 1992, *Norbert Beyrard*; contra: TGI Lyon, 25 January 1994, *Textipar*).

5. Sovereign States' immunity from execution. In France, sovereign States benefit from immunity against enforcement of judicial decisions, including awards. However, if a sovereign State signs an arbitration clause which contains an express undertaking to carry out the award, such as the undertaking contained in art. 28(6) of the ICC Arbitration Rules, French courts will consider that State to have waived its immunity from execution of the award in France (Cour de cassation, 6 July 2000, *Creighton*). In any event, assets belonging to a State may only be seized in France on the basis of an arbitral award, if these assets were used by that State for an economical and commercial purpose connected with the transaction at issue in the award (Cour de cassation, 14 March 1984, *Eurodif*).

[Form of the enforcement order; refusal must be reasoned]

Article 1478

The enforcement order (exequatur) shall be affixed to the original of the arbitral award.
The order refusing exequatur shall be reasoned.

1. Order granting enforcement. When granted, the enforcement order requested pursuant to art. 1498 is merely stamped by the President of the First Instance Court with jurisdiction on the original or on the certified copy of the award filed with the President's clerk (greffe). As discussed under art. 1502 below, an order to enforce a foreign award may be appealed to the Court of Appeal. An order to enforce an international award rendered in France may not be appealed. However, it is still open for a party to ask the Court of Appeal to set aside an international award rendered in France pursuant to art. 1504. Setting aside proceedings are discussed in art. 1504, notes 1-2.

2. Order refusing enforcement. Pursuant to art. 1478, in case the judge decides to refuse enforcement or recognition of an award, that decision must be reasoned. This is true whether the international award at issue is a foreign award or an international award rendered in France. If the President of the First Instance Court with jurisdiction refuses to grant an enforcement order on an award, he must render a decision and reason that decision. As discussed above, the President of the First Instance Court may only refuse to recognise or enforce an international award under art. 1498, either because the decision at issue is not an award or because enforcement of all or part of that award would be manifestly contrary to French international public policy (see art. 1498, notes 4-9). As discussed under art. 1501 below, the judge's decision refusing enforcement may be appealed to the Court of Appeal.

[Provisional execution of awards]

Article 1479

Rules on provisional execution of judgments shall apply to arbitral awards.

In case of appeal or setting aside procedure, the First President or the judge in charge of the procedure when the matter is referred to him or her, may affix the enforcement order (exequatur) to the arbitral award and grant provisional execution. He or she may also order provisional execution under the conditions provided for in articles 525 and 526; his or her decision shall amount to exequatur.

1. General. Art. 1479 was originally applicable only with respect to domestic arbitration but was made applicable to international arbitration by art. 1500. In practice, the provisions suspending execution of international awards in France may be overcome by orders made pursuant to art. 1479 providing that an award is provisionally executable in France (see art. 1506, note 1). Orders for the provisional execution of an award may be made with respect to both international awards rendered in France and foreign awards (see art. 1498, notes 1-3).

2. Provisional execution in France of international awards. Orders for the provisional execution of an award may be made by the arbitral tribunal in its award. An express decision of the arbitrators to that effect in the award is still necessary. For instance, art. 28(6) of the ICC Rules of Arbitration, which provides that 'the parties undertake to carry out any award without delay and

French Code of Civil Procedure (Book IV), art. 1502

shall be deemed to have waived their right to any form of recourse insofar as such waiver can validly be made', does not amount to the granting of provisional execution to ICC awards in France (Cour de cassation, 4 July 2007, *Groupe Antoine Tabet*). Alternatively, once an appeal under art. 1501 or 1502, or a setting aside action under art. 1504 is filed with the Court of Appeal, an order for provisional execution may be granted by either the First President of the Court of Appeal or the judge in charge of the procedure (juge de la mise en état). The First President or the judge in charge of the procedure will only grant an order for provisional execution where he finds such order to be necessary and compatible with the nature of the dispute (Cour d'appel Paris, 13 December 2005, *Lassus*). If the arbitral tribunal rejected a party's request for provisional execution of the award, the French judge may nevertheless grant provisional execution if these conditions are satisfied, and evidence is provided to the judge that there is urgency in granting provisional execution. In the case that provisional execution is granted, execution against a party in France may be made immediately upon service to that party of the award bearing a French judge's enforcement order (exequatur). Moreover, if provisional execution of an award was granted, the first President of the Court of Appeal with jurisdiction over enforcement of the award may terminate provisional execution if he considers the provisional execution unlawful or that the award's provisional execution would have 'clear excessive consequences'.

[Appeal against a refusal to grant an enforcement order]

Article 1501

A court decision refusing recognition or enforcement of an award may be appealed.

1. General. Pursuant to art. 1501, parties may appeal the decision of the President of the First Instance Court refusing enforcement of an international award. This is true whether the award is an international award rendered in France or a foreign award (see art. 1498, note 2). The Court of Appeal is the court with jurisdiction over the judge who refused recognition and enforcement (see art. 1503). On appeal, the Court of Appeal will only review whether the President of the First Instance Court reasoned his decision and correctly refused enforcement or recognition because the decision is not an award or because the enforcement of the award would manifestly be contrary to French international public policy (see art. 1498, notes 6-9).

[Appeal against the granting of an enforcement order]

Article 1502

An appeal against a court decision granting recognition or enforcement is only available on the following grounds:

French Code of Civil Procedure (Book IV), art. 1502

(1) **Where the arbitrator has rendered an award in the absence of an arbitration agreement or on the basis of an arbitration agreement that is void or that has expired;**
(2) **Where the arbitral tribunal was improperly constituted or the sole arbitrator improperly appointed;**
(3) **Where the arbitrator has rendered an award without complying with the mission conferred upon him or her;**
(4) **Where due process was not complied with; or**
(5) **Where the recognition or enforcement is contrary to international public policy.**

1. General. As discussed in art. 1478, note 1, it is not possible to appeal decisions granting recognition and enforcement of international awards rendered in France (see art. 1498, note 2 and art. 1504, note 1). It is, however, possible to appeal decisions granting enforcement of foreign awards. Art. 1502 sets forth the grounds for appealing decisions granting the enforcement of foreign awards. The grounds for appeal under art. 1502 are exclusive; there are no other grounds for appeal of an enforcement order granted on a foreign award.

2. Grounds for appeal may not be modified. The grounds for appeal set forth in art. 1502 are limitative and the parties may not agree to expand them. For example, where an arbitration agreement provides that the award shall be subject to appeal before a national court, then that provision of the arbitration agreement will be considered null and void by the French courts without affecting the parties' arbitration agreement in any other manner (Cour de cassation, 13 March 2007, *Chefaro*). Parties may also not agree to further restrict the grounds for appeal in art. 1502. Having said this, a party's conduct in the course of the arbitration may be considered, by the French courts, as amounting to a waiver of that parties' right to appeal against the enforcement order of a foreign award upon the grounds provided for in art. 1502(1) to (4) (see note 4).

3. The setting aside or suspension of a foreign award at the seat of arbitration. Under French international arbitration law, all international awards are international judicial decisions that are not in and of themselves related to any national legal order (Cour de cassation, 29 June 2007, *Putrabali*). Accordingly, French courts consider that the validity of an international award should be examined in light of the rules applicable at the place where its recognition and enforcement are sought. As a consequence, the setting aside of a foreign award by a court at the seat of arbitration is not, in and of itself, a ground for denying enforcement of that award in France. A foreign award set aside at the seat of arbitration may still be recognised and enforced in France (Cour de cassation, 9 October 1984, *Norsolor* and Cour de cassation, 23 March 1994, *Hilmarton*). Moreover, once the enforcement order granted in France of such an award is res judicata in France, a new award rendered between the same parties with regard to the same matter will not be recognised or enforced in France (Cour de cassation, 29 June 2007, *Putrabali*). Similarly, the filing of an action to set aside a foreign award at the seat of arbitration does not affect the recognition and enforcement of that award in France. In the same vein, the suspension of a foreign award at its seat of arbitration is not a ground for non-enforcement of that award in France (Cour de cassation, 10 March 1993, *Polish Ocean Lines*).

4. Timely objection and waiver. In order for an appeal based on any of the grounds provided in art. 1502(1) to (4) to be admissible before the Court of Appeal, the party bringing the appeal must have raised appropriate objections as soon as possible during the arbitration proceedings. Otherwise, that party may be deemed to have waived its right to complain before the Court of Appeal. For example, the participation of a party in an arbitration without objection amounts to a waiver of that party's right to claim that the arbitration clause is null and void (Cour de cassation, 21 November 2002, *Gromelle*). In the same manner, a party that starts an arbitration without objecting to jurisdiction is estopped from later raising a claim that no arbitration agreement exists (Cour de cassation, 6 July 2005, *Golshani*). By contrast, the signing of terms of reference indicating that a party objects to jurisdiction does not constitute any such waiver (Cour de cassation, 6 January 1987, *SPP*). In the same vein, the failure of a party to timely object that the tribunal was irregularly constituted amounts to a waiver of that party's right to later complain that it was so constituted (Cour d'appel Paris, 11 July 2002, *Beugnet Acquitaine*). Likewise, the failure to timely object that an arbitrator lacked independence also amounts to a waiver (Cour d'appel Paris, 22 February 2007, *Worms*). Similarly, a party that participates in the arbitration without objecting that the time limit for rendering the award has expired waives its right to later complain on that basis (Cour de cassation, 6 July 2005, *Al Amiouny*). Having said this, a party may only waive its rights under art. 1502 by failing to object, if that party had knowledge of the fact justifying its complaint (Cour d'appel Paris, 6 May 2004, *Malecki*) and if the rules applicable to the arbitration procedure would have afforded an opportunity to remedy the alleged irregularity. Where the rules would not have afforded any such opportunity, a party's failure to object does not constitute a waiver for the purposes of art. 1502 (Cour d'appel Paris, 21 January 1997, *Nu Swift*). With respect to appeal under art. 1502(5) on the grounds that enforcement of a foreign award would be contrary to French international public policy, waiver by non-objection is only possible in part. The right to appeal based on alleged violations of procedural French international public policy may be waived for lack of timely objection during the arbitration. However, the right to appeal based on allegations that enforcement of the award would violate substantive French international public policy cannot be waived, and a party is under no obligation to have raised its substantive international public policy concerns with the arbitral tribunal to be able to appeal an enforcement order on such ground before the Court of Appeal (Cour d'appel Paris, 14 June 2001, *Tradigrain*).

French Code of Civil Procedure (Book IV), art. 1502

5. The Court of Appeal will not review an award's reasoning. Appeal of international awards is not available under French international arbitration law. Hence, French courts regularly dismiss applications filed under art. 1502, where the appealing party relies on alleged deficiencies in the arbitral tribunal's reasoning in the award. Such arguments are simply inadmissible before the Courts of Appeal (Cour d'appel Paris, 18 January 2007, *France Animation*). Unless the rules applicable to the arbitration procedure provide that the award shall be reasoned, the failure to reason an international award is not, in and of itself, a ground to refuse enforcement (Cour de cassation, 22 November 1966, *Gerstlé*). If the rules applicable to the arbitration provide that the award shall be reasoned, the French courts will merely verify that the award is reasoned, without regard to what the quality of the reasoning may be. Indeed, erroneous or internally inconsistent reasoning does not render an award unenforceable in France (Cour de cassation, 14 June 2000, *IAIGC*).

6. Extent of the Court of Appeal's review. In deciding an appeal under art. 1502, the Court of Appeal has the power to examine any evidence and factual or legal submissions that it considers relevant to determine whether the appeal should succeed on any of the grounds specified in art. 1502. Moreover, the Court of Appeal has the power to review de novo any issue that may provide a basis for appeal under art. 1502 regarding jurisdiction or the regular constitution of the tribunal (Cour de cassation, 6 January 1987, *SPP*) or violations of procedural international public policy (Cour d'appel Paris, 23 March 2006, *SNF*). Having said this, the Court of Appeal generally tends to give deference to findings of arbitral tribunals, particularly with respect to questions of fact.

7. Sanctions for abuse of rights. In recent years, the Paris Court of Appeal increasingly sanctions parties who frivolously seek to block enforcement or recognition of international awards under art. 1502 (21 January 1997, *Nu Swift*, and 6 May 2004, *Babel Production*), or file claims under this provision that are found to be clearly inadmissible and filed for the sake of generating adverse publicity (Cour d'appel Paris, 18 February 1986, *Ojjeh*).

[Article 1502(1)]

8. Scope of art. 1502(1). Art. 1502(1) provides that a party may appeal against an enforcement order on a foreign award rendered in the absence of an arbitration agreement, or on the basis of an arbitration agreement that is void or that has expired. This may be the case where the Court of Appeal finds that the arbitration agreement is null and void, does not exist, or where the arbitration agreement excludes the dispute settled in the award from the arbitral tribunal's jurisdiction.

9. Form of the arbitration agreement. Under French international arbitration law, an arbitration agreement does not need to be in writing and does not need to be signed by the parties to the arbitration.

10. Separability of the arbitration agreement. Under French international arbitration law, arbitration agreements are separable from the main contract that contains, or refers to them (Cour de cassation, 7 May 1963, *Gosset*). That is to say that the existence, validity and scope of the arbitration agreement is to be evaluated independently from the enforceability of the main contract, and that issues affecting the validity of the contract that contains or refers to the arbitration agreement at stake does not necessarily impair the existence, validity and scope of the arbitration agreement (Cour de cassation, 6 December 1988, *Navimpex*). Arbitration agreements are nevertheless considered ancillary to the contract that contains or refers to the arbitration agreement at stake. As a consequence, arbitration agreements are generally transferred to assignees of all or part of the contract that contains or refers to the arbitration agreement at stake, at the time of assignment (Cour de cassation, 8 February 2000, *Taurus Films,* Cour d'appel Paris, 20 April 1988, *Clark*), unless that arbitration agreement was expressly said to be non-assignable. Moreover, the invalidity of the assignment of all or part of the contract that contains or refers to the arbitration agreement at stake does not necessarily prevent transfer of that agreement in accordance with the rule set forth in *Taurus Films* (Cour de cassation, 28 May 2002, *Ciments d'Abidjan*).

11. No law applicable to the existence and efficiency of an arbitration agreement. When evaluating an appeal based on art. 1502(1), the Court of Appeal will not refer to any national law other than the mandatory rules of French law and French international public policy (Cour de cassation, 30 March 2004, *Uni-Kod*). The Court of Appeal will only examine whether there was a 'common intention of the parties' to arbitrate the dispute settled in the award, and whether any mandatory rules of French law or French international public policy may affect the existence, validity or scope of the arbitration agreement (Cour de cassation, 8 July 2009, *Soerin*). In particular, the French domestic arbitration rules found in the French Civil Code, which prohibit individuals from entering into arbitration agreements in non-business related disputes, are not applicable in the context of an international arbitration (Cour de cassation, 28 January 2003, *Vivendi*). In addition, according to the Cour de cassation, French domestic arbitration rules also found in the French Civil Code, which prohibit French public entities from entering into arbitration agreements, do not to apply where the contractual relationship at stake involves international commerce (Cour de cassation, 2 May 1966, *Galakis*).

12. The 'common intent of the parties' to arbitrate. French courts are liberal in finding a 'common intent of the parties' to arbitrate. Common intent may be found where a party, against which an arbitration clause is invoked, was aware at the time of entering into a contract and accepted by silence the incorporation in the contract, of general conditions or a standard contract that contained an arbitral clause. Such a written reference may, for instance, be found in a confirmation telex or an invoice (Cour de cassation, 9 November 1993, *Bomar Oil*, and Cour d'appel Paris, 13 September 2007,

Comptoir Commercial Blidéen). Similarly, entities that are directly involved in the performance of a contract which contains or refers to an arbitration clause, as well as in the dispute that may result from that contract, are bound by that arbitration clause (Cour de cassation, 27 March 2007, *ABS*). The consistent and repeated practice of the parties to provide for arbitration in their successive contracts may also constitute evidence of a 'common intent to arbitrate' disputes that later arise out of contracts between them that contain no dispute resolution clause (Cour d'appel Paris, 18 March 1983, *Van Dijk*). Similarly, where a chain of contracts operates successive transfer of merchandise property, the arbitration agreement contained in one of these contracts is transmitted together with the contractual rights at issue, unless evidence is provided that there was reasonable ignorance of the arbitration clause on the part of the party against whom that clause is invoked (Cour de cassation, 27 March 2007, *ABS*). Of note, insurers of cargo have been found to be bound by an arbitration clause contained in the underlying transportation contract to which they were not parties, and were even barred from alleging that they had no knowledge of the existence of that arbitration clause (Cour de cassation, 22 November 2005, *Axa Corporate Solutions*). As to the parties' common intent with respect to the scope of their agreement to arbitrate, the language of the clause will be critical. A broadly worded clause will generally be found to cover both contract and tort claims arising out of or in connection with the contract at issue (Cour d'appel Paris, 19 May 2005, *Sucres et Denrées*). However, a tribunal that issues an award on matters falling outside the terms of a restrictive arbitration clause runs the risk that the award will not be enforced in light of art. 1502(1) (Cour d'appel Paris, 22 May 2003, *Caviartrade*). Similarly, an award may be found unenforceable under art. 1502(1) where an arbitral tribunal settles in a single arbitration a dispute concerning two separate contracts that respectively contain different arbitration clauses providing for arbitration at different seats (Cour d'appel Paris, 16 November 2006, *Empresa de Telecommunicaciones de Cuba*).

13. Expiry of the arbitration agreement. There is no requirement under French international arbitration law that an award be rendered within a specific time limit. Therefore, appeal pursuant to art. 1502(1), based on the expiry of the arbitration agreement, first requires that either the law of the seat of arbitration or the rules agreed by the parties to govern the arbitration require the tribunal to render its award within a specific time limit. Where the seat of arbitration is in France and the parties have agreed that the arbitral tribunal is to render its award within a specific time limit, then any party or member of the tribunal may ask the judge with jurisdiction over the seat of arbitration to extend that time limit prior to its expiry (Cour de cassation, 7 March 2000, *Adidas-Salomon*). Of note, in such a case, arbitrators may be held personally liable for damages a party suffers from the setting aside of an award rendered after the expiry of the applicable time limit (TGI Paris, 29 November 1989, *République de Guinée* and Cour de cassation, 6 December 2005, *Juliet*).

[Article 1502(2)]

14. Irregular constitution of the tribunal. Art. 1502(2) allows for appeal against orders enforcing foreign awards in cases where the arbitral tribunal was irregularly constituted. An arbitral tribunal may be irregularly constituted in a variety of ways. The tribunal is said to be irregularly constituted if: it was not constituted in accordance with the parties' agreement (Cour de cassation, 4 December 1990, *Gas del Estado*), e.g. the parties may have specified a particular procedure to be followed in the constitution of the tribunal, or particular criteria an arbitrator must satisfy to be eligible to sit on the tribunal; where the parties did not have the opportunity to participate in an equal manner in the constitution of the tribunal (Cour de cassation, 7 January 1992, *Dutco*); if an arbitrator on the tribunal was not and did not remain independent (Cour d'appel Paris, 6 April 1990, *Icco*), or failed to disclose facts or circumstances that raise reasonable concerns with respect to that arbitrator's independence or impartiality (see art. 1493, notes 6 and 7); where an arbitral institution wrongfully rejected a challenge against an arbitrator on the tribunal (Cour d'appel Paris, 3 July 2007, *Clal MSX*).

[Article 1502(3)]

15. Failure to comply with the tribunal's mission. Art. 1502(3) allows for appeal against an order enforcing a foreign award where the arbitral tribunal has rendered an award without complying with the mission conferred upon it by the parties. An arbitral tribunal may fail to comply with its mission in a variety of ways. The arbitral tribunal may fail to follow the rules agreed by the parties to govern the arbitration procedure. For example, if the rules agreed upon by the parties require that the award be reasoned, an arbitral tribunal that fails to produce a reasoned award fails to fulfil its mission (Cour d'appel Paris, 14 January 1997, *Chromalloy*). Similarly, an arbitral tribunal vested with powers of amiable compositeur that does not use those powers, fails to fulfil its mission (Cour de cassation, 18 October 2001, *Eurovia*, Cour d'appel Paris, 17 December 2009, *Gothaer*). Where the parties have agreed that certain rules of law shall apply to the merits of their dispute, art. 1502(3) may come into play where the arbitral tribunal entirely disregards those rules of law when making its award. In this regard, it is not necessary for the arbitral tribunal to make reference to the particular legal provisions upon which it relies in reaching its decisions (Cour d'appel Paris, 11 December 1997, *Consavio International*). In practice, it is usually sufficient for the arbitral tribunal merely to make reference to the applicable rules of law in its award. In no event will the Court of Appeal examine whether the applicable rules of law were correctly applied by the arbitral tribunal (Cour de cassation, 22 October 1991, *Compania Valenciana de Cementos Portland*).

16. Infra petita and ultra petita. An arbitral tribunal may also fail to fulfil its mission because it fails to decide all of the claims before it (infra petita), or decides matters beyond those submitted by the parties (ultra petita). Awards that are infra petita do not run foul of art. 1502(3), because in such a situation, the claim may be again submitted to the tribunal. Moreover, the tribunal's failure to decide upon each and every legal or factual argument raised by the parties in the course of an arbitration is not sufficient to trigger the application of art. 1502(3). Awards that are ultra petita do provide a basis for appeal of an order of enforcement of a foreign award under art. 1502(3), but only with respect to that part of the award that is ultra petita (Cour d'appel Paris, 28 May 1993, *SGI*). The arbitral tribunal's substantive mission is defined by the subject matter of the parties' dispute, which is itself determined by the parties' submissions during the course of the arbitration. As a consequence, claims that are not expressly set out in terms of reference do not necessarily fall outside the arbitrators' mission (Cour de cassation, 6 March 1996, *Farhat Trading*).

17. Breach of the duty of collegiality. A principle of collegiality, not expressly mentioned in the CPC, generally requires that all arbitrators composing the arbitral tribunal be afforded the opportunity to participate in the tribunal's deliberations (Cour d'appel Paris, 1 July 1997, *Comilog*, Cour d'appel Paris, 16 January 2003, *Intelcam*). A violation of this principle may serve as a basis under art. 1502(3) and (5) to appeal an enforcement order of a foreign award (Cour d'appel Paris, 6 May 2004, *Malecki*).

18. Awards finding the arbitral tribunal lacks jurisdiction. An appeal against an enforcement order on a foreign award deciding that the tribunal lacks jurisdiction must be brought under art. 1502(3) (Cour d'appel Paris, 21 June 1990, *Honeywell Bull*, Cour d'appel Paris, 26 October 1995, *Voight*). This is because art. 1502(1) only addresses the situation where the arbitral tribunal wrongfully retained jurisdiction, and because an arbitral tribunal that has wrongfully declined jurisdiction fails to fulfil its mission to decide the merits of the parties' dispute as agreed by the parties in their arbitration agreement.

[Article 1502(4)]

19. Failure of the tribunal to comply with due process. Art. 1502(4) allows appeal against enforcement orders on foreign awards where due process was not complied with during the arbitration procedure. As a matter of both French international arbitration law and French international public policy, all parties must be afforded due process throughout the arbitration (Cour d'appel Paris, 12 June 2003, *Citel*, Cour d'appel Paris, 27 November 1987, *Sulzer*). Because due process forms part of French international public policy, an alleged denial of due process may also provide grounds for appeal of an enforcement order under art. 1502(5) (see notes 20 and 21). Under French law, due process requires that every party to an arbitration be given a reasonable opportunity to present its case. This means that all information submitted to the tribunal by a party to the arbitration must be provided to all other parties as well (Cour d'appel Paris, 17 December 2009, *Fichtner*). It also means that every party must have a reasonable opportunity to present its factual and legal arguments, and a reasonable opportunity to respond to the arguments put forth by the other parties, before the arbitral tribunal decides on any issue in the case. These requirements apply to decisions taken by way of procedural order or award. Furthermore, in situations where the arbitral tribunal believes that there is any factual or legal issue material to the case that has not been raised by the parties, the arbitral tribunal should raise the issue with the parties, and invite their comments before taking any decision with respect to that issue (Cour d'appel Paris, 14 June 2007, *Ciech*, Cour d'appel Paris, 3 December 2009, *Engel*). Due process under French law also embodies the principle of equal treatment of the parties, such that no party may be put at a material disadvantage vis-à-vis the other parties to the case (Cour d'appel Paris, 12 June 2003, *Citel*). However, this principle of equal treatment does not require that the arbitral tribunal grant each party the exact same number of days to file their respective submissions (Cour d'appel Paris, 15 June 2006, *Prodoil Gabon*).

[Article 1502(5)]

20. French international public policy: general. Pursuant to art. 1502(5), a party may appeal against an enforcement order on a foreign award where recognition or enforcement of the award would be contrary to French international public policy (see art. 1498, note 6). This article thus addresses both violations of French substantive international public policy and French procedural international public policy. The laws of the seat of the arbitration and the rules of law applicable to the merits of the dispute are irrelevant to the Court of Appeal when examining whether recognition or enforcement of an award would be contrary to substantive French international public policy. In order for an appeal to be sustained under art. 1502(5), the breach of substantive international public policy at stake must be actual, blatant and concrete (Cour de cassation, 21 March 2000, *Verhoeft*, Cour de cassation, 4 June 2008, *SNF*, see also Cour d'appel Paris, 18 November 2004, *Thalès*, Cour d'appel Paris, 23 March 2006, *SNF*).

21. Procedural international public policy. Appeals based on allegations that enforcement or recognition of the award would be contrary to French procedural public policy may be brought pursuant to art. 1502(5). In order to succeed on this ground, the appealing party must show that the breach at issue actually caused it harm (Cour d'appel Paris, 21 January 1997, *Nu Swift*). Enforcement of an award may be contrary to French procedural public policy in a variety of circumstances, including where an arbitrator lacked impartiality or independence, or a party was denied due process. These violations of French procedural international public policy would also normally provide a basis for appeal under art. 1502(2) and (4), respectively (see notes 14 and 19). Art. 1502(5) has also been invoked successfully where an arbitrator sat in two parallel arbitrations and provided erroneous information to one of the tribunals with respect to the other arbitration which influenced that tribunal's award on jurisdiction. The award rendered by that tribunal was eventually not enforced in France because the Court of Appeal found that the arbitrator's breach of a duty of loyalty created an imbalance among the parties. The Court of Appeal held that imbalance to violate 'rights of defence' which form part of the procedural international public policy (Cour de cassation, 24 March 1998, *Excelsior Films*). In a case involving alleged bribery, a tribunal found in its award that certain documents constituted evidence that the purpose of the contract at issue was not for bribery. Once the award was rendered, a party asserted that it had just discovered that these documents were in fact false and that therefore the award gave effect to a contract for bribery which was against French substantive international public policy. The Court of Appeal found the award unenforceable on the grounds that the submission of false documents in the course of an arbitral procedure constituted a fraud that was, in and of itself, a breach of French procedural international public policy (Cour d'appel Paris, 30 September 1993, and Cour de cassation, 19 December 1995, *Westman*).

22. Substantive French international public policy. Art. 1502(5) also provides a ground for appeal of an order of enforcement of a foreign award where enforcement or recognition of the award would be contrary to French substantive international public policy at the time the Court of Appeal exercises its powers (Cour d'appel Paris, 23 March 2006, *SNF*). It is the solution reached in the award and not the award's reasoning that the Court of Appeal will examine in light of French substantive international public policy (Cour de cassation, 15 March 1988, *Grands Moulins de Strasbourg*). The tribunal's disregard or misapplication of a French rule of international public policy does not in and of itself constitute the violation envisaged under art. 1502(5) (Cour de cassation, 23 February 1994, *Multitrade*). Rather, the Court of Appeal will focus on whether recognition or enforcement of the award in France would violate French international public policy. To sustain an appeal on this ground, the violation of French substantive international public policy must be actual, blatant and concrete (Cour de cassation, 21 March 2000, *Verhoeft*, Cour de cassation, 4 June 2008, *SNF*, see also Cour d'appel Paris, 18 November 2004, *Thalès*). As discussed in note 6, the Court of Appeal has the power to review de novo any issue that may provide a basis for appeal of a foreign award's enforcement order on grounds of French substantive international public policy (Cour d'appel Paris, 23 March 2006, *SNF*). Having said this, as a matter of practice, the Court of Appeal regularly gives deference to the findings of the arbitral tribunal, particularly with respect to questions of fact. Cases where the Court of Appeal has denied enforcement on the grounds of a violation of French substantive international public policy are rare. Corruption and bribery are contrary to French substantive international public policy (Cour de cassation, 19 December 1995, *Westman*). European competition law is part of the European Union member states' international public policy (CJCE, 1 June 1999, *Eco Swiss*). As France is a member state of the

European Union, European competition law is part of France's substantive international public policy. Certain European regulatory provisions on the protection of consumers are also part of French substantive international public policy and may affect the validity of the arbitration agreement itself (ECJ, 26 October 2006, *Mostaza Claro*). Certain French rules on bankruptcy proceedings are also part of French international public policy (Cour de cassation, 5 February 1991, *Almira Films*). Specifically, if a French party files for bankruptcy during the course of an arbitration, the arbitral tribunal should suspend the proceedings for the time it takes to join the receiver into the arbitration. In addition, the arbitral tribunal may be prevented from ordering that party to pay debts that were owed prior to its filing for bankruptcy (Cour de cassation, 2 June 2004, *Alstom Power*, two cases). The arbitral tribunal may still decide how much the bankrupt party owes; it is simply prevented from ordering that party to pay that amount (Cour de cassation, 6 May 2009, *Liquidator of Jean Lion*).

[Court with jurisdiction and deadline for appeal regarding enforcement orders]

Article 1503

An appeal under articles 1501 or 1502 shall be brought before the Court of Appeal with jurisdiction over the judge who made the decision. It may be brought within one month from service of the judge's decision.

1. General. Art. 1503 specifies where and when parties may bring appeals under arts. 1501 and 1502. Execution of the award in France is suspended while the one-month time limit provided for in art. 1503 is running, unless the award was granted provisional execution (see art. 1479, notes 1-2 and art. 1506, note 1).

2. Time limit for appeal. Under art. 1503, an appeal under arts. 1501 or 1502 must be brought to the Court of Appeal with jurisdiction over the President of the First Instance Court who granted or denied the enforcement order over the award, within one month from service of the President's decision. When the party upon whom the enforcement or recognition decision has been served is domiciled outside France, that time limit may be extended by two more months. If no appeal is filed within the time limit specified in art. 1503, then the decision of the President of the First Instance Court becomes final.

3. Service of the decision of the President of the First Instance Court. Art. 1503 provides that the one month time limit for appeal starts running as from service of the decision of the President of the First Instance Court to enforce a foreign award. Under French law, service requires that delivery of the decision be made on the parties by a French bailiff (huissier de justice) upon the request of a party. Hence, where the President of the First Instance Court has ordered enforcement of an international award under art. 1498, the bailiff must serve a copy of the award bearing the enforcement order stamped by the President of the First Instance Court on the party against whom enforcement is sought, before the time limit set forth in art. 1503 starts running.

[Setting aside of international awards rendered in France]

Article 1504

An arbitral award rendered in France in an international arbitration may be the subject of an action to set aside on the grounds provided for under article 1502.

There is no recourse available against an order granting enforcement of such an award. However, the action for setting aside constitutes, within the limits of such action before the Court of Appeal and as of right, an action against the enforcement judge's order or termination of that judge's jurisdiction.

1. International awards rendered in France may only be set aside on the grounds provided under art. 1502. Art. 1504 allows a party to ask the Court of Appeal to set aside an international award rendered in France (setting aside is also sometimes referred to as 'annulment'). Art. 1504 only applies to international awards rendered in France. It does not apply to foreign awards. Foreign awards may not be set aside by the French courts. Art. 1504 allows the setting aside of an international award rendered in France on the grounds provided under art. 1502 (see art. 1502), and only on these grounds. These grounds are interpreted and applied in setting aside proceedings under art. 1504 in exactly the same way as they are interpreted and applied for appeals under art. 1502 (see art. 1502). Thus, circumstances that would lead the Court of Appeal to sustain or reject an appeal related to the enforcement order of a foreign award under art. 1502 would also lead the Court of Appeal to sustain or reject an action to set aside an international award rendered in France under art. 1504. An action to set aside an international award rendered in France may be brought by any party named in the award as from the rendering of the award. In other words, an action to set aside may be brought even before an enforcement order has been made with respect to the award (see art. 1505, note 1). When an action to set aside an international award rendered in France is filed after the enforcement order was granted on that award, it has, for all practical purposes, the same effect as an appeal on the enforcement order, were the appeal allowed (which it is not). Thus, although no appeal is available against the decision allowing enforcement of an international award rendered in France, a party may still escape enforcement of that award in France by having the award set aside.

2. An action to set aside a partial award on jurisdiction rendered in France does not suspend the arbitration. Where an arbitral tribunal sitting in France renders a partial award finding it has jurisdiction, an action to set aside that award does not require the tribunal to suspend its work (Cour d'appel Paris, 9 July 1992, *GECI*). Having said this, if the Court of Appeal does set that award aside under arts. 1504 and 1502(1) for lack of jurisdiction, the decision of the Court of Appeal deprives the arbitral tribunal of jurisdiction as soon as the Court of Appeal's decision is final. As a consequence, any other award that the arbitral tribunal may have rendered in the meantime, is considered set aside by the Court of Appeal's decision setting aside the partial award on jurisdiction (Cour d'appel Paris, 18 November 2004, *Caviartrade II*).

[Court with jurisdiction and deadline for appeal applicable to the setting aside of international awards rendered in France]

Article 1505

An action to set aside under article 1504 shall be brought before the Court of Appeal having jurisdiction over the place where the award was rendered. This action is admissible as from the rendering of the award; it is no longer admissible if not filed within one month from service of the award bearing exequatur.

1. General. Art. 1505 specifies where and when parties may bring an action to set aside an international award rendered in France under art. 1504. An action to set aside an international award rendered in France must be brought before the Court of Appeal having jurisdiction over the place where the award was rendered. The action may be brought as from the rendering of the award. If a President of a First Instance Court issued an enforcement order with respect to an award, the action to set aside that award must be filed within one month from service of the decision of the President of the First Instance Court (see art. 1503, note 3). If this time limit expires without a setting aside action having been filed, the award may be immediately executed in France.

[Suspension of execution]

Article 1506

Execution of the arbitral award is suspended during the time limit for filing the actions foreseen under articles 1501, 1502 and 1504. An action filed within that time limit also suspends execution.

1. General. Pursuant to art. 1506, execution of an award in France is suspended pending expiry of the time limit for filing an appeal under art. 1501 or 1502, or an action to set aside under 1504 (see art. 1498, notes 2 and 3, art. 1479, notes 1 and 2, and arts. 1503 and 1505). In addition, if an appeal or action to set aside is timely filed in France, its filing also suspends execution of the award in France. By contrast, the filing of an action to set aside a foreign award in the country where the foreign award was rendered does not suspend execution of the award in France. An international award may therefore only be executed in France after one month has elapsed from the date the award bearing a French judge's enforcement order was served by a French bailiff (huissier) on the party against whom the award is to be enforced, provided that during this period, no action was filed either against the enforcement order in the case of a foreign award or for the setting aside of the award in the case of an international award rendered in France. The provisions in art. 1506 suspending execution of international awards in France may be overcome by orders for provisional execution made pursuant to art. 1479 (see art. 1479, notes 1-2).

[No appeal available against international awards]

Article 1507

The provisions of Title IV of this Book, except those of sub-article 1 of article 1487 and of article 1490, shall not apply to recourse proceedings.

1. General. French domestic arbitration law allows for awards rendered in domestic arbitration to be appealed or deprived of enforcement in France under specific circumstances (see Introductory remarks, notes 1 and 4). The purpose of art. 1507 is to make clear that these provisions of French domestic arbitration law do not apply to international awards, be they international awards rendered in France or foreign awards. No appeal is available under French international arbitration law against international awards (see art. 1498, note 2, art. 1502, note 5 and art. 1504, notes 1 and 2).

[Procedure before the Court of Appeal]

Article 1487

The appeal and the recourse for setting aside are filed, heard and decided upon in accordance with the rules governing ordinary litigation before the Court of Appeal.

1. General. Art. 1487 was originally drafted for domestic arbitration and subsequently made applicable to international arbitration by art. 1507 (see art. 1507, note 1). Art. 1487 does not provide any additional grounds for recourse in connection with international awards, nor does art. 1487 affect the grounds set forth in art. 1502. According to art. 1487, the procedural rules generally applicable before the French Courts of Appeal are to be followed in cases of appeal under art. 1501 or 1502, and in actions to set aside under art. 1504. For instance, according to the rules generally applicable in the Court of Appeal, parties before the Court of Appeal must use the services of a lawyer specialised in appellate procedures and licensed to appear before the Court of Appeal (avoué). It also means that, for instance, decisions of the Court of Appeal rendered in matters concerning international arbitration may be subject to recourse before the Supreme Court (Cour de cassation).

[Rejection of appeal or action to set aside, confers exequatur]

Article 1490

The rejection of an appeal or of an action to set aside confers exequatur upon the arbitral award or to its provisions that have not been set aside by the court.

1. General. Art. 1490 was originally drafted for application in domestic arbitration and subsequently expressly made applicable to international arbitration by art. 1507 (see art. 1507, note 1). Art. 1490 speaks to both international awards rendered in France and foreign awards, but in slightly different ways. With respect to foreign awards, art. 1490 provides that if an appeal against an order of enforcement is rejected by the Court of Appeal, the rejection of the appeal constitutes an order of enforcement for the foreign award. This may have been implied, but art. 1490 makes it express. Similarly, with respect to international awards rendered in France, art. 1490 provides that if the Court of Appeal rejects an action for setting aside an award, the rejection of the setting aside action constitutes an order of enforcement for the award in France. Again, this may have been implied, but art. 1490 makes it express.

SWISS PRIVATE INTERNATIONAL LAW ACT
(CHAPTER 12: INTERNATIONAL ARBITRATION), 1989

(In force as from 1 January 1989)

[Introductory remarks]

1. Legislative history. Chapter 12 of the PILA entered into force on 1 January 1989; and has been amended only in a few respects since then. By creating chapter 12 PILA, the Swiss legislator produced a short and concise arbitration act that confined itself to rules of prime importance. The main characteristics of this law on international arbitration are its liberality and its wide scope for party autonomy. Where the parties do not make use of this autonomy, the discretion of the arbitral tribunal for structuring and organising the arbitral proceedings is equally far reaching. The law stipulates only a few mandatory general rules which are necessary in order to keep the arbitral process in balance and in accordance with the basic rules of due process. The intervention of the state courts is kept to a minimum; while assistance and cooperation is provided if so required, setting aside proceedings before the Federal Supreme Court are possible on only very limited grounds. While drafted more or less at the same time as the UNCITRAL Model Law, chapter 12 PILA stands alone and is independent from the UNCITRAL Model Law. There are, however, no fundamental differences between the two.

2. Chapter 12 PILA and the Intercantonal Concordat. Until 1 January 1989, all domestic and international arbitration proceedings were governed by the Intercantonal Concordat on Arbitration of 1969 that was concluded between the Swiss cantons. Compared to chapter 12 PILA, the Concordat is not quite as liberal, and contains a number of mandatory rules that restrict the powers of the arbitral tribunal and the freedom of the parties. Nowadays, chapter 12 PILA constitutes the lex arbitri for all international arbitrations, provided that the requirements of art. 176 are fulfilled. Where they are not fulfilled, the Concordat applies. When the Federal Code of Civil Procedure enters into force in 2011, and replaces the cantonal Codes of Civil Procedure, it will also contain a chapter on arbitration that will replace the Concordat.

3. Case law and academic sources. Arbitration and, in particular, international arbitration have a long-standing tradition in Switzerland. With simple, pragmatic and flexible statutes, a large body of case law has emerged that provides guidance on the interpretation and application of the relevant rules of law and confirms the Swiss judiciary's restraint in interfering with international arbitration. The broad spectrum of precedents by the Federal Supreme Court and a large number of academic sources, which are frequently consulted by arbitrators, counsel and the judiciary, provide for reliability and predictability; this, together with Switzerland's political stability and the nation's historical neutrality, has made Switzerland one of the preferred centres for international arbitration.

Swiss Private International Law Act (Chapter 12), art. 176

[Scope of application; seat of the arbitral tribunal]

Article 176

(1) The provisions of this chapter shall apply to arbitral tribunals which have their seat in Switzerland, provided that, at the time of the conclusion of the arbitration agreement, at least one of the parties had neither its domicile nor its habitual residence in Switzerland.

(2) The provisions in this chapter shall not apply where the parties have excluded their application in writing and agreed that the cantonal provisions on arbitration shall apply exclusively. [*New version of paragraph 2 entering into force in 2011*: The parties can exclude the application of this chapter and agree on the application of the third part of the Federal Code of Civil Procedure by making an explicit declaration in the arbitration agreement or in a later agreement.]

(3) The seat of the arbitral tribunal shall be determined by the parties, or by the arbitration institution designated by them, or, failing both, by the arbitrators.

1. Requirements of the applicability of chapter 12. Art. 176 determines that the provisions of chapter 12 PILA apply to arbitral tribunals (see note 2) with their seat in Switzerland (see note 3) if, at the time of the conclusion of the arbitration agreement, at least one of the parties was not domiciled or resident in Switzerland (see note 4) and provided that the parties did not validly exclude chapter 12 PILA (see note 5).

2. Applicability to arbitral tribunals. Chapter 12 PILA applies only to arbitral tribunals and not to expert determinations, valuations and audits. The concept of arbitration is not defined in the PILA but is taken to mean private jurisdiction sanctioned by the state, based on the parties' agreement to have their dispute adjudicated by a private tribunal, and resulting in decisions comparable to those of state courts (see ATF 4P.299/2006 reason 3; ATF 5P.427/2000 reason 1b). Arbitration must be distinguished from expert determinations (on this distinction, see in particular ATF 4A_438/2008 reason 3.2), valuations, audits and decisions of other institutions which are not directly enforceable and have no res judicata effect. The intention of the parties (see ATF 107 Ia 318 reason 5a), the independence and impartiality of the tribunal (see ATF 5P.427/2000 reason 1b) and the tribunal's powers (see ATF 4P.299/2006 reason 3), as well as the purpose of the proceedings (final decision on claims, as opposed to the mere examination of single preliminary questions, see ATF 126 III 529 reason 3), are decisive for this distinction. Chapter 12 PILA applies to institutional and ad hoc arbitral tribunals.

3. Seat of the arbitration. An arbitral tribunal is subject to chapter 12 PILA only if the seat of the arbitration is in Switzerland (for the determination of the seat see note 6). The seat of the arbitration determines the nationality of an arbitral award, as per art. I New York Convention. It is also relevant for the determination of the court that provides assistance if so required (see, e.g., arts. 179(2), 180(3), 183(2)), and for setting aside proceedings in Switzerland. Hearings and deliberations can be held elsewhere, in which case the law of that state will have to be consulted, since some states apply their law to any arbitration proceedings that are physically held there.

4. Domicile or habitual residence outside Switzerland. Chapter 12 PILA only applies if at least one of the parties to the arbitration does not have its domicile, seat or habitual residence in Switzerland at the time the arbitration agreement is concluded. A business establishment outside Switzerland is not sufficient to fulfil this requirement (Berti-Ehrat, n 35 ad art. 176). The domicile of a company is the statutory seat or, failing such designation, the place of actual management (art. 21(1) and (2) PILA). The domicile of a person is the place where he resides with the intent of permanently settling there (art. 20(1)(a) PILA), whereas the habitual residence is the place where he lives for an extended period (e.g. a couple of months) even if this period was limited from the outset (art. 20(1)(b) PILA). The Swiss legislator uses these purely formal criteria for reasons of clarity and simplicity (Botschaft, at 459). The international nature of the subject-matter is irrelevant (see ATF 4P.115/2003 reason 2.1). Changes of domicile, seat or habitual residence after the conclusion of the arbitration agreement are also irrelevant (see ATF 4P.113/2001 reason 3; ATF, 27 October 1995, reason 2a). The Federal Supreme Court has held, in an often criticised decision, that in cases where the foreign party to an arbitration agreement does not participate in the proceedings, i.e. when only those parties with their domicile or seat in Switzerland appear in the arbitration, chapter 12 PILA does not apply (see ATF 4P.54/2002 reason 3). Furthermore, parties that are all domiciled in Switzerland at present are not allowed to choose to submit their dispute to chapter 12 PILA (see ATF 4P.54/2002 reason 2). This, however, will change when the new Swiss Federal Code of Civil Procedure (FCCP) enters into force 2011, as art. 353(2) FCCP explicitly allows parties to agree on the applicability of chapter 12 PILA.

5. Exclusion of chapter 12 PILA. Art. 176(2) states that the parties may exclude the application of chapter 12 PILA and may elect instead to use the Intercantonal Concordat or, as of 2011, the third part of the FCCP that will replace the Concordat. It is not enough for the parties to explicitly agree in writing that they wish to exclusively apply the Concordat/the third part of the FCCP; it must also be clear from the wording of the agreement that they wish to exclude chapter 12 PILA (see ATF 4P.243/2000 reason 2b; ATF 116 II 721 reason 4). If the parties only agree on the applicability of the Concordat/ the third part of the FCCP, this constitutes an agreement on the applicable arbitration rules, as provided for by art. 182(1) (see ATF 4P.140/2000 reason 2b). If the parties exclude chapter 12 PILA, they exclude all procedural provisions contained therein, but not the substantive provisions and conflict of laws rules, such as art. 178(2) and art. 187 (Basel Commentary-Ehrat/ Pfiffner, n 48-49 ad art. 176 with further examples). In practice, parties rarley exclude chapter 12 PILA.

6. Determination of the seat of arbitration. According to art. 176(3), the parties can determine the seat of arbitration. This determination actually implies a fundamental choice of law, as it simultaneously determines the applicable lex arbitri, i.e. the PILA or the Intercantonal Concordat/the third part of the FCCP (see Introductory Remarks, note 2). If the parties fail to establish the seat of arbitration but do choose a set of arbitration rules, these rules may directly determine the seat of the arbitration (e.g. art. 31 CIETAC Rules, art. 2 Vienna Rules) or, more commonly, provide for the determination of the seat by the arbitral institution (e.g. art. 14(1) ICC Rules, art. 16(1) Swiss Rules). If the parties have failed to agree on either the seat or on a set of arbitration rules, the arbitrators may establish the seat. However, constitution of the arbitral tribunal may be difficult if the parties have not determined the seat beforehand (see art. 179, note 4).

[Arbitrability]

Article 177

(1) Any dispute involving an economic interest may be the subject of an arbitration.

(2) A party which is a state, a state-dominated enterprise, or a state-controlled organisation cannot invoke its own law in order to contest its capacity to arbitrate or the arbitrability of a dispute covered by the arbitration agreement.

1. General. Art. 177 provides broad access to international arbitration by liberally defining the arbitrability of the subject matter of the dispute ('objective arbitrability') as well as addressing the capacity of a state-controlled party to arbitrate ('subjective arbitrability'). Both aspects are preconditions for a valid arbitration agreement.

2. Arbitrability of the dispute. Unlike art. II(1) New York Convention, art. 177(1) establishes a substantive rule with a definition of the requirements for arbitrability. Any disputes involving an economic interest are arbitrable, i.e. all claims that have an economic value for at least one party, be it an asset or a liability (see ATF 1P.113/2000 reason 1b; ATF 118 II 353 reason 3b). It does not matter whether the applicable law allows the parties to dispose of the claim in dispute (Berti-Briner, n 8 ad art. 177). Art. 74 of the new Federal Supreme Court Act, as well as art. 44 of the former Federal Law on Judicial Organization, provide a similar test for the admissibility of appeals to the Federal Supreme Court, and precedents in this context may give valuable guidance with regard to defining the notion of economic interest. Even where the claim is related to a non-arbitrable right, such as a personal right of a party, the dispute can still be subject to arbitration if the party seeks protection from economic consequences and if the economic aspect is predominant, for example if an athlete is suspended because of doping (see Gerichtspräsident Thun, 1 December 2005, at 56 et seq.; see also ATF 4P.230/2000 reason 1).

3. Restrictions. As a principle, Swiss or foreign provisions stipulating the compulsory jurisdiction of a state court (mandatory fora) are not taken into account. Under this liberal approach, the only restriction to the arbitrability of economic interests is the principle of public policy (see ATF 118 II 353 reason 3c; Basel Commentary-Briner, n 12, 18 ad art. 177), as developed by the Federal Supreme Court in the application of art. 190(2)(e) (see art. 190, note 10 et seq.). The abuse of Switzerland as a 'safe haven' for international arbitration is restricted by the general rule prohibiting the abuse of law and by possible difficulties to be encountered in the recognition and enforcement of the ensuing award in a foreign country (see ATF 118 II 353 reason 3d). This is because art. V(2)(a) New York Convention allows any state to deny enforcement of an arbitral award if the matter was not arbitrable under the law of the enforcement state.

4. Non-arbitrable preliminary questions. If the dispute is subject to arbitration, the arbitral tribunal is both entitled and obliged to decide upon preliminary questions which would, as such, not be arbitrable. For example, if a party brings a contractual claim, the arbitral tribunal must decide upon the (in)validity of the contract under antitrust law, regardless of the state authorities' exclusive competence (see ATF 118 II 193 reason 5), or upon the invalidity of the contract due to the violation of criminal law provisions (see ATF 133 III 139 reason 5). The arbitral tribunal's decision does not bind the competent authorities.

5. Examination ex officio. It is controversial whether the arbitral tribunal must examine ex officio the arbitrability of the dispute or whether the parties must raise an objection in this respect (see Basel Commentary-Briner, n 20 ad art. 177; Berger/Kellerhals, *Schiedsgerichtsbarkeit*, n 247; Kaufmann-Kohler/Rigozzi, *LDIP*, n 193). The Federal Supreme Court once ruled that the parties had to challenge the arbitrability of the dispute before pleading on the merits (see ATF, 15 March 1993, reason 5). Respondents are therefore advised to make such a challenge before the arbitral tribunal at the earliest possible opportunity (see ATF 130 III 66 reason 4.3).

6. Consequences of non-arbitrability. If the dispute is not arbitrable, the arbitral tribunal in Switzerland must declare itself not legally competent to arbitrate, as otherwise its award will be set aside under art. 190(2)(b). Furthermore, if an arbitral tribunal with its seat abroad renders an award in a matter that is not arbitrable under art. 177, Swiss courts will deny recognition of the award in Switzerland under art. V(2)(a) New York Convention (Berti-Patocchi/Jermini, n 122 ad art. 194).

7. State-controlled party. Art. 177(2) bars a state from using its legislative power to prevent an arbitration in disputes with an individual (see ATF, 13 October 1992, reason 7b). Art. 177(2) provides that a state cannot invoke its own law in order to challenge either the arbitrability of the dispute or its own capacity to enter into an arbitration agreement or to be a party to the arbitration. This also applies to companies and organisations that are owned or controlled (legally or de facto) by a state. Art. 177(2) constitutes a substantive rule of Swiss international arbitration law. It is not permissible to take foreign law into consideration here, except in clear cases of bad faith (see Basel Commentary-Briner, n 27 ad art. 177).

8. Subjective arbitrability of parties that are not state-controlled. Art. 177 does not address the capacity of a non-state party to be a party to the arbitration. Subjective arbitrability becomes an issue particularly in case of insolvency of a party. The Swiss Federal Supreme Court had to decide a case where one of the respondents in the arbitration became insolvent after the commencement of the arbitration. The arbitral tribunal had denied in an interim award subjective arbitrability with respect to this party based on the domestic insolvency law at the place of incorporation, which was at the same time the place of insolvency. Under this law, the arbitration clause lost its effects as of the date when insolvency was declared. The Swiss Federal Supreme Court upheld the interim award. It held that subjective arbitrability depends on the preliminary question of legal capacity under the applicable substantive law. The substantive law applicable to a company's legal capacity is the law under which it is organised (i.e. the law of its incorporation) or, if the company has not been validly organised under this law, the law of the state in which the company is effectively managed (art. 155(c) PILA; ATF 4A_428/2008 reason 3.2). According to this decision, the law governing the insolvency of a company (lex concursus) will have an impact on subjective arbitrability only if it is also the law under which the company is incorporated. That being said, one should not overestimate the decision, which the Federal Supreme Court did not include in its official collection of precedents, but should await future developments. Instead of applying the law of incorporation, one could consider that the problem concerns in fact the validity of the arbitration agreement and apply the law designated by Art. 178(2), which favours the validity of the arbitration agreement. Another possible alternative would be to hold that the effect of an insolvency on pending arbitration proceedings is subject to the lex arbitri, in line with Article 15 of the EC Insolvency Regulation No. 1346/2000

[Arbitration agreement]

Article 178

(1) As regards its form, an arbitration agreement is valid if made in writing, by telegram, telex, fax or any other means of communication which permits it to be evidenced by a text.

Swiss Private International Law Act (Chapter 12), art. 178

(2) As regards its substance, an arbitration agreement is valid if it conforms either to the law chosen by the parties, the law governing the subject matter of the dispute, in particular the principal contract, or Swiss law.
(3) The arbitration agreement cannot be contested on the grounds that the principal contract is not valid or that the arbitration agreement concerns a dispute which has not yet arisen.

1. Requirements for a valid arbitration agreement. The PILA explicitly and implicitly contains the following mandatory requirements for a valid arbitration agreement: mutual consent on the necessary content (see note 4), written form (see notes 2 and 3), arbitrability of the subject matter and subjective arbitrability (art. 177) and determinability of the arbitral tribunal (see note 5). Art. 178(2) contains a conflict of laws rule for all other substantive requirements and issues (see note 7). If the arbitration agreement does not fulfil all of the requirements, it is invalid and the arbitral tribunal must decline its jurisdiction. Otherwise its award can be set aside under art. 190(2) (b).

2. Form requirement. Art. 178(1) requires the arbitration agreement to be in writing and allows the parties to use any means of communication which permits the arbitration agreement to be evidenced by a text. It must be proved that the parties exchanged declarations which are attributable to each party and which form a binding agreement. The text does not need to bear a signature in order to comply with the requirement of written form (e.g. ZCC Award, 7 August 2006, para. 53; Berger/Kellerhals, *Schiedsgerichtsbarkeit*, n 396 with references; but see ATF 121 III 38 reason 3 on art. II New York Convention, which states that, strictly speaking, arbitration agreements contained in the agreement itself require a signature, whereas those concluded by exchange of documents do not. However, the Federal Supreme Court held in this specific case that the arbitration agreement contained in the bill of lading itself was valid despite the lack of one signature). Under the current standards of technology, the requirement of visual perceptibility and physical reproducibility is fulfilled in an exchange of e-mails (Basel Commentary-Wenger/Müller, n 13 ad art. 178). With regard to the issue of form, the parties cannot choose to apply any law other than that of the Swiss seat of arbitration (Besson, *Arbitration in Switzerland* at 773 with further references; Kaufmann-Kohler/Rigozzi, *LDIP*, n 208).

3. Art. 178(1) and art. II(2) New York Convention. As a general rule, form is governed by art. 178(1) when arbitral tribunals with their seat in Switzerland are called to rule upon their jurisdiction, or when the Federal Supreme Court reviews the arbitration agreement in the context of an application to set aside the arbitral award pursuant to art. 190(2)(b). However, form is governed by art. II New York Convention when Swiss courts are required to rule upon the recognition and enforcement of a foreign arbitral award or when a Swiss court is seized of an action in spite of the existence of an arbitration agreement providing for arbitration seated abroad. The Federal Supreme Court has ruled that there are no differences between the formal requirements of the New York Convention and art. 178 (see ATF 121 III 38 reason 2c; see also Commercial Court St. Gallen, ASA Bulletin 2007, 393 reason II.1).

4. Necessary content of the arbitration agreement and pathological agreements. A valid arbitration agreement requires the parties to agree that existing or future disputes arising in respect of a defined contractual or non-contractual legal relationship will be resolved by a private tribunal instead of a state court (see ATF 130 III 66 reason 3.1; art. 176, note 2). The general principles of contract interpretation, in particular art. 18 Swiss Code of Obligations, also apply to arbitration agreements (see ATF 4P.226/2004 reason 4.2; ATF 116 Ia 56 reason 3a). The Federal Supreme Court consistently takes a rather restrictive approach in making sure that the parties' true intention was to waive their right to proceedings before a state court (see ATF 129 III 675 reason 2.3). However, once the consent to arbitrate has been established, the scope of the arbitration agreement will be broadly construed and it will be assumed that the parties want an all-embracing jurisdiction (see ATF 116 Ia 56 reason 3b, see also note 8). If an arbitration agreement complies with the above-mentioned requirements and allows the determination of the arbitral tribunal (see note 5), but is otherwise incomplete, unclear or contradictory (pathological arbitration agreement), it must be construed in a way that respects the parties' will to submit their dispute to arbitration (see ATF 130 III 66 reason 3.1). Thus, the arbitration agreement is to be construed pursuant to the principle of favor validitatis, and not in a manner that renders it invalid or ineffective (see ATF 4P.226/2004 reason 4.2).

5. Determinability of the arbitral tribunal. For an arbitration agreement to be valid, the Federal Supreme Court requires that it be possible to determine upon which arbitral tribunal the parties agreed (see ATF 130 III 66 reason 3.1; ATF 129 III 675 reason 2.3; for an example, see CCIG case no. 193, 21 October 2002). Should the parties have failed to designate an authority that would be of assistance in the constitution process, they must have determined a seat of arbitration in order to obtain state court assistance under art. 179(2) (see ATF 130 III 66 reason 3.2). The wording 'arbitration in Zurich' is sufficient to enable a constitution of the arbitral tribunal, whereas problems arise if the parties only agreed on 'arbitration in Switzerland' (see art. 179, note 4; see also ZCC Award, 7 August 2006, paras. 71-72). In any event, the parties should strive to express their consent in an unequivocal manner, beyond the bare minimum of the essentialia of an arbitration agreement, and to restrict room for interpretation.

6. Arbitration agreement by reference. An arbitration agreement can be concluded by reference to another document containing an arbitration clause (for example earlier agreements, general business conditions, standard contractual terms and conditions or by-laws of companies and professional associations). The arbitration agreement by reference is formally valid if the parties exchange written declarations that refer to the other document and if this document, which contains the arbitration clause, is also in the written form required by art. 178(1) (see ATF 4P.126/2001 reason 2c; ATF 4P.230/2000 reason 2a). Furthermore, the prerequisites for the substantive validity of the arbitration agreement according to art. 178(2) must be met, i.e. the declarations must also constitute an effective agreement on the arbitration clause. A global reference to a text containing an arbitration agreement constitutes a valid agreement under Swiss law if it can be shown in good faith that, in the specific circumstances at hand, an arbitration agreement is not an unusual provision and would not be something that the party would not and could not have expected at the time of the conclusion of the agreement.

7. Substantive validity. Art. 178(2) constitutes a conflict of laws rule providing that it is sufficient for an arbitration agreement to be valid under the substantive rules of any of the three laws listed in art. 178(2). The purpose of this provision is to ensure, as far as possible, the validity of an arbitration agreement. Art. 178(2) does not indicate which specific issues come under the concept of 'substantive validity' of the arbitration agreement. The scope of application generally includes, inter alia, the conclusion of the arbitration agreement (offer, acceptance, consent in cases where arbitration clauses are incorporated by reference, deficiencies of intent and possible deficiencies of consent, such as error, duress, misrepresentation), possible preconditions to arbitration (e.g. preceding mediation, see art. 186, note 4), performance issues (e.g. delay, impossibility, exceptio non adimpleti contractus), and the scope of the arbitration agreement (e.g. the binding force on non-signatories or assignees). All validity aspects must be covered by the application of one sole law and not by applying any of the three possible laws selectively to individual issues. It is controversial whether it is only national legal systems or also non-national rules of law (e.g. lex mercatoria) that can be applied under art. 178(2) (see Basel Commentary-Wenger/Müller, n 26 ad art. 178).

8. The scope of the arbitration agreement. The common arbitration clause ('all disputes arising from the contract' or 'in connection with the contract') is to be understood broadly. It covers disputes regarding the conclusion and binding effect of the contract, its performance and its interpretation, and claims resulting from its termination, as well as tort claims if they are related to claims arising from an alleged breach of the contract or are otherwise linked to the contract (see ATF 4A_452/2007 reason 2.5.1; ATF 116 Ia 56 reason 3b; ICC case no. 12363/ACS, 23 December 2003, at 467). However, such a clause does not automatically cover claims arising from another contract, even where there are elements connecting the two contracts (see ATF 4A_452/2007 reason 2.5.2). Unless the parties have agreed otherwise, an arbitral tribunal also has jurisdiction to adjudicate counterclaims, provided that the principal claim and the counterclaim stem from the same legal relationship. With regard to set-off defences, the situation may be more complex; where both claims stem from the same legal relationship, the jurisdiction of the arbitral tribunal is not an issue (see art. 186, note 3).

9. Non-signatories. As a general rule, the arbitration agreement binds only those parties that originally agreed to it (see ATF 129 III 727 reason 5.3). Under specific circumstances there are exceptions to this rule, and the arbitration agreement may be extended to third parties pursuant to one of the laws applicable under art. 178(2) (see ATF 4C.40/2003 reason 4.1; for an overview over the Swiss case law see Zuberbühler, *Non-Signatories*, at 19 et seq.). Successors in title are bound by the agreement if the succession is valid under the applicable law and covers the arbitration clause. Under Swiss law, for example, the arbitration clause is automatically transferred with the assignment of the principal claim (see ATF 128 III 50 reason 2b). Furthermore, where a guarantor assumes a contractual debt (either in replacement of the original debtor or as jointly and severally liable co-debtor), the arbitration clause covering the contractual debt also binds the guarantor, unless he explicitly excludes to be bound when assuming the debt (ATF 134 III 565 reason 3.2). The surety or guarantor is not automatically bound in case of other forms of securities, such as surety bonds or bank guarantees. A non-signatory may be bound by the agreement if he has close connections to one of the contracting parties, for example by legal or actual domination of the contracting party, by participating in the contract negotiations or by interfering in the performance of the contract in a manner that demonstrates his intent to be bound by the arbitration clause (see ATF 4A_376/2008 reason 8, setting aside an award that had refused a joinder of several non-signatories; ATF 4P.48/2005 reason 3.4.1; ATF 129 III 727 reason 5.3.2). An arbitration agreement can also be considered binding upon a non-signatory party if circumventing the arbitration agreement would constitute an abuse of law (justifying, e.g., the piercing of the corporate veil, see ATF 4A_160/2009 reason 4.3). Unilateral arbitration provisions can be valid, for example, in a will, in a foundation, in prize contests and for competitions, but restrictions may apply in specific cases (Basel Commentary-Wenger/Müller, n 63 et seq. ad art. 178).

10. Art. 178(2) and art. V(1)(a) New York Convention. For the question of recognition and enforcement of an arbitral award, art. V(1)(a) New York Convention contains a different choice of law clause for the substantive validity of the arbitration agreement than that of art. 178. Art. V(1)(a) New York Convention refers to the law chosen by the parties or, failing such a choice, the law of the country where the award was made. If an arbitration agreement is valid only under the law applicable to the dispute, but not under the other two possible laws referred to in art. 178(2), there are different possible outcomes with regard to the recognition and enforcement of the award. These differences can be resolved by interpreting the term 'the law of the country where the award was made' (art. V(1)(a) New York Convention) to include the conflict rules of that country, so that, for an award rendered in Switzerland, all alternatives under art. 178(2) would be taken into consideration (Basel Commentary-Wenger/Müller, n 24 ad art. 178).

11. The principle of autonomy/separability of the arbitration agreement. Art. 178(3) contains two rules. First, it contains the principle of autonomy/separability, according to which the arbitral tribunal must examine the validity of the arbitration clause separately from the main contract in which the arbitration clause is found. The validity or invalidity of the contract does not necessarily affect the validity or invalidity of the arbitration agreement and vice versa. Thus, a party cannot object to an arbitration clause based on the assertion that the underlying contract is null and void, unless the reason for nullity also affects the arbitration agreement (see ATF 119 II 380 reason 4a). Secondly, art. 178(3) provides that arbitration agreements can be concluded for future disputes and do not have to be re-confirmed once the dispute has arisen.

[Arbitral tribunal: constitution]
Article 179

(1) The arbitrators shall be appointed, dismissed or replaced in accordance with the agreement of the parties.

(2) In the absence of such an agreement, the matter may be referred to the court where the arbitral tribunal has its seat; the court shall apply, by analogy, the provisions of cantonal law concerning the appointment, dismissal or replacement of arbitrators. [*New version of the last part of this sentence entering into force in 2011*: **the court shall apply, by analogy, the provisions of the Federal Code of Civil Procedure concerning the appointment, dismissal or replacement of arbitrators.**]

(3) Where a court is called upon to appoint an arbitrator, it must comply with such request, unless a summary examination shows that no arbitration agreement exists between the parties.

1. Constitution of the arbitral tribunal. Art. 179 applies to the constitution of the arbitral tribunal, i.e. to questions such as the number of arbitrators, the requirements and the procedure for their appointment, dismissal or replacement. The resignation of an arbitrator is not governed by art. 179, but by the arbitral contract between the parties and the arbitrator (see notes 8 and 9). Art. 179(1) leaves the constitution of the arbitral tribunal to the parties. If the parties do not agree or if the constitution fails for other reasons, such as the inability to agree on a sole arbitrator or the chairperson, art. 179(2) offers assistance from the state courts. Furthermore, prevailing legal opinion suggests that the expression 'in the absence of such an agreement' as used in art. 179(2) should be broadly interpreted so that the state court can also be invoked, for example, when the private appointing authority chosen by the parties refuses to make a decision on the appointment of arbitrators, or where the appointing authority no longer exists (Basel Commentary-Peter/Legler, n 20/21 ad art. 179; Berger/Kellerhals, *Schiedsgerichtsbarkeit*, n 754; for the Intercantonal Concordat, see ATF 110 Ia 59 reason 3b). Art. 179(3) provides for the parties' possibility of choosing a Swiss court as appointing authority.

2. Party autonomy. Art. 179(1) establishes the priority of the parties' agreement. The parties can agree on the constitution of the arbitral tribunal either individually or by reference to a set of arbitration rules that normally contain detailed provisions on the tribunal's constitution. If a group of claimants or respondents in multi-party arbitration proceedings cannot agree on the nomination of 'their' arbitrator, some arbitration rules provide for the institution appointing all the arbitrators (see, e.g., art. 8(4) and (5) Swiss Rules, art. 10(2) ICC Rules). If the arbitration rules are silent on this point, it is unclear whether the principle of equal treatment of the parties would require that all arbitrators be appointed by the competent authority (see Berger/Kellerhals, *Schiedsgerichtsbarkeit*, n 773; Basel Commentary-Peter/Legler, n 13 ad art. 179; Kaufmann-Kohler/Rigozzi, *LDIP*, n 330 et seq.). The Federal Supreme Court has, in the past, implicitly denied such a requirement (see ATF, 16 May 1983).

3. State court assistance. For cases where state court assistance is provided (see note 1), art. 179(2) requires the cantonal procedural rules to apply by analogy to the procedure. The Cantons are free to set up their own rules or to declare applicable arts. 12, 22, 23 and 45 of the Intercantonal Concordat (see Introductory Remarks, note 2). When the Federal Code of Civil Procedure (FCCP) enters into force in 2011, the court has to apply, by analogy, the provisions of the FCCP. In referring to an application 'by analogy', art. 179(2) indicates that the particular nature of international arbitration must be observed when applying the cantonal rules or the FCCP. In international arbitration, the competent court is under an obligation to act (Berti-Peter/Legler, n 34 ad art. 179), unless a summary assessment (i.e. prima facie examination) of the case reveals that there is no arbitration agreement between the parties (Obergericht Zürich, 19 November 2004, reason 5). However, the competent court must conduct a full examination of whether the requirements for state court assistance have been met or whether the parties have validly agreed on another mechanism for the constitution of the arbitral tribunal (Obergericht Zürich, 19 November 2004, reason 5). In cases where the defaulting respondent appoints an arbitrator after the claimant has filed a request for state court assistance, Swiss courts will usually give preference to the respondent's choice, but order the respondent to bear the costs for the state proceedings (e.g. Tribunal de première instance Genève, 21 March 2007; Kantonsgericht Wallis, 27 April 2006, reason 2c and 3b; see for an overview Ehle, *Belated Nomination* at 392 et seq.).

4. Competent court. Art. 179(2) vests the authority to appoint the arbitrators in the court at the seat of the arbitration. Because of Switzerland's federal structure, each Canton determines which of its courts has jurisdiction if the seat is located in this Canton. For example, the Obergericht is competent in the Canton of Zurich (§ 239(2) Zurich Code of Civil Procedure) and the Tribunal de première instance in the Canton of Geneva (art. 461B(1)(a) Geneva Code of Civil Procedure). Problems may arise if the seat has not been clearly determined. If the parties have used a clause such as 'arbitration in Switzerland', art. 179 applies, but the identity of the competent court within Switzerland is not clear and the consequences are uncertain. Some courts, tribunals and legal commentators take the view that arbitration proceedings in Switzerland must be ruled out in such cases (e.g. Tribunal de première instance Genève, 18 June 2008, with critical comment by Hirsch at 168-169; ZCC Award, 7 August 2006, paras. 73-75; Basel Commentary-Ehrat/Pfiffner, n 29-32 ad art. 176). In order to uphold the arbitration agreement, three possible solutions should be favoured: art. 2(2) of the Intercantonal Concordat (as of 2011: art. 355(2) FCCP) applies by analogy, with the result that a Swiss court could only constitute the arbitral tribunal if it had jurisdiction in the absence of the arbitration agreement (Lalive/Poudret/Reymond, *L'Arbitrage*, n 9 ad art. 179); or the competent court of the Canton with which the dispute has sufficient connections can constitute the arbitral tribunal (Kaufmann-Kohler/Rigozzi, *LDIP*, n 311); or any competent cantonal court that is so requested can constitute the arbitral tribunal (at least if the respondent refused an invitation by the claimant to specify the Canton in which the seat should be located), thus construing art. 179(3) as vesting this authority in the competent court of any Swiss Canton (e.g. Berger/Kellerhals, *Schiedsgerichtsbarkeit*, n 704; Berti-Peter/Legler, n 3 ad art. 179; Besson, *Arbitration in Switzerland* at 774-775).

5. State court as appointing authority. If the parties agreed that a Swiss court should appoint the arbitrators, art. 179(3) obliges the court to do so. The court's power to examine whether an arbitration agreement exists between the parties is restricted (see note 3; ATF 118 Ia 20 reason 2a). The court should not examine the scope of the arbitration agreement (Basel Commentary-Peter/Legler, n 41 ad art. 179; however, ATF 118 Ia 20 reason 5b upheld a lower court's refusal to appoint an arbitrator where there was no doubt that the arbitration agreement did not cover the alleged claims).

6. Remedies to set aside decisions of the appointing authority. A direct challenge is admissible against court decisions based on art. 179(3) refusing an appointment (see ATF 118 Ia 20 reason 2): until 2011, there are first the cantonal rights of appeal, if any (for instance, no appeal is possible in the canton of Geneva, see ATF 4A_215/2008). As of 2011, there will be no appeal before another cantonal court (see art. 356(2) FCCP). In the last instance, the parties can bring an appeal in civil matters before the Federal Supreme Court (ATF 4A_215/2008 reason 1.1). This also applies to the case of art. 179(2) (see ATF 121 I 81 reason 1; Berti-Peter/Legler, n 33 ad art. 179). On the other hand, court decisions appointing arbitrators are not subject to appeal to the Federal Supreme Court and can only be re-examined on a motion to set aside a subsequent interim award on jurisdiction or to set aside the final award (see ATF 115 II 294 reason 3). The decision of an appointing institutional body cannot directly be challenged (see ATF, 16 May 1983) and can only become the subject of a challenge in setting aside proceedings directed against a subsequent interim award on jurisdiction or against the final award (art. 190(3) and (2)(a); see art. 190, note 4).

7. Repetition of the proceedings in case of a replacement. If an arbitrator is replaced, the PILA does not address the issue of whether procedural steps in which the replaced arbitrator participated remain valid or need to be repeated. In the absence of a specific agreement by the parties or of a provision in institutional rules with respect to this question (see art. 14 Swiss Rules and art. 12(4) ICC Rules), the appropriate solution seems to be to leave the decision to the newly composed arbitral tribunal after it has heard the parties (Berti-Peter/Legler, n 32 ad art. 179; Berti-Wirth, n 19 ad art. 189; Kaufmann-Kohler/Rigozzi, *LDIP*, n 412). In any event, the right to be heard requires that the procedural steps for establishing the facts be repeated if the documentation relating to these steps is inadequate, since the new arbitrator would otherwise have no opportunity to hear and examine the parties' case (Basel Commentary-Wirth, n 24 ad art. 189).

8. The arbitral contract. Under Swiss law, the legal relationship between the arbitrators and the parties is deemed to be contractual in nature. Arbitrators and parties are bound by an arbitral contract, the so-called receptum arbitri, a sui generis contract, with elements of a mandate agreement as per art. 394 et seq. of the Swiss Code of Obligations. However, this is not a pure type of mandate and cannot, for example, be terminated by simple notice at any time. The arbitral contract is normally terminated with the rendering of the arbitral award, unless other specific grounds apply, for instance, a successful challenge of the arbitrator. In the absence of a choice of law, the arbitral contract should be governed by the law of the seat of the arbitral tribunal, as this establishes the closest connection and provides a uniform framework for all arbitrators.

9. Resignation of an arbitrator. The arbitral contract governs the conditions under which an arbitrator can voluntarily resign. Under Swiss law, an arbitrator can only resign for important reasons (see ATF 117 Ia 166 reason 6c). After an arbitrator has resigned, the remaining arbitrators cannot continue the proceedings until a new arbitrator has been appointed, unless the parties explicitly empower them to do so. For the question of repetition of the proceedings, see note 7. If one arbitrator refuses to participate in the deliberations or refuses to vote without sufficient justification and without having formally resigned, the other arbitrators can continue the deliberations and render an award, provided that the refusing arbitrator has the opportunity to participate at all times (see ATF 128 III 234 reason 3b).

Swiss Private International Law Act (Chapter 12), art. 180

[Arbitral tribunal: challenge to an arbitrator]

Article 180

(1) An arbitrator may be challenged:
  (a) if he does not meet the qualifications agreed upon by the parties;
  (b) if there exists a ground for challenge provided by the rules of arbitration agreed upon by the parties;
  (c) if circumstances exist that give rise to justifiable doubts as to his independence.

(2) A party may challenge an arbitrator whom it has appointed, or in whose appointment it participated, only on grounds which come to that party's attention after the appointment. The ground for challenge must be communicated without delay to the arbitral tribunal and the other party.

(3) To the extent that the parties have not made provisions for the challenge procedure, the court at the seat of the arbitral tribunal shall make the final decision.

1. Scope of application and system of the provision. Art. 180(1) comprehensively lists the grounds for challenge. It applies to challenges against all arbitrators (sole arbitrator, chairperson and co-arbitrators), irrespective of whether the appointment was made by the parties, by party-appointed arbitrators, by an arbitration institution or by a court. In formulating the grounds for a challenge, the provision gives priority to party autonomy. It is primarily the responsibility of the parties to establish the grounds for challenge (art. 180(1) (a) and (b)) and the challenge procedure (art. 180(3)) by agreeing individually on these issues, e.g., in the arbitration agreement, by reference to the rules of an arbitration institution or otherwise (e.g. by reference to a national law such as the Intercantonal Concordat or the third part of the FCCP). The only exception to the broad freedom granted to the parties is contained in art. 180(1)(c), namely the requirement of independence of an arbitrator, which the parties cannot waive.

2. Independence. Art. 30(1) of the Swiss Federal Constitution expressly guarantees that all legal disputes will be adjudicated by an independent and impartial court. Both objective independence and subjective impartiality are required, as both concepts are intrinsically linked. The standards that were developed under art. 30(1) Federal Constitution and under art. 6(1) of the European Convention on Human Rights also apply under art. 180(1)(c) (see ATF 4P.208/2004 reason 4.1). However, one must take into account the characteristics of international arbitration (see ATF 4P.4/2007 reason 3.1), for example the fact that contact between arbitrators and counsel is frequent in international arbitration due to the economic and professional background and the private nature of arbitration (see ATF 129 III 445 reason 4.2.2.2). The

von Segesser and Schramm

wording in art. 180(1)(c), 'if circumstances exist that give rise to justifiable doubts as to [the arbitrator's] independence', requires that each case must be considered individually and that an examination must address the question of whether concrete facts objectively justify an assumption of a lack of independence (see ATF 129 III 445 reason 4.2.2.2; ATF 118 II 359 reason 3c). Circumstances must exist that objectively corroborate mistrust. The parties' subjective perception is not relevant; the perception of a reasonable observer is decisive. However, since the standard is based on objective circumstances creating mistrust, it is not necessary for the arbitrator to actually be biased, only to be objectively and possibly perceived as such (see ATF 4P.4/2007 reason 3.1; ATF 117 Ia 182 reason 3b). The arbitrator must remain independent throughout the arbitration proceedings. The requirement of independence also applies to experts appointed by the tribunal (see ATF 126 III 249 reason 3c). The Federal Supreme Court has once held that stricter standards apply to the chairperson and the sole arbitrator than to co-arbitrators (see ATF, 30 June 1994, reason 4; left open in ATF 4P.188/2001 reason 2b; see Basel Commentary-Peter/Besson, n 14 ad art. 180; Kaufmann-Kohler/Rigozzi, *LDIP*, n 362/3). Nowadays, in international arbitrations, such a differentiation is considered irrelevant.

3. Independence: significant factors constituting lack of independence. The following significant factors, drawn from legal commentators and case law, illustrate some cases in which an arbitrator is not considered to be independent or impartial: a relationship of subordination with a party (e.g. executive position with one of the parties, an official in a government/administration which is a party, a member of the law firm representing a party); a significant economic affiliation (e.g. a member of the board of a company being in the same group as one of the parties. Mandates for a party in the past are only deemed to constitute a substantial economic affiliation if economic ties are ongoing, because of, e.g., the promise or concrete prospect of additional remuneration or subsequent mandates, see ATF 4P.188/2001 reason 2d); ongoing professional connections (e.g. if an arbitrator or one of his partners in a law firm is a regular advisor to a party); the representation of one party's counterparty in another matter that is still ongoing or that ended recently (ATF 135 I 14 reason 4.3); strong positive or negative emotional ties between the arbitrator and one party or its counsel (see ATF 1P.99/2000 reason 3); publication of remarks on a prior award by a subsequently designated arbitrator if the remarks show that he has already formed an opinion on the concrete case and is unlikely to change his mind (see ATF 133 I 89 reason 3.3). The IBA Guidelines on Conflicts of Interest in International Arbitration may provide further guidance as they reflect an internationally recognised practice (see ATF 4A_506/2007 reason 3.3.2.2).

4. Independence: insufficient circumstances. According to the Federal Supreme Court, the following circumstances are not sufficient to raise justifiable doubts regarding the arbitrator's independence or impartiality:

where an arbitrator and a counsel have been or are simultaneously working together as arbitrators in another arbitration (see ATF 4P.105/2006 reason 4; ATF 129 III 445 reason 4.2.2.2); where an arbitrator and a counsel are simultaneously and jointly representing a third party in criminal proceedings completely unrelated to the arbitration (ATF 4A_586/2008 reason 3.2); where an arbitrator and a counsel are members of the same professional or social association (see ATF 4A_506/2007 reason 3.3.2.2); where the arbitrator gives both parties his preliminary view on the case (see ATF 4P.196/2003 reason 3.2.1); where the arbitrator makes legal mistakes, as long as these are not flagrant or repeated (see ATF 4P.129/2002 reason 5.2); where a party has the arbitrator shadowed (see ATF 4P.208/2004 reason 4); or where a party challenges the scale of the arbitrator's fees with the consequence that they are then significantly reduced (see ATF 4P.263/2002 reason 5). The Federal Supreme Court has, furthermore, held that the Court of Arbitration for Sport is independent even in cases where the International Olympic Committee is a party (see ATF 129 III 445 reason 3.3). In a case where the arbitral tribunal stigmatised, in a partial award, the behaviour of one of the parties in a personalised and metaphoric way, the Federal Supreme Court rejected doubts made regarding the tribunal's impartiality. It held that despite the inappropriate language in the partial award, the conduct of the arbitral proceedings showed that the arbitrators would continue the proceedings properly and with care (see ATF 4P.4/2007 reason 3.3).

5. Duty to disclose. The arbitral contract with the parties (see art. 179, note 8) imposes on arbitrators the duty to disclose to the arbitral tribunal and the parties, without delay, any circumstances that could justify a challenge (see ATF 111 Ia 72 reason 2c). However, non-disclosure in and of itself does not provide grounds for a challenge; the undisclosed facts themselves must justify the challenge (see ATF 4P.188/2001 reason 2f). If the arbitrator has disclosed circumstances that could justify a challenge and the concerned party does not challenge the arbitrator within reasonable time, it waives this right as it is precluded from challenging the arbitrator at a later stage (see note 8).

6. Arbitrator appointed by a party. Art. 180(2) deals with situations where a party challenges an arbitrator whom it has appointed or in whose appointment it has participated. Because of the principle of 'venire contra factum proprium', the party may base its challenge only on grounds which it became aware of after the appointment. The party has the duty to inform the arbitral tribunal and the other party of the ground for challenge without delay (see note 8).

7. Challenge procedure. According to art. 180(3), the challenge procedure is to be derived directly or indirectly from the parties' agreement, depending on whether they have reached an individual agreement or chosen to submit the arbitral proceedings to institutional arbitration rules. The state court at the seat of the arbitration only has jurisdiction to decide on the challenge if and insofar as the parties have not agreed on the procedure. The competent courts are the Obergericht in the Canton of Zurich (§ 239(2) Zurich Code of Civil Procedure) and the Tribunal de première instance in the Canton of Geneva (art. 461B(1)(b) Geneva Code of Civil Procedure). The state court must apply the rules and grounds for challenge provided for by art. 180 (Basel Commentary-Peter/Besson, n 32 ad art. 180). If the tribunal as a whole is challenged and the challenge is clearly inadmissible or unfounded, the arbitral tribunal itself is competent to reject the challenge (see ATF 129 III 445 reason 4.2.2). A challenge procedure does not per se hinder the continuation of the arbitration proceedings (see ATF 128 III 234 reason 3b/bb).

8. Duty to challenge. A party must challenge the arbitrator as soon as it becomes aware of grounds for challenge, otherwise it is precluded from invoking such grounds at a later stage of the proceedings or in a motion to set aside the award under art. 190(2)(a). There is some debate as to whether information that is easily available (e.g. on the internet) should be considered as having been available to the parties. The Federal Supreme Court held that a party must verify the arbitrators' independence when the arbitral tribunal is constituted and that a party is precluded from basing its claim on information that was easily available at that time (see ATF 4A_506/2007 reason 3.2; see also the obiter dicta in ATF 4P.105/2006 reason 4, ATF 4P.188/2001 reason 2c). This is true even if the arbitrator has violated his duty to disclose this information. The more advanced the arbitral proceedings, the stricter the requirements that must be applied to a party's duty to challenge the arbitrator; a challenge may have to be made on grounds of which the party has not yet gained full and certain knowledge (see ATF 126 III 249 reason 3c with further references).

9. Appeal against a challenge decision. Decisions by an arbitration institution on the challenge to an arbitrator cannot be appealed directly and can only be challenged indirectly by a motion to set aside the arbitral award under art. 190(2)(a) (see ATF 128 III 330 reason 2.2; ATF 118 II 359 reason 3b). If a state court decides on the challenge, art. 180(3) explicitly provides that the decision is final. This not only excludes any direct appeal but also any appeal against the arbitral award on these grounds (see ATF 128 III 330 reason 2.2; this decision is criticised, e.g., by Poudret, *Tribunal fédéral*, at 698 with further references).

[Lis pendens]
Article 181

The arbitral proceedings are pending as soon as one of the parties submits a claim to the arbitrator or arbitrators designated in the arbitration agreement, or, in the absence of any such designation in the arbitration agreement, as soon as one of the parties initiates the procedure for the constitution of the arbitral tribunal.

1. Purpose of the provision. Art. 181 determines the point in time at which the arbitration proceedings become pending. The main procedural effect of pendency is to render other proceedings in the same matter inadmissible, depending on the procedural law applied by the court or arbitral tribunal seized of the matter (for Switzerland, see note 4). Other possible procedural effects of the pendency, depending on the rules applicable under arts. 182 and 183, include restrictions on amending the claim and on adding or substituting parties, an obligation to continue the proceedings or a transfer to the arbitral tribunal of the authority to issue interim measures. With respect to the substance of the dispute, possible effects of the pendency of the proceedings are the interruption of the running of the statute of limitations and the compliance with any time limits for bringing actions, depending on the law applicable under art. 187 (see note 5).

2. Time of lis pendens. In the rare event that the parties have already designated the arbitrator(s) in their arbitration agreement, the proceedings are deemed pending as soon as the claimant files its request with all of the designated arbitrators. If the parties have agreed on institutional arbitration without designating the arbitrator(s), lis pendens occurs once the claimant takes the first step that is necessary under the chosen arbitration rules for the constitution of the arbitral tribunal (art. 179(1)). If the parties have agreed on ad hoc arbitration without designating the arbitrator(s), the proceedings are deemed pending as soon as one party requests the constitution of the arbitral tribunal in accordance with the parties' agreement (for example by sending the other party a request for arbitration, including the appointment of its arbitrator or a proposal for a sole arbitrator, see ATF 4P.129/2002 reason 3.3) or, in the absence of such an agreement, as soon as one party requests the court to constitute an arbitral tribunal under art. 179(2).

3. Contents of the request for arbitration. Art. 181 does not stipulate what requirements the request for arbitration must meet in order to cause lis pendens. This issue is primarily governed by the parties' agreement or by the arbitration rules they chose. In the absence of any such agreement or rules, a request that identifies the subject of the party's claims is considered sufficient to trigger lis pendens (Lalive/Poudret/Reymond, *L'Arbitrage*, n 2 and 3 ad art. 181; see also Basel Commentary-Vogt, n 9 ad art. 181). With regard to the requirements an application must meet in order to be effective under the applicable substantive law, see note 5.

4. Procedural effects of pendency in Switzerland. Art. 181 does not address the effects of pendency before an arbitral tribunal with its seat in Switzerland on subsequent proceedings before a state court or another arbitral tribunal. According to an obiter dictum of the Federal Supreme Court, and according to the majority of legal commentators, the rules applicable to pendency before state courts must be applied by analogy (see ATF 121 III 495 reason 6c; Basel Commentary-Wenger/Schott, n 16 ad art. 186; Berger/Kellerhals, *Schiedsgerichtsbarkeit*, n 638, 948/949, 952/953). A Swiss state court thus has to stay the proceedings until the arbitral tribunal first seized of the dispute has decided on its jurisdiction, and it must renounce its jurisdiction if the arbitral tribunal ultimately asserts jurisdiction (see Basel Commentary-Berti, n 9-10 ad art. 7; Berger/Kellerhals, *Schiedsgerichtsbarkeit*, n 638, 949, 952). Until recently, this also applied to arbitral tribunals with their seat in Switzerland. However, with the entry into force of art. 186(1bis) on 1 March 2007, arbitral tribunals with their seat in Switzerland may continue proceedings even if the same dispute is pending before another arbitral tribunal (see art. 186, note 5). Although pendency before an arbitral tribunal with its seat in Switzerland might not preclude subsequent proceedings before a foreign state court, recognition and enforcement of the foreign state court's decision in Switzerland may be refused (see Liatowitsch/Bernet in *Zivilprozess*, at 161-162). For the converse situation, i.e. the effects of pendency before a state court for arbitral tribunals with their seat in Switzerland, see art. 186, note 5.

5. Substantive effects of pendency under Swiss law. As art. 181 does not contain a conflict of laws rule, the substantive law applicable under art. 187 determines whether bringing a claim before an arbitral tribunal with its seat in Switzerland interrupts the running of the statute of limitations, or is in compliance with a given deadline. Under Swiss substantive law, the standard referred to in note 3 would, in most instances, not be sufficient to interrupt the running of the statute of limitations, since the application for commencing arbitration proceedings would have to incorporate a specific statement of claim noting the amounts claimed (see Basel Commentary-Vogt, n 18 ad art. 181). If a claim is brought before an arbitral tribunal that lacks jurisdiction and if the period of limitation has in the meantime expired, the claimant can still file the claim with the competent court or arbitral tribunal within sixty days of the arbitral tribunal declining jurisdiction (art. 139 Swiss Code of Obligations). Where arbitration proceedings serve a validation purpose, such as validating a freezing order rendered under the Swiss Debt Enforcement and Bankruptcy Law, specific requirements and deadlines must be observed.

[Procedure: principle]

Article 182

(1) The parties may, directly or by reference to existing rules of arbitration, determine the arbitral procedure; they may also submit the arbitral procedure to a procedural law of their choice.

(2) If the parties have not determined the procedure, it shall, to the extent necessary, be determined by the arbitral tribunal, either directly or by reference to a statute or to existing rules of arbitration.

(3) Regardless of the procedure chosen, the arbitral tribunal shall ensure equal treatment of the parties and their right to be heard in adversarial proceedings.

1. Scope of application. Art. 182 addresses procedural rules, which must be clearly distinguished from the general provisions of the law governing the arbitration (lex arbitri). If a procedural issue arises before an arbitral tribunal seated in Switzerland, art. 182 applies as part of the lex arbitri and determines the procedural rule to be applied. 'Arbitral procedure' under art. 182 encompasses all procedural aspects, such as exchanges of memoranda, time limits, communication between the arbitral tribunal and the parties, the language of the proceedings, the costs and advances on costs (see also note 2 and art. 189, note 8), the involvement of third parties (subject to jurisdiction), interim measures (see art. 183), the taking of evidence (see also art. 184), the production of documents, the confidentiality of the proceedings, the staying of the proceedings (see ATF 133 III 139 reason 6), the admissibility of counterclaims and set-offs (art. 186, note 3) and other issues.

2. Priority of party autonomy. Art. 182(1) stipulates the priority of party autonomy. The parties may stipulate how the arbitration shall be conducted according to their needs and wishes. They can either agree on individual rules tailored to their specific case, on institutional arbitration rules, on independent arbitration rules (e.g. UNCITRAL Arbitration Rules) or on national procedural law. There is, however, some controversy regarding whether the chosen national procedural law only applies to procedural questions in a strict sense, excluding, for example, the question of costs (see ATF 4P.280/2005 reason 2.2.1). Neither art. 182(1) nor the New York Convention prescribe a particular form for a procedural agreement, which can become effective tacitly or implicitly. While it may be difficult to establish with certainty an implicit agreement, the tribunal should, in any case, consider in its own ruling any indications of the parties' tacit understanding (Basel Commentary-Schneider, n 5 ad art. 182). Usually, the agreement on the procedure reflects the parties' intent that it should also bind the arbitral tribunal. If the chosen institutional rules change before the arbitration starts and if the old version does not cover the effects of such a change, the new version of the rules will only become applicable if tacitly or implicitly agreed upon by the parties. Thus, the parties' intent has to be established. In this respect it can be assumed that parties that agree to arbitration under the rules of an association they both belong to (such as FIFA), agree to be bound by the rules in force at the time the arbitration starts, including possible amendments (see ATF 4P.253/2003 reason 5.4). The violation of procedural rules agreed upon by the parties does not per se constitute a reason to set aside the award (see art. 190, note 14), but can be pleaded as a defence in recognition and enforcement proceedings pursuant to art. V(1)(d) New York Convention.

3. Discretion of the arbitral tribunal. The arbitral tribunal's authority to determine the procedure is subsidiary to the parties' agreement. According to art. 182(2), the arbitral tribunal can either establish its own rules, or apply a set of arbitration rules or of procedural law, or a combination thereof. With regard to the calculation of time limits, the arbitral tribunal can refer to the European Convention on the Calculation of Time-Limits of 16 May 1972, which has been ratified by Switzerland and which, according to its art. 1(1)(b), applies to the calculation of time limits 'by an arbitral body, where such body has not determined the method of calculating the time-limit'. The arbitral tribunal is not under any obligation to follow any national procedural laws. It can set the procedural rules either in advance or once an individual matter arises. Although formal deliberations are not necessary, decisions on procedural issues, with the exception of those which concern solely the practical course of the proceedings and do not have any impact on the rights of the parties, must be taken with the participation of all the members of the tribunal (Basel Commentary-Schneider, n 43 ad art. 182). The arbitral tribunal's discretion is limited in two main respects: first, the arbitral tribunal must guarantee the equal treatment of the parties, and second, it must respect the parties' right to be heard in an adversarial procedure (art. 182(3); see note 5 et seq.). Furthermore, the arbitral tribunal must respect the requirements set out by the New York Convention, which limit, for example, the arbitral tribunal's discretion to accept counterclaims that do not fall under the arbitration agreement (see art. 186, note 3).

4. Procedural orders by the arbitral tribunal. If the arbitral tribunal decides on a procedural question, it often issues a procedural order. To the extent that such a decision does not concern questions of jurisdiction, art. 188 et seq. do not apply in principle (but see art. 189, note 1) and there is no direct appeal against the decision. The arbitral tribunal can reverse procedural orders, as they do not constitute res judicata (Basel Commentary-Schneider, n 41 et seq. ad art. 182).

5. Procedural public policy. Art. 182(3) is mandatory in nature and forms a central part of procedural public policy in Switzerland. It lays down the principles of equal treatment of the parties and the right to be heard in adversarial proceedings. The arbitral tribunal must guarantee these principles at all times. In cases of violation, the arbitral award can be set aside under art. 190(2)(d), provided that the aggrieved party raised a sufficiently specific objection during the arbitration proceedings (see, e.g., ATF 4P.129/2002 reason 7.1 with further references). In addition, recognition and enforcement of the award abroad can be refused pursuant to art. V(1)(b) and (2)(b) New York Convention.

6. Equal treatment of the parties. The arbitral tribunal must determine and conduct the proceedings in a way which grants the parties the same opportunity to present their case (see, e.g., ATF 4P.117/2004 reason 2.1). It must treat the parties equally in procedural situations which are comparable (see ATF 4P.207/2002 reason 3), for example regarding time limits or the examination of witnesses. The question of whether the factual situations are similar or dissimilar requires careful examination (see ATF 4P.207/2002 reason 3 regarding the parties' requests to produce documents). The arbitral tribunal must not grant to one party something that it has refused the other and vice versa (Berti-Schneider, n 65 ad art. 182). A party may not argue a violation of equal treatment when, in reality, it is merely criticising the weighing of evidence by the arbitral tribunal (see ATF 4P.140/2004 reason 2.1). It does not violate the equal treatment of the parties if the arbitral tribunal accepts a belated submission by one party if this does not violate the terms of reference and if the arbitral tribunal did not reject a belated submission by the other party (see ATF 4A_244/2007 reason 6.3; ATF 134 III 186 unpublished reason 7.1). The situation might be different if the submissions had to be filed simultaneously and the late filing allowed one party to review the other party's submission.

7. Right to be heard. The right to be heard broadly corresponds with the right guaranteed by art. 29(2) of the Swiss Federal Constitution. It is not congruent with the procedural guarantees under art. 6(1) ECHR, which is not directly applicable in voluntary arbitrations (see ATF 4P.105/2006 reason 7.3). The right to be heard under art. 182(3) encompasses the parties' right to examine the files that will constitute the basis of the arbitral award, to present legal arguments, to express their opinion on any facts that are essential for the decision, to participate in the hearings personally or via a representative, to offer relevant evidence and to comment on the results of the taking of evidence (see ATF 4P.235/2001 reason 3e; ATF 127 III 576 reason 2c). The right to be heard also encompasses the arbitral tribunal's obligation to examine and to address the relevant problems: The right to be heard is violated if the arbitral tribunal does not take into consideration a party's arguments that are relevant for the outcome of the decision, i.e. if the award is completely silent on these arguments and does not even implicitly address them (see ATF 133 III 235 reason 5.2). However, the right to be heard does not impose on the arbitral tribunal the duty to discuss all arguments invoked by the parties. For example, the arbitral tribunal may implicitly reject arguments that are objectively irrelevant (see ATF 133 III 235 reason 5.2). If a mistake by the arbitral tribunal (for example overlooking or misunderstanding part of the file) leads to a wrong decision, the right to be heard is violated if the mistake makes it impossible for a party to present and prove its case regarding this specific issue and if the party is thus in the same position as it would have been in if it had not been heard at all (see ATF 127 III 576 reason 2d-f). For the right to be heard related to the taking of evidence, see art. 184, note 4.

8. Right to be heard: counter-examples. The right to be heard does not include a party's right to make an oral statement (see ATF 4A_160/2007 reason 4.1; ATF 117 II 346 reason 1b/aa, but see Basel Commentary-Schneider, n 90 ad art. 182), to a decision which contains the reasons for the decision (see ATF 128 III 234 reason 4b; under the Federal Supreme Court Act (FSCA) ATF 134 III 186 reason 6.1; see art. 189, note 6), or to a substantively correct decision (see ATF 127 III 576 reason 2d). The right to be heard does not oblige the arbitral tribunal to explicitly deal in its award with a party's differing view (see ATF 4P.140/2004 reason 2.2.4) or to address facts and arguments that the parties did not previously duly submit (see ATF 4P.26/2005 reason 3.3). The arbitral tribunal does not have to consult the parties regarding its legal evaluation of the facts unless the evaluation is surprising in the sense that the parties did not invoke the legal grounds on which the arbitral tribunal based its decision, and cannot reasonably have been expected to foresee them (see ATF 4A_400/2008 reason 3; ATF 130 III 35 reason 5 – both decisions set aside the award). The Federal Supreme Court exercises restraint in examining whether a legal evaluation was surprising (see, e.g., ATF 4P.134/2006 reason 6 with further references). The arbitral tribunal neither has to draw the parties' attention to the facts that it considers decisive for its decision, nor has to inform a party that it considers the evidence produced by this party insufficient for proving a relevant fact (see ATF 4A_450/2007 reason 4.2.2). The right to be heard does not preclude default proceedings, provided that the defaulting party had an opportunity to present its case, was duly notified of the consequences of the default and did not present a valid excuse for its default (see Berger/Kellerhals, *Schiedsgerichtsbarkeit*, n 1067; Kaufmann-Kohler/Rigozzi, *LDIP*, n 483/4). The right to be heard is, in principle, not affected by a decision to stay or not to stay the proceedings (see ATF 133 III 139 reason 6.1). In summary, the right to be heard is not violated if it has been established that the procedural conditions allowed the parties to present their arguments and that the arbitral tribunal took note of them (see ATF 4P.318/2001 reason 2.1).

9. Adversarial proceedings. Key requirements for adversary proceedings are that every party must have the right to comment on its opponent's submissions, to examine and evaluate the opponent's evidence and to offer evidence in rebuttal (see ATF 130 III 35 reason 5). This right is not unlimited and does not include the right to rebut ad infinitum the other party's arguments (see ATF 4P.104/2004 reason 5.3.1). The arbitral tribunal may request the parties to file post-hearing briefs simultaneously if the briefs are only meant to include the parties' evaluation of the results of the hearing and legal aspects of the case discussed during the proceedings without new allegations or evidence (see ATF 4P.104/2004 reason 5.3.1). According to legal commentators, the principle of adversarial proceedings not only includes a right, but also leads to the parties' obligation, to substantiate their counter-submissions and contestations of factual assertions (Berti-Schneider, n 61 ad art. 182).

[Procedure: provisional and protective measures]

Article 183

(1) Unless the parties have agreed otherwise, the arbitral tribunal may, at the request of one party, order provisional or protective measures.

(2) If the party concerned does not voluntarily comply with these measures, the arbitral tribunal may request the assistance of the state court; the court shall apply its own law.

(3) The arbitral tribunal or the state court may make the granting of provisional or protective measures conditional upon the provision of appropriate security.

1. Authority of the arbitral tribunal. The lex arbitri decides whether the arbitral tribunal is competent to issue provisional and protective measures. Art. 183 vests arbitral tribunals to which chapter 12 PILA applies (see art. 176, note 1 et seq.) with the authority to grant such measures, provided that the parties have not previously agreed on procedural rules which would exclude such authority. The arbitral tribunal's competence is not exclusive (see note 2). As art. 183 does not give the arbitral tribunal the power to enforce its orders, it provides for collaboration with the Swiss courts.

2. Authority of the state courts. Before the arbitral tribunal is constituted, the state courts have exclusive authority to order interim relief. Once the arbitral tribunal has been constituted, and unless there is an agreement by the parties to the contrary, the majority view in Switzerland is that both the arbitral tribunal and the state courts are competent to issue provisional and protective measures (Berti-Berti, n 5 ad art. 183). A request for interim relief submitted to a state court does not jeopardise the jurisdiction of the arbitral tribunal. Unlike an arbitral tribunal's order, the order of a state court can be directly enforced and may therefore be more effective, especially if enforcement abroad is necessary (see note 7). Although orders for provisional and protective measures do not have the effect of lis pendens or res judicata, arbitral tribunals and state courts will not order the requested interim relief for reasons of efficiency and procedural economy if the same request is already pending before another court or tribunal or if the other court or tribunal has already granted or denied the interim relief, unless a change in circumstances and/or facts justifies doing so (see Berger/Kellerhals, *Schiedsgerichtsbarkeit*, n 1170; Kaufmann-Kohler/Rigozzi, *LDIP*, n 571 et seq.).

3. Requirements for an order of provisional and protective measures. Art. 183 does not contain any requirements for interim relief. Such requirements are subject to art. 182, which leaves the parties free to agree on them. In the absence of any such agreement, the arbitral tribunal may exercise broad discretion in determining these requirements (art. 182(2)). According to international best practice, the following requirements must usually be met (see, e.g., Kaufmann-Kohler/Rigozzi, *LDIP*, n 582 et seq.): prima facie jurisdiction of the arbitral tribunal; plausible proof that without the interim relief, substantial harm may be caused which cannot be adequately compensated by damages; plausible proof that such possible harm would substantially outweigh the harm the interim measure may cause the other party against whom the order is directed; a reasonable possibility that the requesting party will succeed on the merits; and provision of a security by the requesting party, if so ordered by the arbitral tribunal (see note 8). While many national laws require urgency for interim measures issued by state courts, urgency is, in general, not required in international arbitration (see, e.g., art. 17A of the revised UNCITRAL Model Law on International Commercial Arbitration; but see note 4). For orders to preserve evidence, the above requirements may not be relevant. If a Swiss court is requested to grant interim relief, it applies its cantonal code of civil procedure (as of 2011: the Federal Code of Civil Procedure, FCCP). Cantonal procedural law normally requires the applicant to make a plausible case that it is in imminent danger of suffering harm that would be difficult to remedy, and that the main claim is well founded on a prima facie basis. This is in line with the requirements of art. 261(1) FCCP.

4. Ex parte orders. If urgency so demands, the arbitral tribunal may grant interim relief ex parte, i.e. upon request by one party and without hearing the other party. Because of art. 182(3), the arbitral tribunal must grant the other party the right to be heard immediately thereafter, and must lift or modify the order where necessary (Basel Commentary-Berti, n 12 ad art. 183; Berger/Kellerhals, *Schiedsgerichtsbarkeit*, n 1153; Kaufmann-Kohler/Rigozzi, *LDIP*, n 584).

5. Subject matter of the order. It is subject to controversy whether the determination of the substance of the interim relief by the arbitral tribunal is governed by art. 182, i.e. subject to the parties' agreement or to the rules set by the arbitral tribunal, whether the arbitral tribunal must apply the law applicable to the main claim (art. 187), or whether it can choose another law with the aim of enhancing the enforcement of the interim measure (see Kaufmann-Kohler/Rigozzi, *LDIP*, n 579; Poudret/Besson, *Comparative Law*, n 624). Possible orders may, for example, incorporate measures which address the parties' behaviour during the proceedings, such as anti-suit injunctions, orders to continue with a contractual performance, orders which prohibit the drawing of a bank guarantee, orders that prohibit behaviour likely to cause personal injury or orders for security for costs (see ICC case no. 12542/EC, 19 December 2003; Ad hoc Arbitration, 27 November 2002). Orders may also have the purpose of securing the enforcement of an award, such as freezing orders, orders to deposit goods that are in the parties' custody or to provide a bank guarantee. As a rule, only state courts can issue orders directed against third parties, e.g., orders for the seizure of assets which are in the third party's custody and which are under dispute in the arbitral proceedings. The prevailing view in Switzerland is that the arbitral tribunal does not have the competence to combine its orders with constraints or punitive sanctions (see Berger/Kellerhals, *Schiedsgerichtsbarkeit*, n 1156; Berti-Berti, n 11 ad art. 183; Kaufmann-Kohler/Rigozzi, *LDIP*, n 587).

6. Enforcement of interim measures in Switzerland. Parties often comply voluntarily with orders for interim relief issued by arbitral tribunals. Where they do not comply, a Swiss court may enforce the order, provided that the arbitral tribunal so requests, and provided that a prima facie examination shows that a valid arbitration agreement exists and that the arbitral tribunal was validly constituted (Basel Commentary-Berti, n 18 ad art. 183; more liberal apparently Kaufmann-Kohler/Rigozzi, *LDIP*, n 594). Whether the parties themselves may also request the enforcement by the state court, or whether the clear wording of art. 183(2) excludes this possibility is a matter of controversy (see Basel Commentary-Berti, n 16 ad art. 183; Berger/Kellerhals, *Schiedsgerichtsbarkeit*, n 1160). The Bezirksgericht in the Canton of Zurich is competent for ordering the enforcement of interim measures rendered by an arbitral tribunal (§ 239(1) Zurich Code of Civil Procedure), as are the ordinary courts in the Canton of Geneva (art. 461E Geneva Code of Civil Procedure), i.e. in most cases, the Tribunal de première instance (art. 27 Loi sur l'organisation judiciaire). The enforcement judge may not examine the substance of the order except in terms of its public policy aspects (Berti-Berti, n 18 ad art. 183). If the measure that the arbitral tribunal has ordered is foreign to the cantonal code of civil procedure (as of 2011: the Federal Code of Civil Procedure), the state court must transform it into an order of its own procedural law that reflects, as closely as possible, the purpose of the original order (Berger/Kellerhals, *Schiedsgerichtsbarkeit*, n 1164; Kaufmann-Kohler/Rigozzi, *LDIP*, n 594).

7. Enforcement of interim measures abroad. If the interim measure rendered by an arbitral tribunal must be enforced abroad, direct enforcement under the New York Convention is problematic. The revised art. 17 of the UNCITRAL Model Law and its adoption into the body of national laws may improve the chances of successful international enforcements. Alternatively, if enforcement of the order abroad is likely to be an issue, the party concerned should request the state court to order an interim measure and have it enforced abroad, for example under the Lugano Convention which provides for the possibility of enforcing interim measures, provided that they have not been ordered ex parte (art. 25 et seq. Lugano Convention; see Berger/Kellerhals, *Schiedsgerichtsbarkeit*, n 1188). Regarding orders issued by the state court under art. 183(2), the prevailing view is that such orders do not fall within the scope of the Lugano Convention (e.g. Poudret/Besson, *Comparative Law*, n 641; but see Kaufmann-Kohler/Rigozzi, *LDIP*, n 592 FN 261).

8. Appropriate security. The arbitral tribunal or the state court may require the applicant to provide security intended to facilitate the enforcement of a possible claim for damages if the interim measure later turns out to be unjustified. The amount of security ordered should be determined in light of the aforementioned purpose. If the interim measure turns out to be unjustified and if the other party has suffered damages, the arbitral tribunal is presumed to have jurisdiction to adjudicate the claim for damages (ICC case no. 12363/ACS, 23 December 2003).

9. Setting aside proceedings. Setting aside proceedings before the Swiss Federal Supreme Court against an interim measure ordered by an arbitral tribunal are inadmissible, regardless of whether the arbitral tribunal orders it in the form of a procedural order or of an award (Berger/Kellerhals, *Schiedsgerichtsbarkeit*, n 1539; Poudret, *Tribunal fédéral*, at 681; Kaufmann-Kohler/Rigozzi,

LDIP, n 721; for a different view see Berger/Kellerhals, *Schiedsgerichtsbarkeit*, n 1540 if the arbitral tribunal wrongly declines or accepts its competence to order interim measures). An appeal in civil matters to the Federal Supreme Court is admissible, in last instance, against the decision of a state court under art. 183(2) (Poudret, *Tribunal fédéral*, at 682). However, the Federal Supreme Court will only examine the violation of constitutional rights (art. 98 FSCA).

[Procedure: taking of evidence]

Article 184

(1) The arbitral tribunal shall itself conduct the taking of evidence.

(2) If the assistance of state authorities is necessary for the taking of evidence, the arbitral tribunal, or a party with the consent of the arbitral tribunal, may request the assistance of the state court at the seat of the arbitral tribunal; the court shall apply its own law.

1. General principle and the subject matter of taking evidence. Based on art. 184(1), the arbitral tribunal has control over the evidentiary proceedings and has broad discretion within the framework constituted by the applicable procedural rules (see note 2 et seq.). The subject matter of evidentiary proceedings is essentially derived from the parties' submissions and requires their substantiated factual allegations and contestations (see ATF, 17 August 1994, reason 3c). The burden of proof is considered a question of substantive law and is thus subject to the law applicable under art. 187 if the parties have not agreed otherwise (Basel Commentary-Schneider, n 11 ad art. 184; Berger/Kellerhals, *Schiedsgerichtsbarkeit*, n 1203 with further references). In most cases, each party shall bear the burden of proof for the facts on which it is basing its case (actori incumbit probatio). The arbitral tribunal must take evidence itself and may not delegate this task to a third person or to individual members of the arbitral tribunal, unless the parties have so agreed.

2. Applicable procedural rules. The procedure of taking evidence is subject to art. 182 (see art. 182, note 2 et seq.). Procedural issues that fall under art. 182 include, for example, the admissibility of evidence, the production of documents, the required form and time limits for offers to introduce evidence, the appointment of experts and the question of written witness statements and oral examination of the witnesses. In international arbitrations, the parties frequently come from different legal systems and traditions regarding the taking of evidence (see, e.g., for the wide differences regarding the concepts of confidentiality and privilege with respect to document production, Heitzmann, *Confidentiality* at 207 et seq.). It is therefore important either that they agree on procedural rules for the evidentiary part of the proceedings or that the arbitral tribunal, after consultation with the parties, issue procedural directions. This can be achieved by reference to institutional rules or to the IBA Rules on the Taking of Evidence in International Commercial Arbitration.

As a rule, international arbitral tribunals in Switzerland do not follow any standard form of evidentiary proceedings, but tend to adopt a broad range of different approaches, depending, inter alia, on the nature of the dispute, the familiarity of the parties and their representatives with procedural issues and the composition of the tribunal (see Roney/Müller in *Handbook*, at 60).

3. Methods of presenting evidence. Evidence can be presented via documents, through the testimony of witnesses of fact (written or oral), via opinions of expert witnesses (written or oral) and by means of inspecting the objects in dispute. The arbitral tribunal has the authority to order the parties to produce documents, unless the parties have agreed otherwise. Where a party refuses to produce documents without justified cause, the arbitral tribunal may infer that such document would be adverse to the interests of that party or it may seek the assistance of a court in order to enforce its order (Basel Commentary-Schneider, n 21 ad art. 184; for the latter possibility see note 5). Third persons and parties can appear as witnesses, and it is up to the tribunal to evaluate the evidentiary weight of their testimony. It is admissible for the parties' counsel to discuss with a witness his testimony prior to his examination, provided that the counsel does not influence the content of the witness's testimony (Basel Commentary-Schneider, n 25 ad art. 184). The examination of witnesses can either follow the Anglo-American pattern, with direct examination, cross-examination and re-examination, or the continental European pattern with an examination by the tribunal, or, alternatively, it can embody a hybrid form of both patterns. Experts can be appointed either by the parties or the tribunal. The Federal Supreme Court has ruled that under certain conditions an arbitral tribunal must appoint an expert (see note 4). The arbitral tribunal may order the inspection of the item that is the object of the dispute (Basel Commentary-Schneider, n 48 ad art. 184).

4. Procedural guarantees. When taking evidence, the arbitral tribunal must respect the parties' right to be treated equally and to be heard in adversarial proceedings (art. 182(3), see art. 182, note 6 et seq.). With regard to the taking of evidence, the right to be heard in adversarial proceedings encompasses the parties' right to offer relevant evidence, to participate in the evidentiary proceedings, to examine and challenge evidence adduced by the adverse party, to present rebuttal evidence of their own and to comment on the results of the taking of evidence, but not the right to comment on the results of the arbitral tribunal's evaluation of the evidence (see, e.g., ATF 130 III 35 reason 5; ATF 4P.114/2003 reason 2.2; ATF 4P.235/2001 reason 3e). The right to be heard includes the right to an opinion by a tribunal-appointed expert if one party makes a timely and formally valid request and advances the costs, provided that the expert opinion is capable of proving the facts and appears necessary because the arbitral tribunal does not have sufficient (technical) knowledge to solve the relevant questions (ATF 4A_2/2007 reason 3; ATF 129 III 727 unpublished reason 4.2). The right to be heard in adversarial proceedings has limitations; it is not violated if a motion to take evidence is dismissed because the fact has already been proven or if the arbitral tribunal has already concluded that the piece of evidence in question would not lead to the tribunal changing its mind (so-called anticipated evaluation of the evidence; see ATF 4A_220/2007 reason 8.1; ATF 4P.23/2006 reason 3.1; see also art. 190, note 14). The right to be heard is also not violated if the taking of evidence (and the legal evaluation thereof) is restricted to issues which are relevant for the decision, if motions to take evidence are refused because they do not follow the applicable formal rules, have been filed after the applicable time limit expired or are deemed inappropriate to the purpose of proving the facts (see, e.g., ATF 4P.23/2006 reason 3.1; see also Geisinger/Frossard, *Challenge and Revision* at 147). Art. 182(3) does not encompass the parties' right to orally examine a witness who has provided a written witness statement (see ATF 4P.196/2003 reason 4.2.2). If the arbitral tribunal overlooks a piece of evidence and thus comes to the wrong conclusion, the right to be heard is deemed to have been violated if the mistake makes it impossible for a party to present and prove its case regarding this specific issue, and if the party is thus in the same position it would have been in had it never been heard in the first place (see ATF 4P.74/2006 reason 4). Consequently, the right to be heard is violated if the arbitral tribunal does not take into consideration a piece of evidence or an offer to produce evidence if this evidence is important for the outcome of the decision (see ATF 133 III 235 reason 5.2).

5. Assistance by Swiss state courts. The arbitral tribunal can only take evidence insofar as the parties and third persons (for example, witnesses and holders of documents) voluntarily comply with its orders. If this is not the case, the arbitral tribunal, or a party with the consent of the arbitral tribunal, can require judicial assistance from the Swiss courts at the seat of the arbitration (art. 184(2)). In the Canton of Zurich, this is the Bezirksgericht (§ 239(1) Zurich Code of Civil Procedure), in the Canton of Geneva, it is the Tribunal de première instance (art. 461B(1)(c) Geneva Code of Civil Procedure). The form of judicial assistance and its requirements are subject to cantonal law, which will be replaced in 2011 by the Federal Code of Civil Procedure (FCCP). The court normally administers the evidence itself (Tribunale di appello Ticino, 12 March 1993) or orders the person concerned to appear before the arbitral tribunal, and to produce a document or the like (see Tribunal de première instance Genève, 9 May 1990). The court can use means of coercion that are available under the cantonal code of civil procedure (see Knoepfler, *Tribunale di appello Ticino*, at 600 et seq.; Basel Commentary-Schneider, n 62 ad art. 184). As of 2011, the FCCP will provide for means of coercion against third parties (for example fines or compulsion, see art. 167 FCCP), but not against the parties to the proceedings (art. 164 FCCP). In cases where assistance must be provided abroad, a request to the cantonal court will be the first step in obtaining international judicial assistance from a foreign court, pursuant to the Hague Convention on the Taking of Evidence Abroad in Civil or Commercial Matters of 18 March 1970 or the Hague Convention on Civil

Procedure of 1 March 1954 (see Basel Commentary-Schneider, n 63/64 ad art. 184; Poudret/Besson, *Comparative Law*, n 673).

[Procedure: other judicial assistance]
Article 185

For any further judicial assistance the court at the seat of the arbitral tribunal shall have jurisdiction.

1. Scope of application. Art. 185 has a catch-all function for international arbitration proceedings subject to chapter 12 PILA (see art. 176(1)) and completes the other statutory provisions which provide for the assistance of the state courts (arts. 179(2) and (3), 180(3), 183(2), 184(2) and 193(2)). It obliges Swiss courts to cooperate with the arbitral tribunal and provides them with jurisdiction if the arbitral tribunal or the parties require assistance. Examples of cooperation by state courts include extending the arbitrators' term of office where this has not been agreed upon by the parties, intervening, upon request, to advance the proceedings, or decisions on whether the proceedings must be repeated if one arbitrator has been substituted.

2. Jurisdiction. The courts at the seat of arbitration have jurisdiction, i.e. the Bezirksgericht in the Canton of Zurich (§ 239(1) Zurich Code of Civil Procedure) and the Tribunal de première instance in the Canton of Geneva (art. 461B(1)(c) Geneva Code of Civil Procedure).

3. Applicable law. The court applies its own cantonal procedural law (as of 2011: the Federal Code of Civil Procedure).

4. Appeal. The means of appeal are governed by cantonal law (as of 2011: the Federal Code of Civil Procedure). A final cantonal decision can be appealed to the Federal Supreme Court, e.g., on grounds that the cantonal court wrongly agreed, or refused, to assist the arbitral tribunal.

[Jurisdiction]
Article 186

(1) The arbitral tribunal shall decide on its own jurisdiction.

(1bis) It shall decide on its jurisdiction notwithstanding an action concerning the same matter between the same parties that is already pending before a state court or another arbitral tribunal, unless there are serious grounds for staying the proceedings.

(2) A plea of lack of jurisdiction must be raised prior to any defence on the merits.

(3) The arbitral tribunal shall, as a rule, decide on its jurisdiction by a preliminary award.

Swiss Private International Law Act (Chapter 12), art. 186

1. Kompetenz-Kompetenz. Art. 186(1), as a mandatory provision of the lex arbitri, contains the principle of Kompetenz-Kompetenz, according to which arbitrators are the judges of their own jurisdiction. This authority of the arbitral tribunal is, however, subject to later examination by the Federal Supreme Court, which can set aside a decision on jurisdiction (see art. 190(2)(b)), or by state courts whose assistance is required in exequatur proceedings for the enforcement of the arbitral award (see art. V(1)(a) and (c) New York Convention). A request to a Swiss state court for a declaratory judgment on the jurisdiction of the arbitral tribunal will in most cases be deemed inadmissible for reasons of lack of a sufficient interest on the part of the requesting party in such a declaration (see Basel Commentary-Wenger/Schott, n 4 ad art. 186). When a party submits its claim to a Swiss state court despite the existence of an arbitration agreement providing for arbitration in Switzerland, the court will decline jurisdiction, unless the arbitration agreement is null and void, inoperative or incapable of being performed, or unless the defendant has made an appearance in the state court proceedings without reservation, or unless the arbitral tribunal cannot be constituted due to the defendant having obstructed its constitution (art. 7 PILA). When deciding whether to refer the parties to arbitration, the court will examine the validity of the arbitration agreement only on a prima facie basis (see ATF 122 III 139 reason 2b; confirmed in ATF 4P.114/2004 reason 7.3). In contrast, if the arbitration agreement provides for arbitration abroad, a Swiss state court seized of the dispute will thoroughly examine whether the arbitration agreement is 'null and void, inoperative or incapable of being performed' within the meaning of art. II(3) New York Convention (see ATF 121 III 38 reason 2b). A state court's negative decision on its own jurisdiction does not prejudice the decision of an arbitral tribunal subsequently seized of the matter (Basel Commentary-Berti, n 10 ad art. 7; Basel Commentary-Wenger/Schott, n 8 ad art. 186). On the other hand, a Swiss state court's decision admitting jurisdiction despite an arbitration clause is binding on an arbitral tribunal in Switzerland and has res judicata effect (see ATF 4P.114/2004 reason 7.3; ATF 120 II 155 reason 3b/bb). The Federal Supreme Court has based this ruling on the fact that it is the state court judge that decides the question of jurisdiction in last instance, as shown in art. 190(2)(b). As this line of reasoning does not seem to be affected by the new art. 186(1bis), it is most likely that the Federal Supreme Court will not change this jurisprudence (see also Basel Commentary-Berti, n 10 ad art. 7). In general, the principle of Kompetenz-Kompetenz precludes a Swiss state court from issuing an anti-arbitration injunction (Tribunal de première instance Genève, 2 May 2005). If proceedings are already pending before an arbitral tribunal, a Swiss state court subsequently seized of the dispute must stay its proceedings (see art. 181, note 4).

2. Jurisdiction of the arbitral tribunal. In its decision on its own jurisdiction, the arbitral tribunal will have to examine whether the arbitration agreement is valid according to art. 178 (see art. 178, notes 1-7), whether the arbitration agreement covers the subject matter of the dispute (see art. 178, note 8), and whether it is binding on the parties to the arbitration (see art. 178, note 9). In multi-party arbitrations, all parties must have consented to arbitration (Basel Commentary-Wenger/Schott, n 32 ad art. 186). The parties' consent is required for the consolidation of two or more arbitral proceedings, unless the parties have agreed on a set of arbitration rules providing for such consolidation under certain circumstances (see, e.g., art. 4 Swiss Rules).

3. Counterclaim and set-off. Unless the parties have agreed otherwise, an arbitral tribunal has jurisdiction to adjudicate counterclaims, provided that the principal claim and the counterclaim are derived from the same legal relationship covered by the arbitration agreement. If the counterclaim arises from a different legal relationship, or is subject to a separate arbitration agreement, the arbitral tribunal only has jurisdiction to hear the counterclaim if the parties agree to this (Basel Commentary-Wenger/Schott, n 39 ad art. 186; see also art. V(1)(c) New York Convention; Karrer in *Festschrift Kellerhals* at 52-53, takes a different view). With regard to set-off defences, the arbitral tribunal has jurisdiction to adjudicate the set-off claim if both claims stem from the same legal relationship, if the set-off claim is undisputed or is already res judicata or if the claimant does not raise any objections to the arbitral tribunal's jurisdiction. In all other situations and in the absence of an agreement by the parties, it is controversial whether the arbitral tribunal has jurisdiction to adjudicate the set-off claim (see, e.g., Basel Commentary-Wenger/Schott, n 42 et seq. ad art. 186; Berger/Kellerhals, *Schiedsgerichtsbarkeit*, n 483 et seq.; Karrer in *Festschrift Kellerhals* at 49 et seq.). The Federal Supreme Court has not yet decided upon this issue. If the set-off is admissible from a procedural point of view, the arbitral tribunal must examine whether it is also substantively admissible. The issue of substantive admissibility and the further conditions of a set-off are governed by the law that is applicable to the principal claim against which the set-off is being declared (see art. 148(2) PILA), as this is the law that has the closest connection as per art. 187(1). However, where the set-off claim is subject to a different law, the admissibility of the set-off should be examined under both laws, as otherwise the admissibility may depend purely on which party files its claim first (Berger/Kellerhals, *Schiedsgerichtsbarkeit*, n 1109). Counter-claims and set-off defences should be submitted at the earliest possible opportunity in the proceedings. The arbitral tribunal may not admit them if they are submitted too late, for example, only with the rejoinder (Berger/Kellerhals, *Schiedsgerichtsbarkeit*, n 1108).

4. Preliminary mediation or conciliation. Often, arbitration clauses provide that the parties shall first try to settle their dispute by way of mediation, conciliation or other ADR methods before resorting to arbitration. When dealing with such clauses, the first step is to determine by way of interpretation whether the pre-arbitral ADR phase is mandatory or merely permissive (see ATF 4A_18/2007 reason 4.3.2). The absence of any time limit for initiating and closing the pre-arbitral ADR phase and/or for initiating the subsequent arbitration is an indication of the non-mandatory character of the ADR phase (see ATF 4A_18/2007 reason 4.3.2; Boog, *Multi-tiered Dispute Resolution* at 106). If the pre-arbitral ADR phase is mandatory, it is controversial which sanctions shall be imposed upon a party that directly commences arbitration proceedings, in particular whether the consequences are procedural in nature (e.g. the arbitral tribunal has to stay the proceedings or lacks jurisdiction ratione temporis) or substantive (e.g. the other party can claim damages for breach of the mediation clause). For details on this controversy see, e.g., Boog, *Multi-tiered Dispute Resolution* at 106 et seq.; Voser, *Schlichtungsklausel*, at 376 et seq. The Federal Supreme Court left the question undecided because it interpreted the clause in question as not imposing a binding obligation upon the parties to first resort to ADR (see ATF 4A_18/2007 reason 4.3.1-4.3.2). In addition, the Federal Supreme Court held that even in case of a mandatory pre-arbitral ADR phase, the respondent in the arbitration would be precluded from challenging the arbitral award for lack of jurisdiction ratione temporis if he actively participated in the arbitration (even if under reservation) and did not start the ADR process himself (see ATF 4A_18/2007 reason 4.3.3; ATF 4P.67/2003 reason 4).

5. Pending proceedings before a state court or another arbitral tribunal. Art. 186(1bis) entered into force on 1 March 2007. In 2001, the Federal Supreme Court held in the *Fomento* decision that the lis pendens rule, which for state courts is stated in art. 9 PILA, also applied to arbitral tribunals with their seat in Switzerland. An arbitral tribunal would thus have to stay its proceedings if a dispute was already pending before a foreign state court, provided that a decision that would be recognisable in Switzerland could be expected within a reasonable period of time (see ATF 127 III 279 reason 2c). The new art. 186(1bis) was introduced as a response to this decision and expressly entitles an arbitral tribunal to declare itself competent and continue the arbitration despite pending actions before a Swiss or foreign state court or before another arbitral tribunal with its seat in or outside Switzerland (see Parliamentary Commission, Feuille Fédérale 2006, at 4684; Basel Commentary-Wenger/Schott, n 7b ad art. 186). As an exception, the arbitral tribunal may stay the proceedings if there are serious reasons to do so. Until now, there have been no precedents giving any indication of what is meant by 'serious reasons' that would justify a staying of the proceedings. Parliamentary discussions and legal writings suggest the following possible situations for staying the proceedings: if the arbitration was only initiated in order to abide by an agreed upon time limit, while proceedings before a foreign state court were already pending; if the defendant in the antecedent court proceedings has either not raised an objection or has raised it late, thus possibly making the arbitration agreement obsolete (as in the facts underlying ATF 127 III 279 where the defendant in the state proceedings did not invoke the arbitration agreement within the delay provided by the lex fori); if the arbitral tribunal considers that the arbitral tribunal first seized of the dispute is more likely to have jurisdiction (see Parliamentary Commission,

Feuille Fédérale 2006, at 4685; Basel Commentary-Wenger/Schott, n 15 ad art. 186).

6. Plea of lack of jurisdiction. In general, the arbitral tribunal must examine its jurisdiction only if the parties make any objections in this respect (art. 186(2)). Such objections must be raised at the earliest possible opportunity (see, e.g., ATF 4P.298/2005 reason 2.3), i.e. prior to or, at the latest, simultaneously with alternative pleadings of defence on the merits (see ATF 128 III 50 reason 2c/aa). Otherwise, the party forfeits its right to have the final award set aside or to avoid the enforcement of the award because of lack of jurisdiction. The Federal Supreme Court held that the same applies with regard to the challenge to arbitrability of the dispute (see ATF 4A_370/2007 reason 5.2.1; ATF, 15 March 1993, reason 5; see also art. 177, note 5). If the parties do not raise any objections, the arbitral tribunal's jurisdiction is deemed to be established. However, paying an advance on costs, filing a power of attorney, requesting a longer time limit, cooperating in the constitution of the arbitral tribunal and participating in agreeing on the procedural rules do not constitute behaviours which are considered to imply acceptance of the jurisdiction of the arbitral tribunal. There is one exception to the general requirement of an objection by a party: the arbitral tribunal must examine its jurisdiction ex officio if one party does not participate in the proceedings (see ATF 120 II 155 reason 3b/bb). Once a party pleads lack of jurisdiction, the Obergericht Zürich has held that the arbitral tribunal must examine only those grounds for lack of jurisdiction that have been alleged by the parties, and that the parties are precluded from invoking other grounds at a later stage (Obergericht Zürich, 22 May 1990, reason 3.3). The Federal Supreme Court has left this question undecided (see ATF 128 III 50 reason 2c/bb/ccc).

7. Preliminary award. In general, the arbitral tribunal decides on its jurisdiction and renders a preliminary award before entering into the substance of the dispute (art. 186(3)). It may delay the decision on jurisdiction until the final award if there are serious reasons to do so, for instance, if the relevant questions of fact or law are closely connected with the substance of the dispute (Basel Commentary-Wenger/Schott, n 63 ad art. 186).

8. Motion to set aside the award on jurisdiction. The parties may challenge the preliminary award on jurisdiction under art. 190(3) and (2)(b) within thirty days from its notification. If they do not, they are deemed to have waived their right to do so (see, e.g., ATF 4P.298/2005 reason 2.3). The Federal Supreme Court will thoroughly examine pleas of lack of jurisdiction, including any substantive preliminary questions that determine jurisdiction or lack thereof, such as a valid assignment of a contract that includes an arbitration agreement (see ATF 128 III 50 reason 2a), but excluding those aspects which go beyond jurisdiction issues and deal with substantive matters, such as the authority to adjudicate punitive or treble damages. The parties can only waive their right to have the jurisdiction award examined under the conditions provided in art. 192(1). In cases of a party challenging a positive preliminary award on jurisdiction, the arbitral tribunal has the discretion to continue or to stay the proceedings until the decision of the Federal Supreme Court is rendered. If a challenge against a negative award on jurisdiction is successful, the decision of the Federal Supreme Court bindingly establishes the competence of the arbitral tribunal to decide on the merits (see ATF 127 III 279 reason 1b; ATF 117 II 94 reason 4).

[Decision on the merits: applicable law]
Article 187

(1) The arbitral tribunal shall decide the dispute according to the rules of law chosen by the parties or, in the absence of such a choice, according to the rules of law with which the dispute has the closest connection.

(2) The parties may authorise the arbitral tribunal to decide ex aequo et bono.

1. Conflict of laws. Art. 187 contains a conflict of laws rule that designates the law applicable to the merits of the case, i.e. to substantive legal issues including, for example, the statute of limitations, interest, the standing to sue and to be sued and the burden of proof. As a principle, this special conflict of laws rule for international arbitration is to be interpreted autonomously and excludes the applicability of the conflict of laws rules that are contained in the other chapters of the PILA and that are addressed to the state courts (Berti-Karrer, n 5 ad art. 187). Art. 187 provides for a choice of law by the parties (see note 2 et seq.) and allows parties to authorise the arbitral tribunal to render a decision ex aequo et bono (see notes 7 and 8). Art. 187 does not refer to trade usages, which are to be taken into account under certain arbitration rules (see, e.g., art. 17(2) ICC Rules, art. 33(3) Swiss Rules, art. 33(3) UNCITRAL Arbitration Rules). Trade usages may, however, form part of the substantive law, in which case they must be considered.

2. Choice of law. According to art. 187(1), the parties are, subject to the prohibition against abuse of law, free to choose the law that applies to the merits. The choice of law can be explicit or implicit, as long as it is clear from the circumstances that the parties are aware that by their conduct they are choosing specific rules of law (Berti-Karrer, n 88 ad art. 187; Kaufmann-Kohler/Rigozzi, *LDIP*, n 609). It is not in and of itself sufficient for both parties to simply plead under the same law; the circumstances must show that they are aware that another law might apply (see ATF 119 II 173 reason 1b on art. 116 PILA; the same principles apply to art. 187, Berti-Karrer, n 88 ad art. 187; Kaufmann-Kohler/Rigozzi, *LDIP*, n 609).

3. Possible choices. The parties have the following options. First, they can choose the applicability of a national law. If the parties do not agree otherwise, the chosen law applies regardless of the conflict of laws rules of the country in question; the so-called renvoi is thus excluded (Kaufmann-Kohler/ Rigozzi, *LDIP*, n 604). The parties' choice of a national law will generally also include any international conventions that form part of that national law, for instance, the Vienna Sales Convention (CISG) in the case of Switzerland (La Spada in *Handbook*, at 122). Secondly, art. 187(1) also allows the parties to choose a non-national law ('rules of law'), as do most sets of arbitration rules. The parties can choose, for example, international conventions, drafts of international conventions, unofficial codifications such as the UNIDROIT Principles of International Commercial Contracts, the rules and by-laws of private organisations (such as the Incoterms or rules of international sport organisations), general principles of law or the lex mercatoria (see Basel Commentary-Karrer, n 88-97 ad art. 187; Kaufmann-Kohler/Rigozzi, *LDIP*, n 636 et seq.). The lex mercatoria has the advantage that it may provide for appropriate and internationalised solutions, though at the risk of a certain unpredictability if it is unclear whether or not a certain rule is part of the lex mercatoria. Thirdly, the parties can choose another set of conflict of laws rules, notably by choosing a set of arbitration rules that contains conflict of laws rules (so-called 'indirect choice of law'; Berti-Karrer, n 92 ad art. 187). Fourthly, the parties can choose different laws for different questions (so-called 'dépeçage'; Berti-Karrer, n 75 ad art. 187). Finally, the parties can choose a law that is in force as of a specific date, which means that future amendments of this law are not to be considered (so-called 'freezing clause' or 'stabilisation clause'; La Spada in *Handbook*, at 122).

4. Limits of the parties' choice of law. When applying the law chosen by the parties, the arbitral tribunal must still respect international public policy as defined by art. 190(2)(e) (see art. 190, note 10 et seq.; Berger/Kellerhals, *Schiedsgerichtsbarkeit*, n 1597 et seq.; Berti-Karrer, n 176 ad art. 187), as otherwise its award can be set aside later. Furthermore, it must examine whether and to what extent it is obliged or authorised to respect interventionist provisions of law which have the character of 'lois d'application immédiate', i.e. mandatory rules that are imposed on the dispute irrespective of the applicable law and that form part of a country's public policy. The problem of the applicability of the 'lois d'application immédiate' is complex and the details are controversial (for details, see, e.g., Basel Commentary-Karrer, n 229 et seq. ad art. 187; Berti-Blessing, n 669 et seq. ad Introduction; Kaufmann-Kohler/Rigozzi, *LDIP*, n 658 et seq.; Voser, *Mandatory Rules*, at 319 et seq.). A distinction must be drawn between the mandatory provisions of the chosen law and the interventionist norms of another law. When applying the law chosen by the parties, the arbitral tribunal generally must respect the applicable mandatory provisions of that law (Berti-Karrer, n 133 ad art. 187). One prominent example is antitrust law; if the parties choose the law of a member state of the EU, the EU antitrust law must be applied (see ATF 118 II 193; the published part of this decision does not show that Belgian law was chosen). For interventionist provisions outside the lex causae, a further distinction must be drawn between the mandatory provisions of Swiss law and those of a third state. As for Swiss mandatory provisions, they must be respected if they form part of the public policy as defined by art. 190(2)(e) (see art. 190, note 10 et seq.). Regarding the interventionist provisions of a third state, it is controversial whether and to what extent the arbitral tribunal may or must respect them. The Federal Supreme Court has held that the arbitral tribunal must apply EU antitrust law if, for example, the parties chose Swiss law but one party alleges the invalidity of the contract because it affects the EU market (see ATF 132 III 389 reason 3.3; see also the extract of an unpublished decision in Berger/Kellerhals, *Schiedsgerichtsbarkeit*, n 1304; the award is set aside if the arbitral tribunal refuses to apply the antitrust law, but not if it applies it incorrectly, see art. 190, notes 5 and 12). Other writers pose stricter requirements for the application of a third country's interventionist norms, for example, an abuse of law (Berti-Karrer, n 137 ad art. 187; for an overview on the different views, see Berti-Karrer, n 147 ad art. 187). In any event, the consideration of mandatory rules presupposes that these rules have a close connection to the dispute and that the arbitrators will consider their application appropriate for reaching a just decision that is recognised both generally and with regard to international public policy. In general, police laws, exchange control regulations and tax laws are not considered to be of such a nature that a direct application in international arbitrations is justified (Berti-Karrer, n 162 ad art. 187). If the arbitral tribunal does not apply the 'lois d'application immédiate', the parties face the risk of the award not being enforceable in the country that issued them.

5. Closest connection test. If the parties have not chosen a law, the arbitral tribunal applies the conflict of laws rule contained in the chosen arbitration rules. Arbitration rules often refer to the (rules of) law with the closest connection to the dispute (see, e.g., art. 23.2 DIS Rules, art. 33(1) Swiss Rules) or require the application of the rules of law that the arbitral tribunal determines to be appropriate (see, e.g., art. 17(1) ICC Rules, art. 22.3 LCIA Rules, art. 33(1) UNCITRAL Arbitration Rules). If no arbitration rules are chosen, art. 187(1) in fine designates the law that has the closest connection to the dispute. When applying the closest connection test, the arbitral tribunal should consider all the circumstances of the substantive dispute and weigh up all the aspects that have a connection to a specific law. It can (but is not obliged to) take guidance in national or international conflict of laws rules that specify the closest connection for certain disputes, especially if such conflict of laws rules are identical in all the states involved (Kaufmann-Kohler/Rigozzi, *LDIP*, n 630). The arbitral tribunal may take into account mandatory rules when certain requirements are fulfilled (see note 4). In order to ensure predictability within the arbitral process, the arbitral tribunal should always bear in mind whether the parties could have anticipated the applicability of the law it wants to apply. Art. 187(1) in fine does not allow for a 'better law approach'; the arbitral tribunal, in other words, may not consider which law it considers more appropriate in substance (Berti-Karrer, n 110 ad art. 187). Unlike some sets of arbitration rules (see, e.g., art. 23.2 DIS Rules), art. 187(1) in fine allows the arbitral tribunal to apply non-national rules of law (Berti-Karrer, n 63 ad art. 187), as do, for instance, art. 17(1) ICC Rules, art. 22.3 LCIA Rules and art. 33(1) Swiss Rules. Preliminary questions, such as the question of whether a person had the capacity to act or to bind a legal entity, should be determined separately under the law with which that particular question has the closest connection (Berti-Karrer, n 58 ad art. 187).

6. Application of the law by the arbitral tribunal. The Federal Supreme Court has held that the arbitral tribunal must apply the designated law ex officio (see, e.g., ATF 4P.260/2000 reason 5b). It can impose on the parties the duty to contribute to the establishment of the law or can request expert opinions on its content (see ATF 4P.242/2004 reason 7.3; Basel Commentary-Karrer, n 169 et seq. ad art. 187). As in many other countries, however, the precise scope and limits of the arbitrators' right and obligation to apply the law ex officio are controversial (see, e.g., Kaufmann-Kohler in *Études Hirsch*, at 73 et seq.). The arbitral tribunal must hear the parties on its legal evaluation of the case only if this evaluation is based on legal grounds not previously invoked by the parties and whose application they could not reasonably have foreseen (ATF 4A_400/2008 reason 3; ATF 130 III 35 reason 5).

7. Decision ex aequo et bono. According to art. 187(2), the parties may authorise (and thus oblige) the arbitral tribunal to decide ex aequo et bono. This authorisation can be explicit or even implicit, provided that it results unequivocally from the circumstances (which is rare). Rendering a decision ex aequo et bono means that the arbitral tribunal may base its decision on the merits on its own perception of justice without being bound by (even mandatory) law (see ATF 4P.114/2001 reason 2c/bb/aaa). The arbitral tribunal must nevertheless render a reasoned award (but see art. 189, note 6).

8. Limits of the decision ex aequo et bono. The same restrictions as for the parties' choice of law apply with respect to international public policy and the 'lois d'application immédiate' (see note 4). Unless the parties have agreed otherwise, the arbitral tribunal is bound by the contract: it may construe it ex aequo et bono, but must not rule against clear contractual provisions even if it considers them unjust, unless the law would also allow the tribunal to do so, for instance, under the concept of clausula rebus sic stantibus (see Berger/Kellerhals, *Schiedsgerichtsbarkeit*, N 1321; Berti-Karrer, n 201 ad art. 187). In any event, the arbitral tribunal must respect the applicable procedural rules and, in particular, the parties' right to be heard and to be treated equally (see ATF 4P.23/2006 reason 2).

[Decision on the merits: partial award]

Article 188

Unless the parties have agreed otherwise, the arbitral tribunal may render partial awards.

1. Power of the arbitral tribunal. Art. 188 gives the arbitral tribunal the power to render partial awards if it deems it appropriate, and thus serves the interests of procedural economy. The parties can agree to waive this power either individually or by reference to a set of arbitration rules that excludes partial awards.

2. Notion of partial awards. It is controversial whether the term 'partial awards' only includes awards on the merits that are final with regard to a quantitatively limited part of the action, for example, final awards on individual claims, awards on individual and independent prayers for relief and awards against only some of the respondents (so-called partial award stricto sensu, see ATF 128 III 191 reason 4a), or whether it also refers to interim awards on substantive or procedural questions that are not final but are merely a step on the way to the final award. Such questions would include, for example, decisions on jurisdiction, the validity of the contract or exceptions raised by the respondent, for instance, the exception of the statute of limitations or of res judicata (on the concept of interim awards, see ATF 130 III 76 reason 3.1.3). The distinction is especially relevant when determining the extent to which awards can be directly subject to setting aside proceedings under art. 190 (see art. 190, notes 3 and 15). The Federal Supreme Court has taken the restrictive view that art. 188 only refers to partial awards stricto sensu (see ATF 130 III 755 reason 1.2).

3. Effects of partial and interim awards. Although only partial awards stricto sensu have res judicata effect, the arbitral tribunal is also bound by interim awards for the rest of the proceedings (see ATF 128 III 191 reason 4a). To the extent that direct setting aside proceedings are admissible against partial or interim awards under art. 190 (see art. 190, notes 3 and 15), the parties must file such motions directly against such awards as they are otherwise deemed to have waived their right to invoke these grounds for challenge against any later awards (see, e.g., ATF 4A_370/2007 reason 2.3.1 with further references). Although it is possible to also award costs in a partial award, this is, in practice, seldom appropriate (Basel Commentary-Wirth, n 19 ad art. 188).

[Decision on the merits: arbitral award]

Article 189

(1) The arbitral award shall be rendered in conformity with the procedure and in the form agreed upon by the parties.

(2) In the absence of such an agreement, the arbitral award shall be rendered by majority vote, or, in the absence of a majority, by the chairperson alone. The award shall be in writing, shall state the reasons for the award, and shall be dated and signed. The signature of the chairperson is sufficient.

Swiss Private International Law Act (Chapter 12), art. 189

1. Notion of arbitral awards. Art. 189 applies to binding awards including final awards, partial awards stricto sensu (on this concept see art. 188, note 2) and also, we submit, to interim awards (for support of this opinion, see Berti-Wirth, n 2 ad art. 189; see also Berger/Kellerhals, *Schiedsgerichtsbarkeit*, n 1331/2). Although they do not, in principle, apply to procedural orders, the provisions of art. 189 should also be applied by analogy to the procedure of rendering more important procedural orders (Berti-Wirth, n 3 ad art. 189; for a different view see, e.g., Berti-Schneider, n 43 ad art. 182).). Moreover, the fact that a decision by an arbitral tribunal is named 'Procedural Order' does not exclude its characterization as an interim award (see art. 190, note 15).

2. Party autonomy. According to art. 189(1), the procedure for rendering the arbitral award and determining its form are subject to the parties' agreement. This agreement can be made prior to or during the arbitration proceedings, either individually or by referring to a set of arbitration rules. As a principle, the parties' agreement prevails over the requirements contained in art. 189(2) (but see note 3). Any agreements under art. 189 prior to the commencement of the arbitration become part of the arbitral contract with the arbitrators (see art. 179, note 8) and thus can only be substantially changed subsequently if the arbitration rules so provide or if the arbitral tribunal agrees to do so (Berti-Wirth, n 4 ad art. 189). With regard to the issues dealt with by art. 189(2) (quorum for decisions, form, date and signature of the award, stating of reasons), an agreement by the parties generally prevails. In the absence of such an agreement, and within the framework of art. 189(2), the arbitral tribunal is free to determine the procedure.

3. Deliberations and voting. Regardless of the parties' agreement, a panel of arbitrators must deliberate on the decision, as this is part of the parties' inalienable right to be heard (see ATF 4P.115/2003 reason 3.2). In the absence of such deliberations, the award can be set aside under art. 190(2)(a/d/e). Unless the parties have agreed otherwise, the arbitrators are free to deliberate and vote personally, by telephone or in writing (for example, by circulating a draft award and collecting comments) as long as all the arbitrators have an opportunity to express their views on all relevant questions and on the other arbitrators' comments (see ATF 4P.115/2003 reason 3.2). If one arbitrator declines to participate in the deliberations or refuses to vote without justification and without having formally resigned (see art. 179, note 9), the other arbitrators can continue their deliberations and render an award, provided that the arbitrator who has declined to participate had the opportunity to be involved at all times (see ATF 128 III 234 reason 3b). Art. 189(2) provides for a majority decision, which means a decision by the majority of the tribunal members. If no majority is reached, the chairperson can decide alone, regardless of his fellow arbitrators' views. The voting and the deliberations must be kept confidential (see ATF, 12 November 1991, reason 1b/bb), unless the parties agree otherwise prior to the appointment of the arbitrators, or unless the arbitrators agree to waive their right to secrecy thereafter (Berti-Wirth, n 21 ad art. 189). It does not, however, violate the confidentiality of the deliberations if one arbitrator (against good practice) informs the parties of the outcome of the deliberations prior to the parties being notified of the award (see ATF 4P.154/2005 reason 6.2).

4. Form and notification. Unless the parties agree otherwise, the award must be rendered in writing. The waiver of a written award may restrict the parties' right to challenge the award, as it will then be impossible, or very difficult, to establish grounds for having the award set aside. The parties must be notified of the award, at which point the period for filing a motion to set aside the award starts. The modalities of the notification are determined by the parties, or by the arbitration rules chosen by them, or, lacking such determination, by the arbitral tribunal (see ATF 4P.273/1999 reason 5a). In practice, delivery by registered mail or by special courier, with acknowledgment of receipt, is standard, even for parties with their domicile abroad (see ATF 4P.273/1999 reason 5a; Basel Commentary-Wirth, n 74 ad art. 189). When communicated orally, the award is only deemed to have been properly conveyed once it has been delivered in writing with the reasons included, unless the parties have explicitly waived the written form and/or the requirement to give reasons. If a party to an arbitration with its seat in Switzerland refuses to accept delivery of the award, judicial assistance of the state courts pursuant to art. 185 may be requested (see Berger/Kellerhals, *Schiedsgerichtsbarkeit*, n 1378).

5. Content. Art. 189(2) only provides for a minimum content of the award, namely the reasons for the decision (see note 6), the date of rendering the award and the signatures of the arbitrators. Signing the decision does not signify the arbitrators' unreserved consent to it, but only their participation and acknowledgement of the finality of the decision (see ATF 4P.154/2005 reason 3.1). The signature of the chairperson or the signature of both or even only one of the co-arbitrators is sufficient for the decision to be legally valid (see ATF 4P.154/2005 reason 3; Berger/Kellerhals, *Schiedsgerichtsbarkeit*, n 1366). In addition to this minimum content, it is advisable for the award to contain the information necessary to ensure its recognition and enforcement, such as the names and domiciles of the persons involved (parties, counsel, arbitrators), the seat of arbitration, the parties' prayers for relief and a summary of their pleadings, a brief description of the proceedings demonstrating that the parties' right to be heard and their equal treatment have been respected, the findings on the arbitral tribunal's jurisdiction, a description of the facts, the decision on each prayer for relief and the reasons for it, and the decision on costs (see note 8).

6. Reasons. Unless the parties have agreed to the contrary, reasons for the award must be included. These can be submitted in a concise fashion and it is sufficient for the arbitral tribunal to address the more important arguments brought forward by the parties and to restrict the stating of its reasons to those arguments which are relevant for its decisions; it does not have to deal with each and every argument as long as it respects the parties' right to be heard (see art. 182, note 7). If the award does not state the reasons even though the parties have not waived this requirement, the consequences are unclear. The Federal Supreme Court has held that omitting to state the reasons does not in itself constitute grounds for having the award set aside (see ATF 130 III 125 reason 2.2; ATF 116 II 373 reason 7b; under the FSCA ATF 4A_244/2007 reason 6.4; see also Berger/Kellerhals, *Schiedsgerichtsbarkeit*, n 1362). Some distinguished writers take a different view, at least with regard to cases where the omission of stated reasons makes an efficient challenge to the award impossible (see, e.g., Basel Commentary-Wirth, n 38/39 ad art. 189). Other writers support the analogous application of art. 112(1) to (3) FSCA, according to which the parties can request the reasons within thirty days after the tribunal notified them of the award or the Federal Supreme Court can make such a request in setting aside proceedings (Poudret, *Tribunal fédéral*, at 695-696).

7. Dissenting opinion. According to the Federal Supreme Court, an arbitrator has no right to attach a dissenting opinion to an arbitral award or to communicate such dissent to the parties together with the award unless the parties' agreement so provides or unless the majority of the arbitral tribunal consents (see ATF, 11 May 1992, reason 2b). This issue, however, is being heavily debated throughout Europe (see Poudret in *Liber Amicorum Reymond*, at 243 et seq.; Kaufmann-Kohler/Rigozzi, *LDIP*, n 692). In a given case, institutional rules or practice may provide further guidance. In any event, the dissenting opinion does not form part of the arbitral award, even if it is formally included (see ATF 4P.196/2003 reason 1.2).

8. Costs. The question of arbitration costs and the parties' costs, and their amount and allocation to the parties, is often dealt with by the arbitration rules agreed upon by the parties. In the absence of such an agreement, the arbitral tribunal's authority to determine the arbitration costs in the strict sense (arbitrators' fees and costs and expenses) is based on art. 182(2) (Basel Commentary-Wirth, n 63 ad art. 189). Subject to an agreement by the parties, the arbitral tribunal has discretion with respect to the allocation of costs, as long as it follows reasonable, objective criteria such as the degree of success obtained by each party in the proceedings, differences in the amount of effort necessary to adjudicate various claims, frivolous or bad-faith motions, delaying tactics or other behaviour causing additional costs (Berti-Wirth, n 56 ad art. 189). With regard to parties' costs, the arbitral tribunal has the authority to render a decision (Berti-Wirth, n 58 ad art. 189). If the parties' agreement or the applicable arbitration rules do not oblige the arbitral tribunal to award parties' costs, the parties must file a motion to this effect, as the arbitral tribunal would otherwise decide ultra petita (Basel Commentary-Wirth, n 68 ad art. 189). The parties should be invited to submit their costs and be granted the opportunity to comment on the cost submission of the other party. The arbitral tribunal has discretion when determining the amount of parties' costs and usually applies the general test of reasonableness. For the impact of contingency fees and pactum de palmario arrangements on the award on costs, see Wehrli, *Contingency Fees*, at 252 et seq. The tribunal can also award a party the costs of in-house counsel (Berti-Wirth, n 60 ad art. 189). The parties' costs, as a rule, will be allocated following the principles referred to above with regard to arbitration costs.

9. Termination of the proceedings based on the parties' declarations or behaviour. If the parties have agreed on a settlement of the dispute, the arbitral tribunal usually renders a decision as requested by the parties or as provided for in the applicable arbitration rules. In the absence of any such agreement, the arbitral tribunal is free either to render a consent award (or an award on agreed terms), or to close the proceedings by means of an order for termination. Either way, it must include a ruling on the costs. Unless applicable procedural rules provide otherwise, the proceedings should be terminated by an award in cases of recognition of the claim by the respondent or of a waiver of the claim by the claimant. Where a withdrawal of the action with the possibility of reintroduction is admissible (see Berti-Wirth, n 47 ad art. 189), the arbitral tribunal may consider issuing a termination order. If one party does not pay the requested advance on costs, the parties' agreement or the applicable arbitration rules determine the consequences (see ATF 4P.2/2003 reason 3). In the absence of such an agreement, and if the other party does not advance the entire costs, the arbitral tribunal will render a resolution not to enter into the proceedings (Berti-Wirth, n 50 ad art. 189; Lalive/Poudret/Reymond, *L'Arbitrage*, n 17 ad art. 182).

[Finality, setting aside: principle]

Article 190

(1) The award is final from the time when it is communicated.

(2) The award may only be set aside:
  (a) if the sole arbitrator was improperly appointed or if the arbitral tribunal was improperly constituted;
  (b) if the arbitral tribunal wrongly accepted or declined jurisdiction;
  (c) if the arbitral tribunal ruled beyond the claims submitted to it, or failed to decide on one of the items of the claim;
  (d) if the principle of equal treatment of the parties or their right to be heard was violated;
  (e) if the award is incompatible with public policy.

(3) Preliminary awards can be challenged only on the grounds of the above paragraphs 2(a) and 2(b); the time limit for filing the challenge runs from the notification of the preliminary award.

1. Overview and scope of application. Swiss law provides for only very limited options for setting aside arbitral awards rendered in Switzerland.

Swiss Private International Law Act (Chapter 12), art. 190

The Federal Supreme Court, as the exclusively competent court, traditionally applies the grounds for challenge contained in art. 190(2) restrictively. Statistics show that the chances of an even partially successful challenge to an arbitral award on the merits are very limited (Dasser, *International Arbitration* at 452-453). The PILA regime for setting aside arbitral awards reflects to a large extent the provisions of art. V New York Convention on the refusal to recognise and enforce awards, and is also broadly in line with art. 34 of the UNCITRAL Model Law. Art. 190 is applicable to awards rendered by arbitral tribunals with their seat in Switzerland, provided that the requirements of art. 176(1) are fulfilled, that the parties have not agreed on the exclusive applicability of cantonal arbitration law/the third part of the FCCP (art. 176(2)) and that they have not waived the right to challenge the award (see art. 192).

2. Final nature of the arbitral award. According to art. 190(1), once the parties have been notified of the award (see art. 189, note 4), it is final and binding under art. V(1)(e) New York Convention. This means that it has res judicata effect and can be enforced, unless the Federal Supreme Court explicitly grants suspensive effect to a motion to set aside the award (see art. 191, note 2). If the parties have not agreed otherwise, the clarification of an unclear award or rectification of errors by the arbitral tribunal remain possible (see ATF 126 III 524 reason 2b). A rectification is not an addition to the initial award, but forms an integral part of it (see ATF 131 III 164 reason 1.1). Motions to set aside the tribunal's decision on rectification are admissible to the same extent as against the initial award, but can only be based on grounds referring exclusively to the rectification (see ATF 131 III 164 reason 1.2). If such an appeal is successful, the rectification will be annulled, but the initial award will remain effective. In contrast, setting aside the original award would render ineffective any awards that rectified or interpreted it (see ATF 131 III 164 reason 1.2.4). If the arbitral award is incomplete, the parties can request an additional award. The additional award may add something to the original award, but cannot withdraw anything that has already been awarded. The additional award is considered to be an independent award, subject to independent setting aside proceedings (Berger/Kellerhals, *Schiedsgerichtsbarkeit*, n 1417).

3. Motion to set aside the award. The grounds for setting aside an arbitral award contained in art. 190(2) are exhaustive (see, e.g., ATF 128 III 50 reason 1a). Grounds not listed in art. 190(2) do not provide the right to challenge. Not subject to challenge are, for example, a clearly incorrect interpretation of a contract (see ATF 4P.134/2006 reason 4-7), the incorrect application of the substantive law, or arbitrariness for example, in findings of facts that allegedly contradict the evidence (see, e.g., ATF 4P.134/2006 reason 3 with further references). In particular, objections directly based on the ECHR are not admissible (see ATF 4P.105/2006 reason 7.3). The principles of the ECHR can, however, fall within the scope of substantive public policy (see ATF 4A_370/2007 reason 5.3.2). Final awards and partial awards stricto sensu (on this concept see art. 188, note 2) can be challenged on the grounds contained in art. 190(2) (see ATF 130 III 755 reason 1.2.2), provided that no previous interim or partial award has already been or could have been challenged on the same grounds (see, e.g., ATF 4P.298/2005 reason 2.3). Interim awards, on the other hand, are subject to art. 190(3) (see notes 15-16). Procedural mistakes must be challenged by objections to the next appealable award, and the aggrieved party must have already duly objected during the proceedings, as otherwise it shall be deemed to have waived its right to object (see ATF 4P.96/2002 reason 4.3.2).

4. Incorrect constitution of the arbitral tribunal (art. 190(2)(a)). The incorrect constitution of an arbitral tribunal will often be an issue when an interim award is challenged (see notes 15-16). The parties must object to the constitution of the arbitral tribunal during the arbitration procedure and within the deadlines provided for by the applicable procedural rules (see, e.g., ATF 4P.196/2003 reason 3.2.1). In principle, Art. 190(2)(a) allows the challenge that one or several arbitrators were incorrectly appointed, dismissed or replaced, i.e. in contravention of the requirements of art. 179. It also allows the challenge that all or some arbitrators were not independent or impartial (see ATF 129 III 445 reason 3.1). An award can thus be set aside if an arbitration institution dismissed a legitimate challenge to one or several arbitrators under art. 180 (see ATF 118 II 359 reason 3b; art. 180, note 9). A motion to set aside is excluded, however, if the challenge was dismissed by a state court (see ATF 128 III 330 reason 2.2). The Federal Supreme Court made an important restriction to the application of art. 190(2)(a): in a case where the arbitration institution dismissed a challenge to an arbitrator, the Federal Supreme Court held that it would not set aside an award under art. 190(2)(a) on the grounds that the dismissal of the challenge violated the parties' agreement, in particular requirements that they had agreed upon (see art. 180(1) (a) and (b)), unless there was a violation of the parties' right to independent and impartial justice (see ATF, 30 June 1994, reason 4; less explicitly ATF 4P.188/2001 reason 2e). The Federal Supreme Court has not yet decided the question whether the same applies with respect to art. 179, i.e. whether it would verify if the constitution of the arbitral tribunal complied in all respects with the procedures agreed by the parties. Art. 190(2)(a) can also be invoked if the constitution of the arbitral tribunal was temporarily incorrect, e.g., if one arbitrator was missing at a hearing (see ATF 4P.154/2005 reason 3.1; for cases where an arbitrator intentionally refuses to participate in the deliberations or the decision, see art. 189, note 3).

5. Wrong decision on jurisdiction (art. 190(2)(b)). A challenge is possible if the arbitral tribunal wrongly declined jurisdiction in a final award, or wrongly accepted jurisdiction in a final or interim award (see note 15), provided that the party duly raised its objections during the arbitration proceedings (see, e.g., ATF 130 III 66 reason 4.3). The decision on jurisdiction under art. 186 is wrong if it violates art. 177 or 178, or if it wrongly extends the scope of the arbitration agreement, for example, if it decides on claims not covered by the arbitration agreement (see art. 178, note 8), or if it wrongly accepts jurisdiction over non-signatories (ATF 4P.298/2005 reason 2.2; see art. 178, note 9). The decision on jurisdiction is also wrong if it was incorrectly based on chapter 12 PILA instead of on cantonal law/the third part of the FCCP and vice versa (see art. 176, note 5). For the consequences of commencing arbitration despite a binding obligation to first resort to mediation or conciliation, see art. 186, note 4. Art. 190(2)(b) applies if the arbitral tribunal declares itself not competent to apply the EU antitrust law even though the contract in dispute affects the EU market and one party has alleged the invalidity of the contract on these grounds (ATF 132 III 389 reason 3.3; see art. 187, note 4). An arbitral tribunal is also competent to examine, and even has a duty to examine, whether a contract violates the applicable criminal law against corruption and money laundering when determining the validity of a contract whose performance is at issue in the arbitration (see ATF 133 III 139 reason 5). Under the new art. 186(1bis), an arbitral award cannot be set aside on the grounds that the arbitral tribunal continued proceedings although the dispute was already pending before a Swiss or foreign state court or another arbitral tribunal (see art. 186, note 5).

6. Decision on jurisdiction by the Federal Supreme Court. The Federal Supreme Court examines the legal grounds for alleged jurisdiction or lack thereof, including substantive preliminary questions, with unfettered powers (see, e.g., ATF 4P.48/2005 reason 3.1). In case foreign law governs a substantive preliminary question, the Federal Supreme Court will also examine the foreign law with unfettered powers. It will follow the clearly prevailing opinion under the foreign law and, in case of controversies between jurisprudence and doctrine, the decisions of the highest court in the foreign country (ATF 4A_428/2008 reason 3.1). The Federal Supreme Court is, however, bound by the facts established by the arbitral tribunal, unless the findings on the facts are themselves subject to an objection under art. 190(2)(d) or (e) (see, e.g., ATF 4P.48/2005 reason 3.1 with further references) or unless the arbitral tribunal's award itself gave rise to a need to introduce new facts (art. 99(1) FSCA; see art. 191, note 5). If the arbitral tribunal wrongly denied jurisdiction, the Federal Supreme Court can bindingly establish the competence of the arbitral tribunal (see ATF 127 III 279 reason 1b).

7. Decision ultra petita or extra petita (art. 190(2)(c)). The award can be set aside if the arbitral tribunal went beyond the claims submitted to it and thus decided ultra petita or extra petita partium. Art. 190(2)(c) guarantees a particular aspect of the right to be heard and aims to protect the other party from an award on claims it had no reason to expect, taking into account the fact that it is the claimant's responsibility and decision to assert its claims and to dispose of them as it chooses (see ATF 4P.154/2005 reason 5). The tribunal only decides ultra petita or extra petita if the award is not covered by the parties' prayers for relief, i.e. if it adjudicates more, or something else, than what has been requested in the prayers for relief (see, e.g., ATF 4P.54/2006 reason 2.1). If the arbitral tribunal is requested to declare that a certain legal relationship does not exist (negative declaratory relief), it does not decide ultra petita or extra petita if it declares that the legal relationship exists instead of simply dismissing the request (see ATF 4A_220/2007 reason 7.2). A so-called catch-all clause, introduced by the claimant with its prayers for relief, may render a later ultra petita objection ineffective unless the respondent objected against this unspecified prayer for relief at the earliest possible opportunity in the arbitration proceedings (see ATF 4P.114/2001 reason 3b). The award cannot be set aside if the tribunal determines higher amounts for some parts of the claim than were requested, as long as the total amount granted remains within the framework of the total amount requested (see ATF 4P.54/2006 reason 2.1). Neither can the award be set aside if the tribunal adjudicated the amount claimed based on different legal grounds, e.g., if it awarded the amount as damages and not as specific performance of the contract (see, e.g., ATF 4P.260/2000 reason 5c). The arbitral tribunal is thus not bound by the legal grounds invoked by the parties, but applies the law ex officio (see ATF 4A_220/2007 reason 7.2), provided that it respects the parties' right to be heard (see art. 182, note 8).

8. Decision infra petita (art. 190(2)(c)). The award can be set aside if it is incomplete, i.e. if the arbitral tribunal failed to decide on a prayer for relief or a formally valid request by the parties (see ATF 128 III 234 reason 4a). It does not constitute grounds for challenge if the arbitral tribunal did not evaluate the prayers for relief on all possible legal grounds or if it globally dismissed 'any other or further claims' (see, e.g., ATF 4P.269/2003 reason 2).

9. Violation of the equal treatment of the parties or the right to be heard. Art. 190(2)(d) covers the violation of the equal treatment of the parties (see art. 182, note 6) and of their right to be heard in adversarial proceedings (see art. 182, note 7 et seq.; for failure to give reasons for a decision, see art. 189, note 6). The motion to set aside requires the aggrieved party to have duly raised a sufficiently specific objection during the arbitration proceedings (see, e.g., ATF 4P.129/2002 reason 7.1 with further references). If the right to be heard is violated, the award is set aside, regardless of the party's chances on the merits (see ATF 127 III 576 reason 2d; for a different view, see, e.g., Berger/Kellerhals, *Schiedsgerichtsbarkeit*, n 1592).

10. Violation of public policy. Art. 190(2)(e) ensures that the arbitral award complies with fundamental legal principles. In recent years, the Federal Supreme Court has not been consistent in deciding whether the notion of public policy refers to Swiss or to universal principles (see ATF 132 III 389 reason 2.2.2). For example, having previously referred to 'the fundamental legal or moral principles that are recognised in all civilised countries' (see ATF 128 III 234 reason 4c), the Federal Supreme Court in 2006 defined public policy as 'the essential and widely recognised values that should, according to the prevailing concepts in Switzerland, form the basis of every legal system' (see ATF 132 III 389 reason 2.2.3). This definition presupposes that the principles in question do not fundamentally differ between different countries within a common culture (see ATF 132 III 389 reason 3). Arbitrariness ('Willkür') does not in itself constitute a violation of public policy (see ATF 132 III 389 reason 2.2.2). The term 'public policy' encompasses procedural public policy and substantive public policy. When filing a motion to set aside an award on the grounds of public policy, the applicant must show in detail which legal principle was violated and how it was violated, and must demonstrate that the principle in question is part of public policy (see, e.g., ATF 4P.23/2006 reason 4.3). It must be established that the result of the decision, not the reasoning behind it, violates public policy (see, e.g., ATF 4P.240/2006 reason 4.1 with further references). Statistics show that until 2005, not a single challenge based on art. 190(2)(e) was successful (Dasser, *International Arbitration* at 455-456).

11. Substantive public policy. The following principles form part of substantive public policy: (i) the principle of pacta sunt servanda, which is violated if the arbitral tribunal applies a contractual provision in contradiction of its own interpretation of it – if, for example, it imposes on a party a contractual obligation it has held to be invalid or if it denies the performance of a contractual obligation it has held to be valid. If the tribunal applies the wrong contractual provision or incorrectly construes or applies the contract, the principle is not violated (see, e.g., ATF 4P.206/2006 reason 4.1; ATF 4P.134/2006 reason 5.2); (ii) the principle of good faith, including the concept of culpa in contrahendo, which is violated if the arbitral tribunal misconstrues the general application and concept of culpa in contrahendo – the Federal Supreme Court cannot, however, examine whether the facts of a given case lead to a liability under culpa in contrahendo (see ATF 4P.88/2006 reason 4.2); (iii) the prohibition against the abuse of rights (see ATF 120 II 155 reason 6a), including the prohibition against venire contra factum proprium (see ATF 4P.143/2001 reason 3c/aa); (iv) the prohibition against discrimination (see ATF 4P.12/2000 reason 5a/aa); (v) the prohibition against expropriation without compensation (see ATF 4P.200/2001 reason 2b); (vi) the protection of legally incapacitated persons (see, e.g., ATF 132 III 389 reason 2.2.1); (vii) the right to terminate the contract for important reasons (see ATF 4P.172/1999 reason 5d); (viii) the prohibition against bribery (see ATF 4P.208/2004 reason 6.1); (ix) the prohibition against serious violations of personal rights (see ATF 4P.12/2000 reason 5b/aa). This list is not exhaustive. In any event, the Federal Supreme Court has stressed that the chances are extremely slight of having an award set aside for reasons of substantive public policy (see ATF 132 III 389 reason 2.1).

12. Substantive public policy: counter-examples. The non-application or wrong application of interventionist provisions (see art. 187, note 4) only constitutes a violation of substantive public policy where such provisions are considered essential and widely recognised values as defined in note 10 et seq. (see ATF 132 III 389 reason 2.2.2). The Federal Supreme Court has held that, because of significant national differences, national and EU antitrust laws do not belong to public policy in the sense of art. 190(2)(e) and, therefore, that the incorrect application of these laws cannot justify setting aside an award (see ATF 132 III 389 reason 3; but see note 5). Regarding punitive damages, the Federal Supreme Court has held that the principle of prohibiting enriching the aggrieved party, and consequently the limitation of the compensation to the actual damage suffered by the party, is part of Swiss public policy. It has left undecided the question of whether this principle also belongs to international public policy in the sense of art. 190(2)(e) (see ATF 4P.7/1998 reason 3c). However, the prevailing view in Swiss legal doctrine is that the granting of punitive damages is not a violation of international public policy (e.g. Berger/Kellerhals, *Schiedsgerichtsbarkeit*, n 1604 with further references; Kaufmann-Kohler/Rigozzi, *LDIP*, n 908). The awarding of compound interest does not violate Swiss public policy (see ATF, 9 January 1995, reason 7), nor does it violate, a fortiori, art. 190(2)(e) (Berger/Kellerhals, *Schiedsgerichtsbarkeit*, n 1604). In a sports arbitration, the Supreme Court held that neither the enforcement of disciplinary sanctions by a private association (here, FIFA; ATF 4P.240/2006 reason 4.2), nor strict liability for doping with a shift in the burden of proof (see ATF 4P.105/2006 reason 8) violates public policy. An allocation of parties' costs that is considered excessive can only violate public policy if it is clearly out of proportion with the necessary costs a party consented to for defending its rights (see ATF 4P.280/2005 reason 2.2.2). Neither arbitrariness ('Willkür') alone, nor a clear violation of the applicable law or a decision ex aequo et bono instead of the application of the chosen law, constitute a violation of public policy, unless the actual outcome of the award is in itself incompatible with public policy (see ATF 4P.253/2004 reason 3.1 with further references; this is controversial in the case of a decision ex aequo et bono, see ATF 4A_370/2007 reason 5.6 with further references). The mere fact of an award being legally unsustainable does not amount to a violation of public policy (see ATF 4P.54/2006 reason 3.1).

13. Procedural public policy. Procedural public policy contains guarantees that ensure, like the guarantees explicitly mentioned in art. 190(a) to (d), an independent consideration of all the applications and allegations that the parties filed in accordance with the applicable procedural rules (see, e.g., ATF 4P.207/2002 reason 2.2). For example, the following principles form part of procedural public policy: the right to a fair procedure (see, e.g., ATF 4P.143/2001 reason 3a/aa); the observance of the res judicata effect of previous awards (see, e.g., ATF 4P.98/2005 reason 5.1 with further references); the requirement that the decision not contravene the reasoning behind the award (see ATF 4P.99/2000 reason 3b/aa); and the independence and impartiality of experts appointed by the tribunal (see ATF 126 III 249 reason 3c). Generally, procedural public policy is violated if a breach of fundamental procedural principles unacceptably contravenes the sense of justice (see, e.g., ATF 4P.143/2001 reason 3a/aa).

14. Procedural public policy: counter-examples. It does not per se constitute a violation of procedural public policy if the arbitral tribunal wrongly evaluates the evidence or wrongly establishes the facts (see, e.g., ATF 4P.48/2005 reason 3.4.2.1). Neither does it per se violate procedural public policy if the arbitral tribunal applies the arbitration rules incorrectly or arbitrarily (see ATF 4P.23/2006 reason 4.2) or if it fails completely to apply a procedural provision (see ATF 4P.280/2005 reason 2.2.1), unless the violated provision is essential for ensuring the fairness of the proceedings, and is, therefore, part of public policy (see ATF 4P.196/2003 reason 5.1). It does not violate procedural public policy if the Court of Arbitration for Sport (CAS) deems an appeal withdrawn because the appellant did not pay the advance of costs within the time limit, provided that the CAS informed the appellant of this consequence beforehand (ATF 4A_600/2008 reason 5.2).

15. Grounds for a challenge to interim awards. Unlike partial awards stricto sensu (see note 3), interim awards (see art. 188, note 2) are subject to art. 190(3) and can thus only directly be challenged on grounds of lack of jurisdiction or wrong constitution of the arbitral tribunal (see ATF 130 III 76 reason 4). This is regardless of whether the interim award deals directly with these issues or whether the arbitral tribunal implicitly took its jurisdiction and correct constitution for granted (see ATF 130 III 76 reason 3.2.1). The Federal Supreme Court follows the same practice under the FSCA and has held that the defendant could not challenge a final award on grounds of lack of jurisdiction since it had not challenged the interim award that took the tribunal's jurisdiction implicitly for granted (see ATF 4A_370/2007 reasons 2.3.1 and 4.2, see also Besson, *Le recours contre la sentence* at 10-12; for a different view see Kaufmann-Kohler/Rigozzi, *LDIP*, n 713 FN 336). With the decision ATF 130 III 76, the Federal Supreme Court put an end to the old jurisprudence according to which interim awards could also be challenged on the grounds listed in art. 190(2)(c) to (e) if they caused irreparable harm to the party concerned (see ATF 116 II 80 reason 3). According to the new practice, an interim award cannot be challenged directly for the reasons contained in art. 190(2)(c) to (e), but only alongside a challenge to the subsequent partial award strico sensu or the final award that has been based on the interim award (see ATF 4P.74/2006 reason 2.1). The fact that a decision by an arbitral tribunal is named "Procedural Order" does not exclude its characterization as an interim award that can be challenged (and has to be challenged if the party wants to avoid being deemed to have waived its objection, see note 3). It is the content of the decision that is decisive for determining whether setting aside proceedings are admissible, not the title of the decision (ATF 4A_210/2008 reason 2.1). For instance, if the "Procedual Order" contains an implicit decision on the tribunal's jurisdiction, it constitutes to this extent an interim award (see ATF 4A_210/2008 reason 2.1).

16. Requirements for the challenge to interim awards. The challenge to interim awards is only subject to the requirements outlined in note 15. Any deviating requirements contained in arts. 90 to 94 FSCA are not applicable (e.g. Besson, *Le recours contre la sentence* at 11-12; Kaufmann-Kohler/Rigozzi, *LDIP*, n 713 et seq.; Poudret, *Tribunal fédéral*, at 678, 689/90, 701). This will be explicitly clarified in an amended version of art. 77(2) FSCA that enters into force in 2011. The aggrieved party must file a motion to set aside the interim award to the extent possible, as it is otherwise deemed to have waived its right to invoke art. 190(2)(a)-(b) (see, e.g., ATF 4P.162/2003 reason 4.3).

17. No appeal against delay or refusal of an arbitral award. The Federal Supreme Court held that, under the FSCA, a challenge based on the duration of the arbitral proceedings (art. 94 ICSA) is inadmissible because art. 190 does not provide for such grounds for appeal (see ATF 4A_160/2007 reason 6; see also Besson, *Le recours contre la sentence* at 11-12). The Federal Code of Civil Procedure will amend art. 77(2) FSCA as of the year 2011 so that the applicability of art. 94 FSCA is expressly excluded.

18. Revision. Art. 190 does not include any provisions on revision. This gap is filled by applying arts. 123-127 FSCA by analogy (see ATF 134 III 286 reason 2.1). Revision of all awards, i.e. final, partial and interim awards, is possible (see ATF 134 III 286 reason 2.2), but not revision of procedural orders (see ATF 4P.237/2005 reason 3.2).

19. Grounds for revision. The Federal Supreme Court admits requests for revision where it is established as a result of criminal proceedings that criminal acts influenced the award to the detriment of the applicant. A conviction by the penal court is not necessary (see ATF 4A_596/2008 reason 4, in which the Federal Supreme Court granted revision based on a foreign investigating magistrate's order to discontinue criminal investigations against a witness who, according to the investigating magistrate, had deceived the arbitral tribunal and thus influenced the award but had passed away in the meantime). If criminal proceedings are not possible, the criminal acts can be proven by other means (art. 123(1) FSCA). Revision is furthermore admissible where the applicant subsequently discovers relevant facts or decisive pieces of evidence that were already in existence when the award was rendered, but that it was unable to plead or adduce in the earlier proceedings despite reasonable diligence (art. 123(2)(a) FSCA), unless such new facts can be introduced in set aside proceedings under art. 99 FSCA (Poudret, *Tribunal fédéral*, at 681; see art. 191, note 5). The new facts and evidence must affect the factual basis of the contested award with the result that they would probably, upon correct legal assessment, lead to an award with a different outcome (see ATF 134 III 286 unpublished reason 4.1; ATF 4P.117/2003 reason 1.2). The new evidence must serve to either prove newly discovered relevant facts on the basis of which revision is sought or relevant facts that were already alleged during the arbitral proceedings but remained unproven (see ATF 4P.117/2003 reason 1.2). More particularly, the new evidence must serve to determine still unproven facts, and not merely to differently assess already known and proven facts (see ATF 134 III 286 unpublished reason 4.1). The requirement that the party be unable to adduce the new evidence in the earlier proceedings despite reasonable diligence is not fulfilled if the evidence was available in the applicant's own domain, for example, in his archives (see ATF 134 III 286 unpublished reason 4.2).

20. Subsequent discovery of incorrect constitution of the tribunal? Under the old Statute on the Organisation of the Federal Judiciary, revision of an arbitral award was not possible on the grounds of subsequent discovery of an incorrect constitution of the arbitral tribunal (e.g. subsequent discovery of lack of independence of an arbitrator), which was held to be subject to art. 190(2)(a) exclusively (see ATF 118 II 199 reason 4). Under the FSCA, it is controversial whether art. 121 FSCA, which provides for such ground for revision, applies by analogy or whether revision is still excluded (see Besson, *Le recours contre la sentence* at 26; Kaufmann-Kohler/Rigozzi, *LDIP*, n 859 for an analogous application of art. 121(a) FSCA; see Berger/Kellerhals, *Schiedsgerichtsbarkeit*, n 1788 for the opposite view). The Federal Supreme Court left the question undecided (see ATF 4A_528/2007 reason 2.4-2.5). In any case, revision is excluded if the applicant could and should have discovered the alleged incorrect constitution of the tribunal during the arbitration proceedings (see ATF 4A_528/2007 reason 2.5) or if the applicant discovered it within the time-limit for challenging the award, even if the challenge is excluded under art. 192 (ATF 4A_234/2008 reason 2.1).

21. Revision proceedings. The applicant must file a motion for revision with the Federal Supreme Court within 90 days of discovering the grounds for revision but not before receipt of the reasoned arbitral award or the closing of the criminal proceedings (art. 124(1)(d) FSCA). After ten years, revision is only admissible in the case of criminal acts (art. 124(2) FSCA). The motion must indicate the changes to be made to the award and the repayments that are being claimed, the grounds for revision and the related evidence, and must also show that the motion was filed in time. The Federal Supreme Court can grant the application suspensive effect (art. 126 FSCA). It serves the motion to the other party and to the arbitral tribunal for their comments (art. 127 FSCA). If the Federal Supreme Court upholds the motion for revision, it will annul the award and refer the matter either back to the former arbitral tribunal or to an arbitral tribunal that will be newly constituted for this purpose (see ATF 4P.102/2006 reason 1; ATF 4P.237/2005 reason 2).

22. Nullity of the award. If an arbitral award is null and void, the nullity can be asserted by a declaratory action or by objection in the course of recognition and enforcement procedures (see ATF 130 III 125 reason 3.1). The award is null and void only in exceptional cases if the shortcomings of the proceedings are unacceptable, for instance, if an arbitral award is rendered without an arbitration agreement and without any proceedings (see ATF 130 III 125 reason 3.1).

[Setting aside: competent authority]
Article 191

Setting aside proceedings may only be brought before the Swiss Federal Supreme Court. The procedure is governed by art. 77 of the Federal Supreme Court Act of 17 June 2005.

1. General. Awards rendered by arbitral tribunals with their seat in Switzerland can only be challenged before the Federal Supreme Court. On 1 January 2007, paragraph 2 of art. 191, which allowed the parties to agree on the jurisdiction of a cantonal court instead of the Federal Supreme Court, was abolished. The procedure before the Federal Supreme Court is governed by art. 77 of the Federal Supreme Court Act (FSCA), which entered into force on 1 January 2007 and replaced the provisions of the Federal Statute on the Organisation of the Federal Judiciary. The Federal Code of Civil Procedure will amend art. 77(2) FSCA as of 2011. For a detailed analysis of the proceedings under the FSCA, see Besson, *Le recours contre la sentence* at 13 et seq. For statistics regarding the duration of set aside proceedings, see Dasser, *International Arbitration* at 456-459.

2. Suspensive effect. The setting aside proceedings do not suspend the challenged award: it remains effective and enforceable, unless the judge in charge of the proceedings grants the suspension upon request or – in theory – ex officio (art. 103(1) and (3) FSCA). The suspension will only be granted to safeguard the legally protected interests of a party from a serious and irreparable damage; if, for example, the award requires the appellant to pay a certain sum, suspension can only be obtained if the payment would cause him financial difficulties, or if the solvency of the creditor is doubtful so that any restitution would seem unlikely (Président ATF, 14 December 1993). The decision is thus subject to a weighing of interests. Furthermore, a suspension may only be granted if a prima facie examination shows the likelihood that the challenge is well-founded (Berti-Berti/Schnyder, n 25 ad art. 191; Kaufmann-Kohler/Rigozzi, *LDIP*, n 781; Poudret, *Tribunal fédéral*, at 683).

3. Deadline for the challenge. The motion to set aside the arbitral award must be filed with the Federal Supreme Court in Lausanne within thirty days of notification of the award (art. 77 together with 100(1) FSCA; see art. 189, note 4). It is sufficient if the brief is delivered to the Swiss mail service by the deadline (art. 48(1) FSCA). Submitting the motion by telefax does not meet the deadline (ATF 4A_258/2008 reason 2). The thirty-day time period does not include court holidays (15 July to 15 August, 18 December to 2 January, and the seven days preceding and following Easter, art. 46(1) FSCA); it cannot be extended (art. 47(1) FSCA). However, an aggrieved party or its representative, who have been prevented from meeting the deadline through no fault of their own, can ask for a new time limit to be established and can challenge the award if both the motion to set it aside and a request for a new time limit (noting the reason for the party's failure to submit on time) are filed within thirty days of whatever event prevented the party from submitting its motion on time (art. 50 FSCA).

4. Further requirements of the challenge. Setting aside proceedings are admissible against final awards, against partial awards stricto sensu (see art. 188, note 2, art. 190, note 3) and, under certain conditions, against interim awards (see art. 190, notes 15-16). The parties to the arbitration can file the motion if they demonstrate a legal interest in having the award set aside (art. 76 FSCA). It has not yet been decided whether the requirement for a minimum amount in dispute in pecuniary matters (CHF 15,000 for matters of labour law and law of tenancy, CHF 30,000 for other matters, art. 74(1) FSCA) also applies to challenges against arbitral awards. The majority of legal commentators deny the applicability of art. 74(1) FSCA (Berger/Kellerhals, *Schiedsgerichtsbarkeit*, n 1622; Besson, *Le recours contre la sentence* at 16-17; Kaufmann-Kohler/Rigozzi, *LDIP* n 737 et seq.; Poudret, *Tribunal fédéral*, at 688-689).

5. Content of the written brief. The brief must be written in German, French or Italian, must identify the challenged arbitral award (which should, preferably, be attached), and must contain the appellant's requests, his signature, the grounds for the challenge and the evidence (art. 42(1) and (3) FSCA). With regard to the grounds for challenge, the brief must set out the grounds for setting aside the award under art. 190(2) and must show in detail which parts of the challenged decision violate which principle laid down in art. 190(2) and in what way (art. 77(3) FSCA; e.g. ATF 4A_160/2007 reason 2.2; ATF 4P.114/2003 reason 1.3). If, for example, the appellant invokes a violation of public policy, he must show in detail which legal principle was violated and how it was violated and must demonstrate that it forms part of public policy (see, e.g., ATF 4P.23/2006 reason 4.3). If the appellant invokes a violation of the right to be heard, he has to demonstrate in detail that the arbitral tribunal did not examine certain (clearly identified) facts, pieces of evidence or arguments that the appellant had submitted in accordance with the procedural rules and that these elements were relevant for the outcome of the case; it is not required that the appellant demonstrate the reasons why the arbitral tribunal omitted these elements. The burden is on the arbitral tribunal or the counterparty to justify the omissions (see, e.g., ATF 4A_18/2007 reason 5.1). The requirement of substantiated objections is of utmost importance; the Federal Supreme Court regularly rejects objections because they have not been sufficiently substantiated (see, e.g., very incisively ATF 4P.32/2007 reason 3.2). Only when the arbitral tribunal's decision on jurisdiction is challenged under art. 190(2)(b) is it sufficient to simply state why this decision is wrong and in violation of the law (see ATF 4P.137/2002 reason 5.1 with further references). However, even in this case the appellant must draw the attention of the Federal Supreme Court to the legal arguments that justify the challenge (see, e.g., ATF 4P.32/2007 reason 3.1). If the arbitral award is based on several independent arguments, the appellant must effectively challenge all of these arguments, since otherwise the Federal Supreme Court will dismiss the motion without examining the merits (see ATF 4P.114/2006 reason 4.4). The appellant's objections and arguments must be based on the facts established by the arbitral tribunal; the appellant cannot simply present his own view of the relevant facts and base his arguments on them (see, e.g., ATF 4A_220/2007 reason 5.2). The Federal Supreme Court can only exceptionally review the facts established by the arbitral tribunal (see note 9). The brief may contain new facts and new evidence only if the arbitral award has given rise to these (art. 99(1) FSCA, see also note 9), i.e. if it is only as a result of the award that the new facts and evidence have become relevant (Besson, *Le recours contre la sentence* at 25; Poudret, *Tribunal fédéral*, at 680 with examples). If, for example, the award states that all the arbitrators participated in the deliberations, the appellant can introduce the new fact that one of the arbitrators did not, in fact, participate. New prayers for relief are inadmissible (art. 99(2) FSCA).

6. Setting aside proceedings. If the motion to set aside the arbitral award is manifestly inadmissible or contains a manifestly inadequate substantiation, it will be dismissed by a single judge (art. 108 FSCA). Otherwise, the Federal Supreme Court notifies the other party and the arbitral tribunal of the motion and sets an appropriate deadline for them to file submissions and observations and to produce the file (art. 102(1) and (2) FSCA). Parties abroad must appoint a representative in Switzerland (art. 39(3) FSCA). After the exchange of briefs (see note 7), the president of the responsible chamber of the Federal Supreme Court can order a hearing (art. 57 FSCA); this is, however, the exception. Otherwise, the Federal Supreme Court, which normally consists of three or, upon request, one or five judges, directly renders its decision. The judges normally decide without oral deliberation; an oral deliberation can, however, be requested by an individual judge (art. 58 FSCA). At any stage of the proceedings, the judge in charge of the proceedings can grant interim measures in order to preserve the status quo or to protect endangered interests (art. 104 FSCA).

7. Setting aside proceedings: second exchange of briefs. There is usually no second exchange of briefs (art. 102(3) FSCA). The Federal Supreme Court will only invite the parties to a second exchange of briefs if the counterparty raised essential new arguments in its answer that the appellant could not have reasonably anticipated (see ATF 4P.114/2006 reason 3.2.1; for details, see Besson, *Le recours contre la sentence* at 19 et seq.). A reservation by the appellant in his first brief to be allowed a second exchange of briefs is premature and will not have any effect (see ATF 4P.114/2006 reason 3.2). The appellant can only request a second exchange of briefs after receiving the counterparty's brief and/or the arbitral tribunal's observations and should do so without delay. The request should show which new arguments the appellant wants to respond to, why they are relevant to the outcome of the decision and why the second exchange of briefs is indispensable to respect the appellant's right to be heard (see ATF 4A_268/2007 reason 2.2; Kaufmann-Kohler/Rigozzi, *LDIP*, n 783). However, the Federal Supreme Court is not consistent regarding whether such a request is advisable. In a case where the appellant had requested a second exchange of briefs, the Federal Supreme Court has held that if the appellant considers it necessary to submit comments on new arguments raised by the counterparty without being invited to do so, he should submit his comments without seeking leave and without any delay (see ATF 4A_137/2007 reason 2.2 with further references).

8. Publicity of the proceedings. If a hearing and/or oral deliberations take place, both are, as a rule, open to the public (art. 59(1) FSCA). However, the Federal Supreme Court can exclude the public if, inter alia, publicity would be against the interests of one party (art. 59(2) FSCA). When ruling on this issue, the Federal Supreme Court takes into account the increased need for confidentiality in many arbitrations (see ATF 4P.74/2006 reason 8.3). The Federal Supreme Court has held that the principle of publicity should not lead to a party waiving its right to a challenge due to a fear of publicity (see ATF 4P.74/2006 reason 8.3). After the Federal Supreme Court has rendered and announced its decision, it makes the outcome (dismissal/approval) with the parties' names at the seat of the Federal Supreme Court publicly available, unless the parties state an interest in keeping their names and the existence of the proceedings confidential (see ATF 4P.74/2006 reason 8.4). Publication of the full decision will then appear on the internet, normally in an anonymised form as long as the knowledge of the parties' names is not necessary for the understanding of the significance of the decision (art. 27(2) FSCA; see ATF 4A_244/2007 reason 2), and unless the parties present an argument against publication that prevails over the public's right to be informed about the jurisprudence of the Federal Supreme Court (see ATF 4P.74/2006 reason 8.5).

9. Scope of examination by the Federal Supreme Court. The Federal Supreme Court only examines the objections under art. 190 to the extent that they have been sufficiently substantiated (see note 5). To this extent, however, the Federal Supreme Court examines the objections with unfettered powers (Besson, *Le recours contre la sentence* at 24; Poudret, *Tribunal fédéral*, at 684). The Court is bound by the facts as established by the arbitral tribunal (arts. 77 together with 105(1) FSCA), unless the establishment of the facts itself violated art. 190(2)(d) and (e) (see ATF 4P.48/2005 reason 3.1 with further references; see also note 5) or unless the Court may take into account new facts and new evidence pursuant to art. 99(1) FSCA (see note 5). Under art. 190(2)(b), the Federal Supreme Court examines the legal grounds for alleged jurisdiction or lack thereof with unfettered powers, including the consideration of any relevant substantive preliminary questions such as a valid assignment of a contract that includes an arbitration agreement (see ATF 128 III 50 reason 2a; art. 190, note 6).

10. Decision by the Federal Supreme Court. If the appellant's motion is upheld, the Federal Supreme Court generally sets aside the arbitral award and refers the matter back to the arbitral tribunal (arts. 77(2) together with 107(2) FSCA). However, if the party objected to the arbitral tribunal's decision on jurisdiction (art. 190(2)(b)), the Federal Supreme Court bindingly establishes the arbitral tribunal's jurisdiction or lack thereof (e.g. ATF 127 III 279 reason 1b). If the Federal Supreme Court establishes the arbitral tribunal's jurisdiction and refers the matter back to the tribunal, the arbitral tribunal is bound by this decision and must decide on the merits (see ATF 117 II 94 reason 4). It has not yet been decided whether the Federal Supreme Court can itself dismiss an arbitrator if his challenge is upheld under art. 190(2)(a) (see ATF 4P.196/2003 reason 2.2; in favour of this possibility are, e.g., Besson, *Le recours contre la sentence* at 22, Kaufmann-Kohler/Rigozzi, *LDIP*, n 779; Poudret, *Tribunal fédéral*, at 686).

[Waiver of setting aside proceedings]

Article 192

(1) If none of the parties have their domicile, their habitual residence, or a business establishment in Switzerland, they may, by an express statement in the arbitration agreement, or in a subsequent written agreement, waive all setting aside proceedings, or limit such proceedings to one or more of the grounds listed in Article 190(2).

(2) If the parties have waived all setting aside proceedings and if the awards are to be enforced in Switzerland, the New York Convention of 10 June 1958 on the Recognition and Enforcement of Foreign Arbitral Awards applies by analogy.

1. Possibility and effect of a waiver. Unlike many other jurisdictions, Swiss law allows a complete waiver of setting aside proceedings either in the arbitration agreement itself, or in a subsequent written agreement, provided that the parties do not have close connections to Switzerland. Although this waiver option has been criticised by a number of legal commentators, the Federal Supreme Court, lacking the authority to examine the constitutionality of a federal statute, is obliged to apply art. 192, and the debtor cannot invoke public policy against the waiver (see ATF 4P.198/2005 reason 2.2). If a foreign 'loi d'application immédiate' (see art. 187, note 4) prohibits the waiver of remedies against arbitral awards, this prohibition will have no effect in Switzerland (see ATF 4P.198/2005 reason 2.1). Unless it is only partial (see note 5), a waiver excludes setting aside proceedings for all grounds listed in art. 190, including an objection that the arbitration clause and the waiver do not cover the dispute (see ATF 134 III 260 reason 3.2.4) or that they do not bind a non-signatory (see ATF 131 III 173 reason 4.1; legal commentators have criticised this decision, see e.g., Besson, *Etendue du contrôle* at 1080; Basel Commentary-Patocchi/Jermini, n 19 ad art. 192 with further reference). In any event, the parties still enjoy some protection, as art. 192(2) calls for an examination of the award under the New York Convention at the enforcement stage (see note 8).

2. Requirements of a waiver. The parties can only waive their right to challenge the arbitral award if they do not have close connections with Switzerland, as defined by art. 192(1) (see note 3); if they explicitly express the waiver, either in the arbitration agreement or subsequently (see note 4); and if the agreement on the waiver is in writing, as defined by art. 178(1). On the face of art. 192(1), there are no further requirements. However, with regard to international sports arbitration, the Federal Supreme Court held that a waiver is not valid if the athlete in question had no choice but to sign the declaration in order to participate in the events of the professional sports organisation (see ATF 133 III 235 reason 4.3.2.2 and 4.4.2; also Kaufmann-Köhler/Rigozzi, *LDIP*, n 766/7). If the parties to a contract include by reference an arbitration agreement contained in another contract between them (arbitration agreement by reference), they automatically also include the waiver contained in this arbitration agreement (see ATF 4P.198/2005 reason 1.3).

3. No close connection to Switzerland. A waiver requires that the parties to the arbitral proceedings have neither a domicile, nor a habitual residence nor a business establishment in Switzerland. The situation at the time of the waiver is decisive (see ATF 4P.113/2001; Basel Commentary-Patocchi/Jermini, n 12 ad art. 192 with references). The nationality of the parties and any connection of the subject matter of the dispute to Switzerland are not relevant. The domicile of a person is the place where he resides with the intent of permanently settling there (art. 20(1)(a) PILA). The habitual residence of a person is the place where he lives for an extended period (e.g. a couple of months), even if this period was limited from the beginning (art. 20(1)(b) PILA). The business establishment of a person is the place where he has the centre of his business activities (art. 20(1)(c) PILA). The domicile of a company is the statutory seat or, failing such designation, the place of actual management (art. 21(1) and (2) PILA). The business establishment of a company is in the state where it has its registered office or a branch (art. 21(3) PILA). If one party has a branch in Switzerland, the possibility of a waiver is excluded even if the dispute has no connection with this branch (Berger/Kellerhals, *Schiedsgerichtsbarkeit*, n 1673 with references). The existence of a subsidiary in Switzerland does not exclude the waiver, as long as the subsidiary is not involved in the proceedings (Berger/Kellerhals, *Schiedsgerichtsbarkeit*, n 1673 FN 239).

4. Explicit waiver. The waiver must be explicit. First, this requires that the parties themselves formulated the waiver. It is not sufficient to globally refer to the by-laws of an organisation, to a set of arbitration rules or to similar documents that contain a waiver (see ATF 133 III 235 reason 4.3.1 with references). In any event, Art. 28(6) ICC Rules of Arbitration is not considered to constitute a waiver. An exception exists with respect to waivers contained in investment treaties where the Federal Supreme Court held that they are also binding on the investor who is not a party to the treaty (see ATF 4P.114/2006 reason 5.4). Secondly, waiver requires that the parties unambiguously express their clear intent to waive all remedies against the arbitral tribunal's awards. Originally, the Federal Supreme Court required the parties to expressly state the excluded remedy (see ATF 116 II 639 reason 2c). However, it has since abolished this strict formulation and now acknowledges that it is a matter of the construction of each single agreement as to whether it unambiguously reflects the parties' intention to obtain a waiver (see ATF 133 III 235 reason 4.3.1; ATF 131 III 173 reason 4.2.3.1; ATF 4P.206/2006 reason 3). Even though it is recommended that the parties explicitly refer to art. 192, it is not mandatory (see ATF 131 III 173 reason 4.2.3.1). The Federal Supreme Court accepted the formulation 'the parties […] exclude all and any rights of appeal from all and any awards insofar as such exclusion can validly be made' (see ATF 131 III 173 reason 4.2.3.2, see for another example ATF 134 III 260 reason 3.2.2). The formulation that the award is 'final and binding' upon the parties is clearly insufficient, even when contained in an investment treaty (see ATF 4P.114/2006 reason 5.3-5.4). The Federal Supreme Court also refused the formulation '[t]he application to the State Courts are [sic] excluded', as the clause did not make clear whether it constituted a waiver in the sense of art. 192, or only excluded the state court's jurisdiction to hear the case (see ATF, 2 July 1997, reason 1a). Either way, the construction is rather restrictive, even in cases where the dispute has no connection to Switzerland (see ATF 4P.114/2006 reason 5.2).

5. Partial waiver. Instead of waiving all remedies against arbitral awards, the parties can exclude just one or more grounds for challenge contained in art. 190(2). For example, they can exclude the challenge to the arbitral tribunal's decision on jurisdiction under art. 190(2)(b) (upheld in ATF 4P.98/2005 reason 4.2). For a valid partial waiver, the parties must explicitly state the grounds for challenge that they want to exclude, either by indicating the corresponding sub-paragraph of art. 190(2), by reproducing the legal text or by any other formulation that allows clear identification of the excluded ground for challenge (see ATF 131 III 173 reason 4.2.3.1 in fine). If the parties have waived their right to invoke one or more grounds for challenge contained in art. 190(2)(a) to (d), they cannot circumvent this waiver by invoking public policy if the waived grounds are part of public policy (see Basel Commentary Patocchi/Jermini, n 26-28 ad art. 192).

6. Challenge to the award despite a possible waiver. If it seems possible that the parties agreed on a waiver under art. 192, the party filing a motion to set aside the arbitral award must present its arguments on this issue in its first brief. If it fails to do so and the counterparty relies on the waiver in its answer, the appellant will normally not, subject to special circumstances, be granted the option of a second exchange of briefs (see ATF 4P.114/2006 reason 3.2.2; see art. 191, note 7). The Federal Supreme Court, ex officio, makes a thorough determination of the existence or non-existence of a valid waiver, since the absence of such waiver is a requirement for entering into the merits (see ATF 4P.114/2006 reason 3.2.2).

7. Waiver of other remedies. It is controversial whether the parties can also waive their right to a revision of the decision (in favour of this possibility, see, e.g., Berger/Kellerhals, *Schiedsgerichtsbarkeit*, n 1812 et seq., against this possibility, see, e.g., Basel Commentary-Patocchi/Jermini, n 22 ad art. 192; for revision, see art. 190, note 18 et seq.). The parties cannot validly waive their right to appeal against court decisions under arts. 179(2), 183(2), 184(2) and 185 (Basel Commentary-Patocchi/Jermini, n 23 ad art. 192; Berger/Kellerhals, *Schiedsgerichtsbarkeit*, n 1684).

8. Protection by the New York Convention. If the parties have waived all remedies against the arbitral tribunal's awards, they are still protected by the New York Convention. When the arbitral award is to be enforced abroad, the foreign court will examine whether it has to refuse recognition and enforcement on the grounds of art. V New York Convention. If the award must be enforced in Switzerland, art. 192(2) declares the New York Convention applicable by analogy. Thus, the competent Swiss court in the course of the enforcement proceedings will refuse the enforcement based on art. V New York Convention if grounds for such refusal exist. However, the grounds for refusal contained in art. V New York Convention and the grounds for challenge stated in art. 190(2) are not congruent, the former being broader in scope than the latter. Where art. V New York Convention provides for a refusal of the enforcement although art. 190(2) would not allow setting aside the award, the majority of legal commentators apply the grounds for denying enforcement under art. V New York Convention only to the extent that these grounds would also lead to a setting aside of the award under art. 190(2) (Basel Commentary-Patocchi/Jermini, n 31 ad art. 192; Berger/Kellerhals, *Schiedsgerichtsbarkeit*, n 1695). Otherwise, the waiver would restrict the possibility of enforcing the award in Switzerland even though this was not the intention of the parties. If the parties have agreed on a partial waiver, the courts in Switzerland will exercise their supervisory function under art. 192(2) by examining whether enforcement may be denied under those grounds under art. V New York Convention that correspond to the grounds waived by the parties (Basel Commentary Patocchi/Jermini, n 35 ad art. 192). In any event, the decision of the state court is subject to cantonal remedies under the cantonal codes of civil procedure (as of 2011: the remedies under the Federal Code of Civil Procedure) and, in the last instance, to the appeal in civil matters under the FSCA.

Swiss Private International Law Act (Chapter 12), art. 193

[Deposit and certificate of enforceability]

Article 193

(1) Each party may at its own expense deposit a copy of the award with the Swiss court at the seat of the arbitral tribunal.

(2) At the request of a party, that court shall certify the enforceability of the award.

(3) At the request of a party, the arbitral tribunal shall certify that the award has been rendered pursuant to the provisions of this Act; such certificate is equivalent to depositing the award with the court.

1. General. Art. 193 provides for acts by the courts and the arbitral tribunal that are aimed at facilitating the enforcement of the arbitral award.

2. Deposit of the award. Depositing the award with the court under art. 193(1) has no legal effect under Swiss law. The parties may wish to deposit the award because it is so required by the law at the foreign place of enforcement, in order to have it safely stored, or to stress the Swiss nature of the award. Which court or judge has the competence is a matter of cantonal law; in the Canton of Zurich it is the Obergericht (§ 239(2) Zurich Code of Civil Procedure), and in the Canton of Geneva it is the president of the Tribunal de première instance (art. 461C Geneva Code of Civil Procedure).

3. Certificate of enforceability. The certificate of enforceability under art. 193(2) attests that the award is binding and enforceable as required by art. V(1)(e) New York Convention. It has declaratory meaning and is not a prerequisite of enforceability, as the award is already final and enforceable as soon as it has been communicated (art. 190(1)). The effects of certification are thus confined to facilitating proof of the formal legal status of the award as far as the Swiss law at the seat of the arbitration is concerned. If the arbitral award is to be enforced in Switzerland, the creditor can enforce it quickly and with little possibility of the debtor objecting if either the certificate under art. 193(2) or any other document that establishes the enforceability of the award is produced (Tribunal cantonal de Fribourg, 24 March 2004, reason 2; Obergericht Solothurn, 27 September 2001, reason 1a). If the creditor produces the certificate, it is binding on the Swiss court of enforcement (Obergericht Solothurn, 27 September 2001, reason 2a). The court can refuse enforcement only if the award is null and void (see art. 190, note 22), not because the applicant fails to produce the arbitration agreement, nor for grounds that could have been raised when challenging the award under art. 190 (see ATF 130 III 125 reason 2). Should setting aside proceedings have been waived under art. 192, the court of enforcement will examine art. 192(2).

4. Issuance of the certificate of enforceability. The certificate is issued by the competent court (see note 2) upon request by one party, provided that: either no motion to set aside the award has been filed within thirty days (see art. 191, note 3); a motion has been filed but has no suspensive effect (see art. 191, note 2); it has been dismissed; or the parties have validly waived their right to challenge under art. 192, in which case the majority of legal commentators take the view that the certifying court should not carry out the examination under art. 192(2) (e.g. Berti-Berti, n 13 ad art. 193; Berger/Kellerhals, *Schiedsgerichtsbarkeit*, n 1836 with further references). The arbitral tribunal itself may also file a request, e.g., for the purposes of enforcing its fees (Obergericht Zürich, 1 December 2005). The certifying court examines whether the award is null and void or has obvious formal errors such as the lack of a signature (Berti-Berti, n 12 ad art. 193), and whether it is indeed an award rather than an expert determination (see ATF 130 III 125 reason 2.1.2). It is a matter of controversy whether the certificate is only to be issued if the subject matter of the dispute is arbitrable under art. 177 (in favour of this requirement Berger/Kellerhals, *Schiedsgerichtsbarkeit*, n 1835; against this requirement Lalive/Poudret/Reymond, *L'Arbitrage*, n 2 ad art. 193).

5. Certificate by the arbitral tribunal. A certificate by the arbitral tribunal that the award has been rendered pursuant to art. 176 et seq. has the same effect as the deposit of the award under art. 193(1). The certification under art. 193(3) has no legal effect apart from documenting the statement of the arbitral tribunal that it proceeded pursuant to the rules of chapter 12 PILA. Whether a deposit of the award with a court is required or whether the certificate of the arbitral tribunal is accepted as equivalent depends on the law at the place of enforcement.

[Foreign arbitral awards]
Article 194
The recognition and enforcement of foreign arbitral awards is governed by the New York Convention of 10 June 1958 on the Recognition and Enforcement of Foreign Arbitral Awards.

Note. As the New York Convention on the Recognition and Enforcement of Foreign Arbitral Awards is dealt with separately in this Commentary, we shall limit our comments to those issues which are specifically related to the practice and procedure in Switzerland.

1. General. Art. 194 constitutes a declaratory reference to the New York Convention for the recognition and enforcement of awards rendered by arbitral tribunals with their seat outside Switzerland. Thus, the recognition and enforcement of a foreign award is completely governed by the New York Convention, which, for Switzerland, applies erga omnes, irrespective of whether or not the award was rendered in a contracting state of the New York Convention (see art. I New York Convention). For an award made in Switzerland, the New York Convention can only become relevant in Swiss enforcement proceedings if the parties have waived the setting aside proceedings pursuant to art. 192 (see art. 192, note 8). Despite the reference to the New York Convention in art. 194 PILA, the New York Convention is not applicable in Switzerland as a national law, but rather as an international treaty. As a consequence, in order to ensure internationally uniform application, Swiss courts are also required to take into account foreign decisions interpreting the New York Convention (Berti-Patocchi/Jermini, n 20 ad art. 194). The New York Convention does not exclude the applicability of other multilateral or bilateral treaties, provided that their application is, in any given case, more favourable to the recognition and enforcement of the award (art. VII(1) New York Convention). For example, a foreign ICSID award must be recognised and enforced under art. 54 of the Washington Convention on the Settlement of Investment Disputes Between States and Nationals of Other States of 18 March 1965 without any form of control by Swiss courts. Bilateral treaties exist with Austria, Belgium, the Czech Republic, Germany, Italy, Liechtenstein, Slovakia, Spain and Sweden (see Zurich Commentary-Siehr, n 1 ad art. 194).

2. Recognition and enforcement under the New York Convention. Recognition of a foreign arbitral award means that the award has the same effect in Switzerland as in the state of origin, in particular the res judicata effect. Recognition and enforcement of an award are subject to the same requirements under the New York Convention. The New York Convention defines what constitutes an arbitral award. A party seeking recognition or enforcement must submit the documents set out in art. IV New York Convention to the competent court. In cases of non-compliance with art. IV(1) New York Convention, Swiss courts are not excessively rule-bound and are reluctant to deny recognition and enforcement for purely formal reasons, such as, e.g., if the authenticity of a photocopy is not disputed (see Cour de Justice de Genève, 15 April 1999, reason 5 with further references; see also ATF 4P.173/2003 reason 2).

3. Grounds for refusal under art. V(2) New York Convention. While the court examines the grounds for refusing recognition and enforcement under art. V(1) New York Convention only upon request of a party, the grounds contained in art. V(2) New York Convention are examined ex officio. Under art. V(2)(a) New York Convention, a foreign arbitral award will not be recognised and enforced in Switzerland if the subject matter of the dispute is not arbitrable. It is controversial whether this refers to the concept of arbitrability under art. 177 (Basel Commentary-Patocchi/Jermini, n 122 ad art. 194; see also Kaufmann-Kohler/Rigozzi, *LDIP*, n 898) or whether recognition and enforcement can only be refused if the non-arbitrability under art. 177 amounts to a violation of public policy (Berger/Kellerhals, *Schiedsgerichtsbarkeit*, n 1917). Swiss courts have not yet ruled upon this question. Under art. V(2)(b) New York Convention, the recognition and enforcement of a foreign award can be refused if they would violate public policy. The notion of public policy under art. V(2)(b) New York Convention comprises both substantive and procedural public policy and must be applied restrictively (see ATF 4P.173/2003 reason 4.1). This means that even if an award rendered in Switzerland could be set aside under art. 190(2)(e), recognition and enforcement can only be refused if the fundamental principles have been violated in an unacceptable manner (see ATF 101 Ia 521 reason 4a). The Federal Supreme Court has ruled that there was no violation of public policy under art. V(2)(b) New York Convention in cases where the arbitral award did not state any reasons for the award (see ATF 101 Ia 521 reason 4), where the arbitral tribunal issued an interim award on jurisdiction in which it ordered the respondent to reimburse the claimant for the respondent's share of the advance on costs which the claimant had fully paid (see ATF 4P.173/2003 reason 4.2) and where a pactum de palmario was agreed upon, i.e. a supplementary remuneration for the attorney should the case in question have succeeded on the merits (see ATF, 9 January 1995, reason 7).

4. Concept of public policy under art. V(2)(b) New York Convention. Traditionally, the Federal Supreme Court has invoked only Swiss public policy and has held that art. V(2)(b) applies where 'the recognition or enforcement of a foreign award violates in an unacceptable way the Swiss concept of justice' (see ATF 4P.173/2003 reason 4.1; ATF, 9 January 1995, reason 7). In 2006, the Federal Supreme Court interpreted public policy under art. 190(2)(e) as an internationalised concept (see art. 190, note 10). As public policy at the stage of recognition and enforcement must generally be interpreted more restrictively, it can be expected that the Federal Supreme Court will now apply the same standard also under art. V(2)(b) New York Convention. The difference between a Swiss and an internationalised concept of public policy can become relevant with regards to, e.g., punitive damages. While a foreign punitive damages award would most likely be recognised and enforced under an internationalised concept of public policy, recognition and enforcement might be refused under a Swiss concept (see art. 190, note 12).

5. Enforcement of awards of a sum of money. In Switzerland, the creditor of a sum of money can already start enforcement proceedings under the Swiss Debt Enforcement and Bankruptcy Law (DEBL) before he has obtained an enforceable judgement or award. The creditor can apply for enforcement proceedings at the place where the debtor has its domicile, seat or branch, has designated special domicile, or has assets for which the creditor has obtained a Swiss freezing order (arts. 46, 50, 52 DEBL). The enforcement office immediately issues and serves the debtor with a summons to pay (art. 69 DEBL), to which the debtor can object within ten days without stating its reasons. If there is no objection, the summons to pay becomes enforceable. If the debtor objects, the proceedings then hinge on whether or not the creditor has already obtained an award. If it has obtained a foreign arbitral award, it can apply to the court to definitively set aside the objection in summary proceedings. The local courts competent in this regard are: the Einzelrichter (single judge; § 213(2) Zurich Code of Civil Procedure) of the

Bezirksgericht in the Canton of Zurich, and the Tribunal de première instance (art. 20(1)(b) Geneva Code of Application of the DEBL) in the Canton of Geneva. In the course of the summary proceedings, the court decides as a preliminary question upon the recognition and enforceability of the award under the New York Convention. If it accepts enforceability, the court sets aside the debtor's objection unless the debtor successfully invokes the statute of limitations or produces documents showing that, since the award was rendered, the debt has been discharged or payment terms have been extended (art. 81 DEBL). As far as the application of the New York Convention is concerned, and if the requirements (e.g. the minimum amount in dispute) are fulfilled, cantonal remedies (as of 2011: the remedies under the Federal Code of Civil Procedure), as well as an appeal in civil matters to the Federal Supreme Court under the Federal Supreme Court Act, are admissible against the decision of the lower instance. If the debtor's objection is definitively set aside, the enforcement proceedings continue by means of seizure of assets or bankruptcy proceedings. If the creditor has not yet obtained an arbitral award but has succeeded in provisionally removing the debtor's objection to the summons to pay, e.g., on the basis of a written acknowledgment of debt, the debtor must start an action on the merits before the arbitral tribunal if it wants to have its objection upheld (see ATF 7B.55/2006 reason 3 and lower instance's decision cited in para. G.b.a).

6. Enforcement of non-monetary awards. The enforcement of awards ordering, e.g., specific performance or injunctions is still subject to cantonal law. Typically, these cantonal rules provide for summary proceedings similar to those applicable to the enforcement of monetary awards. When the Federal Code of Civil Procedure (FCCP) enters into force in 2011, these cases will be treated uniformly throughout Switzerland. Under the FCCP, the court carries out, in summary proceedings (art. 339(2) FCCP), the same examination of the enforceability of the award as in the case of a monetary award (note 5). In addition, the debtor can invoke the statute of limitations or forfeiture of the claims or can produce documents showing that, since the award was rendered, he has discharged the debt or the creditor has extended the performance terms (art. 341(3) FCCP). If the award orders the losing party to take certain actions, the court can order means of coercion or fines, or it can threaten a fine in case of non-compliance under art. 292 of the Swiss Criminal Code (art. 343 FCCP). If the award orders the losing party to make a declaration of intent (for example, to declare its consent to a transaction), the court may order that the award replace the party's declaration (art. 344 FCCP).

LIST OF ABBREVIATIONS

1950 Act	Arbitration Act 1950 (c. 27)
1975 Act	Arbitration Act 1975 (c. 3)
1979 Act	Arbitration Act 1979 (c. 42)
Australia Act	ICSID Implementation Act 1990 (Act No. 107 of 1990)
BIT(s)	Bilateral Investment Treaty(ies)
Canadian SIA	State Immunity Act 1982
CaS	Causa Sport. Die Sport-Zeitschrift für nationales und internationales Recht sowie für Wirtschaft (Zurich)
CCIG	Chambre de commerce, d'industrie et des services de Genève [Geneva Chamber of Commerce and Industry]
CPR	Civil Procedure Rules
DA	Decision on Annulment
DAC	Department of Trade & Industry Departmental Advisory Committee on *International Commercial Arbitration*
DAC Reports	Report on the Arbitration Bill of the Departmental Advisory Committee on Arbitration Law, chaired by The Rt. Hon. Lord Justice Saville, February 1996 / Supplementary Report on the Arbitration Act 1996, January 1997
DEBL	Swiss Debt Enforcement and Bankruptcy Law of 11 April 1889
Denmark Act	Act No. 466 of December 15, 1967, on Recognition and Execution of Orders Concerning Certain International Investment Disputes
DI	Decision on Interpretation
DJ	Decision on Jurisdiction
DPI	Decision on Preliminary Issues
DPM	Decision on Protective Measures
DS	Decision on Request for a Continued Stay of Enforcement/Execution of the Award
DSR	Decision on Supplementation and Rectification
ECHR	European Convention for the Protection of Human Rights and Fundamental Freedoms (1950) and 11 protocols.
EU	European Union
FA	Final Award
FCCP	Swiss Federal Code of Civil Procedure (enters into force in 2011)

List of Abbreviations

FIFA	Fédération Internationale de Football Association [International Federation of Association Football]
FSCA	Swiss Federal Supreme Court Act of 17 June 2005
ICC	International Chamber of Commerce
ICJ	International Court of Justice
ICSID	International Centre for Settlement of Investment Disputes
IHK	Internationale Handelskammer [International Chamber of Commerce]
ILM	International Legal Materials
IMF	International Monetary Fund
IOC	International Olympic Committee
Ireland Act	Arbitration Act 1980
LCIA	London Court of International Arbitration
LDIP	Loi fédérale du 18 décembre 1987 sur le droit international privé [Swiss Private International Law Act]
Model Law	UNCITRAL Model Law on International Commercial Arbitration, adopted by the United Nations Commission on International Trade Law on June 21, 1985
New York Convention	Convention on the Recognition and Enforcement of Foreign Arbitral Awards, New York, June 10, 1958
NYC	1958 New York Convention on the Recognition and Enforcement of Foreign Arbitral Awards
NZ Act	Arbitration (International Investment Disputes) Act, 1979, (Act No. 39 of 1979) as amended by the Arbitration (International Investment Disputes) Amendment Act 2000 (Act No. 52 of 2000)
PCA	Permanent Court of Arbitrators, Den Haag, Netherlands
PILA	Swiss Private International Law Act of 18 December 1987
SCC	Stockholm Chamber of Commerce
Swiss Rules	Swiss Rules of International Arbitration, as of January 2006
UK	United Kingdom of Great Britain and Northern Ireland
UK Act	Arbitration (International Investment Disputes) Act 1966
UK SIA	State Immunity Act 1978
UN	United Nations
UNCITRAL	United Nations Commission on International Trade Law

List of Abbreviations

US Act	Convention on the Settlement of Investment Disputes Act of 1966 (22 U.S.C. sec. 1650-1650a)
US FSIA	Foreign Sovereign Immunity Act 1976
VCLT	Vienna Convention on the Law of Treaties 1969
VCSS	Vienna Convention on Succession of States in Respect of Treaties 1978
ZR	Blätter für Zürcherische Rechtsprechung (Zurich)

LIST OF REFERENCES

Publications

Alexandrov, *Enforcement*	Stanimir A. Alexandrov, 'Enforcement of ICSID Awards: Articles 53 and 54 of the ISCID Convention', 25 Transnational Dispute Management (22 September 2008)
Amerasinghe, *State Responsibility*	C.F. Amerasinghe, State Responsibility for Injuries to Aliens (1967)
Analytical Commentary	Analytical Commentary on Draft Text of a Model Law on International Commercial Arbitration
Baldwin/Kantor/Nolan, *Limits to Enforcement*	Edward Baldwin, Mark Kantor and Michael Nolan, 'Limits to Enforcement of ICSID Awards', 23 Journal of International Arbitration (February 2006)
Basel Commentary-Author	Heinrich Honsell, Nedim Peter Vogt, Anton K Schnyder and Stephen V Berti (eds.), Basler Kommentar, Internationales Privatrecht (2nd edn, Helbing Lichtenhahn 2007)
Berger/Kellerhals, *Schiedsgerichtsbarkeit*	Bernhard Berger and Franz Kellerhals, Internationale und interne Schiedsgerichtsbarkeit in der Schweiz (Staempfli 2006)
Berti-Author	Stephen V Berti (ed.), International Arbitration in Switzerland: An Introduction to and a Commentary on Articles 176-194 of the Swiss Private International Law Statute (Kluwer Law International, Helbing & Lichtenhahn 2000)
Besson, *Arbitration in Switzerland*	Sébastien Besson, '"Arbitration in Switzerland" – Note on an Award rendered in an Arbitration under the Swiss Rules of International Arbitration', ASA Bulletin 25 (2007) 769
Besson, *Etendue du contrôle*	Sébastien Besson, 'Etendue du contrôle par le juge d'une exception d'arbitrage; renonciation aux recours contre la sentence arbitrale: deux questions choisies de droit suisse de l'arbitrage international', Revue de l'arbitrage (2005) 1071

List of References

Besson, *Le recours contre la sentence*	Sébastien Besson, 'Le recours contre la sentence arbitrale internationale selon la nouvelle LTF (aspects procéduraux)', ASA Bulletin 25 (2007) 2
Böckstiegel/Kröll/Nacimiento, *Arbitration In Germany*	K.-H. Böckstiegel, S. Kröll, P. Nacimiento (eds), Arbitration In Germany – The Model Law In Practice (2007)
Boog, *Multi-tiered Dispute Resolution*	Christopher Boog, 'How to Deal with Multi-tiered Dispute Resolution Clauses – Note on the Swiss Federal Supreme Court's Decision 4A_18/2007', ASA Bulletin 26 (2008) 103
Botschaft	Botschaft zum Bundesgesetz über das internationale Privatrecht [Commentary by the Swiss executive regarding the PILA] of 10 November 1982, Bundesblatt (1983) 263
Broches Article	Aron Broches, 'Awards Rendered Pursuant to the ICSID Convention: Binding Force, Finality, Recognition, Enforcement, Execution', 2 ICSID Rev.-FILJ (1987)
Broches, *Explanatory Notes and Survey*	Aron Broches, 'Convention on the Settlement of Investment Disputes between States and Nationals of Other States of 1965: Explanatory Notes and Survey of its Application', 18 Yearbook of Commercial Arbitration (1993)
Broches, *The Convention*	Aron Broches, 'The Convention on the Settlement of Investment Disputes between States and Nationals of Other States', 136 Receuil des Cours (1972)
Brownlie, *Principles*	Ian Brownlie, Principles of Public International Law (6th edn, Oxford University Press 2003)
Casey, *Crunch Time*	Michael Casey, 'Crunch Time In Key ICSID Case As Argentina Stalls CMS Payout', Dow Jones International News (16 January 2008)
Code of Conduct	2004 Code of Conduct of the Bar of England and Wales, available at <www.barcouncil.org.uk>
Contracting States and Measures Taken by Them	Contracting States and Measures Taken by Them for the Purpose of the Convention, ICSID Document ICSID/8

List of References

DAC Report	Report on the Arbitration Bill of the Departmental Advisory Committee on Arbitration Law, chaired by The Rt. Hon. Lord Justice Saville, February 1996 (full text reprinted in Mustill & Boyd Companion Volume)
DAC Suppl.	Supplementary Report on the Arbitration Act 1996, January 1997 (full text reprinted in Mustill & Boyd Companion Volume)
Dasser, *International Arbitration*	Felix Dasser, 'International Arbitration and Setting Aside Proceedings in Switzerland: A Statistical Analysis', ASA Bulletin 25 (2007) 444
Di Pietro/Platte, *Enforcement of International Arbitration Awards*	Domenico Di Pietro and Martin Platte, Enforcement of International Arbitration Awards (Cameron May 2001)
Dolzer/Stevens, *Bilateral Investment Treaties*	Rudolf Dolzer and Margrete Stevens, Bilateral Investment Treaties (Brill 2005)
Ehle, *Belated Nomination*	Bernd Ehle, 'Belated Nomination of Arbitrator Before the Swiss juge d'appui: Three Recent Decisions', ASA Bulletin 26 (2008) 392
Ethics for International Arbitrators	International Bar Association, 1987 Ethics for International Arbitrators, available at <www.ibanet.org>
Gaillard, *Aspects Philosophiques*	Emmanuel Gaillard, 'Aspects Philosophiques de L'Arbitrage International', 329 Recueil des cours (2008)
Gaillard, *NYLJ*	Emmanuel Gaillard, 'The Denunciation of the ICSID Convention', 237:122 New York Law Journal (26 June 2007)
Gaillard, *Representations of International Arbitration*	Emmanuel Gaillard, 'The Representations of International Arbitration', 238 New York Law Journal 67 (2007)
Gaillard/Savage, *On International Commercial Arbitration*	Emmanuel Gaillard and John Savage (eds.), Fouchard Gaillard Goldmann on International Commercial Arbitration (Kluwer 1999)

List of References

Geisinger/Frossard, *Challenge and Revision*	Elliott Geisinger and Viviane Frossard, 'Challenge and Revision of the Award', Gabrielle Kaufmann-Kohler and Blaise Stucki (eds.), International Arbitration in Switzerland, A Handbook for Practitioners (Kluwer Law International/Schulthess 2004), pp. 135-165
Guidelines on Conflicts of Interest in International Arbitration	International Bar Association, 2004 Guidelines on Conflicts of Interest in International Arbitration, available at <www.ibanet.org>
Guo, *Validity and Performance of Arbitration Agreement*	Guo Xiaowen, 'The Validity and Performance of Arbitration Agreement in China', 1 J Int'l Arb 53 (1994)
Harris/Planterose/Tecks, *Arbitration Act*	Bruce Harris, Rowan Planterose and Jonathan Tecks, The Arbitration Act 1996: A Commentary (4th edn, WileyBlackwell 2007)
Heilbron, *Practical Guide*	Hilary Heilbron, A Practical Guide to Arbitration (Informa Law 2008)
Heitzmann, *Confidentiality*	Pierre Heitzmann, 'Confidentiality and Privileges in Cross-Border Legal Practice: The Need for a Global Standard?', ASA Bulletin 26 (2008) 205
History	Convention on the Settlement of Investment Disputes between States and Nationals of Other States: Documents Concerning the Origin and the Formation of the Convention (ICSID, 1968)
Holtzmann/Neuhaus, *A Guide to the UNCITRAL Model Law*	Howard M. Holtzmann and Joseph E. Neuhaus, A Guide to the UNCITRAL Model Law on International Commercial Arbitration: Legislative History and Commentary (Kluwer Law International 1995)
Hu, *Arbitration Ex Aequo et Bono in China*	Li Hu, 'Arbitration Ex Aequo et Bono in China', 1 Arbitration in China (2000)
ILA	ILA Committee on International Commercial Arbitration, Public Policy as a Bar to the Enforcement of International Arbitral Awards, London Conference Report (2000) and related report by Audley Sheppard and Pierre Mayer

List of References

Karrer in *Festschrift Kellerhals*	Pierre Karrer, 'Verrechnung und Widerklage vor Schiedsgericht', Monique Jametti Greiner (ed.), Rechtsetzung und Rechtsdurchsetzung, Festschrift für Franz Kellerhals (Stämpfli 2005), pp. 49-54
Kaufmann-Kohler in *Études Hirsch*	Gabrielle Kaufmann-Kohler, '"Iura novit arbiter" – Est-ce bien raisonnable? Réflexions sur le statut du droit de fond devant l'arbitre international', Anne Héritier Lachat and Laurent Hirsch (eds.), De lege ferenda, Études pour le Professeur Alain Hirsch (Éditions Slatkine 2004), pp. 71-78
Kaufmann-Kohler/ Rigozzi, *LDIP*	Gabrielle Kaufmann-Kohler and Antonio Rigozzi, Arbitrage international: Droit et pratique à la lumière de la LDIP (Schulthess 2006)
Knoepfler, *Tribunale di appello Ticino*	François Knoepfler, 'Comment on Tribunale di appello Ticino, 12 March 1993', SchwZIER 8 (1998) 600
Kousoulis, *Arbitration*	S. Kousoulis, Arbitration, (Sakkoulas 2004)
La Spada in *Handbook*	Fabrizio La Spada, 'The Law Governing the Merits of the Dispute and Awards ex Aequo et Bono', Gabrielle Kaufmann-Kohler and Blaise Stucki (eds.), International Arbitration in Switzerland, A Handbook for Practitioners (Kluwer/Schulthess 2004), pp. 115-134
Lalive, *Public Policy*	Lalive, 'Transnational (or Truly International) Public Policy and International Arbitration', ICCA Congress series no. 3
Lalive/Poudret/ Reymond, *L'Arbitrage*	Pierre Lalive, Jean-François Poudret and Claude Reymond, Le Droit de L'Arbitrage Interne et International en Suisse (Payot 1989)
Lew/Mistelis/ Kroll, *Comparative and International Commercial Arbitration*	Julian D.M. Lew, Loukas Mistelis and Stefan M. Kroll, Comparative and International Commercial Arbitration, (Kluwer 2003)
Liatowitsch/Bernet in *Zivilprozess*	Manuel Liatowitsch and Martin Bernet, 'Probleme bei parallelen Verfahren vor staatlichen Gerichten und vor Schiedsgerichten', Karl Spühler (ed.), Internationales Zivilprozess- und Verfahrensrecht IV, (Schulthess 2005), pp. 139-167

List of References

Lucio, *UNCITRAL Model Law*	S.E. Lucio, 'The UNCITRAL Model Law on International Commercial Arbitration', 17 U. Miami Inter-Am. L. Rev. (1986) 322
Mantilla-Serrano/Adam, *UNCITRAL Model Law*	Fernando Mantilla-Serrano and John Adam, 'UNCITRAL Model Law: Missed Opportunities for Enhanced Uniformity', 31 UNSW Law Journal (2008) 309
Merkin, *Arbitration Act*	Robert Merkin and Louis Flannery, Arbitration Act 1996 (4th rev. edn, Informa Law 2008)
Merkin, *Arbitration Law*	Robert Merkin, Arbitration Law (3rd rev. edn, Informa Business Publishing 2004)
Mistelis/Brekoulakis, *Arbitrability*	Loukas Mistelis and Stavros Brekoulakis (eds), Arbitrability – International and Comparative Perspectives (Kluwer 2009)
Moser/Yuen, *The New CIETAC Rules*	Michael Moser and Peter Yuen, 'The New CIETAC Arbitration Rules', 21 Arb Int'l 394 (2005)
Mustill/Boyd, *Commercial Arbitration Companion*	Lord Mustill and Stewart Boyd, Commercial Arbitration: 2001 Companion Volume to the Second Edition (Butterworths 2001)
Mustill/Boyd, *Law and Practice of Commercial Arbitration*	Lord Michael Mustill and Stewart Boyd, The Law and Practice of Commercial Arbitration in England (2nd edn, Butterworth 1989)
Notes	'Official Annotations to the Rules of Procedure for Arbitration Proceedings 1968', ICSID Reports 1, 63
Notes to Institution Rules	'Official Annotations to the Rules of Procedure for the Institution of Conciliation and Arbitration Proceedings 1968', ICSID Reports 1, 51
Parliamentary Commission, Feuille Fédérale 2006	'Parlamentarische Initiative – Änderung von Artikel 186 des Bundesgesetzes über das Internationale Privatrecht', Bericht der Kommission für Rechtsfragen des Nationalrates vom 17. Februar 2006, Feuille Fédérale (2006), pp. 4677-4688

Paulsson, *Disregarding LSAS*	Paulsson, 'The Case for Disregarding LSAS (Local Standard Annulments) Under the New York Convention', 7 Am Rev Int'l Arb 99 (1996)
Paulsson, *ICSID's Achievements and Prospects*	Jan Paulsson, 'ICSID's Achievements and Prospects', ICSID Review – Foreign Investment Law Journal (1991)
Paulsson, *May a State Invoke its Internal Law*	Jan Paulsson, 'May a State Invoke its Internal Law to Repudiate Consent to Arbitration?', 2 Arbitration International (1986)
Poudret in *Liber Amicorum Reymond*	Jean-François Poudret, 'Légitimité et opportunité de l'opinion dissidente dans le silence de la loi?', in Liber Amicorum Claude Reymond – Autour de l'arbitrage (LexisNexis Litec 2004), pp. 243-253
Poudret, *Tribunal fédéral*	Jean-François Poudret, 'Les recours au Tribunal fédéral suisse en matière d'arbitrage international (Commentaire de l'art. 77 LTF)', ASA Bulletin 25 (2007) 669
Poudret/Besson, *Comparative Law*	Jean-François Poudret and Sébastien Besson, Comparative Law of International Arbitration (2nd edn, Sweet & Maxwell/Schulthess 2007)
Poudret/Besson, *Droit Comparé de l'Arbitrage International*	Jean-Francois Poudret, Sébastien Besson, Droit Comparé de l'Arbitrage International (Schulthess 2003)
Redfern/Hunter, *Law and Practice of International Commercial*	Alan Redfern, Martin Hunter, Nigel Blackaby and Constantine Partasides, Law and Practice of International Commercial Arbitration (4th edn, Sweet and Maxwell 2004)
Report of the Executive Directors	Report of the Executive Directors of the International Bank for Reconstruction and Development on the Convention on the Settlement of Investment Disputes between States and Nationals of Other States
Report of the Secretary-General A/CN.9/264	

List of References

Report of the Working
Group A/CN.9/246-6
March 1984

Reports	ICSID reports: reports of cases decided under the Convention on the Settlement of Investment Disputes between States and Nationals of Other States, 1965 and related decisions on international protection of investments (ICSID 1993)
Roney/Müller in *Handbook*	David P Roney and Anna K Müller, 'The Arbitral Procedure', Gabrielle Kaufmann-Kohler and Blaise Stucki (eds.), International Arbitration in Switzerland, A Handbook for Practitioners (Kluwer Law International/Schulthess 2004), pp. 49-68
Rules on the Taking of Evidence	International Bar Association, 1999 Rules on the Taking of Evidence, available at <www.ibanet.org>
Russell/Gill/Gearing, *Russell on Arbitration*	David St. John Sutton, Judith Gill, Matthew Gearing, Russell on Arbitration (23rd edn, Sweet & Maxwell 2007).
Sanders, *UNCITRAL's Model Law*	Pieter Sanders, 'UNCITRAL's Model Law on International and Commercial Arbitration: Present Situation and Future', 21 Arb. Int'l (2005) 443
Schreuer, *Commentary*	Christoph Schreuer, The ICSID Convention: A Commentary (Cambridge University Press 2001)
Schreuer, *Consent to Arbitration*	Christoph Schreuer, 'Consent to Arbitration', <www.unctad.org/en/docs/edmmisc232add2_en.pdf> (2003) and updated in 2007 in 2 Transnational Dispute Management 5 (2005/2007)
Shackleton, *Arbitration Law Reports*	Stewart Shackleton, Arbitration Law Reports and Review 2001-2006 (Oxford University Press)
Shaleva, *The Public Policy Exception*	Vesselina Shaleva, 'The "Public Policy" Exception to the Recognition and Enforcement of Arbitral Awards in the Theory and Jurisprudence of the Central and East European States and Russia', 19 Arbitration International (2003)

List of References

Shihata/Parra, *The Experience of ICSID*	I.F.I. Shihata and A.R. Parra, 'The Experience of the International Centre for Settlement of Investment Disputes', 14 ICSID Review – Foreign Investment Law Journal (1999)
Tackaberry/Marriot, *Bernstein's Handbook*	John Tackaberry, QC and Arthur Marriott, QC, Bernstein's Handbook of Arbitration and Dispute Resolution Practice (4th edn, Sweet & Maxwell 2003)
Tao, *Arbitration Law*	Jingzhou Tao, Arbitration Law and Practice in China (Kluwer Law International 2004)
Tao, *Art. 16 and 18 of the PRC Arbitration Law*	Jingzhou Tao, 'Art. 16 and 18 of the PRC Arbitration Law: The Great Wall of China for Foreign Arbitration Institutions', 3 Arb Int'l (2007)
Tao, *Document Production*	Jingzhou Tao, Document Production in Chinese International Arbitration Proceedings, ICCA Congress Series 14 (2007)
Tweeddale/Tweeddale, *Arbitration of Commercial Disputes*	Andrew Tweeddale and Keren Tweeddale, Arbitration of Commercial Disputes: International and English Law and Practice (Oxford University Press 2007)
UN HFCMT	United Nations Handbook on Final Clauses of Multilateral Treaties (UN 2003), Sales No. E.04.V.3.
Van den Berg, *Consolidated*	Albert Jan van den Berg, Consolidated Commentary on New York Convention (1986), 301 Procedure for Enforcement, in General
Van den Berg, *New York*	Albert Jan van den Berg, The New York Arbitration Convention of 1958. Towards a Uniform Judicial Interpretation (Kluwer Law and Taxation 1981)
Voser, *Mandatory Rules*	Nathalie Voser, 'Mandatory Rules of Law as a Limitation on the Law Applicable in International Commercial Arbitration', Am. Rev. Int'l Arb. 7 (1996) 319
Voser, *Schlichtungsklausel*	Nathalie Voser, 'Sanktion bei Nichterfüllung einer Schlichtungsklausel', ASA Bulletin 20 (2002) 376

List of References

Wehrli, *Contingency Fees*	Daniel Wehrli, 'Contingency Fees / Pactum De Palmario – "Civil Law Approach"', ASA Bulletin 26 (2008) 241
Whitesell/Silva-Romero, *L'arbitrage à pluralité de parties ou de contrat*	Anne-Marie Whitesell and Eduardo Silva-Romero, 'L'arbitrage à pluralité de parties ou de contrat: l'expérience récent de la CCI', L'arbitrage complexe – ICC Bulletin, Special Supplement (2003)
Zhao, *CIETAC Rules, Explanations and Applications Guidelines*	Jing Zhao, CIETAC Rules, Explanations and Applications Guidelines (Law Press China 2005)
Zhou, *Arbitration Agreements*	Jian Zhou, 'Arbitration Agreements in China: Battles on Designation of Arbitral Institution and Ad Hoc Arbitration', 23 J Int'l Arb (2006)
Zuberbühler, *Non-Signatories*	Tobias Zuberbühler, 'Non-Signatories and the Consensus to Arbitrate', ASA Bulletin 26 (2008) 18
Zurich Commentary-Author	Daniel Girsberger, Anton Heini, Max Keller, Jolanta Kren Kostkiewicz, Kurt Siehr, Frank Vischer and Paul Volken (eds.), Zürcher Kommentar zum IPRG (2nd edn, Schulthess 2004)

Reports

Report of the Secretary-General on the Preliminary Draft Set of Arbitration Rules, UNCITRAL, 8th Session, UN Doc A/CN.9/97 (1974)

Report of the Secretary-General on the Revised Draft Set of Arbitration Rules, UNCITRAL, 9th Session, Addendum 1 (Commentary), UN Doc A/CN.9/112/Add.1 (1975)

Summary Record of the 2nd Meeting of the Committee of the Whole (II), UNCITRAL, 9th Session, UN Doc A/CN.9/9/C.2/SR.2, (1976)

Summary Record of the 4th Meeting of the Committee of the WHOLE (II), UNCITRAL, 9th Session, UN Doc A/CN.9/9/C.2/SR.4 (1976).

Summary Record of the 5th Meeting of the Committee of the Whole (II), UNCITRAL, 9th Session, UN Doc A/CN.9/9/C.2/SR.5

List of References

Summary Record of the 9th Meeting of the Committee of the Whole (II), UNCITRAL, 9th Session, UN Doc A/CN.9/9/C.2/SR.9 (1976)

Summary Record of the 13th Meeting of the Committee of the Whole (II), UNCITRAL, 9th Session, UN Doc A/CN.9/9/C.2/SR.13 (1976)

Summary Record of the 15th Meeting of the Committee of the Whole (II), UNCITRAL, 9th Session, UN Doc A/CN.9/9/C.2/SR.15 (1976)

UNCITRAL, Report on Eighth Session (1975), UN Doc A/10017

UNCITRAL, Report on Ninth Session (1976), UN Doc A/31/17

Legislation

Arbitration Law	Arbitration Law of the People's Republic of China, adopted at the Ninth Meeting of the Standing Committee of the Eighth National People's Congress on 31 August 1994 promulgated by Order No. 31 of the President of the People's Republic of China on 31 August 1994 and effective as of 1 September 1995
BAC Rules 2001	Arbitration Rules of the Beijing Arbitration Commission adopted on 25 April 2001 and effective as of 1 August 2001
CIETAC Arbitration Rules of 1988	CIETAC Arbitration Rules (1988), adopted by the Third Session of the First National Congress of the China Council for the Promotion of International Trade on 12 September 1988 and effective as of 1 January 1989
CIETAC Financial Arbitration Rules	CIETAC Financial Disputes Arbitration Rules, adopted on 4 April 2003 by the CCPIT / CCOIC effective from 8 May 2003, and revised on 1 May 2005
CIETAC Rules of 1994	Arbitration Rules of CIETAC adopted on 17 March 1994 and effective as of 1 June 1994
CIETAC Rules of 1998	Arbitration Rules of CIETAC adopted on 28 April 1998 and effective as of 10 May 1998
CIETAC Rules of 2000	Arbitration Rules of CIETAC adopted on 5 September 2000 and effective as of 1 October 2000
CIETAC Rules of 2005	Arbitration Rules of CIETAC adopted on 11 January 2005 and effective as of 1 May 2005

List of References

Civil Procedure Law	Civil Procedure Law of the People's Republic of China adopted at the Fourth Session of the Seventh NPC, effective from 9 April 1991 and amended on 28 October 2007
Contract Law	Contract Law of the People's Republic of China adopted by the Second Session of the Ninth NPC on 15 March 1999, and effective from 1 October 1999
Decision concerning the Establishment of a Foreign Trade Arbitration Commission	Decision of the Government Administration Council of the Central People's Government Concerning the Establishment of a Foreign Trade Arbitration Commission within the China Council for the Promotion of International Trade, adopted on 6 May 1954 at the 215th Session of the Government Administration Council and promulgated on and effective from the same date
English Arbitration Act	1996 English Arbitration Act, published and available at <www.hmso.gov.uk>
English Judgments Act	1838 Judgments Act, available at <www.statutelaw.gov.uk>
Ethical Rules for Arbitrators	Ethical Rules for Arbitrators issued by CIETAC and CMAC and adopted in 1991, and subsequently revised in 1993 and 1994
IBA Rules on Evidence	IBA Rules on the Taking of Evidence in International Commercial Arbitration, adopted by a resolution of the IBA Council on 1 June 1999
New York Convention	1958 New York Convention on the Recognition and Enforcement of Foreign Arbitral Awards, available at <www.uncitral.org>
Notice Concerning the Conversion of the FTAC into the FETAC	Notice Concerning the Conversion of the Foreign Trade Arbitration Commission into the Foreign Economic and Trade Arbitration Commission, promulgated by the State Council on, and effective from 26 February 1980
Official Reply Concerning the Renaming of the FETAC as the CIETAC	Official Reply Concerning the Renaming of the Foreign Economic and Trade Arbitration Commission as the China International Economic and Trade Arbitration Commission and the Amendment to Its Arbitration Rules; promulgated by the State Council on, and effective from 21 June 1988

List of References

Provisional Rules of Arbitral Procedure of the Foreign Trade Arbitration Commission	Provisional Rules of Arbitral Procedure of the Foreign Trade Arbitration Commission of the China Council for the Promotion of International Trade, adopted by the Fourth Session of CCPIT on 31 March 1956
Recommendation regarding the interpretation of article II, paragraph 2, and article VII, paragraph 1, of the Convention	Recommendation regarding the interpretation of article II, paragraph 2, and article VII, paragraph 1, of the Convention, adopted by the United Nations Commission on International Trade Law on 7 July 2006 on its 39th session
Regulations concerning the Encouragement of Investment by Overseas Chinese and Hong Kong and Macao Compatriots	Regulations of the State Council concerning the Encouragement of Investment by Overseas Chinese and Hong Kong and Macao Compatriots, adopted by the State Council and effective as of 19 August 1990
Regulations for the Encouragement of Investment by Taiwanese Compatriots	Regulations of the State Council for the Encouragement of Investment by Taiwanese Compatriots, adopted by the State Council and effective as of 3 July 1988
Rome Convention	1980 Rome Convention (80/934/EEC), available at <www.eur-lex.europa.eu>
SPC Judicial Interpretations of September 2006	The Supreme People's Court's Interpretations of Certain Issues Concerning the Application of the Arbitration Law of the People's Republic of China, adopted at the 1375th Meeting of the Adjudication Committee of the Supreme People's Court on 26 December 2005 and effective as of 8 September 2006

List of References

SPC Provisions on Evidence	Several Provisions of the Supreme People's Court on the Evidence for Civil Actions, dated 21 December 2001, adopted by the 1201st Session of the Judicial Committee of the Supreme People's Court on 6 December 2001, and effective from 1 April 2002
UNCITRAL Model Law	1985 UNCITRAL Model Law on International Commercial Arbitration, United Nations Document A/40/17 annex 1, available at <www.uncitral.org>
WIPO expedited rules	1994 WIPO Expedited Arbitration Rules, World Intellectual Property Organisation arbitration, available at <www.wipo.int>
WIPO rules	1994 WIPO Arbitration Rules, World Intellectual Property Organisation arbitration, available at <www.wipo.int>
Zueblin	Letter of Reply of the Supreme People's Court to the Request for Instructions on the Case concerning the Application of German Zueblin International GmbH and Wuxi Woke General Engineering Rubber Co., Ltd for Determining the Validity of the Arbitration Agreement, of 8 July 2004 in (23 Min Si Ta Zi (2003))

Case law

A v *B*	*A* v *B* EWHC 2006 (Comm)
A/18 case	Case No. A/18, Decision No. DEC 32-A18-FT, Iran-US Claims Tribunal, Filed on 6 April 1984
AARP v *Sri Lanka*	*Asian Agricultural Products Limited* v *Sri Lanka* (ICSID Case No. ARB/87/3), FA, 27 June 1990
ABB AG v *Hoctief Airport GmbH*	*ABB AG* v *Hoctief Airport GmbH* [2006] EWHC 388 (QBD)
ABB Lummus Global Ltd v *Keppel Fels Ltd*	*ABB Lummus Global Ltd* v *Keppel Fels Ltd* 2 Lloyd's Rep. 24 (QBD) (Com)
Accentuate Ltd v *Asigra*	*Accentuate Ltd* v *Asigra Inc*. [2009] EWHC 2655 (QB)

List of References

Ad hoc Arbitration, 27 November 2002	*Ad hoc* Arbitration of the Arbitral Tribunal in Zurich, Procedural Order No. 14, 27 November 2002, *ABC AG (in prov. Nachlassstundung), Claimant,* v *Mr. X, Respondent,* 23 ASA Bulletin 108 (2005)
Adriano Gardella v *Cote d'Ivoire*	*Adriano Gardella S.p.A* v *Cote d'Ivoire* (ICSID Case No. ARB/74/1) FA, 29 August 1977
Adviso	*Adviso NV (Netherlands Antilles)* v *Korea Overseas Construction Corp.*, XXI YBCA 612 (1996)
AEG Insurance Services Ltd v *European Reinsurance Co. of Zurich*	*AEG Insurance Services Ltd* v *European Reinsurance Co. of Zurich* [2003] UKPC 11
Aggeliki Charis Compania v *Pagnan SA ('The Angelic Grace')*	*Aggeliki Charis Compania* v *Pagnan SA ('The Angelic Grace')* (1995) 1 Lloyd's Rep. 87
AGIP v *Congo*	*AGIP* v *People's Republic of the Congo* (ICSID Case No. ARB/77/1), FA, 30 November 1979
Agrimex Ltd v *Tradigrain SA*	*Agrimex Ltd* v *Tradigrain SA* [2003] EWHC 1656 (Comm)
Agrimpex SA	Greece, Areios Pagos, Decision No. 88 of 14 December 1977, *Agrimpex SA* v *J F Braun & Sons Inc.*, IV YBCA 269 (1979)
Aguas Argentinas v *Argentina*	*Suez, Sociedad General de Aguas de Barcelona S.A. and Vivendi Universal S.A* v *Argentine Republic* (ICSID Case No. ARB/03/19), Order in Response to a Petition for Transparency and Participation as *Amicus Curiae,* 19 May 2005
Aguas del Tunari v *Bolivia*	*Aguas del Tunari S.A.* v *Republic of Bolivia* (ICSID Case No. ARB/02/3), DJ, 21 October 2005
Ahmonseto v *Egypt* (DA)	*Ahmonseto, Inc. and others* v *Arab Republic of Egypt* (ICSID Case No. ARB/02/15), DA, pending
AIG v *Kazkhstan*	*AIG Capital Partners Inc.* v *Republic of Kazakhstan,* [2005] EWHC 2239 (Comm)

List of References

Al Hadha Trading v *Tradigrain SA*	*Al Hadha Trading Co.* v *Tradigrain SA* [2002] 2 Lloyd's Rep 512 (Merc Ct)
Alcoa Minerals v *Jamaica*	*Alcoa Minerals of Jamaica, Inc.* v *Jamaica* (ICSID Case No. ARB/74/2), DJ, 6 July 1975
Algahanim Industries v *Skandia*	*Algahanim Industries Inc.* v *Skandia* [2002] 2 All ER (Comm) 30
Ali Shipping Corporation v *'Shipyard Trogir'*	*Ali Shipping Corporation* v *'Shipyard Trogir'* [1998] 1 Lloyd's Rep. 643, CA
Allianz SpA v *West Tankers*	*Allianz SpA* v *West Tankers Inc.* (2009) All ER (EC) 491
Allianz Versicherungs AG v *Fortuna* (*'The Baltic Universal'*)	*Allianz Versicherungs AG* v *Fortuna Co. Inc.* (*'The Baltic Universal'*) [1999] 1 Lloyd's Rep. 497
Ambatielos Case	*Ambatielos Case* (*Greece* v *UK*) 1953 ICJ Rep. 10
Ambatielos Claim	Award of 1956, 12 UNRIAA 83, 103-04 (1963)
Amco v *Indonesia* (DPM)	*Amco Asia Corporation and others* v *Republic of Indonesia* (ICSID Case No. ARB/81/1), DPM, 9 December 1983
Amco v *Indonesia* (DSR)	*Amco Asia Corporation and others* v *Republic of Indonesia* (ICSID Case No. ARB/81/1), DSR, 17 October 1990
Amco v *Indonesia* (I)	*Amco Asia Corporation and others* v *Republic of Indonesia* (Case No. ARB/81/1), FA, 20 November 1984
Amco v *Indonesia* (I) (DA)	*Amco Asia Corporation and others* v *Republic of Indonesia* (ICSID Case No. ARB/81/1), DA, 16 May 1986
Amco v *Indonesia* (I) (DJ)	*Amco Asia Corporation and others* v *Republic of Indonesia* (Case No. ARB/81/1), DJ, 25 September 1983
Amco v *Indonesia* (I) (Stay Decision)	*Amco Asia Corporation and others* v *Republic of Indonesia* (ICSID Case No. ARB/81/1), DS, not published but summarised in *Amco* v *Indonesia* (I) (DA)

List of References

Amco v *Indonesia* (II)	*Amco Asia Corporation and others* v *Republic of Indonesia* (ICSID Case No. ARB/81/1), FA, unpublished
Amco v *Indonesia* (II) (DA)	*Amco Asia Corporation and others* v *Republic of Indonesia* (ICSID Case No. ARB/81/1), DA, unpublished
Amco v *Indonesia* (II) (Stay Decision)	*Amco Asia Corporation and others* v *Republic of Indonesia* (ICSID Case No. ARB/81/1), DS, 2 March 1991
Amec Civil Engineering Ltd v *Secretary of State for Transport*	*Amec Civil Engineering Ltd* v *Secretary of State for Transport* [2005] EWCA Civ 291
American Bell	*American Bell International Inc.,* v *The Islamic Republic of Iran*, Award No. 255-48-3 (19 Sep 1986)
American Bell (Decision)	*American Bell International Inc.* v *Iran*, Dec. No. 58-48-3 (19 Mar 1987)
American International Group	*American International Group, Inc.* v *Iran*, Award No. AT 93-2-2
AMF Corporation	*Refusal to File Claim of AMF Corporation*, Decision No. DEC 17-REF20-FT (8 Dec 1982)
Amoco International Finance	*Amoco International Finance Corporation* v *National Iranian Oil Company*, Case No. 56, Chamber Three, Order of 22 Feb 1984, at 1-2
AMT v *Congo*	*American Manufacturing and Trading, Inc.* v *Democratic Republic of the Congo* (ICSID Case No. ARB/93/1) FA, 21 February 1997
AMT v *Congo* (Revision)	*American Manufacturing and Trading, Inc.* v *Democratic Republic of the Congo* (ICSID Case No. ARB/93/1) Revision Proceeding, settled
Anaconda-Iran	*Anaconda-Iran, Inc.,* v *The Islamic Republic of Iran, et al.*, Case No. 167, Chamber Three, Order of 11 Oct 1984
Andrews v *Bradshaw*	*Andrews* v *Bradshaw* (2000) BLR 6

List of References

Anhydro	Cour de cassation, 7 June 1989, *Anhydro* v *Caso Pillet et al.*, 61 (1992), with note Derains
AOOT Kalmneft v Glenmore International	*AOOT Kalmneft* v *Glenmore International* [2002] 1 All ER 76 (QBD)
Apollo v *Berg* (United States)	*Apollo Computer Inc.* v *Berg* 886 F 2d (1st Cir 1989)
Appelationsgericht Basel 6 September 1968	Appelationsgericht Basel, 6 September 1968, *Swiss Corp. X AG* v *German firm Y*, I YBCA 200 (1976)
Arab National Bank v *El-Abdali*	*Arab National Bank* v *El-Abdali* [2005] EWHC 2381 (Comm)
Ares v *Georgia*	*Ares International S.r.l. and MetalGeo S.r.l.* v *Georgia* (ICSID Case No. ARB/05/23), DSR, 8 July 2008
Argentine water arbitrations	*Aguas Provinciales de Santa Fe, S.A., Suez, Sociedad General de Aguas de Barcelona, S.A.* v *Argentine Republic* (Case No. ARB/03/17); *Aguas Argentinas, S.A., Suez, Sociedad General de Aguas de Barcelona, S.A. and Vivendi Universal, S.A.* v *Argentine Republic* (Case No. ARB/03/19); *AWG Limited* v *Argentine Republic* (UNCITRAL Proceeding initiated in 2003 under UK-Argentina BIT), Challenge Decision of May 12 2008
ASM Shipping Ltd v *Harris*	*ASM Shipping Ltd* v *Harris* [2007] EWHC 1513 (Comm)
ASM Shipping Ltd v *TTMI Ltd*	*ASM Shipping Ltd of India* v *TTMI Ltd of England* [2005] EWHC 2238 (Comm), [2006] 2 All ER (Comm) 122, [2005] All ER (D) 271 (Nov), [2006] 1 Lloyd's Rep. 375 *TTMI Ltd of England* v *ASM Shipping Ltd of India* [2005] EWHC 2666 (Comm), [2006] 1 Lloyd's Rep 401, [2005] All ER (D) 334 (Nov) *ASM Shipping Ltd of India* v *TTMI Ltd of England* [2007] EWHC 927 (Comm), [2007] 2 Lloyd's Rep 155, [2007] All ER (D) 195 (Apr) *ASM Shipping Ltd of India* v *TTMI Ltd of England*, 'The Amer Energy' [2009] 1 Lloyd's Rep 293

List of References

Assimina Maritime Ltd v *Pakistan Shipping Corporation*	*Assimina Maritime Ltd* v *Pakistan Shipping Corporation ('The Tasman Spirit')* [2004] EWHC 2972 (QB)
Astra SA v *Yasuda*	*Astra SA Insurance and Reinsurance Co.* v *The Yasuda Fire & Marine Insurance Company of Europe* (1999) CLC 950
AT & T Corp. v *Saudi Cable Co.*	*AT &T Corp* v *Saudi Cable Co.* [2000] 2 Lloyd's Rep 127 (CA)
ATF 101 Ia 521	Tribunal Fédéral, 12 December 1975, *Provenda S.A.* v *Alimenta S.A. et Cour de Justice de Genève*, ATF 101 Ia 521
ATF 107 Ia 318	Tribunal Fédéral, 13 May 1981, *Impresa Zanetta & Moretti* v *Comune di Vacallo e II Camera civile del Tribunale di appello del Cantone Ticino,* ATF 107 Ia 318
ATF 110 Ia 59	Tribunal Fédéral, 16 April 1984, *X.* v *Y.,* ATF 110 Ia 59
ATF 111 Ia 72	Tribunal Fédéral, 14 March 1985, *Société Z.* v *L.*, ATF 111 Ia 72
ATF 115 II 294	Tribunal Fédéral, 11 September 1989, *X.* v *Président de la Cour de justice du canton de Genève,* ATF 115 II 294
ATF 116 Ia 56	Tribunal Fédéral, 15 March 1990, *X.* v *Y.*, ATF 116 Ia 56
ATF 116 II 373	Tribunal Fédéral, 21 August 1990, *I.* v *C. SA und IHK-Schiedsgericht*, ATF 116 II 373
ATF 116 II 639	Tribunal Fédéral, 19 December 1990, *S.* v *K. Ltd und IHK-Schiedsgericht Zürich*, ATF 116 II 639
ATF 116 II 721	Tribunal Fédéral, 9 November 1990, *S. AG* v *H. Ltd und Obergericht des Kantons Zürich,* ATF 116 II 721
ATF 116 II 80	Tribunal Fédéral, 6 February 1990, *B. AG* v *H. et Tribunal arbitral*, ATF 116 II 80
ATF 117 Ia 166	Tribunal Fédéral, 30 April 1991, *Gesellschaft X.* v *Y. AG,* ATF 117 Ia 166

List of References

ATF 117 Ia 182	Tribunal Fédéral, 21 August 1991, *W.* v *Staatsanwaltschaft und Präsident des Kassationsgerichts des Kantons Zürich*, ATF 117 Ia 182
ATF 117 II 346	Tribunal Fédéral, 1 July 1991, *U.* v *Epoux G.*, ATF 117 II 346
ATF 117 II 94	Tribunal Fédéral, 9 April 1991, *C.S. Ltd* v *C., C.S.A. und IHK-Schiedsgericht Zürich*, ATF 117 II 94
ATF 118 Ia 20	Tribunal Fédéral, 27 February 1992, *F. Anstalt* v *T. Company Ltd*, ATF 118 Ia 20
ATF 118 II 193	Tribunal Fédéral, 28 April 1992, *G. S.A.* v *V. S.p.A. et Tribunal arbitral*, ATF 118 II 193
ATF 118 II 199	Tribunal Fédéral, 11 March 1992, *P.* v *société S.*, ATF 118 II 199
ATF 118 II 353	Tribunal Fédéral, 23 June 1992, *Fincantieri-Cantieri Navali Italiani S.p.A. et Oto Melara S.p.A.* v *M. et Tribunal arbitral*, ATF 118 II 353
ATF 118 II 359	Tribunal Fédéral, 18 August 1992, *K.* v *X. und IHK-Schiedsgericht*, ATF 118 II 359
ATF 119 II 173	Tribunal Fédéral, 28 April 1993, *Bank Kreiss AG* v *Schweizerische Kreditanstalt*, ATF 119 II 173
ATF 119 II 380	Tribunal Fédéral, 2 September 1993, *National Power Corporation* v *Westinghouse International Projects Compagny, Westinghouse Electric S.A., Westinghouse Electric Corporation, Burns & Roe, Enterprises Inc. et Tribunal arbitral*, ATF 119 II 380
ATF 120 II 155	Tribunal Fédéral, 19 April 1994, *Emirats Arabes Unis et consorts* v *Westland Helicopters Limited et Tribunal arbitral*, ATF 120 II 155
ATF 121 I 81	Tribunal Fédéral, 20 March 1995, *X. Inc.* v *S. et consorts et Tribunal de première instance du canton de Genève*, ATF 121 I 81
ATF 121 III 38	Tribunal Fédéral, 16 January 1995, *Compagnie de Navigation et Transports SA* v *MSC Mediterranean Shipping Company SA*, ATF 121 III 38

ATF 121 III 495	Tribunal Fédéral, 20 December 1995, *Société G.* v *X. AG et Tribunal arbitral*, ATF 121 III 495
ATF 122 III 139	Tribunal Fédéral, 29 April 1996, *Fondation M.* v *Banque X.*, ATF 122 III 139
ATF 122 III 492	Tribunal Fédéral, 1 November 1996, *Société P.* v *A.,* ATF 122 III 492
ATF 126 III 249	Tribunal Fédéral, 28 April 2000, *Egemetal Demir Celik Sanayi ve Ticaret A.S.* v *Fuchs Systemtechnik GmbH und ICC Schiedsgericht,* case no. 4P.42/2000, ATF 126 III 249
ATF 126 III 524	Tribunal Fédéral, 2 November 2000, *Philipp Holzmann AG et Nord France S.A.* v *l'Entreprise Industrielle S.A.*, case no. 4P.166/2000, ATF 126 III 524
ATF 126 III 529	Tribunal Fédéral, 21 November 2000, *A.* v *Bank X.*, ATF 126 III 529
ATF 127 III 279	Tribunal Fédéral, 14 May 2001, *Fomento de Construcciones y Contratas S.A.* v *Colon Container Terminal S.A.*, case no. 4P.37/2001, ATF 127 III 279
ATF 127 III 576	Tribunal Fédéral, 10 September 2001, *X. GmbH* v *Y. SA und Schiedsgericht Zürich*, case no. 4P.72/2001, ATF 127 III 576
ATF 128 III 191	Tribunal Fédéral, 3 April 2002, *X. Inc., un pseudonyme de Y. Inc.* v *Z. Corporation et Tribunal arbitral*, case no. 4P.282/2001, ATF 128 III 191
ATF 128 III 234	Tribunal Fédéral, 1 February 2002, *X. Ltd* v *Y. BV*, case no. 4P.226/2001, ATF 128 III 234
ATF 128 III 330	Tribunal Fédéral, 3 July 2002, *A.* v *B. und Ad hoc Schiedsgericht Basel*, case no. 4P.77/2002, ATF 128 III 330
ATF 128 III 50	Tribunal Fédéral, 16 October 2001, *Société X.* v *société O.*, case no. 4P.176/2001, ATF 128 III 50
ATF 129 III 445	Tribunal Fédéral, 27 May 2003, *A. et B.* v *Comité International Olympique, Fédération Internationale de Ski et Tribunal Arbitral du Sport*, case no. 4P.267/2002, ATF 129 III 445

List of References

ATF 129 III 675	Tribunal Fédéral, 8 July 2003, *D. d.o.o.* v *Bank C. sowie Schiedsgericht der Zürcher Handelskammer*, case no. 4P.67/2003, ATF 129 III 675
ATF 130 III 125	Tribunal Fédéral, 9 December 2003, *Jean Nachmann* v *Eitan German, Judith German, Joachim German und Obergericht des Kantons Zürich*, case no. 5P.315/2003, ATF 130 III 125
ATF 130 III 35	Tribunal Fédéral, 30 September 2003, *A.* v *B. Ltd et cons. ainsi que Tribunal arbitral de Zurich*, case no. 4P.100/2003, ATF 130 III 35
ATF 130 III 66	Tribunal Fédéral, 21 November 2003, *A. AG* v *B. N.V. sowie Schiedsgericht der Zürcher Handelskammer,* case no. 4P.162/2003, ATF 130 III 66
ATF 130 III 76	Tribunal Fédéral, 18 September 2003, *A.* v *B. sowie ad hoc UNCITRAL Schiedsgericht Genf*, case no. 4P.74/2003, ATF 130 III 76
ATF 131 III 164	Tribunal Fédéral, 12 January 2005, *A.* v *B. et Tribunal arbitral CCI*, case no. 4P.219/2004, ATF 131 III 164
ATF 131 III 173	Tribunal Fédéral, 4 February 2005, *A.* v *B., C. et tribunal arbitrl CNUDCI*, case no. 4P.236/2004, ATF 131 III 173
ATF 132 III 389	Tribunal Fédéral, 8 March 2006, *X. S.p.A.* v *Y. S.r.l. et Tribunal arbitral CCI, Lausanne*, case no. 4P.278/2005, ATF 132 III 389
ATF 133 I 89	Tribunal Fédéral, 7 November 2006, *Swiss International Air Lines AG* v *Swiss Pilots Association*, case no. 4P.247/2006, ATF 133 I 89
ATF 133 III 235	Tribunal Fédéral, 22 March 2007, *X.* v *ATP Tour et Tribunal Arbitral du Sport (TAS)*, case no. 4P.172/2006, ATF 133 III 235
ATF 134 III 186	Tribunal Fédéral, 22 January 2008, *A.C. SE, A.D. Ltd, A.E. Ltd, J. Ltd* v *K. SAS*, case no. 4A_468/2007, partially published as ATF 134 III 186
ATF 134 III 260	Tribunal Fédéral, 6 March 2008, *X. SpA* v *Y.*, case no. 4A_500/2007, ATF 134 III 260

List of References

ATF 134 III 286	Tribunal Fédéral, 14 March 2008, *X. AG* v *Y. Corporation*, case no. 4A_42/2008, partially published as ATF 134 III 286
ATF 134 III 565	Tribunal Fédéral, 18 August 2008, *X. Ltd* v *Y. et Z. S.p.A*, case no. 4A_128/2008, ATF 134 III 565
ATF 135 I 14	Tribunal Fédéral, 6 October 2008, *X.* v *Y.*, case no. 5A_201/2008, ATF 135 I 14
ATF 1P.113/2000	Tribunal Fédéral, 20 September 2000, *Republik Polen* v *SaarPapierVertriebs GmbH*, ATF 1P.113/2000
ATF 1P.99/2000	Tribunal Fédéral, 20 March 2000, *O.* v *N.S. und L.S.*, ATF 1P.99/2000
ATF 4A_137/2007	Tribunal Fédéral, 20 July 2007, *X.* v *Y.*, ATF 4A_137/2007
ATF 4A_160/2007	Tribunal Fédéral, 28 August 2007, *X.* v *Y. et Tribunal Arbitral du Sport (TAS)*, ATF 4A_160/2007
ATF 4A_160/2009	Tribunal Fédéral, 25 August 2009, *A.* v *B.*, case no. 4A_160/2009
ATF 4A_18/2007	Tribunal Fédéral, 6 June 2007, *X. Ltd* v *Y. et Tribunal Arbitral OMPI*, ATF 4A_18/2007
ATF 4A_2/2007	Tribunal Fédéral, 28 March 2007, *X. GmbH* v *A. und Schiedsgericht der Zürcher Handelskammer*, ATF 4A_2/2007
ATF 4A_210/2008	Tribunal Fédéral, 29 October 2008, *X. SA* v *Y. Limited*, ATF 4A_210/2008
ATF 4A_215/2008	Tribunal Fédéral, 23 September 2008, *X. en liquidation* v *Y.*, ATF 4A_215/2008
ATF 4A_220/2007	Tribunal Fédéral, 21 September 2007, *Dame Y.* v *Z. et tribunal arbitral ad hoc à Berne*, ATF 4A_220/2007
ATF 4A_234/2008	Tribunal Fédéral, 14 August 2008, *X.* v *Y.*, ATF 4A_234/2008
ATF 4A_244/2007	Tribunal Fédéral, 22 January 2008, *A.C. SE, A.D. Ltd, A.E. Ltd, J. Ltd* v *K. SAS*, ATF 4A_244/2007

List of References

ATF 4A_258/2008	Tribunal Fédéral, 7 October 2008, *X.* v *Y. et Z.*, ATF 4A_258/2008
ATF 4A_268/2007	Tribunal Fédéral, 14 November 2007, *X.* v *Y.*, ATF 4A_268/2007
ATF 4A_370/2007	Tribunal Fédéral, 21 February 2008, *X.* v *Association A. et SASP B.*, ATF 4A_370/2007
ATF 4A_376/2008	Tribunal Fédéral, 5 December 2008, *A.* v *B. Ltd*, ATF 4A_376/2008
ATF 4A_400/2008	Tribunal Fédéral, 9 February 2009, *X.* v *Y.*, ATF 4A_400/2008
ATF 4A_428/2008	Tribunal Fédéral, 31 March 2009, *Vivendi S.A. et al.* v *Deutsche Telekom AG et al.*, ATF 4A_428/2008
ATF 4A_438/2008	Tribunal Fédéral, 17 November 2008, *X. AG et Y. SA* v *A.*, ATF 4A_438/2008
ATF 4A_450/2007	Tribunal Fédéral, 9 January 2008, *X. SA* v *Y., Inc.*, ATF 4A_450/2007,
ATF 4A_452/2007	Tribunal Fédéral, 29 February 2008, *X. GmbH* v *Y. Corporation*, ATF 4A_452/2007
ATF 4A_506/2007	Tribunal Fédéral, 20 March 2008, *X.* v *Association Y.*, ATF 4A_506/2007
ATF 4A_528/2007	Tribunal Fédéral, 4 April 2008, *Club X.* v *Y. S/A* ATF 4A_528/2007
ATF 4A_586/2008	Tribunal Fédéral, 12 June 2009, *X. SA* v *Y.*, case no. 4A_586/2008
ATF 4A_596/2008	Tribunal Fédéral, 6 October 2009, *X.* v *société Y. en liquidation et Z. Limitada*, case no. 4A_596/2008
ATF 4A_600/2008	Tribunal Fédéral, 20 February 2009, *X.* v *Y.*, ATF 4A_600/2008
ATF 4C.40/2003	Tribunal Fédéral, 19 May 2003, *X. SA* v *Y. AG*, ATF 4C.40/2003
ATF 4P.102/2006	Tribunal Fédéral, 29 August 2006, *A.* v *B. und ICC Schiedsgericht Genf*, ATF 4P.102/2006

List of References

ATF 4P.104/2004	Tribunal Fédéral, 18 October 2004, *A. Ltd* v *Republic of Turkey, Ministry of Energy and Natural Resources und ICC Schiedsgericht Genf*, ATF 4P.104/2004
ATF 4P.105/2006	Tribunal Fédéral, 4 August 2006, *X.* v *Y., Fédération Française d'Equitation, Emirates International Endurance Racing, the Organising Committee of the FEI Endurance World Championship 2005 und Fédération Equestre Internationale*, ATF 4P.105/2006
ATF 4P.113/2001	Tribunal Fédéral, 11 September 2001, *A.A., B.A. e C.A.* v *Comunione dei comproprietari della proprietà per piani concernente la part. n. JJJ RFD di Ponte Capriasca nonché E. e arbitro unico*, ATF 4P.113/2001
ATF 4P.114/2001	Tribunal Fédéral, 19 December 2001, *N.V. Belgische Scheepvaartmaatschappij-Compagnie Maritime Belge* v *N.V. Distrigas et Tribunal arbitral CCI à Genève*, ATF 4P.114/2001
ATF 4P.114/2003	Tribunal Fédéral, 14 July 2003, *A.* v *X. Ltd et Tribunal arbitral de la Chambre de Commerce et d'Industrie de Genève CCIG*, ATF 4P.114/2003
ATF 4P.114/2004	Tribunal Fédéral, 13 September 2004, *A.* v *B.C., D.C., Fondazione X., arbitro unico E.*, ATF 4P.114/2004
ATF 4P.114/2006	Tribunal Fédéral, 7 September 2006, *Tschechische Republik* v *X. und Schiedsgericht UNCITRAL Genf*, ATF 4P.114/2006
ATF 4P.115/2003	Tribunal Fédéral, 16 October 2003, *X. S.A.L, Y. S.A.L. et A.* v *Z. Sàrl et Tribunal arbitral CCI*, ATF 4P.115/2003, partially published as ATF 129 III 727
ATF 4P.117/2003	Tribunal Fédéral, 16 October 2003, *X. S.A.L., Y. S.A.L. et A.* v *Z. Sàrl et Tribunal arbitral CCI à Genève*, ATF 4P.117/2003
ATF 4P.117/2004	Tribunal Fédéral, 6 October 2004, *A. BV* v *B. et Tribunal arbitral CCI*, ATF 4P.117/2004, partially published as ATF 130 III 755

List of References

ATF 4P.12/2000	Tribunal Fédéral, 14 June 2000, *Dumez-GTM S.A. v Campenon Bernard SGE Snc, Hochtief AG, SPIE Batignolles T.P. S.A. et Tribunal arbitral à Genève*, ATF 4P.12/2000
ATF 4P.124/2001	Tribunal Fédéral, 7 August 2001, *X. SpA v Y. & Company, Z. SA et und Tribunal arbitral*, ATF 4P.124/2001
ATF 4P.126/2001	Tribunal Fédéral, 18 December 2001, *LUKoil-Permnefteorgsintez* v *MIR Müteahhitlik ve Ticaret A.S./MIR Constructing and Trading Co. Inc et Tribunal arbitral,* ATF 4P.126/2001
ATF 4P.129/2002	Tribunal Fédéral, 26 November 2002, *A. Ltd, B. Ltd, C, D* v *X. AG und Schiedsgericht Samstagern*, ATF 4P.129/2002, available at <www.bger.ch>, also published in 21 ASA Bulletin 402 (2003)
ATF 4P.134/2006	Tribunal Fédéral, 7 September 2006, *X.* v *Y. Holding Ltd und ICC Schiedsgericht Zürich*, ATF 4P.134/2006
ATF 4P.137/2002	Tribunal Fédéral, 4 July 2003, *A. Ltd* v *B und IHK Schiedsgericht Genf*, ATF 4P.137/2002
ATF 4P.140/2000	Tribunal Fédéral, 10 November 2000, *Union Internationale des Transport Routiers (IRU)* v *Kravag, La Concorde, Generali France Assurances et Préservatrice Foncière Tiard*, ATF 4P.140/2000
ATF 4P.140/2004	Tribunal Fédéral, 18 November 2004, *A. SA* v *B. Inc. und ICC Schiedsgericht Zürich*, ATF 4P.140/2004
ATF 4P.143/2001	Tribunal Fédéral, 18 September 2001, *Özmak Makina Ve Elektrik Sanayi A.S.* v *Voest Alpine Industrieanlagenbau GmbH et Tribunal arbitral CCI à Genève*, ATF 4P.143/2001
ATF 4P.154/2005	Tribunal Fédéral, 10 November 2005, *République X.* v *Y., Z. et Tribunal arbitral CNUDCI*, ATF 4P.154/2005
ATF 4P.168/2006	Tribunal Fédéral, 19 February 2007, *B.* v *A. et Tribunal arbitral ad hoc à Zurich*, ATF 4P.168/2006, partially published as ATF 133 III 139

List of References

ATF 4P.172/1999	Tribunal Fédéral, 17 February 2000, *Rhône-Poulenc Rorer Pharmaceuticals Inc.* v *Roche Diagnostic Corporation*, ATF 4P.172/1999
ATF 4P.173/2003	Tribunal Fédéral, 8 December 2003, *A. SA* v *B. Co. Limited, C. SA et Cour de justice du canton de Genève*, ATF 4P.173/2003
ATF 4P.188/2001	Tribunal Fédéral, 15 October 2001, *X. S.A.* v *la sentence arbitrale rendue le 19 juin 2001 par un tribunal arbitral siégeant à Genève sous l'égide de la CCI*, ATF 4P.188/2001
ATF 4P.196/2003	Tribunal Fédéral, 7 January 2004, *X. Ltd* v *Y. GmbH, Z. GmbH et Tribunal arbitral CCI à Berne*, ATF 4P.196/2003
ATF 4P.198/2005	Tribunal Fédéral, 31 October 2005, *X. AS* v *Y. Corporation und Schiedsgericht der Zürcher Handelskammer*, ATF 4P.198/2005
ATF 4P.2/2003	Tribunal Fédéral, 12 March 2003, *A., einfache Gesellschaft, bestehend aus 1.B., 2.C., 2.D., 4.E., 5.F.* v *G. und Schiedsgericht der Zürcher Handelskammer*, ATF 4P.2/2003
ATF 4P.200/2001	Tribunal Fédéral, 1 March 2002, *Saar Papier Vertriebs GmbH* v *Republik Polen und Schiedsgericht Zürich*, ATF 4P.200/2001
ATF 4P.206/2006	Tribunal Fédéral, 30 March 2007, *X. Ltd, Y. Corps, Z.* v *A.*, ATF 4P.206/2006
ATF 4P.207/2002	Tribunal Fédéral, 10 December 2002, *X.* v *Y. AG und Schiedsgericht der Zürcher Handelskammer*, ATF 4P.207/2002
ATF 4P.208/2004	Tribunal Fédéral, 14 December 2004, *A. Ltd* v *B. Ltd und ICC Schiedsgericht Genf*, ATF 4P.208/2004
ATF 4P.226/2004	Tribunal Fédéral, 9 March 2005, *A.* v *B. und Schiedsgericht der Genfer Industrie- und Handelskammer (CCIG)*, ATF 4P.226/2004

List of References

ATF 4P.23/2006	Tribunal Fédéral, 27 March 2006, *Rückversicherungs-Gesellschaft X. AG* v *Versicherungs-Gesellschaft Y und Vertragliches Schiedsgericht Basel*, ATF 4P.23/2006
ATF 4P.230/2000	Tribunal Fédéral, 7 February 2001, *Stanley Roberts* v *Fédération Internationale de Basketball*, ATF 4P.230/2000
ATF 4P.235/2001	Tribunal Fédéral, 4 April 2002, *A. GmbH* v *B. AG und Schiedsgericht der Handelskammer Deutschland-Schweiz*, ATF 4P.235/2001
ATF 4P.237/2005	Tribunal Fédéral, 2 February 2006, *X. GmbH* v *Y. Ltd und Schiedsgericht Zürcher Handelskammer*, ATF 4P.237/2005
ATF 4P.240/2006	Tribunal Fédéral, 5 January 2007, *X. S.A.D.* v *Fédération Internationale de Football Association (FIFA) und Tribunal Arbitral du Sport (TAS)*, ATF 4P.240/2006
ATF 4P.242/2004	Tribunal Fédéral, 27 April 2005, *D. d.o.o.* v *Bank C. und Schiedsgericht der Zürcher Handelskammer*, ATF 4P.242/2004
ATF 4P.243/2000	Tribunal Fédéral, 8 January 2001, *Imuna s.p.* v *Octapharma AG und Obergericht des Kantons Zürich*, ATF 4P.243/2000
ATF 4P.253/2003	Tribunal Fédéral, 25 March 2004, *A.* v *B. und Tribunal Arbitral du Sport (TAS)*, ATF 4P.253/2003
ATF 4P.253/2004	Tribunal Fédéral, 8 April 2005, *X. Ltd* v *Y. SA et Tribunal arbitral CCI*, ATF 4P.253/2004
ATF 4P.26/2005	Tribunal Fédéral, 23 March 2005, *X.* v *A. et B. et Tribunal Arbitral du Sport (TAS)*, ATF 4P.26/2005
ATF 4P.260/2000	Tribunal Fédéral, 2 March 2001, *Bank Saint Petersburg PLC* v *ATA Insaat Sanayi ve Ticaret Ltd und Schiedsgericht CCIG Genf*, ATF 4P.260/2000
ATF 4P.263/2002	Tribunal Fédéral, 10 June 2003, *A. Ltd* v *B. SA, C. GmbH et Tribunal Arbitral Chambre de Commerce de Zürich*, ATF 4P.263/2002

List of References

ATF 4P.269/2003	Tribunal Fédéral, 6 May 2004, *Sportverein X.* v *Fédération Internationale de Football Association (FIFA), A., Club Y. und Court of Arbitration for Sport (CAS)*, ATF 4P.269/2003
ATF 4P.273/1999	Tribunal Fédéral, 20 June 2000, *A. & V. Sport Ltd* v *la sentence arbitrale rendue le 6 septembre 1999 par un tribunal arbitral siégeant à Lausanne (…)*, ATF 4P.273/1999
ATF 4P.280/2005	Tribunal Fédéral, 9 January 2006, *X.* v *Y. et Arbitre unique*, ATF 4P.280/2005
ATF 4P.298/2005	Tribunal Fédéral, 19 January 2006, *A.* v *B. und ICC Schiedsgericht Zürich*, ATF 4P.298/2005
ATF 4P.299/2006	Tribunal Fédéral, 14 December 2006, *Garage A. et fils* v *Z. AG,* ATF 4P.299/2006
ATF 4P.318/2001	Tribunal Fédéral, 31 May 2002, *Union X.* v *Y. Minerals and Metals Limited und IHK-Schiedsgericht Zürich*, ATF 4P.318/2001
ATF 4P.32/2007	Tribunal Fédéral, 11 April 2007, *X.* v *Y. et Tribunal Arbitral CCI,* ATF 4P.32/2007
ATF 4P.4/2007	Tribunal Fédéral, 26 September 2007, *Sàrl X.* v *Y. AG et Tribunal arbitral de la Cour pour l'Arbitrage International en matière de Commerce et d'Industrie (CARICI),* ATF 4P.4/2007
ATF 4P.48/2005	Tribunal Fédéral, 20 September 2005, *X. SA* v *Y. Banka, Z. und Schiedsgericht Lugano*, ATF 4P.48/2005
ATF 4P.54/2002	Tribunal Fédéral, 24 June 2002, *A. AG* v *B. SA und Schiedsgericht IHK Zürich,* ATF 4P.54/2002
ATF 4P.54/2006	Tribunal Fédéral, 11 May 2006, *A.* v *B. und Einzelschiedsrichter*, ATF 4P.54/2006
ATF 4P.7/1998	Tribunal Fédéral, 17 July 1998, *Entreprise nationale des engrais et des produits phytosanitaires ASMIDAL* v *Compagnie française d'études et de construction TECHNIP et CLE S.A. et Tribunal arbitral CCI à Genève*, case no. 4P.7/1998, 20 ASA Bulletin 660 (2002)

List of References

ATF 4P.74/2006	Tribunal Fédéral, 19 June 2006, *X. Gesellschaft und Y. Gesellschaft* v *Z. Gesellschaft und ICC Schiedsgericht Zürich*, ATF 4P.74/2006
ATF 4P.88/2006	Tribunal Fédéral, 10 July 2006, *X. AG* v *Y. und Schiedsgericht CCIG Genf*, ATF 4P.88/2006
ATF 4P.96/2002	Tribunal Fédéral, 9 January 2007, *X. Sàrl* v *Masse en faillite de Y. SA et Tribunal arbitral ad hoc à Zurich*, ATF 4P.96/2002
ATF 4P.98/2005	Tribunal Fédéral, 10 November 2005, *La République X.* v *Y., Z. et Tribunal arbitral CNUDCI*, ATF 4P.98/2005
ATF 4P.99/2000	Tribunal Fédéral, 10 November 2001, *Sadri Sener Insaat Ve Ticaret A.S.* v *You One Engineering & Construction Company Ltd und Schiedsgericht IHK Genf*, ATF 4P.99/2000
ATF 5P.427/2000	Tribunal Fédéral, 4 December 2000, *Andreea Raducan* v *Comité International Olympique et Tribunal arbitral du sport*, ATF 5P.427/2000
ATF 7B.55/2006	Tribunal Fédéral, 21 September 2006, *Fédération de Russie* v *Commission de surveillance des offices des poursuites et des faillites du canton de Genève*, ATF 4P.173/2003
ATF, 11 May 1992	Tribunal Fédéral, 11 May 1992, *D.* v *A.*, 10 ASA Bulletin 381 (1992)
ATF, 12 November 1991	Tribunal Fédéral, 12 November 1991, *B. Moser* v *BMY, division de Harsco Corporation*, 10 ASA Bulletin 264 (1992)
ATF, 13 October 1992	Tribunal Fédéral, 13 October 1992, *Etat X* v *sociétés Y et Z,* 11 ASA Bulletin 68 (1993)
ATF, 15 March 1993	Tribunal Fédéral, 15 March 1993, *G.* v *Fédération Equestre Internationale,* 11 ASA Bulletin 398 (1993)
ATF, 16 May 1983	Tribunal Fédéral, 16 May 1983, *République arabe d'Egypte* v *Westland Helicopters Ltd et autres*, partially published in 2 ASA Bulletin 203 (1984)

List of References

ATF, 17 August 1994	Tribunal Fédéral, 17 August 1994, *Türkiye Elektrik Kurumu (TEK)* v *Osuuskunta METEX Andelslag (Metex)*, 13 ASA Bulletin 198 (1995)
ATF, 2 July 1997	Tribunal Fédéral, 2 July 1997, *L. Ltd à Gibraltar* v *The Foreign Trade Association of the Republic of U. et Tribunal arbitral CCIG à Genève*, case no. 4P.265/1996, 15 ASA Bulletin 494 (1997)
ATF, 27 October 1995	Tribunal Fédéral, 27 October 1995, *X und XX* v *Y*, 14 ASA Bulletin 277 (1996)
ATF, 30 June 1994	Tribunal Fédéral, 30 June 1994, *Hitachi Ltd* v *SMS Schloemann Siemag Aktiengesellschaft,* 15 ASA Bulletin 99 (1997)
ATF, 9 January 1995	Tribunal Fédéral, 9 January 1995, *Inter Maritime Management SA* v *Russin & Vecchi*, 19 ASA Bulletin 294 (2001)
Athletic Union of Constantinople v *National Basketball Association*	*Athletic Union of Constantinople* v *National Basketball Association* [2002] 1 Lloyd's 305 (QB)
Athletic Union of Constantinople v *National Basketball Association (No. 2)*	*Athletic Union of Constantinople* v *National Basketball Association and others (No. 2)* [2002] EWCA Civ 830
Atlanska Plovidba v *Consignaciones Asturianas SA*	*Atlanska Plovidba and Anor* v *Consignaciones Asturianas SA* [2004] 2 Lloyd's Rep 109
Atlantic Richfield	*Atlantic Richfield Company* v *The Islamic Republic of Iran*, Award No. ITM 50-396-1 (8 May 1985)
Aucoven v *Venezuela*	*Autopista Concesionada de Venezuela, C.A.* v *Bolivarian Republic of Venezuela* (ICSID Case No. ARB/00/5) DJ, 27 September 2001
Audi-NSU	Belgium, Cour de cassation, 28 June 1979, *Audi-NSU Auto Union AG* v *Adelin Petit & Cie (Belgium)*, V YBCA 257 (1980)
Avco	*Iran Aircraft Industries, et al.* v *Avco Corp.*, 980 F 2d 141, 146 (1992)

List of References

Azou Shipping v *Baltic Shipping (No. 2)*	*Azov Shipping Co.* v *Baltic Shipping Co. (No. 2)* [1999] 1 All ER 716 (QBD (Com)
Azov Shipping v *Baltic Shipping*	*Azov Shipping Co.* v *Baltic Shipping Co.* [1999] 2 Lloyd's Rep 159
Azpetrol v *Azerbaijan*	*Azpetrol International Holdings B.V., Azpetrol Group B.V. and Azpetrol Oil Services Group B.V.* v *Republic of Azerbaijan* (ICSID Case No. ARB/06/15), DPM, 6 October 2008
Azurix v *Argentina*	*Azurix Corp.* v *Argentine Republic* (ICSID Case No. ARB/01/12), DA, 1 September 2009
Azurix v *Argentina* (DJ)	*Azurix Corp.* v *Argentine Republic* (ICSID Case No. ARB/01/12), DJ, 8 December 2003
Azurix v *Argentina* (Stay Decision)	*Azurix Corp.* v *Argentine Republic* (ICSID Case No. ARB/01/12), DS, 28 December 2007
Baker Marine v *Chevron*	*Baker Marine Ltd* v *Chevron Ltd and Chevron Corp Inc*, 191 F 3d 194 (2d Cir 1999)
Banro v *Congo*	*Banro American Resources, Inc. and Société Aurifère du Kivu et du Maniema S.A.R.L.* v *Democratic Republic of the Congo* (ICSID Case No. ARB/98/7), FA, 1 September 2000
Barcelona Traction	*Barcelona Traction, Light and Power Co.* (*Belgium* v *Spain*) 1970 ICJ Rep 3
Baruch-Foster	*Imperial Ethiopian Government* v *Baruch-Foster Corp.*, 535 F 2d 334, 336 (5th Cir 1976)
Base Metal v *OJSC*	*Base Metal Trading Ltd* v *OJSC 'Novokuznetsky Aluminium Factory'*, 6 March 2002, XXVII YBCA 902 (2002) (4th Cir 6 March 2002)
Bauer & Grobmann	Corte di Appello Naples, 18 May 1982, *Bauer & Grobmann OHG* v *Fratello Cerrone Alfredo e Raffaele*, X YBCA 461 (1985)
Bawejem Ltd v *MC Fabrications Ltd*	*Bawejem Ltd* v *MC Fabrications Ltd* [1999] All ER Comm 377 (CA)
Bay Hotel and Resort Ltd v *Cavailier Construction Co. Ltd*	*Bay Hotel and Resort Ltd* v *Cavailier Construction Co. Ltd* [2001] UKPC 34

BayObLG 9 September 1999	Bayerisches Oberstes Landesgericht, Germany, 4 Z SchH 03/99, 9 September 1999
BayOLG 16 March 2000	Bayerisches Oberlandesgericht, 16 March 2000, RPS 2/2000, Beilage 12 zu Heft 50 BetriebsBerater 15 (2000)
Behring International	*Behring International, Inc.* v *Iranian Air Force*, Dec. No. 27-382-3
Belair LLC v *Basel LLC*	*Belair LLC* v *Basel LLC* [2009] EWHC 725 (Comm)
Benaim (UK) Ltd v *Davies Middleton & Davies Ltd (No. 2)*	*Benaim (UK) Ltd* v *Davies Middleton & Davies Ltd (No. 2)* [2005] EWHC 1370 (TCC)
Bendone-Derossi International	*Bendone-Derossi International* v *The Islamic Republic of Iran*, Award No. ITM 40-375-1 (7 Jun 1984)
Benteler v *Belgian State*	*Benteler* v *Belgian State*, ad hoc, FA, 18 November 1983
Benvenuti v *Congo*	*S.A.R.L Benvenuti & Bonfant* v *People's Republic of Congo* (ICSID Case No. ARB/77/2), FA, 8 August 1980
Benvenuti v *Congo* (France)	Cour d'appel Paris, 26 June 1981, *SARL Benvenuti & Bonfant* v *People's Republic of the Congo*
Bernuth Lines Ltd v *High Seas Shipping Ltd*	*Bernuth Lines Ltd* v *High Seas Shipping Ltd ('The Eastern Navigator')* [2005] EWHC 3020 (Comm)
BGH 17 August 2000	Bundesgerichtshof, 17 August 2000, 53 NJW 3650 (2001) 3651
BGH 18 January 1990	Bundesgerichtshof, 18 January 1990, XVII YBCA 503 (1992)
BGH 2 November 2000	Germany, Bundesgerichtshof, 2 November 2000, ZIP 2270 (2000) 2271
BGH 23 April 1998	Bundesgerichtshof, 23 April 1998, XXIVb YBCA 928 (1999)
BGH 1 February 2001	Bundesgerichtshof, Germany, 1 February 2001, XXIX Yearbook 700 (2004)

List of References

BGH 24 September 1998	Bundesgerichtshof, Germany, 24 September 1998, NJW 282 (1999)
BGH 4 March 1999	Bundesgerichtshof, Germany, 4 March 1999, III ZR 72/98, NJW 1999, 2370
BGH 6 June 2002	Bundesgerichtshof, Germany, 6 June 2002, III ZB 44/01, SchiedsVZ, 2003, 39
Birse Construction v *St David Ltd*	*Birse Construction Ltd* v *St David Ltd* [1999] BLR 194 *Birse Construction Ltd* v *St David Ltd* (2000) 78 ConLR 121, [2000] All ER (D) 1913
Bitwater v *Tanzania*	*Biwater Gauff (Tanzania) Limited* v *United Republic of Tanzania* (ICSID Case No. ARB/05/22), FA, 24 July 2008
Biwater v *Tanzania* Procedural Order No. 1	*Biwater Gauff (Tanzania) Limited* v *United Republic of Tanzania* (ICSID Case No. ARB/05/22), Procedural Order No. 1, 31 March 2006
Biwater v *Tanzania* Procedural Order No. 3	*Biwater Gauff (Tanzania) Limited* v *United Republic of Tanzania* (ICSID Case No. ARB/05/22), Procedural Order No. 3, 29 September 2006
Biwater v *Tanzania* Procedural Order No. 5	*Biwater Gauff (Tanzania) Limited* v *United Republic of Tanzania* (ICSID Case No. ARB/05/22), Procedural Order No. 5, 2 February 2007
Bomar Oil NV v *Entreprise d'Actvitiés Pétrolières*	*Bomar Oil NV (Neth. Antilles)* v *ETAP – l'Entreprise Tunisienne d'Activités Pétrolières (Tunisia)*, 9 November 1993, Cour de Cassation [French Supreme Court], XX YBCA 660-662 (1995), Revue de l'arbitrage (1991) pp. 293-300, with note C. Kessedjian, pp. 300-304; for the facts see the Court of Appeal: 23 January 1991, Cour d'Appel [Court of Appeal], Versailles, XVII YBCA 488-490 (1992)
Bompard (France)	Cour d'appel Paris, 22 May 1991, *Bompard* v *Consorts C. et al.*, Rev Arb (1996) p. 476
Braes of Doune Wind Farm (Scotland) Ltd v *Alfred McAlpine*	*Braes of Doune Wind Farm (Scotland) Limited* v *Alfred McAlpine Business Services Limited* [2008] EWHC 426

List of References

Brasoil (France)	Cour d'appel Paris, 1 July 1999, *Braspetro Oil Services (Brasoil)* v *The Management and Implementation Authority of the Great Man-Made River Project (GMRA)* XXIVa YBCA (1999), p. 296
Bridas v *Turkmenistan*	*Bridas S.A.P.I.C.* v *Government of Turkmenistan* 447 F 3d 411 (5th Cir 2006).
British Telecommunications plc v *SAE Group Inc.*	*British Telecommunications plc* v *SAE Group Inc.* [2009] EWHC 252 (TCC)
Broda Agro Trade Cyprus v *Alfred C Toepfer*	*Broda Agro Trade (Cyprus) Ltd* v *Alfred C Toepfer International GmbH* [2009] EWHC 3318 (Comm)
Brunner	Cour de cassation, 10 September 1998, *Thomson CSF* v *Brunner Sociedade Civil de Administracao Limitada* and *Frontier AG Bern*, Rev Arb 583 (2001), with note Racine
Brussels, 25 January 1996	Judgment 25 January 1996, XXII YBCA 643 (Court of First Instance, Brussels) (1997)
BV Bureau Wijsmuller	*BV Bureau Wijsmuller* v *United States of America*, III YBCA 290 (1978) (SDNY, 1976)
C v *D*	*C* v *D* [2007] EWHC Civ 1282
Cable TV v *St. Kitts and Nevis*	*Cable Television of Nevis, Ltd and Cable Television of Nevis Holdings, Ltd* v *Federation of St. Kitts and Nevis* (ICSID Case No. ARB/95/2), Award, 13 January 1997
Cadmus Investment v *Amec Building Ltd*	*Cadmus Investment Co.* v *Amec Building Ltd* [1998] ADRLJ 72
Camera di Esecuzione Tessin	Camera di Esecuzione e Fallimenti Canton Tessin, 19 June 1990, *K S AG* v *CC SA*, XX YBCA 762 (1995)
Cameroon Airlines v *Transnet Ltd*	*Cameroon Airlines* v *Transnet Ltd* [2004] EWHC 1829 (QBD)
Canfor Corp.	*Canfor Corporation* v *United States of America*, Procedural Order No. 3 (NAFTA Chapter Eleven, 13 Nov 2003)

List of References

Canfor Corp. (Decision)	*Canfor Corporation* v *United States of America*, Decision on the Place of Arbitration, Filing of a Statement of Defence and Bifurcation of the Proceedings (NAFTA Chapter Eleven, 23 Jan 2004)
Carter v *Harold Simpson Associates*	*Carter* v *Harold Simpson Associates (Architects) Ltd* [2004] UKPC 29
Casado and Allende Foundation v *Chile*	*Victor Pey Casado and Presidente Allende Foundation* v *Republic of Chile* (ICSID Case No. ARB/98/2), DPM, 25 September 2001
Casado and Allende Foundation v *Chile* (Revision)	*Víctor Pey Casado and President Allende Foundation* v *Republic of Chile* (ICSID Case No. ARB/98/2), Revision proceeding, 18 November 2009
Cascade	*Refusal to Accept the Claim of Cascade Overview Development Enterprises, Inc.,* Decision No. DEC 4-REF1-FT (4 May 1982)
Case No. A/1 (Issue II)	*Iran* v *United States*, Case A/1 (Issue II), Decision (14 May 1982)
Case No. A/1 (Issues I, III and IV)	*Iran-United States*, Case No. A/1 (Issues, I, III and IV), Decision of 30 Jul 1982
Case No. A/27	*The Islamic Republic of Iran* v *The United States of* America, Case No. A/27, Full Tribunal, Order of 5 Aug 1998
Case No. A/33	*The United States of America* v *The Islamic Republic of Iran*, Case No. A/33, Full Tribunal, Order of 28 Feb 2002
CCIG case no. 193, 21 October 2002	Geneva Chamber of Commerce and Industry (CCIG), case no. 193, *X (Azerbaijan), Claimant* v *Y (Lithuania), Respondent*, Interim Award of 21 October 2002, 24 ASA Bulletin 61 (2006)
CDC v *Seychelles*	*CDC Group plc* v *Republic of Seychelles* (ICSID Case No. ARB/02/14), DA, 29 June 2005
CDC v *Seychelles* (Stay Decision)	*CDC Group plc* v *Republic of Seychelles* (ICSID Case No. ARB/02/14), DS, 14 July 2004

List of References

Cekobank v ICC (France)	Tribunal de grande instance Paris, 8 October 1986, *Ceskolovenska Obchodni Banka A.S. (Cekobanka)* v *Chambre de Commerce International (CCI),* Rev Arb (1987), p. 367
Cetelem SA v Roust Holdings Ltd	*Cetelem SA v Roust Holdings Ltd* [2005] EWCA Civ 618
CGU International Insurance plc v Astra Zeneca Insurance	*CGU International Insurance plc and others* v *Astra Zeneca Insurance Co. Ltd* [2006] EWCA Civ 1340
Challenge Decision of 11 January 1995	Challenge Decision of 11 January 1995
Champion Trading v Egypt	*Champion Trading Company and Ameritrade International, Inc.* v *Arab Republic of Egypt* (ICSID Case No. ARB/02/9), DJ, 21 October 2003
Cherafat	*Gloria Jean Cherafat et al.* v *The Islamic Republic of Iran*, Decision No. DEC 106-277-2 (25 Jun 1992)
Chevron v Bangladesh	*Chevron Block Twelve and Chevron Blocks Thirteen and Fourteen* v *People's Republic of Bangladesh* (ICSID Case No. ARB/06/10)
Chevron v National Iranian Oil	*Chevron Research Co.* v *National Iranian Oil Co.*, Case No. 19, Chamber One, Order of 19 Nov 1982
China Leasing v Shenzhen Zhongji	*China Leasing Company Ltd* v *Shenzhen Zhongji Industry and Development Centre*, quoted in Li Hu, Enforcement of the International Commercial Arbitral award – with Special Reference to the Enforcement of the Arbitral Award in the PRC (Law Press of China 2000)
China Nanhai Oil Joint Service	Hong Kong, Supreme Court, 13 July 1994, *China Nanhai Oil Joint Service Corp.* v *Gee Tai Holdings Co. Ltd*, XX YBCA 671 (1995)
China Nonferrous v Xinquan Trade	*China Nonferrous Metal Import/Export Henan Co.* v *Xinquan Trade (Private) Co. Ltd*, quoted in Jian Zhou, 'Arbitration Agreements in China: Battles on Designation of Arbitral Institution and Ad Hoc Arbitration', 23 J Int'l Arb 155 (2006)

List of References

Chloe Z Fishing Co.	*Chloe Z Fishing Co., Inc. (US) and others (US)* v *Odyssey Re (London) Limited, formerly known as Sphere Drake Insurance, PLC (UK) and another (UK)*, 109 F. Supp., 2d p. 1236 et seq.; 2000 US Dist. LEXIS 12645, 26 April 2000, XXVI YBCA 910-938 (2001) (US S.D. Cal. 2000)
Christian Mutual Insurance, Central United Life Insurance, Connecticut Reassurance v *Ace Bermuda Insurance*	Court of Appeal, Bermuda, 6 December 2002, *Christian Mutual Insurance Company, Central United Life Insurance Company, Connecticut Reassurance Corporation* v *Ace Bermuda Insurance Ltd*, [2002] Bda LR 1
Chromalloy	*Chromalloy Aeroservices Inc (US)* v *The Arab Republic of Egypt*, 939 F Supp 907, XXII YBCA 1001 (1997) (DDC 1996)
City of Moscow v *Bankers Trust Co.*	*City of Moscow* v *Bankers Trust Co.* [2004] EWCA Civ 314
City of Prince George v *A.L .Sims & Sons*	B.C. Court of Appeal, 4 July 1995, *The City of Prince George* v *A.L .Sims & Sons Ltd*, 9 B.C.L.R.3d 368
City Oriente (DPM)	*City Oriente Limited* v *República del Ecuador y Empresa Estatal Petroleos del Ecuador (Petroecuador)*, (ICSID Case No. ARB/06/21), DPM, 19 November 2007
City Oriente v *Petroecuador*	*City Oriente Limited* v *República del Ecuador y Empresa Estatal Petroleos del Ecuador (Petroecuador)*, (ICSID Case No. ARB/06/21), Decision on Revocation of Provisional Measures, 13 May 2008
CJCE, *Eco Swiss*	CJCE, 1 June 1999, *Eco Swiss China Time Ltd* v *Benetton International*, Rev Arb 631 (1999), with note Jarrosson
CLOUT Case No. 10	*Navigation Sonamar Inc.* v *Algoma Steamships Limited and others*, Superior Court of Quebec, Canada, 16 April 1987
CLOUT Case No. 12	*D. Frampton & Co. Ltd* v *Sylvio Thibeault and Navigation Harvey & Frères Inc.*, Federal Court of Canada, 7 April 1988

List of References

CLOUT Case No. 13	*Deco Automotive Inc.* v *G.P.A. Gesellschaft Für Pressenautomation mbH*, Ontario District Court, Canada 27 October 1989
CLOUT Case No. 16	*Quintette Coal Limited* v *Nippon Steel Corp. et al.*, British Columbia Court of Appeal, Canada, 24 October 1990
CLOUT Case No. 20	*Fung Sang Trading Limited* v *Kai Sun Sea Products and Food Company Limited*, High Court of Hong Kong, 29 October 1991
CLOUT Case No. 28	*BWV Investments Ltd* v *Saskferco Products Inc., UHDE-GmbH, et al.*, Saskatchewan Court of Queen's Bench, Canada, 19 March 1993
CLOUT Case No. 29	*Kanto Yakin Kogyo Kabushiki-Kaisha* v *Can-Eng Manufacturing Ltd*, Ontario Court of Justice, Canada, 30 January 1992
CLOUT Case No. 30	*Robert E. Schreter* v *Gasmac Inc.*, Ontario Court, Canada, 13 February 1992,
CLOUT Case No. 31	*Gulf Canada Resources Ltd* v *Arochem International Ltd*, British Columbia Court of Appeal, Canada, 10 March 2002
CLOUT Case No. 32	*Mind Star Toys Inc.* v *Samsung Co. Ltd*, Ontario Court, Canada, 30 April 1992
CLOUT Case No. 37	*Arcata Graphics Buffalo Ltd* v *Movie (Magazine) Corp.*, Ontario Court, Canada, 12 March 1993
CLOUT Case No. 38	*China State Construction Engineering Corporation, Guangdong Branch* v *Madiford Limited*, High Court of Hong Kong, 2 March 1991
CLOUT Case No. 40	*Pacific International Lines (PTE) Ltd & Another* v *Tsinlien Metals and Minerals Co. Ltd*, High Court of Hong Kong, 30 July 1992
CLOUT Case No. 42	*Interbulk (Hong Kong) Ltd* v *Safe Rich Industries Ltd*, High Court of Hong Kong, 2 March 1992
CLOUT Case No. 43	*Hissan Trading Co. Ltd* v *Orkin Shipping Corporation*, High Court of Hong Kong, 8 September 1992

List of References

CLOUT Case No. 44	*William Company* v *Chu Kong Agency Co. Ltd and Guangzhou Ocean Shipping Company*, High Court of Hong Kong, 17 February 1993
CLOUT Case No. 57	*Lucky-Goldstar International (H.K.) Limited* v *Ng Moo Kee Engineering Limited*, High Court of Hong Kong, 5 May 1993
CLOUT Case No. 59	*China Ocean Shipping Company* v *Mitrans Maritime Panama S.A.*, High Court of Hong Kong, 28 September 1993
CLOUT Case No. 63	*Joong and Shipping Co. Limited* v *Choi Chong-sick (alias Choi Chong-sik) and Chu Ghin Ho trading as Chang Ho Company*, High Court of Hong Kong, 31 March 1994
CLOUT Case No. 64	*H. Small Limited* v *Goldroyce Garment Limited*, High Court of Hong Kong, 13 May 1994
CLOUT Case No. 66	*Jean Charbonneau* v *Les Industries A.C. Davie Inc. et al.*, Superior Court of Quebec, Canada, 14 March 1989
CLOUT Case No. 67	*AAMCO Transmissions Inc.* v *Kunz*, Saskatchewan Court of Appeal, Canada, 17 September 1991
CLOUT Case No. 68	*Delphi Petroleum Inc.* v *Derin Shipping and Training Ltd*, Federal Court of Canada, 3 December 1993
CLOUT Case No. 71	*Trade Fortune Inc.* v *Amagalmated Mill Supplies Ltd*, British Columbia Supreme Court, Canada, 25 February 1994
CLOUT Case No. 76	*China Nanhai Oil Joint Service Corporation, Shenzhen Branch* v *Gee Tai Holdings Co. Ltd*, High Court of Hong Kong, 13 July 1994
CLOUT Case No. 77	*Vibroflotation A.G.* v *Express Builders Co. Ltd*, High Court of Hong Kong, 15 August 1994
CLOUT Case No. 78	*Astel-Peiniger Joint Venture* v *Argos Engineering & Heavy Industries Co. Ltd*, High Court of Hong Kong, 18 August 1994

List of References

CLOUT Case No. 87	*Gay Constructions PTY Ltd and Spaceframe Buildings (North Asia) Ltd* v *Caledonian Techmore (Building) Limited and Hanison Construction Co. Ltd (as a third party)*, High Court of Hong Kong, 17 November 1994
CLOUT Case No. 88	*Nanjing Cereals, Oils and Foodstuffs Import & Export Corporation* v *Luckmate Commodities Trading Ltd*, High Court of Hong Kong, 16 December 1994
CLOUT Case No. 108	*D. Heung & Associates, Architects & Engineers* v *Pacific Enterprises (Holdings) Company Limited*, High Court of Hong Kong, 4 May 1995
CLOUT Case No. 109	*Private Company "Triple V" Inc.* v *Star (Universal) Co. Ltd and Sky Jade Enterprises Group Ltd*, Court of Appeal, Hong Kong, 7 July 1995
CLOUT Case No. 111	*Borowski* v *Heinrich Fiedler Perforiertechnik GmbH*, Alberta Court of Queen's Bench, Canada, 12 August 1994
CLOUT Case No. 117	*Murmansk Trawl Fleet* v *Bimman Realty Inc.*, Ontario Court of Justice, Canada, 19 December 1994
CLOUT Case No. 118	*Bab Systems, Inc.* v *McLurg*, Ontario Court of Justice, Canada, 21 December 1994
CLOUT Case No. 119	*ABN Amro Bank Canada* v *Krupp Mak Maschinenbau GmbH*, Ontario Court of Justice, Canada, 23 December 1994
CLOUT Case No. 146	Moscow City Court, Russian Federation, 10 November 1994
CLOUT Case No. 147	Moscow City Court, Russian Federation, 13 December 1994
CLOUT Case No. 148	Moscow City Court, Russian Federation, 10 February 1995
CLOUT Case No. 149	Moscow City Court, Russian Federation, 18 September 1995
CLOUT Case No. 177	*MMTC* v *Sterlite Industries (India) Ltd*, Supreme Court of India, 18 November 1996

List of References

CLOUT Case No. 178	*Siderurgica Mendes Junior S.A.* v *"Icepearl" (The)*, British Columbia Supreme Court, Canada, 31 January 1996
CLOUT Case No. 179	*The City of Prince George* v *A.L. Sims & Sons Ltd*, British Columbia Court of Appeal, Canada, 4 July 1995
CLOUT Case No. 182	*International Civil Aviation Organization (ICAO)* v *Tripal Systems Pty. Ltd*, Superior Court of Quebec, Canada, 9 September 1994
CLOUT Case No. 208	*Vanol Far East Marketing Pte. Ltd* v *Hin Leong Trading Pte. Ltd*, High Court of Singapore, 27 May 1996
CLOUT Case No. 267	*Zimbabwe Electricity Supply Commission* v *Genius Joel Maposa*, Harare High Court of Zimbabwe, 29 March and 9 December 1998
CLOUT Case No. 323	*Zimbabwe Electricity Supply Authority* v *Genius Joel Maposa*, Zimbabwe Supreme Court, 21 October and 21 December 1999
CLOUT Case No. 342	*Conforce (Pvt.) Limited* v *The City of Harare*, Harare High Court, Zimbabwe 1 March and 5 April 2000
CLOUT Case No. 349	*Harper* v *Kvaerner Fjellstrand Shipping A.S.*, British Columbia Supreme Court, Canada, 13 September 1991
CLOUT Case No. 353	*TLC Multimedia Inc.* v *Core Curriculum Technologies Inc.*, Supreme Court of British Columbia, Canada, 6 July 1998
CLOUT Case No. 354	*Silver Standard Resources Inc.* v *Joint Stock Company Geolog, Cominco Ltd and Open Type Stock Company Dukat GOK*, British Columbia Court of Appeal, Canada, 11 December 1998
CLOUT Case No. 365	*Schiff Food Products Inc.* v *Naber Seed & Grain Co. Ltd*, Saskatchewan Court of Queen's Bench, Canada, 1 October 1996
CLOUT Case No. 367	*NetSys Technology Group AB* v *Open Text Corp.*, Ontario Superior Court of Justice, Canada, 29 July 1999

List of References

CLOUT Case No. 370	*Bitumat Ltd* v *Multicom Ltd*, High Court of Zimbabwe, 24 and 31 May 2000
CLOUT Case No. 371	Hanseatisches Oberlandesgericht Bremen, Germany, 30 September 1999
CLOUT Case No. 372	Oberlandesgericht Rostock, Germany, 28 October 1999
CLOUT Case No. 374	Oberlandesgericht Düsseldorf, Germany, 23 March 2000
CLOUT Case No. 375	Bayerisches Oberstes Landesgericht, Germany, 15 December 1999
CLOUT Case No. 381	*Fibreco Pulp Inc.* v *Star Shipping A/S*, Federal Court of Canada, 24 May 2000
CLOUT Case No. 383	*Deco Automotive Inc.* v *G.P.A. Gesellschaft Für Pressenautomation mbH*, Ontario District Court, 27 October 1989
CLOUT Case No. 384	*Skorimpex Foreign Trade Co.* v *Lelovic Co.*, Ontario Court of Justice, Canada, 26 April 1991
CLOUT Case No. 385	*Murmansk Trawl Fleet* v *Bimman Realty Inc.*, Ontario Court of Justice, Canada, 19 December 1994
CLOUT Case No. 386	*ATM Compute GmbH* v *DY 4 Systems, Inc.*, Ontario Court of Justice, Canada, 8 June 1995
CLOUT Case No. 390	*Re Carter et al. and McLaughlin et al.*, Ontario Court, Canada, 1 February 1996
CLOUT Case No. 391	*Re Corporacion Transnacional de Inversiones, S.A. de C.V. et al. and STET International, S.p.A. et al.*, Superior Court of Justice, Canada, 22 September 1999
CLOUT Case No. 392	*Compagnie nationale Air France* v *Libyan Arab Airlines*, Supreme Court of Quebec, Canada, 15 February 2000
CLOUT Case No. 402	Highest Regional Court of Bavaria, Germany, 16 March 2000
CLOUT Case No. 403	Highest Regional Court of Bavaria, 15 December 1999

List of References

CLOUT Case No. 404	Federal Supreme Court, Germany, 14 September 2000
CLOUT Case No. 406	Bundesgerichtshof, Germany, II ZR 373/98, 3 April 2000
CLOUT Case No. 407	Bundesgerichtshof, Germany, III ZB 55/99, 2 November 2000
CLOUT Case No. 436	Bayerisches Oberstes Landesgericht, Germany, 24 February 1999
CLOUT Case No. 441	Oberlandesgericht Köln, Germany, 20 July 2000
CLOUT Case No. 455	Hanseatisches Oberlandesgericht Hamburg, Germany, 4 September 1998
CLOUT Case No. 508	*United Laboratories, Inc.* v *Abraham*, Ontario Superior Court of Justice, Canada, 8 October 2002
CMA CGM SA v *Beteiligungs-KG MS Northern Pioneer Schiffahrtsgesellschaft*	*CMA CGM SA* v *Beteiligungs-KG MS Northern Pioneer Schiffahrtsgesellschaft MBH & Co.* [2003] 1 Lloyd's Rep 212
CME Czech Republic	*CME Czech Republic BV (The Netherlands)* v *The Czech Republic*, Final Award (*Ad Hoc* UNCITRAL Proceedings, 14 Mar 2003)
CMS v *Argentina* (DA)	*CMS Gas Transmission Company* v *The Argentine Republic* (ICSID Case No. ARB/01/8), DA, 25 September 2007
CMS v *Argentina* (DPM)	*CMS Gas Transmission Company* v *The Argentine Republic* (ICSID Case No. ARB/01/8), DPM, 16 August 2004
CMS v *Argentina* (FA)	*CMS Gas Transmission Company* v *The Argentine Republic* (ICSID Case No. ARB/01/8), FA, 12 May 2005
CMS v *Argentina* (NY and Switzerland)	*CMS Gas Transmission Company* v *Argentina* (ICSID Case No. ARB/01/8), decision on jurisdiction, 17 July 2003, 42 ILM 788 (2003), <ita.law.uvic.ca/documents/cms-argentina_000.pdf>; Award of 12 May 2005; 44 ILM 1205 (2005), <ita.law.uvic.ca/documents/CMS_FinalAward_000.pdf>; Annulment decision, 25 September 2007, <ita.law.uvic.ca/documents/CMSAnnulment Decision.pdf>

List of References

CMS v *Argentina* (Stay Decision)	*CMS Gas Transmission Company* v *The Argentine Republic* (ICSID Case No. ARB/01/8), DS, 1 September 2006
CNTIC v *Swiss Industrial Resources*	*China National Technical Import Corporation* v *Swiss Industrial Resources Company Incorporated*, 1 Gazette of the Supreme People's Court of the PRC (1989)
Colliers International Property Consultants v *Colliers Jordan Lee Jafaar Sdn Bhd*	*Colliers International Property Consultants* v *Colliers Jordan Lee Jafaar Sdn Bhd* [2008] EWHC 1524 (Comm)
Commerce and Industry Insurance Co. of Canada v *Lloyd's Underwriters*	*Commerce & Industry Insurance Co. of Canada* v *Lloyd's Underwriters & Others* [2002] 1 WLR 1323
Commonwealth Coatings v *Continental Casualty*	*Commonwealth Coatings Corp.* v *Continental Casualty Co.*, 393 US 145, 149 (1968)
Compagnie de Saint Gobain-Pont	France, Cour d'appel Paris, 10 May 1971, *Compagnie de Saint Gobain-Pont à Mousson* v *The Fertilizer Corporation of India Ltd*, I YBCA 184 (1976)
Compania des Desarollo de Santa Elena SA v *Costa Rica*	*Compania del Desarollo de Santa Elena S.A.* v *Republic of Costa Rica* (ICSID Case No. ARB/96/1), FA, 17 February 2000
Computer Sciences Corporation	*Computer Sciences Corporation* v *The Islamic Republic of Iran*, Award No. 221-65-1 (16 April 1986)
Contec v *Remote Solution*	*Contec Corp.* v *Remote Solution Co.*, 398 F 3d 205, 208 (2d Cir 2005)
Continental Casualty v *Argentina* (DJ)	*Continental Casualty Company* v *Argentine Republic* (ICSID Case No. ARB/03/9), DJ, 22 February 2006
Corfu Channel	*Corfu Channel* (*United Kingdom* v *Albania*) (Merits) 1949 ICJ Rep 4
Corte d'Appello di Napoli 13 December 1974	Corte d'Appello di Napoli, 13 December 1974, Ditte Frey, Milota, Seitelberger v Ditte F. Cuccaro

List of References

Corte di Cassazione 22 February 1992	Corte di Cassazione, 22 February 1992, XVIII YBCA 433 (1993)
Corte di Cassazione 3 April 1987	Corte di Cassazione 3 April 1987, SpA Abati Legnami v Fritz Häupl, No. 3221
Corte di Cassazione 7 June 1995	Corte di Cassazione, 7 June 1995, XXII YBCA 727 (1997)
Cour d'appel Paris, *ABCI*	Cour d'appel Paris, 11 April 2002, *ABC International* v *Diverseylever*, Rev Arb 143 (2003), with note Bensaude, XXVII YBCA 209 (2003)
Cour d'appel Paris, *AGRR*	Cour d'appel Paris, 1 March 2007, *AGRR Prévoyance* v *ESG*, Rev Arb 643 (2007)
Cour d'appel Paris, *Almira Films*	16 February 1989, *Almira Films* v *Pierrel ès qual.*, Rev Arb 711 (1989), with note Idot
Cour d'appel Paris, *Asmidal*	Cour d'appel Paris, 2 April 1998, *Technip* v *Asmidal*, Rev Arb 820 (1999), with note Leurent
Cour d'appel Paris, *Babel Production*	Cour d'appel Paris, 6 May 2004, *Carthago Films* v *Babel Production*, Rev Arb 661 (2006), with note Lécuyer
Cour d'appel Paris, *Bachelier*	Cour d'appel Paris, 3 July 2007, *Leizer* v *Bachelier*, Rev Arb 821 (2007), with note Chantebout
Cour d'appel Paris, *Beugnet Acquitaine*	Cour d'appel Paris, 11 July 2002, *Beugnet Acquitaine* v *DV Construction*, Rev Arb 283 (2004), with note Bandrac
Cour d'appel Paris, *Brasoil*	Cour d'appel Paris, 1 July 1999, *Braspetro Oil Services (Brasoil)* v *GMRA*, Rev Arb 834 (1999), with note Jarrosson, XXIV YBCA 296 (1999)
Cour d'appel Paris, *Carthago Films*	Cour d'appel Paris, 29 mars 2001, *Carthago Films* v *Babel Production*, Rev Arb 543 (2001), with note Bureau
Cour d'appel Paris, *Caviartrade*	Cour d'appel Paris, 22 May 2003, *Ess Food* v *Caviartrade*, Rev Arb 1252 (2003), with note Train
Cour d'appel Paris, *Caviartrade II*	Cour d'appel Paris, 18 November 2004, *Ess Food* v *Caviartrade*, Rev Arb 755 (2006), with note Duprey

List of References

Cour d'appel Paris, *Central Timber Business*	Cour d'appel Paris, 15 May 2003, *Central Timber Business* v *Best Charity Corporation*, Rev Arb 131 (2004)
Cour d'appel Paris, *Chromalloy*	Cour d'appel Paris, 14 January 1997, *République Arabe d'Egypte* v *Chromalloy Aero Services*, Rev Arb 395 (1997), with note Fouchard
Cour d'appel Paris, *Ciech*	Cour d'appel Paris, 14 June 2007, *Ciech* v *Comexport Companhia de Comercio Exterior*, Rev Arb 644 (2007)
Cour d'appel Paris, *Citel*	Cour d'appel Paris, 12 June 2003, *Citel* v *Mungovan* Rev Arb 894 (2004), with note Bensaude
Cour d'appel Paris, *Clal MSX*	Cour d'appel Paris, 3 July 2007, *Clal MSX* v *Inwon*, Rev Arb 647 (2007)
Cour d'appel Paris, *Clark*	Cour d'appel Paris, 20 April 1988, *Clark International France* v *Sud Matériel Services et al.*, Rev Arb 570 (1988), with note Goutal
Cour d'appel Paris, *Comilog*	Cour d'appel Paris, 1 July 1997, *Agence Transcongolaise des Télécommunications – Chemin de Fer Congo Océan* v *Compagnie Minière de l'Ogoué (Comilog)*, Rev Arb 131 (1998), with note Hascher, XXIV YBCA 281 (1999)
Cour d'appel Paris, *Comptoir Commercial Blidéen*	Cour d'appel Paris, 13 September 2007, *Comptoir Commercial Blidéen* v *Union Invivo*, Rev Arb 649 (2007)
Cour d'appel Paris, *Consavio International*	Cour d'appel Paris, 11 December 1997, *Cubano* v *Consavio International Ltd*, Rev Arb 124 (1999), with note Bureau
Cour d'appel Paris, *Crédirente*	Cour d'appel Paris, 29 November 2007, *Société française de rentes et de financements crédirente* v *Compagnie Générale de Garantie*, Rev Arb 933 (2007)
Cour d'appel Paris, *Empresa de telecommunicaciones de Cuba*	Cour d'appel Paris, 16 November 2006, *Empresa de Telecommunicaciones de Cuba* v *Telefonica Antilla*, Rev Arb 1084 (2006)

List of References

Cour d'appel Paris, *Engel*	Cour d'appel Paris, 3 December 2009, *Engel Austria GmbH* v *Don Trade*, Mealey's International Arbitration Report, A View From Paris, Vol. 24, # 3, March 2010
Cour d'appel Paris, *Fichtner*	Cour d'appel Paris, 17 December 2009, *Fichtner GmbH & Co. KG* v *Lksur SA*, Mealey's International Arbitration Report, A View From Paris, Vol. 24, # 3, March 2010
Cour d'appel Paris, *Fincantieri*	Cour d'appel Paris, 15 June 2006, *Legal Department du Ministère de la Justice de la République d'Irak* v *Fincantieri Cantieri Navali Itialiani, Finmecanica* and *Armamenti e Aeropsazio*, Rev Arb 87 (2007), with note Bollée
Cour d'appel Paris, *France Animation*	Cour d'appel Paris, 18 January 2007, *Ed. Glénats* v *France Animation*, Rev Arb 134 (2007)
Cour d'appel Paris, *Fremarc*	Cour d'appel Paris, 2 April 2003, *Fremarc* v *ITM Entreprises*, Rev Arb 1231 (2003), with note Gaillard
Cour d'appel Paris, *Gastrolouvre*	Cour d'appel Paris, 10 October 2002, *Culioli* v *Gastrolouvre* and *Cibela* Rev Arb 1277 (2003), with note Lacabarats
Cour d'appel Paris, *GECI*	Cour d'appel Paris, 9 July 1992, *Industrialexport-Import* v *GECI* and *GFC*, Rev Arb 303 (1993), with note Jarrosson
Cour d'appel Paris, *GECI* II	Cour d'appel Paris, 19 December 1995, *GECI* and *GFE* v *Industrial Expert*, Rev Arb 110 (1996), with note Hory
Cour d'appel Paris, *Gothaer*	Cour d'appel Paris, 17 December 2009, *Gothaer Finanzholding AG* v *Liquidators of ICD*, Mealey's International Arbitration Report, A View From Paris, Vol. 24, # 3, March 2010
Cour d'appel Paris, *Gutzwiller*	Cour d'appel Paris, 4 December 2003, *Azran* v *Gutzwiller*, Rev Arb 907 (2004), with note Betto
Cour d'appel Paris, *Honeywell Bull*	Cour d'appel Paris, 21 June 1990, *Compagnie Honeywell Bull* v *Computation Bull de Venezuela*, Rev Arb 96 (1991), with note Delvolvé

List of References

Cour d'appel Paris, *Icco*	Cour d'appel Paris, 6 April 1990, *Philipp Brothers* v Icco, Rev Arb 880 (1990), with note Boisséson
Cour d'appel Paris, *Intelcam*	Cour d'appel Paris, 16 January 2003, *Intelcam* v *France Telecom*, Rev Arb 369 (2004), with note Jaeger
Cour d'appel Paris, *Intrafor*	Cour d'appel Paris, 12 March 1985, *Intrafor Cafor* and *Subtec Middle East Company* v *Gagnant* et al., Rev Arb 299 (1985), with note Loquin
Cour d'appel Paris, *J&P Avax*	Cour d'appel Paris, 12 February 2009, *J&P Avax* v *Tecnimont*, Mealey's International Arbitration Report, A View From Paris, Vol. 24, # 5, May 2009
Cour d'appel Paris, *KFTCIC*	Cour d'appel Paris, 28 June 1991, *KFTCIC* v *Icori Estero*, Rev Arb 568 (1992), with note Bellet
Cour d'appel Paris, *L'Oréal*	Cour d'appel Paris, 9 April 1992, *Annahold BV et al.* v *L'Oréal*, Rev Arb 483 (1996), with note Fouchard
Cour d'appel Paris, *Labinal*	Cour d'appel Paris, 19 May 1993, *Labinal* v *Mors and Westland Aerospace*, Rev Arb 645 (1993), with note Jarrosson
Cour d'appel Paris, *Lassus*	Cour d'appel Paris, 13 December 2005, *Lassus* v *Falero et al.*, Rev Arb 321 (2007)
Cour d'appel Paris, *Limak*	Cour d'appel Paris, 23 October 2008, *Limak Insaat San Vetic* v *Weatherford Kopp GmbH*, Mealey's International Arbitration Report, A View From Paris, Vol. 24, # 2, February 2009
Cour d'appel Paris, *LTDC*	Cour d'appel Paris, 27 October 1994, *Lebanese Traders Distributors et Consultants LTDC* v *Reynolds*, Rev Arb 709 (1994), with note Mayer
Cour d'appel Paris, *Malecki*	Cour d'appel Paris, 6 May 2004, *Malecki* v *Long*, J Int'l Arb 81 (2006), with note Bensaude
Cour d'appel Paris, *Minhal*	Cour d'appel Paris, 28 November 1996, *CN France* v *Minhal France*, Rev Arb 380 (1997), with note Loquin
Cour d'appel Paris, *Mytileneos Holdings*	Cour d'appel Paris, 1 February 2005, *Mytileneos Holdings* v *The Authority for Privatization and State Equity Administration*, Rev Arb 709 (2005), with note Hory

List of References

Cour d'appel Paris, *Norbert Beyrard*	Cour d'appel Paris, 9 July 1992, *Norbert Beyrard France* v *République de Côte d'Ivoire*, Rev Arb 133 (1994), with note Théry
Cour d'appel Paris, *Nu Swift*	Cour d'appel Paris, 21 January 1997, *Nu Swift* v *White Knight* et al., Rev Arb 429 (1997), with note Derains
Cour d'appel Paris, *Nuovo Pignone*	Cour d'appel Paris, 25 October 2006, *Nuovo Pignone* v *Dalkia et al.*, Rev Arb 343 (2007)
Cour d'appel Paris, *Ojjeh*	Cour d'appel Paris, 18 February 1986, *Aiita* v *Ojjeh*, Rev Arb 583 (1986), with note Fécheux
Cour d'appel Paris, *Opinter*	Cour d'appel Paris, 5 January 1985, *Opinter France* v *Dacomex*, Rev Arb 87 (1986), with note Metzger
Cour d'appel Paris, *Otor*	Cour d'appel Paris, 7 October 2004, *Otor Participations* v *Carlyle (Luxembourg) Holdings*, J Int'l Arb 357 (2005), with note Bensaude
Cour d'appel Paris, *Prodoil Gabon*	Cour d'appel Paris, 15 June 2006, *République du Gabon* v *Prodoil Gabon*, Rev Arb 1002 (2006), with note Garaud and Taffin
Cour d'appel Paris, *Raffineries de Pétrole D'homs et de Banias*	Cour d'appel Paris, 15 May 1985, *Raffineries de Pétrole D'homs et de Banias* v *Chambre de Commerce Internationale*, Rev Arb 141 (1985), with note Fouchard
Cour d'appel Paris, *Rose*	Cour d'appel Paris, 5 June 2003, *Rose* v *Waterfront*, RTD com 2003.700, with note Loquin
Cour d'appel Paris, *Sardisud*	Cour d'appel Paris, 25 March 1994, *Sardisud et al.* v *Technip*, Rev Arb 391 (1994), with note Jarrosson
Cour d'appel Paris, *SGI*	Cour d'appel Paris, 28 May 1993, *Société Générale pour l'Industrie* v *Ewbank and Partners Ltd*, Rev Arb 664 (1993), with note Bureau
Cour d'appel Paris, *SNF*	Cour d'appel Paris, 23 March 2006, *SNF SAS* v *Cytec Industries BV*, Rev Arb 100 (2007), with note Bollée, XXXII YBCA 282 (2006)

List of References

Cour d'appel Paris, *SNPC*	Cour d'appel Paris, 29 April 2003, *Société Nationale des Pétroles du Congo (SNPC)* and *République du Congo* v *Total Fina Elf E & P Congo*, Rev Arb 1296 (2003), with note Jarrosson, XXIX YBCA 203 (2004)
Cour d'appel Paris, *Société ivoirienne de Raffinage*	Cour d'appel Paris, 31 January 2008, *Société ivoirienne de Raffinage* v *Teekay Shipping Norway AS et al.*, Rev Arb 163 (2008)
Cour d'appel Paris, *Soubaigne*	Cour d'appel Paris, 15 March 1984, *Soubaigne* v *Limmareds Skogar*, Rev Arb 285 (1985), with note Loquin
Cour d'appel Paris, *Sucres et Denrées*	Cour d'appel Paris, 19 May 2005, *Sucres et Denrées* v *Talsy Shipping Co. Ltd*, Rev Arb 925 (2006), with note Bensaude
Cour d'appel Paris, *Sulzer*	Cour d'appel Paris, 27 November 1987, *CCM Sulze*r v *Somagec, Saers et al.*, Rev Arb 62 (1989), with note Couchez
Cour d'appel Paris, *Synergie*	Cour d'appel Paris, 18 March 2004, *Synergie* v *SC Connect*, Rev Arb 917 (2004), with note Ziadé and Garaud
Cour d'appel Paris, *Taurus Films*	Cour d'appel Paris, 4 November 1997, *Taurus Films* v *Les Films du Jeudi*, Rev Arb 704 (1998), with note Derains
Cour d'appel Paris, *Thalès*	Cour d'appel Paris, 18 November 2004, *Thalès* v *Euromissiles*, Rev Arb 529 (2005), with note Radicati de Brozolo; J Int'l Arb 22(3) 239 (2005), with note Bensaude
Cour d'appel Paris, *Thales International*	Cour d'appel Paris, 8 November 2006, *Thales International Middle East Regional Agency* v *Wegliszweski*, Rev Arb 345 (2007)
Cour d'appel Paris, *Tradigrain*	Cour d'appel Paris, 14 June 2001, *Compagnie Commerciale André* v *Tradigrain* France, Rev Arb 773 (2001), with note Seraglini
Cour d'appel Paris, *Van Dijk*	Cour d'appel Paris, 18 March 1983, *Quemener et Fils* v *Van Dijk France*, Rev Arb 491 (1983), with note Robert

List of References

Cour d'appel Paris, *Vanoverbeke*	Cour d'appel Paris, 15 January 2004, *Centrale fotovista* v *Vanoverbeke et al.*, Rev Arb 907 (2004), with note Betto
Cour d'appel Paris, *Voight*	Cour d'appel Paris, 26 October 1995, *SNCFT* v *Voight*, Rev Arb 553 (1997), with note Cohen
Cour d'appel Paris, *Westman*	Cour d'appel Paris, 30 September 1993, *European Gas Turbine* v *Westman International Ltd*, Rev Arb 371 (1995), with note Bureau, XX YBCA 198 (1995)
Cour d'appel Paris, *Worms*	Cour d'appel Paris, 22 February 2007, *Worms services maritimes* v *CMA CGM*, Rev Arb 142 (2007)
Cour d'appel, *BAII*	Cour d'appel Paris, 18 January 2001, *BAII recouvrement et al.*, v *Inter-Arab Investment Guarantee Corporation*, Rev Arb 935 (2002), with note Jeuland
Cour de cassation, *ABS*	Cour de cassation, 27 March 2007, *Alcatel Business Systems (ABS)* v *Amkor Technology et al.*, Rev Arb 785 (2007), with note El Adhab
Cour de cassation, *Adidas-Salomon*	Cour de cassation, 7 March 2000, *Adidas-Salomon* v *Ventex*, Rev Arb 447 (2000), with note Lacabarats
Cour de cassation, *Al Amiouny*	Cour de cassation, 6 July 2005, *AIC Al Amiouny international contracting* v *Skanska*, Rev Arb 429 (2006), with note Pic
Cour de cassation, *Alix*	Cour de cassation, 23 January 2007, *Cofief* and *Codix* v *Alix*, Rev Arb 290 (2007), with note Teynier and Pic
Cour de cassation, *Almira Films*	Cour de cassation 5 February 1991, *Almira Films* v *Pierrel ès qual.*, Rev Arb 625 (1991), with note Idot
Cour de cassation, *Alstom Power*	Cour de cassation, 2 June 2004, *Industry et al.* v *Alstom Power Turbomachines*, and *Gaussin* v *Alstom Power Turbomachines*, Rev Arb 596 (2004), with note Ancel
Cour de cassation, *Anhydro*	Cour de cassation, 7 June 1989, *Anhydro* v *Caso Pillet et al.*, 61 (1992), with note Derains

List of References

Cour de cassation, *Asecna*	Cour de cassation, 17 October 2000, *Asecna* v *N'Doye*, Rev Arb 648 (2000), with note Mayer, XXVI YBCA 767 (2001)
Cour de cassation, *Axa Corporate Solutions*	Cour de cassation, 22 November 2005, *Axa Corporate Solutions et al.* v *Nemesis Shipping Corporate Ltd et al.*, Rev Arb 437 (2006), with note Cachard
Cour de cassation, *BAII*	Cour de cassation, 30 June 2004, *International Bank PLC et al.* v *BAII recouvrement*, Rev Arb 645 (2005), with note Libchaber
Cour de cassation, *Bomar Oil*	Cour de cassation, 9 November 1993, *Bomar Oil* v *Entreprise Tunisienne d'Activités Pétrolières (ETAP)*, Rev Arb 108 (1994), with note Kessedjian, XX YBCA 660 (1995)
Cour de cassation, *Brunner*	Cour de cassation, 10 September 1998, *Thomson CSF* v *Brunner Sociedade Civil de Administracao Limitada* and *Frontier AG Bern*, Rev Arb 583 (2001), with note Racine
Cour de cassation, *C et al.*	Cour de cassation, 28 November 2007, *C et al.* v *S et al.*, Rev Arb 932 (2007)
Cour de cassation, *Cementos Portland*	Cour de cassation, 22 October 1991, *Compania Valencia de Cementos Portland* v *Primary Coal*, Rev Arb 457 (1992), with note Lagarde, XVIII YBCA 137 (1993)
Cour de cassation, *Chays Frères*	Cour de cassation, 25 April 2006, *CSF* v *Chays Frères et al.*, Rev Arb 79 (2007), with note El Adhab
Cour de cassation, *Chefaro*	Cour de cassation, 13 March 2007, *Chefaro International BV* v *Barrère et al.*, Rev Arb 499 (2007), with note Jaeger
Cour de cassation, *Ciments d'Abidjan*	Cour de cassation, 28 May 2002, *Burkinabé des ciments et matériaux* v *Ciments d'Abidjan,* Rev Arb 397 (2003), with note Cohen
Cour de cassation, *Convert*	Cour de cassation, 14 December 1983, *Convert* v *Droga*, Rev Arb 483 (1984), with note Rondeau-Rivier

List of References

Cour de cassation, *Creighton*	Cour de cassation, 6 July 2000, *Creighton* v *Ministère des Finances de l'Etat du Qatar*, Rev Arb 114 (2000), with note Leboulanger, XXV YBCA 458 (2000)
Cour de cassation, *Creighton*	Cour de cassation, 16 March 1999, *Etat du Qatar* v *Creighton Ltd*, Rev Arb 308 (1999), with note Henry, XXV YBCA 451 (2000)
Cour de cassation, *Dalico*	Cour de cassation, 20 December 1993, *Municipalité de Khoms El Mergeb* v *Dalico*, Rev Arb 116 (1994), with note Gaudemet-Tallon
Cour de cassation, *Dutco*	Cour de cassation, 7 January 1992, *BKMI* and *Siemens* v *Dutco*, Rev Arb 470 (1992), with note Bellet
Cour de cassation, *Encore*	Cour de cassation, 1 July 2009, *Encore Orthopedics Inc.* v *Liquidators of Akthea SAS*, Mealey's International Arbitration Report, A View From Paris, Vol. 24, # 12, December 2009
Cour de cassation, *Eurodif*	Cour de cassation, 14 March 1984, *Eurodif et al.,* v *République Islamique d'Iran*, Rev Arb 69 (1985), with note Couchez
Cour de cassation, *Eurodif II*	Cour de cassation, 28 June 1989, *Eurodif* v *République Islamique d'Iran*, Rev Arb 653 (1989), with note Fouchard
Cour de cassation, *Eurovia*	Cour de cassation, 18 October 2001, *Grenobloise d'Investissements* v *Eurovia et al.*, Rev Arb 358 (2002), with note Jarrosson
Cour de cassation, *Excelsior Films*	Cour de cassation, 24 March 1998, *Excelsior Films* v *UGC-PH*, Rev Arb 255 (1999), with note Fouchard, XXIV YBCA 643 (1999)
Cour de cassation, *Farhat Trading*	Cour de cassation, 6 March 1996, *Farhat Trading Company* v *Daewoo*, Rev Arb 69 (1997), with note Arnaldez
Cour de cassation, *FMT Productions*	Cour de cassation, 20 December 2000, *Prodexport* v *FMT Productions*, Rev Arb 1341 (2003), with note Legros

List of References

Cour de cassation, *Galakis*	Cour de cassation, 2 May 1966, *Trésor Public* v *Galakis*, 93 JDI 648 (1966), with note Level, Rev Arb 99 (1966), with note Caribier
Cour de cassation, *Gas del Estado*	Cour de cassation, 4 December 1990, *ETPM and Ecofisa* v *Gas del Estado*, Rev Arb 81 (1991), with note Fouchard
Cour de cassation, *Generali France*	Cour de cassation, 11 July 2006, *Generali France Assurances et al* v *Universal Legend*, Rev Arb 977 (2006), with note Cachard
Cour de cassation, *Gerstlé*	Cour de cassation, 22 November 1966, *Gerstlé* v *Merry Hull*, Rev Arb 9 (1967)
Cour de cassation, *Golshani*	Cour de cassation, 6 July 2005, *Golshani* v *Gouvernement de la République islamique d'Iran*, Rev Arb 993 (2005), with note Pinsolle
Cour de cassation, *Gosset*	Cour de cassation, 7 May 1963, *Ets. Raymond Gosset* v *Carapelli*, 91 JDI 82 (1964), with note Bredin
Cour de cassation, *Grands Moulins de Strasbourg*	Cour de cassation, 15 March 1988, *Grands Moulins de Strasbourg* v *Compagnie Continentale France*, Rev Arb 115 (1990), with note Idot XVI YBCA 129 (1991)
Cour de cassation, *Grands Moulins de Strasbourg II*	Cour de cassation, 19 November 1991, *Grands Moulins de Strasbourg* v *Compagnie Continentale France*, Rev Arb 76 (1992), with note Idot, XVIII YBCA 140 (1993)
Cour de cassation, *Gromelle*	Cour de cassation, 21 November 2002, *Gromelle* v *Institut International des Techniques d'Organisation*, Rev Arb 283 (2004), with note Bandrac
Cour de cassation, *Groupe Antoine Tabet*	Cour de cassation, 4 July 2007, *République du Congo* v *Groupe Antoine Tabet et al.*, Rev Arb 441 (2008) with note Callé
Cour de cassation, *Hanin*	Cour de cassation, 15 February 2001, *Halbout* and *Matenec HG* v *Hanin*, Rev Arb 135 (2001), with note Loquin
Cour de cassation, *Hilmarton*	Cour de cassation, 23 March 1994, *Hilmarton* v *Omnium de Traitement et de Valorisation*, Rev Arb 327 (1994), with note Jarrosson, XX YBCA 663 (1995)

List of References

Cour de cassation, *IAIGC*
Cour de cassation, 14 June 2000, *Inter Arab Investment Guarantee Corporation (IAIGC)* v *Banque Arabe et internationale d'investissement (BAII)*, Rev Arb 729 (2001), with note Lécuyer, XXVI YBCA 270 (2001)

Cour de cassation, *Jules Vernes*
Cour de cassation, 7 June 2006, *Copropriété Maritime Jules Vernes et al.*, v *ABS – American Bureau of Shipping*, Rev Arb 945 (2006), with note Gaillard, XXXII YBCA 290 (2007)

Cour de cassation, *Juliet*
Cour de cassation, 6 December 2005, *Juliet et al.* v *X et al.*, Rev Arb 126 (2006), with note Jarrosson

Cour de cassation, *Liquidator of Jean Lion*
Cour de cassation, 6 May 2009, *Liquidator of Jean Lion* v *Income*, Mealey's International Arbitration Report, A View From Paris, Vol. 24, # 8, August 2009

Cour de cassation, *Lopez-Alberti*
Cour de cassation, 9 October 2001, *Kis* v *Lopez-Alberdi*, Rev Arb 347 (2002), with note Clay

Cour de cassation, *Metu*
Cour de cassation, 1 December 1999, *Metu System Meinig KG and Metu System France* v *Sulzer Infra*, Rev Arb 96 (2000), with note Fouchard

Cour de cassation, *Motokov*
Cour de cassation, 12 October 2006, *Same Deutz-Fahr group* v *Motokov France*, Rev Arb 429 (2008), with note Cuniberti

Cour de cassation, *Multitrade*
Cour de cassation, 23 February 1994, *André* v *Multitrade*, Rev Arb 683 (1994), with note Mayer

Cour de cassation, *Navimpex*
Cour de cassation, 6 December 1988, *Navimpex Centrala Navala* v *Wiking Trader*, Rev Arb 641 (1989), with note Goldman

Cour de cassation, *Nigioni*
Cour de cassation, 20 June 2006, *Prodim* v *Nigioni*, Rev Arb 463 (2007), with note Ortscheidt

Cour de cassation, *NIOC*
Cour de cassation, 1 February 2005, *State of Israel* v *National Iranian Oil Company*, Rev Arb 693 (2006), with note Muir Watt, XXX YBCA 125 (2005)

Cour de cassation, *Noga*
Cour de cassation, 9 December 2003, *Gouvernement de la Fédération de Russie* v *Noga*, Rev Arb 336 (2004), with note Bollée

List of References

Cour de cassation, *Norsolor*	Cour de cassation, 9 October 1984, *Pabalk Ticaret Sirkiti* v *Norsolor*, Rev Arb 431 (1985), with note Goldman, XI YBCA 484 (1986)
Cour de cassation, *Painchaud*	Cour de cassation, 6 February 2007, *Prodim* v *Painchaud*, Rev Arb 138 (2007)
Cour de cassation, *Polish Ocean Lines*	Cour de cassation, 10 March 1993, *Polish Ocean Lines* v *Jolasry*, Rev Arb 255 (1993), with note Hascher, XIX YBCA 662 (1994)
Cour de cassation, *Putrabali*	Cour de cassation, 29 June 2007, *Putrabali and Putrabali Adyamulia* v *Rena holding*, Rev Arb 506 (2007), with note Gaillard, XXXII YBCA 299 (2007)
Cour de cassation, *Quatro Children's Book*	Cour de cassation, 16 October 2001, *Quatro Children's Book* v *Editions du Seuil* and *Editions Phidal Inc.*, Rev Arb 919 (2002), with note Cohen
Cour de cassation, *Royal Mougins*	Cour de cassation, 7 March 2002, *Royal Mougins* v *Benedetti*. Rev Arb 214 (2002)
Cour de cassation, *Soerni*	Cour de cassation, 8 July 2009, *SOERNI* v *ASB Air Sea Broker Ltd*, Mealey's International Arbitration Report, A View From Paris, Vol. 24, # 12, December 2009
Cour de cassation, *SNF*	Cour de cassation, 4 June 2008, *SNF* v *Cytec Industries BV*, Rev Arb 346 (2008), with note Fadlallah
Cour de cassation, *Sofidif*	Cour de cassation, 8 March 1988, *Sofidif et al.* v *OIAETI et al.*, Rev Arb 481 (1989), with note Jarrosson
Cour de cassation, *SPP*	Cour de cassation, 6 January 1987, *Southern Pacific Properties Ltd* and *Southern Properties, (SPP)* v *République Arabe d'Egypte*, Rev Arb 469 (1987), with note Leboulanger, XIII YBCA 152 (1988)
Cour de cassation, *Taurus Films*	Cour de cassation, 8 February 2000, *Taurus Films* v *Les Films du Jeudi*, Rev Arb 280 (2000), with note Bureau

List of References

Cour de cassation, *Uni-Kod*	Cour de cassation, 30 March 2004, *Uni-Kod* v *Ouralkali*, Rev Arb 959 (2005), with note Seraglini, XXX YBCA 1200 (2005)
Cour de cassation, *UOP NV*	Cour de cassation, 20 February 2007, *UOP NV* v *BP France et al.*, Rev Arb 139 (2007)
Cour de cassation, *Verhoeft*	Cour de cassation, 21 March 2000, *Moreau* v *Verhoeft*, Rev Arb 805 (2001), with note Derains
Cour de cassation, *Vinexpo*	Cour de cassation, 14 November 2007, *Salon international de l'alimentation* v *Vinexpo*, Rev Arb 453 (2008), with note Train
Cour de cassation, *Vivendi*	Cour de cassation, 28 January 2003, *Nègre* v *Vivendi*, Rev Arb 1337 (2003), with note Legros
Cour de cassation, *Wasteels*	Cour de cassation, 10 May 1988, *Wasteels* v Ampafrance, Rev Arb 51 (1989), with note Jarrosson
Cour de cassation, *Westman*	Cour de cassation, 19 December 1995, *Westman International Ltd* v *European Gas Turbine*, Rev Arb 49 (1996), with note Bureau
Cour de cassation, *Zanzi*	Cour de cassation, 5 January 1999, *Zanzi* v *de Coninck et al.*, Rev Arb 260 (1999), with note Fouchard
Cour de Justice de Genève, 15 April 1999	Cour de Justice de Genève, 15 April 1999, *R. SA* v *A. Ltd*, published in François Knoepfler and Philippe Schweizer, *Arbitrage international: Jurisprudence Suisse commentée depuis l'entrée en vigueur de la LDIP* (Schulthess 2003), pp. 475-478
Court of Cassation Dubai 25 June 1994	Court of Cassation Dubai, 25 June 1994, 1 Int ALR N-62 (1998)
Credit Suisse Fides Trust SA v *Cuoghi*	*Credit Suisse Fides Trust SA* v *Cuoghi* [1998] 1 WLR 474 (HL)
CSOB v *Slovakia*	*Československa obchodní banka, a.s.* v *Slovakia* (ICSID Case No. ARB/97/4), DJ, 24 May 1999, FA, 29 December 2004

List of References

Cubic (France)	Cour de cassation, 20 February 2001, *Société Cubic Defense Systems, Inc.* v *Chambre de Commerce International (CCI)*, Rev Arb (2001), p. 511 note Clay
Cuflet Chartering v *Caroussel Shipping*	*Cuflet Chartering* v *Carousel Shipping* [2001]1 Lloyd's Rep 707 (QBD)
Cyrus Petroleum	*The Cyrus Petroleum Ltd* v *The Islamic Republic of Iran*, Case No. 624, Chamber One, Order of 30 May 1985
Cyrus Petroleum (Award)	*The Cyrus Petroleum Ltd* v *The Islamic Republic of Iran*, Award No. 230-624-1 (2 May 1986)
Czech Republic v *European Media Ventures*	*Czech Republic* v *European Media Ventures* [2007] EWHC 2851 (Comm)
Dadras	*Dadras International* v *The Islamic Republic of Iran*, Case Nos. 213 and 215, Order of 22 July 1994
Dalimpex v *Janicki*	Ontario Superior Court of Justice, 27 June 2000, Canada, *Dalimpex Ltd* v *Janicki*, (2003) 228 D.L.R. (4th) 179
Dallah v *Pakistan*	Dallah Real Estate and Tourism Holding Company v The Ministry of Religious Affairs, Government of Pakistan [2009] EWCA Civ 755
Dalmia Dairy Industries v *National Bank of Pakistan* (England)	*Dalmia Dairy Industries Ltd* v *National Bank of Pakistan*, [1978] 2 Lloyd's Rep 223 (High Court) (QBD)
Dalmine SpA	Corte di cassazione, 23 April 1997, *Dalmine SpA* v *M & M Sheet Metal Forming Machinery AG*, XXIVa YBCA 709 (1999)
Dames & Moore	*Dames & Moore* v *The Islamic Republic of Iran*, Decision No. DEC 36-54-3
Danco International BVIO v *Faucon Investment Co.*	

List of References

Dardana Ltd v *Yukos Oil*	*Dardana Ltd* v *Yukos Oil Co.* [2002] EWCA Civ 543
Dardana v *Yuganskneftegaz*	*Dardana Ltd* v *Yuganskneftegaz, 2003 WL 122257 (2nd Cir, 2003)*
Dardana v *Yukos*	*Dardana Ltd* v *Yukos Oil Co.* and *Petroalliance Services Co. Ltd* v *Same*, [2002] 2 Lloyd's Rep 326 (CA)
Decision of the Appointing Authority in the Challenge of Judge Bengt Broms	Decision of the Appointing Authority in the Challenge of Judge Bengt Broms (30 Sep 2004)
Decision of the Appointing Authority on the Objections by Iran to Judge Mangård	Decision of the Appointing Authority, Ch M J A Moons on the Objections by Iran to Judge Mangård, 5 March 1982
Decision of the Appointing Authority on the Second Challenge by Iran of Judge Briner	Decision of the Appointing Authority on the Second Challenge by Iran of Judge Briner, 19 Sep 1989
Decision of the District Court of the Hague re. *Telekom Malaysia Berhad*	District Court of the Hague, 18 October 2004 (Challenge No. 13/2004; Petition No. HA/RK/2004.667)
Decision on the Challenge by Iran to Judge Arangio-Ruiz	Decision of the Appointing Authority on the Challenge by Iran to Judge Arangio-Ruiz, 24 Sep 1991
DIPENTA v *Algeria*	*Consortium Groupement L.E.S.I. – DIPENTA* v *People's Democratic Republic of Algeria* (ICSID Case No. ARB/03/8)
Dolphin Tankers SRL v *China Shipbuilding Trading Co.*	*Dolphin Tankers SRL* v *China Shipbuilding Trading Co.* [209] EWHC 2216 (Comm)
DST v *R'AS al-Khaimah*	*Deutsche Schachtbau-und Tiefbohrgesellschaft mbH* v *R'AS al-Khaimah National Oil Co.* [1987] 3 WLR 1023 (CA)

List of References

DST v *RAK National Oil*	*Deutsche Schachtbau-und Tiefbohrgesellschaft* v *R'AS al-Khaimah National Oil Co*. [1987] 3 WLR 1023 (CA)
DST v *Rakoil*	*Deutsche Schachtbau- und Tiefbohrgesellscaft mbH* v *Ras Al Khaimah National Oil Company* [1987] 2 Lloyd's Rep 246, 254.
Dubai Islamic Bank PJSC v *Paymentech Merchant Services*	*Dubai Islamic Bank PJSC* v *Paymentech Merchant Services Inc*. [2001] 1 All ER 514 (QBD (Com.)
Duke Energy Electroquil v *Ecuador*	*Duke Energy Electroquil Partners & Electroquil S.A.* v *Republic of Ecuador* (ICSID Case No. ARB/04/19), FA, 18 August 2008
Durham County Council v *Darlington Borough Council*	*Durham County Council* v *Darlington Borough Council* [2003] EWHC 2598 (Admin)
Dutco (France)	Cour de cassation, 7 January 1992, *Siemens AG and BKMI Industrienlagen GmbH* v *Dutco Construction Company,* Rev Arb (1992), p.470
East Timor	*East Timor (Portugal* v *Australia)*, ICJ, Judgment of 30 June 1995
Eastern Mediterranean Maritime	Corte di Appello Florence, 27 January 1988, *Eastern Mediterranean Maritime Ltd* v *SpA Cerealtoscana*, XV YBCA 496 (1990)
ECJ, *Mostaza*	ECJ, 26 October 2006, *Elisa Maria Mostaza Claro* v *Centro Móvil Milenium SL*, C-168/05 Rev Arb 109 (2007), with note Bollée
Eco Swiss China Time v *Benetton*	Hoge Raad, 21 March 1997, *Eco Swiss China Time Ltd (Hong Kong)* v *Benetton International NV (Netherlands)*, Ned Jur 207 1059 (1998); European Court of Justice, C-126/97, 1 June 1999, *Eco Swiss Time Ltd* v *Benetton International NV*, [1999] 2 All ER (Comm) 44, [1999] ECR I-3055, ECJ
Ecuador v *Occidental* (UK)	*Republic of Ecuador* v *Occidental Exploration and Production Co*., [2005] EWCA Civ 1116
Ecuador v *Occidental Exploration*	*Republic of Ecuador* v *Occidental Exploration and Production Company* [2007] EWCA Civ 616

List of References

Edo Corporation v *Ultra Electronics Ltd*	*Edo Corporation* v *Ultra Electronics Ltd* [2009] EWHC 682 (Ch)
Enron Metals v *HIH Casualty*	*Enron Metals & Commodity Ltd (In administration)* v *HIH Casualty & General Insurance Ltd (In provisional liquidation)* (2005) [2005] EWHC 485 (Ch)
Enron v *Argentina* (DA)	*Enron Creditors Recovery Corporation (formerly Enron Corporation) and Ponderosa Assets, L.P.* v *Argentine Republic* (ICSID Case No. ARB/01/3), pending
Enron v *Argentina* (DSR)	*Enron Creditors Recovery Corporation (formerly Enron Corporation) and Ponderosa Assets, L.P.* v *Argentine Republic* (ICSID Case No. ARB/01/3), DSR, 25 October 2007
Enron v *Argentina* (Stay Decision)	*Enron Creditors Recovery Corporation (formerly Enron Corporation) and Ponderosa Assets, L.P.* v *Argentine Republic* (ICSID Case No. ARB/01/3), Decision on the Argentine Republic's Request for a Continued Stay of Enforcement of the Award, 7 October 2008
Equatorial Traders Ltd v *Louis Dreyfus Trading Ltd*	*Equatorial Traders Ltd* v *Louis Dreyfus Trading Ltd* [2002] 2 Lloyd's Rep 638
Esso Australia Resources Ltd v *Plowman*	Australian High Court's decision in *Esso Australia Resources Ltd and others* v *Plowman (Minister for Energy and Minerals)* [1995] 128 ALR 391.
ET Plus SA v *Welter*	*ET Plus SA* v *Welter* [2005] EWHC 2115 (Comm)
Ethyl Corporation	*Ethyl Corporation* v *The Government of Canada*, Partial Award on Jurisdiction (NAFTA Chapter 11, 24 June 1998)
ETI Telecom v *Bolivia*	*E.T.I. Euro Telecom International N.V.* v *Plurinational State of Bolivia* (ICSID Case No. ARB/07/28).
ETI Telecom v *Bolivia* (UK)	*ETI Telecom International NV* v *Republic of Bolivia, Empresa Nacional de Telecomunicaciones Entel SA*, [2008] EWCA Civ 880

List of References

Eureko	*The Republic of Poland* v *Eureko B.V., Stephen M. Schwebel, Yves L.Fortier and Jerzy Rajski*, Brussels Court of Appeal, 17th Section, Docket no. 2007/AR/70
Eurodif (France)	Cour de cassation, 28 June 1989, *Eurodif* v *République Islamique d'Iran,* Rev Arb (1989), p. 653
Eurodif II	Cour de cassation, 28 June 1989, *Eurodif* v *République Islamique d'Iran*, Rev Arb 653 (1989), with note Fouchard
European Gas Turbine	Cour d'appel Paris, 30 September 1993, *European Gas Turbines SA* v *Westman International Ltd*, Rev Arb 359 (1994), XX YBCA 198 (1995)
Eurosteel Ltd v *Stinnes AG*	*Eurosteel Ltd* v *Stinnes AG* [2000] I All ER (Comm) 964
Exeter City AFC Ltd v *Football Conference Ltd*	*Exeter City AFC Ltd* v *Football Conference Ltd* [2004] EWHC 831 (Ch)
Fedax v *Venezuela* (DJ)	*Fedax N.V.* v *Venezuela* (ICSID Case No. ARB/96/3), DJ, 11 July 1997
Fedders Corporation	*Fedders Corporation* v *Loristan Refrigeration Industries,* Decision No. DEC 51-250-3 (28 Oct 1986)
Federal Insurance Co. v *Transamerica Occidental Life Insurance Co.*	*Federal Insurance Co.* v *Transamerica Occidental Life Insurance Co.* [1999] 2 Lloyd's Rep 286 (QBD)
Fence Gate Ltd v *NEL Construction Ltd*	*Fence Gate Limited* v *NEL Construction Ltd* [2001] 1 All ER (D) 214 (QBD)
Fertilizer Corporation of India	*Fertilizer Corporation of India* v *IDI Management*, 517 F Supp 948, 957-58, VII YBCA 382 (1982) (SD Ohio, 1981)
Fidelity Management SA v *Myriad International Holdings BV*	*Fidelity Management SA* v *Myriad International Holdings BV* [2005] EWHC 1193 (QBD)

List of References

Finnish Ships Arbitration	*Finnish Ships Arbitration (Finland* v *United Kingdom)*, 3 RIAA 1479 (1934)
Fiona Trust v *Privalov*	*Fiona Trust & Holding Corporation & 20 Ors* v *Yuri Privalov & 17 Ors* [2007] UKHL 40
First Options of Chicago v *Kaplan*	*First Options of Chicago, Inc.* v *Kaplan*, 514 US 938, 944 (1995)
Fitzroy Engineering Ltd	*Fitzroy Engineering Ltd* v *Flame Engineering Ltd*, 1994 US Dist LEXIS 17781 (ND Ill, 2 December 1994)
FNCB v *Bancec*	*First National City Bank* v *Banco Para El Comercio Exterior de Cuba* 462 US 611, 626-627 (1983)
Ford Aerospace	*Ford Aerospace & Communications Corp., et al.* v *Air Force of the Islamic Republic of Iran*, Decision No. DEC 47-159-3 (2 Oct 1986)
Foremost Tehran Inc.	*Foremost Tehran Inc.* v *The Islamic Republic of Iran*, Case Nos. 37 and 231, Chamber One, Order of 15 Sep 1983
Fougerolle	Syrian Administrative Tribunal Damascus, 31 March 1988, *Fougerolle SA* v *Ministry of Defence of the Syrian Arab Republic*, XV YBCA 515 (1990)
Fraport v *Philippines* (DA)	*Fraport AG Frankfurt Airport Services Worldwide* v *Republic of the Philippines* (ICSID Case No. ARB/03/25), DA, pending
Frederica Lincoln Riahi	*Frederica Lincoln Riahi* v *The Government of the Islamic Republic of Iran*, Case No. 485, Chamber One, Order of 4 May 2000
Gannet Shipping Ltd v *Eastrade Commodities Inc.*	*Gannet Shipping Ltd* v *Eastrade Commodities Inc.* [2002] 1 Lloyd's Rep 713
Gater Assets Ltd v *NAK Naftogaz Ukrainiy*	*Gater Assets Ltd* v *NAK Naftogaz Ukrainiy* [2008] EWHC 1108 (Comm)
Gater Assets Ltd v *Nak Naftogaz Ukrainiy*	*Gater Assets Ltd* v *Nak Naftogaz Ukrainy* [2007] EWCA Civ 988

List of References

Gbangbola v *Smith & Sherriff Ltd*	*Gbangbola* v *Smith & Sheriff Ltd* [1998] 3 All ER 730, QBD (ORB)
Generation Ukraine v *Ukraine*	*Generation Ukraine Inc.* v *Ukraine* (ICSID Case No. ARB/00/9)
Generica	*Generica Ltd* v *Pharmaceuticals Basics Inc.*, XXIII YBCA 1076 (1998) 1078-9 (7th Cir 1997)
Geneva CA, 14 April 1983	Geneva Court of Appeal, 14 April 1983, XII YBCA 502 (1987)
Genin v *Estonia*	*Alex Genin and others* v *Republic of Estonia* (ICSID Case No. ARB/99/2), DSR, 4 April 2002
Gerichtspräsident Thun, 1 December 2005	Gerichtspräsident Thun, 1 December 2005, *X* v *Fédération Internationale de Ski*, case no. Z 05 1735/1932, CaS 50 (2006)
Glamis Gold	*Glamis Gold Ltd* v *United States of America*, Agreement on Certain Procedural Matters (NAFTA Chapter Eleven)
Glamis Gold (Procedural Order)	*Glamis Gold, Ltd* v *United States of America* UNCITRAL (NAFTA) Procedural Order No. 1, 3 March 2005
Glencore Grain Ltd v *Agros Trading Co.*	*Glencore Grain Ltd* v *Agros Trading Co.* [1999] 2 Lloyd's Rep 410 (CA)
Glencore International AG v *Beogradska Plovidba*	*Glencore International AG* v *Beogradska Plovidba* [1996] Lloyd's Rep 311, HC
Glencore v *Shivnath Rai Harnarain*	*Glencore Grain Rotterdam BV* v *Shivnath Rai Harnarain Co.*, 284 F 3d 1114, XXVII YBCA 922 (2002) (9th Cir 2002)
Global Gold Mining v *Robinson* (United States)	*Global Gold Mining LLC* v *Peter M Robinson*, 533 F Supp 2d 442 (SDNY 2008)
Gold Coast Ltd v *Naval Gijon SA*	*Gold Coast Ltd* v *Naval Gijon SA (The Hull 53)* [2006] EWHC 1044 (Comm)
Good Challenger Nevegante SA v *Metalimportexport SA*	*Good Challenger Nevegante SA* v *Metalimportexport SA* [2003] EWCA Civ 1668

List of References

Grimaldi Compagnia di Navigazione v *Sekihyo Lines*	*Grimaldi Compagnia di Navigazione SpA* v *Sekihyo Lines Ltd* [1998] 3 All ER 943
Gruen	*Gruen Associates, Inc.* v *Iran Housing Company*, Award No. 61-188-2 (27 Jul 1983)
Guangdong New Technology	*In Guangdong New Technology Import & Export Corp. Jiangmen Branch (PR China)* v *Chiu Shing Trading as BC Property & Trading Co.*, XVIII YBCA 385 (1993) (Supreme Court Hong Kong, 23 August 1991)
Guinea-Bissau v *Senegal*	Arbitral Award of 31 July 1989 (*Guinea-Bissau* v *Senegal*), 1991 ICJ Reports 53
Guinee v *Hammermills*	*Compagnie des Bauxites de Guinee* v *Hammermills, Inc.*, 1992 WL 122712 (DDC 1992)
Hackwood v *Areen Design Services*	*Hackwood Ltd* v *Areen Design Services Ltd* [2005] EWHC 2322 (TCC)
Halki Shipping Corp. v *Sopex*	*Halki Shipping Corp.* v *Sopex Oils Ltd (The 'Halki')* [1998] 1 Lloyd's Rep 49, affirmed [1998] 1 Lloyd's Rep 465 (CA)
Hålogaland Court of Appeal 16 August 1999	Norway, Hålogaland Court of Appeal, 16 August 1999, Charterer (Norway) v Shipowner (Russian Federation), XXVII YBCA 519 (2002)
Halpern v *Halpern*	*Halpern & Ors* v *Halpern & Anor* [2007] EWCA Civ 291
Harbour and General Works Ltd v *The Environment Agency*	*Harbour and General Works Ltd* v *The Environment Agency* [1999] 1 All ER (Comm) 953
Harold Birnbaum	*Harold Birnbaum* v *The Islamic Republic of Iran*, Decision No. DEC 124-967-2 (14 Dec 1995)
Harris International Telecommunications	*Harris International Telecommunications, Inc.*, v *The Islamic Republic of Iran*, Award No. 323-409-1 (2 Nov 1987)
Harris International Telecommunications (Decision)	*Harris International Telecommunications, Inc.*, v *Islamic Republic of Iran*, Decision No. DEC 73-409-1 (26 Jan 1988)

Harry L Reynolds	*Harry L Reynolds Jr* v *International Amateur Athletic Federation*, XXI YBCA 715 (1996)
Hebei	*Hebei Import & Export Corp.* v *Polytek Engineering Co. Ltd* [1999] 1 HKLRD 552
Heifer International Inc. v *Helge Christiansen*	*Heifer International Inc.* v *Helge Christiansen & Ors* [2007] EWHC 3015 (TCC)
Helnan Hotels v *Egypt*	*Helnan International Hotels A/S* v *Arab Republic of Egypt*, (ICSID Case No. ARB/05/19), FA, 3 July 2008
Henry Boot Ltd v *Alstom Combined Cycles*	*Henry Boot Ltd* v *Alstom Combined Cycles* [2005] EWCA Civ 814
Hillcourt (Docklands) Ltd v *Telia Sonera AB*	*Hillcourt (Docklands) Ltd* v *Telia Sonera AB* [2006] EWHC 508 (Ch)
Hilmarton	France, Cour de cassation, 23 March 1994, *Hilmarton* v *Omnium de Traitement et de Valorisation (OTV)*, XX YBCA 663 (1995)
Himpurna	*Himpurna California Energy Ltd* v *Republic of Indonesia*, Interim Award (*Ad Hoc* UNCITRAL Proceeding, 26 Sep 1999)
Himpurna (Final)	*Himpurna California Energy Ltd* v *Republic of Indonesia*, Final Award (*Ad Hoc* UNCITRAL Proceeding, Oct 16, 1999), reprinted in XXV YCA 186 (2000) 194, 198, para. 43
Hiscox v *Outhwaite*	*Hiscox* v *Outhwaite* (HL) [1991] 3 WLR 297
Hiscox v *Outhwaite*	*Hiscox* v *Outhwaite (No. 1)* [1992] 1 AC 562
HOK Sport v *Aintree Racecourse*	*HOK Sport Ltd (Formerly Lobb Partnership Ltd)* v *Aintree Racecourse Co. Ltd* [2002] (QBD) EWHC 3094
Holiday Inns v *Morocco* (DJ)	*Holiday Inns S.A.* v *Morocco* (ICSID Case No. ARB/72/1), DJ, 1 July 1973, 1 ICSID Reports 645
Home of Homes Ltd v *Hammersmith and Fulham LBC*	*Home of Homes Ltd* v *Hammersmith and Fulham LBC* [2004] 92 Con LR 48 TCC

List of References

Hood Corporation	*Hood Corporation* v *The Islamic Republic of Iran*, Decision No. DEC 34-100-3 (1 Mar 1985)
Hrvatska Elektroprivreda v *The Republic of Slovenia*	*Hrvatska Elektroprivreda* v *The Republic of Slovenia*, ICSID Case No. ARB/05/24, Tribunal's ruling regarding the participation of David Mildon QC in further stages of proceedings, 6 May 2008
Hunt v *Mobile Corporation* (United States)	*Hunt* v *Mobile Oil Corp.*, 583 F Supp 1092 (SDNY 1984)
Hussmann (Europe) Ltd v *Al Ameen Development & Trade*	*Hussmann (Europe) Ltd* v *Al Ameen Development & Trade Co. & Ors* [2000] 2 Lloyd's Rep 83 (QBD)
Hussmann (Europe) Ltd v *Pharaon*	*Hussman (Europe) Ltd* v *Pharaon* [2003] EWCA Civ 266
Hussmann v *Ahmed Pharaon*	*Hussmann (Europe) Ltd* v *Ahmed Pharaon* [2003] EWCA Civ 266
Huyton v *Jakil*	*Huyton SA* v *Jakil SpA* [1999] 2 Lloyd's Rep 83 (CA)
ICC case no. 12363/ACS, 23 December 2003	ICC case no. 12363/ACS, Partial Award of 23 December 2003 on the issue of jurisdiction in an arbitration between *Claimant (Germany)* v *Respondent (Italy)*, place of arbitration: Geneva, 24 ASA Bulletin 462 (2006)
ICC case no. 12542/EC, 19 December 2003	ICC case no. 12542/EC, Procedural Order No. 1 on the Respondent's request for security of 19 December 2003, place of arbitration: Geneva, 23 ASA Bulletin 685 (2005)
ICC Case No. 6474	Partial award ICC Case No. 6474, XXV YBCA 11 (2000)
IMP Group	District Court Moscow, 21 April 1997, *IMP Group (Cyprus) Ltd* v *Aeroimp*, XXIII YBCA 745 (1998)
In Re S & R Co. of Kingston v *Latona Trucking, Inc.*	*In Re S & R Co. of Kingston* v *Latona Trucking, Inc.*, 159 F 3d 80, 84 (2d Cir 1998)
Inceysa v *El Salvador*	*Inceysa Vallisoletana S.L.* v *Republic of El Salvador* (ICSID Case No. ARB/03/26), FA, 2 August 2006

Inceysa v *El Salvador* (DSR)	*Inceysa Vallisoletana S.L.* v *Republic of El Salvador* (ICSID Case No. ARB/03/26), DSR, 16 November 2006
Inco Europe Ltd v *First Choice Distribution*	*Inco Europe Ltd* v *First Choice Distribution* [2000] 1 Lloyd's Rep 467 (HL)
Industrial Risk Insurers	*Industrial Risk Insurers and Barnard & Burk Group Inc. and Barnard and Burk Engineers and Constructors Inc.* v *MAN Gutehoffnungshütte GmbH*, 141 F 3d 1434, XXIVa YBCA 819 (1999) (11th Cir 1998)
Intelcam v *SA France Telecom* (France)	Cour d'appel Paris, 16 January 2003, *Sociétés des Telecommunications Internationales du Cameroun (Intelcam)* v *SA France Télécom,* Rev Arb (2004)
Interagua v *Argentina*	*Suez, Sociedad General de Aguas de Barcelona S.A. and Interagua Servicios Integrales de Agua S.A.* v *Argentine Republic* (ICSID Case No. ARB/03/17)
Inter-Arab Investment Guarantee Corp.	Belgium, Cour d'appel Brussels, 24 January 1997, *Inter-Arab Investment Guarantee Corporation* v *Banque Arabe et Internationale d'Investissements*, XXII YBCA 643 (1997)
International Bulk Shipping v *Minmetals Trading*	*International Bulk Shipping Services Ltd* v *Minerals & Metals Trading Corpn of India & Ors* [1996] 2 Lloyd's Rep. 474
International Technical Products	*International Technical Products Corp.* v *Iran*, Award No. P 186-302-3 (19 Aug 1985)
Intrend International	*Intrend International, Inc.* v *The Imperial Iranian Air Force*, Award No. 59-220-2 (27 Jul 1983)
Ioan Micula v *Romania* (DJ)	*Ioan Micula, Viorel Micula and others* v *Romania* (ICSID Case No. ARB/05/20), Decision on Jurisdiction and Admissibility, 24 September 2008
IPCO (Nigeria) Ltd v *Nigerian National Petroleum Corporation*	*IPCO (Nigeria) Ltd* v *Nigerian National Petroleum Corporation* [2008] EWCA Civ 1157

List of References

Iran Aircraft Industries	*Iran Aircraft Industries* v *AVCO Corporation*, 980 F 2d 141, XVIII YBCA 596 (1993) (2d Cir, 1992)
Iran v *Gould*	*Ministry of Defense of Islamic Republic of Iran* v *Gould, Inc.*, 887 F.2d 1357, 1364 n. 11 (9th Cir. 1989), cert. denied, 494 US 1016 (1990)
Irvani v *Irvani*	*Irvani* v *Irvani* [2000] 1 Lloyd's Rep 412 (CA)
ISEC v *Bridas* (United States)	*International Standard Electric Corporation (ISEC)* v *Bridas Sociedad Anonima Petrolera, Industrial y Comercial*, 745 F Supp 172 (SDNY 1990), XVII YBCA 639 (1992), p. 639
James Associates v *Anhui Machinery & Equipment*	*James Associates (USA) Ltd* v *Anhui Machinery & Equipment Import and Export Corp.*, 171 F Supp 2d 1146, 1147 (D Colo 2001)
James Lazenby & Co. v *McNicholas Construction Co.*	*James Lazenby & Co.* v *McNicholas Construction Co.* [1995] 3 All ER 820
Japan Supreme Court 11 July 1997	Japan, Supreme Court, 11 July 1997, 5(o) Heisei 1762, 51 Minshu 2573, 1624 Hanrei Jiho 90, 958 Hanrei Times 93
Japan Time v *Kienzle France & ICC* (France)	Cour d'appel Paris, 11 July 1980, *Japan Time* v *Kienzle France and International Chamber of Commerce (ICC)* (unpublished)
Joy Mining v *Egypt* (DA)	*Joy Mining Machinery Limited* v *Arab Republic of Egypt* (ICSID Case No. ARB/03/11), Order taking note of discontinuance, 16 December 2005
Kaiser Bauxite v *Jamaica* (DJ)	*Kaiser Bauxite* v *Jamaica* (ICSID Case No. ARB/74/3), DJ, 6 July 1975
Kajo Erzeugnisse	Austria, Oberster Gerichtshof, 20 October 1993/23 February 1998, *Kajo-Erzeugnisse Essenzen GmbH (Austria)* v *DO Zdravilisce Radenska (Slovenia)*, XXIVa YBCA 919 (1999)
Kanoria v *Guinness*	*Kanoria* v *Guinness* [2006] EWCA Civ 222
Kantonsgericht Wallis, 27 April 2006	Kantonsgericht Wallis, Präsident der Schieds-gerichtskammer Mr Jacques Berthouzoz, 27 April 2006, case no. C2 06 10, *S.* v *B.*, published in 26 ASA Bulletin 406 (2008)

Karaha Bodas v Perusahaan Pertambangan Minyak Dan Gus Bumi Negara	*Karaha Bodas Co.* v *Perusahaan Pertambangan Minyak Dan Gus Bumi Negara*, 364 F 3d 274 (5th Cir. 2004)
Kastner v *Jason*	*Kastner* v *Jason* [2004] EWCA (Civ) 1599
Kazakhstan v *Istil Group*	*Republic of Kazakhstan* v *Istil Group Inc. (No. 3)* [2007] EWHC 2729 (Comm), [2007] EWCA Civ 471
Kenya Railways v *Antares Pte Ltd*	*Kenya Railways* v *Antares Pte Ltd (The Antares)* [1987] 1 Lloyd's Rep 424
Klöckner v *Cameroon* (I)	*Klöckner Industrie-Anlagen GmbH and others* v *United Republic of Cameroon and Société Camerounaise des Engrais* (ICSID Case No. ARB/81/2), FA, 21 October 1983
Klöckner v *Cameroon* (I) (DA)	*Klöckner Industrie-Anlagen GmbH and others* v *United Republic of Cameroon and Société Camerounaise des Engrais* (ICSID Case No. ARB/81/2), DA, 3 May 1985
Klöckner v *Cameroon* (II)	*Klöckner Industrie-Anlagen GmbH and others* v *United Republic of Cameroon and Société Camerounaise des Engrais* (ICSID Case No. ARB/81/2), FA, unpublished
Klöckner v *Cameroon* (II) (DA)	*Klöckner Industrie-Anlagen GmbH and others* v *United Republic of Cameroon and Société Camerounaise des Engrais* (ICSID Case No. ARB/81/2), DA, 17 May 1990
Kohn v *Wagschal*	*Kohn* v *Wagschal* [2007] EWCA Civ 1022
L Brown and Sons Ltd v *Crosby Homes (North West) Ltd*	*L Brown and Sons Ltd* v *Crosby Homes (North West) Ltd* [2008] EWHC 817
Laminoires	*Laminoirs-Trefileries-Cableries de Lens SA* v *Southwire Co.*, 484 F Supp 1063 (ND Ga 1980)
Lampart	Italian Supreme Court in *Lampart Vegypary Gepgyar (Hungary)* v *srl Campomarzio Impianti (Italy)*, XXIVa YBCA 699 (1999)

List of References

Larsen	*Larsen* v *The Hawaiian Kingdom*, Award (Permanent Court of Arbitration, 5 Feb 2001)
Law Debenture Trust Corporation v *Elektrim Finance*	*Law Debenture Trust Corporation* v *Elektrim Finance BV* [2005] EWHC 1412 (Ch)
Lawal v *Northern Spirit Ltd*	*Lawal* v *Northern Spirit Ltd* [2003] UKHL 35
Legality of the use of nuclear weapons, *ICJ Advisory Opinion*	'Legality of the Threat or Use of Nuclear Weapons', Advisory Opinion of 8 July 1996, General List No. 95 (1995-1998), <www.icj-cij.org/docket/index.php?p1=3&p2=4&k=e1&case=95&code=unan&p3=4>
LESI v *Algeria*	*LESI, S.p.A. and Astaldi, S.p.A.* v *People's Democratic Republic of Algeria* (ICSID Case No. ARB/05/3), FA, pending
Lesotho Highlands Development Authority v *Impregilo SpA*	*Lesotho Highlands Development Authority* v *Impregilo SpA* [2005] UKHL 43
Lesotho Highlands Development Authority v *Impregilo SpA*	*Lesotho Highlands Development Authority* v *Impregilo SpA* [2005] UKHL 43
LETCO v *Liberia*	*Liberian Eastern Timber Corporation* v *Republic of Liberia* (ICSID Case No. ARB/83/2), FA, 31 March 1986, rectified on 14 May 1986
LETCO v *Liberia* (DC)	*Liberian Eastern Timber Corporation* v *Republic of Liberia*, U.S. District Court for the District of Columbia, 16 April 1987, 659 F Supp 606 (DDC 1987)
LETCO v *Liberia* (DSR)	*Liberian Eastern Timber Corporation* v *Republic of Liberia* (ICSID Case No. ARB/83/2), DSR, 10 June 1986
LETCO v *Liberia* (NY)	*Liberian Eastern Timber Corporation* v *Republic of Liberia*, U.S. District Court for the Southern District of New York, 5 September 1986 and *Liberian Eastern Timber Corporation* v *Republic of Liberia*, U.S. District Court for the Southern District of New York, 12 December 1986, 650 F Supp 73 (SDNY 1986)

List of References

LG&E v *Argentina* (DA)	*LG&E Energy Corp., LG&E Capital Corp. and LG&E International Inc.* v *Argentine Republic* (ICSID Case No. ARB/02/1), DA, pending
LG&E v *Argentina* (DSR)	*LG&E* v *Argentina* (ICSID Case No. ARB/02/1), DSR, 8 July 2008
Libananco Holdings v *Turkey* (DPI)	*Libananco Holdings Co. Limited* v *Turkey* (ICSID Case No. ARB/06/8), DPI, 23 June 2008
Liberty Reinsurance Canada v *QBE Insurance and Reinsurance*	Ontario Superior Court of Justice, Canada, 20 September 2002, *Liberty Reinsurance Canada* v *QBE Insurance and Reinsurance (Europe) Ltd*, (2002), 42 C.C.L.I. (3d) 249 (Ont. S.C.J.)
Locabail (UK) Ltd v *Bayfield Properties Ltd*	*Locabail (UK) Ltd* v *Bayfield Properties Ltd* [2000] QB 451 (CA)
Loewen Group v *USA*	*The Loewen Group, Inc. and Raymond L. Loewen* v *United States of America* (ICSID Case No. ARB(AF)/98/3), DSR, 13 September 2004
Lopez-Alberti	Cour de cassation, 9 October 2001, *Kis* v *Lopez-Alberdi*, Rev Arb 347 (2002), with note Clay
Lucchetti v *Peru* (DA)	*Industria Nacional de Alimentos, S.A. and Indalsa Perú, S.A. (formerly Empresas Lucchetti, S.A. and Lucchetti Perú, S.A.)* v *Republic of Peru,* (ICSID Case No. ARB/03/4), DA, 5 September 2007
Lucchetti v *Peru* (DSR)	*Industria Nacional de Alimentos, S.A. and Indalsa Perú, S.A. (formerly Empresas Lucchetti, S.A. and Lucchetti Perú, S.A.)* v *Republic of Peru,* (ICSID Case No. ARB/03/4), DSR, 30 November 2007
Maffezini v *Spain*	*Emilio Agustín Maffezini* v *Kingdom of Spain* (ICSID Case No. ARB/97/7), Procedural Order No. 2, 28 October 1999
Maffezini v *Spain* (DSR)	*Emilio Agustín Maffezini* v *Kingdom of Spain* (ICSID Case No. ARB/97/7), DSR, 31 January 2001
Maffezini v *Spain* (DJ)	*Emilio Agustín Maffezini* v *Kingdom of Spain* (ICSID Case No. ARB/97/7, DJ, 25 January 2000

List of References

Malaysian Salvors v *Malaysia* (DA)	*Malaysian Historical Salvors, SDN, BHD* v *Malaysia* (ICSID Case No. ARB/05/10), DA, pending
Malek	*Reza Said Malek* v *The Islamic Republic of Iran*, Award No. ITL 68-193-3 (23 Jun 1988)
Margauld Ltd v *Exide Technologies*	*Margulead Ltd* v *Exide Technologies* [2004] EWHC 1019 (Comm)
Marklands v *Virgin Retail*	*Marklands Ltd* v *Virgin Retail Ltd* [2003] (QBD) EWHC 3428 (Ch)
MCI v *Ecuador* (DA)	*M.C.I. Power Group, L.C. and New Turbine, Inc.* v *Republic of Ecuador* (ICSID Case No. ARB/03/6), DA, pending
Meadows Indemnity	*Meadows Indemnity Co. Ltd* v *Baccala & Shoop Insurance Services, Inc., et al.*, 760 F. Supp. 1036 (E.D.N.Y. 1991)
Melton Medes Ltd v *Securities and Investment Board*	*Melton Medes Ltd* v *Securities and Investment Board* [1995] 3 All ER 880 (ChD)
Methanex (Award)	*Methanex Corp.* v *The United States of America*, Award (NAFTA Chapter Eleven, 3 Aug 2005), 26-29 (Part II, Chapter I)
Methanex (Decision)	*Methanex Corporation* v *United States of America*, Decision on Petitions from Third Persons to Intervene as *Amici Curiae* (NAFTA Chapter Eleven, 15 Jan 2001)
Methanex (Letter)	Letter from the Tribunal to the Parties dated 25 September 2002, paras. 1-3, *Methanex Corp.* v *The United States of America*
Methanex (Partial)	*Methanex Corporation* v *The United States of America*, Partial Award on Jurisdiction (NAFTA Chapter Eleven, 7 Aug 2002)
Methanex v *United States*	*Methanex* v *United States*, Decision on *Amici Curiae*, UNCITRAL (NAFTA), Order on Amicus and Article 1128 Submissions, 19 March 2004

List of References

Meyer	*George J Meyer Manufacturing Division of Figgie International, Inc.* v *Zamzam Bottling Company*, Case No. 299, Chamber One, Order of 22 Mar 1984
MHS v *Malaysia*	*Malaysian Historical Salvors, SDN, BHD* v *Malaysia* (ICSID Case No. ARB/05/10) Decision on Jurisdiction, 17 May 2007
Mihaly v *Sri Lanka*	*Mihaly International Corporation* v *Democratic Socialist Republic of Sri Lanka* (ICSID Case No. ARB/00/2), Award, 15 March 2002
Millicom	*In the Matter of the Arbitration between Millicom International* v *Motorola Inc and Proempres Panama SA*, 2002 WL 472042, XXVII YBCA 948 (2002) (SDNY 28 March 2002)
MINE v *Guinea* (DA)	*Maritime International Nominees Establishment* v *Republic of Guinea* (ICSID Case No. ARB/84/4), DA, 22 December 1989
MINE v *Guinea* (FA)	*Maritime International Nominees Establishment* v *Republic of Guinea* (ICSID Case No. ARB/84/4), FA, 6 January 1988
MINE v *Guinea* (Geneva)	Tribunal de première instance, Geneva, 13 March 1986, *MINE* v *Guinea*
MINE v *Guinea* (Stay Decision)	*Maritime International Nominees Establishment* v *Republic of Guinea* (ICSID Case No. ARB/84/4), DS, 12 August 1988
Minermet SpA Milan v *Luckyfield Shipping Corp.*	*Minermet SpA Milan* v *Luckyfield Shipping Corp SA* [2004] EWHC 729 (Comm)
Minister of Public Works of the Kuwait State Government v *Sir Frederick Snow & Partners*	*Minister of Public Works of the Kuwait State Government* v *Sir Frederick Snow & Partners (a firm)* [1984] AC 426
Ministry of Defense and Support	*The Ministry of Defense and Support for the Armed Forces of The Islamic Republic of Iran* v *Cubic Defense Systems Inc. (US)*, 29 F 2d 1168, XXIVa YBCA 875 (1999) (SD Cal 1998)

List of References

Minmetals Germany GmbH v *Ferco Steel Ltd*	*Minmetals German GmbH* v *Ferco Steel Limited* [1999] CLC 647 (QBD)
Mitchell v *Congo*	*Patrick Mitchell* v *Democratic Republic of the Congo* (ICSID Case No. ARB/99/7), DA, 1 November 2006
Mitchell v *Congo* (Stay Decision)	*Patrick Mitchell* v *Democratic Republic of the Congo* (ICSID Case No. ARB/99/7), DS, 30 November 2004
Mobil Cerro Negro Ltd v *Petroleos De Venezuela SA*	*Mobil Cerro Negro Ltd* v *Petroleos de Venezuela SA* [2008] EWHC 532 (Comm)
Mobil v *NZ*	*Mobil Oil Corporation and Others* v *New Zealand* (ICSID Case No. ARB/87/2), FA, 4 May 1989
Mobil v *NZ* (NZ)	High Court, Wellington, 1 July 1987, *Attorney-General* v *Mobil Oil NZ Ltd* [1989] 2 NZLR 649
Monde Re v *Naftogaz*	*Monegasque de Reassurances SAM (Monde Re)* v *NAK Naftogaz of Ukraine and State of Ukraine (2nd Cir 15 November 2002)*
MTD v *Chile* (DA)	*MTD Equity Sdn. Bhd. and MTD Chile S.A.* v *Republic of Chile* (ICSID Case No. ARB/01/7), DA, 21 March 2007
MTD v *Chile* (Stay Decision)	*MTD Equity Sdn. Bhd. and MTD Chile S.A.* v *Republic of Chile* (ICSID Case No. ARB/01/7), DS, 1 June 2005
Musawi v *RE International (UK) Ltd*	*Musawi* v *RE International (UK) Ltd and Ors* [2007] EWHC 2981 (Ch)
Mylcrist Builders Ltd v *Buck*	*Mylcrist Buliders Ltd* v *Mrs G Buck* [2008] EWHC 2172 (TCC)
Nagusina Naviera v *Allied Maritime Inc.*	*Nagusina Naviera* v *Allied Maritime Inc.* [2002] EWCA Civ 1147
Nanhai West Shipping v *Hong Kong United Dockyards*	High Court, Hong Kong, 11 December 1996, *Nanhai West Shipping Co.* v *Hong Kong United Dockyards Ltd*, [1996] 2 HKC 639

List of References

National Ability SA v *Tinna Oils & Chemicals Ltd*	*National Ability SA* v *Tinna Oils & Chemicals Ltd* [2009] EWCA Civ 1330
National Electricity	Bulgarian Supreme Court's decision in *National Electricity Company AD (Bulgaria)* v *ECONBERG Ltd (Croatia)*, XXV YBCA 678 (2000)
National Grid v *The Republic of Argentina*	*National Grid* v *The Republic of Argentina*, (LCIA Case No. UN 7949) Decision on the Challenge to Mr Judd L. Kessler, 2008
National Navigation Co. v *Endessa Generacion SA*	*National Navigation Co.* v *Endessa Generacion SA* [2009] EWVA Civ 1397
National Oil v *Libyan Sun Oil*	*National Oil Corp.* v *Libyan Sun Oil Co.*, 733 F. Supp. 800, 813 (D Del 1990)
National Westminster Bank plc v *Rabobank Nederland*	*National Westminster Bank plc* v *Rabobank Nederland* [2007] EWHC 3163 (Comm)
Nazari	*Mohsen Asgari Nazari* v *The Government of the Islamic Republic of Iran*, Award No. 559-221-1 (24 Aug 1994)
Newfield Construction v *Tomlinson*	*Newfield Construction Ltd* v *Tomlinson & Anor* [2004] EWHC 3051 (QBD)
Nisshin Shipping v *Cleaves*	*Nisshin Shipping & Co. Ltd* v *Cleaves & Co. Ltd* [2005] EWHC 2602 (Comm)
Noble China v *Lei Kat Cheong*	Ontario Court of Justice, Canada, 13 November 1998, *Noble China Inc.* v *Lei Kat Cheong*, (1998), 42 O.R. (3d) 69
Noble Energy and Machalapower v *Ecuador* (DJ)	*Noble Energy, Inc. and Machalapower Cia. Ltd* v *Ecuador and Consejo Nacional de Electricidad* (ICSID Case No. ARB/05/12), DJ, 5 March 2008
Noble Ventures v *Romania* (DSR)	*Noble Ventures, Inc.* v *Romania* (ICSID Case No. ARB/01/11), DSR, 19 May 2006
Noble Ventures v *Romania* (FA)	*Noble Ventures, Inc.* v *Romania* (ICSID Case No. ARB/01/11), FA, 12 October 2005

List of References

Norbrook Laboratories v *A Tank & Anor*	*Norbrook Laboratories Ltd* v *A Tank and Anor* [2006] EWHC 1055 (QBD)
Norsk Hydro ASA v *State Property Fund of Ukraine*	*Norsk Hydro ASA* v *State Property Fund of Ukraine* [2002] EWHC 2120 (Admin)
Norsk Hydro v *Ukraine*	*Norsk Hydro ASA* v *State Property Fund of Ukraine* [2002] EWHC 2120 (Comm.)
North Range Shipping Ltd v *Seatrans Shipping Corporation*	*North Range Shipping Ltd* v *Seatrans Shipping Corporation (the 'Western Triumph')* [2002] EWCA Civ 405
Norwegian Court of Appeal	Hålogaland Court of Appeal, 16 August 1999
Nottebohm	*Nottebohm* case (*Liechtenstein* v *Guatemala*) 1955 ICJ Rep 4
Occidental Exploration v *Ecuador*	*Occidental Exploration and Production Company* v *The Republic of Ecuador*, LCIA Case No. UN3467, Final Award of 1 July 2004
Occidental v *Ecuador*	*Occidental Exploration & Production Co.* v *Ecuador* [2005] EWCA Civ 116
Occidental v *Ecuador* (DJ)	*Occidental Petroleum Corporation and Occidental Exploration and Production Company* v *Republic of Ecuador* (ICSID Case No. ARB/06/11), DJ, 9 September 2008
Occidental v *Ecuador* (DPM)	*Occidental Petroleum Corporation and Occidental Exploration and Production Company* v *Republic of Ecuador* (ICSID Case No. ARB/06/11), DPM, 17 August 2007
Oceanografia SA de CV v *DSND Subsea AS*	*Oceanografia SA de CV* v *DSND Subsea AS* [2006] EWHC 1360 (Comm)
OG Basel 3 June 1971	Obergericht Basel, 3 June 1971, Dutch seller v Swiss buyer, IV YBCA 309 (1978)
OG Solothurn, 27 September 2001	Obergericht Solothurn, Zivilkammer, 27 September 2001, ZKREK.2001.79, Solothurnische Gerichtspraxis 23 No. 9 (2001)

List of References

OG Zürich, 1 December 2005	Obergericht des Kantons Zürich, III. Zivilkammer, 1 December 2005, 24 ASA Bulletin 797 (2006)
OG Zürich, 19 November 2004	Obergericht des Kantons Zürich, III. Zivilkammer, 19 November 2004, 23 ASA Bulletin 540 (2005)
OG Zürich, 22 May 1990	Obergericht Zürich, 22 May 1990, 90 ZR 9 No. 4 (1991)
OGH 17 November 1965	Oberster Gerichtshof, 17 November 1965, German party v Austrian party, 3 Ob 128/65; 9 ZfRV 123 (1968), I YBCA 182 (1976)
OLG Celle 4 September 2003	Oberlandesgericht Celle, Germany, 4 September 2003, XXX Yearbook 528 (2005)
OLG Frankfurt am Main 6 September 2001	Oberlandesgericht Frankfurt am Main, Germany, 6 September 2001, 3 Sch 2/00, unreported
OLG Hamburg 8 November 2001	Oberlandesgericht Hamburg, Germany, 8 November 2001, 6 Sch 04/0
OLG Hamburg 21 February 2002	Oberlandesgericht Haumburg, Germany, 21 February 2002, 10 Sch 08/01
OLG Naumburg 19 December 2001	Oberlandesgericht Naumburg, Germany, 19 December 2001, 10 SchH 03/01, SchiedsVZ 2003, 134
OLG Nuremberg 30 November 2005	Oberlandesgericht, Nuremberg, Germany, 30 November 2005, IPRax 468 (2006)
OLG Stuttgart 20 December 2001	Oberlandesgericht Stuttgart, Germany, 20 December 2001, 1 Sch 13/01
OLG Stuttgart 4 June 2002	Oberlandesgericht Stuttgart, Germany, 4 June 2002, 1 Sch 22/01, unreported
OLG Dresden 20 October 1998	Oberlandesgericht Dresden, 20 October 1998, 11 Sch 4/98, unreported
OLG Hamburg 30 July 1998	Oberlandesgericht Hamburg, *Charterer* v *Shipowner*, 30 July 1998, XXV YBCA 714 (2000)
OLG Hamburg 3 April 1975	Oberlandesgericht Hamburg, 3 April 1975, *US firm* v *German firm*, II YBCA 241 (1977)
OLG Hamburg 30 June 1998	Oberlandesgericht Hamburg, 30 June 1998, 6 Sch 3/98, unreported

List of References

Olguin v Paraguay	*Eudoro Olguín v Republic of Paraguay* (ICSID Case No. ARB/98/5) DJ, 8 August 2000.
Ommium de Traitement et de Valorisation SA v Hilmartion Ltd	*Omnium de Traitement et de Valorisation SA v Hilmarton Ltd* [1999] 2 Lloyd's Rep 222 (QBD)
Owerri Commercial	Gerechtshof The Hague, 4 August 1993, *Owerri Commercial Inc. v Dielle Srl*, XIX YBCA 703 (1994)
Pacific Reinsurance v Ohio Reinsurance	*Pacific Reinsurance Management Corp. v Ohio Reinsurance Management Corp.*, 935 F 2d 1019, 1025 (9th Cir 1991)
Pacol Ltd v Joint Stock Co. Rossakhar	Pacol Ltd v Joint Stock Co. Rossakhar [1999] 2 All ER 778 (QBD)
Paklito v Klockner	*Paklito Investment Ltd v Klockner East Asia Ltd* [1993] 2 Hong Kong Law Reports 39; 15 January 1993, Supreme Court of Hong Kong, High Court, No. MP 2219; XIX YBCA 664-674 (1994)
Pan American v Argentina	*Pan American Energy LLC and BP Argentina Exploration Company v Argentine Republic* (ICSID Case No. ARB/03/13), Decision on Preliminary Objections, 27 July 2006
Parsons	*Parsons and Whittemore Overseas Co. Inc. v Société générale de l'industrie du papier (RAKTA)*, 508 F 2d 969, 974, I YBCA 205 (1976) (2d Cir 1974)
Parviz Karim-Panahi	*Parviz Karim-Panahi v The Government of the United States of America*, Decision No. DEC 108-182-2 (27 Oct 1992)
Patel v Patel	*Patel v Patel* [2000] QB 551
Paushok v Mongolia	*Paushok v Mongolia*, Order on interim measures, 2 September 2008
People's Insurance Company of China v Vysanthi Shipping Co. Ltd	*People's Insurance Company of China v Vysanthi Shipping Co. Ltd* [2003] EWHC 1655 (Comm)

List of References

Permasteelisa Japan UK v *Bouygesstroi*	*Permasteelisa Japan UK* v *Bouygesstroi* [2007] All ER (D) 97 (TCC)
Peterson Farms v *C&M Farming Ltd*	*Peterson Farms Inc.* v *C&M Farming Ltd* [2004] EWHC 121 (Comm.)
Petrolane	*Petrolane, Inc.* v *Islamic Republic of Iran*, Decision No. DEC 101-131-2 (25 Nov 1991)
Petroships Pte Ltd v *Petec Trading*	*Petroships Pte Ltd of Singapore* v *Petec Trading & Investment Corp of Vietnam ('The Pertro Trader')* [2001] 2 Lloyd's Rep 348
Phesco v *Canac*	Quebec Superior Court, 14 November 2000, Canada, *Phesco Inc.* v *Canac Inc.*
Philip Alexander Securities and Futures Ltd v *Bamberger*	*Philip Alexander Securities and Futures Limited* v *Bamberger* [1997] ILPr 104 (CA)
Philippe Gruslin v *Malaysia* (DA)	*Philippe Gruslin* v *Malaysia* (ICSID Case No. ARB/99/3), DA, discontinued
Picker	*Picker International Corporation* v *Islamic Republic of Iran*, Decision No. DEC 48-10173-3 (7 Oct 1986)
Pirtek (UK) Ltd v *Deanswood Ltd*	*Pirtek (UK) Ltd* v *Deanswood Ltd* [2005] EWHC 2301 (Comm)
Plama Consortium Limited v *Bulgaria*	*Plama Consortium Limited* v *Republic of Bulgaria* (ICSID Case No. ARB/03/24), DPM, 6 September 2005
Plama Consortium Limited v *Bulgaria* (DJ)	*Plama Consortium Limited* v *Republic of Bulgaria* (ICSID Case No. ARB/03/24), DJ, 8 February 2005
Polytek	*Polytek Engineering Co. Ltd* v *Hebei Import and Export Corp., XXII YBCA 666 (1998) (High Court Hong Kong, 16 January 1998)*
Porter v *Magill*	*Porter* v *Magill* [2002] 2 AC 357
Positive Software Solutions v *New Century Mortgage*	*Positive Software Solutions Inc.* v *New Century Mortgage Corp.*, No. 04-11432, 476 F 3d 278 (5th Cir 2007)

List of References

Premium Nafta Products v *Fili Shipping*	*Premium Nafta Products* v *Fili Shipping Co.* [2007] UKHL 40
Président ATF, 14 December 1993	Ordonnance du Président de la 1ère Cour civile du Tribunal Fédéral suisse, 14 December 1993, *Emirats Arabes Unis et cons.* v *Westland Helicopters Limited*, 12 ASA Bulletin 52 (1994)
Primetrade AG v *Ytthan Ltd*	*Primetrade AG* v *Ytthan Ltd* [2005] EWHC 2399 (Comm)
Profilati Italia Srt v *Painewebber Inc.*	*Profilati Italia Srl* v *Painewebber Inc.* [2001] 1 All ER 1065 (QBD)
Protech Projects Construction v *Al-Kharafi & Sons*	*Protech Projects Construction (Pty) Ltd* v *Al-Kharafi & Sons* [2005] EWHC 2165 (Comm)
Qualcomm v *Nokia*	*Qualcomm Inc.* v *Nokia Corp.*, 466 F 3d 1366, 1373 (Fed Cir 2006)
Queensland, 29 October 1993	Supreme Court of Queensland, 29 October 1993, XX YBCA 628 (1995)
R v *Bow Street Metropolitan Stipendiary Magistrate, ex parte Pinochet (No. 2)*	*R* v *Bow Street Metropolitan Stipendiary Magistrate, ex parte Pinochet (No. 2)* [1999] 2 WLR 272 (HL)
R v *V*	*R* v *V* [2008] EWHC 1531 (Comm)
R. SA v *A. Ltd*	*R. SA* v *A. Ltd, XXVI YBCA 863 (2001)*
Raffineries de petrol d'Homs et de Banias v *Chambre de commerce international* (France)	Cour d'appel Paris, 15 May 1985, *Raffineries de pétrole d'Homs et de Banias* v *Chambre de commerce international*, Rev Arb (1985), p. 141
RC Pillar & Sons v *Edwards*	*RC Pillar & Sons* v *Edwards* [2001] CILL 1799
REDEC (France)	Tribunal de grande instance Paris, 13 July 1988, *REDEC et Pharaon* v *Uzinexport Import and Chambre de Commerce Internationale,* Rev Arb (1989), p. 97

List of References

Reichhold Norway ASA v *Goldman Sachs International*	*Reichhold Norway ASA* v *Goldman Sachs International* [1999] 2 Lloyd's Rep 567
Reliance Industries Ltd v *Enron Oil & Gas India Ltd*	*Reliance Industries Ltd* v *Enron Oil & Gas India Ltd* [2002] 1 Lloyd's Rep 645 (QB)
Repsol v *Petroecuador* (Stay Decision)	*Repsol YPF Ecuador S.A.* v *Empresa Estatal Petróleos del Ecuador (Petroecuador)* (ICSID Case No. ARB/01/10), DS, 22 December 2005
Repsol v *Petroecaudor*	*Repsol YPF Ecuador S.A.* v *Empresa Estatal Petróleos del Ecuador (Petroecuador)* (ICSID Case No. ARB/01/10), DA, 8 January 2007
Reservations to the Convention on Genocide *ICJ Advisory Opinion*	Reservations to the Convention on Genocide *ICJ Advisory Opinion*, 1951
Resort Condominiums	Supreme Court Queensland, 29 October 1993, *Resort Condominiums International Inc.* v *Ray Bolwell and Resort Condominiums Pty Ltd*, (1994) 9(4) Mealey's IAR A1, XX YBCA 628 (1995)
Reynolds v *Jamaica*	*Reynolds Jamaica Mines Limited and Reynolds Metals Company* v *Jamaica* (ICSID Case No. ARB/74/4)
Reza Said Malek	*Reza Said Malek* v *The Islamic Republic of Iran*, Award No. 534-193-3 (11 Aug 1992)
RFC v *Morocco*	*Consortium RFCC* v *Kingdom of Morocco* (ICSID Case No. ARB/00/6), DA, 18 January 2006
Richard D Harza	*Richard D Harza* v *The Islamic Republic of Iran*, Award No. 232-97-2 (2 May 1986)
RM Investment & Trading Co.	*RM Investment & Trading Co. Pvt. Limited (India)* v *Boeing Company and another (US)*, 10 February 1994, Supreme Court of India, XXII YBCA 710-714 (1997)
Road Management Services (A13) plc v *London Power Networks plc*	*Road Management Services (A13) plc* v *London Power Networks plc* [2003] BLR 303 (TCC)

List of References

Rompetrol Group NV v Romania	ICSID Case No. ARB/06/03, Decision on the participation of a counsel, 14 January 2010
Rompetrol v Romania	*The Rompetrol Group N.V. v Romania* (ICSID Case No. ARB/06/3), Decision on Respondent's Preliminary Objections on Jurisdiction and Admissibility, 18 April 2008
RosInvest v Russian Federation	*RosInvest Co. UK Ltd v Russian Federation* (Award on Jurisdiction, October 2007)
Rosseel	*Rosseel NV v Oriental Commercial Shipping (UK) Ltd*, XVI YBCA 615 (English High Court 1990) (1991)
Rosseel NV v Oriental Commercial & Shipping Co. (UK) Ltd	*Rosseel NV v Oriental Commercial & Shipping Co. (UK) Ltd and Others* [1991] 2 Lloyd's Rep 625
Roylance v General Medical Council	*Roylance v General Medical Council* [1999] 3 WLR 541 (PC)
Rustal Trading Ltd v Gill & Duffus SA	*Rustal Trading Ltd v Gill & Duffus SA* [2000] 1 Lloyd's Rep 14 (QB)
Salini v Jordan	*Salini Costruttori SpA and Italstrade SpA v Hashemite Kingdom of Jordan* (ICSID Case No. ARB/02/13), DJ, 29 November 2004
Salini v Morocco (DJ)	*Salini Construtorri SpA and Italstrade SpA v Kingdom of Morocco* (ICSID Case No. ARB/00/4), DJ, 23 July 2001
Sam Ming Forestry Economic Co.	*Hong Kong, Sam Ming Forestry Economic Co. v Lam Pun Hing*, (2000) 15(1) Mealey's IAR 12 (HCHK)
Sanghi Polyesters v The International Investor	*Sanghi Polyesters Ltd (India) v The International Investor* [2000] 1 Lloyd's Rep 480
Sapphire	*Sapphire International Petroleums v National Iranium Oil Company* (Calvin sole arb, 15 Mar 1963)
SC Rolinay Sea Star SRL v Petromin SA	*SC Rolinay Sea Star SRL v Compagnia de Navigatie Maritimie Petromin SA* [1999] 2 Lloyd's Rep 481 (QBD)

List of References

SD Myers	*SD Myers, Inc.* v *Government of Canada*, Final Award on Costs (NAFTA Chapter Eleven, 30 Dec 2002)
Sea Trade Marine Corp. v *Hellenic Mutual War Risks Association (Bermuda) Ltd ('The Athena')*	*Sea Trade Maritime Corporation* v *Hellenic Mutual War Risks Association (Bermuda) Ltd (The 'Athena')* [2006] EWHC 2530 (Comm)
SEB Trygg Holding v *Manches*	*SEB Trygg Holding* v *Manches & Ors* [2005] EWHC 35 (Comm)
SEDITEX v *Madagascar I*	*SEDITEX Engineering Beratungsgesellschaft für die Textilindustrie mbH* v *Madagascar*, (ICSID Case No. CONC/82/1)
SEDITEX v *Madagascar II*	*SEDITEX Engineering Beratungsgesellschaft für die Textilindustrie m.b.H.* v *Madagascar* (ICSID Case No. CONC/94/1)
Sempra v *Argentina* (DA)	*Sempra Energy International* v *Argentine Republic* (ICSID Case No. ARB/02/16), Annulment Proceedings, pending
Sempra v *Argentina* (FA)	*Sempra Energy International* v *Argentine Republic* (ICSID Case No. ARB/02/16), FA, 28 September 2007
Serbia v *Imagesat*	*Serbia* v *Imagesat International NV* [2009] EWHC 2853 (Comm)
SESAM v *CAR*	*Shareholders of SESAM* v *Central African Republic* (ICSID Case No. CONC/07/1)
Sesotris SAE	*Sesotris SAE* v *Transportes Navales, 727 F Supp 737*, XVI YBCA 640 (1991) (District Court, D Mass, 1989)
Seven Seas	*Seven Seas Shipping (UK) Ltd* v *Tondo Limitada*, XXV YBCA 987 (2000) 989 (US District Court)
SGS v *Pakistan*	*SGS Société Générale de Surveillance S.A.* v *Islamic Republic of Pakistan* (ICSID Case No. ARB/01/13), Procedural Order No. 2, 16 October 2002

List of References

SGS v Pakistan (DJ)	*SGS Société Générale de Surveillance S.A.* v *Islamic Republic of Pakistan* (ICSID Case No. ARB/01/13), DJ, 6 August 2003
SGS v Philippines	*SGS Société Générale de Surveillance S.A.* v *Republic of the Philippines* (ICSID Case No. ARB/02/6), DJ, 29 January 2004
Shahin Shaine Ebrahimi	*Shahin Shaine Ebrahimi, et al.* v *The Government of the Islamic Republic of Iran*, Case Nos. 44, 46, 47, Chamber Three, Order of 14 Dec 1992
Shalson v DF Keane Ltd	*Shalson* v *DF Keane Ltd* [2003] EWHC 599 (Ch)
Shell Egypt v Dana Gas	*Shell Egypt West Manzala GmbH & Anor* v *Dana Gas Egypt Ltd* [2009] EWHC 2097 (Comm)
Sherk Enterprises	Corte di cassazione, 12 May 1977, *Sherk Enterprises AG* v *Société des Grandes Marques*, IV YBCA 286 (1979)
Siag v Egypt	*Waguih Elie George Siag and Clorinda Vecci* v *The Arab Republic of Egypt,* (ICSID Case No. ARB/05/15), DJ, 11 April 2007
Siemens v Argentina	*Siemens AG* v *Argentine Republic* (ICSID Case No. ARB/02/8), DA, pending
Siemens v Argentina (DJ)	*Siemens AG* v *Argentine Republic* (ICSID Case No. ARB/02/8), DJ, 3 August 2004
Siemens v Argentina (Revision)	*Siemens AG* v *Argentine Republic* (ICSID Case No. ARB/02/8), Revision Proceedings, pending
Simer SpA	Corte di Appello Trento, 14 January 1981, *General Organisation of Commerce and Industrialisation of Cereals of the Arab Republic of Syria* v *SpA Simer*, VIII YBCA 352 (1983)
Sinclair v Woods of Winchester Ltd	*Sinclair* v *Woods of Winchester Ltd* [2005] EWHC 1631 (TCC)
Sinochem International Oil v Fortune Oil	*Sinochem International Oil (London) Co. Ltd* v *Fortune Oil Co. Ltd* [2000] 1 Lloyd's Rep 682 (QBD)

List of References

Smith v *Kvaerner Cementation Foundations Ltd*	*Smith* v *Kvaerner Cementation Foundations Ltd* [2006] EWCA Civ 242
SOABI v *Senegal*	*Société Ouest Africaine des Bétons Industriels* v *Senegal* (ICSID Case No. ARB/82/1), FA, 25 February 1988
SOABI v *Senegal* (France)	Cour de cassation, 11 June 1991, *Société Ouest Africaine des Bétons Industriels* v *Senegal*, 6 ICSID Rev – FILJ 598 (1991)
SOABI v *Senegal* (President's Declaration)	*Société Ouest Africaine des Bétons Industriels* v *Senegal* (ICSID Case No. ARB/82/1), President's Declaration, 1 August 1984
Socadec SA v *Pan Africa Impex Co. Ltd*	*Socadec SA* v *Pan Afric Impex Co. Ltd* [2003] EWHC 2086
Société Arabe des Engrais Phosphates et Azotes	Corte di cassazione, 9 March 1996, No. 4342, *Société Arabe des Engrais Phosphates et Azotes – SAEPA (Tunisia) and Société Industrielle d'Acide Phosphorique et d'Engrais – SIAPE (Tunisia)* v *Gemanco srl (Italy)*, XXII YBCA 737 (1997) 742
Societè d'Investissement Kal	*Société d'Investissement Kal (Tunisia)* v *(1), Taieb Haddad (Tunisia) and (2), Hans Barett, Tunisia*, 10 November 1993, Cour de Cassation [Supreme Court], XXIII YBCA 770-773 (1998)
Société Farhat Trading Company v *Société Daewoo* (France)	Cour de cassation, 6 March 1996, *Société Farhat Trading Company* v *Société Daewoo Industrial Company Ltd*, Rev Arb (1997), p. 69
Société Nihon Plast v *Takata-Petri* (France)	Cour d'appel Paris, 4 March 2004, *Société Nihon Plast Co. Ltd* v *Takata-Petri Aktiengesellschaft*, Rev Arb (2004), p. 452
Société Panalpina World Transports Holdings v *Société Transco* (France)	Cour d'appel Paris, 28 November 2002, *Société Panalpina World Transports Holdings AG* v *Société Transco*, Rev Arb (2003), p. 59
Soinco SACI v *Novokuznetsk Aluminium Plant*	*Soinco SACI* v *Novokuznetsk Aluminium Plant* [1998] 2 Lloyd's Rep 337 (CA)

List of References

Sojuznefteexport	*Sojuznefteexport (SNE)* v *Joc Oil Ltd*, (1990) XV YBCA 384 (Court of Appeal of Bermuda, 7 July 1989)
Soleimany v *Soleimany*	*Soleimany* v *Soleimany* [1999] QB 785, [1999] 3 All ER 847, [1998] 3 WLR 811
Sonatrach (Mass)	*Société Nationale Algérienne pour la Recherche, la Production, le Transport, la Transformation et la Commercialisation des Hydrocarbures (Sonatrach) (Algeria)* v *Distrigas Corp. (US)*, 80 Bankruptcy Reporter 606; 1987 US Dist. LEXIS 11805; 18 Collier Bankr. Cas. 2d (MB) 865, 17 March 1987, XX YBCA 795-804 (1995) (US Dist. Ct Mass.)
Sonatrach (SDNY)	*Société Nationale pour la Recherche, la Production, le Transport, la Transformation et la Commercialisation des Hydrocarbures (Sonatrach) (Algeria)* v *Shaheen Natural Resources Company Inc. (US)*, 15 November 1983, X YBCA 540-548 (1985) (US Dist. Ct SDNY)
Soufraki v *UAE* (DA)	*Hussein Nuaman Soufraki* v *United Arab Emirates* (ICSID Case No. ARB/02/7), DA, 5 June 2007
Soufraki v *UAE* (DJ)	*Hussein Nuaman Soufraki* v *United Arab Emirates* (ICSID Case No. ARB/02/7), DJ, 7 July 2004
Soufraki v *UAE* (DSR)	*Hussein Nuaman Soufraki* v *United Arab Emirates* (ICSID Case No. ARB/02/7), DSR, 13 August 2007
Sphere Drake Insurance v *American Reliable Insurance*	*Sphere Drake Insurance* v *American Reliable Insurance Co.* [2004] EWHC 796 (Comm)
SPP v *Egypt* (DA)	*Southern Pacific Properties (Middle East) Limited* v *Arab Republic of Egypt* (ICSID Case No. ARB/84/3), FA, 20 May 1992
SPP v *Egypt* (DJ)	*Southern Pacific Properties (Middle East) Limited* v *Arab Republic of Egypt* (ICSID Case No. ARB/84/3), DJ, 27 November 1985, 3 ICSID Reports

List of References

SPP v *Egypt* (Stay Decision)	*Southern Pacific Properties (Middle East) Limited* v *Arab Republic of Egypt* (ICSID Case No. ARB/84/3), DS, not published
Starrett Housing	*Starett Housing Corp.* v *Iran*, Case No. 24 (8 Dec 1982)
Starrett Housing (Award)	*Starrett Housing Corporation* v *The Government of the Islamic Republic of Iran*, Award No. 314-24-1 (14 Aug 1987)
Stretford v *Football Association*	*Stretford* v *Football Association* [2007] EWCA Civ 238
Sumitomo Heavy Industries v *Oil and Natural Gas Commission*	*Sumitomo Heavy Industries* v *Oil and Natural Gas Commission* [1994] 1 Lloyd's Rep. 24 (QBD (Com.)
Sumukan v *Commonwealth Secretariat*	*Sumukan* v *Commonwealth Secretariat* [2007] EWCA Civ 1148
Sun Company, Inc.	*Sun Company, Inc.* v *National Iranian Oil Company*, Joint Request for Arbitral Award on Agreed Terms (28 Sep 1992)
Sun Life Assurance Co. of Canada v *Lincoln National Life Insurance Co.*	*Sun Life Assurance Company of Canada* v *The Lincoln National Life Insurance Co.* [2004] EWCA Civ 1660
Supreme Court of New South Wales, *Cockatoo Dockyard*	*Commonwealth of Australia* v *Cockatoo Dockyard Pty Ltd* [1995] 36 NSWLR 662.
Svenska Petroleum Exploration AB v *Lithuania*	*Svenska Petroleum Exploration AB* v *Government of the Republic of Lithuania and Anor* [2005] EWHC 9 (Comm)
Svenska v *Lithuania*	*Svenska Petroleum Exploration AB* v *Government of the Republic of Lithuania and another (No. 2)*, [2006] EWCA Civ 1529
Sylvania	*Sylvania Technical Systems, Inc.* v *The Islamic Republic of Iran*, Case No. 64, Chamber One, Order of 10 May 1983

List of References

Syska v *Vivendi*	*Syska* v *Vivendi Universal SA* [2009] EWCA Civ 677
Tajik Aluminium Plant v *Hydro Aluminium SA*	*Tajik Aluminium Plant* v *Hydro Aluminium SA* [2006] EWHC 1135 (Comm)
Tame Shipping Ltd v *Easy Navigation Ltd*	*Tame Shipping Ltd* v *Easy Navigation Ltd (the 'Easy Rider')* [2004] EWHC 1862
Tang Boon Jek Jeffrey v *Tan Poh Leng Stanley*	Court of Appeal, Singapore, 22 June 2001, *Tang Boon Jek Jeffrey* v *Tan Poh Leng Stanley*, [2001] 3 SLR 237
Tanzania Electric v *Independent Power Tanzania*	*Tanzania Electric Supply Company Limited* v *Independent Power Tanzania Limited* (ICSID Case No. ARB/98/8), DI, pending
Taylor Woodrow Holdings Ltd v *Barnes & Elliot*	*Taylor Woodrow Holdings Ltd and another* v *Barnes & Elliot* [2006] EWHC 1693 (TCC)
Telekom Malaysia Berhad	District Court of the Hague, 18 October 2004 (Challenge No. 13/2004; Petition No. HA/RK/2004.667)
Termorio v *Electranta*	*Termorio Sa Esp Group Llc* v *Electranta Sp*, 487 F 3d 928 (2007)
Tesoro v *Trinidad & Tobago*	*Tesoro Petroleum Corporation* v *Trinidad and Tobago* (ICSID Case No. CONC/83/1)
Texaco Iran	*Texaco Iran, Ltd* v *National Iranian Oil Company and the Islamic Republic of Iran*, Case No. 72, Chamber Three, Order of 9 Sep 1983
TG v *Niegria*	*TG World Petroleum Limited* v *Republic of Niger* (ICSID Case No. CONC/03/1)
TGI Lyon, *Textipar*	TGI Lyon, 25 January 1994, *Textipar* and *Cofid* v *P Roche*, Rev Arb 525 (1994), with note Rondeau-Rivier
TGI Paris, *Chérifienne des Pétroles*	TGI Paris, 18 January 1991, *Chérifienne des Pétroles* v *Mannesmann Industria Iberica*, Rev Arb 503 (1996), with note Fouchard

List of References

TGI Paris, *Philipp Brothers*	TGI Paris, 28 October 1988, 14 and 29 June 1989, 15 July 1989, *Philipp Brothers* v *Drexel Burnham Lambert Limited et al.*, Rev Arb 497 (1990), with note Pluyette and Boisséson
TGI Paris, *République de Guinée*	TGI Paris, 29 November 1989, *Omnium de Travaux* v *République de Guinée*, Rev Arb 525 (1990)
The Dredging and Construction Co. Ltd v *Delta Civil Engineering Co. Ltd*	*The Dredging and Construction Co. Ltd* v *Delta Civil Engineering Co. Ltd* [2000] CLC 213
Thomas Earl Payne	*Thomas Earl Payne* v *The Islamic Republic of Iran*, Case No. 335, Chamber Two, Order of 14 Feb 1986
Three Rivers District Council v *Bank of England*	*Three Rivers District Council & Ors* v *Governor and Company of the Bank of England* [2004] UKHL 48
Through Transport v *New India Assurance*	*Through Transport Mutual Insurance Association (Eurasia) Ltd* v *New India Assurance Co. Ltd* [2005] EWHC 455 (Comm)
Tilia Sonera Ab v *Hilcourt Docklands Ltd*	*Tilia Sonera Ab* v *Hilcourt Docklands Ltd* [2003] EWHC 3540 (Civ)
Togo Electricité v *Togo*	*Togo Electricité* v *Republic of Togo* (ICSID Case No. CONC/05/1)
Tokios Tokelés v *Ukraine*	*Tokios Tokelés* v *Ukraine* (ICSID Case No. ARB/02/18), Procedural Order No. 1, 1 July 2003
Tokios Tokelés v *Ukraine* (DJ)	*Tokios Tokelés* v *Ukraine* (ICSID Case No. ARB/02/18), DJ, 29 April 2004
Tongyuan (USA) International Trading Corp. v *Uni-Clan Ltd*	*Tongyuan (USA) International Trading Group* v *Uni-Clan Limited*, 19 January 2001 (QBD) unreported
Torch Offshore LLC v *Cable Shipping Inc.*	*Torch Offshore LLC* v *Cable Shipping Inc.* [2004] EWHC 787 (Comm)
Totem Marine v *North American Towing*	*Totem Marine* v *North American Towing*, 607 F 2d 649, 653 (5th Cir 1979)

List of References

Tradax Export SA v *Volkswagenwerk AG*	*Tradax Export SA* v *Volkswagenwerk AG* [1970] 1 Lloyd's Rep 62 (CA)
Tradex v *Albania*	*Tradex Hellas S.A.* v *Republic of Albania* (ICSID Case No. ARB/94/2), FA, 29 April 1999
Tradex v *Albania* (DJ)	*Tradex Hellas S.A.* v *Republic of Albania* (ICSID Case No. ARB/94/2), DJ, 24 December 1996
Transcatalana de Commercio SA v *Incobrasa Industrial e Commercial Brazileira SA*	*Transcatalana de Commercio SA* v *Incobrasa Industrial e Commercial Brazileira SA* [1995] 1 Lloyd's Rep 215
Transgabonais v *Gabon* (DA)	*Compagnie d'Exploitation du Chemin de Fer Transgabonais* v *Gabonese Republic* (ICSID Case No. ARB/04/5), DA, pending
Trans-Global Petroleum v *Jordan*	*Trans-Global Petroleum, Inc.* v *Hashemite Kingdom of Jordan* (ICSID Case No. ARB/07/25), Decision on the Respondent's Objection under Rule 41(5) of the ICSID Arbitration Rules, 12 May 2008
Trib. Com Paris, *Chomat*	Trib. Com Paris, 6 July 2004, *Chomat* v *A.*, Rev Arb 709 (2005), with note Hory
Tribunal cantonal de Fribourg, 24 March 2004	Tribunal cantonal de Fribourg, IIe Cour d'appel, 24 March 2004, Revue Fribourgeoise de Jurisprudence 11 (2004)
Tribunal de première instance Genève, 18 June 2008	Tribunal de première instance of Geneva, 18 June 2008, case no. C/24208/2007-15-SS JTPI/8755/08, *Jean-Marc X.* v *Chris Y. et Brian Z.*, published in 27 ASA Bulletin 161 (2009)
Tribunal de première instance Genève, 2 May 2005	République et Canton de Genève, Tribunal de première instance, 2 May 2005, *Air (PTY) Ltd* v *International Air Transport Association (IATA) et C. SA en liquidation*, case no. C/1043/2005-15SP, 23 ASA Bulletin 728 (2005), with English translation at 739 *et seq.*
Tribunal de première instance Genève, 21 March 2007	Tribunal de première instance of Geneva, 15ème Chambre, 21 March 2007, case no. JTPI/4437/07, *A. Ltd* v *B. AG*, published in 26 ASA Bulletin 411 (2008)

List of References

Tribunal de première instance Genève, 9 May 1990	Président du Tribunal de première instance Genève, ordonnance of 9 May 1990, ICC case no. 6286, seat of arbitration: Geneva, 8 ASA Bulletin 283 (1990)
Tribunale di appello Ticino, 12 March 1993	Tribunale di appello Ticino, Seconda camera civile, 12 March 1993, *I. SA* v *E.*, partially translated into French in 8 SchwZIER 599 (1998) with comments by François Knoepfler at 600-602
Tsavliris Salvage v *The Grain Board of Iraq*	*Tsavliris Salvage (International) Ltd* v *The Grain Board of Iraq* [2008] EWHC 612 (Comm)
Union de Cooperativas Agricolas Epis Centre (France)	Spain, Tribunal Supremo, 17 February 1998, Union de Cooperativas Agricolas Epis Centre (France) v La Palentina SA (Spain), XXVII YBCA 533(2002)
Union Discount Co. Ltd v *Zoller*	*Union Discount Co. Ltd* v *Zoller* [2001] EWCA Civ 1755
Union Trans-Pacific Co. Ltd v *Orient Shipping Rotterdam BV*	*Union Trans-Pacific Co. Ltd* v *Orient Shipping Rotterdam BV* [2002] EWHC 1451
United Tyre Company v *Born*	*United Tyre Company* v *Born* [2004] EWCA Civ 1236
UPS	*United Parcel Service of America, Inc.* v *Government of Canada*, Award on Jurisdiction (NAFTA Chapter Eleven, 22 Nov 2002)
UPS (Decision)	*United Parcel Service of America Inc.* v *Government of Canada*, Decision on Petitions for Intervention and Participation as *Amicus Curiae* (NAFTA Chapter Eleven, 17 Oct 2001)
Vacuum Salt v *Ghana*	*Vacuum Salt Products Ltd* v *Republic of Ghana* (ICSID Case No. ARB/92/1), FA, 16 February 1994
Van der Giessen-De Noord Shipbuilding Division BV v *Imtech Marine & Offshore BV*	*Van der Giessen-De-Noord Shipbuilding Division BV* v *Imtech Marine & Offshore BV* [2008] EWHC 2904

List of References

Varo	*Varo International Corporation* v *The Government of the Islamic Republic of Iran*, Award No. 482-275-1 (21 Jun 1990)
Vee Networks Ltd v Econet Wireless International Ltd	*Vee Networks Ltd* v *Econet Wireless International Ltd* [2004] EWHC 2909 (Comm)
Vertex Data Science Ltd v Powergen Retail Ltd	*Vertex Data Science Ltd* v *Powergen Retail Ltd* [2006] EWHC 1340 (Comm)
Vieira v *Chile* (DA)	*Sociedad Anónima Eduardo Vieira* v *Republic of Chile* (ICSID Case No. ARB/04/7), DA, pending
Vivendi v *Argentina* (DSR)	*Compañía de Aguas del Aconquija S.A. and Vivendi Universal S.A.* v *Argentine Republic* (ICSID Case No. ARB/97/3), DSR, 28 May 2003
Vivendi v *Argentina* (I)	*Compañía de Aguas del Aconquija S.A. and Vivendi Universal S.A.* v *Argentine Republic* (ICSID Case No. ARB/97/3), FA, 21 November 2000
Vivendi v *Argentina* (I) (DA)	*Compañía de Aguas del Aconquija S.A. and Vivendi Universal S.A.* v *Argentine Republic* (ICSID Case No. ARB/97/3), DA, 3 July 2002
Viviendi v *Argentina* (II)	*Compañía de Aguas del Aconquija S.A. and Vivendi Universal S.A.* v *Argentine Republic* (ICSID Case No. ARB/97/3), FA, unpublished
Viviendi v *Argentina* (II) (DA)	*Compañía de Aguas del Aconquija S.A. and Vivendi Universal S.A.* v *Argentine Republic* (ICSID Case No. ARB/97/3), Second Annulment Proceedings, pending
Vrinera Marine Co. Ltd v Eastern Rich Operations Inc.	*Vrinera Marine Co. Ltd* v *Eastern Rich Operations Incorporated (the 'Vakis T')* [2004] (QBD) EWHC 1752 (Comm)
Walker v *Rowe*	*Walker* v *Rowe* [2000] 1 Lloyd's Rep 116
Walkinshaw v *Diniz*	*Walkinshaw & Ors* v *Diniz* [2002] EWCA Civ 180
Warborough Investments Ltd v S Robinson & Sons (Holdings) Ltd	*Warborough Investments Ltd* v *S Robinson & Sons (Holdings) Ltd* [2003] EWCA Civ 751

List of References

Wealands v CLC Contractors Ltd	*Wealands v CLC Contractors Ltd* (1999) 2 Lloyd's Rep 739, CA
Wena v Egypt	*Wena Hotels Limited v the Arab Republic of Egypt* (ICSID Case No. ARB/98/4), Decision on the Claimant's Application for Interpretation of the Arbitral Award dated 8 December 2000, 31 October 2005
Wena v Egypt (DA)	*Wena Hotel Limited v Arab Republic of Egypt* (ICSID Case No. ARB/98/4), DA, 5 February 2002
Wena v Egypt (Stay Decision)	*Wena Hotel Limited v Arab Republic of Egypt* (ICSID Case No. ARB/98/4), DS, 5 April 2001
West Tankers	*West Tankers (aka 'The Front Conor')* [2009] 3 WLR 696 (ECJ)
West Tankers v Ras Riunione	*West Tankers v Ras Riunione Adriatico Sicurta SpA* [2007] EWHC 2184 (Comm)
Westacre Investments Inc. v Jugo-Import-SDPR Holding Co. Ltd	*Westacre Investments Inc. v Jugo-Import-SDPR Holding Co. Ltd* [1999] 3 All ER 864 (CA)
Westacre v Jugo-Import-SPDR	*Westacre Investments Inc v Jugo-Import-SPDR Holding Co. Ltd and Others* [1999] 2 Lloyd's Rep 65 (CA), [2000] QB 288 (England, CA)
Westco Airconditioning v Sui Chong Construction & Engineering	Court of First Instance, Hong Kong, 3 February 1998, *Westco Airconditioning Ltd v Sui Chong Construction & Engineering Co.*, [1998] 1 HKC 254,
Westinghouse	*Westinghouse Electric Corporation v The Islamic Republic of Iran Air Force*, Award No. 579-389-2 (20 Mar 1997)
Westland (Switzerland)	Tribunal Federal, 19 July 1988, *Westland Helicopters Ltd v The Arab Republic of Egypt, The Arab Organization for Industrialization and The Arab British Helicopter Company,* XVI YBCA (1991), p. 174
Westland Helicopters Ltd v Sheikh Salah Al-Hejailan	*Westland Helicopters Ltd v Sheikh Salah Al-Hejailan* [2004] EWHC 1625 (Comm)

List of References

Wicketts v *Brine Builders*	*Wicketts and Anor* v *Brine Builders and Anor* [2001] CILL 1805
Will-Drill Resources v *Samson Resources*	*Will-Drill Resources, Inc.* v *Samson Resources Co.*, 352 F 3d 211 (5th Cir 2003)
Wintershall	*Wintershall AG (FR Germany), International Ocean Resources, Inc. (formerly Koch Qatar, Inc.) (US), Veba Oel AG (FR Germany), Deutsche Schachtbau- und Tiefbohrgesellschaft mbH (FR Germany), Gulfstream Resources Canada Ltd (Canada)* v *The Government of Qatar*, Final Award (Ad Hoc UNCITRAL Proceedings, 31 May 1988)
Wintershall (Partial)	*Wintershall AG (FR Germany), International Ocean Resources, Inc. (formerly Koch Qatar, Inc.) (US), Veba Oel AG (FR Germany), Deutsche Schachtbau- und Tiefbohrgesellschaft mbH (FR Germany), Gulfstream Resources Canada Ltd (Canada)* v *The Government of Qatar*. Partial Award on Liability (Ad Hoc UNCITRAL Proceeding, 5 Feb 1988)
World Duty Free v *Kenya*	*World Duty Free Company Limited* v *Republic of Kenya* (ICSID Case No. ARB/00/7), FA, 4 October 2006
World Trade Corporation v *C Czarnikow Sugar Ltd*	*World Trade Corporation* v *C. Czarnikow Sugar Ltd* [2004] EWHC 2332 (Comm)
Yukos Oil v *Dardana*	*Yukos Oil Co.* v *Dardana Ltd* [2002] EWCA Civ 543
Zaporozhye Shareholders Society v *Ashly Ltd*	*Zaporozhye Production Aluminium Plan Open Shareholders Society* v *Ashly Ltd* [2002] EWHC 1410 (Comm)
ZCC Award	Zurich Chamber of Commerce, Award of 7 August 2006, Swiss Rules of International Arbitration, *A UK Limited* v *B SPA, Italy, Sole Arbitrator: Ian L. Meakin,* published in 25 ASA Bulletin 755 (2007)
Zealander v *Laing Homes*	*Zealander and Anor* v *Laing Homes Ltd* [1999] CILL 1510 (TCC)

Zestafoni G Nikoladze Ferroalloy Plant v *Ronly Holdings*   *JSC Zestafoni G Nikoladze Ferroalloy Plant* v *Ronly Holdings Ltd* [2004] EWHC 245 (Comm.)

Zhinvali v *Georgia*   *Zhinvali Development Ltd* v *Republic of Georgia* (ICSID Case No. ARB/00/1), FA, 24 January 2003

Zhongchen International Project Contracting Co. Ltd v *Beijing Jiangong Group LLC*   *Zhongchen International Project Contracting Co. Ltd* v *Beijing Jiangong Group LLC*, dated 14 April 2001 issued by the Beijing No. 2 Intermediate Court <www.bjac.org.cn>

Zwiebel v *Konig*   *Zwiebel* v *Konig* [2009] EWCA Civ 892

INDEX

A
AAA-ICDR International Arbitration Rules, 2009
applicability of, art. 1
  ICDR's role, 469
  international and AAA arbitration rules, 468–469
  mandatory rules, 469
commencement of arbitration
  amendments to claims, art. 4, 473
  notice of arbitration and statement of claim, art. 2, 470–471
  statement of defence and counterclaim, art. 3, 472–473
general conditions
  applicable laws and remedies, art. 28, 493–494
  awards, decisions and rulings, art. 26, 491–492
  closure of hearing, art. 24, 491
  compensation of arbitrators, art. 32, 496
  conduct of arbitration, art. 16, 484–485
  confidentiality, art. 34, 498
  costs, art. 31, 495–496
  default, art. 23, 490–491
  deposit of costs, art. 33, 497
  emergency measures of protection, art. 37, 499–500
  evidence, art. 19, 486–487
  exclusion of liability, art. 35, 498
  experts, art. 22, 489–490
  form and effect of award, art. 27, 492–493
  hearings, art. 20, 487–488
  interim measures of protection, art. 21, 488–489
  interpretation correction of award, art. 30, 495
  interpretation of rules, art. 36, 498–499
  jurisdiction, art. 15, 483–484
  language, art. 14, 482–483
  notices, art. 18, 486
  place of arbitration, art. 13, 481–482
  representation, art. 12, 481
  settlement for termination, art. 29, 494–495
  waiver of rules, art. 25, 491
  written statements, art. 17, 485–486
guidelines on exchanges of information
  costs and compliance, 506
  electronic documents, 505
  inspections, 505
  parties, 505
  privileges and professional ethics, 506
  procedures, 505–506
  purpose, 504
initial filing fee, 507–508
refund schedule, 511
tribunal
  administrator's authority, art.9, 479–480
  arbitrator replacement, art. 10, 480
  arbitrator's appointment, art. 6, 474–476
  authority of two arbitrators, art. 11, 480–481
  challenge of arbitrators, art. 8, 478–479

Index

impartiality and independence of arbitrators, art. 7, 476–478
number of arbitrators, art. 5, 473–474

Administrative Council, ICSID Convention, 1965
Chairman of Council, art. 5, 39–40
composition of, art. 4, 39
decisions, art. 7, 43–45
powers of chairman, art. 5, 40
remuneration from centre, art. 8, 45–46
role of Council, art. 6, 40–43

American Arbitration Association (AAA). *See* AAA-ICDR International Arbitration Rules, 2009

Amiable composition
arbitration clauses, 444
generally, 886

Anti-suit injunctions, 118–119, 737, 768, 788, 789, 795

Arbitrability. *See also* Public Policy
anti-trust and competition law, 905, 915, 947, 948, 957, 960
bribery and corruption, 648, 904, 959
generally, 1, 6, 21, 588, 658, 673, 731, 914
insolvency law, 916
securities transactions, 658, 920

Arbitration agreement
assignment, 8–9, 78, 323, 660, 732, 733, 899, 920, 945, 968
consent to, 36, 52, 72–80, 88, 89, 91, 92, 101, 112, 115–117, 120, 148, 158, 168, 169, 232, 277, 596, 918

enforce/honour of, 1, 2, 5, 21, 270, 360, 420, 441, 638, 743, 874
extension to non-signatories, 323, 604, 919, 920, 957, 969
generally, 322, 521, 595, 598, 599, 605, 670, 730
law applicable, 6, 103–108, 172, 403, 407, 431, 432, 450, 467, 493–494, 498, 549, 662–664, 724, 727, 791, 851, 884–885
null and void, inoperative or incapable of being performed, 604
privity, 732
separability, 483, 484, 613, 722, 724, 731–733, 764, 795, 921
validity, 6, 8, 16, 200, 201, 362, 433, 479, 562, 563, 602, 622, 626, 672, 880, 915, 919, 921
validity, formal, 16, 603

Arbitral award
CIETAC arbitration rules, 2005
additional award, art. 48, 565–566
correction of, art. 47, 564–565
execution of award, art. 49, 566–567
fees, art. 46, 564
interlocutory and partial award, art. 44, 562–563
rendering, art. 43, 560–562
scrutiny of draft award, art. 45, 563–564
time limits, art. 42, 559
English Arbitration Act (C. 23), 1996
additional award, Sec. 57, 805–807

Index

date of, Sec. 54, 802–803
different issues/time, Sec. 47, 793–794
effect of, Sec. 58, 807–808
extension time for making award, Sec. 50, 798–799
from of, Sec. 52, 800–801
interest, Sec. 49, 796–797
notification, Sec. 55, 803
place where award treated as made, Sec. 53, 801–802
remedies, Sec. 48, 794–796
rules applicable to substance of dispute, Sec. 46, 791–793
settlement, Sec. 51, 799–800
withhold award in non-payment, Sec. 56, 804–805

ICC Rules of arbitration
advance on costs of arbitration, art. 30, 375–381
award by consent, art. 26, 365
correction and interpretation, art. 29, 372–373
decision on costs of arbitration, art. 31, 381–385
extension of time, art. 24, 361–362
making of award, art. 25, 363–364
notification, deposit and enforceability, art. 28, 369–371
scrutiny of award by Court, art. 27, 366–368

ICSID Convention, 1965
annulment of, art. 52, 133–141
application, art. 48, 120–121
award written and signed, art. 48, 121–122
binding force of, art. 53, 141
decide by majority, art. 48, 121
dispatch, supplement and rectification, art. 49, 124–126
enforcement of, art. 54, 144–147
individual opinions, art. 48, 122–123
publication of, art. 48, 123
questions and reasons, art. 48, 122
revision of, art. 51, 128–131

ICSID rules
interpretation, revision and annulment, 294–302
preparation, Rule 46, 288
rendering and publishing, Rule 48, 290–292
Rule 47, 289–290
supplementary decisions and rectification, Rule 49, 293–294

LCIA Rules
court appeal, 453
currency and interest, 452
issuing an award, 452
settlement, 452–453
unanimous decision, 452
written award and reasons, 452

New York Convention (1958)
characteristics, 10
domestic and foreign awards, 11–12
jurisdiction, 11
presumption of validity, 10
procedural requirements, 10–11
reference to law of forum, 10

Swiss Private International Law Act, 1989
content, 952
costs, 953–954

1081

deliberations and voting, 951–952
dissenting opinion, 953
form and notification, 952
notion of, 951
party autonomy, 951
proceedings, termination of, 954
reasons, 952–953
UNCITRAL arbitration rules, 1976
additional award, art. 37, 223–225
applicable law, art. 33, 218–219
apportionment of costs, art. 40, 228–229
arbitration cost, art. 38, 225–226
arbitrators' fees, art. 39, 226–228
correction of, art. 36, 222–223
decisions, art. 31, 215–216
deposit of costs, art. 41, 229–230
form and effect of, art. 32, 216–218
interpretations, art. 35, 221–222
settlement for termination, art. 34, 219–221

Arbitral proceedings
CIETAC Arbitration Rules, 2005
acceptance of case, art. 11, 527
amendments to claim/counterclaim, art. 14, 530–531
arbitral tribunal investigation, art. 37, 553–554
arbitrator replacement, art. 27, 542–544
challenge, art. 26, 540–542
commencement, art. 9, 525
conciliation with arbitration, art. 40, 555–557
conduct of hearing, art. 29, 545–546
confidentiality, art. 33, 549–550
continuing arbitration, art. 28, 544–545
counterclaim, art. 13, 529–530
default, art. 34, 550–551
disclosure, art. 25, 539–540
duties of the arbitrator(s), art. 19, 534
evidence preservation, art. 18, 533
evidence, art. 36, 552–553
examination of evidence, art. 39, 554–555
expert's and appraiser's report, art. 38, 554
multi-party, art. 24, 538–539
number of arbitrators, art. 20, 534–535
oral hearing notice, art. 30, 546–547
oral hearing records, art. 35, 551–552
panel of arbitrators, art. 21, 535–536
place of arbitration, art. 31, 547–548
place of oral hearing, art. 32, 548–549
property preservation, art. 17, 532–533
representation, art. 16, 532
request for arbitration, art. 10, 525–526
sole arbitrator, art. 23, 537–538
statement of defence, art. 12, 527–529

submissions copies, art. 15, 531
three arbitrators, art. 22, 536–537
withdrawal and dismissal, art. 41, 558–559
English Arbitration Act (C. 23), 1996
appoint experts, legal advisers, Sec. 37, 776–777
concurrent hearings, Sec. 35, 774–775
court powers, 783–791
duty of parties, Sec. 40, 781
duty of tribunal, Sec. 33, 769–770
legal representation, Sec. 36, 775–776
party's default, Sec. 41, 781–783
powers exercisable by tribunal, Sec. 38, 777–779
powers to grant awards, Sec. 39, 779–780
procedural and evidential matters, Sec. 34, 770–773
ICC Rules of Arbitration
applicable rules of law, art. 17, 350–351
closing of proceedings, art. 22, 359
conservatory and interim measures, art. 23, 359–361
establishing the case facts, art. 20, 356–357
file transmission, art. 13, 344
hearings, art. 21, 358
language of arbitration, art. 16, 348–349
new claims, art. 19, 354–355
place of arbitration, art. 14, 345–346
rules governing the proceedings, art. 15, 347–348
terms of reference, art. 18, 352–354
UNCITRAL Arbitration Rules, 1976
amendments to claim/ defence, art. 20, 198–200
closure of hearings, art. 29, 213–214
default, art. 28, 211–213
evidence, art. 24, 204–205
experts, art. 27, 209–211
further written statements, art. 22, 202
general provisions, art. 15, 190–192
hearings, art. 25, 205–207
interim measures, art. 26, 208–209
jurisdiction of arbitral tribunal, art, 21, 200–201
language, art. 17, 194–195
place of arbitration, art. 16, 192–193
statement of claim, art. 18, 195–196
statement of defence, art.19, 196–198
time periods, art. 23, 203–204
waiver of rules, art. 30, 214–215

Arbitral tribunal
AAA-ICDR International Arbitration Rules, 2009
administrator's authority, art.9, 479–480
arbitrator replacement, art. 10, 480
arbitrator's appointment, art. 6, 474–476
authority of two arbitrators, art. 11, 480–481
challenge of arbitrators, art. 8, 478–479

impartiality and independence of arbitrators, art. 7, 476–478
number of arbitrators, art. 5, 473–474

English Arbitration Act (C. 23), 1996
appointment of arbitrators, Sec. 16, 745–746
arbitrator death, Sec. 26, 759–760
Chairman, Sec. 20, 749–750
court agreed qualification, Sec. 19, 749
decision-making no chairman/umpire, Sec. 22, 752–753
default to appoint sole arbitrator, Sec. 17, 746–747
definition, Sec. 15, 744–745
failure of appointment procedure, Sec. 18, 747–749
filling of vacancy, Sec. 27, 760–761
immunity of arbitrator, Sec. 29, 763–764
liability to pay fees and expenses, Sec. 28, 761–763
removal of arbitrator by court, Sec. 24, 754–758
resignation of arbitrator, Sec. 25, 758–759
revocation of authority, Sec. 23, 753–754
umpire, Sec. 21, 751–752

ICSID Convention, 1965
ancillary claims, art. 46, 114–115
applicable law, art. 42, 103–108
decision on jurisdiction, art. 41, 100–103
evidence, art. 43, 108–110
party fails to appear, art. 45, 112–114
procedural rules, art. 44, 110–112
provisional measures, art. 47, 116–120

Swiss Private International Law Act, 1989
appointing authority decisions, remedies, 923–924
arbitral contract, 924
arbitrator appointment by a party, 927
arbitrator resignation, 924
challenge decision, appeal against, 928
challenge procedure, 927–928
competent court, 923
constitution, 921–922
duty to challenge, 928
duty to disclose, 927
independence, 925–927
party autonomy, 922
proceedings repetition, 924
scope of application and system of provision, 925
state court, appointing authority, 923

UNCITRAL Arbitration Rules, 1976
appointment by appointing authority, art. 8, 180–181
arbitrator replacement, art. 13, 188–189
challenge decision, art. 12, 186–187
disclosure, art. 9, 181–183
notification of challenge, art. 11, 185–186
number of arbitrators, art. 5, 176–177
repetition of hearings, art. 14, 189–190

sole arbitrator appointment, art. 6, 177–179
standard for challenge, art. 10, 183–185
three-person panel appointment, art. 7, 179–180
UNCITRAL Model Law on International Commercial Arbitration, 1985/2006
appointment of arbitrators, art. 11, 607–609
appointment of substitute arbitrator, art. 15, 612–613
challenge procedure, art. 13, 610–611
failure/impossibility, art. 14, 611–612
grounds for challenge, art. 12, 609–610
number of arbitrators, art. 10, 606–607

Arbitration agreement
CIETAC Arbitration Rules, 2005
objection to, art. 6, 522–524
severability of, 521–522
types of, 521
written form, 521
English Arbitration Act (C. 23), 1996
definition, Sec. 6, 730–731
discharged by death of a party, Sec. 8, 733–734
separability, Sec. 7, 732–733
New York Convention, 1958
agreement in writing, 7
assignment, 8–9
content, 5–6
incorporation by reference, 7–8
matter capable of settlement, 6
null and void, 9–10
scope, 5
People's Republic of China Arbitration Law, 1994
invalidity of, art. 17, 673
priority of court jurisdiction, art. 20, 677–678
severability, art. 19, 676–677
unclear designation of arbitration commission, art. 18, 674–676
validity requirements, art. 16, 670–672
Swiss Private International Law Act, 1989
art. 178(1) and art. II(2) New York Convention, 917–918
art. 178(2) and art. V(1)(a) New York Convention, 920–921
by reference, 918–919
determinability, 918
form requirement, 917
non-signatories, 920
pathological agreements, 918
principle of autonomy/ separability, 921
requirements, 917
scope of, 919–920
substantive validity, 919
UNCITRAL Model Law on International Commercial Arbitration, 1985/2006
definition and form of, art. 7, 595–601
interim measures by court, art. 9, 605–606
substantive claim, art. 8, 601–605

Arbitration commissions and association, People's Republic of China arbitration law, 1994
China Arbitration Association (CAA), art. 15, 669–670

Index

geographical organisation, art. 10, 666–667
independence, art. 14, 669
key personnel, art. 12, 667–668
minimum requirements for arbitrators, art. 13, 668–669
minimum requirements, art. 11, 667

Arbitration costs and fees, International Chamber of Commerce (ICC) Rules of Arbitration, 1998

advance on costs, art. 1, 396–397
costs and fees, art. 2, 397–398
ICC as appointing authority, art. 3, 398
scales of administrative expenses and arbitrator's fees, art. 4, 398–400

Arbitration procedure, People's Republic of China Arbitration Law, 1994

arbitrator replacement, art. 37, 688–689
arbitrator's appointment, art. 31, 684–685
arbitrator's liability, art. 38, 689
challenge withdrawal of arbitrator, art. 34, 686–687
competent authority, art. 36, 688
content of request for arbitration, art. 23, 679
decision of arbitration commission, art. 24, 679–680
notice of arbitration, art. 25, 680–681
notification of constitution, art. 33, 685–686
number of arbitrators, art. 30, 684
power of attorney, art. 24, 683–684
primary jurisdiction of courts, art. 26, 681–682
property preservation measures, art. 28, 682–683
request for arbitration, art. 21, 678
requirement of written application, art. 22, 678
right to counterclaim, art. 27, 682
subsidiary appointing authority, art. 32, 685
withdrawal procedure, art. 35, 687–688

Arbitration pursuant and agreement, English Arbitration Act (C. 23), 1996

general principles, Sec. 1, 722–723
mandatory and non-mandatory provisions, Sec. 4, 727–728
scope of application, Sec. 2, 723–725
seat of, Sec. 3, 725–727
written agreements, Sec. 5, 728–730

Arbitration, ICSID Convention, 1965

appointment by Chairman, art. 38
 appoint arbitrators, 96
 by acceptance, 97
 consultation, 96
 content of request, 96
 designations, 96
 nationality of arbitrators, 97
 request of party, 96
 time limit, 95–96
composition, constitution of tribunal, art. 37
 acceptance, replacement of arbitrator, 94
 appointing authority, 94

Index

arbitrators numbers, 94
formalities, 93
president designation, 94
procedure for, 93
timing, 94
interpretation, recognition, enforcement of award, art. 50
application, 127
award, 128
decision effect, 127–128
enforcement of stay, 128
request for, 127
nationality of arbitrators, art. 38, 97–98
powers, functions of tribunal
ancillary claims, art. 46, 114–115
applicable law, art. 42, 103–108
decision on jurisdiction, art. 41, 100–103
evidence, art. 43, 108–110
party fails to appear, art. 45, 112–114
procedural rules, art. 44, 110–112
provisional measures, art. 47, 116–120
qualities of arbitrators, art. 40
appointment by Chairman, 99
appointment by parties, 99
improper appointment, 100
post-appointment, 99–100
request for arbitration, art. 36
acknowledgement, 90
application, 88
content, 89
effect of registration, 92
format, 89
lodging fee, 89–90
notification, 92
optional information, 89
refusal of registration, 91–92
registration, 91
respondent's observations, 91
Secretary-General's power, 91
sending request, 90
submission of request, 88–89
supplement and amending request, 90–91
supporting documentation, 89
time limits, 90
withdrawal of, 92
revision art. 51, 128–131

B

Bad faith, 282, 423, 464, 493, 754, 757, 763, 835, 836, 916, 953
Bankruptcy, 733–734, 889, 905, 930, 975, 976

C

China Arbitration Association (CAA), 669–670, 714–715
China International Economic and Trade Arbitration Commission. *See* **CIETAC Arbitration Rules, 2005**
CIETAC Arbitration Rules, 2005
arbitral award
additional award, art. 48, 565–566
correction of, art. 47, 564–565
execution of award, art. 49, 566–567
fees, art. 46, 564
interlocutory and partial award, art. 44, 562–563
rendering, art. 43, 560–562

1087

Index

scrutiny of draft award, art. 45, 563–564
time limits, art. 42, 559
arbitral proceedings
   acceptance of case, art. 11, 527
   amendments to claim/counterclaim, art. 14, 530–531
   arbitral tribunal investigation, art. 37, 553–554
   arbitrator replacement, art. 27, 542–544
   challenge, art. 26, 540–542
   commencement, art. 9, 525
   conciliation with arbitration, art. 40, 555–557
   conduct of hearing, art. 29, 545–546
   confidentiality, art. 33, 549–550
   continuing arbitration, art. 28, 544–545
   counterclaim, art. 13, 529–530
   default, art. 34, 550–551
   disclosure, art. 25, 539–540
   duties of the arbitrator(s), art. 19, 534
   evidence preservation, art. 18, 533
   evidence, art. 36, 552–553
   examination of evidence, art. 39, 554–555
   expert's and appraiser's report, art. 38, 554
   multi-party, art. 24, 538–539
   number of arbitrators, art. 20, 534–535
   oral hearing notice, art. 30, 546–547
   oral hearing records, art. 35, 551–552
   panel of arbitrators, art. 21, 535–536
   place of arbitration, art. 31, 547–548
   place of oral hearing, art. 32, 548–549
   property preservation, art. 17, 532–533
   representation, art. 16, 532
   request for arbitration, art. 10, 525–526
   sole arbitrator, art. 23, 537–538
   statement of defence, art. 12, 527–529
   submissions copies, art. 15, 531
   three arbitrators, art. 22, 536–537
   withdrawal and dismissal, art. 41, 558–559
bona fide cooperation, art. 7, 524
domestic arbitration
   acceptance, art. 60, 572–573
   application, art. 59, 572
   arbitral tribunal formation, art. 61, 573
   context reference, art. 66, 575
   notice of oral hearing, art. 63, 573–574
   oral hearing records, art. 64, 574
   statement of defence and counterclaim, art. 62, 573
   time limits for rendering award, art. 65, 575
general provisions, rules, art. 1, 513–514
jurisdiction, art. 3, 517–518
name and structure, art. 2, 514–516
objection to, art. 6, 522–524
scope of application, art. 4, 518–520
summary procedure

Index

application, art. 50, 567
arbitral tribunal formation, art. 52, 568
change of procedure, art. 57, 571
conduct of hearing, art. 54, 569
context reference, art. 58, 571
Notice of Arbitration, art. 51, 567–568
oral hearing, art. 55, 570
statement of defence and counterclaim, art. 53, 568–569
time limits for rendering award, art. 56, 570–571
supplementary provisions
arbitration fees and actual expenses, art. 69, 577–578
effectiveness, art. 71, 579
interpretation, art. 70, 578
language, art. 67, 575–576
service of documents, art. 68, 576–577
waiver of the right to object, art. 8, 524

Commencement of proceedings, English Arbitration Act (C. 23), 1996
limitation acts apply, Sec. 13
apply to legal proceedings, 742
enforcement of award, 742–743
foreign limitation periods, 742
new claims, 742
Scott v Avery clauses, 743
set aside and nullified award, 743
parties' agreement, Sec. 14, 743–744

time extensions, Sec. 12, 739–741

Conciliation, ICSID Convention, 1965
Chairman appointment, art. 30, 83
commission's report, art. 34, 85–87
Conciliation Commission, composition, art. 29, 82–83
conciliation proceedings, art. 32, 84
conciliators' qualities, art. 31, 83–84
non-invocation in subsequent proceedings, art. 34, 87–88
request for, art. 28, 81
rule of conciliation procedure, art. 33, 84–85

Conduct of arbitral proceedings, UNCITRAL Model Law on International Commercial Arbitration, 1985/2006
commencement, art. 21, 627–628
court assistance in taking evidence, art. 27, 634–635
default of a party, art. 25, 631–633
hearings and written proceedings, art. 24, 630–631
language, art. 22, 628–629
parties equal treatment, art. 18, 623–624
place of arbitration, art. 20, 626–627
rules of procedure determination, art. 19, 625
statements of claim and defence, art. 23, 629–630

1089

Index

tribunal-appointed experts, art. 26, 633–634
Confidentiality
generally, 206, 462
privileges, 123, 242, 357, 392, 487, 498, 549, 721
Consumer agreements, English Arbitration Act (C. 23), 1996
consumer as a legal person, Sec. 90, 852–853
unfair arbitration agreement, Sec. 91, 853–854
unfair terms in regulations, Sec. 89, 851–852
Cost of arbitration, English Arbitration Act (C. 23), 1996
arbitrators' fees and expenses, 809
award of costs, Sec. 61, 810–812
effect of agreement, Sec. 62, 812
legal cost, 809
limit of recoverable costs, Sec. 65, 816
pay costs in any event, Sec. 60, 810
recoverable costs, Sec. 63, 812–814
recoverable fees and expenses, Sec. 64, 814–815
Court powers and award, English Arbitration Act (C. 23), 1996
appeal, Sec. 69, 825–828
effect of court order, appeal, Sec. 71, 831–832
enforcement of award, Sec. 66, 816–819
serious irregularity, challenging award, Sec. 68, 821–825
substantive jurisdiction, Sec. 67, 819–821
supplementary provisions, Sec. 70, 828–830
Courts, national
anti-suit injunction, 118–119, 737, 768, 788, 789
arbitrators, appointment, 55, 97, 98, 233, 391, 608, 805
assistance-intervention, 208, 609
jurisdiction, decline, 880–882, 942
jurisdiction, insolvency, 734
relationship to arbitration, 5, 184, 209, 326, 327, 339, 594, 606, 721, 924
review of arbitration agreement, 603, 625, 636
review of award,1-37, 10–11
stay of proceedings, 9, 24, 63, 78, 131, 147, 594, 597, 725, 734–739, 764, 849, 944, 946

D
Departmental Advisory Committee (DAC) Reports, 721–724, 726, 727, 729–733, 735, 738, 740–744, 746–751, 753, 755, 757–760, 762–764, 766, 768–771, 774–776, 779–782, 784, 785, 790, 791, 793, 794, 797–804, 806, 807, 809, 810, 812, 813, 815–817, 820, 822, 826, 831–838, 840–842, 845–859, 861, 863, 864, 867, 869, 871, 872
Dissolution of company, 733, 734

E
English Arbitration Act (C. 23), 1996
applicable laws, 719

Index

appointment of judges as arbitrators, Sec. 93, 854–855
arbitral proceedings
   appoint experts, legal advisers, Sec. 37, 776–777
   concurrent hearings, Sec. 35, 774–775
   determination of preliminary law, Sec. 45, 789–791
   duty of parties, Sec. 40, 781
   duty of tribunal, Sec. 33, 769–770
   enforcement of peremptory orders, Sec. 42, 783–784
   exercisable of court powers, Sec. 44, 786–789
   legal representation, Sec. 36, 775–776
   party's default, Sec. 41, 781–783
   power grant awards, Sec. 39, 779–780
   powers exercisable by tribunal, Sec. 38, 777–779
   procedural and evidential matters, Sec. 34, 770–773
   securing attendance of witnesses, Sec. 43, 785–786
arbitral tribunal
   appointment of arbitrators, Sec. 16, 745–746
   arbitrator death, Sec. 26, 759–760
   Chairman, Sec. 20, 749–750
   court agreed qualification, Sec. 19, 749
   decision-making no chairman/umpire, Sec. 22, 752–753
   default to appoint sole arbitrator, Sec. 17, 746–747
   definition, Sec. 15, 744–745
   failure of appointment procedure, Sec. 18, 747–749
   filling of vacancy, Sec. 27, 760–761
   immunity of arbitrator, Sec. 29, 763–764
   liability to pay fees and expenses, Sec. 28, 761–763
   removal of arbitrator by court, Sec. 24, 754–758
   resignation of arbitrator, Sec. 25, 758–759
   revocation of authority, Sec. 23, 753–754
   umpire, Sec. 21, 751–752
arbitration agreement
   definition, Sec. 6, 730–731
   discharged by death of a party, Sec. 8, 733–734
   separability, Sec. 7, 732–733
arbitration pursuant and agreement
   general principles, Sec. 1, 722–723
   mandatory and non-mandatory provisions, Sec. 4, 727–728
   scope of application, Sec. 2, 723–725
   seat of, Sec. 3, 725–727
   written agreements, Sec. 5, 728–730
award
   additional award, Sec. 57, 805–807
   date of, Sec. 54, 802–803
   different issues/time, Sec. 47, 793–794
   effect of, Sec. 58, 807–808
   extension time for making award, Sec. 50, 798–799
   from of, Sec. 52, 800–801
   interest, Sec. 49, 796–797

Index

notification, Sec. 55, 803
place where award treated as made, Sec. 53, 801–802
remedies, Sec. 48, 794–796
rules applicable to substance of dispute, Sec. 46, 791–793
settlement, Sec. 51, 799–800
withhold award in non-payment, Sec. 56, 804–805
commencement of act, Sec. 109, 871
commencement of proceedings
apply limitation acts, Sec. 13, 741–743
parties' agreement, Sec. 14, 743–744
time extensions, Sec. 12, 739–741
consequential amendments and repeals, Sec. 107, 869–870
consumer agreements
consumer as a legal person, Sec. 90, 852–853
unfair arbitration agreement, Sec. 91, 853–854
unfair terms in regulations, Sec. 89, 851–852
cost of arbitration
arbitrators' fees and expenses, 809
award of costs, Sec. 61, 810–812
effect of agreement, Sec. 62, 812
legal cost, 809
limit of recoverable costs, Sec. 65, 816
pay costs in any event, Sec. 60, 810
recoverable costs, Sec. 63, 812–814
recoverable fees and expenses, Sec. 64, 814–815
court powers
determination, Sec. 45, 789–791
enforcement of peremptory orders, Sec. 42, 783–784
in support of arbitral proceedings, Sec. 44, 786–789
securing evidence from witness, Sec. 43, 785–786
court powers and award
appeal, Sec. 69, 825–828
effect of order of court, appeal, Sec. 71, 831–832
enforcement of award, Sec. 66, 816–819
serious irregularity, challenging award, Sec. 68, 821–825
substantive jurisdiction, Sec. 67, 819–821
supplementary provisions, Sec. 70, 828–830
Crown application, Sec. 106, 868–869
domestic agreement
exclude court jurisdiction, Sec. 87, 850
modification of Part I, Sec. 85, 848–849
power to repeal, Sec. 88, 850–851
staying of legal proceedings, Sec. 86, 849–850
enforcement of Geneva Convention awards, Sec. 99, 858–859
European Convention on Human Rights, 722
extent provision of act, Sec. 108, 870–871
history of, 719–720

immunity of arbitral institutions, Sec. 74, 835–836
joinder, consolidation, 721–722
jurisdiction of High Court and county court, Sec. 105, 867–868
jurisdiction of tribunal
  competence to rule, Sec. 30, 764–765
  determination of, Sec. 32, 767–769
  substantive jurisdiction, Sec. 31, 765–767
loss of right to object, Sec. 73, 833–835
new arbitration regime, 722
New York Convention awards
  produced evidence, Sec. 102, 862–863
  pursuance of agreement, Sec. 100, 859–860
  recognition and enforcement of, Sec. 101, 860–862
  refusal, Sec. 103, 863–866
  saving by other basis, Sec. 104, 867
payment of solicitors' costs, Sec. 75, 836
philosophy of, 720–721
privacy, confidentiality, 721
saving for rights of person, Sec. 72, 832–833
short title, Sec. 110, 871–872
small claims arbitration, Sec. 92, 854
sources of, 719
statutory arbitrations
  adaptation of general provisions, Sec. 95, 856
  adaptation of specific provisions, Sec. 96, 856–857
  application of Part I, Sec. 94, 855–856
  excluded provisions, Sec. 97, 857–858
  Secretary of State to make provision, Sec. 98, 858
stay of legal proceedings
  anti-suit injunctions, 737
  arbitration agreement, 735
  consumer contracts, 737
  counterclaim, 736
  definition of, 735
  discretion, 735–736
  interpleader issue, Sec. 10, 737–738
  notice, application, 735
  null and void, inoperative perform, 736
  parties, 735
  pre-condition to arbitration, 736
  retention of security, Sec. 11, 738–739
  right of appeal, 737
  Scott v Avery clauses, 737
  taken steps, 736
supplementary
  definition of minor, Sec. 82, 845–846
  form, time period and content of notice, Sec. 80, 841–843
  governed by common law, Sec. 81, 843–845
  list of expressions, Part I, Sec. 83, 847
  proceedings, extend time limits for, Sec. 79, 840–841
  reckoning periods of time, Sec. 78, 839–840
  service of documents, Sec. 77, 838–839
  service of notices, Sec. 76, 836–838
  transitional provisions, Sec. 84, 848
territorial scope, 719

English Civil Procedure Act, 1833, 720
English common law, 763, 844, 845
European Convention on Human Rights, 184, 722, 821, 827, 925

F
Foreign arbitral awards
 New York Convention (1958)
  arbitrators, jurisdiction, 18–19
  award binding, 20
  award suspension, 20–21
  incapacity, 16–17
  invalidity of arbitration agreement, 15–16
  irregular procedure, 19–20
  overview, 15
  public policy violation, 21–23
  violation of due process, 17–18
 Swiss Private International Law Act, 1989
  enforcement of awards, 975–976
  public policy, 975
  recognition and enforcement, 974
  refusal under art. V(2) New York Convention, 974–975
Foreign-related arbitration, People's Republic of China arbitration law, 1994
 arbitration commissions, art. 66, 708
 competence of CCOIC, art. 73, 713
 evidence preservation, art. 68, 709–710
 lack of jurisdiction rationae loci, art. 72, 713
 non-enforcement, art. 71, 712–713
 panel of arbitrators, art. 67, 708–709
 records of hearings, art. 69, 710
 set aside procedure, art. 70, 710–712
 special provisions, art. 65, 707
Formation of arbitral tribunal, People's Republic of China arbitration law, 1994
 arbitrator replacement, art. 37, 688–689
 arbitrators appointment, art. 31, 684–685
 arbitrators liability, art. 38, 689
 challenge withdrawal of arbitrator, art. 34, 686–687
 competent authority, art. 36, 688
 notification of constitution, art. 33, 685–686
 number of arbitrators, art. 30, 684
 subsidiary appointing authority, art. 32, 685
 withdrawal procedure, art. 35, 687–688
French Code of Civil Procedure, 1981
 amiable composition, art. 1497, 886–887
 appeal against granting enforcement order, art. 1502
  art. 1502(1), 898–900
  art. 1502(2), 901
  art. 1502(3), 901–902
  art. 1502(4), 902–903
  art. 1502(5), 903–905
  award's reasoning, 898
  Court of Appeal's review, 898
  foreign award suspension, 896–897

sanctions for abuse of rights, 898
timely objection and waiver, 897
appeal against refusing enforcement order, art. 1501, 895
applicability of French provisions, art. 1495, 875
application procedure, art. 1457 and 1444, 879–880
constitution of arbitral tribunals, art. 1493
application procedure, art. 1493, 878
disclosure duty, 877–878
issues, 877
most diligent party, 877
objections and challenges, 878
parties agreement, reference in, 876–877
President of the Paris First Instance Court, 876
Court of Appeal with jurisdiction, art. 1503, 905–906
Court of Appeal, art. 1487, 908–909
CPC provisions and French case law, 873
CPC provisions and International Conventions, 873–874
definition of international arbitration, art. 1492, 874–875
form of the enforcement order, art. 1478, 893–894
formalities for execution of awards, art. 1477, 892–893
French international arbitration law, 874
international and domestic arbitration, 873
international awards, art. 1498

France and foreign awards, 887–888
French arbitration law, 888–889
French international public policy, 889
judge's review, 889–890
recognition, enforcement and execution, 888
Kompetenz-Kompetenz, art. 1458 and 1466
arbitral tribunal's decision, 883
disputes, 881–883
provisional measures, 883
law applicable to merits, art. 1496, 884–885
procedural rules during the arbitration proceedings, art. 1494, 883–884
provisional execution of awards, art. 1479, 894–895
rejection of appeal, art. 1490, 909
rendering of award, art. 1505, 907
Res judicata effects of awards, art. 1476, 892
setting aside of international awards, art. 1504, 906–907
suspension of execution, art. 1506, 907–908
translation of foreign awards, art. 1499, 891

G

Geneva Convention awards, 844, 858–859, 867
Good faith, 36, 85–87, 104, 155, 351, 388, 499, 524, 591, 663, 852, 919, 959
Groups of companies, 323, 732, 846, 922

H
Hearing and award, People's Republic of China Arbitration Law, 1994
administration by arbitration commission, art. 41, 690–691
appraisal, art. 44, 692–693
compulsory recording of domestic arbitration, art. 48, 695
conciliation procedure and result, art. 51, 696–697
content and binding effect of conciliation statement, art. 52, 697–698
content and form of, art. 54, 698–699
correction and supplementation, art. 56, 700
cross-examination, art. 45, 693–694
decision making, art. 53, 698
default of one party, art. 42, 691
evidence preservation, art. 46, 694
evidence, art. 43, 691–692
legal effect of, art. 57, 700
mediation and consent awards, art. 49, 695–696
oral hearings, art. 39, 690
partial award, art. 55, 699–700
private hearings, art. 40, 690
repudiation of conciliation settlement, art.50, 696
right to debate, art. 47, 694–695
House of Lords, 431, 453, 720, 722, 731, 737, 765, 802, 844, 860, 870

I
IBA. *See* **International Bar Association (IBA)**
ICSID Convention, 1965
administrative Council
Chairman of Council, art. 5, 39–40
composition of, art. 4, 39
decisions, art. 7, 43–45
powers of Chairman, art. 5, 40
remuneration from centre, art. 8, 45–46
role of Council, art. 6, 40–43
amendment
conventional amendments, art. 65, 160–161
decision of, art. 66, 161
arbitration
ancillary claims, art. 46, 114–115
annulment of award, art. 52, 131–141
applicable law, art. 42, 103–108
appointment by Chairman, art. 38, 95–97
award, art. 48, 120–123
binding force of award, art. 53, 141–143
composition, constitution of tribunal, art. 37, 92–94
default of party, art. 45, 112–114
enforcement of award, art. 54, 143–147
evidence, art. 43, 108–110
interpretation of award, art. 50, 126–128
jurisdiction on tribunal decisions, art. 41, 101–103
nationality of arbitrators, art. 39, 97–98
procedural rules, art. 44, 110–112
provisional measures, art. 47, 116–120
qualities of arbitrators, art. 40, 99–100
request for, art. 36, 88–92

revision of award, art. 51, 128–131
sovereign immunity, art. 55, 147–149
supplementation, rectification, art. 49, 123–126
conciliation
appointment by Chairman, art. 30, 83
commission's report, art. 34, 85–87
Conciliation Commission, composition, art. 29, 82–83
conciliation proceedings, art. 32, 84
conciliators' qualities, art. 31, 83–84
non-invocation in subsequent proceedings, art. 34, 87–88
request for, art. 28, 81
rule of conciliation procedure, art. 33, 84–85
cost of proceedings
apportionment of expenses, art. 61, 155–156
charges of centre, art. 59, 153
expenses, fees, art. 60, 153–154
disputes between Contracting States, 159–160
disqualification of conciliators and arbitrators
decision of disqualify, art. 58, 152
proposal, art. 57, 151–152
establishment, organisation
Centre establishment, art. 1, 37
seat of Centre, art. 2, 38
structure of Centre, art. 3, 39
final provisions

consequences of notice, art. 71, 166–167
consequences of notice, art. 72, 167–169
denounce of Convention, art. 71, 166–167
depositary of Convention, art. 73, 169
implementing legislation, art. 69, 163–164
notification, art. 75, 170
ratification, acceptance, art. 68, 162–163
registration of Convention, art. 74, 170
signature of Convention, art. 67, 162
territorial exclusion, art. 70, 164–166
financing of Centre
expenditure of Centre, art. 17, 58–60
legal personality, art. 18, 60
immunity of Centre, art. 20, 61
jurisdiction of Centre
agencies of Contracting State, 70
Contracting State, 70
diplomatic protection, art. 27, 79–81
directness requirement, 69
excluded disputes, 68
exclusive remedy, art. 26, 77–79
existence of dispute, 67
investment concept, 69–70
judicial persons, 72–73
judicial persons under foreign control, 73–74
legal nature, 67–68
list of exclusions, 68–69
national of another Contracting State, 71
nationality of natural persons, 72

Index

natural persons, 71–72
parties' consent, 74–77
State designation requirement, 70–71
Panels
designations, art. 13, 54–55
purpose of, art. 12, 53
qualities of members, art. 14, 55–56
serving of both Panels, art. 16, 57–58
terms of members, art. 15, 57
place of proceedings
proceedings at another place, art. 63, 157–159
seat of Centre, art. 62, 157
preamble, 33–36
replacement of conciliators, arbitrators, art. 56
expiry of term on Panel, 150–151
filling vacancies, 150
principle of immutability, 149–150
vacancy, 150
Secretariat
composition of, art. 9, 46–47
General and Deputy Secretary, art. 10, 47–48
Secretary-General's role, art. 11, 48–52
status, privileges, immunities of Centre
archives and official communications of Centre, art. 23, 63–64
exemptions of tax, art. 24, 64–65
immunity from legal process, art. 20, 61
immunity of parties, witnesses, art. 22, 62–63
immunity of persons appointed by the Centre, art. 21, 61–62

Insolvency Act 1986, 733, 734
Insolvency of company, 734, 916
Interim measures
arbitration tribunals, power to grant, 209, 360, 617, 779, 780
court ordered, 621–623
emergency and, 309, 419, 500
enforcement of, 620–623, 926, 936–937
ex parte, 622, 936, 937
generally, 208, 450, 488, 605, 616
International Bar Association (IBA)
Guidelines on Conflicts of Interest, 182, 242, 340, 412, 479–480, 542, 926
rules of evidence, 110, 191, 205, 269, 271, 272, 437, 438, 442, 553, 692, 938
International Centre for Dispute Resolution (ICDR). *See* **AAA-ICDR International Arbitration Rules, 2009**
International Centre for Settlement of Investment Disputes (ICSID) Arbitration Rules
award
interpretation, revision and annulment, 294–302
preparation, Rule 46, 288
rendering and publishing, Rule 48, 290–292
Rule 47, 288–290
supplementary decisions and rectification, Rule 49, 292–294
final provisions, Rule 56, 302–303
general procedural provisions
copies of instruments, Rule 23, 257–258

correction of errors, Rule 25, 259
cost of proceeding, Rule 28, 261–262
pre-hearing conference, Rule 21, 255–256
preliminary procedural consultation, Rule 20, 253–255
procedural languages, Rule 22, 256–257
procedural orders, Rule 19, 253
supporting documentation, Rule 24, 258–259
time limits, Rule 26, 259–260
waiver, Rule 27, 260–261
procedures
ancillary claims, Rule 40, 278–279
defaulting party, Rule 42, 283–285
parties failure discontinuance, 286–287
party request for discontinuance, Rule 44, 286
preliminary objections, Rule 41, 279–283
provisional measures, Rule 39, 275–278
settlement and discontinuance, Rule 43, 284–285
tribunal establishment
acceptance of appointments, Rule 5, 239–240
appointment by Chairman of Administrative Council, Rule 4, 237–238
appointment of arbitrator tribunal, Rule 3, 235–237
constitution, Rule 6, 240–242
disqualification of arbitrator, Rule 9, 244–245
filling vacancy on tribunal, Rule 11, 246
general obligations, Rule 1, 231–233
incapacity of arbitrators, Rule 8, 243–244
method of constituting tribunal, Rule 2, 234–235
newly appointed arbitrator, Rule 12, 246
replacement of arbitrators, Rule 7, 242–243
vacancy on tribunal, Rule 10, 245
working of tribunal, ICSID Rules
decisions of tribunal, Rule 16, 250–251
deliberations of tribunal, Rule 15, 249–250
incapacity of the president, Rule 17, 251
representation of the parties, Rule 18, 252–253
sessions of tribunal, Rule 13, 247–249
sittings of tribunal, Rule 14, 249
written and oral procedures
arbitration Rule 31, 263–265
arbitration Rule 32, 265–267
closure of proceeding, Rule 38, 274
examination of witnesses and experts, Rule 35, 269–270
marshalling of evidence, Rule 33, 267
normal procedures, Rule 29, 262–263
principles, Rule 34, 268–269
submission by non-disputing party, Rule 37, 271–274
transmission of request, Rule 30, 262

Index

visits and inquiries, Rule 37, 271–274
witnesses and experts, Rule 36, 270–271

International Centre for Settlement of Investment Disputes. *See* **ICSID Convention, 1965**

International Chamber of Commerce (ICC) Rules of Arbitration, 1998

arbitral proceedings
applicable rules of law, art. 17, 349–351
closing of proceedings, art. 22, 358–359
conservatory and interim measures, art. 23, 359–361
establishing the case facts, art. 20, 355–357
hearing, art. 21, 357–358
language of arbitration, art. 16, 348–349
new claims, art. 19, 354–355
place of arbitration, art. 14, 345–346
rules governing the proceedings, art. 15, 346–348
terms of reference, art. 18, 351–354
transmission of file, art 13, 343–344

arbitration costs and fees
advance on costs, art. 1, 396–397
costs and fees, art. 2, 397–398
ICC as appointing authority, art. 3, 398
scales of administrative expenses and arbitrator's fees, art. 4, 398–400

awards
award by consent, art. 26, 364–365
correction and interpretation, art. 29, 371–373
decisions on costs of arbitration, art. 31, 381–385
making of award, art. 25, 362–364
notification, deposit and enforceability, art. 28, 369–371
provisional advance, art. 30, 374–381
scrutiny by Court, art. 27, 365–368
time limit, art. 24, 361–362

commencing the arbitration
answer to the request, art. 5, 317–321
appointment and confirmation of arbitrator, art. 9, 332–336
challenge of arbitrators, art. 11, 338–340
effect of arbitration agreement, art. 6, 321–325
general provision, art. 7, 326–329
multiple parties, art, 10, 336–338
number of arbitrators, art. 8, 329–332
replacement of arbitrators, art. 12, 341–343
request for arbitration, art. 4, 313–317

exclusion of liability, art. 34, 388–389
general rule, art. 35, 390
internal rules of International Court of Arbitration
Committee of Court, art. 4, 394–395
confidential character, art. 1, 393
Court Secretariat, art. 5, 395

members of Court and ICC National Committees, art. 3, 394
participation of members, art. 2, 393–394
scrutiny of arbitral awards, art. 6, 395
introductory provisions
definition, art. 2, 309–310
International Court of Arbitration, art. 1, 306–309
written of communication, art. 3, 310–313
modified time limits, art. 32, 386–387
waiver, art. 33, 387–389
International Court of Arbitration, internal rules
Committee of Court, art. 4, 394–395
confidential character, art. 1, 393
Court Secretariat, art. 5, 395
members of Court and ICC National Committees, art. 3, 394
participation of members, art. 2, 393–394
scrutiny of arbitral awards, art. 6, 395

J

Jurisdiction of Centre, (ICSID) Convention, 1965
agencies of Contracting State, 70
Contracting State, 70
defines limit of, 70–71
diplomatic protection, art. 27
informal diplomatic exchanges., 80–81
international claims, 80
non-compliance with awards, 80
scope, 80
temporal aspects, 80
directness requirement, 69
excluded disputes, 68
exclusive remedy, art. 26
Fork-in-the-road clauses, 79
judicial remedies, 78
local remedies, 78–79
parties' consent, 78
scope, 77–78
settle dispute in domestic courts, 79
existence of dispute, 67
investment concept, 69–70
judicial persons
critical dates, 74
determination of nationality, 73
indirect foreign control, 73–74
judicial persons under foreign control, 73–74
legal nature, 67–68
list of exclusions, 68–69
national of another Contracting State, 71
nationality of natural persons, 72
natural persons
critical dates, 72
determination of nationality, 72
parties' consent
irrevocability of, 76
nation clauses, 75–76
prohibition of indirect withdrawal, 76–77
scope of, 75
time of, 76
State designation requirement, 70–71
Jurisdiction of tribunal, English Arbitration Act (C. 23), 1996

Index

competence to rule, Sec. 30, 764–765
determination of, Sec. 32, 767–769
substantive jurisdiction, Sec. 31, 765–767

Jurisdiction, Swiss Private International Law Act, 1989
arbitral tribunal, 942–943
counterclaim and set-off, 943
Kompetenz-Kompetenz, 942
lack of jurisdiction plea, 945
pending proceedings, before state court, 944–945
preliminary award, 945–946
preliminary mediation/conciliation, 943–944

L

Limitation Act, 1980, 742, 743, 817, 861
Lis pendens, 79, 928–930, 935, 944
London Court of International Arbitration (LCIA) Rules
additional powers of arbitral tribunal, art. 22
  amiable composition, 444
  apply to state court, 443
  choice of law, 443–444
  correction of mistakes, 443
  disclosure of documents, 442
  inspection of property, 442
  joinder of third party, 443
  rules of evidence, 442–443
  time limits, 442
  tribunal's enquiries, 442
  written statements, 442
arbitration and legal costs, art. 28
  basic rule, 459
  joint and several liability, 460–461
  non-LCIA arbitrations, 460
  party's legal costs, 460
  schedule, 455–459
award, art. 26
  court appeal, 453
  currency and interest, 452
  issuing an award, 452
  settlement, 452–453
  unanimous decision, 452
  written award and reasons, 452
communications between parties and tribunal, art. 13, 425–426
conduct of proceedings, art. 14
  chairman's power, 427–428
  parties' freedom and duty, 427
  tribunal's general duties and discretion, 427
confidentiality, art. 30
  English Court of appeal, 463
  extent of, 462–463
correction of awards and additional awards, art. 27
  errors, 454
  form of correction, 454
  procedure and time limits, 454
decisions by LCIA Court, art 29, 461
deposits, art. 24
  account payment, 447
  consequences of default, 447
  interim and final payment, 446–447
  registrar's authority, 447
  security for costs, 447
  tribunal's duty, 447
exclusion of liability, art. 31
  confidentiality, arbitration, 464
  scope, 464

Index

expedited formation, art. 418
  history of the rule, 419
  procedure, 419
  use in practice, 420
  written agreement, 419
experts to the arbitral tribunal, art. 21
  appointment, 439
  fees, 439
  impartiality and independence, 439
  oral evidence of parties, 439
  parties' duty, 439
  questioning tribunal's expert, 439
features, 401–402
formation of arbitral tribunal, art. 5
  advice on merits/dispute outcomes, 412
  appointment, 414–415
  arbitrator's fees, 412–413
  arbitrator's résumé, 412
  declaration, 413
  independence and impartiality, 411–412
  number of arbitrators, 413–414
  timing of appointment, 413
general rules, art. 32, 464–465
hearings, art. 19
  costs, 435
  in private, 436
  list of questions, 436
  right to be heard, 435
  timing and location, 435–436
interim and conservatory measures, art. 25
  cross-indemnities, 449
  enforcement of tribunal orders, 450
  freedom to apply to state court, 450
  interim measures, 450
  orders for security, 449
  orders to preserve property, 449–450
jurisdiction of arbitral tribunal, art. 23
  application to a state court, 446
  Kompetenz-Kompetenz, 445
  origin of rule, 445
  timing of pleas, 445–446
  timing of tribunal's decision, 446
language of arbitration, art. 17
  basic rule, 433
  translations, 433–434
  tribunal's power, 433
  use of English, 433
majority power to continue proceedings, art. 12
  arbitrators' decision, 425
  history and purpose of rule, 425
nationality of arbitrators, art. 6
  exception, general rule, 415–416
  general rule, 415
  meaning of nationality, 416
nomination and replacement of arbitrators, art. 11, 423–424
notices and periods of time, art. 4
  address for service, 409
  calculating time periods, 409–410
  communication, 409
  exception for party/party communications, 410
  permitted methods of service, 409
  tribunal's powers, 410
party and other nominations, art. 7
  arbitrator appointment, 417

Index

compliance with art. 5(3), 417
delay in nominating, arbitrator, 417
joint nomination, 417
right to nominate, 416–417
party representation, art. 18, 434
place of hearings, art. 16
  applicable procedural law, 432
  geographical location, 431–432
  scope of rule, 431
  terminology, 431
preamble, 402
registrar, art. 3
  communications to another party, 408
  structure and function, 407
request for arbitration, art. 1
  arbitration agreement, 404–405
  content, 403
  copies, 404
  incomplete request, 404
  limitation, 403
response, art. 2
  content, 406
  copies, 406
  pleading, 405–406
  timing and default, 406
revocation of arbitrator's appointment, art. 10
  impartiality, 421
  party's statutory right, 422–423
  procedure, 422
  resignation of arbitrator, 421
  unfit to act, 421–422
seat of arbitration, art. 16
  applicable procedural law, 432
  parties decision, 431
  scope of rule, 430
  terminology, 430
submission of written statements and documents, art. 15
  agreement to amend timetable, 430
  amendments, 430
  background to rule, 429
  communicating through registrar, 430
  contents of written statements, 429–430
  documents, samples and exhibits, 430
  party's default, 430
  timetable, 429
  timing of Claimant's Statement of Case, 429
  timing of respondent's defence, 429
three or more parties, art. 8, 417–418
witnesses, art. 20
  form of witness evidence, 437
  non-appearance of, 437–438
  notice of witness evidence, 437
  preparation of, 438
  questioning of, 437
  tribunal's power, 437
Loss of right, 240, 781, 820, 824, 833–835

M
Mandatory Rules
applicable law and, 187, 347, 389, 450, 452, 461, 469, 636
generally, 217, 347, 636, 947
insolvency law, 916
lex arbitri, 192, 911
procedural, 347, 350, 624
waiver of, 214–215, 593

Index

Multi-party arbitration. *See also* **Arbitrability; Arbitration agreement; Groups of companies; Lis pendens; Res judicata**
arbitration agreement, extension to non-signatories, 323, 919, 920, 957
concurrent hearings, 774–775, 856, 857
consent to, 943
consolidation of proceedings, 774–775, 856, 922
generally, 538
groups of companies, 323, 732, 846, 922
joinder, 418, 538–539
multi-contracts, 7, 65, 309, 324
parallel proceedings, 80, 101
series-group of contracts
shareholders, 415, 416, 436, 438, 875

N

New York Convention (1958)
accession, art. IX, 27
arbitral awards, obligation, art. III
   characteristics, 10
   domestic and foreign awards, 11–12
   jurisdiction, 11
   presumption of validity, 10
   procedural requirements, 10–11
   reference to law of forum, 10
arbitration agreements, art. II
   agreement in writing, 7
   assignment, 8–9
   content, 5–6
   incorporation by reference, 7–8
   matter capable of settlement, 6
   null and void, 9–10
   scope, 5
denunciation, art. XIII, 30–31
deposit of third instrument, art. XII, 30
discretion of national courts, art. VI, 23–24
favourable laws, art. VII, 24–26
federal/non-unitary States, art. XI, 29–30
foreign arbitral awards, art. V
   arbitrators, jurisdiction, 18–19
   award binding, 20
   award suspension, 20–21
   incapacity, 16–17
   invalidity of arbitration agreement, 15–16
   irregular procedure, 19–20
   overview, 15
   public policy violation, 21–23
   violation of due process, 17–18
formalities, art. IV
   applications, 14
   authenticated award/original arbitration agreement, 12–13
   liberal approach, 14
   requirements, 13
   time for document submission, 13
   translation of originals, 13
history and status, 1–2
notification, art. XV, 32
official languages, art. XVI, 32
reciprocity, art. XIV, 31
scope of application, art. 1
   arbitral award, 3
   reservations, 4–5
   territorial criterion, 3
signature, ratification, art. VIII, 26
sources, 2

territorial application declaration, art. X
  application of Convention, 28–29
  dependent territories, 27–28
  depositary of Convention, 28
  operation, 28
  timing of notice, 28

P
Party autonomy
  arbitration proceedings, 401, 625, 723, 922
  intro, general, 537, 625, 723, 885, 911, 922, 925, 951

People's Republic of China Arbitration Law, 1994
  application and acceptance
    alteration claim and right to counterclaim, art. 27, 682
    arbitration commission decision, art. 24, 679–680
    content of request for arbitration, art. 23, 679
    notice of arbitration, art. 25, 680–681
    power of attorney, art. 24, 683–684
    primary jurisdiction of courts, art. 26, 681–682
    property preservation measures, art. 28, 682–683
    request for arbitration, art. 21, 678
    requirement of written application, art. 22, 678
  application for setting aside arbitral award
    domestic award, art. 58, 701–702
    limitation period, art. 59, 702–703
    re-arbitration, art. 61, 703–704
    time frame, request for cancellation, art. 60, 703
  arbitration agreement
    invalidity of, art. 17, 673
    priority of court jurisdiction, art. 20, 677–678
    severability, art. 19, 676–677
    unclear designation of arbitration commission, art. 18, 674–676
    validity requirements, art. 16, 670–672
  arbitration commissions and association
    China Arbitration Association (CAA), art. 15, 669–670
    geographical organisation, art. 10, 666–667
    independence, art. 14, 669
    key personnel, art. 12, 667–668
    minimum requirements for arbitrators, art. 13, 668–669
    minimum requirements, art. 11, 667
  enforcement
    grounds for non-enforcement, art. 63, 705–706
    priority of cancellation procedure, art. 64, 706–707
    right to enforce award, art. 62, 704–705
  foreign-related arbitration
    arbitration commissions, art. 66, 708
    competence of CCOIC, art. 73, 713
    evidence preservation, art. 68, 709–710
    lack of jurisdiction rationae loci, art. 72, 713

Index

non-enforcement, art. 71, 712–713
panel of arbitrators, art. 67, 708–709
records of hearings, art. 69, 710
set aside procedure, art. 70, 710–712
special provisions, art. 65, 707
formation of arbitral tribunal
arbitrator replacement, art. 37, 688–689
arbitrators appointment, art. 31, 684–685
arbitrators liability, art. 38, 689
challenge withdrawal of arbitrator, art. 34, 686–687
competent authority, art. 36, 688
notification of constitution, art. 33, 685–686
number of arbitrators, art. 30, 684
subsidiary appointing authority, art. 32, 685
withdrawal procedure, art. 35, 687–688
general provisions
aim, art. 1, 657–658
applicable law, art. 7, 662–664
arbitrable disputes, art. 2, 658–659
arbitration agreement, art. 4, 660–661
court jurisdiction, art. 5, 661
finality of arbitral award, art. 9, 665–666
independence of arbitration, art. 8, 664–666
non-arbitrable disputes, art. 3, 659–660
parties' autonomy, art. 6, 661–662
hearing and award
administration by arbitration commission, art. 41, 690–691
appraisal, art. 44, 692–693
compulsory recording of domestic arbitration, art. 48, 695
conciliation procedure and result, art. 51, 696–697
content and binding effect of conciliation statement, art. 52, 697–698
content and form of, art. 54, 698–699
correction and supplementation, art. 56, 700
cross-examination, art. 45, 693–694
decision making, art. 53, 698
default of one party, art. 42, 691
evidence preservation, art. 46, 694
evidence, art. 43, 691–692
legal effect of, art. 57, 700
mediation and consent awards, art. 49, 695–696
oral hearings, art. 39, 690
partial award, art. 55, 699–700
private hearings, art. 40, 690
repudiation of conciliation settlement, art.50, 696
right to debate, art. 47, 694–695
supplementary provisions
arbitration fees, art.76, 715
effectiveness of law, art. 80, 717
formulation of arbitration rules, art. 75, 714–715

labour and agricultural disputes, art. 77, 715–716
limitation period, art. 74, 714
priority of arbitration law, art. 78, 716
reorganisation of arbitration commissions, art. 79, 716–717
Permanent Court of Arbitration (PCA), 157, 172, 178, 180, 184, 225, 226, 248
Place of arbitration. *See* **Seat of arbitration**
Provisional and conservatory measures. *See* **Interim measures**
Public policy
arbitrability, 21, 614, 915
illegality, 22, 844, 866
international, 17, 21–23, 865, 882, 884, 886–890, 897, 899, 902–905, 948, 949, 960
international procedural, 624, 884, 886, 898, 903, 904

Q
Question of law, 780, 789–791, 794, 825–827, 845–847

R
Remittance award, 831
Res judicata, 141, 145, 559, 639, 650, 808, 891–892, 896, 942, 950, 955, 974
Rome Convention, 464, 636, 778, 793

S
Scotland Arbitration Act, 2010, 719, 724, 871
Seat of arbitration
applicable law, procedural, 10, 432

Separability, 483, 484, 613–614, 722, 724, 731–733, 795, 899, 921
Statutory arbitrations, English Arbitration Act (C. 23), 1996
adaptation of general provisions, Sec. 95, 856
adaptation of specific provisions, Sec. 96, 856–857
application of Part I, Sec. 94, 855–856
excluded provisions, Sec. 97, 857–858
Secretary of State to make provision, Sec. 98, 858
Swiss Private International Law Act, 1989
applicable law, art. 187
arbitral tribunal, 949
choice of law, 946
closest connection test, 948–949
conflict of laws, 946
decision ex aequo et bono, 949
parties choice of law limits, 947–948
possible choices, 946–947
arbitrability, art. 177
consequences, non-arbitrability, 915
disputes, 914–915
examining ex officio, 915
non-arbitrable preliminary questions, 915
restrictions, 915
state-controlled party, 916
subjective arbitrability, 916
arbitral award, art. 189
content, 952
costs, 953–954
deliberations and voting, 951–952
dissenting opinion, 953

form and notification, 952
notion of, 951
party autonomy, 951
arbitral tribunal, art. 179
appointing authority decisions, remedies, 923–924
arbitral contract, 924
arbitrator resignation, 924
competent court, 923
constitution, 921–922
party autonomy, 922
proceedings repetition, 924
state court, appointing authority, 923
arbitral tribunal, art. 180
arbitrator appointment by a party, 927
challenge decision, appeal against, 928
challenge procedure, 927–928
duty to challenge, 928
duty to disclose, 927
independence, 925–927
scope of application and system of provision, 925
arbitration agreement, art. 178
art. 178(1) and art. II(2) New York Convention, 917–918
art. 178(2) and art. V(1)(a) New York Convention, 920–921
by reference, 918–919
determinability, 918
form requirement, 917
non-signatories, 920
pathological agreements, 918
principle of autonomy/separability, 921
requirements, 917
scope of, 919–920
substantive validity, 919

case law and academic sources, 911
chapter 12 PILA and Intercantonal Concordat, 911
competent authority, art. 191
content of written brief, 965–966
deadline, 964–965
decision, FSC, 968
publicity of proceedings, 967
requirements, 965
scope of examination, FSC, 967–968
setting aside proceedings, 966–967
suspensive effect, 964
deposit and certificate of enforceability, art. 193, 972–973
foreign arbitral awards, art. 194
enforcement of awards, 975–976
public policy, 975
recognition and enforcement, 974
refusal under art. V(2) New York Convention, 974–975
judicial assistance, art. 185, 941
jurisdiction, art. 186
arbitral tribunal, 942–943
counterclaim and set-off, 943
Kompetenz-Kompetenz, 942
lack of jurisdiction plea, 945
pending proceedings, before state court, 944–945
preliminary award, 945–946
preliminary mediation/conciliation, 943–944
legislative history, 911
lis pendens, art. 181
pendency procedural effects, Switzerland, 929–930

Index

provision, purpose of, 929
request for arbitration,
  contents of, 929
Swiss substantive law, 930
time of, 929
partial award, art. 188, 949–950
principle, art. 182
  adversarial proceedings, 934
  discretion, arbitral tribunal,
    931–932
  parties equal treatment,
    932–933
  party autonomy priority, 931
  procedural orders, arbitral
    tribunal, 932
  procedural public policy,
    932
  right to be heard, 933–934
  scope of application, 931
principle, art. 190
  arbitral award, final nature
    of., 955
  decision infra petita, 958
  decision ultra petita/extra
    petita, 957–958
  equal treatment of the
    parties, violation of, 958
  Federal Supreme Court
    decision, 957
  incorrect constitution,
    arbitral tribunal, 956
  interim awards, challenge to,
    961–962
  jurisdiction, wrong decision
    on, 956–957
  nullity of award, 963–964
  overview and scope of
    application, 954–955
  procedural public policy,
    960–961
  public policy violation,
    958–959
  revision, 962–963
  setting aside award, 955–956
  subsequent discovery, incorrect constitution, 963
  substantive public policy,
    959–960
provisional and protective
  measures, art. 183
  appropriate security, 937
  arbitral tribunal authority,
    935
  ex parte orders, 936
  interim measures abroad,
    937
  interim measures enforcement, Switzerland,
    936–937
  orders, subject matter of,
    936
  requirements, 935–936
  setting aside proceedings,
    937–938
  state courts authority, 935
scope of application, art.176
  arbitral tribunals, applicability to, 912
  chapter12 PILA exclusion,
    913–914
  determination, 914
  domicile/habitual residence,
    913
  requirements, 912
  seat of the arbitration,
    912–913
taking of evidence, art. 184
  general principle and subject
    matter, 938
  presenting evidence
    methods, 939
  procedural guarantees,
    939–940
  procedural rules, 938–939
  Swiss state courts, assistance
    by, 940–941
waiver of set aside proceedings,
  art. 192
  explicit waiver, 969–970

Index

partial waiver, 970
possibility and effect of, 968–969
protection by New York Convention, 971
requirements, 969

T
Tribunal establishment, ICSID Rules
acceptance of appointments, Rule 5
  arbitrator's failure, 239
  communications through Secretary-General, 239
  form of acceptance, 239
  loss of right, arbitrator, 240
  refusal, arbitrator rights, 239–240
appointment by Chairman of Administrative Council, Rule 4
  failure, 237–238
  obligation to appoint, 238
  obligation to consult, 238
  request to Chairman, 238
  thirty-day time limit, 238
appointment of tribunal, Rule 3
  art. 37(2)(b) default rule, 236
  communication with Secretary-General, 237
  nationality, 236–237
  procedure, 236
  time limits, 236
constitution, Rule 6
  confidentiality, 242
  declaration, 241
  impartiality, 241–242
  prohibited appointments, 242
  tribunal composition, 241
disqualification of arbitrator, Rule 9
  procedural steps, 245
  timing of proposal, 245
filling vacancy on tribunal, Rule 11, 246
general obligations, Rule 1
  arbitration request, 232–233
  impartiality of arbitrators, 233
  nationality of arbitrators, 233
  parties agreement, 233
  possible dispatch, 232
incapacity of arbitrators, Rule 8
  disqualification, 243–244
  resignation and procedures, 243
method of constituting tribunal, Rule 2
  agreement failure, 235
  communication with Secretary-General, 235
  purpose, 234
  time limits, 234–235
newly appointed arbitrator, Rule 12, 246
replacement of arbitrators, Rule 7
  agreement, 243
  Rules 1, 5 and 6, according to, 243
vacancy on tribunal, Rule 10, 245

Tribunal, AAA-ICDR International Arbitration Rules, 2009
administrator's authority, art.9, 479–480
arbitrator replacement, art. 10, 480
arbitrators appointment, art. 6
  ICDR's authority for selection, 476
  parties' right to agree, 475
  selection of arbitrators, multiple parties, 476

time limit for agreement, 475
authority of two arbitrators, art. 11, 480–481
challenge of arbitrators, art. 8, 478–479
impartiality and independence of arbitrators, art. 7
ex parte communications, 477–478
notice of appointment, 477
requirement, 477
scope of interview, 478
number of arbitrators, art. 5, 473–474

U

UNCITRAL Arbitration Rules, 1976
arbitral proceedings
amendments to claim/defence, art. 20, 198–200
closure of hearings, art. 29, 213–214
default, art. 28, 211–213
evidence, art. 24, 204–205
experts, art. 27, 209–211
further written statements, art. 22, 202
general provisions, art. 15, 190–192
hearings, art. 25, 205–207
jurisdiction of arbitral tribunal, art, 21, 200–201
language, art. 17, 194–195
place of arbitration, art. 16, 192–193
protection, interim measures, art. 26, 208–209
statement of claim, art. 18, 195–196
statement of defence, art.19, 196–198
time periods, art. 23, 203–204
waiver of rules, art. 30, 214–215
award
additional award, art. 37, 223–225
applicable law, art. 33, 218–219
apportionment of costs, art. 40, 228–229
arbitration cost, art. 38, 225–226
arbitrators' fees, art. 39, 226–228
correction of, art. 36, 222–223
decisions, art. 31, 215–216
deposit of costs, art. 41, 229–230
form and effect of, art. 32, 216–218
interpretations, art. 35, 221–222
settlement for termination, art. 34, 219–221
composition of arbitral tribunal
appointment by appointing authority, art. 8, 180–181
arbitrator replacement, art. 13, 188–189
challenge decision, art. 12, 186–187
disclosure, art. 9, 181–183
notification of challenge, art. 11, 185–186
number of arbitrators, art. 5, 176–177
repetition of hearings, art. 14, 189–190
sole arbitrator appointment, art. 6, 177–179
standard for challenge, art. 10, 183–185
three-person panel appointment, art. 7, 179–180
introductory rules

Index

notice and calculation of time periods, art. 2, 172–173
notice of arbitration, art. 3, 173–175
representation and assistance, art. 4, 175–176
scope of application, art. 1, 171–172

UNCITRAL Model Law on International Commercial Arbitration, 1985/2006
arbitration agreement
definition and form of, art. 7, 595–601
interim measures by court, art. 9, 605–606
substantive claim, art. 8, 601–605
composition of arbitral tribunal
appointment of arbitrators, art. 11, 607–609
appointment of substitute arbitrator, art. 15, 612–613
challenge procedure, art. 13, 610–611
failure/impossibility, art. 14, 611–612
grounds for challenge, art. 12, 609–610
number of arbitrators, art. 10, 606–607
conduct of arbitral proceedings
commencement, art. 21, 627–628
court assistance in taking evidence, art. 27, 634–635
default of a party, art. 25, 631–633
hearings and written proceedings, art. 24, 630–631
language, art. 22, 628–629
parties equal treatment, art. 18, 623–624
place of arbitration, art. 20, 626–627
rules of procedure determination, art. 19, 625
statements of claim and defence, art. 23, 629–630
tribunal-appointed experts, art. 26, 633–634
court-ordered interim measures, art. 17J
ex parte interim measures, 622
interim measures enforcement, 623
new provisions, 622
preliminary orders, 622–623
purpose of the 2006 amendments, 621–622
general provisions
arbitration assistance and supervision, art. 6, 594–595
definitions and rules of interpretation, art. 2, 590–591
extent of court intervention, art. 5, 593–594
international origin and general principles, art. 2A, 591
receipt of written communications, art. 3, 591–592
scope of application, art. 1, 582–589
waiver of right to object, art. 4, 593
interim measures
conditions for granting, art. 17A, 617–618
power of arbitral tribunal, art. 17, 616–617

1113

jurisdiction of arbitral tribunal, art. 16
  Kompetenz-Kompetenz and separability, 613–614
  objection against, 614
  tribunal's decision, 615–616
making of award
  and termination of proceedings, art. 32, 642
  correction and interpretation of award, art. 33, 642–643
  decision making by panel of arbitrators, art. 29, 638–639
  form and contents of award, art. 31, 640–641
  rules applicable to substance of dispute, art. 28, 635–638
  settlement, art. 30, 639
preliminary orders
  applications and conditions for, art. 17B, 618
  specific regime for, art. 17C, 618–619
provisions to interim measures and preliminary orders
  costs and damages, art. 17G, 620
  disclosure, art. 17F, 619
  modification, suspension, termination, art. 17D, 619
  provision of security, art. 17E, 619
recognition and enforcement of awards, art. 35
  grounds for refusing, art. 36, 650–655
  new article 35(2), 649–650
recognition and enforcement of interim measures, 620–621
recourse against award, art. 34
  application for setting aside, 644–646

constitution of tribunal, 647
inarbitrability, 647–648
incapacity, invalidity of arbitration agreement, 646
public policy, 648–649
remission, 649
tribunal acts, 647
violation of due process, 646–647

United Nations Commission on International Trade Law (UNCITRAL). *See* **UNCITRAL Arbitration Rules, 1976**

V

Vienna Convention on the Law of Treaties (1969), 105, 163, 914

W

Washington Convention, 1965, 720

Working of tribunal, ICSID Rules
  decisions of tribunal, Rule 16
    correspondence decisions, 251
    majority votes, 250
  deliberations of tribunal
    attendance, 250
    confidentiality, 250
  incapacity of the president, Rule 17, 251
  representation of the parties, Rule 18, 252–253
  sessions of tribunal, Rule 13
    definition, 247
    failure of party, 249
    initial and subsequent, date fixing, 247
    meeting place of tribunal, 248

parties and members
    notification, 248
  sixty-day time limit, 248
sittings of tribunal, Rule 14
  date and time fixing, 249
  quorum, 249
Written and oral procedures, ICSID Rule
  arbitration Rule 31, 263–265
  arbitration Rule 32, 265–267
  closure of proceeding, Rule 38, 274
  examination of witnesses and experts, Rule 35, 269–270
  marshalling of evidence, Rule 33, 267
  normal procedures, Rule 29, 262–263
  principles, Rule 34
    duty of parties, 269
    expenditure incurred by parties, 269
    form of request, 268–269
    power of tribunal, 268
    tribunal to visit place, 269
  submission by non-disputing party, Rule 37
    applications, 273
    April 2006 amendments, 273
    considerations, 273–274
  transmission of request, Rule 30, 262
  visits and inquiries, Rule 37
    arrangements, 272
    content of order, 272
    discretion of tribunal, 272
    form of order, 272
  witnesses and experts, Rule 36, 270–271